Econometric Analysis

Third Edition

William H. Greene

New York University

Prentice Hall, Upper Saddle River, New Jersey 07458

Executive Editor: Leah Jewell
Editorial Assistant: Kristen Kaiser
Editor-in-Chief: James Boyd
Marketing Manager: Susan McLaughlin
Production Editor: Judith Leale
Production Coordinator: Renee Pelletier
Managing Editor: Carol Burgett
Manufacturing Buyer: Kenneth J. Clinton
Manufacturing Supervisor: Arnold Vila
Manufacturing Manager: Vincent Scelta
Cover Design: Bruce Kenselaar
Composition: Progressive Information Technologies

Library of Congress Cataloging-in-Publication Data

Greene, William H. 1951–
Econometric analysis / William H. Greene.—3rd ed.
p. cm.
Includes bibliographical references and indexes.
ISBN 0-02-346602-2
1. Econometrics.
HB139.G74 1997 96-32586
330′.01′5195—dc20 CIP

Prentice-Hall International (UK) Limited, London
Prentice-Hall of Australia Pty. Limited, Sydney
Prentice-Hall Canada, Inc., Toronto
Prentice-Hall Hispanoamericana, S.A., Mexico
Prentice-Hall of India Private Limited, New Delhi
Prentice-Hall of Japan, Inc., Tokyo
Simon & Schuster Asia Pte. Ltd., Singapore
Editora Prentice-Hall do Brasil, Ltda., Rio de Janeiro

Printed in the United States of America

10 9 8 7 6 5 4 3 2

For
Lesley, Elizabeth, Allison, and Julianna

Brief Contents

Contents

Preface

This third edition of *Econometric Analysis* is intended for a one-year graduate course in econometrics for social scientists. The prerequisites for the course should include calculus, basic mathematical statistics, and an introduction to the paradigm of econometrics at the level of, say, Gujarati's *Basic Econometrics* (McGraw-Hill, 1995), Maddala's *Introduction to Econometrics* [Macmillan (now Prentice Hall), 1992], or Griffiths, Hill, and Judge's *Learning and Practicing Econometrics* (John Wiley and Sons, 1993). Self-contained (for our purposes) summaries of the matrix algebra, statistical theory, and mathematical statistics used later in the book are given in Chapters 2 through 4. Chapter 5 is mostly new and contains a description of numerical methods that will be useful to practicing econometricians. The formal presentation of econometrics begins in Chapters 6 through 10 with discussion of the fundamental building block, the linear multiple regression model. Chapters 11 through 16 present familiar extensions of the single linear equation model, including nonlinear regression, panel data models, the generalized regression model, and systems of equations. We end in the last four chapters with discussions of current topics in applied econometrics including GMM estimation methods, Lagrange multiplier tests, time-series analysis, and the analysis of qualitative and limited dependent variable models.

This book has two objectives. The first is to introduce students to *applied econometrics,* including basic techniques in regression analysis and some of the rich variety of models that are used when the linear model proves inadequate or inappropriate. The second objective is to present students with sufficient *theoretical background* that they will recognize new variants of the models that they learn about here as merely natural extensions that fit within a common body of principles. This is why I have spent what might seem to be a large amount of effort explaining the mechanics of GMM estimation, nonlinear least squares, and maximum likelihood estimation, for example, of GARCH models. To meet the second objective, this book also contains a fair amount of theoretical material, such as that on maximum likelihood estimation and on asymptotic results for regression models. Modern software has made complicated modeling very easy to do, and an understanding of the underlying theory is important.

Readers of my second edition will see that this work is a major revision. I had three purposes in undertaking this revision. The first was to respond to the many readers who generously wrote to me with interesting suggestions for my "next edition." Had I followed all their suggestions, I would have (a lifetime of work later) produced an enormous reference work in econometrics. But the four volumes of the *Handbook of Econometrics* already run to over 3000 pages, and volumes 1 and 2 of the *Handbook of Applied Econometrics* will soon appear, so this is hardly necessary. Nonetheless, when I was given the opportunity to do this revision by my publisher, I found the invitation irresistible. This has involved extending some topics that were already present in the second edition and adding many new ones. In fact, a revision of the earlier material on time series was essential. Second, it became obvious to me that the second edition could greatly benefit from some reorganization and some editing. I hope that this will make the flow of the book more logical. Finally, the literature in econometrics has continued to evolve, and my third objective is to continue to grow with it. This is inherently difficult to do with a textbook. Most of the literature is written by professionals for other professionals, and this is a textbook written for students who are in the early stages of their training. But I do hope to provide a bridge to that literature.

There are four components to this revision.

1. New topics in computational methods. I have added a new chapter on numerical methods that includes discussions of digital computing, random number generation, bootstrap sampling, Monte Carlo integration, importance sampling, the Gibbs sampler, numerical quadrature, and optimization methods. The last of these was covered in the previous edition, but I have added a discussion of the EM algorithm to show students an important application of the link between the theoretical specification and the computation of numerical estimates.

2. Estimation methods. I have expanded the treatments of both the maximum likelihood and GMM estimators. Chapter 6 now contains considerably more discussion of asymptotic results for the linear model. This discussion is fairly general so that it, with the earlier material on ML and GMM estimation, can be extended to, for example, discrete choice models without further development. Theoretical background and several applications of two-step estimation have also been added. Finally, the discussion of Bayesian estimation of the linear model has been expanded and moved to Chapter 6 with the other basic material on the multiple linear regression model.

3. Specific models and techniques. This edition contains new material on several models that are used in the econometrics literature. These include time-series models including unit roots, VARs, and cointegration, Box–Jenkins ARMA models (mainly as a stepping-stone to the literature on unit roots and VARs, not as a method of building forecasting models as such), the nested logit model, various specifications for panel data including dynamic panels and robust estimation in a panel data setting, new material on binary choice including a nonparametric, kernel estimator, and newly developed models for count data.

4. Reorganization. To improve the flow of the book, I have rearranged or moved several chapters. The new chapter on numerical methods follows Chapter 4 on statistical inference. This chapter also includes all of what was Chapter 12 on optimization in the second edition, so that all of the "tools" are now gathered at the beginning of the book. Chapter 5 on the bivariate regression model has been eliminated, since most of it was repeated, more compactly, in Chapter 6. The discussion of the linear regression model begins in Chapter 6 with multiple regression. This chapter now also includes all of the previous Chapter 10 on asymptotics as well as the part of the previous Chapter 8 on instrumental variables estimation. There is now an extensive treatment of asymptotic theory in Chapter 6. Some of the material on hypothesis testing in the old Chapter 6 that overlapped with Chapter 7 has been moved to Chapter 7 to improve the organization of this material. The material on the linear regression model has been consolidated a bit. Chapter 6 is now quite long, but the arrangement is somewhat more natural than it was in the second edition. The previous chapter on covariance structures and panel data is now specialized in panel data models, mostly fixed and random effects. Some new material on robust estimation of covariance matrices and dynamic models has been added to this chapter. All the material on covariance structures has been moved to the next chapter on sets of regression equations, where the model of groupwise covariance structures and the random coefficients model have been reoriented as special cases of the seemingly unrelated regressions model. The chapter on simultaneous equations now follows, I believe more naturally, immediately after the chapter on sets of regressions. The two chapters on time-series models, followed by the two chapters on qualitative and limited dependent variables, now appear as the latter chapters in the book, more or less in the fashion of a topics section. As before, the heading "advanced topics" is inappropriate here. These chapters document the mainstream of two major areas of research.

Many authors have used the term *explosion* in the literature to describe the most clearly visible evolution in econometrics, the new methods in time-series analysis and empirical macroeconomics. It has seemed to some observers that the term was more apt than the authors might have intended; for some time, the literature seemed to be huge, but fragmented and everywhere at once. But the field seems to have found an equilibrium, and the current body of literature documents an exciting new paradigm. I have included in this edition a considerable expansion of the sections on unit roots, VARs, and cointegration. But this constitutes only the barest introduction to this literature, and I have no illusions that this will satisfy critics of the earlier editions who looked here for a comprehensive, intermediate-level introduction. That more than one correspondent thought that perhaps a second volume might be a feasible approach for this text suggests how difficult that would be to provide. Fortunately, a half dozen new books are now available for the reader who wishes to continue studies in this area. A good place to begin is Enders (1995), followed by Hamilton (1994). There are too many survey papers to list fully—another mini-growth industry—but two that are noteworthy are Stock (1994) and Watson (1994). Others are listed in Chapters 17 and 18.

Another sea of change in econometrics is the appearance of robust methods for estimation and testing. This is dominated by robust covariance matrix estimates, GMM estimation, and the redemption of the Wald statistic. It has been but a decade or less since pure significance tests were rendered déclassé under the assault of a wave of Lagrange multiplier tests. But recent developments in GMM estimation and distribution free estimation have brought the Wald statistic back from its ignominious fate. In this edition, I have attempted to apply many of the newer methods in estimation, including two-step and GMM estimation and LM and conditional moment testing, in a variety of settings. Likewise, the reader will find numerous applications of robust covariance estimation and hypothesis testing using several methods.

I have attempted to keep the mathematical level consistent throughout. This has meant liberal use of matrix algebra, but it has required little in the way of advanced distribution theory. I give proofs only when they are particularly revealing about some underlying principle that will appear in other contexts or provide students with a useful tool for their work. White's proof of the limiting distribution of the Wald statistic in Chapter 6 is an example. In contrast, a proof of the central limit theorem, although obviously of great utility in its own right, is a one-shot deal. For those who are teaching at a relatively high level and who desire more of a theorem/proof format, I suggest Peter Schmidt's *Econometrics* (Marcel Dekker, 1976) as a very handy adjunct. Also, Davidson and MacKinnon (1993) present many of the topics that we cover at a higher, more theoretical level, but with an appealing operational flavor.

One feature that distinguishes this work from its predecessors is its greater emphasis on nonlinear models, including full chapters on nonlinear regression and nonlinear optimization. [Davidson and MacKinnon (1993) are a noteworthy, but more advanced exception.] Computer software now in wide use has made estimation of nonlinear models as routine as estimation of linear ones, and the recent literature reflects that progression. The purpose of these chapters is to bring the textbook treatment in line with current practice. I have also included two long chapters on limited dependent variable models. These nonlinear models are now common in the applied literature. I have written these chapters because there is still no other source that presents these topics at a level elementary enough to initiate the newcomer but complete enough to enable a diligent student to use the information to undertake a serious empirical study. This book contains a fair amount of material that will extend beyond many first courses in econometrics, including, perhaps, the aforementioned chapters on limited dependent variables, the section in Chapter 20 on duration models, and some of the discussion of time series. Once again, I have included these in the hope of providing a heretofore missing bridge to the professional literature in these areas.

With the current state of microcomputers, students can be given realistic data sets and challenging empirical analyses as a routine part of their econometrics training. To this end, I have included in this book a large number of data sets, many of which have been used in studies already in the literature. In addition, the appendix to Chapter 16 contains a yearly data set on a number of macroeconomic variables. These could be used, for example, to update Klein's Model I or, for the more ambitious, to estimate a new model.

There are many computer programs that students can use in an econometrics course. The most important features are ease of use and flexibility; the same program can easily be used for many different types of analyses. Most of these programs are available in both mainframe and microcomputer versions. The programs vary in size and complexity, cost, and the amount of programming required of the user. Journals such as the *American Statistician* and the *Journal of Applied Econometrics* present frequent surveys and reviews of econometric software. An intriguing development of recent years has been the worldwide dissemination of routines written for other packages such as Gauss and LIMDEP via various list servers and the World Wide Web. (For example, the CodEc project offers a freely distributed library of documentation and many kinds of programs to users of the Internet.)

It is a pleasure to express my appreciation to those who have influenced this work. My gratitude to Arthur Goldberger continues, for his encouragement, guidance, and always interesting correspondence. Dennis Aigner and Laurits Christensen were also influential in shaping my views on econometrics. The number of students and colleagues whose suggestions have helped to produce what you find here is far too large to allow me to thank them all individually. The several collaborators to the second edition, whose contributions I have retained in this one, include Aline Quester, David Hensher, Donald Waldman, Martin Evans, and Paul Wachtel. This work has also benefited at several stages from the careful reading of many reviewers, including Badi Baltagi, University of Houston; Diane Belleville of New York University; Leonard Carlson, Emory University; Chris Cornwell, University of Georgia; Michael Ellis, Wesleyan University; K. Rao Kadiyala, Purdue University; William Lott, University of Connecticut; Edward Mathis, Villanova University; Thad Mirer, State University of New York at Albany; Terry G. Seaks, University of North Carolina at Greensboro; Donald Snyder, California State University at Los Angeles; Houston Stokes, University of Illinois at Chicago; Mark Watson, Harvard University; Kenneth West, University of Wisconsin; Ed Greenberg, Washington University at St. Louis; Edward Dwyer, Clemson University; Frank Chaloupka, City University of New York; Arnold Zellner, University of Chicago; Dimitrios Thomakos at Columbia University; Paul Ruud, University of California at Berkeley; Neal Beck, University of California at San Diego; Anil Bera, University of Illinois; and Miguel Herce, University of North Carolina. I would also like to thank Leah Jewell at Prentice Hall, and Donna King at Progressive Publishing Alternatives, for their contributions to the completion of this book. As always, I owe the greatest debt to my wife, Lynne, and to my daughters, Lesley, Allison, Elizabeth, and Julianna.

William H. Greene

Examples

Theorems and Useful Results

THEOREM 3.10:	Distribution of $\mathbf{x}'\mathbf{\Sigma}^{-1}\mathbf{x}$ When $\mathbf{x}$ Is Standard Normal
THEOREM 3.11:	Independence of a Linear and a Quadratic Form
EXERCISE 3.18:	Hermite Polynomials
EXERCISE 3.19:	Orthogonal Polynomials
EXERCISE 3.21:	Factorial Moments
EXERCISE 3.26:	Probability Generating Function
EXERCISE 3.27:	Moment Generating Function
EXERCISE 3.28:	Moment Generating Function for a Sum of Random Variables
THEOREM 4.1:	Sampling Distribution of the Sample Mean
THEOREM 4.2:	Cramér–Rao Lower Bound
THEOREM 4.3:	Convergence in Quadratic Mean
THEOREM 4.4:	Chebychev's Inequality
THEOREM 4.5:	Markov's Inequality
THEOREM 4.6:	Consistency of the Sample Mean
COROLLARY TO THEOREM 4.6:	Consistency of a Mean of Functions
THEOREM 4.7:	Slutsky Theorem
THEOREM 4.8:	Jensen's Inequality
THEOREM 4.9:	Rules for Probability Limits
THEOREM 4.10:	Rules for Limiting Distributions
THEOREM 4.11:	Central Limit Theorem (Univariate)
THEOREM 4.12:	Central Limit Theorem with Unequal Variances
THEOREM 4.13:	Lindberg–Levy Central Limit Theorem
THEOREM 4.14:	Lindberg–Feller Central Limit Theorem
THEOREM 4.15:	Limiting Normal Distribution of a Function
THEOREM 4.16:	Limiting Normal Distribution of a Set of Functions
THEOREM 4.17:	Asymptotic Distribution of a Nonlinear Function
THEOREM 4.18:	Properties of an MLE
THEOREM 4.19:	Asymptotic Distribution of the Two-Step MLE
THEOREM 4.20:	Distribution of the Likelihood Ratio Test Statistic
THEOREM 4.21:	Distribution of the Wald Test Statistic
THEOREM 4.22:	Distribution of the Lagrange Multiplier Statistic
EXERCISE 4.14:	Even Moments of the Standard Normal Distribution
In SECTION 5.4.2b:	Sterling's Approximation to the Factorial Function
THEOREM 6.1:	Orthogonal Regression
THEOREM 6.2:	Orthogonal Partitioned Regression
THEOREM 6.3:	Frisch–Waugh Theorem
EQUATION (6-30):	Diagonal Elements of a Moment Matrix
EQUATION (6-31):	Change in Sum of Squares When a Variable Is Added to a Regression
EQUATION (6-36):	Effect on R^2 When a Variable Is Added to a Regression
EQUATION (6-37):	Effect on R^2 When a Variable Is Added to a Regression
THEOREM 6.4:	Individual Regression Coefficients
THEOREM 6.5:	Regression with a Constant Term

Definitions

CHAPTER 1
Introduction

1.1. ECONOMETRICS

In the first issue of *Econometrica,* the Econometric Society stated that

> its main object shall be to promote studies that aim at a unification of the theoretical-quantitative and the empirical-quantitative approach to economic problems and that are penetrated by constructive and rigorous thinking similar to that which has come to dominate the natural sciences.
>
> But there are several aspects of the quantitative approach to economics, and no single one of these aspects taken by itself, should be confounded with econometrics. Thus, econometrics is by no means the same as economic statistics. Nor is it identical with what we call general economic theory, although a considerable portion of this theory has a definitely quantitative character. Nor should econometrics be taken as synonomous *[sic]* with the application of mathematics to economics. Experience has shown that each of these three viewpoints, that of statistics, economic theory, and mathematics, is a necessary, but not by itself a sufficient, condition for a real understanding of the quantitative relations in modern economic life. It is the *unification* of all three that is powerful. And it is this unification that constitutes econometrics.[1]

Frish and his society responded to an unprecedented accumulation of statistical information. They saw a need to establish a body of principles that could organize what would otherwise become a bewildering mass of data. Neither the pillars nor the objectives of econometrics have changed in the years since this editorial appeared. Econometrics is the field of economics that concerns itself with the application of mathematical statistics and the tools of statistical inference to the empirical measurement of relationships postulated by economic theory.

---

[1]Frish (1933).

1.2. ECONOMETRIC MODELING

Economic theory is typically crisp and unambiguous. Models of demand, production, and aggregate consumption all postulate precise, *deterministic* relationships. Dependent and independent variables are identified, a functional form is specified, and in most cases, at least a qualitative statement is made about effects that occur when independent variables in the model change. Of course, the model is only a simplification of reality. It will include the salient features of the relationship of interest, but will leave unaccounted for influences that might well be present but are, for our purposes, unimportant. Naturally, people may differ on just how minimal some influences really are, and in the end, this may be yet another empirical question. Still, only the most optimistic analyst would expect to find an exact correspondence between his or her model and its real-world counterpart.

No model could hope to encompass the myriad essentially random aspects of economic life. For example, no matter how elegant or complete a model of production might be, it has no way of coping with the possibility that a snowy day might necessitate a plant closing and show up as an outlier in an otherwise immaculately constructed body of data on production costs. It is thus necessary to incorporate stochastic elements in our empirical models. As a consequence, observations on the dependent variable will display variation attributable not only to differences in variables we have explicitly accounted for, but also to the randomness of human behavior and the interaction of countless minor influences that we have not. It is understood that the introduction of a random "disturbance" into a deterministic model is not intended merely to paper over its inadequacies. It is essential to examine the results of the study, in a sort of postmortem, to ensure that the allegedly random, unexplained factor is truly unexplainable. If it is not, the model is, in fact, inadequate. To pursue our example, ignoring (or being unaware of) a snowstorm is one thing; neglecting regional differences in the unit prices of the factors of production is quite another. Without such omissions, the stochastic element endows the model with its statistical properties. Observations on the variable(s) under study are thus taken to be the outcomes of a random process. With a sufficiently detailed stochastic structure and adequate data, our analysis will become a matter of deducing the properties of a probability distribution. The tools and methods of mathematical statistics will provide the operating principles.

A model (or theory) can never truly be confirmed unless it is made so broad as to include every possibility. But we may subject it to ever more rigorous scrutiny and, in the face of contradictory evidence, refute it. A deterministic theory will be invalidated by a single errant observation. The introduction of stochastic elements into the model changes it from an exact statement to a probabilistic description about expected outcomes and carries with it an important implication. Only a preponderance of contradictory evidence can convincingly invalidate the probabilistic model, and what constitutes a "preponderance of evidence" is a matter of interpretation. Thus, the probabilistic model is both less precise and, perhaps not necessarily to the good, more robust.

The role of theory in econometrics cannot be overstated. The belief that we may scrutinize a set of nonexperimental data and expect some complex truth to be revealed to us if we only spend enough time manipulating the numbers is hopelessly optimistic. In an experimental setting, we are free to choose the values of the stimuli and move them in whatever way we wish to elicit a change in the response variable. What remains is only to quantify the observed relationship. In the realm of economics, we are only passive observers of the economy. The notion of a controlled experiment is almost unheard of. At best, we can expect to sample observations from a large population and to assume that the conditions needed to employ our tools of statistical inference are met. Theory plays the role of organizer of the data. With no theoretical basis, the result of the exercise is most likely to be an ambiguous catalog of possibilities.

The process of econometric analysis departs from the specification of a theoretical relationship. We initially proceed on the optimistic assumption that we can obtain precise measurements on all the variables in our correctly specified model. If the ideal conditions are met at every step, the subsequent analysis will probably be routine. Unfortunately, they rarely are. Some of the difficulties one can expect to encounter are the following:

1. The data may be badly measured or may correspond only vaguely to the variables in the model. "The interest rate" is one example.
2. Some of the variables may be inherently unmeasurable. "Expectations" are a case in point.
3. The theory may make only a rough guess as to the correct functional form, if it makes any at all, and we may be forced to choose from an embarrassingly long menu of possibilities.
4. The assumed stochastic properties of the random terms in the model may be demonstrably violated. This may call into question the methods of estimation and inference procedures we have used.
5. Some relevant variables may be missing from the model.

The ensuing steps of the analysis consist of coping with these problems and attempting to cull whatever information is likely to be present in such obviously imperfect data. The methodology is that of mathematical statistics and econometric theory. The product is an econometric model.

1.3. THEORETICAL AND APPLIED ECONOMETRICS

A distinction is usually made between theoretical and applied econometrics. A rough line can be drawn between the development of techniques and the application of those techniques in a particular setting. Theorists also analyze the consequences of applying particular methods when the assumptions that justify them are not met. But the distinction is often artificial. It is common for new techniques to be developed in the field, in response to a particular problem in a specific study, rather than in the laboratory.[2] This book is oriented to techniques that are usable (and used) in the field. Still, the emphasis is on methods, rather than on specific results.[3] The numerous examples are presented to illustrate techniques rather than to produce new empirical evidence. In a few instances, we have attempted to replicate (sometimes without success) earlier studies, while in others we have repeated studies already in the literature with more recent data. The interested reader may wish to extend these studies with newer or different data sets.

1.4. PLAN OF THE BOOK

The remainder of this book is organized into four parts.

Chapters 2 through 5 survey the tools used in econometrics: Chapter 2 is on matrix algebra, Chapter 3 is on probability and distribution theory, and Chapter 4 is on statistical inference. Since it is assumed that the reader has some previous training in each of these topics, these summaries are fairly brief and are included primarily for those who desire a refresher or a convenient reference. We do not anticipate that these sections can substitute for a course in any of these subjects. The intent of these chapters is to provide a reasonably concise summary of the results, nearly all of which are explicitly used elsewhere in the book. Finally, Chapter 5 describes some of the background and techniques of computation in econometrics, including some of the technical aspects of nonlinear optimization. With the increased power of desktop computers, once highly sophisticated and exotic techniques are becoming routine. It is becoming ever more important for the applied econometrician to be familiar with some of the basic aspects of numerical analysis. Chapter 5 describes some of the aspects of computation in econometrics that form the mechanics of the modern technology of estimation and inference.

Chapters 6 through 11 present basic and some relatively advanced results for the classical linear and nonlinear regression models. Chapters 6 and 7 discuss the essentials of estimation and inference in the linear model. Most of the asymptotic theory used later in the book is presented in Chapter 6 as well. Chapter 8 discusses extensions of the classical model that show, among other things, that the linear model is not nearly so restrictive as its appearance might suggest. Chapter 9, on multicollinearity, measurement error, and missing data, raises some issues that impede the simple, mechanical application of the theo-

[2]In the abstract, there is an intellectual appeal to a technique that is developed to solve a particular problem, as opposed to one that is devised and then sent off to find a problem to solve.

[3]A number of excellent works are devoted to applied econometrics, among them Bridge (1971), Desai (1976), and Berndt (1990).

retical model to real-world data. Chapter 10 is devoted to nonlinear regression models.

From Chapter 11 onward, the restrictions of the classical model are progressively relaxed and the model itself is progressively extended. Chapter 11 presents some general theoretical results for the classical model. These principles are then used in two standard applications, heteroscedasticity in Chapter 12 and autocorrelation in Chapter 13. The combination of these two phenomena is treated in Chapter 14 in our discussion of panel data.

The remaining chapters survey more or less advanced topics in econometrics. (But, since most of the methods discussed there are, in fact, widely used by practitioners throughout the profession, perhaps *further* topics would be better than *advanced.*) Chapter 15 discusses the multivariate regression model and the estimation of systems of demand equations. Chapter 16 discusses simultaneous equations models. Interest in this topic is marked by an ebb and flow. Empirical applications of simultaneous equations models—for example, as envisioned by the Cowles Commission—have received progressively less emphasis and far less attention in the applied econometrics literature in recent years. Interestingly enough, theoretical research on the topic continues unabated and regularly produces important insights, which are often more useful in other frameworks. Chapters 17 and 18 present topics that are primarily the staples of empirical macroeconomics, time-series analysis, models with lagged variables, unit roots, VARs, and cointegration. Chapters 19 and 20 present three subjects that are more prevalent in microeconometrics, models with discrete dependent variables, limited dependent variable models, and models of duration.

CHAPTER 2

Matrix Algebra

2.1. INTRODUCTION

This chapter is the first of four devoted to mathematical and statistical tools used in econometrics. It presents most of the matrix results used in this book; the few additional results that become necessary later will be developed in passing. By using matrix algebra, the fundamental results in econometrics can be presented in an elegant, compact, and uncluttered format. But, more important, we find that many diverse and seemingly complex results have a common structure and a surprising simplicity. The set of theorems and techniques we require are collected here, in one place, so that later in the book we can use them without interrupting the discussion to derive them. For those students who have not used matrix algebra for a while (or have not yet encountered the subject), this chapter also provides a reasonably concise summary.[1]

2.2. SOME TERMINOLOGY

A **matrix** is a rectangular array of numbers, denoted

$$\mathbf{A} = [a_{ik}] = [\mathbf{A}]_{ik} = \begin{bmatrix} a_{11} & a_{12} & \cdots & a_{1K} \\ a_{21} & a_{22} & \cdots & a_{2K} \\ & & \vdots & \\ a_{n1} & a_{n2} & \cdots & a_{nK} \end{bmatrix}. \tag{2-1}$$

[1]For a more complete description of the topic, some sources to consider are Dhrymes (1974), Bellman (1970), Hadley (1961), Strang (1988), and for a large collection of useful results, Rao (1973).

TABLE 2.1 Matrix of Macroeconomic Data

	Column				
	1	*2*	*3*	*4*	*5*
Row	*Year*	*Consumption (billions of dollars)*	*GNP (billions of dollars)*	*GNP Deflator*	*Discount Rate (N.Y. Fed., avg.)*
1	1972	737.1	1185.9	1.0000	4.50
2	1973	812.0	1326.4	1.0575	6.44
3	1974	808.1	1434.2	1.1508	7.83
4	1975	976.4	1549.2	1.2579	6.25
5	1976	1084.3	1718.0	1.3234	5.50
6	1977	1204.4	1918.3	1.4005	5.46
7	1978	1346.5	2163.9	1.5042	7.46
8	1979	1507.2	2417.8	1.6342	10.28
9	1980	1667.2	2633.1	1.7864	11.77

Source: Data from the *Economic Report of the President*, U.S. Government Printing Office, Washington, D.C., 1983.

Note how the typical element is used to denote the matrix. A subscripted element of a matrix is always read as $a_{\text{row, column}}$. An example is given in Table 2.1. In these data, the rows are identified with years and the columns with particular variables.

A **vector** is an ordered set of numbers arranged either in a row or a column. In view of the preceding, a **row vector** is also a matrix with one row, whereas a **column vector** is a matrix with one column. Thus, the five variables observed for 1972 constitute a row vector, whereas the time series of values for consumption is a column vector.

A matrix can also be viewed as a set of column vectors, which would be a natural interpretation of the sample data set, or, of course, as a set of row vectors.[2] The **dimensions** of a matrix are the numbers of rows and columns it contains. "$\mathbf{A}$ is an $n \times K$ matrix" (read "n by K") will always mean that $\mathbf{A}$ has n rows and K columns. If n equals K, then $\mathbf{A}$ is a **square matrix.** Several particular types of square matrices occur frequently in econometrics.

- A **symmetric matrix, A**, is one in which $a_{ik} = a_{ki}$ for all i and k. For example,

$$\mathbf{A} = \begin{bmatrix} 1 & 3 & 7 \\ 3 & 5 & 2 \\ 7 & 2 & 1 \end{bmatrix}.$$

[2]Henceforth, we shall denote a matrix by a boldfaced capital letter, as with **A** in (2-1), and a vector as a boldfaced lowercase letter, as in **a**. Unless otherwise noted, a vector will always be assumed to be a *column vector.*

- A **diagonal matrix** is a square matrix whose only nonzero elements appear on the main diagonal, moving from upper left to lower right.
- A **scalar matrix** is a diagonal matrix with the same value in all diagonal elements.
- An **identity matrix** is a scalar matrix with ones on the diagonal. This is always denoted **I**. A subscript is sometimes included to indicate its size, or **order.** For example,

$$\mathbf{I}_3 = \begin{bmatrix} 1 & 0 & 0 \\ 0 & 1 & 0 \\ 0 & 0 & 1 \end{bmatrix}. \qquad \textbf{(2-2)}$$

- A **triangular matrix** is one that has only zeros either above or below the main diagonal. If the zeros are above the diagonal, the matrix is lower triangular.

2.3. ALGEBRAIC MANIPULATION OF MATRICES

Matrices provide a convenient way of collecting sets of equations and equations involving sums of values. This section outlines some basic arithmetic operations of matrix algebra.

2.3.1. Equality of Matrices

Matrices (or vectors) **A** and **B** are equal if and only if they have the same dimensions and each element of **A** equals the corresponding element of **B**.

$$\mathbf{A} = \mathbf{B} \text{ if and only if } a_{ik} = b_{ik} \text{ for all } i \text{ and } k.$$

2.3.2. Transposition

The **transpose** of a matrix **A**, denoted **A′**, is obtained by creating the matrix whose kth row is the kth column of the original matrix. Thus, if **B** = **A′**, each column of **A** will appear as the corresponding row of **B**. If **A** is $n \times K$, **A′** is $K \times n$. For example,

$$\mathbf{A} = \begin{bmatrix} 1 & 2 & 3 \\ 5 & 1 & 5 \\ 6 & 4 & 5 \\ 3 & 1 & 4 \end{bmatrix}, \qquad \mathbf{A}' = \begin{bmatrix} 1 & 5 & 6 & 3 \\ 2 & 1 & 4 & 1 \\ 3 & 5 & 5 & 4 \end{bmatrix}.$$

An equivalent definition of the transpose of a matrix is

$$\mathbf{B} = \mathbf{A}' \Leftrightarrow b_{ik} = a_{ki} \quad \text{for all } i \text{ and } k \qquad \textbf{(2-3)}$$

The definition of a symmetric matrix implies that

$$\text{if } \mathbf{A} \text{ is symmetric, } \mathbf{A} = \mathbf{A}'. \qquad \textbf{(2-4)}$$

For any **A**,

$$(\mathbf{A}')' = \mathbf{A}. \qquad \textbf{(2-5)}$$

Finally, the transpose of a column vector, **a**, is a row vector:

$$\mathbf{a}' = [a_1 \quad a_2 \quad \cdots \quad a_n].$$

2.3.3. Matrix Addition

The operation of addition is extended to matrices by defining

$$\mathbf{C} = \mathbf{A} + \mathbf{B} = [a_{ik} + b_{ik}]. \tag{2-6}$$

Matrices cannot be added unless they have the same dimensions, in which case they are said to be **conformable for addition.** A **zero matrix** or **null matrix** is one whose elements are all zero. In the addition of matrices, the zero matrix plays the same role as the scalar 0 in scalar addition; that is,

$$\mathbf{A} + \mathbf{0} = \mathbf{A}. \tag{2-7}$$

We also extend the operation of subtraction to matrices precisely as if they were scalars by performing the operation element by element. Thus,

$$\mathbf{A} - \mathbf{B} = [a_{ik} - b_{ik}]. \tag{2-8}$$

It follows that matrix addition is commutative,

$$\mathbf{A} + \mathbf{B} = \mathbf{B} + \mathbf{A}, \tag{2-9}$$

and associative,

$$(\mathbf{A} + \mathbf{B}) + \mathbf{C} = \mathbf{A} + (\mathbf{B} + \mathbf{C}), \tag{2-10}$$

and that

$$(\mathbf{A} + \mathbf{B})' = \mathbf{A}' + \mathbf{B}'. \tag{2-11}$$

2.3.4. Matrix Multiplication

Matrices are multiplied by using the **inner product.** The inner product (or **dot product**) of two vectors, **a** and **b**, is a scalar and is written

$$\mathbf{a}'\mathbf{b} = a_1 b_1 + a_2 b_2 + \cdots + a_n b_n. \tag{2-12}$$

Note that the inner product is written as the transpose of vector **a** times vector **b**, a row vector times a column vector. For example,

$$\mathbf{a}'\mathbf{b} = [1 \quad 3 \quad 4] \begin{bmatrix} 3 \\ 8 \\ 2 \end{bmatrix} = 1(3) + 3(8) + 4(2) = 35.$$

In (2-12), each term $a_j b_j$ equals $b_j a_j$; hence

$$\mathbf{a}'\mathbf{b} = \mathbf{b}'\mathbf{a}. \tag{2-13}$$

For an $n \times K$ matrix **A** and a $K \times T$ matrix **B**, the product matrix,

$$\mathbf{C} = \mathbf{AB}, \tag{2-14}$$

is an $n \times T$ matrix whose ikth element is the inner product of row i of $\mathbf{A}$ and column k of $\mathbf{B}$. We need a notation for the ith row of a matrix. In nearly all of what follows, we will use $\mathbf{a}_i$ to denote the ith column. To avoid confusion, we will use $\mathbf{a}^i$ to denote the ith row of $\mathbf{A}$. Thus,

$$\mathbf{C} = \mathbf{AB} \Rightarrow c_{ik} = \mathbf{a}^i\mathbf{b}_k. \qquad \textbf{(2-15)}$$

To multiply two matrices, the number of columns in the first must be the same as the number of rows in the second, in which case, they are **conformable for multiplication.**[3] For example,

$$\begin{aligned}\mathbf{AB} &= \begin{bmatrix} 1 & 3 & 2 \\ 4 & 5 & -1 \end{bmatrix}\begin{bmatrix} 2 & 4 \\ 1 & 6 \\ 0 & 5 \end{bmatrix} \\ &= \begin{bmatrix} 1(2) + 3(1) + 2(0) & 1(4) + 3(6) + 2(5) \\ 4(2) + 5(1) + (-1)(0) & 4(4) + 5(6) + (-1)(5) \end{bmatrix} \\ &= \begin{bmatrix} 5 & 32 \\ 13 & 41 \end{bmatrix}.\end{aligned}$$

Multiplication of matrices is generally not commutative. For example, in the preceding calculation, $\mathbf{AB}$ is a 2×2 matrix, whereas

$$\begin{aligned}\mathbf{BA} &= \begin{bmatrix} 2(1) + 4(4) & 2(3) + 4(5) & 2(2) + 4(-1) \\ 1(1) + 6(4) & 1(3) + 6(5) & 1(2) + 6(-1) \\ 0(1) + 5(4) & 0(3) + 5(5) & 0(2) + 5(-1) \end{bmatrix} \\ &= \begin{bmatrix} 18 & 26 & 0 \\ 25 & 33 & -4 \\ 20 & 25 & -5 \end{bmatrix}.\end{aligned}$$

In other cases, $\mathbf{AB}$ may exist, but $\mathbf{BA}$ may be undefined or, if it does exist, may have different dimensions, as in the preceding example. In general, however, even if $\mathbf{AB}$ and $\mathbf{BA}$ do have the same dimensions, they will not be equal. In view of this, we define **premultiplication** and **postmultiplication** of matrices. In the product $\mathbf{AB}$, $\mathbf{B}$ is *premultiplied* by $\mathbf{A}$, while $\mathbf{A}$ is *postmultiplied* by $\mathbf{B}$.

The product of a matrix and a vector is written

$$\mathbf{c} = \mathbf{Ab}.$$

The number of elements in $\mathbf{b}$ must equal the number of columns in $\mathbf{A}$; the result is a vector with a number of elements equal to the number of rows in $\mathbf{A}$. For example,

$$\begin{bmatrix} 5 \\ 4 \\ 1 \end{bmatrix} = \begin{bmatrix} 4 & 2 & 1 \\ 2 & 6 & 1 \\ 1 & 1 & 0 \end{bmatrix}\begin{bmatrix} a \\ b \\ c \end{bmatrix}.$$

---

[3]A simple way to check the conformability of two matrices for multiplication is to write down the dimensions of the operation, for example, $(n \times K)$ times $(K \times T)$. The inner dimensions must be equal; the result has dimensions equal to the outer values.

We can interpret this in two ways. First, it is a compact way of writing the three equations

$$\begin{aligned} 5 &= 4a + 2b + 1c, \\ 4 &= 2a + 6b + 1c, \\ 1 &= 1a + 1b + 0c. \end{aligned}$$

Second, by writing the set of equations as

$$\begin{bmatrix} 5 \\ 4 \\ 1 \end{bmatrix} = a\begin{bmatrix} 4 \\ 2 \\ 1 \end{bmatrix} + b\begin{bmatrix} 2 \\ 6 \\ 1 \end{bmatrix} + c\begin{bmatrix} 1 \\ 1 \\ 0 \end{bmatrix},$$

we see that the right-hand side is a **linear combination** of the columns of the matrix where the coefficients are the elements of the vector. For the general case,

$$\begin{aligned} \mathbf{c} &= \mathbf{Ab} \\ &= b_1\mathbf{a}_1 + b_2\mathbf{a}_2 + \cdots + b_K\mathbf{a}_K. \end{aligned} \tag{2-16}$$

In the calculation of a matrix product $\mathbf{C} = \mathbf{AB}$, each column of $\mathbf{C}$ is a linear combination of the columns of $\mathbf{A}$, where the coefficients are the elements in the corresponding column of $\mathbf{B}$. That is,

$$\mathbf{C} = \mathbf{AB} \Leftrightarrow \mathbf{c}_k = \mathbf{Ab}_k. \tag{2-17}$$

Let $\mathbf{e}_k$ be a column vector that has 0s everywhere except for a 1 in the kth position. Then $\mathbf{Ae}_k$ is a linear combination of the columns of $\mathbf{A}$ in which the coefficient on every column but the kth is 0, whereas that on the kth is 1. The result is

$$\mathbf{a}_k = \mathbf{Ae}_k. \tag{2-18}$$

Combining this result with (2-17) produces

$$\begin{aligned} (\mathbf{a}_1 \quad \mathbf{a}_2 \quad \cdots \quad \mathbf{a}_n) &= \mathbf{A}(\mathbf{e}_1 \quad \mathbf{e}_2 \quad \cdots \quad \mathbf{e}_n) \\ &= \mathbf{A}\begin{bmatrix} 1 & 0 & 0 & \cdots & 0 \\ 0 & 1 & 0 & \cdots & 0 \\ & & \vdots & & \\ 0 & 0 & 0 & \cdots & 1 \end{bmatrix} \\ &= \mathbf{AI} = \mathbf{A}. \end{aligned} \tag{2-19}$$

In matrix multiplication, the identity matrix is analogous to the scalar 1. For any matrix or vector $\mathbf{A}$, $\mathbf{AI} = \mathbf{A}$. In addition, $\mathbf{IA} = \mathbf{A}$, although if $\mathbf{A}$ is not a square matrix, the two identity matrices are of different orders.

A conformable matrix of zeros produces the expected result: $\mathbf{A0} = \mathbf{0}$.

Some general rules for matrix multiplication are as follows:

- **Associative law:** $(\mathbf{AB})\mathbf{C} = \mathbf{A}(\mathbf{BC})$. **(2-20)**
- **Distributive law:** $\mathbf{A}(\mathbf{B} + \mathbf{C}) = \mathbf{AB} + \mathbf{AC}$. **(2-21)**

(Note the order of multiplication of the matrices in the second rule: **BA** and **CA** may not be defined.)

- **Transpose of a product:** $(\mathbf{AB})' = \mathbf{B}'\mathbf{A}'.$ **(2-22)**

By direct extension,

$$(\mathbf{ABC})' = \mathbf{C}'\mathbf{B}'\mathbf{A}'. \quad \textbf{(2-23)}$$

Finally, **scalar multiplication** of a matrix is the operation of multiplying every element of the matrix by a given scalar. For scalar c and matrix $\mathbf{A}$,

$$c\mathbf{A} = [ca_{ik}]. \quad \textbf{(2-24)}$$

Note how this operation is used in (2-16).

2.3.5. Sums of Values

Matrices and vectors provide a particularly convenient way to represent sums of values. A useful device is the vector $\mathbf{i}$, which contains a column of 1s. The sum of the elements in any vector $\mathbf{x}$ is

$$\sum_{i=1}^{n} x_i = x_1 + x_2 + \cdots + x_n = \mathbf{i}'\mathbf{x}. \quad \textbf{(2-25)}$$

If all elements in $\mathbf{x}$ are equal to the same constant a, then $\mathbf{x} = a\mathbf{i}$ and

$$\sum_{i=1}^{n} x_i = \mathbf{i}'(a\mathbf{i}) = a(\mathbf{i}'\mathbf{i}) = na. \quad \textbf{(2-26)}$$

For any constant a and vector $\mathbf{x}$,

$$\sum_{i=1}^{n} ax_i = a\sum_{i=1}^{n} x_i = a\mathbf{i}'\mathbf{x}. \quad \textbf{(2-27)}$$

If $a = 1/n$, we obtain the arithmetic mean

$$\bar{x} = \frac{1}{n}\sum_{i=1}^{n} x_i = \frac{1}{n}\mathbf{i}'\mathbf{x}, \quad \textbf{(2-28)}$$

from which it follows that

$$\sum_{i=1}^{n} x_i = \mathbf{i}'\mathbf{x} = n\bar{x}.$$

Sums of squares and cross products are obtained easily with the inner product operation. The sum of squares of the elements in a vector $\mathbf{x}$ is

$$\sum_{i=1}^{n} x_i^2 = \mathbf{x}'\mathbf{x}; \quad \textbf{(2-29)}$$

the sum of the products of the elements in vectors **x** and **y** is

$$\sum_{i=1}^{n} x_i y_i = \mathbf{x}'\mathbf{y}. \tag{2-30}$$

By the definition of matrix multiplication,

$$[\mathbf{X}'\mathbf{X}]_{ij} = [\mathbf{x}_i'\mathbf{x}_j] \tag{2-31}$$

is the inner product of the ith and jth columns of **X**. Thus, for example, for the data set given in Table 2.1, if we define **X** as the 9×3 matrix containing (year, consumption, GNP), then

$$\begin{aligned}[\mathbf{X}'\mathbf{X}]_{23} &= \sum_{i=1}^{9} \text{consumption}_i \text{GNP}_i \\ &= 737.1(1185.9) + \cdots + 1667.2(2633.1) = 19{,}743{,}711.34.\end{aligned}$$

If **X** is $n \times K$,

$$\mathbf{X}'\mathbf{X} = \sum_{i=1}^{n} \mathbf{x}^{i\prime}\mathbf{x}^{i},$$

where $\mathbf{x}^{i\prime}$ is the transpose of the ith row of **X**. This form shows that the $K \times K$ matrix $\mathbf{X}'\mathbf{X}$ is the sum of n $K \times K$ matrices, each formed from a single row (year) of **X**. For the example given earlier, this is the sum of nine 3×3 matrices, each formed from one row (year) of the original data matrix. Suppose that $\mathbf{X}'\mathbf{X}$ for the nine years of data was already in hand, and a tenth year of data was obtained. The matrix of sums of squares and cross products can be updated just by adding a 3×3 matrix to the $\mathbf{X}'\mathbf{X}$ already computed. When there is no ambiguity or when it is obvious from the context, we often write products such as the one above as

$$\mathbf{X}'\mathbf{X} = \sum_{i=1}^{n} \mathbf{x}_i\mathbf{x}_i',$$

where $\mathbf{x}_i$ is now a column vector that is the transpose of the ith row of **X**.

2.3.6. A Useful Idempotent Matrix

A fundamental matrix in statistics is the one that is used to transform data to deviations from their mean. First,

$$\begin{aligned}\mathbf{i}\overline{x} &= \mathbf{i}\frac{1}{n}\mathbf{i}'\mathbf{x} \\ &= \begin{bmatrix} \overline{x} \\ \overline{x} \\ \vdots \\ \overline{x} \end{bmatrix} = \frac{1}{n}\mathbf{i}\mathbf{i}'\mathbf{x}.\end{aligned} \tag{2-32}$$

The matrix $(1/n)\mathbf{ii}'$ is an $n \times n$ matrix with every element equal to $1/n$. The set of values in deviations form is thus

$$\begin{bmatrix} x_1 - \bar{x} \\ x_2 - \bar{x} \\ \vdots \\ x_n - \bar{x} \end{bmatrix} = [\mathbf{x} - \mathbf{i}\bar{x}] = \left[\mathbf{x} - \frac{1}{n}\mathbf{ii}'\mathbf{x}\right]. \tag{2-33}$$

Since $\mathbf{x} = \mathbf{Ix}$,

$$\begin{aligned} \left[\mathbf{x} - \frac{1}{n}\mathbf{ii}'\mathbf{x}\right] &= \left[\mathbf{Ix} - \frac{1}{n}\mathbf{ii}'\mathbf{x}\right] \\ &= \left[\mathbf{I} - \frac{1}{n}\mathbf{ii}'\right]\mathbf{x} \\ &= \mathbf{M}^0\mathbf{x}. \end{aligned} \tag{2-34}$$

Henceforth, the symbol $\mathbf{M}^0$ will be used only for this matrix. Its diagonal elements are all $(1 - 1/n)$, and its off-diagonal elements are $-1/n$.

The matrix $\mathbf{M}^0$ is primarily useful in computing sums of squared deviations. Some computations are simplified by the result

$$\begin{aligned} \mathbf{M}^0\mathbf{i} &= \left[\mathbf{I} - \frac{1}{n}\mathbf{ii}'\right]\mathbf{i} \\ &= \mathbf{i} - \frac{1}{n}\mathbf{i}(\mathbf{i}'\mathbf{i}) \\ &= \mathbf{0}. \end{aligned}$$

This implies that $\mathbf{i}'\mathbf{M}^0 = \mathbf{0}'$. The sum of deviations about the mean is then

$$\sum_{i=1}^{n}(x_i - \bar{x}) = \mathbf{i}'[\mathbf{M}^0\mathbf{x}] = \mathbf{0}'\mathbf{x} = 0. \tag{2-35}$$

For a single variable $\mathbf{x}$, the sum of squared deviations about the mean is

$$\begin{aligned} \sum_{i=1}^{n}(x_i - \bar{x})^2 &= \sum_{i=1}^{n}(x_i^2 - 2\bar{x}x_i + \bar{x}^2) \\ &= \left(\sum_{i=1}^{n}x_i^2\right) - n\bar{x}^2. \end{aligned} \tag{2-36}$$

In matrix terms,

$$\begin{aligned} \sum_{i-l}^{n}(x_i - \bar{x})^2 &= (\mathbf{x} - \bar{x}\,\mathbf{i})'(\mathbf{x} - \bar{x}\,\mathbf{i}) \\ &= (\mathbf{M}^0\mathbf{x})'(\mathbf{M}^0\mathbf{x}) \\ &= \mathbf{x}'\mathbf{M}^{0\prime}\mathbf{M}^0\mathbf{x}. \end{aligned}$$

Two properties of $\mathbf{M}^0$ are useful at this point. First, since all off-diagonal elements of $\mathbf{M}^0$ equal $-1/n$, $\mathbf{M}^0$ is symmetric. Second, as can easily be verified by multiplication, $\mathbf{M}^0$ is equal to its square; $\mathbf{M}^0\mathbf{M}^0 = \mathbf{M}^0$.

DEFINITION 2.1: Idempotent Matrix. *An **idempotent** matrix is one that is equal to its square, that is,* $\mathbf{M}^2 = \mathbf{MM} = \mathbf{M}$. *If* $\mathbf{M}$ *is a symmetric idempotent matrix (most of the idempotent matrices we shall encounter are), then* $\mathbf{M}'\mathbf{M} = \mathbf{M}$.

Thus, $\mathbf{M}^0$ is an idempotent matrix. Combining results, we obtain

$$\sum_{i=1}^{n}(x_i - \bar{x})^2 = \mathbf{x}'\mathbf{M}^0\mathbf{x}. \qquad \textbf{(2-37)}$$

Consider constructing a matrix of sums of squares and cross products in deviations from the column means. For two vectors $\mathbf{x}$ and $\mathbf{y}$,

$$\sum_{i=1}^{n}(x_i - \bar{x})(y_i - \bar{y}) = (\mathbf{M}^0\mathbf{x})'(\mathbf{M}^0\mathbf{y}), \qquad \textbf{(2-38)}$$

so

$$\begin{bmatrix} \sum_{i=1}^{n}(x_i - \bar{x})^2 & \sum_{i=1}^{n}(x_i - \bar{x})(y_i - \bar{y}) \\ \sum_{i=1}^{n}(y_i - \bar{y})(x_i - \bar{x}) & \sum_{i=1}^{n}(y_i - \bar{y})^2 \end{bmatrix} = \begin{bmatrix} \mathbf{x}'\mathbf{M}^0\mathbf{x} & \mathbf{x}'\mathbf{M}^0\mathbf{y} \\ \mathbf{y}'\mathbf{M}^0\mathbf{x} & \mathbf{y}'\mathbf{M}^0\mathbf{y} \end{bmatrix}. \qquad \textbf{(2-39)}$$

If we put the two column vectors $\mathbf{x}$ and $\mathbf{y}$ in an $n \times 2$ matrix $\mathbf{Z} = [\mathbf{x}, \mathbf{y}]$, then $\mathbf{M}^0\mathbf{Z}$ is the $n \times 2$ matrix in which the two columns of data are in mean deviation form. Then

$$(\mathbf{M}^0\mathbf{Z})'(\mathbf{M}^0\mathbf{Z}) = \mathbf{Z}'\mathbf{M}^0\mathbf{M}^0\mathbf{Z} = \mathbf{Z}'\mathbf{M}^0\mathbf{Z}.$$

2.4. GEOMETRY OF MATRICES

Matrix algebra is extremely useful in the formulation and solution of sets of linear equations. At the same time, the algebraic results have a geometrical basis that is very helpful in understanding the calculations. Before developing the mathematical results, it is useful to digress to a geometric treatment of matrices and vectors.

2.4.1. Vector Spaces

The K elements of a column vector

$$\mathbf{a} = \begin{bmatrix} a_1 \\ a_2 \\ \vdots \\ a_K \end{bmatrix}$$

can be viewed as the coordinates of a point in a K-dimensional space, as shown in Figure 2.1 for two dimensions, or as the definition of the line segment connecting the origin and this point.

Two basic operations are defined for vectors, **scalar multiplication** and **addition.** A scalar multiple of a vector, **a**, is another vector, say **a***, whose coordinates are the scalar multiple of **a**'s coordinates. Thus, in Figure 2.1,

$$\mathbf{a} = \begin{bmatrix} 1 \\ 2 \end{bmatrix}, \qquad \mathbf{a}^* = 2\mathbf{a} = \begin{bmatrix} 2 \\ 4 \end{bmatrix}, \qquad \mathbf{a}^{**} = -\frac{1}{2}\mathbf{a} = \begin{bmatrix} -\frac{1}{2} \\ -1 \end{bmatrix}.$$

The set of all possible scalar multiples of **a** is the line through **0** and **a**. Any scalar multiple of **a** is a segment of this line. The sum of two vectors **a** and **b** is a third vector whose coordinates are the sums of the corresponding coordinates of **a** and **b**. For example,

$$\mathbf{c} = \mathbf{a} + \mathbf{b} = \begin{bmatrix} 1 \\ 2 \end{bmatrix} + \begin{bmatrix} 2 \\ 1 \end{bmatrix} = \begin{bmatrix} 3 \\ 3 \end{bmatrix}.$$

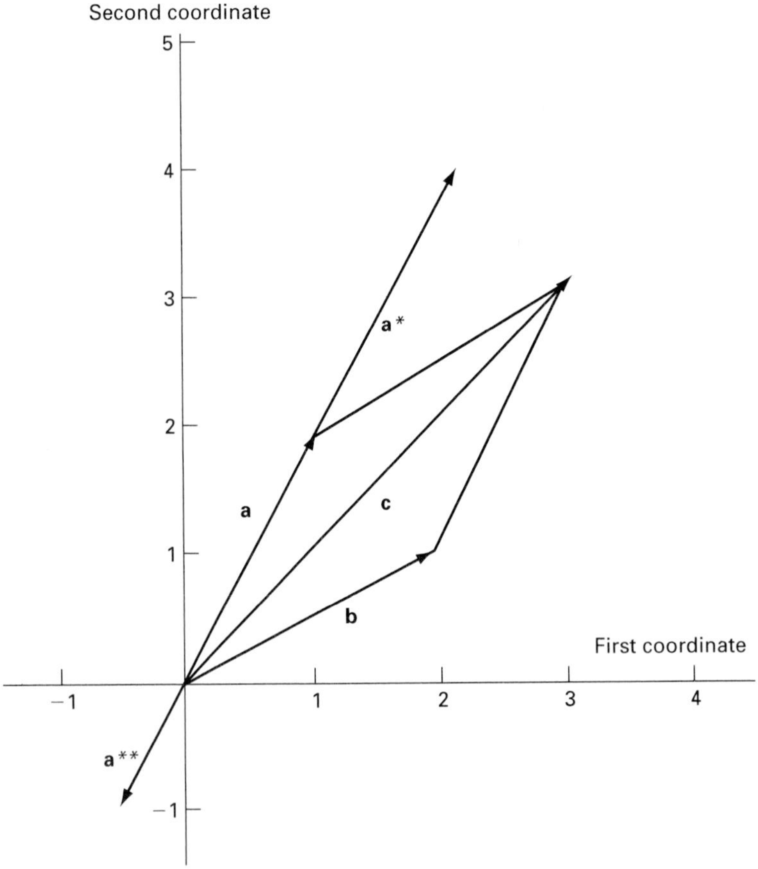

FIGURE 2.1 Vector Space.

Geometrically, **c** is obtained by moving in the distance and direction defined by **b** from the tip of **a** or, because addition is commutative, from the tip of **b** in the distance and direction of **a**. This is a geometric interpretation of the operations of scalar multiplication and addition of matrices applied to vectors.

The two-dimensional plane is the set of all vectors with two real-valued coordinates. We label this set $\mathbf{R}^2$. It has two important properties.

- $\mathbf{R}^2$ *is closed under scalar multiplication;* every scalar multiple of a vector in the plane is also in the plane.
- $\mathbf{R}^2$ *is closed under addition;* the sum of any two vectors in the plane is always a vector in the plane.

DEFINITION 2.2: Vector Space. *A **vector space** is any set of vectors that is closed under scalar multiplication and addition.*

Another example is the set of all real numbers, that is $\mathbf{R}^1$, the set of vectors with one real element. In general, that set of K-element vectors all of whose elements are real numbers is a K-dimensional vector space, denoted $\mathbf{R}^K$. The preceding examples are drawn in $\mathbf{R}^2$.[4]

2.4.2. Linear Combinations of Vectors and Basis Vectors

In Figure 2.2, $\mathbf{c} = \mathbf{a} + \mathbf{b}$ and $\mathbf{d} = \mathbf{a}^* + \mathbf{b}$. But since $\mathbf{a}^* = 2\mathbf{a}$, $\mathbf{d} = 2\mathbf{a} + \mathbf{b}$. Also, $\mathbf{e} = \mathbf{a} + 2\mathbf{b}$ and $\mathbf{f} = \mathbf{b} + (-\mathbf{a}) = \mathbf{b} - \mathbf{a}$. As this exercise suggests, any vector in $\mathbf{R}^2$ could be obtained as a **linear combination** of **a** and **b**.

DEFINITION 2.3: Basis Vectors. *A set of vectors in a vector space is a **basis** for that vector space if any vector in the vector space can be written as a linear combination of them.*

As is clear from Figure 2.2, any pair of two-element vectors, including **a** and **b**, that point in different directions will form a basis for $\mathbf{R}^2$. Consider an arbitrary set of vectors in $\mathbf{R}^2$, **a**, **b**, and **c**. If **a** and **b** are a basis, we can find numbers α_1 and α_2 such that $\mathbf{c} = \alpha_1\mathbf{a} + \alpha_2\mathbf{b}$. Let

$$\mathbf{a} = \begin{bmatrix} a_1 \\ a_2 \end{bmatrix}, \quad \mathbf{b} = \begin{bmatrix} b_1 \\ b_2 \end{bmatrix}, \quad \mathbf{c} = \begin{bmatrix} c_1 \\ c_2 \end{bmatrix}.$$

Then

$$\begin{aligned} c_1 &= \alpha_1 a_1 + \alpha_2 b_1, \\ c_2 &= \alpha_1 a_2 + \alpha_2 b_2. \end{aligned} \qquad \textbf{(2-40)}$$

[4] The definition extends to $\mathbf{C}^K$, the set of vectors whose elements are complex pairs. We shall not require complex vectors in this book.

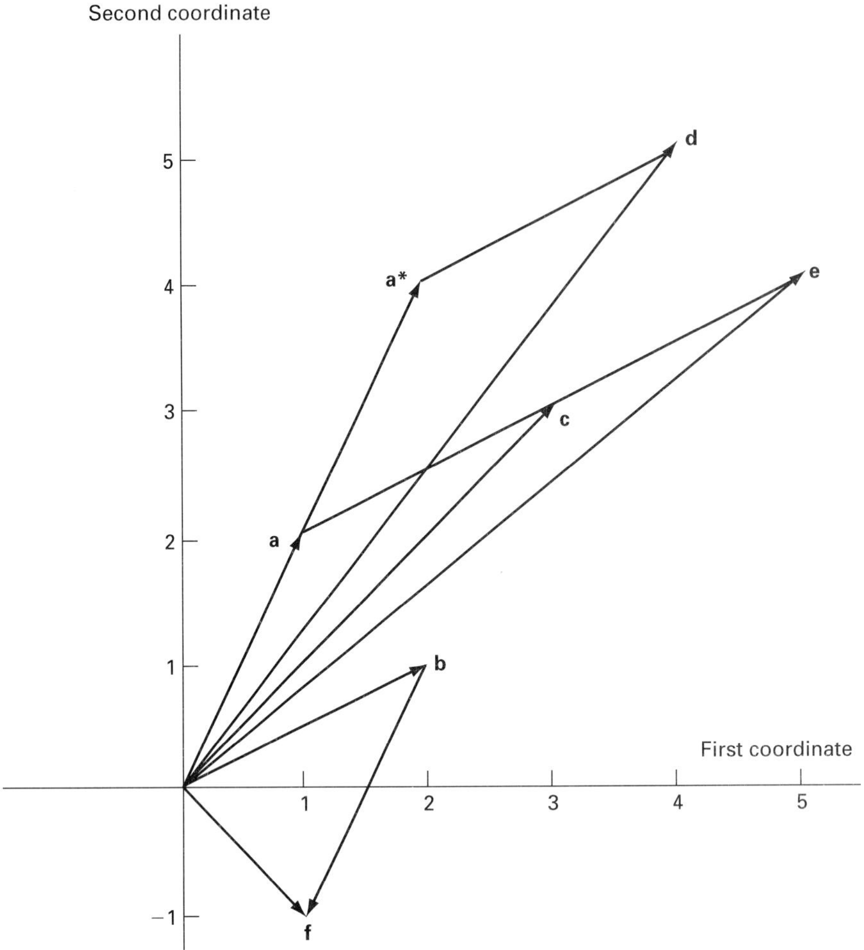

FIGURE 2.2 Linear Combinations of Vectors.

The solutions to this pair of equations are

$$\alpha_1 = \frac{b_2c_1 - b_1c_2}{a_1b_2 - b_1a_2}, \qquad \alpha_2 = \frac{a_1c_2 - a_2c_1}{a_1b_2 - b_1a_2}. \tag{2-41}$$

This gives a unique solution unless $(a_1b_2 - b_1a_2) = 0$. If $(a_1b_2 - b_1a_2) = 0$, then $a_1/a_2 = b_1/b_2$, which means that **b** is just a multiple of **a**. This returns us to our original condition, that **a** and **b** point in different directions. The implication is that if **a** and **b** are any pair of vectors for which the denominator in (2-41) is not zero, then any other vector **c** can be formed as a *unique* linear combination of **a** and **b**. The basis of a vector space is not unique, since any set of vectors that satisfies the definition will do. But for any particular basis, only one linear combination of them will produce another particular vector in the vector space.

2.4.3. Linear Dependence

As the preceding should suggest, K vectors are required to form a basis for $\mathbf{R}^K$. Although the basis for a vector space is not unique, not every set of K vectors will suffice. In Figure 2.2, **a** and **b** form a basis for $\mathbf{R}^2$, but **a** and **a*** do not. The difference between these two pairs is that **a** and **b** are linearly independent, whereas **a** and **a*** are linearly dependent.

DEFINITION 2.4: Linear Dependence. *A set of vectors is* ***linearly dependent*** *if any one of the vectors in the set can be written as a linear combination of the others.*

Since **a*** is a multiple of **a**, **a** and **a*** are linearly dependent. For another example, if

$$\mathbf{a} = \begin{bmatrix} 1 \\ 2 \end{bmatrix}, \quad \mathbf{b} = \begin{bmatrix} 3 \\ 3 \end{bmatrix}, \quad \mathbf{c} = \begin{bmatrix} 10 \\ 14 \end{bmatrix},$$

then

$$2\mathbf{a} + \mathbf{b} - \frac{1}{2}\mathbf{c} = \mathbf{0},$$

so **a**, **b**, and **c** are linearly dependent. Any of the three possible pairs of them, however, are linearly independent.

DEFINITION 2.5: Linear Independence. *A set of vectors is* ***linearly independent*** *if and only if the only solution to*

$$\alpha_1\mathbf{a}_1 + \alpha_2\mathbf{a}_2 + \cdots + \alpha_K\mathbf{a}_K = \mathbf{0}$$

is

$$\alpha_1 = \alpha_2 = \cdots = \alpha_K = 0.$$

The preceding implies the following equivalent definition of a basis.

DEFINITION 2.6: Basis for a Vector Space. *A basis for a vector space of K dimensions is any set of K linearly independent vectors in that space.*

Since any $(K + 1)$st vector can be written as a linear combination of the K basis vectors, it follows that any set of more than K vectors in $\mathbf{R}^K$ must be linearly dependent.

2.4.4. Subspaces

DEFINITION 2.7: Spanning Vectors. *The set of all linear combinations of a set of vectors is the vector space that is* ***spanned*** *by those vectors.*

For example, by definition, the space spanned by a basis for $\mathbf{R}^K$ is $\mathbf{R}^K$. An implication of this is that if **a** and **b** are a basis for $\mathbf{R}^2$ and **c** is another vector in $\mathbf{R}^2$, the space spanned by [**a, b, c**] is, again, $\mathbf{R}^2$. Of course, **c** is superfluous. Nonetheless, any vector in $\mathbf{R}^2$ can be expressed as a linear combination of **a**, **b**, and **c**. (The linear combination will not be unique. Suppose, for example, that **a** and **c** are also a basis for $\mathbf{R}^2$.)

Consider the set of three coordinate vectors whose third element is zero. In particular,

$$\mathbf{a}' = [a_1\ a_2 0] \quad \text{and} \quad \mathbf{b}' = [b_1\ b_2 0].$$

Vectors **a** and **b** do not span the three-dimensional space $\mathbf{R}^3$. Every linear combination of **a** and **b** has a third coordinate equal to zero; thus, for instance, $\mathbf{c}' = [1 \quad 2 \quad 3]$ could not be written as a linear combination of **a** and **b**. If $(a_1 b_2 - a_2 b_1)$ is not equal to zero [see (2-41)], however, then *any vector whose third element is zero can be expressed as a linear combination of* **a** *and* **b**. So, although **a** and **b** do not span $\mathbf{R}^3$, they do span something, the set of vectors in $\mathbf{R}^3$ whose third element is zero. This is a plane (the "floor" of the box in a three-dimensional figure). This plane in $\mathbf{R}^3$ is a **subspace,** in this instance, a two-dimensional subspace. Note that *it is not* $\mathbf{R}^2$; it is the set of vectors in $\mathbf{R}^3$ whose third coordinate is 0. Any plane in $\mathbf{R}^3$, regardless of how it is oriented, forms a two-dimensional subspace. Any two independent vectors that lie in that subspace will span it. But without a third vector that points in some other direction, we cannot span any more of $\mathbf{R}^3$ than this two-dimensional part of it. By the same logic, any line in $\mathbf{R}^3$ is a one-dimensional subspace, in this case, the set of all vectors in $\mathbf{R}^3$ whose coordinates are multiples of those of the vector that define the line. A subspace is a vector space in all the respects in which we have defined it. We emphasize that it is *not* a vector space of lower dimension. For example, $\mathbf{R}^2$ is not a subspace of $\mathbf{R}^3$. The essential difference is the number of dimensions in the vectors. The vectors in $\mathbf{R}^3$ that form a two-dimensional subspace are still three-element vectors; they all just happen to lie in the same plane.

The space spanned by a set of vectors in $\mathbf{R}^K$ has at most K dimensions. If this space has fewer than K dimensions, it is a subspace, or **hyperplane.** But the important point in the preceding discussion is that *every set of vectors spans some space;* it may be the entire space in which the vectors reside, or it may be some subspace of it.

2.4.5. Rank of a Matrix

We view a matrix as a set of column vectors. The number of columns in the matrix equals the number of vectors in the set, and the number of rows equals the number of coordinates in each column vector.

DEFINITION 2.8: Column Space. *The* ***column space*** *of a matrix is the vector space that is spanned by its column vectors.*

If the matrix contains K rows, its column space might have K dimensions. But, as we have seen, it might have fewer dimensions; the column vectors might be linearly dependent, or there might be fewer than K of them. Consider the matrix

$$\mathbf{A} = \begin{bmatrix} 1 & 5 & 6 \\ 2 & 6 & 8 \\ 7 & 1 & 8 \end{bmatrix}.$$

It contains three vectors from $\mathbf{R}^3$, but the third is the sum of the first two, so the column space of this matrix cannot have three dimensions. Nor does it have only one, since the three columns are not all scalar multiples of one another. Hence it has two, and the column space of this matrix is a two-dimensional subspace of $\mathbf{R}^3$.

DEFINITION 2.9: Column Rank. *The* ***column rank*** *of a matrix is the dimension of the vector space that is spanned by its columns.*

It follows that the column rank of a matrix is equal to the largest number of linearly independent column vectors it contains. The column rank of $\mathbf{A}$ is 2. For another specific example, consider

$$\mathbf{B} = \begin{bmatrix} 1 & 2 & 3 \\ 5 & 1 & 5 \\ 6 & 4 & 5 \\ 3 & 1 & 4 \end{bmatrix}.$$

It can be shown (we shall see how later) that this matrix has a column rank equal to 3. Since each column of $\mathbf{B}$ is a vector in $\mathbf{R}^4$, the column space of $\mathbf{B}$ is a three-dimensional subspace of $\mathbf{R}^4$.

Consider, instead, the set of vectors obtained by using the *rows* of $\mathbf{B}$ instead of the columns. The new matrix would be

$$\mathbf{C} = \begin{bmatrix} 1 & 5 & 6 & 3 \\ 2 & 1 & 4 & 1 \\ 3 & 5 & 5 & 4 \end{bmatrix}.$$

This matrix is composed of four column vectors from $\mathbf{R}^3$. (Note that $\mathbf{C}$ is $\mathbf{B}'$.) The column space of $\mathbf{C}$ is at most $\mathbf{R}^3$, since four vectors in $\mathbf{R}^3$ must be linearly dependent. In fact, the column space of $\mathbf{C}$ *is* $\mathbf{R}^3$. Although this is not the same as the column space of $\mathbf{B}$, it does have the same dimension. Thus, the column rank of $\mathbf{C}$ and the column rank of $\mathbf{B}$ are the same. But the columns of $\mathbf{C}$ are the rows of $\mathbf{B}$. Thus, the column rank of $\mathbf{C}$ equals the row **rank** of $\mathbf{B}$. That the column and row ranks of $\mathbf{B}$ are the same is not a coincidence. The general results (which are equivalent) are as follows.

THEOREM 2.1: Equality of Row and Column Rank. *The **column rank** and **row rank** of a matrix are equal. By the definition of row rank and its counterpart for column rank, we obtain the corollary,*

*The **row space** and **column space** of a matrix have the same dimension.*

(2-42)

Theorem 2.1 holds regardless of the actual row and column rank. If the column rank of a matrix happens to equal the number of columns it contains, the matrix is said to have **full column rank. Full row rank** is defined likewise. Since the row and column ranks of a matrix are always equal, we can speak unambiguously of the **rank of a matrix.** For either the row rank or the column rank (and, at this point, we shall drop the distinction),

$$\text{rank}(\mathbf{A}) = \text{rank}(\mathbf{A}') \leq \min(\text{number of rows, number of columns}). \quad \textbf{(2-43)}$$

In most contexts, we shall be interested in the columns of the matrices we manipulate. We shall use the term *full rank* to describe a matrix whose rank is equal to the number of columns it contains.

Of particular interest will be the distinction between **full rank** and **short rank matrices.** The distinction turns of the solutions to $\mathbf{Ax} = \mathbf{0}$. If a nonzero $\mathbf{x}$ for which $\mathbf{Ax} = \mathbf{0}$ exists, $\mathbf{A}$ does not have full rank. Equivalently, if the nonzero $\mathbf{x}$ exists, the columns of $\mathbf{A}$ are linearly dependent and at least one of them can be expressed as a linear combination of the others. For example, a nonzero set of solutions to

$$\begin{bmatrix} 1 & 3 & 10 \\ 2 & 3 & 14 \end{bmatrix} \begin{bmatrix} x_1 \\ x_2 \\ x_3 \end{bmatrix} = \begin{bmatrix} 0 \\ 0 \end{bmatrix}$$

is any multiple of $\mathbf{x}' = (2, 1, -\frac{1}{2})$.

In a product matrix $\mathbf{C} = \mathbf{AB}$, every column of $\mathbf{C}$ is a linear combination of the columns of $\mathbf{A}$, so each column of $\mathbf{C}$ is in the column space of $\mathbf{A}$. It is possible that the set of columns in $\mathbf{C}$ could span this space, but it is not possible for them to span a higher-dimensional space. At best, they could be a full set of linearly independent vectors in $\mathbf{A}$'s column space. We conclude that the column rank of $\mathbf{C}$ could not be greater than that of $\mathbf{A}$. Now, apply the same logic to the rows of $\mathbf{C}$, which are all linear combinations of the rows of $\mathbf{B}$. For the same reason that the column rank of $\mathbf{C}$ cannot exceed the column rank of $\mathbf{A}$, the row rank of $\mathbf{C}$ cannot exceed the row rank of $\mathbf{B}$. Since row and column ranks are always equal, we conclude that

$$\text{rank}(\mathbf{AB}) \leq \min(\text{rank}(\mathbf{A}), \text{rank}(\mathbf{B})). \quad \textbf{(2-44)}$$

A useful corollary of (2-44) is:

If $\mathbf{A}$ is $M \times n$ and $\mathbf{B}$ is a square matrix of rank n, $\text{rank}(\mathbf{AB}) = \text{rank}(\mathbf{A})$.

(2-45)

The proof is left as an exercise.

Another application that plays a central role in the development of regression analysis is, for any matrix **A**,

$$\text{rank}(\mathbf{A}) = \text{rank}(\mathbf{A}'\mathbf{A}) = \text{rank}(\mathbf{A}\mathbf{A}'). \qquad \textbf{(2-46)}$$

2.4.6. Determinant of a Matrix

The vectors of the matrix

$$\mathbf{A} = [\mathbf{a} \quad \mathbf{b}] = \begin{bmatrix} 4 & 2 \\ 1 & 3 \end{bmatrix}$$

are shown in Figure 2.3. The area of the parallelogram formed by the columns of **A** can be obtained by manipulating congruent triangles. The result is $4(3) - 1(2) = 10$. This area is the **determinant** of **A**.[5] If the columns of **A** were linearly dependent—that is, if one were a scalar multiple of the other—the two vectors would lie on the same line. The "parallelogram" would collapse to a line and would have zero area. This implies that *if the columns of a matrix are linearly dependent, its determinant is zero.* Recalling our earlier discussion of linear dependence in $\mathbf{R}^2$, we see that this is the case of $(a_1b_2 - b_1a_2) = 0$ in (2-41). (The determinant of **A** is, in fact, $a_1b_2 - b_1a_2$.)

Consider the same exercise in $\mathbf{R}^3$. If we complete the parallelograms in all dimensions for a set of three-dimensional vectors, we shall form a solid, that is, a parallelotope. The determinant will be the volume of this solid. But if the columns of the matrix are linearly dependent, the columns will all lie in the same plane (or on the same line). The "solid" thus formed will collapse to a plane or a line and will have no volume; again, the determinant will be zero. This general result carries over to higher dimensions as well.

PROPOSITION. *The determinant of a matrix is nonzero if and only if it has full rank.*

Full rank and short rank matrices can be distinguished by whether or not their determinants are nonzero. There are some settings in which the value of the determinant is also of interest, so we now consider some algebraic results.

It is most convenient to begin with a diagonal matrix

$$\mathbf{D} = \begin{bmatrix} d_1 & 0 & 0 & \cdots & 0 \\ 0 & d_2 & 0 & \cdots & 0 \\ & & & \vdots & \\ 0 & 0 & 0 & \cdots & d_K \end{bmatrix}.$$

[5]Strictly speaking, the area is the absolute value of the determinant. Since we are concerned with geometric results at this point, we shall neglect the sign. Later, in an algebraic context, the sign of the determinant will be important. Note that *the determinant is defined only for square matrices.*

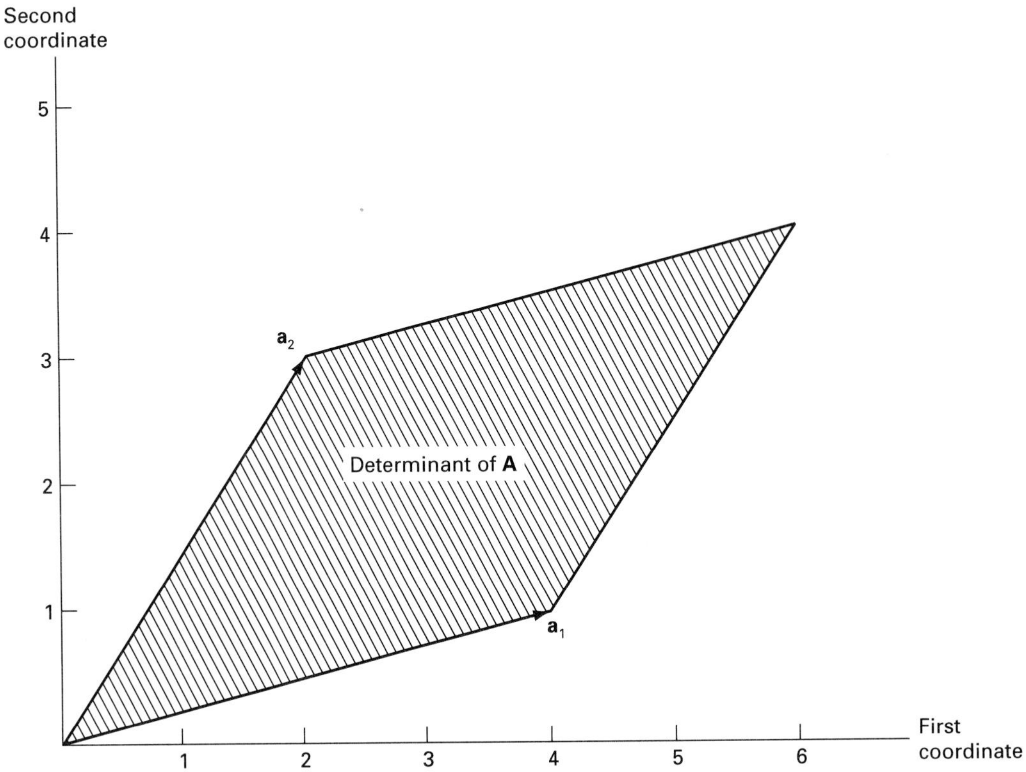

FIGURE 2.3 Determinant of a Matrix.

The column vectors of **D** define a "box" in $\mathbf{R}^K$ whose sides are all at right angles to one another.[6] Its "volume," or determinant, is simply the product of the lengths of the sides, which we denote

$$|\mathbf{D}| = d_1 d_2 \cdots d_K = \prod_{i=1}^{K} d_i. \tag{2-47}$$

A special case is the identity matrix, which has, regardless of K, $|\mathbf{I}_K| = 1$. Multiplying **D** by a scalar c is equivalent to multiplying the length of each side of the box by c, which would multiply its volume by c^K. Thus,

$$|c\mathbf{D}| = c^K |\mathbf{D}|. \tag{2-48}$$

Continuing with this admittedly special case, we suppose that only one column of **D** is multiplied by c. In two dimensions, this would make the box wider but not higher, or vice versa. Hence, the "volume" (area) would also be multiplied

[6]Each column vector defines a segment on one of the axes.

by c. Now, suppose that each side of the box were multiplied by a different c, the first by c_1, the second by c_2, and so on. The volume would, by an obvious extension, now be $c_1 c_2 \cdots c_K|\mathbf{D}|$. The matrix with columns defined by $[c_1\mathbf{d}_1 \; c_2\mathbf{d}_2 \; \ldots]$ is just $\mathbf{DC}$, where $\mathbf{C}$ is a diagonal matrix with c_i as its ith diagonal element. The computation just described is, therefore,

$$|\mathbf{DC}| = |\mathbf{D}| \cdot |\mathbf{C}|. \tag{2-49}$$

(The determinant of $\mathbf{C}$ is the product of the c_is since $\mathbf{C}$, like $\mathbf{D}$, is a diagonal matrix.) In particular, note what happens to the whole thing if one of the c_is is zero.

Thus far, we have considered only diagonal matrices. We now consider the general case. The absolute value of a determinant is still the volume of the parallelotope built up from the columns of the matrix. We have already seen the result for 2×2 matrices:

$$\begin{vmatrix} a & c \\ b & d \end{vmatrix} = ad - bc. \tag{2-50}$$

Notice that it is a function of all the elements of the matrix. This will be true, in general. For more than two dimensions, the determinant can be obtained by using an **expansion by cofactors.** Using *any* row, say i, we obtain

$$|\mathbf{A}| = \sum_{j=1}^{K} a_{ij}(-1)^{i+j}|\mathbf{A}_{ij}|, \quad i = 1, \ldots, K, \tag{2-51}$$

where $\mathbf{A}_{ij}$ is the matrix obtained from $\mathbf{A}$ by deleting row i and column j. The determinant of $\mathbf{A}_{ij}$ is called a **minor** of $\mathbf{A}$.[7] When the correct sign, $(-1)^{i+j}$, is added, it becomes a **cofactor.** This operation can be done using any column as well. For example, a 4×4 determinant becomes a sum of four 3×3s, whereas a 5×5 is a sum of five 4×4s, each of which is a sum of four 3×3s, and so on. Obviously, it is a good idea to base (2-51) on a row or column with many zeros in it, if possible. In practice, this rapidly becomes a heavy burden. It is unlikely, though, that the reader will ever calculate any determinants over 3×3 without a computer. A 3×3, however, might be computed on occasion; if so, the following shortcut will prove useful:

$$\begin{vmatrix} a_{11} & a_{12} & a_{13} \\ a_{21} & a_{22} & a_{23} \\ a_{31} & a_{32} & a_{33} \end{vmatrix} = a_{11}a_{22}a_{33} + a_{12}a_{23}a_{31} + a_{13}a_{32}a_{21} - a_{31}a_{22}a_{13} - a_{21}a_{12}a_{33} - a_{11}a_{23}a_{32}.$$

Although (2-48) and (2-49) were given for diagonal matrices, they hold for general matrices $\mathbf{C}$ and $\mathbf{D}$. One special case of (2-48) to note is that of $c = -1$. Multiplying a matrix by -1 does not necessarily change the sign of its de-

[7]If i equals j, the determinant is a **principal minor.**

terminant. It does so only if the order of the matrix is odd. By using the expansion by cofactors formula, an additional result can be shown:

$$|\mathbf{A}| = |\mathbf{A}'|. \tag{2-52}$$

2.4.7. A Least Squares Problem

Given a vector **y** and a matrix **X**, we are interested in expressing **y** as a linear combination of the columns of **X**. There are two possibilities. If **y** lies in the column space of **X**, we shall be able to find a vector **b** such that

$$\mathbf{y} = \mathbf{Xb}. \tag{2-53}$$

Figure 2.4 illustrates such a case for three dimensions in which the two columns of **X** both have a third coordinate equal to zero. Only **y**'s whose third coordinate is zero, such as $\mathbf{y}^0$ in the figure, can be expressed as **Xb** for some **b**. For the general case, assuming that **y** is, indeed, in the column space of **X**, we can find the coefficients **b** by solving the set of equations in (2-53). Procedures for doing so are discussed in the next section.

Suppose, however, that **y** is not in the column space of **X**. In the context of this example, suppose that **y**'s third component is not zero. Then there is no **b** such that (2-53) holds. We can, however, write

$$\mathbf{y} = \mathbf{Xb} + \mathbf{e}, \tag{2-54}$$

where **e** is the difference between **y** and **Xb**. By this construction, we find an **Xb** that is in the column space of **X**, and **e** is the difference, or "residual." Figure 2.4 shows two examples, **y** and **y***. For the present, we consider only **y**. We are interested in finding the **b** such that **y** is as close as possible to **Xb** in the sense that **e** is as short as possible.

DEFINITION 2.10: Length of a Vector. *The length, or **norm,** of a vector* **e** *is*

$$\|\mathbf{e}\| = \sqrt{\mathbf{e}'\mathbf{e}}. \tag{2-55}$$

The problem is to find the **b** for which

$$\|\mathbf{e}\| = \|\mathbf{y} - \mathbf{Xb}\|$$

is as small as possible. The solution is that **b** that makes **e** perpendicular, or *orthogonal,* to **Xb**.

DEFINITION 2.11: Orthogonal Vectors. *Two vectors* **a** *and* **b** *are **orthogonal,** written* $\mathbf{a} \perp \mathbf{b}$, *if and only if*

$$\mathbf{a}'\mathbf{b} = \mathbf{b}'\mathbf{a} = 0.$$

Returning once again to our fitting problem, we find that the **b** we seek is that for which

$$\mathbf{e} \perp \mathbf{Xb}.$$

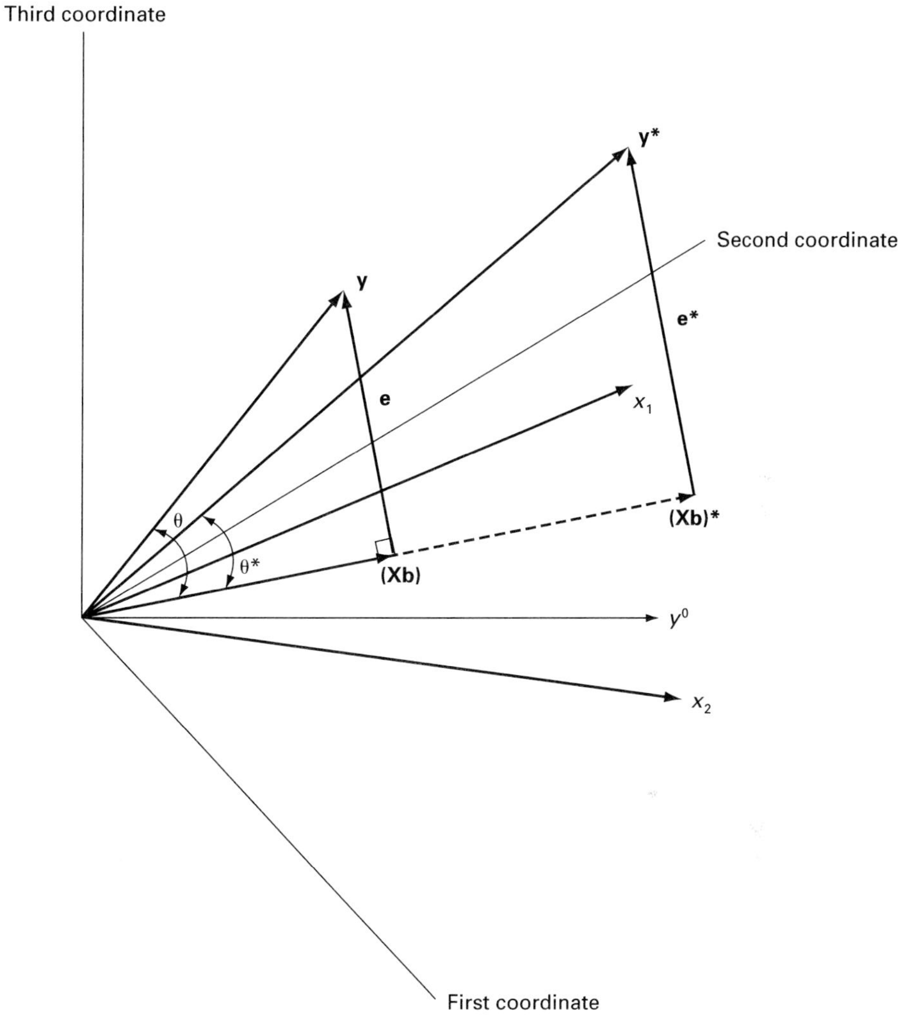

FIGURE 2.4 Least Squares Projections.

Expanding this set of equations gives the requirement

$$\begin{aligned}(\mathbf{Xb})'\mathbf{e} &= \mathbf{0}\\ &= \mathbf{b}'\mathbf{X}'\mathbf{y} - \mathbf{b}'\mathbf{X}'\mathbf{Xb}\\ &= \mathbf{b}'[\mathbf{X}'\mathbf{y} - \mathbf{X}'\mathbf{Xb}]\end{aligned}$$

or, since **b** is not **0**, the set of equations

$$\mathbf{X}'\mathbf{y} = \mathbf{X}'\mathbf{Xb}.$$

The means of solving such a set of equations is the subject of Section 2.5.

In Figure 2.4, the linear combination **Xb** is called the **projection** of **y** into the column space of **X**. The figure is drawn so that although **y** and **y*** are different, they have the same projection. The question we wish to pursue here is: Which vector, **y** or **y***, is closer to its projection in the column space of **X**? Superficially, it would appear that **y** is closer, since **e** is shorter than **e***. Yet **y*** is much more nearly parallel to its projection than **y**, so the only reason that its residual vector is longer is that **y*** is longer compared with **y**. A measure of comparison that would be unaffected by the length of the vectors is the angle between the vector and its projection. By this measure, θ^* is considerably smaller than θ, which would reverse the earlier conclusion.

THEOREM 2.2: The Cosine Law. *The angle θ between two vectors* **a** *and* **b** *satisfies*

$$\cos\theta = \frac{\mathbf{a}'\mathbf{b}}{\|\mathbf{a}\| \cdot \|\mathbf{b}\|}.$$

The two vectors in the calculation would be **y** or **y*** and **Xb** or (**Xb**)*. A zero cosine implies that the vectors are orthogonal. If the cosine is one, the angle is zero, which means that the vectors are the same. (They would be if **y** were in the column space of **X**.) By dividing by the lengths, we automatically compensate for the length of **y**. By this measure, we find that **y** is closer to its projection, **Xb** than **y*** is to its, (**Xb**)*.

2.5. SOLUTION OF A SYSTEM OF LINEAR EQUATIONS

Consider the set of n linear equations

$$\mathbf{Ax} = \mathbf{b}, \tag{2-56}$$

in which the K elements of **x** constitute the unknowns. **A** is a known matrix of coefficients, and **b** is a specified vector of values. We are interested in knowing whether a solution exists; if so, how to obtain it; and finally, if it does exist, whether it is unique.

2.5.1. Systems of Linear Equations

For most of our applications, we shall consider only square systems of equations, that is, those in which **A** is a square matrix. In what follows, therefore, we take n to equal K. Since the number of rows in **A** is the number of equations, whereas the number of columns in **A** is the number of variables, this is the familiar case of "n equations in n unknowns."

There are two types of systems of equations.

DEFINITION 2.12: Homogeneous Equation System. *A homogeneous system is of the form* $\mathbf{Ax} = \mathbf{0}$.

By definition, a nonzero solution to such a system will exist if and only if **A** does not have full rank. If so, then for at least one column of **A**, we can write the preceding as

$$\mathbf{a}_j = -\sum_{i \neq j} \frac{x_i}{x_j} \mathbf{a}_i.$$

This means, as we know, that the columns of **A** are linearly dependent and that $|\mathbf{A}| = \mathbf{0}$.

Definition 2.13: Nonhomogeneous Equation System. *A nonhomogeneous system of equations is of the form* $\mathbf{Ax} = \mathbf{b}$, *where* **b** *is a nonzero vector.*

The vector **b** is chosen arbitrarily and is to be expressed as a linear combination of the columns of **A**. Since **b** has K elements, this will be possible only if the columns of **A** span the entire K-dimensional space, $\mathbf{R}^K$.[8] Equivalently, we shall require that the columns of **A** be linearly independent or that $|\mathbf{A}|$ not be equal to zero.

2.5.2. Inverse Matrices

To solve the system $\mathbf{Ax} = \mathbf{b}$ for $\mathbf{x}$, something akin to division by a matrix is needed. Suppose that we could find a square matrix **B** such that $\mathbf{BA} = \mathbf{I}$. If the equation system is premultiplied by this **B**, the following would be obtained:

$$\mathbf{BAx} = \mathbf{Ix} = \mathbf{x} = \mathbf{Bb}. \tag{2-57}$$

If the matrix **B** exists, it is the **inverse** of **A**, denoted

$$\mathbf{B} = \mathbf{A}^{-1}.$$

From the definition,

$$\mathbf{A}^{-1}\mathbf{A} = \mathbf{I}.$$

In addition, by premultiplying by **A**, postmultiplying by $\mathbf{A}^{-1}$, and then canceling terms, we find

$$\mathbf{AA}^{-1} = \mathbf{I}$$

as well.

If the inverse exists, it must be unique. Suppose that it is not and that **C** is a different inverse of **A**. Then $\mathbf{CAB} = \mathbf{CAB}$, but $(\mathbf{CA})\mathbf{B} = \mathbf{IB} = \mathbf{B}$ and $\mathbf{C}(\mathbf{AB}) = \mathbf{C}$, which would be a contradiction if **C** did not equal **B**. Since, by (2-57), the solution is $\mathbf{x} = \mathbf{A}^{-1}\mathbf{b}$, the solution to the equation system is unique as well.

We now consider the calculation of the inverse matrix. For a 2×2 matrix,

$$\mathbf{AB} = \mathbf{I}$$

[8] If **A** does not have full rank, the nonhomogeneous system will have solutions for *some* vectors **b**, namely, any **b** in the column space of **A**. But we are interested in the case in which there are solutions for *all* nonzero vectors **b**, which requires **A** to have full rank.

implies that

$$\begin{bmatrix} a_{11} & a_{12} \\ a_{21} & a_{22} \end{bmatrix} \begin{bmatrix} b_{11} & b_{12} \\ b_{21} & b_{22} \end{bmatrix} = \begin{bmatrix} 1 & 0 \\ 0 & 1 \end{bmatrix}$$

or

$$\begin{aligned} a_{11}b_{11} + a_{12}b_{21} &= 1 \\ a_{11}b_{12} + a_{12}b_{22} &= 0 \\ a_{21}b_{11} + a_{22}b_{21} &= 0 \\ a_{21}b_{12} + a_{22}b_{22} &= 1. \end{aligned}$$

The solutions are

$$\begin{aligned} \begin{bmatrix} b_{11} & b_{12} \\ b_{21} & b_{22} \end{bmatrix} &= \frac{1}{a_{11}a_{22} - a_{12}a_{21}} \begin{bmatrix} a_{22} & -a_{12} \\ -a_{21} & a_{11} \end{bmatrix} \\ &= \frac{1}{|\mathbf{A}|} \begin{bmatrix} a_{22} & -a_{12} \\ -a_{21} & a_{11} \end{bmatrix}. \end{aligned} \quad \textbf{(2-58)}$$

Notice the presence of the reciprocal of $|\mathbf{A}|$ in $\mathbf{A}^{-1}$. This is not specific to the 2×2 case. We infer from it that if the determinant is zero, the inverse does not exist.

DEFINITION 2.14: Nonsingular Matrix. *A matrix whose inverse exists is **nonsingular**.*

The simplest inverse matrix to compute is that of a diagonal matrix. If

$$\mathbf{D} = \begin{bmatrix} d_1 & 0 & 0 & \cdots & 0 \\ 0 & d_2 & 0 & \cdots & 0 \\ & & \vdots & & \\ 0 & 0 & 0 & \cdots & d_K \end{bmatrix},$$

then

$$\mathbf{D}^{-1} = \begin{bmatrix} 1/d_1 & 0 & 0 & \cdots & 0 \\ 0 & 1/d_2 & 0 & \cdots & 0 \\ & & \vdots & & \\ 0 & 0 & 0 & \cdots & 1/d_K \end{bmatrix},$$

which shows, incidentally, that $\mathbf{I}^{-1} = \mathbf{I}$.

We shall use a^{ij} to indicate the ijth element of $\mathbf{A}^{-1}$. The general formula for computing an inverse matrix is

$$a^{ij} = \frac{|\mathbf{C}_{ji}|}{|\mathbf{A}|}, \quad \textbf{(2-59)}$$

where $|\mathbf{C}_{ji}|$ is the jith cofactor of $\mathbf{A}$. It follows, therefore, that for $\mathbf{A}$ to be nonsingular, $|\mathbf{A}|$ must be nonzero. Notice the reversal of the subscripts. For anything larger than a 3×3 matrix, (2-59) represents a formidable computation. (But that is why we have computers.)

Some computational results involving inverses are[9]

$$|\mathbf{A}^{-1}| = \frac{1}{|\mathbf{A}|}, \tag{2-60}$$

$$(\mathbf{A}^{-1})^{-1} = \mathbf{A}, \tag{2-61}$$

$$(\mathbf{A}^{-1})' = (\mathbf{A}')^{-1}. \tag{2-62}$$

$$\text{If } \mathbf{A} \text{ is symmetric, } \mathbf{A}^{-1} \text{ is symmetric.} \tag{2-63}$$

When both inverse matrices exist,

$$(\mathbf{AB})^{-1} = \mathbf{B}^{-1}\mathbf{A}^{-1}. \tag{2-64}$$

Note the condition preceding (2-64). It may be that **AB** is a square, nonsingular matrix when neither **A** nor **B** are even square. (Consider, for example, $\mathbf{A}'\mathbf{A}$.) Extending (2-64), we have

$$(\mathbf{ABC})^{-1} = \mathbf{C}^{-1}(\mathbf{AB})^{-1} = \mathbf{C}^{-1}\mathbf{B}^{-1}\mathbf{A}^{-1}. \tag{2-65}$$

Recall that for a data matrix **X**, $\mathbf{X}'\mathbf{X}$ is the sum of the *outer products* of the rows **X**. Suppose that we have already computed $\mathbf{S} = (\mathbf{X}'\mathbf{X})^{-1}$ for a number of years of data, such as those given at the beginning of this chapter. The following result, which is called an **updating formula,** shows how to compute the new **S** that would result when a new row is added to **X**:

$$[\mathbf{A} \pm \mathbf{bb}']^{-1} = \mathbf{A}^{-1} \mp \left[\frac{1}{1 \pm \mathbf{b}'\mathbf{A}^{-1}\mathbf{b}}\right]\mathbf{A}^{-1}\mathbf{bb}'\mathbf{A}^{-1}. \tag{2-66}$$

Note the reversal of the sign in the inverse. Two more general forms of (2-66) that are occasionally useful are

$$[\mathbf{A} \pm \mathbf{bc}']^{-1} = \mathbf{A}^{-1} \mp \left[\frac{1}{1 \pm \mathbf{c}'\mathbf{A}^{-1}\mathbf{b}}\right]\mathbf{A}^{-1}\mathbf{bc}'\mathbf{A}^{-1}. \tag{2-66a}$$

$$[\mathbf{A} \pm \mathbf{BCB}']^{-1} = \mathbf{A}^{-1} \mp \mathbf{A}^{-1}\mathbf{B}[\mathbf{C}^{-1} \pm \mathbf{B}'\mathbf{A}^{-1}\mathbf{B}]\mathbf{B}'\mathbf{A}^{-1}. \tag{2-66b}$$

2.5.3. Nonhomogeneous Systems of Equations

For the nonhomogeneous system

$$\mathbf{Ax} = \mathbf{b},$$

if **A** is nonsingular, the unique solution is[10]

$$\mathbf{x} = \mathbf{A}^{-1}\mathbf{b}.$$

---

[9]The proofs of most of these results are obvious and are left as exercises.

[10]Computationally, there are simpler (albeit equivalent) ways of obtaining **x** that do not require explicit computation of $\mathbf{A}^{-1}$. See Johnston (1984, pp. 138–140) or Strang (1988).

2.6. PARTITIONED MATRICES

In formulating the elements of a matrix—for example, in structuring sets of equations—it is sometimes useful to group some of the elements in **submatrices.** For example, we might write

$$\mathbf{A} = \left[\begin{array}{cc|c} 1 & 4 & 5 \\ 2 & 9 & 3 \\ \hline 8 & 9 & 6 \end{array}\right] = \begin{bmatrix} \mathbf{A}_{11} & \mathbf{A}_{12} \\ \mathbf{A}_{21} & \mathbf{A}_{22} \end{bmatrix}.$$

A is a **partitioned matrix.** The subscripts of the submatrices are defined in the same fashion as those for the elements of a matrix. A common special case is the **block diagonal matrix:**

$$\mathbf{A} = \begin{bmatrix} \mathbf{A}_{11} & 0 \\ 0 & \mathbf{A}_{22} \end{bmatrix},$$

where $\mathbf{A}_{11}$ and $\mathbf{A}_{22}$ are square matrices.

2.6.1. Addition and Multiplication of Partitioned Matrices

Addition and multiplication extend to partitioned matrices. For conformably partitioned matrices **A** and **B**,

$$\mathbf{A} + \mathbf{B} = \begin{bmatrix} \mathbf{A}_{11} + \mathbf{B}_{11} & \mathbf{A}_{12} + \mathbf{B}_{12} \\ \mathbf{A}_{21} + \mathbf{B}_{21} & \mathbf{A}_{22} + \mathbf{B}_{22} \end{bmatrix} \tag{2-67}$$

and

$$\begin{aligned} \mathbf{AB} &= \begin{bmatrix} \mathbf{A}_{11} & \mathbf{A}_{12} \\ \mathbf{A}_{21} & \mathbf{A}_{22} \end{bmatrix} \begin{bmatrix} \mathbf{B}_{11} & \mathbf{B}_{12} \\ \mathbf{B}_{21} & \mathbf{B}_{22} \end{bmatrix} \\ &= \begin{bmatrix} \mathbf{A}_{11}\mathbf{B}_{11} + \mathbf{A}_{12}\mathbf{B}_{21} & \mathbf{A}_{11}\mathbf{B}_{12} + \mathbf{A}_{12}\mathbf{B}_{22} \\ \mathbf{A}_{21}\mathbf{B}_{11} + \mathbf{A}_{22}\mathbf{B}_{21} & \mathbf{A}_{21}\mathbf{B}_{12} + \mathbf{A}_{22}\mathbf{B}_{22} \end{bmatrix}. \end{aligned} \tag{2-68}$$

In all these, the matrices must be conformable for the operations involved. For addition, the dimensions of $\mathbf{A}_{ij}$ and $\mathbf{B}_{ij}$ must be the same. For multiplication, the number of columns in $\mathbf{A}_{ij}$ must equal the number of rows in $\mathbf{B}_{jk}$ for all pairs i and j. That is, all the necessary matrix products of the submatrices must be defined.

Two cases frequently encountered are of the form

$$\begin{aligned} \begin{bmatrix} \mathbf{A}_1 \\ \mathbf{A}_2 \end{bmatrix}' \begin{bmatrix} \mathbf{A}_1 \\ \mathbf{A}_2 \end{bmatrix} &= [\mathbf{A}_1' \quad \mathbf{A}_2'] \begin{bmatrix} \mathbf{A}_1 \\ \mathbf{A}_2 \end{bmatrix} \\ &= [\mathbf{A}_1'\mathbf{A}_1 + \mathbf{A}_2'\mathbf{A}_2] \end{aligned} \tag{2-69}$$

and

$$\begin{bmatrix} \mathbf{A}_{11} & \mathbf{0} \\ \mathbf{0} & \mathbf{A}_{22} \end{bmatrix}' \begin{bmatrix} \mathbf{A}_{11} & \mathbf{0} \\ \mathbf{0} & \mathbf{A}_{22} \end{bmatrix} = \begin{bmatrix} \mathbf{A}_{11}'\mathbf{A}_{11} & \mathbf{0} \\ \mathbf{0} & \mathbf{A}_{22}'\mathbf{A}_{22} \end{bmatrix}. \tag{2-70}$$

2.6.2. Determinants of Partitioned Matrices

The determinant of a block diagonal matrix is obtained analogously to that of a diagonal matrix:

$$\begin{vmatrix} \mathbf{A}_{11} & \mathbf{0} \\ \mathbf{0} & \mathbf{A}_{22} \end{vmatrix} = |\mathbf{A}_{11}| \cdot |\mathbf{A}_{22}|. \tag{2-71}$$

The result for a general 2×2 partitioned matrix is

$$\begin{vmatrix} \mathbf{A}_{11} & \mathbf{A}_{12} \\ \mathbf{A}_{21} & \mathbf{A}_{22} \end{vmatrix} = |\mathbf{A}_{22}| \cdot |\mathbf{A}_{11} - \mathbf{A}_{12}\mathbf{A}_{22}^{-1}\mathbf{A}_{21}| = |\mathbf{A}_{11}| \cdot |\mathbf{A}_{22} - \mathbf{A}_{21}\mathbf{A}_{11}^{-1}\mathbf{A}_{12}|. \tag{2-72}$$

The result for matrices larger than 2×2 is extremely cumbersome and will not be necessary for our work.

2.6.3. Inverses of Partitioned Matrices

The inverse of a block diagonal matrix is

$$\begin{bmatrix} \mathbf{A}_{11} & \mathbf{0} \\ \mathbf{0} & \mathbf{A}_{22} \end{bmatrix}^{-1} = \begin{bmatrix} \mathbf{A}_{11}^{-1} & \mathbf{0} \\ \mathbf{0} & \mathbf{A}_{22}^{-1} \end{bmatrix}, \tag{2-73}$$

which can be verified by direct multiplication.

For the general 2×2 partitioned matrix, one form of the **partitioned inverse** is

$$\begin{bmatrix} \mathbf{A}_{11} & \mathbf{A}_{12} \\ \mathbf{A}_{21} & \mathbf{A}_{22} \end{bmatrix}^{-1} = \begin{bmatrix} \mathbf{A}_{11}^{-1}(\mathbf{I} + \mathbf{A}_{12}\mathbf{F}_2\mathbf{A}_{21}\mathbf{A}_{11}^{-1}) & -\mathbf{A}_{11}^{-1}\mathbf{A}_{12}\mathbf{F}_2 \\ -\mathbf{F}_2\mathbf{A}_{21}\mathbf{A}_{11}^{-1} & \mathbf{F}_2 \end{bmatrix}, \tag{2-74}$$

where

$$\mathbf{F}_2 = (\mathbf{A}_{22} - \mathbf{A}_{21}\mathbf{A}_{11}^{-1}\mathbf{A}_{12})^{-1}.$$

This can be checked most easily by postmultiplying $\mathbf{A}$ by the inverse. In view of the symmetry of the calculation, the upper left block could also be written as

$$\mathbf{F}_1 = (\mathbf{A}_{11} - \mathbf{A}_{12}\mathbf{A}_{22}^{-1}\mathbf{A}_{21})^{-1}.$$

2.6.4. Deviations from Means

A useful application of the preceding is the following calculation: Suppose that we begin with a column vector of n values $\mathbf{x}$ and let

$$\mathbf{A} = \begin{bmatrix} n & \sum_{i=1}^{n} x_i \\ \sum_{i=1}^{n} x_i & \sum_{i=1}^{n} x_i^2 \end{bmatrix} = \begin{bmatrix} \mathbf{i}'\mathbf{i} & \mathbf{i}'\mathbf{x} \\ \mathbf{x}'\mathbf{i} & \mathbf{x}'\mathbf{x} \end{bmatrix}.$$

We are interested in the lower right-hand element of $\mathbf{A}^{-1}$. Upon using the definition of $\mathbf{F}_2$ in (2-74), this is

$$\begin{aligned}\mathbf{F}_2 &= [\mathbf{x}'\mathbf{x} - (\mathbf{x}'\mathbf{i})(\mathbf{i}'\mathbf{i})^{-1}(\mathbf{i}'\mathbf{x})]^{-1} \\ &= \left\{\mathbf{x}'\left[\mathbf{I}\mathbf{x} - \mathbf{i}\left(\frac{1}{n}\right)\mathbf{i}'\mathbf{x}\right]\right\}^{-1} \\ &= \left\{\mathbf{x}'\left[\mathbf{I} - \left(\frac{1}{n}\right)\mathbf{i}\mathbf{i}'\right]\mathbf{x}\right\}^{-1} \\ &= [\mathbf{x}'\mathbf{M}^0\mathbf{x}]^{-1}.\end{aligned}$$

Therefore, the lower right-hand value in the inverse matrix is

$$(\mathbf{x}'\mathbf{M}^0\mathbf{x})^{-1} = \frac{1}{\sum_{i=1}^{n}(x_i - \bar{x})^2} = a^{22}.$$

Now, suppose that we replace $\mathbf{x}$ with $\mathbf{X}$, a matrix with several columns. We seek the lower right block of $[\mathbf{Z}'\mathbf{Z}]^{-1}$, where $\mathbf{Z} = [\mathbf{i}, \mathbf{X}]$. The analogous result is

$$\begin{aligned}(\mathbf{Z}'\mathbf{Z})^{22} &= [\mathbf{X}'\mathbf{X} - \mathbf{X}'\mathbf{i}(\mathbf{i}'\mathbf{i})^{-1}\mathbf{i}'\mathbf{X}]^{-1} \\ &= [\mathbf{X}'\mathbf{M}^0\mathbf{X}]^{-1},\end{aligned}$$

which implies that the $K \times K$ matrix in the lower right of $(\mathbf{Z}'\mathbf{Z})^{-1}$ is the inverse of the $K \times K$ matrix whose jkth element is $\Sigma_{i=1}^{n}(x_{ij} - \bar{x}_j)(x_{ik} - \bar{x}_k)$. Thus, when a data matrix contains a column of ones, the elements of the inverse of the matrix of sums of squares and cross products will be computed from the original data in the form of deviations from the respective column means.

2.6.5. Kronecker Products

A calculation that helps to condense the notation when dealing with sets of regression models (see Chapter 15) is the **Kronecker product.** For general matrices $\mathbf{A}$ and $\mathbf{B}$,

$$\mathbf{A} \otimes \mathbf{B} = \begin{bmatrix} a_{11}\mathbf{B} & a_{12}\mathbf{B} & \cdots & a_{1K}\mathbf{B} \\ a_{21}\mathbf{B} & a_{22}\mathbf{B} & \cdots & a_{2K}\mathbf{B} \\ & & \vdots & \\ a_{n1}\mathbf{B} & a_{n2}\mathbf{B} & \cdots & a_{nK}\mathbf{B} \end{bmatrix}. \quad \textbf{(2-75)}$$

For example,

$$\begin{bmatrix} 3 & 0 \\ 5 & 2 \end{bmatrix} \otimes \begin{bmatrix} 1 & 4 \\ 4 & 7 \end{bmatrix} = \begin{bmatrix} 3\begin{bmatrix} 1 & 4 \\ 4 & 7 \end{bmatrix} & 0\begin{bmatrix} 1 & 4 \\ 4 & 7 \end{bmatrix} \\ 5\begin{bmatrix} 1 & 4 \\ 4 & 7 \end{bmatrix} & 2\begin{bmatrix} 1 & 4 \\ 4 & 7 \end{bmatrix} \end{bmatrix}.$$

Notice that there is no requirement for conformability in this operation. The Kronecker product can be computed for any pair of matrices. If $\mathbf{A}$ is $K \times L$ and $\mathbf{B}$ is $m \times n$, then $\mathbf{A} \otimes \mathbf{B}$ is $(Km) \times (Ln)$.

For the Kronecker product,

$$[\mathbf{A} \otimes \mathbf{B}]^{-1} = [\mathbf{A}^{-1} \otimes \mathbf{B}^{-1}], \qquad \textbf{(2-76)}$$

which can be verified by direct multiplication. If **A** is $M \times M$ and **B** is $n \times n$, then

$$|\mathbf{A} \otimes \mathbf{B}| = |\mathbf{A}|^M |\mathbf{B}|^n,$$
$$(\mathbf{A} \otimes \mathbf{B})' = \mathbf{A}' \otimes \mathbf{B}'$$

and (see Section 2.7.7)

$$\text{trace}\,(\mathbf{A} \otimes \mathbf{B}) = \text{tr}(\mathbf{A})\text{tr}(\mathbf{B}).$$

2.7. CHARACTERISTIC ROOTS AND VECTORS

A useful set of results for analyzing a square matrix **A** arises from the solutions to the set of equations

$$\mathbf{Ac} = \lambda\mathbf{c}. \qquad \textbf{(2-77)}$$

The pairs of solutions are the **characteristic vectors c** and characteristic roots λ. If **c** is any solution vector, $k\mathbf{c}$ is also for any value of k. To remove the indeterminancy, **c** is **normalized** so that

$$\mathbf{c}'\mathbf{c} = 1.$$

The solution then consists of λ and the $n - 1$ unknown elements in **c**.

2.7.1. The Characteristic Equation

Solving (2-77) can, in principle, proceed as follows. First, (2-77) implies that

$$\mathbf{Ac} = \lambda\mathbf{Ic}$$

or that

$$(\mathbf{A} - \lambda\mathbf{I})\mathbf{c} = \mathbf{0}.$$

This is a homogeneous system that has a nonzero solution only if the matrix $(\mathbf{A} - \lambda\mathbf{I})$ is singular or has a zero determinant. Therefore, if λ is a solution,

$$|\mathbf{A} - \lambda\mathbf{I}| = 0. \qquad \textbf{(2-78)}$$

This polynomial in λ is the **characteristic equation** of **A**. For example, if

$$\mathbf{A} = \begin{bmatrix} 5 & 1 \\ 2 & 4 \end{bmatrix},$$

then

$$\begin{aligned} |\mathbf{A} - \lambda\mathbf{I}| &= \begin{vmatrix} 5 - \lambda & 1 \\ 2 & 4 - \lambda \end{vmatrix} \\ &= (5 - \lambda)(4 - \lambda) - 2(1) \\ &= \lambda^2 - 9\lambda + 18. \end{aligned}$$

The two solutions are $\lambda = 6$ and $\lambda = 3$.

In solving the characteristic equation, there is no guarantee that the characteristic roots will be real. In the preceding example, if the 2 in the lower right-hand corner of the matrix were -2 instead, the solution would be a pair of complex values. The same problem can emerge in the general $n \times n$ case. The characteristic roots of a symmetric matrix are real, however.[11] This result will be convenient because most of our applications will involve the characteristic roots and vectors of symmetric matrices.

For an $n \times n$ matrix, the characteristic equation is an nth-order polynomial in λ. Its solutions may be n distinct values, as in the preceding example, or may contain repeated values of λ, as in

$$\begin{vmatrix} 2-\lambda & 0 \\ 0 & 2-\lambda \end{vmatrix} = (2-\lambda)^2 \Rightarrow \lambda_1 = \lambda_2 = 2,$$

and may contain some zeros as well, as in

$$\begin{vmatrix} 1-\lambda & 2 \\ 2 & 4-\lambda \end{vmatrix} = \lambda^2 - 5\lambda = 0 \Rightarrow \lambda_1 = 5 \text{ and } \lambda_2 = 0.$$

2.7.2. Characteristic Vectors

With λ in hand, the characteristic vectors are derived from the original problem,

$$\mathbf{Ac} = \lambda\mathbf{c}$$

or

$$(\mathbf{A} - \lambda\mathbf{I})\mathbf{c} = \mathbf{0}.$$

For the first example, we have

$$\begin{bmatrix} 5-\lambda & 1 \\ 2 & 4-\lambda \end{bmatrix} \begin{bmatrix} c_1 \\ c_2 \end{bmatrix} = \begin{bmatrix} 0 \\ 0 \end{bmatrix}. \quad \textbf{(2-79)}$$

The two values for λ are 6 and 3. Inserting these values in (2-79) yields the following:

- For $\lambda = 6$, $-c_1 + c_2 = 0$ and $2c_1 - 2c_2 = 0$, or $c_1 = c_2$.
- For $\lambda = 3$, $2c_1 + c_2 = 0$ and $2c_1 + c_2 = 0$, or $c_1 = -\frac{1}{2}c_2$.

Neither pair determines the values of c_1 and c_2. But this was to be expected; it was the reason $\mathbf{c}'\mathbf{c} = 1$ was specified at the outset. So, for example, if $\lambda = 6$, any vector $\mathbf{c}$ with equal elements will satisfy (2-79). The additional equation $\mathbf{c}'\mathbf{c} = 1$, however, produces complete solutions for both vectors:

[11] A proof may be found in Theil (1971).

$$\text{For } \lambda = 6, \mathbf{c} = \begin{bmatrix} 1/\sqrt{2} \\ 1/\sqrt{2} \end{bmatrix}.$$

$$\text{For } \lambda = 3, \mathbf{c} = \begin{bmatrix} 1/\sqrt{5} \\ -2/\sqrt{5} \end{bmatrix}.$$

These are the only vectors that satisfy both (2-79) and $\mathbf{c}'\mathbf{c} = 1$.

2.7.3. General Results for Characteristic Roots and Vectors

A $K \times K$ symmetric matrix has K distinct characteristic vectors, $\mathbf{c}_1, \mathbf{c}_2, \ldots, \mathbf{c}_K$. The corresponding characteristic roots, $\lambda_1, \lambda_2, \ldots, \lambda_K$, although real, need not be distinct. The characteristic vectors of a symmetric matrix are orthogonal.[12] This implies that for every $i \neq j$, $\mathbf{c}_i'\mathbf{c}_j = 0$.[13] It is convenient to collect the K-characteristic vectors in a $K \times K$ matrix whose ith column is the $\mathbf{c}_i$ corresponding to λ_i,

$$\mathbf{C} = [\mathbf{c}_1 \quad \mathbf{c}_2 \quad \cdots \quad \mathbf{c}_K],$$

and the K-characteristic roots in the same order, in a diagonal matrix,

$$\mathbf{\Lambda} = \begin{bmatrix} \lambda_1 & 0 & 0 & \cdots & 0 \\ 0 & \lambda_2 & 0 & \cdots & 0 \\ & & & \vdots & \\ 0 & 0 & 0 & \cdots & \lambda_K \end{bmatrix}.$$

Then, the full set of equations

$$\mathbf{A}\mathbf{c}_i = \lambda_i \mathbf{c}_i$$

is contained in

$$\mathbf{AC} = \mathbf{C\Lambda}. \qquad \textbf{(2-80)}$$

Since the vectors are orthogonal and $\mathbf{c}_i'\mathbf{c}_i = 1$, we have

$$\mathbf{C}'\mathbf{C} = \begin{bmatrix} \mathbf{c}_1'\mathbf{c}_1 & \mathbf{c}_1'\mathbf{c}_2 & \cdots & \mathbf{c}_1'\mathbf{c}_K \\ \mathbf{c}_2'\mathbf{c}_1 & \mathbf{c}_2'\mathbf{c}_2 & \cdots & \mathbf{c}_2'\mathbf{c}_K \\ & & \vdots & \\ \mathbf{c}_K'\mathbf{c}_1 & \mathbf{c}_K'\mathbf{c}_2 & \cdots & \mathbf{c}_K'\mathbf{c}_K \end{bmatrix}. \qquad \textbf{(2-81)}$$

$$= \mathbf{I}.$$

[12]For proofs of these propositions, see Hadley (1961) or Strang (1988).

[13]This is not true if the matrix is not symmetric. For instance, it does not hold for the characteristic vectors computed in the first example. For nonsymmetric matrices, there is also a distinction between "right" characteristic vectors, $\mathbf{Ac} = \lambda\mathbf{c}$, and "left" characteristic vectors, $\mathbf{d}'\mathbf{A} = \lambda\mathbf{d}'$, which may not be equal.

Result (2-81) implies that

$$\mathbf{C}' = \mathbf{C}^{-1}. \tag{2-82}$$

Consequently,

$$\mathbf{CC}' = \mathbf{CC}^{-1} = \mathbf{I} \tag{2-83}$$

as well, so the rows as well as the columns of **C** are orthogonal.

2.7.4. Diagonalization and Spectral Decomposition of a Matrix

By premultiplying (2-80) by $\mathbf{C}'$ and using (2-81), we can extract the characteristic roots of **A**.

Definition 2.15: Diagonalization of a Matrix. *The **diagonalization** of a matrix* **A** *is*

$$\mathbf{C}'\mathbf{AC} = \mathbf{C}'\mathbf{C}\mathbf{\Lambda} = \mathbf{I}\mathbf{\Lambda} = \mathbf{\Lambda}. \tag{2-84}$$

Alternatively, by *post*multiplying (2-80) by $\mathbf{C}'$ and using (2-83), we obtain a useful representation of **A**.

Definition 2.16: Spectral Decomposition of a Matrix. *The spectral decomposition of* **A** *is*

$$\mathbf{A} = \mathbf{C\Lambda C}' = \sum_{k=1}^{K} \lambda_k \mathbf{c}_k \mathbf{c}_k'. \tag{2-85}$$

In this representation, the $K \times K$ matrix **A** is written as a sum of K rank one matrices. This is also called the **eigenvalue** (or, "own" value) decomposition of **A**. In this connection, the term *signature* of the matrix is sometimes used to describe the characteristic roots and vectors. Yet another pair of terms for the parts of this decomposition are the **latent roots** and **latent vectors** of **A**.

2.7.5. Rank of a Matrix

The diagonalization result enables us to obtain the rank of a matrix very easily.[14] To do so, we can use the following result.

Theorem 2.3: Rank of a Product. *For any matrix* **A** *and nonsingular matrices* **B** *and* **C**, *the rank of* **BAC** *is equal to the rank of* **A**. *The proof is simple. By (2-45),* $rank(\mathbf{BAC}) = rank[(\mathbf{BA})\mathbf{C}] = rank(\mathbf{BA})$. *By (2-43),* $rank(\mathbf{BA}) = rank(\mathbf{A}'\mathbf{B}')$, *and applying (2-45) again,* $rank(\mathbf{A}'\mathbf{B}') = rank(\mathbf{A}')$ *since* $\mathbf{B}'$ *is nonsingular if* **B** *is nonsingular (once again, by 2-43). Finally, applying (2-43) again to obtain* $rank(\mathbf{A}') = rank(\mathbf{A})$ *gives the result.*

---

[14] Recall that when we last considered this problem, we had to try to identify the largest set of linearly independent columns. This might be hopelessly cumbersome if **A** has, say, 20 columns, which would be common in regression analysis.

Since $\mathbf{C}$ and $\mathbf{C}'$ are nonsingular, we can use them to apply this result to (2-84). By an obvious substitution,

$$\text{rank}(\mathbf{A}) = \text{rank}(\mathbf{\Lambda}). \quad \textbf{(2-86)}$$

Finding the rank of $\mathbf{\Lambda}$ is trivial. Since $\mathbf{\Lambda}$ is a diagonal matrix, its rank is just the number of nonzero values on its diagonal. By extending this result, we can prove the following theorems. (Proofs are brief and are left for the reader.)

THEOREM 2.4: Rank of a Symmetric Matrix. *The rank of a symmetric matrix is the number of nonzero characteristic roots it contains.*

Note how this result enters the spectral decomposition given above. If any of the characteristic roots are zero, the number of rank one matrices in the sum is reduced correspondingly. It would appear that this simple rule will not be useful if $\mathbf{A}$ is not square. But recall that

$$\text{rank}(\mathbf{A}) = \text{rank}(\mathbf{A}'\mathbf{A}). \quad \textbf{(2-87)}$$

Since $\mathbf{A}'\mathbf{A}$ is always square, we can use it instead of $\mathbf{A}$. Indeed, we can use it even if $\mathbf{A}$ is square, which leads to a fully general result.

THEOREM 2.5: Rank of a Matrix. *The rank of any matrix* $\mathbf{A}$ *equals the number of nonzero characteristic roots in* $\mathbf{A}'\mathbf{A}$.

This result is useful because it provides a simple way to find the rank of a nonsymmetric matrix. Computationally, finding the characteristic roots of nonsymmetric matrices is rather difficult and involves complex arithmetic. But symmetric matrices, because of their real roots, are much simpler to analyze.

Since the row rank and column rank of a matrix are equal, we should be able to apply Theorem 2.5 to $\mathbf{A}\mathbf{A}'$ as well. This requires, however, an additional result.

THEOREM 2.6: Roots of an Outer Product Matrix. *The nonzero characteristic roots of* $\mathbf{A}\mathbf{A}'$ *are the same as those of* $\mathbf{A}'\mathbf{A}$.

The proof is left as an exercise. A useful special case the reader can examine is the characteristic roots of $\mathbf{a}\mathbf{a}'$ and $\mathbf{a}'\mathbf{a}$, where $\mathbf{a}$ is an $n \times 1$ vector.

If a characteristic root of a matrix is zero, then we have $\mathbf{A}\mathbf{c} = \mathbf{0}$. This means that if the matrix has a zero root, it must be singular. Otherwise, no nonzero $\mathbf{c}$ would exist. In general, therefore, a matrix is singular; that is, it does not have full rank if and only if it has at least one zero root.

2.7.6. Condition Number of a Matrix

As the preceding might suggest, there is a discrete difference between full rank and short rank matrices. In analyzing data matrices such as the one in Section 2.2, however, we shall often encounter cases in which a matrix is not quite short ranked, as it has all nonzero roots, but it is close. That is, by some measure, we can come very close to being able to write one column as a linear combination of the others. This is an important case; we shall examine it at length in our discussion of multicollinearity. Our definitions of rank and determinant will fail to indicate this possibility, but an alternative measure, the **condition number,** is designed for that purpose. Formally, the condition number for a square matrix **A** is

$$\gamma = \left[\frac{\text{maximum root}}{\text{minimum root}}\right]^{1/2}.$$

For nonsquare matrices **X**, such as the data matrix in the example, we use $\mathbf{A} = \mathbf{X}'\mathbf{X}$. As a further refinement, because the characteristic roots are affected by the scaling of the columns of **X**, we scale the columns to have length 1 by dividing each column by the square root of its norm [see (2-55)]. For the **X** in Section 2.2, the largest characteristic root of **A** is 4.9255 and the smallest is 0.0001543. Therefore, the condition number is 178.67, which is extremely large. (Values greater than 20 are large.) That the smallest root is close to zero compared with the largest means that this matrix is nearly singular. Matrices with large condition numbers are difficult to invert accurately.

2.7.7. Trace of a Matrix

The **trace** of a square $K \times K$ matrix is the sum of its diagonal elements:

$$\text{tr}(\mathbf{A}) = \sum_{i=1}^{K} a_{ii}. \tag{2-88}$$

Some easily proven results are

$$\text{tr}(c\mathbf{A}) = c(\text{tr}(\mathbf{A})), \tag{2-89}$$

$$\text{tr}(\mathbf{A}') = \text{tr}(\mathbf{A}), \tag{2-90}$$

$$\text{tr}(\mathbf{A} + \mathbf{B}) = \text{tr}(\mathbf{A}) + \text{tr}(\mathbf{B}), \tag{2-91}$$

$$\text{tr}(\mathbf{I}_K) = K. \tag{2-92}$$

A particularly useful result is the trace of a product matrix:

$$\text{tr}(\mathbf{AB}) = \text{tr}(\mathbf{BA}). \tag{2-93}$$

See, for example, the two product matrices after (2-15). Two useful applications of (2-93) are

$$\mathbf{a}'\mathbf{a} = \text{tr}(\mathbf{a}'\mathbf{a}) = \text{tr}(\mathbf{aa}')$$

and

$$\text{tr}(\mathbf{A}'\mathbf{A}) = \sum_{i=1}^{K} \mathbf{a}_i'\mathbf{a}_i = \sum_{i=1}^{K}\sum_{j=1}^{K} a_{ij}^2.$$

The permutation rule can be extended to any *cyclic* permutation in a product:

$$\text{tr}(\mathbf{ABCD}) = \text{tr}(\mathbf{BCDA}) = \text{tr}(\mathbf{CDAB}) = \text{tr}(\mathbf{DABC}). \tag{2-94}$$

By using (2-84), we obtain

$$\begin{aligned}\operatorname{tr}(\mathbf{C}'\mathbf{A}\mathbf{C}) &= \operatorname{tr}(\mathbf{A}\mathbf{C}\mathbf{C}') = \operatorname{tr}(\mathbf{A}\mathbf{I})\\ &= \operatorname{tr}(\mathbf{A}) = \operatorname{tr}(\mathbf{\Lambda}).\end{aligned} \tag{2-95}$$

Since $\mathbf{\Lambda}$ is diagonal with the roots of $\mathbf{A}$ on its diagonal, the general result is the following.

THEOREM 2.7: Trace of a Matrix. *The trace of a matrix equals the sum of its characteristic roots.* **(2-96)**

2.7.8. Determinant of a Matrix

Recalling how tedious the calculation of a determinant promised to be, we find that the following is particularly useful. Since

$$\begin{aligned}\mathbf{C}'\mathbf{A}\mathbf{C} &= \mathbf{\Lambda},\\ |\mathbf{C}'\mathbf{A}\mathbf{C}| &= |\mathbf{\Lambda}|.\end{aligned} \tag{2-97}$$

Using a number of earlier results, we have, for orthogonal matrix $\mathbf{C}$,

$$\begin{aligned}|\mathbf{C}'\mathbf{A}\mathbf{C}| &= |\mathbf{C}'|\cdot|\mathbf{A}|\cdot|\mathbf{C}| = |\mathbf{C}'|\cdot|\mathbf{C}|\cdot|\mathbf{A}| = |\mathbf{C}'\mathbf{C}|\cdot|\mathbf{A}|\\ &= |\mathbf{I}|\cdot|\mathbf{A}| = 1\cdot|\mathbf{A}|\\ &= |\mathbf{A}|\\ &= |\mathbf{\Lambda}|.\end{aligned} \tag{2-98}$$

Since $|\mathbf{\Lambda}|$ is just the product of its diagonal elements, this implies the following.

THEOREM 2.8: Determinant of a Matrix. *The determinant of a matrix equals the product of its characteristic roots.* **(2-99)**

Notice that we get the expected result if any of these roots is zero. Since the determinant is the product of the roots, it follows that a matrix is singular if and only if its determinant is zero and, in turn, if and only if it has at least one zero characteristic root.

2.7.9. Powers of a Matrix

We often use expressions involving powers of matrices, such as $\mathbf{AA} = \mathbf{A}^2$. For positive integer powers, these expressions can be computed by repeated multiplication. But this does not show how to handle a problem such as finding a $\mathbf{B}$ such that $\mathbf{B}^2 = \mathbf{A}$, that is, the square root of a matrix. The characteristic roots and vectors provide a simple solution.

Consider first

$$\begin{aligned}\mathbf{AA} &= \mathbf{A}^2\\ &= (\mathbf{C\Lambda C}')(\mathbf{C\Lambda C}')\\ &= \mathbf{C\Lambda C}'\mathbf{C\Lambda C}'\\ &= \mathbf{C\Lambda I\Lambda C}'\\ &= \mathbf{C\Lambda\Lambda C}'\\ &= \mathbf{C\Lambda}^2\mathbf{C}'.\end{aligned} \tag{2-100}$$

Two results follow. Since $\mathbf{\Lambda}^2$ is a diagonal matrix whose nonzero elements are the squares of those in $\mathbf{\Lambda}$, this implies the following.

For any symmetric matrix, the characteristic roots of $\mathbf{A}^2$ *are the squares of those of* $\mathbf{A}$, *and the characteristic vectors are the same.* **(2-101)**

The proof is obtained by observing that the last line in (2-100) is the eigenvalue decomposition of the matrix $\mathbf{B} = \mathbf{AA}$. Since $\mathbf{A}^3 = \mathbf{AA}^2$ and so on, (2-101) extends to any positive integer. By convention, for any $\mathbf{A}$, $\mathbf{A}^0 = \mathbf{I}$. Thus, for any symmetric matrix $\mathbf{A}$, $\mathbf{A}^K = \mathbf{C\Lambda}^K\mathbf{C}'$, $K = 0, 1, \ldots$. Hence, the characteristic roots of $\mathbf{A}^K$ are λ^K, whereas the characteristic vectors are the same as those of $\mathbf{A}$. If $\mathbf{A}$ is nonsingular, so that all of its roots λ_i are nonzero, this can be extended to negative powers as well.

If $\mathbf{A}^{-1}$ exists, then

$$\begin{aligned}\mathbf{A}^{-1} &= (\mathbf{C\Lambda C}')^{-1}\\ &= (\mathbf{C}')^{-1}\mathbf{\Lambda}^{-1}\mathbf{C}^{-1}\\ &= \mathbf{C\Lambda}^{-1}\mathbf{C}',\end{aligned} \tag{2-102}$$

where we have used the earlier result, $\mathbf{C}' = \mathbf{C}^{-1}$. This gives an important result that is useful for analyzing inverse matrices.

THEOREM 2.9: Characteristic Roots of an Inverse Matrix. *If* $\mathbf{A}^{-1}$ *exists, the characteristic roots of* $\mathbf{A}^{-1}$ *are the reciprocals of those of* $\mathbf{A}$, *and the characteristic vectors are the same.*

By extending the notion of repeated multiplication, we have a more general result.

THEOREM 2.10: Characteristic Roots of a Matrix Power. *For any nonsingular symmetric matrix* $\mathbf{A} = \mathbf{C\Lambda C}'$, $\mathbf{A}^K = \mathbf{C\Lambda}^K\mathbf{C}'$, $K = \ldots, -2, -1, 0, 1, 2, \ldots$.

We now turn to the general problem of how to compute the square root of a matrix. In the scalar case, the value would have to be nonnegative. The matrix analog to this requirement is that all the characteristic roots are nonnegative. Consider, then, the candidate

$$\begin{aligned}\mathbf{A}^{1/2} &= \mathbf{C\Lambda}^{1/2}\mathbf{C}'\\ &= \mathbf{C}\begin{bmatrix}\sqrt{\lambda_1} & 0 & \cdots & 0\\ 0 & \sqrt{\lambda_2} & \cdots & 0\\ & & \vdots & \\ 0 & 0 & \cdots & \sqrt{\lambda_n}\end{bmatrix}\mathbf{C}'.\end{aligned} \tag{2-103}$$

This satisfies the requirement for a square root, since

$$\begin{aligned}\mathbf{A}^{1/2}\mathbf{A}^{1/2} &= \mathbf{C\Lambda}^{1/2}\mathbf{C}'\mathbf{C\Lambda}^{1/2}\mathbf{C}' = \mathbf{C\Lambda C}'\\ &= \mathbf{A}.\end{aligned} \tag{2-104}$$

If we continue in this fashion, we can define the powers of a matrix more generally, still assuming that all the characteristic roots are nonnegative. For example, $\mathbf{A}^{1/3} = \mathbf{C}\mathbf{\Lambda}^{1/3}\mathbf{C}'$. If all the roots are strictly positive, we can go one step further and extend the result to any real power. For reasons that will be made clear in the next section, we say that a matrix with positive characteristic roots is **positive definite.** It is the matrix analog to a positive number.

DEFINITION 2.17: Real Powers of a Positive Definite Matrix. *For a **positive definite** matrix* $\mathbf{A}$, $\mathbf{A}^r = \mathbf{C}\mathbf{\Lambda}^r\mathbf{C}'$, *for any real number, r.* **(2-105)**

The characteristic roots of $\mathbf{A}^r$ are the rth power of those of $\mathbf{A}$, and the characteristic vectors are the same.

If $\mathbf{A}$ is only **nonnegative definite**—that is, has roots that are either zero or positive—(2-105) holds only for nonnegative r.

2.7.10. Idempotent Matrices

Idempotent matrices are equal to their squares [see (2-37) to (2-39)]. In view of their importance in econometrics, we collect a few results related to idempotent matrices at this point. First, (2-101) implies that if λ is a characteristic root of an idempotent matrix, $\lambda = \lambda^K$ for all nonnegative integers K. As such, if $\mathbf{A}$ is a symmetric idempotent matrix, all its roots are 1 or 0. Assume that all the roots of $\mathbf{A}$ are 1. Then $\mathbf{\Lambda} = \mathbf{I}$, and $\mathbf{A} = \mathbf{C}\mathbf{\Lambda}\mathbf{C}' = \mathbf{C}\mathbf{I}\mathbf{C}' = \mathbf{C}\mathbf{C}' = \mathbf{I}$. If the roots are not all 1, one or more are 0. Consequently, we have the following results for symmetric idempotent matrices:[15]

- *The only full rank, symmetric idempotent matrix is the identity matrix* **I**. **(2-106)**
- *All symmetric idempotent matrices except the identity matrix are singular.* **(2-107)**

The final result on idempotent matrices is obtained by observing that the count of the nonzero roots of $\mathbf{A}$ is also equal to their sum. By combining Theorems 2.5 and 2.7 with the result that for an idempotent matrix, the roots are all 0 or 1, we obtain this result:

- *The rank of a symmetric idempotent matrix is equal to its trace.* **(2-108)**

2.7.11. Factoring a Matrix

In some applications, we shall require a matrix $\mathbf{P}$ such that

$$\mathbf{P}'\mathbf{P} = \mathbf{A}^{-1}.$$

One choice is

$$\mathbf{P} = \mathbf{\Lambda}^{-1/2}\mathbf{C}';$$

hence,

$$\begin{aligned}\mathbf{P}'\mathbf{P} &= (\mathbf{C}')'(\mathbf{\Lambda}^{-1/2})'\mathbf{\Lambda}^{-1/2}\mathbf{C}' \\ &= \mathbf{C}\mathbf{\Lambda}^{-1}\mathbf{C}',\end{aligned}$$

[15]Not all idempotent matrices are symmetric. We shall not encounter any asymmetric ones in our work, however.

as desired.[16] Thus, the **spectral decomposition** of **A**, $\mathbf{A} = \mathbf{C\Lambda C}'$ is a useful result for this kind of computation.

The **Cholesky factorization** of a symmetric positive definite matrix is an alternative representation that is useful in regression analysis. Any symmetric positive definite matrix **A** may be written as the product of a lower triangular matrix **L** and its transpose (which is an **upper triangular matrix**) $\mathbf{L}' = \mathbf{U}$. Thus, $\mathbf{A} = \mathbf{LU}$. This is the Cholesky decomposition of **A**. The square roots of the diagonal elements of **L**, d_i, are the **Cholesky values** of **A**. By arraying these in a diagonal matrix **D**, we may also write $\mathbf{A} = \mathbf{LD}^{-1}\mathbf{D}^2\mathbf{D}^{-1}\mathbf{U} = \mathbf{L}^*\mathbf{D}^2\mathbf{U}^*$. This is similar to the spectral decomposition in (2-85). The usefulness of this formulation arises when the inverse of **A** is required. Once **L** is computed, finding $\mathbf{A}^{-1} = \mathbf{U}^{-1}\mathbf{L}^{-1}$ is also straightforward as well as extremely fast and accurate. Most recently developed econometric software uses this technique for inverting positive definite matrices.

A third type of decomposition of a matrix is useful for numerical analysis when the inverse is difficult to obtain because the columns of **A** are "nearly" collinear. Any matrix $n \times K$ matrix **A** for which $n \geq K$ can be written in the form

$$\mathbf{A} = \mathbf{UWV}',$$

where **U** is an orthogonal $n \times K$ matrix—that is, $\mathbf{U}'\mathbf{U} = \mathbf{I}_K$—**W** is a $K \times K$ diagonal matrix such that $w_i \geq 0$, and **V** is a $K \times K$ matrix such that $\mathbf{V}'\mathbf{V} = \mathbf{I}_K$. This is called the **singular value decomposition** (SVD) of **A**, and w_i are the singular values of **A**.[17] (Note that if **A** is square, the spectral decomposition is a singular value decomposition.) As with the Cholesky decomposition, the usefulness of the SVD arises in inversion, in this case, of $\mathbf{A}'\mathbf{A}$. By multiplying it out, we obtain that $(\mathbf{A}'\mathbf{A})^{-1}$ is simply $\mathbf{VW}^{-2}\mathbf{V}'$. Once the SVD of **A** is computed, the inversion is trivial. The other advantage of this format is its numerical stability, which is discussed at length in Press et al. (1986).

2.7.12. The Generalized Inverse of a Matrix

Inverse matrices are fundamental in econometrics. Although we shall not require them much in our treatment in this book, there are more general forms of inverse matrices than we have considered thus far. A **generalized inverse** of a matrix **A** is another matrix $\mathbf{A}^+$ that satisfies the following requirements:

1. $\mathbf{AA}^+\mathbf{A} = \mathbf{A}$.
2. $\mathbf{A}^+\mathbf{AA}^+ = \mathbf{A}^+$.
3. $\mathbf{A}^+\mathbf{A}$ is symmetric.
4. $\mathbf{AA}^+$ is symmetric.

---

[16]We say that this is "one" choice because if **A** is symmetric, as it will be in all our applications, there are other candidates. The reader can easily verify that $\mathbf{C\Lambda}^{-1/2}\mathbf{C}' = \mathbf{A}^{-1/2}$ works as well.

[17]Discussion of the singular value decomposition (and listings of computer programs for the computations) may be found in Press et al. (1986).

A unique $\mathbf{A}^+$ can be found for any matrix, whether $\mathbf{A}$ is singular or not, or even if $\mathbf{A}$ is not square.[18] The unique matrix that satisfies all four requirements is called the **Moore–Penrose inverse** or **pseudoinverse** of $\mathbf{A}$. If $\mathbf{A}$ happens to be square and nonsingular, the generalized inverse will be the familiar ordinary inverse. But if $\mathbf{A}^{-1}$ does not exist, $\mathbf{A}^+$ can still be computed.

An important special case is the overdetermined system of equations

$$\mathbf{Ab} = \mathbf{y},$$

where $\mathbf{A}$ has n rows, $K < n$ columns, and column rank equal to $R \leq K$. Suppose that R equals K, so that $(\mathbf{A}'\mathbf{A})^{-1}$ exists. Then the Moore–Penrose inverse of $\mathbf{A}$ is

$$\mathbf{A}^+ = (\mathbf{A}'\mathbf{A})^{-1}\mathbf{A}',$$

which can be verified by multiplication. A solution to the system of equations can be written

$$\mathbf{b} = \mathbf{A}^+\mathbf{y}.$$

Readers familiar with regression will recognize this as the least squares solution

Now suppose that $\mathbf{A}$ does not have full rank. The previous solution cannot be computed. An alternative solution can be obtained, however. We continue to use the matrix $\mathbf{A}'\mathbf{A}$. In the spectral decomposition of Section 2.7.9, if $\mathbf{A}$ has rank R, there are R terms in the summation in (2-85). In (2-102), the spectral decomposition using the reciprocals of the characteristic roots is used to compute the inverse. To compute the Moore–Penrose inverse, we apply this calculation to $\mathbf{A}'\mathbf{A}$, using only the nonzero roots, then postmultiply the result by $\mathbf{A}'$. Let $\mathbf{C}_1$ be the R characteristic vectors corresponding to the nonzero roots, which we array in the diagonal matrix, $\mathbf{\Lambda}_1$. Then the Moore–Penrose inverse is

$$\mathbf{A}^+ = \mathbf{C}_1\mathbf{\Lambda}_1^{-1}\mathbf{C}_1'\mathbf{A}',$$

which is very similar to the previous solution.

If $\mathbf{A}$ is a square matrix with rank $R \leq K$, the Moore–Penrose inverse is computed precisely as in the preceding equation without postmultiplying by $\mathbf{A}'$. Thus, for a symmetric matrix $\mathbf{A}$,

$$\mathbf{A}^+ = \mathbf{C}_1\mathbf{\Lambda}_1^{-1}\mathbf{C}_1',$$

where $\mathbf{\Lambda}_1$ is a diagonal matrix containing the reciprocals of the *nonzero* roots of $\mathbf{A}$.

[18]A proof of uniqueness, with several other results, may be found in Theil (1983).

2.8. QUADRATIC FORMS AND DEFINITE MATRICES

Many optimization problems involve double sums of the form

$$q = \sum_{i=1}^{n} \sum_{j=1}^{n} x_i x_j a_{ij}. \qquad \textbf{(2-109)}$$

This **quadratic form** can be written

$$q = \mathbf{x}'\mathbf{A}\mathbf{x},$$

where $\mathbf{A}$ is a symmetric matrix. In general, q may be positive, negative, or zero; it depends on $\mathbf{A}$ and $\mathbf{x}$. There are some matrices, however, for which q will be positive regardless of $\mathbf{x}$, and others for which q will always be negative (or nonnegative or nonpositive). For a given matrix $\mathbf{A}$,

1. If $\mathbf{x}'\mathbf{A}\mathbf{x} > (<)\ 0$ for all nonzero $\mathbf{x}$, then $\mathbf{A}$ is **positive (negative) definite.**
2. If $\mathbf{x}'\mathbf{A}\mathbf{x} \geq (\leq)\ 0$ for all nonzero $\mathbf{x}$, then $\mathbf{A}$ is **nonnegative definite** or **positive semidefinite** (nonpositive definite).

It might seem that it would be impossible to check a matrix for definiteness, since $\mathbf{x}$ can be chosen arbitrarily. But we have already used the set of results necessary to do so. Recall that a symmetric matrix can be decomposed into

$$\mathbf{A} = \mathbf{C}\boldsymbol{\Lambda}\mathbf{C}'.$$

Therefore, the quadratic form can be written as

$$\mathbf{x}'\mathbf{A}\mathbf{x} = \mathbf{x}'\mathbf{C}\boldsymbol{\Lambda}\mathbf{C}'\mathbf{x}.$$

Let $\mathbf{y} = \mathbf{C}'\mathbf{x}$. Then

$$\begin{aligned}\mathbf{x}'\mathbf{A}\mathbf{x} &= \mathbf{y}'\boldsymbol{\Lambda}\mathbf{y} \\ &= \sum_{i=1}^{n} \lambda_i y_i^2. \end{aligned} \qquad \textbf{(2-110)}$$

If λ_i is positive for all i, then regardless of $\mathbf{y}$—that is, regardless of $\mathbf{x}$—q will be positive. This was the case identified earlier as a positive definite matrix. Continuing this line of reasoning, we obtain the following theorem.

THEOREM 2.11: Definite Matrices. *Let* $\mathbf{A}$ *be a symmetric matrix. If all the characteristic roots of* $\mathbf{A}$ *are positive (negative), then* $\mathbf{A}$ *is* ***positive definite (negative definite).*** *If some of the roots are zero, then* $\mathbf{A}$ *is* ***nonnegative (nonpositive) definite*** *if the remainder are positive (negative). If* $\mathbf{A}$ *has both negative and positive roots, then* $\mathbf{A}$ *is* ***indefinite.***

The preceding statements give, in each case, the "if" parts of the theorem. To establish the "only if" parts, assume that the condition on the roots does not hold. This must lead to a contradiction. For example, if some λ can be negative, then $\mathbf{y}'\boldsymbol{\Lambda}\mathbf{y}$ could be negative for some $\mathbf{y}$, so $\mathbf{A}$ cannot be positive definite.

2.8.1. Nonnegative Definite Matrices

A case of particular interest is that of nonnegative definite matrices. The previous theorem implies a number of related results.

- If $\mathbf{A}$ is nonnegative definite, then $|\mathbf{A}| \geq 0$. **(2-111)**

  Proof: The determinant is the product of the roots, which are positive.

  The converse, however, is not true. For example, a 2×2 matrix with two negative roots is clearly not positive definite, but it does have a positive determinant.

- If $\mathbf{A}$ is positive definite, so is $\mathbf{A}^{-1}$. **(2-112)**

  Proof: The roots are the reciprocals of those of $\mathbf{A}$, which are, therefore positive.

- The identity matrix $\mathbf{I}$ is positive definite. **(2-113)**

  Proof: $\mathbf{x}'\mathbf{I}\mathbf{x} = \mathbf{x}'\mathbf{x} > 0$ if $\mathbf{x} \neq \mathbf{0}$.

A very important result for regression analysis is

- If $\mathbf{A}$ is $n \times K$ with full rank and $n > K$, then $\mathbf{A}'\mathbf{A}$ is positive definite and $\mathbf{A}\mathbf{A}'$ is nonnegative definite. **(2-114)**

  Proof: By assumption, $\mathbf{Ax} \neq \mathbf{0}$. So $\mathbf{x}'\mathbf{A}'\mathbf{A}\mathbf{x} = (\mathbf{Ax})'(\mathbf{Ax}) = \mathbf{y}'\mathbf{y} = \Sigma_i y_i^2 > 0$.

A similar proof establishes the nonnegative definiteness of $\mathbf{A}\mathbf{A}'$. The difference in the latter case is that because $\mathbf{A}$ has more rows than columns there is an $\mathbf{x}$ such that $\mathbf{A}'\mathbf{x} = \mathbf{0}$. Thus, in the proof, we only have $\mathbf{y}'\mathbf{y} \geq 0$. The case in which $\mathbf{A}$ does not have full column rank is the same as that of $\mathbf{A}\mathbf{A}'$.

- If $\mathbf{A}$ is positive definite and $\mathbf{B}$ is a nonsingular matrix, then $\mathbf{B}'\mathbf{A}\mathbf{B}$ is positive definite. **(2-115)**

  Proof: $\mathbf{x}'\mathbf{B}'\mathbf{A}\mathbf{B}\mathbf{x} = \mathbf{y}'\mathbf{A}\mathbf{y} > 0$, where $\mathbf{y} = \mathbf{Bx}$. But $\mathbf{y}$ cannot be $\mathbf{0}$ because $\mathbf{B}$ is nonsingular.

Finally, note that for $\mathbf{A}$ to be negative definite, all $\mathbf{A}$'s characteristic roots must be negative. But, in this case, $|\mathbf{A}|$ is positive if $\mathbf{A}$ is of even order and negative if $\mathbf{A}$ is of odd order.

2.8.2. Idempotent Quadratic Forms

Quadratic forms in idempotent matrices play an important role in the distributions of many test statistics. As such, we shall encounter them fairly often. Two central results are of interest.

- Every symmetric idempotent matrix is nonnegative definite. **(2-116)**

  Proof: All roots are 1 or 0; hence, the matrix is nonnegative definite by definition.

Combining this with some earlier results yields a result used in determining the sampling distribution of most of the standard test statistics.

- If $\mathbf{A}$ is symmetric and idempotent, $n \times n$ with rank J, then every quadratic form in $\mathbf{A}$ can be written $\mathbf{x}'\mathbf{A}\mathbf{x} = \Sigma_{i=1}^{J} y_i^2$. **(2-117)**

  Proof: This is (2-110) with $\lambda = 1$ or 0.

2.8.3. Ranking Matrices

It is not obvious how one can compare two matrices. As a starting point, of course, the matrices must be of the same dimensions. A useful, although not always conclusive, comparison is based on

$$d = \mathbf{x}'\mathbf{A}\mathbf{x} - \mathbf{x}'\mathbf{B}\mathbf{x}.$$

If this is always positive, regardless of the choice of $\mathbf{x}$, then at least by this criterion we could say that

$$\mathbf{A} > \mathbf{B}. \tag{2-118}$$

The reverse would apply if d is always negative. For some matrices, the result might be ambiguous. It follows from the definition that

$$d > 0 \text{ implies that } \mathbf{A} - \mathbf{B} \text{ is positive definite,}$$

as

$$d = \mathbf{x}'(\mathbf{A} - \mathbf{B})\mathbf{x}.$$

For example,

$$\mathbf{A} = \begin{bmatrix} 3 & -1 \\ -1 & 49 \end{bmatrix}, \qquad \mathbf{B} = \begin{bmatrix} 2 & 5 \\ 5 & 13 \end{bmatrix}.$$

Is $\mathbf{A} > \mathbf{B}$?

$$\mathbf{A} - \mathbf{B} = \begin{bmatrix} 1 & -6 \\ -6 & 36 \end{bmatrix}.$$

The characteristic roots of this rank 1 matrix are 37 and 0. Therefore, $\mathbf{A} - \mathbf{B}$ is nonnegative definite. For this $\mathbf{A}$ and $\mathbf{B}$, a quadratic form in $\mathbf{A}$ will always be at least as large as the one in $\mathbf{B}$ that uses the same $\mathbf{x}$.

A particular case of the general result is:

> If $\mathbf{A}$ is positive definite and $\mathbf{B}$ is nonnegative definite, then $\mathbf{A} + \mathbf{B} > \mathbf{A}$. **(2-119)**

Consider, for example, the "updating formula" introduced in (2-66). This uses a matrix

$$\mathbf{A} = \mathbf{B}'\mathbf{B} + \mathbf{b}\mathbf{b}' > \mathbf{B}'\mathbf{B}.^{19}$$

[19] The earlier example is constructed using this result.

Finally, in comparing matrices, it may be more convenient to compare their inverses. The result analogous to a familiar result for scalars is:

$$\text{If } \mathbf{A} > \mathbf{B}, \text{ then } \mathbf{B}^{-1} > \mathbf{A}^{-1}. \qquad \textbf{(2-120)}$$

[See Goldberger (1964, Chapter 2).]

2.9. CALCULUS AND MATRIX ALGEBRA

Many problems in econometrics involve the extension of some familiar results from calculus to a multivariate setting. Examples include the formulation of approximating functions, maximization or minimization of a function of many variables, and the analysis of transformations from one set of variables to another. This section presents the basic set of results used later in the book in the discussion of these problems.[20] Each of the four parts begins with the basic result from the univariate calculus and then proceeds to the extension to the multivariate case.

2.9.1. Differentiation and the Taylor Series

A variable y is a function of another variable x written

$$y = f(x), \qquad y = g(x), \qquad y = y(x), \qquad \text{and so on,}$$

if each value of x is associated with a single value of y. In this relationship, y and x are sometimes labeled the **dependent variable** and the **independent variable,** respectively. Assuming that the function $f(x)$ is continuous and differentiable, we obtain the following derivatives:

$$f'(x) = \frac{dy}{dx},$$

$$f''(x) = \frac{d^2y}{dx^2},$$

and so on.

A frequent use of the derivatives of $f(x)$ is in the **Taylor series approximation.** A Taylor series is a polynomial approximation to $f(x)$. Letting x^0 be an arbitrarily chosen expansion point

$$f(x) \approx f(x^0) + \sum_{i=1}^{P} \frac{1}{i!} \frac{d^i f(x^0)}{d(x^0)^i} (x - x^0)^i. \qquad \textbf{(2-121)}$$

The choice of the number of terms is arbitrary; the more that are used, the more accurate the approximation will be. The approximations used most frequently in econometrics are the **linear approximation,**

$$\begin{aligned} f(x) &\simeq [f(x^0) - f'(x^0)x^0] + f'(x^0)x \\ &= \beta_1 + \beta_2 x \end{aligned} \qquad \textbf{(2-122)}$$

and the **quadratic approximation,**

---

[20]For a complete exposition, see Magnus and Neudecker (1988).

$$f(x) \simeq [f^0 - f'^0x^0 + \frac{1}{2}f''^0(x^0)^2] + [f'^0 - f''^0x^0]x + \tfrac{1}{2}f''^0x^2 \qquad \textbf{(2-123)}$$
$$= \beta_1 + \beta_2 x + \beta_3 x^2,$$

where the superscript indicates that the function is evaluated at x^0.

We can regard a function $y = f(x_1, x_2, \ldots, x_n)$ as a **scalar-valued function** of a vector; that is, $y = f(\mathbf{x})$. The vector of partial derivatives, or **gradient vector,** or simply **gradient,** is

$$\frac{\partial f(\mathbf{x})}{\partial \mathbf{x}} = \begin{bmatrix} \partial y/\partial x_1 \\ \partial y/\partial x_2 \\ \vdots \\ \partial y/\partial x_n \end{bmatrix} = \begin{bmatrix} f_1 \\ f_2 \\ \vdots \\ f_n \end{bmatrix}. \qquad \textbf{(2-124)}$$

The vector $\mathbf{g}(\mathbf{x})$ or $\mathbf{g}$ is used to represent the gradient vector. Notice that it is a column vector. The shape of the derivative is determined by the denominator of the derivative.

A **second derivatives matrix** or **Hessian matrix** is computed as

$$\mathbf{H} = \begin{bmatrix} \partial^2 y/\partial x_1 \partial x_1 & \partial^2 y/\partial x_1 \partial x_2 & \cdots & \partial^2 y/\partial x_1 \partial x_n \\ \partial^2 y/\partial x_2 \partial x_1 & \partial^2 y/\partial x_2 \partial x_2 & \cdots & \partial^2 y/\partial x_2 \partial x_n \\ \vdots & \vdots & \vdots & \vdots \\ \partial^2 y/\partial x_n \partial x_1 & \partial^2 y/\partial x_n \partial x_2 & \cdots & \partial^2 y/\partial x_n \partial x_n \end{bmatrix}. \qquad \textbf{(2-125)}$$
$$= [f_{ij}].$$

In general, $\mathbf{H}$ is a square, symmetric matrix. (The symmetry is obtained for continuous functions from Young's theorem.) Each row and column of $\mathbf{H}$ is the derivative of the gradient vector with respect to one of the variables. Therefore,

$$\mathbf{H} = \left[\frac{\partial(\partial y/\partial \mathbf{x})}{\partial x_1} \quad \frac{\partial(\partial y/\partial \mathbf{x})}{\partial x_2} \quad \cdots \quad \frac{\partial(\partial y/\partial \mathbf{x})}{\partial x_n}\right]$$
$$= \frac{\partial(\partial y/\partial \mathbf{x})}{\partial(x_1 \quad x_2 \quad \cdots \quad x_n)}$$
$$= \frac{\partial(\partial y/\partial \mathbf{x})}{\partial \mathbf{x}'}$$
$$= \frac{\partial^2 y}{\partial \mathbf{x} \partial \mathbf{x}'}.$$

The first-order, or linear Taylor series, approximation is

$$y \approx f(\mathbf{x}^0) + \sum_{i=1}^{n} f_i(\mathbf{x}^0)(x_i - x_i^0)$$
$$= f(\mathbf{x}^0) + \left[\frac{\partial f(\mathbf{x}^0)}{\partial \mathbf{x}^0}\right]'(\mathbf{x} - \mathbf{x}^0)$$
$$= f(\mathbf{x}^0) + \mathbf{g}(\mathbf{x}^0)'(\mathbf{x} - \mathbf{x}^0) \qquad \textbf{(2-126)}$$
$$= [f(\mathbf{x}^0) - \mathbf{g}(\mathbf{x}^0)'\mathbf{x}^0] + \mathbf{g}(\mathbf{x}^0)'\mathbf{x}$$
$$= [f^0 - \mathbf{g}^{0\prime}\mathbf{x}^0] + \mathbf{g}^{0\prime}\mathbf{x}$$
$$= \beta_1 + \boldsymbol{\beta}_2'\mathbf{x}.$$

The second-order, or quadratic, approximation adds the second-order terms in the approximation,

$$\frac{1}{2}\sum_{i=1}^{n}\sum_{j=1}^{n} f_{ij}^{0}(x_i - x_i^0)(x_j - x_j^0) = \frac{1}{2}(\mathbf{x} - \mathbf{x}^0)'\,\mathbf{H}^0(\mathbf{x} - \mathbf{x}^0),$$

to the preceding one. Collecting terms in the same manner as in (2-126), we have

$$y \simeq \beta_1 + \boldsymbol{\beta}_2'\mathbf{x} + \frac{1}{2}\mathbf{x}'\boldsymbol{\Gamma}_3\mathbf{x}, \qquad \textbf{(2-127)}$$

where

$$\beta_1 = f^0 - \mathbf{g}^{0\prime}\mathbf{x}^0 + \frac{1}{2}\mathbf{x}^{0\prime}\mathbf{H}^0\mathbf{x}^0,$$
$$\boldsymbol{\beta}_2 = -\mathbf{g}^0 + \mathbf{H}^0\mathbf{x}^0,$$
$$\boldsymbol{\Gamma}_3 = \mathbf{H}^0.$$

A linear function can be written

$$y = \mathbf{a}'\mathbf{x} = \mathbf{x}'\mathbf{a} = \sum_{i=1}^{n} a_i x_i,$$

so

$$\frac{\partial(\mathbf{a}'\mathbf{x})}{\partial\mathbf{x}} = \mathbf{a}. \qquad \textbf{(2-128)}$$

Note, in particular, that $\partial(\mathbf{a}'\mathbf{x})/\partial\mathbf{x} = \mathbf{a}$, not $\mathbf{a}'$. In a set of linear functions

$$\mathbf{y} = \mathbf{A}\mathbf{x},$$

each element y_i of $\mathbf{y}$ is

$$y_i = \mathbf{a}^i\mathbf{x},$$

where $\mathbf{a}^i$ is the ith row of $\mathbf{A}$. Therefore,

$$\frac{\partial y_i}{\partial\mathbf{x}} = \mathbf{a}^{i\prime}$$
$$= \text{transpose of } i\text{th row of } \mathbf{A},$$

and

$$\begin{bmatrix} \partial y_1/\partial\mathbf{x}' \\ \partial y_2/\partial\mathbf{x}' \\ \vdots \\ \partial y_n/\partial\mathbf{x}' \end{bmatrix} = \begin{bmatrix} \mathbf{a}^1 \\ \mathbf{a}^2 \\ \vdots \\ \mathbf{a}^n \end{bmatrix}.$$

Collecting all terms, we find that $\partial\mathbf{A}\mathbf{x}/\partial\mathbf{x}' = \mathbf{A}$, whereas the more familiar form will be

$$\frac{\partial\mathbf{A}\mathbf{x}}{\partial\mathbf{x}} = \mathbf{A}'. \qquad \textbf{(2-129)}$$

A quadratic form is written

$$\mathbf{x}'\mathbf{A}\mathbf{x} = \sum_{i=1}^{n} \sum_{j=1}^{n} x_i x_j a_{ij}. \tag{2-130}$$

For example,

$$\mathbf{A} = \begin{bmatrix} 1 & 3 \\ 3 & 4 \end{bmatrix},$$

so that

$$\mathbf{x}'\mathbf{A}\mathbf{x} = 1x_1^2 + 4x_2^2 + 6x_1x_2.$$

Then

$$\begin{aligned} \frac{\partial \mathbf{x}'\mathbf{A}\mathbf{x}}{\partial \mathbf{x}} &= \begin{bmatrix} 2x_1 + 6x_2 \\ 6x_1 + 8x_2 \end{bmatrix} \\ &= \begin{bmatrix} 2 & 6 \\ 6 & 8 \end{bmatrix} \begin{bmatrix} x_1 \\ x_2 \end{bmatrix} = 2\mathbf{A}\mathbf{x}, \end{aligned} \tag{2-131}$$

which is the general result when $\mathbf{A}$ is a symmetric matrix. If $\mathbf{A}$ is not symmetric, then

$$\frac{\partial(\mathbf{x}'\mathbf{A}\mathbf{x})}{\partial \mathbf{x}} = (\mathbf{A} + \mathbf{A}')\mathbf{x}. \tag{2-132}$$

Referring to the preceding double summation, we find that for each term, the coefficient on a_{ij} is $x_i x_j$. Therefore,

$$\frac{\partial(\mathbf{x}'\mathbf{A}\mathbf{x})}{\partial a_{ij}} = x_i x_j.$$

The square matrix whose ijth element is $x_i x_j$ is $\mathbf{x}\mathbf{x}'$, so

$$\frac{\partial(\mathbf{x}'\mathbf{A}\mathbf{x})}{\partial \mathbf{A}} = \mathbf{x}\mathbf{x}'. \tag{2-133}$$

Derivatives involving determinants appear in maximum likelihood estimation. From the cofactor expansion in (2-51),

$$\frac{\partial|\mathbf{A}|}{\partial a_{ij}} = (-1)^{i+j}|\mathbf{C}_{ji}|,$$

where $|\mathbf{C}_{ji}|$ is the jith cofactor in $\mathbf{A}$. The inverse of $\mathbf{A}$ can be computed using

$$\mathbf{A}_{ij}^{-1} = \frac{(-1)^{i+j}|\mathbf{C}_{ij}|}{|\mathbf{A}|}$$

(note the reversal of the subscripts), which implies that

$$\frac{\partial \ln|\mathbf{A}|}{\partial a_{ij}} = \frac{(-1)^{i+j}|\mathbf{C}_{ji}|}{|\mathbf{A}|}$$

or, collecting terms,

$$\frac{\partial \ln |\mathbf{A}|}{\partial \mathbf{A}} = \mathbf{A}^{-1\prime}.$$

Since the matrices for which we shall make use of this calculation will be symmetric in our applications, the transposition will be unnecessary.

2.9.2. Optimization

Many problems involve finding the x where $f(x)$ is maximized or minimized. Since $f'(x)$ is the slope of $f(x)$, either optimum must occur where $f'(x) = 0$. Otherwise, the function will be increasing or decreasing at x. This implies the **first-order** or **necessary condition for an optimum:**

$$\frac{dy}{dx} = 0. \tag{2-134}$$

The same condition is necessary for both a maximum and a minimum. For a maximum, the function must be concave; for a minimum, it must be convex. This leads to a **sufficient condition for an optimum:**

$$\begin{aligned} &\text{For a maximum, } \frac{d^2y}{dx^2} < 0; \\ &\text{for a minimum, } \frac{d^2y}{dx^2} > 0. \end{aligned} \tag{2-135}$$

Some functions, such as the sine and cosine functions, have many **local optima,** that is, many minima and maxima. A function such as $\sin x/|x|$, which is a damped sine wave, does as well but differs in that although it has many local maxima, it has one, at $x = 0$, at which $f(x)$ is greater than it is at any other point. Thus, $x = 0$ is the **global maximum,** whereas the other maxima are only **local maxima.** Certain functions, such as a quadratic, have only a single optimum. These functions are **globally concave** if the optimum is a maximum and **globally convex** if it is a minimum.

For maximizing or minimizing a function of several variables, the first-order conditions are

$$\frac{\partial f(\mathbf{x})}{\partial \mathbf{x}} = \mathbf{0}. \tag{2-136}$$

This is interpreted in the same manner as the necessary condition in the univariate case. At the optimum, it must be true that no small change in any variable leads to an improvement in the function value. In the single-variable case, d^2y/dx^2 must be positive for a minimum and negative for a maximum. In the multivariate case, we attach a similar condition to the second derivatives matrix of the objective function. The second-order conditions for an optimum are that at the optimizing value,

$$\mathbf{H} = \frac{\partial^2 f(\mathbf{x})}{\partial\mathbf{x}\partial\mathbf{x}'} \tag{2-137}$$

must be positive definite for a minimum and negative definite for a maximum.

In a single-variable problem, the second-order condition can usually be verified by inspection. This will not generally be true in the multivariate case. As discussed earlier, checking the definiteness of a matrix is, in general, a relatively difficult problem. For most of the problems encountered in econometrics, however, the second-order condition will be implied by the structure of the problem. That is, the matrix **H** will usually be of such a form that it is always definite.

For an example of the preceding, consider the problem

$$\text{maximize}_{\mathbf{x}}\ R = \mathbf{a}'\mathbf{x} - \mathbf{x}'\mathbf{A}\mathbf{x},$$

where

$$\mathbf{a}' = (5 \quad 4 \quad 2)$$

and

$$\mathbf{A} = \begin{bmatrix} 2 & 1 & 3 \\ 1 & 3 & 2 \\ 3 & 2 & 5 \end{bmatrix}.$$

Using some now familiar results, we obtain

$$\begin{aligned} \frac{\partial R}{\partial \mathbf{x}} &= \mathbf{a} - 2\mathbf{A}\mathbf{x} \\ &= \begin{bmatrix} 5 \\ 4 \\ 2 \end{bmatrix} - \begin{bmatrix} 4 & 2 & 6 \\ 2 & 6 & 4 \\ 6 & 4 & 10 \end{bmatrix} \begin{bmatrix} x_1 \\ x_2 \\ x_3 \end{bmatrix} = \mathbf{0}. \end{aligned} \tag{2-138}$$

The solutions are

$$\begin{bmatrix} x_1 \\ x_2 \\ x_3 \end{bmatrix} = \begin{bmatrix} 4 & 2 & 6 \\ 2 & 6 & 4 \\ 6 & 4 & 10 \end{bmatrix}^{-1} \begin{bmatrix} 5 \\ 4 \\ 2 \end{bmatrix} = \begin{bmatrix} 11.25 \\ 1.75 \\ -7.25 \end{bmatrix}.$$

The sufficient condition is that

$$\frac{\partial^2 R(\mathbf{x})}{\partial \mathbf{x}\, \partial \mathbf{x}'} = -2\mathbf{A} = \begin{bmatrix} -4 & -2 & -6 \\ -2 & -6 & -4 \\ -6 & -4 & -10 \end{bmatrix} \tag{2-139}$$

must be negative definite. The three characteristic roots of this matrix are -15.746, -4, and -0.25403. Since all three roots are negative, the matrix is negative definite, as required.

In the preceding, it was necessary to compute the characteristic roots of the Hessian to verify the sufficient condition. For a general matrix of order larger than 2, this will normally require a computer. Suppose, however, that **A** is of the form

$$\mathbf{A} = \mathbf{B}'\mathbf{B},$$

where **B** is some known matrix. Then, as shown earlier, we know that **A** will always be positive definite (assuming that **B** has full rank). It is not necessary to calculate the characteristic roots of **A** to verify the sufficient conditions.

2.9.3. Constrained Optimization

It is often necessary to solve an optimization problem subject to some constraints on the solution. One method is merely to "solve out" the constraints. For example, in the maximization problem considered earlier, suppose that the constraint $x_1 = x_2 - x_3$ is imposed on the solution. For a single constraint such as this one, it is possible merely to substitute the right-hand side of this equation for x_1 in the objective function and solve the resulting problem as a function of the remaining two variables. For more general constraints, however, or when there is more than one constraint, the method of Lagrange multipliers provides a more straightforward method of solving the problem. We

$$\begin{aligned} \text{maximize}_{\mathbf{x}}\, f(\mathbf{x}) \text{ subject to } \; & c_1(\mathbf{x}) = 0 \\ & c_2(\mathbf{x}) = 0 \\ & \quad\vdots \\ & c_J(\mathbf{x}) = 0. \end{aligned} \tag{2-140}$$

The Lagrangean approach to this problem is to find the stationary points—that is, the points at which the derivatives are zero—of

$$L^*(\mathbf{x}, \boldsymbol{\lambda}) = f(\mathbf{x}) + \sum_{j=1}^{J} \lambda_j c_j(\mathbf{x}). \tag{2-141}$$

The solutions satisfy the equations

$$\begin{aligned} \frac{\partial L^*}{\partial \mathbf{x}} &= \frac{\partial f(\mathbf{x})}{\partial \mathbf{x}} + \frac{\partial \boldsymbol{\lambda}'\mathbf{c}(\mathbf{x})}{\partial \mathbf{x}} = \mathbf{0}\,(n \times 1), \\ \frac{\partial L^*}{\partial \boldsymbol{\lambda}} &= \mathbf{c}(\mathbf{x}) = \mathbf{0}\,(J \times 1). \end{aligned} \tag{2-142}$$

The second term in $\partial L^*/\partial \mathbf{x}$ is

$$\begin{aligned} \frac{\partial \boldsymbol{\lambda}'\mathbf{c}(\mathbf{x})}{\partial \mathbf{x}} &= \frac{\partial \mathbf{c}(\mathbf{x})'\boldsymbol{\lambda}}{\partial \mathbf{x}} \\ &= \left[\frac{\partial \mathbf{c}(\mathbf{x})'}{\partial \mathbf{x}}\right]\boldsymbol{\lambda} \\ &= \mathbf{C}'\boldsymbol{\lambda}, \end{aligned} \tag{2-143}$$

where **C** is the matrix of derivatives of the constraints with respect to **x**. The jth row of the $J \times n$ matrix $\mathbf{C}$ is the vector of derivatives of the jth constraint, $c_j(\mathbf{x})$, with respect to $\mathbf{x}'$. Upon collecting terms, the first-order conditions are

$$\begin{aligned}\frac{\partial L^*}{\partial \mathbf{x}} &= \frac{\partial f(\mathbf{x})}{\partial \mathbf{x}} + \mathbf{C}'\boldsymbol{\lambda} = \mathbf{0},\\ \frac{\partial L^*}{\partial \boldsymbol{\lambda}} &= \mathbf{c}(\mathbf{x}) = \mathbf{0}.\end{aligned} \quad \textbf{(2-144)}$$

There is one very important aspect of the constrained solution to consider. In the unconstrained solution, we have $\partial f(\mathbf{x})/\partial \mathbf{x} = \mathbf{0}$. From (2-144), we obtain for a constrained solution,

$$\frac{\partial f(\mathbf{x})}{\partial \mathbf{x}} = -\mathbf{C}'\boldsymbol{\lambda}, \quad \textbf{(2-145)}$$

which will not equal $\mathbf{0}$ unless $\boldsymbol{\lambda} = \mathbf{0}$. This has two important implications:

- The constrained solution *must* be inferior to the unconstrained solution. This is implied by the nonzero gradient at the constrained solution.
- If the Lagrange multipliers are zero, then the constrained solution will equal the unconstrained solution.

To continue the example begun earlier, suppose that we add the following conditions:

$$\begin{aligned}x_1 - x_2 + x_3 &= 0,\\ x_1 + x_2 + x_3 &= 0.\end{aligned}$$

To put this in the format of the general problem, write the constraints as $\mathbf{c}(\mathbf{x}) = \mathbf{Cx} = \mathbf{0}$, where

$$\mathbf{C} = \begin{bmatrix} 1 & -1 & 1 \\ 1 & 1 & 1 \end{bmatrix}.$$

The Lagrangean function is

$$R^*(\mathbf{x}, \boldsymbol{\lambda}) = \mathbf{a}'\mathbf{x} - \mathbf{x}'\mathbf{A}\mathbf{x} + \boldsymbol{\lambda}'\mathbf{C}\mathbf{x}.$$

Note the dimensions and arrangement of the various parts. In particular, $\mathbf{C}$ is a 2×3 matrix, with one row for each constraint and one column for each variable in the objective function. The vector of Lagrange multipliers thus has two elements, one for each constraint. The first-order conditions are

$$\mathbf{a} - 2\mathbf{A}\mathbf{x} + \mathbf{C}'\boldsymbol{\lambda} = \mathbf{0} \qquad \text{(three equations)}$$

and

$$\mathbf{Cx} = \mathbf{0} \quad \text{(two equations).} \quad \textbf{(2-146)}$$

These may be combined in the single equation

$$\begin{bmatrix} -2\mathbf{A} & \mathbf{C}' \\ \mathbf{C} & \mathbf{0} \end{bmatrix} \begin{bmatrix} \mathbf{x} \\ \boldsymbol{\lambda} \end{bmatrix} = \begin{bmatrix} -\mathbf{a} \\ \mathbf{0} \end{bmatrix}.$$

Using the partitioned inverse of (2-74) produces the solutions

$$\boldsymbol{\lambda} = -[\mathbf{CA}^{-1}\mathbf{C}']\mathbf{CA}^{-1}\mathbf{a} \qquad \textbf{(2-147)}$$

and

$$\mathbf{x} = \frac{1}{2}\mathbf{A}^{-1}[\mathbf{I} - \mathbf{C}'(\mathbf{CA}^{-1}\mathbf{C}')^{-1}\mathbf{CA}^{-1}]\mathbf{a}. \qquad \textbf{(2-148)}$$

The two results, (2-147) and (2-148), yield analytic solutions for $\boldsymbol{\lambda}$ and $\mathbf{x}$. For the specific matrices and vectors of the example, these are $\boldsymbol{\lambda} = [-0.5 \quad -7.5]'$, and the constrained solution vector is $\mathbf{x}^* = [1.5 \quad 0 \quad -1.5]'$. Note that in computing the solution to this sort of problem, it is not necessary to use the rather cumbersome form of (2-148). Once $\boldsymbol{\lambda}$ is obtained from (2-147), the solution can be inserted in (2-146) for a much simpler computation. The solution

$$\mathbf{x} = \frac{1}{2}\mathbf{A}^{-1}\mathbf{a} + \frac{1}{2}\mathbf{A}^{-1}\mathbf{C}'\boldsymbol{\lambda}$$

suggests a useful result for the constrained optimum:

$$\text{constrained solution} = \text{unconstrained solution} + [2\mathbf{A}]^{-1}\mathbf{C}'\boldsymbol{\lambda}. \qquad \textbf{(2-149)}$$

Finally, by inserting the two solutions in the original function, we find that $R = 24.375$ and $R^* = 2.25$, which illustrates again that the constrained solution (in this *maximization* problem) is inferior to the unconstrained solution.

2.9.4. Transformations

If a function is strictly monotonic, then it is a **one-to-one function.** Each y is associated with exactly one value of x, and vice versa. In this case, an **inverse function** exists, which expresses x as a function of y, written

$$y = f(x) \quad \text{and} \quad x = f^{-1}(y).$$

An example is the inverse relationship between the log and the exponential functions.

The slope of the inverse function,

$$J = \frac{dx}{dy} = \frac{df^{-1}(y)}{dy} = f^{-1\prime}(y),$$

is the **Jacobian** of the transformation from x to y. For example, if

$$y = a + bx,$$

then

$$x = -\frac{a}{b} + \left[\frac{1}{b}\right]y$$

is the inverse transformation and

$$J = \frac{dx}{dy} = \frac{1}{b}.$$

Looking ahead to the statistical application of this concept, we observe that if $y = f(x)$ were *vertical,* then this would no longer be a functional relationship. The same x would be associated with more than one value of y. In this case, at this value of x, we would find that $J = 0$, indicating a singularity in the function.

If $\mathbf{y}$ is a column vector of functions, $\mathbf{y} = \mathbf{f}(\mathbf{x})$, then

$$\mathbf{J} = \frac{\partial \mathbf{x}}{\partial \mathbf{y}'} = \begin{bmatrix} \partial x_1/\partial y_1 & \partial x_1/\partial y_2 & \cdots & \partial x_1/\partial y_n \\ \partial x_2/\partial y_1 & \partial x_2/\partial y_2 & \cdots & \partial x_2/\partial y_n \\ & & \vdots & \\ \partial x_n/\partial y_1 & \partial x_n/\partial y_2 & \cdots & \partial x_n/\partial y_n \end{bmatrix}.$$

Consider the set of linear functions $\mathbf{y} = \mathbf{A}\mathbf{x} = \mathbf{f}(\mathbf{x})$. The inverse transformation is $\mathbf{x} = \mathbf{f}^{-1}(\mathbf{y})$, which will be either

$$\mathbf{x} = \mathbf{A}^{-1}\mathbf{y},$$

if $\mathbf{A}$ is nonsingular, or

$$x = \mathbf{0},$$

if $\mathbf{A}$ is singular. Let $\mathbf{J}$ be the matrix of partial derivatives of the inverse functions:

$$\boldsymbol{J} = \left[\frac{\partial x_i}{\partial y_j}\right].$$

The absolute value of the determinant of $\mathbf{J}$,

$$\text{abs}(|\boldsymbol{J}|) = \left|\frac{\partial \mathbf{x}}{\partial \mathbf{y}'}\right|,$$

is the **Jacobian** of the transformation from $\mathbf{x}$ to $\mathbf{y}$. In the nonsingular case,

$$\text{abs}(|\boldsymbol{J}|) = \text{abs}(|\mathbf{A}^{-1}|) = \frac{1}{\text{abs}(|\mathbf{A}|)}.$$

In the singular case, all the partial derivatives will be zero, as will the Jacobian. In this instance, a zero Jacobian implies that $\mathbf{A}$ is singular or, equivalently, that the transformations from $\mathbf{x}$ to $\mathbf{y}$ are functionally dependent. The singular case is analogous to the single-variable case.

Clearly, if the vector $\mathbf{x}$ is given, then $\mathbf{y} = \mathbf{A}\mathbf{x}$ can be computed from $\mathbf{x}$. Whether $\mathbf{x}$ can be deduced from $\mathbf{y}$ is another question. Evidently, it depends on the Jacobian. If the Jacobian is not zero, then the inverse transformations exist, and we can obtain $\mathbf{x}$. If not, then we cannot obtain $\mathbf{x}$.

EXERCISES

1. For the matrices

$$\mathbf{A} = \begin{bmatrix} 1 & 3 & 3 \\ 2 & 4 & 1 \end{bmatrix}, \qquad \mathbf{B} = \begin{bmatrix} 2 & 4 \\ 1 & 5 \\ 6 & 2 \end{bmatrix},$$

compute **AB**, **A′B′**, and **BA**.

2. Prove that tr(**AB**) = tr(**BA**), where **A** and **B** are any two matrices that are conformable for both multiplications. They need not be square.
3. Prove that $\text{tr}(\mathbf{A}'\mathbf{A}) = \Sigma_{i=1}^{n}\Sigma_{j=1}^{n}a_{ij}^2$.
4. Expand the matrix product $\mathbf{X} = \{[\mathbf{AB} + (\mathbf{CD})'][(\mathbf{EF})^{-1} + \mathbf{GH}]\}'$. Assume that all matrices are square and that **E** and **F** are nonsingular.
5. Prove that for n $K \times 1$ column vectors $\mathbf{x}_i$, $i = 1, \ldots, n$, and some nonzero vector **a**,

$$\sum_{i=1}^{n} (\mathbf{x}_i - \mathbf{a})(\mathbf{x}_i - \mathbf{a})' = \mathbf{X}'\mathbf{M}^0\mathbf{X} + n(\bar{\mathbf{x}} - \mathbf{a})(\bar{\mathbf{x}} - \mathbf{a})'$$

where the ith row of **X** is $\mathbf{x}_i'$ and $\mathbf{M}^0$ is defined in (2-34).

6. Let **A** be any square matrix whose columns are $[\mathbf{a}_1\ \mathbf{a}_2\ \ldots\ \mathbf{a}_M]$, and let **B** be any rearrangement of the columns of the $M \times M$ identity matrix. What operation is performed by the multiplication **AB**? What about **BA**?
7. Consider the 3×3 case of the matrix **B** in Exercise 6. For example,

$$\mathbf{B} = \begin{bmatrix} 0 & 1 & 0 \\ 0 & 0 & 1 \\ 1 & 0 & 0 \end{bmatrix}.$$

Compute $\mathbf{B}^2$ and $\mathbf{B}^3$. Repeat for a 4×4 matrix. Can you generalize your finding?

8. Calculate $|\mathbf{A}|$, tr(**A**), and $\mathbf{A}^{-1}$ for

$$\mathbf{A} = \begin{bmatrix} 1 & 4 & 7 \\ 3 & 2 & 5 \\ 5 & 2 & 8 \end{bmatrix}.$$

9. Obtain the Cholesky decomposition of the matrix

$$\mathbf{A} = \begin{bmatrix} 25 & 7 \\ 7 & 13 \end{bmatrix}.$$

10. A symmetric positive definite matrix **A** can also be written as **A** = **UL**, where **U** is an upper triangular matrix and **L** = **U′**. This is not the Cholesky decomposition, however. Obtain this decomposition of the matrix in Exercise 9.

11. What operation is performed by postmultiplying a matrix by a diagonal matrix? What about premultiplication?

12. Are the following quadratic forms positive for all values of $\mathbf{x}$?
(a) $y = x_1^2 - 28x_1x_2 + (11x_2)^2$.
(b) $y = 5x_1^2 + x_2^2 + 7x_3^2 + 4x_1x_2 + 6x_1x_3 + 8x_2x_3$.

13. Prove that $\text{tr}(\mathbf{A} \otimes \mathbf{B}) = \text{tr}(\mathbf{A})\text{tr}(\mathbf{B})$.

14. A matrix $\mathbf{A}$ is *nilpotent* if $\lim_{K\to\infty}\mathbf{A}^K = \mathbf{0}$. Prove that a necessary and sufficient condition for a symmetric matrix to be nilpotent is that all of its characteristic roots be less than one in absolute value. (For an application, see Section 16.9.2.)

15. Compute the characteristic roots of

$$\mathbf{A} = \begin{bmatrix} 2 & 4 & 3 \\ 4 & 8 & 6 \\ 3 & 6 & 5 \end{bmatrix}.$$

16. Suppose that $\mathbf{A} = \mathbf{A}(z)$, where z is a scalar. What is $\partial(\mathbf{x}'\mathbf{A}\mathbf{x})/\partial z$? Now, suppose that each element of $\mathbf{x}$ is also a function of z. Once again, what is $\partial(\mathbf{x}'\mathbf{A}\mathbf{x})/\partial z$?

17. Show that the solutions to the determinantal equations $|\mathbf{B} - \lambda\mathbf{A}| = 0$ and $|\mathbf{A}^{-1}\mathbf{B} - \lambda\mathbf{I}| = 0$ are the same. How do the solutions to this equation relate to those of the equation $|\mathbf{B}^{-1}\mathbf{A} - \mu\mathbf{I}| = 0$? (For an application of the first of these equations, see Section 16.5.2d.)

18. Using the matrix $\mathbf{A}$ in Exercise 9, find the vector $\mathbf{x}$ that minimizes $y = \mathbf{x}'\mathbf{A}\mathbf{x} + 2x_1 + 3x_2 - 10$. What is the value of y at the minimum? Now, minimize y subject to the constraint $x_1 + x_2 = 1$. Compare the two solutions.

19. What is the Jacobian for the following transformations?

$$y_1 = \frac{x_1}{x_2},$$
$$\ln y_2 = \ln x_1 - \ln x_2 + \ln x_3,$$
$$y_3 = x_1x_2x_3.$$

20. Prove that exchanging two columns of a square matrix reverses the sign of its determinant. [Hint: Use a permutation matrix. See Exercise 6.]

21. Suppose that $\mathbf{x} = \mathbf{x}(z)$, where z is a scalar. What is $\partial[\mathbf{x}'\mathbf{A}\mathbf{x}/\mathbf{x}'\mathbf{B}\mathbf{x}]/\partial z$?

22. Suppose that $\mathbf{y}$ is an $n \times 1$ vector and $\mathbf{X}$ is an $n \times K$ matrix. The projection of $\mathbf{y}$ into the column space of $\mathbf{X}$ is defined in the text after equation (2-55). Now, consider the projection of $\mathbf{y}^* = c\mathbf{y}$ into the column space of $\mathbf{X}^* = \mathbf{XP}$, where c is a scalar and $\mathbf{P}$ is a nonsingular $K \times K$ matrix. Find the projection of $\mathbf{y}^*$ into the column space of $\mathbf{X}^*$. Prove that the cosine of the angle between $\mathbf{y}^*$ and its projection into the column space of $\mathbf{X}^*$ is the same as that between $\mathbf{y}$ and its projection into the column space of $\mathbf{X}$. How do you interpret this result?

23. For the matrix

$$\mathbf{X}' = \begin{bmatrix} 1 & 1 & 1 & 1 \\ 4 & -2 & 3 & -5 \end{bmatrix}$$

compute $\mathbf{P} = \mathbf{X}(\mathbf{X}'\mathbf{X})^{-1}\mathbf{X}'$ and $\mathbf{M} = (\mathbf{I} - \mathbf{P})$. Verify that $\mathbf{MP} = \mathbf{0}$. Let

$$\mathbf{Q} = \begin{bmatrix} 1 & 3 \\ 2 & 8 \end{bmatrix}.$$

[Hint: Show that **M** and **P** are idempotent.]

(a) Compute the **P** and **M** based on **XQ** instead of **X**.

(b) What are the characteristic roots of **M** and **P**?

24. Suppose that **A** is an $n \times n$ matrix of the form

$$\mathbf{A} = (1 - \rho)\mathbf{I} + \rho\mathbf{ii}',$$

where **i** is a column of ones and $0 < \rho < 1$. Write out the format of **A** explicitly for $n = 4$. Find all the characteristic roots and vectors of **A**. [Hint: There are only two distinct characteristic roots, which occur with multiplicity 1 and $n - 1$. Every **c** of a certain type is a characteristic vector of **A**.] For an application that uses a matrix of this type, see Section 14.4 on the random effects model.

25. Find the inverse of the matrix in Exercise 24. [Hint: Use (2-66).]

26. Prove that every matrix in the sequence of matrices

$$\mathbf{W}_{i+1} = \mathbf{W}_i + \mathbf{d}_i\mathbf{d}_i',$$

where $\mathbf{W}_0 = \mathbf{I}$, is positive definite. For an application, see Section 5.5. For an extension, prove that every matrix in the sequence of matrices defined in (5-22) is positive definite if $\mathbf{W}_0 = \mathbf{I}$.

27. What is the inverse matrix of the following?

$$\mathbf{P} = \begin{bmatrix} \cos(x) & \sin(x) \\ -\sin(x) & \cos(x) \end{bmatrix}.$$

What are the characteristic roots of **P**?

28. Derive the off diagonal block of $\mathbf{A}^{-1}$ in Section 2.6.4.

29. (This requires a computer.) For the $\mathbf{X}'\mathbf{X}$ matrix at the end of Section 6.4.1,

(a) Compute the characteristic roots of $\mathbf{X}'\mathbf{X}$.

(b) Compute the condition number of $\mathbf{X}'\mathbf{X}$. (Do not forget to scale the columns of the matrix so that the diagonal elements are 1.)

CHAPTER 3

Probability and Distribution Theory

3.1. INTRODUCTION

This chapter reviews the distribution theory used later in the book. Since a previous course in statistics is assumed, most of the results will be stated without proof. The more advanced results in the later sections will be developed in greater detail.

3.2. RANDOM VARIABLES

We view our observation on some aspect of the economy as the **outcome** of a random experiment. The outcomes of the experiment are assigned unique numeric values. The assignment is one to one; each outcome gets one value, and no two distinct outcomes receive the same value. This outcome variable, X, is a **random variable** because, until the experiment is performed, it is uncertain what value X will take. Probabilities are associated with outcomes to quantify this uncertainty. We usually use capital letters for the "name" of a random variable and lowercase letters for the values it takes. Thus, the probability that X takes a particular value x might be denoted $\text{Prob}(X = x)$.

A random variable is **discrete** if the set of outcomes is either finite in number or countably infinite. The random variable is **continuous** if the set of outcomes is infinitely divisible and, hence, not countable. These definitions will correspond to the types of data we observe in practice. Counts of occurrences will provide observations on discrete random variables, whereas measurements such as time or income will give observations on continuous random variables.

3.2.1. Probability Distributions

A listing of the values x taken by a random variable X and their associated probabilities is a **probability distribution,** $f(x)$. For a discrete random variable,

$$f(x) = \text{Prob}(X = x). \quad \textbf{(3-1)}$$

The axioms of probability require that

1. $0 \leq \text{Prob}(X = x) \leq 1.$
2. $\Sigma_x f(x_i) = 1.$ **(3-2)**

EXAMPLE 3.1 Poisson Model for a Discrete Outcome

Let X be the number of customers to arrive at a teller's window at a bank in a randomly chosen time span of given length. A frequently used model is the **Poisson distribution:**

$$f(x) = \frac{e^{-\lambda}\lambda^x}{x!}, \quad x = 0, 1, 2, \ldots, \quad \textbf{(3-3)}$$

where λ is the average number of persons to arrive in a given time span. Note that regardless of the value of λ, the probability model is, in fact, at odds with the physical phenomenon being described. The number of persons must, of course, be finite. But, for large values of x, the probabilities assigned by this model become arbitrarily small.

For the continuous case, the probability associated with any particular point is zero, and we can only assign positive probabilities to intervals in the range of x. The **probability density function (pdf)** is defined so that $f(x) \geq 0$ and

1. $\text{Prob}(a \leq x \leq b) = \int_a^b f(x)\,dx \geq 0.$ **(3-4)**

This is the area under $f(x)$ in the range from a to b. For a continuous variable,

2. $\int_{-\infty}^{+\infty} f(x)\,dx = 1.$ **(3-5)**

If the range of x is not infinite, it is understood that $f(x) = 0$ anywhere outside the appropriate range. Since the probability associated with any individual point is 0,

$$\begin{aligned}\text{Prob}(a \leq x \leq b) &= \text{Prob}(a \leq x < b)\\ &= \text{Prob}(a < x \leq b)\\ &= \text{Prob}(a < x < b).\end{aligned}$$

3.2.2. Cumulative Distribution Function

For any random variable x, the probability that x is less than or equal to a is denoted $F(a)$. $F(x)$ is the **cumulative distribution function (cdf).** For a discrete random variable,

$$F(x) = \sum_{X \le x} f(x) = \text{Prob}(X \le x). \tag{3-6}$$

In view of the definition of $f(x)$,

$$f(x_i) = F(x_i) - F(x_{i-1}). \tag{3-7}$$

For a continuous random variable,

$$F(x) = \int_{-\infty}^{x} f(t)\, dt \tag{3-8}$$

and

$$f(x) = \frac{dF(x)}{dx}. \tag{3-9}$$

In both the continuous and discrete cases, $F(x)$ must satisfy the following properties:

1. $0 \le F(x) \le 1$.
2. If $x > y$, $F(x) \ge F(y)$.
3. $F(+\infty) = 1$.
4. $F(-\infty) = 0$.

From the definition of the cdf,

$$\text{Prob}(a < x \le b) = F(b) - F(a). \tag{3-10}$$

Any valid pdf will imply a valid cdf, so there is no need to verify these conditions separately.

3.3. EXPECTATIONS OF A RANDOM VARIABLE

Definition 3.1: Mean of a Random Variable. *The* ***mean,*** *or* ***expected value,*** *of a random variable is*

$$E[x] = \begin{cases} \sum_x xf(x) & \text{if } x \text{ is discrete,} \\ \int_x xf(x)\, dx & \text{if } x \text{ is continuous.} \end{cases} \tag{3-11}$$

The notation Σ_x or $\int_x$, used henceforth, means the sum or integral over the entire range of values of x. The mean is usually denoted μ. It is a weighted average of the values taken by x, where the weights are the respective probabilities. It is not necessarily a value actually taken by the random variable. For example, the expected number of heads in one toss of a fair coin is $\frac{1}{2}$.

Other **measures of central tendency** are the **median,** which is the value m such that $\text{Prob}(X \leq m) \geq \frac{1}{2}$ and $\text{Prob}(X \geq m) \leq \frac{1}{2}$, and the **mode,** which is the value of x at which $f(x)$ takes its maximum. The first of these measures is more frequently used than the second. Loosely speaking, the median corresponds more closely than the mean to the middle of a distribution. It is unaffected by extreme values. In the discrete case, the modal value of x has the highest probability of occurring.

Let $g(x)$ be a function of x. The function that gives the expected value of $g(x)$ is denoted

$$E[g(x)] = \begin{cases} \sum_i g(x_i)\text{Prob}(X = x_i) & \text{if } X \text{ is discrete,} \\ \int_{-\infty}^{+\infty} g(x)f(x)\,dx & \text{if } X \text{ is continuous.} \end{cases} \quad \textbf{(3-12)}$$

If $g(x) = a + bx$ for constants a and b,

$$E[a + bx] = a + bE[x].$$

One important case is the expected value of a constant a, which is just a.

DEFINITION 3.2: Variance of a Random Variable. *The **variance** of a random variable is*

$$\begin{aligned} \text{Var}[x] &= E[(x - \mu)^2] \\ &= \begin{cases} \sum_x (x - \mu)^2 f(x) & \text{if } x \text{ is discrete,} \\ \int_x (x - \mu)^2 f(x)\,dx & \text{if } x \text{ is continuous.} \end{cases} \end{aligned} \quad \textbf{(3-13)}$$

Var[x], which must be positive, is usually denoted σ^2. This is a measure of the dispersion of a distribution. Computation of the variance is simplified by using the following important result:

$$\text{Var}[x] = E[x^2] - \mu^2. \quad \textbf{(3-14)}$$

A convenient corollary to (3-14) is

$$E[x^2] = \sigma^2 + \mu^2. \quad \textbf{(3-15)}$$

By inserting $y = a + bx$ in (3-13) and expanding, we find that

$$\text{Var}[a + bx] = b^2\,\text{Var}[x], \quad \textbf{(3-16)}$$

which implies, for any constant a, that

$$\text{Var}[a] = 0. \quad \textbf{(3-17)}$$

To describe a distribution, we usually use σ, the positive square root, which is the **standard deviation** of x. The standard deviation can be interpreted as having the same units of measurement as x and μ. For any random variable x and any positive constant k, the **Chebyshev inequality** states that

$$\text{Prob}(\mu - k\sigma \leq x \leq \mu + k\sigma) \geq 1 - \frac{1}{k^2}. \qquad \textbf{(3-18)}$$

(See Theorem 4.4, Section 4.4.1.)

Two other measures often used to describe a probability distribution are

$$\text{skewness} = E[(x - \mu)^3]$$

and

$$\text{kurtosis} = E[(x - \mu)^4].$$

Skewness is a measure of the asymmetry of a distribution. For symmetric distributions,

$$f(\mu - x) = f(\mu + x)$$

and

$$\text{skewness} = 0.$$

For asymmetric distributions, the skewness will be positive if the "long tail" is in the positive direction. Kurtosis is a measure of the thickness of the tails of the distribution. A shorthand expression for other **central moments** is

$$\mu_r = E[(x - \mu)^r].$$

Since μ_r tends to explode as r grows, the normalized measure, μ_r/σ^r, is often used for description. Two common measures are

$$\text{skewness coefficient} = \frac{\mu_3}{\sigma^3}$$

and

$$\text{degree of excess} = \frac{\mu_4}{\sigma^4} - 3.$$

The second is based on the normal distribution, which has excess of zero.

For any two functions $g_1(x)$ and $g_2(x)$,

$$E[g_1(x) + g_2(x)] = E[g_1(x)] + E[g_2(x)]. \qquad \textbf{(3-19)}$$

For the general case of a possibly nonlinear $g(x)$,

$$E[g(x)] = \int_x g(x)f(x)\,dx \qquad \textbf{(3-20)}$$

and

$$\text{Var}[g(x)] = \int_x (g(x) - E[g(x)])^2 f(x)\,dx. \qquad \textbf{(3-21)}$$

(For convenience, we shall omit the equivalent definitions for discrete variables in the following discussion and use the integral to mean either integration or summation, whichever is appropriate.)

A device used to approximate $E[g(x)]$ and $\text{Var}[g(x)]$ is the linear Taylor series approximation:

$$\begin{aligned} g(x) &\simeq [g(x^0) - g'(x^0)x^0] + g'(x^0)x \\ &= \beta_1 + \beta_2 x \\ &= g^*(x). \end{aligned} \tag{3-22}$$

If the approximation is reasonably accurate, the mean and variance of $g^*(x)$ will be approximately equal to the mean and variance of $g(x)$. A natural choice for the expansion point is $x^0 = \mu = E(x)$. Inserting this in (3-22) gives

$$g(x) \simeq [g(\mu) - g'(\mu)\mu] + g'(\mu)x, \tag{3-23}$$

so that

$$E[g(x)] \simeq g(\mu) \tag{3-24}$$

and

$$\text{Var}[g(x)] \simeq [g'(\mu)]^2 \text{Var}[x]. \tag{3-25}$$

A point to note in view of (3-22) to (3-24) is that $E[g(x)]$ will generally not equal $g(E[x])$. For the special case in which $g(x)$ is concave—that is, where $g''(x) < 0$—we know from **Jensen's inequality** that $E[g(x)] \leq g(E[x])$. (See Theorem 4.8.) For example, $E[\log(x)] \leq \log(E[x])$.

3.4. SOME SPECIFIC PROBABILITY DISTRIBUTIONS

Certain experimental situations naturally give rise to specific probability distributions. In the majority of cases in economics, however, the distributions used are merely models of the observed phenomena. Although the normal distribution, which we shall discuss at length, is the mainstay of econometric research, economists have used a wide variety of other distributions. A few are discussed here.[1]

3.4.1. The Normal Distribution

The general form of a normal distribution with mean μ and standard deviation σ is

$$f(x \mid \mu, \sigma^2) = \frac{1}{\sigma\sqrt{2\pi}} e^{-1/2\,[(x-\mu)^2/\sigma^2]}. \tag{3-26}$$

[1]A much more complete listing appears in Maddala (1977, Chaps. 3 and 18) and in most mathematical statistics textbooks. See also Poirier (1995) and Stuart and Ord (1989).

This is usually denoted $x \sim N[\mu, \sigma^2]$. The standard notation $x \sim f(x)$ is used to state that "x has probability distribution $f(x)$." Among the most useful properties of the normal distribution is its preservation under linear transformation.

$$\text{If } x \sim N[\mu, \sigma^2], (a + bx) \sim N[a + b\mu, b^2\sigma^2]. \tag{3-27}$$

One particularly convenient transformation is $a = -\mu/\sigma$ and $b = 1/\sigma$. The resulting variable

$$z = \frac{x - \mu}{\sigma}$$

has the **standard normal distribution,** denoted $N[0, 1]$, with density

$$\phi(z) = \frac{1}{\sqrt{2\pi}} e^{-z^2/2}. \tag{3-28}$$

The specific notation $\phi(z)$ is often used for this distribution and $\Phi(z)$ for its cdf. It follows from the definitions above that if $x \sim N[\mu, \sigma^2]$, then

$$f(x) = \frac{1}{\sigma}\phi\left[\frac{x - \mu}{\sigma}\right].$$

Tables of the standard normal cdf appear in most statistics and econometrics textbooks. Because the form of the distribution does not change under a linear transformation, it is not necessary to tabulate the distribution for other values of μ and σ. For any normally distributed variable,

$$\text{Prob}(a < x < b) = \text{Prob}\left(\frac{a - \mu}{\sigma} < \frac{x - \mu}{\sigma} < \frac{b - \mu}{\sigma}\right), \tag{3-29}$$

which can always be read from a table of the standard normal distribution. In addition, because the distribution is symmetric, $\Phi(-z) = 1 - \Phi(z)$. Hence, it is not necessary to tabulate both the negative and positive halves of the distribution.

3.4.2. The Chi-Squared, *t*, and *F* Distributions

The chi-squared, t, and F distributions are derived from the normal distribution. They arise in econometrics as sums of n or n_1 and n_2 other variables. These three distributions have associated with them one or two "degrees of freedom" parameters, which for our purposes will be the number of variables in the relevant sum.

The first of the essential results is

- If $z \sim N[0, 1]$, $x = z^2 \sim$ chi-squared[1]—that is, **chi-squared** with one degree of freedom—denoted

$$z^2 \sim \chi^2[1]. \tag{3-30}$$

This is a skewed distribution with mean 1 and variance 2. The second is

- If $x_1, \ldots, x_n$ are n *independent* chi-squared[1] variables, then

$$\sum_{i=1}^{n} x_i \sim \text{chi-squared}[n]. \quad \textbf{(3-31)}$$

The mean and variance of a chi-squared variable with n degrees of freedom are n and $2n$, respectively. A number of useful corollaries can be derived using (3-30) and (3-31).

- If $z_i, i = 1, \ldots, n$, are independent $N[0, 1]$ variables,

$$\sum_{i=1}^{n} z_i^2 \sim \chi^2[n]. \quad \textbf{(3-32)}$$

- If $z_i, i = 1, \ldots, n$, are independent $N[0, \sigma^2]$ variables,

$$\sum_{i=1}^{n} (z_i/\sigma)^2 \sim \chi^2[n]. \quad \textbf{(3-33)}$$

- If x_1 and x_2 are independent chi-squared variables with n_1 and n_2 degrees of freedom, respectively,

$$x_1 + x_2 \sim \chi^2[n_1 + n_2]. \quad \textbf{(3-34)}$$

This can be generalized to the sum of an arbitrary number of independent chi-squared variables.

Unlike the normal distribution, a separate table is required for the chi-squared distribution for each value of n. Typically, only a few percentage points of the distribution are tabulated for each n. Table 4 in the appendix of this book gives upper (right) tail areas for a number of values.

- If x_1 and x_2 are two *independent* chi-squared variables with degrees of freedom parameters n_1 and n_2, respectively, the ratio

$$F[n_1, n_2] = \frac{x_1/n_1}{x_2/n_2} \quad \textbf{(3-35)}$$

  has the ***F* distribution** with n_1 and n_2 degrees of freedom.

The two degrees of freedom parameters n_1 and n_2 are the numerator and denominator degrees of freedom, respectively. Tables of the F distribution must be computed for each pair of values of (n_1, n_2). As such, only one or two specific values, such as the 95 percent and 99 percent upper tail values, are tabulated in most cases.

- If z is an $N[0, 1]$ variable and x is $\chi^2[n]$ and is independent of z, the ratio

$$t[n] = \frac{z}{\sqrt{x/n}} \quad \textbf{(3-36)}$$

  has the ***t* distribution** with n degrees of freedom.

The t distribution has the same shape as the normal distribution but has thicker tails.[2] This distribution is tabulated in the same manner as the chi-squared distribution, with several specific cutoff points corresponding to specified tail areas for various values of the degrees of freedom parameter.

Comparing (3-35) with $n_1 = 1$ and (3-36), we see the useful relationship between the t and F distributions:

- If $t \sim t[n], t^2 \sim F[1, n]$.

3.4.3. Distributions with Large Degrees of Freedom

The chi-squared, t, and F distributions usually arise in connection with sums of sample observations. The degrees of freedom parameter in each case grows with the number of observations. We often deal with larger degrees of freedom than are shown in the tables. Thus, the standard tables are often inadequate. In all cases, however, there are **limiting distributions** that we can use when the degrees of freedom parameter grows large. The simplest case is the t distribution. The t distribution with infinite degrees of freedom is equivalent to the standard normal distribution. Beyond about 100 degrees of freedom, they are almost indistinguishable.

For degrees of freedom greater than 30, a commonly used approximation for the distribution of the chi-squared variable x is

$$z = (2x)^{1/2} - (2n - 1)^{1/2}, \tag{3-37}$$

which is approximately standard normally distributed. Thus,

$$\text{Prob}(\chi^2[n] \le a) \simeq \Phi[(2a)^{1/2} - (2n - 1)^{1/2}].$$

EXAMPLE 3.2 Approximation to the Chi-Squared Distribution

If x is chi-squared with 70 degrees of freedom,

$$\begin{aligned}\text{Prob}(x \le 85) &\simeq \text{Prob}(z < \sqrt{170} - \sqrt{139})\\ &= \text{Prob}(z < 1.249) = 0.8942.\end{aligned}$$

The correct value from the chi-squared distribution is 0.89409.

As used in econometrics, the F distribution with a large-denominator degrees of freedom is common. As n_2 becomes infinite, the denominator of F converges identically to 1, so we can treat the variable

$$x = n_1 F \tag{3-38}$$

as a chi-squared variable with n_1 degrees of freedom. Since the numerator degree of freedom will typically be small, this approximation will suffice for the types of applications we are likely to encounter.[3] If not, the approximation given earlier for the chi-squared distribution can be applied to $n_1 F$.

---

[2]The special case of $t[1]$, which is the ratio of two standard normal variables, is the Cauchy distribution.

[3]See Johnson and Kotz (1970) for other approximations.

3.4.4. Size Distributions—The Lognormal Distribution

In modeling size distributions, such as the distribution of firm sizes in an industry or the distribution of income in a country, the **lognormal distribution,** denoted $LN[\mu, \sigma^2]$, has been particularly useful.[4]

$$f(x) = \frac{1}{\sqrt{2\pi}\,\sigma x} e^{-1/2\,(\ln x - \mu/\sigma)^2}, \quad x \geq 0.$$

A lognormal variable x has

$$E[x] = e^{\mu + \sigma^2/2}$$

and

$$\text{Var}[x] = e^{2\mu + \sigma^2}(e^{\sigma^2} - 1).$$

The relation between the normal and lognormal distributions is

$$\text{If } y \sim LN[\mu, \sigma^2], \ln y \sim N[\mu, \sigma^2].$$

A useful result for transformations is given as follows:

If x has a lognormal distribution with mean θ and variance λ^2,
$\ln x \sim N(\mu, \sigma^2)$, where $\mu = \ln \theta^2 - \frac{1}{2}\ln(\theta^2 + \lambda^2)$ and $\sigma^2 = \ln(1 + \lambda^2/\theta^2)$.

Since the normal distribution is preserved under linear transformation,

$$\text{if } y \sim LN[\mu, \sigma^2], \text{ then } y^r \sim LN[r\mu, r^2\sigma^2],$$

and

$$\text{if } y_1 \sim LN[\mu_1, \sigma_1^2] \text{ and } y_2 \sim LN[\mu_2, \sigma_2^2], \text{ then } y_1 y_2 \sim LN[\mu_1 + \mu_2, \sigma_1^2 + \sigma_2^2].$$

3.4.5. The Gamma and Exponential Distributions

The **gamma distribution** has been used in a variety of settings, including the study of income distribution[5] and production functions.[6] The general form of the distribution is

$$f(x) = \frac{\lambda^P}{\Gamma(P)} e^{-\lambda x} x^{P-1}, \quad x \geq 0, \lambda > 0, P > 0. \tag{3-39}$$

Many familiar distributions are special cases, including the exponential ($P = 1$) and chi-squared ($\lambda = \frac{1}{2}, P = n/2$). The **Erlang distribution** results if P is a positive integer. The mean is P/λ, and the variance is P/λ^2.

3.4.6. The Beta Distribution

Distributions for models are often chosen on the basis of the range within which the random variable is constrained to vary. The lognormal distribution, for example, is sometimes used to model a variable that is always nonnegative.

---

[4]A study of applications of the lognormal distribution appears in Aitchison and Brown (1969).

[5]Salem and Mount (1974).

[6]Greene (1980a).

For a variable constrained between 0 and $c > 0$, the **beta distribution** has proved useful. Its density is

$$f(x) = \frac{\Gamma(\alpha + \beta)}{\Gamma(\alpha)\Gamma(\beta)} \left(\frac{x}{c}\right)^{\alpha-1} \left(1 - \frac{x}{c}\right)^{\beta-1} \left(\frac{1}{c}\right). \tag{3-40}$$

This functional form is extremely flexible in the shapes it will accommodate. It is symmetric if $\alpha = \beta$, asymmetric otherwise, and can be hump-shaped or U-shaped. The mean is $c\alpha/(\alpha + \beta)$, and the variance is $c^2\alpha\beta/[(\alpha + \beta + 1)(\alpha + \beta)^2]$. The beta distribution has been applied in the study of labor force participation rates.[7]

3.4.7. The Logistic Distribution

The normal distribution is ubiquitous in econometrics. But researchers have found that for some microeconomic applications, there does not appear to be enough mass in the tails of the normal distribution; observations that a model based on normality would classify as "unusual" seem not to be very unusual at all. One approach has been to use thicker-tailed symmetric distributions. The **logistic distribution** is one candidate; the cdf for a logistic random variable is denoted

$$F(x) = \Lambda(x) = \frac{1}{1 + e^{-x}}.$$

The density is $f(x) = \Lambda(x)[1 - \Lambda(x)]$. The mean and variance of this distribution are zero and $\pi^2/3$.

3.4.8. Discrete Random Variables

Modeling in economics frequently involves random variables that take integer values. In these cases, the distributions listed thus far only provide approximations that are sometimes quite inappropriate. We can build up a class of models for discrete random variables from the **Bernoulli distribution** for a single binomial outcome (trial)

$$\begin{aligned} \text{Prob}(x = 1) &= \alpha \\ \text{Prob}(x = 0) &= 1 - \alpha, \end{aligned}$$

where $0 \leq \alpha \leq 1$. The modeling aspect of this specification would be the assumptions that the success probability α is constant from one trial to the next and that successive trials are independent. If so, then the distribution for x successes in n trials is the **binomial distribution,**

$$\text{Prob}(X = x) = \binom{n}{x} \alpha^x (1 - \alpha)^{n-x}, \quad x = 0, 1, \ldots, n.$$

[7]Heckman and Willis (1976).

The mean and variance of x are $n\alpha$ and $n\alpha(1 - \alpha)$, respectively. If the number of trials becomes large at the same time that the success probability becomes small so that the mean $n\alpha$ is stable, the limiting form of the binomial distribution is the **Poisson distribution,**

$$\text{Prob}(X = x) = \frac{e^{-\lambda}\lambda^x}{x!}.$$

The Poisson distribution has seen wide use in econometrics in, for example, modeling patents, crime, recreation demand, and demand for health services.

3.5. THE DISTRIBUTION OF A FUNCTION OF A RANDOM VARIABLE

We considered finding the expected value of a function of a random variable. It is fairly common to analyze the random variable itself, which results when we compute a function of some random variable. There are three types of transformation to consider. One discrete random variable may be transformed into another; a continuous variable may be transformed into a discrete one, and one continuous variable may be transformed into another.

The simplest case is the first one. The probabilities associated with the new variable are computed according to the laws of probability. If y is derived from x and the function is one to one, then the probability that $Y = y(x)$ equals the probability that $X = x$. If several values of x yield the same value of y, then $\text{Prob}(Y = y)$ is the sum of the corresponding probabilities for x.

The second type of transformation is illustrated by the way individual data on income are typically obtained in a survey. Income in the population can be expected to be distributed according to some skewed, continuous distribution such as the one shown in Figure 3.1.

Data are normally reported categorically, as shown in the lower part of the figure. Thus, the random variable corresponding to observed income is a discrete transformation of the actual underlying continuous random variable. Suppose, for example, that the transformed variable y is the mean income in the respective interval. Then

$$\begin{aligned}
\text{Prob}(Y = \mu_1) &= P(-\infty < X \leq a),\\
\text{Prob}(Y = \mu_2) &= P(a < X \leq b),\\
\text{Prob}(Y = \mu_3) &= P(b < X \leq c),
\end{aligned}$$

and so on, which illustrates the general procedure.

If x is a continuous random variable with pdf $f_x(x)$, and if $y = g(x)$ is a continuous monotonic function of x, the density of y is obtained by using the change of variable technique to find the cdf of y:

$$\text{Prob}(y \leq b) = \int_{-\infty}^{b} f_x(g^{-1}(y))\,|g^{-1\prime}(y)|\,dy.$$

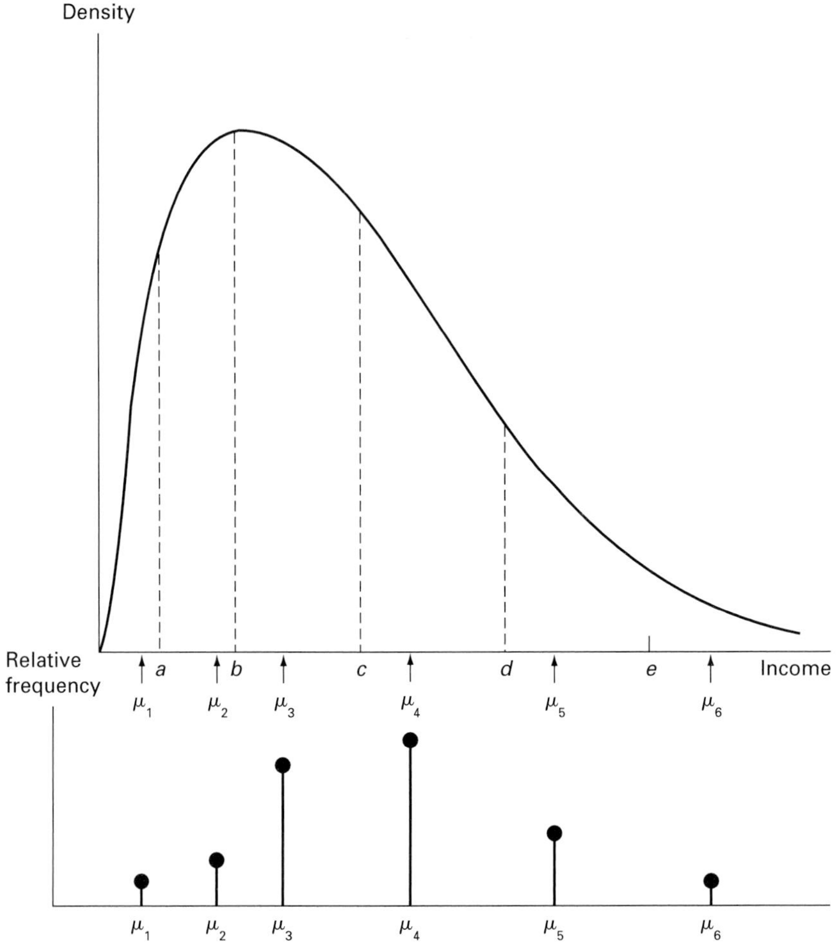

FIGURE 3.1 Censored Distribution.

This can now be written as

$$\text{Prob}(y \leq b) = \int_{-\infty}^{b} f_y(y)\, dy.$$

Hence,

$$f_y(y) = f_x(g^{-1}(y))\,|g^{-1\prime}(y)|. \tag{3-41}$$

To avoid the possibility of a negative pdf if $g(x)$ is decreasing, we use the absolute value of the derivative in the previous expression. The term $|g^{-1\prime}(y)|$ is the Jacobian of the transformation from x to y. The Jacobian must be nonzero for the density of y to be nonzero. In words, the probabilities associated with intervals in the range of y must be associated with intervals in the range of x. If the Jacobian is zero, the function $y = g(x)$ is vertical, and hence all values of y in the given range are associated with the same value of x. This single point must have probability zero.

EXAMPLE 3.3 Linear Transformation of a Normal Variable

If $x \sim N[\mu, \sigma^2]$, what is the distribution of $y = x/\sigma - \mu/\sigma$?

$$y = \frac{x}{\sigma} - \frac{\mu}{\sigma} \Rightarrow x = \sigma y + \mu \Rightarrow f^{-1\prime}(y) = \frac{dx}{dy} = \sigma.$$

Thus,

$$f_y(y) = \frac{1}{\sqrt{2\pi}\,\sigma} e^{-[(\sigma y + \mu) - \mu]^2/(2\sigma^2)} |\sigma|,$$

which is the density of a normally distributed variable with mean 0 and standard deviation 1.

3.6. JOINT DISTRIBUTIONS

The **joint density function** for two random variables X and Y denoted $f(x, y)$ is defined so that

$$\begin{aligned} \text{Prob}(a \le x \le b, c \le y \le d) &= \int_a^b \int_c^d f(x, y)\, dy\, dx \\ &= \sum_{a \le x \le b}\ \sum_{c \le y \le d} f(x, y). \end{aligned} \quad \textbf{(3-42)}$$

The counterparts of the requirements for a univariate probability density are

$$\begin{aligned} &f(x, y) \ge 0 \\ &\sum_x \sum_y f(x, y) = 1 && \text{if } x \text{ and } y \text{ are discrete,} \\ &\int_x \int_y f(x, y)\, dy\, dx = 1 && \text{if } x \text{ and } y \text{ are continuous.} \end{aligned} \quad \textbf{(3-43)}$$

The cumulative probability is likewise the probability of a joint event:

$$\begin{aligned} F(x, y) &= \text{Prob}(X \le x, Y \le y) \\ &= \begin{cases} \sum_{X \le x}\ \sum_{Y \le y} f(x, y) & \text{in the discrete case} \\ \int_{-\infty}^{x} \int_{-\infty}^{y} f(t, s)\, ds\, dt & \text{in the continuous case.} \end{cases} \end{aligned} \quad \textbf{(3-44)}$$

3.6.1. Marginal Distributions

A **marginal probability density** or marginal probability distribution is defined with respect to an individual variable. To obtain the marginal distributions from the joint density, it is necessary to sum or integrate out the other variable:

$$f_x(x) = \begin{cases} \sum_y f(x, y) & \text{in the discrete case} \\ \int_y f(x, t)\, dt & \text{in the continuous case} \end{cases} \tag{3-45}$$

and similarly for $f_y(y)$.

Two random variables are statistically independent if and only if their joint density is the product of the marginal densities:

$$f(x, y) = f_x(x) f_y(y) \Longleftrightarrow x \text{ and } y \text{ are independent.} \tag{3-46}$$

If (and only if) x and y are independent, then the cdf factors as well as the pdf:

$$F(x, y) = F_x(x) F_y(y) \tag{3-47}$$

or

$$\text{Prob}(X \leq x, Y \leq y) = \text{Prob}(X \leq x)\text{Prob}(Y \leq y).$$

3.6.2. Expectations in a Joint Distribution

The means, variances, and higher moments of the variables in a joint distribution are defined with respect to the marginal distributions. For the mean of x in a discrete distribution,

$$\begin{aligned} E[x] &= \sum_x x f_x(x) \\ &= \sum_x x \left[\sum_y f(x, y) \right] \\ &= \sum_x \sum_y x f(x, y). \end{aligned} \tag{3-48}$$

The means of the variables in a continuous distribution are defined likewise, using integration instead of summation:

$$\begin{aligned} E[x] &= \int_x x f_x(x)\, dx \\ &= \int_x \int_y x f(x, y)\, dy\, dx. \end{aligned} \tag{3-49}$$

Variances are computed in the same manner:

$$\begin{aligned} \text{Var}[x] &= \sum_x (x - E[x])^2 f_x(x) \\ &= \sum_x \sum_y (x - E[x])^2 f(x, y). \end{aligned} \tag{3-50}$$

3.6.3. Covariance and Correlation

For any function $g(x, y)$,

$$E[g(x, y)] = \begin{cases} \sum_x \sum_y g(x, y) f(x, y) & \text{in the discrete case,} \\ \int_x \int_y g(x, y) f(x, y)\, dy\, dx & \text{in the continuous case.} \end{cases} \quad \textbf{(3-51)}$$

The covariance of x and y is a special case:

$$\begin{aligned} \text{Cov}[x, y] &= E[(x - \mu_x)(y - \mu_y)] \\ &= E[xy] - \mu_x \mu_y \\ &= \sigma_{xy}. \end{aligned} \quad \textbf{(3-52)}$$

If x and y are independent, $f(x, y) = f_x(x) f_y(y)$ and

$$\begin{aligned} \sigma_{xy} &= \sum_x \sum_y f_x(x) f_y(y)(x - \mu_x)(y - \mu_y) \\ &= \sum_x (x - \mu_x) f_x(x) \sum_y (y - \mu_y) f_y(y) \\ &= E[x - \mu_x] E[y - \mu_y] \\ &= 0. \end{aligned}$$

The sign of the covariance will indicate the direction of covariation of X and Y. Its magnitude depends on the scales of measurement, however. In view of this, a preferable measure is the correlation coefficient:

$$\begin{aligned} r[x, y] &= \rho_{xy} \\ &= \frac{\sigma_{xy}}{\sigma_x \sigma_y}, \end{aligned} \quad \textbf{(3-53)}$$

where σ_x and σ_y are the standard deviations of x and y, respectively. The correlation coefficient has the same sign as the covariance but is always between -1 and 1 and is thus unaffected by any scaling of the variables.

Variables that are uncorrelated are not necessarily independent. For example, in the discrete distribution $f(-1, 1) = f(0, 0) = f(1, 1) = \frac{1}{3}$, the correlation is zero, but $f(1, 1)$ does not equal $f_x(1) f_y(1) = (\frac{1}{3})(\frac{2}{3})$. An important exception is the joint normal distribution discussed subsequently, in which lack of correlation does imply independence.

Some general results regarding expectations in a joint distribution, which can be verified by applying the appropriate definitions, are

$$E[ax + by + c] = aE[x] + bE[y] + c, \quad \textbf{(3-54)}$$

$$\begin{aligned} \text{Var}[ax + by + c] &= a^2 \text{Var}[x] + b^2 \text{Var}[y] + 2ab\, \text{Cov}[x, y] \\ &= \text{Var}[ax + by], \end{aligned} \quad \textbf{(3-55)}$$

and

$$\text{Cov}[ax + by, cx + dy] = ac\, \text{Var}[x] + bd\, \text{Var}[y] + (ad + bc)\text{Cov}[x, y]. \quad \textbf{(3-56)}$$

If X and Y are uncorrelated,

$$\begin{aligned}\text{Var}[x + y] &= \text{Var}[x - y] \\ &= \text{Var}[x] + \text{Var}[y].\end{aligned} \tag{3-57}$$

For any two functions $g_1(x)$ and $g_2(y)$, if x and y are independent,

$$E[g_1(x)g_2(y)] = E[g_1(x)]E[g_2(y)]. \tag{3-58}$$

3.6.4. Distribution of a Function of Bivariate Random Variables

The result for a function of a random variable in (3-41) must be modified for a joint distribution. Suppose that x_1 and x_2 have a joint distribution $f_x(x_1, x_2)$ and that y_1 and y_2 are two monotonic functions of x_1 and x_2:

$$y_1 = y_1(x_1, x_2)$$

and

$$y_2 = y_2(x_1, x_2).$$

Since the functions are monotonic, the inverse transformations,

$$x_1 = x_1(y_1, y_2)$$

and

$$x_2 = x_2(y_1, y_2)$$

exist. The Jacobian of the transformations is the absolute value of the determinant of the matrix of partial derivatives,

$$J = \text{abs}\begin{vmatrix} \partial x_1/\partial y_1 & \partial x_1/\partial y_2 \\ \partial x_2/\partial y_1 & \partial x_2/\partial y_2 \end{vmatrix} = \text{abs}\left|\frac{\partial \mathbf{x}}{\partial \mathbf{y}'}\right|.$$

Then the joint distribution of y_1 and y_2 is

$$f_y(y_1, y_2) = f_x[x_1(y_1, y_2), x_2(y_1, y_2)]\text{abs}|\mathbf{J}|.$$

The Jacobian must be nonzero for the transformation to exist. A zero Jacobian implies that the two transformations are functionally dependent.

EXAMPLE 3.4 Linear Transformations

Suppose that x_1 and x_2 are independently distributed $N[0, 1]$, and the transformations are

$$\begin{aligned}y_1 &= \alpha_1 + \beta_{11}x_1 + \beta_{12}x_2, \\ y_2 &= \alpha_2 + \beta_{21}x_1 + \beta_{22}x_2.\end{aligned}$$

What is the joint distribution of y_1 and y_2? It is simpler to write the transformations as

$$\mathbf{y} = \mathbf{a} + \mathbf{Bx}.$$

The inverse transformation is

$$\mathbf{x} = \mathbf{B}^{-1}(\mathbf{y} - \mathbf{a}),$$

so the Jacobian is

$$J = \text{abs}|\mathbf{B}^{-1}| = \frac{1}{\text{abs}|\mathbf{B}|}.$$

The joint distribution of **x** is the product of the marginal distributions since they are independent. Thus,

$$f_x(\mathbf{x}) = (2\pi)^{-1}e^{-(x_1^2+x_2^2)/2} = (2\pi)^{-1}e^{-\mathbf{x}'\mathbf{x}/2}.$$

Inserting the results for $\mathbf{x}(\mathbf{y})$ and J into $f_y(y_1, y_2)$ gives

$$f_y(\mathbf{y}) = (2\pi)^{-1}\frac{1}{\text{abs}|\mathbf{B}|}e^{-(\mathbf{y}-\mathbf{a})'(\mathbf{B}\mathbf{B}')^{-1}(\mathbf{y}-\mathbf{a})/2}.$$

This **joint normal distribution** is the subject of Section 3.8.

3.7. CONDITIONING IN A BIVARIATE DISTRIBUTION

Conditioning and the use of conditional distributions play a pivotal role in econometric modeling. We consider some general results for a bivariate distribution. (All these results can be extended directly to the multivariate case.)

In a bivariate distribution, there is a **conditional distribution** over y for each value of x. The conditional densities are

$$f(y\,|\,x) = \frac{f(x, y)}{f_x(x)} \tag{3-59}$$

and

$$f(x\,|\,y) = \frac{f(x, y)}{f_y(y)}.$$

It follows from (3-46) that:

If x and y are independent, $f(y\,|\,x) = f_y(y)$ and $f(x\,|\,y) = f_x(x)$. **(3-60)**

The interpretation is that if the variables are independent, the probabilities of events relating to one variable are unrelated to the other. The definition of conditional densities implies the important result

$$\begin{aligned} f(x, y) &= f(y\,|\,x)f_x(x) \\ &= f(x\,|\,y)f_y(y). \end{aligned} \tag{3-61}$$

3.7.1. Regression — The Conditional Mean

A **conditional mean** is the mean of the conditional distribution and is defined by

$$E[y \mid x] = \begin{cases} \int_y y f(y \mid x)\, dy & \text{if } y \text{ is continuous,} \\ \sum_y y f(y \mid x) & \text{if } y \text{ is discrete.} \end{cases} \quad \textbf{(3-62)}$$

The conditional mean function $E[y|x]$ is called the **regression** of y on x.

EXAMPLE 3.5 Regression in an Exponential Distribution

Consider the conditional distribution

$$f(y|x) = \frac{1}{\alpha + \beta x} e^{-y/(\alpha+\beta x)}, \quad y \geq 0, 0 \leq x \leq 1.$$

Note that the conditional density of y is a function of x. The conditional mean can be derived by integration by parts (or more simply, by using results for the gamma function) or by noting that this is an exponential distribution with $\lambda = 1/(\alpha + \beta x)$. The mean of an exponential distribution with parameter λ is $1/\lambda$. Therefore,

$$E[y|x] = \alpha + \beta x.$$

A random variable may always be written as

$$\begin{aligned} y &= E[y|x] + (y - E[y|x]) \\ &= E[y|x] + \epsilon. \end{aligned}$$

EXAMPLE 3.6 Poisson Regression

In their 1984 study, Hausman et al. (1984) suggest that the Poisson distribution (see Example 3.1) is a reasonable model for the distribution of the number of patents granted to firms in any given year (P):

$$f(P) = \frac{\lambda^P e^{-\lambda}}{P!}, \quad P = 0, 1, 2, \ldots.$$

It is known, however, that the more spent on research and development (R), the greater, on average, the number of patents received. This interaction should affect the distribution of P. How R is distributed across firms is a side issue that may or may not be of any interest. But we are interested in how R and the average number of patents interact. Since the mean value of patents received is λ, suppose that we make the preceding a conditional distribution and specify that

$$\lambda = \alpha + \beta R = E[P|R].$$

We would expect β to be positive. Thus,

$$f(P \mid R) = \frac{(\alpha + \beta R)^P e^{-(\alpha+\beta R)}}{P!},$$

which captures the effect we sought. The observation of a large number of patents may reflect a high value from the Poisson process or may follow from an unusually high value of R.

3.7.2. Conditional Variance

A conditional variance is the variance of the conditional distribution:

$$\begin{aligned}\operatorname{Var}[y \mid x] &= E[(y - E[y \mid x])^2 \mid x] \\ &= \int_y (y - E[y \mid x])^2 f(y \mid x)\, dy, \quad \text{if } y \text{ is continuous}\end{aligned} \qquad \textbf{(3-63)}$$

or

$$\operatorname{Var}[y \mid x] = \sum_y (y - E[y \mid x])^2 f(y \mid x), \quad \text{if } y \text{ is discrete.}$$

The computation can be simplified by using

$$\operatorname{Var}[y \mid x] = E[y^2 \mid x] - (E[y \mid x])^2. \qquad \textbf{(3-64)}$$

EXAMPLE 3.7 Conditional Variance in a Poisson Model

The Poisson distribution of Example 3.6 illustrates a pitfall that occasionally arises in specifying an econometric model. In a Poisson distribution, the mean is equal to the variance. We have not ruled out the possibility that $\alpha + \beta R$ could be negative for some values of α and β. Not only is this an invalid parameter for the Poisson distribution in any event, but beyond this, it allows a negative variance. This is a common error of specification.[8]

The conditional variance is called the **scedastic function** and, like the regression, is generally a function of x. Unlike the conditional mean function, however, it is common for the conditional variance not to vary with x. We shall examine a particular case. This does not imply, however, that $\operatorname{Var}[y \mid x]$ equals $\operatorname{Var}[y]$, which will usually not be the case. It implies only that the conditional variance is a constant. The case in which the conditional variance does not vary with x is called **homoscedasticity** (same variance).

3.7.3. Relationships Among Marginal and Conditional Moments

Some useful results for the moments of a conditional distribution are given in the following theorems:

[8]See Example 4.23 for the first of several applications of an alternative specification. The model is also examined at length in Chapter 19.

THEOREM 3.1: Law of Iterated Expectations. $E[y] = E_x[E[y\,|\,x]]$. **(3-65)**

The notation $E_x[\cdot]$ indicates the expectation over the values of x.

EXAMPLE 3.8 Uniform-Exponential Mixture Distribution

In the distribution of Example 3.5, assume that x is uniformly distributed between 0 and 1. Then the marginal distribution of x is $f(x) = 1$, and the joint distribution is

$$f(x, y) = f(x\,|\,y)f(x).$$

Then

$$E[y] = \int_0^\infty \int_0^1 y\left(\frac{1}{\alpha + \beta x}\right)e^{-y/(\alpha+\beta x)}\,dx\,dy.$$

But $E[y\,|\,x] = \alpha + \beta x$, so

$$\begin{aligned} E[y] &= E_x[E[y\,|\,x]] \\ &= E[\alpha + \beta x] \\ &= \alpha + \beta E[x]. \end{aligned} \quad \textbf{(3-66)}$$

Since x has a uniform distribution between 0 and 1, $E[x] = \frac{1}{2}$. Therefore,

$$E[y] = \alpha + \beta(\tfrac{1}{2}).$$

In any bivariate distribution,

$$\begin{aligned} \text{Cov}[x, y] &= \text{Cov}[x, E[y\,|\,x]] \\ &= \int_x (x - E[x])E[y\,|\,x]f_x(x)\,dx. \end{aligned}$$

EXAMPLE 3.9 Covariance in a Mixture Distribution

To continue Example 3.8,

$$\text{Cov}[x, y] = \int_0^\infty \int_0^1 \frac{(x - \frac{1}{2})[y - (\alpha + (\beta/2))]}{\alpha + \beta x}\,e^{-y/(\alpha+\beta x)}\,dx\,dy,$$

which can, in principle, be computed directed. However,

$$\begin{aligned} \text{Cov}[x, y] &= \text{Cov}[x, E[y\,|\,x]] \\ &= \text{Cov}[x, \alpha + \beta x] \\ &= \beta\,\text{Var}[x] = \beta[\tfrac{1}{12}]. \end{aligned} \quad \textbf{(3-67)}$$

The preceding examples provide an additional result for the special case in which the conditional mean function is linear in x.

THEOREM 3.2: Moments in a Linear Regression. *If* $E[y|x] = \alpha + \beta x$, *then*

$$\alpha = E[y] - \beta E[x] \tag{3-68}$$

and

$$\beta = \frac{\text{Cov}[x, y]}{\text{Var}[x]}. \tag{3-69}$$

The proof follows from (3-66) and (3-67). The following theorem also appears in various forms in regression analysis.

THEOREM 3.3: Decomposition of Variance. *In a joint distribution,*

$$\text{Var}[y] = \text{Var}_x[E[y|x]] + E_x[\text{Var}[y|x]]. \tag{3-70}$$

The notation $\text{Var}_x[\cdot]$ indicates the variance over the distribution of x. This states that in a bivariate distribution, the variance of y decomposes into the variance of the conditional mean function plus the expected variance around the conditional mean. For an application, see the proof of Theorem 20.3 in Section 20.3.

EXAMPLE 3.10 Decomposition of Variance

The variance of y in Example 3.5 remains to be derived. As before, the direct integration of the joint distribution is somewhat difficult. But

$$\begin{aligned}\text{Var}_x[E[y|x]] &= \text{Var}[\alpha + \beta x] = \beta^2\text{Var}[x]\\ &= \frac{\beta^2}{12},\end{aligned}$$

and since the variance of the exponential variable is $1/\lambda^2$,

$$\begin{aligned}E_x[\text{Var}[y|x]] &= E[(\alpha + \beta x)^2]\\ &= \alpha^2 + \beta^2 E[x^2] + 2\alpha\beta E[x]\\ &= \alpha^2 + \beta^2(\tfrac{1}{3}) + 2\alpha\beta(\tfrac{1}{2}).\end{aligned}$$

The unconditional variance is the sum of the two parts:

$$\text{Var}[y] = \alpha(\alpha + \beta) + \frac{5\beta^2}{12}.$$

By rearranging (3-70), we obtain the following important results.

THEOREM 3.4: Residual Variance in a Regression. *In any bivariate distribution,*

$$E_x[\text{Var}[y|x]] = \text{Var}[y] - \text{Var}_x[E[y|x]]. \tag{3-71}$$

On average, conditioning reduces the variance of the variable subject to the conditioning. For example, if y is homoscedastic, we have the unambiguous result that the variance of the conditional distribution(s) is less than or equal to the unconditional variance of y. Going a step further, we have the result that appears prominently in the bivariate normal distribution (Section 3.8).

THEOREM 3.5: Linear Regression and Homoscedasticity. *In a bivariate distribution, if* $E[y|x] = \alpha + \beta x$ *and if* $\text{Var}[y|x]$ *is a constant, then*

$$\text{Var}[y|x] = \text{Var}[y](1 - \text{Corr}^2[y, x]) = \sigma_y^2(1 - \rho_{xy}^2).$$

The proof is straightforward using Theorems 3.2 to 3.4.

EXAMPLE 3.11 Conditional Variance in a Poisson Regression

For the patents–research and development (R&D) relationship in Example 3.6, suppose that R is a constant fraction of firm size and that firm sizes have a lognormal distribution. Then R will have a lognormal distribution as well. The density, mean, and variance of the distribution are given in Section 3.4.4. Assume that $\mu = 0$ and $\sigma = 1$. Then

$$E[R] = \sqrt{e} = 1.65 \quad \text{and} \quad \text{Var}[R] = 4.65.$$

Assume, as well, that $\alpha = 1$ and $\beta = 2$. Then

$$\begin{aligned} E[P|R] &= 1 + 2R, \\ E[P] &= 1 + 2E[R] = 4.30, \\ \text{Var}_R[E[P|R]] &= 4\,\text{Var}[R] = 18.6, \\ \text{Var}[P|R] &= 1 + 2R, \\ E_R[\text{Var}[P|R]] &= 4.30, \\ \text{Var}[P] &= 18.6 + 4.30 = 22.9. \end{aligned}$$

Note that $\text{Var}[P]$ is substantially greater than $E[\text{Var}[P|R]]$.

3.7.4. The Analysis of Variance

The variance decomposition result implies that in a bivariate distribution, variation in y arises from two sources:

1. Variation because $E[y|x]$ varies with x:

$$\textbf{regression variance} = \text{Var}_x[E[y|x]]. \tag{3-72}$$

2. Variation because, in each conditional distribution, y varies around the conditional mean:

$$\textbf{residual variance} = E_x[\text{Var}[y|x]]. \tag{3-73}$$

Thus,

$$\text{Var}[y] = \text{regression variance} + \text{residual variance}. \tag{3-74}$$

In analyzing a regression, we shall usually be interested in which of the two parts of the total variance, $\text{Var}[y]$, is the larger one. For example, in the patents-R&D relationship, which explains more of the variance in the number of patents received, variation in the amount of R&D (regression variance) or random variation in patents received within the Poisson distribution (residual variance)? A natural measure is the ratio

$$\textbf{coefficient of determination} = \frac{\text{regression variance}}{\text{total variance}}. \tag{3-75}$$

EXAMPLE 3.12 Analysis of Variance in a Poisson Model

For the decomposition in Example 3.11,

$$\text{coefficient of determination} = \frac{18.6}{22.9} = 0.812.$$

In the setting of a linear regression, (3-75) arises from another relationship that emphasizes the interpretation of the correlation coefficient.

$$\text{If } E[y|x] = \alpha + \beta x, \text{ then the coefficient of determination} = \text{COD} = \rho^2, \tag{3-76}$$

where ρ^2 is the squared correlation between x and y. We conclude that the correlation coefficient (squared) is a measure of the proportion of the variance of y accounted for by variation in the mean of y given x. It is in this sense that correlation can be interpreted as a **measure of linear association** between two variables.

3.8. THE BIVARIATE NORMAL DISTRIBUTION

A bivariate distribution that embodies many of the features described earlier is the bivariate normal. This is the joint distribution of two normally distributed variables. The density is

$$\begin{aligned} f(x, y) &= \frac{1}{2\pi\sigma_x\sigma_y\sqrt{1-\rho^2}} e^{-1/2[(\epsilon_x^2 + \epsilon_y^2 2\rho\epsilon_x\epsilon_y)/(1\rho^2)]} \\ \epsilon_x &= \frac{x - \mu_x}{\sigma_x} \\ \epsilon_y &= \frac{y - \mu_y}{\sigma_y}. \end{aligned} \tag{3-77}$$

The parameters μ_x, σ_x, μ_y, and σ_y are the means and standard deviations of the marginal distributions of x and y, respectively. The additional parameter ρ is the correlation between x and y. The covariance is

$$\sigma_{xy} = \rho\sigma_x\sigma_y. \tag{3-78}$$

The density is defined only if ρ is not 1 or -1. This, in turn, requires that the two variables not be linearly related. If x and y have a bivariate normal distribution, denoted

$$(x, y) \sim N_2[\mu_x, \mu_y, \sigma_x^2, \sigma_y^2, \rho],$$

- The marginal distributions are normal:

$$f_x(x) = N[\mu_x, \sigma_x^2],$$
$$f_y(y) = N[\mu_y, \sigma_y^2]. \tag{3-79}$$

- The conditional distributions are normal:

$$f(y \mid x) = N[\alpha + \beta x, \sigma_y^2(1 - \rho^2)]$$
$$\alpha = \mu_y - \beta\mu_x \tag{3-80}$$
$$\beta = \frac{\sigma_{xy}}{\sigma_x^2},$$

  and likewise for $f(x \mid y)$.
- x and y are independent if and only if $\rho = 0$. The density factors into the product of the two marginal normal distributions if $\rho = 0$.

Two things to note about the conditional distributions beyond their normality are their linear regression functions and their constant conditional variances. The conditional variance is less than the unconditional variance, which is consistent with the results of the previous section.

3.9. MULTIVARIATE DISTRIBUTIONS

The extension of the results for bivariate distributions to more than two variables is direct. It is made much more convenient by using matrices and vectors. The term ***random vector*** applies to a vector whose elements are random variables. The joint density is $f(\mathbf{x})$, whereas the cdf is

$$F(\mathbf{x}) = \int_{-\infty}^{x_n}\int_{-\infty}^{x_{n-1}} \cdots \int_{-\infty}^{x_1} f(\mathbf{x})\, dx_1 \cdots dx_{n-1}\, dx_n. \tag{3-81}$$

Note that the cdf is an n-fold integral. The marginal distribution of any one (or more) of the n variables is obtained by integrating or summing over the other variables.

3.9.1. Moments

The expected value of a vector or matrix is the vector or matrix of expected values. A mean vector is defined as

$$\boldsymbol{\mu} = \begin{bmatrix} \mu_1 \\ \mu_2 \\ \vdots \\ \mu_n \end{bmatrix} = \begin{bmatrix} E[x_1] \\ E[x_2] \\ \vdots \\ E[x_n] \end{bmatrix} = E[\mathbf{x}]. \tag{3-82}$$

Define the matrix

$$(\mathbf{x}-\boldsymbol{\mu})(\mathbf{x}-\boldsymbol{\mu})' = \begin{bmatrix} (x_1-\mu_1)(x_1-\mu_1) & (x_1-\mu_1)(x_2-\mu_2) & \cdots & (x_1-\mu_1)(x_n-\mu_n) \\ (x_2-\mu_2)(x_1-\mu_1) & (x_2-\mu_2)(x_2-\mu_2) & \cdots & (x_2-\mu_2)(x_n-\mu_n) \\ \vdots & & \vdots & \\ (x_n-\mu_n)(x_1-\mu_1) & (x_n-\mu_n)(x_2-\mu_2) & \cdots & (x_n-\mu_n)(x_n-\mu_n) \end{bmatrix}.$$

The expected value of each element in the matrix is the covariance of the two variables in the product. (The covariance of a variable with itself is its variance.) Thus,

$$\begin{aligned} E[(\mathbf{x}-\boldsymbol{\mu})(\mathbf{x}-\boldsymbol{\mu})'] &= \boldsymbol{\Sigma} \\ &= \begin{bmatrix} \sigma_{11} & \sigma_{12} & \cdots & \sigma_{1n} \\ \sigma_{21} & \sigma_{22} & \cdots & \sigma_{2n} \\ \vdots & & \vdots & \\ \sigma_{n1} & \sigma_{n2} & \cdots & \sigma_{nn} \end{bmatrix} \\ &= E[\mathbf{x}\mathbf{x}'] - \boldsymbol{\mu}\boldsymbol{\mu}', \end{aligned} \tag{3-83}$$

which is the **covariance matrix** of the random vector $\mathbf{x}$. Henceforth, we shall denote the covariance matrix of a random vector in boldface, as in

$$\text{Var}[\mathbf{x}] = \boldsymbol{\Sigma}.$$

By dividing σ_{ij} by $\sigma_i\sigma_j$, we obtain the **correlation matrix:**

$$\mathbf{R} = \begin{bmatrix} 1 & \rho_{12} & \rho_{13} & \cdots & \rho_{1n} \\ \rho_{21} & 1 & \rho_{23} & \cdots & \rho_{2n} \\ \vdots & \vdots & \vdots & & \vdots \\ \rho_{n1} & \rho_{n2} & \rho_{n3} & \cdots & 1 \end{bmatrix}.$$

3.9.2. Sets of Linear Functions

Our earlier results for the mean and variance of a linear function can be extended to the multivariate case. For the mean,

$$\begin{aligned} E[a_1x_1 + a_2x_2 + \cdots + a_nx_n] &= E[\mathbf{a}'\mathbf{x}] \\ &= a_1E[x_1] + a_2E[x_2] + \cdots + a_nE[x_n] \\ &= a_1\mu_1 + a_2\mu_2 + \cdots + a_n\mu_n \\ &= \mathbf{a}'\boldsymbol{\mu}. \end{aligned} \tag{3-84}$$

For the variance,

$$\begin{aligned} \text{Var}[\mathbf{a}'\mathbf{x}] &= E[(\mathbf{a}'\mathbf{x} - E[\mathbf{a}'\mathbf{x}])^2] \\ &= E[\{\mathbf{a}'(\mathbf{x} - E[\mathbf{x}])\}^2] \\ &= E[\mathbf{a}'(\mathbf{x}-\boldsymbol{\mu})(\mathbf{x}-\boldsymbol{\mu})'\mathbf{a}] \end{aligned}$$

as $E[\mathbf{x}] = \boldsymbol{\mu}$ and $\mathbf{a}'(\mathbf{x} - \boldsymbol{\mu}) = (\mathbf{x} - \boldsymbol{\mu})'\mathbf{a}$. Since $\mathbf{a}$ is a vector of constants,

$$\begin{aligned}\text{Var}[\mathbf{a}'\mathbf{x}] &= \mathbf{a}'E[(\mathbf{x} - \boldsymbol{\mu})(\mathbf{x} - \boldsymbol{\mu})']\mathbf{a} \\ &= \mathbf{a}'\boldsymbol{\Sigma}\mathbf{a} \\ &= \sum_{i=1}^{n}\sum_{j=1}^{n} a_i a_j \sigma_{ij}.\end{aligned} \tag{3-85}$$

Since it is the expected value of a square, we know that a variance cannot be negative. As such, the preceding quadratic form is nonnegative, and the symmetric matrix $\boldsymbol{\Sigma}$ must be nonnegative definite.

In the set of linear functions $\mathbf{y} = \mathbf{A}\mathbf{x}$, the ith element of $\mathbf{y}$ is $y_i = \mathbf{a}^i\mathbf{x}$, where $\mathbf{a}^i$ is the ith row of $\mathbf{A}$. Therefore,

$$E[y_i] = \mathbf{a}^i\boldsymbol{\mu}.$$

Collecting the results in a vector, we have

$$E[\mathbf{A}\mathbf{x}] = \mathbf{A}\boldsymbol{\mu}. \tag{3-86}$$

For two row vectors $\mathbf{a}^i$ and $\mathbf{a}^j$,

$$\text{Cov}[\mathbf{a}^i\mathbf{x}, \mathbf{a}^j\mathbf{x}] = \mathbf{a}^i\boldsymbol{\Sigma}\mathbf{a}^{j\prime}.$$

Since $\mathbf{a}^i\boldsymbol{\Sigma}\mathbf{a}^j$ is the ijth element of $\mathbf{A}\boldsymbol{\Sigma}\mathbf{A}'$,

$$\text{Var}[\mathbf{A}\mathbf{x}] = \mathbf{A}\boldsymbol{\Sigma}\mathbf{A}'. \tag{3-87}$$

This will be either nonnegative definite or positive definite, depending on the column rank of $\mathbf{A}$.

3.9.3. Nonlinear Functions

Consider a set of possibly nonlinear functions of $\mathbf{x}$, $\mathbf{y} = \mathbf{g}(\mathbf{x})$. Each element of $\mathbf{y}$ can be approximated with a linear Taylor series. Let $\mathbf{j}^i$ be the row vector of partial derivatives of the ith function with respect to the n elements of $\mathbf{x}$:

$$\mathbf{j}^i = \frac{\partial g_i(\mathbf{x})}{\partial \mathbf{x}'} = \frac{\partial y_i}{\partial \mathbf{x}'}. \tag{3-88}$$

Then, proceeding in the now familiar way, we use $\boldsymbol{\mu}$, the mean vector of $\mathbf{x}$, as the expansion point, so that $\mathbf{j}^i$ is the row vector of partial derivatives evaluated at $\boldsymbol{\mu}$. Then

$$g_i(\mathbf{x}) \simeq g_i(\boldsymbol{\mu}) + \mathbf{j}^i(\mathbf{x} - \boldsymbol{\mu}). \tag{3-89}$$

From this we obtain

$$E[g_i(\mathbf{x})] \simeq g_i(\boldsymbol{\mu}), \tag{3-90}$$

$$\text{Var}[g_i(\mathbf{x})] \simeq \mathbf{j}^i\boldsymbol{\Sigma}\mathbf{j}^{i\prime}, \tag{3-91}$$

and

$$\text{Cov}[g_i(\mathbf{x}), g_j(\mathbf{x})] \simeq \mathbf{j}^i\boldsymbol{\Sigma}\mathbf{j}^{j\prime}. \tag{3-92}$$

These can be collected in a convenient form by arranging the row vectors $\mathbf{j}^i$ in a matrix $\mathbf{J}$. Then, corresponding to the preceding equations, we have

$$E[\mathbf{g}(\mathbf{x})] \simeq \mathbf{g}(\boldsymbol{\mu}), \quad \textbf{(3-93)}$$

$$\textbf{Var}[\mathbf{g}(\mathbf{x})] \simeq \mathbf{J\Sigma J}'. \quad \textbf{(3-94)}$$

The matrix $\mathbf{J}$ in the last preceding line is $\partial\mathbf{y}/\partial\mathbf{x}'$.

3.10. THE MULTIVARIATE NORMAL DISTRIBUTION

The foundation of most multivariate analysis in econometrics is the multivariate normal distribution. Let the vector $(x_1, x_2, \ldots, x_n)' = \mathbf{x}$ be the set of n random variables, $\boldsymbol{\mu}$ their mean vector, and $\boldsymbol{\Sigma}$ their covariance matrix. The general form of the joint density is

$$f(\mathbf{x}) = (2\pi)^{-n/2}\,|\boldsymbol{\Sigma}|^{-1/2}e^{(-1/2)(\mathbf{x}-\boldsymbol{\mu})'\boldsymbol{\Sigma}^{-1}(\mathbf{x}-\boldsymbol{\mu})}. \quad \textbf{(3-95)}$$

If $\mathbf{R}$ is the correlation matrix of the variables and $\mathbf{R}_{ij} = \sigma_{ij}/(\sigma_i\sigma_j)$,

$$f(\mathbf{x}) = (2\pi)^{-n/2}(\sigma_1\sigma_2\cdots\sigma_n)^{-1}\,|\mathbf{R}|^{-1/2}e^{(-1/2)\boldsymbol{\epsilon}'\mathbf{R}^{-1}\boldsymbol{\epsilon}}, \quad \textbf{(3-96)}$$

where $\epsilon_i = (x_i - \mu_i)/\sigma_i$.[9]

Two special cases are of interest. If all the variables are uncorrelated, $\rho_{ij} = 0$ for $i \neq j$. Thus, $\mathbf{R} = \mathbf{I}$, and the density becomes

$$\begin{aligned} f(\mathbf{x}) &= (2\pi)^{-n/2}(\sigma_1\sigma_2\cdots\sigma_n)^{-1/2}e^{-\boldsymbol{\epsilon}'\boldsymbol{\epsilon}/2} \\ &= f(x_1)f(x_2)\cdots f(x_n) = \prod_{i=1}^{n} f(x_i). \end{aligned} \quad \textbf{(3-97)}$$

As in the bivariate case, if normally distributed variables are uncorrelated, they are independent. If $\sigma_i = \sigma$ and $\boldsymbol{\mu} = \mathbf{0}$, then $x_i \sim N[0, \sigma^2]$ and $\epsilon_i = x_i/\sigma$, and the density becomes

$$f(\mathbf{x}) = (2\pi)^{-n/2}(\sigma^2)^{-n/2}e^{-\mathbf{x}'\mathbf{x}/(2\sigma^2)}. \quad \textbf{(3-98)}$$

Finally, if $\sigma = 1$,

$$f(\mathbf{x}) = (2\pi)^{-n/2}e^{-\mathbf{x}'\mathbf{x}/2}. \quad \textbf{(3-99)}$$

This is the **multivariate standard normal,** or **spherical normal distribution.**

3.10.1. Marginal and Conditional Normal Distributions

Let $\mathbf{x}_1$ be any subset of the variables, including a single variable, and let $\mathbf{x}_2$ be the remaining variables. Partition $\boldsymbol{\mu}$ and $\boldsymbol{\Sigma}$ likewise so that

$$\boldsymbol{\mu} = \begin{bmatrix} \boldsymbol{\mu}_1 \\ \boldsymbol{\mu}_2 \end{bmatrix} \quad \text{and} \quad \boldsymbol{\Sigma} = \begin{bmatrix} \boldsymbol{\Sigma}_{11} & \boldsymbol{\Sigma}_{12} \\ \boldsymbol{\Sigma}_{21} & \boldsymbol{\Sigma}_{22} \end{bmatrix}.$$

[9]This result is obtained by constructing $\boldsymbol{\Delta}$, the diagonal matrix with σ_i as its ith diagonal element. Then, $\mathbf{R} = \boldsymbol{\Delta}^{-1}\boldsymbol{\Sigma}\boldsymbol{\Delta}^{-1}$, which implies that $\boldsymbol{\Sigma}^{-1} = \boldsymbol{\Delta}^{-1}\mathbf{R}^{-1}\boldsymbol{\Delta}^{-1}$. Inserting this in (3-95) yields (3-96). Note that the ith element of $\boldsymbol{\Delta}^{-1}(\mathbf{x} - \boldsymbol{\mu})$ is $(x_i - \mu_i)/\sigma_i$.

Then the marginal distributions are also normal. In particular, we have the following theorem.

THEOREM 3.6: Marginal and Conditional Normal Distributions. *If* $[\mathbf{x}_1, \mathbf{x}_2]$ *have a joint multivariate normal distribution, then the marginal distributions are*

$$\mathbf{x}_1 \sim N(\boldsymbol{\mu}_1, \boldsymbol{\Sigma}_{11}) \tag{3-100}$$

and

$$\mathbf{x}_2 \sim N(\boldsymbol{\mu}_2, \boldsymbol{\Sigma}_{22}). \tag{3-101}$$

The conditional distribution of $\mathbf{x}_1$ *given* $\mathbf{x}_2$ *is normal as well:*

$$\mathbf{x}_1 | \mathbf{x}_2 \sim N(\boldsymbol{\mu}_{1.2}, \boldsymbol{\Sigma}_{11.2}) \tag{3-102}$$

where

$$\boldsymbol{\mu}_{1.2} = \boldsymbol{\mu}_1 + \boldsymbol{\Sigma}_{12}\boldsymbol{\Sigma}_{22}^{-1}(\mathbf{x}_2 - \boldsymbol{\mu}_2) \tag{3-102a}$$
$$\boldsymbol{\Sigma}_{11.2} = \boldsymbol{\Sigma}_{11} - \boldsymbol{\Sigma}_{12}\boldsymbol{\Sigma}_{22}^{-1}\boldsymbol{\Sigma}_{21}. \tag{3-102b}$$

Proof: We partition $\boldsymbol{\mu}$ and $\boldsymbol{\Sigma}$ as shown above and insert the parts in (3-95). To construct the density, we use (2-72) to partition the determinant,

$$|\boldsymbol{\Sigma}| = |\boldsymbol{\Sigma}_{22}||\boldsymbol{\Sigma}_{11} - \boldsymbol{\Sigma}_{12}\boldsymbol{\Sigma}_{22}^{-1}\boldsymbol{\Sigma}_{21}|,$$

and (2-74) to partition the inverse,

$$\begin{bmatrix} \boldsymbol{\Sigma}_{11} & \boldsymbol{\Sigma}_{12} \\ \boldsymbol{\Sigma}_{21} & \boldsymbol{\Sigma}_{22} \end{bmatrix}^{-1} = \begin{bmatrix} \boldsymbol{\Sigma}_{11.2}^{-1} & -\boldsymbol{\Sigma}_{11.2}^{-1}\mathbf{B} \\ -\mathbf{B}'\boldsymbol{\Sigma}_{11.2}^{-1} & \boldsymbol{\Sigma}_{22}^{-1} + \mathbf{B}'\boldsymbol{\Sigma}_{11.2}^{-1}\mathbf{B} \end{bmatrix}.$$

For simplicity, we let

$$\mathbf{B} = \boldsymbol{\Sigma}_{12}\boldsymbol{\Sigma}_{22}^{-1}.$$

Inserting these in (3-95) and collecting terms produces the joint density as a product of two terms:

$$f(\mathbf{x}_1, \mathbf{x}_2) = f_{1.2}(\mathbf{x}_1|\mathbf{x}_2)f_2(\mathbf{x}_2).$$

The first of these is a normal distribution with mean $\boldsymbol{\mu}_{1.2}$ and variance $\boldsymbol{\Sigma}_{11.2}$, whereas the second is the marginal distribution of $\mathbf{x}_2$. The conditional mean vector is a linear function of the unconditional mean and the conditioning variables, and the conditional covariance matrix is constant and is smaller (in the sense discussed in Section 2.8.3) than the unconditional covariance matrix. Notice that the conditional covariance matrix is the inverse of the upper left block of $\boldsymbol{\Sigma}^{-1}$; that is, this is of the form shown in (2-74) for the partitioned inverse of a matrix. An important special case is that in which $\mathbf{x}_1$ is a single variable y and $\mathbf{x}_2$ is K variables. Then the conditional distribution is a multivariate version of that in (3-80) with $\boldsymbol{\beta} = \boldsymbol{\Sigma}_{\mathbf{xx}}^{-1}\boldsymbol{\sigma}_{\mathbf{x}y}$, where $\boldsymbol{\sigma}_{\mathbf{x}y}$ is the vector of covariances of y with $\mathbf{x}_2$.

3.10.2. Linear Functions of a Normal Vector

Any linear function of a vector of joint normally distributed variables is also normally distributed. The mean vector and covariance matrix of $\mathbf{Ax}$, where $\mathbf{x}$ is normally distributed, follow the general pattern given earlier. Thus,

$$\text{If } \mathbf{x} \sim N[\boldsymbol{\mu}, \boldsymbol{\Sigma}],\ \mathbf{Ax} + \mathbf{b} \sim N[\mathbf{A}\boldsymbol{\mu} + \mathbf{b}, \mathbf{A}\boldsymbol{\Sigma}\mathbf{A}']. \tag{3-103}$$

If $\mathbf{A}$ does not have full rank, $\mathbf{A\Sigma A}'$ is singular and the density does not exist. Nonetheless, the individual elements of $\mathbf{Ax} + \mathbf{b}$ will still be normally distributed, and the joint *distribution* of the full vector is still a multivariate normal.

3.10.3. Quadratic Forms in a Standard Normal Vector

The earlier discussion of the chi-squared distribution gives the distribution of $\mathbf{x}'\mathbf{x}$ if $\mathbf{x}$ has a standard normal distribution. It follows from (2-36) that

$$\mathbf{x}'\mathbf{x} = \sum_{i=1}^{n} x_i^2 = \sum_{i=1}^{n} (x_i - \bar{x})^2 + n\bar{x}^2. \tag{3-104}$$

We know from (3-32) that $\mathbf{x}'\mathbf{x}$ has a chi-squared distribution. It seems natural, therefore, to invoke (3-34) for the two parts on the right-hand side of (3-104). It is not yet obvious, however, that either of the two terms has a chi-squared distribution or that the two terms are independent, as required. To show these conditions, it is necessary to derive the distributions of **idempotent quadratic forms** and to show when they are independent.

To begin, the second term is the square of $\sqrt{n}\,\bar{x}$, which can easily be shown to have a standard normal distribution. Thus, the second term is the square of a standard normal variable and has chi-squared distribution with one degree of freedom. But the first term is the sum of n nonindependent variables, and it remains to be shown that the two terms are independent.

Definition 3.3: Orthonormal Quadratic Form. *A particular case of (3-103) is the following:*

If $\mathbf{x} \sim N[\mathbf{0}, \mathbf{I}]$ *and* $\mathbf{C}$ *is a square matrix such that* $\mathbf{C}'\mathbf{C} = \mathbf{I}$, *then* $\mathbf{C}'\mathbf{x} \sim N[\mathbf{0}, \mathbf{I}]$.

Consider, then, a quadratic form in a standard normal vector $\mathbf{x}$:

$$q = \mathbf{x}'\mathbf{A}\mathbf{x}. \tag{3-105}$$

Let the characteristic roots and vectors of $\mathbf{A}$ be arranged in a diagonal matrix $\boldsymbol{\Lambda}$ and an orthogonal matrix $\mathbf{C}$, as in Section 2.7.3. Then

$$q = \mathbf{x}'\mathbf{C}\boldsymbol{\Lambda}\mathbf{C}'\mathbf{x}. \tag{3-106}$$

By definition, $\mathbf{C}$ satisfies the requirement that $\mathbf{C}'\mathbf{C} = \mathbf{I}$. Thus, the vector $\mathbf{y} = \mathbf{C}'\mathbf{x}$ has a standard normal distribution. Consequently,

$$\begin{aligned} q &= \mathbf{y}'\boldsymbol{\Lambda}\mathbf{y} \\ &= \sum_{i=1}^{n} \lambda_i y_i^2. \end{aligned} \tag{3-107}$$

If λ_i is always 1 or 0,

$$q = \sum_{j=1}^{J} y_i^2, \qquad \textbf{(3-108)}$$

which has a chi-squared distribution. The sum is taken over the $j = 1, \ldots,$ J elements associated with the roots that are equal to 1. A matrix whose characteristic roots are all 0 or 1 is idempotent. Therefore, we have proved the next theorem.

THEOREM 3.7: Distribution of an Idempotent Quadratic Form in a Standard Normal Vector. *If* $\mathbf{x} \sim N[\mathbf{0}, \mathbf{I}]$ *and* $\mathbf{A}$ *is idempotent, then* $\mathbf{x}'\mathbf{A}\mathbf{x}$ *has a chi-squared distribution with degrees of freedom equal to the number of unit roots of* $\mathbf{A}$, *which is equal to the rank of* $\mathbf{A}$.

The rank of a matrix is equal to the number of nonzero characteristic roots it has. Therefore, the degrees of freedom in the preceding chi-squared distribution equals J, the rank of $\mathbf{A}$.

We can apply this result to the earlier sum of squares. The first term is

$$\sum_{i=1}^{n} (x_i - \bar{x})^2 = \mathbf{x}'\mathbf{M}^0\mathbf{x},$$

where $\mathbf{M}^0$ was defined in (2-34) as the matrix that transforms data to mean deviation form:

$$\boldsymbol{M}^0 = \left[\mathbf{I} - \frac{1}{n}\mathbf{i}\mathbf{i}'\right].$$

Since $\mathbf{M}^0$ is idempotent, the sum of squared deviations from the mean has a chi-squared distribution. The degrees of freedom equals the rank $\mathbf{M}^0$, which is not obvious except for the useful result in (2-108), that

- The rank of an idempotent matrix is equal to its trace. **(3-109)**

Each diagonal element of $\mathbf{M}^0$ is $1 - (1/n)$; hence, the trace is $n[1 - (1/n)] = n - 1$. Therefore, we have an application of Theorem 3.7.

- If $\mathbf{x} \sim N(\mathbf{0}, \mathbf{I})$, $\sum_{i=1}^{n}(x_i - \bar{x})^2 \sim \chi^2[n - 1]$. **(3-110)**

We have already shown that the second term in (3-110) has a chi-squared distribution with one degree of freedom. It is instructive to set this up as a quadratic form as well:

$$\begin{aligned} n\bar{x}^2 &= \mathbf{x}'\left[\frac{1}{n}\mathbf{i}\mathbf{i}'\right]\mathbf{x} \\ &= \mathbf{x}'[\mathbf{j}\mathbf{j}']\mathbf{x}, \end{aligned} \qquad \textbf{(3-111)}$$

where

$$\mathbf{j} = \left(\frac{1}{\sqrt{n}}\right)\mathbf{i}.$$

The matrix in brackets is the outer product of a nonzero vector, which always has rank one. You can verify that it is idempotent by multiplication. Thus, $\mathbf{x}'\mathbf{x}$ is the sum of two chi-squared variables, one with $n - 1$ degrees of freedom and the other with one. It is now necessary to show that the two terms are independent. To do so, we will use the next theorem.

THEOREM 3.8: Independence of Idempotent Quadratic Forms. *If* $\mathbf{x} \sim N[\mathbf{0}, \mathbf{I}]$ *and* $\mathbf{x}'\mathbf{A}\mathbf{x}$ *and* $\mathbf{x}'\mathbf{B}\mathbf{x}$ *are two idempotent quadratic forms in* $\mathbf{x}$*, then* $\mathbf{x}'\mathbf{A}\mathbf{x}$ *and* $\mathbf{x}'\mathbf{B}\mathbf{x}$ *are independent if* $\mathbf{AB} = \mathbf{0}$. **(3-112)**

As before, we show the result for the general case and then specialize it for the example. Since both $\mathbf{A}$ and $\mathbf{B}$ are symmetric and idempotent, $\mathbf{A} = \mathbf{A}'\mathbf{A}$ and $\mathbf{B} = \mathbf{B}'\mathbf{B}$. The quadratic forms are therefore

$$\mathbf{x}'\mathbf{A}\mathbf{x} = \mathbf{x}'\mathbf{A}'\mathbf{A}\mathbf{x} = \mathbf{x}_1'\mathbf{x}_1, \text{ where } \mathbf{x}_1 = \mathbf{A}\mathbf{x} \text{ and } \mathbf{x}'\mathbf{B}\mathbf{x} = \mathbf{x}_2'\mathbf{x}_2, \text{ where } \mathbf{x}_2 = \mathbf{B}\mathbf{x}. \tag{3-113}$$

Both vectors have zero mean vectors, so the covariance matrix of $\mathbf{x}_1$ and $\mathbf{x}_2$ is

$$E(\mathbf{x}_1\mathbf{x}_2') = \mathbf{AIB}' = \mathbf{AB} = \mathbf{0}.$$

Since $\mathbf{A}\mathbf{x}$ and $\mathbf{B}\mathbf{x}$ are linear functions of a normally distributed random vector, they are, in turn, normally distributed. Their zero covariance matrix implies that they are statistically independent.[10] This establishes the independence of the two quadratic forms. For the case of $\mathbf{x}'\mathbf{x}$, the two matrices are $\mathbf{M}^0$ and $[\mathbf{I} - \mathbf{M}^0]$. You can show that $\mathbf{M}^0[\mathbf{I} - \mathbf{M}^0] = \mathbf{0}$ just by multiplying.

3.10.4. The *F* Distribution

The normal family of distributions (chi-squared, F, and t) can all be derived as functions of idempotent quadratic forms in a standard normal vector. The F distribution is the ratio of two independent chi-squared variables, each divided by its respective degrees of freedom. Let $\mathbf{A}$ and $\mathbf{B}$ be two idempotent matrices with ranks r_a and r_b, and let $\mathbf{AB} = \mathbf{0}$. Then

$$\frac{\mathbf{x}'\mathbf{A}\mathbf{x}/r_a}{\mathbf{x}'\mathbf{B}\mathbf{x}/r_b} \sim F[r_a, r_b]. \tag{3-114}$$

If $\text{Var}[\mathbf{x}] = \sigma^2\mathbf{I}$ instead, this is modified to

$$\frac{(\mathbf{x}'\mathbf{A}\mathbf{x}/\sigma^2)/r_a}{(\mathbf{x}'\mathbf{B}\mathbf{x}/\sigma^2)/r_b} \sim F[r_a, r_b]. \tag{3-115}$$

3.10.5. A Full Rank Quadratic Form

Finally, consider the general case,

$$\mathbf{x} \sim N[\boldsymbol{\mu}, \boldsymbol{\Sigma}].$$

[10]Note that both $\mathbf{x}_1 = \mathbf{A}\mathbf{x}$ and $\mathbf{x}_2 = \mathbf{B}\mathbf{x}$ have singular covariance matrices. Nonetheless, every element of $\mathbf{x}_1$ is independent of every element of $\mathbf{x}_2$, so the vectors are independent.

We are interested in the distribution of

$$q = (\mathbf{x} - \boldsymbol{\mu})'\boldsymbol{\Sigma}^{-1}(\mathbf{x} - \boldsymbol{\mu}). \tag{3-116}$$

First, the vector can be written as $\mathbf{z} = \mathbf{x} - \boldsymbol{\mu}$, and $\boldsymbol{\Sigma}$ is the covariance matrix of $\mathbf{z}$ as well as of $\mathbf{x}$. Therefore, we seek the distribution of

$$q = \mathbf{z}'\boldsymbol{\Sigma}^{-1}\mathbf{z} = \mathbf{z}'(\text{Var}[\mathbf{z}])^{-1}\mathbf{z}, \tag{3-117}$$

where $\mathbf{z}$ is normally distributed with mean $\mathbf{0}$. This is a quadratic form, but not necessarily in an idempotent matrix.[11] Since $\boldsymbol{\Sigma}$ is positive definite, it has a square root. Define the symmetric matrix $\boldsymbol{\Sigma}^{1/2}$ so that $\boldsymbol{\Sigma}^{1/2}\boldsymbol{\Sigma}^{1/2} = \boldsymbol{\Sigma}$. Then

$$\boldsymbol{\Sigma}^{-1} = \boldsymbol{\Sigma}^{-1/2}\boldsymbol{\Sigma}^{-1/2}$$

and

$$\begin{aligned}\mathbf{z}'\boldsymbol{\Sigma}^{-1}\mathbf{z} &= \mathbf{z}'\boldsymbol{\Sigma}^{-1/2\prime}\boldsymbol{\Sigma}^{-1/2}\mathbf{z}\\ &= (\boldsymbol{\Sigma}^{-1/2}\mathbf{z})'(\boldsymbol{\Sigma}^{-1/2}\mathbf{z})\\ &= \mathbf{w}'\mathbf{w}.\end{aligned}$$

Now $\mathbf{w} = \mathbf{A}\mathbf{z}$, so

$$E(\mathbf{w}) = \mathbf{A}E[\mathbf{z}] = \mathbf{0}$$

and

$$\text{Var}[\mathbf{w}] = \mathbf{A}\boldsymbol{\Sigma}\mathbf{A}' = \boldsymbol{\Sigma}^{-1/2}\boldsymbol{\Sigma}\boldsymbol{\Sigma}^{-1/2} = \boldsymbol{\Sigma}^{0} = \mathbf{I}.$$

This provides an important result.

THEOREM 3.9: Distribution of a Standardized Normal Vector. *If* $\mathbf{x} \sim N[\boldsymbol{\mu}, \boldsymbol{\Sigma}]$, *then* $\boldsymbol{\Sigma}^{-1/2}(\mathbf{x} - \boldsymbol{\mu}) \sim N[\mathbf{0}, \mathbf{I}]$.

The simplest special case is that in which $\mathbf{x}$ has only one variable, so that the transformation is just $(x - \mu)/\sigma$. Combining this with (3-32) concerning the sum of squares of standard normals, we have the following theorem.

THEOREM 3.10: Distribution of $\mathbf{x}'\boldsymbol{\Sigma}^{-1}\mathbf{x}$ When $\mathbf{x}$ Is Standard Normal. *If* $\mathbf{x} \sim N[\boldsymbol{\mu}, \boldsymbol{\Sigma}]$, *then* $(\mathbf{x} - \boldsymbol{\mu})'\boldsymbol{\Sigma}^{-1}(\mathbf{x} - \boldsymbol{\mu}) \sim \chi^2[n]$.

3.10.6. Independence of a Linear and a Quadratic Form

The t distribution is used in many forms of hypothesis tests. In some situations, it arises as the ratio of a linear to a quadratic form in a normal vector. To establish the distribution of these statistics, we use the following result.

THEOREM 3.11: Independence of a Linear and a Quadratic Form. *A linear function* $\mathbf{Lx}$ *and an idempotent quadratic form* $\mathbf{x}'\mathbf{Ax}$ *in a standard normal vector are statistically independent if* $\mathbf{LA} = \mathbf{0}$.

---

[11] It will be idempotent only in the special case of $\boldsymbol{\Sigma} = \mathbf{I}$.

The proof follows the same logic as that for two quadratic forms. Write $\mathbf{x}'\mathbf{A}\mathbf{x}$ as $\mathbf{x}'\mathbf{A}'\mathbf{A}\mathbf{x} = (\mathbf{A}\mathbf{x})'(\mathbf{A}\mathbf{x})$. The covariance matrix of the variables $\mathbf{Lx}$ and $\mathbf{Ax}$ is $\mathbf{LA} = \mathbf{0}$, which establishes the independence of these two random vectors. The independence of the linear function and the quadratic form follows since functions of independent random vectors are also independent.

The t distribution is defined as the ratio of a standard normal variable to the square root of a chi-squared variable divided by its degrees of freedom:

$$t[J] = \frac{N[0, 1]}{\{\chi^2[J]/J\}^{1/2}}.$$

A particular case is

$$t[n-1] = \frac{\sqrt{n}\,\bar{x}}{\left[\dfrac{1}{n-1}\sum_{i=1}^{n}(x_i - \bar{x})^2\right]^{1/2}} = \frac{\sqrt{n}\,\bar{x}}{s},$$

where s is the standard deviation of the values of $\mathbf{x}$. The distribution of the two variables in $t[n-1]$ was shown earlier; we need only show that they are independent. But

$$\sqrt{n}\,\bar{x} = \frac{1}{\sqrt{n}}\mathbf{i}'\mathbf{x} = \mathbf{j}'\mathbf{x}$$

and

$$s^2 = \frac{\mathbf{x}'\mathbf{M}^0\mathbf{x}}{n-1}.$$

It suffices to show that $\mathbf{M}^0\mathbf{j} = \mathbf{0}$, which follows from

$$\mathbf{M}^0\mathbf{i} = [\mathbf{I} - \mathbf{i}(\mathbf{i}'\mathbf{i})^{-1}\mathbf{i}']\mathbf{i} = \mathbf{i} - \mathbf{i}(\mathbf{i}'\mathbf{i})^{-1}(\mathbf{i}'\mathbf{i}) = \mathbf{0}.$$

EXERCISES

1. How many different five-card poker hands can be dealt from a deck of 52 cards?
2. Compute the probability of being dealt four of a kind in a poker hand.
3. Suppose that a lottery ticket costs \$1 per play. The game is played by drawing six numbers without replacement from the numbers 1 to 48. If you guess all six numbers, you win the prize. Now, suppose that N = the number of tickets sold and P = the size of the prize. N and P are related by

$$N = 5 + 1.2P$$
$$P = 1 + 0.4N.$$

N and P are in millions. What is the expected value of a ticket in this game? (Don't forget that you might have to share the prize with other winners.)

4. If x has a normal distribution with mean 1 and standard deviation 3, what are the following?
(a) Prob$[|x| > 2]$.
(b) Prob$[x > -1 | x < 1.5]$.

5. Approximately what is the probability that a random variable with chi-squared distribution with 264 degrees of freedom is less than 297?

6. *Chebychev inequality.* For the following two probability distributions, find the lower limit of the probability of the indicated event using the Chebychev inequality (3-18) and the exact probability using the appropriate table.
(a) $x \sim$ normal$[0,3^2]$, and $-4 < x < 4$.
(b) $x \sim$ chi-squared, 8 degrees of freedom, $0 < x < 16$.

7. Use the following joint probability distribution,

		X = 0	X = 1	X = 2
Y	0	0.05	0.1	0.03
	1	0.21	0.11	0.19
	2	0.08	0.15	0.08

to complete the following.
(a) Compute the following probabilities:

(1) Prob$[Y < 2]$.
(2) Prob$[Y < 2, X > 0]$.
(3) Prob$[Y = 1, X \geq 1]$.

(b) Find the marginal distributions of X and Y.
(c) Calculate $E[X], E[Y], \text{Var}[X], \text{Var}[Y], \text{Cov}[X, Y]$, and $E[X^2Y^3]$.
(d) Calculate $\text{Cov}[Y, X^2]$.
(e) What are the conditional distributions of Y given $X = 2$ and of X given $Y > 0$?
(f) Find $E[Y|X]$ and $\text{Var}[Y|X]$. Obtain the two parts of the variance decomposition.

8. *Minimum mean squared error predictor.* For the joint distribution in Exercise 7, compute $E[y - E[y|x]]^2$. Now, find the a and b that minimize the function $E[y - a - bx]^2$. Given the solutions, verify that

$$E[y - E[y|x]]^2 \leq E[y - a - bx]^2.$$

The result is fundamental in least squares theory. Verify that the a and b that you found satisfy (3-68) and (3-69).

9. Suppose that x has an exponential distribution $f(x) = \theta e^{-\theta x}, x \geq 0$. (For an application, see Examples 3.5, 3.8, and 3.10.) Find the mean, variance, skewness, and kurtosis of x. [Hints: The latter two are defined in Section 3.3. The gamma integral in Section 5.3.4 will be useful for finding the raw moments.]

10. For the random variable in Exercise 9, what is the probability distribution of the random variable $y = e^{-x}$? What is $E[y]$? Prove that the distribution of this y is a special case of the beta distribution in (3-40).

11. If the probability density of y is $\alpha y^2(1 - y)^3$ for y between 0 and 1, what is α? What is the probability that y is between 0.25 and 0.75?

12. Suppose that x has the following discrete probability distribution:

X	*1*	*2*	*3*	*4*
Prob$[X = x]$	0.1	0.2	0.4	0.3

Find the exact mean and variance of X. Now, suppose that $Y = 1/X$. Find the exact mean and variance of Y. Find the mean and variance of the linear and quadratic approximations to $Y = f(X)$. Are the mean and variance of the quadratic approximation closer to the true mean than those of the linear approximation?

13. *Interpolation in the chi-squared table.* To find a percentage point in the chi-squared table that is between two values, we interpolate linearly between the *reciprocals* of the degrees of freedom. The chi-squared distribution is defined for noninteger values of the degrees of freedom parameter [see (3-39)], but your table does not contain critical values for noninteger values. Using linear interpolation, find the 99% critical value for a chi-squared variable with degrees of freedom parameter 11.3. (For an application of this calculation, see Section 8.5.1. and Example 8.7.)

14. Suppose that x has a standard normal distribution. What is the pdf of the following random variable?

$$y = \frac{1}{(2\pi)^{1/2}} e^{-x^2/2}$$

[Hints: You know the distribution of $z = x^2$ from (3-30). The density of this z is given in (3-39). Solve the problem in terms of $y = g(z)$.]

15. *The fundamental probability transformation.* Suppose that the continuous random variable x has cumulative distribution $F(x)$. What is the probability distribution of the random variable $y = F(x)$? [Observation: This result forms the basis of the simulation of draws from many continuous distributions. See Section 5.3.2.]

16. *Random number generators.* Suppose that x is distributed uniformly between 0 and 1 so that $f(x) = 1, 0 \leq x \leq 1$. Let θ be some positive constant.

What is the pdf of $y = -(1/\theta)\ln x$? [Hint: See Section 3.5.] Does this suggest a means of simulating draws from this distribution if one has a random number generator that will produce draws from the uniform distribution? To continue, suggest a means of simulating draws from a logistic distribution, $f(x) = e^{-x}/(1 + e^{-x})^2$.

17. Suppose that x_1 and x_2 are distributed as independent standard normal. What is the joint distribution of $y_1 = 2 + 3x_1 + 2x_2$ and $y_2 = 4 + 5x_1$? Suppose that you were able to obtain two samples of observations from independent standard normal distributions. How would you obtain a sample from the bivariate normal distribution with means 1 and 2 variances 4 and 9 and covariance 3?

18. The density of the standard normal distribution, denoted $\phi(x)$, is given in (3-28). The function based on the ith derivative of the density given by

$$H_i = [(-1)^i d^i\phi(x)/dx^i]/\phi(x), \quad i = 0, 1, 2, \ldots,$$

is called a **Hermite polynomial.** By definition, $H_0 = 1$.

(a) Find the next three Hermite polynomials.

(b) A useful device in this context is the differential equation

$$d^r\phi(x)/dx^r + xd^{r-1}\phi(x)/dx^{r-1} + (r-1)d^{r-2}\phi(x)/dx^{r-2} = 0.$$

Use this result and the results of part a to find H_4 and H_5.

19. *Continuation of orthogonal polynomials.* The Hermite polynomials are orthogonal if x has a standard normal distribution. That is, $E[H_iH_j] = 0$ if $i \neq j$. Prove this for the H_1, H_2, and H_3 you obtained above.

20. If x and y have means μ_x and μ_y, variances σ_x^2 and σ_y^2, and covariance σ_{xy}, what is the approximation of the covariance matrix of the two random variables $f_1 = x/y$ and $f_2 = xy$?

21. *Factorial moments.* For finding the moments of a distribution such as the Poisson, a useful device is the factorial moment. (The Poisson distribution is given in Example 3.1.) The density is

$$f(x) = e^{-\lambda}\lambda^x/x!, \quad x = 0, 1, 2, \ldots$$

To find the mean, we can use

$$\begin{aligned} E[x] &= \sum_{x=0}^{\infty} xf(x) = \sum_{x=0}^{\infty} xe^{-\lambda}\lambda^x/x! \\ &= \sum_{x=1}^{\infty} e^{-\lambda}\lambda^{x-1}/(x-1)! \\ &= \lambda\sum_{y=0}^{\infty} e^{-\lambda}\lambda^y/y! \\ &= \lambda, \end{aligned}$$

since the probabilities sum to 1. To find the variance, we can extend this method by finding $E[x(x-1)]$, and likewise for other moments. Use this method to find the variance and third central moment of the Poisson distribution. (Note that device is used to transform the factorial in the denominator in the probability.)

22. If x has a normal distribution with mean μ and standard deviation σ, what is the probability distribution of $y = e^x$?

23. If y has a lognormal distribution, what is the probability distribution of y^2?

24. Suppose that y, x_1, and x_2 have a joint normal distribution with parameters $\boldsymbol{\mu}' = [1, 2, 4]$ and covariance matrix

$$\boldsymbol{\Sigma} = \begin{bmatrix} 2 & 3 & 1 \\ 3 & 5 & 2 \\ 1 & 2 & 6 \end{bmatrix}.$$

(a) Compute the intercept and slope in the function $E[y|x_1]$, $\text{Var}[y|x_1]$, and the coefficient of determination in this regression. [Hint: See Section 3.10.1.]

(b) Compute the intercept and slopes in the conditional mean function $E[y|x_1, x_2]$. What is $E[y|x_1 = 2.5, x_2 = 3.3]$? What is $\text{Var}[y|x_1 = 2.5, x_2 = 3.3]$?

25. What is the density of $y = 1/x$ if x has a chi-squared distribution?

26. *Probability-generating function.* For a discrete random variable x, the function

$$E[t^x] = \sum_{x=0}^{\infty} t^x \text{Prob}[X = x]$$

is called the **probability-generating function** because in the function, the coefficient on t^i is $\text{Prob}[X = i]$. Suppose that x is the number of the repetition of an experiment with probability π of success upon which the first success occurs. The density of x is the *geometric distribution,*

$$\text{Prob}[X = x] = (1 - \pi)^{x-1}\pi.$$

What is the probability-generating function?

27. *Moment-generating function (MGF).* For the random variable X, with probability density function $f(x)$, if the function

$$M(t) = E[e^{tx}]$$

exists, it is the **moment-generating function.** Assuming the function exists, it can be shown that

$$d^r M(t)/dt^r \big|_{t=0} = E[x^r].$$

Find the moment-generating functions for

(a) The exponential distribution of Exercise 9.

(b) The Poisson distribution of Exercise 21.

28. *Moment-generating function for a sum of random variables.* When it exists, the moment-generating function has a one-to-one correspondence with the distribution. Thus, for example, if we begin with some random variable and find that a transformation of it has a particular MGF, we may infer that the function of the random variable has the distribution associated with that MGF. A useful application is the following:

If x and y are independent, the MGF of $x + y$ is $M_x(t)M_y(t)$.

(a) Use this result to prove that the sum of Poisson random variables has a Poisson distribution.
(b) Use the result to prove that the sum of chi-squared variables has a chi-squared distribution. [Note that you must first find the MGF for a chi-squared variate. The density is given in (3-39).]
(c) The MGF for the standard normal distribution is $M_z = e^{-t^2/2}$. Find the MGF for the $N[\mu, \sigma^2]$ distribution, then find the distribution of a sum of normally distributed variables.

CHAPTER 4

Statistical Inference

4.1. INTRODUCTION

The probability distributions discussed in Chapter 3 serve as models for the underlying processes that produce our observed data. The goal of statistical inference in econometrics is to use the principles of mathematical statistics to combine these theoretical distributions and the observed data into an empirical model of the economy. This analysis takes place in one of two frameworks, classical or Bayesian. The overwhelming majority of empirical study in econometrics has been done in the classical framework. Our focus, therefore, will be on classical methods of inference. Bayesian methods will be discussed briefly in Chapter 6 and in a few applications at various places in the book.[1]

4.2. SAMPLES AND SAMPLING DISTRIBUTIONS

The classical theory of statistical inference centers on rules for using the sampled data effectively. These rules, in turn, are based on the properties of samples and sampling distributions.

4.2.1. Random Sampling

A sample of n observations on one or more variables, denoted $\mathbf{x}_1, \mathbf{x}_2, \ldots, \mathbf{x}_n$, is a **random sample** if the n observations are drawn independently from the same population, or probability distribution, $f(\mathbf{x}_i, \boldsymbol{\theta})$. The sample may be univariate if $\mathbf{x}_i$ is a single random variable or multivariate if each observation contains several variables. The sample of observations, denoted $[\mathbf{x}_1, \mathbf{x}_2, \ldots, \mathbf{x}_n]$

[1]An excellent reference is Leamer (1978). A summary of the results as they apply to econometrics is contained in Zellner (1971) and in Judge et al. (1985). For some recent applications, see Poirier (1991). A recent textbook with a heavy Bayesian emphasis is Poirier (1995).

or $\{\mathbf{x}_i\}_{i=1,\ldots,n}$, is said to be **independent, identically distributed,** which we denote *i.i.d.* The vector $\boldsymbol{\theta}$ contains one or more unknown parameters. Data are generally drawn in one of two settings. A **cross section** is a sample of a number of observational units all drawn at the same point in time. A **time series** is a set of observations drawn on the same observational unit at a number of (usually evenly spaced) points in time. Many recent studies have been based on time-series cross section, which generally consist of the same cross section observed at several points in time. Since the typical data set of this sort consists of a large number of cross-sectional units observed at a few points in time, the common term **panel data set** is usually more fitting for this sort of study.

4.2.2. Descriptive Statistics

Before attempting to estimate parameters of a population or fit models to data, we normally examine the data themselves. One place to begin is with a **scatter diagram,** which is useful in a bivariate sample if the sample contains a reasonable number of observations. Figure 4.1 shows an example for a small data set. In most cases, and particularly if the number of observations in the sample is large, however, we shall use some summary statistics to describe the sample data. Of most interest are measures of **location**—that is, the center of the data—and **scale,** or the dispersion of the data. If the sample contains data on more than one variable, we are also interested in measures of association among the variables.

A few measures of central tendency are as follows:

$$\begin{aligned} \textbf{mean: } \bar{x} &= \frac{1}{n}\sum_{i=1}^{n} x_i, \\ \textbf{median: } m &= \text{middle ranked observation}, \\ \textbf{sample midrange: } \text{midrange} &= \frac{\text{maximum} - \text{minimum}}{2}. \end{aligned} \tag{4-1}$$

The dispersion of the sample observations is usually measured by the

$$\textbf{standard deviation: } s_x = \left[\frac{\sum_{i=1}^{n}(x_i - \bar{x})^2}{n-1}\right]^{1/2}. \tag{4-2}$$

Other measures, such as the average absolute deviation from the sample mean, are also used, although less frequently. If the sample is a multivariate one, the degree of linear association among the variables can be measured by the pairwise measures

$$\textbf{covariance: } s_{xy} = \frac{\sum_{i=1}^{n}(x_i - \bar{x})(y_i - \bar{y})}{n-1}, \tag{4-3}$$

$$\textbf{correlation: } r_{xy} = \frac{s_{xy}}{s_x s_y}.$$

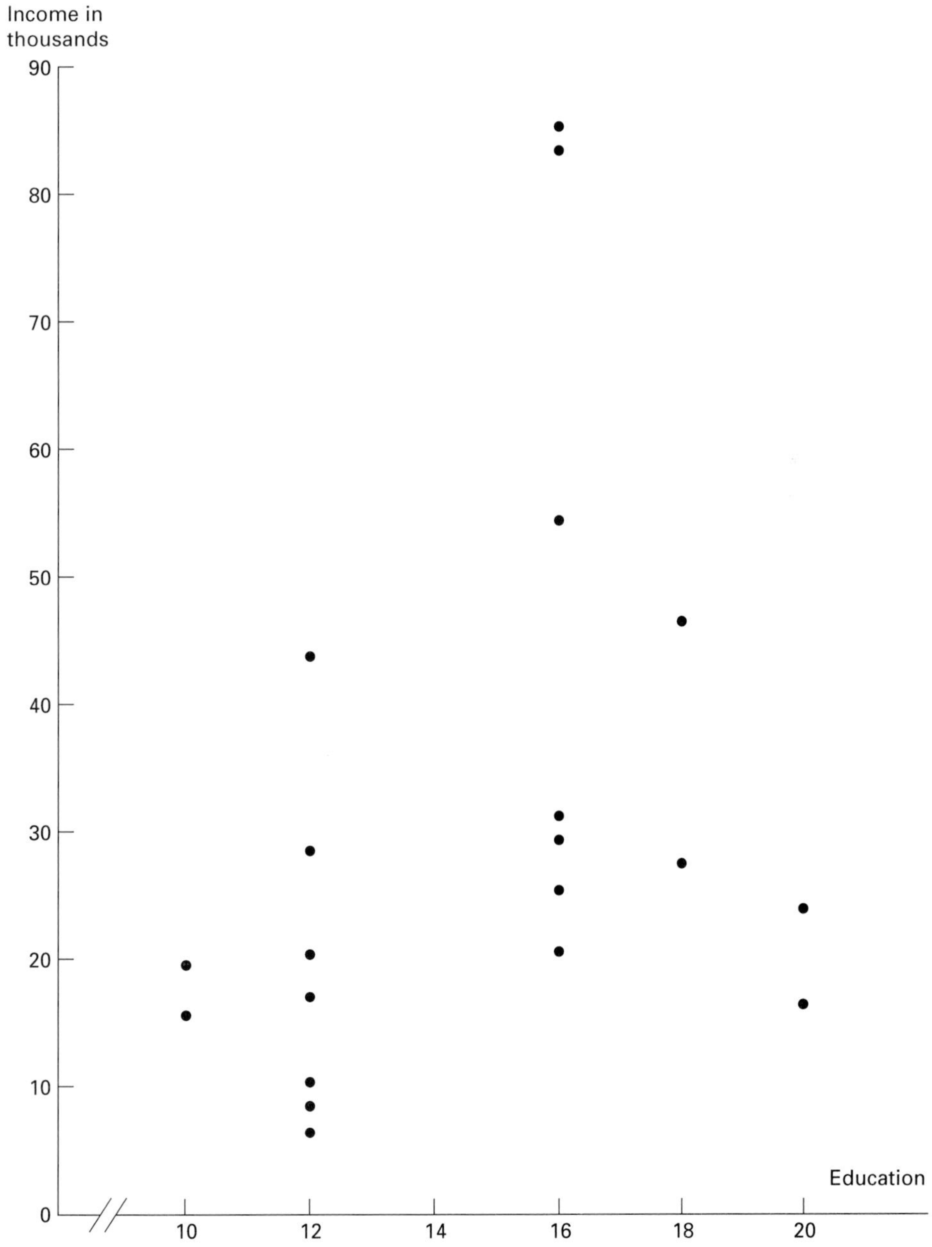

FIGURE 4.1 Scatter Diagram.

If the sample contains data on several variables, it is sometimes convenient to arrange the covariances or correlations in a

$$\textbf{covariance matrix: } \mathbf{S} = [s_{ij}] \tag{4-4}$$

or

$$\textbf{correlation matrix: R} = [r_{ij}].$$

Some useful algebraic results for any two variables $(x_i, y_i), i = 1, \ldots, n$, and constants a and b are

$$s_x^2 = \frac{\sum_{i=1}^{n} x_i^2 - n\bar{x}^2}{n - 1}, \tag{4-5}$$

$$s_{xy} = \frac{\sum_{i=1}^{n} x_i y_i - n\bar{x}\,\bar{y}}{n - 1}, \tag{4-6}$$

$$-1 \le r_{xy} \le 1,$$

$$r_{ax,by} = \frac{ab}{|ab|} r_{xy}, \; a, b \neq 0, \tag{4-7}$$

$$s_{ax} = |a| \, s_x, \tag{4-8}$$

$$s_{ax,by} = |ab| \, s_{xy}.$$

Note that these algebraic results parallel the theoretical results for bivariate probability distributions.

EXAMPLE 4.1 Descriptive Statistics for a Random Sample

Table 4.1 is a (hypothetical) sample of observations on income and education. A scatter diagram appears in Figure 4.1. It suggests a weak positive association between income and education in these data.

Means:

$$\bar{I} = \tfrac{1}{20}(20.5 + \cdots + 84.9) = 31.28,$$
$$\bar{E} = \tfrac{1}{20}(12 + \cdots + 16) = 14.6.$$

TABLE 4.1 Observations on Income and Education

Observation	*Income*	*Education*	*Observation*	*Income*	*Education*
1	20.5	12	11	55.8	16
2	31.5	16	12	25.2	20
3	47.7	18	13	29.0	12
4	26.2	16	14	85.5	16
5	44.0	12	15	15.1	10
6	8.28	12	16	28.5	18
7	30.8	16	17	21.4	16
8	17.2	12	18	17.7	20
9	19.9	10	19	6.42	12
10	9.96	12	20	84.9	16

Note: Income in thousands, education in years.

Standard deviations:

$$s_I = \sqrt{\tfrac{1}{19}[(20.5 - 31.28)^2 + \cdots + (84.9 - 31.28)^2]} = 22.37,$$
$$s_E = \sqrt{\tfrac{1}{19}[(12 - 14.6)^2 + \cdots + (16 - 14.6)^2]} = 3.119.$$

Covariance:

$$\tfrac{1}{19}[20.5(12) + \cdots + 84.9(16) - 20(31.28)(14.6)] = 23.59.$$

Correlation:

$$\frac{23.59}{(22.37)(3.119)} = 0.338.$$

The positive correlation is consistent with our observation of the scatter diagram.

4.2.3. Sampling Distributions

The measures described in the preceding section summarize the data in a random sample. Each measure has a counterpart in the population, that is, the distribution from which the data were drawn. Sample quantities such as the means and the correlation coefficient correspond to population expectations, whereas the values in Table 4.2 parallel the population **pdf** and **cdf.** In the setting of a random sample, we expect these quantities to mimic the population, although not perfectly. The precise manner in which these quantities reflect the population values defines the sampling distribution of a sample statistic.

Definition 4.1: Statistic. *A statistic is any function computed from the data in a sample.*

If another sample were drawn under identical conditions, different values would be obtained for the observations, as each one is a random variable. Consequently, the statistic is also a random variable with a probability distribution called a **sampling distribution.** For example, the following shows an exact result for the sampling behavior of a widely used statistic.

Theorem 4.1: Sampling Distribution of the Sample Mean. *If $x_1, \ldots, x_n$ are a random sample from a population with mean μ and variance σ^2, then $\bar{x}$ is a random variable with mean μ and variance σ^2/n.*

TABLE 4.2 Income Distribution

Range	*Relative Frequency*	*Cumulative Frequency*
<\$10,000	0.15	0.15
10,000–25,000	0.30	0.45
25,000–50,000	0.40	0.85
>50,000	0.15	1.00

Proof: $\bar{x} = (1/n) \Sigma_i x_i$. $E[\bar{x}] = (1/n) \Sigma_i \mu = \mu$. The observations are independent, so $\text{Var}[\bar{x}] = (1/n)^2 \text{Var}[\Sigma_i x_i] = (1/n^2)\Sigma_i \sigma^2 = \sigma^2/n$.

Notice that the fundamental result in Theorem 4.1 does not assume a distribution for x_i.

EXAMPLE 4.2 Sampling Distribution of a Sample Mean

Figure 4.2 shows a frequency plot of the means of 1000 random samples of four observations drawn from a chi-squared distribution with one degree of freedom, which has mean 1 and variance 2.

We are often interested in how a statistic behaves in a large sample or as the sample size increases. The following illustrates one such case.

EXAMPLE 4.3 Sampling Distribution of the Sample Minimum

If $x_1, \ldots, x_n$ are a random sample from an exponential distribution with $f(x) = \theta e^{-\theta x}$, the sampling distribution of the sample minimum in a sample of n observations, denoted $x_{(1)}$, is

$$f(x_{(1)}) = (n\theta)e^{-(n\theta)x_{(1)}}.$$

The proof is considered in the exercises. Since $E[x] = 1/\theta$ and $\text{Var}[x] = 1/\theta^2$, by analogy $E[x_{(1)}] = 1/(n\theta)$ and $\text{Var}[x_{(1)}] = 1/(n\theta)^2$. Thus, in increasingly larger samples, the minimum will be arbitrarily close to 0. [The Chebyshev inequality in (4-17) can be used to prove this intuitively appealing result.]

Sampling distributions are used to make inferences about the population. To consider a perhaps obvious example, because the sampling distribution of the mean of a set of normally distributed observations has mean μ, the sample mean is a natural candidate for an estimate of μ. The observation that the sample "mimics" the population is a statement about the sampling distributions of the sample statistics. Consider, for example, the sample data collected in Figure 4.2. The sample mean of four observations clearly has a sampling distribution, which appears to have a mean roughly equal to the population mean. This is the departure point for our theory of parameter estimation.

4.3. POINT ESTIMATION OF PARAMETERS

Our objective is to use the sample data to infer the value of a parameter or set of parameters, which we denote θ. A **point estimate** is a statistic computed from a sample that gives a single value for θ. The **standard error** of the estimate is the standard deviation of the sampling distribution of the statistic; the square of this quantity is the **sampling variance.** An **interval estimate** is a range of val-

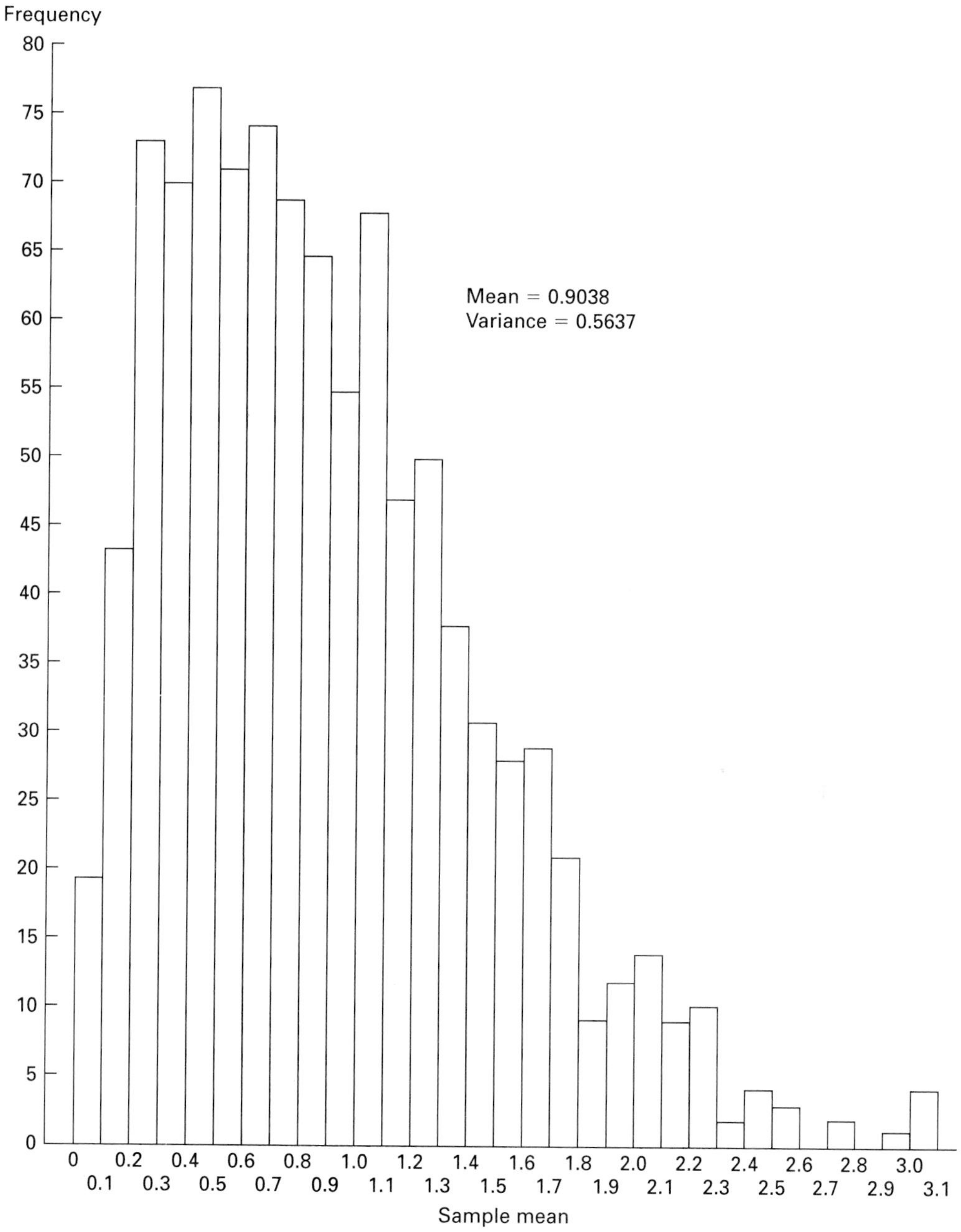

FIGURE 4.2 Sampling Distribution of Means of 1000 Samples of Size 4 from Chi-squared [1].

ues that will contain the true parameter with a preassigned probability. There will be a connection between the two types of estimates; generally, if $\hat{\theta}$ is the point estimate, the interval estimate will be $\hat{\theta} \pm$ a measure of sampling error.

An **estimator** is a rule or strategy for using the data to estimate the parameter. It is defined before the data are drawn. Obviously, some estimators are better than others. To take a simple example, your intuition should convince you that the sample mean would be a better estimator of the population mean than the sample minimum; the minimum is almost certain to underestimate the mean. Nonetheless, the minimum is not entirely without virtue; it is easy to compute, and ease of computation is occasionally a relevant criterion. The search for good estimators constitutes much of econometrics. Estimators are compared on the basis of a variety of attributes. **Finite sample properties** of estimators are those attributes that can be compared regardless of the sample size. Some estimation problems involve characteristics that are not known in finite samples. In these instances, estimators are compared on the basis on their large sample, or **asymptotic properties.** We consider these in turn.

4.3.1. Estimation in a Finite Sample

The following are some finite sample estimation criteria for estimating a single parameter. The extensions to the multiparameter case are direct. We shall consider them in passing where necessary.

DEFINITION 4.2: Unbiased Estimator. *An estimator of a parameter θ is **unbiased** if the mean of its sampling distribution is θ. Formally,*

$$E[\hat{\theta}] = \theta$$

or

$$E[\hat{\theta} - \theta] = \text{Bias}[\hat{\theta} | \theta] = 0$$

implies that $\hat{\theta}$ is unbiased. Note that this implies that the expected sampling error is zero. If $\boldsymbol{\theta}$ is a vector of parameters, the estimator is unbiased if the expected value of every element of $\hat{\boldsymbol{\theta}}$ equals the corresponding element of $\boldsymbol{\theta}$.

If samples of size n are drawn repeatedly and $\hat{\theta}$ is computed for each one, the average value of these estimates will tend to equal θ. For example, the average of the 1000 sample means underlying Figure 4.2 is 0.9038, which is reasonably close to the population mean of 1. The sample minimum is clearly a biased estimator of the mean; it will almost always underestimate the mean, so it will do so on average as well.

Unbiasedness is a desirable attribute, but it is rarely used by itself as an estimation criterion. One reason is that there are many unbiased estimators that are poor uses of the data. For example, in a sample of size n, the first observation drawn is an unbiased estimator of the mean that clearly wastes a great deal of information. A second criterion used to choose among unbiased estimators is efficiency.

DEFINITION 4.3: Efficient Unbiased Estimator. *An unbiased estimator $\hat{\theta}_1$ is more **efficient** than another unbiased estimator $\hat{\theta}_2$ if the sampling variance of $\hat{\theta}_1$ is less than that of $\hat{\theta}_2$. That is,*

$$\text{Var}[\hat{\theta}_1] < \text{Var}[\hat{\theta}_2].$$

In the multiparameter case, the comparison is based on the covariance matrices of the two estimators; $\hat{\boldsymbol{\theta}}_1$ *is more efficient than* $\hat{\boldsymbol{\theta}}_2$ *if* $\text{Var}[\hat{\boldsymbol{\theta}}_2] - \text{Var}[\hat{\boldsymbol{\theta}}_1]$ *is a nonnegative definite matrix.*

By this criterion, the sample mean is obviously to be preferred to the first observation as an estimator of the population mean. If σ^2 is the population variance,

$$\text{Var}[x_1] = \sigma^2 > \text{Var}[\bar{x}] = \frac{\sigma^2}{n}.$$

In discussing efficiency, we have restricted the discussion to unbiased estimators. Clearly, there are biased estimators that have smaller variances than the unbiased ones we have considered. Any constant has a variance of zero. Of course, using a constant as an estimator is not likely to be an effective use of the sample data. Focusing on unbiasedness may still preclude a tolerably biased estimator with a much smaller variance, however. A criterion that recognizes this possible tradeoff is the mean-squared error.

DEFINITION 4.4: Mean-Squared Error. *The mean-squared error of an estimator is*

$$\begin{aligned} \text{MSE}[\hat{\theta}] &= E[(\hat{\theta} - \theta)^2] \\ &= \text{Var}[\hat{\theta}] + (\text{Bias}[\hat{\theta}])^2 && \text{if } \theta \text{ is a scalar,} \\ &= \text{Var}[\hat{\boldsymbol{\theta}}] + \text{Bias}[\hat{\boldsymbol{\theta}}]\,\text{Bias}[\hat{\boldsymbol{\theta}}]' && \text{if } \boldsymbol{\theta} \text{ is a vector.} \end{aligned} \tag{4-9}$$

Figure 4.3 illustrates the effect. On average, the biased estimator will be closer to the true parameter than will the unbiased estimator.

EXAMPLE 4.4 Mean-Squared Error of the Sample Variance

In sampling from a normal distribution, the most frequently used estimator for σ^2 is

$$s^2 = \frac{\sum_{i=1}^{n} (x_i - \bar{x})^2}{n - 1}.$$

It is straightforward to show that s^2 is unbiased, so

$$\text{Var}[s^2] = \frac{2\sigma^4}{n - 1} = \text{MSE}\,[s^2].$$

[A proof is based on the distribution of the idempotent quadratic form $(\mathbf{x} - \mathbf{i}\mu)'\mathbf{M}^0(\mathbf{x} - \mathbf{i}\mu)$, which we discussed in Section 3.10.3.] A less frequently used estimator is

$$\hat{\sigma}^2 = \frac{1}{n} \sum_{i=1}^{n} (x_i - \bar{x})^2 = [(n - 1)/n]s^2.$$

This estimator is slightly biased downward:

$$E[\hat{\sigma}^2] = \frac{(n - 1)E(s^2)}{n} = \frac{(n - 1)\sigma^2}{n},$$

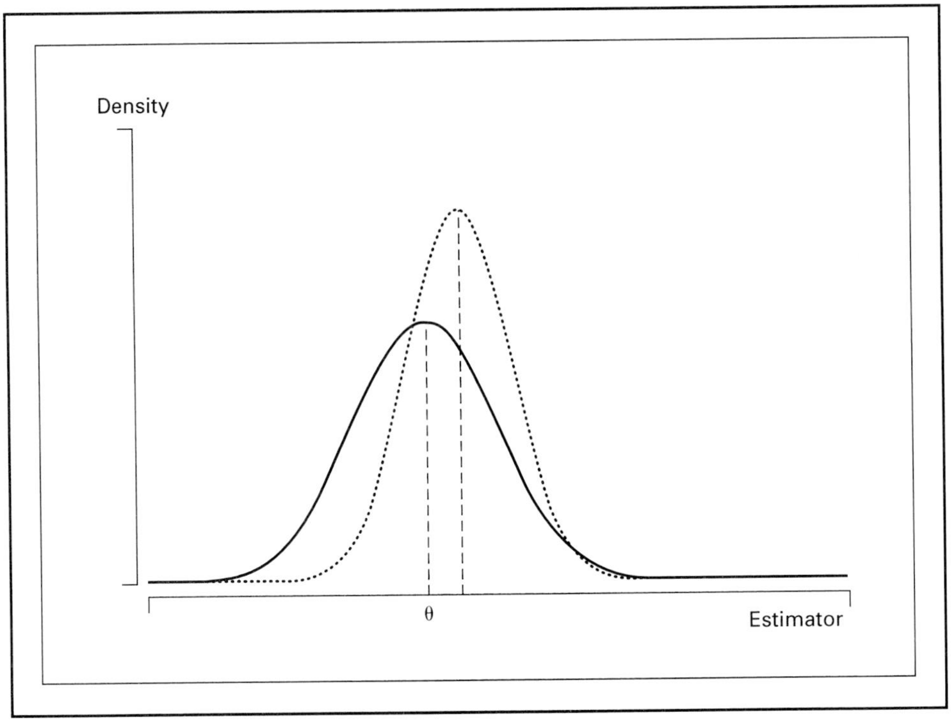

FIGURE 4.3 Sampling Distributions.

so its bias is

$$E[\hat{\sigma}^2 - \sigma^2] = \text{Bias}[\hat{\sigma}^2] = \frac{-1}{n}\sigma^2.$$

But it has a smaller variance than s^2:

$$\text{Var}[\hat{\sigma}^2] = \left[\frac{n-1}{n}\right]^2\left[\frac{2\sigma^4}{n-1}\right] < \text{Var}[s^2].$$

To compare the two estimators, we can use the difference in their mean-squared errors:

$$\text{MSE}[\hat{\sigma}^2] - \text{MSE}[s^2] = \sigma^4\left[\frac{2n-1}{n^2} - \frac{2}{n-1}\right] < 0.$$

The biased estimator is a bit more precise. The difference will be negligible in a large sample, but, for example, it is about 10 percent in a sample of 16.

Which of these criteria should be used in a given situation depends on the particulars of that setting and our objectives in the study.

EXAMPLE 4.5 Quadratic Loss Function

In a **decision theoretic** setting, the purpose of estimating the parameter is to use the data to formulate a decision. The decision depends on the estimated parameter and will be erroneous if $\hat{\theta}$ does not equal the true parameter. The cost of the decision, or **loss,** will depend on the estimate and the true value of θ. Since $\hat{\theta}$ is random, so is the loss. Suppose that the cost associated with a decision is proportional to the square of the difference between the estimate and the true parameter. To minimize the expected loss, we would choose the estimator with the minimum mean-squared error.

Unfortunately, the MSE criterion is rarely operational; minimum mean-squared error estimators, when they exist at all, usually depend on unknown parameters. Thus, we are usually less demanding. A commonly used criterion is **minimum variance unbiasedness.**

4.3.2. Efficient Unbiased Estimation

In a random sample of n observations, the density of each observation is $f(x_i, \theta)$. Since the n observations are independent, their joint density is

$$\begin{aligned} f(x_1, x_2, \ldots, x_n, \theta) &= f(x_1, \theta)f(x_2, \theta)\cdots f(x_n, \theta) \\ &= \prod_{i=1}^{n} f(x_i, \theta) = L(\theta \mid x_1, x_2, \ldots, x_n). \end{aligned} \tag{4-10}$$

The function $L(\theta|\mathbf{X})$ is the likelihood function for θ given the data $\mathbf{x}$. It is frequently abbreviated to $L(\theta)$. Where no ambiguity can arise, we shall abbreviate it further to L.

EXAMPLE 4.6 Likelihood Function for the Exponential Distribution

If $x_1, \ldots, x_n$ are a sample of n observations from an exponential distribution with parameter θ,

$$\begin{aligned} L(\theta) &= \prod_i \theta e^{-\theta x_i} \\ &= \theta^n e^{-\theta \sum_{i=1}^{n} x_i}. \end{aligned}$$

EXAMPLE 4.7 Likelihood Function for the Normal Distribution

If $x_1, \ldots, x_n$ are a sample of n observations from a normal distribution with mean μ and standard deviation σ,

$$\begin{aligned} L(\mu, \sigma) &= \prod_i (2\pi\sigma^2)^{-1/2} e^{-[1/(2\sigma^2)](x_i - \mu)^2} \\ &= (2\pi\sigma^2)^{-n/2} e^{-[1/(2\sigma^2)]\Sigma_i (x_i - \mu)^2}. \end{aligned} \tag{4-11}$$

The likelihood function is the cornerstone for most of our theory of parameter estimation. An important result for efficient estimation is the following.

THEOREM 4.2: Cramér–Rao Lower Bound. *Assuming that the density of x satisfies certain regularity conditions, the variance of an unbiased estimator of a parameter θ will always be at least as large as*

$$
\begin{aligned}
[I(\theta)]^{-1} &= \left(-E\left[\frac{\partial^2 \ln L(\theta)}{\partial \theta^2}\right]\right)^{-1} \\
&= \left(E\left[\left(\frac{\partial \ln L(\theta)}{\theta}\right)^2\right]\right)^{-1}.
\end{aligned} \tag{4-12}
$$

The quantity $I(\theta)$ is the information number for the sample. We will prove the result that the negative of the expected second derivative equals the expected square of the first derivative in the next section. Proof of the main result of the theorem is quite involved. See, for example, Stuart and Ord (1989).

The regularity conditions are technical in nature. [See Theil (1971, Chap. 8).] Loosely, they are conditions imposed on the density of the random variable that appears in the likelihood function which will ensure that the Lindberg–Levy central limit theorem will apply to the sample of observations on the random vector $\mathbf{y} = \partial \ln f(x\,|\,\boldsymbol{\theta})/\partial \boldsymbol{\theta}$. Among the conditions are finite moments of x up to order 3. An additional condition normally included in the set is that the range of the random variable be independent of the parameters. We will reexamine the likelihood function and these conditions in the next section.

In some cases, the second derivative of the log likelihood is a constant, so the Cramér–Rao bound is simple to obtain. For instance, in sampling from an exponential distribution, from Example 4.6,

$$
\begin{aligned}
\ln L &= n \ln \theta - \theta \sum_{i=1}^{n} x_i, \\
\frac{\partial \ln L}{\partial \theta} &= \frac{n}{\theta} - \sum_{i=1}^{n} x_i,
\end{aligned}
$$

so $\partial^2 \ln L/\partial \theta^2 = -n/\theta^2$ and the variance bound is $[I(\theta)]^{-1} = \theta^2/n$. In most situations, the second derivative is a random variable with a distribution of its own. The following examples show two such cases.

EXAMPLE 4.8 Variance Bound for the Poisson Distribution

For the Poisson distribution,

$$
\begin{aligned}
f(x) &= \frac{e^{-\theta}\theta^x}{x!}, \\
\ln L &= -n\theta + \left(\sum_{i=1}^{n} x_i\right)\ln \theta - \sum_{i=1}^{n} \ln(x_i!), \\
\frac{\partial \ln L}{\partial \theta} &= -n + \frac{\sum_{i=1}^{n} x_i}{\theta}, \\
\frac{\partial^2 \ln L}{\partial \theta^2} &= \frac{-\sum_{i=1}^{n} x_i}{\theta^2}.
\end{aligned}
$$

The sum of n identical Poisson variables has a Poisson distribution with parameter equal to n times the parameter of the individual variables. Therefore, the actual distribution of the first derivative will be that of a linear function of a Poisson distributed variable. Since $E[\Sigma_{i=1}^{n} x_i] = nE[x_i] = n\theta$, the variance bound for the Poisson distribution is $[I(\theta)]^{-1} = \theta/n$. (Note, as well, that the same result implies that $E[\partial \ln L/\partial\theta] = 0$, which is a result we will use in the next section.)

Consider, finally, a multivariate case. If $\boldsymbol{\theta}$ is a vector of parameters, $\mathbf{I}(\boldsymbol{\theta})$ is the **information matrix.** The Cramér–Rao theorem states that the difference between the covariance matrix of any unbiased estimator and the inverse of the information matrix,

$$\begin{aligned}[\mathbf{I}(\boldsymbol{\theta})]^{-1} &= \left(-E\left[\frac{\partial^2 \ln L(\boldsymbol{\theta})}{\partial\boldsymbol{\theta}\,\partial\boldsymbol{\theta}'}\right]\right)^{-1} \\ &= \left\{E\left[\left(\frac{\partial \ln L(\boldsymbol{\theta})}{\partial\boldsymbol{\theta}}\right)\left(\frac{\partial \ln L(\boldsymbol{\theta})}{\partial\boldsymbol{\theta}'}\right)\right]\right\}^{-1},\end{aligned} \tag{4-13}$$

will be a nonnegative definite matrix.

EXAMPLE 4.9 Information Matrix for the Normal Distribution

For random sampling from a normal distribution, the log-likelihood and its derivatives are

$$\begin{aligned}\ln L(\mu, \sigma^2) &= -\frac{n}{2}\ln(2\pi) - \frac{n}{2}\ln\sigma^2 - \frac{1}{2\sigma^2}\sum_{i=1}^{n}(x_i-\mu)^2, \\ \frac{\partial \ln L}{\partial\mu} &= \frac{1}{\sigma^2}\sum_{i=1}^{n}(x_i-\mu), \\ \frac{\partial \ln L}{\partial\sigma^2} &= -\frac{n}{2\sigma^2} + \frac{1}{2\sigma^4}\sum_{i=1}^{n}(x_i-\mu)^2, \\ \frac{\partial^2 \ln L}{\partial\mu^2} &= -\frac{n}{\sigma^2}, \\ \frac{\partial^2 \ln L}{\partial(\sigma^2)^2} &= \frac{n}{2\sigma^4} - \frac{1}{\sigma^6}\sum_{i=1}^{n}(x_i-\mu)^2, \\ \frac{\partial^2 \ln L}{\partial\mu\,\partial\sigma^2} &= -\frac{1}{\sigma^4}\sum_{i=1}^{n}(x_i-\mu).\end{aligned}$$

The information matrix contains the negatives of the expected values of the second derivatives:

$$\mathbf{I}(\mu, \sigma^2) = \begin{bmatrix} n/\sigma^2 & 0 \\ 0 & n/2\sigma^4 \end{bmatrix}.$$

The inverse is the variance bound for unbiased estimation of μ and σ^2 of a normal distribution:

$$[\mathbf{I}(\mu, \sigma^2)]^{-1} = \begin{bmatrix} \sigma^2/n & 0 \\ 0 & 2\sigma^4/n \end{bmatrix}. \quad \textbf{(4-14)}$$

The normal distribution is somewhat unusual in its diagonal information matrix.

If $\hat{\mu}$ and $\hat{\sigma}^2$ are any pair of unbiased estimators for μ and σ^2 and $\mathbf{V}$ is their 2×2 covariance matrix, then $\mathbf{V} - [\mathbf{I}(\mu, \sigma^2)]^{-1}$ is a nonnegative definite matrix. Consider the two unbiased estimators

$$\hat{\mu} = \bar{x} = \frac{1}{n}\mathbf{i}'\mathbf{x},$$

$$\hat{\sigma}^2 = s^2 = \frac{\sum_{i=1}^{n}(x_i - \bar{x})^2}{n-1} = \frac{\mathbf{x}'\mathbf{M}^0\mathbf{x}}{n-1}.$$

The mean and variance of $\bar{x}$ were given in Theorem 4.1. The independence of $\bar{x}$ and s^2 was shown in Section 3.10.6. Thus, their covariance is 0, and

$$\begin{aligned}\text{Var}[\bar{x}, s^2] - [\mathbf{I}(\mu, \sigma^2)]^{-1} &= \begin{bmatrix} \sigma^2/n & 0 \\ 0 & 2\sigma^4/(n-1) \end{bmatrix} - \begin{bmatrix} \sigma^2/n & 0 \\ 0 & 2\sigma^4/n \end{bmatrix} \\ &= \begin{bmatrix} 0 & 0 \\ 0 & 2\sigma^4/[n(n-1)] \end{bmatrix},\end{aligned} \quad \textbf{(4-15)}$$

which is a nonnegative definite matrix. Note that the mean attains the variance bound whereas the variance estimator does not.

In most settings, numerous estimators are available for the parameters of a distribution. The usefulness of the Cramér–Rao bound is that if one of these is known to attain the variance bound, there is no need to consider any other to seek a more efficient estimator. Regarding the use of the variance bound, we emphasize that if an unbiased estimator attains it, that estimator is efficient. If a given estimator does not attain the variance bound, however, we do not know, except in a few special cases, whether this estimator is efficient or not. It may be that no unbiased estimator can attain the Cramér–Rao bound, which can leave the question of whether a given unbiased estimator is efficient or not unanswered.

We note, finally, that in some cases we further restrict the set of estimators to linear functions of the data.

DEFINITION 4.5: Minimum Variance Linear Unbiased Estimator (MVLUE). *An estimator is the minimum variance linear unbiased estimator or* ***best linear unbiased estimator (BLUE)*** *if it is a linear function of the data and has minimum variance among linear unbiased estimators.*

In a few instances, such as the normal mean, there will be an efficient linear unbiased estimator; $\bar{x}$ is efficient among all unbiased estimators, both linear and nonlinear. In other cases, such as the normal variance, there is no linear unbiased estimator. This criterion is useful because we can sometimes find an MVLUE without having to specify the distribution at all. Thus, by limiting ourselves to a somewhat restricted class of estimators, we free ourselves from having to assume a particular distribution.

4.4. LARGE-SAMPLE DISTRIBUTION THEORY[2]

In most cases, whether an estimator is exactly unbiased, or what its exact sampling variance is in samples of a given size, will be unknown. But we may be able to obtain approximate results about the behavior of the distribution of an estimator as the sample becomes large. For example, it is well known that the distribution of the mean of a sample tends to approximate normality as the sample size grows, regardless of the distribution of the individual observations. Knowledge about the limiting behavior of the distribution of an estimator can be used to infer an approximate distribution for the estimator in a finite sample. To describe how this is done, it is necessary, first, to present some results on convergence of random variables.

4.4.1. Convergence in Probability

Limiting arguments in this discussion will be with respect to the sample size n. Let x_n be a random variable indexed by the size of a sample.

DEFINITION 4.6: Convergence in Probability. *The random variable* x_n ***converges in probability*** *to a constant c if* $\lim_{n\to\infty} \text{Prob}(|x_n - c| > \epsilon) = 0$ *for any positive* ϵ.

Convergence in probability implies that the values that the variable may take that are not close to c become increasingly unlikely as n increases. To consider one example, suppose that the random variable x_n takes two values, 0 and n, with probabilities $1 - (1/n)$ and $(1/n)$, respectively. As n increases, the second point will become ever more remote from any constant but, at the same time, will become increasingly less probable. In this example, x_n converges in probability to 0. The crux of this form of convergence is that all the probability of the distribution becomes concentrated at points close to c. If x_n converges in probability to c, we write

$$\text{plim}\, x_n = c. \tag{4-16}$$

We will make frequent use of a special case of convergence in probability, **convergence in mean square** or **convergence in quadratic mean.**

[2] An up-to-date summary of many recent developments in large-sample theory appears in White (1984).

THEOREM 4.3: Convergence in Quadratic Mean. *If x_n has mean μ_n and variance σ_n^2 such that the ordinary limits of μ_n and σ_n^2 are c and 0 respectively, then x_n converges in mean square to c, and*

$$\text{plim } x_n = c.$$

A proof of this result can be based on a useful theorem.

THEOREM 4.4: Chebychev's Inequality. *If x_n is a random variable and c_n and ϵ are constants, then* $\text{Prob}(|x_n - c_n| > \epsilon) \leq E[(x_n - c_n)^2]/\epsilon^2$.

To establish this inequality, we use another result [see Goldberger (1991, p. 31)].

THEOREM 4.5: Markov's Inequality. *If y_n is a nonnegative random variable and δ is a positive constant, then* $\text{Prob}[y_n \geq \delta] \leq E[y_n]/\delta$.

Proof: $E[y_n] = \text{Prob}[y_n < \delta]E[y_n | y_n < \delta] + \text{Prob}[y_n \geq \delta]E[y_n | y_n \geq \delta]$. Since y_n is nonnegative, both terms must be nonnegative, so $E[y_n] \geq \text{Prob}[y_n \geq \delta]E[y_n | y_n \geq \delta]$. Since $E[y_n | y_n \geq \delta]$ must be greater than δ, $E[y_n] \geq \text{Prob}[y_n \geq \delta]\delta$. This is the result.

Now, to prove Theorem 4.4, let y_n be $(x_n - c)^2$ and δ be ϵ^2 in Theorem 4.5. Then $(x_n - c)^2 > \delta$ implies that $|x_n - c| > \epsilon$. Finally, we will use a special case of the Chebychev inequality, where $c = \mu_n$, so that we have

$$\text{Prob}(|x_n - \mu_n| > \epsilon) \leq \sigma_n^2/\epsilon^2. \tag{4-17}$$

Taking the limits of μ_n and σ_n^2 in (4-17), we see that if

$$\lim_{n\to\infty} E[x_n] = c \quad \text{and} \quad \lim_{n\to\infty} \text{Var}[x_n] = 0, \tag{4-18}$$

then

$$\text{plim } x_n = c.$$

We have shown that convergence in mean square implies convergence in probability. Mean-square convergence implies that the distribution of x_n collapses to a spike at plim x_n, as shown in Figure 4.4. We will study a different form of convergence in Chapter 6, where we will need more general results. For the applications in the chapter, convergence in mean square will be sufficient.

EXAMPLE 4.10 Convergence of the Sample Minimum in Exponential Sampling

As noted in Example 4.3, in sampling from an exponential distribution, for the sample minimum $x_{(1)}$,

$$\lim_{n\to\infty} E[x_{(1)}] = \lim_{n\to\infty} \frac{1}{n\theta} = 0$$

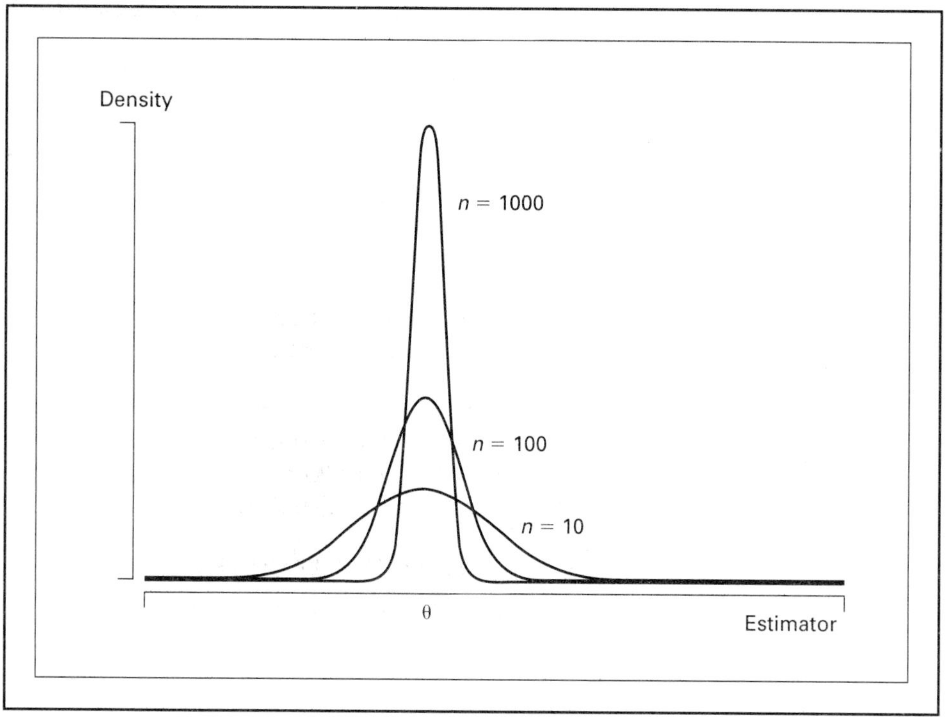

FIGURE 4.4 Quadratic Convergence to a Constant, θ.

and

$$\lim_{n\to\infty} \text{Var}[x_{(1)}] = \lim_{n\to\infty} \frac{1}{(n\theta)^2} = 0.$$

Therefore,

$$\text{plim}\, x_{(1)} = 0.$$

Note, in particular, that the variance is divided by n^2. Thus, this estimator converges very rapidly to 0.

Convergence in probability does not imply convergence in mean square. Consider the simple example given earlier in which x_n equals either 0 or n with probabilities $1 - (1/n)$ and $(1/n)$. The exact expected value of x_n is 1 for all n, which is not the probability limit. Indeed, if we let $\text{Prob}(x_n = n^2) = (1/n)$ instead, the mean of the distribution explodes, but the probability limit is still zero. Again, the point $x_n = n^2$ becomes ever more extreme but, at the same time, becomes ever less likely. The conditions for convergence in mean square are usually easier to verify than those for the more general form. Fortunately, we shall rarely encounter circumstances in which it will be necessary to show convergence in probability in which we cannot rely upon convergence in mean square. Our most frequent use of this concept will be in formulating consistent estimators.

DEFINITION 4.7: Consistent Estimator. *An estimator $\hat{\theta}$ of a parameter θ is a **consistent** estimator of θ if and only if*

$$\text{plim}\, \hat{\theta} = \theta. \tag{4-19}$$

THEOREM 4.6: Consistency of the Sample Mean. *The mean of a random sample from any population with finite mean μ and finite variance σ^2 is a consistent estimator of μ.*

Proof: $E[\bar{x}] = \mu$ and $\text{Var}[\bar{x}] = \sigma^2/n$. Therefore, $\bar{x}$ converges in mean square to μ, or $\text{plim}\, \bar{x} = \mu$.

Theorem 4.6 is broader than it might appear at first.[3]

COROLLARY TO THEOREM 4.6: Consistency of a Mean of Functions. *In random sampling, for any function $g(x)$, if $E[g(x)]$ and $Var[g(x)]$ are finite constants,*

$$\text{plim}\, \frac{1}{n} \sum_{i=1}^{n} g(x_i) = E[g(x)]. \tag{4-20}$$

Proof: Define $y_i = g(x_i)$ and use Theorem 4.6.

EXAMPLE 4.11 Estimating a Function of the Mean

In sampling from a normal distribution with mean μ and variance 1,

$$E[e^x] = e^{\mu + 1/2} \quad \text{and} \quad \text{Var}[e^x] = e^{2\mu + 2} - e^{2\mu + 1}.$$

(See Section 3.4.4 on the lognormal distribution.) Hence,

$$\text{plim}\, \frac{1}{n} \sum_{i=1}^{n} e^{x_i} = e^{\mu + 1/2}.$$

A particularly convenient result is the following.

THEOREM 4.7: Slutsky Theorem. *For a continuous function $g(x_n)$ that is not a function of n,*

$$\text{plim}\, g(x_n) = g(\text{plim}\, x_n). \tag{4-21}$$

The Slutsky theorem highlights a comparison between the expectation of a

[3]The conditions for the theorem are also a bit stronger than necessary. We have used a mean-square convergence proof for consistency. The Kinchine theorem (Theorem 6.14) requires only that the observations be i.i.d. and that the mean be a finite constant to provide convergence *in probability*. With the additional assumption about the variance, we get the stronger result.

random variable and its probability limit. Suppose that $g(x_n)$ is a concave function. Then, the following theorem holds.

Theorem 4.8: Jensen's Inequality. *If $g(x_n)$ is a concave function of x_n, then $g(E[x_n]) \geq E[g(x_n)]$.*

Therefore, although the expected value of a function of x_n may not equal the function of the expected value—it exceeds it if the function is concave—the probability limit of the function *is* equal to the function of the probability limit. (See Section 3.3 for an application.)

The generalization of Theorem 4.7 to a function of several random variables is direct, as illustrated in the next example.

EXAMPLE 4.12 Probability Limit of a Function of $\bar{x}$ and s^2

In random sampling from a population with mean μ and variance σ^2, the exact expected value of $\bar{x}^2/s^2$ will be difficult, if not impossible, to derive. But, by the Slutsky theorem,

$$\text{plim}\,\frac{\bar{x}^2}{s^2} = \frac{\mu^2}{\sigma^2}.$$

Some implications of the Slutsky theorem are now summarized.

Theorem 4.9: Rules for Probability Limits. *If x_n and y_n are random variables with* plim $x_n = c$ *and* plim $y_n = d$, *then*

$$\text{plim}(x_n + y_n) = c + d, \quad \textbf{(sum rule)} \quad \textbf{(4-22)}$$

$$\text{plim}\, x_n y_n = cd, \quad \textbf{(product rule)} \quad \textbf{(4-23)}$$

$$\text{plim}\, x_n/y_n = c/d \quad \text{if } d \neq 0. \quad \textbf{(ratio rule)} \quad \textbf{(4-24)}$$

If $\mathbf{W}_n$ is a matrix whose elements are random variables and if plim $\mathbf{W}_n = \mathbf{\Omega}$, *then*

$$\text{plim}\,\mathbf{W}_n^{-1} = \mathbf{\Omega}^{-1}. \quad \textbf{(matrix inverse rule)} \quad \textbf{(4-25)}$$

If $\mathbf{X}_n$ and $\mathbf{Y}_n$ are random matrices with plim $\mathbf{X}_n = \mathbf{A}$ *and* plim $\mathbf{Y}_n = \mathbf{B}$,

$$\text{plim}\,\mathbf{X}_n\mathbf{Y}_n = \mathbf{AB}. \quad \textbf{(matrix product rule)} \quad \textbf{(4-26)}$$

4.4.2. Convergence in Distribution — Limiting Distributions

A second form of convergence is **convergence in distribution.** Let x_n be a sequence of random variables indexed by the sample size, and assume that x_n has cdf $F_n(x)$.

Definition 4.8: Convergence in Distribution. *x_n converges in distribution to a random variable x with cdf $F(x)$ if $\lim_{n\to\infty}|F_n(x) - F(x)| = 0$ at all continuity points of $F(x)$.*

This is a statement about the probability distribution associated with x_n; it does not imply that x_n converges at all. To take a trivial example, suppose that the exact distribution of the random variable x_n is

$$\text{Prob}(x_n = 1) = \frac{1}{2} + \frac{1}{n+1},$$

$$\text{Prob}(x_n = 2) = \frac{1}{2} - \frac{1}{n+1}.$$

As n increases without bound, the two probabilities converge to $\frac{1}{2}$, but x_n does not converge to a constant.

DEFINITION 4.9: Limiting Distribution. *If x_n converges in distribution to x, where $F(x)$ is the cdf of x, then $F(x)$ is the* ***limiting distribution*** *of x. This is written*

$$x_n \xrightarrow{d} x.$$

The limiting distribution is often given in terms of the pdf, or simply the parametric family. For example, "the limiting distribution of x_n is standard normal."

EXAMPLE 4.13 Limiting Distribution of t_{n-1}

Consider a sample of size n from a standard normal distribution. A familiar inference problem is the test of the hypothesis that the population mean is zero. The test statistic usually used is the t statistic:

$$t_{n-1} = \frac{\bar{x}}{s/\sqrt{n}},$$

where

$$s^2 = \frac{\sum_{i=1}^{n} (x_i - \bar{x})^2}{n-1}.$$

The exact distribution of the random variable t_{n-1} is t with $n - 1$ degrees of freedom. The density is different for every n:

$$f(t_{n-1}) = \frac{\Gamma(n/2)}{\Gamma[(n-1)/2]}[(n-1)\pi]^{-1/2}\left[1 + \frac{t_{n-1}^2}{n-1}\right]^{-n/2} \qquad \textbf{(4-27)}$$

as is the cdf, $F_{n-1}(t) = \int_{-\infty}^{t} f_{n-1}(x)\,dx$. This distribution has mean 0 and variance $(n-1)/(n-3)$. As n grows to infinity, t_{n-1} converges to the standard normal, which is written

$$t_{n-1} \xrightarrow{d} N[0, 1].$$

DEFINITION 4.10: Limiting Mean and Variance. *The* ***limiting mean*** *and* ***variance*** *of a random variable are the mean and variance of the limiting distribution, assuming that the limiting distribution and its moments exist.*

For the random variable with $t[n]$ distribution, the exact mean and variance are 0 and $n/(n-2)$, whereas the limiting mean and variance are 0 and 1. The example might suggest that the limiting mean and variance are 0 and 1, that is, that the moments of the limiting distribution are the ordinary limits of the moments of the finite sample distributions. This is almost always true, but it need not be. It is possible to construct examples in which the exact moments do not even exist, even though the moments of the limiting distribution are well defined.[4] Even in such cases, we can usually derive the mean and variance of the limiting distribution.

Limiting distributions, like probability limits, can greatly simplify the analysis of a problem. Some results that combine the two concepts are as follows.[5]

THEOREM 4.10: Rules for Limiting Distributions.

1. *If* $x_n \xrightarrow{d} x$ *and* $\text{plim}\, y_n = c$, *then*

$$x_n y_n \xrightarrow{d} cx. \tag{4-28}$$

This means that the limiting distribution of $x_n y_n$ *is the distribution of* cx. *Also,*

$$x_n + y_n \xrightarrow{d} x + c, \tag{4-29}$$

$$x_n / y_n \xrightarrow{d} x/c, \quad \text{if } c \neq 0. \tag{4-30}$$

2. *If* $x_n \xrightarrow{d} x$ *and* $g(x_n)$ *is a continuous function,* $g(x_n) \xrightarrow{d} g(x)$. **(4-31)**

This result is analogous to the Slutsky theorem for probability limits. For an example, consider the t_n *random variable discussed earlier. The exact distribution of* t_n^2 *is* $F[1, n]$. *But as* $n \to \infty$, t_n *converges to a standard normal variable. According to this result, the limiting distribution of* t_n^2 *will be that of the square of a standard normal, which is chi-squared with one degree of freedom. We conclude, therefore, that*

$$F[1, n] \xrightarrow{d} \textit{chi-squared}\, [1]. \tag{4-32}$$

We encountered this result in our earlier discussion of limiting forms of the standard normal family of distributions.

3. *If* y_n *has a limiting distribution and* $\text{plim}(x_n - y_n) = 0$, *then* x_n *has the same limiting distribution as* y_n.

The last result combines convergence in distribution and in probability. It may be possible to establish this property by using mean-square convergence.[6]

We are ultimately interested in finding a way to describe the statistical properties of estimators when their exact distributions are unknown. The concepts of consistency and convergence in probability are important. But the the-

---

[4]See, for example, Maddala (1977a, p. 150).

[5]For proofs and further discussion, see, for example, Greenberg and Webster (1983).

[6]Lucid discussion of this topic may be found in Greenberg and Webster (1983, pp. 12–13).

ory of limiting distributions given earlier is not yet adequate. We rarely deal with estimators that are not consistent for something, though perhaps not always the parameter we are trying to estimate. As such,

$$\text{if plim } \hat{\theta}_n = \theta, \text{ then } \hat{\theta}_n \xrightarrow{d} \theta.$$

That is, the limiting distribution of $\hat{\theta}_n$ is a spike. This is not very informative, nor is it at all what we have in mind when we speak of the statistical properties of an estimator. (To endow our finite sample estimator $\hat{\theta}_n$ with the zero sampling variance of the spike at θ would be optimistic in the extreme.)

As an intermediate step, then, to a more reasonable description of the statistical properties of an estimator, we use a **stabilizing transformation** of the random variable to one that does have a well-defined limiting distribution. To jump to the most common application, whereas

$$\text{plim } \hat{\theta}_n = \theta,$$

we often find that

$$z_n = \sqrt{n}\,(\hat{\theta} - \theta) \xrightarrow{d} f(z),$$

where $f(z)$ is a well-defined distribution with a mean and a positive variance. The single most important theorem in econometrics provides an application of this proposition. A basic form of the theorem is as follows.

THEOREM 4.11: Central Limit Theorem (Univariate). *If $x_1, \ldots, x_n$ are a random sample from a probability distribution with finite mean μ and finite variance σ^2 and $\bar{x}_n = (1/n)\sum_{i=1}^n x_i$,*

$$\sqrt{n}\,(\bar{x}_n - \mu) \xrightarrow{d} N[0, \sigma^2].$$

This is the **Lindberg–Levy** variant for the mean of a univariate distribution. A proof appears in Rao (1973, p. 127). The result is quite remarkable as it holds regardless of the form of the parent distribution. For a striking example, return to Figure 4.2. The distribution from which the data were drawn in that figure does not even remotely resemble a normal distribution. In samples of only four observations, however, the force of the central limit theorem is clearly visible in the sampling distribution of the means.

The Lindberg–Levy theorem is one of several forms of this extremely powerful result.[7] For our purposes, an important extension allows us to relax the assumption of equal variances. A more general form of the Lindberg–Levy theorem is the following.

THEOREM 4.12: Central Limit Theorem with Unequal Variances. *Suppose that*

[7]See, for example, Greenberg and Webster (1983) and Rao (1973).

$\{x_i\}$, $i = 1, \ldots, n$, is a set of random variables with finite means μ_i and finite positive variances σ_i^2. Let

$$\overline{\sigma}_n^2 = \frac{1}{n}(\sigma_1^2 + \sigma_2^2 + \cdots).$$

If no single term dominates this average variance, which we could state as $\lim_{n\to\infty} \max(\sigma_i)/(n\overline{\sigma}_n) = 0$, *and if the average variance converges to a finite constant,* $\overline{\sigma}^2 = \lim_{n\to\infty} \overline{\sigma}_n^2$, *then*

$$\sqrt{n}\,(\overline{x}_n - \overline{\mu}_n) \xrightarrow{d} N[0, \overline{\sigma}^2].$$

This is the **Lindberg–Feller** variant of the central limit theorem. In practical terms, the theorem states that sums of random variables, regardless of their form, will tend to be normally distributed. The result is yet more remarkable in that *it does not require the variables in the sum to come from the same underlying distribution. It requires, essentially, only that the mean be a mixture of many random variables, none of which is large compared with their sum.* Since nearly all the estimators we construct in econometrics fall under the purview of the central limit theorem, it is obviously an important result.

For later purposes, we will require multivariate versions of these theorems. Proofs of the following may be found, for example, in Greenberg and Webster (1983) or Rao (1973) and references cited there.

THEOREM 4.13: Lindberg–Levy Central Limit Theorem. *If $\mathbf{x}_1, \ldots, \mathbf{x}_n$ are a random sample from a multivariate distribution with finite mean vector $\boldsymbol{\mu}$ and finite positive definite covariance matrix $\mathbf{Q}$, then*

$$\sqrt{n}\,(\overline{\mathbf{x}}_n - \boldsymbol{\mu}) \xrightarrow{d} N[\mathbf{0}, \mathbf{Q}],$$

where

$$\overline{\mathbf{x}}_n = \frac{1}{n}\sum_{i=1}^{n} \mathbf{x}_i.$$

The extension of the Lindberg–Feller theorem to unequal covariance matrices requires some intricate mathematics. The following is an informal statement of the relevant conditions. Further discussion and references appear in Fomby et al. (1984) and Greenberg and Webster (1983).

THEOREM 4.14: Lindberg–Feller Central Limit Theorem. *Suppose that $\mathbf{x}_1, \ldots, \mathbf{x}_n$ are a sample of random vectors such that $E[\mathbf{x}_i] = \boldsymbol{\mu}_i$, $\text{Var}[\mathbf{x}_i] = \mathbf{Q}_i$, and all mixed third moments of the multivariate distribution are finite. Let*

$$\overline{\boldsymbol{\mu}}_n = \frac{1}{n}\sum_{i=1}^{n} \boldsymbol{\mu}_i,$$

$$\overline{\mathbf{Q}}_n = \frac{1}{n}\sum_{i=1}^{n} \mathbf{Q}_i.$$

We assume that

$$\lim_{n\to\infty} \overline{\mathbf{Q}}_n = \mathbf{Q},$$

where $\mathbf{Q}$ *is a finite, positive definite matrix, and that for every i,*

$$\lim_{n\to\infty} (n\overline{\mathbf{Q}}_n)^{-1}\mathbf{Q}_i = \lim_{n\to\infty}\left(\sum_{i=1}^{n}\mathbf{Q}_i\right)^{-1}\mathbf{Q}_i = \mathbf{0}.$$

We allow the means of the random vectors to differ, although in the cases that we will analyze, they will generally be identical. The second assumption states that individual components of the sum must be finite and diminish in significance. There is also an implicit assumption that the sum of matrices is nonsingular. Since the limiting matrix is nonsingular, the assumption must hold for large enough n, which is all that concerns us here. With these in place, the result is

$$\sqrt{n}\,(\overline{\mathbf{x}}_n - \overline{\boldsymbol{\mu}}_n) \xrightarrow{d} N[\mathbf{0}, \mathbf{Q}].$$

At several points in Chapter 3, we used a linear Taylor series approximation to analyze the distribution and moments of a random variable. We are now able to justify this usage. We complete the development of Theorem 4.7 (probability limit of a function of a random variable), Theorem 4.10(2) (limiting distribution of a function of a random variable), and the central limit theorems, with a useful result that is known as "the delta method." For a single random variable (sample mean or otherwise), we have the following theorem.

THEOREM 4.15: Limiting Normal Distribution of a Function. *If* $\sqrt{n}(z_n - \mu) \xrightarrow{d} N[0, \sigma^2]$ *and if* $g(z_n)$ *is a continuous function not involving n, then*

$$\sqrt{n}[g(z_n) - g(\mu)] \xrightarrow{d} N[0, \{g'(\mu)\}^2\sigma^2]. \qquad \textbf{(4-33)}$$

Notice that the mean and variance of the limiting distribution are the mean and variance of the linear approximation:

$$g(z_n) \simeq g(\mu) + g'(\mu)(z_n - \mu).$$

The multivariate version of this theorem will be used at many points in the text.

THEOREM 4.16: Limiting Normal Distribution of a Set of Functions. *If* $\mathbf{z}_n$ *is a* $K \times 1$ *sequence of vector-valued random variables such that* $\sqrt{n}(\mathbf{z}_n - \boldsymbol{\mu}_n) \xrightarrow{d} N[\mathbf{0}, \boldsymbol{\Sigma}]$ *and if* $\mathbf{c}(\mathbf{z}_n)$ *is a set of J continuous functions of* z_n *not involving n, then*

$$\sqrt{n}[\mathbf{c}(\mathbf{z}_n) - \mathbf{c}(\boldsymbol{\mu}_n)] \xrightarrow{d} N[0, \mathbf{C}\boldsymbol{\Sigma}\mathbf{C}'], \qquad \textbf{(4-34)}$$

where $\mathbf{C}$ *is the* $J \times K$ *matrix* $\partial\mathbf{c}(\mathbf{z}_n)/\partial\mathbf{z}_n'$. *The jth row of* $\mathbf{C}$ *is the vector of partial derivatives of the jth function with respect to* $\mathbf{z}_n$.

4.4.3. Asymptotic Distributions

The theory of limiting distributions is only a means to an end. We are interested in the behavior of the estimators themselves. The limiting distributions obtained through the central limit theorem all involve unknown parameters, generally the ones we are trying to estimate. Moreover, our samples are always finite. Thus, we depart from the limiting distributions to derive the asymptotic distributions of the estimators.

DEFINITION 4.11: Asymptotic Distribution. *An asymptotic distribution is a distribution that is used to approximate the true finite sample distribution of a random variable.*

By far the most common means of formulating an asymptotic distribution (at least by econometricians) is to construct it from the known limiting distribution of a function of the random variable. If

$$\sqrt{n}[(\bar{x}_n - \mu)/\sigma] \xrightarrow{d} N[0, 1],$$

then approximately, or asymptotically, $x_n \sim N[\mu, \sigma^2/n]$, which we write as

$$x_n \xrightarrow{a} N[\mu, \sigma^2/n].$$

The statement that $\bar{x}_n$ is asymptotically normally distributed with mean μ and variance σ^2/n says only that this normal distribution provides an approximation to the true distribution, not that the true distribution is exactly normal.

EXAMPLE 4.14 Asymptotic Distribution of the Mean of an Exponential Sample

In sampling from an exponential distribution with parameter θ, the *exact* distribution of $\bar{x}$ is that of $\theta/(2n)$ times a chi-squared variable with $2n$ degrees of freedom. The *asymptotic* distribution is $N[\theta, \theta^2/n]$. The exact and asymptotic distributions are shown in Figure 4.5 for the case of $\theta = 1$ and $n = 16$.

Extending the definition, suppose that $\hat{\boldsymbol{\theta}}$ is an estimate of the parameter vector $\boldsymbol{\theta}$. The asymptotic distribution of the vector $\hat{\boldsymbol{\theta}}$ is obtained from the limiting distribution:

$$\sqrt{n}(\hat{\boldsymbol{\theta}} - \boldsymbol{\theta}) \xrightarrow{d} N[\mathbf{0}, \mathbf{V}] \qquad \textbf{(4-35)}$$

implies that

$$\hat{\boldsymbol{\theta}} \xrightarrow{a} N\left[\boldsymbol{\theta}, \frac{1}{n}\mathbf{V}\right]. \qquad \textbf{(4-36)}$$

This is read "$\hat{\boldsymbol{\theta}}$ is asympototically normally distributed, with mean vector $\boldsymbol{\theta}$ and covariance matrix $(1/n)\mathbf{V}$." The covariance matrix of the asymptotic distribution is the **asymptotic covariance matrix** and is denoted

$$\text{Asy. Var}[\hat{\boldsymbol{\theta}}] = \frac{1}{n}\mathbf{V}.$$

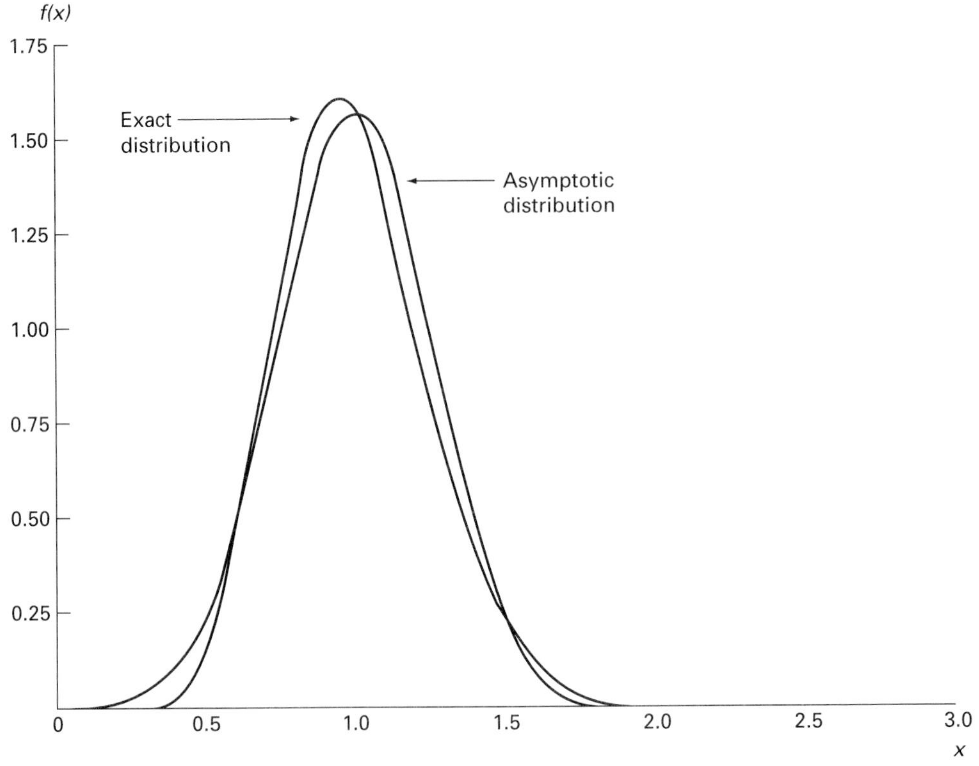

FIGURE 4.5 True Versus Asymptotic Distribution.

Note, once again, the logic used to reach the result; (4-35) holds exactly as $n \to \infty$. We assume that it holds approximately for finite n, which leads to (4-36).

DEFINITION 4.12: Asymptotic Normality and Asymptotic Efficiency. *An estimator $\hat{\boldsymbol{\theta}}$ is asymptotically normal if (4-35) holds. The estimator is asymptotically efficient if the covariance matrix of any other consistent, asymptotically normally distributed estimator exceeds $(1/n)\mathbf{V}$ by a nonnegative definite matrix.*

For most estimation problems, these are the criteria used to choose an estimator.

EXAMPLE 4.15 Asymptotic Inefficiency of the Median in Normal Sampling

In sampling from a normal distribution with mean μ and variance σ^2, both the mean $\bar{x}$ and the median M of the sample are consistent estimators of μ. Since the limiting distributions of both estimators are spikes at μ, they can only be compared on the basis of their asymptotic properties. The necessary results are

$$\bar{x} \xrightarrow{a} N[\mu, \sigma^2/n] \quad \text{and} \quad M \xrightarrow{a} N[\mu, (\pi/2)\sigma^2/n]. \tag{4-37}$$

Therefore, the mean is more efficient by a factor of $\pi/2$. (But, see example 5.4 for a finite sample result.)

4.4.4. Asymptotic Distribution of a Nonlinear Function

Theorems 4.15 and 4.16 for functions of a random variable have counterparts in asymptotic distributions.

THEOREM 4.17: Asymptotic Distribution of a Nonlinear Function. *If* $\sqrt{n}(\hat{\theta} - \theta) \xrightarrow{d} N[0, \sigma^2]$ *and if* $g(\theta)$ *is a continuous function not involving* n, *then* $g(\hat{\theta}) \xrightarrow{a} N[g(\theta), \{g'(\theta)\}^2\sigma^2]$. *If* $\hat{\boldsymbol{\theta}}$ *is a vector of parameter estimates such that* $\hat{\boldsymbol{\theta}} \xrightarrow{a} N[\boldsymbol{\theta}, (1/n)\mathbf{V}]$, *and if* $\mathbf{c}(\boldsymbol{\theta})$ *is a set of* J *continuous functions not involving* n, *then* $\mathbf{c}(\hat{\boldsymbol{\theta}}) \xrightarrow{a} N[\mathbf{c}(\boldsymbol{\theta}), (1/n)\mathbf{C}(\boldsymbol{\theta})\mathbf{V}\mathbf{C}(\boldsymbol{\theta})']$, *where* $\mathbf{C}(\boldsymbol{\theta}) = \partial\mathbf{c}(\boldsymbol{\theta})/\partial\boldsymbol{\theta}'$.

EXAMPLE 4.16 Asymptotic Distribution for a Function of Two Estimates

Suppose that b and t are estimates of parameters β and θ such that

$$\begin{bmatrix} b \\ t \end{bmatrix} \xrightarrow{a} N\left[\begin{pmatrix} \beta \\ \theta \end{pmatrix}, \begin{pmatrix} \sigma_{\beta\beta} & \sigma_{\beta\theta} \\ \sigma_{\theta\beta} & \sigma_{\theta\theta} \end{pmatrix}\right].$$

Find the asymptotic distribution of $c = b/(1 - t)$. Let $\gamma = \beta/(1 - \theta)$. By the Slutsky theorem, c is consistent for γ. We shall require

$$\frac{\partial\gamma}{\partial\beta} = \frac{1}{1 - \theta} = \gamma_\beta,$$

$$\frac{\partial\gamma}{\partial\theta} = \frac{\beta}{(1 - \theta)^2} = \gamma_\theta.$$

Let $\boldsymbol{\Sigma}$ be the 2×2 asymptotic covariance matrix given previously. Then the asymptotic variance of c is

$$\text{Asy. Var}[c] = (\gamma_\beta \quad \gamma_\theta)'\boldsymbol{\Sigma}\begin{pmatrix} \gamma_\beta \\ \gamma_\theta \end{pmatrix} = \gamma_\beta^2\sigma_{\beta\beta} + \gamma_\theta^2\sigma_{\theta\theta} + 2\gamma_\beta\gamma_\theta\sigma_{\beta\theta}.$$

This is the variance of the linear approximation:

$$\hat{\gamma} \simeq \gamma + \gamma_\beta(b - \beta) + \gamma_\theta(t - \theta).$$

4.4.5. Asymptotic Expectations

The asymptotic mean and variance of a random variable are usually the mean and variance of the asymptotic distribution. Thus, for an estimator with the limiting distribution defined in

$$\sqrt{n}(\hat{\boldsymbol{\theta}} - \boldsymbol{\theta}) \xrightarrow{d} N[\mathbf{0}, \mathbf{V}],$$

the asymptotic expectation is $\boldsymbol{\theta}$ and the asymptotic variance is $(1/n)\mathbf{V}$. This implies, among other things, that the estimator is "asymptotically unbiased."

At the risk of clouding the issue a bit, it is necessary to reconsider one aspect of the previous description. We have deliberately avoided the use of consistency even though, in most instances, that is what we have in mind. The description thus far might suggest that consistency and asymptotic unbiasedness are the same. Unfortunately (because it is a source of some confusion), they are not. They are if the estimator is consistent and asymptotically normally distributed, or CAN. They may differ in other settings, however. There are at least three possible definitions of asymptotic unbiasedness:

1. The mean of the limiting distribution of $\sqrt{n}(\hat{\theta} - \theta)$ is 0.
2. $\lim_{n\to\infty} E[\hat{\theta}] = \theta$. **(4-38)**
3. $\text{plim}\ \hat{\theta} = \theta$.

In most cases encountered in practice, the estimator in hand will have all three properties, so there is no ambiguity. It is not difficult to construct cases in which the left-hand sides of all three definitions are different, however.[8] There is no general agreement among authors as to the precise meaning of asymptotic unbiasedness, perhaps because the term is misleading at the outset; *asymptotic* refers to an approximation, whereas *unbiasedness* is an exact result.[9] Nonetheless, the majority view seems to be that (2) is the proper definition of asymptotic unbiasedness.[10] Note, though, that this definition relies on quantities that are generally unknown and that may not exist.

A similar problem arises in the definition of the asymptotic variance of an estimator. One common definition is

$$\text{Asy. Var}[\hat{\theta}] = \frac{1}{n}\lim_{n\to\infty} E[\{\sqrt{n}(\hat{\theta} - \lim_{n\to\infty} E[\hat{\theta}])\}^2].^{11} \quad \textbf{(4-39)}$$

This is a **leading term approximation,** and it will be sufficient for nearly all applications. Note, however, that like definition 2 of asymptotic unbiasedness, it relies on unknown and possibly nonexistent quantities.

EXAMPLE 4.17 Asymptotic Moments of the Sample Variance

The exact expected value and variance of the variance estimator

$$m_2 = \frac{1}{n}\sum_{i=1}^{n}(x_i - \bar{x})^2 \quad \textbf{(4-40)}$$

are

$$E[m_2] = \frac{(n-1)\sigma^2}{n} \quad \textbf{(4-41)}$$

---

[8]See, for example, Maddala (1977a, p. 150).

[9]See, for example, Theil (1971, p. 377).

[10]Many studies of estimators analyze the "asymptotic bias" of, say, $\hat{\theta}$ as an estimator of a parameter θ. In most cases, the quantity of interest is actually plim $[\hat{\theta} - \theta]$. See, for example, Greene (1980b) and another example in Johnston (1984, p. 312).

[11]Kmenta (1986, p. 165).

and

$$\text{Var}[m_2] = \frac{\mu_4 - \sigma^4}{n} - \frac{2(\mu_4 - 2\sigma^4)}{n^2} + \frac{\mu_4 - 3\sigma^4}{n^3}, \qquad \textbf{(4-42)}$$

where $\mu_4 = E[(x - \mu)^4]$. [See Goldberger (1964, pp. 97–99).]

The leading term approximation would be

$$\text{Asy. Var}[m_2] = \frac{1}{n}(\mu_4 - \sigma^4).$$

The formal definition given in (4-39) is adequate if the exact variance is "of order $1/n$."

DEFINITION 4.13: Order 1/*n*. *c_n is of order $1/n$, denoted $O(1/n)$, if* plim nc_n *is a nonzero constant.*

DEFINITION 4.14: Order Less Than 1/*n*. *c_n is of order less than $1/n$, denoted $o(1/n)$, if* plim nc_n *equals* 0.

For example, the variance of the sample minimum in Example 4.3 is $o(1/n)$ because n times this variance still converges to zero. In sampling from an exponential distribution, the variance of the sample minimum is $O(1/n^2)$. If we use the definition just given, the asymptotic variance is 0, which would be a poor approximation to the variance in a finite sample.

The point of this discussion is to emphasize the need for care and precision in formulating asymptotic distributions. The central limit theorem and the surrounding results allow the simple formulation of the correct asymptotic distribution in the vast majority of cases encountered in econometrics. There are relatively common situations, particularly in theoretical econometrics, however, in which some caution is warranted.

4.5. EFFICIENT ESTIMATION — MAXIMUM LIKELIHOOD

The principle of **maximum likelihood** provides a means of choosing an asymptotically efficient estimator for a parameter or a set of parameters. The logic of the technique is best illustrated in the setting of a discrete distribution. Consider a random sample of 10 observations from a Poisson distribution: 5, 0, 1, 1, 0, 3, 2, 3, 4, and 1. The density for each observation is

$$f(x_i, \theta) = \frac{e^{-\theta}\theta^{x_i}}{x_i!}.$$

Since the observations are independent, their joint density, which was identified in Section 4.3.2 as the **likelihood** for the sample, is

$$\begin{aligned} f(x_1, x_2, \ldots, x_{10} \mid \theta) &= \prod_{i=1}^{10} f(x_i, \theta) \\ &= \frac{e^{-10\theta}\, \theta^{\Sigma_{i=1}^{10} x_i}}{\prod_{i=1}^{10} x_i!} \\ &= \frac{e^{-10\theta}\, \theta^{20}}{207,360}. \end{aligned}$$

The last line gives the probability of observing *this particular sample,* assuming that a Poisson distribution with as yet unknown parameter θ generated the data. What value of θ would make this sample most probable? Figure 4.6 plots this function for various values of θ. It has a single mode at $\theta = 2$, which would be the maximum likelihood estimate, or MLE, of θ.

Consider maximizing the function directly. Since the log function is monotonically increasing and easier to work with, we usually maximize $\ln L(\theta)$ instead:

$$\begin{aligned} \ln L(\theta) &= -10\theta + 20 \ln \theta - 12.242, \\ \frac{d \ln L(\theta)}{d\theta} &= -10 + \frac{20}{\theta} = 0 \Rightarrow \hat{\theta} = 2, \end{aligned}$$

and

$$\frac{d^2 \ln L(\theta)}{d\theta^2} = \frac{-20}{\theta^2} < 0 \Rightarrow \text{this is a maximum.}$$

The solution is the same as before. Figure 4.6 also plots the log of L to illustrate the result.

In a continuous distribution, the analogy to the probability of observing the given sample is not exact, since a particular sample has probability zero. The principle is the same for either, however. The joint density of the n observations, which may be univariate (x_i) or multivariate ($\mathbf{x}_i$), is the product of the individual densities. This joint density is the **likelihood function,** defined as a function of the unknown parameter vector, $\boldsymbol{\theta}$:

$$\begin{aligned} f(\mathbf{x}_1, \ldots, \mathbf{x}_n, \boldsymbol{\theta}) &= \prod_{i=1}^{n} f(\mathbf{x}_i, \boldsymbol{\theta}) \\ &= L(\boldsymbol{\theta} \mid \mathbf{X}), \end{aligned} \quad \textbf{(4-43)}$$

where $\mathbf{X}$ is used to indicate the sample data. It is usually simpler to work with the log of the likelihood function:

$$\ln L(\boldsymbol{\theta} \mid \mathbf{X}) = \sum_{i=1}^{n} \ln f(\mathbf{x}_i, \boldsymbol{\theta}). \quad \textbf{(4-44)}$$

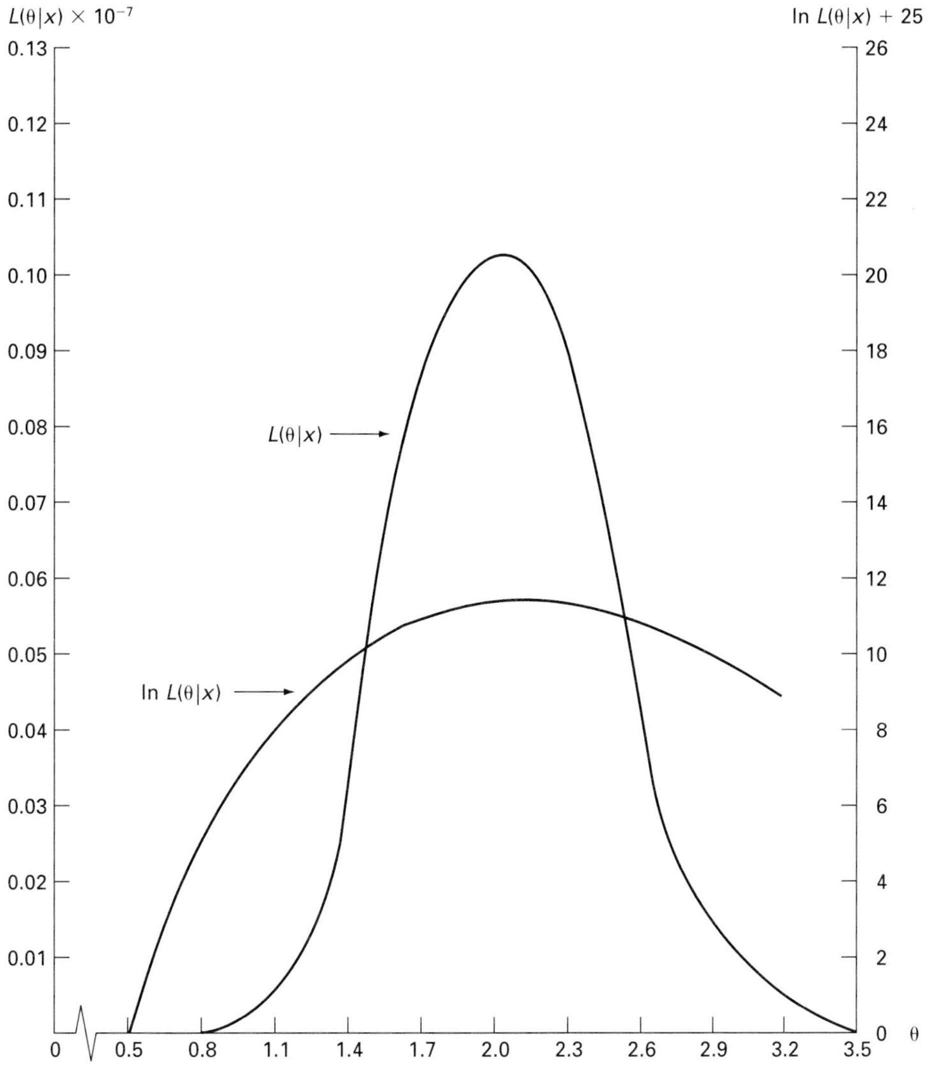

FIGURE 4.6 Likelihood and Log-likelihood Functions for a Poisson Distribution.

The values of the parameters that maximize this function are the maximum likelihood estimates, generally denoted $\hat{\boldsymbol{\theta}}$. Since the logarithm is a monotonic function, the values that maximize L are the same as those that maximize $\ln L$. The likelihood function and its logarithm, evaluated at $\boldsymbol{\theta}$, are usually denoted L and $\ln L$, respectively. The necessary condition for maximizing $\ln L(\boldsymbol{\theta})$ is

$$\frac{\partial \ln L(\boldsymbol{\theta})}{\partial \boldsymbol{\theta}} = \mathbf{0}. \tag{4-45}$$

This is called the **likelihood equation.**

EXAMPLE 4.18 Poisson Likelihood Function

In sampling from a Poisson population,

$$\ln L(\theta) = -n\theta + (\ln \theta) \sum_{i=1}^{n} x_i - \sum_{i=1}^{n} \ln(x_i!),$$

$$\frac{\partial \ln L(\theta)}{\partial \theta} = -n + \frac{1}{\theta} \sum_{i=1}^{n} x_i = 0 \Rightarrow \hat{\theta} = \bar{x}.$$

EXAMPLE 4.19 Likelihood for the Normal Distribution

In sampling from a normal distribution with mean μ and variance σ^2, the log-likelihood function and the likelihood equations for μ and σ^2 are

$$\ln L(\mu, \sigma^2) = -\frac{n}{2}\ln(2\pi) - \frac{n}{2}\ln \sigma^2 - \frac{1}{2}\sum_{i=1}^{n}\left[\frac{(x_i - \mu)^2}{\sigma^2}\right], \quad \textbf{(4-46)}$$

$$\frac{\partial \ln L}{\partial \mu} = \frac{1}{\sigma^2}\sum_{i=1}^{n}(x_i - \mu) = 0, \quad \textbf{(4-47)}$$

$$\frac{\partial \ln L}{\partial \sigma^2} = -\frac{n}{2\sigma^2} + \frac{1}{2\sigma^4}\sum_{i=1}^{n}(x_i - \mu)^2 = 0. \quad \textbf{(4-48)}$$

To solve the likelihood equations, multiply (4-47) by σ^2 and solve for $\hat{\mu}$; then insert this solution in (4-48) and solve for σ^2. The solutions are

$$\hat{\mu} = \frac{1}{n}\sum_{i=1}^{n} x_i = \bar{x}$$

and **(4-49)**

$$\hat{\sigma}^2 = \frac{1}{n}\sum_{i=1}^{n}(x_i - \bar{x})^2.$$

Note that this is the biased estimator discussed in Example 4.4. MLEs are consistent but not necessarily unbiased.

EXAMPLE 4.20 Multivariate Normal Mean Vector

Consider, finally, sampling from a multivariate normal distribution with mean vector, $\boldsymbol{\mu} = (\mu_1, \mu_2, \ldots, \mu_M)$ and covariance matrix $\sigma^2\mathbf{I}$. (The M random variables each have a different mean but a common variance, σ^2, and they are uncorrelated.) The sample consists of n multivariate observations, $\mathbf{x}_1, \ldots, \mathbf{x}_n$. The density for each observation, from (3-95), is

$$\begin{aligned} f(\mathbf{x}_i) &= (2\pi)^{-M/2}|\sigma^2\mathbf{I}|^{-1/2}e^{-1/2(\mathbf{x}_i-\boldsymbol{\mu})'[\sigma^2\mathbf{I}]^{-1}(\mathbf{x}_i-\boldsymbol{\mu})} \\ &= (2\pi)^{-M/2}(\sigma^2)^{-M/2}e^{-[1/(2\sigma^2)](\mathbf{x}_i-\boldsymbol{\mu})'(\mathbf{x}_i-\boldsymbol{\mu})}. \end{aligned}$$

Taking logs and summing over the sample gives the log-likelihood for n observations:

$$\ln L = \frac{-nM}{2}\ln(2\pi) - \frac{nM}{2}\ln\sigma^2 - \frac{1}{2\sigma^2}\sum_{i=1}^{n}(\mathbf{x}_i - \boldsymbol{\mu})'(\mathbf{x}_i - \boldsymbol{\mu}).$$

To obtain the maximum likelihood estimators, we require

$$\frac{\partial \ln L}{\partial \boldsymbol{\mu}} = \frac{1}{\sigma^2}\sum_{i=1}^{n}(\mathbf{x}_i - \boldsymbol{\mu}),$$
$$\frac{\partial \ln L}{\partial \sigma^2} = \frac{-nM}{2\sigma^2} + \frac{1}{2\sigma^4}\sum_{i=1}^{n}(\mathbf{x}_i - \boldsymbol{\mu})'(\mathbf{x}_i - \boldsymbol{\mu}).$$

Solving the first set of equations gives, as might be expected,

$$\hat{\mu}_m = \bar{x}_m = \frac{1}{n}\sum_{i=1}^{n} x_{im}.$$

Inserting this solution in the second condition gives

$$\hat{\sigma}^2 = \frac{\sum_{i=1}^{n}\sum_{m=1}^{M}(x_{im} - \bar{x}_m)^2}{nM} = \frac{1}{M}\sum_{m=1}^{M}\frac{1}{n}\sum_{i=1}^{n}(x_{im} - \bar{x}_m)^2 = \frac{1}{M}\sum_{m=1}^{M}\hat{\sigma}_m^2.$$

4.5.1. Properties of Maximum Likelihood Estimators

Maximum likelihood estimators (MLEs) are most attractive because of their large-sample or asymptotic properties. If we assume that the regularity conditions discussed below are met by $f(\mathbf{x}, \boldsymbol{\theta})$, we have the following theorem.

THEOREM 4.18: Properties of an MLE. *Under regularity, the maximum likelihood estimator (MLE) has the following asymptotic properties:*

M1. **Consistency:** $\operatorname{plim} \hat{\boldsymbol{\theta}}_{\mathrm{ML}} = \boldsymbol{\theta}$.

M2. **Asymptotic normality:** $\hat{\boldsymbol{\theta}} \xrightarrow{a} N[\boldsymbol{\theta}, \{\mathbf{I}(\boldsymbol{\theta})\}^{-1}]$, where $\mathbf{I}(\boldsymbol{\theta}) = -E[\partial^2 \ln L/\partial\boldsymbol{\theta}\,\partial\boldsymbol{\theta}']$.

M3. **Asymptotic efficiency:** $\hat{\boldsymbol{\theta}}$ is asymptotically efficient and achieves the Cramér–Rao lower bound for consistent estimators, given in M2, Theorem 4.2, (4-12), and (4-13).

M4. **Invariance:** The maximum likelihood estimator of $\boldsymbol{\gamma} = \mathbf{c}(\boldsymbol{\theta})$ is $\mathbf{c}(\hat{\boldsymbol{\theta}})$.

The MLE is usually preferred on the basis of its large sample properties. Indeed, the finite sample properties are sometimes less than optimal. For example, the MLE may be biased; the MLE of σ^2 in sampling from a normal distribution is biased downward. [See (4-49) and Example 4.4.] The occasional statement that the properties of the MLE are *only* optimal in large samples is not true, however. It can be shown that when sampling is from an exponential family of distributions (see Section 4.6), there will exist sufficient statistics. If so, MLEs will be functions of them, which means that when minimum variance unbiased estimators exist, they will be MLEs. [See Stuart and Ord (1989).] Most applications in econometrics do not involve exponential families, so the appeal of the MLE remains primarily its asymptotic properties.

To sketch proofs of these results, we first obtain some useful properties of probability density functions. We assume that $(\mathbf{x}_1, \ldots, \mathbf{x}_n)$ is a random sample from the multivariate or univariate population with density function $f(\mathbf{x}_i \mid \boldsymbol{\theta})$ and that the following **regularity conditions** hold. [Our statement of these is informal. More rigorous treatments may be found in Greenberg and Webster (1983), Theil (1971), and Rao (1973), for example.]

R1. The first three derivatives of $\ln f(\mathbf{x}_i, \boldsymbol{\theta})$ with respect to $\boldsymbol{\theta}$ are finite for almost all $\mathbf{x}$ and for all $\boldsymbol{\theta}$. This ensures the existence of a certain Taylor series approximation and the finite variance of the derivatives of $\ln L$.

R2. The conditions necessary to obtain the expectations of the first and second derivatives of $\ln f(\mathbf{x}_i, \boldsymbol{\theta})$ are met.

R3. For all values of $\boldsymbol{\theta}$, $|\partial^3 \ln f(\mathbf{x}_i, \boldsymbol{\theta})/\partial\theta_j\, \partial\theta_k\, \partial\theta_l|$ is less than a function that has a finite expectation. This will allow us to truncate the Taylor series.

With these conditions, we will obtain the following fundamental characteristics of $f(\mathbf{x}_i, \boldsymbol{\theta})$.

D1. $\ln f(\mathbf{x}_i, \boldsymbol{\theta})$, $\mathbf{g}_i = \partial \ln f(\mathbf{x}_i, \boldsymbol{\theta})/\partial\boldsymbol{\theta}$, and $\mathbf{H}_i = \partial^2 \ln f(\mathbf{x}_i, \boldsymbol{\theta})/\partial\boldsymbol{\theta}\, \partial\boldsymbol{\theta}'$, $i = 1, \ldots, n$, are all random samples of random variables. This follows from our assumption of random sampling.

D2. $E[\mathbf{g}_i] = \mathbf{0}$.

D3. $\text{Var}[\mathbf{g}_i] = -E[\mathbf{H}_i]$.

Proof of D2: For the moment, we allow the range of $\mathbf{x}_i$ to depend on the parameters; for each element, x_{ik}, $L(\boldsymbol{\theta}) \le x_{ik} \le U(\boldsymbol{\theta})$. (Consider, for example, finding the maximum likelihood estimate of θ for a continuous uniform distribution with range $[0, \theta]$.) In the following, the single integral $\int \ldots d\mathbf{x}$, is used to indicate the multiple integration over all the elements of $\mathbf{x}_i$. By definition,

$$\int_{L(\boldsymbol{\theta})}^{U(\boldsymbol{\theta})} f(\mathbf{x} \mid \boldsymbol{\theta})\, d\mathbf{x} = 1.$$

Now, differentiate this expression with respect to $\boldsymbol{\theta}$. Leibnitz's theorem gives

$$\frac{\partial \int_{L(\boldsymbol{\theta})}^{U(\boldsymbol{\theta})} f(\mathbf{x} \mid \boldsymbol{\theta})\, d\mathbf{x}}{\partial \boldsymbol{\theta}} = \int_{L(\boldsymbol{\theta})}^{U(\boldsymbol{\theta})} \frac{\partial f(\mathbf{x} \mid \boldsymbol{\theta})}{\partial \boldsymbol{\theta}}\, d\mathbf{x} + f(U(\boldsymbol{\theta}) \mid \boldsymbol{\theta}) \frac{\partial U(\boldsymbol{\theta})}{\partial \boldsymbol{\theta}} - f(L(\boldsymbol{\theta}) \mid \boldsymbol{\theta}) \frac{\partial L(\boldsymbol{\theta})}{\partial \boldsymbol{\theta}} = \mathbf{0}.$$

If the second and third terms go to zero, then we may interchange the operations of differentiation and integration. The necessary condition is that at the limits, the density vanish. (Note that the example given above violates this condition.) A sufficient condition is that the range of the observed random variable, $\mathbf{x}_i$, does not depend on the parameters, which means that $\partial L(\boldsymbol{\theta})/\partial\boldsymbol{\theta} = \partial U(\boldsymbol{\theta})/\partial\boldsymbol{\theta} = \mathbf{0}$.[12] This, then, is regularity condition R2. The latter is usually assumed, and we will assume it in what follows. So,

$$\begin{aligned}\frac{\partial \int f(\mathbf{x}, \boldsymbol{\theta})\, d\mathbf{x}}{\partial \boldsymbol{\theta}} &= \int \frac{\partial f(\mathbf{x}, \boldsymbol{\theta})}{\partial \boldsymbol{\theta}}\, d\mathbf{x} \\ &= \int \frac{\partial \ln f(\mathbf{x}, \boldsymbol{\theta})}{\partial \boldsymbol{\theta}} f(\mathbf{x}, \boldsymbol{\theta})\, d\mathbf{x} \\ &= E\left[\frac{\partial \ln f(\mathbf{x}, \boldsymbol{\theta})}{\partial \boldsymbol{\theta}}\right] \\ &= \mathbf{0}.\end{aligned}$$

This proves D2.

Since we may interchange the operations of integration and differentiation, we differentiate under the integral once again to obtain

$$\int \left[\frac{\partial^2 \ln f(\mathbf{x}, \boldsymbol{\theta})}{\partial \boldsymbol{\theta}\, \partial \boldsymbol{\theta}'} f(\mathbf{x}, \boldsymbol{\theta}) + \frac{\partial \ln f(\mathbf{x}, \boldsymbol{\theta})}{\partial \boldsymbol{\theta}} \frac{\partial f(\mathbf{x}, \boldsymbol{\theta})}{\partial \boldsymbol{\theta}'}\right] d\mathbf{x} = \mathbf{0}.$$

But

$$\frac{\partial f(\mathbf{x} \mid \boldsymbol{\theta})}{\partial \boldsymbol{\theta}'} = f(\mathbf{x} \mid \boldsymbol{\theta}) \frac{\partial \ln f(\mathbf{x} \mid \boldsymbol{\theta})}{\partial \boldsymbol{\theta}'},$$

and the integral of a sum is the sum of integrals. Therefore,

$$-\int \left[\frac{\partial^2 \ln f(\mathbf{x} \mid \boldsymbol{\theta})}{\partial \boldsymbol{\theta}\, \partial \boldsymbol{\theta}'}\right] f(\mathbf{x} \mid \boldsymbol{\theta})\, d\mathbf{x} = \int \left[\frac{\partial \ln f(\mathbf{x} \mid \boldsymbol{\theta})}{\partial \boldsymbol{\theta}} \frac{\partial \ln f(\mathbf{x} \mid \boldsymbol{\theta})}{\partial \boldsymbol{\theta}'}\right] f(\mathbf{x} \mid \boldsymbol{\theta})\, d\mathbf{x} = [\mathbf{0}].$$

The left-hand side of the equation is the negative of the expected second derivatives matrix. The right-hand side is the expected square (outer product) of the first derivative vector. But, since this vector has expected value $\mathbf{0}$ (we just showed this), the right-hand side is the variance of the first derivative vector. This gives us D3:

$$\text{Var}\left[\frac{\partial \ln f(\mathbf{x} \mid \boldsymbol{\theta})}{\partial \boldsymbol{\theta}}\right] = E\left[\left(\frac{\partial \ln f(\mathbf{x} \mid \boldsymbol{\theta})}{\partial \boldsymbol{\theta}}\right)\left(\frac{\partial \ln f(\mathbf{x} \mid \boldsymbol{\theta})}{\partial \boldsymbol{\theta}'}\right)\right] = -E\left[\frac{\partial^2 \ln f(\mathbf{x} \mid \boldsymbol{\theta})}{\partial \boldsymbol{\theta}\, \partial \boldsymbol{\theta}'}\right].$$

---

[12] Alternatively, if the density equals zero at the terminal points, the condition will be met as well. For example, if the left-hand limit in the density in Figure 3.1 were not zero but some $L(\theta)$, that density would meet the condition. The general condition is $\lim_{x_k \to L(\boldsymbol{\theta})} f(\mathbf{x}, \boldsymbol{\theta}) = \lim_{x_k \to U(\boldsymbol{\theta})} f(\mathbf{x}, \boldsymbol{\theta}) = 0$, which includes all cases including $L(\boldsymbol{\theta}) = -\infty$ and/or $U(\boldsymbol{\theta}) = +\infty$.

We can now sketch a derivation of the asymptotic properties of the MLE. The log-likelihood is

$$\ln L = \sum_{i=1}^{n} \ln f(\mathbf{x}_i, \boldsymbol{\theta}).$$

Therefore,

$$\partial \ln L/\partial\boldsymbol{\theta} = \mathbf{g} = \sum_{i=1}^{n} \mathbf{g}_i$$

and

$$\partial^2 \ln L/\partial\boldsymbol{\theta}\,\partial\boldsymbol{\theta}' = \mathbf{H} = \sum_{i=1}^{n} \mathbf{H}_i.$$

It follows from D1 and D2 that

$$E[\partial \ln L/\partial\boldsymbol{\theta}] = E[\mathbf{g}] = \mathbf{0}.$$

By taking $E[\mathbf{g}\mathbf{g}'] = E[\Sigma_{i=1}^{n}\Sigma_{j=1}^{n}\,\mathbf{g}_i\mathbf{g}_j']$ and, because of D1, dropping terms with unequal subscripts to obtain $E[\mathbf{g}\mathbf{g}'] = E[\Sigma_{i=1}^{n}\,\mathbf{g}_i\mathbf{g}_i'] = E[\Sigma_{i=1}^{n}\,(-\mathbf{H}_i)] = -E[\mathbf{H}]$, we find that

$$\text{Var}[\partial \ln L/\partial\boldsymbol{\theta}] = \text{Var}[\mathbf{g}] = -\,E[\partial^2 \ln L/\partial\boldsymbol{\theta}\,\partial\boldsymbol{\theta}'] = -\,E[\mathbf{H}].$$

A proof of the consistency of the MLE requires some fairly intricate mathematics. A widely cited derivation is that of Cramér (1948). [See, as well, Rao (1973).] We will take it as given and use his result that under regularity,

$$\text{plim}\ \hat{\boldsymbol{\theta}} = \boldsymbol{\theta}.$$

At the maximum likelihood estimator, the gradient of the log-likelihood equals zero (by definition), so

$$\mathbf{g}(\hat{\boldsymbol{\theta}}) = \mathbf{0}.$$

Expand this set of equations in a second-order Taylor series around the true parameters $\boldsymbol{\theta}$:

$$\mathbf{g}(\hat{\boldsymbol{\theta}}) = \mathbf{g}(\boldsymbol{\theta}) + \mathbf{H}(\boldsymbol{\theta})(\hat{\boldsymbol{\theta}} - \boldsymbol{\theta}) + \tfrac{1}{2}\{\mathbf{T}(\boldsymbol{\theta}^*, \hat{\boldsymbol{\theta}}, \boldsymbol{\theta})\} = \mathbf{0}.$$

The third term is a vector-valued function that involves the third derivatives of $\ln L$ evaluated at a point $\boldsymbol{\theta}^*$ that is between $\hat{\boldsymbol{\theta}}$ and $\boldsymbol{\theta}$ and product terms in $(\hat{\theta}_j - \theta_j)(\hat{\theta}_l - \theta_l)$. (This is the Lagrange form of the remainder term.) We will return to this shortly. We then rearrange this function and multiply the result by $\sqrt{n}$ to obtain

$$\sqrt{n}(\hat{\boldsymbol{\theta}} - \boldsymbol{\theta}) = -\,[\mathbf{H}(\boldsymbol{\theta})]^{-1}[\sqrt{n}\mathbf{g}(\boldsymbol{\theta})] - \tfrac{1}{2}\sqrt{n}[\mathbf{H}(\boldsymbol{\theta})]^{-1}\{\mathbf{T}(\boldsymbol{\theta}^*, \hat{\boldsymbol{\theta}}, \boldsymbol{\theta})\}.$$

Regularity condition R3 ensures that the third derivatives will converge to finite constants. Because $\text{plim}(\hat{\boldsymbol{\theta}} - \boldsymbol{\theta}) = \mathbf{0}$, the product terms in this part of the expansion will converge to zero. Therefore, the large sample behavior of the right-hand side will not involve $\{\mathbf{T}(\boldsymbol{\theta}^*, \hat{\boldsymbol{\theta}}, \boldsymbol{\theta})\}$. If the limiting distribution exists, then

$$\sqrt{n}(\hat{\boldsymbol{\theta}} - \boldsymbol{\theta}) \xrightarrow{d} [\mathbf{H}(\boldsymbol{\theta})]^{-1}[\sqrt{n}\mathbf{g}(\boldsymbol{\theta})].$$

By dividing $\mathbf{H}(\boldsymbol{\theta})$ and $\mathbf{g}(\boldsymbol{\theta})$ by n, we obtain

$$\sqrt{n}(\hat{\boldsymbol{\theta}} - \boldsymbol{\theta}) \xrightarrow{d} [(1/n)\mathbf{H}(\boldsymbol{\theta})]^{-1}[\sqrt{n}\bar{\mathbf{g}}].$$

We may apply the Lindberg–Levy central limit theorem (4.13) to $[\sqrt{n}\bar{\mathbf{g}}]$, since it is $\sqrt{n}$ times the mean of a random sample; we have invoked D1 again. The limiting variance of $[\sqrt{n}\bar{\mathbf{g}}]$ is $-E[\mathbf{H}(\boldsymbol{\theta})]$, so

$$\sqrt{n}\bar{\mathbf{g}}(\boldsymbol{\theta}) \xrightarrow{d} N\{\mathbf{0}, -E[\mathbf{H}(\boldsymbol{\theta})]\}.$$

By virtue of Theorem 4.2, $\text{plim}[(1/n)\mathbf{H}(\boldsymbol{\theta})] = E[\mathbf{H}(\boldsymbol{\theta})]$. Since this is a constant matrix, we can combine results to obtain

$$[(1/n)\mathbf{H}(\boldsymbol{\theta})]^{-1}\sqrt{n}\bar{\mathbf{g}}(\boldsymbol{\theta}) \xrightarrow{d} N[\mathbf{0}, \{E[\mathbf{H}(\boldsymbol{\theta})]\}^{-1}\{-E[\mathbf{H}(\boldsymbol{\theta})]\}\{E[\mathbf{H}(\boldsymbol{\theta})]\}^{-1}],$$

or

$$\sqrt{n}(\hat{\boldsymbol{\theta}} - \boldsymbol{\theta}) \xrightarrow{d} N[\mathbf{0}, -\{E[\mathbf{H}(\boldsymbol{\theta})]\}^{-1}].$$

This gives the asymptotic distribution of the MLE:

$$\hat{\boldsymbol{\theta}} \xrightarrow{a} N[\boldsymbol{\theta}, \{\mathbf{I}(\boldsymbol{\theta})\}^{-1}].$$

This completes M1 through M3.

Last, the invariance property, M4, is a mathematical result of the method of computing MLEs; it is not a statistical result as such. More formally, the MLE is invariant to *one-to-one* transformations of $\boldsymbol{\theta}$. Any transformation that is not one to one either renders the model inestimable if it is one to many or imposes restrictions if it is many to one. Some theoretical aspects of this feature are discussed in Davidson and MacKinnon (1993, pp. 253–255). For the practitioner, the result can be extremely useful. For example, when a parameter appears in a likelihood function in the form $1/\theta_j$, it is usually worthwhile to reparameterize the model in terms of $\gamma_j = 1/\theta_j$. In an important application, Olsen (1978) used this result to great advantage. (See Example 20.6.) For example, suppose that the normal log-likelihood in Example 4.19 is parameterized in terms of the **precision parameter,** $\theta^2 = 1/\sigma^2$. The log-likelihood becomes

$$\ln L(\mu, \theta^2) = -(n/2)\ln(2\pi) + (n/2)\ln\theta^2 - \frac{1}{2}\sum_{i=1}^{n}\theta^2(x_i - \mu)^2.$$

The MLE for μ is clearly still $\bar{x}$. But the likelihood equation for θ^2 is now

$$\partial \ln L(\mu, \theta^2)/\partial\theta^2 = \frac{1}{2}\left[n/\theta^2 - \sum_{i=1}^{n}\theta^2(x_i - \mu)^2\right] = 0,$$

which has solution $\hat{\theta}^2 = n/\sum_{i=1}^{n}(x_i - \hat{\mu})^2 = 1/\hat{\sigma}^2$, as expected. There is a second implication. If it is desired to analyze a function of an MLE, the function of $\hat{\boldsymbol{\theta}}$ will, itself, be the MLE.

These four properties explain the prevalence of the maximum likelihood technique in econometrics. The second one greatly facilitates hypothesis testing and the construction of interval estimates. The third one is a particularly powerful result. The MLE has the minimum variance achievable by a consistent estimator.

EXAMPLE 4.21 Information Matrix for a Multivariate Normal Distribution

For the likelihood function in Example 4.20, the second derivatives are

$$\frac{\partial^2 \ln L}{\partial \boldsymbol{\mu}\, \partial \boldsymbol{\mu}'} = \frac{-n}{\sigma^2}\mathbf{I},$$

$$\frac{\partial^2 \ln L}{\partial (\sigma^2)^2} = \frac{nM}{2\sigma^4} - \frac{1}{\sigma^6}\sum_{i=1}^{n}(\mathbf{x}_i - \boldsymbol{\mu})'(\mathbf{x}_i - \boldsymbol{\mu}),$$

$$\frac{\partial^2 \ln L}{\partial \boldsymbol{\mu}\, \partial \sigma^2} = \frac{-1}{\sigma^4}\sum_{i=1}^{n}(\mathbf{x}_i - \boldsymbol{\mu}).$$

For the asymptotic variance of the maximum likelihood estimator, we need the expectations of these derivatives. The first is nonstochastic, and the third has expectation $\mathbf{0}$, as $E[\mathbf{x}_i] = \boldsymbol{\mu}$. That leaves the second, which you can verify has expectation $-nM/(2\sigma^4)$ because each of the n terms $(\mathbf{x}_i - \boldsymbol{\mu})'(\mathbf{x}_i - \boldsymbol{\mu})$ has expected value $M\sigma^2$. Collecting these in the information matrix, reversing the sign, and inverting the matrix gives the asymptotic covariance matrix for the maximum likelihood estimators:

$$\left\{-E\left[\frac{\partial^2 \ln L}{\partial \boldsymbol{\theta}\, \partial \boldsymbol{\theta}'}\right]\right\}^{-1} = \begin{bmatrix} \sigma^2\mathbf{I}/n & \mathbf{0} \\ \mathbf{0} & 2\sigma^4/(nM) \end{bmatrix}.$$

The asymptotic covariance matrix for estimating a single mean and the variance of a normal distribution is given in (4-14) in Example 4.9. Notice that the preceding expression is analogous for the means but differs in the divisor for the variance. In this case, instead of one estimator of σ^2, we have M, which explains the difference.

4.5.2. Estimating the Asymptotic Variance of the Maximum Likelihood Estimator

The asymptotic covariance matrix of the maximum likelihood estimator is a matrix of parameters that must be estimated. (That is, it is a function of the $\boldsymbol{\theta}$ that is being estimated.) If the form of the expected values of the second derivatives of the log likelihood is known,

$$[\mathbf{I}(\boldsymbol{\theta})]^{-1} = \left\{-E\left[\frac{\partial^2 \ln L(\boldsymbol{\theta})}{\partial \boldsymbol{\theta}\, \partial \boldsymbol{\theta}'}\right]\right\}^{-1} \qquad \textbf{(4-50)}$$

can be evaluated at $\hat{\boldsymbol{\theta}}$ to estimate the covariance matrix for the MLE. This estimator will rarely be available. The second derivatives of the log-likelihood will almost always be complicated nonlinear functions of the data, whose exact expected values will be unknown. There are, however, two alternatives. A second estimator is

$$[\hat{\mathbf{I}}(\hat{\boldsymbol{\theta}})]^{-1} = \left(-\frac{\partial^2 \ln L(\hat{\boldsymbol{\theta}})}{\partial\hat{\boldsymbol{\theta}}\,\partial\hat{\boldsymbol{\theta}}'}\right)^{-1}. \tag{4-51}$$

This is computed simply by evaluating the actual (not expected) second derivatives matrix of the log-likelihood function at the maximum likelihood estimates. It is straightforward to show that this amounts to estimating the expected second derivatives of the density with the sample mean of this quantity. Result (4-20) can be used to justify the computation. The only shortcoming of this estimator is that the second derivatives can be complicated to derive and program for a computer. A third estimator based on the result that the expected second derivatives matrix is the covariance matrix of the first derivatives vector is

$$\begin{aligned}[\hat{\hat{\mathbf{I}}}(\hat{\boldsymbol{\theta}})]^{-1} &= \left[\sum_{i=1}^{n} \hat{\mathbf{g}}_i \hat{\mathbf{g}}_i'\right]^{-1} \\ &= [\hat{\mathbf{G}}'\hat{\mathbf{G}}]^{-1},\end{aligned} \tag{4-52}$$

where

$$\hat{\mathbf{g}}_i = \frac{\partial \ln f(\mathbf{x}_i, \hat{\boldsymbol{\theta}})}{\partial\hat{\boldsymbol{\theta}}}$$

and

$$\hat{\mathbf{G}} = [\hat{\mathbf{g}}_1, \hat{\mathbf{g}}_2, \ldots, \hat{\mathbf{g}}_n]'.$$

$\hat{\mathbf{G}}$ is an $n \times K$ matrix with ith row equal to the transpose of the ith vector of derivatives of the log-likelihood function. For a single parameter, this estimator is just the reciprocal of the sum of squares of the first derivatives. This estimator is extremely convenient, in most cases, because it does not require any computations beyond those required to solve the likelihood equation. It has the added virtue that it is always nonnegative definite. For some extremely complicated log-likelihood functions, sometimes because of rounding error, the *observed* Hessian can be indefinite, even at the maximum of the function. This is known as the **BHHH** estimator[13] and the **outer product of gradients,** or **OPG,** estimator.

EXAMPLE 4.22 Variance Estimators for an MLE

The sample data in Table 4.1 are generated by a model of the form

$$f(y_i, x_i, \beta) = \frac{1}{\beta + x_i} e^{-y_i/(\beta + x_i)},$$

[13]It appears to have been advocated first in the econometrics literature in Berndt et al. (1974).

where y = income and x = education. To find the maximum likelihood estimate of β, we maximize

$$\ln L(\beta) = -\sum_{i=1}^{n} \ln(\beta + x_i) - \sum_{i=1}^{n} \frac{y_i}{\beta + x_i}.$$

The likelihood equation is

$$\frac{\partial \ln L(\beta)}{\partial \beta} = -\sum_{i=1}^{n} \frac{1}{\beta + x_i} + \sum_{i=1}^{n} \frac{y_i}{(\beta + x_i)^2} = 0, \qquad \textbf{(4-53)}$$

which has the solution $\hat{\beta} = 15.60275$. To compute the asymptotic variance of the MLE, we require

$$\frac{\partial^2 \ln L(\beta)}{\partial \beta^2} = \sum_{i=1}^{n} \frac{1}{(\beta + x_i)^2} - 2\sum_{i=1}^{n} \frac{y_i}{(\beta + x_i)^3}. \qquad \textbf{(4-54)}$$

Since $E(y_i) = \beta + x_i$ is known, the exact form of the expected value in (4-54) is known. Inserting $\beta + x_i$ for y_i in (4-54) and taking the reciprocal yields the first variance estimate, 44.255. Simply inserting $\hat{\beta} = 15.60275$ in (4-54) and taking the reciprocal gives the second estimate, 46.164. Finally, by computing the reciprocal of the sum of squares of first derivatives of the densities evaluated at $\hat{\beta}$,

$$[\hat{\hat{\mathbf{I}}}(\hat{\beta})]^{-1} = \frac{1}{\sum_{i=1}^{n} [-1/(\hat{\beta} + x_i) + y_i/(\hat{\beta} + x_i)^2]^2},$$

we obtain the BHHH estimate, 100.512.

None of the three estimators given here is preferable to the others on statistical grounds; all are asymptotically equivalent. In most cases, the BHHH estimator will be the easiest to compute. One caution is in order. As the example illustrates, these estimators can give different results in a finite sample. This is an unavoidable finite sample problem that can, in some cases, lead to different statistical conclusions. The example is a case in point. Using the usual procedures, we would reject the hypothesis that $\beta = 0$ if either of the first two variance estimators were used, but not if the third were used.

4.6. TWO-STEP ESTIMATION[14]

The applied literature contains a large and increasing number of models in which one model is embedded in another. This produces what are broadly

[14]This material is relatively advanced for this point in the text and, unavoidably, uses some of the developments that will be constructed more fully quite a bit later. We will use two-step estimation in some of the applications in Chapter 20. It is presented here as a natural extension of the material in the preceding section of this chapter.

known as "two-step" estimation problems. Consider an (admittedly contrived) example in which we have the following.

> **Model 1.** Expected number of children $= E[y_1 | \mathbf{x}_1, \boldsymbol{\theta}_1]$.
>
> **Model 2.** Decision to enroll in job training $= y_2$, a function of $(\mathbf{x}_2, \boldsymbol{\theta}_2, E[y_1 | \mathbf{x}_1, \boldsymbol{\theta}_1])$.

There are two parameter vectors, $\boldsymbol{\theta}_1$ and $\boldsymbol{\theta}_2$, and note that the first appears in the second model, though not the reverse. In such a situation, there are two ways to proceed. **Full information maximum likelihood (FIML)** estimation would involve forming the joint distribution $f(y_1, y_2 | \mathbf{x}_1, \mathbf{x}_2, \boldsymbol{\theta}_1, \boldsymbol{\theta}_2)$ of the two random variables, then maximizing the full log-likelihood function,

$$\ln L = \sum_{i=1}^{n} f(y_{i1}, y_{i2} | \mathbf{x}_{i1}, \mathbf{x}_{i2}, \boldsymbol{\theta}_1, \boldsymbol{\theta}_2).$$

A second, or two-step, **limited information maximum likelihood (LIML)** procedure, for this kind of model, could be done by estimating the parameters of model 1, since it does not involve $\boldsymbol{\theta}_2$, then maximizing a conditional log-likelihood function using the estimates from step 1:

$$\ln \hat{L} = \sum_{i=1}^{n} f[y_{i1} | \mathbf{x}_{i1}, \boldsymbol{\theta}_1, (\mathbf{x}_{i2}, \hat{\boldsymbol{\theta}}_2)].$$

There are at least two reasons one might proceed in this fashion. First, it may be straightforward to formulate the two separate log-likelihoods, but very complicated to derive the joint distribution. This situation frequently arises when the two variables being modeled are from different kinds of populations, such as one discrete and one continuous (which is a very common case in this framework). The second reason is that maximizing the separate log-likelihoods may be fairly straightforward, but maximizing the joint log-likelihood may be numerically complicated or difficult.[15] We will consider a few examples. Although we will encounter FIML problems at various points later in the book, for now, we will present some basic results for two-step estimation. Proofs of the results given here are complicated, so they will be omitted.[16]

Suppose, then, that our model consists of the two *marginal* distributions, $f_1(y_1 | \mathbf{x}_1, \boldsymbol{\theta}_1)$ and $f_2(y_2 | \mathbf{x}_1, \mathbf{x}_2, \boldsymbol{\theta}_1, \boldsymbol{\theta}_2)$. Estimation proceeds in two steps.

1. Estimate $\boldsymbol{\theta}_1$ by maximum likelihood in model 1. Let $\hat{\mathbf{V}}_1$ be any of the estimators of the asymptotic covariance matrix of this estimator that were discussed in Section 4.5.2.

---

[15] There is a third possible motivation. If either model is misspecified, then the FIML estimates of both models will be inconsistent. But if only the second is misspecified, at least the first will be estimated consistently. Of course, this is only "half a loaf," but that may be better than none.

[16] An important reference on this subject that gives some of the background is Murphy and Topel (1985).

2. Estimate $\boldsymbol{\theta}_2$ by maximum likelihood in model 2, with $\hat{\boldsymbol{\theta}}_1$ inserted in place of $\boldsymbol{\theta}_1$ as if it were known. Let $\hat{\mathbf{V}}_2$ be any appropriate estimator of the asymptotic covariance matrix of $\hat{\boldsymbol{\theta}}_2$.

The argument for consistency of $\hat{\boldsymbol{\theta}}_2$ is essentially that if $\boldsymbol{\theta}_1$ *were* known, all our results for MLEs would apply for estimation of $\boldsymbol{\theta}_2$, and since plim $\hat{\boldsymbol{\theta}}_1 = \boldsymbol{\theta}_1$, asymptotically, this line of reasoning is correct. But the same line of reasoning is not sufficient to justify using $\hat{\mathbf{V}}_2$ as the estimator of the asymptotic covariance matrix of $\hat{\boldsymbol{\theta}}_2$. Some correction is necessary to account for an estimate of $\boldsymbol{\theta}_1$ being used in estimation of $\boldsymbol{\theta}_2$. The essential result is the following.

Theorem 4.19: Asymptotic Distribution of the Two-Step MLE [Murphy and Topel (1985)]. *If the standard regularity conditions are met for both log-likelihood functions, then the second-step maximum likelihood estimator of $\boldsymbol{\theta}_2$ is consistent and asymptotically normally distributed with asymptotic covariance matrix*

$$\mathbf{V}_2^* = \mathbf{V}_2 + \mathbf{V}_2[\mathbf{C}\mathbf{V}_1\mathbf{C}' - \mathbf{R}\mathbf{V}_1\mathbf{C}' - \mathbf{C}\mathbf{V}_1\mathbf{R}']\mathbf{V}_2,$$

where

$$\begin{aligned}
\mathbf{V}_1 &= \text{Asy. Var}[\hat{\boldsymbol{\theta}}_1] \quad \text{based on } \ln L_1, \\
\mathbf{V}_2 &= \text{Asy. Var}[\hat{\boldsymbol{\theta}}_2] \quad \text{based on } \ln L_2 \,|\, \boldsymbol{\theta}_1, \\
\mathbf{C} &= E\left[\left(\frac{\partial \ln L_2}{\partial \boldsymbol{\theta}_2}\right)\left(\frac{\partial \ln L_2}{\partial \boldsymbol{\theta}_1'}\right)\right], \\
\mathbf{R} &= E\left[\left(\frac{\partial \ln L_2}{\partial \boldsymbol{\theta}_2}\right)\left(\frac{\partial \ln L_1}{\partial \boldsymbol{\theta}_1'}\right)\right].
\end{aligned}$$

The correction of the asymptotic covariance matrix at the second step requires some additional computation. The matrices **R** and **C** are obtained by summing the individual observations on the cross products of the derivatives. These are estimated with

$$\hat{\mathbf{C}} = \frac{1}{n}\sum_{i=1}^{n}\left(\frac{\partial \ln f_{i2}}{\partial \hat{\boldsymbol{\theta}}_2}\right)\left(\frac{\partial \ln f_{i2}}{\partial \hat{\boldsymbol{\theta}}_1'}\right) \quad \text{and} \quad \hat{\mathbf{R}} = \frac{1}{n}\sum_{i=1}^{n}\left(\frac{\partial \ln f_{i2}}{\partial \hat{\boldsymbol{\theta}}_2}\right)\left(\frac{\partial \ln f_{i1}}{\partial \hat{\boldsymbol{\theta}}_1'}\right).$$

An example demonstrates.

EXAMPLE 4.23 Two-Step ML Estimation

Continuing the example at the beginning of this section, we suppose that y_{i2} is a binary indicator of the choice whether to enroll in the program ($y_{i2} = 1$) or not ($y_{i2} = 0$) and that the probabilities of the two outcomes are

$$\text{Prob}[y_{i2} = 1] = \frac{e^{\mathbf{x}_i'\boldsymbol{\beta} + \gamma E[y_{i1}]}}{1 + e^{\mathbf{x}_i'\boldsymbol{\beta} + \gamma E[y_{i1}]}}$$

and $\text{Prob}[y_{i2} = 0] = 1 - \text{Prob}[y_{i2} = 1]$, where **x** is some covariates that might influence the decision, such as marital status or age. This is a **logit** model. We will develop this model more fully in Chapter 19. The *expected value* of y_{i1} appears in the probability. (Remark: The expected, rather than the actual, value was chosen deliberately. The models would differ substantially. In our case, we might view the difference as that between an ex ante decision and an ex post one.) Suppose that the number of children can be described by a Poisson distribution (see Section 3.4.7 and Examples 3.6 through 3.8) dependent on some variables $\mathbf{z}_i$ such as education, age, and so on. Then

$$\text{Prob}[y_{i1} = j] = \frac{e^{-\lambda_i}\lambda_i^j}{j!}, \quad j = 0, 1, \ldots,$$

and suppose, as is customary, that

$$E[y_{i1}] = \lambda_i = e^{\mathbf{z}_i'\boldsymbol{\delta}}.$$

The models involve $\boldsymbol{\theta} = [\boldsymbol{\delta}, \boldsymbol{\beta}, \gamma]$, where $\boldsymbol{\theta}_1 = \boldsymbol{\delta}$. In fact, it is unclear what the joint distribution of y_1 and y_2 might be, but two-step estimation is straightforward. For model 1, the log-likelihood and its first derivatives are

$$\begin{aligned}
\ln L_1 &= \sum_{i=1}^{n} \ln f_1(y_{i1} \mid \mathbf{z}_i, \boldsymbol{\delta}) \\
&= \sum_{i=1}^{n} -\lambda_i + y_{i1} \ln \lambda_i - \ln y_{i1}! \\
&= \sum_{i=1}^{n} -e^{\mathbf{z}_i'\boldsymbol{\delta}} + y_{i1}(\mathbf{z}_i'\boldsymbol{\delta}) - \ln y_{i1}!, \\
\frac{\partial \ln L_1}{\partial \boldsymbol{\delta}} &= \sum_{i=1}^{n} (y_{i1} - \lambda_i)\mathbf{z}_i \\
&= \sum_{i=1}^{n} u_i \mathbf{z}_i.
\end{aligned}$$

Computation of the estimates is developed in Chapter 19. (This particular model is quite simple to estimate.) Any of the three estimators of $\mathbf{V}_1$ is also easy to compute, but the BHHH estimator is most convenient, so we use

$$\hat{\mathbf{V}}_1 = \sum_{i=1}^{n} \hat{u}_i^2 \mathbf{z}_i \mathbf{z}_i'.$$

[In this and the succeeding summations, we are actually estimating expectations of the various matrices. Since they will ultimately cancel in the final results, we have omitted terms of $(1/n)$ in all of the summations.]

We can write the density function for the second model as

$$f_2(y_{i2} \mid \mathbf{x}_i, \mathbf{z}_i, \boldsymbol{\beta}, \gamma, \boldsymbol{\delta}) = P_i^{y_{i2}} \times (1 - P_i)^{1-y_{i2}},$$

where $P_i = \text{Prob}[y_{i2} = 1]$ as given earlier. Then

$$\ln L_2 = \sum_{i=1}^{n} y_{i2} \ln P_i + (1 - y_{i2}) \ln(1 - P_i).$$

For convenience, let $\mathbf{x}_i^* = [\mathbf{x}_i', \exp(\mathbf{z}_i'\hat{\boldsymbol{\delta}})]'$, and recall that $\boldsymbol{\theta}_2 = [\boldsymbol{\beta}, \gamma]'$. Then

$$\ln L_2 = \sum_{i=1}^{n} y_{i2}[\mathbf{x}_i^{*\prime}\boldsymbol{\theta}_2 - \ln(1 + \exp(\mathbf{x}_i^{*\prime}\boldsymbol{\theta}_2))] + (1 - y_{i2})[-\ln(1 + \exp(\mathbf{x}_i^{*\prime}\boldsymbol{\theta}_2))].$$

So, at the second step, we create the additional variable, append it to $\mathbf{x}_i$, and estimate the logit model as if $\boldsymbol{\delta}$ (and this additional variable) were actually observed instead of estimated. The maximum likelihood estimates of $[\boldsymbol{\beta}, \gamma]$ are obtained by maximizing this function. (See Chapter 19.) After a bit of manipulation, we find the convenient result that[17]

$$\frac{\partial \ln L_2}{\partial \boldsymbol{\theta}_2} = \sum_{i=1}^{n} (y_{2i} - P_i)\mathbf{x}_i^* = \sum_{i=1}^{n} v_i \mathbf{x}_i^*.$$

Once again, any of the three estimators could be used for estimating the asymptotic covariance, but the BHHH estimator is convenient, so we use

$$\hat{\mathbf{V}}_2 = \sum_{i=1}^{n} \hat{v}_i^2 \mathbf{x}_i^* \mathbf{x}_i^{*\prime}.$$

For the final step, we must correct the asymptotic covariance matrix using $\hat{\mathbf{C}}$ and $\hat{\mathbf{R}}$. What remains to derive—the few lines are left for the reader—is

$$\frac{\partial \ln L_2}{\partial \boldsymbol{\delta}} = \sum_{i=1}^{n} v_i(\gamma e^{\mathbf{z}_i'\boldsymbol{\delta}})\mathbf{z}_i.$$

So, using our estimates,

$$\hat{\mathbf{C}} = \sum_{i=1}^{n} \hat{v}_i^2(\hat{\gamma} e^{\mathbf{z}_i'\hat{\boldsymbol{\delta}}})\hat{\mathbf{x}}_i^* \mathbf{z}_i',$$

$$\hat{\mathbf{R}} = \sum_{i=1}^{n} \hat{u}_i \hat{v}_i \hat{\mathbf{x}}_i^* \mathbf{z}_i'.$$

We can now compute the correction. We will continue this application in Chapter 20 after developing the two probability models in more detail.

In many applications, the covariance of the two gradients $\mathbf{R}$ converges to zero. Note, for example, in our application above, $\mathbf{R} = \Sigma_{i=1}^{n} u_i v_i \mathbf{x}_i^* \mathbf{z}_i'$. The two "residuals," u and v, may well be uncorrelated. This must be checked on a model-by-model basis, but in such an instance, the third and fourth terms in $\mathbf{V}_2^*$ vanish asymptotically, and what remains is the simpler alternative,

$$\mathbf{V}_2^{**} = \mathbf{V}_2 + \mathbf{V}_2\mathbf{C}\mathbf{V}_1\mathbf{C}'\mathbf{V}_2.$$

[17] It is an interesting result that in both models, the derivatives are equal to the difference between the actual value and the mean, times the covariates. It is a result that reappears in many models.

We will examine some additional applications of this technique (including an empirical implementation of the preceding example) later in the book. Perhaps the most common application of two-step maximum likelihood estimation in the current literature involves inserting a prediction of one variable into a function that describes the behavior of another. This is common in regression analysis. We will take up the special case of two-step least squares in Chapter 10.

4.7. CONSISTENT ESTIMATION — THE METHOD OF MOMENTS

In some situations, all that is required is a consistent estimator of a parameter; efficiency is secondary. Examples include the correlation coefficient in the AR(1) regression model, the disturbance covariance matrix in a multiple equation model, the correlation coefficient in the sample selection model, and the disturbance variances in some heteroskedastic regressions.

A technique used in many such cases is the **method of moments.** The basis of this method is as follows. In random sampling, a sample statistic will converge in probability to some constant. For example, $(1/n)\ \Sigma_i x_i^2$ will converge in mean square to the variance plus the square of the mean of the distribution of x_i. This constant will, in turn, be a function of the unknown parameters of the distribution. To estimate K parameters, $\theta_1, \ldots, \theta_K$, we compute K statistics, $m_1, \ldots, m_K$, whose probability limits are known functions of the parameters. These K moments are equated to the K functions, and the functions are inverted to express the parameters as functions of the moments. The estimators are consistent by virtue of the Slutsky theorem [(4-21) and Theorem 4.3].

This section will develop this technique in some detail, partly to present it in its own right and partly as a prelude to the discussion of the generalized method of moments, or GMM, estimation technique discussed in Section 11.5. The results in this section have been applied in standard problems in estimating the parameters of distributions. Recent econometric applications have extended the method of moments to problems involving regressions and much more involved models than we will consider here. The extension to GMM estimation is treated in Chapter 11.

4.7.1. Random Sampling and Estimating the Parameters of Distributions

Consider random sampling from a distribution $f(x \mid \theta_1, \ldots, \theta_K)$ with finite moments $E[x^k]$. The sample consists of n observations, $x_1, \ldots, x_n$. The kth "raw" or **uncentered moment** is

$$m'_k = \frac{1}{n} \sum_{i=1}^{n} x_i^k.$$

By substituting $z_i = x_i^k$, we obtain the following results. By (3-14) and Theorem 4.1,

$$E[m_k'] = \mu_k' = E[x_i^k]$$

and

$$\text{Var}[m_k'] = \frac{1}{n}\text{Var}[x_i^k] = \frac{1}{n}(\mu_{2k}' - \mu_k'^2).$$

By Theorem 4.3,

$$\text{plim } m_k' = \mu_k' = E[x_i^k].$$

Finally, by Theorem 4.4,

$$\sqrt{n}(m_k' - \mu_k') \xrightarrow{d} N[0, \mu_{2k}' - \mu_k'^2].$$

By convention,

$$\mu_1' = E[x_i] = \mu.$$

In general, μ_k' will be a function of the underlying parameters. By computing K raw moments and equating them to these functions, we obtain K equations that can be solved to provide estimates of the K unknown parameters.

EXAMPLE 4.24 Method of Moments Estimator for $N[\mu, \sigma^2]$

In random sampling from $N[\mu, \sigma^2]$,

$$\text{plim } \frac{1}{n}\sum_{i=1}^{n} x_i = \text{plim } m_1' = E[x_i] = \mu$$

and

$$\text{plim } \frac{1}{n}\sum_{i=1}^{n} x_i^2 = \text{plim } m_2' = \text{Var}[x_i] + \mu^2 = \sigma^2 + \mu^2.$$

Equating the right- and left-hand sides of the probability limits gives moment estimators

$$\hat{\mu} = m_1' = \bar{x}$$

and

$$\hat{\sigma}^2 = m_2' - m_1'^2 = \frac{1}{n}\sum_{i=1}^{n}(x_i - \bar{x})^2.$$

Note that $\hat{\sigma}^2$ is biased, although both estimators are consistent.

EXAMPLE 4.25 Mixture of Normal Distributions

Quandt and Ramsey (1978) analyzed the problem of estimating the parameters of a mixture of normal distributions. Suppose that each observation in a random sample is drawn from one of two different normal distributions. The probability that the observation is drawn from the first distribution, $N[\mu_1, \sigma_1^2]$, is λ, and the probability that it is drawn from the second is $(1 - \lambda)$. The density is

$$f(x) = \lambda N[\mu_1, \sigma_1^2] + (1 - \lambda)N[\mu_2, \sigma_2^2], \quad 0 \le \lambda \le 1$$
$$= \frac{\lambda}{(2\pi\sigma_1^2)^{1/2}} e^{-1/2[(x-\mu_1)/\sigma_1]^2} + \frac{1-\lambda}{(2\pi\sigma_2^2)^{1/2}} e^{-1/2[(x-\mu_2)/\sigma_2]^2}.$$

The sample mean and second through fifth **central moments,**

$$m_k = \frac{1}{n}\sum_{i=1}^{n}(x_i - \bar{x})^k, \quad k = 2, 3, 4, 5,$$

provide five equations in five unknowns that can be solved (via a ninth-order polynomial) for consistent estimators of the five parameters. Note that $m_1 = 0$ and $m_2 = \hat{\sigma}^2$. Because $\bar{x}$ converges in probability to μ, the theorems given above for m'_k as an estimator of μ'_k apply as well to m_k as an estimator of

$$\mu_k = E[(x_i - \mu)^k].$$

Although the moments based on powers of x provide a natural source of information about the parameters, other functions of the data may also be useful. Let $g_k(\cdot)$ be any continuous function not involving the sample size n, and let

$$\bar{g}_k = \frac{1}{n}\sum_{i=1}^{n} g_k(x_i), \quad k = 1, 2, \ldots, K.$$

These are also "moments" of the data. It follows from Theorem 4.3 that

$$\text{plim}\, \bar{g}_k = E[g_k(x)] = \gamma_k(\theta_1, \ldots, \theta_K).$$

We assume that $\gamma_k(\cdot)$ involves some or all of the parameters of the distribution. With K parameters to be estimated, the K **moment equations,**

$$\bar{g}_1 - \gamma_1(\theta_1, \ldots, \theta_K) = 0,$$
$$\bar{g}_2 - \gamma_2(\theta_1, \ldots, \theta_K) = 0,$$
$$\vdots$$
$$\bar{g}_K - \gamma_K(\theta_1, \ldots, \theta_K) = 0,$$

provide K equations in K unknowns, $\theta_1, \ldots, \theta_K$. If they are independent, **method of moments estimators** are obtained by solving the system of equations for

$$\hat{\theta}_k = \hat{\theta}_k[\bar{g}_1, \ldots, \bar{g}_K].$$

EXAMPLE 4.25 (Continued)

For the mixed normal distribution,

$$E[e^{tx_i}] = \lambda e^{t\mu_1 + t^2\sigma_1^2/2} + (1-\lambda)e^{t\mu_2 + t^2\sigma_2^2/2} = \Lambda_t,$$

where t is any value not necessarily an integer. Quandt and Ramsey suggest choosing five values of t that are not too close together, and using the statistics

$$M_t = \frac{1}{n}\sum_{i=1}^{n} e^{tx_i}$$

to estimate the parameters. The moment equations are $M_t - \Lambda_t = 0$. They label this the **"method of moment-generating functions."** (See Exercise 27 in Chapter 3.)

As Example 4.25 suggests, there may be more than one set of moments that one can use for estimating the parameters, or there may be more moment equations available than are necessary.

EXAMPLE 4.26 Gamma Distribution

In sampling from the gamma distribution (see Section 3.4.5),

$$f(x) = \frac{\lambda^P}{\Gamma(P)} e^{-\lambda x} x^{P-1}, \quad x > 0, P > 0, \lambda > 0,$$

$$\text{plim}\,\frac{1}{n}\sum_{i=1}^{n} x_i = \frac{P}{\lambda},$$

$$\text{plim}\,\frac{1}{n}\sum_{i=1}^{n} x_i^2 = \frac{P(P+1)}{\lambda^2},$$

$$\text{plim}\,\frac{1}{n}\sum_{i=1}^{n} \ln x_i = \frac{d\ln\Gamma(P)}{dP} - \ln\lambda = \Psi(P) - \ln\lambda,$$

$$\text{plim}\,\frac{1}{n}\sum_{i=1}^{n} \frac{1}{x_i} = \frac{\lambda}{P-1}.$$

The functions $\Gamma(P)$ and $\Psi(P)$ are discussed in Section 5.4.2b. Any two of these could be used to estimate λ and P. The set could also be expanded since, for example,

$$\text{plim}\, m'_k = \mu'_k = \left[\frac{\Gamma(P+k)}{\lambda^{P+k}}\right]\left[\frac{\lambda^P}{\Gamma(P)}\right] = \frac{\prod_{j=1}^{k}(P+k-j)}{\lambda^k},$$

$$\text{plim}\, m'_{-k} = \mu'_{-k} = \frac{\lambda^k}{\prod_{j=1}^{k}(P-j)}.$$

In most cases, method of moments estimators are not efficient. The exception is in random sampling from **exponential families** of distributions.

DEFINITION 4.15: Exponential Family. *An exponential (parametric) family of distributions is one whose log-likelihood is of the form*

$$\ln L(\boldsymbol{\theta} \mid \mathbf{X}) = a(\mathbf{X}) + b(\boldsymbol{\theta}) + \sum_{j=1}^{K} c_j(\mathbf{X}) s_j(\boldsymbol{\theta}),$$

where $a(\cdot)$, $b(\cdot)$, $c(\cdot)$, and $s(\cdot)$ are functions. The members of the "family" are distinguished by the different parameter values.

If the log-likelihood function is of this form, then the functions $c_j(\cdot)$ are called **sufficient statistics.**[18] When sufficient statistics exist, the method of moments estimator(s) will be functions of them. Also, in this case, the method of moments estimators will be the maximum likelihood estimators, so, of course, they will be efficient, at least asymptotically.

EXAMPLE 4.26 (Continued)

The log-likelihood function for the gamma distribution is

$$\ln L = n[P \ln \lambda - \ln \Gamma(P)] - \lambda \sum_{i=1}^{n} x_i + (P-1) \sum_{i=1}^{n} \ln x_i .$$

This is an exponential family with $a(\mathbf{X}) = 0$, $b(\boldsymbol{\theta}) = n[P \ln \lambda - \ln \Gamma(P)]$, and two sufficient statistics, $\Sigma_{i=1}^{n} x_i$ and $\Sigma_{i=1}^{n} \ln x_i$. The method of moments estimators based on $\Sigma_{i=1}^{n} x_i$ and $\Sigma_{i=1}^{n} \ln x_i$ would be the maximum likelihood estimators.

For the income data in Table 4.1, the four moments listed above are

$$\frac{1}{n}\sum_{i=1}^{n}\left[x_i, x_i^2, \ln x_i, \frac{1}{x_i}\right] = [31.278, 1453.957, 3.221387, 0.0500141]$$
$$= (m_1', m_2', m_*', m_{-1}').$$

Denote the estimated parameters as $\boldsymbol{\theta} = (P, \lambda)$. The method of moments estimators of P and λ based on pairs of these moments are as follows:

$$\begin{aligned}
\hat{\boldsymbol{\theta}}(m_1', m_2') &= (2.05682, 0.065759), & \hat{\boldsymbol{\theta}}(m_1', m_*') &= (2.4097, 0.07704137),\\
\hat{\boldsymbol{\theta}}(m_1', m_{-1}') &= (2.77198, 0.0886239), & \hat{\boldsymbol{\theta}}(m_2', m_*') &= (2.4806, 0.079835),\\
\hat{\boldsymbol{\theta}}(m_{-1}', m_2') &= (2.609045, 0.080745), & \hat{\boldsymbol{\theta}}(m_{-1}', m_*') &= (3.0358, 0.1018119).
\end{aligned}$$

The maximum likelihood estimates are $\hat{\boldsymbol{\theta}}(m_1', m_*') = (2.4097, 0.07704137)$.

4.7.2. Computing the Variance of a Method of Moments Estimator

In a few cases, the exact variance of the method of moments estimator can be obtained. For example, in sampling from the normal distribution, the variance of $\hat{\mu}$ is σ^2/n whereas the variance of $\hat{\sigma}^2$ is $[(n-1)/n]^2 2\sigma^4/(n-1)$. (See Example 4.4.) If sampling is not from the normal distribution, the exact variance of

[18]Stuart and Ord (1989, pp. 1–29) give a discussion of sufficient statistics and exponential families of distributions.

the sample mean will still be σ^2/n, whereas an asymptotic variance for the moment estimator of the population variance can be based on the leading term in (4-42). But these are particularly simple cases. Method of moments estimators are usually more complicated than simple sums and sums of squares.

EXAMPLE 4.27 Characterizing the "Normality" of a Distribution

Two useful parameters are

$$\theta_1 = \text{skewness coefficient} = \frac{E[(x-\mu)^3]}{(\text{Var}[x])^{3/2}} = \frac{\mu_3}{\sigma^3}$$

and

$$\theta_2 = \text{kurtosis coefficient} = \frac{E[(x-\mu)^4]}{(\text{Var}[x])^2} = \frac{\mu_4}{\sigma^4}.$$

The sample values of $c_1 = m_3/m_2^{3/2}$ and $c_2 = m_4/m_2^2$ are often compared with the population values for the normal distribution, 0 and 3, respectively, to characterize departure from normality. (The quantity $\theta_2 - 3$ is called the "degree of excess"; see Section 3.3.) These statistics are based on three central moments (see Example 4.24), m_2, m_3, and m_4. To obtain an asymptotic covariance matrix for $[c_1, c_2]$, we can proceed as follows. First, obtain the asymptotic covariance matrix for the three sample moments. Second, use result (3-94) of Section 3.9.3 and Section 4.4.4 on nonlinear functions to obtain the appropriate asymptotic covariance. The following result from Stuart and Ord (1983, p. 230) will be useful:

$$\begin{aligned} n\,(\text{Asy. Cov}[m_j, m_k]) &= \lim_{n\to\infty} n\,\text{Cov}[m_j, m_k] \\ &= \mu_{j+k} - \mu_j\mu_k + jk\mu_2\mu_{j-1}\mu_{k-1} - j\mu_{j-1}\mu_{k+1} - k\mu_{j+1}\mu_{k-1}. \end{aligned}$$

Since these are central moments, $m_1 = \mu_1 = 0$. For the six terms for $j, k = 2, 3, 4$, this formula gives

$$\begin{aligned} \text{Asy. Var}[m_2] &= \frac{1}{n}[\mu_4 - \mu_2^2], \\ \text{Asy. Var}[m_3] &= \frac{1}{n}[\mu_6 - \mu_3^2 - 6\mu_4\mu_2 + 9\mu_2^3], \\ \text{Asy. Var}[m_4] &= \frac{1}{n}[\mu_8 - \mu_4^2 - 8\mu_5\mu_3 + 16\mu_2\mu_3^2], \\ \text{Asy. Cov}[m_2, m_3] &= \frac{1}{n}[\mu_5 - 4\mu_3\mu_2], \\ \text{Asy. Cov}[m_2, m_4] &= \frac{1}{n}[\mu_6 - \mu_2\mu_4 - 4\mu_3^2], \\ \text{Asy. Cov}[m_3, m_4] &= \frac{1}{n}[\mu_7 - \mu_3\mu_4 + 12\mu_2^2\mu_3 - 3\mu_2\mu_5 - \mu_4\mu_3]. \end{aligned}$$

We would estimate these with the sample moments $m_2, \ldots, m_8$ and collect them in a 3×3 matrix:

$$\mathbf{V} = \text{Est. Asy. Cov}[m_2, m_3, m_4].$$

The necessary matrix of derivatives is

$$\mathbf{J} = \begin{bmatrix} \partial\theta_1/\partial m_2 & \partial\theta_1/\partial m_3 & \partial\theta_1/\partial m_4 \\ \partial\theta_2/\partial m_2 & \partial\theta_2/\partial m_3 & \partial\theta_2/\partial m_4 \end{bmatrix} = \begin{bmatrix} -3/2\mu_2^{-5/2}\mu_3 & \mu_2^{-3/2} & 0 \\ -2\mu_2^{-3}\mu_4 & 0 & \mu_2^{-2} \end{bmatrix}.$$

Then the estimate of the asymptotic covariance matrix for the estimators of θ_1 and θ_2 would be $\mathbf{JVJ}'$.

There are cases in which no explicit expression is available for the variance of the underlying sample moment. For instance, in Example 4.25, the underlying sample statistic is

$$M_t = \frac{1}{n}\sum_{i=1}^{n} e^{tx_i}.$$

The exact variance of M_t is known only if t is an integer. But if sampling is random, a consistent estimator for the variance of M_t can easily be computed since M_t is a sample mean:

$$M_t = \frac{1}{n}\sum_{i=1}^{n} z_i = \bar{z}.$$

Therefore, we can estimate the variance of M_t with $1/n$ times the sample variance of the observations on z. We can also obtain an estimate of the covariance of M_t and M_s with $1/n$ times the sample covariance of the individual terms. In particular,

$$\text{Est. Asy. Cov}[M_t, M_s] = \frac{1}{n}\frac{1}{n-1}\sum_{i=1}^{n} [(e^{tx_i} - M_t)(e^{sx_i} - M_s)].$$

When the moments are computed as

$$\bar{g}_k = \frac{1}{n}\sum_{i=1}^{n} g_k(\mathbf{x}_i), \quad k = 1, \ldots, K,$$

where $\mathbf{x}_i$ may be an observation on a vector of variables, an appropriate estimate of the asymptotic covariance matrix for $[\bar{g}_1, \ldots, \bar{g}_k]$ can be computed using

$$\mathbf{V} = \frac{1}{n}\frac{1}{n-1}\sum_{i=1}^{n} [(g_j(\mathbf{x}_i) - \bar{g}_j)(g_k(\mathbf{x}_i) - \bar{g}_k)], \quad j, k = 1, \ldots, K. \tag{4-55}$$

This provides the asymptotic covariance matrix for the moments used in computing the estimated parameters. This estimator could have been used in Example 4.26. We would have computed $\mathbf{V}$ equal to $(1/n)$ times the sample covariance matrix of x^2, x^3, and x^4.

To complete the computation, refer back to the moment equations

$$\overline{m}_k = \overline{g}_k - \gamma_k(\theta_1, \theta_2, \ldots, \theta_k) = 0, \quad k = 1, \ldots, K.$$

Let $\mathbf{G}$ be the $K \times K$ matrix whose kth row is the vector of partial derivatives

$$\mathbf{G}^k = \frac{\partial \overline{g}_k}{\partial \boldsymbol{\theta}'}.$$

Now, expand the set of solved moment equations around the true values of the parameters $\boldsymbol{\theta}$ in a linear Taylor series. The linear approximation is

$$\overline{\mathbf{g}} \approx \gamma(\boldsymbol{\theta}) + \mathbf{G}(\boldsymbol{\theta})(\hat{\boldsymbol{\theta}} - \boldsymbol{\theta}).$$

Therefore,

$$(\hat{\boldsymbol{\theta}} - \boldsymbol{\theta}) \approx \mathbf{G}(\boldsymbol{\theta})^{-1}[\overline{\mathbf{g}} - \gamma(\boldsymbol{\theta})] = \mathbf{G}(\boldsymbol{\theta})^{-1}\overline{\mathbf{m}}.$$

The arguments needed to characterize the large sample behavior of the estimator of $\hat{\boldsymbol{\theta}}$ are discussed in Chapter 6. We have from Theorem 4.11 (the central limit theorem) that $\overline{\mathbf{g}} - \gamma(\boldsymbol{\theta})$ is asymptotically normally distributed with mean vector $\mathbf{0}$ and asymptotic covariance matrix equal to $1/n$ times plim$(n\mathbf{V})$. Under fairly general conditions, we can use (3-87) for the variance of a set of linear functions. Thus, the asymptotic covariance matrix for the method of moments estimator may be estimated with

$$\text{Est. Asy. Var}[\hat{\boldsymbol{\theta}}] = (\hat{\mathbf{G}}^{-1})\mathbf{V}(\hat{\mathbf{G}}^{-1})'. \tag{4-56}$$

EXAMPLE 4.26 (Continued)

Using the estimates $\hat{\boldsymbol{\theta}}(m_1', m_*') = (2.4097, 0.07704137)$,

$$\hat{\mathbf{G}} = \begin{bmatrix} -1/\hat{\lambda} & \hat{P}/\hat{\lambda}^2 \\ -\hat{\Psi} & 1/\hat{\lambda} \end{bmatrix} = \begin{bmatrix} -12.98004 & 405.9897 \\ -0.51264 & 12.98004 \end{bmatrix}.$$

[The function Ψ' is $d^2 \ln \Gamma(P)/dP^2 = (\Gamma\Gamma'' - \Gamma'^2)/\Gamma^2$. With $\hat{P} = 2.4097$, $\hat{\Gamma} = 1.250091$, $\hat{\Psi} = 0.657886$, and $\hat{\Psi}' = 0.512640$.][19] The matrix $\mathbf{V}$ is $1/n$ times the sample covariance matrix of x and $\ln x$:

$$\mathbf{V} = \begin{bmatrix} 25.034 & 0.7155 \\ 0.7155 & 0.023873 \end{bmatrix}.$$

The product in (4-56) is

$$\hat{\mathbf{G}}^{-1}\mathbf{V}(\hat{\mathbf{G}}')^{-1} = \begin{bmatrix} 0.38927 & 0.014587 \\ 0.014587 & 0.00068673 \end{bmatrix}.$$

[19] Ψ' is the **digamma** function. Values for $\Gamma(P)$, $\Psi(P)$, and $\Psi'(P)$ are tabulated in Abramovitz and Stegun (1971).

For the maximum likelihood estimator, the estimate of the asymptotic covariance matrix based on the expected (and actual) Hessian is

$$\frac{1}{n}[-\mathbf{H}]^{-1} = \frac{1}{n}\begin{bmatrix} \Psi' & -1/\lambda \\ -1/\lambda & P/\lambda^2 \end{bmatrix}^{-1} = \begin{bmatrix} 0.51203 & 0.01637 \\ 0.01637 & 0.00064654 \end{bmatrix}.$$

The Hessian has the same elements as **G** because we chose to use the sufficient statistics for the moment estimators, so the moment equations that we differentiated are, apart from a sign change, also the derivatives of the log-likelihood. The estimates of the two variances are 0.51203 and 0.00064654, respectively, which agrees reasonably well with the estimates above. The difference would be due to sampling variability in a finite sample.

4.8. INTERVAL ESTIMATION

Regardless of the properties of an estimator, the estimate obtained will vary from sample to sample, and there is some probability that it will be quite erroneous. A point estimate will not provide any information on the likely range of error. The logic behind an **interval estimate** is that we use the sample data to construct an interval, [lower $(\mathbf{X})$, upper $(\mathbf{X})$], such that we can expect this interval to contain the true parameter in some specified proportion of samples, or equivalently, with some desired level of confidence. Clearly, the wider the interval, the more confident we can be that it will, in any given sample, contain the parameter being estimated.

The theory of interval estimation is based on a **pivotal quantity,** which is a function of both the parameter and a point estimate that has a known distribution. Consider the following examples.

EXAMPLE 4.28 Confidence Intervals for the Normal Mean

In sampling from a normal distribution with mean μ and standard deviation σ,

$$z = \frac{\sqrt{n}(\bar{x} - \mu)}{s} \sim t[n-1]$$

and

$$c = \frac{(n-1)s^2}{\sigma^2} \sim \chi^2[n-1].$$

Given the pivotal quantity, we can make probability statements about events involving the parameter and the estimate. Let $p(g, \theta)$ be the constructed random variable, for example, z or c. Given a prespecified **confidence level,** $1 - \alpha$, we can state that

$$\text{Prob}(\text{lower} \le p(g, \theta) \le \text{upper}) = 1 - \alpha, \qquad \textbf{(4-57)}$$

where lower and upper are obtained from the appropriate table. This statement is then manipulated to make equivalent statements about the endpoints of the intervals. For example, the following statements are equivalent:

$$\text{Prob}\left(-z \le \frac{\sqrt{n}(\bar{x} - \mu)}{s} \le z\right) = 1 - a,$$

$$\text{Prob}\left(\bar{x} - \frac{zs}{\sqrt{n}} \le \mu \le \bar{x} + \frac{zs}{\sqrt{n}}\right) = 1 - \alpha.$$

The second of these is a statement about the interval, not the parameter; that is, it is the interval that is random, not the parameter. We attach a probability, or $100(1 - \alpha)$ percent confidence level, to the interval itself; in repeated sampling, an interval constructed in this fashion will contain the true parameter $100(1 - \alpha)$ percent of the time.

In general, the interval constructed by this method will be of the form

$$\text{lower}(\mathbf{X}) = \hat{\theta} - e_1,$$
$$\text{upper}(\mathbf{X}) = \hat{\theta} + e_2,$$

where $\mathbf{X}$ is the sample data, e_1 and e_2 are sampling errors, and $\hat{\theta}$ is a point estimate of θ. It is clear from the preceding example that if the sampling distribution of the pivotal quantity is either t or standard normal, which will be true in the vast majority of cases we encounter in practice, then the confidence interval will be

$$\hat{\theta} \pm C_{1-\alpha/2}[\text{se}(\hat{\theta})], \tag{4-58}$$

where se(·) is the (known or estimated) standard error of the parameter estimate and $C_{1-\alpha/2}$ is the value from the t or standard normal distribution that is exceeded with probability $1 - \alpha/2$. The usual values for α are 0.10, 0.05, or 0.01.

EXAMPLE 4.29 Estimated Confidence Interval for a Normal Mean

In a sample of 25,

$$\bar{x} = 1.63 \quad \text{and} \quad s = 0.51.$$

Construct a 95 percent confidence interval for μ. Assuming that the sample of 25 is from a normal distribution,

$$\text{Prob}\left(-2.064 \le \frac{5(\bar{x} - \mu)}{s} \le 2.064\right) = 0.95,$$

where 2.064 is the critical value from a t distribution with 24 degrees of freedom. Thus, the confidence interval is $1.63 \pm [2.064(0.51)/5]$ or [1.4195, 1.8405].

Remark: Had the parent distribution not been specified, it would have been natural to use the standard normal distribution instead, perhaps relying on the central limit theorem. But a sample size of 25 is small enough that the more conservative t distribution might still be preferable.

The theory does not prescribe exactly how to choose the endpoints for the confidence interval. An obvious criterion is to minimize the width of the interval. If the sampling distribution is symmetric, the symmetric interval is the best one. If the sampling distribution is not symmetric, however, this procedure will not be optimal.

EXAMPLE 4.30 Confidence Interval for a Variance

The chi-squared distribution is used to construct a confidence interval for the variance of a normal distribution. Using the data from Example 4.28, we find that the usual procedure would use

$$\text{Prob}\left(12.4 \leq \frac{24s^2}{\sigma^2} \leq 39.4\right) = 0.95,$$

where 12.4 and 39.4 are the 0.025 and 0.975 cutoff points from the chi-squared (24) distribution. This leads to the 95 percent confidence interval [0.1581, 0.5032]. By making use of the asymmetry of the distribution, a narrower interval can be constructed. Allocating 4 percent to the left-hand tail and 1 percent to the right instead of 2.5 percent to each, the two cutoff points are 13.4 and 42.9, and the resulting 95 percent confidence interval is [0.1455, 0.4659].[20]

Finally, the confidence interval can be manipulated to obtain a confidence interval for a function of a parameter. For example, based on the preceding, a 95 percent confidence interval for σ would be $[\sqrt{0.1581}, \sqrt{0.5032}] = [0.3976, 0.7094]$.

4.9. HYPOTHESIS TESTING

The second major group of statistical inference procedures is hypothesis tests. The classical testing procedures are based on constructing a statistic from a random sample that will enable the analyst to decide, with reasonable confidence, whether or not the data in the sample would have been generated by a hypothesized population. The formal procedure involves a statement of the hypothesis, usually in terms of a "null" or maintained hypothesis and an "alternative," conventionally denoted H_0 and H_1, respectively. The procedure itself is a rule, stated in terms of the data, that dictates whether the null hypothesis should be rejected or not. For example, the hypothesis might state a parameter is equal to a specified value. The decision rule might state that the hypothesis should be rejected if a sample estimate of that parameter is too far away from

[20]Formal conditions for finding the narrowest interval are considered in Exercise 19.

that value (where "far" remains to be defined). The classical, or Neyman–Pearson, methodology involves partitioning the sample space into two regions. If the observed data (i.e., the test statistic) fall in the **rejection region** (sometimes called the **critical region**), the null hypothesis is rejected; if they fall in the **acceptance region,** it is not.

4.9.1. Testing Procedures

Since the sample is random, the test statistic, however defined, is also random. The same test procedure can lead to different conclusions in different samples. As such, there are two ways such a procedure can be in error:

1. **Type I error.** The procedure may lead to rejection of the null hypothesis when it is true.
2. **Type II error.** The procedure may fail to reject the null hypothesis when it is false. To continue the previous example, there is some probability that the estimate of the parameter will be quite far from the hypothesized value, even if the hypothesis is true. This might cause a type I error.

DEFINITION 4.16: Size of a Test. *The probability of a type I error is the* ***size*** *of the test. This is conventionally denoted* α *and is also called the* ***significance level.***

The size of the test is under the control of the analyst. It can be changed just by changing the decision rule. Indeed, the type I error could be eliminated altogether just by making the rejection region very small. But this would come at a cost. By eliminating the probability of a type I error—that is, by making it unlikely that the hypothesis is rejected—we must increase the probability of a type II error. Ideally, we would like both probabilities to be as small as possible. It is clear, however, that there is a tradeoff between the two. The best we can hope for is that for a given probability of type I error, the procedure we choose will have as small a probability of type II error as possible.

DEFINITION 4.17: Power of a Test. *The* ***power*** *of a test is the probability that it will correctly lead to rejection of a false null hypothesis:*

$$\text{power} = 1 - \beta = 1 - \text{Prob(type II error)}. \qquad \textbf{(4-59)}$$

For a given significance level α, we would like β to be as small as possible. Since β is defined in terms of the alternative hypothesis, it depends on the value of the parameter.

EXAMPLE 4.31 Testing a Hypothesis About a Mean

For testing $H_0: \mu = \mu^0$ in a normal distribution with known variance σ^2, the decision rule is to reject the hypothesis if the absolute value of the z statistic, $\sqrt{n}(\bar{x} - \mu^0)/\sigma$, exceeds the predetermined critical value. For a test at the 5 percent significance level, we set the critical value at 1.96. The power of the test, therefore, is the probability that the absolute value of the test statistic will exceed 1.96 given that the true value of μ is, in fact, not μ^0. This depends on the alternative value of μ, as shown in Figure 4.7. Notice that for this test the

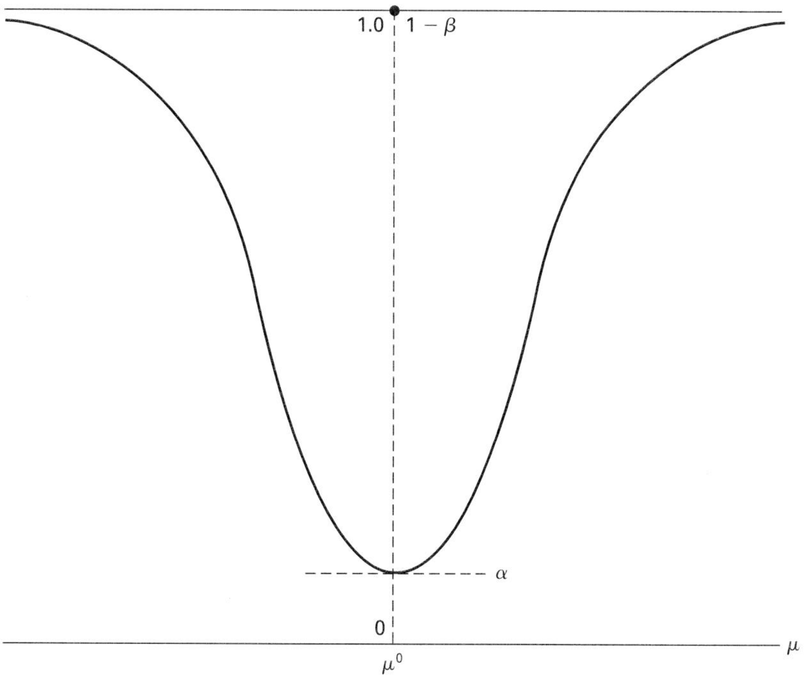

FIGURE 4.7 Power Function for a Test.

power is equal to the size at the point where μ equals μ^0. As might be expected, the test becomes more powerful the farther the true mean is from the hypothesized value.

Testing procedures, like estimators, can be compared using a number of criteria.

Definition 4.18: Most Powerful Test. *A test is* ***most powerful*** *if it has greater power than any other test of the same size.*

This is a very strong requirement. Since the power depends on the alternative hypothesis, we might require that the test be **uniformly most powerful (UMP),** that is, have greater power than any other test of the same size for all admissible values of the parameter. There are few situations in which a UMP test is available. We usually must be less stringent in our requirements. Nonetheless, the criteria for comparing hypothesis testing procedures are generally based on their respective power functions. A common and very modest requirement is that the test be unbiased.

Definition 4.19: Unbiased Test. *A test is* ***unbiased*** *if its power* $(1 - \beta)$ *is greater than or equal to its size* α *for all values of the parameter.*

If a test is **biased,** then for some values of the parameter, we are more likely to accept the null hypothesis when it is false than when it is true.

The use of the term *unbiased* here is unrelated to the concept of an unbiased estimator. Fortunately, there is little chance of confusion. Tests and estimators are clearly connected, however. The following criterion derives, in general, from the corresponding attribute of a parameter estimate.

DEFINITION 4.20: Consistent Test. *A test is* ***consistent*** *if its power goes to one as the sample size grows to infinity.*

EXAMPLE 4.32 Consistent Test About a Mean

A confidence interval for the mean of a normal distribution is $\bar{x} \pm t_{1-\alpha/2}(s/\sqrt{n})$, where $\bar{x}$ and s are the usual consistent estimators for μ and σ, n is the sample size, and $t_{1-\alpha/2}$ is the correct critical value from the t distribution with $n - 1$ degrees of freedom. For testing $H_0{:}\mu = \mu_0$ versus $H_1{:}\mu \neq \mu_0$, let the procedure be to reject H_0 if the confidence interval does not contain μ_0. Since $\bar{x}$ is consistent for μ, one can discern if H_0 is false as $n \to \infty$, with probability 1, because $\bar{x}$ will be arbitrarily close to the true μ. Therefore, this test is consistent.

As a general rule, a test will be consistent if it is based on a consistent estimator of the parameter.

4.9.2. Tests Based on Confidence Intervals

There is an obvious link between interval estimation and the sorts of hypothesis tests we have been discussing here. The confidence interval gives a range of plausible values for the parameter. Therefore, it stands to reason that if a hypothesized value of the parameter does not fall in this range of plausible values, the data are not consistent with the hypothesis, and it should be rejected. Consider, then, testing

$$H_0{:}\theta = \theta_0,$$
$$H_1{:}\theta \neq \theta_0.$$

We form a confidence interval based on $\hat{\theta}$ as described earlier:

$$\hat{\theta} - C_{1-\alpha/2}[\text{se}(\hat{\theta})] < \theta < \hat{\theta} + C_{1-\alpha/2}[\text{se}(\hat{\theta})].$$

H_0 is rejected if θ_0 exceeds the upper limit or is less than the lower limit. Equivalently, H_0 is rejected if

$$\left|\frac{\hat{\theta} - \theta_0}{\text{se}(\hat{\theta})}\right| > C_{1-\alpha/2}.$$

In words, the hypothesis is rejected if the estimate is too far from θ_0, where the distance is measured in standard error units. The critical value is taken from the t or standard normal distribution, whichever is appropriate.

EXAMPLE 4.33 Testing a Hypothesis About a Mean with a Confidence Interval

For the results in Example 4.28, test $H_0 : \mu = 1.98$ versus $H_1 : \mu \neq 1.98$, assuming sampling from a normal distribution:

$$t = \left| \frac{\bar{x} - 1.98}{s/\sqrt{n}} \right| = \left| \frac{1.63 - 1.98}{0.102} \right| = 3.43.$$

The 95 percent critical value for $t(24)$ is 2.064. Therefore, reject H_0. If the critical value for the standard normal table of 1.96 is used instead, the same result is obtained.

If the test is one-sided, as in

$$H_0 : \theta \geq \theta_0,$$
$$H_1 : \theta < \theta_0,$$

the critical region must be adjusted. Thus, for this test, H_0 will be rejected if a point estimate of θ falls sufficiently below θ_0. (Tests can usually be set up by departing from the decision criterion "What sample results are inconsistent with the hypothesis?")

EXAMPLE 4.34 One-Sided Test About a Mean

A sample of 25 from a normal distribution yields $\bar{x} = 1.63$ and $s = 0.51$. Test

$$H_0 : \mu \leq 1.5,$$
$$H_1 : \mu > 1.5.$$

Clearly, no observed $\bar{x}$ less than or equal to 1.5 will lead to rejection of H_0. Using the borderline value of 1.5 for μ, we obtain

$$\text{Prob}\left(\frac{\sqrt{n}(\bar{x} - 1.5)}{s} > \frac{5(1.63 - 1.5)}{0.51} \right) = \text{Prob}(t_{24} > 1.27).$$

This is approximately 0.11. This is not unlikely by the usual standards. Hence, at a significant level of 0.11, we would not reject the hypothesis.

4.9.3. Three Asymptotically Equivalent Test Procedures

The next several sections will discuss the most commonly used test procedures: the likelihood ratio, Wald, and Lagrange multiplier tests. [Extensive discussion of these procedures is given in Godfrey (1988).] We consider maximum likelihood estimation of a parameter θ and a test of the hypothesis $H_0 : c(\theta) = 0$. The logic of the tests can be seen in Figure 4.8.[21] The figure plots the log-likelihood

[21]See Buse (1982). Note that the scale of the vertical axis would be different for each curve. As such, the points of intersection have no significance.

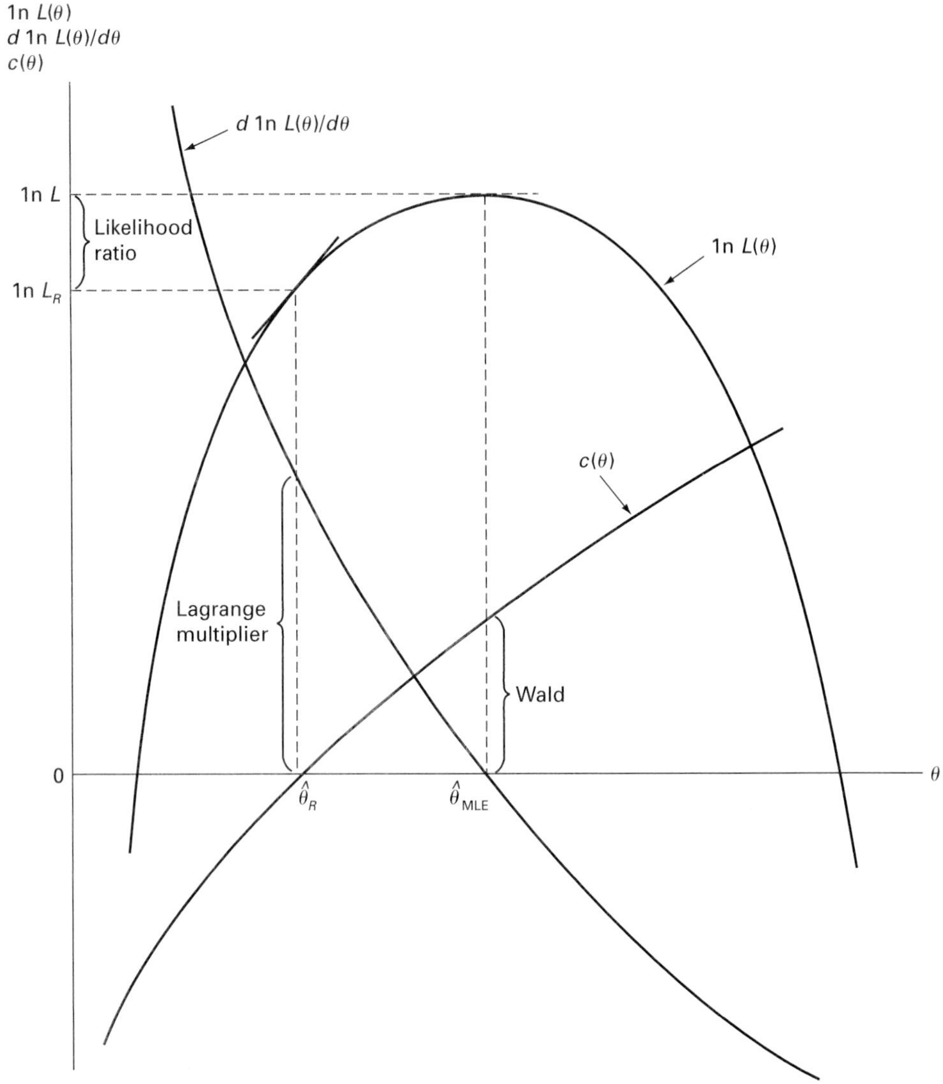

FIGURE 4.8 Three Bases for Hypothesis Tests.

function ln $L(\theta)$, its derivative with respect to θ, d ln $L(\theta)/d\theta$, and the constraint $c(\theta)$. There are three approaches to testing the hypothesis suggested in the figure:

- **Likelihood ratio test.** If the restriction $c(\theta) = 0$ is valid, imposing it should not lead to a large reduction in the log-likelihood function. Therefore, we base the test on the difference, ln L − ln L_R, where L is the value of the likelihood function at the unconstrained value of θ and L_R is the value of the likelihood function at the restricted estimate.

- **Wald test.** If the restriction is valid, $c(\hat{\theta}_{\text{MLE}})$ should be close to zero since the MLE is consistent. Therefore, the test is based on $c(\hat{\theta}_{\text{MLE}})$. We reject the hypothesis if this is significantly different from zero.
- **Lagrange multiplier test.** If the restriction is valid, the restricted estimator should be near the point that maximizes the log likelihood. Therefore, the slope of the log-likelihood function should be near zero at the restricted estimator. The test is based on the slope of the log-likelihood at the point where the function is maximized subject to the restriction.

These three tests are asymptotically equivalent, but they can behave rather differently in a small sample. Unfortunately, their small-sample properties are unknown, except in a few special cases. As a consequence, the choice among them is typically made on the basis of ease of computation. The likelihood ratio test requires calculation of both restricted and unrestricted estimators. If both are simple to compute, this will be a convenient way to proceed. The Wald test requires only the unrestricted estimator, and the Lagrange multiplier test requires only the restricted estimator. In some problems, one of these estimators may be much easier to compute than the other. For example, a linear model is simple to estimate but becomes nonlinear and cumbersome if a nonlinear constraint is imposed. In this case, the Wald statistic might be preferable. Alternatively, restrictions sometimes amount to the removal of nonlinearities, which would make the Lagrange multiplier test the simpler procedure.

4.9.3a. The Likelihood Ratio Test. Let $\boldsymbol{\theta}$ be a vector of parameters to be estimated, and let H_0 specify some sort of restriction on these parameters. Let $\hat{\boldsymbol{\theta}}_U$ be the maximum likelihood estimate of $\boldsymbol{\theta}$ obtained without regard to the constraints, and let $\hat{\boldsymbol{\theta}}_R$ be the constrained maximum likelihood estimator. If $\hat{L}_U$ and $\hat{L}_R$ are the likelihood functions evaluated at these two estimates, then the **likelihood ratio** is

$$\lambda = \frac{\hat{L}_R}{\hat{L}_U}. \tag{4-60}$$

This function must be between 0 and 1. Both likelihoods are positive, and $\hat{L}_R$ cannot be larger than $\hat{L}_U$. (A restricted optimum is never superior to an unrestricted one.) If λ is too small, doubt is cast on the restrictions.

An example from a discrete distribution helps to fix these ideas. In estimating from a sample of 10 from a Poisson distribution at the beginning of Section 4.5, we found the MLE of the parameter θ to be 2. At this value, the likelihood, which is the probability of observing the sample we did, is 0.104×10^{-8}. Are these data consistent with $H_0\colon \theta = 1.8$? $L_R = 0.936 \times 10^{-9}$, which is, as expected, smaller. This particular sample is somewhat less probable under the hypothesis.

The formal test procedure is based on the following result.

THEOREM 4.20: Distribution of the Likelihood Ratio Test Statistic. *Under regularity, the large sample distribution of $-2 \ln \lambda$ is chi-squared, with degrees of freedom equal to the number of restrictions imposed.*

The null hypothesis is rejected if this value exceeds the appropriate critical value from the chi-squared tables. Thus, for the Poisson example,

$$-2 \ln \lambda = -2 \ln\left(\frac{0.0936}{0.104}\right) = 0.21072.$$

This chi-squared statistic with one degree of freedom is not significant at any conventional level, so we would not reject the hypothesis that $\theta = 1.8$ on the basis of this test.[22]

It is tempting to use the likelihood ratio test to test a simple null hypothesis against a simple alternative. For example, we might be interested in the Poisson setting in testing $H_0: \theta = 1.8$ against $H_1: \theta = 2.2$. But the test cannot be used in this fashion. The degrees of freedom of the chi-squared statistic for the likelihood ratio test equals the reduction in the number of dimensions in the parameter space that results from imposing the restrictions. In testing a simple null hypothesis against a simple alternative, this is zero.[23] Second, one sometimes encounters an attempt to test one distributional assumption against another with a likelihood ratio test; for example, a certain model will be estimated assuming a normal distribution and then assuming a t distribution. The ratio of the two likelihoods is then compared to determine which distribution is preferred. This is also inappropriate. The parameter spaces, and hence the likelihood functions of the two cases, are unrelated.

4.9.3b. The Wald Test. A practical shortcoming of the likelihood ratio test is that it usually requires estimation of both the restricted and unrestricted parameter vectors. In complex models, one or the other of these estimates may be very difficult to compute. Fortunately, there are two alternative testing procedures, the Wald test and the Lagrange multiplier test, that circumvent this problem. Both tests are based on an estimator that is asymptotically normally distributed.

These two tests are based on the distribution of the full rank quadratic form considered at the end of Section 3.10.5. Specifically,

$$\text{If } \mathbf{x} \sim N_J[\boldsymbol{\mu}, \boldsymbol{\Sigma}], (\mathbf{x} - \boldsymbol{\mu})'\boldsymbol{\Sigma}^{-1}(\mathbf{x} - \boldsymbol{\mu}) \sim \text{chi-squared}[J]. \qquad \textbf{(4-61)}$$

In the setting of a hypothesis test, under the hypothesis that $E(\mathbf{x}) = \boldsymbol{\mu}$, the quadratic form has the chi-squared distribution. If the hypothesis that $E(\mathbf{x}) = \boldsymbol{\mu}$ is false, however, the quadratic form just given will, on average, be larger than it would be if the hypothesis were true.[24] This condition forms the basis for the test statistics discussed in this and the next section.

---

[22]Of course, our use of the large-sample result in a sample of 10 might be questionable.

[23]Note that because both likelihoods are restricted in this instance, there is nothing to prevent $-2 \ln \lambda$ from being negative.

[24]If the mean is not $\boldsymbol{\mu}$, the statistic in (4-61) will have a **noncentral chi-squared distribution.** This distribution has the same basic shape as the central chi-squared distribution, with the same degrees of freedom, but lies to the right of it. Thus, a random draw from the noncentral distribution will tend, on average, to be larger than a random observation from the central distribution.

Let $\hat{\boldsymbol{\theta}}$ be the vector of parameter estimates obtained without restrictions. We hypothesize a set of restrictions

$$H_0: \mathbf{c}(\boldsymbol{\theta}) = \mathbf{q}.$$

If the restrictions are valid, then at least approximately $\hat{\boldsymbol{\theta}}$ should satisfy them. If the hypothesis is erroneous, however, $\mathbf{c}(\hat{\boldsymbol{\theta}}) - \mathbf{q}$ should be farther from $\mathbf{0}$ than would be explained by sampling variability alone. The device we use to formalize this notation is the Wald test.

THEOREM 4.21: Distribution of the Wald Test Statistic. *The Wald statistic is*

$$\mathrm{W} = [\mathbf{c}(\hat{\boldsymbol{\theta}}) - \mathbf{q}]'(\mathrm{Var}[\mathbf{c}(\hat{\boldsymbol{\theta}}) - \mathbf{q}])^{-1}[\mathbf{c}(\hat{\boldsymbol{\theta}}) - \mathbf{q}]. \tag{4-62}$$

Under H_0, in large samples, W has a chi-squared distribution with degrees of freedom equal to the number of restrictions [i.e., the number of equations in $\mathbf{c}(\hat{\boldsymbol{\theta}}) - \mathbf{q} = \mathbf{0}$]. A derivation of the limiting distribution of the Wald statistic appears in Chapter 6.

This test is analogous to the chi-squared statistic in (4-61) if $\mathbf{c}(\hat{\boldsymbol{\theta}}) - \mathbf{q}$ is normally distributed, with a hypothesized mean of $\mathbf{0}$. A large value of W leads to rejection of the hypothesis. Note, finally, that W only requires computation of the unrestricted model. One must still compute the covariance matrix appearing in the preceding quadratic form. This is the variance of a possibly nonlinear function, which we treated earlier.

$$\begin{aligned} \mathrm{Var}[\mathbf{c}(\hat{\boldsymbol{\theta}}) - \mathbf{q}] &= \mathbf{C}\,\mathrm{Var}[\hat{\boldsymbol{\theta}}]\mathbf{C}', \\ \mathbf{C} &= \left[\frac{\partial \mathbf{c}(\hat{\boldsymbol{\theta}})}{\partial \hat{\boldsymbol{\theta}}'}\right]. \end{aligned} \tag{4-63}$$

That is, $\mathbf{C}$ is the $J \times K$ matrix whose jth row is the derivatives of the jth constraint with respect to the K elements of $\boldsymbol{\theta}$. A common application occurs in testing a set of linear restrictions.

For testing a set of linear restrictions $\mathbf{R}\boldsymbol{\theta} = \mathbf{q}$, the Wald test would be based on

$$\begin{aligned} H_0: \mathbf{c}(\boldsymbol{\theta}) - \mathbf{q} &= \mathbf{R}\boldsymbol{\theta} - \mathbf{q} = \mathbf{0}, \\ \mathbf{C} &= \left[\frac{\partial \mathbf{c}(\hat{\boldsymbol{\theta}})}{\partial \hat{\boldsymbol{\theta}}'}\right] = \mathbf{R}, \\ \mathrm{Var}[\mathbf{c}(\hat{\boldsymbol{\theta}}) - \mathbf{q}] &= \mathbf{R}\,\mathrm{Var}[\hat{\boldsymbol{\theta}}]\,\mathbf{R}', \end{aligned} \tag{4-64}$$

and

$$\mathrm{W} = [\mathbf{R}\hat{\boldsymbol{\theta}} - \mathbf{q}]'[\mathbf{R}\,\mathrm{Var}(\hat{\boldsymbol{\theta}})\mathbf{R}']^{-1}[\mathbf{R}\hat{\boldsymbol{\theta}} - \mathbf{q}].$$

The degrees of freedom is the number of rows in $\mathbf{R}$.

EXAMPLE 4.35 Wald Test for a Restriction

If $\mathbf{c}(\boldsymbol{\theta}) - \mathbf{q}$ is a single restriction, the Wald test will be the same as the test based on the confidence interval developed previously. If the test is

$$H_0: \theta = \theta_0 \quad \text{versus} \quad H_1: \theta \neq \theta_0,$$

then the earlier test is based on

$$z = \frac{|\hat{\theta} - \theta_0|}{s(\hat{\theta})}, \tag{4-65}$$

where s is the estimated asymptotic standard error. The test statistic is compared to the appropriate value from the standard normal table. The Wald test will be based on

$$\begin{aligned} W &= [(\hat{\theta} - \theta_0) - 0](\text{Var}[(\hat{\theta} - \theta_0) - 0])^{-1}[(\hat{\theta} - \theta_0) - 0] \\ &= \frac{(\hat{\theta} - \theta_0)^2}{\text{Var}[\hat{\theta}]} \\ &= z^2. \end{aligned} \tag{4-66}$$

Here W has a chi-squared distribution with one degree of freedom, which is the distribution of the square of the standard normal test statistic in (4-65).

EXAMPLE 4.36 Testing a Hypothesis About a Mean

For sampling from a normal distribution, the Wald statistic for testing the hypothesis that the mean takes a particular value is simply the square of the t statistic in Example 4.32 or the t ratio, which uses s^2 instead of σ^2 if σ^2 is unknown. Consider the multivariate example in Example 4.20, in which we obtained the maximum likelihood estimate of a vector of means. Suppose that we wished to test the hypothesis that the means of the M distributions were all equal. There are two cases to consider. First, we might have a particular value μ^0 in mind. Using the results from that example and the covariance matrix we derived in Example 4.21, the Wald statistic would be

$$\begin{aligned} W &= (\bar{\mathbf{x}} - \mu^0\mathbf{i})'\left(\frac{\hat{\sigma}^2}{n}\mathbf{I}\right)^{-1}(\bar{\mathbf{x}} - \mu^0\mathbf{i}) \\ &= \left(\frac{n}{s^2}\right)(\bar{\mathbf{x}} - \mu^0\mathbf{i})'(\bar{\mathbf{x}} - \mu^0\mathbf{i}), \end{aligned}$$

where $\bar{\mathbf{x}}$ is the vector of sample means. This statistic would be asymptotically distributed as chi-squared with M degrees of freedom. A slightly less restrictive hypothesis is that the means are equal, but we do not have a specific value in mind. This imposes only $M - 1$ restrictions. The statistic is the same one, except that μ^0 must be replaced with a consistent estimator of the common mean, for which we can use

$$\bar{\bar{x}} = \frac{1}{nM}\sum_{i=1}^{n}\sum_{j=1}^{M} x_{ij}.$$

To summarize, the Wald test is based on measuring the extent to which the unrestricted estimates fail to satisfy the hypothesized restrictions. There are two shortcomings of the Wald test. First, it is a pure significance test. The alternative hypothesis does not enter the computation. As such, its power may be limited in some settings. In fact, the test statistic tends to be rather large in applications. The second shortcoming is not shared by either of the other test statistics discussed here. The Wald test is not invariant to the formulation of the restrictions. For example, for a test of the hypothesis that a function $\theta = \beta/(1 - \gamma)$ equals a specific value θ_0 there are two approaches one might choose. A Wald test based directly on $\theta - \theta_0 = 0$ would use a statistic based on the variance of this nonlinear function. An alternative approach would be to analyze the linear restriction $\beta - \theta_0(1 - \gamma) = 0$, which is an equivalent, but linear, restriction. The Wald statistics for these two tests could be different. These two shortcomings have been widely viewed as compelling arguments against use of the Wald test. But, in its favor, the Wald test does not rely on a strong distributional assumption, as do the likelihood ratio and Lagrange multiplier tests. The recent econometrics literature is replete with applications that are based on distribution free estimation procedures, such as the GMM method. As such, in recent years, the Wald test has enjoyed a redemption of sorts.

4.9.3c. The Lagrange Multiplier Test. The third test procedure is the **Lagrange multiplier (LM)** or **efficient score** (or just **score**) test. It is based on the restricted model instead of the unrestricted model. Suppose that we maximize the log-likelihood subject to the set of constraints $\mathbf{c}(\boldsymbol{\theta}) - \mathbf{q} = \mathbf{0}$. Let $\boldsymbol{\lambda}$ be a vector of Lagrange multipliers and define the Lagrangean function

$$\ln L^*(\boldsymbol{\theta}) = \ln L(\boldsymbol{\theta}) + \boldsymbol{\lambda}'\mathbf{c}(\boldsymbol{\theta}).$$

The solution to the constrained maximization problem is the root of

$$\begin{aligned} \frac{\partial \ln L^*}{\partial \boldsymbol{\theta}} &= \frac{\partial \ln L(\boldsymbol{\theta})}{\partial \boldsymbol{\theta}} + \mathbf{C}'\boldsymbol{\lambda} = \mathbf{0}, \\ \frac{\partial \ln L^*}{\partial \boldsymbol{\lambda}} &= \mathbf{c}(\boldsymbol{\theta}) = \mathbf{0}, \end{aligned} \tag{4-67}$$

where $\mathbf{C}'$ is the transpose of the matrix in the second line of (4-63). If the restrictions are valid, imposing them will not lead to a significant difference in the maximized value of the likelihood function. In the first-order conditions, this will mean that the second term in the derivative vector will be small. In particular, $\boldsymbol{\lambda}$ will be small. We could test this directly; that is, test $H_0 : \boldsymbol{\lambda} = \mathbf{0}$, which leads to the Lagrange multiplier test. There is an equivalent simpler formulation, however. At the restricted maximum, the derivatives of the log-likelihood function are

$$\frac{\partial \ln L(\hat{\boldsymbol{\theta}})}{\partial \hat{\boldsymbol{\theta}}} = -\hat{\mathbf{C}}'\hat{\boldsymbol{\lambda}} = \hat{\mathbf{g}}_R. \tag{4-68}$$

If the restrictions are valid, at least within the range of sampling variability, $\hat{\mathbf{g}}_R = \mathbf{0}$. That is, the derivatives of the log-likelihood evaluated at the **restricted** parameter vector will be approximately zero. The vector of first derivatives of the log-likelihood is the vector of **efficient scores.** Since the test is based on this vector, it is called the **score test** as well as the Lagrange multiplier test. The variance of the first derivative vector is the information matrix, which we have used to compute the asymptotic covariance matrix of the MLE. The test statistic is based on reasoning analogous to that underlying the Wald test statistic.

THEOREM 4.22: Distribution of the Lagrange Multiplier Statistic. *The Lagrange multiplier test statistic is*

$$\mathrm{LM} = \left(\frac{\partial \ln L(\hat{\boldsymbol{\theta}}_R)}{\partial \hat{\boldsymbol{\theta}}_R}\right)' [\mathbf{I}(\hat{\boldsymbol{\theta}}_R)]^{-1} \left(\frac{\partial \ln L(\hat{\boldsymbol{\theta}}_R)}{\partial \hat{\boldsymbol{\theta}}_R}\right). \tag{4-69}$$

Under the null hypothesis, LM has a chi-squared distribution with degrees of freedom equal to the number of restrictions. All terms are computed at the restricted estimator.

The LM statistic has a useful form. Let $\hat{\mathbf{g}}_{iR}$ denote the ith term in the gradient of the log-likelihood function. Then,

$$\begin{aligned}\hat{\mathbf{g}}_R &= \sum_{i=1}^{n} \hat{\mathbf{g}}_{iR} \\ &= \mathbf{i}'\hat{\mathbf{G}}_R,\end{aligned}$$

where $\hat{\mathbf{G}}_R$ is the $n \times K$ matrix with ith row equal to $\hat{\mathbf{g}}'_{iR}$ and $\mathbf{i}$ is a column of ones. [See (4-52).] If we use the BHHH (outer product of gradients) estimator in (4-52) to estimate the Hessian, then

$$[\hat{\mathbf{I}}(\hat{\boldsymbol{\theta}})]^{-1} = [\hat{\mathbf{G}}'_R\mathbf{G}_R]^{-1}$$

and

$$\mathrm{LM} = \mathbf{i}'\hat{\mathbf{G}}_R[\hat{\mathbf{G}}'_R\mathbf{G}_R]^{-1}\hat{\mathbf{G}}'_R\,\mathbf{i}.$$

Now, since $\mathbf{i}'\mathbf{i}$ equals n, $\mathrm{LM} = n(\mathbf{i}'\mathbf{G}_R[\hat{\mathbf{G}}'_R\,\mathbf{G}_R]^{-1}\hat{\mathbf{G}}'_R\,\mathbf{i}/n) = nR_{\mathbf{i}}^2$, which is n times the uncentered multiple correlation coefficient in a linear regression of a column of ones on the derivatives of the log-likelihood function computed at the restricted estimator. We will encounter this result in various forms at several points in the book.[25]

---

[25]See especially Section 6.8.3.

4.9.4. An Example of the Test Procedures

Consider, again, the data in Table 4.1. In Example 4.22, the parameter β in the model

$$f(y_i, x_i, \beta) = \frac{1}{\beta + x_i} e^{-y_i/(\beta + x_i)} \tag{4-70}$$

was estimated by maximum likelihood. This exponential density is a restricted form of a more general gamma distribution:

$$f(y_i, x_i, \beta, \rho) = \frac{(\beta + x_i)^{-\rho}}{\Gamma(\rho)} y_i^{\rho - 1} e^{-y_i/(\beta + x_i)}. \tag{4-71}$$

The restriction is $\rho = 1$.[26] We consider testing

$$H_0: \rho = 1 \quad \text{versus} \quad H_1: \rho \neq 1$$

using the various procedures developed previously. The log-likelihood and its derivatives are

$$\ln L(\beta, \rho) = -\rho \sum_{i=1}^{n} \ln(\beta + x_i) - n \ln \Gamma(\rho) - \sum_{i=1}^{n} \frac{y_i}{\beta + x_i} + (\rho - 1) \sum_{i=1}^{n} \ln y_i,$$

$$\frac{\partial \ln L}{\partial \beta} = -\rho \sum_{i=1}^{n} \frac{1}{\beta + x_i} + \sum_{i=1}^{n} \frac{y_i}{(\beta + x_i)^2},$$

$$\frac{\partial \ln L}{\partial \rho} = -\sum_{i=1}^{n} \ln(\beta + x_i) - \frac{n\Gamma'(\rho)}{\Gamma(\rho)} + \sum_{i=1}^{n} \ln y_i,$$

$$\frac{\partial^2 \ln L}{\partial \beta^2} = \rho \sum_{i=1}^{n} \frac{1}{(\beta + x_i)^2} - 2\sum_{i=1}^{n} \frac{y_i}{(\beta + x_i)^3},$$

$$\frac{\partial^2 \ln L}{\partial \rho^2} = \frac{-n[\Gamma(\rho)\Gamma''(\rho) - (\Gamma'(\rho))^2]}{(\Gamma(\rho))^2},$$

$$\frac{\partial^2 \ln L}{\partial \beta\, \partial \rho} = -\sum_{i=1}^{n} \frac{1}{\beta + x_i}.$$

Maximum likelihood estimates are obtained by equating the two first derivatives to zero, with and without the restriction. The results are shown in Table 4.3.

Confidence Interval Test. A 95 percent confidence interval for ρ based on the unrestricted estimates is

$$3.151 \pm 1.96\sqrt{0.6625} = [1.556, 4.746].$$

This does not contain $\rho = 1$; therefore, the hypothesis is rejected.

---

[26]The gamma function $\Gamma(\rho)$ and the gamma distribution are described in Sections 3.4.5 and 5.4.2b.

TABLE 4.3 Maximum Likelihood Estimates

Quantity	*Unrestricted Estimate*	*Restricted Estimate*
β	−4.719	15.603
ρ	3.151	1.000
$\ln L$	−82.916	−88.436
$\partial \ln L/\partial\beta$	0.000	0.000
$\partial \ln L/\partial\rho$	0.000	7.914
$\partial^2 \ln L/\partial\beta^2$	−8.8534	−0.02166
$\partial^2 \ln L/\partial\rho^2$	−0.436	−32.894
$\partial^2 \ln L/\partial\beta\,\partial\rho$	−0.242	−0.6689
$\text{Var}[\hat{\beta}]$	5.773	46.164
$\text{Var}[\hat{\rho}]$	0.6625	0.000
$\text{Cov}[\hat{\beta}, \hat{\rho}]$	−1.747	0.000

Likelihood Ratio Test. The likelihood ratio test statistic is

$$\lambda = -2[-88.436 - (-82.916)] = 11.04.$$

The table value for the test, with one degree of freedom, is 3.842. The hypothesis is again rejected.

Wald Test. The Wald test is based on the unrestricted estimates. For this restriction,

$$\begin{aligned} c(\theta) - q &= \rho - 1, \\ dc(\hat{\rho})/d\hat{\rho} &= 1, \\ \hat{\text{Var}}[c(\hat{\rho}) - q] &= \hat{\text{Var}}[\hat{\rho}] = 0.6625, \\ W &= (3.151 - 1)[0.6625]^{-1}(3.151 - 1) = 6.984. \end{aligned}$$

The critical value is the same as the previous one; hence, H_0 is again rejected. Note that the Wald test statistic is the square of the corresponding test statistic that would be used in the confidence interval test, $|3.151 - 1|/(0.6625)^{1/2} = 2.626$.

Lagrange Multiplier Test. The Lagrange multiplier test is based on the restricted estimates

$$\text{LM} = [0.000 \quad 7.914]\begin{bmatrix} 0.02166 & 0.6689 \\ 0.6689 & 32.894 \end{bmatrix}^{-1}\begin{bmatrix} 0.000 \\ 7.914 \end{bmatrix} = 5.120.$$

The conclusion is the same as before.

Note that the latter three test statistics have substantially different values. It is possible to reach different conclusions depending on which one is used. For example, if the test had been carried out at the 1 percent significance level instead of the 5 percent level, the critical value from the chi-squared table would be 6.635. The hypothesis would then have been rejected if the test were based on the likelihood ratio or the Wald test statistics, but not if it were based on the LM statistic. Asymptotically, all three tests are equivalent. In a finite sample, however, differences such as these are to be expected, particularly in a small sample such as ours.[27] Unfortunately, there is no clear rule for how to proceed in such a case. Its possibility, however, does highlight the problem of relying on a particular significance level and drawing a firm reject/accept conclusion based on sample evidence.

EXERCISES

1. The following sample is drawn from a normal distribution with mean μ and standard deviation σ:

$$\mathbf{x} = 1.3, 2.1, 0.4, 1.3, 0.5, 0.2, 1.8, 2.5, 1.9, 3.2.$$

Compute the mean, median, variance, and standard deviation of the sample.

2. Using the data in the previous exercise, test the following hypotheses:

$$\mu \geq 2.0.$$
$$\mu \leq 0.7.$$
$$\sigma^2 = 0.5.$$

Using a likelihood ratio test, test the following hypothesis

$$\mu = 1.8, \quad \sigma^2 = 0.8.$$

3. Suppose that the following sample is drawn from a normal distribution with mean μ and standard deviation σ:

$$\mathbf{y} = 3.1, -0.1, 0.3, 1.4, 2.9, 0.3, 2.2, 1.5, 4.2, 0.4.$$

Test the hypothesis that the mean of the distribution that produced these data is the same as the mean that produced the data in Exercise 1. Test the hypothesis assuming that the variances are the same. Test the hypothesis that the variances are the same using an F test and using a likelihood ratio test. (Do not assume that the means are the same.)

4. A common method of simulating random draws from the standard normal distribution is to compute the sum of 12 draws from the uniform [0, 1] distribution and subtract 6. Can you justify this procedure?

5. Using the data in Exercise 1, form confidence intervals for the mean and standard deviation.

6. Based on a sample of 65 observations from a normal distribution, you obtain a *median* of 34 and a standard deviation of 13.3. Form a confidence in-

---

[27]For further discussion of this problem, see Berndt and Savin (1977).

terval for the mean. [Hint: Use the asymptotic distribution. See Example 4.15.] Compare your confidence interval with the one you would have obtained had the estimate of 34 been the sample mean instead of the sample median.

7. The random variable x has a continuous distribution $f(x)$ and cumulative distribution function $F(x)$. What is the probability distribution of the sample maximum? [Hint: In a random sample of n observations, x_1, $x_2, \ldots, x_n$, if z is the maximum, then every observation in the sample is less than or equal to z. Use the cdf.]

8. Assume that the distribution of x is $f(x) = 1/\theta, 0 \leq x \leq \theta$. In random sampling from this distribution, prove that the sample maximum is a consistent estimator of θ. Note: You can prove that the maximum is the maximum likelihood estimator of θ. But the usual properties do not apply here. Why not? [Hint: Attempt to verify that the expected first derivative of the log-likelihood with respect to θ is zero.]

9. In random sampling from the exponential distribution $f(x) = (1/\theta)e^{-x/\theta}$, $x > 0$, $\theta > 0$, find the maximum likelihood estimator of θ and obtain the asymptotic distribution of this estimator.

10. Suppose that in a sample of 500 observations from a normal distribution with mean μ and standard deviation σ, you are told that 35% of the observations are less than 2.1 and 55% of the observations are less than 3.6. Estimate μ and σ.

11. For random sampling from a normal distribution with nonzero mean μ and standard deviation σ, find the asymptotic joint distribution of the maximum likelihood estimators of σ/μ and μ^2/σ^2.

12. The random variable x has the following distribution: $f(x) = e^{-\lambda}\lambda^x/x!$, $x = 0, 1, 2, \ldots$. The following random sample is drawn: 1, 1, 4, 2, 0, 0, 3, 2, 3, 5, 1, 2, 1, 0, 0. Carry out a Wald test of the hypothesis that $\lambda = 2$.

13. Based on random sampling of 16 observations from the exponential distribution of Exercise 9, we wish to test the hypothesis that $\theta = 1$. We will reject the hypothesis if $\bar{x}$ is greater than 1.2 or less than 0.8. We are interested in the power of this test.

(a) Using the asymptotic distribution of $\bar{x}$, graph the asymptotic approximation to the true power function.

(b) Using the result discussed in Example 4.17, describe how to obtain the true power function for this test.

14. For the normal distribution $\mu_{2k} = \sigma^{2k}(2k)!/(k!2^k)$ and $\mu_{2k+1} = 0$, $k = 0, 1, \ldots$. Use this result to show that in Example 4.26, $\theta_1 = 0$, $\theta_2 = 3$, and

$$\mathbf{JVJ'} = \begin{bmatrix} 6 & 0 \\ 0 & 24 \end{bmatrix}.$$

15. *Testing for normality.* One method that has been suggested for testing whether the distribution underlying a sample is normal is to refer the statistic

$$L = n[\text{skewness}^2/6 + (\text{kurtosis} - 3)^2/24]$$

to the chi-squared distribution with two degrees of freedom. Using the data in Exercise 1, carry out the test.

16. *Mixture distribution.* Suppose that the joint distribution of the two random variables x and y is

$$f(x, y) = \frac{\theta e^{-(\beta+\theta)y}(\beta y)^x}{x!}, \quad \beta, \theta > 0, y \geq 0, x = 0, 1, 2, \ldots .$$

(a) Find the maximum likelihood estimators of β and θ and their asymptotic joint distribution.

(b) Find the maximum likelihood estimator of $\theta/(\beta + \theta)$ and its asymptotic distribution.

(c) Prove that $f(x)$ is of the form

$$f(x) = \gamma(1 - \gamma)^x, \quad x = 0, 1, 2, \ldots ,$$

and find the maximum likelihood estimator of γ and its asymptotic distribution.

(d) Prove that $f(y \mid x)$ is of the form

$$f(y \mid x) = \frac{\lambda e^{-\lambda y}(\lambda y)^x}{x!}, \quad y \geq 0, \lambda > 0.$$

Prove that $f(y \mid x)$ integrates to 1. Find the maximum likelihood estimator of λ and its asymptotic distribution. [Hint: In the conditional distribution, just carry the x's along as constants.]

(e) Prove that

$$f(y) = \theta e^{-\theta y}, \quad y \geq 0, \theta > 0.$$

Find the maximum likelihood estimator of θ and its asymptotic variance.

(f) Prove that

$$f(x \mid y) = \frac{e^{-\beta y}(\beta y)^x}{x!}, \quad x = 0, 1, 2, \ldots , \beta > 0.$$

Based on this distribution, what is the maximum likelihood estimator of β?

17. Suppose that x has the Weibull distribution

$$f(x) = \alpha\beta x^{\beta-1}e^{-\alpha x^{\beta}}, \quad x > 0, \alpha, \beta > 0.$$

(a) Obtain the log-likelihood function for a random sample of n observations.

(b) Obtain the likelihood equations for maximum likelihood estimation of α and β. Note that the first provides an explicit solution for α in terms of the data and β. But, after inserting this in the second, we obtain only an implicit solution for β. How would you obtain the maximum likelihood estimators?

(c) Obtain the second derivatives matrix of the log-likelihood with respect to α and β. The exact expectations of the elements involving β involve the derivatives of the gamma function and are quite messy analytically. Of course, your exact result provides an empirical estimator. How would you estimate the asymptotic covariance matrix for your estimators in part b?

(d) Prove that $\alpha\beta$ Cov$[\ln x, x^{\beta}] = 1$. [Hint: The expected first derivatives of the log-likelihood function are zero.]

18. The following data were generated by the Weibull distribution of Exercise 17:

1.3043	0.49254	1.2742	1.4019	0.32556	0.29965	0.26423
1.0878	1.9461	0.47615	3.6454	0.15344	1.2357	0.96381
0.33453	1.1227	2.0296	1.2797	0.96080	2.0070	

(a) Obtain the maximum likelihood estimates of α and β, and estimate the asymptotic covariance matrix for the estimates.

(b) Carry out a Wald test of the hypothesis that $\beta = 1$.

(c) Obtain the maximum likelihood estimate of α under the hypothesis that $\beta = 1$.

(d) Using the results of parts a and c, carry out a likelihood ratio test of the hypothesis that $\beta = 1$.

(e) Carry out a Lagrange multiplier test of the hypothesis that $\beta = 1$.

19. We consider forming a confidence interval for the variance of a normal distribution. As shown in Example 4.29, the interval is formed by finding c_{lower} and c_{upper} such that $\text{Prob}[c_{\text{lower}} < \chi^2[n-1] < c_{\text{upper}}] = 1 - \alpha$. The endpoints of the confidence interval are then $(n-1)s^2/c_{\text{upper}}$ and $(n-1)s^2/c_{\text{lower}}$. How do we find the narrowest interval? Consider simply minimizing the width of the interval $c_{\text{upper}} - c_{\text{lower}}$ subject to the constraint that the probability contained in the interval is $(1 - \alpha)$. Prove that for symmetric and asymmetric distributions alike, the narrowest interval will be such that the density is the same at the two endpoints.

20. Using the results in Example 4.25 and Section 4.6.2, estimate the asymptotic covariance matrix of the method of moments estimators of P and λ based on m_1' and m_2'. [Note: You will need to use the data in Table 4.1 to estimate $\mathbf{V}$.]

CHAPTER 5

Computation and Optimization

5.1. INTRODUCTION

The computation of empirical estimates by econometricians involves using digital computers and software written either by the researchers themselves or by others. It is also a surprisingly balanced mix of art and science. It is important for software users to be aware of how results are obtained, not only to understand routine computations, but also to be able to explain the occasional strange and contradictory results that do arise. Users of computer software can also benefit from an understanding of the limitations of programs they are using.[1] This chapter will describe some of the basic elements of computing and a number of tools that are used for computation of estimates.[2] We begin in Section 5.2 with a discussion of digital computing. The focus here is on the way that approximations used in digital computers affect the accuracy of computation in econometrics. Section 5.3 presents a few issues that arise in data generation, including the input of "live" data and the generation of artificial data using Monte Carlo methods. Section 5.4 then describes some techniques for computing certain quantities that are recurrent in econometric applications, in-

[1]It is one of the interesting aspects of the development of econometric methodology that the dissemination of certain techniques has proceeded in discrete jumps with the development of software. Noteworthy examples include the appearance, both around 1970, of G. K. Joreskog's LISREL [Joreskog and Sorbom (1981)] program, which spawned a still-growing industry in linear structural modelling, and TSP [Hall (1982)], which was among the first computer programs to accept symbolic representations of econometric models and which provided a significant advance in econometric practice with its LSQ procedure.

[2]Save for a few brief comments at the end of the chapter, this discussion is not intended to teach the reader how to write computer programs. For those who expect to do so, there are whole libraries of useful sources. Three very useful works are Kennedy and Gentle (1980), Abramovitz and Stegun (1971), and especially Press et al. (1986). The third of these provides a wealth of expertly written programs and a large amount of information about how to do computation efficiently and accurately.

cluding simulated data sets, sums, integrals, and derivatives. Some of these integrals are complicated functions that cannot be computed just by plugging a value into a formula; most do not have closed forms. In many cases, finding an optimum value of a function or estimating a covariance matrix involves computing exceedingly complicated derivatives of functions. Section 5.5 assembles all these tools in a discussion of optimization of functions. Some examples are given in Section 5.6.

5.2. DIGITAL COMPUTING

Digital computing refers to the method by which computers represent numerical values by assembling strings of binary digits, or bits (which take the value 0 or 1) to produce numbers. This is in contrast to *analog* computing, by which the representation of values is achieved with measurable continuous variables (analogs), such as length or voltage. (Readers old enough to remember what one looks like will recognize a slide rule as an analog computer.) The fundamental differences between the two types of computing are that analog computing is exact (at least in theory, although in practice only to within the precision of the device that measures the analog), but extremely slow and expensive, whereas digital computing is always only approximate but very fast and inexpensive. For our purposes, the crucial aspect of this comparison is that the approximation that digital computers do has implications for the accuracy of computation.

In a digital computer, any integer can be represented exactly with a single sign bit and a sufficiently long string of bits multiplying positive powers of two. Using $m + 1$ bits, which we label $b_0, b_1, \ldots, b_m$, an integer I may be written

$$I = [2b_m - 1] \times \sum_{i=0}^{m-1} b_i 2^i.$$

The range of values is thus $\pm 2^m - 1$. Computers differ on the number of bits used, but most use 16 or 32, which makes the ranges of values $\pm 32{,}767$ and $\pm 2{,}147{,}483{,}647$, respectively. One obvious limitation (among several) of integer-based computation is that no noninteger value can be represented this way.[3] For this reason, integers are only used for purposes such as indexing loops and pointing to locations such as where in a matrix a certain result should be placed. For manipulating real numbers, such as data (including those that take integer values) and the results of computations, we use a scientific notation, or **floating-point format,**

$$R = \text{sign} \times \text{mantissa} \times \text{base}^{\text{sign} \times \text{exponent}},$$

instead. The base can be any integer, although modern computers almost always use 16. The **mantissa** is a number in the interval (0, 1). The **range** of values

[3] Of course, a larger value can be represented with more bits. To continue our earlier distinction, note that the analog computer has no counterpart for measuring an integer except as a special case.

that can be stored is dependent on the range of the exponent, whereas the **precision** of the value depends on the number of digits in the mantissa. Both of these depend on how the number is stored and on how many bits in total are used to store the result. We can illustrate this format with a **single precision** number. On most computers this is a **double word** of 32 bits. One might represent R in 32 bit (single precision) with 6 bits for the exponent, including one for its sign, one for the sign of R, and the remaining 25 bits for the mantissa. The base 16 exponent ranges from -32 to $+32$, so the decimal value ranges in $\pm$ mantissa $\times 10^{\pm 38}$. The mantissa is

$$M = \sum_{i=1}^{25} b_i 2^{-i}.$$

Since 2^{-25} is approximately 3×10^{-8}, no number with more than eight significant digits can be represented exactly in this format. Using all 25 available bits for the mantissa produces an accuracy of somewhere between seven and eight digits. This rather overstates the case, in fact, since in practice, most computers use only 21 or 22 bits for the mantissa, so the accuracy is reduced to six to seven digits. Exponents are also represented differently to produce a range of about $10^{\pm 30}$.[4] No number with more than seven digits can be represented exactly, and, moreover, not all numbers within this precision can be. [Of course, the approximation can be quite close (to within six-digit accuracy).] Greater accuracy can be obtained by using more bits in the exponent and mantissa. **Double precision** values typically use 50 or 51 bits, which gives from 15 to 16 significant digits and decimal exponents that range in ± 308.

This may all sound like esoterica, but there are several implications for the computer user. Obviously, the range of values limits the sizes of numbers that can be stored and analyzed, although probably not in a substantive way for econometricians. But it also suggests several kinds of approximations that computers will do as they manipulate your data, and these approximations ultimately translate into rounding error and affect the accuracy of computations. We consider them in the next section.

5.3. DATA INPUT AND GENERATION

The data used in an econometric study can be broadly characterized as either real or simulated. "Real" data consist of actual measurements on some physical phenomenon such as the level of activity of an economy or the behavior of real consumers. For present purposes, the defining characteristic of such data is that they are generated outside the context of the empirical study and are gathered for the purpose of measuring some aspect of their real-world counterpart, such

[4]Our description is necessarily simplistic and purely illustrative. Modern computers use a different but similar representation of real numbers. One way that they are modified is so that integer values *can* be represented exactly.

as an elasticity of some aspect of consumer behavior. The alternative is simulated data, produced by the analyst with a random number generator, usually for the purpose of studying the behavior of econometric estimators for which the statistical properties are unknown or impossible to derive. This section will consider a few aspects of the manipulation of data with a computer. Section 5.3.1 begins the discussion with consideration of the accuracy of real data input into computer programs. The remainder of Section 5.3 is devoted to the use of randomly generated data by Monte Carlo methods. Section 5.3.4 describes **bootstrapping,** a technique that combines Monte Carlo methods with the analysis of real data.

5.3.1. Data Input

Before you can begin to analyze a data set, it must be moved "into the computer." The first implication of our discussion above is that there is an implicit restriction on the kinds of data that can be moved; they are limited to the precision that is being employed by the computer program. This varies from one to the next, but most take account of the following consideration: Even on modern computers with large amounts of memory, the physical memory of the machine is scarce for some purposes. Economic data are rarely accurate to more than six digits, so it would be enormously wasteful to store them in double precision. Most programs do not, although they do manipulate them in double precision (we turn to this issue below). Users should be aware of the convention in use by the program they are using. They may find that some data, such as lengthy identification numbers in a cross section or flow variables in a macroeconomic time series, are read into their computer with restricted accuracy because of this limitation. Occasionally, some trailing digits of a variable are lost on input.

There is an additional, subtle problem that can arise with modern software. To free the user from having to input data in fixed format (neat, compulsively lined-up columns), many programs treat numerical input as a string of characters that must be translated to a number. This enables them to read lines of data that contain numbers correctly placed logically but arranged freely on a line. Thus, a program might "read" a value by "parsing" it one character at a time, finding first some digits to the left of a decimal point, then the decimal point, then some digits to the right of a decimal point. At each step, the digit is multiplied by an appropriate power of 10 and then added to an accumulating result. Since there is an approximation needed at each step, as we discussed above, the end result can be surprising. It is not uncommon to find that a value such as 1.25 on input is displayed *after* input as 1.249998973. The difference is not large, but it might be unexpected.

5.3.2. Generating Pseudo–Random Numbers

Monte Carlo methods and Monte Carlo studies of estimators are enjoying a flowering in the econometrics literature. In these studies, data are generated internally in the computer using **pseudo–random number generators.** These are computer programs that generate sequences of values that appear to be strings of draws from a specified probability distribution. There are many types of random number generators, but most take advantage of the inherent inaccuracy of the digital representation of real numbers. The method of generation is usually by the following steps:

0. Set a seed.
1. Update the seed by $\text{seed}_j = \text{seed}_{j-1} \times \text{value}$.
2. $x = \text{seed} \times \text{value}$.
3. Transform x if necessary, then move x to desired place in memory.
4. Return to step 1.

EXAMPLE 5.1 Random Number Generator

The following simple pseudo–random number generator has been used in many computer programs:

$$P = 2147483647.0 \text{ (exactly)},$$
$$Q = 2147483655.0,$$
$$R = 16807.0.$$

Set initial value of the seed, then use

$$\text{seed} = \text{Mod}(R \times \text{seed}, P)$$
$$x = \text{seed}/Q.$$

The modulus function Mod(a, b) is the remainder after a is divided by b. Mod(11, 3) = 2, and so forth. This generator will produce several million pseudorandom draws from $U[0, 1]$ before recycling. For example, if the seed is set at 1234567.0, the first three values produced by this random number generator are

0.662177215034496,
0.212494543526572,
0.395806354111692.

5.3.2a. Sampling from a Standard Uniform $U[0, 1]$ Population. When sampling from a standard uniform $U[0, 1]$ population, the sequence is a kind of difference equation, since given the initial seed, x_j is ultimately a function of x_{j-1}. In most cases, the result at step 2 is a pseudodraw from the continuous uniform distribution in the range 0 to 1. This can then be transformed to a draw from another distribution by using the fundamental probability transformation. (See Exercises 15 and 16 in Chapter 3.)

There are several reasons that the sequence of draws is not truly a random sample from the uniform (or any other) distribution. First, the draws are not independent; they are a difference series, although if the generator is well constructed, the sequences it generates will pass randomness tests. Second, the draws are not truly random at all because they can be replicated just by resetting the seed to its initial value.[5] Third, the assumed distribution is only approximate. Fourth, regardless of how the generator is constructed, the random number generator will ultimately cycle back to its initial value and repeat the sequence. This may not happen until millions or billions of values have been drawn. But since many Monte Carlo studies require billions of values, this is not a trivial consideration. Finally, the choice of the seed itself is a problem. One method often used is to count the number of clock ticks since midnight on a system clock. On some systems, this allows 1000 ticks per second, which allows a large, albeit still finite, number of possible sequences.

5.3.2b. Sampling from Continuous Distributions. As soon as the sequence of $U[0, 1]$ values is obtained, there are several ways to transform them to the desired distribution. A common approach is to use the fundamental probability transform. For continuous distributions, this is done by treating the draw F as if F were $F(x)$, where F is the cdf of x. For example, if we desire draws from the exponential distribution with known θ, $F(x) = 1 - \exp(-\theta x)$. The inverse transform is $x = (-1/\theta)\ln(1 - F)$. For example, for a draw of 0.4 with $\theta = 5$, the associated x would be 0.1022. One of the most common applications is the draws from the standard normal distribution, which is complicated because there is no closed form for $\Phi^{-1}(F)$. There are several ways to proceed. The first is to approximate the inverse function. One well-known approximation is given in Abramovitz and Stegun (1971):

$$\Phi^{-1}(F) = x \approx \frac{c_0 + c_1 T + c_2 T^2}{1 + d_1 T + d_2 T^2 + d_3 T^3},$$

where $T = \ln(1/H^2)$ and $H = F$ if $F > 0.5$ and $1 - F$ otherwise. The sign is then reversed if $F < 0.5$. A second method is to transform the $U[0, 1]$ values directly to a standard normal value. The Box–Muller (1958) method is $z = (-2 \ln x_1)^{1/2} \cos(2\pi x_2)$, where x_1 and x_2 are two independent $U[0, 1]$ draws. A second $N[0, 1]$ draw can be obtained from the same two values by replacing cos with sin in the transformation. Sequences of draws from the standard normal distribution can be transformed easily into draws from other distributions by making use of the results in Section 3.4.2. The square of a standard normal has chi-squared [1], and the sum of K chi-squareds is chi-squared $[K]$. From this relationship, it is possible to produce samples from the chi-squared, t, F, and beta distributions. A related problem is obtaining draws from the truncated normal distribution. An obviously inefficient (albeit effective) method of draw-

---

[5] We will forgo the opportunity at this point to digress into philosophical questions of Newtonian versus quantum physics, the Heisenberg principle, and the current state of the universe. More down-to-earth considerations make this a positive feature of random number generation. Current trends in the econometrics literature dictate that readers of empirical studies be able to replicate applied work. Sometimes this requires authors to make their data available to interested researchers. In other cases, in Monte Carlo work, at least in principle, data can be replicated efficiently merely by providing the random number generator and the seed instead.

ing values from the truncated normal $[\mu, \sigma^2]$ distribution in the range $[L, U]$ is simply to draw F from the $U[0, 1]$ distribution, transform it first to a standard normal variate as discussed previously, then to the $N[\mu, \sigma^2]$ variate by using $x = \mu + \sigma\Phi^{-1}(F)$. Finally, the value x is retained if it falls in the range $[L, U]$ and discarded otherwise. This method will require, on average, $1/[\Phi(U) - \Phi(L)]$ draws per observation, which could be substantial. A direct transformation that requires only one draw is as follows. Let $P_j = \Phi[(j - \mu)/\sigma], j = L, U$. Then

$$x = \mu + \sigma\Phi^{-1}[P_L + F \times (P_U - P_L)]. \tag{5-1}$$

5.3.2c. Sampling from a Multivariate Normal Population. Samples from multivariate distributions can often be generated this way as well. The most common application involves draws from a multivariate normal distribution with specified mean $\boldsymbol{\mu}$ and covariance matrix $\boldsymbol{\Sigma}$. To sample from this K-variate distribution, we begin with a draw, $\mathbf{z}$, from the K-variate standard normal distribution just by stacking K independent draws from the univariate standard normal distribution. Let $\mathbf{T}$ be the square root of $\boldsymbol{\Sigma}$ such that $\mathbf{TT}' = \boldsymbol{\Sigma}$.[6] The desired draw is then just $\mathbf{x} = \boldsymbol{\mu} + \mathbf{Tz}$. A draw from a Wishart distribution of order K (which is a multivariate generalization of the chi-squared distribution) can be produced by computing $\mathbf{X}'\mathbf{M}^0\mathbf{X}$, where each row of $\mathbf{X}$ is a draw from the multivariate normal distribution. Note that the Wishart is a matrix-variate random variable and that a sample of M draws from the Wishart distribution ultimately requires $M \times N \times K$ draws from the standard normal distribution, however generated.

5.3.2d. Sampling from a Discrete Population. Discrete distributions, such as the Poisson, present a different problem. There is no obvious inverse transformation for most of these. One inefficient, albeit unfortunately, unavoidable method for some distributions is to draw the F, then search sequentially for the discrete value which has cdf equal to or greater than F. This makes intuitive sense, but can involve a lot of computation. The **rejection method** described by Press et al. (1986, pp. 203–209) will be more efficient (although not more accurate) for some distributions.

5.3.2e. The Gibbs Sampler. The following problem is pervasive in Bayesian statistics and econometrics, although it has many applications in classical problems as well. We are given a joint density $f(x, y_1, y_2, \ldots, y_K)$. We are interested in studying the characteristics, such as the mean, of the marginal distribution,

$$f(x) = \int_{y_K} \cdots \int_{y_1} f(x, y_1, y_2, \ldots, y_K)\, dy_1 \ldots dy_K.$$

[6]In practice, this is usually done with a Cholesky decomposition in which $\mathbf{T}$ is a lower triangular matrix. See Section 2.7.11.

The direct approach, actually doing the integration to obtain the marginal density, may be infeasible or at least complicated enough to seem so. But the **Gibbs sampler,** a technique that has begun to enjoy a surge of activity in the econometrics literature, allows one to generate random draws from the marginal density $f(x)$ without having to compute it.[7,8] The theory is presented in Casella and George (1992), among others. We will briefly sketch the mechanics of the technique and examine an application to a bivariate distribution.

Consider a two-variable case, $f(x, y)$ in which $f(x|y)$ and $f(y|x)$ are known. A "Gibbs sequence" of draws, $y_0, x_0, y_1, x_1, y_2, \ldots, y_M, x_M$, is generated as follows. First, y_0 is specified "manually." Then x_0 is obtained as a random draw from the population $f(x|y_0)$. Then y_1 is drawn from $f(y|x_1)$, and so on. The iteration is, generically, as follows.

1. Draw x_j from $f(x|y_j)$.
2. Draw y_{j+1} from $f(y|x_j)$.
3. Exit or return to step 1.

Note that the sequence of values are not independent; they are a **Markov chain.** If enough iterations are completed, the final observation x_M is a draw from $f(x)$ and likewise for y_M.[9] Characteristics of the marginal distributions, such as the means, variances, or values of the densities, can then be studied just by using corresponding averages of the functions of the observations.

EXAMPLE 5.2 Gibbs Sampler for a Bivariate Distribution

Suppose that the joint distribution of x and y is

$$f(x, y) \propto \binom{n}{x} y^{x+\alpha-1}(1-y)^{n-x+\beta-1}, x = 0, 1, \ldots, n, 0 < y < 1,$$

and we are interested in the marginal distribution of x. The marginal distribution of x is, in fact, a rather messy **beta-binomial** distribution. But there is no need to examine it directly. The conditional distributions are $f(x|y) =$ binomial(n, y) and $f(y|x) =$ beta$(x + \alpha, n - x + \beta)$. The Gibbs sequence can be generated by starting y at a value, say 0.5. A random draw from the binomial distribution can be obtained by summing n draws from the Bernoulli distribution with probability equal to y. Generate $d =$ a $U[0, 1]$ deviate, and set $z = \mathbf{1}\,(d \le y)$. Generating the beta-distributed variate is more difficult. For integer values of α and β, the following relationship can be used. If X and Y have

[7]A very readable introduction to the technique, on which we have based most of this discussion, is Casella and George (1992).

[8]The technique lends itself naturally to Bayesian applications, which is where most of the applications are to be found. See, for example, Albert and Chib (1993a,b), Chib (1992), Chib and Greenberg (1995), Chib (1992), Carlin and Chib (1995). There are classical applications as well, as surveyed in Tanner (1993) and Gelfand and Smith (1992).

[9]Determining when to stop the sequence is an interesting and yet unsolved problem. See Casella and George (1992, pp. 172–173), Raferty and Lewis (1992), Roberts (1992), and Zellner and Min (1992).

gamma distributions with parameters $\lambda_X = \lambda_Y = 1$, $P_X = \alpha$, and $P_Y = \beta$, then $X/(X + Y)$ has a beta distribution with parameters α and β. Now, we need to generate gamma variates with parameters $x + \alpha$ and $n - x + \beta$. For integer P, the desired gamma variate can be obtained as the sum of P independent exponentially distributed variates. These, in turn, can be generated just by summing the logs of independent $U[0, 1]$ variates, which solves our problem. For noninteger values, the generation is much more difficult. Approximation formulas for inverting the incomplete beta function (i.e., the cdf) are given in Abramovitz and Stegun (1971, p. 945).

EXAMPLE 5.3 Gibbs Sampling and Data Augmentation

Nearly all this book is devoted to classical or "frequentist" methods of estimation and inference. We will take an occasional detour into Bayesian econometrics, however, as our first brush with the subject, we will examine an intriguing application of the Gibbs sampler in the context of a model of discrete choice by Albert and Chib (1993a). We will wait until the end of Chapter 6 to develop some generalities about Bayesian estimation, so it should be noted that the following example is intended to illustrate the Gibbs sampler, not to introduce the Bayesian paradigm per se. Also, since full development of the discrete choice model must wait until Chapter 19, our discussion of it here will be quite vague.

The **probit model** developed in Chapter 19 describes how to fit a model for a binary outcome, which we denote $y_i = 1$ if some outcome occurs and $y_i = 0$ if not. For example, y_i might indicate whether a consumer decides to take some action ($y_i = 1$) or not ($y_i = 0$). We develop a model for the probability that $y_i = 1$ based on a vector of covariates $\mathbf{x}_i$ and a parameter vector $\boldsymbol{\beta}$. Now, under a Bayesian approach to this statistical application, we treat $\boldsymbol{\beta}$ as a random variable with a distribution that we would like to study by drawing a sample, $(\mathbf{X}, \mathbf{y})$. Before we draw any data, we have a **prior** belief about this distribution, which has the density $\pi(\boldsymbol{\beta})$, a mean called the **prior mean** $\boldsymbol{\beta}_0$, and a **prior covariance matrix** $\boldsymbol{\Sigma}_0$. The purpose of drawing the data is to revise our prior beliefs to incorporate the new information that they (the data) contain. The updated distribution is called the **posterior distribution,** denoted $\pi(\boldsymbol{\beta}\,|\,\text{data})$. Among the interesting things about the posterior that we would like to study is its mean, the **posterior mean.** This is the counterpart to a fixed-parameter vector that we might estimate. Presumably, the posterior mean will not equal $\boldsymbol{\beta}_0$.

Albert and Chib show the form of the posterior density and conclude that integrating it to obtain the posterior mean would be hopeless. They obtain a more appealing form, however, by *augmenting* $(\mathbf{X}, \mathbf{y})$ with a set of variables z_i that are drawn from an underlying continuous distribution with mean that depends on $\boldsymbol{\beta}$ such that $y_i = 1$ when $z_i > 0$ and $y_i = 0$ otherwise. They then form the *joint* posterior distribution for $\boldsymbol{\beta}$ and $\mathbf{z}$, $\pi(\boldsymbol{\beta}, \mathbf{z}\,|\,\mathbf{X}, \mathbf{y})$. The clever result that emerges is that the **conditional posterior** distribution for $\boldsymbol{\beta}\,|\,\mathbf{z}$ has a simple normal distribution with an easily computable mean, and the conditional posterior distributions for the observations in $\mathbf{z}|\boldsymbol{\beta}$ are easily computed truncated normal distributions. Therefore, the Gibbs sampling approach that we have been discussing will allow us to study the marginal posterior distribution for $\boldsymbol{\beta}$ by iterating a sampling procedure between these two conditional distributions.

5.3.3. Monte Carlo Studies

Simulated data generated by the methods of the previous section have various uses in econometrics. One of the more common applications is the derivation of the properties of estimators or in obtaining comparisons of the properties of estimators. For example, in time-series settings, most of the known results for characterizing the sampling distributions of estimators are asymptotic, large-sample results. But the typical time series is not very long, and descriptions that rely on T, the number of observations going to infinity, may not be very accurate. Exact, finite sample properties are usually intractable, however, which leaves the analyst with only the choice of learning about the behavior of the estimators experimentally.

In the typical application, one would either compare the properties of two or more estimators while holding the sampling conditions fixed or study how the properties of an estimator are affected by changing conditions such as the sample size or the value of an underlying parameter.

EXAMPLE 5.4 Monte Carlo Study of the Mean versus the Median

In Example 4.15, we compared the asymptotic distributions of the sample mean and the sample median in random sampling from the normal distribution. The basic result is that both estimators are consistent, but the mean is more efficient by a factor of

$$\frac{\text{Asy. Var[Median]}}{\text{Asy. Var[Mean]}} = \frac{\pi}{2}.$$

This is a useful result, but it does not tell which is the better estimator in small samples, nor does it suggest how the estimators would behave in some other distribution. It is known that the mean is affected by outlying observations whereas the median is not. The effect is averaged out in large samples, but the small sample behavior might be very different. To investigate the issue, we constructed the following experiment: We sampled n observations from the t distribution with d degrees of freedom by sampling $d+1$ values from the standard normal distribution and then computing

$$t_{ir} = \frac{z_{ir,d+1}}{\sqrt{\frac{1}{d}\sum_{l=1}^{d} z_{ir,l}^2}}, \quad i = 1, \ldots, n.$$

The t distribution with a low value of d was chosen because it has very thick tails and because large, outlying values have high probability. For each value of n and d, we generated $R = 100$ replications. For each of the 100 replications, we

TABLE 5.1 Mean Squared Errors, Ratio, Median to Mean

	Degrees of Freedom		
Observations	***3***	***6***	***10***
10	0.2952	0.9161	1.0317
25	0.8903	0.9308	1.0880
100	1.0000	1.1986	1.3451

obtained the mean and median. Since both are unbiased, we compared the mean squared errors, using

$$M_{n,d} = \frac{\frac{1}{R}\sum_{r=1}^{R}(\text{median} - 0)^2}{\frac{1}{R}\sum_{r=1}^{R}(\bar{x} - 0)^2}.$$

Table 5.1 shows the results of the Monte Carlo experiment. The results confirm what intuition would suggest. As the sample size increases, the sample mean becomes the better estimator. Likewise, as the degrees of freedom parameter increases, which brings the distribution closer to the normal distribution, the sample mean once again becomes more efficient. What might be surprising is the apparent overwhelming advantage of the median in small samples when the distribution is very nonnormal.

The preceding is a very small, straightforward application of the technique. In the typical substantive study, there are many more parameters to be varied and more dimensions upon which the results are to be studied. One of the practical problems in this setting is how to organize the results. There is a tendency in Monte Carlo work to proliferate tables. It is incumbent on the analyst to collect the results in an easy-to-use fashion. For example, this requires some judgment on how finely one should vary the parameters of interest. One useful possibility that will often mimic the thought process of the reader is to collect the results of bivariate tables such as the preceding in carefully designed contour plots. For example, our experimental results could have been presented in a figure such as Figure 5.1. This device would allow as fine a gradation of the degrees of freedom parameter as desired, although one must decide how informative the greater detail really would be.

There are any number of situations in which Monte Carlo simulation offers the only possibility of learning about finite sample properties of estimators. Still, there are a number of problems with Monte Carlo studies. To achieve any level of generality, the number of parameters that must be varied and hence the amount of information that must be distilled can become enormous. Second, they are limited by the design of the experiments, so the results they pro-

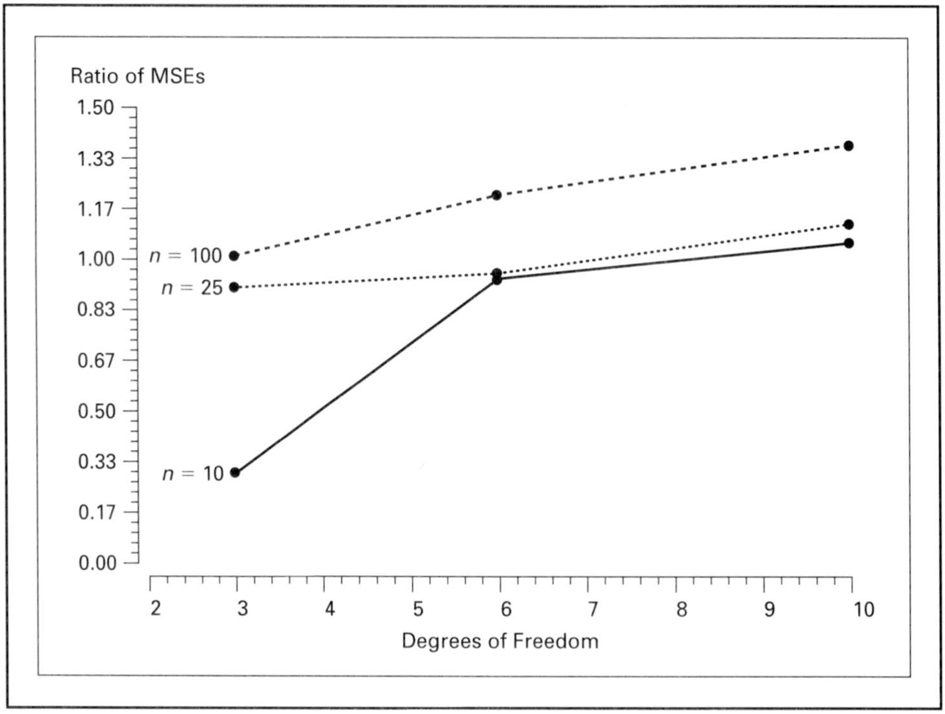

FIGURE 5.1 Monte Carlo Results.

duce are rarely generalizable. For our example, we may have learned something about the t distribution. But the results that would apply in other distributions remain to be described. And, unfortunately, real data will rarely conform to any specific distribution, so no matter how many other distributions we analyze, our results would still only be suggestive. In more general terms, this problem of **specificity** [Hendry (1984)] limits most Monte Carlo studies to quite narrow ranges of applicability. There are very few that have proved general enough to have provided a general, widely cited result.[10]

5.3.4. Bootstrapping

The technique of **bootstrapping** is used to obtain a description of the sampling properties of empirical estimators using the sample data themselves, rather than broad theoretical results. Suppose that $\hat{\boldsymbol{\theta}}_n$ is an estimate of a parameter vector $\boldsymbol{\theta}$ based on a sample $\mathbf{X} = (\mathbf{x}_1, \ldots, \mathbf{x}_n)$. An approximation to the statistical properties of $\hat{\boldsymbol{\theta}}_n$ can be obtained by studying a sample of bootstrap estimators $\hat{\boldsymbol{\theta}}(b)_m$, $b = 1, \ldots, B$, obtained by sampling m observations, *with*

[10] Two that have withstood the test of time are Griliches and Rao (1969) and Kmenta and Gilbert (1968).

replacement, from $\mathbf{X}$ and recomputing $\hat{\boldsymbol{\theta}}$ with each sample. (The bootstrap sample size, m, may be larger or smaller than n.[11]) This is done a total of B times, and the desired sampling characteristic is computed from

$$\hat{\boldsymbol{\Theta}} = [\hat{\boldsymbol{\theta}}(1)_m, \ldots, \hat{\boldsymbol{\theta}}(B)_m].$$

For example, if it were known that the estimator were consistent and if n were reasonably large, one might approximate the asymptotic covariance matrix of the estimator $\hat{\boldsymbol{\theta}}$ by using

$$\text{Est. Asy. Var}[\hat{\boldsymbol{\theta}}] = \frac{1}{B}\sum_{b=1}^{B}[\hat{\boldsymbol{\theta}}(b)_m - \hat{\boldsymbol{\theta}}_n][\hat{\boldsymbol{\theta}}(b)_m - \hat{\boldsymbol{\theta}}_n]'.$$

This technique was developed by Efron (1979) and has been appearing with increasing frequency in the applied econometrics literature. [See, for example, Veall (1987, 1992), Vinod (1993), and Vinod and Raj (1994).] An application of this technique to a model of binary choice is described in Section 19.5.3.

5.4. COMPUTATION IN ECONOMETRICS

The preceding showed how a number is translated from a symbol on a page to a physical entity in a computer that can be manipulated as part of a statistical study. This section will discuss some aspects of data manipulation.

5.4.1. Summation and Multiplication

The large majority of the time and effort in computation in econometric estimation is the accumulation of sums of observations, squares and cross products, and functions of observations. Most of the remainder consists of fairly straightforward matrix manipulations, including addition and subtraction, multiplication, and inversion. The latter usually involve matrices of quite manageable dimensions. In terms of the arithmetic operations, our concern here is with only a single aspect of digital computation. Using scientific notation, addition and subtraction are accomplished (essentially) by first converting one base or the other so that the two are equal, then adding or subtracting the resulting mantissas. Now, recall that in single precision, a mantissa will not have more than seven significant digits. Therefore, there are many combinations of operations that will result in lost digits. Consider, for example, summing the squares of a dollar denominated income variable. Suppose that an observation is 12,515, which can be represented in full precision (if not exactly) in single pre-

[11]A tip on sampling observations: One can sample an observation from the discrete uniform distribution $[1, 2, \ldots, n]$ by multiplying n by a draw from the continuous $U[0, 1]$ distribution. The naive application of j = the integer part of $U \times n$, however (once again, because of the nature of digital computing), will eliminate the nth observation from the pool because this uses truncation rather than rounding. In a small sample, this could be substantive. The appropriate draw is obtained as $INT(U \times n + 0.5)$, where n is represented as a floating-point number, not an integer, for purpose of the computation.

cision. The square is 156,635,225, which in single precision will lose the last three significant digits. As in an earlier case, the error is small, but not trivial. But notice what happens if the square of this value is added to the square of a number less than 10. The second value will disappear from the result. A solution to this is to do such computations in double precision. But computer programs differ in how this is to be done. For example, if your data set contains a variable *INCOME* and you wish to create a second variable *INCOMESQ* as the square of the first, what most programs do is the following:

1. "Read" *INCOME* in single precision, at full accuracy.
2. During transformation, convert the observation on *INCOME* to double precision and compute $INCOME^2$.
3. Store $INCOME^2$ once again as single precision.

The unfortunate upshot is that the computer will know the true value of income squared at one point but forget the trailing digits immediately. There is little one can do to avoid this problem. But it does bring one consequence of which users should be aware. The identical computations with different computer programs will occasionally produce slightly different results. Sometimes this is a result of different methods. But another explanation is the mode of data storage. A program that stores data in double precision will get a slightly different answer, even for routine computations such as least squares coefficients, from one that stores data in single precision if data are transformed in such a way as to result in lost digits.

Another related problem arises when data are of different scales. Normally, one would not add three-digit numbers to nine-digit numbers. But consider a regression that contains income, income squared, and number of children. The moment matrix, $\mathbf{X}'\mathbf{X}$, which must be inverted, is manipulated by any inversion routine by various rearrangements of linear combinations of its columns. One would be hard pressed to find a commercial statistical package that did not use double precision for the inversion, but any equation that involves two diagonal elements of this matrix will involve numbers of order 10^{18} and 10^2. The total will be completely dominated by the former and will be inherently unstable as a result, possibly even in double precision. The problem can impede conversion of iterative computations and can produce apparent singularities in perfectly well behaved problems. The solution from the point of view of a computer user is to avoid mixing variables of very different orders of magnitude in the same equation. The practical solution involves nothing more than simply scaling variables of large orders of magnitude by some power of 10. Coefficients will adjust correspondingly, and nothing will be lost.

A final consideration is, once again, a consequence of approximation in a digital computer. When should a computer program decide that a matrix is singular? In theory, the answer is when its determinant is zero, or when a Cholesky value or a pivot value is zero if using Gaussian elimination for inversion. But recall that in a digital computer, rounding error often obscures the true value of a quantity. This is an especially common problem in matrix inversion, particularly when the matrices being inverted are large. Cholesky inversion is very accurate. But in the process of computing this matrix, the quantity that will reveal the singularity of a matrix is computed as a product, so it will never be exactly zero. Programs that do this calculation will test the product, or sum of logs, against some small value instead. As a consequence, simply scaling a matrix, or one or more of its columns, can affect this test. As a computer user, the practical implication is that this is likely to become a problem, once again, when data are of very different magnitudes and when data are of very large scale. The strategy is, as before, to scale the data.

At this point, we will turn from problems in computation to methods. The final observation is that if you are writing programs of your own, aside from using effective algorithms, you should be using double precision for any manipulations when possible. If you are using third-party software, this is almost certainly a nonissue; expert programmers have been well aware of these considerations for decades, and modern software is almost surely going to be satisfactorily accurate, given well-conditioned data to begin with.

5.4.2. Computing Integrals

One advantage of computers is their ability to compute approximations to complex functions such as logs and exponents rapidly. The basic functions, such as these, trigonometric functions, and so forth, are standard parts of the libraries of programs that accompany all scientific computing installations.[12] But one of the very common applications that often requires some high-level creativity by econometricians is the evaluation of integrals that do not have simple closed forms and that do not typically exist in "system libraries." We will consider several of these in this section. We will not go into detail on the nuts and bolts of how to compute integrals with a computer; rather, we will turn directly to the most common applications in econometrics.

5.4.2a. The Standard Normal Cumulative Distribution Function. The standard normal cumulative distribution function (cdf) is ubiquitous in econometric models. Yet this most homely of applications must be computed by approximation. There are a number of ways to do so.[13] Recall that what we desire is

$$\Phi(x) = \int_{-\infty}^{x} \phi(t)\, dt, \quad \text{where } \phi(x) = \frac{1}{\sqrt{2\pi}} e^{-x^2/2}.$$

One way to proceed is to use a Taylor series:

$$\Phi(x) \approx \sum_{i=0}^{M} \frac{1}{i!} \frac{d^i \Phi(x_0)}{dx_0^i} (x - x_0)^i.$$

[12]Of course, at some level, these must have been programmed as approximations by someone.

[13]Many system libraries provide a related function, the *error function*, $\text{erf}(x) = (2/\sqrt{\pi}) \int_0^\infty e^{-t^2}\, dt$. If this is available, the normal cdf can be obtained as $\Phi(x) = \frac{1}{2} + \frac{1}{2}\,\text{erf}(x/\sqrt{2})$.

The normal cdf has some advantages for this approach. First, the derivatives are simple and not integrals. Second, the function is **analytic;** as $M \to \infty$, the approximation converges to the true value. Third, the derivatives have a simple form, which we have met before; they are the Hermite polynomials that appear in Exercise 18 of Chapter 3, and they can be computed by a simple recursion. The 0th term in the expansion above is $\Phi(x)$ evaluated at the expansion point. The first derivative of the cdf is the pdf, so the terms from 2 onward are the derivatives of $\phi(x)$, once again evaluated at x_0. The derivatives of the standard normal pdf obey the recursion

$$\phi^i/\phi(x) = x\phi^{i-1}/\phi(x) + (i-1)\phi^{i-2}/\phi(x),$$

where ϕ^i is $d^i\phi(x)/dx^i$. The 0 and 1 terms in the sequence are 1 and $-x$. The next term is $x^2 - 1$, followed by $3x - x^3$ and $x^4 - 6x^2 + 3$, and so on. The approximation can be made more accurate by adding terms. Consider using a fifth-order Taylor series approximation around the point $x = 0$, where $\Phi(0) = 0.5$ and $\phi(0) = 0.3989423$. Evaluating the derivatives at 0 and assembling the terms produces the approximation

$$\Phi(x) \approx \tfrac{1}{2} + 0.3989423[x - x^3/6 + x^5/40].$$

[Some of the terms (every other one, in fact) will conveniently drop out.] Figure 5.2 shows the actual values (F) and approximate values (FA) over the

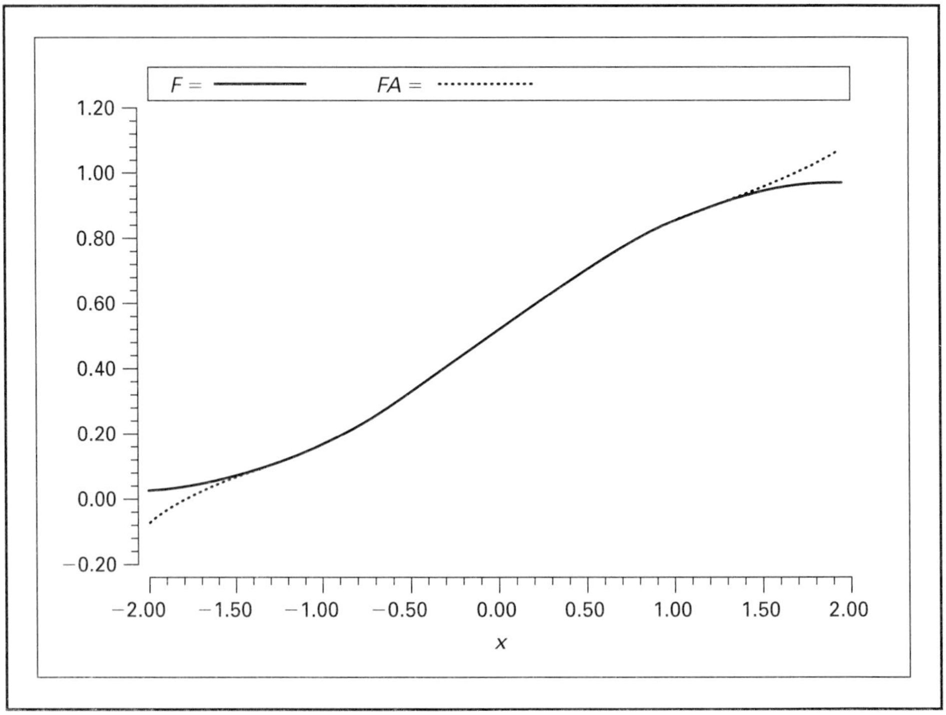

FIGURE 5.2 Approximation to Normal cdf.

range −2 to 2. The figure shows two important points. First, the approximation is remarkably good over most of the range. Second, as is usually true for Taylor series approximations, the quality of the approximation deteriorates as one gets far from the expansion point.

Unfortunately, it is the tail areas of the standard normal distribution that are usually of interest, so the preceding is likely to be problematic. An alternative approach that is used much more often is a polynomial approximation reported by Abramovitz and Stegun (1971, p. 932):

$$\Phi(-|x|) = \phi(x) \sum_{i=1}^{5} a_i t^i + \epsilon(x), \quad \text{where } t = 1/[1 + a_0|x|].$$

(The complement is taken if x is positive.) The error of approximation is less than $\pm 7.5 \times 10^{-8}$ for all x. (Note that the error exceeds the function value at $|x| > 5.7$, so this is the operational limit of this approximation.)

5.4.2b. The Gamma and Related Functions. The standard normal cdf is probably the most common application of numerical integration of a function in econometrics. Another very common application is the class of gamma functions. For positive constant P, the gamma function is

$$\Gamma(P) = \int_0^{\infty} t^{P-1} e^{-t}\, dt.$$

The gamma function obeys the recursion $\Gamma(P) = (P-1)\Gamma(P-1)$, so for integer values of P, $\Gamma(P) = (P-1)!$. This suggests that the gamma function can be viewed as a generalization of the factorial function for noninteger values. Another convenient value is $\Gamma(\frac{1}{2}) = \sqrt{\pi}$. By making a change of variable, it can be shown that for positive constants a, c, and P,

$$\int_0^{\infty} t^{P-1} e^{-at^c}\, dt = \int_0^{\infty} t^{-(P+1)} e^{-a/t^c}\, dt = \left(\frac{1}{c}\right) a^{-P/c}\, \Gamma\left(\frac{P}{c}\right).$$

As a generalization of the factorial function, the gamma function will usually overflow for the sorts of values of P that normally appear in applications. The log of the function should normally be used instead. The function $\ln \Gamma(P)$ can be approximated remarkably accurately with only a handful of terms and is very easy to program. A number of approximations appear in the literature; they are generally modifications of **Sterling's approximation** to the factorial function $P! \approx (2\pi P)^{1/2} P^P e^{-P}$, so

$$\ln \Gamma(P) \approx (P - 0.5)\ln P - P + 0.5\ln(2\pi) + C + \epsilon(P),$$

where C is the correction term [see, e.g., Abramovitz and Stegun (1971, p. 257), Press et al. (1986, p. 157), or Rao (1973, p. 59)] and $\epsilon(P)$ is the approximation error.[14]

[14]For example, one widely used formula is $C = z^{-1}/12 - z^{-3}/360 - z^{-5}/1260 + z^{-7}/1680 - q$, where $z = P$ and $q = 0$ if $P > 18$, or $z = P + J$ and $q = \ln[P(P+1)(P+2)\cdots(P+J-1)]$, where $J = 18 - \text{int}(P)$, if not.

The derivatives of the gamma function are

$$\frac{d^r\Gamma(P)}{dP^r} = \int_0^\infty (\ln P)^r t^{P-1} e^{-t} dt.$$

The first two derivatives of $\ln \Gamma(P)$ are denoted $\Psi(P) = \Gamma'/\Gamma$ and $\Psi'(P) = (\Gamma\Gamma'' - \Gamma'^2)/\Gamma^2$ and are known as the **digamma** and **trigamma** functions.[15] The beta function, denoted $\beta(a, b)$,

$$\beta(a, b) = \int_0^1 t^{a-1}(1 - t)^{b-1}\, dt = \frac{\Gamma(a)\Gamma(b)}{\Gamma(a + b)},$$

is related.

5.4.2c. Approximating Integrals by Quadrature. The digamma and trigamma functions, and the gamma function for noninteger values of P and values that are not integers plus $\frac{1}{2}$, do not exist in closed form and must be approximated. Most other applications will also involve integrals for which no simple computing function exists. The simplest approach to approximating

$$F(x) = \int_L^U f(x)\, dx$$

is likely to be a variant of Simpson's rule, or the trapezoid rule. For example, one approximation [see Press et al. (1986, p. 108)] is

$$F(x) \approx \Delta[\tfrac{1}{3}f_1 + \tfrac{4}{3}f_2 + \tfrac{2}{3}f_3 + \tfrac{4}{3}f_4 + \cdots + \tfrac{2}{3}f_{N-2} + \tfrac{4}{3}f_{N-1} + \tfrac{1}{3}f_N],$$

where f_j is the function evaluated at N equally spaced points in $[L, U]$ including the endpoints and $\Delta = (L - U)/(N - 1)$. There are a number of problems with this method, most notably that it is difficult to obtain satisfactory accuracy with a moderate number of points.

Gaussian quadrature is a popular method of computing integrals. The general approach is to use an approximation of the form

$$\int_L^U W(x)f(x)\, dx \approx \sum_{j=1}^{M} w_j f(a_j),$$

where $W(x)$ is viewed as a "weighting" function for integrating $f(x)$, w_j is the **quadrature weight,** and a_j is the **quadrature abscissa.** Different weights and abscissas have been derived for several weighting functions. Two weighting functions common in econometrics are

$$W(x) = x^c e^{-x},\ x \in [0, \infty),$$

[15] Tables of specific values for the gamma, digamma, and trigamma functions appear in Abramovitz and Stegun (1971).

for which the computation is called **Gauss-Laguerre quadrature,** and

$$W(x) = e^{-x^2}, x \in (-\infty, \infty),$$

for which the computation is called **Gauss–Hermite quadrature.** The theory for deriving weights and abscissas is given in Press et al. (1986, pp. 121–125). Tables of weights and abscissas for many values of M are given by Abramovitz and Stegun (1971).

EXAMPLE 5.5 Probabilities for a Discrete Choice Model

In "A Heteroscedastic Extreme Value Model of Intercity Mode Choice," Bhat (1995) derives a model for the choice among J discrete alternatives in which the probability that an individual i will make choice j is

$$\text{Prob}(j) = \int_{-\infty}^{\infty} \prod_{l \neq j} F[\theta_l(\boldsymbol{\beta}'\mathbf{x}_l - \boldsymbol{\beta}'\mathbf{x}_j - (\ln u)/\theta_j)]e^{-u}\, du,$$

where

$$\text{F}(t) = \exp(-e^{-t}).$$

This (horrendous) integral has no closed form but is handled easily in Bhat's study by using Gauss–Hermite quadrature.

EXAMPLE 5.6 The Bivariate Normal CDF

A longstanding challenge in applied econometrics has been to obtain a fast and accurate method of computing cumulative probabilities for the bivariate normal distribution. One approach used in some computer programs is based on a quadrature method.[16] We are interested in

$$F(x, y) = \int_{Y<y} \int_{X<x} p(X, Y)\, dX\, dY,$$

where $p(x, y)$ is the bivariate normal pdf. [See (3-77).] One approach is to write $p(x, y) = p(x \mid y)p(y)$:

$$\begin{aligned} F(x, y) &= \int_{Y<y} \int_{X<x} p(X \mid Y)p(Y)\, dX\, dY \\ &= \int_{Y<y} \left[\int_{X<x} p(X \mid Y)\, dX \right] p(Y)\, dY. \end{aligned}$$

The inner integral is

$$\int_{-\infty}^{x} \frac{1}{\sqrt{1-\rho^2}} \phi\left(\frac{X - \rho Y}{\sqrt{1-\rho^2}}\right) dX = \Phi(x \mid Y) = h(Y).$$

[16]For instance, the 1995 LIMDEP, Econometric Software.

The univariate normal density is $p(y) = (2\pi)^{-1/2}\exp(-\frac{1}{2}y^2)$, so the full expression to be evaluated is

$$F(x, y) = \int_{-\infty}^{y} \frac{h(Y)}{\sqrt{2\pi}} e^{-Y^2/2}\, dY.$$

This is amenable to quadrature methods. (Note that since the integral is incomplete, a weighting somewhat different from the Gauss–Hermite quadrature method is used.)

5.4.2d. Monte Carlo Integration. The quadrature methods have proved very useful in empirical research and are surprisingly accurate even for a small number of points. There are integrals that defy treatment in this form, however. Recent work has brought many advances in techniques for evaluating complex integrals by using Monte Carlo methods rather than direct numerical approximations.

EXAMPLE 5.7 Fractional Moments of the Truncated Normal Distribution

The following function appeared in Greene's (1990) study of the stochastic frontier model:

$$h(r, \epsilon) = \frac{\displaystyle\int_0^{\infty} z^r \frac{1}{\sigma}\phi\left[\frac{z - (-\epsilon - \theta\sigma^2)}{\sigma}\right] dz}{\displaystyle\int_0^{\infty} \frac{1}{\sigma}\phi\left[\frac{z - (-\epsilon - \theta\sigma^2)}{\sigma}\right] dz}.$$

If we let $\mu = -(\epsilon + \theta\sigma^2)$, we see that the denominator is just $\Phi[(z - \mu)/(\sigma)]$, which is a value from the standard normal cdf. But the numerator is complex. It does not fit into a form that lends itself to Gauss–Laguerre integration because the exponential function involves both z and z^2. An alternative form that has potential is obtained by making the change of variable to $w = (z - \mu)/\sigma$. This produces the right weighting function. But now the range of integration is not $-\infty$ to $+\infty$; it is $-\mu/\sigma$ to $+\infty$. There is another approach. Suppose that z is a random variable with $N[\mu, \sigma^2]$ distribution. Then the density of the truncated normal (at zero) distribution for z is

$$f(z \mid z > 0) = \frac{f(z)}{\text{Prob}[z > 0]} = \frac{\dfrac{1}{\sigma}\phi\left[\dfrac{z - \mu}{\sigma}\right]}{\displaystyle\int_0^{\infty} \frac{1}{\sigma}\phi\left[\frac{z - \mu}{\sigma}\right] dz}.$$

This is exactly the weighting function that appears in $h(r, \epsilon)$, and the function being weighted is z^r. Therefore, $h(r, \epsilon)$ is the expected value of z^r given that z is greater than zero. That is, $h(r, \epsilon)$ is a possibly fractional moment—we do not restrict r to integer values—from the truncated (at zero) normal distribution when the untruncated variable has mean $-(\epsilon + \theta\sigma^2)$ and variance σ^2.

Now that we have identified the function, how do we compute it? We have already concluded that the familiar quadrature methods will not suffice. (And, no one has previously derived closed forms for the fractional moments of the normal distribution, truncated or not.) But we can use (4-30), the corollary to Theorem 4.2. If we can draw a random sample of observations from this truncated normal distribution $\{z_i\}$, then the sample mean of $w_i = z_i^r$ will converge in probability (mean square) to its population counterpart. [The remaining detail is to establish that this expectation is finite, which it is for the truncated normal distribution; see Amemiya (1973b).] Since we showed earlier how to draw observations from a truncated normal distribution, this remaining step is simple.

The preceding is a fairly straightforward application of **Monte Carlo integration.** In certain cases, an integral can be approximated by computing the sample average of a set of function values. The approach taken here was to interpret the integral as an expected value. We then had to establish that the mean we were computing was finite. Our basic statistical result for the behavior of sample means implies that with a large enough sample, we can approximate the integral as closely as we like.

The general approach is widely applicable in Bayesian econometrics and has begun to appear in classical statistics and econometrics as well.[17] For direct application in a straightforward class of problems, we consider the general computation

$$F(x) = \int_L^U f(x)g(x)\,dx,$$

where $g(x)$ is a continuous function in the range $[L, U]$. (We could achieve greater generality by allowing more complicated functions, but for current purposes, we limit ourselves to straightforward cases.) Now, suppose that $g(x)$ is nonnegative in the entire range $[L, U]$. To normalize the weighting function, we suppose, as well, that

$$K = \int_L^U g(x)\,dx$$

is a known constant. Then $h(x) = g(x)/K$ is a probability density function in the range because it satisfies the axioms of probability.[18] Let

$$H(x) = \int_L^x h(t)\,dt.$$

---

[17]See Geweke (1986, 1988, 1989) for discussion and applications. A number of other references are given in Poirier (1995, p. 654).

[18]In many applications, K will already be part of the desired integral.

Then $H(L) = 0, H(U) = 1, H'(x) = h(x) > 0$, and so on. Then

$$\int_L^U f(x)g(x)\,dx = K\int_L^U f(x)\frac{g(x)}{K}\,dx = KE_{h(x)}\,[f(x)],$$

where we use the notation $E_{h(x)}[f(x)]$ to denote the expected value of the function $f(x)$ when x is drawn from the population with probability density function $h(x)$. We assume that this expected value is a finite constant. This defines the computation. We now assume that we are able to draw (pseudo)random samples from the population $h(x)$. Since K is a known constant and the means of random samples are unbiased and consistent estimators of their population counterparts, the sample mean of the functions,

$$\hat{F}(x) = K \times \frac{1}{n}\sum_{i=1}^{n} f(x_i^h),$$

where x_i^h is a random draw from $h(\cdot)$, is an unbiased and consistent estimator of the integral.

Suppose that the problem is well defined as above but that it is not possible to draw random samples from the population $h(\cdot)$. If there is another probability density function that resembles $h(\cdot)$, say, $I(x)$, then there may be an alternative strategy. We can rewrite our computation in the form

$$F(x) = K\int_L^U f(x)h(x)\,dx = K\int_L^U \left[\frac{f(x)h(x)}{I(x)}\right] I(x)\,dx.$$

Then we can interpret our integral as the expected value of $[f(x)h(x)]/I(x)$ when the population has density $I(x)$. The new density $I(x)$ is called an **importance function.** The same strategy works if certain fairly benign conditions are imposed on the importance function. [See Geweke (1989).] The range of variation is an important consideration, for example. If the range of x is, say, $(-\infty, +\infty)$ and we choose an importance function that is nonzero only in the range $(0, +\infty)$, our strategy is likely to come to some difficulties.

EXAMPLE 5.8 Mean of a Lognormal Distribution

Consider computing the mean of a lognormal distribution. If $x \sim N[0, 1]$, then e^x is distributed as lognormal and has density

$$g(x) = \frac{1}{x\sqrt{2\pi}}e^{-1/2(\ln x)^2}, \quad x0$$

(see Section 3.4.4). The expected value is $\int xg(x)\,dx$, so $f(x) = x$. Suppose that we did not know how to draw a random sample from this lognormal distribution (by just exponentiating our draws from the standard normal distribution) [or that the true mean is $\exp(0.5) = 1.648$]. Consider using a $\chi^2[1]$ as an importance function, instead. This chi-squared distribution is a gamma distribution with parameters $P = \lambda = \frac{1}{2}$ [see (3-39)], so

$$I(x) = \frac{\frac{1}{2}^{1/2}}{\Gamma(\frac{1}{2})} x^{-1/2} e^{-1/2x}.$$

After a bit of manipulation, we find

$$\frac{f(x)g(x)}{I(x)} = q(x) = e^{1/2[x-(\ln x)^2]} x^{-1/2}.$$

Therefore, to estimate the mean of this lognormal distribution, we can draw a random sample of values x_i from the $\chi^2[1]$ distribution, which we can do by squaring the draws in a sample from the standard normal distribution, then computing the average of the sample of values, $q(x_i)$.

We carried out this experiment with 1000 draws from a standard normal distribution. The mean of our sample was 1.6974, compared with a true mean of 1.648, so the error was less than 3%.

5.4.2e. Multivariate Normal Probabilities and Simulated Moments. The computation of bivariate normal probabilities as shown in Example 5.6 requires a large amount of computing effort. Quadrature methods have been developed for trivariate probabilities as well, but the amount of computing effort needed at this level is enormous. For integrals of level greater than three, satisfactory (in terms of speed and accuracy) direct approximations remain to be developed. Our work thus far does suggest an alternative approach. Suppose that $\mathbf{x}$ has a K-variate normal distribution with mean vector $\mathbf{0}$ and covariance matrix $\mathbf{\Sigma}$. (No generality is sacrificed by the assumption of a zero mean, since we could just subtract a nonzero mean from the random vector wherever it appears in any result.) We wish to compute the K-variate probability, $\text{Prob}[a_1 < x_1 < b_1,\ a_2 < x_2 < b_2, \ldots, a_K < x_K < b_K]$. This is a well-defined problem for which our Monte Carlo integration technique is well suited. As a first approach, consider sampling R observations, $\mathbf{x}_r$, $r = 1, \ldots, R$, from this multivariate normal distribution, using the method described in Section 5.3.2. Now, define

$$d_r = \mathbf{1}[a_1 < x_{r1} < b_1, a_2 < x_{r2} < b_2, \ldots, a_K < x_{rK} < b_K].$$

(That is, $d_r = 1$ if the condition is true and 0 otherwise.) Based on our earlier results, it follows that

$$\text{plim}\,\bar{d} = \text{plim}\,\frac{1}{R}\sum_{r=1}^{R} d_r = \text{Prob}[a_1 < x_1 < b_1, a_2 < x_2 < b_2, \ldots, a_K < x_K < b_K].^{19}$$

This method is valid in principle, but in practice it has proved to be unsatisfactory for several reasons. For large-order problems, it requires an enormous

---

[19]This method was suggested by Lerman and Manski (1981).

number of draws from the distribution to give reasonable accuracy. Also, even with large numbers of draws, it appears to be problematic when the desired tail area is very small. Nonetheless, the idea is sound, and recent research has built on this idea to produce some quite accurate and efficient simulation methods for this computation. A survey of the methods is given in McFadden and Ruud (1994).[20]

Among the simulation methods examined in the survey, the GHK smooth recursive simulator appears to be the most accurate.[21] The method is surprisingly simple. The general approach uses

$$\text{Prob}[a_1 < x_1 < b_1, a_2 < x_2 < b_2, \ldots, a_K < x_K < b_K] \approx \frac{1}{R}\sum_{r=1}^{R}\prod_{k=1}^{K} Q_{rk},$$

where Q_{rk} are easily computed univariate probabilities. The probabilities Q_{rk} are computed according to the following recursion: We first factor $\mathbf{\Sigma}$ using the Cholesky factorization $\mathbf{\Sigma} = \mathbf{LL}'$, where $\mathbf{L}$ is a lower triangular matrix (see Section 2.7.11.) The elements of $\mathbf{L}$ are l_{km}, where $l_{km} = 0$ if $m > k$. Then we begin the recursion with

$$Q_{r1} = \Phi(b_1/l_{11}) - \Phi(a_1/l_{11}).$$

Note that $l_{11} = \sigma_{11}$, so this is just the marginal probability, $\text{Prob}[a_1 < x_1 < b_1]$. Now, generate a random observation ϵ_{r1} from the truncated standard normal distribution in the range

$$A_{r1} \text{ to } B_{r1} = a_1/l_{11} \text{ to } b_1/l_{11}.$$

(Note, again, the range is standardized since $l_{11} = \sigma_{11}$.) The draw can be obtained from a $U[0, 1]$ observation using (5-1). For steps $k = 2, \ldots, K$, compute

$$A_{rk} = \left[a_k - \sum_{m=1}^{k-1} l_{km}\epsilon_{rm}\right]/l_{kk},$$

$$B_{rk} = \left[b_k - \sum_{m=1}^{k-1} l_{km}\epsilon_{rm}\right]/l_{kk}.$$

Then

$$Q_{rk} = \Phi(B_{rk}) - \Phi(A_{rk}),$$

and in preparation for the next step in the recursion, we generate a random draw from the truncated standard normal distribution in the range A_{rk} to B_{rk}.

---

[20]A symposium on the topic of simulation methods appears in *Review of Economic Statistics,* Vol. 76, November, 1994. See, especially, McFadden and Ruud (1994), Stern (1994), Geweke et al. (1994), and Breslaw (1994).

[21]See Geweke (1989), Hajivassiliou (1990), and Keane (1994). Details on the properties of the simulator are given in Börsch-Supan and Hajivassiliou (1990).

This process is replicated R times, and the estimated probability is the sample average of the simulated probabilities.

The GHK simulator has been found to be impressively fast and accurate for fairly moderate numbers of replications. Its main usage has been in computing functions and derivatives for maximum likelihood estimation of models that involve multivariate normal integrals. We will revisit this in the context of the method of simulated moments when we examine the probit model in Chapter 19.

5.4.3. Computing Derivatives

For certain functions, the programming of derivatives may be quite difficult. Numeric approximations can be used, although it should be borne in mind that analytic derivatives obtained by formally differentiating the functions involved are to be preferred. First derivatives can be approximated by using

$$\frac{\partial F(\boldsymbol{\theta})}{\partial \theta_i} \simeq \frac{F(\cdots \theta_i + \epsilon \cdots) - F(\cdots \theta_i - \epsilon \cdots)}{2\epsilon}.$$

The choice of ϵ is a remaining problem. Extensive discussion may be found in Quandt (1983).

There are three drawbacks to this means of computing derivatives compared with using the analytic derivatives. A possible major consideration is that it may substantially increase the amount of computation needed to obtain a function and its gradient. In particular, $K + 1$ function evaluations (the criterion and K derivatives) are replaced with $2K + 1$ functions. The latter may be more burdensome than the former, depending on the complexity of the partial derivatives compared with the function itself. The comparison will depend on the application. But in most settings, careful programming that avoids superfluous or redundant calculation can make the advantage of the analytic derivatives substantial. Second, the choice of ϵ can be problematic. If it is chosen too large, the approximation will be inaccurate. If it is chosen too small, there may be insufficient variation in the function to produce a good estimate of the derivative. A compromise that is likely to be effective is to compute ϵ_i separately for each parameter, as in

$$\epsilon_i = \text{Max}[\alpha|\theta_i|, \gamma]$$

[see Goldfeld and Quandt (1971)]. The values α and γ should be relatively small, such as 10^{-5}. Third, although numeric derivatives computed in this fashion are likely to be reasonably accurate, in a sum of a large number of terms, say several thousand, enough approximation error can accumulate to cause the numerical derivatives to differ significantly from their analytic counterparts. Second derivatives can also be computed numerically; in addition to the preceding problems, however, it is generally not possible to ensure negative definiteness of a Hessian computed in this manner. Unless the choice of ϵ is made extremely carefully, an indefinite matrix is a possibility. In general, the use of numeric derivatives should be avoided if the analytic derivatives are available.

5.5. OPTIMIZATION

Nonlinear optimization (e.g., maximizing log-likelihood functions) is an intriguing practical problem. Theory provides few hard and fast rules, and there are relatively few cases in which it is obvious how to proceed. This section introduces some of the terminology and underlying theory of nonlinear optimization.[22] We begin with a general discussion on how to search for a solution to a nonlinear optimization problem and describe some specific commonly used methods. We then consider some practical problems that arise in optimization. An example is given in the final section.

Consider maximizing the quadratic function

$$F(\boldsymbol{\theta}) = a + \mathbf{b}'\boldsymbol{\theta} - \tfrac{1}{2}\boldsymbol{\theta}'\mathbf{C}\boldsymbol{\theta},$$

where **C** is a positive definite matrix. The first-order condition for a maximum is

$$\frac{\partial F(\boldsymbol{\theta})}{\partial \boldsymbol{\theta}} = \mathbf{b} - \mathbf{C}\boldsymbol{\theta} = \mathbf{0}. \quad \textbf{(5-2)}$$

This set of *linear* equations has the unique solution

$$\boldsymbol{\theta} = \mathbf{C}^{-1}\mathbf{b}. \quad \textbf{(5-3)}$$

This is a linear optimization problem. Note that it has a **closed-form solution;** for any a, **b**, and **C**, the solution can be computed directly.[23] In the more typical situation,

$$\frac{\partial F(\boldsymbol{\theta})}{\partial \boldsymbol{\theta}} = \mathbf{0} \quad \textbf{(5-4)}$$

is a set of nonlinear equations that cannot be solved explicitly for $\boldsymbol{\theta}$.[24] The techniques considered in this section provide systematic means of searching for a solution.

We consider the general problem of maximizing a function of several variables:

$$\text{maximize}_{\theta}\, F(\boldsymbol{\theta}), \quad \textbf{(5-5)}$$

where $F(\boldsymbol{\theta})$ may be a log-likelihood or some other function. Minimization of

---

[22] There are numerous excellent references that offer a more complete exposition. Among these are Quandt (1983), Bazaraa and Shetty (1979), and Fletcher (1980).

[23] Notice that the constant a is irrelevant to the solution. Many maximum likelihood problems are presented with the preface "neglecting an irrelevant constant." For example, the log-likelihood for the normal linear regression model contains a term $-(n/2)\ln(2\pi)$ that can be discarded.

[24] See, for example, the normal equations for the nonlinear least squares estimators of Chapter 11.

$F(\boldsymbol{\theta})$ is handled by maximizing $-F(\boldsymbol{\theta})$. Two special cases are

$$F(\boldsymbol{\theta}) = \sum_{i=1}^{n} f_i(\boldsymbol{\theta}), \tag{5-6}$$

which is typical for maximum likelihood problems, and the **least squares problem,**[25]

$$f_i(\boldsymbol{\theta}) = -(y_i - f(\mathbf{x}_i, \boldsymbol{\theta}))^2. \tag{5-7}$$

We will treat the nonlinear least squares problem in detail in Chapter 11. An obvious way to search for the $\boldsymbol{\theta}$ that maximizes $F(\boldsymbol{\theta})$ is by trial and error. If $\boldsymbol{\theta}$ has only a single element and it is known approximately where the optimum will be found, a **grid search** will be a feasible strategy. The Box–Cox model of Section 10.4 is often estimated by scanning the range of -2 to 2 for the optimal value of λ.[26] Another example is a common time-series problem in which a one-dimensional search for a correlation coefficient is made in the interval $(-1, 1)$. The grid search can proceed in the obvious fashion—that is, . . . , $-0.1, 0, 0.1, 0.2$, . . . , then $\hat{\theta}_{\text{max}} - 0.1$ to $\hat{\theta}_{\text{max}} + 0.1$ in increments of 0.01, and so on—until the desired precision is achieved.[27] If $\boldsymbol{\theta}$ contains more than one parameter, a grid search is likely to be extremely costly, particularly if little is known about the parameter vector at the outset. Nonetheless, relatively efficient methods have been devised. Quandt (1983) and Fletcher (1980) contain further details.

There are also systematic, derivative-free methods of searching for a function optimum that resemble in some respects the algorithms that we will examine in the next section. The **downhill simplex** (and other simplex) methods[28] have been found to be very fast and effective for some problems. A recent entry in the econometric literature is the method of **simulated annealing.**[29] These derivative-free methods, particularly the latter, are often very effective in problems with many variables in the objective function. But they usually require far more function evaluations than the methods based on derivatives that are considered below. Since the problems typically analyzed in econometrics involve relatively few parameters but often quite complex functions involving large numbers of terms in a summation, on balance, the gradient methods are usually going to be preferable.[30]

---

[25]Least squares is, of course, a minimizing problem. The negative of the criterion is used to maintain consistency with the general formulation.

[26]It should be remembered, however, that nothing prevents λ from being outside this range. For example, if a Box–Cox model is fit to the production data in Table 7.1, two minima of the sum of squares can be found: a local minimum at 0.29 and a global minimum at 1.7.

[27]There are more efficient methods of carrying out a one-dimensional search, for example, the **golden section** method. See Press et al. (1986, Chapter 10).

[28]See Nelder and Mead (1965) and Press et al. (1986).

[29]See Goffe, Ferrier, and Rodgers (1994) and Press et al. (1986, pp. 326–334).

[30]Goffe, Ferrier, and Rodgers (1994) did find that the method of simulated annealing was quite adept at finding the best among multiple solutions. This is frequently a problem for derivative-based methods, as they usually have no method of distinguishing between a local optimum and a global one.

5.5.1. Algorithms

A more effective means of solving most nonlinear maximization problems is by an **iterative algorithm:**

Beginning from initial value $\boldsymbol{\theta}_0$, at entry to iteration t, if $\boldsymbol{\theta}_t$ is not the optimal value for $\boldsymbol{\theta}$, compute direction vector $\boldsymbol{\Delta}_t$, step size λ_t, then

$$\boldsymbol{\theta}_{t+1} = \boldsymbol{\theta}_t + \lambda_t \boldsymbol{\Delta}_t. \tag{5-8}$$

Figure 5.3 illustrates the structure of an iteration for a hypothetical function of two variables. The direction vector $\boldsymbol{\Delta}_t$ is shown in the figure with $\boldsymbol{\theta}_t$. The dashed line is the set of points $\boldsymbol{\theta}_t + \lambda_t \boldsymbol{\Delta}_t$. Different values of λ_t lead to different contours; for this $\boldsymbol{\theta}_t$ and $\boldsymbol{\Delta}_t$, the best value of λ_t is about 0.5.

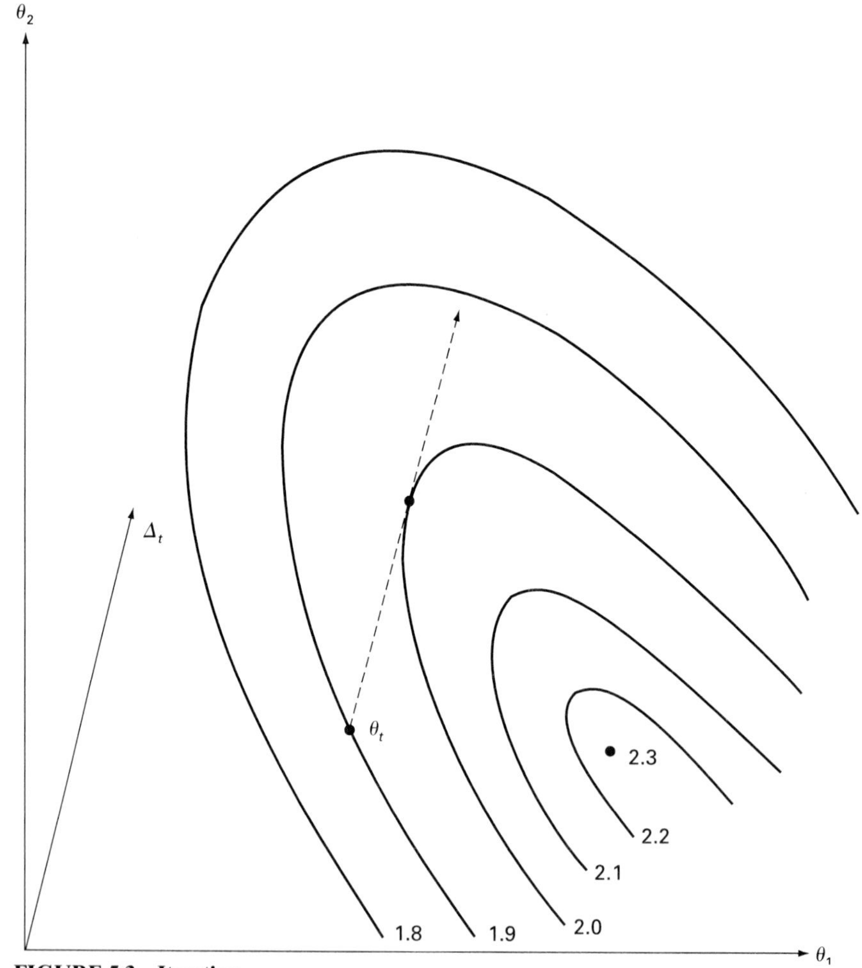

FIGURE 5.3 Iteration.

Notice in Figure 5.3 that for a given direction vector $\mathbf{\Delta}_t$ and current parameter vector $\boldsymbol{\theta}_t$, a secondary optimization is required to find the best λ_t. Translating from Figure 5.3, we obtain the form of this problem as shown in Figure 5.4. This subsidiary search is called a **line search,** as we search along the line $\boldsymbol{\theta}_t + \lambda_t \mathbf{\Delta}_t$ for the optimal value of $F(.)$. The formal solution to the line search problem would be the λ_t that satisfies

$$\frac{\partial F(\boldsymbol{\theta}_t + \lambda_t \mathbf{\Delta}_t)}{\partial \lambda_t} = \mathbf{g}(\boldsymbol{\theta}_t + \lambda_t \mathbf{\Delta}_t)' \mathbf{\Delta}_t = 0, \tag{5-9}$$

where $\mathbf{g}$ is the vector of partial derivatives of $F(.)$ evaluated at $\boldsymbol{\theta}_t + \lambda_t \mathbf{\Delta}_t$. In general, this will also be a nonlinear problem. In most cases, adding a formal search for λ_t will be too expensive, as well as unnecessary. Some approximate or ad hoc method will usually be chosen. It is worth emphasizing that finding the λ_t that maximizes $F(\boldsymbol{\theta}_t + \lambda_t \mathbf{\Delta}_t)$ at a given iteration does not generally lead to the overall solution in that iteration. This is clear in Figure 5.4, where the optimal value of λ_t leads to $F(.) = 2.0$, at which point we reenter the iteration.

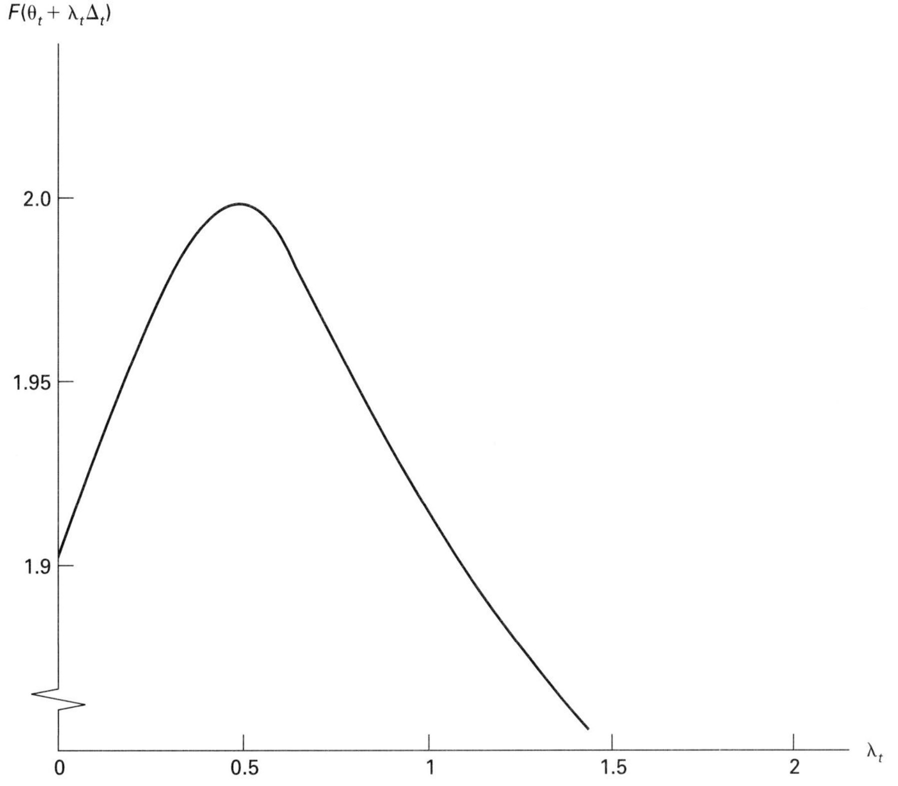

FIGURE 5.4 Line Search.

5.5.2. Gradient Methods

The most commonly used algorithms are **gradient methods,** in which

$$\boldsymbol{\Delta}_t = \mathbf{W}_t \mathbf{g}_t, \tag{5-10}$$

where $\mathbf{W}_t$ is a positive definite matrix and $\mathbf{g}_t$ is the **gradient** of $F(\boldsymbol{\theta}_t)$:

$$\mathbf{g}_t = \mathbf{g}(\boldsymbol{\theta}_t) = \frac{\partial F(\boldsymbol{\theta}_t)}{\partial \boldsymbol{\theta}_t}. \tag{5-11}$$

These methods are motivated partly by the following. Consider a linear Taylor series approximation to $F(\boldsymbol{\theta}_t + \lambda_t \boldsymbol{\Delta}_t)$ around $\lambda = 0$:

$$F(\boldsymbol{\theta}_t + \lambda_t \boldsymbol{\Delta}_t) \simeq F(\boldsymbol{\theta}_t) + \lambda_t \mathbf{g}(\boldsymbol{\theta}_t)' \boldsymbol{\Delta}_t. \tag{5-12}$$

Let $F(\boldsymbol{\theta}_t + \lambda_t \boldsymbol{\Delta}_t)$ equal F_{t+1}. Then,

$$F_{t+1} - F_t \simeq \lambda_t \mathbf{g}_t' \boldsymbol{\Delta}_t.$$

If $\boldsymbol{\Delta}_t = \mathbf{W}_t \mathbf{g}_t$,

$$F_{t+1} - F_t \simeq \lambda_t \mathbf{g}_t' \mathbf{W}_t \mathbf{g}_t.$$

If $\mathbf{g}_t$ is not $\mathbf{0}$ and λ_t is small enough, $F_{t+1} - F_t$ must be positive. This means that if $F(\boldsymbol{\theta})$ is not already at its maximum, we can always find a step size such that a gradient-type iteration will lead to an increase in the function. (Recall that $\mathbf{W}_t$ is assumed to be positive definite.)

In the following, we will omit the iteration index t, except where it is necessary to distinguish one vector from another. The following are some commonly used algorithms.[31]

Steepest Ascent. The simplest algorithm to employ is the **steepest ascent** method, which uses

$$\mathbf{W} = \mathbf{I} \text{ so that } \boldsymbol{\Delta} = \mathbf{g}. \tag{5-13}$$

As its name implies, the direction is the one of greatest increase of $F(.)$. Another virtue is that the line search has a straightforward solution; at least near the maximum, the optimal λ is

$$\lambda = \frac{-\mathbf{g}'\mathbf{g}}{\mathbf{g}'\mathbf{H}\mathbf{g}}, \tag{5-14}$$

where

$$\mathbf{H} = \frac{\partial^2 F(\boldsymbol{\theta})}{\partial \boldsymbol{\theta}\, \partial \boldsymbol{\theta}'}.$$

[31]A more extensive catalog may be found in Judge et al. (1985, Appendix B). Those mentioned here are some of the more commonly used ones and are chosen primarily because they illustrate many of the important aspects of nonlinear optimization.

Therefore, the steepest ascent iteration is

$$\boldsymbol{\theta}_{t+1} = \boldsymbol{\theta}_t - \frac{\mathbf{g}_t'\mathbf{g}_t}{\mathbf{g}_t'\mathbf{H}_t\mathbf{g}_t}\mathbf{g}_t. \tag{5-15}$$

Computation of the second derivatives matrix may be extremely burdensome. Also, if $\mathbf{H}_t$ is not negative definite, which is likely if $\boldsymbol{\theta}_t$ is far from the maximum, the iteration may diverge. A systematic line search can bypass this problem. This algorithm usually converges very slowly, however, so other techniques are usually used.

Newton's Method. The template for most gradient methods in common use is Newton's method. The basis for **Newton's method** is a linear Taylor series approximation. Expanding the first-order conditions,

$$\frac{\partial F(\boldsymbol{\theta})}{\partial \boldsymbol{\theta}} = \mathbf{0},$$

equation by equation, in a linear Taylor series around an arbitrary $\boldsymbol{\theta}^0$ yields

$$\frac{\partial F(\boldsymbol{\theta})}{\partial \boldsymbol{\theta}} \simeq \mathbf{g}^0 + \mathbf{H}^0(\boldsymbol{\theta} - \boldsymbol{\theta}^0) = \mathbf{0}, \tag{5-16}$$

where the superscript indicates that the term is evaluated at $\boldsymbol{\theta}^0$. Solving for $\boldsymbol{\theta}$ and then equating $\boldsymbol{\theta}$ to $\boldsymbol{\theta}_{t+1}$ and $\boldsymbol{\theta}^0$ to $\boldsymbol{\theta}_t$, we obtain the iteration

$$\boldsymbol{\theta}_{t+1} = \boldsymbol{\theta}_t - \mathbf{H}_t^{-1}\mathbf{g}_t. \tag{5-17}$$

Thus, for Newton's method,

$$\mathbf{W} = -\mathbf{H}^{-1}, \qquad \boldsymbol{\Delta} = -\mathbf{H}^{-1}\mathbf{g}, \qquad \lambda = 1. \tag{5-18}$$

Newton's method will converge very rapidly in many problems. If the function is quadratic, this method will reach the optimum in one iteration from any starting point. [Consider, for example, the optimization problem posed in (5-2).] If the criterion function is globally concave, as it is in a number of problems that we shall examine later, it is probably the best algorithm available. This method is very well suited to maximum likelihood estimation.

Alternatives to Newton's Method. Newton's method is very effective in some settings, but it can perform very poorly in others. If the function is not approximately quadratic or if the current estimate is very far from the maximum, it can cause wide swings in the estimates and even fail to converge at all. A number of algorithms have been devised to improve upon Newton's method. An obvious one is to include a line search at each iteration rather than use $\lambda = 1$. Two problems remain, however. At points distant from the optimum, the second derivatives matrix may not be negative definite, and, in any event, the computational burden of computing $\mathbf{H}$ may be excessive.

The **quadratic hill-climbing method** proposed by Goldfeld et al. (1966)

deals directly with the first of these problems. In any iteration, if **H** is not negative definite, it is replaced with

$$\mathbf{H}_\alpha = \mathbf{H} - \alpha\mathbf{I}, \tag{5-19}$$

where α is a positive number chosen large enough to ensure the negative definiteness of $\mathbf{H}_\alpha$. Another suggestion is that of Greenstadt (1967), which uses, at every iteration,

$$\mathbf{H}_\pi = -\sum_{i=1}^{n} |\pi_i| \mathbf{c}_i\mathbf{c}_i', \tag{5-20}$$

where π_i is the ith characteristic root of **H** and $\mathbf{c}_i$ is its associated characteristic vector. Other proposals have been made to ensure the negative definiteness of the required matrix at each iteration.[32] The computational complexity of these methods remains a problem, however.

Quasi-Newton Methods: Davidon–Fletcher–Powell. A very effective class of algorithms has been developed that eliminates second derivatives altogether and has excellent convergence properties, even for ill-behaved problems. These are the **quasi-Newton methods,** which form

$$\mathbf{W}_{t+1} = \mathbf{W}_t + \mathbf{E}_t,$$

where $\mathbf{E}_t$ is a positive definite matrix.[33] As long as $\mathbf{W}_0$ is positive definite—**I** is commonly used—$\mathbf{W}_t$ will be positive definite at every iteration. In the **Davidon–Fletcher–Powell (DFP) method,** after a sufficient number of iterations, $\mathbf{W}_{t+1}$ will be an approximation to $-\mathbf{H}^{-1}$. Let

$$\boldsymbol{\delta}_t = \lambda_t\boldsymbol{\Delta}_t \quad \text{and} \quad \boldsymbol{\gamma}_t = \mathbf{g}(\boldsymbol{\theta}_{t+1}) - \mathbf{g}(\boldsymbol{\theta}_t). \tag{5-21}$$

The DFP **variable metric algorithm** uses

$$\mathbf{W}_{t+1} = \mathbf{W}_t + \frac{\boldsymbol{\delta}_t\boldsymbol{\delta}_t'}{\boldsymbol{\delta}_t'\boldsymbol{\gamma}_t} + \frac{\mathbf{W}_t\boldsymbol{\gamma}_t\boldsymbol{\gamma}_t'\mathbf{W}_t}{\boldsymbol{\gamma}_t'\mathbf{W}_t\boldsymbol{\gamma}_t}. \tag{5-22}$$

Notice that in the DFP algorithm, the change in the first derivative vector is used in **W**; an estimate of the inverse of the second derivatives matrix is being accumulated.

The variable metric algorithms are those that update **W** at each iteration while preserving its definiteness. For the DFP method, the accumulation of $\mathbf{W}_{t+1}$ is of the form

$$\mathbf{W}_{t+1} = \mathbf{W}_t + \mathbf{aa}' + \mathbf{bb}' = \mathbf{W}_t + [\mathbf{a} \quad \mathbf{b}][\mathbf{a} \quad \mathbf{b}]'.$$

The two-column matrix $[\mathbf{a} \quad \mathbf{b}]$ will have rank two; hence this is called a **rank two update** or **rank two correction.** The **Broyden–Fletcher–Goldfarb–Shanno**

[32]See, for example, Goldfeld and Quandt (1971).

[33]See Fletcher (1980).

(BFGS) method is a rank three correction that subtracts $v\mathbf{dd}'$ to the **DFP** update, where $v = (\gamma_t'\mathbf{W}_t\gamma_t)$ and

$$\mathbf{d}_t = \left(\frac{1}{\delta_t'\gamma_t}\right)\delta_t - \left(\frac{1}{\gamma_t'\mathbf{W}_t\gamma_t}\right)\mathbf{W}_t\gamma_t.$$

There is some evidence that this method is more efficient than DFP. Other methods, such as **Broyden's method,** involve a rank one correction instead. Any method that is of the form

$$\mathbf{W}_{t+1} = \mathbf{W}_t + \mathbf{QQ}'$$

will preserve the definiteness of $\mathbf{W}$, regardless of the number of columns in $\mathbf{Q}$.

The DFP and BFGS algorithms are extremely effective and are among the most widely used gradient methods. An important practical consideration to keep in mind is that although $\mathbf{W}_t$ accumulates an estimate of the negative inverse of the second derivatives matrix for both algorithms, in maximum likelihood problems it rarely converges to a very good estimate of the covariance matrix of the estimator and should generally not be used as one.

5.5.3. Aspects of Maximum Likelihood Estimation

Newton's method is often used for maximum likelihood problems. For solving a maximum likelihood problem, the **method of scoring** replaces $\mathbf{H}$ with

$$\overline{\mathbf{W}} = (-E[\mathbf{H}(\boldsymbol{\theta})])^{-1}, \qquad \textbf{(5-23)}$$

which will be recognized as the asymptotic variance of $\sqrt{n}$ times the maximum likelihood estimator. There is some evidence that where it can be used, this method performs better than Newton's method. The exact form of the expectation of the Hessian of the log likelihood is rarely known, however.[34] Newton's method, which uses actual instead of expected second derivatives, is generally used instead.

One-Step Estimation. A convenient variant of Newton's method is the **one-step maximum likelihood estimator.** It has been shown that if $\boldsymbol{\theta}^0$ is *any* consistent initial estimator of $\boldsymbol{\theta}$ and $\mathbf{H}^*$ is $\mathbf{H}$ or $\overline{\mathbf{H}}$, or any other asymptotically equivalent estimator of $\text{Var}[\sqrt{n}(\hat{\boldsymbol{\theta}}_{\text{MLE}} - \boldsymbol{\theta})]$, then

$$\boldsymbol{\theta}^1 = \boldsymbol{\theta}^0 + (\mathbf{H}^*)^{-1}\mathbf{g}^0 \qquad \textbf{(5-24)}$$

is an estimator of $\boldsymbol{\theta}$ that has the same asymptotic properties as the maximum likelihood estimator.[35] (Note that it is *not* the maximum likelihood estimator. As such, for example, it should not be used as the basis for likelihood ratio tests.)

[34]Amemiya (1981) provides a number of examples.

[35]See, for example, Rao (1973).

The EM Algorithm. The **expectation-maximization (EM)** algorithm was suggested in 1977 by Dempster, Laird, and Rubin (DLR) as a method of solving maximum likelihood problems. The method has an intuitively appealing structure and is particularly well suited to some familiar problems in econometrics.

The EM method is used in the following setting.[36] Let y^* denote a "latent" random variable, and let y denote its observed counterpart, where y is some *many-to-one* transformation of y^*, $t(y^*)$; the method is applicable to models in which the transformation implies that some information is "lost." The example below will demonstrate. Let $f(y_i \mid \boldsymbol{\theta}, \mathbf{x}_i)$ denote the density for the observed random variable, given the parameters to be estimated $\boldsymbol{\theta}$ and other data $\mathbf{x}$ that enter the distribution, and let $f(y_i^* \mid \boldsymbol{\theta}, \mathbf{x}_i)$ denote the same for y^*. The maximum likelihood estimator of $\boldsymbol{\theta}$ is the vector $\hat{\boldsymbol{\theta}}$ that maximizes the log-likelihood function for the *observed* data.

$$\ln L = \sum_{i=1}^{n} \ln f(y_i \mid \boldsymbol{\theta}, \mathbf{x}_i).$$

At iteration l, we have in hand an estimate $\hat{\boldsymbol{\theta}}_l$. The EM method proceeds iteratively in these two steps:

E step: Form $H(\boldsymbol{\theta} \mid \hat{\boldsymbol{\theta}}_l, \mathbf{y}, \mathbf{X}) = E\left[\sum_{i=1}^{n} \ln f(y_i^* \mid \boldsymbol{\theta}, y_i, \mathbf{x}_i)\right]$.

M step: Maximize $H(\boldsymbol{\theta} \mid \hat{\boldsymbol{\theta}}_l, \mathbf{y}, \mathbf{X})$ to obtain $\hat{\boldsymbol{\theta}}_{l+1}$.

The **E** step involves forming a log-likelihood function for the latent data *as if they were observed,* then taking its expectation. In some cases, this is equivalent to forming a sort of prediction for y^*, then maximizing the likelihood using that prediction. Moreover, in some cases involving the normal distribution, the **M** step involves simple least squares regression of these predictions on the variables in $\mathbf{x}$, which is what makes this approach so intuitively appealing. It has been shown [see Ruud (1991), Boyles (1983), and Wu (1983)] that under the right conditions (regularity for the log-likelihood, DLR's conditions for the data-generation process), this method will converge to the maximum likelihood estimator.

EXAMPLE 5.9 Consumer Choice

Suppose that we are observing a consumer's decision whether to buy or lease a new car. Then y^* might represent the difference in utilities of the two choices, $y^* = U(\text{buy}) - U(\text{lease})$. Since utility is never observed directly, all we could observe is the decision, which we assume favors the option with the greater utility. Thus, $y =$ "buy" if $y^* > 0$ and $y =$ "lease" if $y^* \leq 0$. If we let $y = 1$ if

[36] There are more general statements of the method. See Ruud (1991). We will introduce the algorithm with one of the more straightforward cases.

$y^* > 0$ and 0 otherwise, we have $y = t(y^*) = \mathbf{1}(y^* > 0) = \text{sgn}(y^*)$, which is a many-to-one transformation that loses all information on the actual magnitude of y^*. Suppose that $y^* \mid \mathbf{x} = \mathbf{x}'\boldsymbol{\theta} + \epsilon$, where ϵ is distributed $N[0, 1]$ and $\mathbf{x}$ is a set of covariates that we believe influence the decision. Then, y^* is distributed as $N[\mathbf{x}'\boldsymbol{\theta}, 1]$.

The observed random variable y takes only two values, 0 and 1, with $\text{Prob}[y_i = 1 \mid \boldsymbol{\theta}, \mathbf{x}_i] = \text{Prob}[y_i^* > 0] = \text{Prob}[\epsilon > -\mathbf{x}_i'\boldsymbol{\theta}] = 1 - \Phi(-\mathbf{x}_i'\boldsymbol{\theta}) = \Phi(\mathbf{x}_i'\boldsymbol{\theta})$, where $\Phi(\cdot)$ is the standard normal PDF, and $\text{Prob}[y_i = 0] = 1 - \text{Prob}[y_i \mid \boldsymbol{\theta}, \mathbf{x}_i]$. Therefore, the log-likelihood function for the observed data is

$$\ln L = \sum_{y=0} \ln\{1 - \Phi(\mathbf{x}_i'\boldsymbol{\theta})\} + \sum_{y=1} \ln \Phi(\mathbf{x}_i'\boldsymbol{\theta}). \qquad \textbf{(5-25)}$$

Maximization of this function is not exceedingly complicated, but it is a nonlinear problem that requires iteration.

For the latent data, $\ln f(y_i^* \mid \boldsymbol{\theta}, \mathbf{x}_i) = -\frac{1}{2}[\ln(2\pi) + (y_i^* - \mathbf{x}_i'\boldsymbol{\theta})^2]$. Therefore,

$$\ln L_* = -\frac{n}{2}\ln(2\pi) - \frac{1}{2}\sum_{i=1}^{n}(y_i^* - \mathbf{x}_i'\boldsymbol{\theta})^2.$$

Taking expectations and moving the expectation inside the summation, we have

$$H(\boldsymbol{\theta} \mid \hat{\boldsymbol{\theta}}_l, \mathbf{y}, \mathbf{X}) = -\frac{n}{2}\ln(2\pi) - \frac{1}{2}\sum_{i=1}^{n} E[(y_i^* - \mathbf{x}_i'\boldsymbol{\theta})^2 \mid \boldsymbol{\theta}_l, y_i, \mathbf{x}_i].$$

Therefore, the **E** step requires us to find this expectation. Unconditionally, $E[(y_i^* - \mathbf{x}_i'\boldsymbol{\theta})^2] = E[\epsilon_i^2] = 1.0$. But, conditioned on y_i, we know more about y_i^*; we know its sign. When $y_i = 1$,

$$E[(y_i^* - \mathbf{x}_i'\boldsymbol{\theta})^2 \mid \hat{\boldsymbol{\theta}}_l, y_i^* > 0, \mathbf{x}_i] = \{E[(y_i^* - \mathbf{x}_i'\boldsymbol{\theta}) \mid \hat{\boldsymbol{\theta}}_l, y_i^* > 0, \mathbf{x}_i]\}^2$$

$$+ \text{Var}[(y_i^* - \mathbf{x}_i'\boldsymbol{\theta}) \mid \hat{\boldsymbol{\theta}}_l, y_i^* > 0, \mathbf{x}_i],$$

and likewise for $y_i^* < 0$ $(y_i = 0)$. If $y_i = 1$, then y_i^* is greater than 0, so conditioned on $y_i = 1$, y_i^* has a truncated normal distribution, which we encountered in Section 5.3.2a and (5-1). The moments of a truncated normal variable are given in Theorem 20.2. Using the theorem, we have

$$\begin{aligned} E[(y_i^* - \mathbf{x}_i'\boldsymbol{\theta}) \mid \hat{\boldsymbol{\theta}}_l, y_i^* > 0, \mathbf{x}_i] &= E[y_i^* \mid \hat{\boldsymbol{\theta}}_l, y_i^* > 0, \mathbf{x}_i] - \mathbf{x}_i'\boldsymbol{\theta} \\ &= \mathbf{x}_i'\hat{\boldsymbol{\theta}}_l + \hat{\lambda}_i^+ - \mathbf{x}_i'\boldsymbol{\theta}, \end{aligned}$$

where

$$\hat{\lambda}_i^+ = \phi(\mathbf{x}_i'\hat{\boldsymbol{\theta}}_l)/\Phi(\mathbf{x}_i'\hat{\boldsymbol{\theta}}_l).$$

Note that $\hat{\lambda}_i^+$ involves $\hat{\boldsymbol{\theta}}_l$ but does not involve $\boldsymbol{\theta}$. The counterpart for $y_i^* \le 0$ is just $\lambda_i^- = -\phi/(1 - \Phi)$, where the argument of the functions is still $\mathbf{x}_i'\hat{\boldsymbol{\theta}}_l$. The variance for the terms when $y_i = 1$ is

$$\text{Var}[(y_i^* - \mathbf{x}_i'\boldsymbol{\theta}) \mid \hat{\boldsymbol{\theta}}_l, y_i^* > 0, \mathbf{x}_i] = 1 - \hat{\lambda}_i^+(\mathbf{x}_i'\hat{\boldsymbol{\theta}}_l + \hat{\lambda}_i^+) = \hat{\delta}_i^+$$

and likewise for $y_i = 0$ (i.e., $y_i^* \le 0$). Assembling all of our parts, we have

$$H(\boldsymbol{\theta} \mid \hat{\boldsymbol{\theta}}_l, \mathbf{y}, \mathbf{X}) = -\frac{n}{2}\ln(2\pi) - \frac{1}{2}\sum_{i=1}^{n}\{[(\mathbf{x}_i'\hat{\boldsymbol{\theta}}_l + \hat{\lambda}_i) - \mathbf{x}_i'\boldsymbol{\theta}]^2 + \hat{\delta}_i\}$$

$$= \text{constant} - \frac{1}{2}\sum_{i=1}^{n}(\hat{y}_i^* - \mathbf{x}_i'\boldsymbol{\theta})^2 - \frac{1}{2}\sum_{i=1}^{n}\hat{\delta}_i.$$

Remember that $\hat{\delta}_i$ does not involve $\boldsymbol{\theta}$, so the first and third terms are irrelevant to the solution. Therefore, to maximize $H(\cdot)$ (the **M** step), we minimize the sum of squared deviations, which means that we linearly regress $\hat{\mathbf{y}}^*$ on $\mathbf{X}$. To summarize, for this model, the EM algorithm is employed as follows, where we start the iterations with some estimate of $\boldsymbol{\theta}$.

E step: Compute $\hat{y}_i^* = \mathbf{x}_i'\hat{\boldsymbol{\theta}}_l + \hat{\lambda}_i$ appropriately for each observation.

M step: Linearly regress $\hat{\mathbf{y}}^*$ on $\mathbf{X}$ to obtain a new $\boldsymbol{\theta}$. Exit or return to the E step.

The process that consists of computing predicted values for the latent data at the E step, then using simple least squares at the M step, recurs in a number of models used in econometrics. The intuitive appeal of this approach has contributed to the popularity of this method. The numerical stability of the EM method has been suggested as one of its virtues [see Haberman (1977)]. The claim that it is a "derivative free" algorithm is untrue, which we can easily show. By differentiating the terms in (5-25), you can show that $\partial \ln f(y_i \mid \mathbf{x}_i, \boldsymbol{\theta})/\partial\boldsymbol{\theta} = \mathbf{x}_i\lambda_i$. That means that, in the final analysis, our iterated least squares algorithm has amounted to using the *gradient method,*

$$\hat{\boldsymbol{\theta}}_{l+1} = \hat{\boldsymbol{\theta}}_l - (\mathbf{X}'\mathbf{X})^{-1}\mathbf{g}_l.$$

This looks rather like Newton's method with $(\mathbf{X}'\mathbf{X})^{-1}$ used as an estimate of $-\mathbf{H}$. Others have observed that the EM method is sometimes slow to converge. We might expect that here, since this estimator of $-\mathbf{H}$ is not necessarily very good and, moreover, is never updated. The other disadvantage is that an estimator of the asymptotic covariance matrix of the estimator of $\boldsymbol{\theta}$ is not produced as a byproduct of the iterations, as in other methods, so one additional computation is often needed after the estimation process.

Example 5.9 demonstrates the mechanics of the EM algorithm in the context of a very simple latent data model. In the end, it turns out that for all its intuitive appeal, essentially nothing is gained by using the EM method here. But there are other cases in which EM does provide some useful insights into the workings of the model and estimator and is a useful way of simplifying the estimation problem. The survey by Ruud (1991) gives a discussion of this.

Covariance Matrix Estimation. In computing maximum likelihood estimators, a commonly used method of estimating $\mathbf{H}$ simultaneously simplifies the calculation of $\mathbf{W}$ and solves the occasional problem of indefiniteness of the Hessian. The method of Berndt et al. (1974) replaces $\mathbf{W}$ with

$$\hat{\mathbf{W}} = \left[\sum_{i=1}^{n} \mathbf{g}_i \mathbf{g}_i'\right] = \mathbf{G}'\mathbf{G}, \tag{5-26}$$

where

$$\mathbf{g}_i = \frac{\partial \ln f(\mathbf{x}_i, \boldsymbol{\theta})}{\partial \boldsymbol{\theta}}.$$

Then, $\mathbf{G}$ is the $n \times K$ matrix with ith row equal to $\mathbf{g}_i'$. This is the third estimator for the variance of the maximum likelihood estimator that we considered in Chapter 4.[37] (See Section 4.5.2.) Although $\hat{\mathbf{W}}$ and other consistent estimators of $-\mathbf{H}$ are asymptotically equivalent, $\hat{\mathbf{W}}$ has the additional virtues that it is always positive definite, and it is only necessary to differentiate the log-likelihood once to compute it.

The Lagrange Multiplier Statistic. The use of $\hat{\mathbf{W}}$ as an estimator of $-\mathbf{H}$ bring another intriguing convenience in maximum likelihood estimation. When testing restrictions on parameters estimated by maximum likelihood, one approach is to use the **Lagrange multiplier** statistic. We will examine this test at length at various points in this book, so we need only sketch it briefly here. The logic of the LM test is as follows. The gradient $\mathbf{g}(\boldsymbol{\theta})$ of the log-likelihood function equals $\mathbf{0}$ at the unrestricted maximum likelihood estimators (that is, at least to within the precision of the computer program in use). If $\hat{\boldsymbol{\theta}}_r$ is an MLE that is computed subject to some restrictions on $\boldsymbol{\theta}$, then we know that $\mathbf{g}(\hat{\boldsymbol{\theta}}_r) \neq \mathbf{0}$. The LM test is used to test whether, at $\hat{\boldsymbol{\theta}}_r$, $\mathbf{g}_r$, is *significantly* different from $\mathbf{0}$ (or whether the deviation of $\mathbf{g}_r$ from $\mathbf{0}$ can be viewed as sampling variation). The covariance matrix of the gradient of the log-likelihood is $-\mathbf{H}$, so the Wald statistic (see Section 4.9.3) for testing this hypothesis is $\mathbf{W} = \mathbf{g}'(-\mathbf{H})^{-1}\mathbf{g}$. Now, suppose that we use $\hat{\mathbf{W}}$ to estimate $-\mathbf{H}$. Let $\mathbf{G}$ be the $n \times K$ matrix with ith row equal to $\mathbf{g}_i'$, and let $\mathbf{i}$ denote an $n \times 1$ column of 1s. Then the LM statistic can be computed as

$$\text{LM} = \mathbf{i}'\mathbf{G}(\mathbf{G}'\mathbf{G})^{-1}\mathbf{G}'\mathbf{i}.$$

Since $\mathbf{i}'\mathbf{i} = n$,

$$\begin{aligned}\text{LM} &= n[\mathbf{i}'\mathbf{G}(\mathbf{G}'\mathbf{G})^{-1}\mathbf{G}'\mathbf{i}/n] \\ &= nR_{\mathbf{i}}^2,\end{aligned}$$

where $R_{\mathbf{i}}^2$ is the *uncentered* R^2 in a regression of a column of 1s on the derivatives of the log-likelihood function.

The Concentrated Log-Likelihood. Many problems in maximum likelihood estimation can be formulated in terms of a partitioning of the parameter vector $\boldsymbol{\theta} = [\boldsymbol{\theta}_1, \boldsymbol{\theta}_2]$ such that at the solution to the optimization problem, $\boldsymbol{\theta}_{2,\text{ML}}$

[37]This is the estimator of the asymptotic covariance matrix used for the Box–Cox model in Example 10.10.

can be written as an explicit function of $\boldsymbol{\theta}_{1,\text{ML}}$. When the solution to the likelihood equation for $\boldsymbol{\theta}_2$ produces

$$\boldsymbol{\theta}_{2,\text{ML}} = \mathbf{t}(\boldsymbol{\theta}_{1,\text{ML}}),$$

then, if it is convenient, we may "concentrate" the log-likelihood function by writing,

$$F^*(\boldsymbol{\theta}_1, \boldsymbol{\theta}_2) = F[\boldsymbol{\theta}_1, \mathbf{t}(\boldsymbol{\theta}_1)] = F_c(\boldsymbol{\theta}_1).$$

The unrestricted solution to the problem $\text{Max}_{\boldsymbol{\theta}_1} F_c(\boldsymbol{\theta}_1)$ provides the full solution to the optimization problem. Once the optimizing value of $\boldsymbol{\theta}_1$ is obtained, the optimizing value of $\boldsymbol{\theta}_2$ is simply $\mathbf{t}(\hat{\boldsymbol{\theta}}_{1,\text{ML}})$. Note that $F^*(\boldsymbol{\theta}_1, \boldsymbol{\theta}_2)$ is a subset of the set of values of the log-likelihood function, namely those values at which the second parameter vector satisfies the first-order conditions.

The most familiar case in which we can concentrate a log-likelihood function arises when we are estimating a variance parameter and a mean of some sort (such as a regression).

EXAMPLE 5.10 Concentrated Log-Likelihood Function

In Example 4.19, we found the maximum likelihood estimators of the mean and variance of a normal population, μ and σ^2. The log-likelihood function is

$$\log L(\mu, \sigma^2) = -\frac{n}{2}[\ln(2\pi) + \ln \sigma^2] - \frac{1}{2\sigma^2}\sum_{i=1}^{n}(x_i - \mu)^2.$$

The solution to the likelihood equation for σ^2 [see (4-49)] implies that however we estimate μ, the estimator will be

$$\hat{\sigma}^2 = \frac{1}{n}\sum_{i=1}^{n}(x_i - \hat{\mu}_{\text{ML}})^2.$$

If we insert this solution back into the log-likelihood function, we obtain the concentrated log-likelihood,

$$\text{Ln } L_c = -\frac{n}{2}\left\{1 + \ln(2\pi) + \ln\left[\frac{1}{n}\sum_{i=1}^{n}(x_i - \hat{\mu}_{\text{ML}})^2\right]\right\}.$$

The solution for μ is, of course, $\bar{x}$, so the solution for σ^2 is the usual one. This is a particularly simple example. In fact, you could concentrate the log-likelihood over μ instead of σ^2. We leave that as an exercise.

We will examine another application in Example 5.11.

5.5.4. Optimization with Constraints

Occasionally, some or all of the parameters of a model are constrained, for example, to be positive in the case of a variance or to be in a certain range, such as a correlation coefficient. Optimization subject to constraints is often yet another art form. The elaborate literature on the general problem provides some guidance—see, for example, Appendix B in Judge et al. (1985)—but applications still, as often as not, require some creativity on the part of the analyst. In this section, we will examine a few of the most common forms of constrained optimization as they arise in econometrics.

Parametric constraints typically come in two forms, which may occur simultaneously in a problem. Equality constraints can be written $\mathbf{c}(\boldsymbol{\theta}) = \mathbf{0}$, where $c_j(\boldsymbol{\theta})$ is a continuous and differentiable function. Typical applications include linear constraints on slope vectors, such as a requirement that a set of elasticities in a log-linear model add to one, exclusion restrictions, which are often cast in the form of interesting hypotheses about whether or not a variable should appear in a model, (i.e., whether a coefficient is zero or not), and equality restrictions, such as the symmetry restrictions in a translog model, which require that parameters in two different equations be equal to each other. Inequality constraints, in general, will be of the form $a_j \leq c_j(\boldsymbol{\theta}) \leq b_j$, where a_j and b_j are known constants (either of which may be infinite). Once again, the typical application in econometrics involves a restriction on a single parameter, such as $\sigma > 0$ for a variance parameter, $-1 \leq \rho \leq 1$ for a correlation coefficient, or $\beta_j \geq 0$ for a particular slope coefficient in a model. We will consider the two cases separately.

In the case of equality constraints, for practical purposes of optimization, there are usually two strategies available. One can use a Lagrangean multiplier approach. The new optimization problem is

$$\text{Max}_{\boldsymbol{\theta},\boldsymbol{\lambda}}\, L(\boldsymbol{\theta}, \boldsymbol{\lambda}) = F(\boldsymbol{\theta}) + \boldsymbol{\lambda}'\mathbf{c}(\boldsymbol{\theta}).$$

The necessary conditions for an optimum are

$$\frac{\partial L(\boldsymbol{\theta}, \boldsymbol{\lambda})}{\partial \boldsymbol{\theta}} = \mathbf{g}(\boldsymbol{\theta}) + \mathbf{C}(\boldsymbol{\theta})'\boldsymbol{\lambda} = \mathbf{0},$$

$$\frac{\partial L(\boldsymbol{\theta}, \boldsymbol{\lambda})}{\partial \boldsymbol{\lambda}} = \mathbf{c}(\boldsymbol{\theta}) = \mathbf{0},$$

where $\mathbf{g}(\boldsymbol{\theta})$ is the familiar gradient of $F(\boldsymbol{\theta})$ and $\mathbf{C}(\boldsymbol{\theta})$ is a $J \times K$ matrix of derivatives with jth row equal to $\partial c_j/\partial \boldsymbol{\theta}'$. The joint solution will provide the constrained optimizer, as well as the Lagrange multipliers, which are often interesting in their own right. The disadvantage of this approach is that it increases the dimensionality of the optimization problem. An alternative strategy is to eliminate some of the parameters by either imposing the constraints directly on the function or by solving out the constraints. For exclusion restrictions, which are usually of the form $\theta_j = 0$, this usually means dropping a variable from a model. Other restrictions can often be imposed just by building them into the model. For example, in a function of θ_1, θ_2, and θ_3, if the restriction is of the form $\theta_3 = \theta_1\theta_2$, θ_3 can be eliminated from the model by a direct substitution.

Inequality constraints are more difficult. For the general case, one suggestion is to transform the constrained problem into an unconstrained one by imposing some sort of penalty function into the optimization criterion that will cause a parameter vector that violates the constraints, or nearly does so, to be an unattractive choice. For example, to force a parameter θ_j to be nonzero, one might maximize the augmented function $F(\boldsymbol{\theta}) - |1/\theta_j|$. This is a feasible approach, but it has the disadvantage that because the penalty is a function of the parameters, different penalty functions will lead to different solutions of the optimization problem. For the most common problems in econometrics, a simpler approach will usually suffice. One can often reparameterize a function so that the new parameter is unconstrained. For example, the "method of squaring" is sometimes used to force a parameter to be positive. If we require θ_j to be positive, we can define $\theta_j = \alpha^2$ and substitute α^2 for θ_j wherever it appears in the model. Then an unconstrained solution for α is obtained. An alternative reparameterization for a parameter that must be positive that is often used is $\theta_j = \exp(\alpha)$. To force a parameter to be between 0 and 1, we can use the func tion $\theta_j = 1/[1 + \exp(\alpha)]$. The range of α is now unrestricted. Experience suggests that a third, less orthodox approach works very well for many problems. When the constrained optimization is begun, there is a starting value $\boldsymbol{\theta}^0$ that begins the iterations. Presumably, $\boldsymbol{\theta}^0$ obeys the restrictions. (If not, and none can be found, the optimization process must be terminated immediately.) The next iterate, $\boldsymbol{\theta}^1$, is a step away from $\boldsymbol{\theta}^0$, by $\boldsymbol{\theta}^1 = \boldsymbol{\theta}^0 + \lambda_0\boldsymbol{\delta}^0$. Suppose that $\boldsymbol{\theta}^1$ violates the constraints. By construction, we know that there is some value $\boldsymbol{\theta}_*^1$ between $\boldsymbol{\theta}^0$ and $\boldsymbol{\theta}^1$ that does not violate the constraint, where "between" means only that a shorter step is taken. Therefore, the next value for the iteration can be $\boldsymbol{\theta}_*^1$. The logic is true at every iteration, so a way to proceed is to alter the iteration so that the step length is shortened when necessary when a parameter violates the constraints.

5.5.5. Some Practical Considerations

The reasons for the good performance of many algorithms, including DFP, are unknown. Moreover, different algorithms may perform differently in given settings. Indeed, for some problems, one algorithm may fail to converge whereas another will succeed in finding a solution without great difficulty. In view of this, computer programs such as GQOPT[38] and Gauss[39] that offer a menu of different preprogrammed algorithms can be particularly useful. It is sometimes worth the effort to try more than one algorithm on a given problem.

Step Sizes. Except for the steepest ascent case, an optimal line search is likely to be infeasible or to require more effort than it is worth in view of the potentially large number of function evaluations required. In most cases, the choice of a step size is likely to be rather ad hoc. But within limits, the most widely used algorithms appear to be robust to inaccurate line searches. For example, one method employed by the widely used TSP computer program[40] is

---

[38]Goldfeld and Quandt (1972).

[39]Edlefson and Jones (1985).

[40]Hall (1982, p. 147).

the method of *squeezing,* which tries $\lambda = 1, \frac{1}{2}, \frac{1}{4}$, and so on until an improvement in the function results. Although this is obviously a bit unorthodox, it appears to be quite effective when used with the Gauss–Newton method for nonlinear least squares problems. (See Chapter 11.) A somewhat more elaborate rule is suggested by Berndt et al. (1974). Choose an ϵ between 0 and $\frac{1}{2}$; then find a λ such that

$$\epsilon < \frac{F(\boldsymbol{\theta} + \lambda\boldsymbol{\Delta}) - F(\boldsymbol{\theta})}{\lambda\mathbf{g}'\boldsymbol{\Delta}} < 1 - \epsilon. \tag{5-27}$$

Of course, which value of ϵ to choose is still open, so the choice of λ remains ad hoc. Moreover, in neither of these cases is there any optimality to the choice; we merely find a λ that leads to a function improvement. Other authors have devised relatively efficient means of searching for a step size without doing the full optimization at each iteration.[41]

Assessing Convergence. Ideally, the iterative procedure should terminate when the gradient is zero. In practice, this will not be possible, primarily because of accumulated rounding error in the computation of the function and its derivatives. In view of this, a number of alternative convergence criteria are used. Most of them are based on the relative changes in the function or the parameters. There is considerable variation in those used in different computer programs, and there are some pitfalls that should be avoided. A critical absolute value for the elements of the gradient or its norm will be affected by any scaling of the function, such as normalizing it by the sample size. Similarly, stopping on the basis of small absolute changes in the parameters can lead to premature convergence when the parameter vector approaches the maximizer. It is probably best to use several criteria simultaneously, such as the proportional change in both the function and the parameters. Belsley (1980) discusses a number of possible stopping rules. One that has proved useful and is immune to the scaling problem is to base convergence on $\mathbf{g}'\mathbf{H}^{-1}\mathbf{g}$.

Multiple Solutions. It is possible for a function to have several local extrema. It is difficult to know a priori whether this is true of the one at hand. But if the function is not globally concave, it may be a good idea to attempt to maximize it from several starting points to ensure that the maximum obtained is the global one. Ideally, a starting value near the optimum can facilitate matters; in some settings, this can be obtained by using a consistent estimate of the parameter for the starting point. The method of moments, if available, is sometimes a convenient device for doing so.

No Solution. Finally, it should be noted that in a nonlinear setting the iterative algorithm can break down, even in the absence of constraints, for at

---

[41]See, for example, Joreskog and Gruvaeus (1970), Powell (1964), Quandt (1983), and Hall (1982).

least two reasons. The first is that the problem being solved may be so numerically complex as to defy solution. The second possibility, which is often neglected, is that the proposed model may simply be inappropriate for the data. In a linear setting, a low R^2 or some other diagnostic test may suggest that the model and data are mismatched, but as long as the full rank condition is met by the regressor matrix, a linear regression can *always* be computed. Nonlinear models are not so forgiving. The failure of an iterative algorithm to find a maximum of the criterion function may be a warning that the model is not appropriate for this body of data.

5.6. EXAMPLES

To illustrate the use of gradient methods, we consider two simple problems.

EXAMPLE 5.11 Function of One Parameter

First, consider maximizing a function of a single variable, $f(\theta) = \ln(\theta) - 0.1\theta^2$. The function is shown in Figure 5.5. The first and second derivatives are

$$f'(\theta) = \frac{1}{\theta} - 0.2\theta,$$

$$f''(\theta) = \frac{-1}{\theta^2} - 0.2.$$

Equating f' to zero yields the simple solution $\theta = \sqrt{5} = 2.236$. At the solution, $f'' = -0.4$, so this is indeed a maximum. To demonstrate the use of an iterative method, we solve this problem using Newton's method. Observe, first, that the second derivative is always negative for any admissible (positive) θ.[42] Therefore, it should not matter where we start the iterations; we shall eventually find the maximum. For a single parameter, Newton's method is

$$\theta_{t+1} = \theta_t - [f_t'/f_t''].$$

The sequence of values that results when 5 is used as the starting value is given in Table 5.2. The path of the iterations is also shown in the table.

EXAMPLE 5.12 Function of Two Parameters—The Gamma Distribution

For random sampling from the gamma distribution,

$$f(y_i, \beta, \rho) = \frac{\beta^\rho}{\Gamma(\rho)} e^{-\beta y_i} y_i^{\rho - 1}.$$

[42]This is a problem in which an inequality restriction, $\theta > 0$, is required. As is common, for our first attempt, however, we shall neglect the constraint.

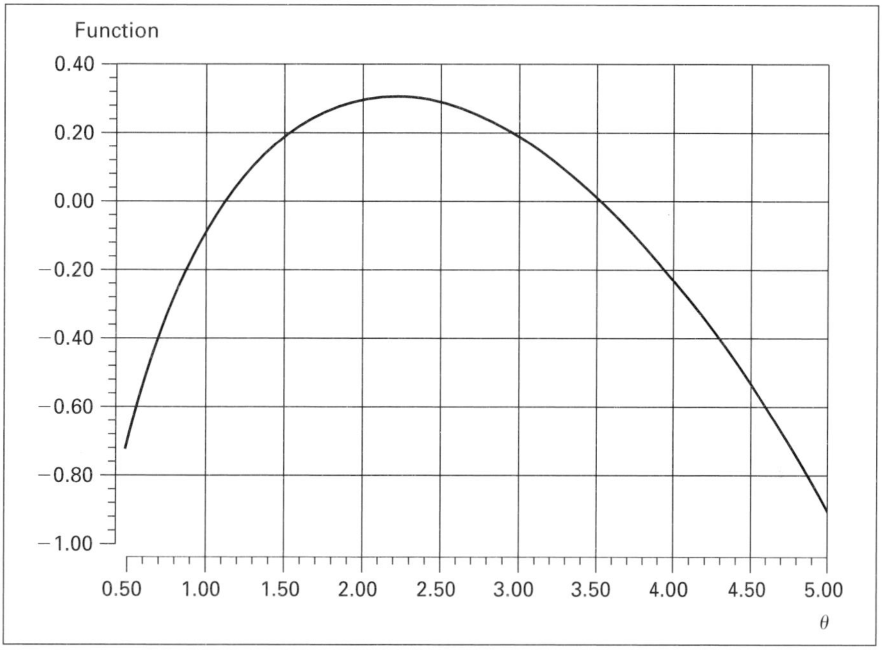

FIGURE 5.5 Function of One Variable Parameter.

The log-likelihood is $\ln L(\beta, \rho) = n\rho \ln \beta - n \ln \Gamma(\rho) - \beta \sum_{i=1}^{n} y_i + (\rho - 1) \sum_{i=1}^{n} \ln y_i$. (See Section 4.8.4.) It is often convenient to scale the log-likelihood by the sample size. Suppose, as well, that we have a sample with

$$\bar{y} = 3 \quad \text{and} \quad \overline{\ln y} = 1.$$

Then the function to be maximized is $F(\beta, \rho) = \rho \ln \beta - \ln \Gamma(\rho) - 3\beta + \rho - 1$. The derivatives are

$$\frac{\partial F}{\partial \beta} = \frac{\rho}{\beta} - 3,$$

TABLE 5.2 Iterations for Newton's Method

Iteration	θ	f	f'	f''
0	5.00000	−0.890562	−0.800000	−0.240000
1	1.66667	0.233048	0.266667	−0.560000
2	2.14286	0.302956	0.030952	−0.417778
3	2.23404	0.304718	0.000811	−0.400363
4	2.23607	0.304719	0.0000004	−0.400000

$$\frac{\partial F}{\partial \rho} = \ln \beta - \frac{\Gamma'}{\Gamma} + 1 = \ln \beta - \Psi(\rho) + 1,$$
$$\frac{\partial^2 F}{\partial \beta^2} = \frac{-\rho}{\beta^2},$$
$$\frac{\partial^2 F}{\partial \rho^2} = \frac{-(\Gamma\Gamma'' - \Gamma'^2)}{\Gamma^2} = -\Psi'(\rho),$$
$$\frac{\partial^2 F}{\partial \beta\, \partial \rho} = \frac{1}{\beta}.$$

Finding a good set of starting values is often a difficult problem. Here we choose three starting points somewhat arbitrarily: $(\rho^0, \beta^0) = (4,1)$ (8,3), and (2,7). The solution to the problem is (5.233, 1.7438). We used Newton's method and DFP with a line search to maximize this function.[43] For Newton's method, $\lambda = 1$. The results are shown in Table 5.3. The two methods were essentially the same when starting from a good starting point (trial 1), but differed substantially when starting from a poorer one (trial 2). Note that DFP and Newton approached the solution from different directions in trial 2. The third starting point shows the value of a line search. At this starting value, the Hessian is extremely large, and the second value for the parameter vector with Newton's method is $(-47.671, -233.35)$, at which point F cannot be computed and this method must be abandoned. Beginning with $\mathbf{H} = \mathbf{I}$ and using a line search, DFP reaches the point (6.63, 2.03) at the first iteration, after which convergence occurs routinely in three more iterations. At the solution, the Hessian is $[(-1.72038, 0.191153)', (0.191153, -0.210579)']$. The diagonal elements of the Hessian are negative and its determinant is 0.32574, so it is negative definite.

[43]The one used is described in Joreskog and Gruvaeus (1970).

TABLE 5.3 Iterative Solutions to Max(ρ, β) $\rho \ln \beta - \ln \Gamma(\rho) - 3\beta + \rho - 1$

	Trial 1				***Trial 2***				***Trial 3***			
	DFP		***Newton***		***DFP***		***Newton***		***DFP***		***Newton***	
Iter.	ρ	β	ρ	β	ρ	β	ρ	β	ρ	β	ρ	β
0	4.000	1.000	4.000	1.000	8.000	3.000	8.000	3.000	2.000	7.000	2.000	7.000
1	3.981	1.345	3.812	1.203	7.117	2.518	2.640	0.615	6.663	2.027	−47.7	−233.
2	4.005	1.324	4.795	1.577	7.144	2.372	3.203	0.931	6.195	2.075	—	—
3	5.217	1.743	5.190	1.728	7.045	2.389	4.257	1.357	5.239	1.731	—	—
4	5.233	1.744	5.231	1.744	5.114	1.710	5.011	1.656	5.251	1.754	—	—
5	—	—	—	—	5.239	1.747	5.219	1.740	5.233	1.744	—	—
6	—	—	—	—	5.233	1.744	5.233	1.744	—	—	—	—

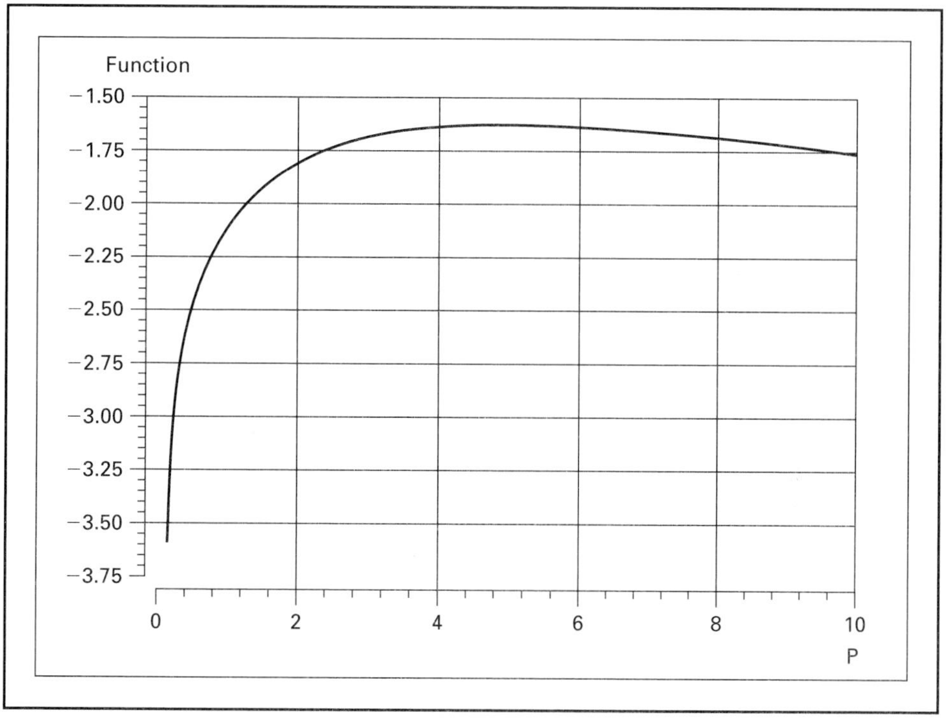

FIGURE 5.6 Concentrated Log-Likelihood.

(The two characteristic roots are −1.7442 and −0.18675). Therefore, this is indeed the maximum of the function.

EXAMPLE 5.13 A Concentrated Log-Likelihood Function

There is another way that the problem in Example 5.12 might have been solved. The first of the necessary conditions implies that at the joint solution for (β, ρ), β will equal $\rho/3$. Suppose that we impose this requirement on the function we are maximizing. This produces the **concentrated** (over β) **log-likelihood function:**

$$\begin{aligned} F_c(\rho) &= \rho \ln(\rho/3) - \ln \Gamma(\rho) - 3(\rho/3) + \rho - 1 \\ &= \rho \ln(\rho/3) - \ln \Gamma(\rho) - 1. \end{aligned}$$

This function could be maximized by an iterative search or by a simple one-dimensional grid search. Figure 5.6 shows the behavior of the function. As expected, the maximum occurs at $\rho = 5.233$. The value of β is found as $5.23/3 = 1.743$.

The concentrated log-likelihood is a useful device in many problems. Note the interpretation of the function plotted in Figure 5.5. The original function of ρ and β is a surface in three dimensions. The curve in Figure 5.5 is a projection of that function; it is a plot of the function values above the line $\beta = \rho/3$. By virtue of the first-order condition, we know that one of these points will be the maximizer of the function. Therefore, we may restrict our search for the overall maximum of $F(\beta, \rho)$ to the points on this line.

EXERCISES

1. Show how to maximize the function

$$f(\beta) = \frac{1}{\sqrt{2\pi}} e^{-(\beta-c)^2/2}$$

with respect to β for a constant c using Newton's method. Show that maximizing $\ln f(\beta)$ leads to the same solution. Plot $f(\beta)$ and $\ln f(\beta)$.

2. Prove that Newton's method for minimizing the sum of squared residuals in the linear regression model will converge to the minimum in one iteration.

3. For the Poisson regression model,

$$\text{Prob}(Y_i = y_i \mid \mathbf{x}_i) = \frac{e^{-\lambda_i}\lambda_i^{y_i}}{y_i!},$$

where

$$\lambda_i = e^{\boldsymbol{\beta}'\mathbf{x}_i},$$

and the log-likelihood function is $\ln L = \Sigma_{i=1}^{n} \ln \text{Prob}(Y_i = y_i \mid \mathbf{x}_i)$.

(a) Insert the expression for λ_i to obtain the log-likelihood function in terms of the observed data.

(b) Derive the first-order conditions for maximizing this function with respect to $\boldsymbol{\beta}$.

(c) Derive the second derivatives matrix of this criterion function with respect to $\boldsymbol{\beta}$. Is this matrix negative definite?

(d) Define the computations for using Newton's method to obtain estimates of the unknown parameters.

(e) Write out the full set of steps in an algorithm for obtaining the estimates of the parameters of this model. Include in your algorithm a test for convergence of the estimates based on Belsley's suggested criterion.

(f) How would you obtain starting values for your iterations?

(g) The following data are generated by the Poisson regression model with $\ln \lambda = \alpha + \beta x$:

y	6	7	4	10	10	6	4	7	2	3	6	5	3	3	4
x	1.5	1.8	1.8	2.0	1.3	1.6	1.2	1.9	1.8	1.0	1.4	0.5	0.8	1.1	0.7

Use your results from parts a through f to compute the maximum likelihood estimates of α and β. Also obtain estimates of the asymptotic covariance matrix of your estimates.

4. Use Monte Carlo integration to plot the function $g(r) = E[x^r | x > 0]$ for the standard normal distribution.

5. For the model in Example 5.10, derive the LM statistic for the test of the hypothesis that $\mu = 0$.

6. In Example 5.8, what is the concentrated over μ log-likelihood function?

CHAPTER 6

The Classical Multiple Linear Regression Model — Specification and Estimation

6.1. INTRODUCTION

An econometric study begins with a set of propositions about some aspect of the economy. The theory specifies a set of precise, deterministic relationships among variables. Familiar examples are demand equations, production functions, and macroeconomic models. The empirical investigation provides estimates of unknown parameters in the model, such as elasticities or the marginal propensity to consume, and usually attempts to measure the validity of the theory against the behavior of observable data. This and the next several chapters develop a number of techniques used in this framework. We begin with a generic linear model and a basic statistical specification. Subsequent chapters will discuss more elaborate specifications and complications that arise in the application of techniques that are based on the simple models presented here.

6.2. THE LINEAR MODEL

The **multiple linear regression model** is used to study the relationship between a dependent variable and several independent variables. The generic form of the linear regression model is

$$\begin{aligned} y_i &= f(x_{i1}, x_{i2}, \ldots, x_{iK}) + \epsilon_i \\ &= \beta_1 x_{i1} + \beta_2 x_{i2} + \cdots + \beta_K x_{iK} + \epsilon_i, \quad i = 1, \ldots, n, \end{aligned} \tag{6-1}$$

where y is the **dependent** or explained variable, $x_1, \ldots, x_K$ are the **independent** or **explanatory** variables, and i indexes the n sample observations. One's theory will specify $f(x_{i1}, x_{i2}, \ldots, x_{iK})$. This is commonly called the **population**

regression equation of y on $x_1, \ldots, x_K$. In this setting, y is the **regressand** and $x_k, k = 1, \ldots, K$, are the **regressors** or **covariates.** The term ϵ is a random **disturbance,** so named because it "disturbs" an otherwise stable relationship. The disturbance arises for several reasons. The primary reason is that we cannot hope to capture every influence on an economic variable in a model, no matter how elaborate. The net effect, which can be positive or negative, of these omitted factors is captured in the disturbance. There are many other contributors to the disturbance in an empirical model. Probably the most significant is errors of measurement. It is easy to theorize about the relationships among precisely defined variables; it is quite another to obtain accurate measures of these variables. For example, the difficulty of obtaining reasonable measures of profits, interest rates, capital stocks, or worse yet, flows of services from capital stocks is a recurrent theme in the empirical literature. At the extreme, there may be no observable counterpart to the theoretical variable. The literature on the permanent income model of consumption [e.g., Friedman (1957)] provides an interesting example.

EXAMPLE 6.1 Keynes's Consumption Function

Consider the following propositions from Keynes's (1936) *General Theory:*

> We shall therefore define what we shall call the propensity to consume as the functional relationship f between X, a given level of income and C the expenditure on consumption out of that level of income, so that $C = f(X)$.[1]
>
> The amount that the community spends on consumption depends (i) partly on the amount of its income, (ii) partly on other objective attendant circumstances, and (iii) partly on the subjective needs and the psychological propensities and habits of the individuals composing it . . . .
>
> The fundamental psychological law upon which we are entitled to depend with great confidence, both a priori from our knowledge of human nature and from the detailed facts of experience, is that men are disposed, as a rule and on the average, to increase their consumption as their income increases, but not by as much as the increase in their income.[2] That is . . . dC/dX is positive and less than unity.
>
> But, apart from short-period changes in the level of income, it is also obvious that a higher absolute level of income will tend as a rule to widen the gap between income and consumption. . . . These reasons will lead, as a rule, to a greater proportion of income being saved as real income increases.

The theory posits a stable relationship between consumption and income, $C = f(X)$, and claims in the third paragraph that the marginal propensity to consume (MPC), dC/dX, is between 0 and 1. The final paragraph asserts that the average propensity to consume (APC), C/X, falls as income rises, or

[1] Keynes's original text denoted the function X, not f, and income Y, not X. We have changed the notation to avoid confusion with the later discussion.

[2] Modern economists are rarely this confident about their theories.

$d(C/X)/dX = (\text{MPC} - \text{APC})/X < 0$. It follows that MPC < APC. The most common formulation of the consumption function is a linear relationship

$$C = \alpha + \beta X$$

that satisfies Keynes's "laws" if β lies between 0 and 1 and α is greater than 0.[3]

These theoretical results provide the basis for an empirical study. Given an appropriate data set, we could investigate whether the linear function just given is a satisfactory description of the relation between consumption and income, and if so, whether α is positive and β is between 0 and 1.

Table 6.1 and Figure 6.1 present aggregate consumption and personal income in constant dollars for the U.S. economy for the 10 years of 1970–1979. It is apparent from the figure that, at least superficially, the data are consistent with the theory. But the linear function is only approximate; in fact, it is unlikely that consumption and income can be connected by any simple relationship. The **deterministic** relationship is clearly inadequate. (Recall the list of three explanations in the second paragraph of the excerpt.) The model is intended only to represent the salient features of this part of the economy. We are not so ambitious as to attempt to capture every influence in the relationship, but only those that are substantial enough to model directly.

The next step is to incorporate in the model the inherent randomness in its real-world counterpart. Thus, we write $C = f(X, \epsilon)$, where ϵ is a stochastic element. It is important not to view ϵ as a catchall for the inadequacies of the model. For example, Figure 6.2 shows the same measured variables as Figure 6.1 for the years 1940 to 1950. The same moderate lack of fit appears. But for the years 1942 to 1945, something is obviously missing. These differences are not the result of random variation; 1942 to 1945 were years of wartime rationing, which prevented consumption from rising to rates historically consistent with these levels of income. This would be incorporated in the model if

TABLE 6.1 Disposable Personal Income and Personal Consumption Expenditures

Year	*Disposable Income*	*Personal Consumption*	*Year*	*Disposable Income*	*Personal Consumption*
1970	751.6	672.1	1975	874.9	779.4
1971	779.2	696.8	1976	906.8	823.1
1972	810.3	737.1	1977	942.9	864.3
1973	864.7	767.9	1978	988.8	903.2
1974	857.5	762.8	1979	1015.7	927.6

Source: Economic Report of the President, U.S. Government Printing Office, Washington, D.C., 1984.
Note: Figures are in billions of 1972 dollars.

[3]For analysis of nonlinear models, see Chapter 10 and, for example, Husby (1971).

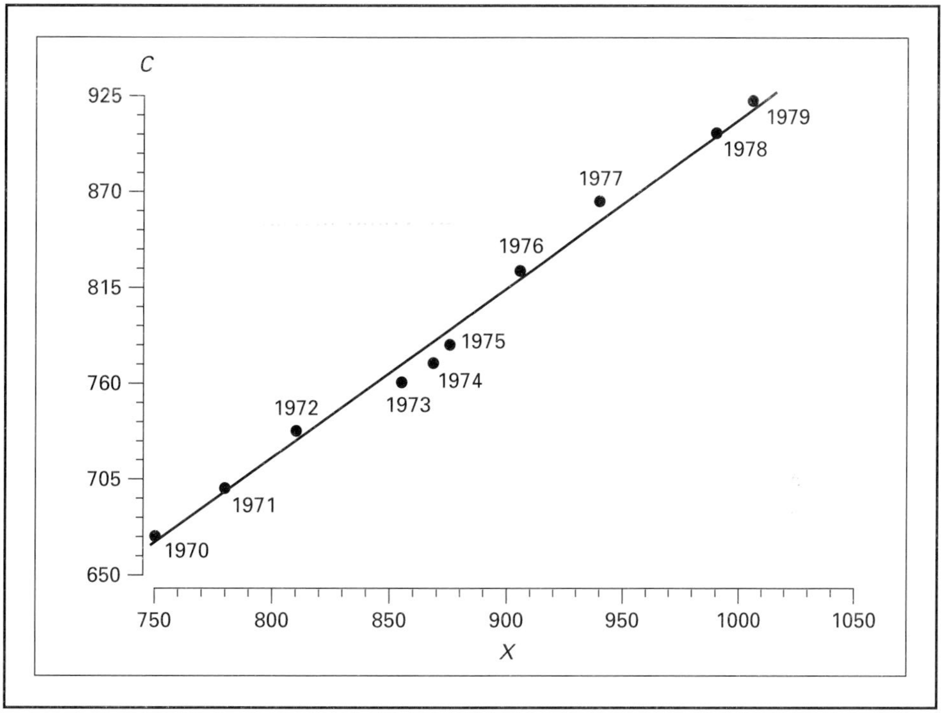

FIGURE 6.1 Consumption Data, 1970–1979.

one intended to apply it to this earlier period. It remains to establish how the stochastic element will be incorporated in the equation. The most frequent approach is to assume that it is *additive.* Thus, we can recast the equation in **stochastic** terms:

$$C = \alpha + \beta X + \epsilon.$$

This is the empirical counterpart to the theoretical model.

We assume that each observation in our sample (C_t, X_t), $t = 1, \ldots, T$, is generated by an underlying process described by $C_t = \alpha + \beta X_t + \epsilon_t$, $t = 1, \ldots, T$. Observed consumption is the sum of two parts, a deterministic part $\alpha + \beta X$ and the random component ϵ. Our objective is to estimate the unknown parameters of the model, use the data to study the validity of the theoretical propositions, and perhaps use the estimated model to predict the value of consumption. How we proceed from here depends crucially on what we assume about the stochastic process that has led to our observations of the data in hand.

One of the most useful aspects of the multiple regression model is its ability to identify the independent effects of a set of variables on a dependent variable.

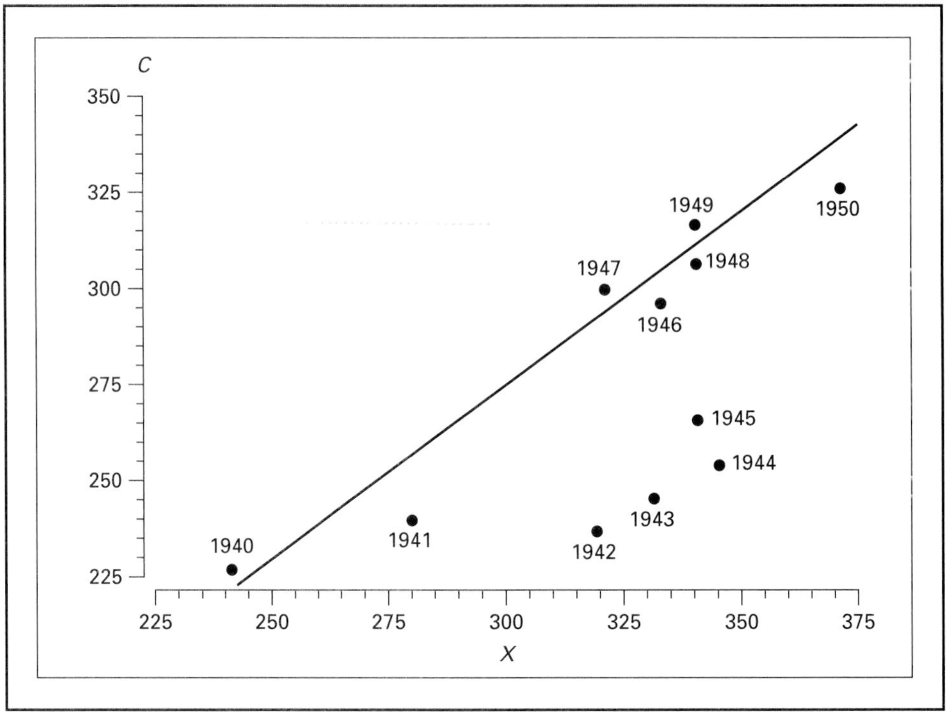

FIGURE 6.2 Consumption Data, 1940–1950.

EXAMPLE 6.2 Income and Education

A number of recent studies have analyzed the relationship between income and education. We would expect, on average, higher levels of education to be associated with higher incomes. The simple regression model

$$\text{income} = \beta_1 + \beta_2 \,\text{education} + \epsilon,$$

however, neglects that most people have higher incomes when they are older than when they are young, regardless of their education. This means that β_2 will overstate the marginal impact of education. If age and education are positively correlated, the regression model will associate all the observed increases in income with increases in education. A better specification would account for the effect of age, as in

$$\text{income} = \beta_1 + \beta_2 \,\text{education} + \beta_3 \,\text{age} + \epsilon.$$

It is often observed that income tends to rise less rapidly in the later earning years than in the early ones. To accommodate this possibility, we might extend the model to

$$\text{income} = \beta_1 + \beta_2 \,\text{education} + \beta_3 \,\text{age} + \beta_4 \,\text{age}^2 + \epsilon.$$

We would expect β_3 to be positive and β_4 to be negative.

The crucial feature of this model is that it allows us to carry out a conceptual experiment that might not be observed in the actual data. In the example, we might like to (and could) compare the incomes of two individuals of the same age with different amounts of "education" even if the data set does not actually contain two such individuals. (How we should measure education is a different, and quite difficult, question that we will not be able to pursue here.)

A large literature has been devoted to an intriguing question on this subject. Education is not truly "independent" in this setting. Highly motivated individuals will choose to pursue more education (for example, by going to college or graduate school) than others. By the same token, highly motivated individuals may do things that, on average, lead them to have higher incomes. If so, does a positive β_2 that suggests an association between income and education really measure the effect of education on income, or does it reflect the effect of some underlying effect on both variables that we have not included in our regression model? We will revisit the issue in Section 20.4.

6.3. ASSUMPTIONS OF THE CLASSICAL LINEAR REGRESSION MODEL

The classical linear regression model consists of a set of assumptions about how a data set will be produced by an underlying "data-generating process." The theory will usually specify a precise, deterministic relationship between the dependent variable and the independent variables. The assumptions of the model concern the following additional issues:

1. Linear functional form of the relationship,
2. Identifiability of the model parameters,
3. Expected value of the disturbance given observed information,
4. Variances and covariances of the disturbances given observed information,
5. Nature of the sample of data on the independent variables, and
6. Probability distribution of the stochastic part of the model.

The assumptions describe the form of the model and relationships among its parts and dictate appropriate estimation and inference procedures. This section will discuss each of these in detail.

6.3.1. Linearity of the Regression Model

Let the column vector $\mathbf{x}_k$ be the n observations on variable x_k, $k = 1, \ldots, K$, and assemble these data in an $n \times K$ data matrix $\mathbf{X}$. In most contexts, the first column of $\mathbf{X}$ is assumed to be a column of 1s so that β_1 is the constant term in the model. Let $\mathbf{y}$ be the n observations, $y_1, \ldots, y_n$, and let ϵ be the column vector containing the n disturbances. The model in (6-1) can now be written

$$\mathbf{y} = \mathbf{x}_1\beta_1 + \cdots + \mathbf{x}_K\beta_K + \boldsymbol{\epsilon}, \quad \textbf{(6-2)}$$

or in the form of Assumption 1.

$$\textsc{Assumption 1:}\ \mathbf{y} = \mathbf{X}\boldsymbol{\beta} + \boldsymbol{\epsilon}. \quad \textbf{(6-3)}$$

A Notational Convention. *Henceforth, to avoid a possibly confusing and cumbersome notation, we will use a boldface* $\mathbf{x}$ *to denote a column* or *a row of* $\mathbf{X}$. *Which applies will be clear from the context. In (6-2),* $\mathbf{x}_k$ *is the kth column of* $\mathbf{X}$. *Subscripts j and k will be used to denote columns (variables). It will often be convenient to refer to a single observation in (6-3), which we would write*

$$y_i = \mathbf{x}_i'\boldsymbol{\beta} + \epsilon_i. \quad \textbf{(6-4)}$$

Subscripts i and t will be used to denote rows (observations) of $\mathbf{X}$. *In (6-4),* $\mathbf{x}_i$ *is a column vector that is the transpose of the ith* $1 \times K$ *row of* $\mathbf{X}$.

Our primary interest is in estimation and inference about the parameter vector $\boldsymbol{\beta}$. Note that the simple regression model in Example 6.1 is a special case in which $\mathbf{X}$ has only two columns, the first of which is a column of 1s. The assumption of linearity of the regression model includes the additive disturbance. For the regression to be linear in the sense described here, it must be of the form in (6-1) either in the original variables or after some suitable transformation. For example, the model

$$y = Ax^{\beta}e^{\epsilon}$$

is linear (after taking logs on both sides of the equation), whereas

$$y = Ax^{\beta} + \epsilon$$

is not. The observed dependent variable is thus the sum of two components, a deterministic element $\alpha + \beta x$ and a random variable ϵ. It is worth emphasizing that neither of the two parts is directly observed because α and β are unknown.

The linearity assumption is not as narrow as it might first appear. In the regression context, *linearity* refers to the manner in which the parameters and the disturbance enter the equation, not necessarily to the relationship between variables. For examples, the equations $y = \alpha + \beta x + \epsilon$, $y = \alpha + \beta\cos(x) + \epsilon$, $y = \alpha + \beta/x + \epsilon$, and $y = \alpha + \beta \ln x + \epsilon$ are all linear in some function of x by the definition we have used here. In the examples, only x has been transformed, but y could have been as well, as in $y = Ax^{\beta}e^{\epsilon}$, which is a linear relationship in the logs of x and y; $\ln y = \alpha + \beta \ln x + \epsilon$. The variety of functions is unlimited. This aspect of the model is used in a number of commonly used functional forms. The **log-linear model** is

$$y = e^{\beta_1}X_2^{\beta_2}X_3^{\beta_3}\cdots X_K^{\beta_K}e^{\epsilon} = e^{\beta_1}\prod_{k=2}^{K} X_k^{\beta_k}e^{\epsilon}.$$

In logs,

$$\ln y = \beta_1 + \beta_2 \ln X_2 + \beta_3 \ln X_3 + \cdots + \beta_K \ln X_K + \epsilon.$$

This is also known as the **constant elasticity** form; as in this equation, the elasticity of y with respect to changes in x is

$$\eta_k = \frac{\partial y/y}{\partial x_k/x_k} = \frac{\partial \ln y}{\partial \ln x_k} = \beta_k,$$

which does not vary with x_k. In contrast, the elasticity in the linear model is

$$\frac{\partial y/y}{\partial x_k/x_k} = \frac{x_k\beta_k}{\mathbf{x}'\boldsymbol{\beta} + \epsilon}.$$

The log-linear form is often used in models of demand and production. Different values of β produce widely varying functions. A **semilog** model is often used to model growth rates:

$$\ln y_t = \mathbf{x}_t'\boldsymbol{\beta} + \delta t + \epsilon_t.$$

In this model, the autonomous (at least not explained by the model itself) proportional, per period growth rate is

$$d \ln y/dt = \delta.$$

Other variations of the general form

$$f(y_i) = g(\mathbf{x}_i'\boldsymbol{\beta} + \epsilon_i)$$

will allow a tremendous variety of functional forms, all of which fit into our definition of a linear model.

Two examples below will discuss functional forms that, like the log-linear model, have seen very wide use in applied econometrics.

EXAMPLE 6.3 The Logistic Model

Sometimes the range and type of variation observed for the dependent variable suggest a particular type of model. In some applications, the regressand is a proportion that displays a particular pattern. In the adoption of new technologies in an industry or new products in a market, when the observed variable is the rate of adoption or saturation rate, a characteristic pattern is that displayed in Figure 6.3.[4] The rate of adoption is slow at first, then rapid as the innovation gains popularity then slow once again as the last market participants finally join. A model that would accommodate this pattern is the **logistic** functional form

$$y_t = \frac{1}{e^{-(\mathbf{x}_t'\boldsymbol{\beta}+\delta t+\epsilon_t)}}.$$

[4]A classic application is Griliches (1957).

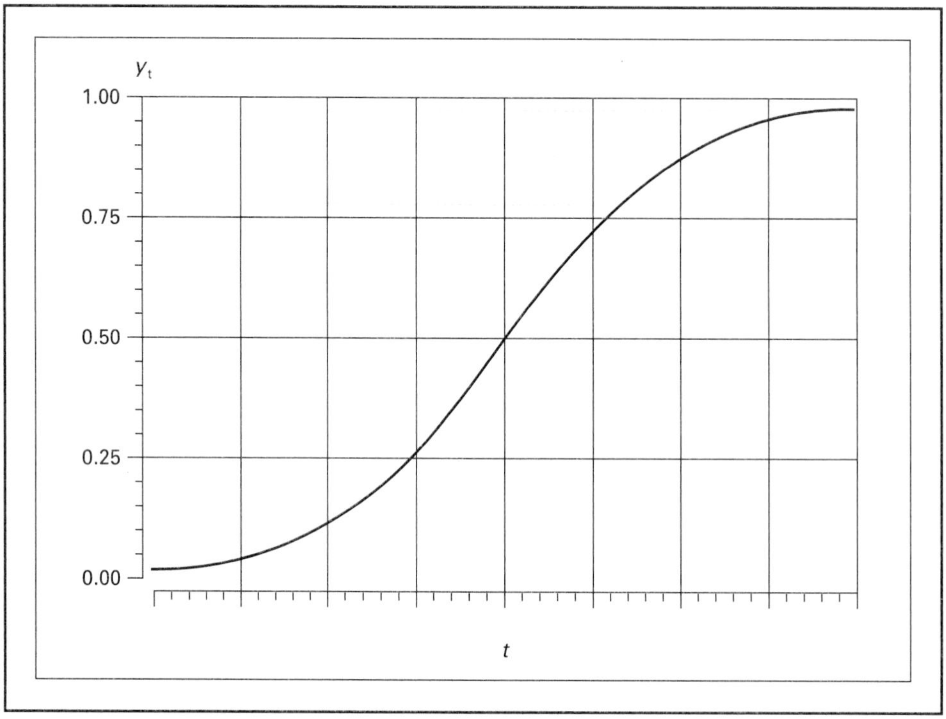

FIGURE 6.3 Logistic Model.

The transformation to linearity is

$$\text{logit}(y_t) = \ln \frac{y_t}{1 - y_t} = \mathbf{x}_t'\boldsymbol{\beta} + \delta t + \epsilon_t.$$

The logistic model is so named because of the logit transformation. We will examine applications of this model in Chapter 19.

The linear regression model is sometimes interpreted as an approximation to some unknown, underlying function. (See Section 2.9.1 for discussion.) By this interpretation, however, the linear model, even with quadratic terms, is fairly limited in that such an approximation is likely to be useful only over a small range of variation of the independent variables. The model discussed in the next example, in contrast, has proved far more effective as an approximating function.

EXAMPLE 6.4 The Translog Model

Modern studies of demand and production are usually done in the context of a **flexible functional form.** Flexible functional forms are used in econometrics because they allow analysts to model **second-order effects** such as elasticities of substitution, which are functions of the second derivatives of production, cost, or utility functions. The linear model restricts these to equal zero, whereas the log-linear model (e.g., the Cobb–Douglas model) restricts the interesting elasticities to the uninteresting values of -1 or $+1$. The most popular functional form is the **translog** model, which is often interpreted as a second-order approximation to an unknown functional form.[5] One way to derive it is as follows: We first write $y = g(x_1, \ldots, x_K)$. Then, $\ln y = \ln g(\ldots) = f(\ldots)$. Since by a trivial transformation $x_k = \exp(\ln x_k)$, we interpret the function as a function of the logarithms of the x's. Thus,

$$\ln y = f(\ln x_1, \ldots, \ln x_K).$$

Now, expand this function in a second-order Taylor series around the point $\mathbf{x} = [1, 1, \ldots, 1]'$ so that at the expansion point, the log of each variable is a convenient zero. [In practice, analysts sometimes "normalize" the measured variables by dividing by their respective sample means. It turns out that the interesting elasticities in this model are unaffected by the normalization. See Berndt and Christensen (1973) for details.] Then

$$\ln y = f(\mathbf{0}) + \sum_{k=1}^{K} [\partial f(\cdot)/\partial \ln x_k]_{|\ln \mathbf{x}=0} \ln x_k + \frac{1}{2}\sum_{k=1}^{K}\sum_{l=1}^{K} [\partial^2 f(\cdot)/\partial \ln x_l \partial \ln x_k]_{|\ln \mathbf{x}=0} \ln x_k \ln x_l + \epsilon.$$

The disturbance in this model is assumed to embody the familiar factors and the error of approximation to the unknown function. Since the function and its derivatives evaluated at the fixed value $\mathbf{0}$ are constants, we interpret them as the coefficients and write

$$\ln y = \beta_0 + \sum_{k=1}^{K} \beta_k \ln x_k + \frac{1}{2}\sum_{k=1}^{K}\sum_{l=1}^{K} \gamma_{kl} \ln x_k \ln x_l + \epsilon.$$

This model is linear by our definition but can, in fact, mimic an impressive amount of curvature when it is used to approximate another function. Among the interesting features of this formulation are that the log-linear model is a special case, $\gamma_{kl} = 0$. Also, there is an interesting test of the underlying theory possible because if the underlying function were assumed to be continuous, then by Young's theorem it must be true that $\gamma_{kl} = \gamma_{lk}$. We will see in Chapter 15 how this feature is studied in practice.

Despite its great flexibility, the linear model does not include all the situations we encounter in practice. For a simple example, there is no transformation that will reduce $y = \alpha + 1/(\beta + x)$ to linearity. The methods we consider in this chapter are not appropriate for estimating the parameters of such a model. Relatively straightforward techniques have been developed for inherently nonlinear models such as this, however. We shall treat them in detail in Chapter 10.

[5] See Berndt and Christensen (1973).

6.3.2. Full Rank

A very important assumption must be made about the regressors. We assume that there are no exact linear relationships among the variables.

ASSUMPTION 2: **X** is an $n \times K$ matrix with rank K. **(6-5)**

This means that **X** has full column rank; the columns of **X** are linearly independent and there are at least K observations. [See (2-42) and the surrounding text.] This assumption is known as an **identification condition.** To see the need for this assumption, consider an example.

EXAMPLE 6.5 Short Rank

Suppose that a cross-section model specifies

$$C = \beta_1 + \beta_2 \text{ nonlabor income} + \beta_3 \text{ salary} + \beta_4 \text{ income} + \epsilon,$$

where income is exactly equal to salary plus nonlabor income. Clearly, there is an exact linear dependency in the model. Now let

$$\beta_2' = \beta_2 + a,$$
$$\beta_3' = \beta_3 + a,$$

and

$$\beta_4' = \beta_4 - a,$$

where a is any number. Then the exact same value appears on the right-hand side of C if we substitute β_2', β_3', and β_4' for β_2, β_3, and β_4. Obviously, there is no way to estimate the parameters of this model. There are certain functions of the parameters that can be estimated in a case such as this. For instance, regardless of the value of a,

$$\beta_2 + \beta_4 = \beta_2' + \beta_4'$$

and

$$\beta_3 + \beta_4 = \beta_3' + \beta_4'.$$

We should be able to estimate a model that is a function of $\gamma_1 = \beta_2 + \beta_4$ and $\gamma_2 = \beta_3 + \beta_4$. By substituting income = nonlabor income + salary in the previous equation, we obtain precisely

$$C = \beta_1 + \gamma_1 \text{ nonlabor income} + \gamma_2 \text{ salary} + \epsilon.$$

If there are fewer than K observations, then **X** cannot have full rank. [See (2-43).] Hence, we make our (redundant) assumption that n is at least as large as K.[6]

[6]See, as well, Goldberger (1991, pp. 248–250) and Gujarati (1995, pp. 226–328) on the subject of micronumerosity.

EXAMPLE 6.6 No Variation in a Regressor

In a two-variable linear model with a constant term, the full rank assumption means that there must be variation in the regressor x. If there is no variation in x_i, all our observations will lie on a vertical line. This does not invalidate the other assumptions of the model; presumably, it is a flaw in the data set. The possibility that this suggests is that we *could* have drawn a sample in which there was variation in x, but in this instance, we did not. Thus, the model still applies, but we cannot learn about it from the data set in hand.

6.3.3. Regression

The disturbance is assumed to have expected value zero at every observation, which we write as

$$E[\epsilon_i \mid \mathbf{X}] = 0. \tag{6-6}$$

For the full set of observations, we write the following.

$$\text{Assumption 3:} \quad E[\boldsymbol{\epsilon} \mid \mathbf{X}] = \begin{bmatrix} E[\epsilon_1 \mid \mathbf{X}] \\ E[\epsilon_2 \mid \mathbf{X}] \\ \vdots \\ E[\epsilon_n \mid \mathbf{X}] \end{bmatrix} = \mathbf{0}. \tag{6-7}$$

There is a subtle point in this discussion that the observant reader might have noted. In (6-6), the left-hand side states, in principle, that the mean of each ϵ_i *conditioned on all observations* $\mathbf{x}_i$ is zero. This conditional mean assumption states, in words, that no observations on $\mathbf{x}$ convey information about the expected value of the disturbance. It is conceivable, for example in a time-series setting, that although $\mathbf{x}_i$ might provide no information about $E[\epsilon_i \mid \cdot]$, $\mathbf{x}_j$ *at some other observation,* such as in the previous time period, might. Our assumption at this point is that there is no information about $E[\epsilon_i \mid \cdot]$ contained in any observation $\mathbf{x}_j$. Later, when we extend the model, we will study the implications of dropping this assumption. We will also assume that the disturbances convey no information about each other. That is, $E[\epsilon_i \mid \epsilon_1, \ldots, \epsilon_{i-1}, \epsilon_{i+1}, \ldots, \epsilon_n] = 0$. In sum, at this point, we have assumed that the disturbances are purely random draws from some population.

The zero conditional mean implies that the unconditional mean is also zero, since

$$E[\epsilon_i] = E_{\mathbf{x}}[E[\epsilon_i \mid \mathbf{x}_i]] = E_{\mathbf{x}}[0] = 0.$$

Since $\text{Cov}[\mathbf{x}, \boldsymbol{\epsilon}] = \text{Cov}[\mathbf{x}, E[\boldsymbol{\epsilon} \mid \mathbf{X}]]$, Assumption 3 implies that $\text{Cov}[\mathbf{X}, \boldsymbol{\epsilon}] = \mathbf{0}$. (Exercise: Is the converse true?)

In most cases, the zero mean assumption is not restrictive. Consider a two-variable model and suppose that the mean of ϵ is $\mu \neq 0$. Then $\alpha + \beta x + \epsilon$ is the same as $(\alpha + \mu) + \beta x + (\epsilon - \mu)$. Letting $\alpha' = \alpha + \mu$ and $\epsilon' = \epsilon - \mu$ produces the original model. For an application, see the discussion of frontier production functions in Example 6.25. If, however, the original model does not contain a constant term, then assuming the disturbance has mean zero is substantive. This does suggest that there is a potential problem in models without constant terms. As a general rule, regression models should not be specified without constant terms unless this is specifically dictated by the underlying theory.[7] Arguably, if we have reason to specify that the mean of the disturbance is something other than zero, we should build it into the systematic part of our regression, leaving in the disturbance only the unknown part of ϵ. Assumption 3 also implies that

$$E[\mathbf{y}\,|\,\mathbf{X}] = \mathbf{X}\boldsymbol{\beta}. \tag{6-8}$$

Assumptions 1 and 3 comprise the *linear regression model.* The **regression** of $\mathbf{y}$ on $\mathbf{X}$ is the conditional mean, $E[y\,|\,\mathbf{x}]$, so that without Assumption 3, $\mathbf{X}\boldsymbol{\beta}$ is *not* the conditional mean function.

The remaining assumptions will more completely specify the characteristics of the disturbances in the model and state the conditions under which the sample observations on $\mathbf{x}$ are obtained.

6.3.4. Spherical Disturbances

The fourth assumption concerns the variances and covariances of the disturbances:

$$\text{Var}[\epsilon_i\,|\,\mathbf{X}] = \sigma^2, \quad \text{for all } i = 1, \ldots, n,$$

and

$$\text{Cov}[\epsilon_i, \epsilon_j\,|\,\mathbf{X}] = 0, \quad \text{for all } i \neq j.$$

Constant variance is labeled **homoscedasticity.** [See McCulloch (1985).] Consider a model that describes the profits of firms in an industry as a function of, say, size. Even accounting for size, measured in dollar terms, the profits of large firms will exhibit greater variation than those of smaller firms. The homoscedasticity assumption would be inappropriate here. Also, survey data on household expenditure patterns often display marked **heteroscedasticity,** even after accounting for income and household size.

Uncorrelatedness across observations is labeled generically **nonautocorrelation.** In Figure 6.1, there is some suggestion that the disturbances might not be truly independent across observations. Although the number of observation is limited, it does appear that, on average, each disturbance tends to be followed by one with the same sign. This "inertia" is precisely what is meant by **autocorrelation,** and it is assumed away at this point. Methods of handling autocorrelation in economic data occupy a large proportion of the literature and will be treated at length in Chapter 13. Note that nonautocorrelation does not imply that observations y_i and y_j are uncorrelated. The assumption is that *devi-*

[7]Models that describe first differences of variables might well be specified without constants. Consider $y_t - y_{t-1}$. If there is a constant term α on the right-hand side of the equation, this means that y_t is a function of αt, which is an explosive regressor. Models with linear time trends merit special treatment in the time-series literature. We will return to this issue in Chapter 18.

ations of observations from their expected values are uncorrelated. The two assumptions imply that

$$E[\boldsymbol{\epsilon\epsilon}' \mid \mathbf{X}] = \begin{bmatrix} E[\epsilon_1\epsilon_1 \mid \mathbf{X}] & E[\epsilon_1\epsilon_2 \mid \mathbf{X}] & \cdots & E[\epsilon_1\epsilon_n \mid \mathbf{X}] \\ E[\epsilon_2\epsilon_1 \mid \mathbf{X}] & E[\epsilon_2\epsilon_2 \mid \mathbf{X}] & \cdots & E[\epsilon_2\epsilon_n \mid \mathbf{X}] \\ \vdots & \vdots & \vdots & \vdots \\ E[\epsilon_n\epsilon_1 \mid \mathbf{X}] & E[\epsilon_n\epsilon_2 \mid \mathbf{X}] & \cdots & E[\epsilon_n\epsilon_n \mid \mathbf{X}] \end{bmatrix}$$

$$= \begin{bmatrix} \sigma^2 & 0 & \cdots & 0 \\ 0 & \sigma^2 & \cdots & 0 \\ & & \vdots & \\ 0 & 0 & \cdots & \sigma^2 \end{bmatrix},$$

which we summarize in the following assumption.

Assumption 4: $E[\boldsymbol{\epsilon\epsilon}'|\mathbf{X}] = \sigma^2\mathbf{I}$. **(6-9)**

By using the variance decomposition formula in (3-70), we find

$$\text{Var}[\boldsymbol{\epsilon}] = E[\text{Var}[\boldsymbol{\epsilon} \mid \mathbf{X}]] + \text{Var}[E[\boldsymbol{\epsilon} \mid \mathbf{X}]] = \sigma^2\mathbf{I}.$$

Once again, we should emphasize that this assumption describes the information about the variances and covariances among the disturbances that is provided by the independent variables. For the present, we assume that there is none. We will also drop this assumption later when we enrich the regression model. We are also assuming that the disturbances themselves provide no information about the variances and covariances. This is a minor issue at this point, but it will become crucial in our treatment of time-series applications. Models such as $\text{Var}[\epsilon_t] = \sigma_t^2 + \alpha\epsilon_{t-1}^2$—this is a "GARCH" model (see Section 18.5)—do not violate our conditional variance assumption, but do assume that $\text{Var}[\epsilon_t | \epsilon_{t-1}] \neq \text{Var}[\epsilon_t]$.

Disturbances that meet the twin assumptions of homoscedasticity and nonautocorrelation are sometimes called **spherical** disturbances.[8]

6.3.5. Nonstochastic Regressors

It is common to assume that $\mathbf{x}_i$ is nonstochastic, as it would be in an experimental situation. Here the analyst chooses the values of the regressors and then observes y_i. This would apply, for example, in an agricultural experiment in which y_i is yield and $\mathbf{x}_i$ is fertilizer concentration and water applied. As a point of departure, we will make that assumption here. The assumption of nonstochastic regressors at this point is largely a convenience. With it, we shall be able to use the results of elementary statistics to obtain our results; the vector $\mathbf{x}_i$ is simply a

[8]The term will describe the multivariate normal distribution; see (3-95). If $\Sigma = \sigma^2\mathbf{I}$ in the multivariate normal density, then the equation $f(\mathbf{x}) = c$ is the formula for a "ball" centered at $\boldsymbol{\mu}$ with radius σ in n-dimensional space. The name *spherical* is used whether or not the normal distribution is assumed; sometimes the "spherical normal" distribution is assumed explicitly.

known constant in the probability distribution of y_i. With this simplification, Assumptions 3 and 4 can be made unconditional, although the counterparts would now simply state that the probability distribution of ϵ_i involves none of the constants in $\mathbf{X}$.

An alternative view is that the observations on $\mathbf{x}_i$ are "fixed in repeated samples," which is equivalent to doing the statistical analysis conditionally on the sample we have observed. Thus, we would only assume that the regression model and its assumptions apply to the particular set of $\mathbf{x}$'s that we have observed. Either treatment allows us to disregard the ultimate source of variation in $\mathbf{x}$ and concentrate on the relationship between y and $\mathbf{x}$.

ASSUMPTION 5: $\mathbf{X}$ is a known $n \times K$ matrix of constants. **(6-10)**

Social scientists are rarely able to analyze experimental data, and relatively few of their models are built around nonrandom regressors. Clearly, for example, in the consumption function, it would be difficult to defend such an asymmetric treatment of aggregate consumption and aggregate income. Since some of our results rely on the assumption that $\mathbf{x}_i$ is a known constant, it is important to consider the implications of a random regressor. If $\mathbf{x}_i$ is taken to be a random vector, Assumptions 1 through 4 become a statement about the joint distribution of y_i and $\mathbf{x}_i$. The development of Section 3.7 would apply. The precise nature of the regressor and how we view the sampling process will be a major determinant of our derivation of the statistical properties of our estimators and test statistics. As we shall see, we can relax the assumption of fixed, nonstochastic regressors at almost no cost. In the end, the crucial assumption is Assumption 3, the uncorrelatedness of $\mathbf{X}$ and $\boldsymbol{\epsilon}$.

6.3.6. Normality

It is convenient to assume that the disturbances are **normally distributed,** with zero mean and constant variance. That is, we add normality of the distribution to Assumptions 3 and 4.

ASSUMPTION 6: $\boldsymbol{\epsilon} | \mathbf{X} \sim N[\mathbf{0}, \sigma^2\mathbf{I}]$. **(6-11)**

In view of our description of the source of $\boldsymbol{\epsilon}$, the conditions of the central limit theorem will generally apply, at least approximately, and the normality assumption will be reasonable in most settings. A useful implication of Assumption 6 is that it implies that observations on ϵ_i are statistically independent as well as uncorrelated. [See point 3 in Section 3.8 and (3-97) and (3-99).] Normality is often viewed as an unnecessary and possibly inappropriate addition to the regression model. Except in those cases in which some alternative distribution is explicitly assumed,[9] however, the normality assumption is probably quite reasonable.

---

[9]See Example 6.24.

TABLE 6.2 Assumptions of the Classical Regression Model

A1. $\mathbf{y} = \mathbf{X}\boldsymbol{\beta} + \boldsymbol{\epsilon}$
A2. $\mathbf{X}$ is $n \times K$ with rank K
A3. $E[\boldsymbol{\epsilon} \mid \mathbf{X}] = \mathbf{0}$
A4. $E[\boldsymbol{\epsilon}\boldsymbol{\epsilon}' \mid \mathbf{X}] = \sigma^2\mathbf{I}$
A5. $\mathbf{X}$ is a nonstochastic matrix
A6. $\boldsymbol{\epsilon} \mid \mathbf{X} \sim N[\mathbf{0}, \sigma^2\mathbf{I}]$

Normality is not necessary to obtain many of the results we use in multiple regression analysis, although it will enable us to obtain several exact statistical results. It does prove useful in constructing test statistics, as shown in Section 6.6.5.[10] Later, it will be possible to relax this assumption and retain most of the statistical results we obtain here.

6.3.7. Summary

The assumptions of the classical regression model are summarized in Table 6.2 and in Figure 6.4, which shows the two-variable case.

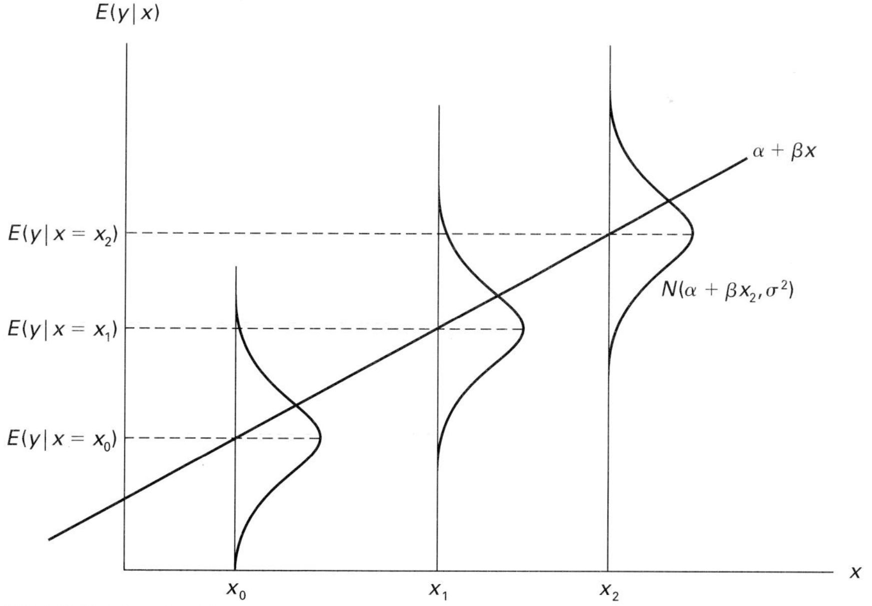

FIGURE 6.4 The Classical Regression Model.

[10] But see also Section 6.7.6.

6.4. LEAST SQUARES REGRESSION

We consider the most common method of estimating the parameters of the linear regression model, **least squares.** The unknown parameters of the stochastic relation $y_i = \mathbf{x}_i'\boldsymbol{\beta} + \epsilon_i$ are the objects of estimation. It is necessary to distinguish between population quantities, such as $\boldsymbol{\beta}$ and ϵ_i, and our sample estimates of them, denoted $\mathbf{b}$ and e_i. The population regression is $E[y_i|\mathbf{x}_i] = \mathbf{x}_i'\boldsymbol{\beta}$, while our estimate of $E[y_i|\mathbf{x}_i]$ is denoted

$$\hat{y}_i = \mathbf{x}_i'\mathbf{b}.$$

The disturbance associated with the ith data point is

$$\epsilon_i = y_i - \mathbf{x}_i'\boldsymbol{\beta}.$$

For any value of $\mathbf{b}$, we shall estimate ϵ_i with the **residual**

$$e_i = y_i - \mathbf{x}_i'\mathbf{b}.$$

From the definitions,

$$\begin{aligned} y_i &= \mathbf{x}_i'\boldsymbol{\beta} + \epsilon_i \\ &= \mathbf{x}_i'\mathbf{b} + e_i. \end{aligned}$$

These are summarized for the two variable regression in Figure 6.5.

The population quantity $\boldsymbol{\beta}$ is a vector of unknown parameters of the probability distribution of y_i whose values we hope to estimate with our sample data. This is a problem of statistical inference. It is instructive, however, to begin by considering the purely algebraic problem of choosing a vector $\mathbf{b}$ so that the fitted line $\mathbf{x}_i'\mathbf{b}$ is close to the data points. The measure of closeness constitutes a **fitting criterion.** Although numerous candidates have been suggested, the one used most frequently is **least squares.**[11]

6.4.1. The Least Squares Coefficient Vector

The least squares coefficient vector minimizes the sum of squared residuals:

$$\sum_{i=1}^{n} \epsilon_{i0}^2 = \sum_{i=1}^{n} (y_i - \boldsymbol{\beta}_0'\mathbf{x}_i)^2, \tag{6-12}$$

where $\boldsymbol{\beta}_0$ is the arbitrary choice for the coefficient vector. The minimization problem is to choose $\boldsymbol{\beta}_0$ to

$$\text{minimize}_{\boldsymbol{\beta}_0}\ S(\boldsymbol{\beta}_0) = \boldsymbol{\epsilon}_0'\boldsymbol{\epsilon}_0 = (\mathbf{y} - \mathbf{X}\boldsymbol{\beta}_0)'(\mathbf{y} - \mathbf{X}\boldsymbol{\beta}_0). \tag{6-13}$$

Expanding this gives

$$\boldsymbol{\epsilon}_0'\boldsymbol{\epsilon}_0 = \mathbf{y}'\mathbf{y} - \boldsymbol{\beta}_0'\mathbf{X}'\mathbf{y} - \mathbf{y}'\mathbf{X}\boldsymbol{\beta}_0 + \boldsymbol{\beta}_0'\mathbf{X}'\mathbf{X}\boldsymbol{\beta}_0 \tag{6-14}$$

[11]We shall have to establish that the practical approach of fitting the line as closely as possible to the data by least squares leads to estimates with good statistical properties. This makes intuitive sense and is, indeed, the case.

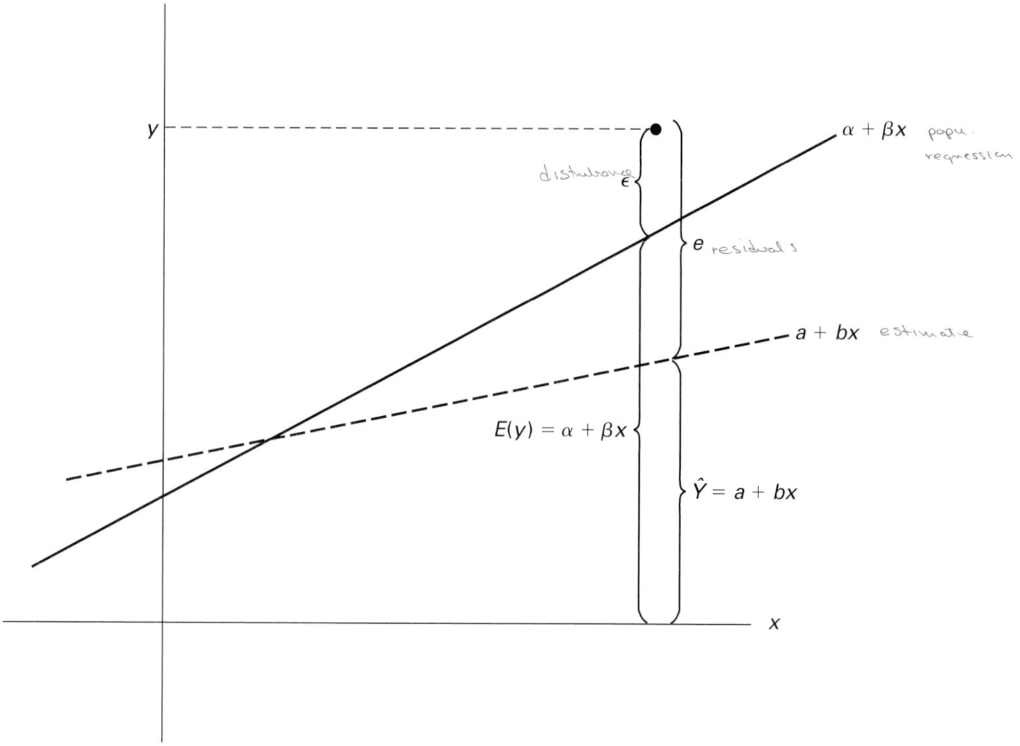

FIGURE 6.5 Population and Sample Regression.

or

$$\begin{aligned} S(\boldsymbol{\beta}_0) &= \mathbf{y}'\mathbf{y} - 2\boldsymbol{\beta}_0'\mathbf{X}'\mathbf{y} + \boldsymbol{\beta}_0'\mathbf{X}'\mathbf{X}\boldsymbol{\beta}_0 \\ &= \mathbf{y}'\mathbf{y} - 2\mathbf{y}'\mathbf{X}\boldsymbol{\beta}_0 + \boldsymbol{\beta}_0'\mathbf{X}'\mathbf{X}\boldsymbol{\beta}_0. \end{aligned}$$

The necessary condition for a minimum is

$$\frac{\partial S(\boldsymbol{\beta}_0)}{\partial \boldsymbol{\beta}_0} = -2\mathbf{X}'\mathbf{y} + 2\mathbf{X}'\mathbf{X}\boldsymbol{\beta}_0 = \mathbf{0}. \qquad \textbf{(6-15)}$$

Let **b** be the solution. Then **b** satisfies the **least squares normal equations,**

$$\mathbf{X}'\mathbf{X}\mathbf{b} = \mathbf{X}'\mathbf{y}.$$

If the inverse of $\mathbf{X}'\mathbf{X}$ exists, which follows from the full rank assumption, the solution is

$$\mathbf{b} = (\mathbf{X}'\mathbf{X})^{-1}\mathbf{X}'\mathbf{y}. \qquad \textbf{(6-16)}$$

For this solution to minimize the sum of squares,

$$\frac{\partial^2 S(\mathbf{b})}{\partial \mathbf{b}\, \partial \mathbf{b}'} = 2\mathbf{X}'\mathbf{X} \qquad \textbf{(6-17)}$$

must be a positive definite matrix. Let $q = \mathbf{c}'\mathbf{X}'\mathbf{X}\mathbf{c}$ for some arbitrary nonzero vector $\mathbf{c}$. Then

$$q = \mathbf{v}'\mathbf{v} = \sum_{i=1}^{n} v_i^2, \quad \text{where } \mathbf{v} = \mathbf{X}\mathbf{c}.$$

Unless every element of $\mathbf{v}$ is zero, q is positive. But if $\mathbf{v}$ could be zero, $\mathbf{v}$ would be a linear combination of the columns of $\mathbf{X}$ that equals $\mathbf{0}$. This contradicts the assumption that $\mathbf{X}$ has full rank. Therefore, if $\mathbf{X}$ has full rank, the least squares solution $\mathbf{b}$ minimizes the sum of squared residuals.

EXAMPLE 6.7 Least Squares in the Two-Variable Model

For any pair of values a and b, the **sum of squared residuals** is

$$\sum_{i=1}^{n} e_i^2 = \sum_{i=1}^{n} (y_i - a - bx_i)^2.$$

The least squares coefficients are the values of a and b that minimize this fitting criterion. The first-order conditions for a minimum are

$$\frac{\partial\left(\sum_{i=1}^{n} e_i^2\right)}{\partial a} = \sum_{i=1}^{n} 2(y_i - a - bx_i)(-1) = 0 \Longrightarrow \sum_{i=1}^{n} e_i = 0$$

and

$$\frac{\partial\left(\sum_{i=1}^{n} e_i^2\right)}{\partial b} = \sum_{i=1}^{n} 2(y_i - a - bx_i)(-x_i) = 0 \Longrightarrow \sum_{i=1}^{n} x_i e_i = 0.$$

Expanding these and collecting terms yields the **normal equations**

$$\begin{aligned} \sum_{i=1}^{n} y_i &= na + \left(\sum_{i=1}^{n} x_i\right)b, \\ \sum_{i=1}^{n} x_i y_i &= \left(\sum_{i=1}^{n} x_i\right)a + \left(\sum_{i=1}^{n} x_i^2\right)b. \end{aligned} \qquad \textbf{(6-18)}$$

To obtain a solution, we divide the first equation in (6-18) by n. The result is

$$\bar{y} = a + b\bar{x}.$$

The least squares regression line passes through the point of means. (If there is no intercept term, this will not be true. This is considered in the exercises.) Now isolate a:

$$a = \bar{y} - b\bar{x}. \qquad \textbf{(6-19)}$$

With a in hand, we can solve (6-18) for b. First, $\Sigma_{i=1}^{n} x_i = n\bar{x}$. Insert this and (6-19) in (6-18) and rearrange the terms:

$$\sum_{i=1}^{n} x_i y_i - n\bar{x}\bar{y} = b\left(\sum_{i=1}^{n} x_i^2 - n\bar{x}^2\right)$$

or[12]

$$b = \frac{\left(\sum_{i=1}^{n} x_i y_i\right) - n\bar{x}\bar{y}}{\left(\sum_{i=1}^{n} x_i^2\right) - n\bar{x}^2} = \frac{\sum_{i=1}^{n} (x_i - \bar{x})(y_i - \bar{y})}{\sum_{i=1}^{n} (x_i - \bar{x})^2}. \qquad \textbf{(6-20)}$$

The matrix of second derivatives with respect to a and b is

$$\begin{bmatrix} \dfrac{\partial^2\left(\sum_{i=1}^{n} e_i^2\right)}{\partial a^2} & \dfrac{\partial^2\left(\sum_{i=1}^{n} e_i^2\right)}{\partial a\, \partial b} \\ \dfrac{\partial^2\left(\sum_{i=1}^{n} e_i^2\right)}{\partial b\, \partial a} & \dfrac{\partial^2\left(\sum_{i=1}^{n} e_i^2\right)}{\partial b^2} \end{bmatrix} = \begin{bmatrix} 2n & 2n\bar{x} \\ 2n\bar{x} & 2\sum_{i=1}^{n} x_i^2 \end{bmatrix}.$$

The two diagonal elements must be positive. The determinant is $4n[(\Sigma_{i=1}^{n} x_i^2) - n\bar{x}^2] = 4n[\Sigma_{i=1}^{n} (x_i - \bar{x})^2]$, which is positive unless all values of x are the same. That violates the full rank assumption, so, the Hessian is positive definite, and a and b are the minimizers of the sum of squares.

For the consumption data in Table 6.1, the normal equations are

$$\begin{aligned} 7934.3 &= 10a + 8792.4b, \\ 7041953.27 &= 8792.4a + 7797822.22b. \end{aligned}$$

The solutions are $a = -67.5806$ and $b = 0.979267$. This is the line plotted in Figure 6.1.

To illustrate the computations in a multiple regression, we consider another example based on the macroeconomic data in Table 6.3.

EXAMPLE 6.8 Investment Equation

To estimate an investment equation, we first convert the investment and GNP series in Table 6.3 to real terms by dividing them by the CPI,[13] and then we scale the two series so that they are measured in trillions of dollars. The other

[12]But recall the discussion in Section 5.4.1. If (6-20) is badly programmed in single precision, the two formulas could give different answers.

[13]Arguably, one might choose a better deflator.

TABLE 6.3 Investment Data[a]

Year	*Nominal GNP*	*Nominal Investment*	*CPI*	*Interest Rate*[a]
1968	873.4	133.3	82.54	5.16
1969	944.0	149.3	86.79	5.87
1970	992.7	144.2	91.45	5.95
1971	1077.6	166.4	96.01	4.88
1972	1185.9	195.0	100.0	4.50
1973	1326.4	229.8	105.75	6.44
1974	1434.2	228.7	115.08	7.83
1975	1549.2	206.1	125.79	6.25
1976	1718.0	257.9	132.34	5.50
1977	1918.3	324.1	140.05	5.46
1978	2163.9	386.6	150.42	7.46
1979	2417.8	423.0	163.42	10.28
1980	2633.1	402.3	178.64	11.77
1981	2937.7	471.5	195.51	13.42
1982	3057.5	421.9	207.23	11.02

Source: Data from the *Economic Report of the President,* U.S. Government Printing Office, Washington, D.C., 1983. CPI 1967 is 79.06.

[a]Average yearly discount rate at the New York Federal Reserve Bank.

variables in the regression are a time trend (1, 2, . . .), the interest rate, and the rate of inflation, computed as the percentage change in the CPI. These produce the data matrices listed in Table 6.4.

Consider first a regression of real investment on a constant, a time trend, and real GNP, which correspond to x_1, x_2, and x_3. The normal equations are

$$\begin{bmatrix} \Sigma_i x_{i1}x_{i1} & \Sigma_i x_{i1}x_{i2} & \Sigma_i x_{i1}x_{i3} \\ \Sigma_i x_{i2}x_{i1} & \Sigma_i x_{i2}x_{i2} & \Sigma_i x_{i2}x_{i3} \\ \Sigma_i x_{i3}x_{i1} & \Sigma_i x_{i3}x_{i2} & \Sigma_i x_{i3}x_{i3} \end{bmatrix} \begin{bmatrix} b_1 \\ b_2 \\ b_3 \end{bmatrix} = \begin{bmatrix} \Sigma_i x_{i1}y_i \\ \Sigma_i x_{i2}y_i \\ \Sigma_i x_{i3}y_i \end{bmatrix}.$$

Inserting the specific variables of the example, we have

$$\begin{aligned} b_1 n \quad &+ b_2\Sigma_i T_i \quad + b_3\Sigma_i G_i \quad = \Sigma_i Y_i, \\ b_1\Sigma_i T_i &+ b_2\Sigma_i T_i^2 \quad + b_3\Sigma_i T_i G_i = \Sigma_i T_i Y_i, \\ b_1\Sigma_i G_i &+ b_2\Sigma_i T_i G_i + b_3\Sigma_i G_i^2 \quad = \Sigma_i G_i Y_i. \end{aligned}$$

A solution can be obtained by first dividing the first equation by n to obtain

$$b_1 = \overline{Y} - b_2\overline{T} - b_3\overline{G}.$$

Insert this in the second and third equations, and rearrange terms to yield a set of two equations:

TABLE 6.4 Data Matrices

Real Investment	*Constant*	*Trend*	*Real GNP*	*Interest Rate*	*Inflation Rate*
(Y)	(1)	(T)	(G)	(R)	(P)
0.161	1	1	1.058	5.16	4.40
0.172	1	2	1.088	5.87	5.15
0.158	1	3	1.086	5.95	5.37
0.173	1	4	1.122	4.88	4.99
0.195	1	5	1.186	4.50	4.16
0.217	1	6	1.254	6.44	5.75
0.199	1	7	1.246	7.83	8.82
$\mathbf{y}$ = 0.163	$\mathbf{X}$ = 1	8	1.232	6.25	9.31
0.195	1	9	1.298	5.50	5.21
0.231	1	10	1.370	5.46	5.83
0.257	1	11	1.439	7.46	7.40
0.259	1	12	1.479	10.28	8.64
0.225	1	13	1.474	11.77	9.31
0.241	1	14	1.503	13.42	9.44
0.204	1	15	1.475	11.02	5.99

Note: Subsequent results are based on these values. Slightly different results are obtained if the raw data in Table 6.3 are input to the computer program and transformed internally.

$$\begin{aligned} b_2\Sigma_i(T_i-\overline{T})^2 \qquad\qquad &+ b_3\Sigma_i(T_i-\overline{T})(G_i-\overline{G}) = \Sigma_i(T_i-\overline{T})(Y_i-\overline{Y}),\\ b_2\Sigma_i(T_i-\overline{T})(G_i-\overline{G}) &+ b_3\Sigma_i(G_i-\overline{G})^2 \qquad\qquad = \Sigma_i(G_i-\overline{G})(Y_i-\overline{Y}). \end{aligned}$$

This shows the nature of the solution for the slopes, which can be computed from the sums of squared deviations and cross products of the variables. Letting lowercase letters indicate variables measured as deviations from the sample means, we find that the least squares solutions for b_2 and b_3 are

$$b_2 = \frac{\Sigma_i t_i y_i \Sigma_i g_i^2 - \Sigma_i g_i y_i \Sigma_i t_i g_i}{\Sigma_i t_i^2 \Sigma_i g_i^2 - (\Sigma_i g_i t_i)^2},$$

$$b_3 = \frac{\Sigma_i g_i y_i \Sigma_i t_i^2 - \Sigma_i t_i y_i \Sigma_i t_i g_i}{\Sigma_i t_i^2 \Sigma_i g_i^2 - (\Sigma_i g_i t_i)^2}.$$

With these solutions in hand, the intercept can now be computed. The sample sums for the variables of this regression are

$$\begin{aligned} \overline{Y} &= 0.20333, & \Sigma_i y_i^2 &= 0.016353, & \Sigma_i t_i y_i &= 1.60400,\\ \overline{T} &= 8, & \Sigma_i t_i^2 &= 280, & \Sigma_i g_i y_i &= 0.066196,\\ \overline{G} &= 1.2873, & \Sigma_i g_i^2 &= 0.359609, & \Sigma_i t_i g_i &= 9.82000. \end{aligned}$$

Therefore, the least squares slopes and intercept in the regression of Y on a constant, T and G are

$$b_1 = -0.50639,$$
$$b_2 = -0.0171984,$$
$$b_3 = 0.653716.$$

Some additional insight is provided by manipulating the solution for, say b_3, the slope on GNP. Suppose that we just regressed investment on GNP, neglecting the time trend. At least some of the correlation we observe will be explainable because both investment and real GNP have an obvious time trend. The slope in this regression would be

$$b_{yg} = \frac{\Sigma_i g_i y_i}{\Sigma_i g_i^2} = 0.184078.$$

Now divide the preceding expression for b_3 by $\Sigma_i t_i^2 \Sigma_i g_i^2$. By manipulating it a bit and using the definition of the sample correlation between G and T, $r_{gt}^2 = (\Sigma_i g_i t_i)^2/(\Sigma_i g_i^2 \Sigma_i t_i^2)$, we obtain

$$b_{yg.t} = \frac{b_{yg}}{1 - r_{gt}^2} - \frac{b_{yt}b_{tg}}{1 - r_{gt}^2} = 0.653791.$$

(The notation used on the left-hand side is interpreted to mean the slope in the regression of y on g "in the presence of t.") The slope in the multiple regression embodies a correction to the slope in the simple regression that accounts for the influence of the additional variable t on both Y and G. For an explicit example of this effect, note what we get in the simple regression of real investment on a time trend: $b_{yt} = 1.604/280 = 0.057286$, a positive number that reflects the upward trend apparent in the data. But in the multiple regression, after we account for the influence of GNP on real investment, the slope on the time trend, as we have seen, is -0.0171984, indicating instead a downward trend. This simple example illustrates the considerable danger of drawing conclusions from a badly specified regression model. The general result for a three-variable regression in which x_1 is a constant term is

$$b_{y2.3} = \frac{b_{y2} - b_{y3}b_{32}}{1 - r_{23}^2}. \qquad \textbf{(6-21)}$$

It is clear from this expression that the magnitudes of $b_{y2.3}$ and b_{y2} can be quite different. They need not even have the same sign. The omission of important variables can be particularly serious.

As a final observation, note what becomes of $b_{yg.t}$ if r_{gt}^2 equals zero. The first term becomes b_{yg}, whereas the second becomes zero. (If G and T are not correlated, the slope in the regression of G on T, b_{gt}, is zero.) Therefore, we conclude the following.

THEOREM 6.1: Orthogonal Regression. *If the variables in a multiple regression are not correlated (i.e., are orthogonal), then the multiple regression slopes are the same as the slopes in the individual simple regressions.*

In practice, you will rarely compute a multiple regression by hand or with a calculator. Computers and easy-to-use software have greatly simplified the process. Still, it helps to see the nature of the calculations involved. For a regression with more than three variables, the calculations proceed along similar lines but are extremely cumbersome. The tools of matrix algebra rapidly become indispensable (as does a computer). Consider, for example, an enlarged model of investment that includes—in addition to the constant, time, trend, and GNP—an interest rate and the rate of inflation. Least squares requires the simultaneous solution of five normal equations. Letting **X** and **y** denote the full data matrices shown previously, the normal equations are

$$(\mathbf{X}'\mathbf{X})\mathbf{b} = \mathbf{X}'\mathbf{y}$$

or

$$\begin{bmatrix} 15.000 & 120.00 & 19.310 & 111.79 & 99.770 \\ 120.000 & 1240.0 & 164.30 & 1035.9 & 875.60 \\ 19.310 & 164.30 & 25.218 & 148.98 & 131.22 \\ 111.79 & 1035.9 & 148.98 & 953.86 & 799.02 \\ 99.770 & 875.60 & 131.22 & 799.02 & 716.67 \end{bmatrix} \begin{bmatrix} b_1 \\ b_2 \\ b_3 \\ b_4 \\ b_5 \end{bmatrix} = \begin{bmatrix} 3.0500 \\ 26.004 \\ 3.9926 \\ 23.521 \\ 20.732 \end{bmatrix}.$$

The solution is

$$\mathbf{b} = (\mathbf{X}'\mathbf{X})^{-1}\mathbf{X}'\mathbf{y};$$

$$\mathbf{b} = \begin{bmatrix} 67.413 & 2.2701 & -66.774 & 0.1242 & -0.071153 \\ 2.2701 & 0.086241 & -2.2575 & -0.006399 & -0.0009444 \\ -66.774 & -2.2575 & 67.094 & -0.16146 & -0.05055 \\ 0.1242 & -0.006399 & -0.16146 & 0.032955 & -0.016652 \\ -0.071153 & -0.0009444 & -0.05055 & -0.016652 & 0.040276 \end{bmatrix} \begin{bmatrix} 3.050 \\ 26.004 \\ 3.993 \\ 23.521 \\ 20.732 \end{bmatrix}$$

or

$$\begin{bmatrix} b_1 \\ b_2 \\ b_3 \\ b_4 \\ b_5 \end{bmatrix} = \begin{bmatrix} -0.50909 \\ -0.016581 \\ 0.67039 \\ -0.002326 \\ -0.0009394 \end{bmatrix}.$$

6.4.2. Algebraic Aspects of the Least Squares Solution

As a prelude to some later results, it is useful to examine some algebraic aspects of the least squares solution. The normal equations are

$$\begin{aligned} \mathbf{X}'\mathbf{X}\mathbf{b} - \mathbf{X}'\mathbf{y} &= -\mathbf{X}'(\mathbf{y} - \mathbf{X}\mathbf{b}) = -\mathbf{X}'\mathbf{e} \\ &= \mathbf{0}. \end{aligned} \qquad \textbf{(6-22)}$$

This means that for every column $\mathbf{x}_k$ of **X**, $\mathbf{x}_k'\mathbf{e} = 0$. If the first column of **X** is a column of ones, there are three implications.

1. *The least squares residuals sum to zero.* This follows from $\mathbf{x}_1'\mathbf{e} = \mathbf{i}'\mathbf{e} = \Sigma_i e_i = 0$.

2. *The regression hyperplane passes through the point of means of the data.* The first normal equation implies that

$$\bar{y} = \bar{\mathbf{x}}'\mathbf{b}.$$

3. *The mean of the fitted values from the regression equals the mean of the actual values.* This follows from point 1 because the fitted values are just

$$\hat{\mathbf{y}} = \mathbf{Xb}.$$

It is important to note that none of these results need hold if the regression does not contain a constant term.

The vector of least squares residuals is

$$\mathbf{e} = \mathbf{y} - \mathbf{Xb}. \tag{6-23}$$

Inserting (6-16) for $\mathbf{b}$ gives

$$\begin{aligned}\mathbf{e} &= \mathbf{y} - \mathbf{X}(\mathbf{X}'\mathbf{X})^{-1}\mathbf{X}'\mathbf{y}\\ &= (\mathbf{I} - \mathbf{X}(\mathbf{X}'\mathbf{X})^{-1}\mathbf{X}')\mathbf{y}\\ &= \mathbf{My}.\end{aligned}$$

The $n \times n$ matrix $\mathbf{M}$ is fundamental in regression analysis. You can easily show that $\mathbf{M}$ is both symmetric ($\mathbf{M} = \mathbf{M}'$) and idempotent ($\mathbf{M} = \mathbf{M}^2$). In view of (6-23), we can interpret $\mathbf{M}$ as a matrix that produces the vector of least squares residuals in the regression of $\mathbf{y}$ on $\mathbf{X}$ when it premultiplies any vector $\mathbf{y}$. It follows that

$$\mathbf{MX} = \mathbf{0}.$$

One way to interpret this result is that if $\mathbf{X}$ is regressed on $\mathbf{X}$, a perfect fit will result and the residuals will be zero.

Finally, (6-23) implies that

$$\mathbf{y} = \mathbf{Xb} + \mathbf{e},$$

which is the sample analog to (6-3). (See Figure 6.5 as well). Our least squares results partition $\mathbf{y}$ into two parts, the fitted values $\hat{\mathbf{y}} = \mathbf{Xb}$ and the residuals $\mathbf{e}$. [See Section 2.4.7, esp. (2-54).] We see from $\mathbf{MX} = \mathbf{0}$ that these two parts are orthogonal. Now, given (6-23),

$$\hat{\mathbf{y}} = \mathbf{y} - \mathbf{e} = [\mathbf{I} - \mathbf{M}]\mathbf{y} = \mathbf{Py}.$$

The matrix $\mathbf{P}$, which is also symmetric and idempotent, is a **projection matrix.** It is the matrix formed from $\mathbf{X}$ such that when a vector $\mathbf{y}$ is premultiplied by $\mathbf{P}$, the result is the fitted values in the least squares regression of $\mathbf{y}$ on $\mathbf{X}$.[14] Given

[14]It creates the projection of the vector $\mathbf{y}$ in the column space of $\mathbf{X}$. This is the problem analyzed in Section 2.4.7.

the earlier results,

$$\mathbf{PX} = \mathbf{X}$$

and

$$\mathbf{PM} = \mathbf{MP} = \mathbf{0}.$$

In manipulating equations involving least squares results, the following equivalent expressions for the sum of squared residuals are often useful:

$$\mathbf{e}'\mathbf{e} = \mathbf{y}'\mathbf{M}'\mathbf{M}\mathbf{y} = \mathbf{y}'\mathbf{M}\mathbf{y} = \mathbf{y}'\mathbf{e} = \mathbf{e}'\mathbf{y},$$
$$\mathbf{e}'\mathbf{e} = \mathbf{y}'\mathbf{y} - \mathbf{b}'\mathbf{X}'\mathbf{X}\mathbf{b},$$

and

$$\mathbf{e}'\mathbf{e} = \mathbf{y}'\mathbf{y} - \mathbf{b}'\mathbf{X}'\mathbf{y} = \mathbf{y}'\mathbf{y} - \mathbf{y}'\mathbf{X}\mathbf{b}.$$

6.4.3. Partitioned Regression and Partial Regression

It is common to specify a multiple regression model when, in fact, interest centers on only one or a subset of the full set of variables. Consider the income equation discussed in Example 6.2. Although we are primarily interested in the association of income and education, age is, of necessity, included in the model. We have already established that it would be erroneous to omit age from the equation. The question we consider here is what computations are involved in obtaining, in isolation, the coefficients of a subset of the variables in a multiple regression (for example, the coefficient of education in the aforementioned regression).

Suppose that the regression involves two sets of variables $\mathbf{X}_1$ and $\mathbf{X}_2$. Thus,

$$\mathbf{y} = \mathbf{X}\boldsymbol{\beta} + \boldsymbol{\epsilon} = \mathbf{X}_1\boldsymbol{\beta}_1 + \mathbf{X}_2\boldsymbol{\beta}_2 + \boldsymbol{\epsilon}.$$

What is the algebraic solution for $\mathbf{b}_2$? The normal equations are

$$\begin{matrix}(1)\\(2)\end{matrix}\begin{bmatrix}\mathbf{X}_1'\mathbf{X}_1 & \mathbf{X}_1'\mathbf{X}_2\\ \mathbf{X}_2'\mathbf{X}_1 & \mathbf{X}_2'\mathbf{X}_2\end{bmatrix}\begin{bmatrix}\mathbf{b}_1\\ \mathbf{b}_2\end{bmatrix} = \begin{bmatrix}\mathbf{X}_1'\mathbf{y}\\ \mathbf{X}_2'\mathbf{y}\end{bmatrix}.$$

A solution can be obtained by using the partitioned inverse matrix of (2-74) in the result

$$\begin{bmatrix}\mathbf{X}_1'\mathbf{X}_1 & \mathbf{X}_1'\mathbf{X}_2\\ \mathbf{X}_2'\mathbf{X}_1 & \mathbf{X}_2'\mathbf{X}_2\end{bmatrix}^{-1}\begin{bmatrix}\mathbf{X}_1'\mathbf{y}\\ \mathbf{X}_2'\mathbf{y}\end{bmatrix} = \begin{bmatrix}\mathbf{b}_1\\ \mathbf{b}_2\end{bmatrix}.$$

Alternatively, (1) and (2) can be manipulated directly to solve for $\mathbf{b}_2$. We first solve (1) for $\mathbf{b}_1$:

$$\begin{aligned}\mathbf{b}_1 &= (\mathbf{X}_1'\mathbf{X}_1)^{-1}\mathbf{X}_1'\mathbf{y} - (\mathbf{X}_1'\mathbf{X}_1)^{-1}\mathbf{X}_1'\mathbf{X}_2\mathbf{b}_2\\ &= (\mathbf{X}_1'\mathbf{X}_1)^{-1}\mathbf{X}_1'(\mathbf{y} - \mathbf{X}_2\mathbf{b}_2).\end{aligned} \tag{6-24}$$

This solution states that $\mathbf{b}_1$ is the set of coefficients in the regression of $\mathbf{y}$ on $\mathbf{X}_1$, minus a correction vector. We digress briefly to examine an important result embedded in (6-24). Suppose that $\mathbf{X}_1'\mathbf{X}_2 = \mathbf{0}$. Then

$$\mathbf{b}_1 = (\mathbf{X}_1'\mathbf{X}_1)^{-1}\mathbf{X}_1'\mathbf{y},$$

which is simply the coefficient vector in the regression of $\mathbf{y}$ on $\mathbf{X}_1$. The general result, which we have just proved is the following theorem.

THEOREM 6.2: Orthogonal Partitioned Regression. *In the multiple linear least squares regression of* $\mathbf{y}$ *on two sets of variables* $\mathbf{X}_1$ *and* $\mathbf{X}_2$, *if the two sets of variables are orthogonal, then the separate coefficient vectors can be obtained by separate regressions of* $\mathbf{y}$ *on* $\mathbf{X}_1$ *alone and* $\mathbf{y}$ *on* $\mathbf{X}_2$ *alone.*

Note that Theorem 6.2 encompasses 6.1. Now, inserting (6-24) in (2) produces

$$\mathbf{X}_2'\mathbf{X}_1(\mathbf{X}_1'\mathbf{X}_1)^{-1}\mathbf{X}_1'\mathbf{y} - \mathbf{X}_2'\mathbf{X}_1(\mathbf{X}_1'\mathbf{X}_1)^{-1}\mathbf{X}_1'\mathbf{X}_2\mathbf{b}_2 + \mathbf{X}_2'\mathbf{X}_2\mathbf{b}_2 = \mathbf{X}_2'\mathbf{y}.$$

After collecting terms,

$$\mathbf{X}_2'[\mathbf{I} - \mathbf{X}_1(\mathbf{X}_1'\mathbf{X}_1)^{-1}\mathbf{X}_1']\mathbf{X}_2\mathbf{b}_2 = \mathbf{X}_2'(\mathbf{I} - \mathbf{X}_1(\mathbf{X}_1'\mathbf{X}_1)^{-1}\mathbf{X}_1')\mathbf{y}.$$

The solution is

$$\begin{aligned}\mathbf{b}_2 &= [\mathbf{X}_2'(\mathbf{I} - \mathbf{X}_1(\mathbf{X}_1'\mathbf{X}_1)^{-1}\mathbf{X}_1')\mathbf{X}_2]^{-1}[\mathbf{X}_2'(\mathbf{I} - \mathbf{X}_1(\mathbf{X}_1'\mathbf{X}_1)^{-1}\mathbf{X}_1')\mathbf{y}] \\ &= (\mathbf{X}_2'\mathbf{M}_1\mathbf{X}_2)^{-1}(\mathbf{X}_2'\mathbf{M}_1\mathbf{y}).\end{aligned} \quad \textbf{(6-25)}$$

Notice that the matrix appearing in the parentheses inside each set of square brackets is the "residual maker" discussed earlier, in this case for a regression on the columns of $\mathbf{X}_1$. Thus, $\mathbf{M}_1\mathbf{X}_2$ is a matrix of residuals; each column of $\mathbf{M}_1\mathbf{X}_2$ is a vector of residuals in the regression of the corresponding column of $\mathbf{X}_2$ on the variables in $\mathbf{X}_1$. By exploiting that $\mathbf{M}_1$, like $\mathbf{M}$, is idempotent, we can rewrite (6-25) as

$$\mathbf{b}_2 = (\mathbf{X}_2^{*\prime}\mathbf{X}_2^*)^{-1}\mathbf{X}_2^{*\prime}\mathbf{y}^*, \quad \textbf{(6-26)}$$

where

$$\mathbf{X}_2^* = \mathbf{M}_1\mathbf{X}_2 \quad \text{and} \quad \mathbf{y}^* = \mathbf{M}_1\mathbf{y}.$$

This result is fundamental in regression analysis.

THEOREM 6.3: Frisch–Waugh Theorem. *The subvector* $\mathbf{b}_2$ *is the set of coefficients obtained when the residuals from a regression of* $\mathbf{y}$ *on* $\mathbf{X}_1$ *alone are regressed on the set of residuals obtained when each column of* $\mathbf{X}_2$ *is regressed on* $\mathbf{X}_1$.

This is commonly called **partialing out** or **netting out** the effect of $\mathbf{X}_1$. It is for this reason that the coefficients in a multiple regression are often called the **partial regression coefficients.** The application of this theorem to the computation suggested at the beginning of this section is as follows. Consider the regression of **y** on a set of variables **X** and an additional variable **z**. Denote the coefficients **b** and c.

THEOREM 6.4: Individual Regression Coefficients. *The coefficient on* **z**, *c, in a multiple regression of* **y** *on* $\mathbf{W} = [\mathbf{X}, \mathbf{z}]$ *is computed as* $c = (\mathbf{z}'\mathbf{M}\mathbf{z})^{-1}(\mathbf{z}'\mathbf{M}\mathbf{y}) = (\mathbf{z}_*'\mathbf{z}_*)^{-1}(\mathbf{z}_*'\mathbf{y}_*)$, *where* $\mathbf{z}_*$ *and* $\mathbf{y}_*$ *are the residual vectors from least squares regressions of* **z** *and* **y** *on* **X**; $\mathbf{z}_* = \mathbf{M}\mathbf{z} = [\mathbf{I} - \mathbf{X}(\mathbf{X}'\mathbf{X})^{-1}\mathbf{X}']\mathbf{z}$ and $\mathbf{y}_* = \mathbf{M}\mathbf{y}$.

In terms of our first example, we could obtain the coefficient on education in the multiple regression by first regressing income and education on age (or age and age squared) and then using the residuals from these regressions in a simple regression. In a classic application of this latter observation, Frisch and Waugh (1933) (who are credited with the result) noted that in a time-series setting, the same results were obtained whether a regression was fitted with a time-trend variable or the data were first "detrended" by netting out the effect of time, as noted earlier, and using just the detrended data in a simple regression.[15]

EXAMPLE 6.9 Deviations from Means—Regression on a Constant

As an application of these results, consider the case in which $\mathbf{X}_1$ is **i**, a column of 1s in the first column of **X**. The solution for $\mathbf{b}_2$ in this case will then be the slopes in a regression with a constant term. The coefficient in a regression of any variable **z** on **i** is $[\mathbf{i}'\mathbf{i}]^{-1}\mathbf{i}'\mathbf{z} = \bar{z}$, the fitted values are $\mathbf{i}\bar{z}$, and the residuals are $z_i - \bar{z}$. When we apply this to our previous results, we find the following.

THEOREM 6.5: Regression with a Constant Term. *The slopes in a multiple regression that contains a constant term are obtained by transforming the data to deviations from their means, then regressing the variable y in deviation form on the explanatory variables, also in deviation form.*

Exercise. What happens in the preceding regression if we neglect to transform **y** to deviation from $\bar{y}$ before we compute the slopes?

Having obtained the coefficients on $\mathbf{X}_2$, how can we recover the coefficients on $\mathbf{X}_1$, the constant term? One way is to repeat the exercise of the previous section while reversing the roles of $\mathbf{X}_1$ and $\mathbf{X}_2$. But there is an easier way. The first of the two normal equations is

$$\mathbf{X}_1'\mathbf{X}_1\mathbf{b}_1 + \mathbf{X}_1'\mathbf{X}_2\mathbf{b}_2 = \mathbf{X}_1'\mathbf{y}.$$

We have already solved for $\mathbf{b}_2$. Therefore, we can use this in a solution for $\mathbf{b}_1$:

$$\mathbf{b}_1 = (\mathbf{X}_1'\mathbf{X}_1)^{-1}\mathbf{X}_1'\mathbf{y} - (\mathbf{X}_1'\mathbf{X}_1)^{-1}\mathbf{X}_1'\mathbf{X}_2\mathbf{b}_2 = (\mathbf{X}_1'\mathbf{X}_1)^{-1}\mathbf{X}_1'(\mathbf{y} - \mathbf{X}_2\mathbf{b}_2). \tag{6-27}$$

If $\mathbf{X}_1$ is just a column of 1s, the first of these produces the familiar result

$$\mathbf{b}_1 = \bar{y} - \bar{x}_2 b_2 - \cdots - \bar{x}_K b_K. \tag{6-28}$$

[15]Recall our earlier investment example.

6.4.4. Partial Regression and Partial Correlation Coefficients

The use of multiple regression involves a conceptual experiment that we might not be able to carry out in practice, the *ceteris paribus* analysis familiar in economics. To pursue an example considered in the introduction to this chapter, a regression equation relating income to age and education enables us to do the conceptual experiment of comparing the incomes of two individuals of the same age with different education levels, *even if the sample contains no such pair of individuals.* It is this characteristic of the regression that is implied by the term *partial regression coefficients.* The way we obtain this result, as we have seen, is first to regress income and education on age and then to compute the residuals from this regression. By construction, age will not have any power in explaining variation in these residuals. Therefore, any correlation between income and education after this "purging" is independent of (or after netting out the effect of) age.

The same principle can be applied to the correlation between two variables. To continue our example, to what extent can we assume that this correlation reflects a direct relationship rather than the fact that both income and education tend, on average, to rise as individuals become older? To find out, we would use a **partial correlation coefficient,** which is computed along the same lines as the partial regression coefficient. In the context of our example, the partial correlation coefficient between income and education, controlling for the effect of age, is obtained as follows.

1. $y_* =$ the residuals in a regression of income on a constant and age.
2. $z_* =$ the residuals in a regression of education on a constant and age.
3. The partial correlation r^*_{yz} is the simple correlation between y_* and z_*.

This might seem to be a formidable amount of computation. There is, however, a convenient shortcut. Once the multiple regression is computed, the t ratio in (6-46) and (6-47) for testing the hypothesis that the coefficient equals zero (e.g., the last column of Table 6.9) can be used to compute

$$r^{*2}_{yz} = \frac{t_z^2}{t_z^2 + \text{degrees of freedom}}. \tag{6-29}$$

The proof of this less than perfectly intuitive result will be useful to illustrate some of our results on partitioned regression and to put into context two very useful results from least squares algebra. As in Theorem 6.4, let $\mathbf{W}$ denote the $n \times (K+1)$ regressor matrix $[\mathbf{X}, \mathbf{z}]$ and let $\mathbf{M} = \mathbf{I} - \mathbf{X}(\mathbf{X}'\mathbf{X})^{-1}\mathbf{X}$. We assume that there is a constant term in $\mathbf{X}$, so that our vectors of residuals $\mathbf{y}_*$ and $\mathbf{z}_*$ will have zero sample means. (See Section 6.4.2.) The residuals from regressions of $\mathbf{y}$ and $\mathbf{z}$ on $\mathbf{X}$ are $\mathbf{y}_* = \mathbf{My}$ and $\mathbf{z}_* = \mathbf{Mz}$. The squared partial correlation is

$$r^{*2}_{yz} = \frac{(\mathbf{z}'_*\mathbf{y}_*)^2}{(\mathbf{z}'_*\mathbf{z}_*)(\mathbf{y}'_*\mathbf{y}_*)}.$$

Let c denote the coefficient on $\mathbf{z}$ in the multiple regression of $\mathbf{y}$ on $\mathbf{W}$. The squared t ratio is

$$t_z^2 = \frac{c^2}{\left[\dfrac{\mathbf{u}'\mathbf{u}}{n-(K+1)}\right](\mathbf{W}'\mathbf{W})^{-1}_{K+1,K+1}}.$$

To obtain the denominator, we have extracted the $(K+1)$ (last) diagonal element of $(\mathbf{W}'\mathbf{W})^{-1}$. The partitioned inverse formula in (2-74) can be applied to the matrix $[\mathbf{X}, \mathbf{z}]'[\mathbf{X}, \mathbf{z}]$. This is the matrix that appears at the beginning of Section 6.4.3, with $\mathbf{X}_1 = \mathbf{X}$ and $\mathbf{X}_2 = \mathbf{z}$. The result is the inverse matrix that appears in (6-26), so we have the first important result.

Diagonal Elements of a Moment Matrix. *If* $\mathbf{W} = [\mathbf{X}, \mathbf{z}]$, *the last diagonal element of* $(\mathbf{W}'\mathbf{W})^{-1}$ *is* $(\mathbf{z}'\mathbf{M}\mathbf{z})^{-1} = (\mathbf{z}_*'\mathbf{z}_*)^{-1}$ *where* $\mathbf{z}_* = \mathbf{M}\mathbf{z}$ *and* $\mathbf{M} = \mathbf{I} - \mathbf{X}(\mathbf{X}'\mathbf{X})^{-1}\mathbf{X}'$. **(6-30)**

Note that this generalizes the application that we saw in Section 2.6.4. If we use this and Theorem 6.4 for c, after a bit of manipulation, we obtain

$$\frac{t_k^2}{t_k^2 + [n-(K+1)]} = \frac{(\mathbf{z}_*'\mathbf{y}_*)^2}{(\mathbf{z}_*'\mathbf{y}_*)^2 + (\mathbf{u}'\mathbf{u})(\mathbf{z}_*'\mathbf{z}_*)}$$
$$= \frac{r_{yz}^{*2}}{r_{yz}^{*2} + (\mathbf{u}'\mathbf{u})/(\mathbf{y}_*'\mathbf{y}_*)},$$

where

$$\mathbf{u} = \mathbf{y} - \mathbf{X}\mathbf{d} - \mathbf{z}c$$

is the vector of residuals when $\mathbf{y}$ is regressed on $\mathbf{X}$ *and* $\mathbf{z}$. Note that unless $\mathbf{X}'\mathbf{z} = \mathbf{0}$, $\mathbf{d}$ will not equal $\mathbf{b} = (\mathbf{X}'\mathbf{X})^{-1}\mathbf{X}'\mathbf{y}$. (See Theorem 6.2.) Moreover, unless $c = 0$, $\mathbf{u}$ will not equal $\mathbf{e} = \mathbf{y} - \mathbf{X}\mathbf{b}$. Now we have shown in Theorem 6.4 that $c = (\mathbf{z}_*'\mathbf{z}_*)^{-1}(\mathbf{z}_*'\mathbf{y}_*)$. We also have, from (6-24), that

$$\mathbf{d} = (\mathbf{X}'\mathbf{X})^{-1}\mathbf{X}'(\mathbf{y} - \mathbf{z}c) = \mathbf{b} - (\mathbf{X}'\mathbf{X})^{-1}\mathbf{X}'\mathbf{z}c.$$

So, inserting this expression for $\mathbf{d}$ in that for $\mathbf{u}$ gives

$$\begin{aligned}\mathbf{u} &= \mathbf{y} - \mathbf{X}\mathbf{b} + \mathbf{X}(\mathbf{X}'\mathbf{X})^{-1}\mathbf{X}'\mathbf{z}c - \mathbf{z}c \\ &= \mathbf{e} - \mathbf{M}\mathbf{z}c \\ &= \mathbf{e} - \mathbf{z}_*c.\end{aligned}$$

Now

$$\mathbf{u}'\mathbf{u} = \mathbf{e}'\mathbf{e} + c^2(\mathbf{z}_*'\mathbf{z}_*) - 2c\mathbf{z}_*'\mathbf{e}.$$

But $\mathbf{e} = \mathbf{M}\mathbf{y} = \mathbf{y}_*$ and $\mathbf{z}_*'\mathbf{e} = \mathbf{z}_*'\mathbf{y}_* = c(\mathbf{z}_*'\mathbf{z}_*)$. Inserting this in $\mathbf{u}'\mathbf{u}$ gives our second useful result.

Change in the Sum of Squares When a Variable Is Added to a Regression. *If*

$\mathbf{e}'\mathbf{e}$ *is the sum of squared residuals when* $\mathbf{y}$ *is regressed on* $\mathbf{X}$ *and* $\mathbf{u}'\mathbf{u}$ *is the sum of squared residuals when* $\mathbf{y}$ *is regressed on* $\mathbf{X}$ *and* $\mathbf{z}$, *then*

$$\mathbf{u}'\mathbf{u} = \mathbf{e}'\mathbf{e} - c^2(\mathbf{z}_*'\mathbf{z}_*), \qquad \textbf{(6-31)}$$

where c *is the coefficient on* $\mathbf{z}$ *in the long regression and* $\mathbf{z}_* = [\mathbf{I} - \mathbf{X}(\mathbf{X}'\mathbf{X})^{-1}\mathbf{X}']\mathbf{z}$, *the vector of residuals when* $\mathbf{z}$ *is regressed on* $\mathbf{X}$.

Returning to our derivation, we note that $\mathbf{e}'\mathbf{e} = \mathbf{y}_*'\mathbf{y}_*$ and $c^2(\mathbf{z}_*'\mathbf{z}_*) = (\mathbf{z}_*'\mathbf{y}_*)^2/(\mathbf{z}_*'\mathbf{z}_*)$. Therefore, $(\mathbf{u}'\mathbf{u})/(\mathbf{y}_*'\mathbf{y}_*) = 1 - r_{yz}^{*2}$, and we have our result.

EXAMPLE 6.10 Partial Correlations

For the data of Example 6.8, the simple correlations between investment and the regressors r_{yk} and partial correlations (given the other variables) r_{yk}^* and between investment and the four regressors are listed in Table 6.5. As is clear from the table, there is no necessary relation between the simple and partial correlation coefficients. One thing worth noting is the signs of the coefficients. The signs of the partial correlation coefficients are the same as the signs of the respective regression coefficients, three of which are negative. All the simple correlation coefficients are positive because of the latent "effect" of time.

TABLE 6.5 Correlations of Investment with Other Variables

	Simple Correlation	*Partial Correlation*
Time	0.7496	−0.9360
GNP	0.8632	0.9680
Interest	0.5871	−0.5166
Inflation	0.4777	−0.0253

6.5. GOODNESS OF FIT AND THE ANALYSIS OF VARIANCE

The original fitting criterion, the sum of squared residuals, also provides a measure of the fit of the regression line to the data. Unfortunately, as can easily be verified, the sum of squared residuals can be scaled arbitrarily just by multiplying the values of y by the desired scale factor. Since the fitted values of the regression are based on the values of $\mathbf{x}$, we might ask instead whether *variation* in $\mathbf{x}$ is a good predictor of *variation* in y. Figure 6.6 shows several possible cases for a simple regression model. The measure of fit described here embodies both the fitting criterion and the covariation of y and $\mathbf{x}$.

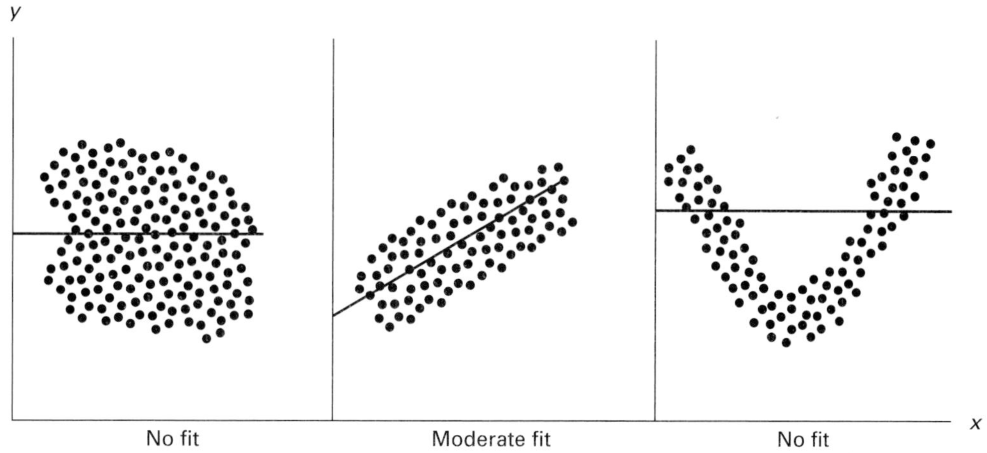

FIGURE 6.6 Sample Data.

Variation of the dependent variable is defined in terms of deviations from its mean, $(y_i - \bar{y})$. The **total variation** in y is the sum of squared deviations:

$$\text{SST} = \sum_{i=1}^{n} (y_i - \bar{y})^2.$$

The squares are used because the sum of deviations is always zero. In terms of the regression equation, we may write the full set of observations as

$$\begin{aligned}\mathbf{y} &= \mathbf{Xb} + \mathbf{e}\\ &= \hat{\mathbf{y}} + \mathbf{e}.\end{aligned}$$

For an individual observation, we have

$$\begin{aligned}y_i &= \hat{y}_i + e_i\\ &= \mathbf{x}_i'\mathbf{b} + e_i.\end{aligned}$$

If the regression contains a constant term, the residuals will sum to zero and the mean of the predicted values of y_i will equal the mean of the actual values. Subtracting $\bar{y}$ from both sides and using this result and result 2 in Section 6.4.2 gives

$$\begin{aligned}y_i - \bar{y} &= \hat{y}_i - \bar{y} + e_i\\ &= (\mathbf{x}_i - \bar{\mathbf{x}})'\mathbf{b} + e_i.\end{aligned}$$

Figure 6.7 illustrates the computation for the two variable regression. Intuitively, the regression would appear to fit well if the deviations of y from its mean are more largely accounted for by deviations of x from its mean than by the residuals. Since both terms in this decomposition sum to zero, to quantify this fit, we use the sums of squares instead. For the full set of observations, we have

$$\mathbf{M}^0\mathbf{y} = \mathbf{M}^0\mathbf{Xb} + \mathbf{M}^0\mathbf{e},$$

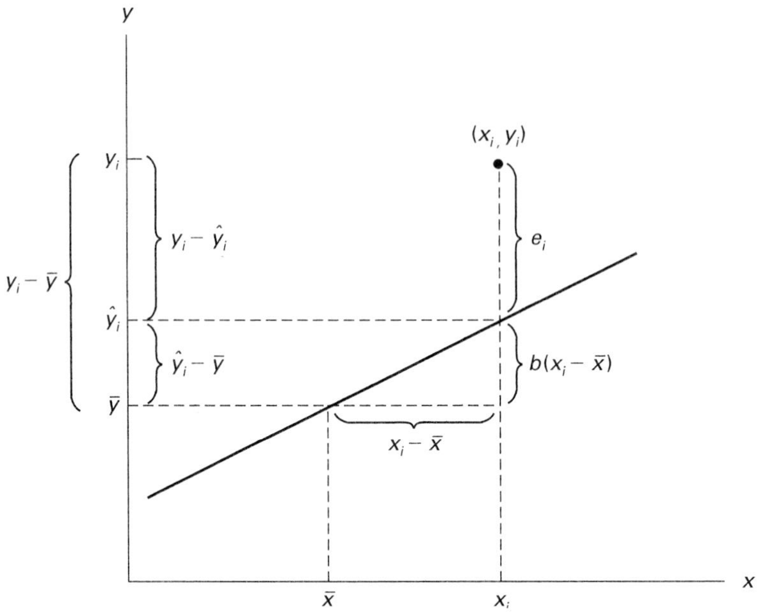

FIGURE 6.7 Decomposition of y_i.

where $\mathbf{M}^0$ is the $n \times n$ idempotent matrix that transforms observations into deviations from sample means. (See Section 2.3.6.) The column of $\mathbf{M}^0\mathbf{X}$ corresponding to the constant term is zero and, since the residuals already have mean zero, $\mathbf{M}^0\mathbf{e} = \mathbf{e}$. Then, since $\mathbf{e}'\mathbf{M}^0\mathbf{X} = \mathbf{e}'\mathbf{X} = \mathbf{0}$, the total sum of squares is

$$\mathbf{y}'\mathbf{M}^0\mathbf{y} = \mathbf{b}'\mathbf{X}'\mathbf{M}^0\mathbf{X}\mathbf{b} + \mathbf{e}'\mathbf{e}.$$

Write this as total sum of squares = regression sum of squares + error sum of squares or

$$\text{SST} = \text{SSR} + \text{SSE}. \tag{6-32}$$

We can now obtain a measure of how well the regression line fits the data by using the

$$\textbf{coefficient of determination:}\ \frac{\text{SSR}}{\text{SST}} = \frac{\mathbf{b}'\mathbf{X}'\mathbf{M}^0\mathbf{X}\mathbf{b}}{\mathbf{y}'\mathbf{M}^0\mathbf{y}} = 1 - \frac{\mathbf{e}'\mathbf{e}}{\mathbf{y}'\mathbf{M}^0\mathbf{y}}. \tag{6-33}$$

The coefficient of determination is denoted R^2. As we have shown, it must be between 0 and 1, and it measures the proportion of the total variation in **y** that is accounted for by variation in the regressors. It takes the value of zero if the regression is a horizontal line, that is, if all the elements of **b** except the constant term are zero. In this case, the predicted values of y are always $\bar{y}$, so deviations of **x** from its mean do not translate into different predictions for y. As such, **x** has no explanatory power. The other extreme, $R^2 = 1$, occurs if the values of **x** and y all lie in the same hyperplane (on a straight line for a two variable regression) so that the residuals are zero. If all the values of y_i lie on a vertical line, R^2 has no meaning and cannot be computed.

Regression analysis is often used for forecasting. In this case, we are interested in how well the regression model predicts movements in the dependent variable. The **coefficient of determination** R^2 is a measure of the fit of the model. An equivalent way to compute R^2 is also useful. First

$$\mathbf{b}'\mathbf{X}'\mathbf{M}^0\mathbf{X}\mathbf{b} = \hat{\mathbf{y}}'\mathbf{M}^0\hat{\mathbf{y}},$$

but $\hat{\mathbf{y}} = \mathbf{X}\mathbf{b}$, $\mathbf{y} = \hat{\mathbf{y}} + \mathbf{e}$, $\mathbf{M}^0\mathbf{e} = \mathbf{e}$, and $\mathbf{X}'\mathbf{e} = \mathbf{0}$, so $\hat{\mathbf{y}}'\mathbf{M}^0\hat{\mathbf{y}} = \hat{\mathbf{y}}'\mathbf{M}^0\mathbf{y}$. If we multiply and divide $R^2 = \hat{\mathbf{y}}'\mathbf{M}^0\hat{\mathbf{y}}/\mathbf{y}'\mathbf{M}^0\mathbf{y}$ by $\hat{\mathbf{y}}'\mathbf{M}^0\hat{\mathbf{y}}$, we obtain

$$R^2 = \frac{[\Sigma_i(y_i - \bar{y})(\hat{y}_i - \hat{\bar{y}})]^2}{[\Sigma_i(y_i - \bar{y})^2][\Sigma_i(\hat{y}_i - \hat{\bar{y}})^2]}, \tag{6-34}$$

which is the squared correlation between the observed values of y and the predictions produced by the estimated regression equation.

EXAMPLE 6.11 Fit of a Consumption Function

For our example of the consumption function, where y is C and x is X, we have

$$\begin{aligned}
&\bar{y} && = 793.43,\\
&\bar{x} && = 879.24,\\
&S_{xx} = \Sigma_i(x_i - \bar{x})^2 && = 64{,}972.12,\\
&S_{yy} = \Sigma_i(y_i - \bar{y})^2 && = 67{,}192.44,
\end{aligned}$$

and

$$S_{xy} = \Sigma_i(x_i - \bar{x})(y_i - \bar{y}) \quad = 65{,}799.34,$$

so

$$\begin{aligned}
&\text{SST} && = 64{,}972.12,\\
&\text{SSR} = b^2S_{xx} && = (65{,}799.34/67{,}192.44)^2 67{,}192.44 = 64{,}435.13,\\
&\text{SSE} = \text{SST} - \text{SSR} && = 536.99,
\end{aligned}$$

and

$$R^2 = b^2S_{xx}/S_{yy} \quad = 0.9917351.$$

Apparently, as seen in Figure 6.1, the regression provides quite a good fit.

We can summarize the calculation of R^2 in an **analysis of variance table,** which might appear as shown in Table 6.6.[16]

[16]This assumes that there is a constant term in the equation.

TABLE 6.6 Analysis of Variance

	Source	*Degrees of Freedom*	*Mean Square*
Regression	$\mathbf{b}'\mathbf{X}'\mathbf{y} - n\bar{y}^2$	$K - 1$[16]	
Residual	$\mathbf{e}'\mathbf{e}$	$n - K$	s^2
Total	$\mathbf{y}'\mathbf{y} - n\bar{y}^2$	$n - 1$	$S_{yy}/(n-1) = s_y^2$
Coefficient of determination		$R^2 = 1 - \mathbf{e}'\mathbf{e}/(\mathbf{y}'\mathbf{y} - n\bar{y}^2)$	

EXAMPLE 6.12 Analysis of Variance for an Investment Equation

The analysis of variance table for the investment equation is given in Table 6.7.

TABLE 6.7 Analysis of Variance for the Investment Equation

	Source	*Degrees of Freedom*	*Mean Square*
Regression	0.0159023	4	0.003976
Residual	0.0004507	10	0.00004507
Total	0.016353	14	0.0011681

$R^2 = 0.0159023/0.016353 = 0.97244.$

There are some problems with the use of R^2 in analyzing goodness of fit. The first concerns the number of degrees of freedom used up in estimating the parameters. *R^2 will never decrease when another variable is added to a regression equation.* Equation (6-31) provides a convenient means for us to establish this result. Once again, we are comparing a regression of $\mathbf{y}$ on $\mathbf{X}$ with sum of squared residuals $\mathbf{e}'\mathbf{e}$ to a regression of $\mathbf{y}$ on $\mathbf{X}$ and an additional variable $\mathbf{z}$, which produces sum of squared residuals $\mathbf{u}'\mathbf{u}$. Recall the vectors of residuals $\mathbf{z}_* = \mathbf{Mz}$ and $\mathbf{y}_* = \mathbf{My} = \mathbf{e}$, which implies that $\mathbf{e}'\mathbf{e} = (\mathbf{y}_*'\mathbf{y}_*)$. Let c be the coefficient on $\mathbf{z}$ in the longer regression. Then $c = (\mathbf{z}_*'\mathbf{z}_*)^{-1}(\mathbf{z}_*'\mathbf{y}_*)$, and inserting this in (6-31) produces

$$\mathbf{u}'\mathbf{u} = \mathbf{e}'\mathbf{e} - (\mathbf{z}_*'\mathbf{y}_*)^2/(\mathbf{z}_*'\mathbf{z}_*) = \mathbf{e}'\mathbf{e}(1 - r_{yz}^{*2}), \tag{6-35}$$

where r_{yz}^{*2} is the partial correlation between $\mathbf{y}$ and $\mathbf{z}$, controlling for $\mathbf{X}$. Now divide through both sides of the equality by $\mathbf{y}'\mathbf{M}^0\mathbf{y}$. From (6-33), $\mathbf{u}'\mathbf{u}/\mathbf{y}'\mathbf{M}^0\mathbf{y}$ is $(1 - R_{\mathrm{X}z}^2)$ for the regression on $\mathbf{X}$ and $\mathbf{z}$ and $\mathbf{e}'\mathbf{e}/\mathbf{y}'\mathbf{M}^0\mathbf{y}$ is $(1 - R_{\mathrm{X}}^2)$. Rearranging the result produces the following.

Change in R^2 When a Variable Is Added to a Regression. *Let $R_{\mathrm{X}z}^2$ be the coefficient of determination in the regression of* $\mathbf{y}$ *on* $\mathbf{X}$ *and an additional variable* $\mathbf{z}$, *let R_{X}^2 be the same for the regression of* $\mathbf{y}$ *on* $\mathbf{X}$ *alone, and let r_{yz}^{*2} be the partial correlation between* $\mathbf{y}$ *and* $\mathbf{z}$, *controlling for* $\mathbf{X}$. *Then*

$$R_{\mathrm{X}z}^2 = R_{\mathrm{X}}^2 + (1 - R_{\mathrm{X}}^2)r_{yz}^{*2}. \tag{6-36}$$

Thus, the R^2 in the longer regression cannot be smaller. It is tempting to exploit this result by just adding variables to the model; R^2 will continue to rise to its limit of 1.[17] In view of this, we sometimes report an **adjusted** R^2 (for degrees of freedom), which is computed as follows:[18]

$$\overline{R}^2 = 1 - \frac{\mathbf{e}'\mathbf{e}/(n-K)}{\mathbf{y}'\mathbf{M}^0\mathbf{y}/(n-1)}.$$

For computational purposes, the connection between R^2 and $\overline{R}^2$ is

$$\overline{R}^2 = 1 - \frac{n-1}{n-K}(1 - R^2).$$

The essential point to observe about this measure is that it may decline when a variable is added to the set of independent variables. Indeed, $\overline{R}^2$ may even be negative. To consider an admittedly extreme case, suppose that $\mathbf{x}$ and $\mathbf{y}$ have a sample correlation of zero. Then the adjusted R^2 will equal $-1/(n-2)$. Whether $\overline{R}^2$ rises or falls depends on whether the contribution of the new variable to the fit of the regression more than offsets the correction for the loss of an additional degree of freedom. The general result (the proof of which is left as an exercise) is as follows.

Change in $\overline{R}^2$ When a Variable Is Added to a Regression. *In a multiple regression, $\overline{R}^2$ will fall (rise) when the variable x is deleted from the regression if the t ratio associated with this variable is greater (less) than* 1. **(6-37)**

A second difficulty with R^2 concerns the constant term in the model. The proof that $0 \le R^2 \le 1$ requires $\mathbf{X}$ to contain a column of 1s. If not, then (1) $\mathbf{M}^0\mathbf{e} \neq \mathbf{e}$ and (2) $\mathbf{e}'\mathbf{M}^0\mathbf{X} \neq \mathbf{0}$, and the third term in the preceding expansion will not drop out. Consequently, when we compute

$$R^2 = 1 - \frac{\mathbf{e}'\mathbf{e}}{\mathbf{y}'\mathbf{M}^0\mathbf{y}},$$

the result is unpredictable. It may be higher or lower than the same figure computed for the regression with a constant term included. It can even be negative. Computer packages differ in their computation of R^2. An alternative computation,

$$R^2 = \frac{\mathbf{b}'\mathbf{X}'\mathbf{y}}{\mathbf{y}'\mathbf{M}^0\mathbf{y}},$$

is equally problematic. Again, this calculation will differ from the one obtained with the constant term included; this time, R^2 may be larger than 1. Some computer packages bypass these difficulties by reporting a third "R^2," the squared sample correlation between the actual values of y and the fitted values from

---

[17]This comes at a cost, however. The parameter estimates become progressively less precise as we do so.

[18]This measure is sometimes advocated on the basis of the unbiasedness of the two quantities in the fraction. Since the ratio is not an unbiased estimator of any population quantity, it is difficult to justify the adjustment on this basis.

the regression. This approach could be deceptive. If the regression contains a constant term, then, as we have seen, all three computations give the same answer. Even if not, this last one will still produce a value between zero and one. But, it is not a proportion of variation explained. On the other hand, for the purpose of comparing models, this squared correlation might well be a useful descriptive device. It is important for users of computer packages to be aware of how the reported R^2 is computed. Indeed, some packages will give a warning in the results when a regression is fit without a constant or by some technique other than linear least squares.

This discussion might suggest that we can produce a higher R^2 simply by choosing whether or not to include a constant term in the model. One ought not to view the inclusion of a constant as an option. Certain models specify that the equation should not contain an intercept. But estimating a model without a constant term amounts to imposing a linear restriction, that is, that the constant term is zero. Arbitrarily assuming that the intercept is zero is no less restrictive than arbitrarily imposing some other linear restriction on the coefficients.

The value of R^2 we obtained for the consumption function seems high in an absolute sense. Is it? Unfortunately, there is no absolute basis for comparison. In fact, in using aggregate time-series data, coefficients of determination this high are routine. In terms of the values one normally encounters in cross sections, an R^2 of 0.5 is relatively high. Still, it is much lower than the one obtained for the consumption function. Coefficients of determination in cross sections of individual data as high as 0.2 are sometimes noteworthy. The point of this discussion is that whether a regression line provides a good fit to a body of data depends on the setting.

Little can be said about the relative quality of fits of regression lines in different contexts. One must be careful, however, even in a single context, to be sure to use the same basis for comparison for competing models. Usually, this concerns how the dependent variable is computed. For example, a perennial question concerns whether a linear or log-linear model fits the data better. Unfortunately, the question cannot be answered with a direct comparison. An R^2 for the linear regression model is different from an R^2 for the log-linear model. Variation in y is different from variation in $\ln y$. To continue the consumption function example, the R^2 in the regression of $\ln C$ on $\ln X$ is 0.99154, which suggests that (albeit only trivially) the linear model fits slightly better ($R^2 =$ 0.99174). It is often useful to compute an analog to the usual R^2 that can be used to compare models, however:

$$R^2 = 1 - \frac{\sum_{i=1}^{n} e_i^2}{S_{yy}}.$$

The residuals can be computed as $y_i - \hat{y}_i$ from any model. To continue the example, if we compute the predicted values from the log-linear model and then use for the fitted values

$$\hat{C} = e^{\widehat{\ln C}},$$

the R^2 for this "regression," computed as previously, is 0.991956, which is a slight improvement over the linear model.

It is worth emphasizing that R^2 is a measure of *linear* association between x and y. For example, the third panel of Figure 6.6 shows data that might arise from the model

$$y_i = \alpha + \beta(x_i - c)^2 + \epsilon_i .$$

(The constant c allows x to be distributed about some value other than zero.) The relationship between y and x in this model is nonlinear, and a linear regression would find no fit.

A final word of caution is in order. The interpretation of R^2 as a proportion of variation explained is dependent on the use of least squares to compute the fitted values. It is always correct to write

$$y_i - \bar{y} = (\hat{y}_i - \bar{y}) + e_i .$$

In computing the sum of squares on the two sides, however, the cross-product term vanishes only if least squares is used to compute the fitted values and if the model contains a constant term.[19] Thus, in our previous example, it is not unambiguous that the log-linear model fits better; the cross-product term has been ignored in computing R^2 for the log-linear model. Thus, it is only in the case of least squares applied to a linear equation that R^2 can be interpreted as the proportion of variation in y explained by variation in x.

6.6. STATISTICAL PROPERTIES OF THE LEAST SQUARES ESTIMATOR IN FINITE SAMPLES

The preceding discussion treated the fitting of the regression to the data as a purely algebraic problem. We can now treat the results as parameter estimates and assess the virtues of least squares on a statistical basis. There are other candidates for estimating β. In a two-variable case, for example, we might use the slope of the line between the points with the largest and smallest values of x or (which would be more difficult) find the a and b that minimize the sum of absolute values of the residuals. The question of which estimator to choose is usually based on the statistical properties of the candidates, such as unbiasedness, efficiency, and precision.[20] These, in turn, frequently depend on the particular distribution that we assume produced the data. It is interesting that a number

[19]An analogous computation can be done without computing deviations from means if the regression does not contain a constant term. Other purely algebraic artifacts will crop up in regressions without a constant, however. For example, the value of R^2 will change when the same constant is added to each observation on y, but it is obvious that nothing fundamental has changed in the regression relationship. One should be wary (even skeptical) in the calculation and interpretation of fit measures for regressions without constant terms.

[20]See Section 4.3.

of desirable properties can be obtained for the least squares estimator even without specifying a particular distribution for the disturbances in the regression. This section will consider exact, finite-sample results. These require fairly strong assumptions, such as nonstochastic regressors and normally distributed disturbances. In the next section, we will turn to the properties of the least squares estimator in more general cases.

6.6.1. Nonstochastic Regressors

If the regressors can be treated as nonstochastic, as they would be in an experimental situation in which the analyst chooses the values in **X**, then the properties of the least squares estimator can be derived by treating **X** as a matrix of constants. Insert (6-3) in (6-6) to obtain

$$\mathbf{b} = (\mathbf{X}'\mathbf{X})^{-1}\mathbf{X}'(\mathbf{X}\boldsymbol{\beta} + \boldsymbol{\epsilon}) = \boldsymbol{\beta} + (\mathbf{X}'\mathbf{X})^{-1}\mathbf{X}'\boldsymbol{\epsilon}. \qquad \textbf{(6-38)}$$

Since we can write $\mathbf{b} = \boldsymbol{\beta} + \mathbf{A}\boldsymbol{\epsilon}$, where **A** is a matrix of constants, **b** is a linear function of the disturbances, or a **linear estimator.** If **X** is nonstochastic, or if $E(\mathbf{X}'\boldsymbol{\epsilon}) = \mathbf{0}$, the expected value of the second term in (6-38) is **0**. Therefore, *regardless of the distribution of* $\boldsymbol{\epsilon}$, *under our other assumptions,* **b** *is a linear, unbiased estimator of* $\boldsymbol{\beta}$. The covariance matrix of the least squares slope estimator is

$$\begin{aligned}
\text{Var}[\mathbf{b}] &= E[(\mathbf{b} - \boldsymbol{\beta})(\mathbf{b} - \boldsymbol{\beta})'] \\
&= E[(\mathbf{X}'\mathbf{X})^{-1}\mathbf{X}'\boldsymbol{\epsilon}\boldsymbol{\epsilon}'\mathbf{X}(\mathbf{X}'\mathbf{X})^{-1}] \\
&= (\mathbf{X}'\mathbf{X})^{-1}\mathbf{X}'E[\boldsymbol{\epsilon}\boldsymbol{\epsilon}']\mathbf{X}(\mathbf{X}'\mathbf{X})^{-1} \\
&= (\mathbf{X}'\mathbf{X})^{-1}\mathbf{X}'(\sigma^2\mathbf{I})\mathbf{X}(\mathbf{X}'\mathbf{X})^{-1} \\
&= \sigma^2(\mathbf{X}'\mathbf{X})^{-1}.
\end{aligned}$$

EXAMPLE 6.13 Sampling Variance in the Two-Variable Regression Model

Suppose that **X** contains only a constant term (column of 1s) and a single regressor **x**. Using the results of Section 2.6.4, we find that

$$\text{Var}[b] = \text{Var}[b - \beta] = \sigma^2/\sum_{i=1}^{n}(x_i - \bar{x})^2.$$

Note, in particular, the denominator of the variance of b. The greater is the variation in x, the smaller this variance. For example, consider the problem of estimating the slopes of the two regressions in Figure 6.8. A more precise result will be obtained for the data in the right-hand panel of the figure. This does not necessarily argue that one should always attempt, if possible, to maximize the variation in x. The greater the range of variation we consider, the more likely it becomes that our assumption of linearity of the regression becomes suspect. Otherwise, greater variation in the explanatory variable is to be preferred.

We will now obtain a general result for the class of linear unbiased estimators of $\boldsymbol{\beta}$. Let $\mathbf{b}_0 = \mathbf{C}\mathbf{y}$ be another linear unbiased estimator of $\boldsymbol{\beta}$, where **C** is

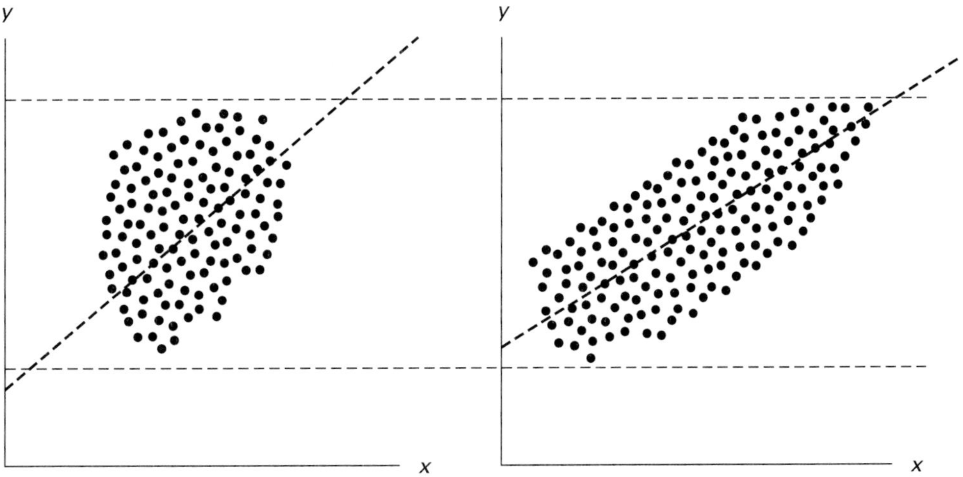

FIGURE 6.8 Effect of Increased Variation in x Given the Same Variation in y.

a $K \times n$ matrix. If $\mathbf{b}_0$ is unbiased,

$$E[\mathbf{Cy}] = E[\mathbf{CX}\boldsymbol{\beta} + \mathbf{C}\boldsymbol{\epsilon}] = \boldsymbol{\beta},$$

which implies that $\mathbf{CX} = \mathbf{I}$. There are many candidates. For example, consider using just the first K (or, any K) linearly independent rows of $\mathbf{X}$. Then $\mathbf{C} = [\mathbf{X}_0^{-1} : \mathbf{0}]$, where $\mathbf{X}_0^{-1}$ is the transpose of the matrix formed from the K rows of $\mathbf{X}$. The covariance matrix of $\mathbf{b}_0$ can be found by replacing $(\mathbf{X}'\mathbf{X})^{-1}\mathbf{X}'$ with $\mathbf{C}$ in (6-38); the result is $\text{Var}[\mathbf{b}_0] = \sigma^2\mathbf{CC}'$. Now let $\mathbf{D} = \mathbf{C} - (\mathbf{X}'\mathbf{X})^{-1}\mathbf{X}'$ so $\mathbf{Dy} = \mathbf{b}_0 - \mathbf{b}$. Then,

$$\text{Var}[\mathbf{b}_0] = \sigma^2[(\mathbf{D} + (\mathbf{X}'\mathbf{X})^{-1}\mathbf{X}')(\mathbf{D} + (\mathbf{X}'\mathbf{X})^{-1}\mathbf{X}')'].$$

We know that $\mathbf{CX} = \mathbf{I} = \mathbf{DX} + (\mathbf{X}'\mathbf{X})^{-1}(\mathbf{X}'\mathbf{X})$, so $\mathbf{DX}$ must equal $\mathbf{0}$. Therefore,

$$\begin{aligned}\text{Var}[\mathbf{b}_0] &= \sigma^2(\mathbf{X}'\mathbf{X})^{-1} + \sigma^2\mathbf{DD}' \\ &= \text{Var}[\mathbf{b}] + \sigma^2\mathbf{DD}'.\end{aligned}$$

The covariance matrix of $\mathbf{b}_0$ equals that of $\mathbf{b}$ plus a nonnegative definite matrix.[21] Therefore, every quadratic form in $\text{Var}[\mathbf{b}_0]$ is larger than the corresponding quadratic form in $\text{Var}[\mathbf{b}]$. This implies a very important property of the least squares coefficient vector.

THEOREM 6.6: Gauss–Markov Theorem. *In the classical linear regression model, the least squares estimator* $\mathbf{b}$ *is the minimum variance linear unbiased estimator of* $\boldsymbol{\beta}$. *For any vector of constants* $\mathbf{w}$, *the minimum variance linear unbiased estimator of* $\mathbf{w}'\boldsymbol{\beta}$ *in the classical regression model is* $\mathbf{w}'\mathbf{b}$, *where* $\mathbf{b}$ *is the least squares estimator.*

---

[21]A quadratic form in $\mathbf{DD}'$ is $\mathbf{q}'\mathbf{DD}'\mathbf{q} = \mathbf{z}'\mathbf{z} \geq 0$.

The proof of the second statement follows from the previous derivation, since the variance of $\mathbf{w}'\mathbf{b}$ is a quadratic form in Var[$\mathbf{b}$], and likewise for any $\mathbf{b}_0$. This proves that each individual slope estimator b_k is the best linear unbiased estimator of β_k. (Let $\mathbf{w}$ be all zeros except for a one in the kth position.) The theorem is much broader than this, however, since the result also applies to every other linear combination of the elements of $\boldsymbol{\beta}$.

We obtained the Gauss–Markov result as a characterization of the least squares estimator. That is, we began with a particular estimator in mind and assessed its statistical properties. An alternative approach would have been to pose the general problem of finding the estimator with the smallest variance, subject to the constraint that the estimator be linear and unbiased. We would have been led, once again, to least squares. Suppose that we drop the assumption of linearity and seek only the minimum variance unbiased estimator? This is a far more difficult problem that requires us to specify a particular distribution for the disturbance. Under normality, linearity is, in fact, superfluous. The least squares estimator has minimum variance among *all* unbiased estimators. As we shall show in Chapter 9, however, there *are* biased estimators with smaller **mean-squared errors** than least squares.[22] If we drop the assumption of normality, many of these results no longer hold. The Gauss–Markov theorem is intact, but without normality, the class of **linear unbiased estimators** itself becomes a bit restrictive. Other "robust" estimators, which may outperform least squares in some circumstances, have been proposed. The conclusion is that least squares is a powerful technique that produces an estimator with desirable statistical properties in many cases. In more general cases than we consider here, however, the field is much broader, and there is room for other estimators to compete favorably with least squares.

6.6.2. Stochastic Regressors

Social scientists are rarely able to analyze experimental data. As such, to achieve much generality for the properties of the least squares estimator, it is necessary to extend the results of the preceding section to cases in which some of or all the independent variables are randomly drawn from some probability distribution. A convenient method of obtaining the statistical properties of $\mathbf{b}$ is to obtain the desired results conditioned on $\mathbf{X}$ first. This is equivalent to the case of nonstochastic regressors. We then find the unconditional result by "averaging" (e.g., by integrating over) the conditional distributions. The crux of the argument is that if we can establish unbiasedness conditionally on an arbitrary $\mathbf{X}$, we can average over $\mathbf{X}$'s to obtain an unconditional result.

As before,

$$\mathbf{b} = \boldsymbol{\beta} + (\mathbf{X}'\mathbf{X})^{-1}\mathbf{X}'\boldsymbol{\epsilon}.$$

---

[22]See Judge et al. (1985) for an extensive discussion.

So, conditioned on the observed **X**,

$$E[\mathbf{b} \mid \mathbf{X}] = \boldsymbol{\beta} + (\mathbf{X}'\mathbf{X})^{-1}\mathbf{X}'E[\boldsymbol{\epsilon} \mid \mathbf{X}] = \boldsymbol{\beta} + (\mathbf{X}'\mathbf{X})^{-1}\mathbf{X}'\mathbf{0} = \boldsymbol{\beta}.$$

A useful device is the law of iterated expectations (Theorem 3.1):

$$\begin{aligned} E[\mathbf{b}] &= E_{\mathbf{X}}[E[\mathbf{b} \mid \mathbf{X}]] \\ &= \boldsymbol{\beta} + E_{\mathbf{X}}[(\mathbf{X}'\mathbf{X})^{-1}\mathbf{X}'E[\boldsymbol{\epsilon} \mid \mathbf{X}]]. \end{aligned}$$

Since $E[\boldsymbol{\epsilon}|\mathbf{X}] = \mathbf{0}$ by Assumption 3, **b** is unbiased unconditionally as well. Thus,

$$E[\mathbf{b}] = E_{\mathbf{X}}[E[\mathbf{b} \mid \mathbf{X}]] = E_{\mathbf{X}}[\boldsymbol{\beta}] = \boldsymbol{\beta}.$$

The unbiasedness of least squares is robust to assumptions about the **X** matrix; it rests only on Assumption 3.

The variance of **b**, again conditioned on **X**, is

$$\text{Var}[\mathbf{b} \mid \mathbf{X}] = \sigma^2(\mathbf{X}'\mathbf{X})^{-1}.$$

For the exact variance, we use the decomposition of variance of (3-70):

$$\text{Var}[\mathbf{b}] = E_{\mathbf{X}}[\text{Var}[\mathbf{b} \mid \mathbf{X}]] + \text{Var}_{\mathbf{X}}[E[\mathbf{b} \mid \mathbf{X}]].$$

The second term is zero since $E[\mathbf{b}|\mathbf{X}] = \boldsymbol{\beta}$ for all **X**, so

$$\text{Var}[\mathbf{b}] = E[\sigma^2(\mathbf{X}'\mathbf{X})^{-1}] = \sigma^2 E[(\mathbf{X}'\mathbf{X})^{-1}].$$

Our earlier conclusion is altered slightly. We must replace $(\mathbf{X}'\mathbf{X})^{-1}$ with its expected value to get the appropriate covariance matrix. This brings a subtle change in the interpretation of these results. The unconditional variance of **b** can only be described in terms of the average behavior of **X**, so to proceed further, it would be necessary to make some assumptions about the variances and covariances of the regressors. We will return to this subject in Section 6.7.

The Gauss–Markov theorem can be established logically from the results of the preceding paragraph. We showed in Section 6.6.1 that

$$\text{Var}[\mathbf{b} \mid \mathbf{X}]\text{Var}[\mathbf{b}_0 \mid \mathbf{X}]$$

for any $\mathbf{b}_0 \neq \mathbf{b}$ and for the specific **X** in our sample. But if this inequality holds for every particular **X**, it must hold for

$$\text{Var}[\mathbf{b}] = E_{\mathbf{X}}[\text{Var}[\mathbf{b} \mid \mathbf{X}]].$$

That is, if it holds for every particular **X**, it must hold over the average value(s) of **X**.

The conclusion, therefore, is that the important results we have obtained thus far for the least squares estimator, unbiasedness, and the Gauss–Markov theorem hold whether or not we regard **X** as stochastic.

THEOREM 6.7: Gauss–Markov Theorem with Stochastic Regressors (Concluded). *In the classical linear regression model, the least squares estimator* **b** *is the minimum variance linear unbiased estimator of* $\boldsymbol{\beta}$ *whether* **X** *is stochastic or nonstochastic.*

6.6.3. Normality and the Distribution of b

Thus far, we have not made any use of Assumption 6, normality of $\boldsymbol{\epsilon}$, in any of our results. The assumption is useful for constructing statistics for testing hypotheses. For the moment, we continue to assume that the regressors are nonstochastic, although this is just a convenience because our assumptions are made conditionally on **X**. The assumption will be reconsidered in Section 6.7.7. In (6-23), **b** is a linear function of the disturbance vector $\boldsymbol{\epsilon}$. If we assume that $\boldsymbol{\epsilon}$ has a multivariate normal distribution, we may use the results of Section 3.10.2 and the mean vector and covariance matrix derived earlier to state that

$$\mathbf{b} \mid \mathbf{X} \sim N[\boldsymbol{\beta}, \sigma^2(\mathbf{X}'\mathbf{X})^{-1}]. \tag{6-39}$$

This is a multivariate normal distribution, so each element of $\mathbf{b}|\mathbf{X}$ is normally distributed:

$$b_k \mid \mathbf{X} \sim N[\beta_k, \sigma^2(\mathbf{X}'\mathbf{X})^{-1}_{kk}]. \tag{6-40}$$

The distribution of **b** is conditioned on **X**. If **X** is nonstochastic, then we would regard this as just the distribution of **b**, with **X** entering as a set of fixed constants. The important thing to note at this point is that the normal distribution of **b** in a finite sample is a consequence of our specific assumption of normally distributed disturbances. Without this assumption, and without some alternative specific assumption about the distribution of $\boldsymbol{\epsilon}$, we will not be able to make any definite statement about the exact distribution of **b**, conditional or otherwise. In an interesting result that we will explore at length in the next section, we *will* be able to obtain an approximate normal distribution for **b**, with or without assuming normally distributed disturbances and whether the regressors are stochastic or not. (Of course, we will have to make *some* additional assumptions about the underlying processes that have produced the data.)

There is an interesting way that assuming normally distributed disturbances does strengthen the results of the previous section. If ϵ_i is normally distributed, then ϵ_i and ϵ_j are statistically independent as well as uncorrelated (see Section 3.10, (3-97 and 3-98)). The joint density of $\boldsymbol{\epsilon}$ is

$$\prod_i f(\epsilon_i) = (2\pi\sigma^2)^{-n/2} e^{-\boldsymbol{\epsilon}'\boldsymbol{\epsilon}/(2\sigma^2)}.$$

This is the likelihood function for $\boldsymbol{\epsilon}$. If we now substitute $\epsilon_i = y_i - \mathbf{x}_i'\boldsymbol{\beta}$ and take logs, we obtain the log-likelihood function for $\mathbf{y}|\mathbf{X}$

$$\ln L(\boldsymbol{\beta}, \sigma^2 \mid \mathbf{y}, \mathbf{X}) = -\frac{n}{2}[\ln(2\pi\sigma^2)] - \frac{1}{2\sigma^2}(\mathbf{y} - \mathbf{X}\boldsymbol{\beta})'(\mathbf{y} - \mathbf{X}\boldsymbol{\beta}).$$

By expanding the sum of squares, we see that the log-likelihood can be written in the form

$$\ln L = a(\mathbf{y} \mid \mathbf{X}) + b(\boldsymbol{\beta}, \sigma^2) + \sum_j c_j(\mathbf{y} \mid \mathbf{X}) s_j(\boldsymbol{\beta}, \sigma^2).$$

This implies that the normal distribution is an **exponential family of distributions**—see the end of Section 4.6.1—and the functions $c_j(\mathbf{y}, \mathbf{X})$ are **sufficient**

statistics, $\mathbf{y'y}$, $\mathbf{X'y}$, and $\mathbf{X'X}$. So, for normally distributed disturbances, $\mathbf{b}$ is an unbiased estimator that is a function of sufficient statistics. This gives us a somewhat stronger version of Theorem 6.7. By the theorem of Rao and Blackwell [see Rao (1973), p. 320], unbiased estimators that are functions of sufficient statistics are efficient among all unbiased estimators. Therefore, the following holds.

THEOREM 6.8: (Based on the Rao–Blackwell Theorem). *In the classical regression model with normally distributed disturbances, the least squares estimator* $\mathbf{b}$ *has the minimum variance of all unbiased estimators.*

What this has done is broaden the class of estimators in which $\mathbf{b}$ is efficient from linear *and* unbiased to *all* unbiased estimators. This is stronger than the Gauss–Markov theorem.

6.6.4. Estimating σ^2 and the Variance of b

If we wish to test hypotheses about $\boldsymbol{\beta}$ or to form confidence intervals, we will require an estimate of the covariance matrix $\text{Var}[\mathbf{b}] = \sigma^2(\mathbf{X'X})^{-1}$. The population parameter σ^2 remains to be estimated. Since σ^2 is the expected value of ϵ_i^2 and e_i is an estimate of ϵ_i, by analogy,

$$\hat{\sigma}^2 = \frac{1}{n}\sum_{i=1}^{n} e_i^2 \tag{6-41}$$

would seem to be a natural estimator. But the least squares residuals are imperfect estimates of their population counterparts; $e_i = y_i - \mathbf{x}_i'\mathbf{b} = \epsilon_i - \mathbf{x}_i'(\mathbf{b} - \boldsymbol{\beta})$. The estimator is distorted (as might be expected) because $\boldsymbol{\beta}$ is not observed directly. The expected square on the right-hand side involves a second term that might not have expected value zero.

The least squares residuals are

$$\mathbf{e} = \mathbf{My} = \mathbf{M}[\mathbf{X}\boldsymbol{\beta} + \boldsymbol{\epsilon}] = \mathbf{M}\boldsymbol{\epsilon},$$

as $\mathbf{MX} = \mathbf{0}$. An estimator of σ^2 will be based on the sum of squared residuals:

$$\mathbf{e'e} = \boldsymbol{\epsilon}'\mathbf{M}\boldsymbol{\epsilon}.$$

The expected value of this quadratic form is

$$E[\mathbf{e'e} \mid \mathbf{X}] = E[\boldsymbol{\epsilon}'\mathbf{M}\boldsymbol{\epsilon} \mid \mathbf{X}].$$

By using the result on cyclic permutations (2-94),

$$E[\text{tr}(\boldsymbol{\epsilon}'\mathbf{M}\boldsymbol{\epsilon}) \mid \mathbf{X}] = E[\text{tr}(\mathbf{M}\boldsymbol{\epsilon}\boldsymbol{\epsilon}') \mid \mathbf{X}].$$

Since $\mathbf{M}$ is fixed—it is a function of $\mathbf{X}$—this is

$$\text{tr}(\mathbf{M}E[\boldsymbol{\epsilon}\boldsymbol{\epsilon}' \mid \mathbf{X}]) = \text{tr}(\mathbf{M}\sigma^2\mathbf{I}) = \sigma^2\text{tr}(\mathbf{M}).$$

The trace of $\mathbf{M}$ is

$$\begin{aligned}\text{tr}[\mathbf{I}_n - \mathbf{X}(\mathbf{X'X})^{-1}\mathbf{X}'] &= \text{tr}(\mathbf{I}_n) - \text{tr}[(\mathbf{X'X})^{-1}\mathbf{X'X}]\\ &= \text{tr}(\mathbf{I}_n) - \text{tr}(\mathbf{I}_K) = n - K.\end{aligned}$$

Therefore,

$$E[\mathbf{e}'\mathbf{e} \mid \mathbf{X}] = (n - K)\sigma^2,$$

so the natural estimator is biased toward zero, although the bias becomes smaller as the sample size increases. An unbiased estimator of σ^2 is

$$s^2 = \frac{\mathbf{e}'\mathbf{e}}{n - K}. \tag{6-42}$$

The estimator is unbiased unconditionally as well, since $E[s^2] = E_{\mathbf{x}}[E[s^2 | \mathbf{X}]] = E_{\mathbf{x}}[\sigma^2] = \sigma^2$.[23] The **standard error of the regression** is s, the square root of s^2. With s^2, we can then compute

$$\text{Est. Var}[\mathbf{b}] = s^2(\mathbf{X}'\mathbf{X})^{-1}.$$

Henceforth, we shall use the notation Est. Var[$\cdot$] to indicate a sample estimate of the sampling variance of an estimator. The square root of the kth diagonal element of this matrix, $\{[s^2(\mathbf{X}'\mathbf{X})^{-1}]_{kk}\}^{1/2}$, is the **standard error** of the estimate b_k. This is often denoted simply "the standard error of b_k."

6.6.5. Testing a Hypothesis About a Coefficient

Let S^{kk} be the kth diagonal element of $(\mathbf{X}'\mathbf{X})^{-1}$. Then, assuming normality,

$$z_k = \frac{b_k - \beta_k}{\sqrt{\sigma^2 S^{kk}}} \tag{6-43}$$

has a standard normal distribution. If σ^2 were known, statistical inference about β_k could be based on z_k. By using s^2 instead of σ^2, we can derive a statistic to use in place of z_k in (6-43). The quantity

$$\frac{(n - K)s^2}{\sigma^2} = \frac{\mathbf{e}'\mathbf{e}}{\sigma^2} = \left(\frac{\boldsymbol{\epsilon}}{\sigma}\right)'\mathbf{M}\left(\frac{\boldsymbol{\epsilon}}{\sigma}\right) \tag{6-44}$$

is an idempotent quadratic form in a standard normal vector $(\boldsymbol{\epsilon}/\sigma)$. Therefore, it has a chi-squared distribution with rank $(\mathbf{M})$ = trace$(\mathbf{M}) = n - K$ degrees of freedom.[24] The chi-squared variable in (6-44) is independent of the standard normal variable in (6-43). To prove this, it suffices to show that

$$\frac{\mathbf{b} - \boldsymbol{\beta}}{\sigma} = (\mathbf{X}'\mathbf{X})'\mathbf{X}'\left(\frac{\boldsymbol{\epsilon}}{\sigma}\right) \tag{6-45}$$

is independent of $(n - K)s^2/\sigma^2$. In Section 3.10.6, we found that a sufficient condition for the independence of a linear form $\mathbf{Lx}$ and an idempotent quadratic form $\mathbf{x}'\mathbf{Ax}$ in a standard normal vector $\mathbf{x}$ is that $\mathbf{LA} = \mathbf{0}$. Letting $\boldsymbol{\epsilon}/\sigma$ equal $\mathbf{x}$, we find that the requirement here would be that $(\mathbf{X}'\mathbf{X})^{-1}\mathbf{X}'\mathbf{M} = \mathbf{0}$. It

---

[23]Note that the Rao–Blackwell theorem that we used in Theorem 6.8 applies to s^2 if we assume normally distributed disturbances.

[24]This was proved in Section 3.10.3a.

does, as can be verified by multiplying it out. The general result is central in the derivation of many test statistics in regression analysis.

THEOREM 6.9: Independence of b and s^2. *If* $\boldsymbol{\epsilon}$ *is normally distributed, the least squares coefficient estimator* **b** *is statistically independent of the residual vector* **e** *and therefore, all functions of* **e**, *including* s^2.

Therefore, the ratio

$$t_k = \frac{(b_k - \beta_k)/\sqrt{\sigma^2 S^{kk}}}{\sqrt{[(n-K)s^2/\sigma^2]/(n-K)}} = \frac{b_k - \beta_k}{\sqrt{s^2 S^{kk}}} \tag{6-46}$$

has a t distribution with $(n - K)$ degrees of freedom.[25] We can use t_k to test hypotheses or form confidence intervals about the individual elements of $\boldsymbol{\beta}$.

A common test is whether a parameter β_k is significantly different from zero. The appropriate test statistic

$$t = \frac{b}{s_b} \tag{6-47}$$

is presented as standard output with the other results by most computer programs. The test is done in the usual way. This is usually labeled the ***t* ratio** for the estimate b_k. If $|b_k - \beta_k|/s_{bk} > t_{\lambda/2}$, where $t_{\lambda/2}$ is the $100(1 - \lambda/2)$ percent critical value from the t distribution with $(n - K)$ degrees of freedom, then the hypothesis is rejected and the coefficient is said to be "statistically significant." The value of 1.96, which would apply for the 5 percent significance level in a large sample, is often used as a benchmark value when a table of critical values is not immediately available. The t ratio for the test of the hypothesis that a coefficient equals zero is a standard part of the regression output of most computer programs.

EXAMPLE 6.14 Investment Equation

To continue the earlier investment example, the matrix $(\mathbf{X}'\mathbf{X})^{-1}$ for the five-variable regression has been given. The sum of squared residuals from that regression is 0.0004507, so the estimate of σ^2 is $s^2 = 0.0004507/(15 - 5) = 0.00004507$. Multiplying $(\mathbf{X}'\mathbf{X})^{-1}$ by this yields the estimated covariance matrix for the least squares slopes shown in Table 6.8. A summary of the regression results is presented in Table 6.9.

There are 15 observations and five coefficients, so the t statistics have 10 degrees of freedom. The 5 percent critical value for a t distribution with 10 degrees of freedom is 2.228. Thus, the individual hypotheses that the first three coefficients are zero are rejected. The last two are not significantly different

[25]See (3-36) in Section 3.4.2. It is the ratio of a standard normal variable to the square root of a chi-squared variable divided by its degrees of freedom.

TABLE 6.8 Estimated Covariance Matrix for b

Constant	*Time*	*Real GNP*	*Interest*	*Inflation*
0.0030391				
0.00010234	0.0000038878			
−0.0030102	−0.00010177	0.0030247		
0.000005592	−0.0000002885	−0.0000072788	0.0000014856	
−0.0000032077	−0.00000002573	−0.000002279	−0.00000075071	0.0000018157

TABLE 6.9 Regression Results for an Investment Equation

Sum of squared residuals:	0.0004507
Standard error of the regression:	0.006713

Variable	*Coefficient*	*Standard Error*	*t ratio*
Constant	−0.50907	0.05513	−9.234
Time	−0.01658	0.001972	−8.409
Real GNP	0.67038	0.054997	12.189
Interest	−0.0023259	0.0012189	1.908
Inflation	−0.000094012	0.0013475	−0.070

from zero by this test. Testing a hypothesis about a particular value of a coefficient other than zero proceeds along the lines developed in Example 4.35. For example, are these data consistent with the hypothesis that each \$1 billion increase in GNP will be associated with an equal increase in investment? The t ratio for testing this hypothesis is $(0.67038 - 1)/0.054997 = -5.9934$, which indicates that the slope on GNP is significantly less than 1.

6.6.6. Confidence Intervals for Parameters

A confidence interval for β_k would be based on (6-46). We could say that

$$\text{Prob}(b_k - t_{\lambda/2}s_{bk}\beta_k b_k + t_{\lambda/2}s_{bk}) = 1 - \lambda,$$

where $1 - \lambda$ is the desired level of confidence and $t_{\lambda/2}$ is the appropriate critical value from the t distribution with $(n - K)$ degrees of freedom.

EXAMPLE 6.15 Confidence Interval for the MPC

In the estimated consumption function, we obtained $b = 0.9793$. To compute the standard error of b, we need $s^2 = 536.99/8 = 67.12375$, $S_{xx} = 67{,}192.45$, which gives Est. $\text{Var}[b] = 0.0009992$ or $s_b = 0.03161$. For a t distribution with $n - 2 = 8$ degrees of freedom, the 95 percent critical value is 2.306. Therefore, a 95 percent confidence interval for β is $0.9793 \pm 2.306(0.03161)$ or $(0.90641, 1.0522)$.

For a one-sided test, we adjust the critical region and use the t_λ critical point from the distribution. Again, values of the sample estimate that are greatly inconsistent with the hypothesis cast doubt upon it.

EXAMPLE 6.16 Test for MPC < 1

Recall Keynes's fundamental principle that the marginal propensity to consume is less than 1. Are the data consistent with the hypothesis that β is less than 1? Consider testing the alternative,

$$H_0 : \beta 1 \quad \text{versus} \quad H_1 : \beta < 1.$$

The appropriate test statistic is

$$t = \frac{0.9793 - 1}{0.03161} = -0.655.$$

This is well above the 0.05 critical point of -2.306. We conclude that H_0 should not be rejected. The data are consistent with the hypothesis that $\beta \geq 1$. They are also consistent with the hypothesis that $\beta < 1$. That is, the estimate is not *significantly* different from 1.

We can also form a confidence interval for the disturbance variance σ^2. Using the same reasoning we used previously, we find that a 95 percent confidence interval for σ^2 would be

$$\frac{(n - K)s^2}{\chi^2_{0.975}} \quad \text{to} \quad \frac{(n - K)s^2}{\chi^2_{0.025}}. \tag{6-48}$$

EXAMPLE 6.17 Confidence Interval for σ^2

Continuing Example 6.14, we obtain a confidence interval for σ^2 that would be based on the chi-squared distribution with $(15 - 5) = 10$ degrees of freedom. The appropriate critical values are 3.25 and 20.48, so that the interval is

$$(15 - 10)\left[\frac{0.00004507}{20.48}\right] < \sigma^2 < (15 - 10)\left[\frac{0.00004507}{3.25}\right]$$

or

$$0.00002201 < \sigma^2 < 0.0001387.$$

We are usually more interested in the standard deviation rather than the variance of ϵ, because it has the same units of measurement as the dependent variable. A 95 percent confidence interval for σ, based on these same results, would be 0.004691 to 0.01178.[26]

---

[26] It is also not the narrowest possible confidence interval for σ^2 because of the asymmetry of the chi-squared distribution. See Exercise 19 in Chapter 4.

6.6.7. Testing the Significance of the Regression

A question that is usually of interest is whether the regression equation as a whole is significant. This is a joint test of the hypotheses that *all* the coefficients except the constant term are zero. If all the slopes are zero, the multiple correlation coefficient is zero as well, so we can base a test of this hypothesis on the value of R^2. The central result needed to carry out the test is the distribution of the statistic

$$F[K-1, n-K] = \frac{R^2/(K-1)}{(1-R^2)/(n-K)}. \quad \textbf{(6-49)}$$

If the hypothesis that $\boldsymbol{\beta}_2 = \mathbf{0}$ (the part of $\boldsymbol{\beta}$ not including the constant) is true, and the disturbances are normally distributed, then this statistic has an F distribution with $K-1$ and $n-K$ degrees of freedom. Large values of F give evidence against the validity of the hypothesis. Note that a large F is induced by a large value of R^2.

Proof of the Distribution of F: Recall that $R^2 = \mathbf{b}'\mathbf{X}'\mathbf{M}^0\mathbf{X}\mathbf{b}/\mathbf{y}'\mathbf{M}^0\mathbf{y}$ and $1 - R^2 = \mathbf{e}'\mathbf{e}/\mathbf{y}'\mathbf{M}^0\mathbf{y}$. Neglecting the term $(n-K)/(K-1)$ for the present, we will examine

$$R^2/(1-R^2) = \mathbf{b}'\mathbf{X}'\mathbf{M}^0\mathbf{X}\mathbf{b}/\mathbf{e}'\mathbf{e}.$$

Write the least squares results as

$$\mathbf{y} = b_1\mathbf{i} + \mathbf{X}\mathbf{J}\mathbf{b}_2 + \mathbf{e},$$

where $\mathbf{i}$ is the column of 1s in $\mathbf{X}$, b_1 is the estimated constant, $\mathbf{b}_2$ is the remaining coefficients, and $\mathbf{J}$ is a $K \times (K-1)$ matrix whose first row is $\mathbf{0}'$ and whose remaining rows are a $(K-1) \times (K-1)$ identity matrix. Thus, $\mathbf{XJ}$ is the last $K-1$ columns of $\mathbf{X}$. Now,

$$\mathbf{M}^0\mathbf{y} = \mathbf{M}^0\mathbf{X}\mathbf{J}\mathbf{b}_2 + \mathbf{e}$$

because $\mathbf{M}^0\mathbf{i} = \mathbf{0}$ (just multiply it out) and $\mathbf{M}^0\mathbf{e} = \mathbf{e}$ ($\mathbf{e}$ already has mean 0). For convenience, let $\mathbf{Z} = \mathbf{M}^0\mathbf{X}\mathbf{J}$, the last $K-1$ columns of $\mathbf{X}$, in mean deviation form. Then

$$\mathbf{M}^0\mathbf{y} = \mathbf{Z}\mathbf{b}_2 + \mathbf{e}$$

and

$$R^2 = \mathbf{b}_2'\mathbf{Z}'\mathbf{Z}\mathbf{b}_2/\mathbf{y}'\mathbf{M}^0\mathbf{y}.$$

We showed earlier that $\mathbf{b} = \boldsymbol{\beta} + (\mathbf{X}'\mathbf{X})^{-1}\mathbf{X}'\boldsymbol{\epsilon}$. Without the constant term, this is $\mathbf{b}_2 = \boldsymbol{\beta}_2 + (\mathbf{Z}'\mathbf{Z})^{-1}\mathbf{Z}'\boldsymbol{\epsilon}$. Under the hypothesis $\boldsymbol{\beta}_2 = \mathbf{0}$, $\mathbf{b}_2 = (\mathbf{Z}'\mathbf{Z})^{-1}\mathbf{Z}'\boldsymbol{\epsilon}$. We will expand this in the numerator of the ratio, use $\mathbf{I} - \mathbf{M}_Z = \mathbf{Z}(\mathbf{Z}'\mathbf{Z})^{-1}\mathbf{Z}'$ and $\mathbf{e} = \mathbf{My} = \mathbf{M}\boldsymbol{\epsilon}$ because $\mathbf{MX} = \mathbf{0}$, and divide both numerator and denominator by σ^2 to obtain

$$R^2/(1 - R^2) = [(\boldsymbol{\epsilon}/\sigma)'(\mathbf{I} - \mathbf{M}_Z)(\boldsymbol{\epsilon}/\sigma)]/[(\boldsymbol{\epsilon}/\sigma)'\mathbf{M}(\boldsymbol{\epsilon}/\sigma)].$$

This is the ratio of two quadratic forms in a vector $(\boldsymbol{\epsilon}/\sigma)$ that has a standard normal distribution. The matrices of the quadratic forms are idempotent, so both numerator and denominator have chi-squared distributions. To obtain the F distribution, we must divide each by their respective degrees of freedom. The degrees of freedom are the ranks of the idempotent matrices, which are $K - 1$ for $\mathbf{I} - \mathbf{M}_Z$ and $n - K$ for $\mathbf{M}$. Multiplication by the term that we have temporarily ignored does this. The remaining detail is to show that the two chi-squared variates are independent, which we can do by showing that $\mathbf{I} - \mathbf{M}_Z$ and $\mathbf{M}$ are orthogonal. Expand $(\mathbf{I} - \mathbf{M}_Z)\mathbf{M}$ to obtain

$$(\mathbf{I} - \mathbf{M}_Z)\mathbf{M} = \mathbf{M}^0\mathbf{XJ}(\mathbf{J}'\mathbf{X}'\mathbf{M}^0\mathbf{XJ})^{-1}\mathbf{J}'\mathbf{X}'\mathbf{M}^0\mathbf{M}.$$

To show that this equals $\mathbf{0}$, it is only necessary to show that $\mathbf{X}'\mathbf{M}^0\mathbf{M}$ equals $\mathbf{0}$. To do so, expand $\mathbf{M}^0$ in the multiplication. Then the first of the two terms in the product is $\mathbf{X}'\mathbf{M}$, which is $\mathbf{0}$, whereas the second is $\mathbf{X}'\mathbf{i}(1/n)\mathbf{i}'\mathbf{M}$. But $\mathbf{i}$ is one of the columns in $\mathbf{X}$, so $\mathbf{i}'\mathbf{M} = \mathbf{0}$ as well.[27] This completes the proof.

The logic of the test is that the F statistic is a measure of the loss of fit (namely, all R^2) that results when we impose the restriction that all of the slopes are zero. If F is large, the hypothesis is rejected.

EXAMPLE 6.18 *F* Test for the Investment Equation

The F ratio for testing the hypothesis that the four slopes in the investment equation are all zero is

$$F[4, 10] = \frac{0.97244/4}{(1 - 0.97244)/10} = 88.211,$$

which is far larger than the 95 percent critical value of 3.48. We conclude that the data are inconsistent with the hypothesis that all the slopes in the investment equation are zero.

We might have expected the preceding result, given the substantial t ratios presented earlier. But this need not always be the case. Examples can be constructed in which the individual coefficients are statistically significant, while jointly they are not.[28] This can be regarded as a pathological case, but the

[27] A more direct approach is to observe that $\mathbf{M}^0\mathbf{XJ}$ is a linear combination of the columns of $\mathbf{X}$ and that $\mathbf{M}$ will be orthogonal to every linear combination of the columns of $\mathbf{X}$. As an exercise, you might determine what $\mathbf{A}$ is in $\mathbf{M}^0\mathbf{XJ} = \mathbf{XA}$. (Hint: Treat the sample means as constants.) In Chapter 7, we will analyze a more general result that produces this one as a special case.

[28] See Maddala (1977a, pp. 123–124).

opposite one, in which none of the coefficients are significantly different from zero while R^2 is highly significant, is relatively common. The problem is that the interaction among the variables may serve to obscure their individual contribution to the fit of the regression, whereas their joint effect may still be significant. We will return to this point in Chapter 9 in our discussion of multicollinearity.

6.6.8. Test Statistics with Stochastic X and Normal ϵ

We now consider the validity of our sample test statistic and inference procedures when X is stochastic. First, consider the conventional t statistic in (6-46) for testing $H_0: \beta_k = \beta_k^0$.

$$t \mid \mathbf{X} = \frac{(b_k - \beta_k^0)}{[s^2(\mathbf{X}'\mathbf{X})_{kk}^{-1}]^{1/2}}.$$

Conditional on $\mathbf{X}$, $t|\mathbf{X}$ has a t distribution with $(n - K)$ degrees of freedom. What interests us, however, is the marginal, that is, the unconditional, distribution of t. As we saw, $\mathbf{b}$ is only normally distributed conditionally on $\mathbf{X}$; the marginal distribution may not be normal because it depends on $\mathbf{X}$. Similarly, because of the presence of the stochastic $\mathbf{X}$, the denominator of the t statistic is not the square root of a chi-square divided by its degrees of freedom, again, except conditional on this $\mathbf{X}$. The surprising result, however, is that *despite these complications,* the *marginal* distribution of t is still t, with $(n - K)$ degrees of freedom, regardless of the distribution of $\mathbf{X}$ or even of whether $\mathbf{X}$ is stochastic or nonstochastic! This intriguing result follows because $f(t|\mathbf{X})$ is not a function of $\mathbf{X}$. The same reasoning can be used to deduce that the usual F ratio used for testing linear restrictions is valid whether $\mathbf{X}$ is stochastic or not. This is a very powerful result. The implication is that

> *If the disturbances are normally distributed, we may carry out tests and construct confidence intervals for the parameters without making any change in our procedures, regardless of whether the regressors are stochastic, nonstochastic, or some mix of the two.*

6.7. LARGE-SAMPLE RESULTS FOR THE CLASSICAL REGRESSION MODEL

The discussion thus far has concerned *finite sample* properties of the least squares estimator. We derived the exact distribution of the least squares estimator and several test statistics under the assumptions of nonstochastic regressors and normally distributed disturbances. These results are independent of the sample size. But the classical regression model with nonstochastic regressors and normally distributed disturbances is a special case that does not include many of the most common applications, for examples, panel data and most time series models. This section will generalize the classical regression model by relaxing these two important assumptions.[29]

The classical regression model is one of relatively few settings in econometrics in which any definite statements can be made about the exact finite sample properties of an estimator. In most cases, the only known properties of our estimators are those that apply to large samples. We are only able to approximate finite-sample behavior by using what we know about large-sample properties. Thus, it is useful at this point to examine the asymptotic behavior of the parameter estimators in the classical regression model so that we can see how the analysis changes when only **asymptotic properties** can be obtained.

The assumptions of the classical normal linear regression model are the following.

A1. $\mathbf{y} = \mathbf{X}\boldsymbol{\beta} + \boldsymbol{\epsilon}$, for observations $i = 1, \ldots, n$.

A2. $\mathbf{X}$ is an $n \times K$ matrix of rank K.

A3. $E[\boldsymbol{\epsilon}|\mathbf{X}] = \mathbf{0}$.

A4. $E[\boldsymbol{\epsilon}\boldsymbol{\epsilon}'|\mathbf{X}] = \sigma^2\mathbf{I}, \sigma^2 < \infty$.

A5. $\mathbf{X}$ is a nonstochastic matrix of constants.

A6. $\boldsymbol{\epsilon}|\mathbf{X}$ is distributed as $N[\mathbf{0}, \sigma^2\mathbf{I}]$.

For convenience, we will briefly review the finite sample results of the previous sections. We then turn to the asymptotic results.

6.7.1. The Finite Sample Properties of Least Squares

Using only A1 through A4, we have established that the least squares estimators of the unknown parameters, $\boldsymbol{\beta}$ and σ^2,

$$\mathbf{b} = (\mathbf{X}'\mathbf{X})^{-1}\mathbf{X}'\mathbf{y} = \boldsymbol{\beta} + (\mathbf{X}'\mathbf{X})^{-1}\mathbf{X}'\boldsymbol{\epsilon}$$

and

$$s^2 = \mathbf{e}'\mathbf{e}/(n - K) = \boldsymbol{\epsilon}'\mathbf{M}\boldsymbol{\epsilon}/(n - K),$$

have the following **exact, finite sample properties:**

FS1. $E[\mathbf{b}|\mathbf{X}] = E[\mathbf{b}] = \boldsymbol{\beta}$. Least squares is unbiased.

FS2. $\text{Var}[\mathbf{b}|\mathbf{X}] = \sigma^2(\mathbf{X}'\mathbf{X})^{-1}$.

FS3. **Gauss–Markov theorem:** The minimum variance linear unbiased estimator of $\mathbf{w}'\boldsymbol{\beta}$ is $\mathbf{w}'\mathbf{b}$.

FS4. $E[s^2|\mathbf{X}] = E[s^2] = \sigma^2$.

FS5. $\text{Cov}[\mathbf{b}, \mathbf{e}|\mathbf{X}] = E[(\mathbf{b} - \boldsymbol{\beta})\mathbf{e}'|\mathbf{X}] = E[(\mathbf{X}'\mathbf{X})^{-1}\mathbf{X}'\boldsymbol{\epsilon}\boldsymbol{\epsilon}'\mathbf{M}|\mathbf{X}] = \mathbf{0}$ as $\mathbf{X}'(\sigma^2\mathbf{I})\mathbf{M} = \mathbf{0}$.

---

[29]Most of this discussion will use our earlier results on asymptotic distributions. It may be helpful to review Section 4.4 before proceeding.

Thus far, A5 plays no role. If $\mathbf{X}$ is allowed to be stochastic, the only change is the unconditional variance in FS2. That would be $\text{Var}[\mathbf{b}] = \sigma^2 E[(\mathbf{X}'\mathbf{X})^{-1}]$. The unconditional covariance in FS5 is $E[\text{Cov}[\mathbf{b}, \mathbf{e}] \mid \mathbf{X}] = \mathbf{0}$. For constructing confidence intervals and testing hypotheses, we derived some additional results that depended explicitly on the normality assumption:

FS6. $\mathbf{b}$ and $\mathbf{e}$ are statistically independent in addition to being uncorrelated. It follows that $\mathbf{b}$ and s^2 are uncorrelated and statistically independent.

FS7. The exact distribution of $\mathbf{b}$, conditioned on $\mathbf{X}$, is $N[\boldsymbol{\beta}, \sigma^2(\mathbf{X}'\mathbf{X})^{-1}]$.

FS8. $(n - K)s^2/\sigma^2$ is distributed exactly as $\chi^2[n - K]$. s^2 has mean σ^2 and variance $2\sigma^4/(n - K)$.

FS9. Based on results FS6 through FS8, the statistic

$$t[n - K] = \frac{b_k - \beta_k}{[s^2(\mathbf{X}'\mathbf{X})^{-1}_{kk}]^{1/2}}$$

has a t distribution with $n - K$ degrees of freedom, independently of $\mathbf{X}$.

FS10. The test statistic for testing the hypothesis that all slopes in the model are zero,

$$F[K - 1, n - K] = \frac{R^2/(K - 1)}{(1 - R^2)/(n - K)}$$

has an F distribution with $K - 1$ and $n - K$ degrees of freedom. (In the next chapter, we will extend this result to more general restrictions.)

Only FS7 depends on whether $\mathbf{X}$ is stochastic or not. If so, the *marginal* distribution of $\mathbf{b}$ depends on that of $\mathbf{X}$. Note the distinction between the properties of $\mathbf{b}$ established using A1 through A4 and the additional inference results obtained with the further assumption of normality of the disturbances. The primary result in the first set is the Gauss–Markov theorem, which holds regardless of the distribution of the disturbances. The important additional results brought by the normality assumption are FS9 and FS10. Under normality (and, perhaps under some other *specific* distributional assumptions) we also showed the following:

FS11. $\mathbf{b}$ is the minimum variance unbiased estimator of $\boldsymbol{\beta}$.

For the basic model of Assumptions A1 through A4, it is straightforward to derive the large-sample properties of the least squares estimator. We shall continue to assume that $\mathbf{X}$ is nonstochastic until Section 6.7.7. The normality assumption is inessential at this point. We will examine its implications in Section 6.8.

6.7.2. Consistency of the Least Squares Estimator of $\boldsymbol{\beta}$

We begin by assuming that

$$\lim_{n\to\infty} \frac{1}{n}\mathbf{X}'\mathbf{X} = \mathbf{Q}, \text{ a positive definite matrix.} \qquad \textbf{(6-50)}$$

If $\mathbf{X}$ is taken to be "fixed in repeated samples," or equivalently, if the assumptions of this regression model are meant to apply only to the $\mathbf{X}$ matrix in hand, then (6-50) implies that $\mathbf{Q} = (1/n)\mathbf{X}'\mathbf{X}$. If, instead, $\mathbf{X}$ is taken to be nonstochastic, but not constant in repeated samples, then (6-50) is a statement about the means of choosing the sample data. It is important to emphasize at this point that this is not meant to characterize anything about an expected value of $\mathbf{X}'\mathbf{X}$, as we have not yet assumed that the rows of $\mathbf{X}$ are stochastic. The least squares estimator may be written

$$\mathbf{b} = \boldsymbol{\beta} + \left(\frac{1}{n}\mathbf{X}'\mathbf{X}\right)^{-1}\left(\frac{1}{n}\mathbf{X}'\boldsymbol{\epsilon}\right) \tag{6-51}$$

If $\mathbf{Q}^{-1}$ exists,

$$\text{plim}\,\mathbf{b} = \boldsymbol{\beta} + \mathbf{Q}^{-1}\,\text{plim}\,\frac{1}{n}\mathbf{X}'\boldsymbol{\epsilon}$$

because the inverse is a continuous function of the original matrix. [We have invoked result (4-23).] We now require the probability limit of the last term. Let

$$\frac{1}{n}\mathbf{X}'\boldsymbol{\epsilon} = \frac{1}{n}\sum_{i=1}^{n}\mathbf{x}_i\epsilon_i = \frac{1}{n}\sum_{i=1}^{n}\mathbf{w}_i = \overline{\mathbf{w}}.$$

Then

$$\text{plim}\,\mathbf{b} = \boldsymbol{\beta} + \mathbf{Q}^{-1}\,\text{plim}\,\overline{\mathbf{w}}.$$

Because $\mathbf{X}$ is a nonstochastic matrix,

$$E[\overline{\mathbf{w}}] = \frac{1}{n}\sum_{i=1}^{n}E[\mathbf{w}_i] = \frac{1}{n}\sum_{i=1}^{n}\mathbf{x}_iE[\epsilon_i] = \frac{1}{n}\mathbf{X}'E[\boldsymbol{\epsilon}] = \mathbf{0}, \tag{6-52}$$

and, since $E[\boldsymbol{\epsilon\epsilon}'] = \sigma^2\mathbf{I}$,

$$\text{Var}[\overline{\mathbf{w}}] = E[\overline{\mathbf{w}}\,\overline{\mathbf{w}}'] = \frac{1}{n}\mathbf{X}'E[\boldsymbol{\epsilon\epsilon}']\mathbf{X}\frac{1}{n}\frac{\sigma^2}{n}\frac{\mathbf{X}'\mathbf{X}}{n}.$$

It then follows that

$$\lim_{n\to\infty}\text{Var}[\overline{\mathbf{w}}] = 0\cdot\mathbf{Q} = \mathbf{0}.$$

Since the mean of $\overline{\mathbf{w}}$ is identically zero and its variance converges to zero, $\overline{\mathbf{w}}$ **converges in mean square to zero,** so plim $\overline{\mathbf{w}} = \mathbf{0}$. Therefore,

$$\text{plim}\,\frac{1}{n}\mathbf{X}'\boldsymbol{\epsilon} = \mathbf{0}, \tag{6-53}$$

so

$$\text{plim}\,\mathbf{b} = \boldsymbol{\beta} + \mathbf{Q}^{-1}\cdot\mathbf{0} = \boldsymbol{\beta}. \tag{6-54}$$

This establishes that **b** is a consistent estimator of $\boldsymbol{\beta}$ in the classical regression model.

This way of proceeding is useful to set the stage for the results derived in the following sections. But although (6-50) is a conventional assumption, it is stronger than necessary and excludes a very common case. If **X** contains a time trend, $(1/n)\mathbf{X}'\mathbf{X}$ will explode as n goes to infinity, not converge to a positive definite matrix.[30] In this case, it would follow from the exact results

$$E[\mathbf{b}] = \boldsymbol{\beta} \Longrightarrow \lim_{n\to\infty} E[\mathbf{b}] = \boldsymbol{\beta},$$
$$\text{Var}[\mathbf{b}] = \sigma^2(\mathbf{X}'\mathbf{X})^{-1} \Longrightarrow \lim_{n\to\infty} \text{Var}[\mathbf{b}] = \mathbf{0}$$

that **b** converges in mean square to $\boldsymbol{\beta}$. Indeed, this case is particularly favorable in that the sampling difference between **b** and $\boldsymbol{\beta}$ converges to zero more rapidly than in the conventional case.[31]

Time-series settings that involve time trends, polynomial time series, and trending variables often pose cases in which the preceding assumptions are too restrictive.[32] A somewhat weaker set of assumptions about **X** that is broad enough to include most of these is the **Grenander conditions:**[33]

G1. For each column of **X**, $\mathbf{x}_k$, if $d_{nk}^2 = \mathbf{x}_k'\mathbf{x}_k$, $\lim_{n\to\infty} d_{nk}^2 = +\infty$. This means that $\mathbf{x}_k$ does not degenerate to a sequence of zeros.[34]

G2. $\text{Lim}_{n\to\infty}\, x_{ik}^2/d_{nk}^2 = 0$ for all $i = 1, \ldots, n$. This implies that no single observation will ever dominate $\mathbf{x}_k'\mathbf{x}_k$, and as $n \to \infty$, individual observations will become less important.

G3. Let $\mathbf{R}_n$ be the sample correlation matrix of the columns of **X**, excluding the constant term if there is one. Then $\lim_{n\to\infty} \mathbf{R}_n = \mathbf{C}$, a positive definite matrix. This implies that the full rank condition will always be met.[35] We have already assumed that **X** has full rank in a finite sample, so this assumption ensures that the condition will never be violated.

The conditions ensure that the data matrix is "well behaved" in large samples in that no single observation dominates the sum of squares and that sums of

---

[30] The diagonal element of $(1/n)\mathbf{X}'\mathbf{X}$ corresponding to the time trend is $(1/n)n(n+1)(2n+1)/6$, which is $O(n^2)$.

[31] Further discussion of this case and several others is given in Schmidt (1976, pp. 85–88). White (1984) examines a number of other cases. It is more difficult to establish consistency of s^2 when **X** contains a time trend. See Schmidt (1976) and Theil (1971) for discussion.

[32] These are sometimes labeled *asymptotically uncooperative regressors.* See, for example, Schmidt (1976, p. 85). An example is a regressor of the form λ^t, where t indexes the time-series observations. It turns out that consistency cannot be established in the presence of this type of variable unless $|\lambda| > 1$, which will cause other problems.

[33] Judge et al. (1985, p. 162).

[34] The regressor λ^t described in the earlier footnote violates this assumption.

[35] The formal statement of this condition, for example, in Judge et al. (1985), is a bit more involved. The preceding is equivalent.

squares continue to grow as the sample size grows, but at a reasonable rate. This is a very weak assumption and is likely to be satisfied by almost any data set encountered in practice.[36]

6.7.3. Asymptotic Normality of the Least Squares Estimator

To derive the asymptotic distribution of the least squares estimator, we shall use the results of Section 4.4.2. We need not assume that the disturbances are normally distributed. We will make use of some basic central limit theorems, however, so in addition to Assumption 4 (uncorrelatedness), we shall assume that the observations are *independent.* For practical purposes, this is a minor subtlety. But, for purposes of later theoretical treatments, we must take into consideration that without a normality assumption, uncorrelatedness does not necessarily imply statistical independence, and without independence, we must use something other than our familiar central limit theorem to establish the asymptotic normality of least squares. We shall return to this point below. As before, we take the simplest case of nonstochastic, "asymptotically cooperative" regressors.

It follows from (6-51) that

$$\sqrt{n}(\mathbf{b} - \boldsymbol{\beta}) = \left(\frac{\mathbf{X}'\mathbf{X}}{n}\right)^{-1}\left(\frac{1}{\sqrt{n}}\right)\mathbf{X}'\boldsymbol{\epsilon}. \tag{6-55}$$

Since the inverse matrix is a continuous function of the original matrix, $\lim_{n\to\infty}(\mathbf{X}'\mathbf{X}/n)^{-1} = \mathbf{Q}^{-1}$. Therefore, if the limiting distribution exists, the limiting distribution of the statistic in (6-55) is the same as that of

$$\left[\lim_{n\to\infty}\left(\frac{\mathbf{X}'\mathbf{X}}{n}\right)^{-1}\right]\left(\frac{1}{\sqrt{n}}\right)\mathbf{X}'\boldsymbol{\epsilon} = \mathbf{Q}^{-1}\left(\frac{1}{\sqrt{n}}\right)\mathbf{X}'\boldsymbol{\epsilon}.^{37} \tag{6-56}$$

Thus, we must establish the limiting distribution of

$$\left(\frac{1}{\sqrt{n}}\right)\mathbf{X}'\boldsymbol{\epsilon} = \sqrt{n}(\overline{\mathbf{w}} - E[\overline{\mathbf{w}}]), \tag{6-57}$$

where $E[\overline{\mathbf{w}}] = \mathbf{0}$. [See (6-52).] We can use the Lindberg–Feller version of the central limit theorem given in Section 4.4.2 to obtain the limiting distribution of $\sqrt{n}\overline{\mathbf{w}}$. Using that formulation,

$$\overline{\mathbf{w}} = \frac{1}{n}\sum_{i=1}^{n}\mathbf{x}_i\epsilon_i$$

[36]White (1984) continues this line of analysis. He also provides additional results on conditions that must be attached to *stochastic* regressors in order to establish the asymptotic properties of least squares. We turn to this subject in Section 6.7.7.

[37]This is a multivariate version of result (4-28).

is the average of n independent random vectors $\mathbf{x}_i\epsilon_i$, with means $\mathbf{0}$ and variances

$$\text{Var}[\mathbf{x}_i\epsilon_i] = \sigma^2\mathbf{x}_i\mathbf{x}_i' = \sigma^2\mathbf{Q}_i. \tag{6-58}$$

The variance of $\sqrt{n}\overline{\mathbf{w}}$ is

$$\begin{aligned}\sigma^2\overline{\mathbf{Q}}_n &= \sigma^2\left(\frac{1}{n}\right)[\mathbf{Q}_1 + \mathbf{Q}_2 + \cdots + \mathbf{Q}_n]\\ &= \sigma^2\left(\frac{1}{n}\right)\sum_{i=1}^{n}\mathbf{x}_i\mathbf{x}_i'\\ &= \sigma^2\left(\frac{\mathbf{X}'\mathbf{X}}{n}\right).\end{aligned} \tag{6-59}$$

As long as the sum is not dominated by any particular term and the regressors are well behaved, which in this case means that (6-50) holds,

$$\lim_{n\to\infty} \sigma^2\overline{\mathbf{Q}}_n = \sigma^2\mathbf{Q}. \tag{6-60}$$

Therefore, we may apply the Lindberg–Feller central limit theorem to the vector $\sqrt{n}\overline{\mathbf{w}}$, as we did in Section 4.4.2 for the univariate case $\sqrt{n}\bar{x}$. This gives the elements we need for a formal result.[38] If:

> $[\epsilon_i], i = 1, \ldots, n$ are independent and identically distributed with mean 0 and variance $\sigma^2 < \infty$, and if the elements x_{ik} of $\mathbf{X}$ are such that $|x_{tk}|$ is finite and $\lim_{n\to\infty}(\mathbf{X}'\mathbf{X}/n) = \mathbf{Q}$, a finite positive definite matrix, then
>
> $$\left(\frac{1}{\sqrt{n}}\right)\mathbf{X}'\boldsymbol{\epsilon} \xrightarrow{d} N[\mathbf{0}, \sigma^2\mathbf{Q}]. \tag{6-61}$$

It then follows that

$$\mathbf{Q}^{-1}\left(\frac{1}{\sqrt{n}}\right)\mathbf{X}'\boldsymbol{\epsilon} \xrightarrow{d} N[\mathbf{Q}^{-1}\mathbf{0}, \mathbf{Q}^{-1}(\sigma^2\mathbf{Q})\mathbf{Q}^{-1}]. \tag{6-62}$$

Or, combining terms,

$$\sqrt{n}(\mathbf{b} - \boldsymbol{\beta}) \xrightarrow{d} N[\mathbf{0}, \sigma^2\mathbf{Q}^{-1}]. \tag{6-63}$$

Using the technique of Section 4.4.3, we then obtain the **asymptotic distribution** for **b**.

THEOREM 6.10: Asymptotic Distribution of b with Nonstochastic Regressors. *If $\{\epsilon_i\}$ are i.i.d. with mean zero and finite variance σ^2 and x_{ik} is such that the*

[38]A more detailed proof is given in Schmidt (1976). Note that the Lindberg–Levy variant does not apply because $\text{Var}[\mathbf{w}_i]$ is not constant.

Grenander conditions are met, then

$$\mathbf{b} \xrightarrow{a} N\left[\boldsymbol{\beta}, \frac{\sigma^2}{n}\mathbf{Q}^{-1}\right]. \tag{6-64}$$

In practice, it is necessary to estimate $(1/n)\mathbf{Q}^{-1}$ with $(\mathbf{X}'\mathbf{X})^{-1}$ and σ^2 with $\mathbf{e}'\mathbf{e}/(n - K)$.

If $\boldsymbol{\epsilon}$ is normally distributed, Result **FS7** given in Section 6.7.1 holds in *every* sample, so it holds asymptotically as well. The important implication of this derivation is that *if the regressors are well behaved, the asymptotic normality of the least squares estimator does not depend on normality of the disturbances;* it is a consequence of the central limit theorem. If the variables in $\mathbf{X}$ are "asymptotically uncooperative," then some other method of proof is required. If the Grenander conditions are met, with the other assumptions, a counterpart to (6-64) can still be obtained. Discussion of this important case appears in Judge et al. (1985, pp. 161–162). We will also consider other more general cases in the sections to follow.

6.7.4. Consistency of s^2 and the Estimator of Asy. Var[b]

To complete the derivation of the asymptotic properties of $\mathbf{b}$, we will require an estimator of Asy. Var$[\mathbf{b}] = (\sigma^2/n)\mathbf{Q}^{-1}$. With (6-50), it is sufficient to restrict attention to s^2, so the purpose here is to assess the consistency of s^2 as an estimator of σ^2. Expanding

$$s^2 = \frac{1}{n - K}\boldsymbol{\epsilon}'\mathbf{M}\boldsymbol{\epsilon}$$

produces

$$s^2 = \frac{1}{n - K}[\boldsymbol{\epsilon}'\boldsymbol{\epsilon} - \boldsymbol{\epsilon}'\mathbf{X}(\mathbf{X}'\mathbf{X})^{-1}\mathbf{X}'\boldsymbol{\epsilon}]$$

$$= \frac{n}{n - k}\left[\frac{\boldsymbol{\epsilon}'\boldsymbol{\epsilon}}{n} - \left(\frac{\boldsymbol{\epsilon}'\mathbf{X}}{n}\right)\left(\frac{\mathbf{X}'\mathbf{X}}{n}\right)^{-1}\left(\frac{\mathbf{X}'\boldsymbol{\epsilon}}{n}\right)\right].$$

The leading constant converges to 1. We can apply (6-50), (6-53) (twice), and the product rule for probability limits (4-23) to assert that the second term in the brackets converges to zero. That leaves

$$\overline{\epsilon^2} = \frac{1}{n}\sum_{i=1}^{n} \epsilon_i^2.$$

Assuming that the disturbances are independent, $\overline{\epsilon^2}$ is the mean of a random sample. If the terms in the sum have finite variance, then Theorem 4.4 will apply. Therefore, we assume that

$$E[\epsilon_i^4] = \phi_\epsilon < \infty.$$

Then the terms in the sum are independent, with mean σ^2 and variance $\phi_\epsilon - \sigma^4$. So, by Theorem 4.3, the first term in brackets converges in probability to σ^2, which gives our result,

$$\text{plim } s^2 = \sigma^2,$$

and, by the product rule,

$$\text{plim } s^2(\mathbf{X}'\mathbf{X}/n)^{-1} = \sigma^2\mathbf{Q}^{-1}.$$

With normally distributed disturbances, the proof is even easier, whether $\mathbf{X}$ is stochastic or not. We already showed that under normality, s^2 is $\sigma^2/(n-K)$ times a chi-squared variable with $n-K$ degrees of freedom. Therefore, $E[s^2|\mathbf{X}] = E[s^2] = \sigma^2$ and $\text{Var}[s^2|\mathbf{X}] = \text{Var}[s^2] = 2\sigma^4/(n-K)$. The mean is σ^2 for any n or $\mathbf{X}$ and the variance converges to 0, so with normally distributed disturbances, s^2 converges in mean square to σ^2.

It follows in either case that the appropriate estimator of the asymptotic covariance matrix of $\mathbf{b}$ is

$$\text{Est. Asy. Var}[\mathbf{b}] = s^2(\mathbf{X}'\mathbf{X})^{-1}.$$

6.7.5. Asymptotic Distribution of a Function of b — The Delta Method

To complete the derivation, we can extend Theorem 4.15 to functions of the least squares estimator. Let $\mathbf{f}(\mathbf{b})$ be a set of J continuous, linear or nonlinear functions of the least squares estimators, and let

$$\mathbf{C} = \frac{\partial \mathbf{f}(\mathbf{b})}{\partial \mathbf{b}'}.$$

$\mathbf{C}$ is the $J \times K$ matrix whose jth row is the vector of derivatives of the jth function with respect to $\mathbf{b}'$. By the Slutsky theorem (4-21),

$$\text{plim } \mathbf{f}(\mathbf{b}) = \mathbf{f}(\boldsymbol{\beta})$$

and

$$\text{plim } \mathbf{C} = \frac{\partial \mathbf{f}(\boldsymbol{\beta})}{\partial \boldsymbol{\beta}'} = \boldsymbol{\Gamma}.$$

Then the following theorem holds.

THEOREM 6.11: Asymptotic Distribution of a Function of b. *If* $\mathbf{f}(\mathbf{b})$ *is a set of continuous functions of* $\mathbf{b}$ *such that* $\boldsymbol{\Gamma} = \partial\mathbf{f}(\boldsymbol{\beta})/\partial\boldsymbol{\beta}'$ *and if Theorem 6.10 holds, then*

$$\mathbf{f}(\mathbf{b}) \xrightarrow{a} N\left[\mathbf{f}(\boldsymbol{\beta}), \boldsymbol{\Gamma}\left(\frac{\sigma^2}{n}\mathbf{Q}^{-1}\right)\boldsymbol{\Gamma}'\right]. \tag{6-65}$$

In practice, the estimator of the asymptotic covariance matrix would be

$$\text{Est. Asy. Var}[\mathbf{f}(\mathbf{b})] = \mathbf{C}[s^2(\mathbf{X}'\mathbf{X})^{-1}]\mathbf{C}'.$$

If any of the functions are nonlinear, the property of unbiasedness that holds for **b** may not carry over to **f**(**b**). Nonetheless, it follows from (10-4) that **f**(**b**) is a consistent estimator of $\mathbf{f}(\boldsymbol{\beta})$, and the asymptotic covariance matrix is readily available.

EXAMPLE 6.19 Asymptotic Distribution of the Constant in a Log-Linear Model

To estimate a log-linear model $Y = AX^{\beta}e^{\epsilon}$, we first write

$$\begin{aligned}\ln Y &= \ln A + \beta \ln X + \epsilon \\ &= \alpha + \beta x + \epsilon.\end{aligned}$$

The parameters can now be estimated by least squares. If ϵ is normally distributed, the exact finite-sample distribution of a, the estimator of α, is

$$a \sim N\left[\alpha, \sigma^2\left\{\frac{1}{n} + \frac{\bar{x}^2}{\Sigma_i(x_i - \bar{x})^2}\right\}\right] = N[\alpha, \sigma_a^2].$$

For estimating $A = e^{\alpha}$, the usual estimator will be e^a. The exact distribution, mean, and variance of e^a can be found by using the results for the lognormal distribution in Section 3.4.4. For this application, if $a \sim N[\alpha, \sigma_a^2]$, then $e^a \sim$ **lognormal** with mean $e^{\alpha + 1/2\sigma_a^2}$ and variance $e^{2\alpha + \sigma_a^2}(e^{\sigma_a^2} - 1)$. A useful way to write this is

$$e^a \sim LN[e^{\alpha}e^{1/2\sigma_a^2}, (e^{\alpha})^2 e^{\sigma_a^2}(e^{\sigma_a^2} - 1)].$$

This gives the *exact distribution* for e^a. We see that e^a is an upward-biased estimator of A, since $E[e^a]/e^{\alpha} = e^{1/2\sigma_a^2} > 1$. But assuming that $\Sigma_i(x_i - \bar{x})^2$ continues to increase as the sample size increases and $\bar{x}^2$ approaches a finite constant, $\sigma_a^2 \to 0$ as $n \to \infty$, then $E[e^a] \to e^{\alpha}$. Likewise, the third term in $\text{Var}[e^a]$ converges to zero as $n \to \infty$, so $\text{Var}[e^a] \to 0$. Therefore, e^a converges in mean square to e^{α}.

Based on (6-65), the *asymptotic distribution* of e^a will be normal (not lognormal) with mean A. The asymptotic variance of a is

$$\kappa^2 = \frac{1}{n}\lim n\sigma_a^2 = \frac{1}{n}\sigma^2\mathbf{Q}^{11},$$

where $\mathbf{Q}^{11} = \lim_{n\to\infty}[1 + \bar{x}^2/((1/n)\Sigma_i(x_i - \bar{x})^2)]$, once again, assuming that the limits exist. So, using (6-65), the asymptotic variance of e^a is

$$(dA/d\alpha)^2 \text{ Asy. Var}[a] = (e^{\alpha})^2\kappa^2.$$

Note the difference between the exact variance given earlier and the variance of the asymptotic normal distribution. We could estimate the asymptotic variance with

$$\text{Est. Asy. Var}[e^a] = (e^a)^2 s_a^2$$

and the exact variance with

$$\text{Est. Var}[e^a] = (e^a)^2 e^{s_a^2}(e^{s_a^2} - 1).$$

The comparison between the true and asymptotic distributions would be similar to that in Figure 4.5.

EXAMPLE 6.20 Estimating an Elasticity

In the linear model $y = \mathbf{x}'\boldsymbol{\beta} + \epsilon$, the elasticity of y with respect to changes in x_k is

$$\eta_k = \frac{\partial \ln y}{\partial \ln x_k} = \beta_k\left(\frac{x_k}{y}\right).$$

This value is often estimated by computing it at the sample means as

$$h_k = b_k \frac{\overline{x}_k}{\overline{\mathbf{x}}'\mathbf{b}}.$$

The denominator is the estimate of $E[y\,|\,\mathbf{x}]$ using the mean values of the regressors. (If the model contains a constant term, this will equal $\overline{y}$.) The finite sample properties of h_k are not likely to be tractable because of the division by $\overline{\mathbf{x}}'\mathbf{b}$. But with (6-65), the large-sample properties should be straightforward. If (6-50) is met, then $\overline{\mathbf{x}}$ will converge to a finite vector, say $\mathbf{q}$ (the last $K - 1$ elements of the first column of $\mathbf{Q}$). It follows from the Slutsky theorem that

$$\text{plim } h_k = \eta_{k|\mathrm{x}=\mathrm{q}}.$$

The sample estimate will converge to the true elasticity, evaluated at the limiting values of the sample means of the regressors. The vector of derivatives is

$$\begin{aligned}\boldsymbol{\gamma} &= \frac{\partial \eta}{\partial \boldsymbol{\beta}} \\ &= \frac{(\mathbf{q}'\boldsymbol{\beta})q_k\mathbf{e}_k - (\beta_k q_k)\mathbf{q}}{(\mathbf{q}'\boldsymbol{\beta})^2} \\ &= \frac{q_k\mathbf{e}_k - \eta_k\mathbf{q}}{\mathbf{q}'\boldsymbol{\beta}},\end{aligned}$$

where $\mathbf{e}_k$ is the kth column of a $K \times K$ identity matrix. (It is a column vector with 1 in the kth position and zeros elsewhere.) The asymptotic distribution would be normal with mean η_k and variance

$$\text{Asy. Var}[h_k] = \boldsymbol{\gamma}'\left[\left(\frac{\sigma^2}{n}\right)\mathbf{Q}^{-1}\right]\boldsymbol{\gamma}.$$

In practice, $(\sigma^2/n)\mathbf{Q}^{-1}$ is estimated with $s^2(\mathbf{X}'\mathbf{X})^{-1}$ and $\hat{\boldsymbol{\gamma}}$ can be computed by adding $\overline{x}_k/\overline{y}$ to the kth element of $(-h_k/\overline{y})\overline{\mathbf{x}}$.

6.7.6. Asymptotic Behavior of the Standard Test Statistics

Without normality of $\boldsymbol{\epsilon}$, the t, F, and chi-squared statistics given earlier do not have these distributions. We can appeal instead to the results of Section 4.4.3.

We have shown that

$$\mathbf{b} \xrightarrow{a} N\left[\beta, \frac{\sigma^2}{n}\mathbf{Q}^{-1}\right].$$

It follows that the asymptotic distribution of

$$\theta_k = \frac{b_k - \beta_k}{[(\sigma^2/n)\mathbf{Q}_{kk}^{-1}]^{1/2}}$$

is standard normal. Since plim $s^2(\mathbf{X}'\mathbf{X}/n)^{-1} = \sigma^2\mathbf{Q}^{-1}$,

$$t_k = \frac{b_k - \beta_k}{[s^2(\mathbf{X}'\mathbf{X})_{kk}^{-1}]^{1/2}}$$

will have the same asymptotic distribution as θ_k. So instead of the t distribution, we can refer the usual statistic for a hypothesis about an element of $\boldsymbol{\beta}$ to the standard normal distribution.

The F statistic for testing the validity of a set of linear restrictions of the form $\mathbf{R}\boldsymbol{\beta} - \mathbf{q} = \mathbf{0}$ is

$$F = \frac{(\mathbf{e}_*'\mathbf{e}_* - \mathbf{e}'\mathbf{e})/J}{\mathbf{e}'\mathbf{e}/(n - K)} = \frac{(\mathbf{Rb} - \mathbf{q})'[\mathbf{R}s^2(\mathbf{X}'\mathbf{X})^{-1}\mathbf{R}']^{-1}(\mathbf{Rb} - \mathbf{q})}{J},$$

where J is the number of restrictions (rows in $\mathbf{R}$) and $\mathbf{e}_*'\mathbf{e}_*$ is the sum of squared residuals that results when the restrictions are imposed.[39] We looked at a special case of F in Section 6.6.7 in which the hypothesized restriction was that all the coefficients in $\boldsymbol{\beta}$ except the constant term equal zero. For this case, $\mathbf{e}_*'\mathbf{e}_*$ is $\Sigma_i(y_i - \bar{y})^2 > \mathbf{e}'\mathbf{e}$, J is $K - 1$, and $\mathbf{R}$ equals $\mathbf{J}'$. (Note the distinction between the matrix $\mathbf{J}$ and the scalar J, which is the number of rows in $\mathbf{R}$.) The t test of the hypothesis that β_k equals a specific value that we examined in Section 6.6.5 is another application in which $\mathbf{R}$ has a single row, and as we shall show in Chapter 7, the test statistic is the square root of F. We will also examine a number of other cases in Chapter 7.

To begin, we maintain the assumption that $\boldsymbol{\epsilon}$ is normally distributed. Then F is distributed as $F[J, n - K]$ regardless of the sample size. But it is instructive to examine the large-sample behavior of the statistic. We will revisit the testing procedure in Chapter 7; our purpose here is to examine the behavior of the test statistic itself. We will show in Chapter 7 that the least squares coefficient vector when computed subject to the set of linear constraints $\mathbf{Rb} - \mathbf{q} = \mathbf{0}$ can be written

$$\mathbf{b}_* = \mathbf{b} - \mathbf{Cm},$$

[39] We will not use this test statistic until Chapter 7, but it is convenient to examine its behavior now with the other least squares results.

where

$$\mathbf{C} = (\mathbf{X}'\mathbf{X})^{-1}\mathbf{R}'[\mathbf{R}(\mathbf{X}'\mathbf{X})^{-1}\mathbf{R}']^{-1},$$
$$\mathbf{m} = \mathbf{Rb} - \mathbf{q},$$

$\mathbf{b}$ is the familiar unconstrained least squares coefficient vector, $(\mathbf{X}'\mathbf{X})^{-1}\mathbf{X}'\mathbf{y}$, and $\mathbf{e}_* = \mathbf{y} - \mathbf{X}\mathbf{b}_*$. Recall that $\mathbf{b} = \boldsymbol{\beta} + (\mathbf{X}'\mathbf{X})^{-1}\mathbf{X}'\boldsymbol{\epsilon}$, and under the hypothesis that the restrictions are valid, $\mathbf{R}\boldsymbol{\beta} - \mathbf{q} = \mathbf{0}$. To obtain another form of F, use $\mathbf{Rb} - \mathbf{q} = \mathbf{R}(\mathbf{b}_* + \mathbf{Cm}) - \mathbf{q} = \mathbf{Cm}$ because the restrictions are imposed on $\mathbf{b}_*$ (so $\mathbf{R}\mathbf{b}_* - \mathbf{q} = \mathbf{0}$). If we substitute this and the expression for $\mathbf{b}$ (which appears in $\mathbf{m}$) in terms of $\boldsymbol{\beta}$, $\mathbf{X}$, and $\boldsymbol{\epsilon}$, we obtain (after some manipulation)

$$F = \frac{(\mathbf{m}'\mathbf{C}'\mathbf{X}'\mathbf{X}\mathbf{C}\mathbf{m})/J}{\mathbf{e}'\mathbf{e}/(n-K)} = \frac{\boldsymbol{\epsilon}'\mathbf{X}(\mathbf{X}'\mathbf{X})^{-1}\mathbf{R}'[\mathbf{R}(\mathbf{X}'\mathbf{X})^{-1}\mathbf{R}']^{-1}\mathbf{R}(\mathbf{X}'\mathbf{X})^{-1}\mathbf{X}'\boldsymbol{\epsilon}/J}{\boldsymbol{\epsilon}'\mathbf{M}\boldsymbol{\epsilon}/(n-K)}.$$

Now, divide the numerator and denominator by σ^2 and write this as

$$JF = \frac{(\boldsymbol{\epsilon}/\sigma)'\mathbf{L}(\boldsymbol{\epsilon}/\sigma)}{[\boldsymbol{\epsilon}'\mathbf{M}\boldsymbol{\epsilon}/(n-K)]/\sigma^2}.$$

The denominator of the fraction is s^2/σ^2. Since plim $s^2 = \sigma^2$, if the statistic JF as given above has a limiting distribution, then it is the same limiting distribution of the statistic that results when the denominator is replaced by its limiting value 1.0. Thus, JF has the same limiting distribution as $\boldsymbol{\Omega} = (\boldsymbol{\epsilon}/\sigma)'\mathbf{L}(\boldsymbol{\epsilon}/\sigma)$. This is a quadratic form in a standard normal vector. You can verify that $\mathbf{L}$ is idempotent by multiplying it out. So, $\boldsymbol{\Omega}$ has a chi-squared distribution. The degrees of freedom equal the rank of $\mathbf{L}$, which equals its trace. To find this, use

$$\begin{aligned}\text{trace}(\mathbf{L}) &= \text{trace}\{\mathbf{X}(\mathbf{X}'\mathbf{X})^{-1}\mathbf{R}'[\mathbf{R}(\mathbf{X}'\mathbf{X})^{-1}\mathbf{R}']^{-1}\mathbf{R}(\mathbf{X}'\mathbf{X})^{-1}\mathbf{X}'\}\\ &= \text{trace}\{[\mathbf{R}(\mathbf{X}'\mathbf{X})^{-1}\mathbf{R}']^{-1}\mathbf{R}(\mathbf{X}'\mathbf{X})^{-1}\mathbf{X}'\mathbf{X}(\mathbf{X}'\mathbf{X})^{-1}\mathbf{R}'\}\\ &= \text{trace}\{\mathbf{I}_J\} = J.\end{aligned}$$

We conclude that $JF \xrightarrow{d} \chi^2(J)$ when $\boldsymbol{\epsilon}$ is normally distributed.

If $\boldsymbol{\epsilon}$ is not normally distributed, then F is no longer distributed as $F[J, n-K]$ because neither the numerator nor the denominator has the necessary chi-squared distribution. The **Wald statistic,** $JF[J, n-K]$, however, does have a chi-squared distribution asymptotically and can be used instead. This is the same result we have for the case of normally distributed disturbances. Under the usual assumptions, the Wald statistic may be used whether or not the disturbances are normally distributed. A proof of this important conclusion will be instructive.[40]

THEOREM 6.12: Limiting Distribution of the Wald Statistic. *If* $\sqrt{n}(\mathbf{b} - \boldsymbol{\beta}) \xrightarrow{d} N[\mathbf{0}, \sigma^2\mathbf{Q}^{-1}]$, *and if* $H_0\!: \mathbf{R}\boldsymbol{\beta} - \mathbf{q} = \mathbf{0}$ *is true, then*

$$W = (\mathbf{Rb} - \mathbf{q})'[\mathbf{R}\, s^2(\mathbf{X}'\mathbf{X})^{-1}\mathbf{R}']^{-1}(\mathbf{Rb} - \mathbf{q}) = JF \xrightarrow{d} \chi^2(J).$$

[40] See White (1984, p. 71).

Proof: Since $\mathbf{R}$ is a matrix of constants,

$$\sqrt{n}\mathbf{R}(\mathbf{b} - \boldsymbol{\beta}) \xrightarrow{d} N[\mathbf{0}, \mathbf{R}(\sigma^2\mathbf{Q}^{-1})\mathbf{R}']. \qquad \textbf{(1)}$$

But $\mathbf{R}\boldsymbol{\beta} = \mathbf{q}$, so

$$\sqrt{n}(\mathbf{Rb} - \mathbf{q}) \xrightarrow{d} N[\mathbf{0}, \mathbf{R}(\sigma^2\mathbf{Q}^{-1})\mathbf{R}']. \qquad \textbf{(2)}$$

For convenience, write this as

$$\mathbf{z} \xrightarrow{d} N[\mathbf{0}, \mathbf{P}]. \qquad \textbf{(2')}$$

In Section 2.7.11, we defined the inverse square root of a positive definite matrix $\mathbf{P}$ as another matrix, say $\mathbf{T}$ such that $\mathbf{T}^2 = \mathbf{P}^{-1}$, and denoted $\mathbf{T}$ as $\mathbf{P}^{-1/2}$. Let $\mathbf{T}$ be the inverse square root of $\mathbf{P}$. Then, by the same reasoning as in (1) and (2),

$$\text{if } \mathbf{z} \xrightarrow{d} N[\mathbf{0}, \mathbf{P}], \mathbf{P}^{-1/2}\mathbf{z} \xrightarrow{d} N[\mathbf{0}, \mathbf{P}^{-1/2}\mathbf{P}\mathbf{P}^{-1/2}] = N[\mathbf{0}, \mathbf{I}]. \qquad \textbf{(3)}$$

We now invoke (4-31) for the limiting distribution of a function of a random variable. The sum of squares of uncorrelated (i.e., independent) standard normal variables is distributed as chi-squared. Thus, the limiting distribution of

$$(\mathbf{P}^{-1/2}\mathbf{z})'(\mathbf{P}^{-1/2}\mathbf{z}) = \mathbf{z}'\mathbf{P}^{-1}\mathbf{z} \xrightarrow{d} \chi^2(J). \qquad \textbf{(4)}$$

Reassembling the parts from before, we have shown that the limiting distribution of

$$n(\mathbf{Rb} - \mathbf{q})'[\mathbf{R}(\sigma^2\mathbf{Q}^{-1})\mathbf{R}']^{-1}(\mathbf{Rb} - \mathbf{q}) \qquad \textbf{(5)}$$

is chi-squared, with J degrees of freedom. Note the similarity of this to the results of Section 3.10.5. Finally, if

$$\text{plim } s^2\left(\frac{1}{n}\mathbf{X}'\mathbf{X}\right)^{-1} = \sigma^2\mathbf{Q}^{-1}, \qquad \textbf{(6)}$$

the statistic obtained by replacing $\sigma^2\mathbf{Q}^{-1}$ by $s^2(\mathbf{X}'\mathbf{X}/n)^{-1}$ in (5) has the same limiting distribution. The n's cancel, and we are left with the same Wald statistic we looked at before. This completes the proof. The Wald statistic can be computed as J times the usual F statistic.

One implication of these asymptotic results is that if the normality assumption of the classical model with normal disturbances is not met, the significance levels assigned to the familiar test statistic will be inappropriate. The exact finite sample distribution of, for example, a t statistic will almost surely be intractable. But the same statistic will be asymptotically distributed as standard normal. This leaves open the question of how to proceed in a moderately sized sample. If the sample is not large, the limiting distributions (e.g., standard normal instead of t) may be overly optimistic. Conservatism may still argue in favor of using the finite-sample distributions, t, F, or chi-squared.

6.7.7. Independent Observations on Stochastic Regressors

The assumption of nonstochastic regressors simplifies the derivation of the statistical properties of the least squares estimator. But as we saw in Sections 6.6.1 and 6.6.3, the important finite-sample results (the Gauss–Markov theorem) do not depend on this assumption, nor do the distributions of the conventional test statistics (t, F, and chi-squared) that are based on normality of the disturbances. (See Section 6.6.8.) For practical purposes, at least as regards the finite-sample results, the assumption of nonstochastic regressors is inessential. This is fortunate because the assumption is restrictive and unrealistic as well. This section will continue the analysis to determine whether any of the asymptotic results must be revised to accommodate stochastic regressors.

We replace Assumption **A5** (nonstochastic **X**) with

AS5. $[\mathbf{x}_i, \epsilon_i], i = 1, \ldots, n$, are an i.i.d. sequence of random variables.

Note that AS5 does not assume that $\mathbf{x}_i$ and ϵ_i are independent. But, with A3: $E[\epsilon_i|\mathbf{x}_i] = 0$, we still have $\text{Cov}[\mathbf{x}_i, \epsilon_i] = \mathbf{0}$. Assume that the rows of **X** are random and independent draws from a multivariate distribution with mean vector $\boldsymbol{\mu}_x$, finite positive definite covariance matrix $\boldsymbol{\Sigma}_{xx}$, and finite fourth moments $\phi_{jklm} = E[x_j x_k x_l x_m]$.[41]

The crucial results needed to establish the consistency and asymptotic normality of **b** with nonstochastic regressors are (6-50), (6-53), and (6-62). If we assume that the regressors are stochastic and replace the ordinary limit in (6-50) with

$$\text{plim}\, \frac{1}{n}\mathbf{X}'\mathbf{X} = \mathbf{Q}, \text{ a positive definite matrix,} \tag{6-66}$$

then the consistency of **b** can be established using the same line of argument as that used in Section 6.7.2. If, in addition, (6-62) continues to hold, then the asymptotic normality of **b** can be shown as well. What remains, then, is to consider the more general conditions under which (6-66), (6-62), and by implication (6-53) will hold.

Now (6-66) can be established by using a mean-squared convergence argument for random sampling from a distribution. The matrix $\overline{\mathbf{Q}}_n$ of (6-59) is the mean of a random sample of $K \times K$ matrices;

$$\overline{\mathbf{Q}}_n = \frac{1}{n}\sum_{i=1}^{n} \mathbf{x}_i\mathbf{x}_i' = \frac{1}{n}\sum_i \mathbf{Q}_i.$$

The population counterpart to $\overline{\mathbf{Q}}_n$ is

$$E[\mathbf{x}_i\mathbf{x}_i'] = \mathbf{Q} = \Sigma_{xx} + \boldsymbol{\mu}_x\boldsymbol{\mu}_x'.$$

A multivariate generalization of Theorem 4.3 and (4-20) can be used to assert

[41] This is general enough to include any nonstochastic elements in **x**, such as the constant term.

that plim $\overline{\mathbf{Q}}_n = \mathbf{Q}$. The jkth element of $\overline{\mathbf{Q}}_n$, which we denote $\overline{\mathbf{Q}}_{n,jk}$, is an unbiased estimator of that element of $\mathbf{Q}$ (i.e., $\mathbf{Q}_{jk}$). (This follows just by applying Theorem 4.1 element by element.) Each pair of elements $(\overline{\mathbf{Q}}_{n,jk}, \overline{\mathbf{Q}}_{n,lm})$ in $\overline{\mathbf{Q}}_n$ will have

$$\text{Cov}[\overline{\mathbf{Q}}_{n,jk}, \overline{\mathbf{Q}}_{n,lm}] = \frac{1}{n}[\phi_{jklm} - \mathbf{Q}_{jk}\mathbf{Q}_{lm}], \tag{6-67}$$

which converges to zero. This establishes (6-66) for the assumption of random sampling of the rows of $\mathbf{X}$. That is, we have replicated (6-50) for the case of random sampling of the observations on $\mathbf{x}_i$ from a distribution with finite mean vector $\boldsymbol{\mu}_x$, covariance matrix Σ_{xx}, and fourth moment ϕ_{jklm}.

Now assume as before that the observations $\epsilon_i|\mathbf{X}$ are a random sample from a distribution with mean 0 and constant variance σ^2 and that ϵ_i is uncorrelated with every $\mathbf{x}_j$ for all pairs of observations. The observations $\mathbf{w}_i = \mathbf{x}_i\epsilon_i$ in

$$\overline{\mathbf{w}} = \frac{1}{n}\mathbf{X}'\boldsymbol{\epsilon}$$

are independent and identically distributed with mean

$$\begin{aligned} E[\mathbf{w}_i] &= \text{Cov}[\mathbf{x}_i, \epsilon_i] + E[\mathbf{x}_i]E[\epsilon_i] \\ &= \text{Cov}[\mathbf{x}_i, E[\epsilon_i \mid \mathbf{x}_i]] + \boldsymbol{\mu}_{\mathbf{x}} E_{\mathbf{x}}[E[\epsilon_i \mid \mathbf{x}_i]] \\ &= \mathbf{0} \end{aligned}$$

since $E[\epsilon_i|\mathbf{x}_i] = 0$. We obtain the covariance matrix for $\mathbf{w}_i$ by using the variance decomposition formula, (3-70);

$$\text{Var}[\mathbf{w}_i] = E[\mathbf{w}_i\mathbf{w}_i'] + E[\mathbf{w}_i]E[\mathbf{w}_i'].$$

The second term is $\mathbf{0}$ since $E[\mathbf{w}_i] = \mathbf{0}$. The first term is

$$\begin{aligned} E[\epsilon_i^2\mathbf{x}_i\mathbf{x}_i'] &= E_{\mathbf{x}}[E[\epsilon_i^2\mathbf{x}_i\mathbf{x}_i' \mid \mathbf{x}_i]] \\ &= E_{\mathbf{x}}[\mathbf{x}_i\mathbf{x}_i'E[\epsilon_i^2 \mid \mathbf{x}_i]] \\ &= \sigma^2 E[\mathbf{x}_i\mathbf{x}_i'] = \sigma^2 \end{aligned}$$

The assumption $E[\epsilon_i|\mathbf{x}_i] = 0$ is crucial at this point. Also, $\text{Var}[\epsilon_i]$ and $\text{Var}[\epsilon_i|\mathbf{x}_i]$ will often differ. When they do, this will lead us to the more general cases of the regression model that we consider in Chapters 12 and 13. For now, though, we emphasize that our assumptions of the classical regression model include these *conditional* moments, $E[\epsilon_i|\mathbf{x}_i] = 0$ and $\text{Var}[\epsilon_i|\mathbf{x}_i] = \sigma^2 < \infty$.

Finally, by a multivariate extension of Theorem 4.1, $E[\overline{\mathbf{w}}] = \mathbf{0}$ and $\text{Var}[\overline{\mathbf{w}}] = (\sigma^2/n)\mathbf{Q}$, which converges to $\mathbf{0}$. This establishes (6-53), once again by mean square convergence. We can use the Lindberg–Levy variant of the central limit theorem (Theorem 4.13) to establish (6-62) and then (6-64) because the terms in $\overline{\mathbf{w}}$ have identical variances. This provides the following.

THEOREM 6.13: Asymptotic Distribution of b with Stochastic Regressors. *If the rows of* $\mathbf{X}$ *are a random sample from a distribution with finite fourth mo-*

ments[42] *and the observations on* ϵ *are a random sample from a distribution with zero mean and constant variance* σ^2 *and are uncorrelated with all observations in* $\mathbf{X}$, *then* $\mathbf{b}$ *is consistent and asymptotically normally distributed as shown in (6-64). If, in addition, the fourth moment of* ϵ_i, ϕ_ϵ *is finite, then* s^2 *is a consistent estimator of* σ^2, *and we can use* $s^2(\mathbf{X}'\mathbf{X})$ *to estimate* Asy. Var$[\mathbf{b}]$.

Note that the proof of the consistency of s^2 as an estimator of σ^2 that was given in Section 6.7.4. does not have to be changed to accommodate stochastic regressors. It is tempting to assert that Theorem 6.13 encompasses the case of nonstochastic regressors, and, from a purely mathematical standpoint, it does. But, in practical terms, the case in which $\mathbf{x}$ is an observation drawn randomly from a population is different from that in which $\mathbf{x}$ is a set of control variates that is predetermined by an analyst as part of an experimental design.

The preceding arguments are general enough to accommodate many cases in which the rows of $\mathbf{X}$ are independent and identically distributed.[43] They are not as general as they might be, however, because we have made a specific assumption about the distributions of $\mathbf{x}_i$ and ϵ_i, namely that they have finite fourth moments. We did this to allow us to use mean square convergence arguments, which have an intuitive appeal. The practical significance of this for econometrics may be minimal. For theoretical purposes, whether this is a restrictive assumption or not is a question without an obvious answer, but in the study of theoretical econometrics, Occam's razor is the tool of choice. There are alternative proofs of consistency and asymptotic normality of $\mathbf{b}$ that rely on weaker assumptions. For the interested reader, and as a bridge both to the theoretical literature and to some of our work later in the book, we will sketch alternative derivations of the consistency results.[44]

We replace $E[x_j x_k x_l x_m] = \phi_{jklm} < \infty$ with

AS5a. $E[x_{ik}^2] = Q_{kk} < \infty$, a finite constant, $k = 1, \ldots, K$.

Since $Q_{kk} = \text{Var}[x_{ik}] + \{E[x_{ik}]\}^2$, AS5a implies that $\mu_k = E[x_{ik}]$ is also a finite constant for all k. This is sufficient to establish that $E[\mathbf{x}_i\mathbf{x}_i']$ is a finite matrix $\mathbf{Q}$. The additional result needed is the following.

$$\textbf{Cauchy–Schwartz Inequality: } E[\,|\,xy\,|\,]\{E[x^2]\}^{1/2}\{E[y^2]\}^{1/2}. \qquad \textbf{(6-68)}$$

---

[42]If some columns of $\mathbf{X}$ are nonstochastic, a mix of the results here and in Section 6.7.3 is easily constructed.

[43]It is possible to relax the assumption of finite σ^2 and still obtain some results for the regression model. But this treatment is for more advanced courses than ours. Brief mention of this possibility appear, for example, in Davidson and MacKinnon (1993) and variously in the work of White (1984, 1994). We differ slightly from White at this point because he does not make an explicit assumption about the disturbance variance whereas we do. *But,* in his derivation on pages 30–31, there is an implicit assumption about the variance of ϵ that allows the analysis to proceed. He touches briefly on the point on page 5, but throughout he maintains the assumption of a finite variance. Since we are concerned at this point only with cases in which the disturbances are i.i.d, his case is the same as ours.

[44]The derivation parallels those in White (1984).

This means that the off-diagonal elements of $\mathbf{Q}$ as well as the diagonal elements must be finite. We must also assume that $\mathbf{Q}$ has full rank and that these off-diagonal elements are constants as well. It will then follow that $\mathbf{Q}$ is positive definite, since it is a covariance matrix. These assumptions are weaker than those we made earlier. With no assumption about the fourth moments of $\mathbf{x}$, we cannot use mean-squared convergence to establish convergence of $(1/n)\mathbf{X}'\mathbf{X}$ to $\mathbf{Q}$. We can, however, use a simpler approach based on the following theorem.

THEOREM 6.14: Kinchine's Theorem (Weak Law of Large Numbers). *Let $\{x_i\}$, $i = 1, 2, \ldots, n$ be a random sample (i.i.d.) and assume that $E[x_i] = \mu$, a finite constant. Then $\bar{x} \xrightarrow{p} \mu$.*

This powerful theorem requires only that the population mean exist and be finite for the sample mean of a random sample to be a consistent estimator of it. By applying the Kinchine theorem element by element, we can conclude that AS5a provides us with $\text{plim}(1/n)\mathbf{X}'\mathbf{X} = \mathbf{Q}$, without a special assumption about the fourth moments.[45] No further assumption about $\mathbf{x}_i\epsilon_i$ is necessary. We know from A3 that $E[\epsilon_i] = E_{\mathbf{x}}[E[\epsilon_i|\mathbf{x}_i]] = 0$ and $\text{Cov}[\mathbf{x}_i, \epsilon_i] = \text{Cov}[\mathbf{x}_i, E[\epsilon_i|\mathbf{x}_i]] = \mathbf{0}$. But $\text{Cov}[\mathbf{x}_i, \epsilon_i] = E[\mathbf{x}_i\epsilon_i] - E[\mathbf{x}_i]E[\epsilon_i]$, so $E[\mathbf{x}_i\epsilon_i] = \mathbf{0}$. This means that the conditions of the theorem are met for $\{\mathbf{x}_i\epsilon_i\}$,which means that

$$\frac{1}{n}\mathbf{X}'\boldsymbol{\epsilon} \xrightarrow{p} \mathbf{0} \Longrightarrow \text{plim}\,\frac{1}{n}\mathbf{X}'\boldsymbol{\epsilon} = \mathbf{0}.$$

Therefore,

$$\mathbf{b} \xrightarrow{p} \boldsymbol{\beta} \Longrightarrow \text{plim}\,\mathbf{b} = \boldsymbol{\beta}.$$

Also, assumption A4 is sufficient to provide

$$s^2 \xrightarrow{p} \sigma^2 \Longrightarrow \text{plim}\,s^2 = \sigma^2.$$

In Section 6.7.4, we assumed a finite fourth moment for ϵ to establish consistency of s^2. We now see that this was stronger than necessary.

We have not established asymptotic normality yet. For the classical regression model with independent observations, the proof of asymptotic normality is essentially unchanged. The Lindberg–Levy theorem (4.4) is general enough in its multivariate form to encompass the case of stochastic regressors that we are examining here. Once again, what we require is that each vector $\mathbf{w}_i$ have finite mean, which it does, 0; finite covariance matrix, which we have shown is $\sigma^2\mathbf{Q}$; and finite third moments, which is an additional assumption. We also require that no term in $(1/n)\mathbf{X}'\mathbf{X}$ dominates the sum. (Note that this does

[45] Note that a special assumption will be necessary for uncooperative regressors, since, for example, for a time trend, the conditions of the theorem will not be met.

not rule out a time trend). Then, we can obtain the limiting distribution of $\overline{\mathbf{w}}$ as before and thereafter, the asymptotic normal distribution of **b**.[46]

Now why do this? The reason is that in the more general cases that we will now consider, we will not be able to establish mean square convergence at all, but we will be able to obtain convergence results based on other assumptions.

6.7.8. Correlation Between $\mathbf{x}_i$ and ϵ_i—Instrumental Variables Estimation

The assumption that $\mathbf{x}_i$ and ϵ_i are uncorrelated has been crucial in the development thus far. But, there are any number of applications in economics in which this assumption is untenable. For example, as we will explore below, in the consumption function, by construction of the national income accounts, the disturbance in the consumption function must be correlated with the current value of income, at least in macroeconomic data. Other examples include models that contain variables that are measured with error and most dynamic models involving expectations. Without this assumption, none of the proofs of consistency given above will hold up, so least squares loses its attractiveness as an estimator. There is an alternative method of estimation called the method of **instrumental variables** (IV). The least squares estimator is a special case, but the IV method is far more general. The method of instrumental variables is developed around the following general extension of the estimation strategy in the classical regression model:

> Suppose that in the classical model $y_i = \mathbf{x}_i'\boldsymbol{\beta} + \epsilon_i$, the K variables $\mathbf{x}_i$ may be correlated with ϵ_i. Suppose, as well, that there exists a set of L variables $\mathbf{z}_i$, where L is at least as large as K, such that $\mathbf{z}_i$ is correlated with $\mathbf{x}_i$ but not with ϵ_i. We cannot estimate $\boldsymbol{\beta}$ consistently by using the familiar least squares estimator. But, we can construct a consistent estimator $\boldsymbol{\beta}$ by using the assumed relationships among $\mathbf{z}_i$, $\mathbf{x}_i$, and ϵ_i.

EXAMPLE 6.21 The Consumption Function

We (and many other authors) have used a macroeconomic version of the consumption function at various points to illustrate least squares estimation of the classical regression model. But, by construction, the model violates the assumptions of the classical regression model. The national income data are assembled around some basic accounting identities, including "$Y = C +$ *investment* + *government spending* + *net exports*." Therefore, although the precise relationship between consumption C, and income Y, $C = f(Y, \epsilon)$, is ambiguous and is a

[46]We depart from White's treatment at this point, as he makes no distinction between the asymptotic distribution and the limiting distribution, although his treatment is largely along the lines discussed here. In the interest of maintaining consistency of the discussion, we prefer to retain the sharp distinction and derive the asymptotic distribution of **b** by first obtaining the *limiting* distribution of $\sqrt{n}(\mathbf{b} - \boldsymbol{\beta})$. By our construction, the limiting distribution of **b** is degenerate, whereas the asymptotic distribution of $\sqrt{n}(\mathbf{b} - \boldsymbol{\beta}) = (\mathbf{X}'\mathbf{X}/n)^{-1}(1/\sqrt{n})\mathbf{X}'\boldsymbol{\epsilon}$ is not useful.

suitable candidate for modeling, it is clear that consumption (and, therefore, ϵ) is one of the main determinants of Y. Indeed, in the U.S. data, over 90 percent of the *level* of income is consumption.[47] The model

$$C_t = \alpha + \beta Y_t + \epsilon_t$$

does not fit our assumptions for the classical model; $\text{Cov}[Y_t, \epsilon_t] \neq 0$. But it is reasonable to assume (at least for now) that ϵ_t is uncorrelated with past values of C and Y. Therefore, in this model, we might consider Y_{t-1} and C_{t-1} as suitable instrumental variables.

We will now construct an estimator for $\boldsymbol{\beta}$ in this extended model. We will maintain assumptions AS5 and AS5a, which will preserve the important result that $\text{plim}(\mathbf{X}'\mathbf{X}/n) = \mathbf{Q}_{xx}$. (We use the subscript to differentiate this from the results given below.) The basic assumptions of the regression model have changed, however. First, A3 is, under our new assumptions,

AI3. $E[\epsilon_i | \mathbf{x}_i] = \eta_i$.

AI3a. $E[\eta_i] = 0$.

We interpret this to mean that the regressors now provide information about the expectations of the disturbances. The zero mean assumption in AI3a is innocent as long as the model contains a constant term (or, if there is no constant term, that this absence is part of the specification, not an improper restriction). The important implication of AI3 is that the disturbances and the regressors are now correlated, which modifies AS5 from the previous section as follows.

AI5b. $\text{Cov}[\mathbf{x}_i, \epsilon_i] = \text{Cov}[\mathbf{x}_i, E[\epsilon_i | \mathbf{x}_i]] = \text{Cov}[\mathbf{x}_i, \eta_i] = \boldsymbol{\gamma}$.

Since $E[\epsilon_i]$ is still zero—$E[\epsilon_i] = E_{\mathbf{x}}[E[\epsilon_i | \mathbf{x}_i]] = E[\eta_i] = 0$—we now have

$$E[\mathbf{x}_i \epsilon_i] = \text{Cov}[\mathbf{x}_i, \eta_i] = \boldsymbol{\gamma}.$$

So, we can apply Theorem 6.14 (Kinchine's theorem) to assert that

$$\text{plim} \frac{1}{n} \mathbf{X}'\boldsymbol{\epsilon} = \boldsymbol{\gamma}.$$

(Notice that the original model results if $\eta_i = 0$.) This new model has an implication for A4. There are now two sources of variation in ϵ, variation around the conditional mean $\text{Var}[\epsilon_i | \mathbf{x}_i] = \sigma^2$ and variation of the conditional mean itself, as follows.

AI3b. $\text{Var}[\eta_i] = \kappa^2 < \infty$.

This means that the unconditional variance of ϵ_i, which will be largely unused in our treatment, is

$$\text{Var}[\epsilon_i] = \sigma^2 + \kappa^2 < \infty.$$

---

[47]Also important for modeling purposes, however, is that most of the *variance* in national income is explained by variation in investment, not consumption.

We will be generally interested only in the conditional variance σ^2, but it is worth keeping in mind that the total variation of ϵ around its overall mean is partly due to variation in the regressors, which we have not seen before. Finally, we must characterize the instrumental variables. We assume the following:

AI7. $[\mathbf{x}_i, \mathbf{z}_i, \epsilon_i], i = 1, \ldots, n$, are an i.i.d. sequence of random variables.
AI7a. $E[x_{ik}^2] = Q_{xx,kk} < \infty$, a finite constant, $k = 1, \ldots, K$.
AI7b. $E[z_{il}^2] = Q_{zz,ll} < \infty$, a finite constant, $l = 1, \ldots, L$.
AI7c. $E[z_{il}x_{ik}] = Q_{zx,lk} < \infty$, a finite constant, $l = 1, \ldots, L, k = 1, \ldots, K$.
AI7d. $E[\epsilon_i | \mathbf{z}_i] = 0$.

Finite means of z_l follows from AI7b. Using the same analysis as in the previous section, we have

$$\text{plim}\,\frac{1}{n}\mathbf{Z}'\mathbf{Z} = \mathbf{Q}_{zz}, \text{ a finite, positive definite (assumed) matrix,}$$

$$\text{plim}\,\frac{1}{n}\mathbf{Z}'\mathbf{X} = \mathbf{Q}_{zx}, \text{ a finite, } L \times K \text{ matrix with rank } K \text{ (assumed),}$$

$$\text{plim}\,\frac{1}{n}\mathbf{Z}'\boldsymbol{\epsilon} = \mathbf{0}.$$

In our statement of the model, the classical regression model that we have assumed thus far is the special case of $\eta_i = 0$; $\boldsymbol{\gamma} = \mathbf{0}$ follows. There is no need to dispense with Assumption 7—it may well continue to be true—but in this special case, it becomes irrelevant.

For this more general model, we lose most of the useful results we had for least squares. The estimator **b** is no longer unbiased;

$$E[\mathbf{b} \mid \mathbf{X}] = \boldsymbol{\beta} + (\mathbf{X}'\mathbf{X})^{-1}\mathbf{X}'\boldsymbol{\eta} \neq \boldsymbol{\beta},$$

so the Gauss–Markov theorem no longer holds. It is also inconsistent;

$$\begin{aligned}\text{plim}\,\mathbf{b} &= \boldsymbol{\beta} + \text{plim}\left(\frac{1}{n}\mathbf{X}'\mathbf{X}\right)^{-1}\text{plim}\left(\frac{1}{n}\mathbf{X}'\boldsymbol{\epsilon}\right)\\ &= \boldsymbol{\beta} + \mathbf{Q}^{-1}\boldsymbol{\gamma} \neq \boldsymbol{\beta}.\end{aligned}$$

(The asymptotic distribution is considered in the exercises.)

We now turn to the instrumental variable estimator. Since $E[\mathbf{z}_i\epsilon_i] = \mathbf{0}$ and all terms have finite variances, we can state that

$$\begin{aligned}\text{plim}\left(\frac{1}{n}\mathbf{Z}'\mathbf{y}\right) &= \left[\text{plim}\left(\frac{1}{n}\mathbf{Z}'\mathbf{X}\right)\right]\boldsymbol{\beta} + \text{plim}\left(\frac{1}{n}\mathbf{Z}'\boldsymbol{\epsilon}\right)\\ &= \left[\text{plim}\left(\frac{1}{n}\mathbf{Z}'\mathbf{X}\right)\right]\boldsymbol{\beta}.\end{aligned}$$

Suppose that **Z** has the same number of variables as **X**. For example, suppose in our consumption function that $\mathbf{x}_t = [1, Y_t]$ while $\mathbf{z}_t = [1, Y_{t-1}]$. We have assumed that the rank of $\mathbf{Z}'\mathbf{X}$ is K, so now $\mathbf{Z}'\mathbf{X}$ is a square matrix. It follows that

$$\left[\text{plim}\left(\frac{1}{n}\mathbf{Z}'\mathbf{X}\right)\right]^{-1}\text{plim}\left(\frac{1}{n}\mathbf{Z}'\mathbf{y}\right) = \boldsymbol{\beta},$$

which leads us to the instrumental variable estimator,

$$\mathbf{b}_{\text{IV}} = (\mathbf{Z}'\mathbf{X})^{-1}\mathbf{Z}'\mathbf{y}.$$

We have already proved that $\mathbf{b}_{\text{IV}}$ is consistent. We now turn to the asymptotic distribution. We will use the same method as in the previous section. First,

$$\sqrt{n}\,(\mathbf{b}_{\text{IV}} - \boldsymbol{\beta}) = \left(\frac{1}{n}\mathbf{Z}'\mathbf{X}\right)^{-1}\frac{1}{\sqrt{n}}\mathbf{Z}'\boldsymbol{\epsilon}.$$

This has the same limiting distribution as $\mathbf{Q}_{zx}^{-1}[(1/\sqrt{n})\mathbf{Z}'\boldsymbol{\epsilon}]$. Our analysis of $(1/\sqrt{n})\mathbf{Z}'\boldsymbol{\epsilon}$ is the same as that of $(1/\sqrt{n})\mathbf{X}'\boldsymbol{\epsilon}$ in the previous section, so it follows that

$$\left(\frac{1}{\sqrt{n}}\mathbf{Z}'\boldsymbol{\epsilon}\right) \xrightarrow{d} N[\mathbf{0}, \sigma^2\mathbf{Q}_{zz}]$$

and

$$\left(\frac{1}{n}\mathbf{Z}'\mathbf{X}\right)^{-1}\left(\frac{1}{\sqrt{n}}\mathbf{Z}'\boldsymbol{\epsilon}\right) \xrightarrow{d} N[\mathbf{0}, \sigma^2\mathbf{Q}_{zx}^{-1}\mathbf{Q}_{zz}\mathbf{Q}_{xz}^{-1}].$$

This completes the derivation for the next theorem.

THEOREM 6.15: Asymptotic Distribution of the Instrumental Variables Estimator. *If Assumptions A1, A2, AI3(a,b), AI4, AS5(a), AI5b, and AI7(a–d) all hold for* $[y_i, \mathbf{x}_i, \mathbf{z}_i, \epsilon_i]$, *where* $\mathbf{z}$ *is a valid set of L instrumental variables, then the asymptotic distribution of the instrumental variables estimator* $\mathbf{b}_{\text{IV}} = (\mathbf{Z}'\mathbf{X})^{-1}\mathbf{Z}'\mathbf{y}$ *is*

$$\mathbf{b}_{\text{IV}} \xrightarrow{a} N[\boldsymbol{\beta}, \sigma^2\mathbf{Q}_{zx}^{-1}\mathbf{Q}_{zz}\mathbf{Q}_{xz}^{-1}], \tag{6-69}$$

where $\mathbf{Q}_{zx} = \text{plim}(\mathbf{Z}'\mathbf{X}/n)$ *and* $\mathbf{Q}_{zz} = \text{plim}(\mathbf{Z}'\mathbf{Z}/n)$.

To estimate the asymptotic covariance matrix, we will require an estimator of σ^2. The natural estimator is

$$\hat{\sigma}^2 = \frac{1}{n}\sum_{i=1}^{n}(y_i - \mathbf{x}_i'\mathbf{b}_{\text{IV}})^2.$$

A correction for degrees of freedom, as in the development in the previous section, is superfluous, as all results here are asymptotic, and $\hat{\sigma}^2$ would not be unbiased in any event. Write the vector of residuals as

$$\mathbf{y} - \mathbf{X}\mathbf{b}_{\text{IV}} = \mathbf{y} - \mathbf{X}(\mathbf{Z}'\mathbf{X})^{-1}\mathbf{Z}'\mathbf{y}.$$

Substitute $\mathbf{y} = \mathbf{X}\boldsymbol{\beta} + \boldsymbol{\epsilon}$ and collect terms to obtain $\hat{\boldsymbol{\epsilon}} = [\mathbf{I} - \mathbf{X}(\mathbf{Z}'\mathbf{X})^{-1}\mathbf{Z}']\boldsymbol{\epsilon}$.

Now,

$$\begin{aligned}\hat{\sigma}^2 &= \frac{1}{n}\hat{\boldsymbol{\epsilon}}'\hat{\boldsymbol{\epsilon}}\\ &= \frac{1}{n}\boldsymbol{\epsilon}'\boldsymbol{\epsilon} + \left(\frac{1}{n}\boldsymbol{\epsilon}'\mathbf{Z}\right)\left(\frac{1}{n}\mathbf{X}'\mathbf{Z}\right)^{-1}\left(\frac{1}{n}\mathbf{X}'\mathbf{X}\right)\left(\frac{1}{n}\mathbf{Z}'\mathbf{X}\right)^{-1}\left(\frac{1}{n}\mathbf{Z}'\boldsymbol{\epsilon}\right)\\ &\quad - 2\left(\frac{1}{n}\boldsymbol{\epsilon}'\mathbf{X}\right)\left(\frac{1}{n}\mathbf{Z}'\mathbf{X}\right)^{-1}\left(\frac{1}{n}\mathbf{Z}'\boldsymbol{\epsilon}\right).\end{aligned}$$

We found earlier that we could (after a bit of manipulation) apply the product result for probability limits to obtain the probability limit of an expression such as this. Without repeating the derivation, we find that $\hat{\sigma}^2$ is a consistent estimator of σ^2, by virtue of the first term. The second and third product terms converge to zero. To complete the derivation, then, we will estimate Asy. Var$[\mathbf{b}_{IV}]$ with

$$\begin{aligned}\text{Est. Asy. Var}[\mathbf{b}_{IV}] &= \frac{1}{n}\left\{\left(\frac{1}{n}\hat{\boldsymbol{\epsilon}}'\hat{\boldsymbol{\epsilon}}\right)\left(\frac{1}{n}\mathbf{Z}'\mathbf{X}\right)^{-1}\left(\frac{1}{n}\mathbf{Z}'\mathbf{Z}\right)\left(\frac{1}{n}\mathbf{X}'\mathbf{Z}\right)^{-1}\right\}\\ &= \hat{\sigma}^2(\mathbf{Z}'\mathbf{X})^{-1}(\mathbf{Z}'\mathbf{Z})(\mathbf{X}'\mathbf{Z})^{-1}.\end{aligned} \quad \textbf{(6-70)}$$

There is a remaining detail. If $\mathbf{Z}$ contains more variables than $\mathbf{X}$, then much of the preceding is unusable, as $\mathbf{Z}'\mathbf{X}$ will be $L \times K$ with rank $K < L$ and will thus not have an inverse. The crucial result in all the preceding is $\text{plim}(\mathbf{Z}'\boldsymbol{\epsilon}/n) = \mathbf{0}$. That is, every column of $\mathbf{Z}$ is asymptotically uncorrelated with $\boldsymbol{\epsilon}$. That also means that every linear combination of the columns of $\mathbf{Z}$ is also uncorrelated with $\boldsymbol{\epsilon}$. This suggests that one approach would be to choose K linear combinations of the columns of $\mathbf{Z}$. Which to choose? One obvious possibility is simply to choose K variables among the L in $\mathbf{Z}$. But intuition correctly suggests that throwing away the information contained in the remaining $L - K$ columns is inefficient. A better choice is the projection of the columns of $\mathbf{X}$ in the column space of $\mathbf{Z}$:

$$\hat{\mathbf{X}} = \mathbf{Z}(\mathbf{Z}'\mathbf{Z})^{-1}\mathbf{Z}'\mathbf{X}.$$

We will return shortly to the virtues of this choice. With this choice of instrumental variables, $\hat{\mathbf{X}}$ for $\mathbf{Z}$, we have

$$\begin{aligned}\mathbf{b}_{IV} &= (\hat{\mathbf{X}}'\mathbf{X})^{-1}\hat{\mathbf{X}}'\mathbf{y}\\ &= [\mathbf{X}'\mathbf{Z}(\mathbf{Z}'\mathbf{Z})^{-1}\mathbf{Z}'\mathbf{X}]^{-1}\mathbf{X}'\mathbf{Z}(\mathbf{Z}'\mathbf{Z})^{-1}\mathbf{Z}'\mathbf{y}.\end{aligned} \quad \textbf{(6-71)}$$

By substituting $\hat{\mathbf{X}}$ in the expression for Est. Asy. Var$[\mathbf{b}_{IV}]$ and multiplying it out, we see that the expression is unchanged. The proofs of consistency and asymptotic normality for this estimator are exactly the same as before, because our proof was generic for any valid set of instruments, and $\hat{\mathbf{X}}$ qualifies.

There are two reasons for using this estimator, one practical, one theoretical.

If any column of $\mathbf{X}$ also appears in $\mathbf{Z}$, then that column of $\mathbf{X}$ is reproduced exactly in $\hat{\mathbf{X}}$. This is easy to show. In the expression for $\hat{\mathbf{X}}$, if the kth column in $\mathbf{X}$ is one of the columns in $\mathbf{Z}$, say the lth, then the kth column in

$(\mathbf{Z}'\mathbf{Z})^{-1}\mathbf{Z}'\mathbf{X}$ will be the lth column of an $L \times L$ identity matrix. This means that the kth column in $\hat{\mathbf{X}} = \mathbf{Z}(\mathbf{Z}'\mathbf{Z})^{-1}\mathbf{Z}'\mathbf{X}$ will be the lth column in $\mathbf{Z}$, which is the kth column in $\mathbf{X}$. This is an important and useful result. Consider what is probably the typical application. Suppose that the regression contains K variables, only one of which, say the kth, is correlated with the disturbances. We have one or more instrumental variables at hand, as well as the other $K - 1$ variables that certainly qualify as instrumental variables in their own right. Then what we would use is $\mathbf{Z} = [\mathbf{X}_{(k)}, z_1, z_2, \ldots]$, where we indicate omission of the kth variable by (k) in the subscript. Another useful interpretation of $\hat{\mathbf{X}}$ is that each column is the set of fitted values when the corresponding column of $\mathbf{X}$ is regressed on all the columns of $\mathbf{Z}$. This is obvious from the definition. It also makes clear why each $\mathbf{x}_k$ that appears in $\mathbf{Z}$ is perfectly replicated. Every $\mathbf{x}_k$ provides a perfect predictor for itself, without any help from the remaining variables in $\mathbf{Z}$. In the example, then, every column of $\mathbf{X}$ except the one that is omitted from $\mathbf{X}_{(k)}$ is replicated exactly, while the one that *is* omitted is replaced in $\hat{\mathbf{X}}$ by the predicted values in the regression of this variable on all the $\mathbf{z}$'s.

Of all the different linear combinations of $\mathbf{Z}$ that we might choose, $\hat{\mathbf{X}}$ is the most efficient in the sense that the asymptotic covariance matrix of an IV estimator based on a linear combination $\mathbf{ZF}$ is smaller when $\mathbf{F} = (\mathbf{Z}'\mathbf{Z})^{-1}\mathbf{Z}'\mathbf{X}$ than with any other $\mathbf{F}$ that uses all L columns of $\mathbf{Z}$; a fortiori, this eliminates linear combinations obtained by dropping any columns of $\mathbf{Z}$. This important result was proved in a seminal paper by Brundy and Jorgenson (1971).

EXAMPLE 6.22 Instrumental Variables Estimation of the Consumption Function

Table 6.10 lists yearly data on consumption C and income Y for the U.S. economy.

TABLE 6.10 Aggregate Income *Y* and Consumption *C*

	Y	*C*		*Y*	*C*		*Y*	*C*
1950	791.8	733.2	1962	1170.2	1069.0	1974	1896.6	1674.0
1951	819.0	748.7	1963	1207.3	1108.4	1975	1931.7	1711.9
1952	844.3	771.4	1964	1291.0	1170.6	1976	2001.0	1803.9
1953	880.0	802.5	1965	1365.7	1236.4	1977	2066.6	1883.8
1954	894.0	822.7	1966	1431.3	1298.9	1978	2167.4	1961.0
1955	944.5	873.8	1967	1493.2	1337.7	1979	2216.2	2004.4
1956	989.4	899.8	1968	1551.3	1405.9	1980	2214.3	2000.4
1957	1012.1	919.7	1969	1599.8	1456.7	1981	2248.6	2024.2
1958	1028.8	932.9	1970	1688.1	1492.0	1982	2261.5	2050.7
1959	1067.2	979.4	1971	1728.4	1538.8	1983	2334.6	2145.9
1960	1091.1	1005.1	1972	1797.4	1621.9	1984	2468.4	2239.9
1961	1123.2	1025.2	1973	1916.3	1689.6	1985	2509.0	2312.6

Source: Data from the *Economic Report of the President,* U.S. Government Printing Office, Washington, D.C., 1986.

TABLE 6.11 Instrumental Variable Estimates of a Consumption Function

	Least Squares		*Instrumental Variables*	
	Coefficient	*Std. Error*	*Coefficient*	*Std. Error*
Constant	9.7325	10.130	8.9214	9.8498
Income	0.89918	0.0060859	0.89969	0.0059184
Sum of squares	11923.1		11925.7	
R^2	0.99848		0.99848	

Least squares and instrumental variables estimates of the consumption function discussed in the previous example are given in Table 6.11. Since lagged values of C and Y are used, both sets of estimates are computed without the first observation.

The differences between the estimates and the standard errors are trivial. Of course, the R^2 for the least squares regression suggests why we observe this. One subtle difference in the results sometimes shows up in widely used computer programs. The least squares standard errors are based on an estimate of σ^2 that is corrected for degrees of freedom. Packages differ on whether a corresponding correction is made for the estimator when an IV estimator is computed. Those above are not so corrected. If the least squares estimates are scaled by $(33/35)^{1/2}$, the values are 9.83631 and 0.0059095, which are almost identical to the IV values. It is not always obvious which estimator has been used by a computer program, and practitioners will find it useful to be aware of the possible differences.

One might question at this point whether this has been much ado about nothing. After all, the differences in the table above are inconsequential. Table 16.6 presents a large number of estimates for a different formulation of the consumption function and a different data set. In that application, the differences between the "OLS" (least squares) and "2SLS" (instrumental variables) estimates are extremely large.

We close this section with some practical considerations in the use of the instrumental variables estimator. By just multiplying out the matrices in the expression, you can show that

$$\begin{aligned}\mathbf{b}_{\text{IV}} &= (\hat{\mathbf{X}}'\mathbf{X})^{-1}\hat{\mathbf{X}}'\mathbf{y} \\ &= (\mathbf{X}'(\mathbf{I}-\mathbf{M}_z)\mathbf{X})^{-1}\mathbf{X}'(\mathbf{I}-\mathbf{M}_z)\mathbf{y} \\ &= (\hat{\mathbf{X}}'\hat{\mathbf{X}})^{-1}\hat{\mathbf{X}}'\mathbf{y}\end{aligned}$$

since $\mathbf{I}-\mathbf{M}_z$ is idempotent. This means that when *(and only when)* $\hat{\mathbf{X}}$ is the set of instruments, the IV estimator is computed by least squares regression of $\mathbf{y}$ on $\hat{\mathbf{X}}$. This suggests (only logically; one need not actually do this in two steps), that $\mathbf{b}_{\text{IV}}$ can be computed in two steps, first by computing $\hat{\mathbf{X}}$, then by the least squares regression. As a practical matter, this is a perfectly valid way to proceed. We will revisit this form of estimator at great length at several points below, particularly in our discussion of simultaneous equations models, under the rubric of "two-stage least squares." One should be careful of this approach, however, in the computation of the asymptotic covariance matrix; $\hat{\sigma}^2$ should not be based on $\hat{\mathbf{X}}$. The estimator

$$s_{\text{IV}}^2 = \frac{1}{n}(\mathbf{y} - \hat{\mathbf{X}}\mathbf{b})'(\mathbf{y} - \hat{\mathbf{X}}\mathbf{b})$$

is inconsistent for σ^2, with or without a correction for degrees of freedom.

An obvious question is where one is likely to find a suitable set of instrumental variables. In many time-series settings, such as the one here, lagged values of the variables in the model provide natural candidates. In other cases, the answer is less than obvious. It should be noted that the asymptotic variance matrix of the IV estimator can be rather large if $\mathbf{Z}$ is not highly correlated with $\mathbf{X}$; the elements of $(\mathbf{Z}'\mathbf{X})^{-1}$ grow large. Unfortunately, there usually is not much choice in the selection of instrumental variables. The choice of $\mathbf{Z}$ is often ad hoc.[48] There is a bit of a dilemma in this result. It would seem to suggest that the best choices of instruments are variables that are highly correlated with $\mathbf{X}$. But the more highly correlated a variable is with the problematic columns of $\mathbf{X}$, the less defensible the claim that these same variables are *uncorrelated* with the disturbances.

6.7.9. Heterogeneity in the Distributions of $\mathbf{x}_i$

Exceptions to the assumptions made above are likely to arise in two settings. In a **panel data set,** the sample will consist of multiple observations on each of many observational units. For example, a study might consist of a set of observations made at different points in time on a large number of families. In this case, the $\mathbf{x}$'s will surely be correlated across observations, at least within observational units. They might even be the same for all the observations on a single family. They are also likely to be a mixture of random variables, such as family income, and nonstochastic regressors, such as a fixed "family effect" represented by a dummy variable. The second case would be a time-series model in which lagged values of the dependent variable appear on the right-hand side of the model.

The panel data set could be treated as follows. Assume for the moment that the data consist of a fixed number of observations, say T, on a set of N families, so that the total number of rows in $\mathbf{X}$ is $n = NT$. The matrix

$$\overline{\mathbf{Q}}_n = \frac{1}{n}\sum_{i=1}^{n} \mathbf{Q}_i$$

[48]Results on "optimal instruments" appear in White (1984) and Hansen (1982).

[see (6-59)], in which n is all the observations in the sample, could be viewed as

$$\overline{\mathbf{Q}}_n = \frac{1}{N}\sum_i \frac{1}{T} \sum_{\substack{\text{observations}\\ \text{for family } i}} \mathbf{Q}_{ij} = \frac{1}{N}\sum_{i=1}^{N} \overline{\mathbf{Q}}_i,$$

where $\overline{\mathbf{Q}}_i$ = average $\mathbf{Q}_{ij}$ for family i. We might then view the set of observations on the ith unit as if they were a single observation and apply our convergence arguments to the number of families increasing without bound. The point is that the conditions that are needed to establish convergence will apply with respect to the number of observational units. The number of observations taken for each observation unit might be fixed and could be quite small.[49] Extensions to the case of unequal-sized groups and other configurations of the data are considered in Chapter 14.

For the general case of heterogeneous $\mathbf{x}_i$, we suppose only that $\mathbf{x}_i$ is drawn from a distribution with mean vector $E[\mathbf{x}_i]$ and covariance matrix $\mathbf{Q}_i = E[\mathbf{x}_i\mathbf{x}_i']$. Now we are faced with an interesting problem. Not only can we not establish (6-50) [convergence of $(1/n)\mathbf{X}'\mathbf{X}$ to a finite matrix]; we do not yet have enough structure to claim that $(1/n)\mathbf{X}'\mathbf{X}$ converges to anything at all! It need not. Our theorems on the convergence of sample means of observations, Theorems 4.3, and 4.4, rely on independent and *identically distributed* observations. Can we still establish the consistency of $\mathbf{b}$? The answer is yes, if we can make an additional, not very restrictive assumption about the distribution of $\mathbf{x}_i$. To do so, we must digress briefly to present some additional results on convergence of sums of random variables. Our assumption is now as follows.

AH5. $[\mathbf{x}_i, \epsilon_i]$ are an independent sequence of random variables.
AH5a. $E[\mathbf{x}_i\mathbf{x}_i'] = \mathbf{Q}_i = \mathbf{\Sigma}_i + \boldsymbol{\mu}_i\boldsymbol{\mu}_i'$, a finite, positive definite matrix.

The results we need to establish that $(1/n)\mathbf{X}'\mathbf{X}$ converges to a finite matrix are **laws of large numbers.** We will examine three, progressively less general. Denote

$$\overline{z}_n = \frac{1}{n}\sum_{i=1}^{n} z_i \quad \text{and} \quad \overline{\mu}_n = \frac{1}{n}\sum_{i=1}^{n} \mu_i.$$

For our application, z_i is a square or cross product $x_{ik}x_{il}$ and μ_i is $\mathbf{Q}_{i,kl}$.

THEOREM 6.16: Markov's Strong Law of Large Numbers. *If $\{z_i\}$ is a sequence of independent random variables with $E[z_i] = \mu_i < \infty$, and if for some $\delta > 0$, $\sum_{i=1}^{\infty} E[|z_i - \mu_i|^{1+\delta}]/i^{1+\delta} < \infty$, then $\overline{z}_n - \overline{\mu}_n$ converges almost surely to 0, which we denote $\overline{z}_n - \overline{\mu}_n \xrightarrow{as} 0$.*

[49]In some models, such as the **probit model with random effects** (Section 19.5.1), the full set of T observations for family i is treated as one multivariate observation. Then results for random sampling are applied to the random sample of N multivariate observations.

There are two new concepts in this definition.[50] First, **almost sure convergence** is a different form of convergence from what we have used thus far. Formally, $\overline{w}_n$ converges almost surely to ω, written $\overline{w}_n \xrightarrow{as} \omega$ if $\text{Prob}[\lim_{n\to\infty} |\overline{w}_n - \omega| < \epsilon] = 1$ for every $\epsilon > 0$. Loosely speaking, the random variable $\overline{w}_n$ converges almost surely to the constant ω if we are assured that for any arbitrarily small ϵ, there is a large enough n such that the probability of the event $[|\overline{w}_{n+1} - \omega| > \epsilon, |\overline{w}_{n+2} - \omega| > \epsilon, \ldots]$ diminishes to zero. This is different from mean-squared convergence, but the important point is that *both mean-squared convergence and almost sure convergence imply convergence in probability.* (The converse is not true.[51]) Second, *the result does not state that the sample mean converges to anything specific. It states that the behavior of the mean of the sample observations is the same as the behavior of the average of the population means.*

The Markov theorem requires that $\mathbf{x}_i$ have moments slightly greater than 2 to be finite. A somewhat weaker form of the theorem is the following.

THEOREM 6.17: Kolmogorov's Strong Law of Large Numbers. *If* $\{z_i\}$ *is a sequence of independent random variables with* $E[z_i] = \mu_i < \infty$, $\text{Var}[z_i] = \sigma_i^2 < \infty$, *and* $\Sigma_{i=1}^{\infty} \sigma_i^2/i^2 < \infty$, *then* $\overline{z}_n - \overline{\mu}_n \xrightarrow{as} 0$.

This is the special case of Markov's theorem with $\delta = 1$. To use the Kolmogorov result, we would require that the variances of x_{ik}^2 satisfy the assumptions, which characterizes the fourth moments. Recall that we made this assumption in our first derivation. Both of these theorems allow the variances to increase, but slowly enough so that the sums of variances will converge. For economic applications, this is probably more general than necessary. A third result, which is slightly less general is the following.

THEOREM 6.18: Chebychev's Weak Law of Large Numbers. *If* $\{z_i\}$ *is a sequence of uncorrelated random variables with* $E[z_i] = \mu_i < \infty$, $\text{Var}[z_i] = \sigma_i^2 < \infty$, *and,* $\lim_{n\to\infty}(1/n^2)\Sigma_{i=1}^{n} \sigma_i^2 < \infty$, *then* $\overline{z}_n - \overline{\mu}_n \xrightarrow{p} 0$.

We can use these results to establish consistency of $\mathbf{b}$ as follows. First, using the same form of analysis as in the previous section, the theorems state that as long as $\mathbf{Q}_i$ meets the assumption of the theorem, $(1/n)\mathbf{X}'\mathbf{X}$ will not explode. The reason is that $(1/n)\Sigma_i\mathbf{Q}_i$ is the average of n finite matrices and is therefore finite. As $n \to \infty$, the difference between $(1/n)\mathbf{X}'\mathbf{X}$ and this finite matrix will converge to $\mathbf{0}$. The important result is that the convergence of $\mathbf{b}$ to $\boldsymbol{\beta}$ is controlled by the behavior of $\overline{\mathbf{w}}$, not $(\mathbf{X}'\mathbf{X}/n)$. By similar reasoning, we have that

[50]The use of the expected absolute deviation differs a bit from the expected squared deviation that we have used heretofore to characterize the spread of a distribution. Consider two examples. If $z \sim N[0, \sigma^2]$, then $E[|z|] = \text{Prob}[z < 0]E[z|z < 0] + \text{Prob}[z \geq 0]E[z|z> = 0] = 0.7989\sigma$. (See Theorem 20.2.) So, finite expected absolute value is the same as finite second moment for the normal distribution. But if z takes values $[0, n]$ with probabilities $[1 - 1/n, 1/n]$, then the variance of z is $(n - 1)$, but $E[|z - \mu_z|]$ is $2 - 2/n$. For this case, finite expected absolute value occurs without finite expected second moment. These are different characterizations of the spread of the distribution.

[51]See Greenberg and Webster (1983).

$\overline{\mathbf{w}}$ converges to $\mathbf{0}$, either in probability or almost surely. Therefore, the large-sample behavior of $\mathbf{b} - \boldsymbol{\beta}$ is that of a finite matrix ($\overline{\mathbf{Q}}_n$) times a vector that converges to $\mathbf{0}$ ($\overline{\mathbf{w}}$). The product must therefore converge to $\mathbf{0}$. This establishes the consistency of $\mathbf{b}$ for $\boldsymbol{\beta}$.

Asymptotic normality in this instance follows, once again, from the Lindberg–Feller central limit theorem. It is necessary to assume independent observations, however. Some discussion appears in White (1984), Rao (1973), and Greenberg and Webster (1983).

6.7.10. Dependent Observations

The second difficult case is that in which there are lagged dependent variables among the variables on the right-hand side. Suppose that the model may be written

$$y_t = \mathbf{z}_t'\boldsymbol{\theta} + \gamma_1 y_{t-1} + \cdots + \gamma_p y_{t-p} + \epsilon_t. \tag{6-72}$$

(Since this is a time-series setting, we use t instead of i to index the observations.) We continue to assume that the disturbances are uncorrelated across observations. Since y_{t-1} is dependent on y_{t-2} and so on, it is clear that although the disturbances are uncorrelated across observations, the regressor vectors, including the lagged y's, surely are not. Also, although $\text{Cov}[\mathbf{x}_t, \epsilon_s] = 0$ if $s \geq t$ ($\mathbf{x}_t = [\mathbf{z}_t, y_{t-1}, \ldots, y_{t-p}]$), $\text{Cov}[\mathbf{x}_t, \epsilon_s] \neq 0$ if $s < t$. Every observation y_t is determined by the entire history of the disturbances. Therefore, we have lost the assumption $E[\boldsymbol{\epsilon}|\mathbf{X}] = \mathbf{0}$; $E[\epsilon_t|\text{previous } \mathbf{x}\text{'s}]$ is not equal to 0. The conditions needed for the finite-sample results we had earlier no longer hold. Without Assumption 3, $E[\boldsymbol{\epsilon}|\mathbf{X}] = \mathbf{0}$, our earlier proof of unbiasedness dissolves, and without unbiasedness, the Gauss–Markov theorem no longer applies. We are left with only asymptotic results for this case.

We should note before proceeding that although the observations thus far suggest that the least squares estimator is biased in this case, they do not suggest that it is *persistently* biased. That is, some estimators, including some that we will encounter in the chapters to follow, are fundamentally flawed because they are inappropriate estimators of the parameters in the model. For the case we are examining here, the bias of least squares consists of a deviation of the expected value of the estimator from the true parameters that will become less substantive as the sample size increases.

This case is considerably more general than the ones we have considered thus far. The theorems we invoked previously do not apply when the observations in the sums are correlated. To establish counterparts to the limiting normal distribution of $(1/\sqrt{n})\mathbf{X}'\boldsymbol{\epsilon}$ and convergence of $(1/n)\mathbf{X}'\mathbf{X}$ to a finite positive definite matrix, it is necessary to make additional assumptions about the regressors. For the disturbances, we assume the following.

a. $E[\epsilon_t|\mathbf{x}_t] = 0$.
b. $E[\epsilon_t^r|\mathbf{x}_t] = \mu_r < \infty$, $r \geq 2$ (for $r = 2$, this implies finite variance). **(6-73)**
c. $E[\epsilon_t \mathbf{x}_{t-s}] = \mathbf{0}$ if $s > 0$.

This states that the disturbance in the current period is a new "innovation"; previous values of y_t do not carry information about the moments of ϵ_t. These are sufficient to produce $(1/n)\mathbf{X}'\boldsymbol{\epsilon} \rightarrow \mathbf{0}$. We replace (6-66) with two assumptions about the right-hand variables. First,

$$\text{plim}\,\frac{1}{T-s}\sum_{t=s+1}^{T} \mathbf{x}_t\mathbf{x}'_{t-s} = \mathbf{Q}(s), \text{ a finite matrix}, \quad s \geq 0 \qquad \textbf{(6-74)}$$

and $\mathbf{Q}(0)$ is nonsingular if $T \geq K$. [Note that $\mathbf{Q} = \mathbf{Q}(0)$.] This is the matrix of cross products of the elements of $\mathbf{x}_t$ with lagged values of $\mathbf{x}_t$. The sum converges to a finite matrix if the series on $\mathbf{x}_t$ is **stationary** and **ergodic.** Heuristically, these mean that the correlation between values of the $\mathbf{x}$'s at different points in time varies only with how far apart in time they are, not specifically with the points in time at which observations are made, and that the correlation between observations made at different points in time fades sufficiently rapidly that sample moments such as $\mathbf{Q}(s)$ above will converge in probability to a population counterpart.[52] Second, we assume that the roots of the polynomial

$$1 - \gamma_1 L - \gamma_2 L^2 - \cdots - \gamma_P L^P = 0 \qquad \textbf{(6-75)}$$

are all outside the unit circle. (See Section 18.2.2 for further details.[53]) These are sufficient to establish the consistency of **b**. The results of Mann and Wald (1943) provide the basis for the asymptotic normal distribution in (6-62). This, then, produces the asymptotic distribution of the least squares estimator.

In sum, the important properties of consistency and asymptotic normality of the least squares estimator are preserved under the assumption of stochastic regressors, provided that additional assumptions are made. In most cases, these assumptions are quite benign, so we conclude that the two asymptotic properties of least squares considered here, consistency and asymptotic normality, are quite robust to different specifications of the regressors.

6.8. NORMALLY DISTRIBUTED DISTURBANCES

The results in Section 6.7 were established under minimal assumptions about the distribution of ϵ, only zero mean, constant variance, finite higher moments, and uncorrelatedness of $\mathbf{x}$ and ϵ in most cases. It would appear that as far as the asymptotic results are concerned, the assumption of normally distributed disturbances is superfluous. We have not established any large-sample counterpart

---

[52]We will examine some cases in later chapters in which this does not occur. To consider a simple example, suppose that $\mathbf{x}$ contains a constant. Then the assumption requires sample means to converge to population parameters. Suppose that all observations are correlated. Then the variance of $\bar{x}$ is $\text{Var}[(1/T)\,\Sigma_t x_t] = (1/T^2)\,\Sigma_t\,\Sigma_s\,\text{Cov}\,[x_t, x_s]$. Since none of the T^2 terms is assumed to be zero, there is no assurance that double sum converges to zero as $T \rightarrow \infty$. But if the correlations diminish with distance in time, then the sum may converge to zero.

[53]More detailed treatments of this issue appear in Chapters 15 and 18 and in Goldberger (1991, Chap. 27).

to the Gauss–Markov theorem, however. That is, it remains to establish whether the large-sample properties of the least squares estimator are optimal by any measure. In this section, we will examine the implications of the normality assumption for the asymptotic properties of least squares. As should be clear from the preceding, the only remaining issue is efficiency, and it will turn out that normality plays a crucial role in this regard.

6.8.1. Asymptotic Efficiency — Maximum Likelihood Estimation

DEFINITION: Asymptotic Efficiency. *An estimator is asymptotically efficient if it is consistent, asymptotically normally distributed, and has an asymptotic covariance matrix that is not larger than the asymptotic covariance matrix of any other consistent, asymptotically normally distributed estimator.*[54]

Asymptotic efficiency will be extremely difficult to verify. There is, however, an indirect strategy. In any "regular" problem, the maximum likelihood estimator is asymptotically efficient by the previous definition.[55] Therefore, to establish that an estimator is asymptotically efficient, one need only show that the estimator in question either (1) *is* the maximum likelihood estimator or (2) has the same asymptotic properties as the maximum likelihood estimator. We shall use both approaches here, the first for the least squares estimator of $\boldsymbol{\beta}$ and the second for the least squares estimator of σ^2. As such, least squares has all the desirable properties of maximum likelihood estimators, including asymptotic efficiency.[56]

The likelihood function for a sample of n independent, identically and normally distributed disturbances is

$$L = (2\pi\sigma^2)^{-n/2} e^{-\boldsymbol{\epsilon}'\boldsymbol{\epsilon}/(2\sigma^2)}. \tag{6-76}$$

The transformation from ϵ_i to y_i is $\epsilon_i = y_i - \mathbf{x}_i'\boldsymbol{\beta}$, so the Jacobian for each observation, $|\partial\epsilon_i/\partial y_i|$, is one.[57] Making the transformation, we find that the likelihood function for the n observations on the observed random variable is[58]

$$\begin{aligned} L &= (2\pi\sigma^2)^{-n/2} e^{(-1/(2\sigma^2))\Sigma_{i=1}^{n}(y_i - \mathbf{x}_i'\boldsymbol{\beta})^2} \\ &= (2\pi\sigma^2)^{-n/2} e^{(-1/(2\sigma^2))(\mathbf{y}-\mathbf{X}\boldsymbol{\beta})'(\mathbf{y}-\mathbf{X}\boldsymbol{\beta})}. \end{aligned} \tag{6-77}$$

---

[54]*Smaller* is defined in the sense of (2-118): The covariance matrix of the less efficient estimator equals that of the efficient estimator plus a nonnegative definite matrix.

[55]By *regular,* we mean a likelihood function that satisfies the regularity conditions discussed in Section 4.5.1.

[56]The general results are presented in Section 4.5.

[57]See (3-41) in Section 3.5.

[58]The analysis is conditioned on $\mathbf{X}$. For now, we take $\mathbf{X}$ to be nonstochastic. For stochastic regressors, the analysis is the same as long as the distribution of $\mathbf{X}$ does not involve $\boldsymbol{\beta}$ or σ^2.

To maximize this function with respect to $\boldsymbol{\beta}$, it will be necessary to maximize the exponent or minimize the familiar sum of squares. Taking logs in (6-77), we obtain the log-likelihood function for the classical regression model:

$$\ln L = -\frac{n}{2}\ln 2\pi - \frac{n}{2}\ln\sigma^2 - \frac{1}{2\sigma^2}(\mathbf{y} - \mathbf{X}\boldsymbol{\beta})'(\mathbf{y} - \mathbf{X}\boldsymbol{\beta}). \quad \textbf{(6-78)}$$

The necessary conditions for maximizing this log-likelihood are

$$\frac{\partial \ln L}{\partial \boldsymbol{\beta}} = \frac{1}{\sigma^2}\mathbf{X}'(\mathbf{y} - \mathbf{X}\boldsymbol{\beta}) = \mathbf{0}$$

and **(6-79)**

$$\frac{\partial \ln L}{\partial \sigma^2} = \frac{-n}{2\sigma^2} + \frac{1}{2\sigma^4}(\mathbf{y} - \mathbf{X}\boldsymbol{\beta})'(\mathbf{y} - \mathbf{X}\boldsymbol{\beta}) = 0.$$

The values that satisfy these equations are

$$\hat{\beta}_{ML} = (\mathbf{X}'\mathbf{X})^{-1}\mathbf{X}'\mathbf{y} = \mathbf{b} \quad \textbf{(6-80)}$$

and

$$\hat{\sigma}^2_{ML} = \frac{\mathbf{e}'\mathbf{e}}{n}.$$

The slope estimator is the familiar one, whereas the variance estimator differs from the least squares value by the divisor of n instead of $n - K$.[59]

The Cramér–Rao bound for the variance of an unbiased estimator is the negative inverse of the expectation of

$$\begin{bmatrix} \partial^2\ln L/\partial\boldsymbol{\beta}\partial\boldsymbol{\beta}' & \partial^2\ln L/\partial\boldsymbol{\beta}\,\partial\sigma^2 \\ \partial^2\ln L/\partial\sigma^2\,\partial\boldsymbol{\beta}' & \partial^2\ln L/\partial(\sigma^2)^2 \end{bmatrix} = \begin{bmatrix} -(1/\sigma^2)\mathbf{X}'\mathbf{X} & -(1/\sigma^4)\mathbf{X}'\boldsymbol{\epsilon} \\ -(1/\sigma^4)\boldsymbol{\epsilon}'\mathbf{X} & n/(2\sigma^4) - \boldsymbol{\epsilon}'\boldsymbol{\epsilon}/\sigma^6 \end{bmatrix}. \quad \textbf{(6-81)}$$

In taking expected values, the off-diagonal term vanishes. Thus, the Cramér–Rao variance bound is

$$[-\mathbf{I}(\boldsymbol{\beta}, \sigma^2)]^{-1} = \begin{bmatrix} \sigma^2(\mathbf{X}'\mathbf{X})^{-1} & \mathbf{0} \\ \mathbf{0}' & 2\sigma^4/n \end{bmatrix}. \quad \textbf{(6-82)}$$

The least squares slope estimator coincides with the maximum likelihood estimator for this model. Therefore, it inherits all the desirable *asymptotic* properties of maximum likelihood estimators. To reiterate:

ML1. It is *consistent,* which we showed earlier.

ML2. It is *asymptotically normally distributed,* with an asymptotic covariance matrix equal to the Cramér–Rao bound for efficient estimation.

ML3. It is *asymptotically efficient.* No other consistent and asymptotically normally distributed estimator has a smaller asymptotic covariance matrix.

ML4. Maximum likelihood estimators are also *invariant.* The maximum likelihood estimator of any continuous function of $\boldsymbol{\beta}$ is that function of the maximum likelihood estimator. Whereas, by the Gauss–Markov theorem, we could assert that

[59]As a general rule, maximum likelihood estimators do not make corrections for degrees of freedom.

the most efficient linear unbiased estimator of $\mathbf{w}'\boldsymbol{\beta}$ is $\mathbf{w}'\mathbf{b}$, we now have a much broader result. At least asymptotically, the most efficient estimator of $\mathbf{g}(\boldsymbol{\beta})$, where $\mathbf{g}(\boldsymbol{\beta})$ is any set of continuous functions, is $\mathbf{g}(\mathbf{b})$. The asymptotic distribution of this continuous function of the maximum likelihood estimator is given by Theorem 6.11, (6-65).

We showed earlier that $s^2 = \mathbf{e}'\mathbf{e}/(n - K)$ is an unbiased estimator of σ^2. Therefore, the maximum likelihood estimator is biased toward zero:

$$E[\hat{\sigma}^2_{ML}] = \frac{n - K}{n}\sigma^2 = \left(1 - \frac{K}{n}\right)\sigma^2 < \sigma^2. \tag{6-83}$$

Despite its small-sample bias, the maximum likelihood estimator of σ^2 has all the desirable asymptotic properties. We see in (6-83) that s^2 and $\hat{\sigma}^2$ differ only by a factor $-K/n$, which vanishes in large samples. Nonetheless, it is instructive to formalize the asymptotic equivalence of the two. From (6-80) and (6-82), we know that

$$\sqrt{n}(\hat{\sigma}^2_{ML} - \sigma^2) \xrightarrow{d} N[0, 2\sigma^4].$$

It follows that the limiting distribution of

$$z_n = \left(1 - \frac{K}{n}\right)\sqrt{n}(\hat{\sigma}^2_{ML} - \sigma^2) + \frac{K}{\sqrt{n}}\sigma^2$$

is that of

$$\left(1 - \frac{K}{n}\right)N[0, 2\sigma^4] + \frac{K}{\sqrt{n}}\sigma^2.$$

But $K/\sqrt{n}$ and K/n vanish as $n \to \infty$, so the limiting distribution of z_n is also $N[0, 2\sigma^4]$. Since

$$z_n = \sqrt{n}(s^2 - \sigma^2),$$

we have shown that the asymptotic distribution of s^2 is the same as that of the maximum likelihood estimator.

6.8.2. Stochastic Regressors

The preceding treats the regressor matrix $\mathbf{X}$ as nonstochastic. If the regressors are stochastic and their distribution involves parameters to be estimated, then the log-likelihood function must be formulated to account for this:

$$\ln L = \ln f(\mathbf{y}, \mathbf{X} \mid \boldsymbol{\beta}, \sigma^2, \boldsymbol{\theta}),$$

where $\boldsymbol{\theta}$ is a collection of unknown parameters in the distribution of $\mathbf{X}$. But if $\boldsymbol{\theta}$ does not involve $\boldsymbol{\beta}$ or σ^2, then the log-likelihood can be factored into

$$\ln L = \ln f_{y|\mathbf{x}}(\mathbf{y} \mid \mathbf{X}, \boldsymbol{\beta}, \sigma^2) + \ln g_{\mathbf{x}}(\mathbf{X} \mid \boldsymbol{\theta}).$$

The two parts of the log-likelihood can be maximized separately so that our earlier treatment of the regression model with nonstochastic regressors remains appropriate. The parameters of the marginal distribution of $\mathbf{X}$ can be estimated separately if desired.

6.8.3. Wald, Lagrange Multiplier, and Likelihood Ratio Test Statistics

In Section 6.7.6, we examined a test statistic for assessing the validity of a set of linear restrictions, $\mathbf{R}\boldsymbol{\beta} - \mathbf{q} = \mathbf{0}$,

$$F = \frac{(\mathbf{e}_*'\mathbf{e}_* - \mathbf{e}'\mathbf{e})/J}{\mathbf{e}'\mathbf{e}/(n-K)} = \frac{(\mathbf{Rb}-\mathbf{q})'[\mathbf{R}s^2(\mathbf{X}'\mathbf{X})^{-1}\mathbf{R}']^{-1}(\mathbf{Rb}-\mathbf{q})}{J}. \qquad \textbf{(6-84)}$$

With normally distributed disturbances, the F test is valid with any sample size. There remains a problem with nonlinear restrictions of the form $\mathbf{f}(\boldsymbol{\beta}) = \mathbf{0}$, since the counterpart to F, which we will examine here, has validity only asymptotically even with normally distributed disturbances. In this section, we will reconsider the Wald statistic and examine two related statistics, the likelihood ratio statistic and the Lagrange multiplier statistic. These are both based on the likelihood function and, like the Wald statistic, are generally valid only asymptotically.

No simplicity is gained by restricting ourselves to linear restrictions at this point, so we will consider general hypotheses of the form

$$H_0: \mathbf{f}(\boldsymbol{\beta}) = \mathbf{0},$$
$$H_1: \mathbf{f}(\boldsymbol{\beta}) \neq \mathbf{0}.$$

The **Wald statistic** for testing this hypothesis would be

$$W = \mathbf{f}(\mathbf{b})'\{\mathbf{G}(\mathbf{b})[s^2(\mathbf{X}'\mathbf{X})^{-1}]\mathbf{G}(\mathbf{b})'\}^{-1}\mathbf{f}(\mathbf{b}) \xrightarrow{d} \chi^2[J], \qquad \textbf{(6-85)}$$

where

$$\mathbf{G}(\mathbf{b}) = [\partial\mathbf{f}(\mathbf{b})/\partial\mathbf{b}'].$$

If the model and the restrictions are linear, then W can be computed simply as JF, where F is defined in (6-84). The second form is useful, as it shows that W can be based only on the original, unrestricted least squares estimator. For more general models or restrictions, the computation in (6-85) will be required instead.

Since we are considering results in this section that are only valid asymptotically, it will be convenient to drop the degrees of freedom correction in s^2. This will make it easier to compare W with the other statistics. Then we have the useful result

$$W = \frac{nJ}{n-K}F. \qquad \textbf{(6-86)}$$

The **likelihood ratio (LR) test** is carried out by comparing the values of the log-likelihood function with and without the restrictions imposed. We leave aside for the present how the restricted estimator $\mathbf{b}_*$ is computed (except for the linear model, which we saw earlier). The test statistic is

$$\text{LR} = -2[\ln L_* - \ln L] \xrightarrow{d} \chi^2[J]. \quad \textbf{(6-87)}$$

The log-likelihood for the regression model is

$$\ln L = -\frac{n}{2}\ln 2\pi - \frac{n}{2}\ln \sigma^2 - \frac{1}{2\sigma^2}(\mathbf{y} - \mathbf{X}\boldsymbol{\beta})'(\mathbf{y} - \mathbf{X}\boldsymbol{\beta}).$$

The first-order conditions imply that regardless of how the slopes are computed, the estimator of σ^2 will be $\hat{\sigma}^2 = (\mathbf{y} - \mathbf{X}\mathbf{b})'(\mathbf{y} - \mathbf{X}\mathbf{b})/n$ and likewise for a restricted estimator $\hat{\sigma}_*^2 = (\mathbf{y} - \mathbf{X}\mathbf{b}_*)'(\mathbf{y} - \mathbf{X}\mathbf{b}_*)/n$. The concentrated log-likelihood will be

$$\ln L_c = -\frac{n}{2}[1 + \ln 2\pi + \ln(\mathbf{e}'\mathbf{e}/n)]$$

and likewise for the restricted case. If we insert these in the definition of LR, we obtain

$$\text{LR} = n \ln[\mathbf{e}_*'\mathbf{e}_*/\mathbf{e}'\mathbf{e}]. \quad \textbf{(6-88)}$$

If the model and restrictions are linear, this can also be written as

$$\text{LR} = n \ln[1 + JF/(n - K)] = n \ln[1 + W/n]. \quad \textbf{(6-89)}$$

This gives another convenient way to compute the test statistic, based only on the unrestricted estimator. (This simplification only arises in the linear model with linear restrictions.) There is a simple comparison for the linear model. Since the log function is concave, we know that $W > \text{LR}$. They will converge asymptotically. For small x, $\ln(1 + x) \approx x$. The term W/n approaches zero from above, so $\lim_{n\to\infty} \text{LR} = W$.

The **Lagrange multiplier (LM)** test is based, essentially, on the gradient of the log-likelihood function. The principle of the test is that if the hypothesis is valid, then at the restricted estimator, the derivatives of the log-likelihood function should be close to zero. There are two ways to carry out the LM test. The log-likelihood function can be maximized subject to a set of restrictions by using

$$\ln L_{\text{LM}} = -\frac{n}{2}\ln 2\pi - \frac{n}{2}\ln \sigma^2 - \frac{1}{2\sigma^2}(\mathbf{y} - \mathbf{X}\boldsymbol{\beta})'(\mathbf{y} - \mathbf{X}\boldsymbol{\beta}) + \boldsymbol{\lambda}'\mathbf{f}(\boldsymbol{\beta}).$$

The first-order conditions for a solution are

$$\frac{\partial \ln L_{\text{LM}}}{\partial \boldsymbol{\beta}} = \frac{1}{\sigma^2}\mathbf{X}'(\mathbf{y} - \mathbf{X}\boldsymbol{\beta}) + \mathbf{G}(\boldsymbol{\beta})'\boldsymbol{\lambda} = \mathbf{0},$$

$$\frac{\partial \ln L_{\text{LM}}}{\partial \sigma^2} = \frac{-n}{2\sigma^2} + \frac{1}{2\sigma^4}(\mathbf{y} - \mathbf{X}\boldsymbol{\beta})'(\mathbf{y} - \mathbf{X}\boldsymbol{\beta}) = \mathbf{0},$$

$$\frac{\partial \ln L_{\text{LM}}}{\partial \boldsymbol{\lambda}} = \mathbf{f}(\boldsymbol{\beta}) = \mathbf{0}.$$

The solutions to these equations give the restricted least squares estimator $\mathbf{b}_*$, the usual variance estimator, now $\mathbf{e}_*'\mathbf{e}_*/n$, and the Lagrange multipliers. There are two ways to compute the test statistic. In the setting of the classical linear regression model, when we actually compute the Lagrange multipliers, a convenient way to proceed is to test the hypothesis that the multipliers equal zero. We will show formally in Chapter 7 the result that for this model, the solution for $\boldsymbol{\lambda}$ is

$$\boldsymbol{\lambda} = [\mathbf{R}(\mathbf{X}'\mathbf{X})^{-1}\mathbf{R}']^{-1}(\mathbf{Rb} - \mathbf{q}). \tag{6-90}$$

This is a linear function of the least squares estimator. If we carry out a *Wald* test of the hypothesis that $\boldsymbol{\lambda}$ equals $\mathbf{0}$, the statistic will be

$$\begin{aligned}\text{LM} &= \boldsymbol{\lambda}'\{\text{Est. Var}[\boldsymbol{\lambda}]\}^{-1}\boldsymbol{\lambda}\\ &= [(\mathbf{Rb} - \mathbf{q})'[\mathbf{R}(\mathbf{X}'\mathbf{X})^{-1}\mathbf{R}']^{-1}]'\{[\mathbf{R}(\mathbf{X}'\mathbf{X})^{-1}\mathbf{R}']^{-1}\mathbf{R}s_*^2(\mathbf{X}'\mathbf{X})^{-1}\mathbf{R}'\\ &\quad\times[\mathbf{R}(\mathbf{X}'\mathbf{X})^{-1}\mathbf{R}']^{-1}\}^{-1}\;[[\mathbf{R}(\mathbf{X}'\mathbf{X})^{-1}\mathbf{R}']^{-1}(\mathbf{Rb} - \mathbf{q})]\\ &= (\mathbf{Rb} - \mathbf{q})'[\mathbf{R}s_*^2(\mathbf{X}'\mathbf{X})^{-1}\mathbf{R}']^{-1}(\mathbf{Rb} - \mathbf{q}).\end{aligned} \tag{6-91}$$

The variance estimator is based on the restricted slopes $\mathbf{e}_*'\mathbf{e}_*/n$. After some manipulation, it can be shown[60] that

$$\text{LM} = \frac{nJ}{(n - K)[1 + JF/(n - K)]}F = \frac{W}{1 + W/n}. \tag{6-92}$$

EXAMPLE 6.23 Test Statistics for the Investment Equation

For the investment equation examined in several earlier examples (e.g., Example 6.12), the coefficient of determination based on 15 observations is 0.97244. The F statistic for testing the hypothesis that the four slopes are zero is $F[4, 10] = (0.97244/4)/(0.02756/10) = 88.211$. The Wald statistic, using (6-86), is 529.267. The likelihood ratio statistic based on (6-89) is 53.871. The Lagrange multiplier statistic based on (6-92) is 14.586. This stretches the results a bit, since we are applying our asymptotic results to 15 observations. Still, there are two familiar results shown. First, the inequality

$$W > \text{LR} > \text{LM}$$

that we see here can be shown theoretically and is widely cited. [See, e.g., Godfrey (1988).] Second, it is common to observe, as we have here, that the Wald statistic far exceeds the other two.

An alternative way to compute the LM statistic often produces interesting results. In most situations, we maximize the log-likelihood function without actually computing a vector of Lagrange multipliers. (The restrictions are usu-

[60]See Godfrey (1988, pp. 49–51).

ally imposed some other way.) An alternative way to compute the statistic is based on the (general) result that under the hypothesis being tested,[61]

$$E[\partial \ln L/\partial \boldsymbol{\beta}] = E[(1/\sigma^2)\mathbf{X}'\boldsymbol{\epsilon}] = \mathbf{0}$$

and

$$\text{Asy. Var}[\partial \ln L/\partial \boldsymbol{\beta}] = [-\partial^2 \ln L/\partial \boldsymbol{\beta}\, \partial \boldsymbol{\beta}']^{-1} = \sigma^2(\mathbf{X}'\mathbf{X})^{-1}.$$

We can test the hypothesis that at the restricted estimator, the derivatives are equal to zero. The statistic would be

$$\text{LM} = \frac{\mathbf{e}_*'\mathbf{X}(\mathbf{X}'\mathbf{X})^{-1}\mathbf{X}'\mathbf{e}_*}{\mathbf{e}_*'\mathbf{e}_*/n} = nR_0^2. \tag{6-93}$$

In this form, the LM statistic is n times the coefficient of determination in a regression of the residuals $e_{i*} = (y_i - \mathbf{x}_i'\mathbf{b}_*)$ on the full set of regressors.

6.8.4. Cases in Which Least Squares Is Inefficient

The result in Section 6.8.1 is useful insofar as it establishes conditions under which least squares is optimal. On the other hand, there is an opposite and much less appealing conclusion to be drawn. That is, since maximum likelihood estimators are asymptotically efficient, the optimality of least squares in large samples depends on the assumption of normality. If any other distribution is specified for $\boldsymbol{\epsilon}$ and it emerges that $\mathbf{b}$ is not the maximum likelihood estimator, it follows directly that least squares is not efficient. In the absence of a specified model, it is rarely appropriate to specify a particular, nonnormal distribution for the disturbance in a regression model. But there are many applications that do specify other distributions.

EXAMPLE 6.24 The Gamma Regression Model

Greene (1980a) considers estimation in a regression model with an asymmetrically distributed disturbance,

$$\begin{aligned} y &= \left(\alpha - \frac{\sqrt{P}}{\sigma}\right) + \mathbf{x}'\boldsymbol{\beta} - \left(\epsilon - \frac{\sqrt{P}}{\sigma}\right) \\ &= \alpha^* + \mathbf{x}'\boldsymbol{\beta} + \epsilon^*, \end{aligned} \tag{6-94}$$

where ϵ has the gamma distribution in Section 3.4.5 [see (3-39)] and $\sigma = \sqrt{P}/\lambda$ is the standard deviation of the disturbance. He shows that the covariance matrix of the least squares estimator of the slope coefficients (not including the constant term) is, as always,

$$\text{Var}[\mathbf{b}] = \sigma^2(\mathbf{X}'\mathbf{M}^0\mathbf{X})^{-1},$$

[61] We are using a shortcut here for the classical regression model. The information matrix for this model is block diagonal. The cross derivative $[\partial^2 \ln L/\partial \boldsymbol{\beta}\, \partial \sigma^2]$ has expected value $\mathbf{0}$. This considerably simplifies the derivation of the LM statistic for this model.

whereas for the maximum likelihood estimator (which is not the OLS estimator),

$$\text{Asy. Var}[\hat{\boldsymbol{\beta}}_{ML}] \simeq \left[\frac{P-2}{P}\right]\sigma^2(\mathbf{X}'\mathbf{M}^0\mathbf{X})^{-1}.$$[62]

But for the asymmetry parameter, this would be the same as the least squares estimator. We conclude that the estimator that accounts for the asymmetric disturbance distribution is more efficient asymptotically.

6.8.5. Alternative Estimation Criteria

As a general rule, least squares treats negative and positive observations symmetrically and involves sums of observations that weight all observations equally. Maximum likelihood estimators make more explicit use of information about the shape of the disturbance distribution and, when appropriate, weight observations according to a more appropriate weighting scheme. To consider another example, if the disturbance were distributed according to the Laplace distribution,

$$f(\epsilon) = \frac{1}{2\sigma}e^{-|\epsilon|/2\sigma},$$

the maximum likelihood estimator of $\boldsymbol{\beta}$ would minimize the sum of absolute values of the residuals instead of the sum of squares.[63] The least squares estimator can be seriously distorted by outlying observations in a relatively small sample, whereas the minimum absolute deviations (MAD) estimator will be considerably less so.

The possibility of disturbance distributions with thicker tails than the normal, particularly in microeconomic data and in applications in finance, has led to the proposal of numerous robust estimators.[64] Most of these can be written in the form

$$S(\mathbf{b}) = \sum_i \eta\left[\frac{y_i - \mathbf{x}_i'\mathbf{b}}{s}\right],$$

where $\eta[\cdot]$ is a weighting function designed to reduce the weight attached to extreme observations. Least squares and MAD are two we have already considered. Alternatives that have been suggested include $\eta(z) = |z|^p$ for alternative values of p between 1 and 2 and some discontinuous ones such as $\eta(z) = -\cos(z) - 1$ if $|z| \leq \pi$ and zero otherwise.[65] Koenker and Bassett

---

[62]The Matrix $\mathbf{M}^0$ produces data in the form of deviations from sample means. (See Section 2.3.6.) In Greene's model, P must be strictly greater than 2.

[63]See L. Taylor (1974).

[64]An extensive survey may be found in Amemiya (1985, pp. 70–80).

[65]Andrews (1974).

(1978) have proposed the following criterion function:

$$S(\mathbf{b}) = t \sum_{+} |y - \mathbf{x}'\mathbf{b}| + (1 - t) \sum_{-} |y - \mathbf{x}'\mathbf{b}|,$$

where t is a predetermined proportion. For certain thick-tailed distributions, this estimator has performed well in Monte Carlo studies. In practice, however, the choice of t is likely to be a problem. These estimators have found little use in econometrics, primarily because of the difficulty in implementing them and their largely ad hoc nature. Tinkering with the outlying observations amounts to letting the computer be the ultimate judge of the estimated relationship and diminishes the role of the underlying theory. Least squares remains by far the estimator of choice for the linear regression model.

6.8.6. Detecting Departures from Normality

This section considers the general problem of using the moments of the least squares residuals to make inference about the distribution of the true disturbances.

The natural estimator of

$$\mu_r = E[\epsilon^r]$$

would be

$$m_r = \frac{1}{n} \sum_{i=1}^{n} e_i^r.$$

The least squares residuals, however, are only imperfect estimates of the true disturbances:

$$e_i = \epsilon_i - \mathbf{x}_i'(\mathbf{b} - \boldsymbol{\beta}).$$

Since plim $\mathbf{b} = \boldsymbol{\beta}$, the larger the sample, the better an estimate this becomes. This is sometimes labeled **pointwise consistency.** It can be shown that the sample of least squares residuals converges to the sample of true disturbances.[66] This implies that if

$$\hat{\mu}_r = \frac{1}{n} \sum_{i=1}^{n} \epsilon_i^r$$

is a consistent estimator of μ_r, then

$$m_r = \frac{1}{n} \sum_{i=1}^{n} e_i^r$$

is also.

The foregoing has been used to devise a test of normality.[67] The normal distribution is symmetric and **mesokurtic.** The symmetry implies that the third

---

[66]See Theil (1971).

[67]Kiefer and Salmon (1983).

moment $E[\epsilon^3]$ is zero. The standard measure of symmetry of a distribution is the skewness coefficient,

$$\sqrt{\beta_1} = \frac{E[\epsilon^3]}{(\sigma^2)^{3/2}}.$$

Kurtosis is a measure of the thickness of the tails of a distribution. The measure is

$$\beta_2 = \frac{E[\epsilon^4]}{(\sigma^2)^2}.$$

The normal distribution is the usual yardstick for this; the mesokurtic value is the kurtosis of the normal distribution, which is 3. Therefore, we might compare a distribution to the normal distribution by comparing this skewness to zero and its kurtosis to three. In practice, the usual measure is the **degree of excess,** $(\beta_2 - 3)$. The device we shall use is a Wald statistic. Under the hypothesis of normality, the test statistic would be

$$W = n\left[\frac{b_1}{6} + \frac{(b_2 - 3)^2}{24}\right] \sim \chi^2[2]. \qquad \textbf{(6-95)}$$

This is asymptotically distributed as chi-squared with two degrees of freedom. Feasible estimators of these parameters are computed using the least squares residuals.[68] The statistic can be referred to the standard chi-squared tables.

This test statistic has been derived as a Lagrange multiplier test in the context of the Pearson distributions by Bera and Jarque (1981, 1982).[69] It should be noted that the test is essentially nonconstructive. A finding of nonnormality does not necessarily suggest what to do next.[70] Note also that failing to reject normality does not confirm it. This remains only a test of symmetry and mesokurtosis.

EXAMPLE 6.25 A Model with a Nonnormal Disturbance

The data listed in Table 7.1 were used by Aigner, Lovell, and Schmidt (1977) to estimate a **stochastic frontier** model. Their model may be written

$$y_i = \alpha + \boldsymbol{\beta}'\mathbf{x}_i + \epsilon_i,$$
$$\epsilon_i = v_i - |u_i|,$$

[68] It is sometimes suggested that the residuals be transformed to remove their finite-sample covariance before these testing procedures are performed. See, for example, Judge et al. (1985, p. 826). Since the tests are valid only asymptotically, when the residuals are uncorrelated anyway, this would not add to the validity of the test procedures. There is some evidence, for example, by Ramsey (1974), that using uncorrelated BLUS residuals [see Theil (1971)] makes matters worse instead of better.

[69] Additional results appear in Kiefer and Salmon (1983).

[70] Proceeding with estimation of Bera and Jarques's more general Pearson type 7 distribution is so cumbersome that empirical implementation is likely to be exceedingly difficult.

where v_i and u_i are normally distributed with zero means and constant variances σ_v^2 and σ_u^2. The distribution of the absolute value of a normally distributed variable is shown in Figure 20.1; it is clearly nonnormal. The difference of the two variables is asymmetric and nonnormal.[71] The asymmetry of the distribution of ϵ_i is a central feature of the model. The degree of asymmetry can be characterized by the parameter $\lambda = \sigma_u/\sigma_v$. The larger λ is, the more pronounced the asymmetry will be. Conversely, if λ equals zero, then $\epsilon_i = v_i$, which has a normal distribution. The expected value of ϵ_i is

$$E[v_i - |u_i|] = \mu_\epsilon = -\left(\frac{2}{\pi}\right)^{1/2} \sigma_u.$$

The model can be written

$$\begin{aligned} y_i &= (\alpha + \mu_\epsilon) + \boldsymbol{\beta}'\mathbf{x}_i + (\epsilon_i - \mu_\epsilon) \\ &= \alpha^* + \boldsymbol{\beta}'\mathbf{x}_i + \epsilon_i^*, \end{aligned}$$

where ϵ_i^* has zero mean and constant variance, but a nonnormal and asymmetric distribution. A test of the model can be based on the least squares residuals.

The results of least squares regression of the log of output (value added) on the logs of capital and labor are given in Table 7.2. Although the least squares estimator is inefficient—it is not the maximum likelihood estimator for this model—it is consistent. The moments of the residuals are

$$\begin{aligned} m_2 &= 0.03154199, \\ m_3 &= 0.004741061, \\ m_4 &= 0.00410284. \end{aligned}$$

The skewness and excess coefficients are

$$\frac{m_3}{(m_2)^{3/2}} = 0.846334$$

and

$$\frac{m_4}{(m_2)^2} - 3 = 1.12388.$$

With 27 observations, the chi-squared statistic is 4.6443. The 5 percent critical value from the chi-squared table for two degrees of freedom is 5.99, so we conclude that the residuals do not depart significantly from normality. As an indirect test of the same hypothesis, Aigner et al.'s estimate of λ is only 0.1, with an asymptotic t ratio of 0.05. Therefore, their results are consistent with these.

---

[71] The density of ϵ is $(2/\pi)^{1/2}\Phi(-\epsilon\lambda/\sigma)(1/\sigma)\phi(\epsilon/\sigma)$, where $\sigma = (\sigma_v^2 + \sigma_u^2)^{1/2}$.

6.9. BAYESIAN ESTIMATION

The results thus far present a bit of a methodological dilemma. They would seem to straitjacket the researcher into a fixed and immutable specification of the model. But in any analysis, there is uncertainty as to the magnitudes and even, on occasion, the signs of coefficients. It is rare that the presentation of a set of empirical results has not been preceded by at least some exploratory analysis. Proponents of the Bayesian methodology argue that the process of estimation is not one of deducing the values of fixed parameters, but rather of continually updating and sharpening our subjective beliefs about the state of the world.[72] Assembled in the Bayesian methodology, these aspects of the theory come together in an appealing format.

The centerpiece of the Bayesian methodology is Bayes's theorem:

$$P(A \mid B) = \frac{P(B \mid A)P(A)}{P(B)}. \qquad \textbf{(6-96)}$$

Paraphrased for our applications here, we would write this as

$$P(\text{parameters} \mid \text{data}) = \frac{P(\text{data} \mid \text{parameters})P(\text{parameters})}{P(\text{data})}. \qquad \textbf{(6-97)}$$

In this setting, the data are viewed as constants whose distributions do not involve the parameters of interest. For the purpose of the study, we treat the data as only a fixed set of additional information to be used in updating our beliefs about the parameters. Thus, we write

$$P(\text{parameters} \mid \text{data}) \propto P(\text{data} \mid \text{parameters})P(\text{parameters}).$$

The symbol $\propto$ means "is proportional to." In the preceding, we have dropped the density of the data, so what remains is not a proper density until it is scaled by what will be an inessential proportionality constant. The first term on the right is the joint distribution of the observed random variables $\mathbf{y}$, given the parameters. As we shall analyze it here, this is the normal distribution we have

---

[72]Indeed, they see the fact that researchers do such exploratory analysis as evidence of this. Consider, for example, "Personally, I find the Bayesian philosophy compelling [see Poirier (1988)]. While I believe that *everyone is a Bayesian deep down inside,* I realize that relatively few researchers are 'out-of-the-closet'" [Poirier (1991, p. 1), emphasis added]. In recent years, Bayesian techniques and treatments have made large inroads into the econometrics literature. Nonetheless, the applications remain dominated by sampling theory (or "frequentist") approaches. There remains some tension between practitioners on ideological grounds, although much less so than previously. Still, consider that the authoritative recent work by Davidson and Mackinnon (1993) devotes less than a paragraph in nearly 800 pages to the Bayesian methodology, whereas another recent econometrics text whose treatment and orientation is more Bayesian than not, Poirier (1995), is replete with exhortative quotations such as "The people who don't know they are Bayesians are called non-Bayesians" (p. 540). Its occasionally zealous undercurrents notwithstanding, this dichotomy continues to be one of the fundamentally interesting issues in econometric methodology. It is made much the more so as Bayesian econometrics has matured in recent years from studies that often merely replicated received sampling theory results in a Bayesian setting to demonstrations of elegant solutions to problems that were heretofore viewed as intractable.

used in our previous analysis. The second term is the **prior beliefs** of the analyst. The left-hand side is the **posterior density** of the parameters, given the current body of data, or our revised beliefs about the distribution of the parameters. The posterior is a mixture of the prior information and the "current information," that is, the data. Once obtained, this posterior density is available to be the prior density function when the next body of data or other usable information becomes available. The principle involved, which appears nowhere in the classical analysis, is one of continual accretion of knowledge about the parameters.

6.9.1. Bayesian Analysis of the Classical Regression Model

The complexity of the algebra involved in Bayesian analysis is often extremely burdensome.[73] For the classical regression model, however, many fairly straightforward results have been obtained. To provide some of the flavor of the techniques, we present the full derivation only for some simple cases. In the interest of brevity, and to avoid the burden of excessive algebra, we refer the reader to one of the several sources that present the full derivation of the more complex cases.[74]

The classical normal regression model we have analyzed thus far is constructed around the conditional multivariate normal distribution $N[\mathbf{X}\boldsymbol{\beta}, \sigma^2\mathbf{I}]$ in (6-77). The interpretation is different here. In the sampling theory setting, this distribution embodies the information about the observed sample data *given* the assumed distribution and the fixed, albeit unknown, parameters of the model. In the Bayesian setting, this function summarizes the information that a particular realization of the data provides about the assumed distribution of the model parameters. To underscore that idea, we rename this joint density the **likelihood for $\boldsymbol{\beta}$ and σ^2 given the data,** so

$$L(\boldsymbol{\beta}, \sigma^2 \,|\, \mathbf{y}, \mathbf{X}) = [2\pi\sigma^2]^{-n/2}\, e^{-[(1/2\sigma^2)(\mathbf{y}-\mathbf{X}\boldsymbol{\beta})'(\mathbf{y}-\mathbf{X}\boldsymbol{\beta})]}. \tag{6-98}$$

For purposes of the results below, some reformulation is useful. Let $d = n - K$ (the degrees of freedom parameter), and substitute

$$\mathbf{y} - \mathbf{X}\boldsymbol{\beta} = \mathbf{y} - \mathbf{X}\mathbf{b} - \mathbf{X}(\boldsymbol{\beta} - \mathbf{b}) = \mathbf{e} - \mathbf{X}(\boldsymbol{\beta} - \mathbf{b})$$

in the exponent. Expanding this produces

$$\left(-\frac{1}{2\sigma^2}\right)(\mathbf{y} - \mathbf{X}\boldsymbol{\beta})'(\mathbf{y} - \mathbf{X}\boldsymbol{\beta}) = \left(-\frac{1}{2}ds^2\right)\left(\frac{1}{\sigma^2}\right) - \frac{1}{2}(\boldsymbol{\beta} - \mathbf{b})'\left(\frac{1}{\sigma^2}\mathbf{X}'\mathbf{X}\right)(\boldsymbol{\beta} - \mathbf{b}).$$

---

[73]Recent work with Monte Carlo integration techniques have enabled researchers to analyze some exceedingly complex problems in the Bayesian context. See, for example, Chib and Greenberg (1995).

[74]These include Judge et al. (1982, 1985), Maddala (1977a), and the canonical reference for econometricians, Zellner (1971). Further topics in Bayesian inference are contained in Zellner (1985). A recent treatment of both Bayesian and sampling theory approaches is Poirier (1995).

After a bit of manipulation (note that $n/2 = d/2 + K/2$), the likelihood may be written

$$L(\boldsymbol{\beta}, \sigma^2 \mid \mathbf{y}, \mathbf{X}) = [2\pi]^{-d/2}[\sigma^2]^{-d/2} e^{-(d/2)(s^2/\sigma^2)} [2\pi]^{-K/2}[\sigma^2]^{-K/2} e^{-(1/2)(\boldsymbol{\beta}-\mathbf{b})'[\sigma^2(\mathbf{X}'\mathbf{X})^{-1}]^{-1}(\boldsymbol{\beta}-\mathbf{b})}.$$

This density embodies all that we have to learn about the parameters from the observed data. Since the data are taken to be constants in the joint density, we may multiply this joint density by the (very carefully chosen), inessential constant function of the observations,

$$A = \frac{\left(\frac{d}{2}s^2\right)^{(d/2)+1}}{\Gamma\left(\frac{d}{2}+1\right)} [2\pi]^{(d/2)+} \mid \mathbf{X}'\mathbf{X} \mid^{-1/2}.$$

For convenience, let $v = d/2$. Then, multiplying $L(\boldsymbol{\beta}, \sigma^2 \mid \mathbf{y}, \mathbf{X})$ by A gives

$$L(\boldsymbol{\beta}, \sigma^2 \mid \mathbf{y}, \mathbf{X}) \propto \frac{[vs^2]^{v+1}}{\Gamma(v+1)} \left(\frac{1}{\sigma^2}\right)^{v} e^{-vs^2(1/\sigma^2)} [2\pi]^{-K/2} \mid \sigma^2(\mathbf{X}'\mathbf{X})^{-1} \mid^{-1/2} \times e^{-1/2(\boldsymbol{\beta}-\mathbf{b})'[\sigma^2(\mathbf{X}'\mathbf{X})^{-1}]^{-1}(\boldsymbol{\beta}-\mathbf{b})}. \qquad \textbf{(6-99)}$$

The likelihood function is proportional to the product of a gamma density for $z = 1/\sigma^2$ with parameters $\lambda = vs^2$ and $P = v + 1$ [see (3-39); this is an **inverted gamma distribution**] and a K-variate normal density for $\boldsymbol{\beta} \mid \sigma^2$ with mean vector $\mathbf{b}$ and covariance matrix $\sigma^2(\mathbf{X}'\mathbf{X})^{-1}$. The reason will be clear shortly.

The departure point for the Bayesian analysis of the model is the specification of a prior distribution. This distribution gives the analyst's prior beliefs about the parameters of the model. One of two approaches is taken. If no prior information is known about the parameters, we can specify a **noninformative prior** that reflects that. We do this by specifying a "flat" prior for the parameter in question:[75]

$$g(\text{parameter}) \propto \text{constant}.$$

There are different ways that one might characterize the lack of prior information. The implication of a flat prior is that within the range of valid values for the parameter, all intervals of equal length—hence, in principle, all values—are equally likely. The second possibility, an **informative prior,** is treated in the next section. The **posterior density** is the result of combining the likelihood function with the prior density. Since it pools the full set of information available to the analyst, *once the data have been drawn,* the posterior density would be interpreted the same way the prior density was before the data were obtained.

---

[75]The fact that this "improper" density might not integrate to one is only a minor difficulty. Any constant of integration would ultimately drop out of the final result. See Zellner (1971, pp. 41–53) for a discussion of noninformative priors.

To begin, we analyze the case in which σ^2 is assumed to be known. This is obviously unrealistic, and we do so only to establish a point of departure. Using (6-97), we construct the **posterior density,**

$$f(\boldsymbol{\beta}\,|\,\mathbf{y}, \mathbf{X}, \sigma^2) = \frac{L(\boldsymbol{\beta}\,|\,\sigma^2, \mathbf{y}, \mathbf{X})g(\boldsymbol{\beta}\,|\,\sigma^2)}{f(\mathbf{y})}$$
$$\propto L(\boldsymbol{\beta}\,|\,\sigma^2, \mathbf{y}, \mathbf{X})g(\boldsymbol{\beta}\,|\,\sigma^2),$$

assuming that the distribution of $\mathbf{y}$ does not depend on $\boldsymbol{\beta}$ or σ^2. Since $g(\boldsymbol{\beta}\,|\,\sigma^2) \propto$ a constant, this is the density in (6-99). For now, write this as

$$f(\boldsymbol{\beta}\,|\,\sigma^2, \mathbf{y}, \mathbf{X}) \propto h(\sigma^2)[2\pi]^{-K/2} \times |\sigma^2(\mathbf{X}'\mathbf{X})^{-1}|^{-1/2}e^{-1/2(\boldsymbol{\beta}-\mathbf{b})'[\sigma^2(\mathbf{X}'\mathbf{X})^{-1}]^{-1}(\boldsymbol{\beta}-\mathbf{b})}, \tag{6-100}$$

where

$$h(\sigma^2) = \frac{[vs^2]^{v+1}}{\Gamma(v+1)}\left[\frac{1}{\sigma^2}\right]^{v} e^{-vs^2(1/\sigma^2)}. \tag{6-101}$$

For the present, we treat $h(\sigma^2)$ simply as a constant that involves σ^2, not as a probability density; (6-100) is *conditional* on σ^2. Thus, the posterior density $f(\boldsymbol{\beta}\,|\,\sigma^2, \mathbf{y}, \mathbf{X})$ is proportional to a multivariate normal distribution with mean $\mathbf{b}$ and covariance matrix $\sigma^2(\mathbf{X}'\mathbf{X})^{-1}$.

This is a familiar result, but it is interpreted differently in this setting. First, we have combined our prior information about $\boldsymbol{\beta}$ (in this case, no information) and the sample information to obtain a *posterior distribution.* Thus, on the basis of the sample data in hand, we obtain a distribution for $\boldsymbol{\beta}$ with mean $\mathbf{b}$ and covariance matrix $\sigma^2(\mathbf{X}'\mathbf{X})^{-1}$. The result is dominated by the sample information, as it should be if there is no prior information. In the absence of any prior information, the mean of the posterior distribution, which is a type of Bayesian point estimate, is the sampling theory estimator.

To generalize the preceding to an unknown σ^2, we specify a noninformative prior distribution for $\ln \sigma$ over the entire real line.[76] By the change of variable formula, if $g(\ln \sigma)$ is constant, $g(\sigma^2)$ is proportional to $1/\sigma^2$.[77] Assuming that $\boldsymbol{\beta}$ and σ^2 are independent, this gives the noninformative joint prior distribution:

$$g(\boldsymbol{\beta}, \sigma^2) = g(\boldsymbol{\beta})g(\sigma^2) \propto \frac{1}{\sigma^2}.$$

We can obtain the **joint posterior distribution** for $\boldsymbol{\beta}$ and σ^2 by using

$$f(\boldsymbol{\beta}, \sigma^2\,|\,\mathbf{y}, \mathbf{X}) = L(\boldsymbol{\beta}\,|\,\sigma^2, \mathbf{y}, \mathbf{X})g(\sigma^2)$$
$$\propto L(\boldsymbol{\beta}\,|\,\sigma^2, \mathbf{y}, \mathbf{X}) \times \frac{1}{\sigma^2}. \tag{6-102}$$

---

[76]See Zellner (1971) for justification of this prior distribution.

[77]Many treatments of this model use σ rather than σ^2 as the parameter of interest. The end results are identical. We have chosen this parameterization because it makes manipulation of the likelihood function with a gamma prior distribution especially convenient. See Zellner (1971, pp. 44–45) for discussion.

For the same reason as before, we multiply $g(\sigma^2)$ by a well-chosen constant, this time $vs^2\Gamma(v+1)/\Gamma(v+2) = vs^2/(v+1)$. Multiplying (6-100) by this constant times $g(\sigma^2)$ and inserting $h(\sigma^2)$ gives the joint posterior for $\boldsymbol{\beta}$ and σ^2, given $\mathbf{y}$ and $\mathbf{X}$:

$$f(\boldsymbol{\beta}, \sigma^2 \mid \mathbf{y}, \mathbf{X}) \propto \frac{[vs^2]^{v+2}}{\Gamma(v+2)} \left[\frac{1}{\sigma^2}\right]^{v+1} e^{-vs^2(1/\sigma^2)}[2\pi]^{-K/2} \left|\sigma^2(\mathbf{X}'\mathbf{X})^{-1}\right|^{-1/2} \times e^{-1/2(\boldsymbol{\beta}-\mathbf{b})'[\sigma^2(\mathbf{X}'\mathbf{X})^{-1}]^{-1}(\boldsymbol{\beta}-\mathbf{b})}.$$

To obtain the marginal posterior distribution for $\boldsymbol{\beta}$, it is now necessary to integrate σ^2 out of the joint distribution (and vice versa to obtain the marginal distribution for σ^2). By collecting the terms, $f(\boldsymbol{\beta}, \sigma^2 \mid \mathbf{y}, \mathbf{X})$ can be written as

$$f(\boldsymbol{\beta}, \sigma^2 \mid \mathbf{y}, \mathbf{X}) \propto A \times \left(\frac{1}{\sigma^2}\right)^{P-1} e^{-\lambda(1/\sigma^2)},$$

where

$$A = \frac{[vs^2]^{v+2}}{\Gamma(v+2)} [2\pi]^{-K/2} \left|(\mathbf{X}'\mathbf{X})^{-1}\right|^{-1/2},$$
$$P = v + 2 + K/2 = (n-K)/2 + 2 + K/2 = (n+4)/2,$$
$$\lambda = vs^2 + \tfrac{1}{2}(\boldsymbol{\beta} - \mathbf{b})'\mathbf{X}'\mathbf{X}(\boldsymbol{\beta} - \mathbf{b}),$$

so, the marginal posterior distribution for $\boldsymbol{\beta}$ is

$$\int_0^\infty f(\boldsymbol{\beta}, \sigma^2 \mid \mathbf{y}, \mathbf{X})\, d\sigma^2 \propto A \int_0^\infty \left(\frac{1}{\sigma^2}\right)^{P-1} e^{-\lambda(1/\sigma^2)}\, d\sigma^2.$$

To do the integration, we have to make a change of variable; $d(1/\sigma^2) = -(1/\sigma^2)^2\, d\sigma^2$, so $d\sigma^2 = -(1/\sigma^2)^{-2}\, d(1/\sigma^2)$. Making the substitution—the sign of the integral changes twice, once for the Jacobian and back again because the integral from $\sigma^2 = 0$ to ∞ is the negative of the integral from $(1/\sigma^2) = 0$ to ∞—we obtain

$$\int_0^\infty f(\boldsymbol{\beta}, \sigma^2 \mid \mathbf{y}, \mathbf{X})\, d\sigma^2 \propto A \int_0^\infty \left(\frac{1}{\sigma^2}\right)^{P-3} e^{-\lambda(1/\sigma^2)}\, d\left(\frac{1}{\sigma^2}\right)$$
$$= A \times \frac{\Gamma(P-2)}{\lambda^{P-2}}.$$

Reinserting the expressions for A, P, and λ produces

$$f(\boldsymbol{\beta} \mid \mathbf{y}, \mathbf{X}) \propto \frac{\dfrac{[vs^2]^{v+2}\Gamma(v+K/2)}{\Gamma(v+2)} [2\pi]^{-K/2} \left|\mathbf{X}'\mathbf{X}\right|^{-1/2}}{[vs^2 + \tfrac{1}{2}(\boldsymbol{\beta} - \mathbf{b})'\mathbf{X}'\mathbf{X}(\boldsymbol{\beta} - \mathbf{b})]^{v+K/2}}. \qquad \textbf{(6-103)}$$

This is proportional to a **multivariate *t* distribution.**[78] This is a generalization of the familiar univariate distribution we have used at various points. This distri-

[78]See, for example, Judge et al. (1985) for details. The expression appears in Zellner (1971, p. 67). Note that the exponent in the denominator is $v + K/2 = n/2$.

bution has a degrees of freedom parameter, $d = n - K$, mean $\mathbf{b}$, and covariance matrix $(d/(d-2))[s^2(\mathbf{X}'\mathbf{X})^{-1}]$. Each element of the K-element vector $\boldsymbol{\beta}$ has a marginal distribution that is the univariate t distribution with degrees of freedom $n - K$, mean b_k, and variance equal to the kth diagonal element of the covariance matrix given earlier. Once again, this is the same as our sampling theory result. The difference is a matter of interpretation. In the current context, the estimated distribution is for $\boldsymbol{\beta}$ and is centered at $\mathbf{b}$.

6.9.2. Point Estimation

The posterior density function embodies the prior and the likelihood and therefore contains all of the researcher's information about the parameters. But for purposes of presenting results, the density is somewhat imprecise, and one normally prefers a point or interval estimate. The natural approach would be to use the mean of the posterior distribution as the estimator. For the noninformative prior, this will be $\mathbf{b}$, the sampling theory estimator.

One might ask at this point, Why bother? These Bayesian point estimates are identical to the sampling theory estimates. All that has changed is our interpretation of the results. This is, however, exactly the way it should be. Remember that we entered this analysis with noninformative priors for $\boldsymbol{\beta}$ and σ^2. Therefore, the only information brought to bear on estimation is the sample data, and it would be peculiar if anything other than the sampling theory estimates emerged at the end. The results do change when our prior brings out of sample information into the estimates, as we shall see below.

The results will also change if we change our motivation for estimating $\boldsymbol{\beta}$. The parameter estimates have been treated thus far as if they were an end in themselves. But in some settings, parameter estimates are obtained so as to enable the analyst to make a decision. Consider then, a **loss function,** $H(\hat{\boldsymbol{\beta}}, \boldsymbol{\beta})$, which quantifies the cost of basing a decision on an estimate $\hat{\boldsymbol{\beta}}$ when the parameter is $\boldsymbol{\beta}$. The expected, or average loss is

$$E_{\beta}[H(\hat{\boldsymbol{\beta}}, \boldsymbol{\beta})] = \int_{\beta} H(\hat{\boldsymbol{\beta}}, \boldsymbol{\beta}) f(\boldsymbol{\beta} \mid \mathbf{y}, \mathbf{X})\, d\boldsymbol{\beta}, \qquad \textbf{(6-104)}$$

where the weighting function is the marginal posterior density. (The joint density for $\boldsymbol{\beta}$ and σ^2 would be used if the loss were defined over both.) The Bayesian point estimate is the parameter vector that minimizes the expected loss. If the loss function is a quadratic form in $(\hat{\boldsymbol{\beta}} - \boldsymbol{\beta})$, then the mean of the posterior distribution is the "minimum expected loss" (MELO) estimator. The proof is simple. For this case,

$$E[H(\hat{\boldsymbol{\beta}}, \boldsymbol{\beta}) \mid \mathbf{y}, \mathbf{x}] = E[\tfrac{1}{2}(\hat{\boldsymbol{\beta}} - \boldsymbol{\beta})'\mathbf{W}(\hat{\boldsymbol{\beta}} - \boldsymbol{\beta}) \mid \mathbf{y}, \mathbf{X}].$$

To minimize this, we can use the result that

$$\begin{aligned} \partial E[H(\hat{\boldsymbol{\beta}}, \boldsymbol{\beta}) \mid \mathbf{y}, \mathbf{X}]/\partial\hat{\boldsymbol{\beta}} &= E[\partial H(\hat{\boldsymbol{\beta}}, \boldsymbol{\beta})/\partial\hat{\boldsymbol{\beta}} \mid \mathbf{y}, \mathbf{X}] \\ &= E[-\mathbf{W}(\hat{\boldsymbol{\beta}} - \boldsymbol{\beta}) \mid \mathbf{y}, \mathbf{X}]. \end{aligned}$$

The minimum is found by equating this derivative to $\mathbf{0}$, whence, since $-\mathbf{W}$ is irrelevant, $\hat{\boldsymbol{\beta}} = E[\boldsymbol{\beta}|\mathbf{y}, \mathbf{X}]$. This kind of loss function would state that errors in the positive and negative direction are equally bad, and large errors are much worse than small errors. If the loss function were a linear function, instead, then the MELO estimator would be the median of the posterior distribution. These are the same in the case of the noninformative prior that we have just examined.

6.9.3. Interval Estimation

The counterpart to a confidence interval in this setting is an interval of the posterior distribution that contains a specified probability. Clearly, it is desirable to have this interval be as narrow as possible. For a unimodal density, this corresponds to an interval within which the density function is higher than any points outside it, which justifies the term ***highest posterior density (HPD) interval***. For the case we have analyzed, which involves a symmetric distribution, we would form the HPD interval for $\boldsymbol{\beta}$ around the least squares estimate $\mathbf{b}$, with terminal values taken from the standard t tables.

6.9.4. Estimation with an Informative Prior Density

Once we leave the simple case of noninformative priors, matters become quite complicated, both at a practical level and, methodologically, in terms of just where the prior comes from. The integration of σ^2 out of the joint posterior in (6-100) is complicated by itself. It is made much more so if the prior distributions of $\boldsymbol{\beta}$ and σ^2 are at all involved. Partly to offset these difficulties, researchers usually use what is called a **conjugate prior,** which is one that has the same form as the conditional density and is therefore amenable to the integration needed to obtain the marginal distributions.[79]

Suppose that we assume that the prior beliefs about $\boldsymbol{\beta}$ may be summarized in a K-variate normal distribution with mean $\boldsymbol{\beta}_0$ and variance matrix $\boldsymbol{\Sigma_\theta}$. Once again, it is illuminating to begin with the case in which σ^2 is assumed to be known. Proceeding in exactly the same fashion as before, we would obtain

[79]Note that our choice of noninformative prior for ln σ led to a convenient prior for σ^2 in our derivation of the posterior for $\boldsymbol{\beta}$. The idea that the prior can be specified arbitrarily in whatever form is mathematically convenient is very troubling; it is supposed to represent the accumulated prior belief about the parameter. On the other hand, it could be argued that the conjugate prior is the posterior of a previous analysis, which could justify its form. The issue of how priors should be specified is one of the focal points of the methodological debate. "Non-Bayesians" argue that it is disingenuous to claim the methodological high ground and then base the crucial prior density in a model purely on the basis of mathematical convenience. In a small sample, this assumed prior is going to dominate the results, while in a large one, the sampling theory estimates will dominate anyway.

the following result: The posterior density of $\boldsymbol{\beta}$ conditioned on σ^2 and the data will be normal with

$$\begin{aligned} E(\boldsymbol{\beta} \mid \sigma^2, \mathbf{y}, \mathbf{X}) &= \{\boldsymbol{\Sigma}_0^{-1} + [\sigma^2(\mathbf{X}'\mathbf{X})^{-1}]^{-1}\}^{-1}\{\boldsymbol{\Sigma}_0^{-1}\boldsymbol{\beta}_0 + [\sigma^2(\mathbf{X}'\mathbf{X})^{-1}]^{-1}\mathbf{b}\} \\ &= \mathbf{F}\boldsymbol{\beta}_0 + (\mathbf{I} - \mathbf{F})\mathbf{b}, \end{aligned} \quad \textbf{(6-105)}$$

where

$$\begin{aligned} \mathrm{F} &= \{\boldsymbol{\Sigma}_0^{-1} + [\sigma^2(\mathbf{X}'\mathbf{X})^{-1}]^{-1}\}^{-1}\boldsymbol{\Sigma}_0^{-1} \\ &= \{[\text{prior variance}]^{-1} + [\text{conditional variance}]^{-1}\}^{-1}[\text{prior variance}] \end{aligned}$$

This is a matrix weighted average of the prior and the least squares (sample) coefficient estimates, where the weights are the inverses of the prior and the conditional covariance matrices.[80] The smaller the variance of the estimator, the larger its weight, which makes sense. Also, still taking σ^2 as known, we can write the variance of the posterior normal distribution as

$$\mathrm{Var}[\boldsymbol{\beta} \mid \mathrm{y}, \mathbf{X}, \sigma^2] = \{\boldsymbol{\Sigma}_0^{-1} + [\sigma^2(\mathbf{X}'\mathbf{X})^{-1}]^{-1}\}^{-1}. \quad \textbf{(6-106)}$$

Notice that the posterior variance combines the prior and conditional variances on the basis of their inverses.[81] We may interpret the noninformative prior as having infinite elements in $\boldsymbol{\Sigma}_0$, which would reduce this to the earlier case.

Once again, it is necessary to account for the unknown σ^2. If our prior over σ^2 is to be informative as well, the resulting distribution can be extremely cumbersome. A conjugate prior for β and σ^2 that can be used is

$$g(\boldsymbol{\beta}, \sigma^2) = g(\boldsymbol{\beta} \mid \sigma^2)g(\sigma^2), \quad \textbf{(6-107)}$$

where $g(\boldsymbol{\beta} \mid \sigma^2)$ is normal, with mean $\boldsymbol{\beta}^0$ and variance $\sigma^2\mathbf{A}$ and **(6-108)**

$$g(\sigma^2) = \frac{[m\sigma_0^2]^{m+1}}{\Gamma(m+1)}\left(\frac{1}{\sigma^2}\right)^m e^{-m\sigma_0^2(1/\sigma^2)}. \quad \textbf{(6-109)}$$

This distribution is an **inverted gamma distribution.** It implies that $1/\sigma^2$ has a gamma distribution. The prior mean for σ^2 is σ_0^2 and the prior variance is $\sigma_0^4/(m-1)$.[82] The product in (6-107) produces what is called a **normal-gamma** prior, which is the natural conjugate prior for this form of the model. By integrating out σ^2, we would obtain the prior marginal for $\boldsymbol{\beta}$ alone, which

[80]Note that it will not follow that individual elements of the posterior mean vector lie between those of $\boldsymbol{\beta}_0$ and $\mathbf{b}$. See Judge et al. (1985, p. 109–110) and Chamberlain and Leamer (1976).

[81]Precisely this estimator was proposed by Theil and Goldberger (1961) as a way of combining a previously obtained estimate of a parameter and a current body of new data. They called this a "mixed estimator."

[82]You can show this by using gamma integrals. Note that the density is a function of $1/\sigma^2 = 1/x$ in the formula of (3-39), so to obtain $E[\sigma^2]$, we use the analog of $E[1/x] = \lambda/(P-1)$ and $E[(1/x)^2] = \lambda^2/[(P-1)(P-2)]$. In the density for $(1/\sigma^2)$, the counterparts to λ and P are $m\sigma_0^2$ and $m+1$.

would be a multivariate t distribution.[83] Combining (6-107) with (6-98) produces the joint posterior distribution for $\boldsymbol{\beta}$ and σ^2. Finally, the marginal posterior distribution for $\boldsymbol{\beta}$ is obtained by integrating out σ^2. It has been shown that this posterior distribution is multivariate t with

$$E[\boldsymbol{\beta} \mid \mathbf{y}, \mathbf{X}] = \{[\bar{\sigma}^2\mathbf{A}]^{-1} + [\bar{\sigma}^2(\mathbf{X}'\mathbf{X})^{-1}]^{-1}\}^{-1}\{[\bar{\sigma}^2\mathbf{A}]^{-1}\boldsymbol{\beta}^0 + [\bar{\sigma}^2(\mathbf{X}'\mathbf{X})^{-1}]^{-1}\mathbf{b}\} \tag{6-110}$$

and

$$\mathrm{Var}[\boldsymbol{\beta} \mid \mathbf{y}, \mathbf{X}] = \left(\frac{j}{j-2}\right)\{[\bar{\sigma}^2\mathbf{A}]^{-1} + [\bar{\sigma}^2(\mathbf{X}'\mathbf{X})^{-1}]^{-1}\}^{-1}, \tag{6-111}$$

where j is a degrees of freedom parameter

$$j = n - K + m \tag{6-112}$$

and $\bar{\sigma}^2$ is the Bayesian estimate of σ^2. The prior degrees of freedom m is a parameter of the prior distribution for σ^2 that would have been determined at the outset. (See the following example.) Once again, it is clear that as the amount of data increases, the posterior density, and the estimates thereof, converge to the sampling theory results.

EXAMPLE 6.26 Bayesian Estimates of a Consumption Function

In Example 6.7, an estimate of the marginal propensity to consume is obtained using 10 observations from 1970 to 1979, with the following results:

estimated MPC:	0.9793,
variance of b:	$0.0316^2 = 0.0009989$,
degrees of freedom:	$10 - 2 = 8$,
estimated σ:	8.192.

A classical 95 percent confidence interval for β based on these estimates is $\langle 0.90641, 1.1251\rangle$, as given earlier. Based on noninformative priors for β and σ^2, we would estimate the posterior density for β to be univariate t with eight degrees of freedom, with mean 0.9793 and variance $(8/6)0.0009989 = 0.0013319$. An HPD interval for β would coincide with the confidence interval.

The 11 observations from 1940 to 1950 give the following results:

estimated MPC:	0.9596,
variance of b:	$0.0895^2 = 0.0081025$,
degrees of freedom:	$11 - 3 = 8$,
estimated σ:	9.0088.

(The second regression includes a binary variable indicating the years 1942–1944.)

[83]Full details of this (lengthy) derivation appear in Judge et al. (1985, pp. 106–110) and in Zellner (1971).

We take the earlier estimate and its estimated distribution as our prior for β and obtain a posterior density for β based on an informative prior instead. We assume for this exercise that σ^2 may be taken as known at the sample value of 8.192. Then

$$\bar{b} = \left[\frac{1}{0.0081025} + \frac{1}{0.0009989}\right]^{-1}\left[\frac{0.9596}{0.0081025} + \frac{0.9793}{0.0009989}\right] = 0.9771.$$

The weights in the average are 0.1109 and 0.8891, which gives an estimated posterior mean of 0.9771. The posterior variance is the inverse in brackets, which is 0.0008881. Since σ^2 is assumed to be known, the posterior distribution is normal with this mean and variance. An HPD interval can be formed in the familiar fashion. Using the posterior standard deviation of 0.0298, we find that a 95 percent HPD interval for β is $0.9771 \pm 1.96(0.0298) = \langle 0.9187, 1.0355\rangle$. Note that this is narrower than the earlier interval; this is the value of the prior information.

6.9.5. Hypothesis Testing

The Bayesian methodology treats the classical approach to hypothesis testing with a large amount of skepticism. Two issues are especially problematic. First, a close examination of only the work we have done in Section 6.7 will show that because we are using consistent estimators, with a large enough sample, we will ultimately reject almost any hypothesis, unless we adjust the significance level of the test downward as the sample size increases. Second, the all-or-nothing approach of either rejecting or not rejecting a hypothesis provides no method of simply sharpening our beliefs. Even the most committed of analysts might be reluctant to discard a strongly held prior based on a single sample of data, yet this is what the sampling methodology mandates. The Bayesian approach to hypothesis testing is much more appealing in this regard. Indeed, the approach might be more appropriately called "comparing hypotheses," since it essentially involves making an assessment of which of two hypotheses has a higher probability of being correct.

The Bayesian approach to hypothesis testing bears large similarity to Bayesian estimation.[84] We have formulated two hypotheses, a "null," denoted H_0, and an alternative, denoted H_1. These need not be complementary, as in H_0: "statement A is true" versus H_1: "statement A is not true," since the intent of the procedure is not to reject one hypothesis in favor of the other. For simplicity, however, we will confine our attention to hypotheses about the parameters in the regression model, which often are complementary. Assume that before we begin our experimentation (data gathering, statistical analysis) we are

[84]For extensive discussion, see Zellner and Siow (1980) and Zellner (1984, pp. 275–305).

able to assign **prior probabilities** $P(H_0)$ and $P(H_1)$ to the two hypotheses. The **prior odds ratio** is simply the ratio

$$\text{Odds}_{\text{prior}} + \frac{P(H_0)}{P(H_1)}.$$

For example, one's uncertainty about the sign of a parameter might be summarized in a prior odds over $H_0: \beta \geq 0$ versus $H_1: \beta < 0$ of $0.5/0.5 = 1$. After the sample evidence is gathered, the prior will be modified, so the posterior is, in general,

$$\text{Odds}_{\text{posterior}} = B_{01} \times \frac{P(H_0)}{P(H_1)}.$$

The value B_{01} is called the **Bayes factor** for comparing the two hypotheses. It summarizes the effect of the sample data on the prior odds. The end result, $\text{Odds}_{\text{posterior}}$, is a new odds ratio that can be carried forward as the prior in a subsequent analysis.

The Bayes factor is computed by assessing the likelihoods of the data observed under the two hypotheses. We return to our first departure point, the likelihood of the data, given the parameters:

$$f(\mathbf{y} \mid \boldsymbol{\beta}, \sigma^2, \mathbf{X}) = [2\pi\sigma^2]^{-n/2} e^{(-1/(2\sigma^2))(\mathbf{y}-\mathbf{X}\boldsymbol{\beta})'(\mathbf{y}-\mathbf{X}\boldsymbol{\beta})}. \quad \textbf{(6-113)}$$

Based on our priors for the parameters, the expected, or average likelihood, assuming that hypothesis j is true ($j = 0, 1$), is

$$f(\mathbf{y} \mid \mathbf{X}, H_j) = E_{\boldsymbol{\beta},\sigma^2}[f(\mathbf{y} \mid \boldsymbol{\beta}, \sigma^2, \mathbf{X}, H_j)]$$

$$= \int_{\sigma^2} \int_{\boldsymbol{\beta}} f(\mathbf{y} \mid \boldsymbol{\beta}, \sigma^2, \mathbf{X}, H_j) g(\boldsymbol{\beta}, \sigma^2) \, d\boldsymbol{\beta} \, d\sigma^2.$$

(This is also the **predictive density** for $\mathbf{y}$.) Therefore, based on the observed data, we use Bayes's theorem to reassess the probability of H_j; the posterior probability is

$$P(H_j \mid \mathbf{y}, \mathbf{X}) = \frac{f(\mathbf{y} \mid \mathbf{X}, H_j) P(H_j)}{f(\mathbf{y})}.$$

The posterior odds ratio is $P(H_0 \mid \mathbf{y}, \mathbf{X})/P(H_1 \mid \mathbf{y}, \mathbf{X})$, so the Bayes's factor is

$$B_{01} = \frac{f(\mathbf{y} \mid H_0)}{f(\mathbf{y} \mid H_1)}.$$

EXAMPLE 6.27 Posterior Odds for the Classical Regression Model

Zellner (1971) analyzes the setting in which there are two possible explanations for the variation in a dependent variable y:

$$\text{model } 0\text{: } y = \mathbf{x}_0'\boldsymbol{\beta}_0 + \epsilon_0$$

and

$$\text{model 1: } y = \mathbf{x}_1'\boldsymbol{\beta}_1 + \epsilon_1.$$

We will briefly sketch his results. We form *informative* priors for $[\boldsymbol{\beta}, \sigma^2]_j, j = 0, 1$, as specified in (6-107) and (6-108), that is, multivariate normal and inverted gamma, respectively. Zellner then derives the Bayes's factor for the posterior odds ratio. The derivation is lengthy and complicated, but for large n, with some simplifying assumptions, a useful formulation emerges. First, assume that the priors for σ_0^2 and σ_1^2 are the same. Second, assume that $[|\mathbf{A}_0^{-1}|/|\mathbf{A}_0^{-1} + \mathbf{X}_0'\mathbf{X}_0|]/[|\mathbf{A}_1^{-1}|/|\mathbf{A}_1^{-1} + \mathbf{X}_1'\mathbf{X}_1|] \to 1$. The first of these would be the usual situation, in which the uncertainty concerns the covariation between y and $\mathbf{x}_i$, not the amount of residual variation (lack of fit). The second concerns the relative amounts of information in the prior ($\mathbf{A}$) versus the likelihood ($\mathbf{X}'\mathbf{X}$). These are the inverses of the covariance matrices, or the **precision matrices.** [Note how these two matrices form the matrix weights in the computation of the posterior mean in (6-105).] Zellner (p. 310) discusses this assumption at some length. With these two assumptions, he shows that as n grows large,[85]

$$B_{01} \approx \left(\frac{s_0^2}{s_1^2}\right)^{-(n+m)/2} = \left(\frac{1 - R_0^2}{1 - R_1^2}\right)^{-(n+m)/2}.$$

Therefore, the result favors the model that provides the better fit using R^2 as the fit measure. If we stretch Zellner's analysis a bit by interpreting model 1 as "the model" and model 0 as "no model" (i.e., the relevant part of $\boldsymbol{\beta}_0 = \mathbf{0}$, so $R^2 = 0$), then the ratio simplifies to

$$B_{01} = (1 - R^2)^{(n+m)/2}.$$

Thus, the better the fit of the regression, the lower the Bayes's factor in favor of model 0 (no model), which makes intuitive sense.

Zellner and Siow (1980) have continued this analysis with noninformative priors for $\boldsymbol{\beta}$ and σ_j^2. Specifically, they use the flat prior for $\ln \sigma$ [see (6-102)] and a multivariate Cauchy prior (which has infinite variances) for $\boldsymbol{\beta}$. Their main result (3.10) is

$$B_{01} = \frac{\frac{1}{2}\sqrt{\pi}}{\Gamma[(k+1)/2]}\left(\frac{n-K}{2}\right)^{k/2}(1 - R^2)^{1/2(n-K-1)}.$$

This is very much like the previous result, with some slight differences due to degrees of freedom corrections and due to the several approximations used to reach the first one.

---

[85]A ratio of exponentials that appears in Zellner's result (his equation 10.50) is omitted. To the order of approximation in the result, this ratio vanishes from the final result. (Personal correspondence from A. Zellner to the author.)

EXERCISES

1. Production data for 22 firms in a certain industry produce the following, where y = ln output and x = ln labor hours input:

$$\bar{y} = 20, \qquad \sum_{i=1}^{n} (y_i - \bar{y})^2 = 100,$$

$$\bar{x} = 10, \qquad \sum_{i=1}^{n} (x_i - \bar{x})^2 = 60,$$

$$\sum_{i=1}^{n} (x_i - \bar{x})(y_i - \bar{y}) = 30.$$

(a) Compute the least squares estimates of α and β in the model $y = \alpha + \beta x + \epsilon$.
(b) Test the hypothesis that $\beta = 1$.
(c) Form a 99% confidence interval for σ^2, the variance of ϵ.

2. Data from a different industry are used to obtain the following estimated regression:

$$\hat{y} = 25 + 0.4 \qquad R^2 = 0.2, \qquad \bar{y} = 35, \qquad n = 12, \qquad \sum_i (x_i - \bar{x})^2 = 100.$$

Test the hypothesis that the slopes are the same in this regression and the one in the previous problem assuming that the disturbance variances are the same. [Hint: For independent samples, there are two approaches. If it can be assumed that the disturbance variances in the two models are equal, the two samples can be pooled to estimate the common σ^2. Determine the pooled moments by manipulating the results above. Then, the statistic $(b_1 - b_2)/\{s^2[(1/(\mathbf{x}_1'\mathbf{M}^0\mathbf{x}_1)) + (1/(\mathbf{x}_2'\mathbf{M}^0\mathbf{x}_2))]\}^{1/2}$ may be referred to the t distribution with $n_1 + n_2 - 4$ degrees of freedom. If the assumption of equal variances is untenable, the statistic $(b_1 - b_2)/\{\text{Est. Var}[b_1] + \text{Est. Var}[b_2]\}^{1/2}$ will be approximately distributed as standard normal.] Carry out the test using both methods.

3. Suppose that you have two independent unbiased estimators of the same parameter θ, say $\hat{\theta}_1$ and $\hat{\theta}_2$, with different variances v_1 and v_2. What linear combination $\hat{\theta} = c_1\hat{\theta}_1 + c_2\hat{\theta}_2$ is the minimum variance unbiased estimator of θ? Use your result to compute the minimum variance unbiased estimator of the common slope in the two regressions in Exercises 1 and 2.

4. For the data in Exercise 1, what is the R^2 in the regression of y on x? Now, suppose that the regression is fit without a constant term, and the computer program computes the R^2 using

$$R^2 = 1 - \frac{\mathbf{e}'\mathbf{e}}{\sum_i (y_i - \bar{y})^2}.$$

What value will be reported? What if it uses

$$R^2 = \frac{b^2 \sum_i (x_i - \bar{x})^2}{\sum_i (y_i - \bar{y})^2}$$

instead? What value will be reported? What is the appropriate value to report?

5. We are interested in studying salary differences between two professions. Our sample consists of 60 individuals from profession A and 40 from B. The average salary in B is 1. The average salary in the entire sample is 0.75. If we compute a least squares regression of salaries on a constant and a variable that is simply 0 for all individuals in A and 1 for those in B, what will be the constant and slope? If the standard deviations of the two samples are 0.2 for profession A and 0.3 for profession B, what are the estimates of the variances and covariance of the two estimates? What is the R^2 in the regression? (For further applications, see Section 8.2.)

6. Suppose that a regression of the balance of trade with a particular country gives results

$$y = 100{,}000 + 0.6x + e, \quad R^2 = 0.4,$$

using yearly observations quoted in 1972 dollars. Suppose that the figures were rescaled to 1982 dollars by multiplying by 0.74. What would have been obtained for the constant and slope? Based on the previous figures, would you be able to determine the least squares results if the figures were quoted in the currency of the other country instead if you knew the exchange rates?

7. Three variables, N, D, and Y, all have zero means and unit variances. A fourth variable is $C = N + D$. In the regression of C on Y, the slope is 0.8. In the regression of C on N, the slope is 0.5. In the regression of D on Y, the slope is 0.4. What is the sum of squared residuals in the regression of C on D? There are 21 observations and all moments are computed using $1/(n - 1)$ as the divisor.

8. Prove that the least squares intercept estimator in the classical regression model is the minimum variance linear unbiased estimator.

9. Suppose that the data for a regression are given in terms of deviations from the sample means. What is the expected value of the slope in the regression of $(y_i - \bar{y})$ on $(x_i - \bar{x})$ if it is computed without a constant term? Suppose that only the data on x are in mean deviation form. Now what is the expected value of the slope estimator? Finally, suppose that only y is in mean deviation form. What is the expected value of the slope estimator in the regression of the centered y's on the uncentered x's, assuming that the true value of the intercept is not zero?

10. Consider the simple regression $y_i = \beta x_i + \epsilon_i$.

(a) What is the minimum mean squared error linear estimator of β? [Hint: Let the estimator be $[\hat{\beta} = \mathbf{c}'\mathbf{y}]$. Choose $\mathbf{c}$ to minimize $\text{Var}[\hat{\beta}] + [E(\hat{\beta} - \beta)]^2$. The answer is a function of the unknown parameters.]

(b) For the estimator in part a, show that ratio of the mean squared error of $\hat{\beta}$ to that of the ordinary least squares estimator b is

$$\frac{\text{MSE}[\hat{\boldsymbol{\beta}}]}{\text{MSE}[b]} = \frac{\tau^2}{(1 + \tau^2)},$$

where

$$\tau^2 = \frac{\beta^2}{[\sigma^2/\mathbf{x}'\mathbf{x}]}.$$

Note that τ is the square of the population analog to the "t ratio" for testing the hypothesis that $\beta = 0$, which is given after (6-47). How do you interpret the behavior of this ratio as $\tau \to \infty$? (For some further discussion of this result and some related issues, see Section 8.5.)

11. Suppose that the classical regression model applies but that the true value of the constant is zero. Compare the variance of the least squares slope estimator computed without a constant term to that of the estimator computed with an unnecessary constant term.

12. The next year's data for the consumption data given in Table 6.1 are \$1026.1 billion and \$931.8 billion for disposable income and consumption, respectively. Reestimate the regression with this new information; then use the updated regression to compute a 95 percent forecast interval for consumption for 1981 assuming that disposable income is forecasted to be \$1037.4 billion.

13. Suppose that the regression model is

$$y_i = \alpha + \beta x_i + \epsilon_i, \quad \text{where } f(\epsilon_i) = (1/\lambda)e^{-\epsilon_i/\lambda}, \epsilon_i 0.$$

This is rather a peculiar model in that all the disturbances are assumed to be positive. Note that the disturbances have $E[\epsilon_i] = \lambda$. Show that the least squares slope is unbiased but that the intercept is biased.

14. For the regression model without a constant term in Exercise 10, prove that the estimator $\bar{y}/\bar{x}$ is unbiased, and show that its variance is greater than that of the ordinary least squares estimator.

15. As a profit maximizing monopolist, you face the demand curve

$$Q = \alpha + \beta P + \epsilon.$$

In the past, you have set the following prices and sold the accompanying quantities:

Q	3	3	7	6	10	15	16	13	9	15	9	15	12	18	21
P	18	16	17	12	15	15	4	13	11	6	8	10	7	7	7

Suppose that your marginal cost is 10. Based on the least squares regression, compute a 95 percent confidence interval for the expected value of the profit maximizing output.

16. For the bivariate distribution in Exercise 16 of Chapter 4, it is shown (claimed) in part f that

$$f(x \mid y) = \frac{e^{-\beta y}(\beta y)^x}{x!}$$

It follows that $E[x \mid y] = \beta y$.

(a) Does this suggest an alternative estimator for β to the maximum likelihood estimator of part a of that problem?

(b) It can also be shown (can you do it?) that in the conditional distribution in part d of that exercise

$$E[y \mid x] = \alpha x, \quad \text{where } \alpha = 1/(\beta + \theta).$$

Does this suggest an alternative estimator to the maximum likelihood estimator of α implied by part a of that exercise? What is the MLE of α for that bivariate distribution? What is its asymptotic distribution?

17. Using the matrices of sums of squares and cross products immediately preceding Section 6.3.3, compute the coefficients in the multiple regression of real investment on a constant, real GNP and the interest rate. The sum of squares of real investment is 0.63652. Compute R^2 and the estimate of the covariance matrix of the estimated slopes and constant term. Test the individual hypotheses that the two slopes are zero. Test the joint hypothesis that both slopes are zero.

18. The following matrix gives the slope in the simple regression of the column variable on the row variable:

$$\begin{matrix} & y & x_1 & x_2 & \\ \mathbf{A} = & \begin{bmatrix} 1 & 0.03 & 0.36 \\ 0.4 & 1 & 0.3 \\ 1.20 & 0.075 & 1 \end{bmatrix} & \begin{matrix} y \\ x_1 \\ x_2 \end{matrix} \end{matrix}$$

For example, if y is regressed on x_1, the slope is 0.4, but, if x_1 is regressed on y, the slope is 0.03. All variables have zero means, so the constant terms in all regressions are zero. What are the two slope coefficients in the multiple regression of y on x_1 and x_2?

19. Assuming that x_1 and x_2 have zero sample means and zero sample correlation, where is the inconsistency in the results given below? (Estimated standard errors of the parameter estimates are given in parentheses.)

$$\begin{aligned} \hat{y} = 3 + &\underset{(0.25)}{2x_1} + \underset{(0.25)}{1x_2}, \quad R^2 = 0.77, \\ & \qquad\qquad\qquad n = 23. \end{aligned}$$

Analysis of Variance			
	Variation	*Degrees of Freedom*	*Mean Square*
Regression	68	2	34
Residual	20	20	1
Total	88	22	4

20. If the interest rate were added to the regression of investment on a constant, the time trend, and GNP that is given after Example 6.8, what would be its coefficient in the multiple regression? [Hint: You will find the necessary sums in the matrix you used for Exercise 17.]

21. For the regression in the previous problem, what is the new value of R^2 after you add the interest to the regression?

22. The data below relate to gasoline consumption in the United States from the years 1960 to 1986:

(a) Compute the multiple regression of G on all the other explanatory variables, including the time trend, and report all results. Do the signs of the estimates agree with your expectations?

(b) Test the hypothesis that at least in regard to demand for gasoline, consumers do not differentiate between changes in the prices of new and used cars.

(c) Estimate the own price elasticity of demand, the income elasticity, and the cross-price elasticity with respect to changes in the price of public transportation.

(d) Reestimate the regression in logarithms so that the coefficients are direct estimates of the elasticities. (Do not use the log of the time trend.) How do your estimates compare with the results in the previous question? Which specification do you prefer?

(e) Notice that the price indices for the automobile market are normalized to 1967 whereas the aggregate price indices are anchored at 1982. Does this discrepancy affect the results? How? If you were to renormalize the indices so that they were all 1.000 in 1982, how would your results change? Note that this would be an application of the principle in Exercise 28. What is the **P** matrix?

The variables are as follows:

G = total gasoline consumption, computed as current dollar expenditure divided by the price index.

P_g = price index for gasoline.

Y = per capita real disposable income.

P_{nc} = price index for new cars.

P_{uc} = price index for used cars.

P_{pt} = price index for public transportation.

P_d = aggregate price index for consumer durable goods.

P_n = aggregate price index for consumer nondurable goods.
P_s = aggregate price index for consumer services.

Year	G	P_g	Y	P_{nc}	P_{uc}	P_{pt}	P_d	P_n	P_s
1960	129.7	.925	6036	1.045	.836	.810	.444	.331	.302
1961	131.3	.914	6113	1.045	.869	.846	.448	.335	.307
1962	137.1	.919	6271	1.041	.948	.874	.457	.338	.314
1963	141.6	.918	6378	1.035	.960	.885	.463	.343	.320
1964	148.8	.914	6727	1.032	1.001	.901	.470	.347	.325
1965	155.9	.949	7027	1.009	.994	.919	.471	.353	.332
1966	164.9	.970	7280	.991	.970	.952	.475	.366	.342
1967	171.0	1.000	7513	1.000	1.000	1.000	.483	.375	.353
1968	183.4	1.014	7728	1.028	1.028	1.046	.501	.390	.368
1969	195.8	1.047	7891	1.044	1.031	1.127	.514	.409	.386
1970	207.4	1.056	8134	1.076	1.043	1.285	.527	.427	.407
1971	218.3	1.063	8322	1.120	1.102	1.377	.547	.442	.431
1972	226.8	1.076	8562	1.110	1.105	1.434	.555	.458	.451
1973	237.9	1.181	9042	1.111	1.176	1.448	.566	.497	.474
1974	225.8	1.599	8867	1.175	1.226	1.480	.604	.572	.513
1975	232.4	1.708	8944	1.276	1.464	1.586	.659	.615	.556
1976	241.7	1.779	9175	1.357	1.679	1.742	.695	.638	.598
1977	249.2	1.882	9381	1.429	1.828	1.824	.727	.671	.648
1978	261.3	1.963	9735	1.538	1.865	1.878	.769	.719	.698
1979	248.9	2.656	9829	1.660	2.010	2.003	.821	.800	.756
1980	226.8	3.691	9722	1.793	2.081	2.516	.892	.894	.839
1981	225.6	4.109	9769	1.902	2.569	3.120	.957	.969	.926
1982	228.8	3.894	9725	1.976	2.964	3.460	1.000	1.000	1.000
1983	239.6	3.764	9930	2.026	3.297	3.626	1.041	1.021	1.062
1984	244.7	3.707	10421	2.085	3.757	3.852	1.038	1.050	1.117
1985	245.8	3.738	10563	2.152	3.797	4.028	1.045	1.075	1.173
1986	269.4	2.921	10780	2.240	3.632	4.264	1.053	1.069	1.224

Source: All data are from the *Economic Report of the President: 1987,* Council of Economic Advisors, 1987.

23. Suppose for purposes of this exercise that the variable Y in Exercise 22 is total expenditure on consumer durables, nondurables, and services rather than total income (which includes savings as well). Suppose as well that E_d, E_n, and E_s are the expenditures on the three categories. As defined, $Y = E_d + E_n + E_s$. Now, consider the expenditure system

$$E_d = \alpha_d + \beta_d Y + \gamma_{dd} P_d + \gamma_{dn} P_n + \gamma_{ds} P_s + \epsilon_d,$$
$$E_n = \alpha_n + \beta_n Y + \gamma_{nd} P_d + \gamma_{nn} P_n + \gamma_{ns} P_s + \epsilon_n,$$
$$E_s = \alpha_s + \beta_s Y + \gamma_{sd} P_d + \gamma_{sn} P_n + \gamma_{ss} P_s + \epsilon_s.$$

If all equations are estimated by ordinary least squares, prove that the sum of the income coefficients will be 1 and the four other column sums in the preceding model will be zero. (Some applications of demand systems such as this are discussed in Section 15.5.)

24. Prove the result in (6-29).

25. Prove that the adjusted R^2 in (6-37) rises (falls) when variable $\mathbf{x}_k$ is deleted from the regression if the square of the t ratio on $\mathbf{x}_k$ in the multiple regression is less (greater) than 1.

26. Consider the multiple regression of $\mathbf{y}$ on K variables $\mathbf{X}$ and an additional variable $\mathbf{z}$. Prove that the true variance of the least squares estimator of the slopes on $\mathbf{X}$ is larger when $\mathbf{z}$ is included in the regression than when it is not. Does the same hold for the sample estimate of this covariance matrix? Why or why not?

27. An estimate of a Cobb–Douglas production function is given in the discussion preceding Example 7.5 in the next chapter. The basic equation is of the form $\ln Y = \alpha + \beta_k \ln K + \beta_l \ln L + \epsilon$. We are interested in the issue of constant returns to scale, which is implied by $\beta_k + \beta_l = 1$. This hypothesis is tested in Example 7.6. For present purposes, construct a confidence region for these two parameters in the manner of Example 7.4. On the same figure, draw the line that represents the set of points for which $\beta_k + \beta_l = 1$.

28. Consider the least squares regression of $\mathbf{y}$ on K variables (with a constant) $\mathbf{X}$. Consider an alternative set of regressors $\mathbf{Z} = \mathbf{XP}$, where $\mathbf{P}$ is a nonsingular matrix. Thus, each column of $\mathbf{Z}$ is a mixture of some of the columns of $\mathbf{X}$. Prove that the residual vectors in the regressions of $\mathbf{y}$ on $\mathbf{X}$ and $\mathbf{y}$ on $\mathbf{Z}$ are identical. What relevance does this have to the question of changing the fit of a regression by changing the units of measurement of the independent variables?

29. Suppose that $\mathbf{b}$ is the least squares coefficient vector in the regression of $\mathbf{y}$ on $\mathbf{X}$ and that $\mathbf{c}$ is any other $K \times 1$ vector. Prove that the difference in the two sums of squared residuals is

$$(\mathbf{y} - \mathbf{Xc})'(\mathbf{y} - \mathbf{Xc}) - (\mathbf{y} - \mathbf{Xb})'(\mathbf{y} - \mathbf{Xb}) = (\mathbf{c} - \mathbf{b})'\mathbf{X}'\mathbf{X}(\mathbf{c} - \mathbf{b}).$$

Prove that this difference is positive.

30. *(Once again.)* Suppose that you estimate a multiple regression first with then without a constant. Whether the R^2 is higher in the second case than the first will depend in part on how it is computed. Using the (relatively) standard method

$$R^2 = 1 - \frac{\mathbf{e}'\mathbf{e}}{\mathbf{y}'\mathbf{M}^0\mathbf{y}},$$

which regression will have a higher R^2? [Hint: Consider Exercise 29.]

31. In the least squares regression of $\mathbf{y}$ on a constant and $\mathbf{X}$, to compute the regression coefficients on $\mathbf{X}$, we can first transform $\mathbf{y}$ to deviations from the mean $\bar{y}$ and, likewise, transform each column of **X** to deviations from the respective column mean; second, regress the transformed **y** on the transformed **X** without a constant. Do we get the same result if we only transform **y**? What if we only transform **X**?

32. What is the result of the matrix product $\mathbf{M}_1\mathbf{M}$ where $\mathbf{M}_1$ is defined in (6-25) and $\mathbf{M}$ is defined in (6-23)?

33. Let e_i be the ith residual in the ordinary least squares regression of **y** on **X** in the classical regression model, and let ϵ_i be the corresponding true disturbance. Prove that $\text{plim}(e_i - \epsilon_i) = 0$.

34. For the simple regression model

$$y_i = \mu + \epsilon_i, \epsilon_i \sim N[0, \sigma^2],$$

prove that the sample mean is consistent and asymptotically normally distributed. Now consider the alternative estimator

$$\hat{\mu} = \sum_i w_i y_i,$$

$$w_i = \frac{i}{(n(n+1)/2)} = \frac{i}{\sum_i i}.$$

Note that $\Sigma_i w_i = 1$. Prove that this is a consistent estimator of μ and obtain its asymptotic variance. [Hint: $\Sigma_i i^2 = n(n+1)(2n+1)/6$.]

35. Example 8.3 presents Nerlove's estimates of a generalized Cobb–Douglas cost function:

$$\log\left(\frac{C}{P_f}\right) = \alpha + \beta \log Q + \gamma \log^2 Y + \delta_k \log\left(\frac{P_k}{P_f}\right) + \delta_l \log\left(\frac{P_l}{P_f}\right) + \epsilon.$$

(Nerlove used common, not natural, logarithms.) The purpose of the generalization was to produce a U-shaped average total cost curve. We are interested in the output at which the cost curve reaches its minimum. That is the point at which

$$\left.\frac{\partial \log C}{\partial \log Q}\right|_{Q=Q^*} = 1$$

or $Q^* = 10^{[(1-\beta)/(2\gamma)]}$. (You can simplify the analysis a bit by using that $10^x = \exp(2.3026x)$. Thus,

$$Q^* = \exp\left(2.3026\left[\frac{1-\beta}{2\gamma}\right]\right).$$

Using the estimates given in the example, compute the estimate of this **efficient scale**. Estimate the asymptotic distribution of this estimate, assuming that the estimate of the asymptotic covariance of $\hat{\beta}$ and $\hat{\gamma}$ is -0.00008.

36. Suppose that y_i is a discrete random variable whose distribution given x_i is

$$\text{Prob}(Y_i = y_i) = \frac{e^{-\beta x_i}(\beta x_i)^{y_i}}{y_i!}, \quad y_i = 0, 1, \ldots .$$

Thus, y_i has a Poisson distribution. We also assume that $x_i > 0$ for all i.

(a) Compute the maximum likelihood estimator of β and its asymptotic distribution. Using the result that the sum of Poisson variables y_i with parameters λ_i is distributed as Poisson with parameter $\Sigma_i \lambda_i$, it is possible to obtain the exact distribution of the maximum likelihood estimator. What is this?

(b) As shown in Chapter 3, $E[y_i|x_i] = \beta x_i$. Therefore, this is a linear regression model. It does not satisfy the assumptions of the classical model, however, since $\text{Var}[y_i|x_i] = \beta x_i$. Nonetheless, it can be shown that the least squares estimator is consistent. Do so. Obtain the asymptotic distribution of the estimator. What assumptions are necessary to ensure your result?

(c) Prove that the asymptotic variance of the maximum likelihood estimator is smaller than that of the least squares estimator. [Hint: The proof will hinge upon the assumption that x_i is strictly positive.]

37. For the principal components estimator in (9-10), prove that the variance estimator

$$q^2 = \frac{(\mathbf{y} - \mathbf{Zd})'(\mathbf{y} - \mathbf{Zd})}{n}$$

is not a consistent estimator of σ^2. Obtain the probability limit of q^2. [Hint: $\mathbf{I} - \mathbf{C}_L\mathbf{C}_L' = \mathbf{C}_M\mathbf{C}_M'$, where $\mathbf{C}_M$ is the matrix of the other $K - L$ characteristic vectors of $\mathbf{X'X}$.]

38. For the classical normal regression model $\mathbf{y} = \mathbf{X}\boldsymbol{\beta} + \boldsymbol{\epsilon}$ with no constant term and K regressors, what is

$$\text{plim } F[K, n - K] = \text{plim } \frac{R^2/K}{(1 - R^2)/(n - K)},$$

assuming that the true value of $\boldsymbol{\beta}$ is zero? What is the exact expected value?

39. The density function for the compound disturbance in the stochastic frontier model is given in a footnote to Example 6.25.

(a) Derive the log-likelihood function and its first derivatives to define the maximum likelihood estimators of β, σ, and λ. Note that a useful shortcut is $d\phi(x)/dx = -x\phi(x)$ and $d\Phi(x)/dx = \phi(x)$.

(b) Show how you would obtain estimates and standard errors for the underlying parameters σ_v^2 and σ_u^2 given estimates of σ and λ and the appropriate estimate of their asymptotic covariance matrix.

40. In the discussion of the instrumental variables estimator in Section 6.7.8, we showed that the least squares estimator $\mathbf{b}$ is biased and inconsistent. Nonetheless, $\mathbf{b}$ does estimate something: plim $\mathbf{b} = \boldsymbol{\theta} = \boldsymbol{\beta} + \mathbf{Q}^{-1}\boldsymbol{\gamma}$. Derive the asymptotic covariance matrix of $\mathbf{b}$, and show that $\mathbf{b}$ is asymptotically normally distributed.

41. For the study that precedes Example 7.5, suppose that an earlier study had produced the following estimated production function:

$$\ln Q = 1.2 + \underset{(0.09)}{0.65} \ln L + \underset{(0.16)}{0.31} \ln K \qquad \text{Est. Cov}[b_L, b_K] = 0.1$$

(estimated standard errors are given in parentheses.) Using these estimates and the estimates in Example 7.5, form the Bayesian estimate of the posterior distribution, assuming a normal prior distribution for the parameters. Assume that σ^2 is known.

CHAPTER 7

Inference and Prediction

7.1. INTRODUCTION

In this chapter, we examine some applications of hypothesis tests using the classical model. The basic statistical theory was developed in Sections 6.6 through 6.8. We will fill in the remaining parts in Section 7.2. This chapter also presents additional statistical results for some tests that do not fit into the classical framework. The final section discusses a second major use of the regression model, prediction.

7.2. TESTING RESTRICTIONS

One common approach to testing a hypothesis is to formulate a statistical model that contains the hypothesis as a restriction on its parameters. A theory is said to have *testable implications* if it implies some testable restrictions on the model. Consider, for example, a simple model of investment,

$$\text{investment} = \beta_1 + \beta_2\,\text{interest} + \beta_3\,\text{inflation} + \epsilon,$$

which states that investors are sensitive to nominal interest rates and the rate of inflation. An alternative theory states that "investors care about real interest rates." The alternative model is

$$\text{investment} = \beta_1 + \beta_2(\text{interest} - \text{inflation}) + \beta_3\,\text{inflation} + \epsilon. \quad \textbf{(7-1)}$$

Although this new model does embody the theory, the equation still contains both nominal interest and inflation. The theory has no testable implication for our model. But consider the stronger hypothesis, "investors care *only* about real interest rates." The resulting equation,

$$\text{investment} = \beta_1 + \beta_2(\text{interest} - \text{inflation}) + \epsilon, \quad \textbf{(7-2)}$$

is now restricted; in the context of the first model, the implication is that $\beta_2 + \beta_3 = 0$. The stronger statement implies something very specific about the parameters in the equation that may or may not be supported by the empirical evidence.

7.2.1. Two Approaches to Testing Hypotheses

Hypothesis testing of the sort suggested above can be approached from two viewpoints. First, having computed a set of parameter estimates, we can ask whether the estimates come reasonably close to satisfying the restrictions implied by the hypothesis. More formally, we can ascertain whether the failure of the estimates to satisfy the restrictions is simply the result of sampling error or is instead systematic. An alternative view of the testing procedure might proceed as follows. Suppose that we impose the restrictions implied by the theory. Since unrestricted least squares is, by definition, "least squares," this imposition must lead to a loss of fit. We can then ascertain whether this loss of fit results merely from sampling error or whether it is so large as to cast doubt on the validity of the restrictions.

7.2.2. Testing a Set of Linear Restrictions

Beginning with the linear regression model

$$\mathbf{y} = \mathbf{X}\boldsymbol{\beta} + \boldsymbol{\epsilon},$$

we consider a set of linear restrictions of the form

$$\begin{aligned} r_{11}\beta_1 + r_{12}\beta_2 + \cdots + r_{1K}\beta_K &= q_1 \\ r_{21}\beta_1 + r_{22}\beta_2 + \cdots + r_{2K}\beta_K &= q_2 \\ &\vdots \\ r_{J1}\beta_1 + r_{J2}\beta_2 + \cdots + r_{JK}\beta_K &= q_J. \end{aligned}$$

These can be combined into the single equation

$$\mathbf{R}\boldsymbol{\beta} = \mathbf{q}.$$

Each row of $\mathbf{R}$ is the coefficients in one of the restrictions. The matrix $\mathbf{R}$ has K columns to be conformable with $\boldsymbol{\beta}$, J rows for a total of J restrictions, and full row rank, so J must be less than or equal to K. The rows of $\mathbf{R}$ must be linearly independent. Although it does not violate the condition, the case of $J = K$ must also be ruled out.[1]

The restriction $\mathbf{R}\boldsymbol{\beta} = \mathbf{q}$ imposes J restrictions on K otherwise free parameters. This means that with the restrictions imposed, there are, in principle, only $K - J$ free parameters remaining. One way to view this is to partition $\mathbf{R}$

[1]If the K slopes satisfy $J = K$ restriction, $\mathbf{R}$ is square and nonsingular and $\boldsymbol{\beta} = \mathbf{R}^{-1}\mathbf{q}$. There is no estimation or inference problem.

into two groups of columns, one with J and one with $K - J$, so that the first set are linearly independent. (There are many ways to do so; any one will do for the present.) Then, with $\boldsymbol{\beta}$ likewise partitioned and its elements reordered in whatever way is needed, we may write

$$\mathbf{R}\boldsymbol{\beta} = \mathbf{R}_1\boldsymbol{\beta}_1 + \mathbf{R}_2\boldsymbol{\beta}_2 = \mathbf{q}.$$

If the J columns of $\mathbf{R}_1$ are independent,

$$\boldsymbol{\beta}_1 = \mathbf{R}_1^{-1}\,[\mathbf{q} - \mathbf{R}_2\boldsymbol{\beta}_2]. \tag{7-3}$$

The implication is that although $\boldsymbol{\beta}_2$ is free to vary, once $\boldsymbol{\beta}_2$ is determined, $\boldsymbol{\beta}_1$ is determined by (7-3). Thus, only the $K - J$ elements of $\boldsymbol{\beta}_2$ are free parameters in the model.

AN IMPORTANT ASSUMPTION: *To develop the test statistics in the next few sections, we will assume normally distributed disturbances. As we saw in Chapter 6, this enables us to obtain the exact distributions of the test statistics. In Section 7.2.6, we will consider the implications of relaxing this assumption and whether it is necessary.*

7.2.3. Testing One Linear Restriction

We shall often be interested in testing hypotheses involving a single linear restriction. We can use a test statistic similar to the one in (6-46). Suppose that the hypothesis is

$$H_0: r_1\beta_1 + r_2\beta_2 + \cdots + r_K\beta_K = \mathbf{r}'\boldsymbol{\beta} = q.$$

(Usually some of the r's will be zero.) The sample estimate of $\mathbf{r}'\boldsymbol{\beta}$ is

$$r_1b_1 + r_2b_2 + \cdots + r_Kb_K = \mathbf{r}'\mathbf{b} = \hat{q}.$$

If $\hat{q}$ differs significantly from q, we conclude that the sample data are not consistent with the hypothesis. Consistent with (6-46), it is natural to base the test on

$$t = \frac{\hat{q} - q}{\text{se}(\hat{q})}.$$

We require an estimate of the standard error of $\hat{q}$. Since $\hat{q}$ is a linear function of $\mathbf{b}$ and we have an estimate of the covariance matrix of $\mathbf{b}$, $s^2(\mathbf{X}'\mathbf{X})^{-1}$, we can estimate the variance of $\hat{q}$ with

$$\text{Est. Var}[\hat{q}] = \mathbf{r}'[s^2(\mathbf{X}'\mathbf{X})^{-1}]\mathbf{r}.$$

The denominator is the square root of this quantity.[2] In words, t is the distance in standard error units between the hypothesized function of the true coeffi-

[2]This is a special case of the more general result to be proved, so we need not derive the distribution separately.

cients and the same function of our estimates of them. If the hypothesis is true, our estimates should reflect that, at least within the range of sampling variability. Thus, if the absolute value of the preceding t ratio is larger than the appropriate critical value, doubt is cast on the hypothesis.

EXAMPLE 7.1 Linear Combination of Coefficients

The introduction to this chapter suggested a theory about the behavior of investors: that they care only about real interest rates. In the investment equation of Example 6.14, we might ask whether it is more appropriate to formulate the regression in terms of the real interest rate rather than to treat the interest rate and the rate of inflation separately.[3] If investors were only interested in the real rate of interest, equal increases in interest rates and the rate of inflation would have no effect on investment. The hypothesis is

$$H_0: \beta_4 + \beta_5 = 0.$$

To form the appropriate test statistic, we require the standard error of $\hat{q} = b_4 + b_5$, which is

$$\begin{aligned} \text{se}(\hat{q}) &= [0.14856 \times 10^{-5} + 0.18157 \times 10^{-5} + 2(-0.75071 \times 10^{-6})]^{1/2} \\ &= 0.001341609. \end{aligned}$$

The t ratio for the test is therefore

$$t = \frac{-0.0023259 + (-0.000094012)}{0.001341609} = -1.80376.$$

Using the same critical value as before (1.96), we conclude that the sum of the two coefficients is not significantly different from zero.

EXAMPLE 7.2 Reparameterizing a Restriction

There will often be more than one way to formulate a restriction in a regression model. One convenient way to parameterize a constraint is to set it up in such a way that the standard test statistics produced by the regression can be used without further computation to test the hypothesis. In the previous example, we could write the regression model as suggested in (7-1):

$$\text{investment} = \cdots + \beta_4 \text{ real interest rate} + \beta_5 \text{ rate of inflation} + \epsilon.$$

Then an equivalent way to test H_0 would be to fit the investment equation with both the real interest rate and the rate of inflation as regressors and to test our theory by simply testing the hypothesis that β_5 equals zero, using the standard t statistic that is routinely computed. When the regression is computed this way, $b_5 = -0.0024199$ and the estimated standard error is 0.0013416, resulting in a t

[3]Once again, the use of the CPI and, here, an ex post rate of inflation is questionable. We retain these variables purely for the sake of a reasonably uncomplicated example.

ratio of -1.804(!). (Exercise: Suppose that the nominal interest rate, rather than the rate of inflation, were included as the extra regressor. What do you think the coefficient and its standard error would be?)

7.2.4. Testing J Linear Restrictions

We now consider a set of J linear restrictions of the form

$$H_0: \mathbf{R}\boldsymbol{\beta} = \mathbf{q}.$$

Each row of $\mathbf{R}$ is a single linear restriction on the coefficient vector. Typically, $\mathbf{R}$ will have only a few rows and numerous zeros in each row. Some examples are as follows.

- One of the coefficients is zero, $\beta_j = 0$:

$$\mathbf{R} = [0 \quad 0 \quad \cdots \quad 1 \quad 0 \quad \cdots \quad 0] \quad \text{and} \quad \mathbf{q} = 0.$$

- Two of the coefficients are equal, $\beta_k = \beta_j$:

$$\mathbf{R} = [0 \quad 0 \quad 1 \quad \cdots \quad -1 \quad \cdots \quad 0] \quad \text{and} \quad \mathbf{q} = 0.$$

- A set of the coefficients sum to one, $\beta_2 + \beta_3 + \beta_4 = 1$:

$$\mathbf{R} = [0 \quad 1 \quad 1 \quad 1 \quad 0 \quad \cdots] \quad \text{and} \quad \mathbf{q} = 1.$$

- A subset of the coefficients are all zero, $\beta_1 = 0, \beta_2 = 0$, and $\beta_3 = 0$:

$$\mathbf{R} = \begin{bmatrix} 1 & 0 & 0 & 0 & \cdots & 0 \\ 0 & 1 & 0 & 0 & \cdots & 0 \\ 0 & 0 & 1 & 0 & \cdots & 0 \end{bmatrix} \quad \text{and} \quad \mathbf{q} = \begin{bmatrix} 0 \\ 0 \\ 0 \end{bmatrix}$$

  or, equivalently,

$$[\mathbf{I}:\mathbf{0}]\boldsymbol{\beta} = \mathbf{0}.$$

- Several constraints hold simultaneously:

$$\beta_2 + \beta_3 = 1, \beta_4 + \beta_6 = 0 \quad \text{and} \quad \beta_5 + \beta_6 = 0,$$

$$\begin{bmatrix} 0 & 1 & 1 & 0 & 0 & 0 \\ 0 & 0 & 0 & 1 & 0 & 1 \\ 0 & 0 & 0 & 0 & 1 & 1 \end{bmatrix} \begin{bmatrix} \beta_1 \\ \beta_2 \\ \beta_3 \\ \beta_4 \\ \beta_5 \\ \beta_6 \end{bmatrix} = \begin{bmatrix} 1 \\ 0 \\ 0 \end{bmatrix}.$$

Given the least squares estimator $\mathbf{b}$, our interest centers on the "discrepancy," vector $\mathbf{m} = \mathbf{R}\mathbf{b} - \mathbf{q}$. It is unlikely that $\mathbf{m}$ will be exactly $\mathbf{0}$. The statistical question is whether the deviation of $\mathbf{m}$ from $\mathbf{0}$ can be attributed to sampling error or whether it is significant. Since $\mathbf{b}$ is normally distributed and $\mathbf{m}$ is a linear function of $\mathbf{b}$, $\mathbf{m}$ is also normally distributed. (See Section 6.7.5.) If the null hypothesis is true, $\mathbf{m}$ has mean vector $\mathbf{0}$ and variance

$$\text{Var}[\mathbf{m}] = \text{Var}[\mathbf{R}\mathbf{b} - \mathbf{q}] = \mathbf{R}\{\text{Var}[\mathbf{b}]\}\mathbf{R}' = \sigma^2\mathbf{R}(\mathbf{X}'\mathbf{X})^{-1}\mathbf{R}'.$$

We can base a test of H_0 on the *Wald criterion:*

$$W = \chi^2[J] = \mathbf{m}'\{\text{Var}[\mathbf{m}]\}^{-1}\mathbf{m}.$$

The statistic W has a chi-squared distribution with J degrees of freedom if the hypothesis is correct.[4] Intuitively, the larger $\mathbf{m}$ is—that is, the worse is the failure of least squares to satisfy the restrictions—the larger the chi-squared statistic. Therefore, a large chi-squared value will weigh against the hypothesis.

The chi-squared statistic is not usable because of the unknown σ^2. We can derive a usable sample statistic similar to the t ratio in (6-46) by using s^2 instead of σ^2. Let

$$F = \frac{(\mathbf{Rb} - \mathbf{q})'[\sigma^2\mathbf{R}(\mathbf{X}'\mathbf{X})^{-1}\mathbf{R}']^{-1}(\mathbf{Rb} - \mathbf{q})/J}{[(n - K)s^2/\sigma^2]/(n - K)}. \tag{7-4}$$

We found the exact distribution of this statistic for a special case, $\mathbf{R} = [\mathbf{0}:\mathbf{I}]$ in Section 6.7.6. We now obtain the general result. Recall that $s^2 = \mathbf{e}'\mathbf{e}/(n - K) = \boldsymbol{\epsilon}'\mathbf{M}\boldsymbol{\epsilon}/(n - K)$. If $\mathbf{R}\boldsymbol{\beta} = \mathbf{q}$, then $\mathbf{Rb} - \mathbf{q} = \mathbf{Rb} - \mathbf{R}\boldsymbol{\beta} = \mathbf{R}(\mathbf{b} - \boldsymbol{\beta}) = \mathbf{R}(\mathbf{X}'\mathbf{X})^{-1}\mathbf{X}'\boldsymbol{\epsilon}$. By using (6-44) and the fact that $\mathbf{M}$ is idempotent, we may write F as

$$F = \frac{\{\mathbf{R}(\mathbf{b} - \boldsymbol{\beta})/\sigma\}'[\mathbf{R}(\mathbf{X}'\mathbf{X})^{-1}\mathbf{R}']^{-1}\{\mathbf{R}(\mathbf{b} - \boldsymbol{\beta})/\sigma\}/J}{[\mathbf{M}(\boldsymbol{\epsilon}/\sigma)]'[\mathbf{M}(\boldsymbol{\epsilon}/\sigma)]/(n - K)}.$$

Since

$$\frac{\mathbf{R}(\mathbf{b} - \boldsymbol{\beta})}{\sigma} = \mathbf{R}(\mathbf{X}'\mathbf{X})^{-1}\mathbf{X}'\left(\frac{\boldsymbol{\epsilon}}{\sigma}\right) = \mathbf{T}\left(\frac{\boldsymbol{\epsilon}}{\sigma}\right),$$

the F statistic is the ratio of two quadratic forms in $(\boldsymbol{\epsilon}/\sigma)$. The numerator is W from above, where $\mathbf{d} = \mathbf{T}(\boldsymbol{\epsilon}/\sigma)$, and is distributed as $1/J$ times chi-squared$[J]$. The denominator is $1/(n - K)$ times an idempotent quadratic form in the standard normal vector $\boldsymbol{\epsilon}/\sigma$, which is also distributed as chi-squared, with $n - K$ degrees of freedom. Since $\mathbf{M}(\boldsymbol{\epsilon}/\sigma)$ and $\mathbf{T}(\boldsymbol{\epsilon}/\sigma)$ are both normally distributed and their covariance $\mathbf{TM}$ is $\mathbf{0}$, the vectors of the quadratic forms are independent. The numerator and denominator of F are functions of independent random vectors and are therefore independent. This completes the proof.

Canceling the two appearances of σ^2 leaves the F statistic for testing a linear hypothesis:

$$F = \frac{(\mathbf{Rb} - \mathbf{q})'[\mathbf{R}(\mathbf{X}'\mathbf{X})^{-1}\mathbf{R}']^{-1}(\mathbf{Rb} - \mathbf{q})/J}{\mathbf{e}'\mathbf{e}/(n - K)},$$

$$= \frac{(\mathbf{Rb} - \mathbf{q})'[s^2\mathbf{R}(\mathbf{X}'\mathbf{X})^{-1}\mathbf{R}']^{-1}(\mathbf{Rb} - \mathbf{q})}{J}.$$

[4]This is an application of the "full rank quadratic form" of Section 3.10.5. But see Theorem 6.12 in Section 6.7.6 as well. We showed that under general conditions, this statistic would converge to a chi-squared variable, whether or not we assumed that the disturbances were normally distributed.

EXAMPLE 7.3 Restricted Investment Equation

In the investment equation estimated earlier, consider a test of the joint hypothesis

$$\begin{aligned} \beta_2 &= 0 \quad \text{(there is no time trend)}, \\ \beta_3 &= 1 \quad \text{(the marginal propensity to invest} = 1), \\ \beta_4 + \beta_5 &= 0 \quad \text{(investors consider the real interest rate)}. \end{aligned}$$

Then

$$\mathbf{R} = \begin{bmatrix} 0 & 1 & 0 & 0 & 0 \\ 0 & 0 & 1 & 0 & 0 \\ 0 & 0 & 0 & 1 & 1 \end{bmatrix} \quad \text{and} \quad \mathbf{q} = \begin{bmatrix} 0 \\ 1 \\ 0 \end{bmatrix}.$$

Based on the sample estimates, we obtain

$$\mathbf{Rb} - \mathbf{q} = \begin{bmatrix} -0.01658 \\ -0.32962 \\ -0.0024199 \end{bmatrix}.$$

The covariance matrix was given in Example 6.14. Inserting these values in F yields

$$F = 1266.3525.$$

The 5 percent critical value for $F[3, 10]$ from the table is 3.71. We conclude, therefore, that these data are not consistent with the hypothesis. This gives no hint as to which of the restrictions is particularly problematic. Based on the individual test statistics, however, we would expect both the first and second hypotheses to be rejected.

7.2.5. A Test Based on a Confidence Region

A confidence interval for a single coefficient is based on a set of values for which the t ratio in (6-46) is less than a specified critical value. It is the set of values for which, at a given level of significance, we would not reject the hypothesis that β equals this value. In a multiple regression model, a joint confidence region for a set of coefficients would be the set of values for which the hypothesis that the set of true coefficients simultaneously equal these values would not be rejected. The test statistic is the F ratio given above. For two coefficients, this would be

$$F[2, n - K] = \tfrac{1}{2}(\mathbf{b} - \boldsymbol{\beta})'(\text{Est. Var}[\mathbf{b}])^{-1}(\mathbf{b} - \boldsymbol{\beta}).$$

(For convenience, we assume that only the two coefficients of interest appear in the vectors and that the estimated covariance matrix is a 2×2 submatrix of the full covariance matrix.) The set of values of β_1 and β_2 for which this quadratic form is less than a tabulated critical value form a joint confidence region for β_1 and β_2.

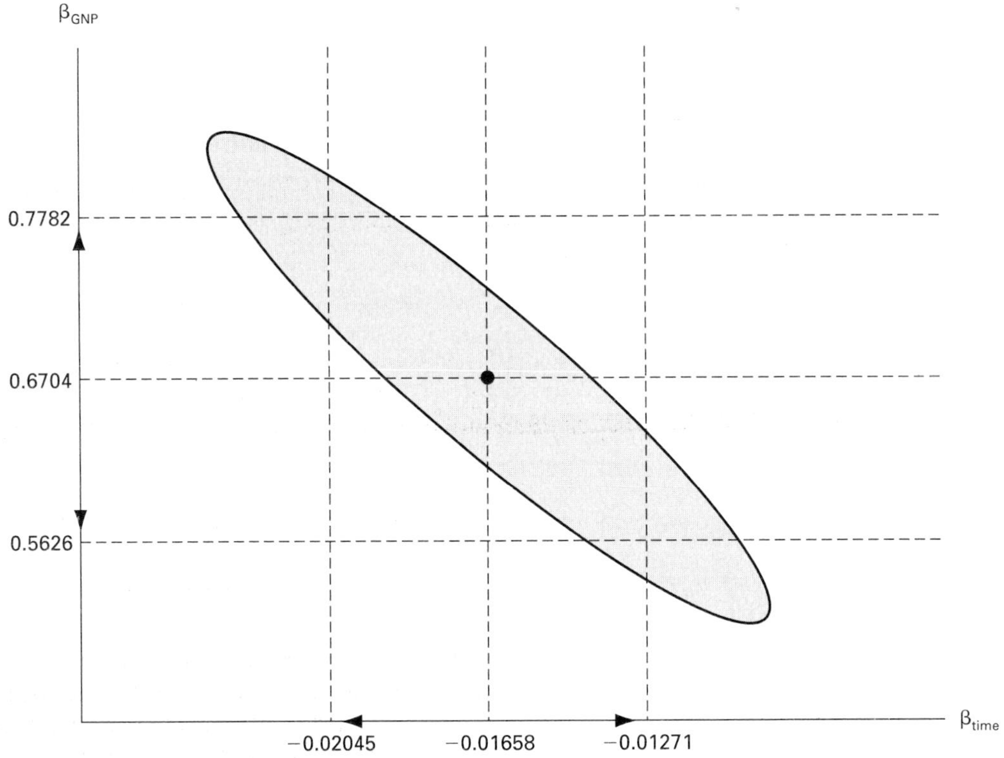

FIGURE 7.1 Joint Confidence Region.

EXAMPLE 7.4 Joint Confidence Region

Figure 7.1 shows a confidence region for β_2 and β_3 for the investment equation. It is the set of values for which the quadratic form

$$\frac{1}{2}\begin{bmatrix} -0.01658 - \beta_1 \\ 0.67038 - \beta_2 \end{bmatrix}' \begin{bmatrix} 0.389 \times 10^{-5} & -0.102 \times 10^{-3} \\ -0.102 \times 10^{-3} & 0.302 \times 10^{-2} \end{bmatrix}^{-1} \begin{bmatrix} 0.01658 - \beta_1 \\ 0.67038 - \beta_2 \end{bmatrix}$$

is less than or equal to the critical $F[2, 10]$ of 4.1. The individual confidence intervals for the coefficients are shown on the axes. Note how the interaction of the two coefficients affects the joint confidence region.

The calculation of the confidence ellipse can be a bit tedious. It can be shown that the simple rectangle formed by the two individual confidence intervals provides a confidence region with probability at least $1 - \alpha_1 - \alpha_2$.[5] Thus, for example, the rectangle in Figure 7.1 contains at least 90 percent of the probability in the estimate of the joint distribution of b_2 and b_3.

---

[5]See Theil (1971, p. 132). The confidence levels chosen for the individual estimates are α_1 and α_2.

7.2.6. Nonnormal Disturbances

With normally distributed disturbances, one can use several test statistics for testing linear restrictions. Note first that the t test of a single linear restriction is a special case of the F test. The relationship is

$$F[1, n - K] = t^2[n - K].$$

We also obtained three asymptotically equivalent test statistics in Section 6.8.3:

$$\text{Wald} \quad W = \frac{nJ}{n - K} F,$$

$$\text{Likelihood ratio} \quad \text{LR} = n \ln\left[1 + \frac{J}{n - K} F\right] \approx \frac{nJ}{n - K} F, \tag{7-5}$$

$$\text{Lagrange multiplier} \quad \text{LM} = \frac{nJ}{n - K} \frac{1}{\left[1 + \dfrac{j}{n - K} F\right]} F \approx \frac{nJ}{n - K} F.$$

In large samples, these are all approximately equal to JF, which is easy to compute. The main result of Section 6.7.6 was that asymptotically, as long as the regressors are reasonably well behaved, the assumption of normality was inessential to the derivation of the statistical properties of these chi-squared statistics. For present purposes, this means that, in general, for testing J linear restrictions, the chi-squared[J] statistic $W = JF$ provides a reasonable approximation to the appropriate (but unknown) exact distribution of the test statistic. For testing one restriction, we can use the standard normal instead of the t distribution to obtain appropriate critical values.

7.3. THE RESTRICTED LEAST SQUARES ESTIMATOR

Suppose, instead, that we explicitly impose the restrictions of the hypothesis in the regression. The restricted least squares estimator is obtained as the solution to

$$\text{Minimize}_{\beta} S(\boldsymbol{\beta}) = (\mathbf{y} - \mathbf{X}\boldsymbol{\beta})'(\mathbf{y} - \mathbf{X}\boldsymbol{\beta}) \quad \text{subject to} \quad \mathbf{R}\boldsymbol{\beta} = \mathbf{q}. \tag{7-6}$$

A Lagrangean function for this problem can be written

$$L^*(\boldsymbol{\beta}, \boldsymbol{\lambda}) = (\mathbf{y} - \mathbf{X}\boldsymbol{\beta})'(\mathbf{y} - \mathbf{X}\boldsymbol{\beta}) + 2\boldsymbol{\lambda}'(\mathbf{R}\boldsymbol{\beta} - \mathbf{q}).^6 \tag{7-7}$$

The solutions $\mathbf{b}_*$ and $\boldsymbol{\lambda}$ will satisfy the necessary conditions

$$\frac{\partial L^*}{\partial \mathbf{b}_*} = -2\mathbf{X}'(\mathbf{y} - \mathbf{X}\mathbf{b}_*) + 2\mathbf{R}'\boldsymbol{\lambda} = \mathbf{0}, \tag{7-8}$$

[6] The value of $\boldsymbol{\lambda}$ will be obtained subsequently. Since $\boldsymbol{\lambda}$ is not restricted, we can formulate the constraints in terms of $2\boldsymbol{\lambda}$. Why this is convenient will be clear shortly.

$$\frac{\partial L^*}{\partial \boldsymbol{\lambda}} = 2(\mathbf{R}\mathbf{b}_* - \mathbf{q}) = \mathbf{0}. \tag{7-9}$$

Dividing through by 2 and expanding terms produces the partitioned matrix equation

$$\begin{bmatrix} \mathbf{X}'\mathbf{X} & \mathbf{R}' \\ \mathbf{R} & \mathbf{0} \end{bmatrix} \begin{bmatrix} \mathbf{b}_* \\ \boldsymbol{\lambda} \end{bmatrix} = \begin{bmatrix} \mathbf{X}'\mathbf{y} \\ \mathbf{q} \end{bmatrix} \tag{7-10}$$

or

$$\mathbf{W}\mathbf{d}_* = \mathbf{v}.$$

Assuming that the partitioned matrix in brackets is nonsingular, the restricted least squares estimator is the upper part of the solution

$$\mathbf{d}_* = \mathbf{W}^{-1}\mathbf{v}. \tag{7-11}$$

If, in addition, $\mathbf{X}'\mathbf{X}$ is nonsingular, then explicit solutions for $\mathbf{b}_*$ and $\boldsymbol{\lambda}$ may be obtained by using the formula for the partitioned inverse (2-74),[7]

$$\begin{aligned} \mathbf{b}_* &= \mathbf{b} - (\mathbf{X}'\mathbf{X})^{-1}\mathbf{R}'[\mathbf{R}(\mathbf{X}'\mathbf{X})^{-1}\mathbf{R}']^{-1}(\mathbf{R}\mathbf{b} - \mathbf{q}) \\ &= \mathbf{b} - \mathbf{C}\mathbf{m} \end{aligned}$$

and

$$\boldsymbol{\lambda} = [\mathbf{R}(\mathbf{X}'\mathbf{X})^{-1}\mathbf{R}']^{-1}(\mathbf{R}\mathbf{b} - \mathbf{q}). \tag{7-12}$$

Greene and Seaks (1991) show that the covariance matrix for $\mathbf{b}_*$ is simply σ^2 times the upper left block of $\mathbf{W}^{-1}$. Once again, in the usual case in which $\mathbf{X}'\mathbf{X}$ is nonsingular, an explicit formulation may be obtained:

$$\text{Var}[\mathbf{b}_*] = \sigma^2(\mathbf{X}'\mathbf{X})^{-1} - \sigma^2(\mathbf{X}'\mathbf{X})^{-1}\mathbf{R}'[\mathbf{R}(\mathbf{X}'\mathbf{X})^{-1}\mathbf{R}']^{-1}\mathbf{R}(\mathbf{X}'\mathbf{X})^{-1}.$$

Thus,

$$\text{Var}[\mathbf{b}_*] = \text{Var}[\mathbf{b}] - \text{a positive definite matrix.}$$

One way to interpret this reduction in variance is as the value of the information contained in the restrictions.

Note that the explicit solution for $\boldsymbol{\lambda}$ involves the discrepancy vector $\mathbf{R}\mathbf{b} - \mathbf{q}$. If the unrestricted least squares estimator satisfied the restriction, the Lagrangean multipliers would equal zero and $\mathbf{b}_*$ would equal $\mathbf{b}$. Of course, this is unlikely. The constrained solution $\mathbf{b}_*$ is equal to the unconstrained solution $\mathbf{b}$ plus a term that accounts for the failure of the unrestricted solution to satisfy the constraints.

---

[7]The general solution given for $\mathbf{d}_*$ may be usable even if $\mathbf{X}'\mathbf{X}$ is singular. Suppose, for example, that $\mathbf{X}'\mathbf{X}$ is 4×4 with rank 3. Then $\mathbf{X}'\mathbf{X}$ is singular. But if there is a parametric restriction on $\boldsymbol{\beta}$, the 5×5 matrix in brackets may still have rank 5. Whether or not $\mathbf{X}'\mathbf{X}$ is singular, (7-10) and (7-11) are likely to be simpler to program for a computer than (7-12). This formulation and a number of related results are given in Greene and Seaks (1991).

7.4. A TEST BASED ON LOSS OF FIT

A different type of hypothesis test focuses on the fit of the regression. Recall that the least squares vector **b** was chosen to minimize the sum of squared deviations. Since R^2 equals $1 - \text{SSE}/S_{yy}$, it follows that the value of **b** is chosen to maximize R^2. One might ask whether choosing some other value for the slopes of the regression leads to a significant loss of fit. For example, for the consumption function in Example 6.7, one might be interested in whether a value of 0.8 as opposed to the least squares value of 0.9793 leads to a substantially worse fit. To develop the test statistic, we consider a single coefficient first, then turn to the general case of J linear restrictions.

First, consider the change in the fit of a multiple regression when a variable is added to the model; a variable z is added to model that contains $K - 1$ variables, $\mathbf{x}$. We showed in Section 6.5 (6-36) that the effect on the fit would be given by

$$R^2_{\mathbf{Xz}} = R^2_{\mathbf{X}} + (1 - R^2_{\mathbf{X}})r^{*2}_{yz},$$

where r^{*2}_{yz} is the partial correlation between y and z, controlling for $\mathbf{x}$. So, as we knew, the fit improves (or, at the least, does not deteriorate). In deriving the partial correlation coefficient between y and z, we obtained the convenient result

$$r^{*2}_{yz} = \frac{t_z^2}{t_z^2 + (n - K)},$$

where t_z^2 is the square of the t ratio for testing the hypothesis that the coefficient on z is zero in the *multiple* regression of $\mathbf{y}$ on $\mathbf{X}$ and $\mathbf{z}$. If we solve the first of these for r^{*2}_{yz} and the second for t_z^2 and then insert the first solution in the second, we obtain the result

$$t_z^2 = \frac{(R^2_{\mathbf{Xz}} - R^2_{\mathbf{X}})/1}{(1 - R^2_{\mathbf{Xz}})/(n - K)}.$$

We saw earlier that for a single restriction, such as $\beta_z = 0$,

$$F[1, n - K] = t^2[n - K],$$

which gives us our result. We have proved it for the case of testing whether a single slope is zero, but, the result above is general. The test statistic for a single linear restriction is the square of the t ratio in Section 7.2.3. By this construction, we see that F is a measure of the loss of fit that results from imposing a restriction.

The counterpart for the general case of J restrictions is the same, as we will now show.[8] The fit of the restricted least squares coefficients will be worse

---

[8]See Section 6.7.6.

than that of the unrestricted solution. Let $\mathbf{e}_*$ equal $\mathbf{y} - \mathbf{X}\mathbf{b}_*$. Then, using a familiar device,

$$\mathbf{e}_* = \mathbf{y} - \mathbf{X}\mathbf{b} - \mathbf{X}(\mathbf{b}_* - \mathbf{b}) = \mathbf{e} - \mathbf{X}(\mathbf{b}_* - \mathbf{b}).$$

The new sum of squared deviations is

$$\mathbf{e}_*'\mathbf{e}_* = \mathbf{e}'\mathbf{e} + (\mathbf{b}_* - \mathbf{b})'\mathbf{X}'\mathbf{X}(\mathbf{b}_* - \mathbf{b}) \geq \mathbf{e}'\mathbf{e}.$$[9]

(The middle term in the expression involves $\mathbf{X}'\mathbf{e}$, which is zero.) The loss of fit is

$$\mathbf{e}_*'\mathbf{e}_* - \mathbf{e}'\mathbf{e} = (\mathbf{R}\mathbf{b} - \mathbf{q})'[\mathbf{R}(\mathbf{X}'\mathbf{X})^{-1}\mathbf{R}']^{-1}(\mathbf{R}\mathbf{b} - \mathbf{q}). \tag{7-13}$$

This appears in the numerator of the F statistic derived earlier. Inserting the remaining parts, we obtain

$$F[J, n - K] = \frac{(\mathbf{e}_*'\mathbf{e}_* - \mathbf{e}'\mathbf{e})/J}{\mathbf{e}'\mathbf{e}/(n - K)}. \tag{7-14}$$

Finally, by dividing the numerator and denominator of F by $\Sigma_i (y_i - \bar{y})^2$, we obtain the general result:

$$F[J, n - K] = \frac{(R^2 - R_*^2)/J}{(1 - R^2)/(n - K)}. \tag{7-15}$$

This form has some intuitive appeal in that the difference in the fits of the two models is directly incorporated in the test statistic. As an example of this approach, consider the earlier joint test that all of the slopes in the model are zero. This is the overall F ratio discussed in Section 6.6.7, where $R_*^2 = 0$.

7.5. EXAMPLES AND SOME GENERAL PROCEDURES

The data in Table 7.1 have been used in several studies of production functions.[10]

Least squares regression of log output (value added) on a constant and the logs of labor and capital produce the estimates of a Cobb–Douglas production function shown in Table 7.2. We will construct several hypothesis tests based on these results.

---

[9] An interesting variation is $\mathbf{e}_*'\mathbf{e}_* = \mathbf{e}'\mathbf{e} + \Sigma_j \lambda_j (\mathbf{R}^j\boldsymbol{\beta} - q_j)$, where $\mathbf{R}^j$ is the jth row of $\mathbf{R}$ (i.e., the coefficients in the jth restriction). This decomposes the increase in the sum of squares into the contributions of the individual discrepancies.

[10] The data are statewide observations on SIC 33, the primary metals industry. They were originally constructed by Hildebrand and Liu (1957) and have subsequently been used by a number of authors, notable Aigner et al. (1977). The 28th data point used in the original study is incomplete; we have used only the remaining 27.

TABLE 7.1 Production Data for SIC 33: Primary Metals

Observation	*Value Added*	*Labor*	*Capital*
1	657.29	162.31	279.99
2	935.93	214.43	542.50
3	1110.65	186.44	721.51
4	1200.89	245.83	1,167.68
5	1052.68	211.40	811.77
6	3406.02	690.61	4,558.02
7	2427.89	452.79	3,069.91
8	4257.46	714.20	5,585.01
9	1625.19	320.54	1,618.75
10	1272.05	253.17	1,562.08
11	1004.45	236.44	662.04
12	598.87	140.73	875.37
13	853.10	145.04	1,696.98
14	1165.63	240.27	1,078.79
15	1917.55	536.73	2,109.34
16	9849.17	1564.83	13,989.55
17	1088.27	214.62	884.24
18	8095.63	1083.10	9,119.70
19	3175.39	521.74	5,686.99
20	1653.38	304.85	1,701.06
21	5159.31	835.69	5,206.36
22	3378.40	284.00	3,288.72
23	592.85	150.77	357.32
24	1601.98	259.91	2,031.93
25	2065.85	497.60	2,492.98
26	2293.87	275.20	1,711.74
27	745.67	137.00	768.59

Note: Data are per establishment, labor is a measure of labor input, and capital is the gross value of plant and equipment. A scale factor used to normalize the capital figure in the original study has been omitted.

EXAMPLE 7.5 Labor Elasticity Equal to 1

For testing the hypothesis that the jth coefficient is equal to a particular value, $\mathbf{R}$ has a single row with a 1 in the jth position. Thus, $\mathbf{R}(\mathbf{X}'\mathbf{X})^{-1}\mathbf{R}'$ is the jth diagonal element of the inverse matrix, and $\mathbf{Rb} - \mathbf{q}$ is $(b_j - q)$. The F statistic is

$$F[1, n - K] = \frac{(b_j - q)^2}{\text{Var}[b_j]}, \tag{7-16}$$

which is the square of the t statistic in (6-47). For the production function, the hypothesis $H_0: \beta_2 = 1$ is rejected on the basis of an F statistic of

$$F[1, 24] = \frac{(0.6030 - 1)^2}{0.01586} = 9.937.$$

The 5 percent critical value from the F table is 4.26.

For testing a single linear restriction of the form

$$H_0: \mathbf{r}'\boldsymbol{\beta} = q,$$

the F statistic is

$$F[1, n - K] = \frac{(\Sigma_j r_j b_j - q)^2}{\Sigma_j \Sigma_k r_j r_k \operatorname{Cov}[b_j, b_k]}. \tag{7-17}$$

EXAMPLE 7.6 Constant Returns to Scale

The hypothesis that the two coefficients of the production function sum to 1 is equivalent to one of constant returns to scale. This is often tested in studies of production. For the preceding data,

$$F[1, 24] = \frac{(0.6030 + 0.3757 - 1)^2}{0.01586 + 0.00728 - 2(0.00961)} = 0.1157.$$

This is substantially less than the critical value given earlier. We would not reject the hypothesis; the data are consistent with the hypothesis of constant returns to scale.

TABLE 7.2 Estimated Production Function

Number of observations	27
Standard error of regression	0.18840
Sum of squared residuals	0.85163
R-squared	0.94346
Adjusted R-squared	0.93875

Variable	*Coefficient*	*Standard Error*	*t ratio*
Constant	1.171	0.3268	3.583
ln labor	0.6030	0.1260	4.787
ln capital	0.3757	0.0853	4.402

Estimated Covariance Matrix of the Estimates

	Constant	*ln Labor*	*ln Capital*
Constant	0.1068		
ln labor	−0.01984	0.01586	
ln capital	0.00189	−0.00961	0.00728

In most cases encountered in practice, it is possible to incorporate the restrictions of a hypothesis directly on the regression and estimate a restricted model.[11] For example, to impose the constraint $\beta_2 = 1$ on the model, we would write

$$\ln Y = \beta_1 + 1.0 \ln L + \beta_3 \ln K + \epsilon$$

or

$$\ln Y - \ln L = \beta_1 + \beta_3 \ln K + \epsilon.$$

Thus, the restricted model is estimated by regressing $\ln Y - \ln L$ on a constant and $\ln K$. Some care is needed if this regression is to be used to compute an F statistic. If the F statistic is computed using the sum of squared residuals [i.e., using (7-14)], no problem will arise. If (7-15) is used instead, however, it may be necessary to account for the restricted regression having a different dependent variable from the unrestricted one. In the example just given, the dependent variable in the unrestricted regression is $\ln Y$, whereas in the restricted regression, it is $\ln Y - \ln L$. The R^2 from the restricted regression is only 0.26979, which would imply an F statistic of 285.96, whereas the correct value is, as we saw earlier, 9.375. If we compute the appropriate R_*^2 using the correct denominator, however, its value is 0.94339 and the correct F value results.

For imposing a set of exclusion restrictions such as $\beta_k = 0$ for one or more coefficients, the obvious approach is simply to omit the variables from the regression and base the test on the sums of squared residuals for the restricted and unrestricted regressions.

EXAMPLE 7.7 Translog Production Function

A generalization of the Cobb–Douglas model used earlier is the *translog* model,[12] which is

$$\ln Y = \beta_1 + \beta_2 \ln L + \beta_3 \ln K + \beta_4(\tfrac{1}{2}\ln^2 L) + \beta_5(\tfrac{1}{2}\ln^2 K) + \beta_6 \ln L \ln K + \epsilon.$$

As we shall analyze further in Chapter 15, this model differs from the Cobb–Douglas model in that it relaxes the Cobb–Douglas's assumption of a unitary elasticity of substitution. The Cobb–Douglas model is obtained by the restriction $\beta_4 = \beta_5 = \beta_6 = 0$. Thus, the restricted regression is simply the one we computed earlier. The results for the unrestricted regression are given in Table 7.3.

The F statistic for the hypothesis of a Cobb–Douglas model is

$$F[3, 21] = \frac{(0.85163 - 0.67993)/3}{0.67993/21} = 1.768.$$

[11]This is not the case when the restrictions are nonlinear. We consider this issue in Chapter 10.

[12]Berndt and Christensen (1973). See Example 6.4 for discussion.

TABLE 7.3 Translog Production Function

Standard error of regression	0.17994
Sum of squared residuals	0.67993
R-squared	0.95486
Adjusted R-squared	0.94411

Variable	*Coefficient*	*Standard Error*	*t ratio*
Constant	0.944216	2.911	0.324
ln L	3.61363	1.548	2.334
ln K	−1.89311	1.016	−1.863
$\frac{1}{2}\ln^2 L$	−0.96406	0.7074	−1.363
$\frac{1}{2}\ln^2 K$	0.08529	0.2926	0.291
$\ln L \times \ln K$	0.31239	0.4389	0.712

Estimated Covariance Matrix for Coefficient Estimates

	Constant	*ln L*	*ln K*	$\frac{1}{2}\ln^2 L$	$\frac{1}{2}\ln^2 K$	*ln L ln K*
Constant	8.472					
ln L	−2.388	2.397				
ln K	−0.3313	−1.231	1.033			
$\frac{1}{2}\ln^2 L$	−0.08760	−0.6658	0.5231	0.5004		
$\frac{1}{2}\ln^2 K$	0.2332	0.03477	0.02637	0.1467	0.08562	
ln L ln K	0.3635	0.1831	−0.2255	−0.2880	−0.1160	0.1927

The critical value from the F table is 3.07, so we would not reject the hypothesis that a Cobb–Douglas model is appropriate.

Note that the coefficient on ln K is now negative. We might conclude that the estimated output elasticity with respect to capital now has the wrong sign. This would be incorrect, however; in the translog model, the capital elasticity of output is

$$\frac{\partial \ln Y}{\partial \ln K} = \beta_3 + \beta_5 \ln K + \beta_6 \ln L.$$

If we insert the coefficient estimates and the mean values for ln K and ln L (not the logs of the means) of 7.44592 and 5.7637, respectively, the result is 0.5425, which is quite in line with our expectations and is fairly close to the value of 0.3757 obtained earlier. The estimated standard error for this linear combination of the least squares estimates is computed as the square root of

$$\text{Est. Var}[b_3 + b_5 \ln K + b_6 \ln L] = \mathbf{w}'(\text{Est. Var}[\mathbf{b}])\mathbf{w},$$

where

$$\mathbf{w} = (0, 0, 1, 0, \overline{\ln K}, \overline{\ln L})'$$

and $\mathbf{b}$ is the full 6×1 least squares coefficient vector. This is 0.1122, which is reasonably close to the earlier estimate of 0.0854.

The F statistic for testing the hypothesis that a subset, say $\boldsymbol{\beta}_2$, of the coefficients are all zero is constructed using

$$\mathbf{R} = (\mathbf{0}:\mathbf{I}), \qquad \mathbf{q} = \mathbf{0},$$

and

$$J = K_2 = \text{the number of elements in } \boldsymbol{\beta}_2.$$

The matrix $\mathbf{R}(\mathbf{X}'\mathbf{X})^{-1}\mathbf{R}'$ is the $K_2 \times K_2$ lower right block of the full inverse matrix. Using our earlier results for partitioned inverses and the results of Section 6.4.3, we have

$$\mathbf{R}(\mathbf{X}'\mathbf{X})^{-1}\mathbf{R}' = (\mathbf{X}_2'\mathbf{M}_1\mathbf{X}_2)^{-1}$$

and

$$\mathbf{Rb} - \mathbf{q} = \mathbf{b}_2.$$

Inserting these in (7-13), we have the loss of fit that results when we drop a subset of the variables from the regression:

$$\mathbf{e}_*'\mathbf{e}_* - \mathbf{e}'\mathbf{e} = \mathbf{b}_2'\mathbf{X}_2'\mathbf{M}_1\mathbf{X}_2\mathbf{b}_2. \qquad \textbf{(7-18)}$$

The procedure for computing the appropriate F statistic amounts simply to comparing the sums of squared deviations from the "short" and "long" regressions, which we saw earlier.

7.6. TESTS OF STRUCTURAL CHANGE

One of the more common applications of the F test is in tests of structural change.[13] In specifying a regression model, we assume that its assumptions apply to all the observations in our sample. It is, however, straightforward to test the hypothesis that some of or all the regression coefficients are different in subsets of the data. To analyze a number of examples, we use the *Longley data,* a data set that is widely used to calibrate regression programs.[14] (See Table 7.4.)

The dependent variable in the regression models will be employment, either total or in one of the two sectors given. The regressors will be a constant, and the set of four variables that is listed at the left of the table.

---

[13]This test is often labeled a *Chow test,* in reference to Chow (1960).

[14]The data are from Longley (1967). Note that the total employment is not the sum of the two sectors given; several sectors from the original data set have been omitted.

TABLE 7.4 The Longley Data

Year	GNP Deflator	GNP (Millions)	Armed Forces	Employment (Thousands) Total	Agricultural	Nonagricultural
1947	83.0	234,289	1590	60,323	8256	38,407
1948	88.5	259,426	1456	61,122	7960	39,241
1949	88.2	258,054	1616	60,171	8017	37,922
1950	89.5	284,599	1650	61,187	7497	39,196
1951	96.2	328,975	3099	63,221	7048	41,460
1952	98.1	346,999	3594	63,639	6792	42,216
1953	99.0	365,385	3547	64,989	6555	43,587
1954	100.0	363,112	3350	63,761	6495	42,271
1955	101.2	397,469	3048	66,019	6718	43,761
1956	104.6	419,180	2857	67,857	6572	45,131
1957	108.4	442,769	2798	68,169	6222	45,278
1958	110.8	444,546	2637	66,513	5844	43,530
1959	112.6	482,704	2552	68,655	5836	45,214
1960	114.2	502,601	2514	69,564	5723	45,850
1961	115.7	518,173	2572	69,331	5463	45,397
1962	116.9	554,894	2827	70,551	5190	46,652

7.6.1. Different Parameter Vectors

The Longley data span the years of the Korean conflict, which ended in 1953. Note the considerable change in the size of the armed forces during the period of this war. It is possible that the relationship between total employment and the variables in $\mathbf{X}$ changed after the war. To test this as a hypothesis, we can proceed as follows. Denote the first 7 years of the data in $\mathbf{y}$ and $\mathbf{X}$ as $\mathbf{y}_1$ and $\mathbf{X}_1$. An unrestricted regression that allows the coefficients to be different in the two periods is

$$\begin{bmatrix} \mathbf{y}_1 \\ \mathbf{y}_2 \end{bmatrix} = \begin{bmatrix} \mathbf{X}_1 & \mathbf{0} \\ \mathbf{0} & \mathbf{X}_2 \end{bmatrix} \begin{bmatrix} \boldsymbol{\beta}_1 \\ \boldsymbol{\beta}_2 \end{bmatrix} + \begin{bmatrix} \boldsymbol{\epsilon}_2 \\ \boldsymbol{\epsilon}_2 \end{bmatrix}. \tag{7-19}$$

Denoting the data matrices as $\mathbf{y}$ and $\mathbf{X}$, we find that the unrestricted least squares estimator is

$$\begin{aligned} \mathbf{b} &= (\mathbf{X}'\mathbf{X})^{-1}\mathbf{X}'\mathbf{y} \\ &= \begin{bmatrix} \mathbf{X}_1'\mathbf{X}_1 & \mathbf{0} \\ \mathbf{0} & \mathbf{X}_2'\mathbf{X}_2 \end{bmatrix}^{-1} \begin{bmatrix} \mathbf{X}_1'\mathbf{y} \\ \mathbf{X}_2'\mathbf{y} \end{bmatrix} = \begin{bmatrix} \mathbf{b}_1 \\ \mathbf{b}_2 \end{bmatrix}, \end{aligned} \tag{7-20}$$

which is least squares applied to the two equations separately. Therefore, the total sum of squared residuals from this regression will be the sum of the two residual sums of squares from the two separate regressions:

$$\mathbf{e}'\mathbf{e} = \mathbf{e}_1'\mathbf{e}_1 + \mathbf{e}_2'\mathbf{e}_2.$$

The restricted coefficient vector can be obtained in two ways. Formally, the restriction $\boldsymbol{\beta}_1 = \boldsymbol{\beta}_2$ is $\mathbf{R}\boldsymbol{\beta} = \mathbf{q}$, where $\mathbf{R} = [\mathbf{I} : -\mathbf{I}]$ and $\mathbf{q} = \mathbf{0}$. The general result given earlier can be applied directly. An easier way to proceed is to build the restriction directly into the model. If the two coefficient vectors are the same, (7-19) may be written

$$\begin{bmatrix} \mathbf{y}_1 \\ \mathbf{y}_2 \end{bmatrix} = \begin{bmatrix} \mathbf{X}_1 \\ \mathbf{X}_2 \end{bmatrix} \boldsymbol{\beta} + \begin{bmatrix} \boldsymbol{\epsilon}_1 \\ \boldsymbol{\epsilon}_2 \end{bmatrix},$$

and the restricted estimator can be obtained simply by stacking the data and estimating a single regression. The residual sum of squares from this regression then forms the basis for the test.

EXAMPLE 7.8 Separate Regressions

Using the data on total employment for this example, we obtain the three estimated regression equations shown in Table 7.5.

The F statistic for testing the restriction that the coefficients in the two equations are the same is

$$F[5, 6] = \frac{(4{,}898{,}596 - 345{,}212 - 800{,}244)/5}{(345{,}212 + 800{,}244)/(7 + 9 - 10)} = 3.932.$$

The tabled critical value is 4.39 for 5 percent significance, so we would not reject the hypothesis that the coefficient vectors are the same in the two periods.

TABLE 7.5 Employment Regressions

Coefficients	*1947–1962*	*1947–1953*	*1954–1962*
Constant	1,169,090	1,678,148	3,776,130
Year	−576.464	−835.193	−1914.17
Deflator	−19.7681	−163.292	−42.4647
GNP	0.0643094	0.0948082	0.11233
Armed forces	−0.0101452	−0.246697	−2.57928
Standard error	667.328	415.459	447.28
Sum of squares	4,898,596	345,212	800,244

7.6.2. Different Constant Terms

The general formulation previously suggested lends itself to many variations that allow a wide range of possible tests. Some important particular cases are suggested by our test data. We might consider the difference between employment in the agricultural and nonagricultural sectors. The figures for the two dependent variables are of a different order of magnitude, however. There are various ways to deal with this problem. One crude way would be to allow for different intercepts in the equation while stacking only the regressors in the restricted equation. Thus, the unrestricted equation is based on least squares regression of each category of employment on a constant and the four regressors, while the restricted regression is a pooled one with 32 observations. The restricted model has a regressor matrix of the form

$$\mathbf{X} = \begin{bmatrix} \mathbf{i} & \mathbf{0} & \mathbf{W} \\ \mathbf{0} & \mathbf{i} & \mathbf{W} \end{bmatrix}.$$

The first two columns of **X** are **dummy variables** that indicate the sector in which the observation falls.

EXAMPLE 7.9 Change in Slope Coefficients

Using the 16 observations on the two dependent variables for the test, we obtain the results shown in Table 7.6. The F statistic is

$$F[4, 22] = \frac{(107{,}780{,}171 - 241{,}184 - 5{,}037{,}866)/4}{(241{,}184 + 5{,}037{,}866)/22}$$
$$= 106.79.$$

This is extremely large and leads to rejection of the hypothesis at any significant level.

TABLE 7.6 Regressions with Separate Constant Terms

Coefficients	*Agricultural*	*Nonagricultural*	*Pooled*
Constant			
Agricultural	201,828	—	626,192
Nonagricultural	—	1,086,740	662,375
Year	−97.5838	−544.519	−321.051
Deflator	−40.5182	−23.3502	−31.9342
GNP	0.000513124	0.0534508	0.026982
Armed forces	−0.208122	0.764720	0.278299
Standard error	148.074	676.748	2036.024
Sum of squares	241,186	5,037,866	107,780,171

7.6.3. Change in a Subset of Coefficients

One factor that might have a strong influence in Example 7.9 is the clear secular trend in the dependent variables. In the cases of agricultural and nonagricultural employment, they are in opposite directions. It might have been more reasonable to allow both the constant term and the time trend (coefficient on "Year") to differ across the two equations. Once again, the unrestricted coefficient vector is the earlier one (separate regressions). The restricted coefficients are computed using a regressor matrix of the form

$$\mathbf{X} = \begin{bmatrix} \mathbf{i} & \mathbf{Year} & \mathbf{0} & \mathbf{0} & \mathbf{W} \\ \mathbf{0} & \mathbf{0} & \mathbf{i} & \mathbf{Year} & \mathbf{W} \end{bmatrix}, \tag{7-21}$$

where **W** contains (replicated for both data series) the last three columns of the original data matrix.

EXAMPLE 7.10 Separate Constants and Time Trends

The F ratio that results from estimating the model in (7-21) is

$$F[3, 22] = \frac{(11{,}917{,}648 - 5{,}279{,}050)/3}{5{,}279{,}050/22} = 9.221.$$

The critical value from the F table is 3.05, so we would still reject the hypothesis. The sample value is substantially reduced, however. Apparently, the difference in the secular trends accounted for much of the difference in the coefficient vectors.

7.6.4. Insufficient Observations

There are circumstances in which the data series are not long enough to estimate one or the other of the separate regressions for a test of structural change. For example, the data presented earlier on the armed forces series suggests that the major employment change, if there was one, occurred in 1951, not 1954. We might naturally consider the same test we did earlier, using the two subperiods 1947 to 1950 and 1951 to 1962. There are five parameters to estimate and only four observations in the first data set, however. Fisher (1970) has shown that in such a circumstance, a valid way to proceed is as follows.

1. Estimate the regression, using the full data set, and compute the restricted residual sum of squared residuals, $\mathbf{e}_*'\mathbf{e}_*$.
2. Use the longer (adequate) subperiod to estimate the regression, and compute the unrestricted sum of squares, $\mathbf{e}'\mathbf{e}$. This latter computation is done under the assumption that with only $n_1 < K$ observations, we could obtain a perfect fit and thus contribute zero to the sum of squares.
3. The F statistic is then computed, using

$$F[n_1, n_2 - K] = \frac{(\mathbf{e}_*'\mathbf{e}_* - \mathbf{e}'\mathbf{e})/n_1}{\mathbf{e}'\mathbf{e}/(n_2 - K)}. \qquad \textbf{(7-22)}$$

Note that the numerator degrees of freedom is n_1, not K.[15] This test has been labeled the Chow *predictive test,* as it is equivalent to extending the restricted model to the shorter subperiod and basing the test on the prediction errors of the model in this period.

EXAMPLE 7.11 Inadequate Degrees of Freedom

Using the total employment series as an example, we find that the F test for stability of the coefficients in the equation across the two subperiods is

$$F[4, 7] = \frac{(4{,}898{,}762 - 3{,}394{,}431)/4}{3{,}394{,}431/(12 - 5)} = 0.776.$$

This is not larger than the critical value of 4.12. Hence, the hypothesis of stability would not be rejected.

[15]One way to view this is that only $n_1 < K$ coefficients are needed to obtain this perfect fit.

7.7. TESTS OF STRUCTURAL CHANGE WITH UNEQUAL VARIANCES

An important assumption made in using the Chow test is that the disturbance variance is the same in both (or all) regressions. In the restricted model, if this is not true, the first n_1 elements of $\boldsymbol{\epsilon}$ have variance σ_1^2, whereas the next n_2 have variance σ_2^2, and so on. The restricted model is, therefore, heteroscedastic, and our results for the classical regression model no longer apply. As analyzed by Schmidt and Sickles (1977), Ohtani and Toyoda (1985), and Toyoda and Ohtani (1986), it is quite likely that we shall overestimate the significance level of our test statistic. (That is, we shall regard as large an F statistic that is actually less than the *appropriate* table value.) Precisely how severe this effect is going to be will depend on the data and the extent to which the variances differ, in ways that are not likely to be obvious.

There are direct ways to deal with this problem. Assuming that we can estimate both (all) the separate regressions, we can examine our estimates of the disturbance variances. With these in hand, for instance, we can test for significant differences.[16] Without any significant difference, we can proceed as described. If, however, there is evidence to suggest that the variances actually are different, there are still simple and appropriate ways to carry out the analysis by explicitly estimating the model, accounting for the heteroscedasticity. This relies on some results that we develop more fully in Section 15.2.1, so we defer until that point a more complete discussion of the procedure.[17]

If the sample is reasonably large, we have a test that is valid whether or not the disturbance variances are the same. To set up the test, we shall use some general results presented in Chapter 4. Suppose that $\hat{\boldsymbol{\theta}}_1$ and $\hat{\boldsymbol{\theta}}_2$ are two normally distributed estimators of a parameter based on independent samples,[18] with covariance matrices $\mathbf{V}_1$ and $\mathbf{V}_2$. Then, under the null hypothesis that the two estimates have the same expected value,

$$\hat{\boldsymbol{\theta}}_1 - \hat{\boldsymbol{\theta}}_2 \text{ has mean } \mathbf{0} \text{ and variance } \mathbf{V}_1 + \mathbf{V}_2.$$

Thus, the Wald statistic,

$$W = (\hat{\boldsymbol{\theta}}_1 - \hat{\boldsymbol{\theta}}_2)'(\mathbf{V}_1 + \mathbf{V}_2)^{-1}(\hat{\boldsymbol{\theta}}_1 - \hat{\boldsymbol{\theta}}_2), \qquad \textbf{(7-23)}$$

has a chi-squared distribution with K degrees of freedom. A test that the difference between the parameters is zero can be based on this statistic. It is straightforward to apply this to our test of common parameter vectors in our regressions. Large values of the statistic lead us to reject the hypothesis. What

[16] We consider this more fully in the discussion of the Goldfeld–Quandt test in Section 12.3.2.

[17] Since the initial test will have some probability of a type II error, there is that probability that we will fail to pick up an actual difference in the disturbance variances and incorrectly estimate the model as if there were none. This potential is a contributor to *pretest bias* and is discussed more fully for this model in Toyoda and Ohtani (1986).

[18] Without the required independence, this test and several similar ones will fail completely. The problem becomes a variant of the famous Behrens–Fisher problem.

remains for us to resolve is whether it is valid to base such a test on *estimates* of $\mathbf{V}_1$ and $\mathbf{V}_2$. Looking ahead to our results in Chapter 12, the test is indeed valid in large samples, so we may use our least squares estimates of the two covariance matrices to compute W.

EXAMPLE 7.12 Wald Test for Structural Change

The test statistic in (7-23) for the regression results in Table 7.5 gives a value of 13.895. The 5 percent critical value from the chi-squared table for 5 degrees of freedom is 11.075. So, on the basis of the Wald test, we would reject the hypothesis that the same coefficient vector applies in the two subperiods 1947 to 1953 and 1954 to 1962. We should note that the Wald statistic is valid only in large samples, and our samples of seven and nine observations hardly meet that standard.

In a small or moderate-sized sample, the Wald test has the unfortunate property that the probability of a type I error is persistently larger than the critical level we use to carry it out. (That is, we shall too frequently reject the null hypothesis that the parameters are the same in the subsamples.) We should be using a larger critical value. Ohtani and Kobayashi (1986) have devised a "bounds" test that gives a partial remedy for the problem.[19]

7.8. ALTERNATIVE TESTS OF MODEL STABILITY

Example 7.11 shows a test of structural change based essentially on the model's ability to predict correctly outside the range of the observations used to estimate it. A similar logic underlies an alternative test of model stability proposed by Brown, Durbin, and Evans (1975) based on **recursive residuals.** The technique is appropriate for time-series data and might be used if one is uncertain about when a structural change might have taken place. The null hypothesis is that the coefficient vector $\boldsymbol{\beta}$ is the same in every period; the alternative is simply that it (or the disturbance variance) is not. The test is quite general in that it does not require a prior specification of when the structural change takes place. The cost, however, is that the power of the test is rather limited compared with that of the Chow test.[20]

[19]See also Kobayashi (1986). An alternative, somewhat more cumbersome test is proposed by Jayatissa (1977). Further discussion is given in Thursby (1982).

[20]The test is frequently criticized on this basis. The Chow test, however, is based on a rather definite piece of information, namely, when the structural change takes place. If this is not known or must be estimated, the advantage of the Chow test diminishes considerably. An intriguing if relatively short thread of literature considered modeling a discrete shift from regime 1, $\mathbf{y}_t = \mathbf{x}_t'\boldsymbol{\beta}_1 + \boldsymbol{\epsilon}_t$ to regime 2, $\mathbf{y}_t = \mathbf{x}_t'\boldsymbol{\beta}_2 + \boldsymbol{\epsilon}_t$ at some unknown point in time t^*. It seems natural for such a framework simply to fit the two models with successive partitions of the full sample and search for the unknown t^*, for example, on the basis of the total sum of squares. The statistical basis for estimating a discrete "parameter" in this fashion is weak at best, however.

Suppose that the sample contains a total of T observations.[21] The tth recursive residual is the ex post prediction error for y_t when the regression is estimated using only the first $t - 1$ observations:

$$e_t = y_t - \mathbf{x}_t'\mathbf{b}_{t-1},$$

where $\mathbf{x}_t$ is the vector of regressors associated with observation y_t and $\mathbf{b}_{t-1}$ is the least squares coefficients computed using the first $t - 1$ observations.[22] The forecast variance of this residual is

$$\sigma_{ft}^2 = \sigma^2[1 + \mathbf{x}_t'(\mathbf{X}_{t-1}'\mathbf{X}_{t-1})^{-1}\mathbf{x}_t]. \tag{7-24}$$

Let the rth scaled residual be

$$w_r = \frac{e_r}{\sqrt{1 + \mathbf{x}'(\mathbf{X}_{r-1}'\mathbf{X}_{r-1})^{-1}\mathbf{x}_r}}. \tag{7-25}$$

Under the hypothesis that the coefficients remain constant during the full sample period, $w_r \sim N[0, \sigma^2]$ and is independent of w_s for all $s \neq r$. Evidence that the distribution of w_r is changing over time weighs against the hypothesis of model stability.

Brown et al. suggest two tests based on w_r. The CUSUM test is based on the cumulated sum of the residuals:

$$W_t = \sum_{r=K+1}^{r=t} \frac{w_r}{\hat{\sigma}^2}, \tag{7-26}$$

where

$$\hat{\sigma}^2 = \frac{\sum_{r=K+1}^{T} (w_r - \overline{w})^2}{T - K - 1}$$

and

$$\overline{w} = \frac{\sum_{r=K+1}^{T} w_r}{T - K}.$$

---

[21]Since we are dealing explicitly with time-series data at this point, it is convenient to use T instead of n for the sample size and t instead of i to index observations.

[22]In principle, this requires the computation of $T - K$ regressions. The difficult part of the computation is $(\mathbf{X}_t'\mathbf{X}_t)^{-1}$. Since $\mathbf{X}_t'\mathbf{X}_t = \mathbf{X}_{t-1}'\mathbf{X}_{t-1} + \mathbf{x}_t\mathbf{x}_t'$, the rank one updating formula of Section 2.5.2, equation (2-66), can be applied, beginning with an initial regression based on K observations. The result is useful and does provide insight into the calculation. [Discussion can be found in Johnston (1984, p. 387).] Using an electronic computer, however, it is unlikely that using the updating formula instead of actually computing the regression will save a noticeable amount of time. It is also possible, depending on how the accumulation is programmed, that this will introduce a new source of accumulated rounding error into the calculations. This may be a problem in a badly conditioned data set such as the Longley data used earlier.

Under the null hypothesis, W_t has a mean of zero and a variance of approximately the number of residuals being summed (as each term has variance 1 and they are independent). The test is performed by plotting W_t against t. Confidence bounds for the sum are obtained by plotting the two lines that connect the points $[K, \pm a(T - K)^{1/2}]$ and $[T, \pm 3a(T - K)^{1/2}]$. Values of a that correspond to various significance levels can be found in their paper. Those corresponding to 95 percent and 99 percent are 0.948 and 1.143, respectively. The hypothesis is rejected if W_t strays outside the boundaries.

An alternative similar test is based on the squares of the recursive residuals. The CUSUM of squares (CUSUMSQ) test uses

$$S_t = \frac{\sum_{r=K+1}^{r=t} w_r^2}{\sum_{r=K+1}^{r=T} w_r^2}. \tag{7-27}$$

Since the residuals are independent, each of the two terms is approximately a sum of chi-squared variables each with one degree of freedom. Therefore, $E[S_t]$ is approximately $(t - K)/(T - K)$. The test is carried out by constructing confidence bounds for $E[S_t]$ at the values of t and plotting S_t and these bounds against t. The appropriate bounds are $E[S] \pm c_0$, where c_0 depends on both $(T - K)$ and the significance level desired.[23] As before, if the cumulated sum strays outside the confidence bounds, doubt is cast on the hypothesis of parameter stability.

A related test proposed by Harvey and Collier (1977) is based directly on the mean. Under the hypothesis of model stability, $\overline{w}$ is normally distributed, with mean zero and variance $\sigma^2/(T - K)$. The test is a familiar t test of the hypothesis that the mean of w_t is zero. The procedure uses

$$t[T - K - 1] = \frac{(\sqrt{T - K})\,\overline{w}}{s}, \tag{7-28}$$

where

$$s^2 = \frac{\sum_{r=K+1}^{r=T} (w_r - \overline{w})^2}{T - K - 1}. \tag{7-29}$$

The statistic is compared to the critical value from the t distribution with $T - K - 1$ degrees of freedom.

EXAMPLE 7.13 Tests of Model Stability

Example 11.4 presents estimates of a model of the demand for money using aggregate U.S. data for 1966 through 1985. Applying the previous tests to the data

[23]Tables may be found in Harvey (1990) and Johnston (1984). For an application, see Galpin and Hawkins (1984).

given in the example, we find the evidence mixed on whether the underlying parameter vector is unchanged for the 20 years.

Figures 7.2 and 7.3 and Table 7.7 show the CUSUM and CUSUMSQ tests based on these data. The CUSUM stays outside the boundaries for the last four observations. The CUSUM of squares is smaller than would be expected for most of the sample. Both tests suggest that the model is not stable over time. The Harvey–Collier test is based on

$$\overline{w} = 120.26$$

and

$$s = 132.08,$$

which gives

$$t[16] = 3.75.$$

This test agrees with the CUSUM test in suggesting that the parameters are not constant across the full 20 years. The CUSUM series suggests that the source of the instability, such as it is, is the last four observations. As a final

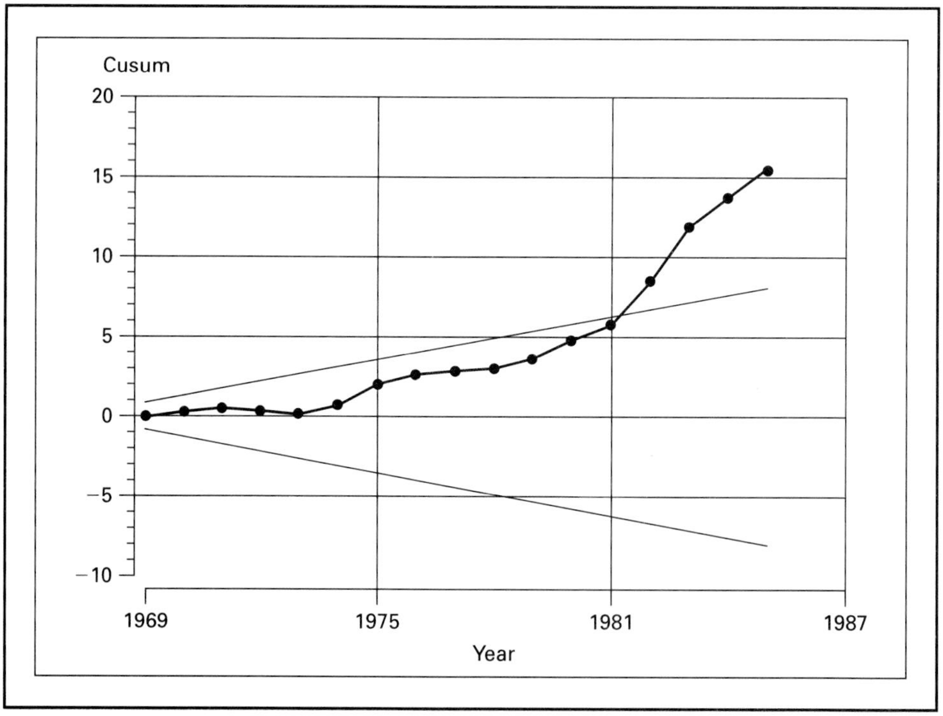

FIGURE 7.2 CUSUM Test.

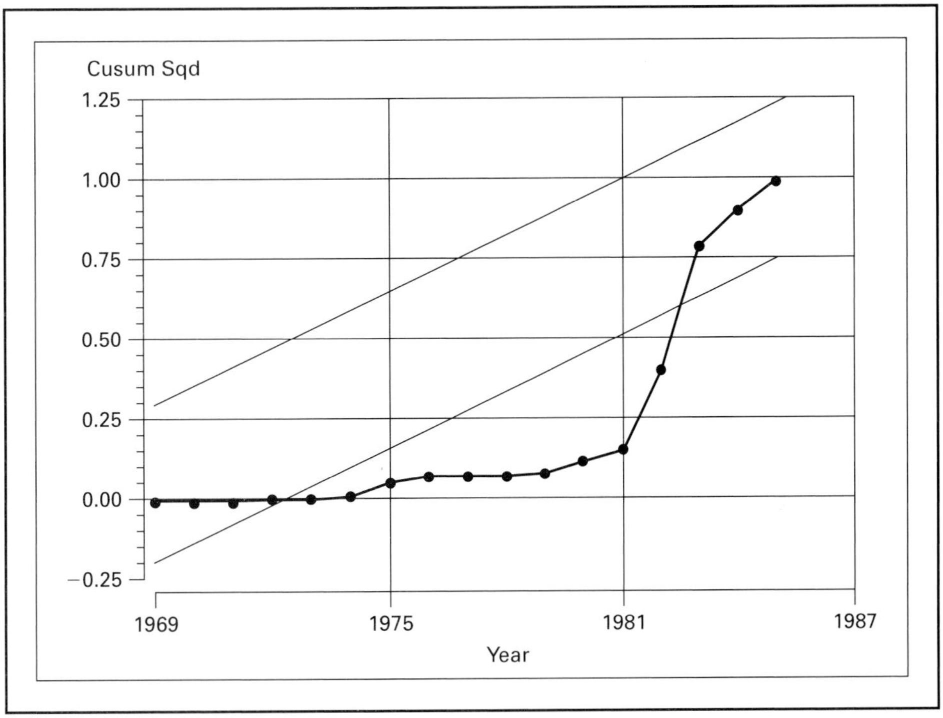

FIGURE 7.3 CUSUM of Squares Test.

check, we compute the Chow test of Example 7.7 for these four observations. The results are

$$F[3, 17] = \frac{[525{,}006.1 - (86{,}545.6 + 1330.8)]/3}{(86{,}545.6 + 1330.8)/(20 - 3 - 3)} = 23.21.$$

This is quite large and agrees with CUSUM and Harvey–Collier tests.

TABLE 7.7 CUSUM Tests

Year	*CUSUM*	*CUSUM²*	*Year*	*CUSUM*	*CUSUM²*
1966	0.000	0.000	1976	2.691	0.072
1967	0.000	0.000	1977	2.970	0.074
1968	0.000	0.000	1978	3.105	0.075
1969	−0.002	0.000	1979	3.748	0.089
1970	0.240	0.002	1980	4.877	0.131
1971	0.463	0.004	1981	5.885	0.165
1972	0.390	0.004	1982	8.601	0.410
1973	0.353	0.004	1983	12.039	0.830
1974	0.809	0.011	1984	13.853	0.912
1975	1.929	0.053	1985	15.48	1.000

7.9. TESTING NONLINEAR RESTRICTIONS

The preceding discussion has relied heavily on the linearity of the regression model. Most of the distributional results, for example, follow either from the normality of a linear function of normally distributed variables or from the F and chi-squared distributions derived from the normal distribution. When we analyze nonlinear functions of the parameters and nonlinear regression models, most of these exact distributional results no longer hold.

The general problem is that of testing a hypothesis that involves a nonlinear function of the regression coefficients:

$$H_0 : c(\boldsymbol{\beta}) = q.$$

We shall look at the case of a single restriction. The more general one, in which $\mathbf{c}(\boldsymbol{\beta}) = \mathbf{q}$ is a set of restrictions, is a simple extension, however. The counterpart to the test statistic we used earlier would be

$$z = \frac{c(\hat{\boldsymbol{\beta}}) - q}{\text{estimated standard error}} \tag{7-30}$$

or its square, which in the preceding were distributed as $t[n - K]$ and $F[1, n - K]$, respectively. The discrepancy in the numerator presents no difficulty. Obtaining an estimate of the sampling variance of $f(\boldsymbol{\beta}) - q$, however, involves the variance of a nonlinear function of $\hat{\boldsymbol{\beta}}$.

We obtained the results we need for this computation in Sections 3.9.3 and 4.4.4. A linear Taylor series approximation to $c(\hat{\boldsymbol{\beta}})$ around the true parameter vector $\boldsymbol{\beta}$ is

$$c(\hat{\boldsymbol{\beta}}) \approx c(\boldsymbol{\beta}) + \left(\frac{\partial c(\boldsymbol{\beta})}{\partial \boldsymbol{\beta}}\right)'(\hat{\boldsymbol{\beta}} - \boldsymbol{\beta}). \tag{7-31}$$

We must rely on consistency rather than unbiasedness here, since, in general, the expected value of a nonlinear function is not equal to the function of the expected value. If $\text{plim}(\hat{\boldsymbol{\beta}}) = \boldsymbol{\beta}$, we are justified in using $c(\hat{\boldsymbol{\beta}})$ as an estimate of $c(\boldsymbol{\beta})$. (The relevant result is the Slutsky theorem.) Assuming that our use of this approximation is appropriate, the variance of the nonlinear function is approximately equal to the variance of the right-hand side, which is, then,

$$\text{Var}[c(\hat{\boldsymbol{\beta}})] \approx \left(\frac{\partial c(\boldsymbol{\beta})}{\partial \boldsymbol{\beta}}\right)' \text{Var}[\hat{\boldsymbol{\beta}}] \left(\frac{\partial c(\boldsymbol{\beta})}{\partial \boldsymbol{\beta}}\right). \tag{7-32}$$

The derivatives in the expression for the variance are functions of the unknown parameters. Since these are being estimated, we use our sample estimates in computing the derivatives. To estimate the variance of the estimator, we can use $s^2(\mathbf{X}'\mathbf{X})^{-1}$, as is familiar. Finally, we rely on Theorem 6.11 in Section

6.7.5 and use the standard normal distribution instead of the t distribution for the test statistic. Using $f(\hat{\boldsymbol{\beta}})$ to estimate $f(\boldsymbol{\beta})$, we can now test a hypothesis in the same fashion we did earlier.

EXAMPLE 7.14 A Long-Run Marginal Propensity to Consume

A consumption function that has different short- and long-run marginal propensities to consume can be written in the form

$$C_t = \alpha + \beta Y_t + \gamma C_{t-1} + \epsilon_t.$$

(This is a *distributed lag* model. We consider these models in more detail in Chapter 16.) In this model, the short-run marginal propensity to consume is β, while the long-run marginal propensity to consume is $\delta = \beta/(1 - \gamma)$. Consider testing the hypothesis that $\delta = 1$.

The data in Table 7.8 are aggregate data on real consumption and GNP (deflated by the CPI) from the *1983 Economic Report of the President.* Least squares regression of consumption on a constant, GNP, and lagged consumption produces the results in Table 7.9.

The estimate of the long-run marginal propensity to consume is

$$d = \frac{b}{1 - c} = \frac{0.400147}{1 - 0.380728} = 0.6461.$$

To compute the estimated variance of d, we require that

$$\frac{\partial \delta}{\partial \beta} = \frac{1}{1 - \gamma} = 1.6149,$$

$$\frac{\partial \delta}{\partial \gamma} = \frac{\beta}{(1 - \gamma)^2} = 1.0434,$$

TABLE 7.8 Consumption and GNP Data

Year	*Consumption*	*GNP*	*Year*	*Consumption*	*GNP*
1963	522.67	832.57	1973	767.85	1254.28
1964	550.36	876.32	1974	771.72	1246.26
1965	578.81	929.40	1975	776.21	1231.58
1966	605.92	984.89	1976	819.93	1298.17
1967	620.16	1011.38	1977	859.98	1369.73
1968	650.47	1058.15	1978	895.16	1438.57
1969	670.35	1087.68	1979	922.29	1479.50
1970	679.83	1085.51	1980	933.27	1473.97
1971	700.14	1122.38	1981	942.77	1502.58
1972	737.10	1185.90	1982	951.60	1475.41

TABLE 7.9 Distributed Lag Model

Variable	*Coefficient*	*Standard Error*	*t ratio*
Constant	−7.69575	11.44	−0.672
Real GNP	0.400147	0.06272	6.380
Cons $(t-1)$	0.380728	0.09479	4.017
R-squared	0.99758		

Estimated Covariance Matrix of Estimates

	Constant	*Real GNP*	$Cons_{t-1}$
Constant	130.972		
Real GNP	−0.43868	0.00393	
Cons $(t-1)$	0.54959	−0.0058961	0.00898

when evaluated at our estimates. The estimated variance is

$$\begin{aligned}\text{Est. Var}[\hat{\delta}] &= 1.6149^2(0.00393) + 1.0434^2(0.00898) \\ &\quad - 2(1.6149)(1.0434)0.0058961 \\ &= 0.000155735.\end{aligned}$$

The square root is 0.012479. To test the hypothesis that the long-run marginal propensity to consume is greater than or equal to 1, we would use

$$z = \frac{0.6461 - 1}{0.012479} = -28.359.$$

Because we are using a large-sample approximation, we refer this to a standard normal table instead of the usual t distribution. Obviously, the hypothesis should be rejected.

We can use this example to illustrate a frequent problem with the Wald test. You may have noticed that we could have tested this hypothesis with a linear restriction, instead. That is,

$$\delta = 1 \Longrightarrow \beta = 1 - \gamma,$$

or $\beta + \gamma - 1 = 0$. Consider what happens when we test this restriction instead, using the results of Section 7.2.3. The estimate is $q = b + c - 1 = 0.400147 + 0.380728 - 1 = -0.219125$. The estimated standard error of this linear function is $[0.00393 + 0.00898 - 2(0.0058961)]^{1/2} = 0.0334335$. The t ratio for the test is -6.5541. This is still statistically significant by conventional measures. But the statistic is far smaller than the earlier one. This sort of result is common with Wald tests. The test statistic is not invariant with respect to the way the hypothesis is formulated. In a borderline case, we could well have reached a different conclusion depending on how the restriction is stated. This does not occur with likelihood ratio or Lagrange multiplier statistics. On the other hand, LR and LM tests require a firm assumption of normality, whereas the Wald test does not. Thus, we see one of the tradeoffs between a more detailed specification and the power of the test procedures that are implied.

The generalization to more than one function of the parameters proceeds along similar lines. Let $\mathbf{c}(\hat{\boldsymbol{\beta}})$ be set of J functions of the estimated parameter vector. The estimate of the sampling covariance matrix of these functions is

$$\text{Est. Var}[\hat{\mathbf{c}}] = \hat{\mathbf{C}}\{\text{Est. Var}[\hat{\boldsymbol{\beta}}]\}\hat{\mathbf{C}}', \tag{7-33}$$

where $\hat{\mathbf{C}}$ is a $J \times K$ matrix of derivatives:

$$\hat{\mathbf{C}} = \frac{\partial \mathbf{c}(\hat{\boldsymbol{\beta}})}{\partial \hat{\boldsymbol{\beta}}'}. \tag{7-34}$$

The jth row of $\mathbf{C}$ is K derivatives of c_j with respect to the K elements of $\hat{\boldsymbol{\beta}}$. For example, the covariance matrix for estimates of the short- and long-run marginal propensity to consume would be obtained using

$$\mathbf{c} = \begin{bmatrix} 0 & 1 & 0 \\ 0 & 1/(1-\gamma) & \beta/(1-\gamma)^2 \end{bmatrix}.$$

The statistic for testing the J hypotheses $\mathbf{c}(\boldsymbol{\beta}) = \mathbf{q}$ is

$$W = (\hat{\mathbf{c}} - \mathbf{q})'\{\text{Est. Var}[\hat{\mathbf{c}}]\}^{-1}(\hat{\mathbf{c}} - \mathbf{q}). \tag{7-35}$$

In large samples, W has a chi-squared distribution with degrees of freedom equal to the number of restrictions. Note that for a single restriction, this is the square of the statistic in (7-30).

The preceding analysis is based on the unrestricted least squares estimates. In the same way that we approached this problem before, we might have examined the loss of fit that results when the restrictions are imposed. But in this case, that would have involved fitting the regression subject to a set of nonlinear restrictions. Although straightforward in principle, this procedure can be more difficult in practice. The test statistic must be changed as well, since the F distribution no longer applies. But with normally distributed disturbances, the likelihood ratio statistic,

$$\lambda = n \ln\left(\frac{\hat{\sigma}_*^2}{\hat{\sigma}^2}\right),$$

where $\hat{\sigma}^2 = \mathbf{e}'\mathbf{e}/n$ and $\hat{\sigma}_*^2 = \mathbf{e}_*'\mathbf{e}_*/n$, is still appropriate. If the normality assumption is untenable, a large sample approximation to the F test can be based on

$$\chi^2[J] = n\frac{R^2 - R_*^2}{1 - R^2}.$$

7.10. CHOOSING BETWEEN NONNESTED MODELS

The classical testing procedures that we have been using have been shown to be most powerful (in the Neyman–Pearson sense) for the types of hypotheses we have considered.[24] Although this is clearly desirable, the requirement that we express the hypotheses in the form of restrictions on the model $\mathbf{y} = \mathbf{X}\boldsymbol{\beta} + \boldsymbol{\epsilon}$,

$$H_0 : \mathbf{R}\boldsymbol{\beta} = \mathbf{q}$$

versus

$$H_1 : \mathbf{R}\boldsymbol{\beta} \neq \mathbf{q},$$

can be limiting. Two common exceptions are the general problem of determining which of two possible sets of regressors is more appropriate and whether a linear or log-linear model is more appropriate for a given analysis. For the present, we are interested in comparing two competing linear models:

$$H_0 : \mathbf{y} = \mathbf{X}\boldsymbol{\beta} + \boldsymbol{\epsilon}_0 \tag{7-36a}$$

and

$$H_1 : \mathbf{y} = \mathbf{Z}\boldsymbol{\gamma} + \boldsymbol{\epsilon}_1 . \tag{7-36b}$$

The classical procedures we have considered thus far provide no means of forming a preference for one model or the other.

Before turning to classical- (frequentist-) based tests in this setting, we should note that the Bayesian approach to this question might be more intellectually appealing. Our procedures will continue to be directed toward an objective of rejecting one model in favor of the other. Yet, in fact, if we have doubts as to which of two models is appropriate, we might well be convinced to concede that possibly neither one is really "the truth." We have rather painted ourselves into a corner with our "left or right" approach. The Bayesian approach to this question treats it as a problem of comparing the two hypotheses rather than testing for the validity of one over the other. We enter our sampling experiment with a set of prior probabilities as to the relative merit of the two hypotheses, which is summarized in a "prior odds ratio," $P_{01} = \text{Prob}[H_0]/\text{Prob}[H_1]$. After gathering our data, we construct the Bayes factor, which summarizes the weight of the sample evidence in favor of one model or the other. After the data have been analyzed, we have our "posterior odds ratio,"

$$P_{01} | \text{data} = \text{Bayes factor} \times P_{01} .$$

The upshot is that ex post, neither model is discarded; we have merely revised our assessment of the comparative likelihood of the two in the face of the sample data. Some of the formalities of this approach are discussed in Section 6.9.5.

[24]See, for example, Stuart and Ord (1989, Chapter 27).

7.10.1. An Encompassing Model

Since H_1 cannot be written as a restriction on H_0, none of the procedures we have considered thus far is appropriate. One possibility is an artificial nesting of the two models. Let $\overline{\mathbf{X}}$ be the set of variables in $\mathbf{X}$ that are not in $\mathbf{Z}$, define $\overline{\mathbf{Z}}$ likewise with respect to $\mathbf{X}$, and let $\mathbf{W}$ be the variables that the models have in common. Then H_0 and H_1 could be combined in a "supermodel":

$$\mathbf{y} = \overline{\mathbf{X}}\overline{\boldsymbol{\beta}} + \overline{\mathbf{Z}}\overline{\boldsymbol{\gamma}} + \mathbf{W}\boldsymbol{\delta} + \boldsymbol{\epsilon}.$$

In principle, H_1 is rejected if it is found that $\overline{\boldsymbol{\gamma}} = \mathbf{0}$ by a conventional F test, whereas H_0 is rejected if it is found that $\overline{\boldsymbol{\beta}} = \mathbf{0}$. There are two problems with this approach. First, $\boldsymbol{\delta}$ remains a mixture of parts of $\boldsymbol{\beta}$ and $\boldsymbol{\gamma}$, and it is not established by the F test that either of these parts is zero. Hence, this test does not really distinguish between H_0 and H_1; it distinguishes between H_1 and a hybrid model. Second, this compound model may have an extremely large number of regressors. In a time-series setting, the problem of collinearity may be severe.

Consider an alternative approach. If H_0 is correct, then $\mathbf{y}$ will, apart from the random disturbance $\boldsymbol{\epsilon}$, be fully explained by $\mathbf{X}$. Suppose we then attempt to estimate $\boldsymbol{\gamma}$ by regression of $\mathbf{y}$ on $\mathbf{Z}$. Whatever set of parameters is estimated by this regression, say $\mathbf{c}$, if H_0 is correct, we should estimate exactly the same coefficient vector if we were to regress $\mathbf{X}\boldsymbol{\beta}$ on $\mathbf{Z}$, since $\boldsymbol{\epsilon}_0$ is random noise under H_0. Since $\boldsymbol{\beta}$ must be estimated, suppose that we use $\mathbf{Xb}$ instead and compute $\mathbf{c}_0$. A test of the proposition that model 0 "encompasses" model 1 would be a test of the hypothesis that $E[\mathbf{c} - \mathbf{c}_0] = \mathbf{0}$. It is straightforward to show [see Davidson and MacKinnon (1993, pp. 384–387)] that the test can be carried out by using a standard F test to test the hypothesis that $\boldsymbol{\gamma}_1 = \mathbf{0}$ in the augmented regression,

$$\mathbf{y} = \mathbf{X}\boldsymbol{\beta} + \mathbf{Z}_1\boldsymbol{\gamma}_1 + \boldsymbol{\epsilon}_1,$$

where $\mathbf{Z}_1$ is the variables in $\mathbf{Z}$ that are not in $\mathbf{X}$.

The general problem of testing nonnested hypotheses has attracted an impressive amount of attention in the theoretical literature.[25] Recent developments have been structured around a common pillar labeled the **encompassing principle** [Mizon and Richard (1986)]. In the large, the principle directs attention to the question of whether a maintained model can explain the features of its competitors, that is, whether the maintained model encompasses the alternative. It turns out that the two tests that we will consider here, Davidson and MacKinnon's J test and the Cox test, are tests of this sort.

7.10.2. The *J* Test

The J test proposed by Davidson and MacKinnon (1981) is similar in spirit to

[25]Recent surveys on this subject are White (1982a, 1983), Gourieroux and Monfort (1994) and Wang (1996). Despite the very large body of theory, the applied literature on nonnested tests, and the received stock of applications is surprisingly sparse.

the nesting strategy but overcomes its practical problems. An alternative to the preceding compound model is

$$\mathbf{y} = (1 - \alpha)\mathbf{X}\boldsymbol{\beta} + \alpha(\mathbf{Z}\boldsymbol{\gamma}) + \boldsymbol{\epsilon}.$$

In this model, a test of $\alpha = 0$ would be a test against H_1. The problem is that α cannot be estimated in this model; it would amount to a redundant scaling of the regression coefficients. Davidson and MacKinnon's J test consists of estimating $\boldsymbol{\gamma}$ by a least squares regression of $\mathbf{y}$ on $\mathbf{Z}$ followed by a least squares regression of $\mathbf{y}$ on $\mathbf{X}$ and $\mathbf{Z}\hat{\boldsymbol{\gamma}}$, the fitted values in the first regression. A valid test, at least asymptotically, of H_1 is to test $H_0: \alpha = 0$. If H_0 is true,

$$\text{plim } \hat{\alpha} = 0.$$

Asymptotically, the ratio $\hat{\alpha}/se(\hat{\alpha})$ (i.e., the usual t ratio) is distributed as standard normal and may be referred to the standard tables to carry out the test. Unfortunately, in testing H_0 versus H_1 and vice versa, all four possibilities (reject both, neither, or either one of the two hypotheses) could occur. This is, however, a finite sample problem. Davidson and MacKinnon show that as $n \to \infty$, if H_1 is true, the probability that $\hat{\alpha}$ will differ significantly from zero approaches 1.

EXAMPLE 7.15 *J* Test for a Consumption Function

Gaver and Geisel (1974) propose two forms of a consumption function:

$$H_0: C_t = \beta_1 + \beta_2 Y_t + \beta_3 Y_{t-1} + \epsilon_{0t}$$

and

$$H_1: C_t = \gamma_1 + \gamma_2 Y_t + \gamma_3 C_{t-1} + \epsilon_{1t}.$$

The first model states that consumption responds to changes in income over two periods, whereas the second states that the effects of changes in income on consumption persist for many periods. (These models are examined further in Chapter 17.) Data on aggregate U.S. consumption and income are given in Example 7.14. Here we apply the J test to these data and the previous two specifications. First, the two models are estimated separately. The least squares regression of C on a constant Y, lagged Y, and the fitted values from the second model produces an estimate of α of 2.74 with a t ratio of 5.21. Thus, H_0 should be rejected in favor of H_1. But reversing the roles of H_0 and H_1, we obtain an estimate of α of -2.70 with a t ratio of -3.55. Thus, H_1 is rejected as well.[26]

7.10.3. The Cox Test

A related set of procedures based on the likelihood ratio test has been devised by Cox (1961, 1962). The versions of the Cox test appropriate for the linear and nonlinear regression models have been derived by Pesaran (1974) and Pesaran

[26]For related discussion of this possibility, see McAleer et al. (1982).

and Deaton (1978). The latter present a test statistic for testing linear versus log-linear models that is extended in Aneuryn-Evans and Deaton (1980). Since in the classical regression model, the least squares estimator is also the maximum likelihood estimator, it is perhaps not surprising that Davidson and MacKinnon (1981, p. 789) find that their test statistic is asymptotically equal to the negative of the Cox–Pesaran and Deaton statistic. The Cox statistic for testing the hypothesis that $\mathbf{X}$ is the correct set of regressors and that $\mathbf{Z}$ is not is

$$\begin{aligned} c_{01} &= \frac{n}{2}\ln\left[\frac{s_z^2}{s_x^2 + (1/n)\mathbf{b}'\mathbf{X}'\mathbf{M}_z\mathbf{X}\mathbf{b}}\right] \\ &= \frac{n}{2}\ln\left[\frac{s_z^2}{s_{zx}^2}\right], \end{aligned} \tag{7-37}$$

where

$$\begin{aligned} \mathbf{M}_z &= \mathbf{I} - \mathbf{Z}(\mathbf{Z}'\mathbf{Z})^{-1}\mathbf{Z}', \\ \mathbf{M}_x &= \mathbf{I} - \mathbf{X}(\mathbf{X}'\mathbf{X})^{-1}\mathbf{X}', \\ \mathbf{b} &= (\mathbf{X}'\mathbf{X})^{-1}\mathbf{X}'\mathbf{y}. \\ s_z^2 &= \frac{1}{n}\mathbf{e}_z'\mathbf{e}_z = \text{mean-squared residual in the regression of } \mathbf{y} \text{ on } \mathbf{Z}, \\ s_x^2 &= \frac{1}{n}\mathbf{e}_x'\mathbf{e}_x = \text{mean-squared residual in the regression of } \mathbf{y} \text{ on } \mathbf{X}, \end{aligned}$$

and

$$s_{zx}^2 = s_x^2 + \frac{1}{n}\mathbf{b}'\mathbf{X}'\mathbf{M}_z\mathbf{X}\mathbf{b}.$$

The hypothesis is tested by comparing

$$\begin{aligned} q &= \frac{c_{01}}{\{\text{Est. Var}[c_{01}]\}^{1/2}} \\ &= \frac{c_{01}}{\sqrt{\dfrac{s_x^2}{s_{zx}^4}\mathbf{b}'\mathbf{X}'\mathbf{M}_z\mathbf{M}_x\mathbf{M}_z\mathbf{X}\mathbf{b}}} \end{aligned} \tag{7-38}$$

with the critical value from the standard normal table. A large value of q is evidence against the null hypothesis (H_0). Although this involves a substantial amount of matrix algebra, there are several shortcuts that will simplify the result:

$$\begin{aligned} \mathbf{X}\mathbf{b} &= \text{fitted values in the regression of } \mathbf{y} \text{ on } \mathbf{X}, \\ \mathbf{M}_z\mathbf{X}\mathbf{b} &= \text{residuals in a regression of } \mathbf{X}\mathbf{b} \text{ on } \mathbf{Z}, \\ \mathbf{b}'\mathbf{X}'\mathbf{M}_z\mathbf{X}\mathbf{b} &= \text{sum of squared residuals in the regression of } \mathbf{X}\mathbf{b} \text{ on } \mathbf{Z}, \\ (\mathbf{b}'\mathbf{X}'\mathbf{M}_z)\mathbf{M}_x(\mathbf{M}_z\mathbf{X}\mathbf{b}) &= \text{sum of squared residuals in the regression of } \mathbf{M}_z\mathbf{X}\mathbf{b} \text{ on } \mathbf{X}. \end{aligned}$$

Therefore, the Cox statistic can be computed simply by computing a set of least squares regressions.

EXAMPLE 7.16 Cox Test for a Consumption Function

We continue the previous example by applying the Cox test to the data of Example 7.14. For purposes of the test, let $\mathbf{X} = [\mathbf{i} \;\; \mathbf{y} \;\; \mathbf{y}_{-1}]$ and $\mathbf{Z} = [\mathbf{i} \;\; \mathbf{y} \;\; \mathbf{c}_{-1}]$. Using the notation of (7-37) and (7-38), we find that

$$\begin{aligned} s_x^2 &= 60.09631, \\ s_z^2 &= 39.36133, \\ \mathbf{b}'\mathbf{X}'\mathbf{M}_z\mathbf{X}\mathbf{b} &= 46.630105, \\ \mathbf{b}'\mathbf{X}'\mathbf{M}_z\mathbf{M}_x\mathbf{M}_z\mathbf{X}\mathbf{b} &= 40.592986, \end{aligned}$$

and

$$s_{zx}^2 = 60.09631 + \frac{46.630105}{19} = 62.50527.$$

Thus,

$$c_{01} = \frac{19}{2} \ln\left(\frac{39.36133}{62.50527}\right) = -4.4003$$

and

$$\text{Est. Var}[c_{01}] = \frac{60.09631(40.592986)}{62.50527^2} = 0.62441.$$

Thus, $q = -5.569$. On this basis, we reject the hypothesis that $\mathbf{X}$ is the correct set of regressors. Note in the previous example that we reached the same conclusion based on a t ratio of 5.21. As expected, the result has the opposite sign from the corresponding J statistic in the previous example. Now we reverse the roles of $\mathbf{X}$ and $\mathbf{Z}$ in our calculations. Letting $\mathbf{d}$ denote the least squares coefficients in the regression of consumption on $\mathbf{Z}$, we find that

$$\begin{aligned} \mathbf{d}'\mathbf{Z}'\mathbf{M}_x\mathbf{Z}\mathbf{d} &= 97.63601, \\ \mathbf{d}'\mathbf{Z}'\mathbf{M}_x\mathbf{M}_z\mathbf{M}_x\mathbf{Z}\mathbf{d} &= 84.99524, \end{aligned}$$

so that

$$s_{xz}^2 = 39.36133 + \frac{97.36601}{19} = 44.50007.$$

Thus,

$$c_{10} = \frac{19}{2} \ln\left(\frac{60.09631}{44.50007}\right) = 2.8543$$

and

$$\text{Est. Var}[c_{10}] = \frac{39.36133(84.99524)}{44.50007^2} = 1.6894.$$

This produces a value of $q = 2.196$, which is considerably smaller (in absolute value) than its counterpart in Example 7.11, −3.55. Since 2.196 is greater than the 5 percent critical value of 1.96, we would once again reject the hypothesis that **Z** is the preferred set of regressors.

7.11. PREDICTION

After the estimation of parameters, the most common use of regression is for prediction. Suppose that we wish to predict the value of y^0 associated with a regressor vector $\mathbf{x}^0$. This would be

$$y^0 = \boldsymbol{\beta}'\mathbf{x}^0 + \epsilon^0.$$

It follows from the Gauss–Markov theorem that

$$\hat{y}^0 = \mathbf{b}'\mathbf{x}^0 \tag{7-39}$$

is the minimum variance linear unbiased estimator of $E[y^0]$. The forecast error is

$$e^0 = y^0 - \hat{y}^0 = (\boldsymbol{\beta} - \mathbf{b})'\mathbf{x}^0 + \epsilon^0.$$

The forecast variance to be applied to this estimate is

$$\begin{aligned}\text{Var}[e^0] &= \sigma^2 + \text{Var}[(\boldsymbol{\beta} - \mathbf{b})'\mathbf{x}^0] \\ &= \sigma^2 + \mathbf{x}^{0\prime}[\sigma^2(\mathbf{X}'\mathbf{X})^{-1}]\mathbf{x}^0.\end{aligned} \tag{7-40}$$

If the regression contains a constant term, an equivalent expression is

$$\text{Var}[e^0] = \sigma^2\left[1 + \frac{1}{n} + \sum_{j=2}^{K}\sum_{k=2}^{K}(x_j^0 - \bar{x}_j)(x_k^0 - \bar{x}_k)(\mathbf{X}'\mathbf{M}^0\mathbf{X})^{jk}\right].$$

This shows that the width of the interval depends on the distance of the elements of $\mathbf{x}^0$ from the center of the data. Intuitively, this makes sense; the farther the forecasted point is from the center of our experience, the greater the degree of uncertainty.

The forecast variance can be estimated by using s^2 in place of σ^2. A confidence interval for y^0 would be formed using

$$\text{forecast interval} = \hat{y}^0 \pm t_{\lambda/2}\text{se}(\hat{y}^0).$$

Figure 7.4 shows the effect for the bivariate case. Note that the forecast variance is composed of three parts. The second and third become progressively smaller as we accumulate more data (i.e., as n increases). But the first term σ^2 is constant, which implies that no matter how much data we have, we can never predict perfectly.

EXAMPLE 7.17 Forecast for Investment

Suppose that we wish to forecast the 1983 value of real investment based on forecasts of (1) real GNP = 1.5 trillion, (2) a discount rate of 10 percent, and

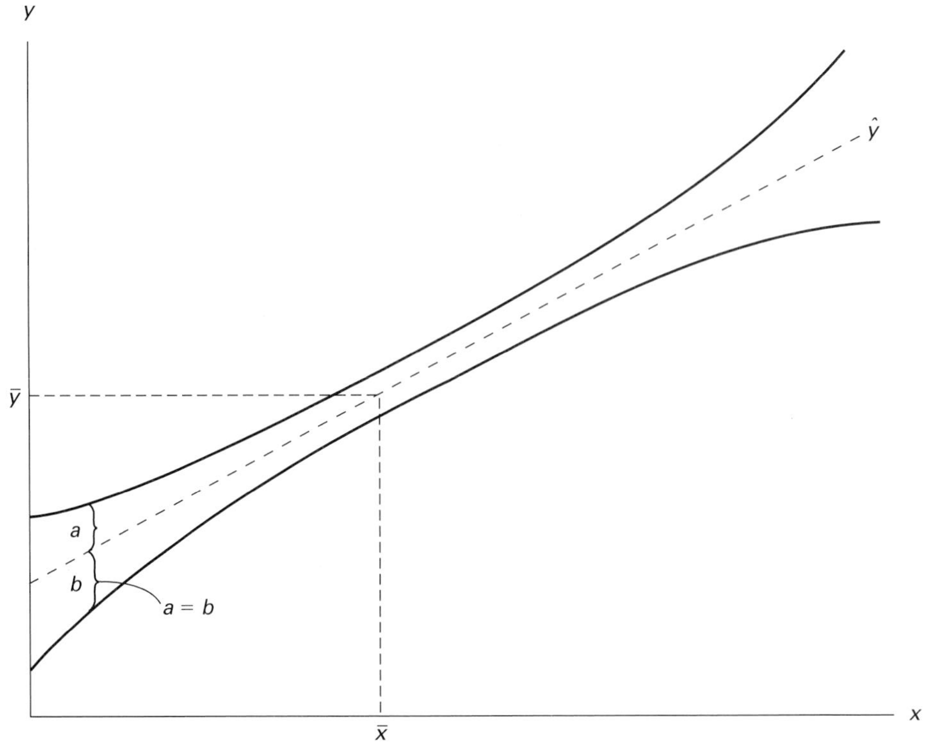

FIGURE 7.4 Forecast Intervals.

(3) inflation of 4 percent, using the regression results in Example 6.5. The forecast is $\mathbf{x}^0\mathbf{b}$:

$$(1, 16, 1.5, 10, 4)(-0.509, -0.017, 0.670, -0.002, -0.0001)' = 0.2036.$$

The estimated variance of this forecast is

$$s^2[1 + \mathbf{x}^{0\prime}(\mathbf{X}'\mathbf{X})^{-1}\mathbf{x}^0] = 0.00009772113.$$

Using the square root of this result, we obtain the forecast interval:

$$0.2036 \pm 2.228(0.009885) = <0.1811, 0.2262>.$$

7.11.1. A Convenient Method of Computing the Forecasts

The preceding might suggest that two sets of computations are necessary to obtain the predictions (7-39) and the associated standard errors (7-40): first, the least squares estimates are obtained, and second, the forecasts and the forecast variances are computed. Salkever (1976) has suggested a convenient method of combining the computations by using an expanded regression. Suppose that the estimation is based on n observations and that we desire to forecast n^0 observations,

$$\mathbf{y}^0 = \mathbf{X}^0\boldsymbol{\beta} + \boldsymbol{\epsilon}^0.$$

We first construct an augmented regression:

$$\begin{bmatrix}\mathbf{y}\\ \mathbf{0}\end{bmatrix} = \begin{bmatrix}\mathbf{X} & \mathbf{0}\\ \mathbf{X}^0 & -\mathbf{I}\end{bmatrix}\begin{bmatrix}\boldsymbol{\beta}\\ \boldsymbol{\gamma}\end{bmatrix} + \begin{bmatrix}\boldsymbol{\epsilon}\\ \boldsymbol{\epsilon}^0\end{bmatrix} \tag{7-41}$$

or

$$\mathbf{y}^* = \mathbf{X}^*\boldsymbol{\beta}^* + \boldsymbol{\epsilon}^*.$$

In (7-41) there are n^0 new observations added and a set of n^0 new variables. Each column in the second part of $\mathbf{X}^*$ is a **dummy variable** that takes the value minus one only for that observation and zero for all others. (Note that the new parameter vector $\boldsymbol{\gamma}$ is $\mathbf{y}^0$.)

Using this expanded regression model, we obtain the following results.

- The least squares regression of $\mathbf{y}^*$ on $\mathbf{X}^*$ produces the coefficient vector $[\mathbf{b}, \mathbf{c}]$, where $\mathbf{b}$ is the original OLS coefficient vector and $\mathbf{c}$ is the predictions for $\mathbf{y}^0$.

  Proof:

$$\mathbf{X}^{*\prime}\mathbf{X}^* = \begin{bmatrix}\mathbf{X}'\mathbf{X} + \mathbf{X}^{0\prime}\mathbf{X}^0 & -\mathbf{X}^{0\prime}\\ -\mathbf{X}^0 & \mathbf{I}\end{bmatrix} \quad\text{and}\quad \mathbf{X}^{*\prime}\mathbf{y}^* = \begin{bmatrix}\mathbf{X}'\mathbf{y}\\ \mathbf{0}\end{bmatrix}.$$

  Using the partitioned inverse formula from Chapter 2, we obtain

$$(\mathbf{X}^{*\prime}\mathbf{X}^*)^{-1} = \begin{bmatrix}(\mathbf{X}'\mathbf{X})^{-1} & (\mathbf{X}'\mathbf{X})^{-1}\mathbf{X}^{0\prime}\\ \mathbf{X}^0(\mathbf{X}'\mathbf{X})^{-1} & \mathbf{I} + \mathbf{X}^{0\prime}(\mathbf{X}'\mathbf{X})^{-1}\mathbf{X}^0\end{bmatrix}.$$

  Postmultiplying $(\mathbf{X}^{*\prime}\mathbf{X}^*)^{-1}$ by $\mathbf{X}^{*\prime}\mathbf{y}^*$ produces the result.

- The residuals from this regression are, for the first T observations, the original least squares residuals and for the last n^0, zero. The first part is obvious, since the coefficient vector is the same. Multiplying out produces

$$\mathbf{y}^* - \mathbf{X}^*\mathbf{b}^* = \begin{bmatrix}\mathbf{e}\\ \mathbf{0}\end{bmatrix}.$$

- The estimated covariance matrix for the expanded vector of coefficient estimates contains, in its upper left block, the covariance matrix for the least squares estimates of $\boldsymbol{\beta}$ and, in its lower right block, the covariance matrix for the forecasts.

  Proof:

$$s^{2*} = \frac{\mathbf{e}^{*\prime}\mathbf{e}^*}{n^* - K^*} = \frac{\mathbf{e}'\mathbf{e} + \mathbf{0}'\mathbf{0}}{n + n^0 - (K + n^0)} = s^2.$$

  Therefore,

$$s^{2*}(\mathbf{X}^{*\prime}\mathbf{X}^*)^{-1} = \begin{bmatrix}s^2(\mathbf{X}'\mathbf{X})^{-1} & *\\ * & s^2[\mathbf{I} + \mathbf{X}^{0\prime}(\mathbf{X}'\mathbf{X})^{-1}\mathbf{X}^0]\end{bmatrix},$$

where * indicates a submatrix for which we have no convenient interpretation. The upper matrix is familiar. The ith diagonal element of the lower matrix is

$$\text{Est. Var}[c_i] = \text{Est. Var}[\hat{y}_i^0] = s^2[1 + \mathbf{x}_i^{0\prime}(\mathbf{X}'\mathbf{X})^{-1}\mathbf{x}_i^0],$$

which is (7-40). This completes the proof.

These results imply that the standard computer output from this expanded regression will contain, in addition to the usual least squares results, the forecasts and estimated forecast variances or standard errors. One thing to note is that the R^2 in the expanded regression will be incorrect. The total sum of squares will be computed using an expanded $\mathbf{y}$ vector containing a set of zeros. It would be possible to patch this up by replacing the zeros in $\mathbf{y}^*$ with $\bar{y}$ from the original data, but then the lower subvector of the coefficient vector would no longer be the least squares predictions.

There is an interesting corollary that follows from the second result. It is not uncommon for researchers to include a dummy variable in a regression to account for something that applies only to a single observation. For example, in time-series studies, an occasional study includes a dummy variable that is one only in a single unusual year, such as the year of a major strike. The result shows what the effect of this variable will be.

A dummy variable that takes the value 1 only for one observation has the effect of deleting that observation from the least squares computations.

7.11.2. Measuring the Accuracy of Forecasts

Various measures have been proposed for assessing the predictive accuracy of forecasting models.[27] Most of these measures are designed to evaluate **ex post forecasts,** that is, forecasts for which the exogenous variables do not have to be forecasted. Two that are based on the residuals from the forecasts are the root mean squared error

$$\text{RMSE} = \sqrt{\frac{1}{n^0}\sum_i (y_i - \hat{y}_i)^2}$$

and the mean absolute error

$$\text{MAE} = \frac{1}{n^0}\sum_i |y_i - \hat{y}_i|,$$

[27]See Theil (1961) and Fair (1984).

where n^0 is the number of periods being forecasted. These have an obvious scaling problem. Several measures that do not are based on the Theil U statistic:[28]

$$U = \sqrt{\frac{(1/n^0)\sum_i (y_i - \hat{y}_i)^2}{(1/n^0)\sum_i y_i^2}}.$$

This measure is related to R^2 but is not bounded by 0 and 1. Large values indicate a poor forecasting performance. An alternative is to compute the measure in terms of the changes in y:

$$U_\Delta = \sqrt{\frac{(1/n^0)\sum_i (\Delta y_i - \Delta \hat{y}_i)^2}{(1/n^0)\sum_i (\Delta y_i)^2}},$$

where $\Delta y_i = y_i - y_{i-1}$ and $\Delta \hat{y}_i = \hat{y}_i - y_{i-1}$, or, in percentage changes, $\Delta y_i = (y_i - y_{i-1})/y_{i-1}$ and $\Delta \hat{y}_i = (\hat{y}_i - y_{i-1})/y_{i-1}$. These measures will reflect the model's ability to track turning points in the data.

EXAMPLE 7.18 Forecasting Performance

Most of the cyclical variation in the investment data we have analyzed is picked up by GNP. Consider a comparison of the predictions of two models, one that includes GNP and one that does not. For these two candidates, the results are listed in Table 7.10. The last of these is particularly pronounced. In a forecasting model, the ability to predict turning points is obviously important. The actual values and predictions from the two competing models presented are shown in Table 7.11. There were declines in real investment in 1970, 1973, 1974, 1980, and 1982. The model including GNP predicted all five turning points. The one omitting GNP missed all five. Figure 7.5 shows the effect.

TABLE 7.10

	With GNP	*Without GNP*
RMSE	0.005482	0.02183
MAE	0.004227	0.01692
U	0.02661	0.10559
U_Δ^a	0.19727	0.89600

[a] U_Δ is computed using the absolute rather than the percentage changes.

[28] Theil (1961).

TABLE 7.11 Investment Forecasts

	1968	*1969*	*1970*	*1971*	*1972*	*1973*	*1974*	*1975*
Actual	0.161	0.172	0.158	0.173	0.195	0.217	0.199	0.163
With GNP	0.171	0.173	0.155	0.165	0.192	0.217	0.191	0.187
Without GNP	0.162	0.168	0.174	0.181	0.187	0.192	0.198	0.205

	1976	*1977*	*1978*	*1979*	*1980*	*1981*	*1982*
Actual	0.195	0.231	0.257	0.259	0.225	0.241	0.204
With GNP	0.199	0.230	0.255	0.259	0.234	0.234	0.205
Without GNP	0.210	0.216	0.222	0.226	0.231	0.236	0.243

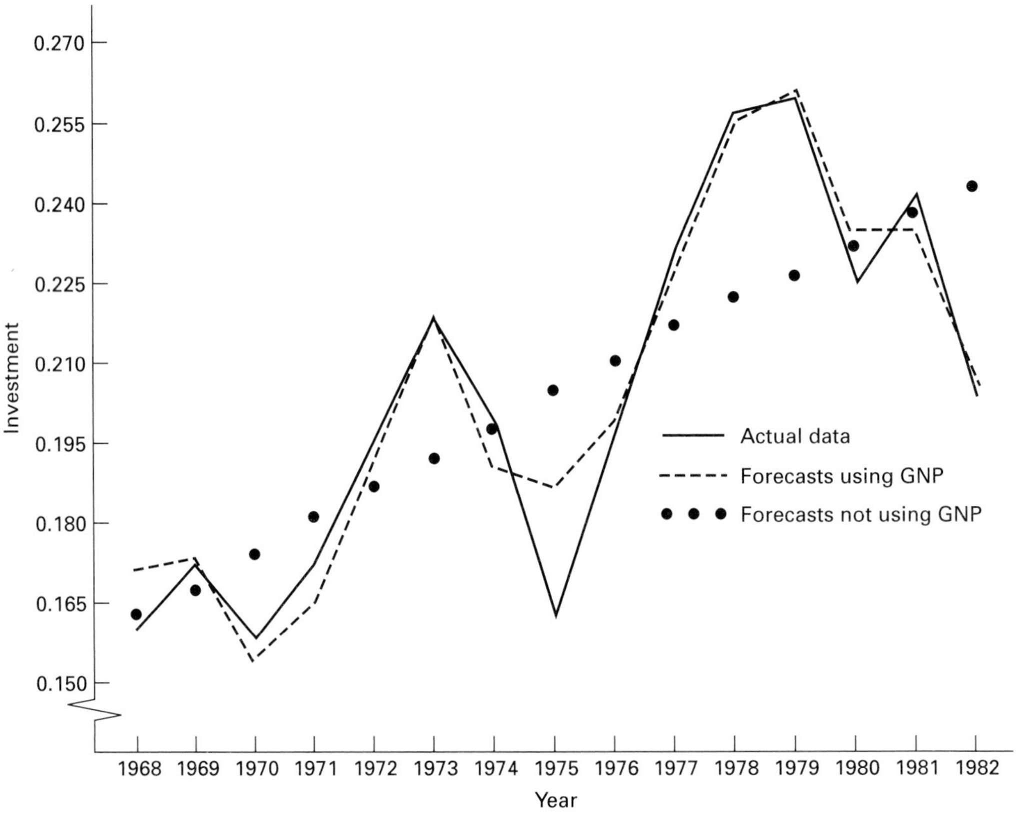

FIGURE 7.5 Model Forecasts.

EXERCISES

1. A multiple regression of y on a constant x_1 and x_2 produces the following results:

$$\hat{y} = 4 + 0.4x_1 + 0.9x_2, R^2 = 8/60, \quad \mathbf{e'e} = 520, \quad n = 29,$$
$$\mathbf{X'X} = \begin{bmatrix} 29 & 0 & 0 \\ 0 & 50 & 10 \\ 0 & 10 & 80 \end{bmatrix}.$$

Test the hypothesis that the two slopes sum to 1.

2. Using the results in Exercise 1, test the hypothesis that the slope on x_1 is zero by running the restricted regression and comparing the two sums of squared deviations.

3. The translog production function in Example 7.7 has constant returns to scale if

$$\frac{\partial \ln Y}{\partial \ln L} + \frac{\partial \ln Y}{\partial \ln K} = 1$$

for all values of K and L. (This model is analyzed in some detail in Chapter 15.

(a) What restrictions on the coefficients produce constant returns to scale? How would you estimate the restricted model? A Cobb–Douglas production function with constant returns to scale is a restriction on the translog model with constant returns to scale. What is the restriction? How would you test the restriction as a hypothesis?

(b) Using the data given in Table 7.1, estimate the translog model subject to the restrictions of constant returns to scale and test the hypothesis. Carry out a test of the hypothesis of a Cobb–Douglas technology assuming constant returns to scale.

4. The gasoline data of Exercise 22 in Chapter 6 span the years of the oil embargo of 1973 and the tumultuous period thereafter. Did the market change sufficiently in 1973 that it is inappropriate to pool the data? The results of that example notwithstanding, regressions of G on a constant, P_g, Y, and P_{pt} produce the following residual sums of squares:

1960–1986	*1960–1973*	*1974–1986*
841.3	40.57	246.51

(a) Carry out a Chow test of the hypothesis that the coefficient vectors are the same in the two subperiods. What are you assuming in making this test?

(b) An alternative hypothesis is that the year 1973 and the few (say, 4) subsequent years that it took to return to normalcy in the market were aberrations. How would you test this hypothesis in the context of the full regression estimated in Exercise 6 of Chapter 6?

(c) Carry out the test in part (b).

5. Two samples of 50 observations each produce the following moment matrices (in each case, **X** is a constant and one variable):

	Sample 1	*Sample 2*
$\mathbf{X}'\mathbf{X}$	$\begin{bmatrix} 50 & 300 \\ 300 & 2100 \end{bmatrix}$	$\begin{bmatrix} 50 & 300 \\ 300 & 2100 \end{bmatrix}$
$\mathbf{y}'\mathbf{X}$	$[300 \quad 2000]$	$[300 \quad 2200]$
$\mathbf{y}'\mathbf{y}$	2100	2500

(a) Test the hypothesis that the same regression coefficients apply in both data sets assuming that the disturbance variances are the same.

(b) Use a Wald test to test the hypothesis that the two coefficient vectors are the same without assuming that the disturbance variances are the same.

6. The regression model to be analyzed is $\mathbf{y} = \mathbf{X}_1\boldsymbol{\beta}_1 + \mathbf{X}_2\boldsymbol{\beta}_2 + \boldsymbol{\epsilon}$, where $\mathbf{X}_1$ and $\mathbf{X}_2$ have K_1 and K_2 columns, respectively. The restriction is $\boldsymbol{\beta}_2 = \mathbf{0}$.

(a) Using (7-12), prove that the restricted estimator is simply $[\mathbf{b}_1, \mathbf{0}]$, where $\mathbf{b}_1$ is the least squares coefficient vector in the regression of $\mathbf{y}$ on $\mathbf{X}_1$.

(b) Prove that if the restriction is $\boldsymbol{\beta}_2 = \boldsymbol{\beta}_2^0$ for a nonzero $\boldsymbol{\beta}_2^0$, the restricted estimator of $\boldsymbol{\beta}_1$ is

$$\mathbf{b}_{1*} = (\mathbf{X}_1'\mathbf{X}_1)^{-1}\mathbf{X}_1'(\mathbf{y} - \mathbf{X}_2\boldsymbol{\beta}_2^0).$$

7. The expression for the restricted coefficient vector in (7-12) may be written in the form

$$\mathbf{b}_* = [\mathbf{I} - \mathbf{CR}]\mathbf{b} + \mathbf{w},$$

where **w** does not involve **b**. What is **C**? Show that covariance matrix of the restricted least squares estimator is

$$\sigma^2(\mathbf{X}'\mathbf{X})^{-1} - \sigma^2(\mathbf{X}'\mathbf{X})^{-1}\mathbf{R}'[\mathbf{R}(\mathbf{X}'\mathbf{X})^{-1}\mathbf{R}']^{-1}\mathbf{R}(\mathbf{X}'\mathbf{X})^{-1}$$

and that this matrix may be written as

$$\text{Var}[\mathbf{b}]\{[\text{Var}(\mathbf{b})]^{-1} - \mathbf{R}'[\text{Var}(\mathbf{Rb})]^{-1}\mathbf{R}\}\text{Var}[\mathbf{b}].$$

8. Prove the result that the restricted least squares estimator never has a larger covariance matrix than the unrestricted least squares estimator.

9. Prove the result that the R^2 associated with a restricted least squares estimator is never larger than that associated with the unrestricted least squares estimator. Conclude that imposing restrictions never improves the fit of the regression.

10. What is the vector $\mathbf{w}$ in Exercise 7?

11. The Lagrange multiplier test of the hypothesis $\mathbf{R}\boldsymbol{\beta} - \mathbf{q} = \mathbf{0}$ is equivalent to a Wald test of the hypothesis that $\boldsymbol{\lambda} = \mathbf{0}$, where $\boldsymbol{\lambda}$ is defined in (7-12). Prove that

$$\chi^2 = \boldsymbol{\lambda}'\{\text{Est. Var}[\boldsymbol{\lambda}]\}^{-1}\boldsymbol{\lambda} = (n - K)\left[\frac{\mathbf{e}_*'\mathbf{e}_*}{\mathbf{e}'\mathbf{e}} - 1\right].$$

Note that the fraction in brackets is the ratio of two estimators of σ^2. By virtue of (7-13) and the preceding discussion, we know that this is greater than 1. Finally, prove that the Lagrange multiplier statistic is simply JF, where J is the number of restrictions being tested and F is the conventional F statistic given in (7-14).

12. Use the Lagrange multiplier test to test the hypothesis in Exercise 1.

13. Using the data and model of Exercise 6 in Chapter 6, carry out a test of the hypothesis that the three aggregate price indices are not significant determinants of the demand for gasoline.

14. Suppose that there are two competing models for the gasoline market of Exercise 22 in Chapter 6. Both models include the constant, time trend, price of gasoline, and income. Model 1 includes the three microeconomic price indices P_{nc}, P_{uc}, and P_{pt}. Model 2 argues that these are just components in the broader categories. Thus, model 2 includes P_d, P_n, and P_s instead. Use the J or Cox test to determine which theory is better. [Hint: The results of Exercise 22(a) in Chapter 6 should give you an idea of what to expect.]

15. The model of Exercise 22 in Chapter 6 may be written in logarithmic terms as

$$\ln G = \alpha + \beta_p \ln P_g + \beta_y \ln Y + \gamma_{nc} \ln P_{nc} + \gamma_{uc} \ln P_{uc} + \gamma_{pt} \ln P_{pt} + \beta\,\text{year} + \delta_d \ln P_d + \delta_n \ln P_n + \delta_s \ln P_s + \epsilon.$$

Consider the hypothesis that the microelasticities are a constant proportion of the elasticity with respect to their corresponding aggregate. Thus, for some positive θ (presumably between 0 and 1),

$$\gamma_{nc} = \theta\delta_d,$$
$$\gamma_{uc} = \theta\delta_d,$$
$$\gamma_{pt} = \theta\delta_s.$$

The first two imply the simple linear restriction $\gamma_{nc} = \gamma_{uc}$. By taking ratios, the first (or second) and third imply the nonlinear restriction

$$\frac{\gamma_{nc}}{\gamma_{pt}} = \frac{\delta_d}{\delta_s} \quad \text{or} \quad \gamma_{nc}\delta_s - \gamma_{pt}\delta_d = 0.$$

(a) Describe in detail how you would test the validity of the restriction.

(b) Using the data in Exercise 22 in Chapter 6, test the restrictions separately and jointly.

16. Prove that under the hypothesis that $\mathbf{R}\boldsymbol{\beta} = \mathbf{q}$, the estimator

$$s_*^2 = \frac{(\mathbf{y} - \mathbf{X}\mathbf{b}_*)'(\mathbf{y} - \mathbf{X}\mathbf{b}_*)}{n - K + J},$$

where J is the number of restrictions, is unbiased for σ^2.

17. Show that in the multiple regression of $\mathbf{y}$ on a constant $\mathbf{x}_1$ and $\mathbf{x}_2$, using (7-3) to impose the restriction $\beta_1 + \beta_2 = 1$ leads to the regression of $\mathbf{y} - \mathbf{x}_1$ on a constant and $\mathbf{x}_2 - \mathbf{x}_1$.

18. Using the results of Example 6.8, compute a 95 percent forecast interval for real investment for 1983 assuming forecasts of 3100 for nominal GNP, 212 for the CPI, and 10.0 for the interest rate.

CHAPTER 8

Functional Form, Nonlinearity, and Specification

8.1. INTRODUCTION

In this chapter, we are concerned with the functional form of the regression model. There are many different types of functions that are "linear" by our definition. By using dummy variables and different arrangements of functions of variables, we can produce an impressive variety of models. Sections 8.2 and 8.3 examine some of the devices used in constructing regression models. Sections 8.4 and 8.5 consider some questions concerning errors in the specification of the model and the dangers of using the same data both to estimate parameters and to determine what form the model will take.

8.2. DUMMY VARIABLES

One of the most useful devices in regression analysis is the binary, or **dummy,** variable. We have used it in two previous applications: in Section 7.11.1 in computing forecasts and in Section 7.6 in constructing Chow tests for structural change. In both cases, these variables were only computational devices. But binary variables are also a convenient means of building discrete shifts of the function into a regression model.

8.2.1. Comparing Two Means

A comparison of the means of a variable in two groups might be formulated as follows:

$$\begin{aligned} &\text{group 1:} \quad y_i = \mu + \epsilon_i, \\ &\text{group 2:} \quad y_i = \mu + \delta + \epsilon_i. \end{aligned}$$

The parameter δ is of particular interest. By defining the variable d as

$$d_i = 0 \text{ if group 1} \quad \text{and} \quad d_i = 1 \text{ if group 2,}$$[1]

these may be combined into the single equation

$$y_i = \mu + \delta d_i + \epsilon_i.$$

If, for example, y_i is income and d_i indicates whether or not the individual attended college, then

$$E[\text{income} \mid \text{did not attend college}] = \mu$$

and

$$E[\text{income} \mid \text{attended college}] = \mu + \delta.$$

In this model, δ is the difference between the expected incomes of the two groups. A test of whether δ is zero is equivalent to a test that this difference is zero or that the means are the same. An alternative model is

$$y_i = \mu_N + \epsilon_i \quad \text{for those who did not attend college}$$

and

$$y_i = \mu_C + \epsilon_i \quad \text{for those who attended college.}$$

By defining $h_i = 1$ if individual i did not attend college and $h_i = 0$ otherwise, so that h_i equals $1 - d_i$, we can combine these equations in

$$y_i = \mu_N h_i + \mu_C d_i + \epsilon_i.$$

Of course, these are the same; in the first formulation,

$$\delta = \mu_C - \mu_N.$$

There is a difference in interpretation, however. A test of $\mu_N = 0$ or $\mu_C = 0$ makes little sense, but the test of $\delta = 0$ is equivalent to a test of $\mu_C = \mu_N$.[2]

Aside from the special nature of the independent variables, these are multiple regression models that we can estimate by least squares. We arrange the observations so that the first n_1 are the individuals who did not attend college and the remaining n_2 are those who did. Denote by $\mathbf{i}_g$ a column of 1s with n_g elements, either n_1 or n_2. Then the first model is

$$\mathbf{y} = \begin{bmatrix} \mathbf{i}_1 & \mathbf{0} \\ \mathbf{i}_2 & \mathbf{i}_2 \end{bmatrix} \begin{bmatrix} \mu \\ \delta \end{bmatrix} + \boldsymbol{\epsilon}.$$

Least squares produces

$$\begin{bmatrix} m \\ d \end{bmatrix} = \begin{bmatrix} n_1 + n_2 & n_2 \\ n_2 & n_2 \end{bmatrix}^{-1} \begin{bmatrix} n_1\bar{y}_1 + n_2\bar{y}_2 \\ n_2\bar{y}_2 \end{bmatrix} = \begin{bmatrix} \bar{y}_1 \\ \bar{y}_2 - \bar{y}_1 \end{bmatrix}.$$

---

[1]The choice of zero and one for the two values is purely for convenience. Any other two values could be used, but the interpretation of the equation is simplest when we use zero and one.

[2]See Suits (1984).

For the second model,

$$\mathbf{y} = \begin{bmatrix} \mathbf{i}_1 & \mathbf{0} \\ \mathbf{0} & \mathbf{i}_2 \end{bmatrix} \begin{bmatrix} \mu_N \\ \mu_C \end{bmatrix} + \boldsymbol{\epsilon}$$

and

$$\mathbf{m} = (\mathbf{X}'\mathbf{X})^{-1}\mathbf{X}'\mathbf{y} = \begin{bmatrix} 1/n_1 & 0 \\ 0 & 1/n_2 \end{bmatrix} \begin{bmatrix} n_1\bar{y}_1 \\ n_2\bar{y}_2 \end{bmatrix} = \begin{bmatrix} \bar{y}_1 \\ \bar{y}_2 \end{bmatrix}.$$

The equation may be written either with an overall intercept and a dummy variable for the effect being analyzed or with no constant term and two dummy variables. What might seem like a third possibility, an overall constant term and separate dummy variables for each group, leads to the **dummy variable trap,** a case of perfect collinearity. If the first model shown were written

$$\text{income}_i = \mu + \delta_N h_i + \delta_C d_i + \epsilon_i,$$

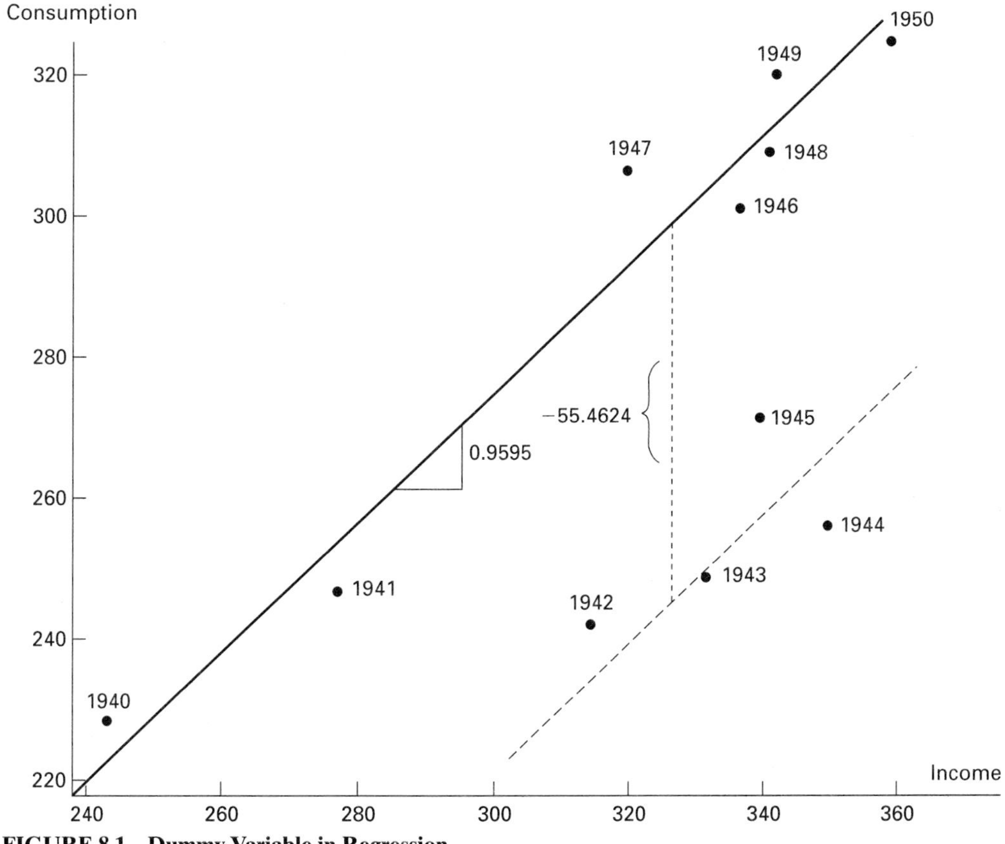

FIGURE 8.1 Dummy Variable in Regression.

the matrix of independent variables would be

$$\mathbf{X} = \begin{bmatrix} \mathbf{i}_1 & \mathbf{i}_1 & \mathbf{0} \\ \mathbf{i}_2 & \mathbf{0} & \mathbf{i}_2 \end{bmatrix}.$$

The second and third columns sum to the first, which makes least squares estimation of the three parameters impossible.

8.2.2. Binary Variables in Regression

Dummy variables are most frequently used in regression equations that also contain other quantitative variables. Recall the consumption data discussed in Example 6.1 and shown in Figure 6.2. There are four data points, the years 1942 to 1945, that lie conspicuously below the regression line for the remaining data. Figure 8.1, on page 381, suggests a means of treating this effect.

EXAMPLE 8.1 Wartime Consumption

Consumption and income data for the years 1940 to 1950 are listed in Table 8.1. The regression model is

$$C_t = \beta_1 + \beta_2 x_t + \beta_3 W_t + \epsilon_t,$$

where x_t is disposable income and W_t is the wartime dummy variable, which takes the value one in the years 1942 to 1945 and zero in other years. (The subscript t is used here to indicate the observation at time t.) The regression results are given in Table 8.2. The regression results confirm that consumption during World War II was significantly below what would have been expected, given income.

TABLE 8.1 Consumption Expenditures

Year	*Disposable Income*	*Personal Consumption*
1940	244.0	229.9
1941	277.9	243.6
1942	317.5	241.1
1943	332.1	248.2
1944	343.6	255.2
1945	338.1	270.9
1946	332.7	301.0
1947	318.8	305.8
1948	335.8	312.2
1949	336.8	319.3
1950	362.8	337.3

Note: Income and consumption are in billions of 1972 dollars.

TABLE 8.2 Consumption Function

Numbers of observations	11
Standard error of regression	9.088
R-squared	0.95283

Variable	*Coefficient*	*Standard Error*	*t ratio*
Constant	−10.065	28.44	−0.354
x	0.959595	0.0895	10.724
W	−55.4624	5.902	−9.397

In more recent applications, researchers in many fields often study the effects of **treatment** on some kind of **response.** Examples include the effect of college on income, as in the preceding example, cross-sex differences in labor supply behavior and in salary structures in industries, and in pre- versus postregime shifts in macroeconomic models, to name but a few. These can all be formulated in regression models involving a single dummy variable:

$$y_i = \boldsymbol{\beta}'\mathbf{x}_i + \delta d_i + \epsilon_i.$$

8.2.3. Several Categories

When there are several categories, a set of binary variables is necessary. Correcting for seasonal factors in macroeconomic data is a common application. Extending the device used earlier, we could write a consumption function for quarterly data as

$$C_t = \beta_1 + \beta_2 x_t + \delta_1 D_{t1} + \delta_2 D_{t2} + \delta_3 D_{t3} + \epsilon_t,$$

where x_t is disposable income. Once again, to avoid the dummy variable trap, we drop the dummy variable for the fourth quarter. (Depending on the application, it might be preferable to have four separate dummy variables and drop the overall constant.)[3] Any of the four quarters (or 12 months) can be used as the base period. The matrix of independent variables for this model is

$$\mathbf{X} = \begin{bmatrix} 1 & 0 & 0 & 0 & x_1 \\ 1 & 1 & 0 & 0 & x_2 \\ 1 & 0 & 1 & 0 & x_3 \\ 1 & 0 & 0 & 1 & x_4 \\ 1 & 0 & 0 & 0 & x_5 \\ \vdots & \vdots & \vdots & \vdots & \vdots \\ 1 & 0 & 0 & 1 & x_T \end{bmatrix}.$$

[3]See Suits (1984) and Greene and Seaks (1991).

The preceding is a means of *deseasonalizing* the data. Consider the alternative formulation:

$$C_t = \beta x_t + \delta_1 D_{t1} + \delta_2 D_{t2} + \delta_3 D_{t3} + \delta_4 D_{t4} + \epsilon_t. \quad \textbf{(8-1)}$$

Using the results from Chapter 6 on partitioned regression, we know that the preceding multiple regression is equivalent to first regressing **C** and **x** on the four dummies and then using the residuals from these regressions in the subsequent regression of deseasonalized consumption on deseasonalized income. Clearly, deseasonalizing in this fashion prior to computing the simple regression of consumption on income is the same as including the set of dummy variables in the regression.

8.2.4. Several Groupings

The case in which several sets of dummy variables are needed is much the same as those we have already considered, with one important exception. Consider a model of statewide per capita expenditure on education y as a function of statewide per capita income x. Suppose that we have observations on all $n = 50$ states for $T = 10$ years. A regression model that allows the expected expenditure to change over time as well as across states would be

$$y_{it} = \alpha + \beta x_{it} + \delta_i + \theta_t + \epsilon_{it}. \quad \textbf{(8-2)}$$

This is essentially the same as the earlier regression model. As before, it is necessary to drop one of the variables in the set of dummy variables to avoid the dummy variable trap. This is necessary even if the overall constant term is dropped. For our example, if the overall constant term is omitted and a total of 50 state dummies and 10 time dummies is retained, a problem of "perfect multicollinearity" remains; the sums of the 50 state dummies and the 10 time dummies are the same, that is, one. One of the variables in one of the sets must be omitted.

EXAMPLE 8.2 Analysis of Variance

The number of incidents of damage to a sample of ships, with the type of ship and the period when it was constructed, is shown in Table 8.3. There are five types of ships and four different periods of construction. On inspection, it seems clear that the means will differ across ship types. Whether they will differ across periods is less clear. The regression results are shown in Table 8.4 (we report only the regression coefficients).

According to the full model, the expected number of incidents for a ship of the base type A built in the base period 1960 to 1964, is 3.4. The other 19 predicted values follow from the previous results and are left as an exercise. The relevant test statistics for differences across ship type and year are as follows:

$$\text{type: } F[4, 12] = \frac{(3925.2 - 660.9)/4}{660.9/12} = 14.82,$$

TABLE 8.3 Ship Damage Incidents

Ship Type	*Period Constructed* 1960–1964	1965–1969	1970–1974	1975–1979
A	0	4	18	11
B	29	53	44	18
C	1	1	2	1
D	0	0	11	4
E	0	7	12	1

Source: Data from McCullagh and Nelder (1983, p. 137).

$$\text{year: } F[3, 12] = \frac{(1090.3 - 660.9)/3}{660.9/12} = 2.60.$$

The 5 percent critical values from the F table with these degrees of freedom are 3.26 and 3.49, respectively, so we would conclude that the average number of incidents varies significantly across ship types but not across years.

TABLE 8.4 Regression Coefficients

	Full Model	*Time Effects*	*Type Effects*	*No Effects*
Constant	3.4	6.0	8.25	10.85
B	27.75	0	27.75	0
C	−7.0	0	−7.0	0
D	−4.5	0	−4.5	0
E	−3.25	0	−3.25	0
65–69	7.0	7.0	0	0
70–74	11.4	11.4	0	0
75–79	1.0	1.0	0	0
R^2	0.84823	0.0986	0.74963	0
$\mathbf{e}'\mathbf{e}$	660.9	3925.2	1090.2	4354.5

8.2.5. Threshold Effects

In most applications, we use dummy variables to account for purely qualitative factors, such as membership in a group, or to represent a particular time period. There are cases, however, in which the dummy variable(s) represents levels of some underlying factor that might have been measured directly if this were possible. For example, education is a case in which we typically observe certain thresholds rather than, say, years of education.[4] Suppose, for example, that our interest is in a regression of the form

$$\text{income} = \beta_1 + \beta_2\,\text{age} + \text{effect of education} + \epsilon.$$

The data on education might consist of the highest level of education attained, such as high school, undergraduate, master's, or Ph.D. An obviously unsatisfactory way to proceed is to use a variable E that is 0 for the first group, 1 for the second, 2 for the third, and 3 for the fourth. That is,

$$\text{income} = \beta_1 + \beta_2\,\text{age} + \beta_3 E + \epsilon.$$

The difficulty with this approach is that it assumes that the increment in income at each threshold is the same; β_3 is the difference between income with a Ph.D. and a master's and between a master's and a bachelor's degree. This is unlikely and unduly restricts the regression. A more flexible model would use three (or four) binary variables, one for each level of education. Thus, we would write

$$\text{income} = \beta_1 + \beta_2\,\text{age} + \delta_1\text{B.A.} + \delta_2\text{M.A.} + \delta_3\text{Ph.D.} + \epsilon.$$

The correspondence between the coefficients and income for a given age is

$$\begin{aligned}
\text{high school:}\quad \text{income} &= \beta_1 + \beta_2\,\text{age},\\
\text{B.A.:}\quad \text{income} &= \beta_1 + \beta_2\,\text{age} + \delta_1,\\
\text{M.A.:}\quad \text{income} &= \beta_1 + \beta_2\,\text{age} + \delta_2,\\
\text{Ph.D.:}\quad \text{income} &= \beta_1 + \beta_2\,\text{age} + \delta_3.
\end{aligned}$$

The differences between, say, δ_3 and δ_2 and between δ_2 and δ_1 are of interest. Obviously, these are simple to compute. An alternative way to formulate the equation that reveals these differences directly is to redefine the dummy variables to be 1 if the individual has the degree, rather than whether the degree is the highest degree obtained. Thus, for someone with a Ph.D., all three binary variables are 1, and so on. The independent variables appear as follows, where individuals with only a high school education are grouped first and those with higher degrees are arranged in order below them:

$$\mathbf{X} = \begin{bmatrix} \mathbf{i}_h & \mathbf{0} & \mathbf{0} & \mathbf{0} & \mathbf{age}_h \\ \mathbf{i}_b & \mathbf{i}_b & \mathbf{0} & \mathbf{0} & \mathbf{age}_b \\ \mathbf{i}_m & \mathbf{i}_m & \mathbf{i}_m & \mathbf{0} & \mathbf{age}_m \\ \mathbf{i}_p & \mathbf{i}_p & \mathbf{i}_p & \mathbf{i}_p & \mathbf{age}_p \end{bmatrix}.$$

By defining the variables in this fashion, the regression is

$$\begin{aligned}
\text{high school:}\quad \text{income} &= \alpha + \beta\,\text{age},\\
\text{B.A.:}\quad \text{income} &= \alpha + \beta\,\text{age} + \delta_1,
\end{aligned}$$

[4]Even this quantitative measure is only a crude measure of amount of education.

$$\text{M.A.:} \quad \text{income} = \alpha + \beta \,\text{age} + \delta_1 + \delta_2,$$
$$\text{Ph.D.:} \quad \text{income} = \alpha + \beta \,\text{age} + \delta_1 + \delta_2 + \delta_3.$$

Instead of the difference between a Ph.D. and the base case, in this model δ_3 is the marginal value of the Ph.D. How equations with dummy variables are formulated is a matter of convenience. All the results can be obtained from a basic equation.[5]

8.2.6. Interactions and Spline Regression

The tests of structural change analyzed in Section 7.6 illustrate another common use of dummy variables. Recall that the data matrix for that model could be formulated as

$$\mathbf{X} = \begin{bmatrix} \mathbf{i}_1 & \mathbf{0} & \mathbf{x}_1 & \mathbf{0} \\ \mathbf{i}_2 & \mathbf{i}_2 & \mathbf{x}_2 & \mathbf{x}_2 \end{bmatrix}.$$

If we let **d** be the second column of this matrix and **i** be a full column of 1's, this data matrix is of the form

$$\mathbf{Z} = [\mathbf{i} \quad \mathbf{d} \quad \mathbf{X} \quad \mathbf{dX}].$$

The last column is just the product of the dummy variable and the other regressors. Consider, for example, a regression model that embodies the proposition that "not only are the salaries of college graduates higher than those of noncollege graduates at any given age, but they rise faster as the individuals grow older."[6] The regression would appear as in Figure 8.2 and could be written

$$S = \beta_1 + \beta_2 \,\text{age} + \beta_3 d + \beta_4 d \,\text{age} + \epsilon.$$

Estimating the parameters is a straightforward application of multiple regression. It is simple to show (we leave it as an exercise) that this is the same as computing two separate regressions. One ambiguity does arise in the estimation of the disturbance variance. If we assume that the two groups have equal disturbance variances, then

$$E[\epsilon^2 \mid d = 0] = \sigma^2$$

and

$$E[\epsilon^2 \mid d = 1] = \sigma^2.$$

In this case, it is most efficient to pool the observations and estimate a single parameter. If the variances differ across groups, however, then pooling the observations will result in one biased estimate of both disturbance variances. In

[5]See Suits (1984).

[6]The first of these propositions may, in fact, be inappropriate. In the earliest earning years, those who go to college are forgoing the income being earned by those of like age who are not in school.

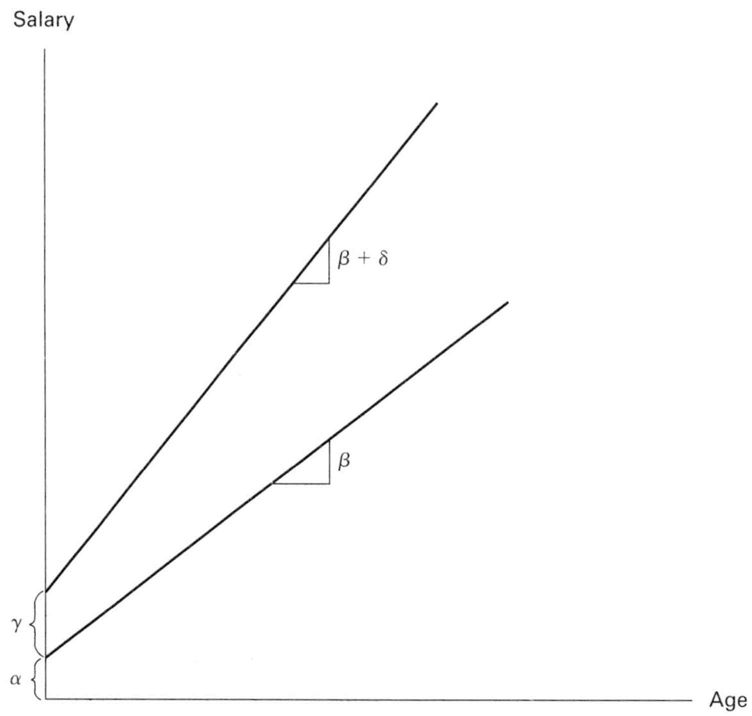

FIGURE 8.2 Shifting Slope and Intercept.

addition, the usual estimate of the covariance matrix of the coefficients will be incorrect. In this instance, the proper approach is to disaggregate the data and use the subsamples separately.

If one is examining income data for a large cross section of individuals of varying ages in a population, certain patterns with regard to some age thresholds will be clearly evident. In particular, throughout the range of values of age, income will be rising, but the slope might change at some distinct milestones, for example, at age 18, when the typical individual graduates from high school, and at age 22, when he or she graduates from college. The **time profile** of income for the typical individual in this population might appear as in Figure 8.3. Based on the discussion in the preceding paragraph, we could fit such a regression model just by dividing the sample into three subsamples, however; this would neglect the continuity of the preceding function. The result would appear more like the dotted figure than the continuous function we had in mind. Restricted regression and what is known as a **spline** function can be used to achieve the desired effect.[7]

[7]An important reference on this subject is Poirier (1974). An often-cited application appears in Garber and Poirier (1974).

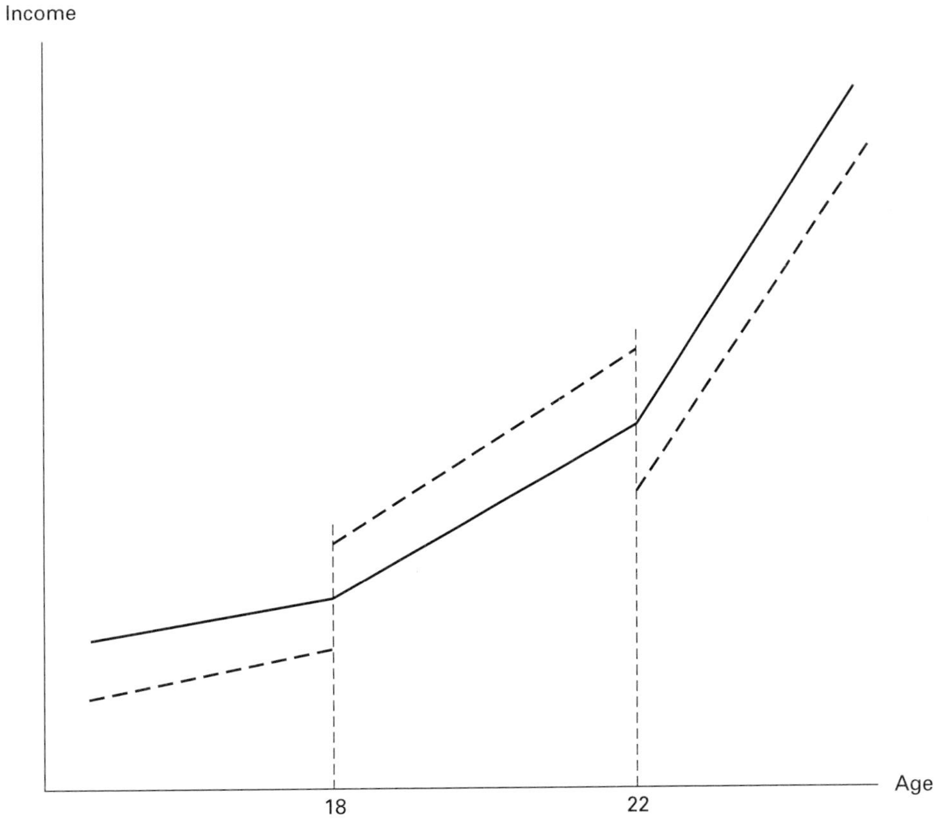

FIGURE 8.3 Spline Function.

The function we wish to estimate is

$$\begin{aligned} \text{income} = \; & \alpha^0 + \beta^0 \text{ age} \quad \text{if age} < 18, \\ & \alpha^1 + \beta^1 \text{ age} \quad \text{if age} \geq 18 \text{ and} < 22, \\ & \alpha^2 + \beta^2 \text{ age} \quad \text{if age} \geq 22. \end{aligned}$$

The threshold values, 18 and 22, are called **knots.** The function is simple enough to specify using dummy variables, as we have done. Let

$$\begin{aligned} d_1 &= 1 \quad \text{if age} \geq t_1^*, \\ d_2 &= 1 \quad \text{if age} \geq t_2^*, \end{aligned}$$

where $t_1^* = 18$ and $t_2^* = 22$. To combine all three equations, we use

$$\text{income} = \beta_1 + \beta_2 \text{ age} + \gamma_1 d_1 + \delta_1 d_1 \text{ age} + \gamma_2 d_2 + \delta_2 d_2 \text{ age} + \epsilon. \qquad \textbf{(8-3)}$$

This is the dashed function in Figure 8.3. The slopes in the three segments are β_2, $\beta_2 + \delta_1$, and $\beta_2 + \delta_1 + \delta_2$. To make the function continuous, we require that the segments join at the knots, that is,

$$\beta_1 + \beta_2 t_1^* = (\beta_1 + \gamma_1) + (\beta_2 + \delta_1) t_1^*$$

and

$$(\beta_1 + \gamma_1) + (\beta_2 + \delta_1)t_2^* = (\beta_1 + \gamma_1 + \gamma_2) + (\beta_2 + \delta_1 + \delta_2)t_2^*.$$

These are linear restrictions on the coefficients. Collecting terms, the first one is

$$\gamma_1 + \delta_1 t_1^* = 0 \text{ or } \gamma_1 = -\delta_1 t_1^*.$$

Doing likewise for the second and inserting these in (8-3), we obtain

$$\text{income} = \beta_1 + \beta_2 \text{ age} + \delta_1 d_1(\text{age} - t_1^*) + \delta_2 d_2(\text{age} - t_2^*).$$

Constrained least squares estimates are obtainable by multiple regression, using the variables

$$x_1 = \text{age},$$
$$x_2 = \text{age} - 18 \quad \text{if age} \geq 18 \text{ and 0 otherwise,}$$

and

$$x_3 = \text{age} - 22 \quad \text{if age} \geq 22 \text{ and 0 otherwise.}$$

We can test the hypothesis that the slope of the function is constant with the joint test of $\delta_1 = 0$ and $\delta_2 = 0$. Whether the individual test, $\delta_1 = 0$ or $\delta_2 = 0$, is meaningful will depend on the context. In our example, the first of these is a test that graduating from high school (actually, reaching 18) does not carry with it any increase in the slope of the earnings function until age 22 is reached.

8.3. NONLINEARITY IN THE VARIABLES

It is useful at this point to write the linear regression model in a very general form: Let $\mathbf{z} = z_1, z_2, \ldots, z_L$ be a set of L independent variables; let $f_1, f_2, \ldots, f_K$ be K independent functions of $\mathbf{z}$; let $g(y)$ be an observable function of y; and retain the usual assumptions about the disturbance. The linear regression model is

$$\begin{aligned} g(y) &= \beta_1 f_1(\mathbf{z}) + \beta_2 f_2(\mathbf{z}) + \cdots + \beta_K f_K(\mathbf{z}) + \epsilon \\ &= \beta_1 x_1 + \beta_2 x_2 + \cdots + \beta_K x_K + \epsilon \\ &= \mathbf{x}'\boldsymbol{\beta} + \epsilon. \end{aligned} \qquad \textbf{(8-4)}$$

By using logarithms, exponentials, reciprocals, transcendental functions, polynomials, products, ratios, and so on, this "linear" model can be tailored to any number of situations.

8.3.1. Functional Forms

A commonly used form of regression model is the log-linear model

$$y = \alpha \prod_k X_k^{\beta_k} e^{\epsilon}$$

or

$$\ln y = \ln \alpha + \sum_k \beta_k \ln X_k + \epsilon$$
$$= \beta_1 + \sum_k \beta_k x_k + \epsilon.$$

In this model, the coefficients are elasticities:

$$\left(\frac{\partial y}{\partial x_k}\right)\left(\frac{x_k}{y}\right) = \frac{\partial \ln y}{\partial \ln x_k} = \beta_k. \quad \textbf{(8-5)}$$

This formulation is particularly useful in studies of demand and production.

A hybrid of the linear and log-linear models is the semilog equation

$$y = e^{\beta_1 + \beta_2 x + \epsilon}$$

or

$$\ln y = \beta_1 + \beta_2 x + \epsilon.$$

A common use of semilog formulation is in exponential growth curves. If x is "time" t, then

$$\frac{d \ln y}{dt} = \beta_2$$
$$= \text{average rate of growth of } y.$$

Macroeconomic models are often formulated with autonomous time trends. For example, aggregate models of productivity will usually include a trend variable, as in

$$\ln\left(\frac{Q}{L}\right)_t = \beta_1 + \beta_2 \ln\left(\frac{K}{L}\right)_t + \delta t + \epsilon_t.$$

This provides an estimate of the "autonomous growth in productivity," usually attributed to technical change. In this equation, δ is the rate of growth of average product not attributable to increases in the use of capital.

Another useful formulation of the regression model is one with **interaction terms.** For example, a model relating braking distance D to speed S and road wetness W might be

$$D = \beta_1 + \beta_2 S + \beta_3 W + \beta_4 SW + \epsilon.$$

In this model,

$$\frac{\partial E[D]}{\partial S} = \beta_2 + \beta_4 W$$
$$\frac{\partial E[D]}{\partial W} = \beta_3 + \beta_4 S,$$

which implies that the marginal effect of higher speed on braking distance is increased when the road is wetter (assuming that β_4 is positive). If it is desired to form confidence intervals or test hypotheses about these marginal effects, the necessary standard error is computed as

$$\text{Var}\left(\frac{\partial \hat{E}\,[D]}{\partial S}\right) = \text{Var}[\hat{\beta}_2] + W^2\text{Var}[\hat{\beta}_4] + 2W\,\text{Cov}[\hat{\beta}_2, \hat{\beta}_4].$$

and likewise for $\partial E[D]/\partial W$. A value must be inserted for W. The sample mean is a natural choice, but for some purposes, a specific value, such as an extreme value of W in this example, might be preferred.

A form of the linear model

$$y = \alpha + \beta g(x) + \epsilon$$

that has appeared in a number of recent studies is the **Box–Cox transformation,**[8]

$$g^{(\lambda)}(x) = \frac{x^\lambda - 1}{\lambda}. \qquad \textbf{(8-6)}$$

The linear model results if λ equals 1, whereas a log-linear or semilog model (depending on how y is measured) results if λ equals 0.[9] Other values of λ produce many different functional forms. For example, if λ equals -1, then the equation will involve the reciprocal of x. The Box–Cox model is a useful formulation that embodies many of the models we have considered as special cases. Of course, in itself, this is only a minor virtue; if λ is known, we merely insert the known value and obtain a model linear in the transformed variables. But, except for the polar cases of λ equal to -1, 0, or 1, it is hard to conceive of situations in which a particular value would be specified a priori. By treating λ as an additional unknown parameter in the equation, we obtain a tremendous amount of flexibility.[10] The cost of doing so is that the model then becomes nonlinear in its parameters. We shall study the model in detail in Chapter 10.

Despite their very complex functional forms, these models are **intrinsically linear** because they can be placed directly in the form of (8-4). As discussed in Chapter 6, the distinguishing feature of the linear model is not the relationship among the variables as such but the way the parameters enter the equation.

---

[8]See Box and Cox (1964) and Zarembka (1974). A survey of the properties of this model appears in Spitzer (1982b). Some further results on estimation appear in Spitzer (1982a).

[9]For λ equal to zero, L'Hôpital's rule can be used to obtain the result of the transformation: $g^{(0)}(x) = [\lim_{\lambda\to 0} d(x^\lambda - 1)/d\lambda]/[\lim_{\lambda\to 0} d\lambda/d\lambda] = \ln x$.

[10]In principle, y could be modified by the Box–Cox transformation as well. Some important issues of specification will arise, however (that is, is the model linear or log-linear? What is the allowable range of the dependent variable?). We defer until Chapter 10 a detailed treatment of the Box–Cox transformation applied to the dependent variable.

8.3.2. Identifying Nonlinearity

If the functional form is not known a priori, there are a few approaches that might help at least to identify any nonlinearity and to provide some information about it from the sample. For example, if the suspected nonlinearity is with respect to a single regressor in the equation, fitting a quadratic or cubic polynomial rather than a linear function may capture some of the nonlinearity. By choosing several ranges for the regressor in question and allowing the slope of the function to be different in each range, a piecewise linear approximation to the nonlinear function can be fit.

EXAMPLE 8.3 Nonlinear Cost Function

In a celebrated study of the U.S. electric power industry, Nerlove (1963) analyzed the production costs of 145 American electric generating companies. At the outset of the study, he fit a Cobb–Douglas cost function of the form

$$\log C = \beta_1 + \beta_q \log Q + \sum_k \beta_k \log P_k + \epsilon,^{11} \tag{8-7}$$

where C is total cost, Q is output, and P_k is the unit price of the kth factor of production (k = labor, fuel, capital). The underlying theory implies that $\Sigma_k \beta_k = 1$. This is imposed by regressing $\log C - \log P_F$ on a constant $\log Q$, $\log P_L - \log P_F$, and $\log P_K - \log P_F$. This first set of results appears at the top of Table 8.5.

TABLE 8.5 Cobb–Douglas Cost Function (Standard Errors in Parentheses)

	$\log Q$	$\log P_L - \log P_F$	$\log P_K - \log P_F$	R^2
All firms	0.721	0.562	−0.003	0.931
	(0.175)	(0.198)	(0.192)	
Group 1	0.398	0.641	−0.093	0.512
	(0.079)	(0.691)	(0.669)	
Group 2	0.668	0.105	0.364	0.635
	(0.116)	(0.275)	(0.277)	
Group 3	0.931	0.408	0.249	0.571
	(0.198)	(0.199)	(0.189)	
Group 4	0.915	0.472	0.133	0.871
	(0.108)	(0.174)	(0.157)	
Group 5	1.045	0.604	−0.295	0.920
	(0.065)	(0.197)	(0.175)	

[11] Readers who attempt to replicate the original study should note that Nerlove used common (base 10) logs in his calculations, not natural logs. This creates some numerical differences.

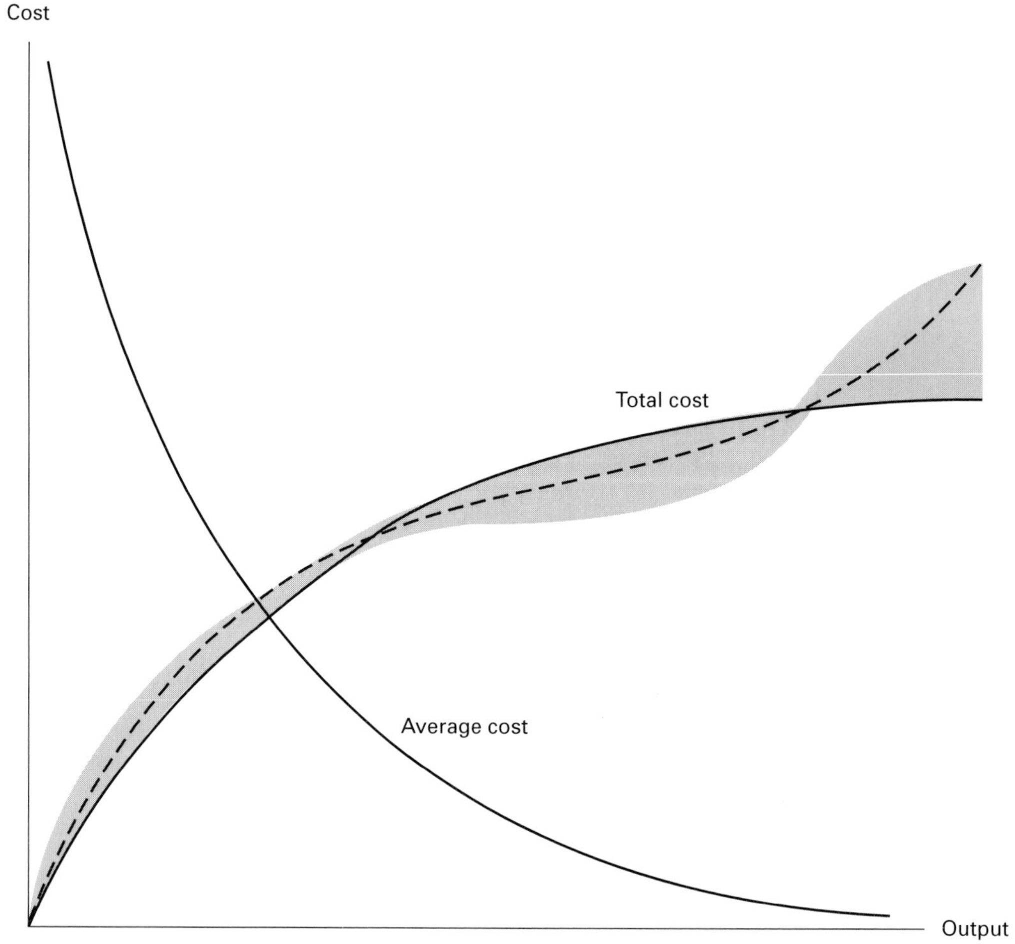

FIGURE 8.4 Cost Functions.

The implied total and average cost functions for these results are shown in Figure 8.4. The striking pattern of the residuals (sketched in the figure) and some thought about the implied form of production suggested that something was missing from the model.[12] In theory, the estimated model implies a continually declining average cost curve, which in turn implies pervasive economies of scale at all levels of output. This conflicts with the textbook notion of a U-shaped average cost curve and appears implausible for the data. Two approaches were used to analyze the model.[13]

[12]A Durbin–Watson test of correlation among the residuals (see Section 13.5.1) revealed substantial autocorrelation. This is to be expected, given the pattern in the figure.

[13]A third approach based on a model of the production function appears in Example 10.8.

TABLE 8.6 Log-Quadratic Cost Function (Standard Errors in Parentheses)

	$\log Q$	$\log^2 Q$	$\log P_L - \log P_F$	$\log P_K - \log P_F$	R^2
All firms	0.151	0.117	0.498	−0.062	0.958
	(0.062)	(0.012)	(0.161)	(0.151)	

By sorting the sample into five groups on the basis of output and fitting separate regressions to each group, Nerlove fit a piecewise linear model. The results are given in the lower rows of the table, where the firms in the successive groups are progressively larger. The results are persuasive that the (log)-linear cost function is inadequate. The output coefficient that rises toward and then crosses 1 is consistent with a U-shaped cost curve as surmised earlier. (See Exercise 35 in Chapter 6.)

A second approach was to expand the cost function to include a quadratic term in log output. This corresponds to a much more general model (the dashed cost curve shown in Figure 8.4) and produced the result given in Table 8.6. Again, a simple t test strongly suggests that increased generality is called for.[14]

The preceding illustrates three useful tools in identifying and dealing with unspecified nonlinearity: analysis of residuals, the use of piecewise linear regression,[15] and the use of polynomials to approximate the unknown regression function.

8.3.3. Intrinsic Linearity and Identification

The log-linear model illustrates an intermediate case of a nonlinear regression model. The equation is intrinsically linear by our definition; by taking logs of

$$Y_i = \alpha X_i^{\beta_2} e^{\epsilon_i},$$

we obtain

$$\ln Y_i = \ln \alpha + \beta_2 \ln X_i + \epsilon_i \tag{8-8}$$

or

$$y_i = \beta_1 + \beta_2 x_i + \epsilon_i.$$

[14] Nerlove inadvertently measured economies of scale from this function as $1/(\beta_q + \delta \log Q)$, where β_q and δ are the coefficients on $\log Q$ and $\log^2 Q$. The correct expression would have been $1/[\partial \log C/\partial \log Q] = 1/[\beta_q + 2\delta \log Q]$. This slip was periodically rediscovered in several later papers.

[15] It may seem that a spline regression might be useful here. There is no theoretical basis for the choice of output knots, in fact, they were chosen simply to have 29 firms in each group.

Although this equation is linear in most respects, something has changed in that it is no longer linear in α. Written in terms of β_1, we obtain a fully linear model. This may not be the form of interest, however. Nothing is lost, of course, since β_1 is just ln α. If β_1 can be estimated, an obvious estimate of α is suggested.

This leads us to a second aspect of intrinsically linear models. Maximum likelihood estimators have an invariance property. In the classical normal regression model, the maximum likelihood estimator of σ is the square root of the maximum likelihood estimator of σ^2. Under some conditions, least squares estimates have the same property. By exploiting this, we can broaden the definition of linearity and include some additional cases that might otherwise be quite complex.

DEFINITION 8.1: Intrinsic Linearity. *In the classical regression model, if the K parameters $\beta_1, \beta_2, \ldots, \beta_K$ can be written as K one-to-one possibly nonlinear functions of a set of K underlying parameters $\theta_1, \theta_2, \ldots, \theta_K$, then the model is intrinsically linear in θ.*

EXAMPLE 8.4 Intrinsically Linear Regression

In Section 4.8.4, we estimated by maximum likelihood the parameters of the model

$$f(y \mid \beta, x) = \frac{(\beta + x)^{-\rho}}{\Gamma(\rho)} y^{\rho-1} e^{-y/(\beta+x)}.$$

In this model, $E[y \mid x] = (\beta\rho) + \rho x$, which suggests another way that we might estimate the two parameters. This is an intrinsically linear regression model, $E[y \mid x] = \beta_1 + \beta_2 x$, in which $\beta_1 = \beta\rho$ and $\beta_2 = \rho$. We can estimate the parameters by least squares, then retrieve the estimate of β using b_1/b_2. Since this is a nonlinear function of the estimated parameters, we use the delta method to estimate the standard error. Using the data from that example, the least squares estimates of β_1 and β_2 (with standard errors in parentheses) are -4.1431 (23.734) and 2.4261 (1.5915). The estimated covariance is -36.979. The estimate of β is $-4.1431/2.4261 = -1.7077$. We estimate the sampling variance of $\hat{\beta}$ with

$$\begin{aligned}
\text{Est. Var}[\hat{\beta}] &= \left(\frac{\partial\hat{\beta}}{\partial b_1}\right)^2 \text{Var}[b_1] + \left(\frac{\partial\hat{\beta}}{\partial b_2}\right)^2 \text{Var}[b_2] + 2\left(\frac{\partial\hat{\beta}}{\partial b_1}\right)\left(\frac{\partial\hat{\beta}}{\partial b_2}\right)\text{Cov}[b_1, b_2] \\
&= \left(\frac{1}{b_2}\right)^2 \text{Var}[b_1] + \left(\frac{-b_1}{b_2^2}\right)^2 \text{Var}[b_2] + 2\left(\frac{1}{b_2}\right)\left(\frac{-b_1}{b_2^2}\right)\text{Cov}[b_1, b_2] \\
&= 8.6889^2.
\end{aligned}$$

Table 8.7 compares the least squares and maximum likelihood estimates of the parameters.

The lower standard errors for the maximum likelihood estimates result from the inefficient (equal) weighting given to the observations by the least squares procedure. The gamma distribution is highly skewed. In addition, we

TABLE 8.7 Estimates of the Regression in a Gamma Model: Least Squares versus Maximum Likelihood

	β		ρ	
	Estimate	*Standard Error*	*Estimate*	*Standard Error*
Least squares	−1.708	8.689	2.426	1.592
Maximum likelihood	−4.719	2.403	3.151	0.663

know from our results in Chapter 4 that this is an exponential family. We found for the gamma distribution that the sufficient statistics for this density were $\Sigma_i\, y_i$ and $\Sigma_i \ln y_i$. The least squares estimator does not use the second of these, whereas an efficient estimator will.

The emphasis here is on "one to one." If the conditions are met, the model can be estimated in terms of the functions $\beta_1, \ldots, \beta_K$, and the underlying parameters derived after these are estimated. The one-to-one correspondence is an **identification condition.** If the condition is met, the underlying parameters of the regression ($\boldsymbol{\theta}$) are said to be **exactly identified** in terms of the parameters of the linear model β. An excellent example is provided by Kmenta (1986, p. 515).

EXAMPLE 8.5 CES Production Function

The constant elasticity of substitution production function may be written

$$\ln y = \ln \gamma - \frac{\nu}{\rho} \ln[\delta K^{-\rho} + (1 - \delta)L^{-\rho}] + \epsilon. \tag{8-9}$$

A Taylor series approximation to this function around the point $\rho = 0$ is

$$\begin{aligned} \ln y &= \ln \gamma + \nu\delta \ln K + \nu(1 - \delta)\ln L \\ &\quad + \rho\nu\delta(1 - \delta)\{-\tfrac{1}{2}[\ln K - \ln L]^2\} + \epsilon \\ &= \beta_1 x_1 + \beta_2 x_2 + \beta_3 x_3 + \beta_4 x_4 + \epsilon, \end{aligned} \tag{8-10}$$

where $x_1 = 1$, $x_2 = \ln K$, $x_3 = \ln L$, $x_4 = -\frac{1}{2}\ln^2(K/L)$, and the transformations are

$$\begin{aligned} \beta_1 &= \ln \gamma, & \gamma &= e^{\beta_1}, \\ \beta_2 &= \nu\delta, & \delta &= \beta_2/(\beta_2 + \beta_3), \\ \beta_3 &= \nu(1 - \delta), & \nu &= \beta_2 + \beta_3, \\ \beta_4 &= \rho\nu\delta(1 - \delta), & \rho &= \beta_4(\beta_2 + \beta_3)/(\beta_2\beta_3). \end{aligned} \tag{8-11}$$

Estimates of β_1, β_2, β_3, and β_4 can be computed by least squares. The estimates of γ, δ, ν, and ρ obtained by the second column of (8-11) are the same as those we would obtain had we found the nonlinear least squares estimates of (8-10) directly. As Kmenta shows, they are not the same as the nonlinear least squares estimates of (8-9) due to the use of the Taylor series approximation to get to (8-10). The full set of estimates appears in Table 8.8. Once again, we use the delta method to construct the estimated covariance matrix for the estimates of $\boldsymbol{\theta} = [\gamma, \delta, \nu, \rho]$. The derivatives matrix is

$$\mathbf{C} = \frac{\partial \boldsymbol{\theta}}{\partial \boldsymbol{\beta}'} = \begin{bmatrix} e^{\beta_1} & 0 & 0 & 0 \\ 0 & \beta_3/(\beta_2 + \beta_3)^2 & -\beta_2/(\beta_2 + \beta_3)^2 & 0 \\ 0 & 1 & 1 & 0 \\ 0 & -\beta_3\beta_4/(\beta_2^2\beta_3) & -\beta_2\beta_4/(\beta_2\beta_3^2) & (\beta_2 + \beta_3)/(\beta_2\beta_3) \end{bmatrix}.$$

The estimated covariance matrix for $\hat{\boldsymbol{\theta}}$ is $\hat{\mathbf{C}}[s^2(\mathbf{X}'\mathbf{X})^{-1}]\hat{\mathbf{C}}'$.

Table 8.8 also presents the nonlinear least squares estimates (see Chapter 10 for discussion). As often happens in this sort of application involving a highly nonlinear model and a moderate sample size, the full nonlinear least squares estimates obtained *without* using the Taylor series approximation differ markedly from the transformed linear least squares estimates. Whereas the former give a more plausible estimate of the capital share parameter δ, it gives a wholly different estimate of ρ. The difference between estimates of 2.451 and

TABLE 8.8 Estimates of CES Production Function

Least Squares Regression of ln Y on 1, ln K, ln L, $-\frac{1}{2}$(ln K − ln L)^2

Sum of Squared Residuals: 0.801802, R^2: 0.94677

	β_1	β_2	β_3	β_4
Estimate	1.4677	−0.1115	1.1002	−0.3045
Standard error	0.40823	0.4162	0.43422	0.25469
t ratio	3.595	−0.268	2.534	−1.196

Transformed Least Squares Coefficients

	γ	δ	ν	ρ
Estimate	4.3394	−0.11277	0.98872	2.4541
Standard error	0.094076	0.46004	0.89248	1.3393
t ratio	46.126	−0.245	1.108	1.832

Nonlinear Least Squares Estimates of Production Function

Sum of Squared Residuals = 0.806604, R^2 = 0.94645

Estimate	3.6165	0.10468	0.99805	−1.0046
Standard error	1.1893	0.18120	0.057518	1.1138
t ratio	3.041	0.578	17.352	−0.902

-1.0046 is that between two completely different production functions. Since these two estimates are supposed to be of the same parameter, a difference this large might raise some concern about the appropriateness of this specification for these data.

Not all models of the form

$$y_i = \beta_1(\boldsymbol{\theta})x_{i1} + \beta_2(\boldsymbol{\theta})x_{i2} + \cdots + \beta_K(\boldsymbol{\theta})x_{ik} + \epsilon_i \tag{8-12}$$

are intrinsically linear. Recall that the condition that the functions be one to one (i.e., that the parameters be exactly identified) was required. For example,

$$y_i = \alpha + \beta x_{i1} + \gamma x_{i2} + \beta\gamma x_{i3} + \epsilon_i$$

is nonlinear. The reason is that if we write it in the form of (8-12), we fail to account for the condition that β_4 equals $\beta_2\beta_3$, which is a nonlinear restriction. In this model, the three parameters α, β, and γ are said to be **overidentified** in terms of the four parameters β_1, β_2, β_3, and β_4. Unrestricted least squares estimates of β_2, β_3, and β_4 can be used to obtain two estimates of each of the underlying parameters, and there is no assurance that these will be the same.

8.4. SPECIFICATION ANALYSIS

Our analysis has been based on the assumption that the correct specification of the regression model is known to be

$$\mathbf{y} = \mathbf{X}\boldsymbol{\beta} + \boldsymbol{\epsilon}.$$

There are numerous types of errors that one might make in the specification of the estimated equation. Perhaps the most common ones are the omission of relevant variables and the inclusion of superfluous variables.

8.4.1. Selection of Variables

Consider an initial model, which we assume contains a constant term and several independent variables:

$$\mathbf{y} = \mathbf{X}_1\boldsymbol{\beta}_1 + \boldsymbol{\epsilon}. \tag{8-13}$$

It is not unusual to begin with some formulation and then contemplate adding more variables to the model. As shown earlier, the effects of a new variable on the coefficients on $\mathbf{X}_1$ are uncertain. The effect on R^2, however, is unambiguous. The change in the residual sum of squares when a set of variables $\mathbf{X}_2$ is added to the regression is

$$\mathbf{e}_{1,2}'\mathbf{e}_{1,2} = \mathbf{e}_1'\mathbf{e}_1 - \mathbf{b}_2'\mathbf{X}_2'\mathbf{M}_1\mathbf{X}_2\mathbf{b}_2,$$

where we use subscript 1 to indicate the regression based on (8-13) and 1,2 to indicate the use of *both* $\mathbf{X}_1$ and $\mathbf{X}_2$. The coefficient vector $\mathbf{b}_2$ is the coefficients on $\mathbf{X}_2$ in the multiple regression of $\mathbf{y}$ on $\mathbf{X}_1$ and $\mathbf{X}_2$. (See Section 6.4.3 for definitions of $\mathbf{b}_2$ and $\mathbf{M}_1$.) Therefore,

$$R_{1,2}^2 = 1 - \frac{\mathbf{e}_1'\mathbf{e}_1 - \mathbf{b}_2'\mathbf{X}_2'\mathbf{M}_1\mathbf{X}_2\mathbf{b}_2}{\mathbf{y}'\mathbf{M}^0\mathbf{y}}$$
$$= R_1^2 + \frac{\mathbf{b}_2'\mathbf{X}_2'\mathbf{M}_1\mathbf{X}_2\mathbf{b}_2}{\mathbf{y}'\mathbf{M}^0\mathbf{y}}.$$

This is greater than R_1^2 unless $\mathbf{b}_2$ equals zero. ($\mathbf{M}_1\mathbf{X}_2$ could not be zero unless $\mathbf{X}_2$ was a linear function of $\mathbf{X}_1$, in which case the regression could not be computed.) This can be manipulated a bit further to obtain

$$R_{1,2}^2 = R_1^2 + \frac{\mathbf{y}'\mathbf{M}_1\mathbf{y}}{\mathbf{y}'\mathbf{M}^0\mathbf{y}} \frac{\mathbf{b}_2'\mathbf{X}_2'\mathbf{M}_1\mathbf{X}_2\mathbf{b}_2}{\mathbf{y}'\mathbf{M}_1\mathbf{y}}.$$

But $\mathbf{y}'\mathbf{M}_1\mathbf{y} = \mathbf{e}_1'\mathbf{e}_1$, so the first term in the product is $1 - R_1^2$. The second is the **multiple correlation** in the regression of $\mathbf{M}_1\mathbf{y}$ on $\mathbf{M}_1\mathbf{X}_2$, or the partial correlation (after the effect of $\mathbf{X}_1$ is removed) in the regression of $\mathbf{y}$ on $\mathbf{X}_2$.[16] Collecting terms, we have

$$R_{1,2}^2 = R_1^2 + (1 - R_1^2)r_{y2.1}^2.$$[17]

Clearly, it would be possible to push R^2 as high as desired just by adding regressors. This problem motivates the use of the **adjusted *R* squared,**

$$\overline{R}^2 = 1 - \frac{n-1}{n-K}(1 - R^2),$$

instead of R^2 as a method of choosing among alternative models.[18] Since $\overline{R}^2$ incorporates a penalty for reducing the degrees of freedom while still revealing an improvement in fit, one possibility is to choose the specification that maximizes $\overline{R}^2$.[19] It can be shown that this is equivalent to minimizing the variance estimator $\mathbf{e}'\mathbf{e}/(n - K)$. It has been suggested that the adjusted R-squared does not penalize the loss of degrees of freedom heavily enough.[20] Two alternatives that have been proposed for comparing models (which we index by j) are

$$\tilde{R}_j^2 = \frac{n + K_j}{n - K_j}(1 - R_j^2),$$

which minimizes Amemiya's (1985) **prediction criterion,**

$$\text{PC}_j = \frac{\mathbf{e}_j'\mathbf{e}_j}{n - K_j}\left(1 + \frac{K_j}{n}\right) = s_j^2\left(1 + \frac{K_j}{n}\right),$$

[16]See Section 6.4.4. We obtained this result earlier for the case of a single additional variable in Section 6.5, result (6-36).

[17]The interpretation of $r_{y2.1}^2$ as a multiple correlation coefficient requires $\mathbf{x}_1$ to contain a constant term.

[18]See Section 6.5.

[19]There is a computer program that will automatically do the complete search among the 2^{K-1} specifications to find the maximum $\overline{R}^2$. In the interest of conserving resources, we leave readers to their own devices to locate it.

[20]See, for example, Amemiya (1985, pp. 50–51).

and Akaike's (1973) **information criterion,**

$$\text{AIC}_j = \ln\left(\frac{\mathbf{e}_j'\mathbf{e}_j}{n}\right) + \frac{2K_j}{n} = \ln\hat{\sigma}^2 + \frac{2K_j}{n}.$$

Although intuitively appealing, these measures are a bit unorthodox in that they have no firm basis in theory. Perhaps a somewhat more palatable alternative is the method of **stepwise regression.**[21] This procedure evaluates each variable in turn on the basis of its significance level and accumulates the model by adding or deleting variables sequentially. At the second step, to say nothing of the latter steps of this procedure, the classical inference procedures break down. Suppose, for example (as is common), that the method is used to ensure that all the variables ultimately included have F statistics (the square of the conventional t ratio) larger than four. It is hardly appropriate to call these F statistics and base inference on them as if they were drawn from an F distribution; it is known a priori that they all will be larger than four. For this reason, economists have tended to avoid stepwise regression methods.

The preceding creates a bit of a methodological dilemma for researchers using the classical procedures. On one hand, there is a presumption that there is a "true model" known a priori. If so, orthodoxy dictates that the researcher will compute only a single regression and report the results. Of course, this is hardly likely, and in practice, some exploratory work is always necessary. There is, however, good reason to be skeptical of a "model" that is constructed entirely by mechanical means.

8.4.2. Omission of Relevant Variables

Suppose that a correctly specified regression model would be

$$\mathbf{y} = \mathbf{X}_1\boldsymbol{\beta}_1 + \mathbf{X}_2\boldsymbol{\beta}_2 + \boldsymbol{\epsilon}, \tag{8-14}$$

where the two parts of $\mathbf{X}$ have K_1 and K_2 columns, respectively. If we regress $\mathbf{y}$ on $\mathbf{X}_1$ without including $\mathbf{X}_2$, the estimator is

$$\begin{aligned}\mathbf{b}_1 &= (\mathbf{X}_1'\mathbf{X}_1)^{-1}\mathbf{X}_1'\mathbf{y} \\ &= \boldsymbol{\beta}_1 + (\mathbf{X}_1'\mathbf{X}_1)^{-1}\mathbf{X}_1'\mathbf{X}_2\boldsymbol{\beta}_2 + (\mathbf{X}_1'\mathbf{X}_1)^{-1}\mathbf{X}_1'\boldsymbol{\epsilon}.\end{aligned} \tag{8-15}$$

Taking the expectation, we see that unless $\mathbf{X}_1'\mathbf{X}_2 = \mathbf{0}$, $\mathbf{b}_1$ is biased:

$$E[\mathbf{b}_1] = \boldsymbol{\beta}_1 + \mathbf{P}_{1.2}\boldsymbol{\beta}_2, \tag{8-16}$$

where

$$\mathbf{P}_{1.2} = (\mathbf{X}_1'\mathbf{X}_1)^{-1}\mathbf{X}_1'\mathbf{X}_2. \tag{8-17}$$

Each column of the $K_1 \times K_2$ matrix $\mathbf{P}_{1.2}$ is the column of slopes in the least squares regression of the corresponding column of $\mathbf{X}_2$ on the columns of $\mathbf{X}_1$.

---

[21]See Draper and Smith (1980) and Maddala (1977a, pp. 124–127) for discussion.

EXAMPLE 8.6 Omitted Variables

If a demand equation is estimated without the relevant income variable, (8-16) shows how the estimated price elasticity will be biased. Letting b be the estimate, we obtain

$$E[b] = \beta + \frac{\text{Cov[price, income]}}{\text{Var[price]}}\gamma,$$

where γ is the income coefficient. In aggregate data, it is unclear whether the missing covariance would be positive or negative. The sign of the bias in b would be the same as this covariance, however, because Var[price] and γ would be positive.

In this development, it is straightforward to deduce the directions of bias when there is a single included variable and one omitted variable. It is important to note, however, that if more than one variable is included, then the terms in the **omitted variable formula** involve multiple regression coefficients, which themselves have the sign of partial, not simple, correlations. For example, in the demand equation of the previous example, if the price of a closely related product had been included as well, then the simple correlation between price and income would be insufficient to determine the direction of the bias in the price elasticity. What would be required is the sign of the correlation between price and income net of the effect of the other price. This might not be obvious, and it would become even less so as more regressors were added to the equation.

The variance of $\mathbf{b}_1$ is that of the third term in (8-15), which is

$$\text{Var}[\mathbf{b}_1] = \sigma^2(\mathbf{X}_1'\mathbf{X}_1)^{-1}. \tag{8-18}$$

If we had computed the correct regression, including $\mathbf{X}_2$, the slopes on $\mathbf{X}_1$ would have been unbiased and would have had a covariance matrix equal to the upper left block of $\sigma^2(\mathbf{X}'\mathbf{X})^{-1}$. This is

$$\text{Var}[\mathbf{b}_{1.2}] = \sigma^2(\mathbf{X}_1'\mathbf{M}_2\mathbf{X}_1)^{-1}, \tag{8-19}$$

where

$$\mathbf{M}_2 = \mathbf{I} - \mathbf{X}_2(\mathbf{X}_2'\mathbf{X}_2)^{-1}\mathbf{X}_2',$$

or

$$\text{Var}[\mathbf{b}_{1.2}] = \sigma^2[\mathbf{X}_1'\mathbf{X}_1 - \mathbf{X}_1'\mathbf{X}_2(\mathbf{X}_2'\mathbf{X}_2)^{-1}\mathbf{X}_2'\mathbf{X}_1]^{-1}.$$

We can compare the covariance matrices of $\mathbf{b}_1$ and $\mathbf{b}_{1.2}$ more easily by comparing their inverses [see result (2-120)]:

$$\text{Var}[\mathbf{b}_1]^{-1} - \text{Var}[\mathbf{b}_{1.2}]^{-1} = (1/\sigma^2)\mathbf{X}_1'\mathbf{X}_2(\mathbf{X}_2'\mathbf{X}_2)^{-1}\mathbf{X}_2'\mathbf{X}_1,$$

which is positive definite. We conclude that although $\mathbf{b}_1$ is biased, it has a smaller variance than $\mathbf{b}_{1.2}$ (since the inverse of its variance is larger).

Suppose, for instance, that $\mathbf{X}_1$ and $\mathbf{X}_2$ are each a single column and that the variables are measured as deviations from their respective means. Then

$$\text{Var}[b_1] = \frac{\sigma^2}{s_{11}}, \quad \text{where } s_{11} = \sum_{i=1}^{n} (x_{i1} - \bar{x}_1)^2,$$

whereas

$$\begin{aligned}\text{Var}[b_{1.2}] &= \sigma^2[\mathbf{x}_1'\mathbf{x}_1 - \mathbf{x}_1'\mathbf{x}_2(\mathbf{x}_2'\mathbf{x}_2)^{-1}\mathbf{x}_2'\mathbf{x}_1]^{-1} \\ &= \frac{\sigma^2}{s_{11}(1 - r_{12}^2)},\end{aligned} \tag{8-20}$$

where

$$r_{12}^2 = \frac{(\mathbf{x}_1'\mathbf{x}_2)^2}{\mathbf{x}_1'\mathbf{x}_1\mathbf{x}_2'\mathbf{x}_2}$$

is the squared sample correlation between $\mathbf{x}_1$ and $\mathbf{x}_2$. The more highly correlated $\mathbf{x}_1$ and $\mathbf{x}_2$ are, the larger the variance of $b_{1.2}$ compared with that of b_1. Therefore, it is possible that b_1 is a more precise estimator based on the **mean-squared-error** criterion.

For statistical inference, it would be necessary to estimate σ^2. Proceeding as usual, we would use

$$s^2 = \frac{\mathbf{e}_1'\mathbf{e}_1}{n - K_1}.$$

But

$$\mathbf{e}_1 = \mathbf{M}_1\mathbf{y} = \mathbf{M}_1(\mathbf{X}_1\boldsymbol{\beta}_1 + \mathbf{X}_2\boldsymbol{\beta}_2 + \boldsymbol{\epsilon}) = \mathbf{M}_1\mathbf{X}_2\boldsymbol{\beta}_2 + \mathbf{M}_1\boldsymbol{\epsilon}.$$

To find the expected value of $\mathbf{e}_1'\mathbf{e}_1$, we use the same approach we used in Section 6.5.1 and that $E[\mathbf{X}_1'\boldsymbol{\epsilon}] = \mathbf{0}$ to drop the middle term in the quadratic form. Thus,

$$\begin{aligned}E[\mathbf{e}_1'\mathbf{e}_1] &= \boldsymbol{\beta}_2'\mathbf{X}_2'\mathbf{M}_1\mathbf{X}_2\boldsymbol{\beta}_2 + \sigma^2\text{tr}(\mathbf{M}_1) \\ &= \boldsymbol{\beta}_2'\mathbf{X}_2'\mathbf{M}_1\mathbf{X}_2\boldsymbol{\beta}_2 + (n - K_1)\sigma^2.\end{aligned} \tag{8-21}$$

The first term in the expectation is the population counterpart to the increase in the residual sum of squares that results when $\mathbf{X}_2$ is dropped from the regression. It is simple to show that the first term is positive, so that s_2 is biased upward. Unfortunately, to take any account of this bias, we would require an estimate of $\boldsymbol{\beta}_2$.

The conclusion from this is that if we omit relevant variables from the regression, our estimates of both $\boldsymbol{\beta}_1$ and σ^2 are biased. It is possible for $\mathbf{b}_1$ to be more precise than $\mathbf{b}_{1.2}$. But even this should be of limited comfort. Since we cannot estimate σ^2, we cannot test hypotheses about $\boldsymbol{\beta}_1$. To make matters worse, even if we had an estimate of σ^2, we could only test hypotheses about $\boldsymbol{\beta}_1 + \mathbf{P}_{1.2}\boldsymbol{\beta}_2$, which is unlikely to be of much interest. As a final observation, note that when the regressors are orthogonal—$(\mathbf{X}_1'\mathbf{X}_2) = \mathbf{0}$—the estimator in the short regression is unbiased. But the estimator of σ^2 is *still* biased upward, so we are still precluded from drawing valid inferences about $\boldsymbol{\beta}_1$. Of course, it is unlikely that in practice the regressors would be orthogonal.

8.4.3. Inclusion of Irrelevant Variables

If the regression model is correctly given by

$$\mathbf{y} = \mathbf{X}_1\boldsymbol{\beta}_1 = \boldsymbol{\epsilon} \tag{8-22}$$

and we estimate it as if (8-14) were correct (i.e., we include some extra variables), it might seem that the same sorts of problems considered earlier would arise. In fact, this is not the case. We can view the omission of a set of relevant variables as equivalent to imposing an incorrect restriction on (8-14). In particular, omitting $\mathbf{X}_2$ is equivalent to *incorrectly* estimating (8-14) subject to the restriction

$$\boldsymbol{\beta}_2 = \mathbf{0}. \tag{8-23}$$

As we discovered, incorrectly imposing a restriction leads to a number of biases. Another way to view this error is to note that it amounts to incorporating incorrect information in our estimation. Suppose, however, that our error is simply a failure to use some information that *is correct.*

The inclusion of the irrelevant variables $\mathbf{X}_2$ in the regression is equivalent to failing to impose (8-23) on (8-14) in estimation. But (8-14) is not incorrect; it simply fails to incorporate (8-23). Therefore, we do not need to prove formally that the least squares estimator of $\boldsymbol{\beta}$ in (8-14) is unbiased *even given* (8-23); we have already proved it. We can assert on the basis of all our earlier results that

$$E[\mathbf{b}] = \begin{bmatrix} \boldsymbol{\beta}_1 \\ \boldsymbol{\beta}_2 \end{bmatrix} = \begin{bmatrix} \boldsymbol{\beta}_1 \\ \mathbf{0} \end{bmatrix}. \tag{8-24}$$

By the same reasoning, s^2 is also unbiased:

$$E\left[\frac{\mathbf{e}'\mathbf{e}}{n - K_1 - K_2}\right] = \sigma^2.$$

Then where is the problem? It would seem that one would generally want to "overfit" the model. From a theoretical standpoint, the difficulty with this view is that the failure to use correct information is always costly. In this instance, the cost is the reduced precision of the estimates. As we have shown, the covariance matrix in the short regression (omitting $\mathbf{X}_2$) is never larger than the covariance matrix for the estimator obtained in the presence of the superfluous variables.[22] Consider again the single-variable comparison given earlier. If $\mathbf{x}_2$ is highly correlated with $\mathbf{x}_1$, incorrectly including it in the regression will greatly inflate the variance of the estimator.

---

[22]There is no loss if $\mathbf{X}_1'\mathbf{X}_2 = \mathbf{0}$, which makes sense in terms of the information about $\mathbf{X}_1$ contained in $\mathbf{X}_2$ (here, none). This is not likely to occur in practice, however.

8.5. BIASED ESTIMATORS AND PRETEST ESTIMATORS

Our focus on unbiased estimators parallels the general attraction among economists for them. It has been amply demonstrated, however, that this approach will almost surely neglect estimators that, although biased, are more precise in an expected squared error sense.[23] Indeed, the famous result of James and Stein (1961) shows that by a squared error loss criterion, there is always a feasible estimator that dominates least squares for every value of $\boldsymbol{\beta}$.[24] From our point of view, the importance of this result will lie in how we can use information drawn from outside the sample data to sharpen our parameter estimates. At several points, we have invoked the general proposition that increased information, good or bad, reduces variance. We have also found, however, that *incorrect* information will induce biases.[25] Here we shall explore further the possibility that when our out-of-sample information is sufficiently close to the truth, the induced bias will be offset by the improvement in the variance of the estimator in its expected squared error.

8.5.1. The Mean-Squared-Error Test

Suppose that we incorporate a set of restrictions $\mathbf{R}\boldsymbol{\beta} = \mathbf{q}$ on the least squares estimator of $\boldsymbol{\beta}$ in the model $\mathbf{y} = \mathbf{X}\boldsymbol{\beta} + \boldsymbol{\epsilon}$. The restricted least squares estimator is

$$\mathbf{b}_* = \mathbf{b} - (\mathbf{X}'\mathbf{X})^{-1}\mathbf{R}'[\mathbf{R}(\mathbf{X}'\mathbf{X})^{-1}\mathbf{R}']^{-1}(\mathbf{R}\mathbf{b} - \mathbf{q}) = \mathbf{b} - \mathbf{W}(\mathbf{R}\mathbf{b} - \mathbf{q}), \tag{8-25}$$

and its covariance matrix is

$$\text{Var}[\mathbf{b}_*] = \sigma^2[(\mathbf{X}'\mathbf{X})^{-1} - (\mathbf{X}'\mathbf{X})^{-1}\mathbf{R}'(\mathbf{R}(\mathbf{X}'\mathbf{X})^{-1}\mathbf{R}')^{-1}\mathbf{R}(\mathbf{X}'\mathbf{X})^{-1}]. \tag{8-26}$$

The covariance matrix of $\mathbf{b}_*$ is equal to that of $\mathbf{b}$ minus a positive definite matrix, so it is smaller in the sense defined in Section 2.8.3. However, unless the restrictions are correct in the population, $\mathbf{b}_*$ is biased: $E[\mathbf{b}_*] = \boldsymbol{\beta} - \mathbf{W}(\mathbf{R}\boldsymbol{\beta} - \mathbf{q})$. It is still possible that the mean-squared error of $\mathbf{b}_*$ is smaller than that of $\mathbf{b}$.

Since $\mathbf{b}$ is unbiased, its mean-squared-error matrix is its covariance matrix:

$$\text{MSE}[\mathbf{b} \mid \boldsymbol{\beta}] = \sigma^2(\mathbf{X}'\mathbf{X})^{-1}.$$

To obtain the mean-squared-error matrix for $\mathbf{b}_*$, we can use (8-26) and the result preceding it:

$$\begin{aligned}\text{MSE}[\mathbf{b}_* \mid \boldsymbol{\beta}] &= \text{Var}[\mathbf{b}_*] + E[\mathbf{b}_* - \boldsymbol{\beta}]E[\mathbf{b}_* - \boldsymbol{\beta}]' \\ &= \sigma^2(\mathbf{I} - \mathbf{W}\mathbf{R})(\mathbf{X}'\mathbf{X})^{-1}(\mathbf{I} - \mathbf{W}\mathbf{R})' + \mathbf{W}(\mathbf{R}\boldsymbol{\beta} - \mathbf{q})(\mathbf{R}\boldsymbol{\beta} - \mathbf{q})'\mathbf{W}'.\end{aligned}$$

---

[23]See, for example, Judge et al. (1985) and the many references cited therein.

[24]See as well the discussions in Judge et al. (1985, pp. 82–92) and Amemiya (1985, pp. 61–63).

[25]See the discussion of specification errors in Section 8.4.

It has been shown that $\mathbf{b}_*$ will be more precise in the sense that MSE[$\mathbf{b} \mid \boldsymbol{\beta}$] − MSE[$\mathbf{b}_* \mid \boldsymbol{\beta}$] is a positive definite matrix if[26]

$$\lambda = \frac{(\mathbf{R}\boldsymbol{\beta} - \mathbf{q})'[\mathbf{R}(\mathbf{X}'\mathbf{X})^{-1}\mathbf{R}']^{-1}(\mathbf{R}\boldsymbol{\beta} - \mathbf{q})}{2\sigma^2} < \frac{1}{2}. \tag{8-27}$$

This is $J/2$ times the population analog to the F statistic that would be used to test the validity of the restrictions. *This implies that if the failure of the true parameters to satisfy the restrictions is not too severe, then the biased estimator will be more precise despite its bias.*

Since λ depends on the unknown parameters we are trying to estimate, (8-27) cannot be computed. It is possible to test the inequality in (8-27) as a hypothesis, but not with the procedures we have used thus far. Under the hypothesis that $(\mathbf{R}\boldsymbol{\beta} - \mathbf{q}) = \mathbf{0}$,

$$\frac{2\hat{\lambda}}{J} = F = \frac{(\mathbf{R}\boldsymbol{\beta} - \mathbf{q})'[\mathbf{R}(\mathbf{X}'\mathbf{X})^{-1}\mathbf{R}']^{-1}(\mathbf{R}\mathbf{b} - \mathbf{q})/\sigma^2}{Js^2/\sigma^2} \tag{8-28}$$

has the familiar F distribution. But if the hypothesis is incorrect, the F distribution no longer applies. The difference arises because the numerator of (8-28) has a chi-squared distribution with J degrees of freedom only if $E[\mathbf{R}\mathbf{b} - \mathbf{q}] = \mathbf{0}$. If not, the numerator has a **noncentral chi-squared** distribution, and the ratio has a **noncentral *F*** distribution. These distributions arise as follows.

1. *Noncentral chi-squared distribution.* If z has a normal distribution with mean μ and standard deviation 1, the distribution of z^2 is *noncentral* chi-squared with parameters 1 and $\mu^2/2$. If μ equals zero, the familiar *central* chi-squared distribution results. The extensions that will enable us to deduce the distribution of F when the restrictions do not hold in the population are:
   a. If $\mathbf{z} \sim N[\boldsymbol{\mu}, \boldsymbol{\Sigma}]$ with J elements, then $\mathbf{z}'\boldsymbol{\Sigma}^{-1}\mathbf{z}$ has a noncentral chi-squared distribution with J degrees of freedom and noncentrality parameter $\boldsymbol{\mu}'\boldsymbol{\Sigma}^{-1}\boldsymbol{\mu}/2$, which we denote $\chi^2_*[J, \boldsymbol{\mu}'\boldsymbol{\Sigma}^{-1}\boldsymbol{\mu}/2]$.
   b. If $\mathbf{z} \sim N[\boldsymbol{\mu}, \mathbf{I}]$ and $\mathbf{M}$ is an idempotent matrix with rank J, then $\mathbf{z}'\mathbf{M}\mathbf{z} \sim \chi^2_*[J, \boldsymbol{\mu}'\mathbf{M}\boldsymbol{\mu}/2]$.
2. *Noncentral F distribution.* If X_1 has a noncentral chi-squared distribution with noncentrality parameter λ and degrees of freedom n_1 and X_2 has a central chi-squared distribution with degrees of freedom n_2 and is independent of X_1, then

$$F_* = \frac{X_1/n_1}{X_2/n_2}$$

   has a noncentral F distribution with parameters n_1, n_2, and λ.[27] Note that in each of these cases, the statistic and the distribution are the familiar ones, except that the effect of the nonzero mean, which induces the noncentrality, is to push the distribution to the right.

[26] See, for example, Fomby et al. (1984, pp. 98–100).

[27] The denominator chi-squared could also be noncentral, but we shall not use any statistics with doubly noncentral distributions.

Thus, the distribution of the sample F statistic in (8-28) is noncentral F with degrees of freedom J and $n - K$ and noncentrality parameter λ, as given in (8-27). If the restrictions are valid, λ will be zero and the familiar central F distribution will result.

A test of the hypothesis that the mean-squared error of the restricted estimator is smaller than that of the unrestricted one can now be constructed. The test of $H_0{:}\lambda \leq \frac{1}{2}$ can be carried out by referring the sample F ratio to the noncentral F distribution with parameters J, $n - K$, and $\frac{1}{2}$. A value of F larger than the critical value in the table is taken as evidence that $\lambda > \frac{1}{2}$. Critical values for the noncentral F distribution have been tabulated by Wallace and Toro-Vizcarrondo (1969). Since this is a three-parameter distribution, the complete tabulation is cumbersome. There is, however, a very simple and accurate approximation that requires only the central F tables given in the appendixes of most textbooks (including this one).

For degrees of freedom J and T, we can approximate the noncentral F critical values by using

$$C_* \approx \left(1 + \frac{1}{J}\right) C, \tag{8-29}$$

where

$$\text{Prob}\left(F\left[J + \frac{1}{J+2}, T\right] > C\right) = 0.05.$$

To find the critical value for noninteger degrees of freedom, it is necessary to interpolate in the F table, which is done using the reciprocals of the degrees of freedom.

EXAMPLE 8.7 Mean-Squared-Error Test (Hypothetical)

A Cobb–Douglas cost function of the form

$$\ln\left(\frac{C}{P_m}\right) = \beta_1 + \beta_2 \ln Q + \beta_3 \ln\left(\frac{P_k}{P_m}\right) + \beta_4 \ln\left(\frac{P_l}{P_m}\right) + \beta_5 \ln\left(\frac{P_e}{P_m}\right)$$

is estimated using 20 observations, where C is cost, Q is output, and P_k, P_l, P_e, and P_m are the unit prices of four factors of production: capital, labor, energy, and materials. The restriction that the function be homogeneous of degree zero in the prices is already imposed. The parameter β_2 is of primary interest. The F statistic for testing the hypothesis that $\beta_3 = \beta_4 = \beta_5 = 0$ is 4.17. Will the estimate of β_2 be improved by imposing the restriction? First, the critical value from the central F distribution for 5 percent significance is 3.29; so, outright, the restrictions are rejected by the familiar standard. But for this test, we require the 5 percent critical value from the noncentral F distribution. This is C^* such that

$$\text{Prob}(F_*[3, 15, \tfrac{1}{2}] > C_*) = 0.05.$$

The neighboring values to the critical value for $F[3.2, 15]$ are 3.29 for $F[3, 15]$

and 3.06 for $F[4, 15]$. Therefore,

$$C = 3.29 - (3.29 - 3.06)\frac{(1/3.2 - 1/3)}{(1/4 - 1/3)} = 3.233,$$

so

$$C_* = (1 + \tfrac{1}{3})3.233 = 4.310.$$

(The corresponding value from the Wallace and Toro-Vizcarrondo tables is 4.315.) Since the test statistic was 4.17, we would conclude that the restricted estimator is more precise, despite the earlier finding.

Because the critical points of the noncentral distribution are always to the right of those for the central distribution, it is worth emphasizing that this test can lead to retention of a set of restrictions when we might reject the restrictions themselves.

Should we use the restricted or the unrestricted estimator? This question is relevant in all the settings we have considered thus far in this chapter. (That is, having tested a set of restrictions and failed to reject them, should we then impose them on the model and reestimate?) It is clear from the preceding that the answer depends on the precision of the estimator in a way that depends on some unknown parameters. Obviously, if we are sure that the restrictions are correct, we should impose them a priori and not concern ourselves with the unrestricted model. If we are sure that the restrictions are incorrect, it is unlikely that the earlier mean-squared-error test would favor the restricted estimator. It is the intermediate case, in which we are uncertain, that is at issue. Unfortunately, the problem becomes yet more complicated, because the process of sequential estimation implied here calls into question any further statistical inference that might be done.

8.5.2. Pretest Estimators

In dealing with the problem of multicollinearity,[28] one of the most tempting (and commonly used) strategies is simply to drop the variable(s) suspected of causing the problem. Consider the simplest case, that of a regression with two independent variables and no constant term. The regression is

$$\mathbf{y} = \beta_1\mathbf{x}_1 + \beta_2\mathbf{x}_2 + \boldsymbol{\epsilon}.$$

Two competing estimators are the **short regression,**

$$b_1 = (\mathbf{x}_1'\mathbf{x}_1)^{-1}\mathbf{x}_1'\mathbf{y},$$

and the **long regression,**

$$b_{1.2} = (\mathbf{x}_1'\mathbf{M}_2\mathbf{x}_1)^{-1}\mathbf{x}_1'\mathbf{M}_2\mathbf{y}.$$

---

[28]This is the subject of Section 9.2. For now, we may view it as an imprecision in the estimation of the parameters that is caused by correlation between the independent variables in a multiple regression.

From our earlier results,

$$E[b_1] = \beta_1 + \beta_2 \frac{\mathbf{x}_1'\mathbf{x}_2}{\mathbf{x}_1'\mathbf{x}_1}$$

and

$$\text{Var}[b_1] = \frac{\sigma^2}{\mathbf{x}_1'\mathbf{x}_1},$$

whereas

$$E[b_{1.2}] = \beta_1$$

and

$$\text{Var}[b_{1.2}] = \frac{\sigma^2}{\mathbf{x}_1'\mathbf{x}_1(1 - r_{12}^2)}.$$

Therefore, b_1 is biased but has a smaller variance. The estimators can be compared on the basis of their mean-squared errors. Using the results of the previous section, we find that the short regression estimator is more precise if the population analog to the F statistic for testing $H_0{:}\beta_2 = 0$ is less than 1. Since this is the square of the usual t ratio for this simple hypothesis, the basis for the mean-squared-error test of (8-27) is

$$\tau^2 = \frac{\beta_2^2}{\sigma^2/(S_{22}(1 - r_{12}^2))}. \tag{8-30}$$

The larger β_2 is, the worse the bias in b_1 and the less likely it is that λ will be less than $\frac{1}{2}$. Thus, b_1 will be a preferable estimator only if this bias is small, as measured by the earlier population t ratio. The test itself can be carried out by referring the square of the t ratio associated with b_2 to $F*[1, n - K, \frac{1}{2}]$.

There are a few ways in which one might proceed at this point. If it is strongly believed that τ is close to zero, it makes sense to omit x_2 from the regression at the outset and use b_1. On the other hand, if one is convinced that x_2 is a significant influence in the regression, it makes little sense even to consider b_1; $b_{1.2}$ is the better estimator. Unfortunately, most of the time, we shall be in neither situation. A third possibility (probably the one used most often) is to use a *sequential estimator.* We first compute the long regression and then choose the estimator on the basis of the t test, where we use t, the sample analog to τ, in

$$b_1^* = \begin{cases} b_1 & \text{if } t^2 < 1, \\ b_{1.2} & \text{if } t^2 \geq 1. \end{cases}$$

This is a "pretest" estimator because it is based on the preliminary regression. It has been analyzed extensively, with some striking results.[29] Remember that

[29]Pretest estimators are examined at length in Judge and Bock (1978, 1983), Feldstein (1973), and Judge et al. (1985).

b_1^* is a function not of the true τ but of the sample statistic t. Therefore, its mean and variance depend on the value of t that is "drawn" in the sample. In particular,

$$E[b_1^*] = E[b_{1.2}]\text{Prob}(t^2 \geq 1) + E[b_1]\text{Prob}(t^2 < 1).$$

Of course, t^2 can be less than 1 even if τ^2 is greater than 1. Since b_1^* is a weighted average of an unbiased estimator and a biased one, it must be biased. The larger is τ^2, the less likely it is that t^2 will be less than 1, so this bias is a decreasing function of τ^2. The variance of b_1^* behaves similarly. The important thing to note is that this variance will not equal either of the variances of the two competing estimators unless τ^2 is zero or infinity.[30]

We have three competing estimators, b_1, $b_{1.2}$, and b_1^*. Two of the three are biased, but none of the three always has the smallest mean-squared error. The comparison is shown in Figure 8.5. When τ^2 is small, b_1 is the best of the three, since its bias is small and its variance is always smaller than that of $b_{1.2}$. When τ^2 is very large, $b_{1.2}$ is the best estimator, which stands to reason. The intermediate

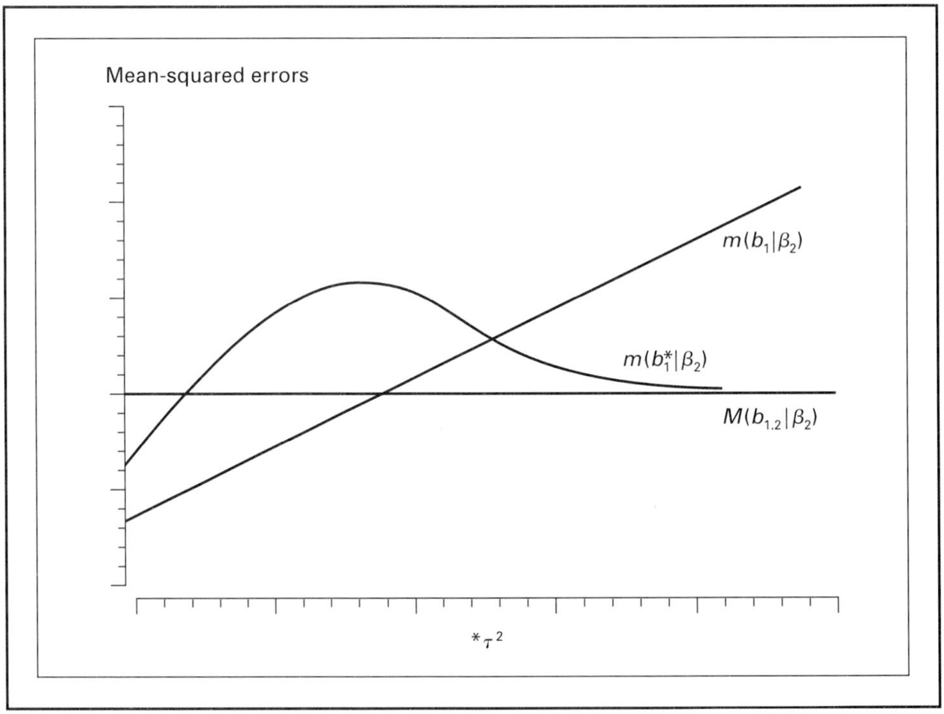

FIGURE 8.5 Mean-Squared Errors.

[30]It is a weighted average of the estimators plus a term that arises out of the noncentral distribution. See Bock et al. (1972).

cases are the problematic ones. Note that b_1^* is never the best of the three estimators, and in the intermediate cases—that is, in those cases in which it is most likely to be used—it is the worst of the three. This simple example illustrates the general principle that allowing the data and the values of sample test statistics to dictate the form of the model can lead to estimators with demonstrably poor statistical properties.

8.5.3. Inequality Restrictions

Prior information about the regression parameters may come in the form of inequality restrictions. For example:

1. The price elasticities in a demand equation must be negative.
2. The marginal propensity to consume is between 0 and 1.
3. To rule out decreasing returns to scale, we would require that the sum of the output elasticities in a production function be greater than or equal to 1.

Estimation subject to inequality restrictions can be formulated as a quadratic programming problem in the framework of the Kuhn–Tucker problem:

$$\text{Minimize}_{\hat{\boldsymbol\beta}} L_I = (\mathbf{y} - \mathbf{X}\hat{\boldsymbol\beta})'(\mathbf{y} - \mathbf{X}\hat{\boldsymbol\beta}) + \boldsymbol\lambda'(\mathbf{R}\hat{\boldsymbol\beta} - \mathbf{q}).$$

The necessary conditions, in which we let $\mathbf{b}_I$ be the solution, are

$$\begin{aligned}\frac{\partial L_I}{\partial \mathbf{b}_I} &= 2\mathbf{X}'\mathbf{X}\mathbf{b}_I - 2\mathbf{b}_I'\mathbf{X}'\mathbf{y} + \mathbf{R}'\boldsymbol\lambda = \mathbf{0},\\ \frac{\partial L_I}{\partial \boldsymbol\lambda} &= \mathbf{R}\mathbf{b}_I - \mathbf{q} \geq \mathbf{0},\\ \boldsymbol\lambda'(\mathbf{R}\mathbf{b}_I - \mathbf{q}) &= \mathbf{0},\\ \boldsymbol\lambda &\leq \mathbf{0}.\end{aligned}$$

As we have seen before, if $\mathbf{Rb} - \mathbf{q} = \mathbf{0}$, where $\mathbf{b} = (\mathbf{X}'\mathbf{X})^{-1}\mathbf{X}'\mathbf{y}$, then $\boldsymbol\lambda$ will equal zero, and this will be a solution. If not, some other solution will be required. Standard algorithms exist for solving the problem, and the computational aspects, although not simple, are at least straightforward.[31] The very difficult matter concerns the sampling properties of the estimator.[32] The following generalities have been obtained.

1. $\mathbf{b}_I$ is biased. It is, as always, a mix of an unbiased and a biased estimator.
2. Var$[\mathbf{b}_I]$ is always less than that of $\mathbf{b}$. This follows from the arguments we have seen before; it is the value of the prior information.
3. MSE$[\mathbf{b}_I \mid \boldsymbol\beta]$ can be less than that of $\mathbf{b}$ but will sometimes be larger.

---

[31]See, for example, Fletcher (1980) and Bazaraa and Shetty (1979).

[32]An illustrative case in a relatively simple setting is analyzed by Thompson (1982). A study that employs some of these results is Goldberger (1986).

There will be some cases in which the solution can be written

$$\begin{aligned}\mathbf{b}_I &= \mathbf{b} \quad \text{if } \mathbf{Rb} - \mathbf{q} \geq \mathbf{0},\\ \mathbf{b}_I &= \mathbf{b}_* \quad \text{if } \mathbf{Rb} - \mathbf{q} < \mathbf{0},\end{aligned}$$

where $\mathbf{b}_*$ is the equality restricted least squares estimator in (8-25). This will always be the case if there is only one constraint, which will be true in most instances analyzed in practice.[33] The estimator **b** fits directly into the pretest estimators we have discussed. The sampling distribution of the inequality restricted estimator is quite complicated, but it has been derived for some cases.[34]

EXAMPLE 8.8 Restricting a Coefficient to Be Positive

Suppose that the constrained regression model is of the form[35]

$$y = \beta_1 + \beta_2 x + \epsilon, \qquad \beta_2 \geq 0, \qquad \epsilon \sim N[0, \sigma^2].$$

The inequality-constrained least squares estimator is

$$\begin{aligned}b_{I2} &= 0 \quad \text{if } b_2 < 0,\\ b_{I2} &= b_2 \quad \text{if } b_2 \geq 0.\end{aligned}$$

Without restrictions, b_2 has the familiar normal distribution with mean β_2 and variance σ^2/S_{xx}, which, for convenience, we denote θ^2. Then b_{I2} is biased unless β_2 equals zero:

$$E[b_{I2}] = 0 \operatorname{Prob}(b_2 < 0) + \beta_2 \operatorname{Prob}(b_2 \geq 0),$$

which is between β_2 and 0. Let τ equal β_2/θ. This is the population t ratio that appeared earlier in (8-29), although here there is no other regressor. Since b_2 is normally distributed, we can use the standard normal distribution to obtain $\operatorname{Prob}(b_2 \geq 0) = \Phi(-\tau)$. Let the density of the standard normal distribution evaluated at $-\tau$ be $\phi(-\tau)$, and denote $\phi(-\tau)/\Phi(-\tau) = \lambda(\tau)$. Thompson (1982) gives the following:[36]

$$\begin{aligned}\text{Bias}[b_{I2}] &= \beta_2 \Phi(-\tau)[\lambda(\tau) - \tau],\\ \text{MSE}[b_{I2}] &= \theta^2 + \theta^2 \Phi(-\tau)[\tau - 1 + \tau\lambda(\tau)].\end{aligned}$$

The bias, as we have seen, is toward zero. The mean-squared error may be greater than or less than θ^2. Note the presence of $\tau - 1$ in the mean-squared error. If τ is greater than 1, the mean-squared error of b_2 is greater than that of $b_{2.1}$, which is what we found earlier in a different problem. If $\tau < 1$, this mixed estimator may have a smaller mean-squared error than that of least squares.

---

[33]If there are several constraints, it is still possible that the solution will appear as given earlier. It is also possible, however, that only some of the constraints will be violated by the least squares estimator. Imposing only these particular constraints may induce failure of the other constraints, which previously were not violated. This complicates the analysis substantially. See Fomby et al. (1984, pp. 104–105) for a discussion.

[34]See Judge and Bock (1978) and Judge and Yancey (1981).

[35]Adding a set of additional regressors would complicate the algebra but would not materially change the solution we shall obtain.

[36]We have simplified Thompson's results a bit.

EXERCISES

1. Use (8-16) to derive the bias that results when the constant term in a regression is inappropriately omitted.
2. In Solow's classic (1957) study of technical change in the U.S. economy, he suggests the following aggregate production function: $q(t) = A(t)f[k(t)]$, where $q(t)$ is aggregate output per workhour, $k(t)$ is the aggregate capital labor ratio, and $A(t)$ is the technology index. Solow considered four static models,

$$q/A = \alpha + \beta \ln k, \qquad q/A = \alpha - \beta/k,$$
$$\ln(q/A) = \alpha + \beta \ln k, \qquad \ln(q/A) = \alpha - \beta/k.$$

(He also estimated a dynamic model, $q(t)/A(t) - q(t-1)/A(t-1) = \alpha + \beta k$.)

(a) Sketch the four functions.

(b) Solow's data for the years 1909 to 1949 are listed below:

Year	*q*	*k*	*A*	*Year*	*q*	*k*	*A*	*Year*	*q*	*k*	*A*
1909	.623	2.06	1.000	1923	.809	2.61	1.196	1937	0.971	2.71	1.415
1910	.616	2.10	.983	1924	.836	2.74	1.215	1938	1.000	2.78	1.445
1911	.647	2.17	1.021	1925	.872	2.81	1.254	1939	1.034	2.66	1.514
1912	.652	2.21	1.023	1926	.869	2.87	1.241	1940	1.082	2.63	1.590
1913	.680	2.23	1.064	1927	.871	2.93	1.235	1941	1.122	2.58	1.660
1914	.682	2.20	1.071	1928	.874	3.02	1.226	1942	1.136	2.64	1.665
1915	.669	2.26	1.041	1929	.895	3.06	1.251	1943	1.180	2.62	1.692
1916	.700	2.34	1.076	1930	.880	3.30	1.197	1944	1.265	2.63	1.812
1917	.679	2.21	1.065	1931	.904	3.33	1.226	1945	1.296	2.66	1.850
1918	.729	2.22	1.142	1932	.879	3.28	1.198	1946	1.215	2.50	1.769
1919	.767	2.47	1.157	1933	.869	3.10	1.211	1947	1.194	2.50	1.739
1920	.721	2.58	1.069	1934	.921	3.00	1.298	1948	1.221	2.55	1.767
1921	.770	2.55	1.146	1935	.943	2.87	1.349	1949	1.275	2.70	1.809
1922	.788	2.49	1.183	1936	.982	2.72	1.429				

Source: Solow (1957, p. 314). Several variables are omitted.

Use these data to estimate the α and β of the four functions listed above. [Note: Your results will not quite match Solow's. See the next problem for resolution of the discrepancy.]

(c) Sketch the functions using your particular estimates of the parameters.

3. In the aforementioned study, Solow states:

> A scatter of q/A against k is shown in Chart 4. Considering the amount of a priori doctoring which the raw figures have undergone, the fit is remarkably tight. Except, that is, for the layer of points which are obviously too high. These maverick observations relate to the seven last years of the period, 1943–1949. From the

way they lie almost exactly parallel to the main scatter, one is tempted to conclude that in 1943 the aggregate production function simply shifted.

(a) Draw a scatter diagram of q/A against k. [Or obtain Solow's original study and examine his. An alternative source of the original paper is the volume edited by Zellner (1968).]

(b) Estimate the four models you estimated in the previous problem including a dummy variable for the years 1943 to 1949. How do your results change? [Note: These results match those reported by Solow, although he did not report the coefficient on the dummy variable.]

(c) Solow went on to surmise that, in fact, the data were fundamentally different in the years before 1943 than during and after. If so, one would guess that the regression should be as well (although whether the change is merely in the data or in the underlying production function is not settled). Use a Chow test to examine the difference in the two subperiods using your four functional forms. Note that with the dummy variable, you can do the test by introducing an interaction term between the dummy and whichever function of k appears in the regression. Use an F test to test the hypothesis.

4. Consider two alternative regressions

$$1.\ y = \alpha_1 D_1 + \alpha_2 D_2 + \alpha_3 D_3 + \alpha_4 D_4 + \epsilon.$$
$$2.\ y = \alpha_1 \quad\ + \alpha_2 D_2 + \alpha_3 D_3 + \alpha_4 D_4 + \epsilon.$$

The variables are quarterly dummy variables [see (8-1)]. There are equal numbers of observations in each quarter. By computing $(\mathbf{X}'\mathbf{X})^{-1}\mathbf{X}'\mathbf{y}$ for the two models, obtain the precise formulas for the least squares coefficients in the two cases. Prove that if there were a term βx in the two equations, the least squares estimates of β would be identical.

5. What restriction on the parameters of (8-1) leads to the model $C_t = \beta_1 + \beta_2 X_t + \delta q_t + \epsilon_t$, where $q_t = 1, 2, 3$ in the second, third, and fourth quarters, respectively? How would you test the restriction?

6. In a classic study of the American automobile market, Griliches (1961b) reports the following regression results:

$$\begin{aligned}\ln \text{Price} = {} & 6.4 + 0.056H + 0.249W + 0.023L + 0.010V + 0.023T \\ & + 0.090A + 0.088P + 0.109B + 0.157C - 0.044D_1 - 0.015D_2 \\ & + 0.019D_3 + 0.044D_4 + 0.044D_5 + 0.023D_6,\end{aligned}$$

where 1954 is the base year and

H = advertised horsepower, in hundreds;
W = shipping weight, in thousands of pounds;
L = overall length, in tens of inches;
V = 1 if the car has a V8 engine and 0 otherwise;
T = 1 if the car is a hard top, 0 if a convertible;

A = 1 if it has an automatic transmission, 0 if not;
P = 1 if power steering is standard, 0 if not;
B = 1 if power brakes are standard, 0 if not;
C = 1 if the car is a "compact," 0 if not;
D_1 = 1 for 1955 model car, 0 otherwise;
D_2 = 1 for 1956 model car, 0 otherwise;
D_3 = 1 for 1957 model car, 0 otherwise;
D_4 = 1 for 1958 model car, 0 otherwise;
D_5 = 1 for 1959 model car, 0 otherwise;
D_6 = 1 for 1960 model car, 0 otherwise.

(The value of 6.4 for the constant term is assumed here. The author did not report the constant terms in his results.)

The regression is estimated using a large sample of prices of cars for the years 1954 to 1960. Since the dependent variable is in logarithms and the coefficients are close to zero, they may be treated as percentage changes. For example, the model predicts that if everything else were held constant, an increase of 100 horsepower increased the cost of a car by 5.6 percent, whereas from 1954 to 1956, the price of a particular car fell by 1.5 percent.

(a) As a benchmark, suppose that an average car in 1954 had 141 horsepower, weighed 3452 pounds, and was 205 inches long (from Griliches, Table 1). Suppose, as well, that in 1954, 25 percent of the cars had V8s, 75 percent were hard tops, 20 percent had automatic transmissions, 10 percent had power steering, 5 percent had power brakes, and 10 percent of the cars sold called be called "compact." (All these are hypothetical; Griliches gives no figures for these.) What does the model predict for the median price of a car? (The prediction would not be the mean. Griliches reports a *geometric* mean of all prices for 1954 of $2360.)

(b) Everything else held constant, how much more would it cost to buy a car with a V8 and power steering in 1955 than without these two features in 1954?

(c) Holding all other features constant, how much did the price of a car rise from 1956 to 1957. From 1956 to 1959?

(d) Suppose that putting a hard top on a car instead of a convertible always added exactly 100 pounds to the weight of the car. How would this affect the interpretation of the coefficients on W and T in the regression?

(e) The R^2 in the regression above was 0.922, using 570 observations. If the R^2 in the regression without $D_1, \ldots$ were 0.919, would the results support the hypothesis that variation in the mix of options and other features was entirely responsible for the variation in car prices in the 7-year period?

(f) Suppose that the preceding data had also been used to compute seven separate regressions, one for each year, with the following results:

	1954	*1955*	*1956*	*1957*	*1958*	*1959*	*1960*	*All*
Observations	65	55	87	95	103	87	78	570
$\mathbf{e}'\mathbf{e}$	104	88	206	144	199	308	211	1425

Test the hypothesis that the same coefficients apply in each year. [Note: The model with the pooled data allows a separate constant for each year. Note as well that you may need an approximate value for the F distribution with large degrees of freedom.]

7. Suppose that estimation of the model in (8-6) produced estimates of 0.34 for β and 0.1 for λ. The means of y and x are 1 and 2, respectively. What is the estimate of the elasticity $(x/y)\ \partial E[y]/\partial x$? (For applications of the Box–Cox regression, see Section 10.4.)

8. Let $\mathbf{b}_* = [\mathbf{X}'\mathbf{X} + k\mathbf{I}]^{-1}\mathbf{X}'\mathbf{y}$. Prove that this is a biased estimator of $\boldsymbol{\beta}$ in the classical regression model. What is its mean-squared-error matrix? (This is a **ridge regression** estimator.)

9. Given the results in part e of Exercise 6, would the estimates of the other parameters in the model be sharpened if the six yearly dummy variables were dropped? Use the noncentral F test (see Example 8.7) to find out. Do this first assuming that there are 30 observations in total. Then use the chi-squared approximation to the distribution of JF with the full 570 observations.

10. *Reverse regression.* A common method of analyzing statistical data to detect discrimination in the workplace is to fit the regression

$$y = \alpha + \boldsymbol{\beta}'\mathbf{x} + \gamma d + \epsilon, \tag{1}$$

where y is the wage rate and d is a dummy variable indicating either membership ($d = 1$) or nonmembership ($d = 0$) in the class toward which it is suggested the discrimination is directed. The regressors $\mathbf{x}$ include factors specific to the particular type of job as well as indicators of the qualifications of the individual. The hypothesis of interest is $H_0{:}\gamma < 0$ versus $H_1{:}\gamma = 0$. The regression seeks to answer the question, "In a given job, are individuals in the class ($d = 1$) paid less than equally qualified individuals not in the class ($d = 0$)?" Consider, however, an alternative possibility. Do individuals in the class in the same job as others, and receiving the same wage, uniformly have higher qualifications? If so, this might also be viewed as a form of discrimination. To analyze this question, Conway and Roberts (1983) suggested the following procedure:

1. Fit (1) by ordinary least squares. Denote the estimates a, $\mathbf{b}$, and c.

2. Compute the set of **qualification indices**

$$\mathbf{q} = a\mathbf{i} + \mathbf{X}\mathbf{b}. \quad \textbf{(2)}$$

Note the omission of $c\mathbf{d}$ from the fitted value.

3. Regress $\mathbf{q}$ on a constant $\mathbf{y}$ and $\mathbf{d}$. The equation is

$$\mathbf{q} = \alpha_* + \beta_*\mathbf{y} + \gamma_*\mathbf{d} + \epsilon_*. \quad \textbf{(3)}$$

The analysis suggests that if $\gamma < 0$, $\gamma_* > 0$.

(a) Prove that the theory notwithstanding, the least squares estimates c and c_* are related by

$$c_* = \frac{(\bar{y}_1 - \bar{y})(1 - R^2)}{(1 - P)(1 - r_{yd}^2)} - c, \quad \textbf{(4)}$$

where

$$\begin{aligned} \bar{y}_1 &= \text{mean of } y \text{ for observations with } d = 1, \\ \bar{y} &= \text{mean of } y \text{ for all observations}, \\ P &= \text{mean of } d, \\ R^2 &= \text{coefficient of determination for (1)}, \\ r_{yd}^2 &= \text{squared correlation between } y \text{ and } d. \end{aligned}$$

[Hint: The model contains a constant term. Thus, to simplify the algebra, assume that all variables are measured as deviations from the overall sample means and use a partitioned regression to compute the coefficients in (3). Second, in (2), use the result that based on the least squares results,

$$\mathbf{y} = a\mathbf{i} + \mathbf{X}\mathbf{b} + c\mathbf{d} + \mathbf{e},$$

so

$$\mathbf{q} = \mathbf{y} - c\mathbf{d} - \mathbf{e}.$$

From here on, we drop the constant term.] Thus, in the regression in (3), you are regressing $[\mathbf{y} - c\mathbf{d} - \mathbf{e}]$ on $\mathbf{y}$ and $\mathbf{d}$. Remember that all variables are in deviation form.

(b) Will the sample evidence necessarily be consistent with the theory? [Hint: Suppose that $c = 0$.]

A symposium on the Conway and Roberts paper appeared in the *Journal of Business and Economic Statistics* in April 1983.

CHAPTER 9

Data Problems

9.1. INTRODUCTION

It is rare that the data one has in hand for estimating a regression model conform exactly to the theory underlying the model. Any number of problems will arise, even in the most carefully designed survey. The most prevalent of these are the following.

1. **Multicollinearity.** The measured variables are too highly intercorrelated to allow precise analysis of their individual effects.
2. **Missing data.** There are gaps in the data set.
3. **Grouped data.** The information contained in the original data has been masked by averaging or some other kind of data aggregation.
4. **Measurement error.** The measured data do not conform to the variables in the model, either because of poor measurement or because the variables in the model are inherently unmeasurable.

All these factors cause problems in estimating and interpreting regression models. This chapter will survey some results in detecting and solving these problems.

9.2. MULTICOLLINEARITY

In our analysis of the classical regression model, we have assumed that the matrix of independent variables $\mathbf{X}$ has full rank; that is, there is no exact linear relationship among the independent variables. For $(\mathbf{X}'\mathbf{X})^{-1}$ to exist, $\mathbf{X}$ must have full column rank. Consider the case of just two explanatory variables and a constant. For either slope coefficient,

$$\text{Var}[b_k] = \frac{\sigma^2}{(1 - r_{12}^2)\sum_{i=1}^{n}(x_{ik} - \bar{x}_k)^2} = \frac{\sigma^2}{(1 - r_{12}^2)S_{kk}}, \quad k = 1, 2. \tag{9-1}$$

If the two variables are perfectly correlated, the variance is infinite. The case of an exact linear relationship among the regressors is a serious failure of the assumptions of the model, not of the data. The more common case is one in which the variables are highly but not perfectly correlated. In this instance, the regression model retains all its assumed properties, although potentially severe statistical problems arise. We consider the two cases in turn.

9.2.1. Perfect Collinearity

We first considered the possibility of perfect collinearity when we laid out the assumptions of the regression model. In a consumption function

$$C = \beta_1 + \beta_2 \text{ nonlabor income} + \beta_3 \text{ salary} + \beta_4 \text{ income} + \epsilon, \tag{9-2}$$

it is not possible to separate individual effects of the components of income and total income. If we let N be nonlabor income, S be salary, and T be total income, then $T = N + S$ for every individual. According to the model,

$$E[C] = \beta_1 + \beta_2 N + \beta_3 S + \beta_4 T.$$

But if we let q be any nonzero value and let $\beta_2' = \beta_2 + q$, $\beta_3' = \beta_3 + q$, and $\beta_4' = \beta_4 - q$,

$$E[C] = \beta_1 + \beta_2' N + \beta_3' S + \beta_4' T.$$

as well for a different set of parameters. Unlike the full rank case, this one allows the same value of $E[C]$ for many different values of the parameters.

It is worth emphasizing that this is a badly specified model, and its failure has nothing to do with the quality of the data involved. The parameters of this regression model are said to be **unidentified.** We shall return to this subject at several points later. In this example, we see the hallmark of what is known as the **identification problem.** For this model, as it is specified, there are an infinite number of possible parameter vectors that are consistent with the same expected value. Thus, no matter how much data we are able to obtain, we cannot estimate the parameters. The full rank assumption can be viewed as an identification assumption; it means that for a given vector $\mathbf{x}$, there is only one set of parameters consistent with a given value of $E(y)$.[1]

9.2.2. Near Multicollinearity

In the short-rank case, the regressor matrix has K columns but only rank $L < K$. It follows from the result given earlier that only L functions of the pa-

---

[1]See Theil (1971) and Schmidt (1976, pp. 43–44) for further discussion.

rameters can be estimated. The significance of this is that in the K columns of $\mathbf{X}$, there are only L independent sources of variation. Hence, the data permit only L estimable functions of the parameters. It is much more common for the variables to be correlated, but not perfectly so. The case of near collinearity or high intercorrelation among the variables is, in contrast, a statistical problem. The difficulty in estimation is not one of identification but of precision. The higher the correlation between the regressors becomes, the less precise our estimates will be.

9.2.3. The Symptoms of Multicollinearity

When the regressors are highly correlated, we often observe the following problems:

- Small changes in the data can produce wide swings in the parameter estimates.
- Coefficients may have very high standard errors and low significance levels even though they are jointly highly significant and the R^2 in the regression is quite high.
- Coefficients will have the wrong sign or an implausible magnitude.

EXAMPLE 9.1 Multicollinearity in the Longley Data

The Longley data analyzed in Section 7.6 are notorious for severe multicollinearity. Look, for example, at the last year of the data set. The last observation does not appear to be unusual. The results listed in Table 9.1, however, in which the earlier regression is reestimated without the last year of the data, suggest how severe the multicollinearity problem is in these data. The change in the results that occurs when 1 year of the data is dropped is dramatic. The last coefficient rises by 600 percent and the third rises by 800 percent. One might reach very different conclusions, depending on when the data were drawn.

TABLE 9.1 Dependent Variable: Total Employment

	1947–1961	*1947–1962*
Constant	1,459,400	1,169,090
Year	−721.76	−576.464
GNP deflator	−181.12	−19.761
GNP	0.091068	0.064394
Armed forces	−0.074937	−0.010145

In the inverse matrix $(\mathbf{X}'\mathbf{X})^{-1}$, the kth diagonal element (where we let k equal one for convenience) is

$$(\mathbf{x}_1'\mathbf{M}_2\mathbf{x}_1)^{-1} = [\mathbf{x}_1'\mathbf{x}_1 - \mathbf{x}_1'\mathbf{X}_2(\mathbf{X}_2'\mathbf{X}_2)^{-1}\mathbf{X}_2'\mathbf{x}_1]^{-1}$$
$$= \left[\mathbf{x}_1'\mathbf{x}_1\left(1 - \frac{\mathbf{x}_1'\mathbf{X}_2(\mathbf{X}_2'\mathbf{X}_2)^{-1}\mathbf{X}_2'\mathbf{x}_1)}{\mathbf{x}_1'\mathbf{x}_1}\right)\right]^{-1} \tag{9-3}$$
$$= \frac{1}{S_{11}(1 - R_{1.}^2)},$$

where $R_{1.}^2$ is the R^2 in the regression of $\mathbf{x}_1$ on all the other independent variables in the regression. Therefore, in the multiple regression, the variance of b_1 is

$$\text{Var}[b_1] = \frac{\sigma^2}{(1 - R_{1.}^2)S_{11}}. \tag{9-4}$$

We can envision a case in which we add a variable to the regression that is highly correlated with $\mathbf{x}_1$. S_{11} will not change at all, whereas R_1^2 will rise and $\text{Var}[b_1]$ will rise correspondingly.

The role of these $R_{k.}^2$'s is considerable. The simple correlations among the variables may not give an adequate indication of the problem. For a particular variable, Leamer (1978, p. 179) suggests the following measure of the effect of multicollinearity:

$$c_2(b_k) = \left\{\frac{\left[\sum_i (x_{ik} - \bar{x}_k)^2\right]^{-1}}{[(\mathbf{X}'\mathbf{X})_{kk}^{-1}]}\right\}^{1/2}. \tag{9-5}$$

This measure is the square root of the ratio of the true variances of b_k when estimated with and without the other variables. If $\mathbf{x}_k$ were uncorrelated with the other variables, $c_2(b_k)$ would be 1. Otherwise, $c_2(b_k)$ is equivalent to $(1 - R_{k.}^2)^{1/2}$, which again suggests the usefulness of the auxiliary coefficients of determination. For example, our results thus far suggest that the coefficient on "armed forces" is being adversely affected by multicollinearity. The three simple correlations of this variable with "year," "GNP deflator," and "GNP," however, are 0.417, 0.465, and 0.446, which are not particularly high. But the corresponding R^2 in the regression of "armed forces" on these three variables is only 0.35616, so, evidently, yet more analysis is called for.[2]

Our primary concern might be the imprecision of our estimates. One suggested rule of thumb is that we should be concerned about multicollinearity if the overall R^2 in the regression is less than any of the individual $R_{i.}^2$'s we have been considering.[3] The *estimated* variance of the kth coefficient (assuming that the constant term is the first) is

$$\text{Est. Var}[b_k] = \frac{s^2}{(1 - R_{k.}^2)S_{kk}} = \frac{(1 - R^2)S_{yy}}{(n - K)(1 - R_{k.}^2)S_{kk}}, \quad k = 2, \ldots, K. \tag{9-6}$$

---

[2]The **multiple correlation** is the square root of this value, 0.5968.

[3]See, for example Klein (1962).

This shows the interaction of the two coefficients of determination. For our sample data, the overall R^2 is 0.97352, whereas the four coefficients of determination for the regressions of each independent variable on the other regressors are 0.99303, 0.98679, 0.99245, and 0.35616. On the basis of this criterion, we conclude that multicollinearity in these data is, indeed, a problem. The auxiliary R^2's of 0.99 for the first three variables are extremely high. Of course, this rule is only suggestive. It gives no indication of how to proceed. The second most volatile of the coefficients was that on "armed forces." But the $R_{k.}^2$ for the "armed forces" variable is only 0.35616, so despite the obvious problem with this coefficient, the rule of thumb appears not to pick it up.

An alternative measure of multicollinearity has been suggested by Belsley et al. (1980). The **condition number** of a matrix is the square root of the ratio of the largest to the smallest characteristic root:

$$\gamma = \left(\frac{\lambda_{\max}}{\lambda_{\min}}\right)^{1/2}. \tag{9-7}$$

Belsley et al. suggest computing this ratio for the moment matrix $\mathbf{X}'\mathbf{X}$. Since the roots are dependent on the scaling of the data, we first normalize the data by dividing each column in $\mathbf{X}$ by $(\mathbf{x}_k'\mathbf{x}_k)^{1/2}$.[4] If the regressors are orthogonal (so that $R_{k.}^2$ will be zero for all k), γ will be 1. The greater the intercorrelation among the variables, the higher the condition number. Belsley et al. suggest that values in excess of 20 suggest potential problems.

EXAMPLE 9.2 Condition Number

The largest and smallest characteristic roots of the normalized 5×5 matrix for the Longley data are 4.91993902 and $0.39929527 \times 10^{-7}$. Thus, the condition number for these data is 11,100.25. This confirms what we have already suspected.

The results thus far suggest that the coefficient on "armed forces" is adversely affected by multicollinearity. But in the regression on the full data set (all 16 observations), the t ratio on the "armed forces" coefficient is -0.033, indicating that this coefficient is not significantly different from zero by any standard. A 95 percent confidence interval for the coefficient would be $[-0.6794, 0.6691]$, which is quite wide. Apparently, the range of variation we observed in this coefficient was simply because it does not really have much explanatory power in the regression, and we merely observed sampling variation.

The point just noted has been the source of some confusion in the literature. It is tempting to conclude that a variable has a low t ratio, or is insignificant, because of multicollinearity. One might (some authors have) then conclude that if the data were not collinear, the coefficient would be significantly different from zero. Of course, this is not necessarily true. Sometimes a coeffi-

[4]For computational purposes, the correct matrix is obtained by the product $\mathbf{S}(\mathbf{X}'\mathbf{X})\mathbf{S}$, where $\mathbf{S}$ is a diagonal matrix with $(\mathbf{x}_k'\mathbf{x}_k)^{-1/2}$ on the diagonals.

cient turns out to be insignificant because the variable does not have any explanatory power in the model. Moreover, in nonexperimental data, the suggestion that the results might be different if the data were not collinear has little practical value.

An additional tool that has been advocated for detecting multicollinearity is Belsley et al.'s (1980) variance decomposition. The covariance matrix of the least squares coefficient vector can be written in terms of its spectral decomposition [see Sections 2.7.4, 2.7.9, and (2-102)],

$$\sigma^2(\mathbf{X}'\mathbf{X})^{-1} = \sigma^2\mathbf{C}\boldsymbol{\Lambda}^{-1}\mathbf{C}' = \sigma^2 \sum_{k=1}^{K} (1/\lambda_k)\mathbf{c}_k\mathbf{c}_k',$$

where λ_k is the kth characteristic root, ordered from largest to smallest, and $\mathbf{c}_k$ is the associated characteristic vector. This suggests a decomposition of the kth diagonal element of Var[$\mathbf{b}$]. Where the columns of $\mathbf{C}$ are the characteristic vectors, we have

$$\text{Var}[b_k] = \sigma^2 \sum_{l=1}^{k} (1/\lambda_l)C_{kl}^2.$$

(That is, the sum for each coefficient is taken along a row of $\mathbf{C}$.) Each variance can then be broken down into the proportion associated with each root by computing

$$\pi_{kl} = \frac{C_{kl}^2/\lambda_l}{(\mathbf{X}'\mathbf{X})_{kk}^{-1}}$$

so that $\Sigma_l\, \pi_{kl} = 1$. These are arranged in a table that reveals (suggests) linear dependence among the regressors associated with a particular characteristic root. Small roots suggest large values of π_{kl}, so the authors suggest looking for two or more large values in a row of the table, or values that exceed 0.5.

9.2.4. Suggested Remedies for the Multicollinearity Problem

Several methods have been proposed for coping with multicollinearity. The obvious remedy (and surely the most frequently used) is to drop variables suspected of causing the problem from the regression. Of course, in so doing, one encounters the problems of specification analyzed in Section 8.4. A number of other approaches have been suggested. Before considering them, it is worth making an observation about our predicament. Under the assumptions of the regression model, the least squares estimator (assuming that it exists) is still the best unbiased estimator of the parameters. The problem with multicollinearity is that "best" is not very good.

One approach to the problem involves the incorporation of additional information. One might argue, however, that if such information were available at the outset, we ought to have used it before discovering the problem of multicollinearity. The situations in which such useful outside information is available are, unfortunately, rare in any event.

Another possibility for improvement within the confines of the model is to find a slightly biased estimator with a much smaller variance, that is, one with a smaller mean-squared error. Unfortunately, the distributions of such estimators, at least the ones that have been devised thus far, depend on unknown parameters. This puts us back where we started. The other "solutions" we shall discuss involve trading an unbiased estimator for a biased one about which our ability to make statistical inferences will be limited.[5]

Two purely mechanical solutions have been proposed for dealing with the most obvious problem of multicollinearity, the large standard errors of the estimates. The **ridge regression estimator** is

$$\mathbf{b}_r = [\mathbf{X}'\mathbf{X} + r\mathbf{D}]^{-1}\mathbf{X}'\mathbf{y}, \tag{9-8}$$

where $\mathbf{D}$ is a diagonal matrix containing the diagonal elements of $\mathbf{X}'\mathbf{X}$ and the scalar r is chosen arbitrarily.[6] In application, r is to be chosen in such a way that the resulting estimates are "stable" with respect to small variations in r. The authors of the technique suggest that a small value, say 0.01, be chosen at the outset and then successively larger values be tried until the coefficients stabilize.[7] In its favor, it is easily shown that although the ridge estimator is biased,

$$E[\mathbf{b}_r] = [\mathbf{X}'\mathbf{X} + r\mathbf{D}]^{-1}\mathbf{X}'\mathbf{X}\boldsymbol{\beta},$$

its covariance matrix,

$$\text{Var}[\mathbf{b}_r] = \sigma^2[\mathbf{X}'\mathbf{X} + r\mathbf{D}]^{-1}\mathbf{X}'\mathbf{X}[\mathbf{X}'\mathbf{X} + r\mathbf{D}]^{-1}, \tag{9-9}$$

is smaller than that of the ordinary least squares estimator.[8]

The ridge estimator may have a smaller mean-squared error than ordinary least squares.[9] Unfortunately, this mean-squared error is a function of the unknown parameters that we are trying to estimate (here, with a clear bias). Thus, this is unlikely to be a useful criterion. Economists have avoided use of this estimator, perhaps because of their aversion to biased estimators and partly because of the difficulty it presents for statistical inference. Unlike our earlier case of omitted variables, in this case, we have an unbiased estimate of σ^2 obtained from the least squares regression with r equal to zero. Still, it is difficult to attach much meaning to hypothesis tests about an estimator that is biased in an unknown direction.

A second approach that offers somewhat more intuitive appeal is that of **principal components.** Referring back to our discussion of exact collinearity, we considered the suggestion that although the data matrix has K columns, it may have fewer than K truly independent sources of information, that is, variation.

---

[5]Nonetheless, this idea has produced a large and insightful literature. A summary for econometrics appears in Judge et al. (1985).

[6]See Hoerl and Kennard (1970) and extensive discussion in Judge et al. (1985, pp. 912–922).

[7]The ridge estimator for the Longley data is extremely volatile. With $r = 0.01$, it bears little resemblance to the least squares estimator. With $r = 0.75, 1.0, \ldots$, the estimator continues to change rapidly.

[8]The proof is left as an exercise.

[9]Schmidt (1976, pp. 48–55) proves that there is always an r such that the trace of the mean-squared-error matrix for the ridge estimator is smaller than that for least squares. Since this r depends on both β and σ^2, it is unlikely to be of much practical use.

We can carry the same reasoning over to the full rank case. Even though the **X** matrix may have full rank, if there is substantial collinearity, we may still believe that there are only a limited number of independent sources of variation. The use of principal components is an attempt to extract from the **X** matrix a small number of variables that, in some sense, account for most of or all the variation in **X**.

Algebraically, we may approach the calculation of principal components as a regression problem. What linear combination of the columns of **X** provides the best fit to all the columns of **X**? The linear combination will be

$$\mathbf{z}_1 = \mathbf{X}\mathbf{c}_1.$$

Since the R^2 in the regression of any column of **X** on $\mathbf{z}_1$ will be the same for any scalar multiple of $\mathbf{c}_1$, we remove the indeterminacy by imposing

$$\mathbf{z}_1'\mathbf{z}_1 = 1.$$[10]

For each column of **X**, $\mathbf{x}_k$, the sum of squared residuals will be

$$\mathbf{e}_k'\mathbf{e}_k = \mathbf{x}_k'[\mathbf{I} - \mathbf{z}_1(\mathbf{z}_1'\mathbf{z}_1)^{-1}\mathbf{z}_1']\mathbf{x}_k = \mathbf{x}_k'[\mathbf{I} - \mathbf{z}_1\mathbf{z}_1']\mathbf{x}_k.$$

Taking all the $\mathbf{x}_k$'s simultaneously, we seek to minimize

$$\sum_{k=1}^{K} \mathbf{e}_k'\mathbf{e}_k = \text{tr}(\mathbf{X}'[\mathbf{I} - \mathbf{z}_1\mathbf{z}_1']\mathbf{X})$$

subject to $\mathbf{z}_1'\mathbf{z}_1 = 1$. This is the same as maximizing the second part of the trace since $\mathbf{X}'\mathbf{X}$ does not involve $\mathbf{c}_1$. We can set this up as a Lagrangean problem; $\mathbf{c}_1$ and λ are the roots of

$$\ell = \text{tr}(\mathbf{X}'\mathbf{z}_1\mathbf{z}_1'\mathbf{X}) + \lambda(1 - \mathbf{z}_1'\mathbf{z}_1).$$

By permuting in the trace and substituting $\mathbf{z}_1 = \mathbf{X}\mathbf{c}_1$, we obtain the equivalent problem which is to find the roots of

$$\ell = \mathbf{c}_1'(\mathbf{X}'\mathbf{X})^2\mathbf{c}_1 + \lambda[1 - \mathbf{c}_1'(\mathbf{X}'\mathbf{X})\mathbf{c}_1].$$

The first-order condition for $\mathbf{c}_1$ is

$$\frac{\partial \ell}{\partial \mathbf{c}_1} = 2(\mathbf{X}'\mathbf{X})^2\mathbf{c}_1 - 2\lambda(\mathbf{X}'\mathbf{X})\mathbf{c}_1 = \mathbf{0}.$$

Now, premultiply both sides of the equation by $\frac{1}{2}(\mathbf{X}'\mathbf{X})^{-1}$ to obtain the result for $\mathbf{c}_1$:

$$(\mathbf{X}'\mathbf{X})\mathbf{c}_1 - \lambda\mathbf{c}_1 = \mathbf{0}.$$

Therefore, $\mathbf{c}_1$ is a characteristic vector of $\mathbf{X}'\mathbf{X}$. Which one? The criterion is

$$\mathbf{c}_1'(\mathbf{X}'\mathbf{X})^2\mathbf{c}_1 = \lambda^2\mathbf{c}_1'\mathbf{c}_1 = \lambda^2$$

---

[10]Since principal components are sensitive to the scaling of the data, the columns of **X** should also be normalized so that $\mathbf{x}_k'\mathbf{x}_k = 1$. This can be done without modifying the original data just by pre- and postmultiplying $\mathbf{X}'\mathbf{X}$ by $[\text{diag}(\mathbf{X}'\mathbf{X})]^{-1/2}$.

since $\mathbf{c}_1'\mathbf{c}_1$ must equal 1. Therefore, to maximize the criterion, we choose the characteristic vector associated with the largest characteristic root. If the total variation in $\mathbf{X}$ is defined to be the trace of $\mathbf{X}'\mathbf{X}$, the proportion of the variation in $\mathbf{X}'\mathbf{X}$ explained by this variable is

$$w_1 = \frac{\lambda_1}{\sum_{k=1}^{K} \lambda_k}.$$

This exercise can be repeated by seeking a second linear combination of the columns of $\mathbf{X}$ with the same criterion, subject to the condition that this second variable be orthogonal to the first. There are K such variables, the kth computed using the characteristic vector corresponding to the kth largest characteristic root.

If we use all K principal components, we end up exactly where we started. This would amount to regressing $\mathbf{y}$ on K linear combinations of the columns of $\mathbf{X}$. The point of the exercise is to use a small number of principal components so that the sum of their contributions is satisfactorily close to 1.

Suppose that of the K columns of $\mathbf{X}$, we use $L < K$ principal components. Thus, we regress $\mathbf{y}$ on $\mathbf{XC}_L$, where $\mathbf{C}_L$ is a $K \times L$ matrix containing L characteristic vectors of $\mathbf{X}'\mathbf{X}$. The estimator is

$$\mathbf{d} = (\mathbf{Z}'\mathbf{Z})^{-1}\mathbf{Z}'\mathbf{y}. \quad \textbf{(9-10)}$$

From the definitions of characteristic roots and vectors,

$$\mathbf{Z}'\mathbf{Z} = \mathbf{C}_L'\mathbf{X}'\mathbf{X}\mathbf{C}_L = \mathbf{\Lambda}_L,$$

where $\mathbf{\Lambda}_L$ is the $L \times L$ matrix that contains the L largest characteristic roots of $\mathbf{X}'\mathbf{X}$ on its diagonal. Also,

$$\mathbf{Z}'\mathbf{y} = \mathbf{C}_L'\mathbf{X}'\mathbf{y} = \mathbf{C}_L'\mathbf{X}'\mathbf{X}\mathbf{b},$$

but

$$\mathbf{C}_L'\mathbf{X}'\mathbf{X} = \mathbf{\Lambda}_L\mathbf{C}_L'.$$

By making the preceding substitutions,

$$\mathbf{d} = \mathbf{C}_L'\mathbf{b}. \quad \textbf{(9-11)}$$

Therefore, if we use L principal components, the resulting coefficient vector in the regression of $\mathbf{y}$ on $\mathbf{Z}$ is a simple function of the least squares coefficients in the regression of $\mathbf{y}$ on $\mathbf{X}$.

Like the ridge estimator, the principal components estimator is a biased estimator that may be more precise than its least squares counterpart. If we insert our estimate $\mathbf{d}$ into the original formulation, we obtain the fitted values

$$\hat{\mathbf{y}} = \mathbf{Z}\mathbf{d} = \mathbf{X}\mathbf{C}_L\mathbf{d},$$

so we may view the principal components estimator of the full coefficient vector as

$$\mathbf{b}_p = \mathbf{C}_L\mathbf{d} = \mathbf{C}_L\mathbf{C}_L'\mathbf{b},$$

where **b** is the original least squares estimator. Since **b** is unbiased, this competing estimator is clearly biased.[11] Its covariance matrix, however, is unambiguously smaller than the variance of **b**.[12]

There are three problems with using this estimator. First, the results are sensitive to the scale of measurement on the variables. The obvious remedy is to standardize the variables, but, unfortunately, this has substantial effects on the computed results. Second, the principal components are not chosen on the basis of any relationship of the regressors to **y**, the variable we are attempting to explain. Last, the calculation makes ambiguous the interpretation of the results. The principal components estimator is a mixture of all the original coefficients. It is unlikely that we shall be able to interpret these combinations in any meaningful way.

9.2.5. Conclusion

Using diagnostic tools such as these for finding multicollinearity could be viewed as an attempt to distinguish a bad model from bad data. But, in fact, the problem only stems from a prior opinion with which the data seem to be in conflict. A finding that suggests that multicollinearity is adversely affecting the estimates seems to suggest that but for this effect, all the coefficients would be statistically significant. Of course, this need not be the case. If the data suggest that a variable is unimportant in a model, the theory notwithstanding, the researcher has ultimately to decide how strong their commitment is to that theory. Suggested "remedies" for multicollinearity might well amount to attempts to force the theory on the data.

9.3. MISSING OBSERVATIONS

It is fairly common for a data set to have gaps, for a variety of reasons. Perhaps the most common occurrence of this problem is in survey data, in which it often happens that respondents simply fail to answer the questions. In a time series, the data may be missing because they do not exist at the frequency we wish to observe them; for example, the model may specify monthly relationships, but some variables are observed only quarterly.

[11]It is not biased if $\mathbf{C}_L\mathbf{C}_L' = \mathbf{I}$. Could this happen?

[12]Fomby et al. (1978) show that we can view the principal components estimator as a restricted least squares estimator with the property that its covariance matrix has a smaller trace than that of any other restricted least squares estimator with the same number of restrictions. The small variance is, of course, a virtue, but because the estimator is biased, the relative size of its mean-squared error remains ambiguous.

There are two possible cases to consider, depending on why the data are missing. One is that the data are simply unavailable, for reasons unknown to the analyst and unrelated to the other observations in the sample being complete. If this is the case, the complete observations in the sample constitute a usable data set, and the only issue is what possibly helpful information could be salvaged from the incomplete observations. Griliches (1986) calls this the **ignorable case** in that, for purposes of estimation, if we are not concerned with efficiency, then we may simply ignore the problem. A second case, which has recently attracted a great deal of attention in the econometrics literature, is that in which the gaps in the data set are not benign but are systematically related to the phenomenon being modeled. This happens most often in surveys when the data are self-selected.[13] For example, if a survey were designed to study expenditure patterns and if high-income individuals tended to withhold information about their income, the gaps in the data set would represent more than just missing information. In this case, the complete observations would be qualitatively different. We treat this second case in Chapter 20, so we shall defer our discussion until later.

The early work on the subject of missing data concentrated primarily on the ignorable case.[14] The data in this instance may usefully be partitioned into three subsets:

$$\mathbf{y} = \mathbf{X}\boldsymbol{\beta} + \boldsymbol{\epsilon}$$

for all observations, but the data are

$$\begin{aligned}&\mathbf{y}_A\mathbf{X}_A \cdots n_A \text{ complete observations,}\\ &—\mathbf{X}_B \cdots n_B \text{ observations missing } \mathbf{y}_B,\end{aligned}$$

and

$$\mathbf{y}_C— \cdots n_C \text{ observations missing } \mathbf{X}_C.$$

In the third case, if $\mathbf{X}_C$ contains multiple regressors, we suppose that only some of the observations on some of the variables are missing. As noted, since this case is ignorable, the least squares regression of $\mathbf{y}_A$ on $\mathbf{X}_A$ produces estimates of $\boldsymbol{\beta}$ that have all the usual properties. The various schemes for dealing with missing data concern how to fill the gaps in some way to use whatever information may be contained in the latter two sets. The question is solely one of efficiency and lost information.

First, consider case B, in which data on $\mathbf{y}$ are missing. Any method devised to use $\mathbf{X}_B$ will have to employ some predictor of $\mathbf{y}_B$, so let $\hat{\mathbf{y}}_B$ be that predictor.

[13]The vast surveys of Americans' opinions about sex by Ann Landers (*Chicago Tribune,* 1984, passim) and Shere Hite (1987) constitute two celebrated studies that were surely tainted by a heavy dose of self-selection bias. The latter was pilloried in numerous publications for purporting to represent the population at large instead of the opinions of those strongly enough inclined to respond to the survey. The first was presented with much greater modesty.

[14]Afifi and Elashoff (1966, 1967), Haitovsky (1968), Anderson (1957), and Kelejian (1969) are a few of the major works.

At this point, we leave unspecified just what that might be; some possibilities will be noted. The least squares slope vector in this "filled" data set is

$$\mathbf{b} = \left[\begin{bmatrix}\mathbf{X}_A \\ \mathbf{X}_B\end{bmatrix}'\begin{bmatrix}\mathbf{X}_A \\ \mathbf{X}_B\end{bmatrix}\right]^{-1}\begin{bmatrix}\mathbf{X}_A \\ \mathbf{X}_B\end{bmatrix}'\begin{bmatrix}\mathbf{y}_A \\ \hat{\mathbf{y}}_B\end{bmatrix}.$$

We can write this as

$$\mathbf{b}_{\mathrm{f}} = [\mathbf{X}_A'\mathbf{X}_A + \mathbf{X}_B'\mathbf{X}_B]^{-1}[\mathbf{X}_A'\mathbf{y}_A + \mathbf{X}_B'\hat{\mathbf{y}}_B].$$

Recall the normal equation for the multiple regression model,

$$\mathbf{X}'\mathbf{X}\mathbf{b} = \mathbf{X}'\mathbf{y}.$$

Let $\mathbf{b}_A$ be the least squares slope in a regression that uses only the observations in group A, and define $\mathbf{b}_B$ likewise for group B, using $\hat{\mathbf{y}}_B$. Then we may write

$$\begin{aligned}\mathbf{b}_{\mathrm{f}} &= [\mathbf{X}_A'\mathbf{X}_A + \mathbf{X}_B'\mathbf{X}_B]^{-1}[\mathbf{X}_A'\mathbf{X}_A\mathbf{b}_A + \mathbf{X}_B'\mathbf{X}_B\mathbf{b}_B] \\ &= \mathbf{F}\mathbf{b}_A + (\mathbf{I} - \mathbf{F})\mathbf{b}_B,\end{aligned} \tag{9-12}$$

where

$$\mathbf{F} = [\mathbf{X}_A'\mathbf{X}_A + \mathbf{X}_B'\mathbf{X}_B]^{-1}\mathbf{X}_A'\mathbf{X}_A.$$

This is a *matrix weighted average* of two least squares estimators. Now

$$E[\mathbf{b}_{\mathrm{f}}] = \mathbf{F}\boldsymbol{\beta} + (\mathbf{I} - \mathbf{F})E[\mathbf{b}_B], \tag{9-13}$$

which will equal $\boldsymbol{\beta}$ only if $\mathbf{b}_B$ is unbiased. A weighted average of an unbiased estimator and some other estimator can be unbiased only if the other estimator is unbiased as well. Therefore, we can draw a conclusion:

Any scheme that purports to obtain an unbiased estimate by filling in missing values of the dependent variable must do so in such a way that a regression using only the filled observations would produce an unbiased estimator.[15]

This may be a tall order. Two schemes that have been suggested are as follows.

1. *Zero-order regression.* Replace the missing values in $\mathbf{y}_B$ with the mean of the complete observations in $\mathbf{y}_A$. Then the estimator using only the filled observations will be

$$\mathbf{b}_B = [\mathbf{X}_B'\mathbf{X}_B]^{-1}\mathbf{X}_B'\mathbf{i}\bar{y}_A,$$

where $\mathbf{i}$ is a column of n_B 1s. But

$$\bar{y}_A = \bar{\mathbf{x}}_A'\boldsymbol{\beta} + \bar{\epsilon}_A,$$

so

$$\mathbf{b}_B = [\mathbf{X}_B'\mathbf{X}_B]^{-1}\mathbf{X}_B'\mathbf{i}\bar{\mathbf{x}}_A\boldsymbol{\beta} + \bar{\epsilon}_A\mathbf{i}].$$

[15] If there are too few incomplete observations to compute the regression, it suffices for the expected value of each y_{Bi} to be $\mathbf{x}_i'\boldsymbol{\beta}$.

The expected value of $\bar{\epsilon}_A$ is zero. Also,

$$\mathbf{X}_B'\mathbf{i} = n_B\bar{\mathbf{x}}_B.$$

But

$$n_B[\mathbf{X}_B'\mathbf{X}_B]^{-1}\bar{\mathbf{x}}_B\bar{\mathbf{x}}_A' \neq \mathbf{I},$$

so this estimator fails the test.[16] There is another, perhaps more intuitive reason for this finding. Consider a simple regression with only a single regressor. If β is not zero, there is some covariation between y and x. Suppose that it is positive. Then high values of x are associated with high values y. But if we replace every missing y_B with $\bar{y}_A$, high values of x_B do not imply higher values of these $\bar{y}$'s, even in expectation. Therefore, the higher the value of x_B, the larger the disturbance at this observation. The regressor and the disturbance are therefore correlated for these observations. When this is the case, the least squares estimator is biased, which is what we found earlier.

2. *First-order regression.* Use group A to estimate $\boldsymbol{\beta}$; then estimate $\mathbf{y}_B$ with $= \mathbf{X}_B\mathbf{b}_A$. This method passes the test of unbiasedness and appears to bring a gain in efficiency. But the gain in efficiency from using these fitted values may be illusory.[17] In finding the variance of the "mixed" estimator, we must account for the additional variation present in the predicted values.

Other suggestions have been made. In general, not much is known about the properties of estimators based on predicted values of y. Those results we do have are largely from simulation studies based on a particular data set or pattern of missing data. The results of these Monte Carlo studies are usually difficult to generalize. The overall conclusion seems to be that in a single-equation regression context, filling in missing values of y is not a good idea.

For the case of missing data in the regressors, it helps to consider the simple regression and multiple regression cases separately. In the first instance, $\mathbf{X}_C$ has two columns: the column of 1s for the constant and a column of blanks where the missing data would be if we had them. As before, several schemes have been suggested for filling the blanks. The zero-order method of replacing each missing x in group C with $\bar{x}_A$ results in no changes and is equivalent to dropping the incomplete data. There are several ways to prove this, but the simplest is to observe that if each of the missing observations is equal to $\bar{x}_A$, then $\bar{x}$ for the full sample is equal to $\bar{x}_A$, and each term in $\Sigma_i\,(x_i - \bar{x})^2$ and $\Sigma_i\,(x_i - \bar{x})(y_i - \bar{y})$ that corresponds to one of these constructed observations is a zero. Therefore, the sample moments upon which the regression is computed are unchanged. Unfortunately, the R^2 will be lower, since even though the numerator in b^2S_{xx}/S_{yy} is unchanged, the denominator is increased by the new observations that have been brought into the sum. We conclude that there is no

[16]The conclusion to the contrary drawn by Kmenta (1986, p. 385) is in error. In his ratio, even if the means are the same, there are different numbers of observations in the numerator and denominator. What he does show is that the estimator is biased toward zero, which makes sense in view of the next result.

[17]See Kosobud (1963) and Kelejian (1969).

gain in the estimation of $\boldsymbol{\beta}$, and the cost is to bring a poor fit for the constructed data. An alternative, *modified zero-order regression* is to fill the second column of $\mathbf{X}_C$ with zeros and add a dummy variable that takes the value 1 for missing observations and zero for complete ones.[18] We leave it as an exercise to show that this is algebraically identical to simply filling the gaps with $\bar{x}_A$. Last, there is the possibility of computing fitted values for the missing x's by a regression of x on y in the complete data. The sampling properties of the resulting estimator are largely unknown, but what evidence there is suggests that this is not a beneficial way to proceed.[19]

Thus far, the picture is quite pessimistic. The best we have done is to present a case in which no harm was done. In a multiple regression, however, there is scope for culling some useful information from the incomplete observations. Consider a regression with just two regressors to illustrate the point.[20] The model is

$$\mathbf{y} = \beta\mathbf{x} + \gamma\mathbf{z} + \boldsymbol{\epsilon}.$$

Suppose that it were valid to posit a linear relationship between $\mathbf{x}$ and $\mathbf{z}$.[21] Then, if

$$\mathbf{x} = \delta\mathbf{z} + \mathbf{u},$$

the model may be written in three equations:

$$\begin{aligned}
\mathbf{y}_A &= \beta\mathbf{x}_A + \gamma\mathbf{z}_A + \boldsymbol{\epsilon}_A, \\
\mathbf{x}_A &= \delta\mathbf{z}_A + \mathbf{u}_A, \\
\mathbf{y}_C &= (\gamma + \beta\delta)\mathbf{z}_C + \boldsymbol{\epsilon}_C + \beta\mathbf{u}_C.
\end{aligned}$$

Each of the first two can be estimated by ordinary least squares. Let $\hat{\mathbf{x}}_C$ be the predicted values of the missing x's obtained by using $\hat{\delta}$ and $\mathbf{z}_C$. Consider combining the two data sets in one regression model:

$$\begin{bmatrix} \mathbf{y}_A - \hat{\beta}\mathbf{x}_A \\ \mathbf{y}_C - \hat{\beta}\hat{\mathbf{x}}_C \end{bmatrix} = \gamma\begin{bmatrix} \mathbf{z}_A \\ \mathbf{z}_C \end{bmatrix} + \mathbf{v}.$$

The compound disturbance $\mathbf{v}$ is a hodgepodge of the original disturbance and the sampling errors in estimation of β, γ, and δ. Assuming (correctly) that $\mathbf{v}$ and $\mathbf{z}$ are uncorrelated (at least asymptotically), γ can be estimated by least squares. At this point, the important thing to note is that although we have done nothing to the original estimate of β, some new information is being used to estimate γ in the second regression, which can be expected to provide added efficiency. Griliches provides additional results. The overall conclusion is that even though there may be a still more efficient way to use the same data, *there*

---

[18]See Maddala (1977a, p. 202).

[19]Afifi and Elashoff (1966) and Haitovsky (1968).

[20]This set of results is presented in much greater detail in Griliches (1986).

[21]In the case of nonstochastic regressors, this will only be descriptive; if the regressors are stochastic, it characterizes their joint distribution.

is some possibility that this estimator may outperform least squares, omitting group C. In a multiple regression, there is information about the covariation between the regressors with complete data and the dependent variable that is not used if these observations are discarded. The problem is to use that information in such a way that the influence of the other variables is partialed out. The preceding illustrates one possibility.

9.4. GROUPED DATA

Reporting agencies often release only group mean data to preserve the anonymity of the constituents. Data are **censored** when a range of values that contains the actual value, rather than the value itself, is given. For example, rather than ask for income, surveys often request only the income category in which a respondent falls. As a practical matter, to ease the burden of computation, it may make sense to analyze group means even if the original ungrouped data are available. Two changes generally occur as a result of this form of data aggregation.

1. The parameter estimates are less efficient, due to the loss of information.
2. The fit of the regression improves, sometimes dramatically.

Suppose that the usual regression model

$$\mathbf{y} = \mathbf{X}\boldsymbol{\beta} + \boldsymbol{\epsilon} \tag{9-14}$$

applies to a full data set and that a preassigned grouping allocates the n observations into G groups, with $n_1, n_2, \ldots, n_G$ observations in them. For the n_g observations in group g, the same model applies, so for them—that is, for these particular rows of (9-14)—

$$\mathbf{y}_g = \mathbf{X}_g\boldsymbol{\beta} + \boldsymbol{\epsilon}_g. \tag{9-15}$$

These n_g observations are collapsed into a single observation $[\overline{y}_g, \overline{x}_{1g}, \ldots, \overline{x}_{Kg}]$ by premultiplying by the $n_g \times 1$ vector, $(1/n_g)\mathbf{i}'$. Applying this to (9-15), we obtain

$$\frac{1}{n_g}\mathbf{i}'\mathbf{y}_g = \frac{1}{n_g}\mathbf{i}'\mathbf{X}_g\boldsymbol{\beta} + \frac{1}{n_g}\mathbf{i}'\boldsymbol{\epsilon}_g,$$

which implies that

$$\overline{y}_g = \overline{\mathbf{x}}_g'\boldsymbol{\beta} + \overline{\epsilon}_g. \tag{9-16a}$$

The same regression model applies to each group mean as well. Assuming that G is larger than K, we can stack these observations in G rows in

$$\overline{\mathbf{y}} = \overline{\mathbf{X}}\boldsymbol{\beta} + \overline{\boldsymbol{\epsilon}}.$$

Each element of $\overline{\boldsymbol{\epsilon}}$ has mean zero, and it is easy to verify that the conditions necessary for least squares to be unbiased are met here. In principle, we need go no further. Least squares continues to be unbiased. Given the convenience of using the smaller number of observations, why not do this routinely?

Each element of $\bar{\boldsymbol{\epsilon}}$ is $\bar{\epsilon}_g = (1/n_g)(\epsilon_{g1} + \epsilon_{g2} + \cdots + \epsilon_{gn_g})$, which has mean zero and variance σ^2/n_g. Therefore, one of the conditions of the classical regression model, equal variances across the disturbances, is not met here unless all the groups have the same number of members. If we just multiply both sides of (9-16a) by $\sqrt{n_g}$, however, then the disturbance, say $\bar{\epsilon}_g^* = \sqrt{n_g}\,\bar{\epsilon}_g$, has variance σ^2 for all g. Therefore, a slightly modified model,

$$\bar{y}_g^* = \bar{\mathbf{x}}_g^{*\prime}\boldsymbol{\beta} + \bar{\epsilon}_g^*, \tag{9-16b}$$

fits all the assumptions of the classical regression model. Least squares regression of $\bar{y}_g^*$ on $\bar{\mathbf{x}}_g^*$ gives the best linear unbiased estimate of $\boldsymbol{\beta}$, given the data (i.e., the group means) in hand.[22] (We emphasize the qualifications because, as we will show, we would do better yet if we had the original data.) Collecting the G observations in $\bar{\mathbf{X}}^*$ and $\bar{\mathbf{y}}^*$, the least squares estimator is

$$\mathbf{b}^* = [\bar{\mathbf{X}}^{*\prime}\bar{\mathbf{X}}^*]^{-1}[\bar{\mathbf{X}}^{*\prime}\bar{\mathbf{y}}^*] = \left[\sum_{g=1}^{G} n_g\bar{\mathbf{x}}_g\bar{\mathbf{x}}_g'\right]^{-1}\left[\sum_{g=1}^{G} n_g\bar{\mathbf{x}}_g\bar{y}_g\right]. \tag{9-17}$$

Note that the efficient estimator is obtained by multiplying each "observation" (i.e., group mean) by the respective group size. In effect, this replicates each group mean observation n_g times.

Obviously, the estimator in (9-17) is different from the one that would result if the original data were used. But it remains to be shown that any loss in efficiency has occurred. Let $\mathbf{H}$ be the $G \times n$ matrix that transforms the entire sample to $\bar{y}_g^*$ and $\bar{\mathbf{x}}_g^*$. $\mathbf{H}$ would appear

$$\mathbf{H} = \begin{bmatrix} (1/\sqrt{n_1})(1\ 1\ \cdots\ 1) & (0\ 0\ \cdots\ 0) & \cdots & (0\ 0\ \cdots\ 0) \\ (0\ 0\ \cdots\ 0) & (1/\sqrt{n_2})(1\ 1\ \cdots\ 1) & \cdots & (0\ 0\ \cdots\ 0) \\ \vdots & \vdots & \cdots & \vdots \\ (0\ 0\ \cdots\ 0) & (0\ 0\ \cdots\ 0) & \cdots & (1/\sqrt{n_g})(1\ 1\ \cdots\ 1) \end{bmatrix}.$$

Since $\bar{\mathbf{X}}^* = \mathbf{HX}$ and the classical regression model applies to (9-16b), the covariance matrix of $\mathbf{b}^*$ in (9-17) is

$$\text{Var}[\mathbf{b}^*] = \sigma^2[\mathbf{X}'\mathbf{H}'\mathbf{HX}]^{-1}. \tag{9-18}$$

To show that this is no smaller than $\sigma^2(\mathbf{X}'\mathbf{X})^{-1}$, the covariance matrix of the estimator for the ungrouped data, it is much easier to show that the inverse of the matrix in (9-18) is *no larger* than $\mathbf{X}'\mathbf{X}$. The difference is

$$\mathbf{X}'\mathbf{X} - \mathbf{X}'\mathbf{H}'\mathbf{HX} = \mathbf{X}'(\mathbf{I} - \mathbf{H}'\mathbf{H})\mathbf{X}. \tag{9-19}$$

[22]This is an example of weighted least squares in a heteroscedastic regression model. The model is analyzed in greater detail in Chapter 12. This particular application is somewhat different from the usual case of heteroscedasticity in that the unequal variances arise as a consequence of the data construction rather than as a part of the structure of the model.

All that must be shown is that $(\mathbf{I} - \mathbf{H}'\mathbf{H})$ is positive semidefinite, which can easily be done by showing that $(\mathbf{I} - \mathbf{H}'\mathbf{H})$ is idempotent. You can do this just by multiplying it out. The conclusion is that the best use of the group means will never be better than using the original data, and it may be worse.

The larger the difference matrix in (9-19), the greater the information loss in the grouped data. The kmth element of this difference matrix is

$$[\mathbf{X}'(\mathbf{I} - \mathbf{H}'\mathbf{H})\mathbf{X}]_{km} = \sum_{g=1}^{G}\left[\left(\sum_{i=1}^{n_g} x_{ik}x_{im}\right) - n_g\bar{x}_k\bar{x}_m\right]. \quad \textbf{(9-20)}$$

This is the within-groups variation in the language of the analysis of variance. It is no surprise that this is the result that emerges. The greater the variation within the groups that is discarded by replacing individual elements with group means, the greater the information loss will be.

Although grouping results in a loss of information in the regressors, it often brings a striking increase in the fit of the regression. Cramer's classic (1964) study on the subject provides a good example. A subset of his results is given in Example 9.3.

EXAMPLE 9.3 Regressions Based on Group Mean Data

The results shown in Table 9.2 are reported in Cramer (1964). The slope estimate is on income in an Engle curve. Essentially, the averaging has the additional effect of averaging out the disturbance variation.[23]

TABLE 9.2 Regressions with Grouped Data

Observations 278
Groups Six of 5, 26, 73, 106, 52, and 16 observations

	Slope		R^2	
Commodity	*Ungrouped*	*Grouped*	*Ungrouped*	*Grouped*
Oranges	16.87	16.84	0.242	0.968
Eggs	139.20	142.06	0.234	0.972
Apples	21.35	21.47	0.165	0.924
Butter	39.14	38.21	0.116	0.784
Cheese	29.01	30.00	0.105	0.876
Soap	3.73	3.55	0.099	0.949
Fish	14.31	15.40	0.036	0.868

[23]Cramer (1964) contains further discussion of this issue.

9.5. MEASUREMENT ERROR AND PROXY VARIABLES

Thus far, it has been assumed (at least implicitly) that the data used to estimate the parameters of our models are true measurements on their theoretical counterparts. In practice, this happens only in the best of circumstances. All sorts of measurement problems creep into the data that must be used in our analyses. Even carefully constructed survey data do not always conform exactly to the variables the analysts have in mind for their regressions. Aggregate statistics such as GNP are only estimates of their theoretical counterparts, and some variables, such as depreciation, the services of capital, and "the interest rate," do not even exist in an agreed-upon theory. At worst, there may be no physical measure corresponding to the variable in our model; intelligence, education, and permanent income are but a few examples. Nonetheless, they all have appeared in very precisely defined regression models.

In this section, we examine some of the received results on regression analysis with badly measured data. The general assessment of the problem is not particularly optimistic. The biases introduced by measurement error can be rather severe. There are almost no known finite-sample results for the models of measurement error; nearly all the results that have been developed are asymptotic. The following presentation will use a few simple asymptotic results for the classical regression model. These are discussed in detail in Section 6.7.[24] For purposes of the discussion, it is useful to summarize the essential result before proceeding.

The properties of the least squares estimator derived in the previous chapters have been obtained by analyzing the identity

$$\mathbf{b} = \boldsymbol{\beta} + [\mathbf{X}'\mathbf{X}]^{-1}\mathbf{X}'\boldsymbol{\epsilon}. \tag{9-21}$$

The unbiasedness property follows from the assumption that

$$\text{Cov}[\mathbf{X}, \boldsymbol{\epsilon}] = \mathbf{0}.$$

When this assumption is not met, it is clear that the second term in the previous equation will not be zero, and $\mathbf{b}$ will no longer estimate $\boldsymbol{\beta}$. We have seen this at several points in our analysis. For example:

1. In the analysis of specification errors in Section 8.4, the bias due to left-out variables can be cast in the framework of correlation between the included $\mathbf{X}_1$ and a disturbance consisting of $\boldsymbol{\epsilon} + \mathbf{X}_2\boldsymbol{\beta}_2$.
2. The problem with certain schemes to fill in missing data on a regressor is that the filled-in data are correlated with the disturbance.

We may write (9-21) as

$$\mathbf{b} - \boldsymbol{\beta} = \left[\frac{\mathbf{X}'\mathbf{X}}{n}\right]^{-1}\left[\frac{\mathbf{X}'\boldsymbol{\epsilon}}{n}\right].$$

---

[24]It may be useful to review the general results in Section 4.4 as well.

Under most conditions, it will follow that

$$\text{plim}[\mathbf{b} - \boldsymbol{\beta}] = \mathbf{Q}_{\mathbf{xx}}\boldsymbol{\sigma}_{\mathbf{x}\epsilon},$$

where $\mathbf{Q}_{\mathbf{xx}}$ is a positive definite matrix and $\boldsymbol{\sigma}_{\mathbf{x}\epsilon}$ is a vector of covariances. If these covariances are not zero, least squares is inconsistent. The topics considered in this section are concerned with situations in which these covariances do not vanish even as $n \to \infty$. In the discussion, since only large-sample results are known, we assume that sample moments such as $\mathbf{X}'\mathbf{X}/n$ will converge in probability to population parameters such as $\mathbf{Q}_{\mathbf{xx}}$. For convenience, results are cast in terms of the probability limits of sample moments. For example, we shall usually write "Cov[x, y]" when "the parameter estimated by $(1/n)\ \Sigma_i x_i y_i$" would be appropriate.

9.5.1. One Badly Measured Variable

The simplest case to analyze is that of a regression model with a single regressor and no constant term. Although this is admittedly unrealistic, it illustrates the essential concepts, and we shall generalize it presently. Assume that the model

$$y^* = \beta x^* + \epsilon \tag{9-22}$$

conforms to all the assumptions of the classical normal regression model. If data on y^* and x^* were available, all the apparatus of the classical model would apply. Suppose, however, that our observed data are only imperfectly measured versions of y^* and x^*. To put this in the context of an example, suppose that y^* is ln(output/labor) and x^* is ln(capital/labor). Neither factor input can be measured with precision, so the observed y and x contain errors of measurement. We assume that

$$y = y^* + v \quad \text{with } v \sim N[0, \sigma_v^2], \tag{9-23a}$$
$$x = x^* + u \quad \text{with } u \sim N[0, \sigma_u^2]. \tag{9-23b}$$

(We adhere to the widely used conventions of using asterisks to indicate unobserved variables and omitting them on the measured variables.) Assume, as well, that u and v are independent of each other and of y^* and x^*. (As we shall see, adding these restrictions is not sufficient to rescue a bad situation.)

As a first step, insert (9-23a) into (9-22), assuming for the moment that only y^* is measured with error:

$$\begin{aligned} y &= \beta x^* + \epsilon + v \\ &= \beta x^* + \epsilon^*. \end{aligned}$$

This conforms completely to the assumptions of the classical regression model. As long as the regressor is measured properly, measurement error on the dependent variable can be absorbed in the disturbance of the regression and ignored. To save some cumbersome notation, therefore, we shall henceforth assume that our measurement error problems concern only the independent variables in the model.

Consider, then, the regression of y on the observed x. By substituting (9-23b) into (9-22), we obtain

$$y = \beta x + [\epsilon - \beta u] = \beta x + w. \tag{9-24}$$

Since x equals $x^* + u$, the regressor in (9-24) is correlated with the disturbance:

$$\text{Cov}[x, w] = \text{Cov}[x^* + u, \epsilon - \beta u] = -\beta\sigma_u^2. \tag{9-25}$$

This violates one of the central assumptions of the classical model, so we can expect the least squares estimator

$$b = \frac{(1/n)\sum_{i=1}^{n} x_i y_i}{(1/n)\sum_{i=1}^{n} x_i^2}$$

to be inconsistent. To find the probability limits, insert (9-22) and (9-23b) and use the Slutsky theorem:

$$\text{plim } b = \frac{\text{plim}(1/n)\sum_{i=1}^{n}(x_i^* + u_i)(\beta x_i^* + \epsilon_i)}{\text{plim}(1/n)\sum_{i=1}^{n}(x_i^* + u_i)^2}.$$

Since x^*, ϵ, and u are mutually independent, this reduces to

$$\text{plim } b = \frac{\beta Q^*}{Q^* + \sigma_u^2} = \frac{\beta}{1 + \sigma_u^2/Q^*}, \tag{9-26}$$

where $Q^* = \text{plim}(1/n)\Sigma_i x_i^{*2}$. As long as σ_u^2 is positive, b is inconsistent, with a persistent bias toward zero. Clearly, the greater the variability in the measurement error, the worse the bias. The effect of biasing the coefficient toward zero is called **attenuation.**

The result makes some sense in view of (9-24). In regressing y on x, we have omitted a variable, u, from the regression. Write (9-24) in a slightly different form:

$$y = \beta x + \theta u + \epsilon. \tag{9-24a}$$

It so happens that θ equals $-\beta$, but neglect that for the moment. Were u an observed variable, the *multiple* regression of y on x and u would produce unbiased estimates of β and θ.[25] Note that both x and u appear in the regression and that both affect y when they vary. In a model that contains only x, the effect of variation of u on y must be transmitted through variation in x. Viewed in this light, the omitted variable formula (8-16) applies directly. In regressing y only on x, the coefficient we obtain is a mixture of that on x (i.e., β) and that on u (i.e., $-\beta$).

[25]They would not be efficient, as they neglect the constraint $\theta = -\beta$, but they *are* unbiased nonetheless.

To this point, we have been unable to estimate β. The problem is one of identification. There are four "parameters" in the model—$\beta, \sigma_\epsilon^2, \sigma_u^2$, and Q^*—and only three pieces of information:

S_{yy}, which estimates plim $S_{yy} = \beta^2 Q^* + \sigma_\epsilon^2$,
S_{xx}, which estimates plim $S_{xx} = Q^* + \sigma_u^2$,
S_{xy}, which estimates plim $S_{xy} = \beta Q^*$.

Using the Slutsky theorem (i.e., the method of moments), we could, at this point, only manipulate our three estimators. As it stands, none of the parameters can be estimated. One approach to estimation is based on assuming that there is an additional known quantity or restriction. For example:

1. If σ_ϵ^2 were known, $(S_{yy} - \sigma_\epsilon^2)/S_{xy}$ would be a consistent estimator of β, and the rest of the puzzle would unfold.
2. If σ_u^2 were known, $S_{xy}/(S_{xx} - \sigma_u^2)$ would be a consistent estimator of β.
3. If $\lambda = \sigma_u^2/Q^*$ were known, $(S_{xy}/S_{xx})(1 + \lambda)$ would be a consistent estimator of β.

Other combinations are possible; the logic is that any known function of the underlying parameters raises the number of known estimators to the number of unknown parameters. Assuming that the unknown parameters are known is a bit utopian, however. Perhaps the third suggestion offers some hope; it is not unusual to have at least some information about the degree of error in a measured variable. Government statistics are often released with a range of error. Otherwise, the appeal of this approach is largely intellectual.

It has been pointed out that the preceding trap was set by locking ourselves into the normal distribution at the outset. If, for example, some other distribution were specified for ϵ and u, perhaps some higher moments—that is, the third moment of y or the product of y^2 and x—could be used to provide additional information about the parameters. It is known that this approach will be fruitless for the normal distribution, but almost any other symmetric distribution solves the identification problem.[26] Of course, assuming that some other particular distribution applies is also somewhat optimistic.

The approach stated in the preceding paragraph does, however, suggest a possibility in a time-series setting. The difficulty we face is that there is not enough information in the contemporaneous variances and covariances of the observed variables to identify the parameters of the model. To take a simple example, suppose that we add to the basic model of (9-22) and (9-23b) that x is a time series characterized by

$$x_t = x_t^* + u_t \tag{9-23c}$$

and

$$x_t^* = \rho x_{t-1}^* + v_t.$$

[26]See Pal (1980). In a much earlier analysis, Riersol (1950) showed that the fundamental problem of identification in this model is peculiar to the bivariate normal distribution.

Then, because the disturbances and measurement errors are uncorrelated across observations—that is, across time—

$$\begin{aligned}\text{plim}\,\frac{1}{T}\sum_{t=2}^{T} x_{t-1}y_t &= \text{plim}\,\frac{1}{T}\sum_{t=2}^{T}(\beta\rho x_{t-1}^* + \beta v_t + \epsilon_t)(x_{t-1}^* + u_{t-1}) \\ &= \beta\rho Q^*\end{aligned} \tag{9-27}$$

and

$$\begin{aligned}\text{plim}\,\frac{1}{T}\sum_{t=2}^{T} x_{t-1}x_t &= \text{plim}\,\frac{1}{T}\sum_{t=2}^{T}(x_{t-1}^* + u_{t-1})(\rho x_{t-1}^* + v_t) \\ &= \rho Q^*.\end{aligned}$$

The ratio $\hat{\beta} = (\Sigma_t x_{t-1}y_t)/(\Sigma_t x_{t-1}x_t)$ provides a consistent estimator of β, after which the remaining parameters can be derived.

9.5.2. Multiple Regression with Measurement Error

In a multiple regression model, matters only get worse. Suppose, to begin, we assume that

$$\mathbf{y} = \mathbf{X}^*\boldsymbol{\beta} + \boldsymbol{\epsilon}$$

and

$$\mathbf{X} = \mathbf{X}^* + \mathbf{U},$$

allowing every observation on every variable to be measured with error. The extension of our earlier results is

$$\begin{aligned}\text{plim}\,\frac{1}{n}\,\mathbf{X}'\mathbf{X} &= \mathbf{Q}^* + \boldsymbol{\Sigma}_{uu}, \\ \text{plim}\,\frac{1}{n}\,\mathbf{X}'\mathbf{y} &= \mathbf{Q}^*\boldsymbol{\beta}.\end{aligned}$$

Hence,

$$\begin{aligned}\text{plim}\,\mathbf{b} &= [\mathbf{Q}^* + \boldsymbol{\Sigma}_{uu}]^{-1}\mathbf{Q}^*\boldsymbol{\beta} \\ &= \boldsymbol{\beta} - [\mathbf{Q}^* + \boldsymbol{\Sigma}_{uu}]^{-1}\boldsymbol{\Sigma}_{uu}\boldsymbol{\beta}.\end{aligned} \tag{9-28}$$

This is a mixture of all the parameters in the model. In the same fashion as before, bringing in outside information could lead to identification. The amount of information necessary is extremely large, however, and this approach is not particularly promising.

There are some particular cases of interest. It is common for only a single variable to be measured with error, and one might speculate that the problems would be isolated to the single coefficient. Unfortunately, this is not the case. For a single bad variable—assume that it is the first—the matrix $\boldsymbol{\Sigma}_{uu}$ is of the form

$$\boldsymbol{\Sigma}_{uu} = \begin{bmatrix} \sigma_u^2 & 0 & \cdots & 0 \\ 0 & 0 & \cdots & 0 \\ & & \vdots & \\ 0 & 0 & \cdots & 0 \end{bmatrix}.$$

It can be shown that for this special case

$$\text{plim } b_1 = \frac{\beta_1}{1 + \sigma_u^2 q^{*11}} \tag{9-29a}$$

(note the similarity of this result to the earlier one) and, for $k \neq 1$,

$$\text{plim } b_k = \beta_k - \beta_1 \left[\frac{\sigma_u^2 q^{*k1}}{1 + \sigma_u^2 q^{*11}} \right], \tag{9-29b}$$

where q^{*k1} is the $(k, 1)$th element in $(\mathbf{Q}^*)^{-1}$.[27] This depends on several unknowns and cannot be estimated. The coefficient on the badly measured variable is still biased toward zero. The coefficients are all biased as well, although in unknown directions. A badly measured variable contaminates all the least squares estimates.[28]

If more than one variable is measured with error, there is very little that can be said.[29] Although expressions can be derived for the biases in a few of these cases, they generally depend on numerous parameters whose signs and magnitudes are unknown and, presumably, unknowable.

9.5.3. The Method of Instrumental Variables

An alternative set of results for estimation in this model (and numerous others) is built around the method of instrumental variables. We developed the general results for this estimator in Section 6.7.8. Consider once again the errors in variables model

$$y = \beta x^* + \epsilon, \qquad x = x^* + u.$$

The parameters, β, σ_ϵ^2, q^*, and σ_u^2 are not identified in terms of the moments of x and y. Suppose, however, that there exists a variable z such that z is correlated with x^* but not with u. For example, in surveys of families, income is notoriously badly reported, partly deliberately and partly because respondents often neglect some minor sources. In fitting consumption functions based on

[27]Use (2-66) to invert $[\mathbf{Q}^* + \boldsymbol{\Sigma}_{uu}] = [\mathbf{Q}^* + (\sigma_u \mathbf{e}_1)(\sigma_u \mathbf{e}_1)']$, where $\mathbf{e}_1$ is the first column of a $K \times K$ identity matrix. The remaining results are then straightforward.

[28]This point is important to remember when the presence of measurement error is suspected. For example, notice that the marginal product of capital estimated in Example 8.3 is negative, which contradicts a firm theoretical result. Nerlove (1963) attributed this finding largely to measurement error in the variable used for the price of capital, but made no note of the likely effects on the other coefficients in the model.

[29]Some firm analytic results have been obtained by Levi (1973), Theil (1961), Klepper and Leamer (1983), Garber and Klepper (1980), and Griliches (1986).

these data, the regressor is thus subject to measurement error. Suppose, however, that one could determine the total amount of checks written by the head(s) of the household. It is quite likely that this z would be highly correlated with both consumption and income, but perhaps not significantly correlated with the errors of measurement. If $\text{Cov}[x^*, z]$ is not zero, the parameters of the model become estimable, as

$$\text{plim}\,\frac{(1/n)\sum_i y_i z_i}{(1/n)\sum_i x_i z_i} = \frac{\beta\,\text{Cov}[x^*, z]}{\text{Cov}[x^*, z]} = \beta. \tag{9-30}$$

It is not always clear where instrumental variables are to be found. For the simple errors in variables model we have discussed here, a few instruments have been devised based only on the data in hand:

$$z = 1 \text{ if } x > \text{median } x \text{ and } -1 \text{ if } x < \text{median } x$$
(if n is even, the middle observation is discarded)[30]

or

$$z = \text{rank of } x.$$ [31]

Notice, for instance, that in the time-series example of (9-23c), the variable x_{t-1} is being used as an instrumental variable.

In a multiple regression framework, if only a single variable is measured with error, the preceding can be applied to that variable and the remaining variables can serve as their own instruments. If more than one variable is measured with error, the first preceding proposal will be cumbersome at best, whereas the second can be applied to each.

For the general case, $\mathbf{y} = \mathbf{X}^*\boldsymbol{\beta} + \boldsymbol{\epsilon}$, $\mathbf{X} = \mathbf{X}^* + \mathbf{U}$, in the **reduced form**, in terms of the observable data,

$$\begin{aligned}\mathbf{y} &= \mathbf{X}\boldsymbol{\beta} + \boldsymbol{\epsilon} - \mathbf{U}\boldsymbol{\beta}\\ &= \mathbf{X}\boldsymbol{\beta} + \mathbf{v},\end{aligned}$$

$$\text{plim}\,\frac{1}{n}\mathbf{X}'\mathbf{v} \neq \mathbf{0},$$

so least squares is not a consistent estimator of $\boldsymbol{\beta}$. Suppose, however, that there exists a matrix of K variables $\mathbf{Z}$ that is not correlated with the disturbances or the measurement error but is correlated with regressors. That is,

$$\text{plim}\,\frac{1}{n}\mathbf{Z}'(\boldsymbol{\epsilon} - \mathbf{U}\boldsymbol{\beta}) = \mathbf{0} - \mathbf{0}\boldsymbol{\beta} = \mathbf{0},$$

[30] This is sometimes called the *method of group averages* because it amounts to passing a line between the group means of two groups of observations, one with small values of x and one with large values.

[31] To the extent that the ranking of x is determined by the size of the measurement error rather than by x^*, this instrument, like the one before it, will fail to satisfy the requirement that it be uncorrelated with the measurement error. The relevant quantity, as we have seen before, is σ_u^2/Q^*.

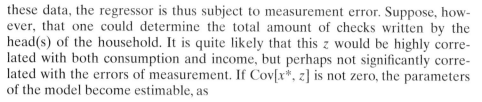

and

$$\text{plim}\,\frac{1}{n}\,\mathbf{Z}'\mathbf{X} = \text{plim}\,\frac{1}{n}\,\mathbf{Z}'\mathbf{X}^* = \mathbf{Q}_{ZX} \neq \mathbf{0}.$$

Then the instrumental variables estimator

$$\mathbf{b}_{\text{IV}} = [\mathbf{Z}'\mathbf{X}]^{-1}\mathbf{Z}'\mathbf{y} \tag{9-31}$$

has

$$\begin{aligned}\text{plim}\,\mathbf{b}_{\text{IV}} &= \text{plim}\left[\frac{1}{n}\,\mathbf{Z}'\mathbf{X}\right]^{-1}\text{plim}\left[\frac{1}{n}\,\mathbf{Z}'(\mathbf{X}\boldsymbol{\beta} + \mathbf{v})\right]\\ &= \boldsymbol{\beta} + \text{plim}\left[\frac{1}{n}\,\mathbf{Z}'\mathbf{X}\right]^{-1}\left[\frac{1}{n}\,\mathbf{Z}'\mathbf{v}\right]\\ &= \boldsymbol{\beta}\end{aligned}$$

and asymptotic covariance matrix,

$$\text{Asy. Var}[\mathbf{b}_{\text{IV}}] = \sigma^2[\mathbf{Z}'\mathbf{X}]^{-1}[\mathbf{Z}'\mathbf{Z}][\mathbf{X}'\mathbf{Z}]^{-1}. \tag{9-32}$$

Asymptotic normality of the estimator can be shown if some additional conditions are attached to the behavior of the columns of **Z**. In general, if they are as well behaved as those of **X**, which is likely, all the necessary results can be obtained.[32]

9.5.4. Proxy Variables

In some situations, a variable in a model simply has no observable counterpart. Education, intelligence, and like factors are perhaps the most common examples. In this instance, unless there is some observable indicator for the variable, the model will have to be treated in the framework of missing variables. Usually, however, such an indicator can be obtained; for the factors just given, years of schooling and test scores of various sorts are familiar examples. The usual treatment of such variables is in the measurement error framework. If, for example,

$$\text{income} = \beta_1 + \beta_2\,\text{education} + \epsilon$$

and

$$\text{years of schooling} = \text{education} + u,$$

then the model of Section 9.5.1 applies directly. The only difference here is that the true variable in the model is "latent." No amount of improvement in reporting or measurement would bring the proxy closer to the variable for which it is proxying.

It is to be emphasized that a proxy variable is not an instrument (or the

[32]White (1984) presents an extensive analysis. See Section 6.7.8 as well.

reverse). In the instrumental variables framework, this implies that we do not regress $\mathbf{y}$ on $\mathbf{Z}$ to obtain the estimates. To take an extreme example, suppose that the full model was

$$\mathbf{y} = \mathbf{X}^*\boldsymbol{\beta} + \boldsymbol{\epsilon},$$
$$\mathbf{X} = \mathbf{X}^* + \mathbf{U},$$
$$\mathbf{Z} = \mathbf{X}^* + \mathbf{W}.$$

That is, we happen to have two badly measured estimates of $\mathbf{X}^*$. The parameters of this model can be estimated without difficulty if $\mathbf{W}$ is uncorrelated with $\mathbf{U}$ and $\mathbf{X}^*$, *but not by regressing* $\mathbf{y}$ on $\mathbf{Z}$. The instrumental variables technique is called for.

When the model contains a variable such as education, the question that naturally arises is: If interest centers on the other coefficients in the model, why not just discard the problem variable?[33] This produces the familiar problem of an omitted variable, compounded by the least squares estimator in the full model being inconsistent anyway. Which estimator is worse? McCallum (1972) and Wickens (1972) show that the asymptotic bias (actually, degree of inconsistency) is worse if the proxy is omitted, even if it is a bad one (has a high proportion of measurement error). This neglects, however, the precision of the estimates. Aigner (1974) analyzed this aspect of the problem and found, as might be expected, that it could go either way. He concluded, however, that "there is evidence to broadly support use of the proxy."

9.5.5. A Specification Test for Measurement Error

Hausman (1978) has devised a test for the presence of errors of measurement. Under the hypothesis of no measurement error, both $\mathbf{b}$, the least squares estimator, and $\mathbf{b}_{\text{IV}}$, the instrumental variables estimator, are consistent estimators of $\boldsymbol{\beta}$, although least squares is efficient whereas the IV estimator is inefficient. But if the hypothesis is false, only $\mathbf{b}_{\text{IV}}$ is consistent. The test, then, examines the difference between $\mathbf{b}$ and $\mathbf{b}_{\text{IV}}$. Under the hypothesis of no measurement error, $\text{plim}(\mathbf{b} - \mathbf{b}_{\text{IV}}) = \mathbf{0}$, whereas if there is measurement error, this plim will be nonzero. We have done similar tests at many points before, using the Wald statistic, which is what Hausman suggests. The innovation of his study is to determine the appropriate covariance matrix to use. Let $\mathbf{V}_1$ be the estimated asymptotic covariance matrix for the IV estimator, and let $\mathbf{V}_0$ be $s^2(\mathbf{X}'\mathbf{X})^{-1}$, where s^2 is the estimate of σ^2 obtained *using the IV estimator.* We know that $\mathbf{V}_1$ is larger than $\mathbf{V}_0$ asymptotically, and our use of the same estimate of σ^2 will ensure this algebraically as well. The Wald statistic is

$$W = (\mathbf{b} - \mathbf{b}_{\text{IV}})'[\mathbf{V}_1 - \mathbf{V}_0]^{-1}(\mathbf{b} - \mathbf{b}_{\text{IV}}) \sim \chi^2[K]. \tag{9-33}$$

As Hausman then shows, this may be referred to a chi-squared table.

[33]This discussion applies to the measurement error and latent variable problems equally.

The algebra simplifies a bit because the same estimate of σ^2 is used for both matrices. Inserting (9-32) and using $\mathbf{q} = \mathbf{b} - \mathbf{b}_{IV}$ reduces (9-33) to

$$W = \frac{\mathbf{q}'\{[\mathbf{X}'\mathbf{Z}(\mathbf{Z}'\mathbf{Z})^{-1}\mathbf{Z}'\mathbf{X}]^{-1} - (\mathbf{X}'\mathbf{X})^{-1}\}^{-1}\mathbf{q}}{s^2} = \frac{\mathbf{q}'\{(\hat{\mathbf{X}}'\hat{\mathbf{X}})^{-1} - (\mathbf{X}'\mathbf{X})^{-1}\}^{-1}\mathbf{q}}{s^2}. \tag{9-34}$$

Each column of $\hat{\mathbf{X}}$ is the set of fitted values when the corresponding column of $\mathbf{X}$ is regressed on all the columns of $\mathbf{Z}$.

For the simple regression model with only a single regressor, the algebra simplifies even further. It can be shown that the test is equivalent to applying a standard test of significance to the coefficient on $\hat{\mathbf{u}}$ in the least squares regression

$$\mathbf{y} = \beta_1 + \beta_2\mathbf{x} + \gamma\hat{\mathbf{u}} + \boldsymbol{\epsilon}^0,$$

where $\hat{\mathbf{u}}$ is the vector of residuals obtained by regressing $\mathbf{x}$ on the instrumental variable $\mathbf{z}$. The results are valid only asymptotically, so the standard normal table is used instead of the t table.

9.6. REGRESSION DIAGNOSTICS AND INFLUENTIAL DATA POINTS

Even in the absence of multicollinearity or other data problems, it is worthwhile to examine one's data and regression results closely for two reasons. First, the identification of outliers in the data is useful, particularly in relatively small cross sections in which the identity and perhaps even the ultimate source of the data point may be known. Second, it may be possible to ascertain which, if any, particular observations are especially influential in the results obtained. As such, the identification of these data points may call for further study. It is worth emphasizing, though, that there is a certain danger in singling out particular observations for scrutiny or even elimination from the sample on the basis of statistical results that are based on those data. At the extreme, this may invalidate the usual inference procedures.[34]

Of particular importance in this analysis is the *hat matrix:*

$$\mathbf{H} = \mathbf{X}(\mathbf{X}'\mathbf{X})^{-1}\mathbf{X}'. \tag{9-35}$$

This matrix appeared earlier as the matrix that projects any $n \times 1$ vector into the column space of $\mathbf{X}$. For any vector $\mathbf{y}$, $\mathbf{Hy}$ is the set of fitted values in the least squares regression of $\mathbf{y}$ on $\mathbf{X}$. The least squares residuals are

$$\mathbf{e} = \mathbf{My} = \mathbf{M}\boldsymbol{\epsilon} = (\mathbf{I} - \mathbf{H})\boldsymbol{\epsilon},$$

[34]See the discussion of pretest estimators in Chapter 8.

so the covariance matrix for the least squares residual vector is

$$E[\mathbf{ee}'] = \sigma^2\mathbf{M} = \sigma^2(\mathbf{I} - \mathbf{H}).$$

To identify which residuals are significantly large, we first standardize them by dividing by the appropriate standard deviations. Thus, we would use[35]

$$\hat{e}_i = \frac{e_i}{[s^2(1 - h_{ii})]^{1/2}} = \frac{e_i}{(s^2\mathbf{M}_{ii})^{1/2}}. \tag{9-36}$$

As a diagnostic tool, Belsley et al. (1980) suggests going one step further. If the regression were estimated without the ith observation, the least squares coefficients would be

$$\mathbf{b}(i) = [\mathbf{X}(i)'\mathbf{X}(i)]^{-1}\mathbf{X}(i)'\mathbf{y}(i),$$

where the (i) notation indicates that the ith observation has been omitted. Using these coefficients, the modified residual would be

$$\begin{aligned} e_i(i) &= y_i - \mathbf{b}(i)'\mathbf{x}_i \\ &= \epsilon_i + [\boldsymbol{\beta} - \mathbf{b}(i)]'\mathbf{x}_i. \end{aligned}$$

Since the ith observation is not used in computing $\mathbf{b}(i)$, the two terms are independent. The appropriate variance is, therefore,

$$\begin{aligned} \text{Var}[e_i(i)] &= \sigma^2[1 + \mathbf{x}_i'(\mathbf{X}(i)'\mathbf{X}(i))^{-1}\mathbf{x}_i] \\ &= \sigma^2[1 + h_{ii}(i)]. \end{aligned} \tag{9-37}$$

The estimate of σ^2 is $s^2(i)$. The standardized residual is approximately distributed as standard normal.[36] Values in excess of two suggest observations that deserve closer scrutiny. The calculation is repeated for each observation.[37]

This approach has some intuitive appeal. If the observation conforms to the model that is estimated with the other observations, this standardized residual should be small. If not, the particular observation may deserve scrutiny as perhaps not conforming to the model. It is worth emphasizing, though, that this interpretation is likely to be a bit problematic in a time-series setting unless one is aware of some unusual event taking place at the time the observation in question was generated. The set of calculations is similar in spirit to the CUSUM and CUSUM of squares tests discussed earlier.

---

[35]Note that only the diagonal elements of $\mathbf{H}$, which are $\mathbf{x}_i'(\mathbf{X}'\mathbf{X})^{-1}\mathbf{x}_i$, are used in these computations. Since $\mathbf{H}$ is an $n \times n$ matrix, this can be an important practical consideration. In a sample of, say, only 500, the entire matrix would occupy two million bytes on a digital computer, yet only 500 elements, requiring 4000 bytes to store in double precision, are useful. Actually computing the full $\mathbf{H}$ matrix instead of the vector of its diagonal elements can be inefficient and, in even moderately sized samples, impractical.

[36]$e_i(i)$ is normally distributed, but in using s^2 instead of σ^2, we lose the normal distribution of the ratio. Nor is this distributed as t, since $e_i(i)$ is not independent of s^2.

[37]This does not require that the regression be recomputed n times. The rank one update formula can be used to do the computation recursively if desired. For each observation, the matrix $\mathbf{X}'\mathbf{X}$ is "updated" by subtracting an observation. If this exercise is to be performed on a large cross section involving many regressors, the economy provided by the updating formula may be worth exploiting.

EXERCISES

1. The following sample moments were computed from 100 observations produced using a random number generator:

$$\begin{array}{cccc} \textbf{one} & \textbf{x1} & \textbf{x2} & \textbf{x3} \end{array}$$

$$\mathbf{X}'\mathbf{X} = \begin{bmatrix} 100 & 123 & 96 & 109 \\ 123 & 252 & 125 & 189 \\ 96 & 125 & 167 & 146 \\ 109 & 189 & 146 & 168 \end{bmatrix}, \qquad \mathbf{X}'\mathbf{y} = \begin{bmatrix} 460 \\ 810 \\ 615 \\ 712 \end{bmatrix},$$

$$(\mathbf{X}'\mathbf{X})^{-1} = \begin{bmatrix} 0.03767 & & & \\ -0.06263 & 1.129 & & \\ -0.06247 & 1.107 & 1.110 & \\ 0.1003 & -2.192 & -2.170 & 4.292 \end{bmatrix}, \qquad \mathbf{y}'\mathbf{y} = 3924.$$

The true model underlying these data is $y = x_1 + x_2 + x_3 + \epsilon$.

(a) Compute the simple correlations among the regressors.

(b) Compute the ordinary least squares coefficients in the regression of y on a constant x_1, x_2, and x_3.

(c) Compute the ordinary least squares coefficients in the regression of y on a constant x_1 and x_2, on a constant x_1 and x_3, and on a constant x_2 and x_3.

(d) Compute Leamer's magnification factor [see (9-5)] associated with each variable.

(e) The regressors are obviously collinear. Which is the problem variable?

2. For the data in Exercise 1, compute the condition number for the moment matrix based on the constant x_1 and x_2.

3. Prove that

$$E[\mathbf{b}'\mathbf{b}] = \boldsymbol{\beta}'\boldsymbol{\beta} + \sigma^2 \sum_{k=1}^{K} \frac{1}{\lambda_k},$$

where $\mathbf{b}$ is the ordinary least squares estimator and λ_k is a characteristic root of $\mathbf{X}'\mathbf{X}$.

4. Prove that the covariance matrix of the principal components estimator $\mathbf{b}_p = \mathbf{C}_L\mathbf{C}_L'\mathbf{b}$ (defined at the end of Section 9.2) is smaller than that of $\mathbf{b}$.

5. Suppose that instead of choosing the principal components in (9-10) on the basis of the variation in $\mathbf{X}$, we compute all the principal components and choose the one that is most highly correlated with $\mathbf{y}$. Show that the principal component $\mathbf{z}_j = \mathbf{X}\mathbf{c}_j$, which is most highly correlated with $\mathbf{y}$, is the one that maximizes $\sqrt{\lambda_j}\,\mathbf{b}'\mathbf{c}_j$, where $\mathbf{b}$ is the least squares estimator of $\boldsymbol{\beta}$, $\mathbf{c}_j$ is a characteristic vector of $\mathbf{X}'\mathbf{X}$, and λ_j is the associated characteristic root.

6. Consider the simple regression $y = \alpha + \beta x + \epsilon$. Assume that some of the observations on x are missing. Prove that filling these observations with zeros and adding a dummy variable to the regression that is 1 for each missing observation and 0 otherwise is equivalent to dropping the incomplete observations.

7. The simple regression model

$$y_{ig} = \beta x_{ig} + \epsilon_{ig}, \qquad E[\epsilon_{ig}] = 0, \qquad \text{Var}[\epsilon_{ig}] = \sigma^2$$

applies to observation i in group g. The observed data consist of group means. The following data are obtained from five groups:

Group	*1*	*2*	*3*	*4*	*5*	*All*
n_g	10	20	15	30	25	100
$\bar{y}_g$	2	4	3	1	5	—
$\bar{x}_g$	1	4	2	1	6	—

The following are three possible estimators of β:

$$\frac{\bar{y}}{\bar{x}} = \frac{\sum_{g=1}^{G} n_g \bar{y}_g / \sum_{g=1}^{G} n_g}{\sum_{g=1}^{G} n_g \bar{x}_g / \sum_{g=1}^{G} n_g} = \frac{\sum_{g=1}^{G} w_g \bar{y}_g}{\sum_{g=1}^{G} w_g \bar{x}_g},$$

$$\frac{\sum_{g=1}^{g} \bar{y}_g \bar{x}_g}{\sum_{g=1}^{G} \bar{x}_g^2} = \text{least squares},$$

$$\frac{\sum_{g=1}^{G} n_g \bar{x}_g \bar{y}_g}{\sum_{g=1}^{G} n_g \bar{x}_g^2} = \text{estimator in (9-17).}$$

(a) Prove that all three estimators are unbiased.

(b) Derive the expression for the sampling variance of each estimator.

(c) Using the previous sample data, compute the three estimators and their sampling variances. Assume that $\sigma^2 = 1$. Which is the most efficient? The least efficient? (The difference you observe between the second and third estimators is that between the ordinary and generalized least squares estimator. This is the subject of Chapter 12.)

(d) Prove that the sampling variance of the third estimator is always less than that of the second.

8. For the model in (9-22) and (9-23), prove that when only x^* is measured with error, the squared correlation between y and x is less than that between y^* and x^*. (Note the assumption that $y^* = y$.) Does the same hold true if y^* is also measured with error?

9. *Reverse regression.* This and the next exercise continue the analysis of Exercise 11 in Chapter 8. In the earlier exercise, interest centered on a particular dummy variable in which the regressors were accurately measured. Here we consider the case in which the crucial regressor in the model is measured with error. The paper by Kamlich and Polachek (1982) is directed toward this issue.

Consider the simple errors in the variables model,

$$y = \alpha + \beta x^* + \epsilon,$$
$$x = x^* + u,$$

where u and ϵ are uncorrelated and x is the erroneously measured, observed counterpart to x^*.

(a) Assume that x^*, u, and ϵ are all normally distributed with means μ^*, 0, and 0, variances σ_*^2, σ_u^2, and σ_ϵ^2, and zero covariances. Obtain the probability limits of the least squares estimates of α and β.

(b) As an alternative, consider regressing x on a constant and y, then computing the reciprocal of the estimate. Obtain the probability limit of this estimate.

(c) Do the "direct" and "reverse" estimators bound the true coefficient?

10. *Reverse regression continued.* Suppose that the model in Exercise 9 is extended to

$$y = \beta x^* + \gamma d + \epsilon,$$
$$x = x^* + u.$$

For convenience, we drop the constant term. Assume that x^*, ϵ, and u are independent normally distributed with zero means. Suppose that d is a random variable that takes the values 1 and 0 with probabilities π and $1 - \pi$ in the population and that is independent of all other variables in the model. To put this in context, the preceding model (and variants of it) have appeared in the literature on discrimination. We view y as a "wage" variable, x^* as "qualifications," and x as some imperfect measure such as education. The dummy variable d is membership ($d = 1$) or nonmembership ($d = 0$) in some protected class. The hypothesis of discrimination turns on $\gamma < 0$ versus $\gamma = 0$.

(a) What is the probability limit of c, the least squares estimator of γ, in the least squares regression of y on x and d? [Hints: The independence of x^* and d is important. Also, plim $\mathbf{d}'\mathbf{d}/n = \text{Var}[d] + E^2[d] = \pi(1 - \pi) + \pi^2 = \pi$. This minor modification does not affect the model substantively, but greatly simplifies the algebra.] Now suppose that x^* and d are not independent. In particular, suppose that $E[x^* | d = 1] = \mu^1$ and $E[x^* | d = 0] = \mu^0$. Repeat the derivation with this assumption.

(b) Consider, instead, a regression of x on y and d. What is the probability limit of the coefficient on d in this regression? Assume that x^* and d are independent.

(c) Suppose that x^* and d are not independent, but γ is, in fact, less than zero. Assuming that both preceding equations still hold, what is estimated by $(\bar{y}|d = 1) - (\bar{y}|d = 0)$? What does this quantity estimate if γ does equal zero?

11. A data set consists of n observations on $\mathbf{X}_n$ and $\mathbf{y}_n$. The least squares estimator based on these n observations is

$$\mathbf{b}_n = (\mathbf{X}_n'\mathbf{X}_n)^{-1}\mathbf{X}_n'\mathbf{y}_n.$$

Another observation, $\mathbf{x}_s$ and y_s, becomes available. Prove that the least squares estimator computed using this additional observation is

$$\mathbf{b}_{n,s} = \mathbf{b}_n + \frac{1}{1 + \mathbf{x}_s'(\mathbf{X}_n'\mathbf{X}_n)^{-1}\mathbf{x}_s}(\mathbf{X}_n'\mathbf{X}_n)^{-1}\mathbf{x}_s(y_s - \mathbf{x}_s'\mathbf{b}_n).$$

Note that the last term is e_s, the residual from the prediction of y_s using the coefficients based on $\mathbf{X}_n$ and $\mathbf{b}_n$. Conclude that the new data change the results of least squares only if the new observation on y cannot be perfectly predicted using the information already in hand.

CHAPTER 10

Nonlinear Regression Models

10.1. INTRODUCTION

To this point, we have considered only linear models that can be estimated by least squares. Although the linear model is flexible enough to allow great variety in the shape of the regression, it still rules out many useful functional forms. In this chapter, we shall examine models that are intrinsically nonlinear in their parameters. Although these models are often difficult to estimate, with the development of easy-to-use software they have become quite common.

10.2. NONLINEAR REGRESSION MODELS

A general form of the regression model is

$$y_i = h(\mathbf{x}_i, \boldsymbol{\beta}) + \epsilon_i.^{1} \tag{10-1}$$

The linear model is obviously a special case, but this includes far more possibilities. For example,

$$y = \beta_1 + \beta_2 e^{\beta_3 x} + \epsilon \tag{10-2}$$

cannot be transformed to linearity. It would appear that

$$y = \beta_1 x_1^{\beta_1} x_2^{\beta_2} e^{\epsilon}$$

is also nonlinear, but for the purposes of our discussion, this is a linear regression model, whereas the first is not. The second can be transformed to linearity by taking logarithms on both sides of the equation.

---

[1]In principle, it could be written in terms of $g(y_i)$. But unless $g(y_i)$ introduces new unknown parameters, as in the Box–Cox model, we can view this as determining the units of measurement of y and retain the less cumbersome notation.

We shall require an operational definition to distinguish these cases. In the context of regression analysis, what will characterize (10-1) as a **nonlinear regression model** is the method used to estimate the parameters. We take as our benchmark the case in which ϵ is normally distributed. Then, using the argument of Chapter 6, the values of the parameters that minimize (one half of) the sum of squared deviations,

$$S(\boldsymbol{\beta}) = \frac{1}{2}\sum_{i=1}^{n}\epsilon_i^2 = \frac{1}{2}\sum_{i=1}^{n}[y_i - h(\mathbf{x}_i, \boldsymbol{\beta})]^2 \tag{10-3}$$

will be the maximum likelihood estimators, as well as the **nonlinear least squares** estimators. The first-order conditions for minimization of $S(\boldsymbol{\beta})$ are

$$\frac{\partial S(\boldsymbol{\beta})}{\partial \boldsymbol{\beta}} = -\sum_{i=1}^{n}[y_i - h(\mathbf{x}_i, \boldsymbol{\beta})]\frac{\partial h(\mathbf{x}_i, \boldsymbol{\beta})}{\partial \boldsymbol{\beta}} = \mathbf{0}. \tag{10-4}$$

In the linear model of Chapter 6, this will be a set of linear equations, that is, the normal equations (6-15). But in this more general case, this will be a set of nonlinear equations that do not have an explicit solution. This will typically require an iterative procedure for solution.

EXAMPLE 10.1 First-Order Conditions for a Nonlinear Model

The first-order conditions for estimating the parameters of (10-2) by least squares are

$$\begin{aligned}
\frac{\partial S(\boldsymbol{\beta})}{\partial \beta_1} &= -\sum_{i=1}^{n}[y_i - \beta_1 - \beta_2 e^{\beta_3 x_i}] &= 0,\\
\frac{\partial S(\boldsymbol{\beta})}{\partial \beta_2} &= -\sum_{i=1}^{n}[y_i - \beta_1 - \beta_2 e^{\beta_3 x_i}]e^{\beta_3 x_i} &= 0,\\
\frac{\partial S(\boldsymbol{\beta})}{\partial \beta_3} &= -\sum_{i=1}^{n}[y_i - \beta_1 - \beta_2 e^{\beta_3 x_i}]\beta_2 x_i e^{\beta_3 x_i} &= 0.
\end{aligned}$$

These equations do not have an explicit solution.

Conceding the potential for ambiguity, we define a nonlinear regression model at this point as follows.

DEFINITION 10.1: Nonlinear Regression Model. *A **nonlinear regression model** is one for which the first-order conditions for least squares estimation of the parameters are nonlinear functions of the parameters.*[2]

[2]Judge et al. (1985, pp. 195–196) adopt a similar approach but take a somewhat broader view of estimation. In their framework, the nonlinearity of the model is defined by the optimization criterion used to define the estimator. Thus, least squares is but one of the possibilities they would consider. The broader definition will be useful when we analyze models for which maximum likelihood techniques are indispensable. But in this chapter, least squares will provide a satisfactory benchmark.

Thus, nonlinearity is defined in terms of the techniques needed to estimate the parameters, not the shape of the regression function. Later we shall broaden our definition to include other techniques besides least squares.

10.2.1. The Linearized Regression

The nonlinear regression model is

$$y = h(\mathbf{x}, \boldsymbol{\beta}) + \epsilon.$$

(To save some notation, we have dropped the observation subscript.) Many of the results that have been obtained for nonlinear regression models are based on a linear Taylor series approximation to $h(\mathbf{x}, \boldsymbol{\beta})$ at a particular value for the parameter vector $\boldsymbol{\beta}^0$:

$$h(\mathbf{x}, \boldsymbol{\beta}) \simeq h(\mathbf{x}, \boldsymbol{\beta}^0) + \sum_{k=1}^{K} \frac{\partial h(\mathbf{x}, \boldsymbol{\beta}^0)}{\partial \beta_k^0}(\beta_k - \beta_k^0). \tag{10-5}$$

This is called the **linearized regression model.** By collecting terms, we obtain

$$h(\mathbf{x}, \boldsymbol{\beta}) \approx \left[h(\mathbf{x}, \boldsymbol{\beta}^0) - \sum_{k=1}^{K} \beta_k^0 \left(\frac{\partial h(\mathbf{x}, \boldsymbol{\beta}^0)}{\partial \beta_k^0}\right)\right] + \sum_{k=1}^{K} \beta_k \left(\frac{\partial h(\mathbf{x}, \boldsymbol{\beta}^0)}{\partial \beta_k^0}\right). \tag{10-6}$$

Let x_k^0 equal the kth partial derivative,[3] $\partial h(\mathbf{x}, \boldsymbol{\beta}^0)/\partial \beta_k^0$. For a given value of $\boldsymbol{\beta}^0$, this is a function only of the data, not of the unknown parameters. We now have

$$\begin{aligned} h(\mathbf{x}, \boldsymbol{\beta}) &\simeq [h^0 - \sum_{k=1}^{K} x_k^0 \beta_k^0] + \sum_{k=1}^{K} x_k^0 \beta_k \\ &= h^0 - \mathbf{x}^{0\prime}\boldsymbol{\beta}^0 + \mathbf{x}^{0\prime}\boldsymbol{\beta} \end{aligned} \tag{10-7}$$

or

$$y \simeq h^0 - \mathbf{x}^{0\prime}\boldsymbol{\beta}^0 + \mathbf{x}^{0\prime}\boldsymbol{\beta} + \epsilon.$$

By placing the known terms on the left-hand side of the equation, we obtain a regression model:

$$\begin{aligned} y^0 &= y - h^0 + \mathbf{x}^{0\prime}\boldsymbol{\beta}^0 \\ &= \mathbf{x}^{0\prime}\boldsymbol{\beta} + \epsilon^0. \end{aligned} \tag{10-8}$$

With a value of $\boldsymbol{\beta}^0$ in hand, we could compute y^0 and $\mathbf{x}^0$ then estimate the parameters of (10-8) by linear least squares.

---

[3]You should verify that for the linear regression model, these derivatives are the independent variables.

EXAMPLE 10.2 Linearized Regression

For the example given in (10-2), the regressors in the linearized equation would be

$$x_1^0 = \frac{\partial h(.)}{\partial \beta_1} = 1,$$

$$x_2^0 = \frac{\partial h(.)}{\partial \beta_2} = e^{\beta_3^0 x},$$

$$x_3^0 = \frac{\partial h(.)}{\partial \beta_3} = \beta_2^0 x e^{\beta_3^0 x}.$$

With a set of values of the parameters $\boldsymbol{\beta}^0$,

$$y^0 = y - h(x, \beta_1^0, \beta_2^0, \beta_3^0) + \beta_1^0 x_1^0 + \beta_2^0 x_2^0 + \beta_3^0 x_3^0$$

could be regressed on the three variables previously defined to estimate β_1, β_2, and β_3.

10.2.2. The Nonlinear Least Squares Estimator

Least squares remains an attractive way to proceed for estimating the parameters. Numerous analytical results have been obtained for the estimator, such as consistency and asymptotic normality.[4] We cannot be sure that nonlinear least squares is the most efficient estimator, however, except in the case of normally distributed disturbances. (This is the same conclusion we drew for the linear model.) Some examples that follow will illustrate the point.

It is necessary to make some assumptions about the regressors. The precise requirements are discussed in some detail in Judge et al. (1985), Amemiya (1985), and Davidson and MacKinnon (1993). In the classical regression model, to obtain our asymptotic results, we assume that the sample moment matrix $(1/n)\mathbf{X}'\mathbf{X}$ converges to a positive definite matrix $\mathbf{Q}$. By analogy, we impose the same condition on the **pseudoregressors** in the linearized model *when they are computed at the true parameter values.* Therefore, for the nonlinear regression model, the analog to (6-66) is

$$\text{plim}\,\frac{1}{n}\mathbf{X}_0'\mathbf{X}_0 = \text{plim}\,\frac{1}{n}\sum_{i=1}^{n}\left(\frac{\partial h(\mathbf{x}_i, \boldsymbol{\beta}^0)}{\partial \boldsymbol{\beta}^0}\right)\left(\frac{\partial h(\mathbf{x}_i, \boldsymbol{\beta}^0)}{\partial \boldsymbol{\beta}^{0\prime}}\right) = \mathbf{Q}_0, \qquad \textbf{(10-9)}$$

where $\mathbf{Q}_0$ is a positive definite matrix. To establish consistency of b in the linear

[4]A complete discussion of the subject can be found in Amemiya (1985). Other important references are Jennrich (1969), Malinvaud (1970), and especially Goldfeld and Quandt (1972). A very lengthy authoritative treatment is the text by Davidson and MacKinnon (1993).

model, we required $\text{plim}(1/n)\mathbf{X}'\boldsymbol{\epsilon} = \mathbf{0}$. We will require the counterpart to this for the pseudoregressors:

$$\text{plim}\,\frac{1}{n}\sum_{i=1}^{n}\mathbf{x}_i^0\epsilon_i = \mathbf{0}.$$

Finally, asymptotic normality can be established under general conditions if

$$\frac{1}{\sqrt{n}}\sum_{i=1}^{n}\mathbf{x}_i\epsilon_i \xrightarrow{d} N[\mathbf{0}, \sigma^2\mathbf{Q}_0].$$

With these in hand, the asymptotic properties of the nonlinear least squares estimator have been derived. They are, in fact, essentially those we have already seen for the linear model, except that in this case we place the derivatives of the linearized function $\mathbf{X}_0$ in the role of the regressors.[5]

The nonlinear least squares criterion function is

$$S(\mathbf{b}) = \frac{1}{2}\sum_{i=1}^{n}[y_i - h(\mathbf{x}_i, \mathbf{b})]^2 = \frac{1}{2}\sum_{i=1}^{n}e_i^2, \tag{10-10}$$

where we have inserted what will be the solution value, **b**. The first-order conditions for a minimum are

$$\mathbf{g}(\mathbf{b}) = -\sum_{i=1}^{n}[y_i - h(\mathbf{x}_i, \mathbf{b})]\frac{\partial h(\mathbf{x}_i, \mathbf{b})}{\partial \mathbf{b}} = \mathbf{0}. \tag{10-11}$$

Notice that at the solution,

$$\mathbf{g}(\mathbf{b}) = -\mathbf{X}_0'\mathbf{e} = \mathbf{0},$$

which is the same as (6-22) for the linear model.

A consistent estimate of σ^2 can be computed using the residuals:

$$\hat{\sigma}^2 = \frac{1}{n}\sum_{i=1}^{n}[y_i - h(\mathbf{x}_i, \mathbf{b})]^2. \tag{10-12}$$

A degrees of freedom correction, $1/(n - K)$, would have no virtue here, as all results are asymptotic in any event.[6] Under normality, the estimator in (10-12) is the maximum likelihood estimator.

Given our assumptions, we have the general result, as follows.

---

[5]This description is a bit informal. The specific results, and additional assumptions necessary to reach these conclusions, are spelled out in detail in Davidson and MacKinnon (1993, Chap. 5) or Amemiya (1985). The overall assessment of the latter study is as follows: "[T]he practical consequence . . . is that all of the results for the linear regression model are asymptotically valid for the nonlinear regression model if we treat **G** as the regressor matrix" (p. 136). His **G** is our $\mathbf{X}_0$.

[6]But users of computer software should be aware that some programs use $1/n$ and others use $1/(n - K)$ in the computation, and in a small sample, the difference can be noticeable.

THEOREM 10.1: Asymptotic Distribution of the Nonlinear Least Squares Estimator. *If the pseudoregressors defined in (10-3) are "well behaved," then*

$$\mathbf{b} \xrightarrow{a} N\left[\boldsymbol{\beta}, \frac{\sigma^2}{n}\mathbf{Q}_0^{-1}\right],$$

where

$$\mathbf{Q}_0 = \text{plim}\,\frac{1}{n}\mathbf{X}^{0\prime}\mathbf{X}^0.$$

The sample estimate of the asymptotic covariance matrix is

$$\text{Est. Asy. Var}[\mathbf{b}] = \hat{\sigma}^2(\mathbf{X}^{0\prime}\mathbf{X}^0)^{-1}. \quad \textbf{(10-13)}$$

Once these are in hand, inference and hypothesis tests can proceed in the same fashion as prescribed in Chapter 7. A minor problem can arise in evaluating the fit of the regression in that

$$R^2 = 1 - \frac{\sum_{i=1}^{n} e_i^2}{\sum_{i=1}^{n}(y_i - \bar{y})^2} \quad \textbf{(10-14)}$$

is no longer guaranteed to be in the range of 0 to 1. It does, however, provide a useful descriptive measure.

10.2.3. Computing the Nonlinear Least Squares Estimator

Minimizing the sum of squares is a standard problem in nonlinear optimization that can be solved by a number of methods. (See Section 5.5.) The method of Gauss–Newton is often used. In the linearized regression model, if a value of $\boldsymbol{\beta}^0$ is available, the linear regression model shown in (10-8) can be estimated by linear least squares. Once a parameter vector is obtained, it can play the role of a new $\boldsymbol{\beta}^0$, and the computation can be done again. The iteration can continue until the difference between successive parameter vectors is small enough to assume convergence. One of the main virtues of this method is that at the last iteration the estimate of $\mathbf{Q}_0^{-1}$ will, apart from the scale factor $\hat{\sigma}^2$, provide the correct estimate of the asymptotic covariance matrix from the parameter estimates.

This iterative solution to the minimization problem is

$$\begin{aligned}
\mathbf{b}_{t+1} &= \left[\sum_{i=1}^{n}\mathbf{x}_i^0\mathbf{x}_i^{0\prime}\right]^{-1}\left[\sum_{i=1}^{n}\mathbf{x}_i^0(y_i - h_i^0 + \mathbf{x}_i^{0\prime}\mathbf{b}_t)\right] \\
&= \mathbf{b}_t + \left[\sum_{i=1}^{n}\mathbf{x}_i^0\mathbf{x}_i^{0\prime}\right]^{-1}\left[\sum_{i=1}^{n}\mathbf{x}_i^0(y_i - h_i^0)\right] \\
&= \mathbf{b}_t + (\mathbf{X}^{0\prime}\mathbf{X}^0)^{-1}\mathbf{X}^{0\prime}\mathbf{e}^0,
\end{aligned}$$

where all terms on the right-hand side are evaluated at $\mathbf{b}_t$ and $\mathbf{e}^0$ is the vector of nonlinear least squares residuals. This algorithm has some intuitive appeal. For each iteration, we update the previous parameter estimates by regressing the nonlinear least squares residuals on the derivatives of the regression functions. The process will have converged (i.e., the update will be $\mathbf{0}$) when $\mathbf{X}^{0\prime}\mathbf{e}^{0}$ is close enough to $\mathbf{0}$. This has a direct counterpart in the normal equations for the linear model $\mathbf{X}'\mathbf{e} = \mathbf{0}$.

EXAMPLE 10.3 A Nonlinear Consumption Function

The linear consumption function analyzed at the beginning of Chapter 6 is a restricted version of the more general consumption function

$$C = \alpha + \beta Y^{\gamma} + \epsilon,$$

in which γ equals 1. With this restriction, the model is linear. If γ is free to vary, however, this becomes a nonlinear regression. The linearized model is

$$C - (\alpha^0 + \beta^0 Y^{\gamma^0}) + \alpha^0 1 + \beta^0 Y^{\gamma^0} + \gamma^0 \beta^0 Y^{\gamma^0} \ln Y$$
$$= \alpha + \beta(Y^{\gamma^0}) + \gamma(\beta^0 Y^{\gamma^0} \ln Y) + \epsilon.$$

After a bit of manipulation, the nonlinear least squares procedure reduces to iterated regression of

$$C^0 = C + \gamma^0 \beta^0 Y^{\gamma^0} \ln Y$$

on

$$\frac{\partial h(.)}{\partial \alpha} = 1,$$
$$\frac{\partial h(.)}{\partial \beta} = Y^{\gamma^0},$$
$$\frac{\partial h(.)}{\partial \gamma} = \beta Y^{\gamma^0} \ln Y.$$

The data on consumption and income listed in Table 10.1 are used to fit the consumption function.

Finding the initial values for a nonlinear procedure can be a problem.[7] Simply trying a convenient set of values can be unproductive. Unfortunately, there are no good rules for starting values, except that they should be as close to the final values as possible (not particularly helpful). When it is possible, an initial consistent estimator of $\boldsymbol{\beta}$ will be a good starting value. In many cases, however, the only consistent estimator available is the one we are trying to compute by least squares. For better or worse, trial and error is the most frequently used procedure. For the present model, a natural set of values can be obtained because a simple linear model is a special case. Thus, we can start α and β at the linear least squares values that would result in the special case of

[7]A lengthy discussion may be found in Draper and Smith (1980, pp. 473–474).

TABLE 10.1 Aggregate Income Y and Consumption C

Year	Y	C	*Year*	Y	C
1950	791.8	733.2	1968	1551.3	1405.9
1951	819.0	748.7	1969	1599.8	1456.7
1952	844.3	771.4	1970	1688.1	1492.0
1953	880.0	802.5	1971	1728.4	1538.8
1954	894.0	822.7	1972	1797.4	1621.9
1955	944.5	873.8	1973	1916.3	1689.6
1956	989.4	899.8	1974	1896.6	1674.0
1957	1012.1	919.7	1975	1931.7	1711.9
1958	1028.8	932.9	1976	2001.0	1803.9
1959	1067.2	979.4	1977	2066.6	1883.8
1960	1091.1	1005.1	1978	2167.4	1961.0
1961	1123.2	1025.2	1979	2212.6	2004.4
1962	1170.2	1069.0	1980	2214.3	2000.4
1963	1207.3	1108.4	1981	2248.6	2024.2
1964	1291.0	1170.6	1982	2261.5	2050.7
1965	1365.7	1236.4	1983	2334.6	2145.9
1966	1431.3	1298.9	1984	2468.4	2239.9
1967	1493.2	1337.7	1985	2509.0	2312.6

Source: Data from the *Economic Report of the President,* U.S. Government Printing Office, Washington, D.C., 1986.

$\gamma = 1$ and use 1 for the starting value for γ. The nonlinear least squares estimates are reported in Table 10.2. The procedures outlined earlier are used at the last iteration to obtain asymptotic standard errors and an estimate of σ^2. It is illustrative to compare these with the estimates for the linear consumption function, as shown in Table 10.2.

TABLE 10.2 Estimated Consumption Functions

	Linear		*Nonlinear*	
Parameter	*Estimate*	*Standard Error*	*Estimate*	*Standard Error*
α	11.1458	9.64	184.97	39.138
β	0.89853	0.00586	0.25197	0.081396
γ	1.000	—	1.1535	0.03925
$\boldsymbol{\epsilon}'\boldsymbol{\epsilon}$	12,068		8421.95	
σ^2	18.939		15.29515	
R^2	0.99856		0.99899	
Var[b]	—		0.006625	
Var[c]	—		0.001541	
Cov[b,c]	—		−0.003195	

For hypothesis testing and confidence intervals, the usual procedures can be used, with the proviso that all results are only asymptotic. As such, for testing a restriction, the chi-squared statistic rather than the F ratio is likely to be more appropriate. For example, for testing the hypothesis that γ is different from 1, an asymptotic t test, based on the standard normal distribution, is carried out, using

$$z = \frac{1.1535 - 1}{0.03925} = 3.911.$$

This is larger than the critical values of 1.96 for the 5 percent significance level, and we thus reject the linear model in favor of the nonlinear regression. We are also interested in the marginal propensity to consume. In this expanded model, $H_0: \gamma = 1$ is a test that the marginal propensity to consume is constant, not that it is 1. (That would be a joint test of both $\gamma = 1$ and $\beta = 1$.) In this model, the marginal propensity to consume is

$$\text{MPC} = \frac{dc}{dY} = \beta\gamma Y^{\gamma-1},$$

which varies with Y. To test the hypothesis that this is 1, we require a particular value of Y. Since it is the most recent value, we choose $Y_{1985} = 2509$. At this value, the MPC is estimated as 0.9676. We estimate its standard error as the square root of

$$\begin{aligned}
&[\partial\text{MPC}/\partial b \quad \partial\text{MPC}/\partial c]\begin{bmatrix} \text{Var}[b] & \text{Cov}[b, c] \\ \text{Cov}[b, c] & \text{Var}[c] \end{bmatrix}\begin{bmatrix} \partial\text{MPC}/\partial b \\ \partial\text{MPC}/\partial c \end{bmatrix} \\
&\qquad = [cY^{c-1} \quad bY^{c-1}(1 + c\ln Y)]\begin{bmatrix} 0.006625 & -0.003195 \\ -0.003195 & 0.001541 \end{bmatrix} \\
&\qquad \times [cY^{c-1} \quad bY^{c-1}(1 + c\ln Y)]' = 0.00032318,
\end{aligned}$$

which gives a standard error of 0.0179772. For testing the hypothesis that the MPC was equal to 1.0 in 1985, we would refer

$$z = \frac{0.9676 - 1}{0.0179772} = -1.80228$$

to a standard normal table. This is not statistically significant, so we would not reject the hypothesis.

The requirement that the matrix in (10-13) converge to a positive definite matrix carries with it the condition that the columns of the regressor matrix $\mathbf{X}^0$ be linearly independent. This is an identification condition analogous to the requirement that the independent variables in the linear model be linearly independent. Nonlinear regression models usually involve several independent variables, and at first blush, it might seem sufficient to examine the data directly if one is concerned with multicollinearity. Unfortunately, because it complicates the analysis, this is not the case.

EXAMPLE 10.4 Multicollinearity in Nonlinear Regression

In the preceding example, there is no question of collinearity in the data matrix $\mathbf{X} = [\mathbf{i}, \mathbf{y}]$; the variation in Y is obvious on inspection. But at the final parameter estimates, the R^2 in the regression is 0.99899 and the correlation between the two pseudoregressors $x_2^0 = Y^\gamma$ and $x_3^0 = \beta Y^\gamma \ln Y$ is 0.999866. The condition number for the normalized matrix of sums of squares and cross products is 385.401. Recall that 20 was the benchmark value for a problematic data set. By the standards discussed in Chapter 9, the collinearity problem in this "data set" is severe.

10.2.4. A Specification Test for Nonlinear Regressions: Testing for Linear Versus Log-Linear Specification

MacKinnon et al. (1983) have extended the J test discussed in Section 7.7 to nonlinear regressions. One result of this analysis is a simple test for linearity versus log-linearity.

The specific hypotheses to be tested are

$$H_0 : y = h^0(\mathbf{x}, \boldsymbol{\beta}) + \epsilon_0$$

versus

$$H_1 : g(y) = h^1(\mathbf{z}, \boldsymbol{\gamma}) + \epsilon_1,$$

where $\mathbf{x}$ and $\mathbf{z}$ are regressor vectors and $\boldsymbol{\beta}$ and $\boldsymbol{\gamma}$ are the parameters. As the authors note, using y instead of, say, $j(y)$ in the first function is nothing more than an implicit definition of the units of measurement of the dependent variable.

An intermediate case is useful. If we assume that $g(y)$ is equal to y, but allow $h^0(.)$ and $h^1(.)$ to be nonlinear, the necessary modification of the J test is straightforward, albeit perhaps a bit more difficult to carry out. For this case, we form the compound model

$$\begin{aligned} y &= (1 - \alpha)h^0(\mathbf{x}, \boldsymbol{\beta}) + \alpha h^1(\mathbf{z}, \boldsymbol{\gamma}) + \epsilon \\ &= h^0(\mathbf{x}, \boldsymbol{\beta}) + \alpha[h^1(\mathbf{z}, \boldsymbol{\gamma}) - h^0(\mathbf{x}, \boldsymbol{\beta})] + \epsilon. \end{aligned} \tag{10-15}$$

Presumably, both $\boldsymbol{\beta}$ and $\boldsymbol{\gamma}$ could be estimated in isolation by nonlinear least squares. Suppose that a nonlinear least squares estimate of $\boldsymbol{\gamma}$ has been obtained. One approach is to insert this in (10-15) and then estimate $\boldsymbol{\beta}$ and α by nonlinear least squares. The J test amounts to testing the significance of the estimate of α. Of course, the model is symmetric in $h^0(.)$ and $h^1(.)$, so their roles could be reversed. The same conclusions drawn earlier would apply here.

Davidson and MacKinnon (1981) propose what may be a simpler alternative. Given an estimate of $\boldsymbol{\beta}$, say $\hat{\boldsymbol{\beta}}$, approximate $h^0(\mathbf{x}, \boldsymbol{\beta})$ with a linear Taylor series at this point. The result is

$$\begin{aligned} h^0(\mathbf{x}, \boldsymbol{\beta}) &\simeq h^0(\mathbf{x}, \hat{\boldsymbol{\beta}}) + \left[\frac{\partial h^0(.)}{\partial \hat{\boldsymbol{\beta}}'}\right]\hat{\boldsymbol{\beta}} \\ &= \hat{h}^0 + \hat{\mathbf{H}}^0 \boldsymbol{\beta}. \end{aligned} \tag{10-16}$$

Using this device, they replace (10-15) with

$$y - \hat{h}^0 = \hat{\mathbf{H}}^0\mathbf{b} + \alpha[h^1(\mathbf{z}, \hat{\gamma}) - h^0(\mathbf{x}, \hat{\boldsymbol{\beta}})] + \epsilon,$$

in which **b** and α can be estimated by linear least squares. As before, the J test amounts to testing the significance of $\hat{\alpha}$. If it is found that $\hat{\alpha}$ is significantly different from zero, H_0 is rejected. For the authors' asymptotic results to hold, any consistent estimate of $\boldsymbol{\beta}$ will suffice for $\hat{\boldsymbol{\beta}}$; the nonlinear least squares estimator that they suggest seems a natural choice.[8]

Now we can generalize the test to allow a nonlinear function, $g(y)$, in H_1. Davidson and MacKinnon require $g(y)$ to be monotonic, continuous and continuously differentiable and not to introduce any new parameters. (This excludes the Box–Cox model, which is considered in Section 10.4.) The compound model that forms the basis of the test is

$$(1 - \alpha)[y - h^0(\mathbf{x}, \boldsymbol{\beta})] + \alpha[g(y) - h^1(\mathbf{z}, \boldsymbol{\gamma})] = \epsilon. \quad \textbf{(10-17)}$$

Again, there are two approaches. As before, if $\hat{\boldsymbol{\gamma}}$ is an estimate of $\boldsymbol{\gamma}$, $\boldsymbol{\beta}$ and α can be estimated by maximum likelihood conditional on this estimate.[9] This promises to be extremely messy, and an alternative is proposed. Rewrite (10-17) as

$$y - h^0(\mathbf{x}, \boldsymbol{\beta}) = \alpha[h^1(\mathbf{z}, \boldsymbol{\gamma}) - g(y)] + \alpha[y - h^0(\mathbf{x}, \boldsymbol{\beta})] + \epsilon.$$

Now use the same linear Taylor series expansion for $h^0(\mathbf{x}, \boldsymbol{\beta})$ on the left-hand side, and replace both y and $h^0(\mathbf{x}, \boldsymbol{\beta})$ with $\hat{h}^0$ on the right. The resulting model is

$$y - \hat{h}^0 = \hat{\mathbf{H}}^0\mathbf{b} + \alpha[\hat{h}^1 - g(\hat{h}^0)] + e. \quad \textbf{(10-18)}$$

As before, with an estimate of $\boldsymbol{\beta}$, this can be estimated by least squares.

This modified form of the J test is labeled the P_E *test.* As the authors discuss, it is probably not as powerful as any of the Wald, Lagrange multiplier, or likelihood ratio tests that we have considered. In their experience, however, it has sufficient power for applied research and is clearly simple to carry out.

The P_E test can be used to test a linear specification against a log-linear model. For this test, both $h^0(.)$ and $h^1(.)$ are linear, whereas $g(y) = \ln y$. Let the two competing models be denoted

$$H_0: y = \mathbf{x}'\boldsymbol{\beta} + \epsilon$$

and

$$H_1: \ln y = \ln(\mathbf{x})'\boldsymbol{\gamma} + \epsilon.$$

[We stretch the usual notational conventions by using $\ln(\mathbf{x})$ for $(\ln x_1, \ldots, \ln x_k)$.] Now let **b** and **c** be the two linear least squares estimates of the parame-

[8]This assumes that H_0 is correct, of course.

[9]Least squares will be inappropriate because of the transformation of y, which will translate to a Jacobian term in the log-likelihood. See the later discussion of the Box–Cox model.

ter vectors. The P_E test for H_1 as an alternative to H_0 is carried out by testing the significance of the coefficient $\hat{\alpha}$ in the model

$$y = \mathbf{x}'\boldsymbol{\beta} + \alpha[\widehat{\ln y} - \ln(\mathbf{x}'\boldsymbol{\beta})] + \epsilon. \tag{10-19}$$

The second term is the difference between predictions of y obtained directly from the log-linear model and obtained as the log of the prediction from the linear model. We can also reverse the roles of the two formulas and test H_0 as the alternative. The compound regression is

$$\ln y = \ln(\mathbf{x})'\boldsymbol{\gamma} + \alpha(\hat{y} - e^{\ln(\mathbf{x})'\mathbf{c}}) + \epsilon. \tag{10-20}$$

EXAMPLE 10.5 Money Demand

A large number of studies have estimated money demand equations, some linear and some log-linear.[10] Yearly data for estimation of a money demand equation are given in Table 10.3. The data are taken from the *1986 Economic Report of the President*. The interest rate is the end of December value of the discount rate at the New York Federal Reserve Bank. The money stock is M2. The GNP is seasonally adjusted and stated in 1982 constant dollars. Results of the P_E test of the linear versus the log-linear model are shown in Table 10.4.

Regressions of M on a constant r and Y, and $\ln M$ on a constant $\ln r$ and $\ln Y$, produce the results given in Table 10.4 (standard errors are given in parentheses). Both models appear to fit quite well,[11] and the pattern of significance of the coefficients is the same in both equations. After computing fitted

TABLE 10.3 Money Demand Data

Year	*Interest* r	*Money* M	*GNP* Y	*Year*	*Interest* r	*Money* M	*GNP* Y
1966	4.5	480.0	2208.3	1976	5.50	1163.6	2826.7
1967	4.19	524.3	2271.4	1977	5.46	1286.6	2958.6
1968	5.16	566.3	2365.6	1978	7.46	1388.9	3115.2
1969	5.87	589.5	2423.3	1979	10.28	1497.9	3192.4
1970	5.95	628.2	2416.2	1980	11.77	1631.4	3187.1
1971	4.88	712.8	2484.8	1981	13.42	1794.4	3248.8
1972	4.50	805.2	2608.5	1982	11.02	1954.9	3166.0
1973	6.44	861.0	2744.1	1983	8.50	2188.8	3277.7
1974	7.83	908.4	2729.3	1984	8.80	2371.7	3492.0
1975	6.25	1023.1	2695.0	1985	7.69	2563.6	3573.5

[10] A comprehensive survey appears in Goldfeld (1973).

[11] The interest elasticity is in line with the received results. The income elasticity is quite a bit larger.

TABLE 10.4 Estimated Money Demand Equations

	a	b_r	c_Y	R^2	s
Linear	−3169.42 (310.8)	−14.9223 (22.59)	1.55815 (0.1434)	0.93526	175.73
P_E test for the linear model, $\hat{\alpha} = -751.21$ (242.21), $t = -3.102$					
Log-linear	−21.992 (1.648)	−.03157 (0.0969)	3.65628 (0.2255)	0.97578	0.0881
P_E test for the loglinear model, $\hat{\alpha} = -0.0001363$ (0.0002067), $t = -0.659$					

values from the two equations, the estimates of α from the two models are as shown in Table 10.4. Referring these to a standard normal table, we reject the linear model in favor of the log-linear model.

The test of linearity vs. log-linearity has been the subject of a number of studies. Godfrey and Wickens (1981) discuss several approaches.

10.2.5. Nonlinear Instrumental Variables Estimation

In Section 6.7.8, we extended the linear regression model to allow for the possibility that the regressors might be correlated with the disturbances. The same problem can arise in nonlinear models. The consumption function estimated in Example 10.3 is almost surely a case in point, and we reestimated it using the instrumental variables technique for linear models in Examples 6.21 and 6.22. In this section, we will extend the method of instrumental variables to nonlinear regression models.

In the nonlinear model,

$$y_i = h(\mathbf{x}_i, \boldsymbol{\beta}) + \epsilon_i,$$

the covariates $\mathbf{x}_i$ may be correlated with the disturbances. We would expect this effect to be transmitted to the pseudoregressors, $\mathbf{x}_i^0 = \partial h(\mathbf{x}_i, \boldsymbol{\beta})/\partial \boldsymbol{\beta}$. If so, then the results that we derived for the linearized regression would no longer hold. Suppose that there are a set of variables $[\mathbf{z}_1, \ldots, \mathbf{z}_L]$ such that

$$\text{plim} \frac{1}{n} \mathbf{Z}'\boldsymbol{\epsilon} = \mathbf{0} \tag{10-21}$$

and

$$\text{plim} \frac{1}{n} \mathbf{Z}'\mathbf{X}^0 = \mathbf{Q}_{ZX}^0 \neq \mathbf{0},$$

where $\mathbf{X}^0$ is the matrix of pseudoregressors in the linearized regression, evaluated at the true parameter values. If the analysis that we did for the linear model in Section 6.7.8 can be applied to this set of variables, then we will be able to construct a consistent estimator for $\boldsymbol{\beta}$ using the instrumental variables.

As a first step, we will attempt to replicate the approach that we used for the linear model. The linearized regression model is given in (10-8),

$$\mathbf{y} = \mathbf{h}(\mathbf{X}, \boldsymbol{\beta}) + \boldsymbol{\epsilon} \approx \mathbf{h}^0 + \mathbf{X}^0(\boldsymbol{\beta}^0 - \boldsymbol{\beta}) + \boldsymbol{\epsilon}$$

or

$$\mathbf{y}^0 \approx \mathbf{X}^0\boldsymbol{\beta} + \boldsymbol{\epsilon},$$

where

$$\mathbf{y}^0 = \mathbf{y} - \mathbf{h}^0 + \mathbf{X}^0\boldsymbol{\beta}.$$

For the moment, we neglect the approximation error in linearizing the model. In (10-21), we have assumed that

$$\text{plim}\, \frac{1}{n}\mathbf{Z}'\mathbf{y}^0 = \text{plim}\, \frac{1}{n}\mathbf{Z}'\mathbf{X}^0\boldsymbol{\beta}. \tag{10-22}$$

Suppose, as we did before, that there are the same number of instrumental variables as there are parameters, that is, columns in $\mathbf{X}^0$. (Note: This need not be the number of variables. See our example above.) Then this suggests the "estimator" used before:

$$\mathbf{b}_{\text{IV}} = (\mathbf{Z}'\mathbf{X}^0)^{-1}\mathbf{Z}'\mathbf{y}^0. \tag{10-23}$$

The logic is sound, but there is a problem with this estimator. The unknown parameter vector $\boldsymbol{\beta}$ appears on both sides of (10-22). [The solution to (10-23), if we can find it, is a **fixed point**.] We might consider the approach we used for our first solution to the nonlinear regression model. That is, with some initial estimator in hand, iterate back and forth between the instrumental variables regression and recomputing the pseudoregressors until the process converges to the fixed point that we seek. Once again, the logic is sound, and in principle, this does produce the estimator we seek.

If we add to our preceding assumptions

$$\frac{1}{\sqrt{n}}\mathbf{Z}'\boldsymbol{\epsilon} \xrightarrow{d} N[\mathbf{0}, \sigma^2\mathbf{Q}_{ZZ}],$$

we will be able to use the same form of the asymptotic distribution for this estimator that we did for the linear case. Before doing so, we must fill in some gaps in the preceding. First, despite its intuitive appeal, the suggested procedure for finding the estimator is very unlikely to be a good algorithm for locating the estimates. Second, we do not wish to limit ourselves to the case in which we have the same number of instrumental variables as parameters. So, we will consider the problem in general terms. The estimation criterion for nonlinear instrumental variables is a quadratic form,

$$\begin{aligned}\text{Min}_{\boldsymbol{\beta}} S(\boldsymbol{\beta}) &= \tfrac{1}{2}\{[\mathbf{y} - \mathbf{h}(\mathbf{X}, \boldsymbol{\beta})]'\mathbf{Z}\}(\mathbf{Z}'\mathbf{Z})^{-1}\{\mathbf{Z}'[\mathbf{y} - \mathbf{h}(\mathbf{X}, \boldsymbol{\beta})]\}\\ &= \tfrac{1}{2}\boldsymbol{\epsilon}(\boldsymbol{\beta})'\mathbf{Z}(\mathbf{Z}'\mathbf{Z})^{-1}\mathbf{Z}'\boldsymbol{\epsilon}(\boldsymbol{\beta}).\end{aligned}$$

The first-order conditions for minimization of this weighted sum of squares are

$$\frac{\partial S(\boldsymbol{\beta})}{\partial \boldsymbol{\beta}} = -\mathbf{X}^{0\prime}\mathbf{Z}(\mathbf{Z}'\mathbf{Z})^{-1}\mathbf{Z}'\boldsymbol{\epsilon}(\boldsymbol{\beta}) = \mathbf{0}.$$

This is the same result we had for the linear model with $\mathbf{X}^0$ in the role of $\mathbf{X}$. You should check that when $\boldsymbol{\epsilon}(\boldsymbol{\beta}) = \mathbf{y} - \mathbf{X}\boldsymbol{\beta}$, this replicates exactly our results for the linear model in Section 6.7.8. This problem, however, is highly nonlinear in most cases, and the repeated least squares approach is unlikely to be effective. But it is a straightforward minimization problem in the frameworks of Chapter 5, and instead, we can just treat estimation here as a problem in nonlinear optimization.

With well-behaved *pseudoregressors* and instrumental variables, we have the general result for the nonlinear instrumental variables estimator; this is discussed at length in Davidson and MacKinnon (1993).

Theorem 10.2: Asymptotic Distribution of the Nonlinear Instrumental Variables Estimator. *With well-behaved instrumental variables and pseudoregressors,*

$$\mathbf{b}_{\text{IV}} \xrightarrow{a} N[\boldsymbol{\beta}, \sigma^2(\mathbf{Q}^0_{ZX})^{-1}\mathbf{Q}_{ZZ}(\mathbf{Q}^0_{XZ})^{-1}].$$

We estimate the asymptotic covariance matrix with

$$\text{Est. Asy. Var}[\mathbf{b}_{\text{IV}}] = \hat{\sigma}^2(\mathbf{Z}'\hat{\mathbf{X}}^0)^{-1}(\mathbf{Z}'\mathbf{Z})(\hat{\mathbf{X}}^{0\prime}\mathbf{Z})^{-1},$$

where $\hat{\mathbf{X}}^0$ *is* $\mathbf{X}^0$ *computed using* $\mathbf{b}_{\text{IV}}$.

As a final observation, note that the "two-stage least squares" interpretation of the instrumental variables estimator for the linear model still applies here, with respect to the IV estimator. That is, at the final estimates, the first-order conditions (normal equations) imply that

$$\mathbf{X}^{0\prime}\mathbf{Z}(\mathbf{Z}'\mathbf{Z})^{-1}\mathbf{Z}'\mathbf{y} = \mathbf{X}^{0\prime}\mathbf{Z}(\mathbf{Z}'\mathbf{Z})^{-1}\mathbf{Z}'\mathbf{X}^0\boldsymbol{\beta},$$

which says that the estimates satisfy the normal equations for a linear regression of $\mathbf{y}$ (not $\mathbf{y}^0$) on the predictions obtained by regressing the columns of $\mathbf{X}^0$ on $\mathbf{Z}$. The interpretation is not quite the same here, because to compute the predictions of $\mathbf{X}^0$, we must have the estimate of $\boldsymbol{\beta}$ in hand. Thus, this two-stage least squares approach does not show *how to compute* $\mathbf{b}_{\text{IV}}$; it shows a characteristic of $\mathbf{b}_{\text{IV}}$.

EXAMPLE 10.6 Instrumental Variables Estimates of the Consumption Function

The consumption function in Example 10.3 was estimated by nonlinear least squares without accounting for the nature of the data that would certainly induce correlation between $\mathbf{X}^0$ and ϵ. See Example 6.21 and 6.22 for discussion. As we did earlier, we will reestimate this model using the technique of instrumental variables. For this application, we will use the one-period lagged value of consumption and one- and two-period lagged values of income as instrumental variables. Table 10.5 reports the nonlinear least squares and instrumen-

TABLE 10.5 Nonlinear Least Squares and Instrumental Variables Estimates

	Instrumental Variables		*Least Squares*	
Parameter	*Estimate*	*Standard Error*	*Estimate*	*Standard Error*
α	254.97	76.844	214.93	43.108
β	0.14110	0.098729	0.20127	0.072909
γ	1.2338	0.085277	1.1806	0.04403
σ	15.585		15.37128	
$\epsilon'\epsilon$	8258.28		8033.39	

tal variables. Since we are using two periods of lagged values, two observations are lost. Thus, the least squares estimates are not the same as those reported earlier. The fairly large change that results when two observations are dropped is indicative of the multicollinearity problem discussed in Example 10.4.

In contrast to our finding for the linear model, we now find that the instrumental variables estimates differ considerably from the least squares estimates. The differences can be a bit deceiving, however. Recall that the MPC in the model is $\beta Y^{\gamma-1}$. The 1985 value for Y that we examined earlier was 2509. At this value, the instrumental variables and least squares estimates of the MPC are 0.87969 and 0.82742, respectively. These do differ noticeably, but perhaps less than the quite large differences in the parameters might have led one to expect. We do note that both of these estimates are considerably lower than the earlier estimate in the linear model of 0.9676.

10.2.6. Two-Step Nonlinear Least Squares Estimation

In Section 4.6, we considered maximum likelihood estimation of a model $f_2(y_2 | \mathbf{x}_1, \mathbf{x}_2, \boldsymbol{\theta}_1, \boldsymbol{\theta}_2)$ in which $\boldsymbol{\theta}_1$ is estimated by maximum likelihood separately, then $\boldsymbol{\theta}_2$ is estimated in a second step, conditionally upon this first step estimate of $\boldsymbol{\theta}_1$. In this section, we consider a special case of this general class of models in which the nonlinear regression model depends on a second set of parameters that is estimated separately.

The model is

$$y = h(\mathbf{x}, \boldsymbol{\beta}, \mathbf{w}, \boldsymbol{\gamma}) + \epsilon.$$

We consider cases in which the auxiliary parameter $\boldsymbol{\gamma}$ is estimated separately in a model that depends on an additional set of variables $\mathbf{w}$. This first step might be a least squares regression, a nonlinear regression, or a maximum likelihood estimation. The parameters $\boldsymbol{\gamma}$ will usually enter $h(\cdot)$ through some function of $\boldsymbol{\gamma}$ and $\mathbf{w}$, such as an expectation. The second step then consists of a nonlinear regression of y on $h(\mathbf{x}, \boldsymbol{\beta}, \mathbf{w}, \mathbf{c})$ in which $\mathbf{c}$ is the first round estimate of $\boldsymbol{\gamma}$. To put this in context, we will develop an example.

EXAMPLE 10.7 Two-Step Estimation of a Credit Scoring Model

Greene (1995c) estimates a model of consumer behavior in which the dependent variable of interest is the number of major derogatory reports recorded in the credit history of a sample of applicants for a type of credit card. In fact, this particular variable is one of the most significant determinants of whether an application for a loan or a credit card will be accepted. This dependent variable y is a discrete variable that at any time, for most consumers, will equal zero, but for a significant fraction who have missed several revolving credit payments, it will take a positive value. The typical values are 0, 1, or 2, but values up to, say, 10 are not unusual. This count variable is modelled using a Poisson regression model. This model appears in Examples 3.6, 3.7, 3.11, and 4.23 and Section 19.8. The probability density function for this discrete random variable is

$$\text{Prob}[y_i = j] = \frac{e^{-\lambda_i}\lambda_i^j}{j!}.$$

The expected value of y_i is λ_i, so depending on how λ_i is specified, despite the unusual nature of the dependent variable, this is a linear or nonlinear regression model. We will consider both cases, the linear model

$$E[y_i \mid \mathbf{x}_i] = \mathbf{x}_i'\boldsymbol{\beta}$$

and the more common log-linear model

$$E[y_i \mid \mathbf{x}_i] = e^{\mathbf{x}_i'\boldsymbol{\beta}},$$

where $\mathbf{x}_i$ might include such covariates as age, income, and typical monthly credit account expenditure. This model is usually estimated by maximum likelihood. But since it is a bona fide regression model, least squares, either linear or nonlinear, is a consistent, if inefficient, estimator.

In Greene's study, a secondary model is fit for the outcome of the credit card application. Let z_i denote this outcome, coded 1 if the application is accepted, 0 if not. For purposes of this exercise, we will model this outcome using a **logit** model (see Example 4.23 and the extensive development in Chapter 19). Thus

$$\text{Prob}[z_i = 1] = P(\mathbf{w}_i, \boldsymbol{\gamma}) = \frac{e^{\mathbf{w}_i'\boldsymbol{\gamma}}}{1 + e^{\mathbf{w}_i'\boldsymbol{\gamma}}},$$

where $\mathbf{w}_i$ might include age, income, whether the applicants own their own homes, and whether they are self-employed; these are the sorts of variables that "credit scoring" agencies examine.

Finally, we suppose that the probability of acceptance enters the regression model as an additional explanatory variable. (We concede that the power of the underlying theory wanes a bit here.) Thus, our nonlinear regression model is

$$E[y_i \mid \mathbf{x}_i] = \mathbf{x}_i'\boldsymbol{\beta} + \delta P(\mathbf{w}_i, \boldsymbol{\gamma}) \quad \text{(linear)}$$

or

$$E[y_i \mid \mathbf{x}_i] = e^{\mathbf{x}_i'\boldsymbol{\beta} + \delta P(\mathbf{w}_i, \gamma)} \quad \text{(loglinear, nonlinear).}$$

The two-step estimation procedure consists of estimation of $\boldsymbol{\gamma}$ by maximum likelihood, then computing $\hat{P} = P(\mathbf{w}_i, \mathbf{c})$, and finally estimating by either linear or nonlinear least squares $[\boldsymbol{\beta}, \delta]$ using $\hat{P}$ as a constructed regressor. We will develop the theoretical background for the estimator, then continue with implementation of the estimator.

The estimation procedure is as follows.

1. Estimate $\boldsymbol{\gamma}$ by least squares, nonlinear least squares, or maximum likelihood. We assume that this estimator, however obtained, denoted $\mathbf{c}$, is consistent and asymptotically normally distributed with asymptotic covariance matrix $\mathbf{V}_c$. Let $\hat{\mathbf{V}}_c$ be any appropriate estimator of $\mathbf{V}_c$.
2. Estimate $\boldsymbol{\beta}$ by nonlinear least squares regression of y on $h(\mathbf{x}, \boldsymbol{\beta}, \mathbf{w}, \mathbf{c})$. Let $\sigma^2\mathbf{V}_b$ be the asymptotic covariance matrix of this estimator of $\boldsymbol{\beta}$, and let $s^2\hat{\mathbf{V}}_b$ be any appropriate estimator of $\sigma^2\mathbf{V}_b = \sigma^2(\mathbf{X}^{0\prime}\mathbf{X}^0)^{-1}$, where $\mathbf{X}^0$ is the matrix of pseudoregressors evaluated at the true parameter values $\mathbf{x}_i^0 = \partial h(\mathbf{x}_i, \boldsymbol{\beta}, \mathbf{w}_i, \boldsymbol{\gamma})/\partial\boldsymbol{\beta}$.

The argument for consistency of $\mathbf{b}$ is the same as that used for the maximum likelihood case. We require, as usual, well-behaved pseudoregressors. As long as $\mathbf{c}$ is consistent for $\boldsymbol{\gamma}$, the large-sample behavior of the estimator of $\boldsymbol{\beta}$ conditioned on $\mathbf{c}$ is the same as that conditioned on $\boldsymbol{\gamma}$, that is, as if $\boldsymbol{\gamma}$ were known. Asymptotic normality is obtained along similar lines (albeit with greater difficulty). The asymptotic covariance matrix for the two step estimator is provided by the following theorem.

THEOREM 10.3: Asymptotic Distribution of the Two-Step Nonlinear Least Squares Estimator [Murphy and Topel (1985)]. *Under the standard conditions assumed for the nonlinear least squares estimator, the second-step estimator of $\boldsymbol{\beta}$ is consistent and asymptotically normally distributed with asymptotic covariance matrix*

$$\mathbf{V}_b^* = \sigma^2\mathbf{V}_b + \mathbf{V}_b[\mathbf{C}\mathbf{V}_c\mathbf{C}' - \mathbf{C}\mathbf{V}_c\mathbf{R}' - \mathbf{R}\mathbf{V}_c\mathbf{C}']\mathbf{V}_b,$$

where

$$\mathbf{C} = n \operatorname{plim} \frac{1}{n}\sum_{i=1}^{n}\mathbf{x}_i^0\left(\frac{\partial h(\mathbf{x}_i, \boldsymbol{\beta}, \mathbf{w}_i, \boldsymbol{\gamma})}{\partial\boldsymbol{\gamma}'}\right)$$

and

$$\mathbf{R} = n \operatorname{plim} \frac{1}{n}\sum_{i=1}^{n}\mathbf{x}_i^0\hat{\epsilon}_i\left(\frac{\partial g(\mathbf{w}_i, \boldsymbol{\gamma})}{\partial\boldsymbol{\gamma}'}\right).$$

The function $\partial g(\cdot)/\partial\boldsymbol{\gamma}$ in the definition of $\mathbf{R}$ is the gradient of the ith term in the log-likelihood function if $\boldsymbol{\gamma}$ is estimated by maximum likelihood. (The precise *form is shown below.) If $\boldsymbol{\gamma}$ appears as the parameter vector in a regression model,*

$$z = f(\mathbf{w}_i, \boldsymbol{\gamma}) + u_i, \qquad \textbf{(10-24)}$$

then $\partial g(.)/\partial\boldsymbol{\gamma}$ will be a derivative of the sum of squared deviations function,

$$\frac{\partial g(.)}{\partial \boldsymbol{\gamma}} = u_i \frac{\partial f(\mathbf{w}_i, \boldsymbol{\gamma})}{\partial \boldsymbol{\gamma}}.$$

If this is a linear regression, then the derivative vector is just $\mathbf{w}_i$.

As in the maximum likelihood case, implementation of the theorem requires that the asymptotic covariance matrix computed as usual for the second-step estimator based on **c** instead of the true $\boldsymbol{\gamma}$ must be corrected for the presence of the estimator **c** in **b**.

Before continuing with the application begun in the previous example, we note how some important special cases are handled. If $\boldsymbol{\gamma}$ enters $h(.)$ as the coefficient vector in a prediction of another variable in a regression model, then we have the following useful results.

Case 1. Linear regression models. If $h(.) = \mathbf{x}_i'\boldsymbol{\beta} + \delta E[z_i | \mathbf{w}_i] + \epsilon_i$, where $E\,[z_i | \mathbf{w}_i] = \mathbf{w}_i'\boldsymbol{\gamma}$, then the two models are just fit by linear least squares as usual. The regression for y includes an additional variable, $\mathbf{w}_i'\mathbf{c}$. Let d be the coefficient on this new variable. Then,

$\mathbf{C} = d\,\Sigma_{i=1}^{n}\, \mathbf{x}_i\mathbf{w}_i'$ and $\mathbf{R} = \Sigma_{i=1}^{n}(e_iu_i)\mathbf{x}_i\mathbf{w}_i'$.

Case 2. Uncorrelated linear regression models. In case 1, if the two regression disturbances are uncorrelated, then $\mathbf{R} = \mathbf{0}$.

Case 2 is general. The terms in **R** vanish asymptotically if the regressions have uncorrelated disturbances, whether either or both of them are linear. This will be quite common.

Case 3. Prediction from a nonlinear model. In cases 1 and 2, if $E[z_i | \mathbf{w}_i]$ is a nonlinear function rather than a linear function, then it is only necessary to change $\mathbf{w}_i$ to $\mathbf{w}_i^0 = \partial E[z_i | \mathbf{w}_i]/\partial\boldsymbol{\gamma}$—a vector of pseudoregressors—in the definitions of **C** and **R**.

Case 4. Subset of regressors. In case 2 (but not in case 1), if **w** contains all the variables that are in **x**, then the appropriate estimator is simply

$$\mathbf{V}_b^* = s_e^2\left(1 + \frac{c^2 s_u^2}{s_e^2}\right)(\mathbf{X}'\mathbf{X})^{-1},$$

where **X** includes all of the variables in **x** as well as the prediction for z.

All these cases carry over to the case of a nonlinear regression function for y. It is only necessary to replace $\mathbf{x}_i$, the actual regressors in the linear model, with $\mathbf{x}_i^0$, the pseudoregressors.

EXAMPLE 10.7 Two-Step Estimation of a Credit Scoring Model (Continued)

For the Poisson regression model, when the conditional mean function is linear, $\mathbf{x}_i^0 = \mathbf{x}_i$. If it is log-linear, then

$$\mathbf{x}_i^0 = \partial\lambda_i/\partial\boldsymbol{\beta} = \partial\exp(\mathbf{x}_i'\boldsymbol{\beta})/\partial\boldsymbol{\beta} = \lambda_i\mathbf{x}_i,$$

which is simple to compute. When $P(\mathbf{w}_i, \boldsymbol{\gamma})$ is included in the model, the pseudoregressor vector includes this variable and the coefficient vector is $[\boldsymbol{\beta}, \delta]$. Then

$$\hat{\mathbf{V}}_b = \frac{1}{n}\sum_{i=1}^{n}[y_i - h(\mathbf{x}_i, \mathbf{w}_i, \mathbf{b}, \mathbf{c})]^2 \times (\mathbf{X}^{0\prime}\mathbf{X}^0)^{-1},$$

where $\mathbf{X}^0$ is computed at $[\mathbf{b}, d, \mathbf{c}]$, the final estimates.

For the logit model, the gradient of the log-likelihood and the estimator of $\mathbf{V}_c$ are given in Example 4.23. These are

$$\partial \ln f(z_i \,|\, \mathbf{w}_i, \boldsymbol{\gamma})/\partial\boldsymbol{\gamma} = [z_i - P(\mathbf{w}_i, \boldsymbol{\gamma})]\mathbf{w}_i$$

and

$$\hat{\mathbf{V}}_c = \sum_{i=1}^{n}[z_i - P(\mathbf{w}_i, \boldsymbol{\gamma})]^2\mathbf{w}_i\mathbf{w}_i'.$$

Note that for this model, we are actually inserting a prediction from a regression model of sorts, since $E[z_i] = P(\mathbf{w}_i, \boldsymbol{\gamma})$. To compute $\mathbf{R}$, we will require

$$\partial h(\cdot)/\partial\boldsymbol{\gamma} = \lambda_i\delta\,\partial P_i/\partial\boldsymbol{\gamma} = \lambda_i\delta P_i(1 - P_i)\mathbf{w}_i.$$

The remaining parts of the corrected covariance matrix are computed using

$$\mathbf{C} = \sum_{i=1}^{n}(\lambda_i\mathbf{x}_i^0)[\lambda_i d P_i(1 - P_i)]\mathbf{w}_i'$$

and

$$\mathbf{R} = \sum_{i=1}^{n}(\lambda_i\mathbf{x}_i^0)(z_i - P_i)\mathbf{w}_i'.$$

(If the regression model is linear, the three occurrences of λ_i are omitted and $\mathbf{x}^0$ becomes just $\mathbf{x}$.)

Data used in the application are listed in Table 10.6. We use the following model:

$$\begin{aligned}\text{Prob}[z_i = 1] &= P(\text{age, income, own rent, self-employed}),\\ E[y_i] &= h(\text{age, income, expend}).\end{aligned}$$

We have used 100 of the 1319 observations used in the original study. Table 10.7 reports the results of the various regressions and computations. The column denoted St.Er.* contains the corrected standard error. The column

TABLE 10.6 Data on Credit Applications

Variables are:

y_1 = number of derogatory reports
y_2 = credit card application accepted (1 = yes)
x_1 = age
x_2 = income
x_3 = average expenditure
x_4 = own own home (1 = yes)
x_5 = self-employed (1 = yes)

y_1	y_2	x_1	x_2	x_3	x_4	x_5	y_1	y_2	x_1	x_2	x_3	x_4	x_5
0	1	38	4.52	124.98	1	0	0	0	50	3.60	0.00	0	0
0	1	33	2.42	9.85	0	0	0	1	24	2.00	93.20	0	0
0	1	34	4.50	15.00	1	0	0	1	21	1.70	105.04	0	0
0	1	31	2.54	137.87	0	0	0	1	24	2.80	34.13	0	0
0	1	32	9.79	546.50	1	0	0	1	26	2.40	41.19	0	0
0	1	23	2.50	92.00	0	0	1	1	33	3.00	169.89	0	0
0	1	28	3.96	40.83	0	0	0	1	34	4.80	1898.03	0	0
0	1	29	2.37	150.79	1	0	0	1	33	3.18	810.39	0	0
0	1	37	3.80	777.82	1	0	0	0	45	1.80	0.00	0	0
0	1	28	3.20	52.58	0	0	0	1	21	1.50	32.78	0	0
0	1	31	3.95	256.66	1	0	2	1	25	3.00	95.80	0	0
0	0	42	1.98	0.00	1	0	0	1	27	2.28	27.78	0	0
0	0	30	1.73	0.00	1	0	0	1	26	2.80	215.07	0	0
0	1	29	2.45	78.87	1	0	0	1	22	2.70	79.51	0	0
0	1	35	1.91	42.62	1	0	3	0	27	4.90	0.00	1	0
0	1	41	3.20	335.43	1	0	0	0	26	2.50	0.00	0	1
0	1	40	4.00	248.72	1	0	0	1	41	6.00	306.03	0	1
7	0	30	3.00	0.00	1	0	0	1	42	3.90	104.54	0	0
0	1	40	10.00	548.03	1	1	0	0	22	5.10	0.00	0	0
3	0	46	3.40	0.00	0	0	0	1	25	3.07	642.47	0	0
0	1	35	2.35	43.34	1	0	0	1	31	2.46	308.05	1	0
1	0	25	1.88	0.00	0	0	0	1	27	2.00	186.35	0	0
0	1	34	2.00	218.52	1	0	0	1	33	3.25	56.15	0	0
1	1	36	4.00	170.64	0	0	0	1	37	2.72	129.37	0	0
0	1	43	5.14	37.58	1	0	0	1	27	2.20	93.11	0	0
0	1	30	4.51	502.20	0	0	1	0	24	4.10	0.00	0	0
0	0	22	3.84	0.00	0	1	0	1	24	3.75	292.66	0	0
0	1	22	1.50	73.18	0	0	0	1	25	2.88	98.46	0	0
0	0	34	2.50	0.00	1	0	0	1	36	3.05	258.55	0	0
0	1	40	5.50	1532.77	1	0	0	1	33	2.55	101.68	0	0
0	1	22	2.03	42.69	0	0	0	0	33	4.00	0.00	0	0
1	1	29	3.20	417.83	0	0	1	1	55	2.64	65.25	1	0
1	0	25	3.15	0.00	1	0	0	1	20	1.65	108.61	0	0
0	1	21	2.47	552.72	1	0	0	1	29	2.40	49.56	0	0
0	1	24	3.00	222.54	0	0	3	0	40	3.71	0.00	0	0
0	1	43	3.54	541.30	1	0	0	1	41	7.24	235.57	1	0

TABLE 10.6 Data on Credit Applications (Continued)

y_1	y_2	x_1	x_2	x_3	x_4	x_5	y_1	y_2	x_1	x_2	x_3	x_4	x_5
0	0	43	2.28	0.00	0	0	0	0	41	4.39	0.00	1	0
0	1	37	5.70	568.77	1	0	0	0	35	3.30	0.00	1	0
0	1	27	3.50	344.47	0	0	0	0	24	2.30	0.00	0	0
0	1	28	4.60	405.35	1	0	1	0	54	4.18	0.00	0	0
0	1	26	3.00	310.94	1	0	2	0	34	2.49	0.00	0	0
0	1	23	2.59	53.65	0	0	0	0	45	2.81	0.00	1	0
0	1	30	1.51	63.92	0	0	0	1	43	2.40	68.38	0	0
0	1	30	1.85	165.85	0	0	4	0	35	1.50	0.00	0	0
0	1	38	2.60	9.58	0	0	2	0	36	8.40	0.00	0	0
0	0	28	1.80	0.00	0	1	0	1	22	1.56	0.00	0	0
0	1	36	2.00	319.49	0	0	1	1	33	6.00	474.15	1	0
0	0	38	3.26	0.00	0	0	1	1	25	3.60	234.05	0	0
0	1	26	2.35	83.08	0	0	0	1	26	5.00	451.20	1	0
0	1	28	7.00	644.83	1	0	0	1	46	5.50	251.52	1	0

marked St.Er. contains the standard errors that would be computed ignoring the two step nature of the computations. For the linear model, we used $\mathbf{e}'\mathbf{e}/n$ to estimate σ^2.

As expected, accounting for the variability in $\mathbf{c}$ increases the standard errors of the second-step estimator. The linear model appears to give quite different results from the nonlinear model. But this can be deceiving. In the linear

TABLE 10.7 Two-Step Estimates of a Credit Scoring Model

	Step 1. $P(w_i, \gamma)$		***Step 2.*** $E[y_i \mid x_i] = x_i'\beta + \delta P_i$			***Step 2.*** $E[y_i \mid x_i] = e^{x_i'\beta + \delta P_i}$		
Variable	***Est.***	***St.Er.***	***Est.***	***St.Er.***	***St.Er.****	***Est.***	***St.Er.***	***Se.Er.****
Constant	2.7236	1.0970	−1.0628	1.1907	1.3952	−6.3199	7.5222	9.14297
Age	−0.7328	0.02961	0.021661	0.018756	0.021579	0.074621	0.10185	0.11606
Income	0.21919	0.14296	0.03473	0.07266	0.086218	0.045272	0.26175	0.33393
Self-empl	−1.9439	1.01270						
Own Rent	0.18937	0.49817						
Expend			−0.000787	0.000368	0.000365	−0.02005	0.016056	0.016125
$P(w_i, \gamma)$			1.0408	1.0653	1.239758	4.6325	6.8179	8.77218
ln L	−53.924							
$\mathbf{e}'\mathbf{e}$			95.5506			86.9421		
s			0.977496			0.93243		
R^2			0.05433			0.13953		
Mean	0.73		0.36			0.36		

model, $\partial E[y_i \mid \mathbf{x}_i, P_i]/\partial \mathbf{x}_i = \boldsymbol{\beta}$, whereas in the nonlinear model, the counterpart is not $\boldsymbol{\beta}$ but $\lambda_i \boldsymbol{\beta}$. The value of λ_i at the mean values of all the variables in the second-step model is roughly 0.36 (the mean of the dependent variable; this is one of the first-order conditions), so the marginal effects in the nonlinear model are [0.0268, 0.016299, 0.00722, 1.6677], respectively, including P_i but not the constant, which are reasonably similar to those for the linear model. To compute an asymptotic covariance matrix for the estimated marginal effects, we would use the delta method from Section 6.7.5. For convenience, let $\mathbf{b}_p = [\mathbf{b}', d]'$, and let $\mathbf{v}_i = [\mathbf{x}_i', \hat{P}_i]'$; this just adds P_i to the regressor vector so we need not treat it separately. Then the vector of marginal effects is

$$\mathbf{m} = \exp(\mathbf{v}_i'\mathbf{b}_p) \times \mathbf{b}_p = \lambda_i \mathbf{b}_p.$$

The matrix of derivatives is

$$\mathbf{G} = \partial \mathbf{m}/\partial \mathbf{b}_p = \lambda_i(\mathbf{I} + \mathbf{b}_p \mathbf{v}_i'),$$

so the estimator of the asymptotic covariance matrix for $\mathbf{m}$ is

$$\text{Est. Asy. Var}[\mathbf{m}] = \mathbf{G}\mathbf{V}_b^* \mathbf{G}'.$$

One might be tempted to treat λ_i as a constant, in which only the first term in the quadratic form would appear, and the computation would amount simply to multiplying the asymptotic standard errors for $\mathbf{b}_p$ by λ_i. This approximation would leave the asymptotic t ratios unchanged, whereas making the full correction will change the entire covariance matrix. The approximation will generally lead to an understatement of the correct standard errors.

Finally, although this treatment is not discussed in detail until Chapter 19, we note at this point that nonlinear least squares is an inefficient estimator in the Poisson regression model; maximum likelihood is the preferred, efficient estimator. Table 10.8 presents the maximum likelihood estimates with both corrected and uncorrected estimates of the asymptotic standard errors of the parameter estimates. (The full discussion of the model is given in Chapter 19.) The corrected standard errors are computed using the methods shown in Example 4.23. A comparison of these estimates with those in the third set of Table 10.7 suggests the clear superiority of the maximum likelihood estimator.

TABLE 10.8 Maximum Likelihood Estimates of Second Step Regression Model

	Constant	*Age*	*Income*	*Expend*	*P*
Estimate	−6.3200	0.073106	0.045236	20.0068969	4.6324
Std.Error	3.9308	0.054246	0.17411	0.00202	3.6618
Corr.Std.Error	4.4736	0.05914	0.226296	0.002192	4.3382

10.3. PARAMETRIC TRANSFORMATIONS OF THE DEPENDENT VARIABLE

Thus far, we have considered models in which the nonlinearity in the parameters was entirely on the right-hand side of the equation. There are models in which parameters appear nonlinearly in functions of the dependent variable as well. The Box–Cox transformation considered in the next section is one example. Another is given here.

EXAMPLE 10.8 A Generalized Production Function

The Cobb–Douglas production function has often been used to study production. Among the assumptions of this model is that the average cost of production increases or decreases monotonically with increases in output. This is in direct contrast to the standard textbook treatment of a U-shaped average cost curve as well as to a large amount of empirical evidence. To relax this assumption, Zellner and Revankar (1970) proposed a generalization of the Cobb–Douglas production function.[12] Their model allows economies of scale to vary with output and to increase and then decrease as output rises:

$$\ln y + \theta y = \ln \gamma + \alpha(1 - \delta)\ln K + \alpha\delta \ln L + \epsilon.$$

Note that the right-hand side of their model is intrinsically linear according to the results of Section 8.3.3. The model as a whole, however, is intrinsically nonlinear due to the parametric transformation of y appearing on the left.

Suppose that, in general, the model is

$$g(y_i, \boldsymbol{\theta}) = h(\mathbf{x}_i, \boldsymbol{\beta}) + \epsilon_i. \quad \textbf{(10-25)}$$

One approach to estimation would be least squares, minimizing

$$S(\boldsymbol{\theta}, \boldsymbol{\beta}) = \sum_{i=1}^{n}[g(y_i, \boldsymbol{\theta}) - h(\mathbf{x}_i, \boldsymbol{\beta})]^2.$$

For this kind of regression model, however, maximum likelihood estimation is more efficient and generally not appreciably more difficult. For normally distributed disturbances, the density of y_i is

$$f(y_i) = \left|\frac{\partial \epsilon_i}{\partial y_i}\right|(2\pi\sigma^2)^{-1/2}e^{-[g(y_i, \boldsymbol{\theta}) - h(\mathbf{x}_i, \boldsymbol{\beta})]^2/(2\sigma^2)}.$$

The Jacobian of the transformation [see (3-41)] is

$$J(y_i, \boldsymbol{\theta}) = \left|\frac{\partial \epsilon_i}{\partial y_i}\right| = \left|\frac{\partial g(y_i, \boldsymbol{\theta})}{\partial y_i}\right| = J_i.$$

---

[12] An alternative approach is to model costs directly with a flexible functional form such as the translog model. This is examined in detail in Chapter 15.

After collecting terms, the log-likelihood function will be

$$\ln L = -\frac{n}{2}\ln 2\pi - \frac{n}{2}\ln \sigma^2 + \sum_{i=1}^{n} \ln J(y_i, \boldsymbol{\theta}) - \frac{1}{2\sigma^2}\sum_{i=1}^{n}[g(y_i, \boldsymbol{\theta}) - h(\mathbf{x}_i, \boldsymbol{\beta})]^2. \tag{10-26}$$

Before proceeding, two aspects of the log-likelihood should be noted. First, it is obvious that but for the Jacobians, nonlinear least squares would be maximum likelihood. If the Jacobian terms involve $\boldsymbol{\theta}$, however, *least squares is not maximum likelihood*. Second, as regards σ^2, this likelihood function is essentially the same as that for the simpler nonlinear regression model of (10-1). The maximum likelihood estimator of σ^2 will be

$$\begin{aligned}\hat{\sigma}^2 &= \frac{1}{n}\sum_{i=1}^{n}[g(y_i, \hat{\boldsymbol{\theta}}) - h(\mathbf{x}_i, \hat{\boldsymbol{\beta}})]^2 \\ &= \frac{1}{n}\sum_{i=1}^{n} e_i^2.\end{aligned} \tag{10-27}$$

The likelihood equations for the unknown parameters are

$$\begin{aligned}\frac{\partial \ln L}{\partial \boldsymbol{\beta}} &= \frac{1}{\sigma^2}\sum_{i=1}^{n}\epsilon_i \frac{\partial h(\mathbf{x}_i, \boldsymbol{\beta})}{\partial \boldsymbol{\beta}} = \mathbf{0}, \\ \frac{\partial \ln L}{\partial \boldsymbol{\theta}} &= \sum_{i=1}^{n}\frac{1}{J_i}\left(\frac{\partial J_i}{\partial \boldsymbol{\theta}}\right) - \left(\frac{1}{\sigma^2}\right)\sum_{i=1}^{n}\epsilon_i \frac{\partial g(y_i, \boldsymbol{\theta})}{\partial \boldsymbol{\theta}} = \mathbf{0}, \\ \frac{\partial \ln L}{\partial \sigma^2} &= \frac{-n}{2\sigma^2} + \frac{1}{2\sigma^4}\sum_{i=1}^{n}\epsilon_i^2 = 0.\end{aligned} \tag{10-28}$$

These will usually be nonlinear, so a solution must be obtained iteratively. One special case that is common is a model in which $\boldsymbol{\theta}$ is a single parameter. Given a particular value of θ, we would maximize (10-26) with respect to $\boldsymbol{\beta}$ by using nonlinear least squares. [It would be simpler yet if, in addition, $h(\mathbf{x}_i, \boldsymbol{\beta})$ were linear so that we could use linear least squares. See the following example.] Therefore, a way to maximize L for all the parameters is to scan over values of θ for the one that, with the associated least squares estimates of $\boldsymbol{\beta}$ and σ^2, gives the highest value of L. (Of course, this requires that we know roughly what values of θ to examine.)

For more general models, a similar method could be used, but this will probably be much more difficult. If $\boldsymbol{\theta}$ is a vector of parameters, direct maximization of L with respect to the full set of parameters may be preferable. (Methods of maximization are discussed in Chapter 5.) There is an additional simplification that may be useful. Whatever values are ultimately obtained for the estimates of $\boldsymbol{\theta}$ and $\boldsymbol{\beta}$, the estimate of σ^2 will be given by (10-27). If we insert this solution in (10-26), we obtain the **concentrated log-likelihood**,

$$\ln L_c = \sum_{i=1}^{n} \ln J(y_i, \boldsymbol{\theta}) - \frac{n}{2}[1 + \ln(2\pi)] - \frac{n}{2}\ln\left[\frac{1}{n}\sum_{i=1}^{n}\epsilon_i^2\right]. \tag{10-29}$$

This is a function only of $\boldsymbol{\theta}$ and $\boldsymbol{\beta}$. We can maximize it with respect to $\boldsymbol{\theta}$ and $\boldsymbol{\beta}$ and obtain the estimate of σ^2 as a by-product.[13]

An estimate of the asymptotic covariance matrix of the maximum likelihood estimators can be obtained by inverting the estimated information matrix. It is quite likely, however, that the Berndt et al. (1974) estimator will be much easier to compute. The log of the density for the ith observation is

$$\ln L_i = \ln J_i - \frac{1}{2}[\ln(2\pi) + \ln \sigma^2] - \frac{1}{2\sigma^2}[g(y_i, \boldsymbol{\theta}) - h(\mathbf{x}_i, \boldsymbol{\beta})]^2.$$

The derivatives of $\ln L_i$ with respect to the unknown parameters are

$$\mathbf{w}_i = \begin{bmatrix} \partial \ln L_i/\partial \boldsymbol{\beta} \\ \partial \ln L_i/\partial \boldsymbol{\theta} \\ \partial \ln L_i/\partial \sigma^2 \end{bmatrix} = \begin{bmatrix} (\epsilon_i/\sigma^2)[\partial h(\mathbf{x}_i, \boldsymbol{\beta})/\partial \boldsymbol{\beta}] \\ (1/J_i)[\partial J_i/\partial \boldsymbol{\theta}] - (\epsilon_i/\sigma^2)[\partial g(y_i, \boldsymbol{\theta})/\partial \boldsymbol{\theta}] \\ (1/(2\sigma^2))[\epsilon_i^2/\sigma^2 - 1] \end{bmatrix}. \qquad \textbf{(10-30)}$$

The covariance matrix for the maximum likelihood estimators is consistently estimated using

$$\text{Est. Asy. Var[MLE]} = \left[\sum_{i=1}^{n} \hat{\mathbf{w}}_i \hat{\mathbf{w}}_i'\right]^{-1}.$$

EXAMPLE 10.8 A Generalized Production Function (Continued)

For Zellner and Revankar's production function, the Jacobian of the transformation from ϵ_i to y_i is $\partial \epsilon_i/\partial y_i = (\theta + 1/y_i)$. Some simplification is achieved by writing this as $(1 + \theta y_i)/y_i$. The log-likelihood is then

$$\ln L = \sum_{i=1}^{n} \ln(1 + \theta y_i) - \sum_{i=1}^{n} \ln y_i - \frac{n}{2}\ln(2\pi) - \frac{n}{2}\ln \sigma^2 - \frac{1}{2\sigma^2}\sum_{i=1}^{n} \epsilon_i^2,$$

where

$$\epsilon_i = (\ln y_i + \theta y_i - \beta_1 - \beta_2 \ln \text{capital}_i - \beta_3 \ln \text{labor}_i).$$

Estimation of this model is straightforward. For a given value of θ, $\boldsymbol{\beta}$ and σ^2 are estimated by linear least squares. Therefore, to estimate the full set of parameters, we can scan over the range of 0 to 1 for θ. The value of θ that, with its associated least squares estimates of $\boldsymbol{\beta}$ and σ^2, maximizes the log-likelihood function provides the least desired estimate. This is the procedure used by Zellner and Revankar. The data used for the study are listed in Table 10.9.[14]

[13]A formal proof that this is a valid way to proceed is given by Amemiya (1985, pp. 125–127).

[14]Zellner and Revankar (1970, p. 249). Full descriptions of the variables are given in the study.

TABLE 10.9 U.S. Annual Survey of Manufactures Data for the Transportation Equipment Industry

State	*Value Added*	*Capital*	*Labor*	*Establishments*
Alabama	126.148	3.804	31.551	68
California	3201.486	185.446	452.844	1372
Connecticut	690.670	39.712	124.074	154
Florida	56.296	6.547	19.181	292
Georgia	304.531	11.530	45.534	71
Illinois	723.028	58.987	88.391	275
Indiana	992.169	112.884	148.530	260
Iowa	35.796	2.698	8.017	75
Kansas	494.515	10.360	86.189	76
Kentucky	124.948	5.213	12.000	31
Louisiana	73.328	3.763	15.900	115
Maine	29.467	1.967	6.470	81
Maryland	415.262	17.546	69.342	129
Massachusetts	241.530	15.347	39.416	172
Michigan	4079.554	435.105	490.384	568
Missouri	652.085	32.840	84.831	125
New Jersey	667.113	33.292	83.033	247
New York	940.430	72.974	190.094	461
Ohio	1611.899	157.978	259.916	363
Pennsylvania	617.579	34.324	98.152	233
Texas	527.413	22.736	109.728	308
Virginia	174.394	7.173	31.301	85
Washington	636.948	30.807	87.963	179
West Virginia	22.700	1.543	4.063	15
Wisconsin	349.711	22.001	52.818	142

Source: A. Zellner and N. Revankar, "Generalized Production Functions," *Review of Economic Studies,* 37, 1970, p. 249.

Note: "Value added," "capital," and "labor" are in millions of 1957 dollars. Data used for the regressions are per establishment.

In their model, Zellner and Revankar report the maximum likelihood estimates of the parameters listed in Table 10.10. For each of their estimates, three estimates of the asymptotic standard error were given. The authors report asymptotic standard errors based on the information matrix (1) and the (inappropriate) least squares standard errors (2). We have reestimated the model by maximum likelihood. The constant and slopes on $\ln K/E$ and $\ln L/E$ are obtained by least squares regression using $(\ln Y/E + \theta Y/E)$ as the dependent variable. The value of θ was located by a grid search, using the log-likelihood, not the sum of squares, as the criterion. A contour of the log-likelihood is

TABLE 10.10 Maximum Likelihood Estimates

	Estimate	*SE(1)*	*SE(2)*
β_1	3.0186	0.4271	0.1346
β_2	0.3354	0.09679	0.1024
β_3	1.1567	0.1781	0.1230
θ	0.135	0.07766	—
σ^2	0.04741	0.01838	—

shown in Figure 10.1.[15] The estimation results are given in Table 10.10.[16] The standard errors are based on the estimator suggested earlier. The second set are the customary least squares results that do not account for θ being estimated with the slopes.

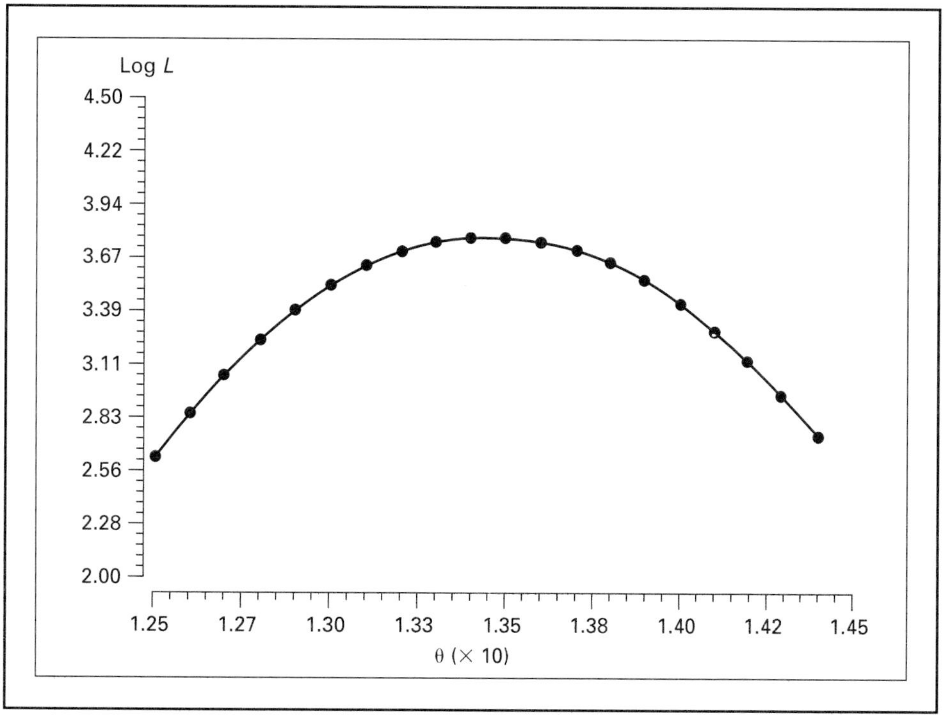

FIGURE 10.1 Log-Likelihood for the Generalized Production Model.

[15]The plot has 10θ on the abscissa and $100(\ln L - 3.6)$ on the ordinate.

[16]These do not agree with the authors' original results. In correspondence, Professor Zhiquang Liu reports that the labor value for Michigan is miscoded in the original paper (they report 590.384). We have reestimated the model with the correction shown in Table 10.9. For purposes of the example, we have not attempted to reconcile the differences.

As usual, there is a problem in interpreting the coefficients in this nonlinear regression model. The slope coefficients of the regression are not the marginal effects. An approximation to the appropriate value can be obtained with

$$\frac{\partial E[y]}{\partial x_j} \simeq \left[\frac{\partial h(\mathbf{x}, \boldsymbol{\beta})}{\partial x_j}\right]\frac{1}{g'(y)}. \tag{10-31}$$

Elasticities are computed using

$$\frac{\partial \ln y}{\partial \ln x_j} \simeq \left[\frac{\partial h(\mathbf{x}, \boldsymbol{\beta})}{\partial x_j}\right]\left[\frac{x_j}{yg'(y)}\right]. \tag{10-32}$$

(Note the similarity to the form for the log-linear model.) If $g(y) = y$, then $yg'(y) = 1$ and we get the familiar result. These functions will vary with the data, so they must be computed at a particular data point. The predicted values and functions of them can be used in place of y and $g'(y)$ on the right-hand side of (10-31) and (10-32). For Zellner and Revankar's generalized Cobb–Douglas production function, we use the result

$$x_j\left[\frac{\partial h(\mathbf{x}, \boldsymbol{\beta})}{\partial x_j}\right] = \frac{\partial h(\mathbf{x}, \boldsymbol{\beta})}{\partial x_j}.$$

Since $h(\mathbf{x}, \boldsymbol{\beta}) = \beta_1 + \beta_2 \ln K + \beta_3 \ln L$, these derivatives are the slope coefficients, β_2 and β_3. To compute a value for y, we insert the means of ln $K(-2.0822)$ and ln $L(-1.0070)$ on the right-hand side to obtain a prediction for $\ln y + \theta y = 1.1593$. The value of y for which $\ln y + 0.135y = 1.1593$ is 2.32802. Finally, for this model,

$$g'(y) = \frac{1}{y} + \theta.$$

So

$$\frac{\partial \ln y}{\partial \ln x_j} = \frac{\beta_j}{1 + \theta y}.$$

Assembling the terms, we obtain estimates of the output elasticities of

$$\text{capital: } \frac{0.3354}{1 + 0.135(2.32802)} = 0.2552,$$

$$\text{labor: } \frac{1.1567}{1 + 0.135(2.32802)} = 0.88801.$$

As a rough check on these values, consider a simple Cobb–Douglas function, which has $\theta = 0$. This can be efficiently estimated by ordinary least squares regression of ln y on a constant ln K and ln L. The slope coefficients in this regression, using the preceding data, are 0.2579 and 0.93299. Once again, the linear regression approximates the nonlinear regression surprisingly closely.

In this study, the parameter θ was of primary interest, so the result in the preceding paragraph is not necessarily a virtue. In the Cobb–Douglas model,

TABLE 10.11 Economies of Scale

State	*Output*	*Economies of Scale*
Florida	0.193	1.45
Louisiana	0.638	1.37
California	2.333	1.13
Maryland	3.219	1.04
Ohio	4.440	0.93
Michigan	7.182	0.76

the economies of scale parameter is the sum of the output elasticities. For these data, that would be 1.136, indicating a fair degree of economies of scale. (It can be shown that this parameter also corresponds to the ratio of average to marginal cost on the cost side, which indicates that average costs are declining throughout the range of y.) For the previous generalized production function, the economies of scale parameter is

$$\alpha = \frac{\beta_K + \beta_L}{1 + \theta y} = \frac{1.492}{1 + 0.135y}.$$

Some representative values for their sample are listed in Table 10.11.

10.4. THE BOX–COX TRANSFORMATION

The Box–Cox transformation was introduced in Chapters 6 and 8 as a method of generalizing the linear model. The transformation is[17]

$$x^{(\lambda)} = \frac{x^\lambda - 1}{\lambda}.$$

As noted earlier, in a regression model, the analysis could be done *conditionally*. For a given value of λ, the model

$$y = \alpha + \sum_{k=1}^{K} \beta_k x_k^{(\lambda)} + \epsilon \qquad \textbf{(10-33)}$$

is a linear regression that can be estimated by least squares.[18] Save for the complexity of the calculations, in principle, each regressor could be transformed by a different value of λ. In most applications, this level of generality becomes ex-

[17]Box and Cox (1964). To be defined for all values of λ, x must be strictly positive.

[18]In most applications, some of the regressors—for example, dummy variables—will not be transformed. For such a variable, say v_k, $v_k^{(\lambda)} = v_k$, and the relevant derivatives in (10-34) and (10-43) will be zero.

cessively cumbersome, and λ is assumed to be the same for all the variables in the model.[19] At the same time, it is also possible to transform y by $y^{(\theta)}$.

EXAMPLE 10.9 Flexible Cost Function

Caves et al. (1980) analyzed the costs of production for railroads providing freight and passenger service. Continuing a long line of literature on the costs of production in regulated industries, a translog cost function (see Example 7.3) would be a natural choice for modeling this multiple-output technology. Several of the firms in the study, however, produced no passenger service, which would preclude the use of the translog model. (This would require the log of zero.) An alternative is the Box–Cox transformation, which is computable for zero output levels. A constraint must still be placed on λ in their model, as $0^{(\lambda)}$ is defined only if λ is strictly positive. As shown in Example 10.10, a positive value of λ is not assured. A question does arise in this context (and other similar ones) as to whether zero outputs should be treated the same as nonzero outputs or whether an output of zero represents a discrete corporate decision distinct from other variation in the output levels. In addition, this is only a partial solution. The zero values of the regressors preclude computation of appropriate standard errors.

10.4.1. Transforming the Independent Variables

If λ in (10-33) is taken to be an unknown parameter, the regression becomes nonlinear in the parameters. Although no transformation will reduce it to linearity, nonlinear least squares is straightforward. In most instances, we can expect to find the least squares value of λ between -2 and 2. Typically, then, λ is estimated by scanning this range in increments of 0.1.

When λ equals zero, the transformation is, by L'Hôpital's rule,

$$\lim_{\lambda \to 0} \frac{x^{\lambda} - 1}{\lambda} = \lim_{\lambda \to 0} \frac{d(x^{\lambda} - 1)/d\lambda}{1} = \lim_{\lambda \to 0} x^{\lambda} \times \ln x = \ln x.$$

If a minimum of the sum of squares is found and greater precision is desired, the area to the right and left of the current optimum can be searched in increments of 0.01, and so on. Once the optimum value of λ is located, the least squares estimates, the mean squared residual, and this value of λ constitute the nonlinear least squares (and, with normality of the disturbance, maximum likelihood) estimates of the parameters.

After determining the optimal value of λ, it is sometimes treated as if it were a *known* value in the least squares results. But, $\hat{\lambda}$ is an estimate of an unknown parameter. It is not hard to show that the least squares standard errors will always underestimate the correct asymptotic standard errors.[20] To get the

[19] See, for example, Seaks and Layson (1983).

[20] See Fomby et al. (1984, pp. 426–431).

appropriate values, we need the derivatives of the right-hand side of (10-33) with respect to α, $\boldsymbol{\beta}$, and λ. In the notation of (10-1), these are

$$\begin{aligned}\frac{\partial h(.)}{\partial \alpha} &= 1,\\ \frac{\partial h(.)}{\partial \beta_k} &= x_k^{(\lambda)},\\ \frac{\partial h(.)}{\partial \lambda} &= \sum_{k=1}^{K} \beta_k \frac{\partial x_k^{(\lambda)}}{\partial \lambda}\\ &= \sum_{k=1}^{K} \beta_k \left[\frac{1}{\lambda}\left(x_k^{\lambda} \ln x_k - x_k^{(\lambda)}\right)\right].\end{aligned} \tag{10-34}$$

We can now use (10-13) to estimate the asymptotic covariance matrix of the parameter estimates. Note that $\ln x_k$ appears in $\partial h(.)/\partial \lambda$. If $x_k = 0$, this cannot be computed.

EXAMPLE 10.10 A More General Money Demand Equation

The estimates of the log-linear money demand equation in Example 10.5 are implicitly a Box–Cox model:

$$\ln M = \alpha + \beta_r r^{(\lambda)} + \beta_Y Y^{(\lambda)} + \epsilon, \tag{10-35}$$

with λ equal to zero. Here we will allow λ to be a free parameter. For a given value of λ, the Box–Cox model is a linear regression model; we can compute $r^{(\lambda)}$ and $Y^{(\lambda)}$ and then obtain the remaining parameters by least squares. Maximum likelihood estimates of all the parameters in the model are obtained by scanning over the range of λ from -1 to 1. The sums of squared deviations, which we denote $S(\boldsymbol{\beta})$, for a range of values of λ are shown in Table 10.12.

At the optimal value of 0.47, the least squares results with the appropriate standard errors are as listed in Table 10.13. The standard errors are computed using the nonlinear least squares results, (10-34) and (10-13). Table 10.13 contains three alternative estimates of the set of standard errors. The LS standard errors are computed by ignoring the variation in the estimate of λ. These are the standard errors that the least squares regression produces automatically when $\ln M$ is regressed on a constant, $r^{(\lambda)}$, and $Y^{(\lambda)}$. Obviously, they would be

TABLE 10.12 Sums of Squared Deviations for Given λ

λ	$s(\beta)$	λ	$s(\beta)$	λ	$s(\beta)$
0.3	0.13016	0.44	0.12723	0.49	0.12721
0.4	0.12732	0.45	0.12721	0.50	0.12721
0.41	0.12729	0.46	0.12721	0.60	0.12753
0.42	0.12726	0.47	0.12720		
0.43	0.12724	0.48	0.12721		

TABLE 10.13 Estimated Money Demand Equations

Variable	Coefficient	Standard Error	t ratio	Alternative Standard Errors LS	ML/BHHH	ML/Hessian
Constant	−0.543	8.048	−0.067	0.3614	15.38	7.713
$r^{(0.47)}$	−0.00607	0.032	−0.177	0.0352	0.0480	0.0344
$Y^{(0.47)}$	0.0867	0.3804	0.228	0.00505	0.7221	0.5303
λ	0.47	0.5510	0.853	0.0000	1.044	1.016

seriously misleading. The standard errors denoted ML/BHHH are computed according to (10-43) through (10-45) without a transformation of the dependent variable. The change to (10-43) is that the Jacobian term, ln y_i, and the first term in the parentheses in $\partial \ln f(y_i)/\partial\lambda$ are omitted. Note that (10-45) also produces an estimated standard error for the estimate of σ^2. This is omitted from Table 10.13. The last column gives the standard errors computed using the actual second derivatives of the log-likelihood function. For this problem, that would be (10-39) without the term $(\lambda - 1)\sum_i \ln y_i$ and without the transformation of y_i in the sum of squares. With the exception of the LS column, the estimators are all appropriate, and all would be the same asymptotically. The differences that are evident are small sample variation; we have used only 20 observations. There is no obvious answer to which is right; all are. The choice is usually based on ease of computation, which would generally favor the one we used first.

It is important to remember that the coefficients in a nonlinear model are not equal to the slopes (i.e., here the demand elasticities) with respect to the variables. In the Box–Cox model,[21]

$$\ln Y = \alpha + \beta\left[\frac{X^\lambda - 1}{\lambda}\right]$$
$$\frac{d\ln Y}{d\ln X} = \beta X^\lambda = \eta. \tag{10-36}$$

Inserting the means for r (7.273) and Y (2849.23), we obtain elasticities of −0.0154 and 3.6454, respectively. These are quite similar to the estimates for the log-linear model in Example 10.5. Standard errors for these estimates can be obtained using the delta method. The derivatives are $\partial\eta/\partial\beta = \eta/\beta$ and

[21]We have used the result $d \ln Y/d \ln X = X d \ln Y/dX$.

$\partial\eta/\partial\lambda = \eta \ln X$. Collecting terms, we obtain

$$\text{Asy. Var}[\hat{\eta}] = (\eta/\beta)^2\{\text{Asy. Var}[\hat{\beta}] + (\beta \ln X)\text{Asy. Var}[\hat{\lambda}] + (2\beta \ln X)\text{Asy. Cov}[\hat{\beta}, \hat{\lambda}]\}.$$

10.4.2. Transforming the Model

It seems a natural generalization at this point to extend (10-33) to

$$y^{(\theta)} = \alpha + \sum_{k=1}^{K} \beta_k x_k^{(\lambda)} + \epsilon \qquad \textbf{(10-37)}$$

or

$$y^{(\theta)} = \boldsymbol{\beta}'\mathbf{x}^{(\lambda)} + \epsilon.$$

This includes the linear and log-linear models as special cases.

Allowing θ to differ from λ is usually taken to be more cumbersome than necessary. The computational burden increases greatly with this level of generality. We shall assume that they are equal. If $\epsilon \sim N[0, \sigma^2]$, the log-likelihood for a sample of n observation is

$$\ln L = -\frac{n}{2}\ln(2\pi) - \frac{n}{2}\ln\sigma^2 - \frac{1}{2\sigma^2}\sum_{i=1}^{n}\epsilon_i^2.$$ [22]

Transforming from the distribution ϵ to that of y, we use the change-of-variable result

$$f_y(y) = \left|\frac{d\epsilon}{dy}\right| f_\epsilon(y).$$

From (10-37),

$$\epsilon = y^{(\lambda)} - \mathbf{x}^{(\lambda)\prime}\boldsymbol{\beta}, \qquad \textbf{(10-38)}$$

so the Jacobian is

$$\left|\frac{d\epsilon}{dy}\right| = y^{\lambda-1}.$$

Making the substitution and multiplying by the Jacobian, we obtain the log-likelihood function for the Box–Cox model:

$$\ln L = -\frac{n}{2}\ln(2\pi) - \frac{n}{2}\ln\sigma^2 + (\lambda - 1)\sum_{i=1}^{n}\ln y_i - \frac{1}{2\sigma^2}\sum_{i=1}^{n}\left(y_i^{(\lambda)} - \boldsymbol{\beta}'\mathbf{x}_i^{(\lambda)}\right)^2. \qquad \textbf{(10-39)}$$

[22]Two useful references on this form of the model are Spitzer (1982a, 1982b). See also Poirier (1978b), Poirier and Melino (1978), and Draper and Cox (1969) for discussion of the implications of this more general model for the allowable values of y. Note that in view of (10-39), y must be positive, and as such, the normality assumption cannot hold exactly. See Poirier and Melino (1978).

As a first step, we "concentrate" the log-likelihood. The maximum likelihood estimator of σ^2 will be the average squared residual. By inserting this result in (10-39), we see that at the maximum of the log-likelihood, the last term will be $-n/2$. So the log-likelihood will collapse to

$$\ln L_c = (\lambda - 1)\sum_i \ln y_i - \frac{n}{2}[\ln(2\pi) + 1] - \frac{n}{2}\ln \hat{\sigma}^2. \tag{10-40}$$

The maximum likelihood estimates of λ and $\boldsymbol{\beta}$ are computed by maximizing this function. The estimate of σ^2 will be a by-product and need not be considered separately. Now, since there is still only one value of λ to be found, we can use the same one-dimensional grid search used in Examples 10.8 and 10.10. It must be remembered, however, that the criterion function is not $S(\boldsymbol{\beta}, \lambda)$ but

$$\ln L_c = (\lambda - 1)\sum_i \ln y_i - \frac{n}{2}[\ln(2\pi) + 1] - \frac{n}{2}\ln\left(\frac{S(\boldsymbol{\beta}, \lambda)}{n}\right).^{23} \tag{10-41}$$

After searching for the appropriate λ, it is necessary to correct the least squares standard errors. The appropriate estimate of the asymptotic covariance matrix for the maximum likelihood estimates was presented in Chapter 4. For this model, the second derivatives of the log-likelihood are quite cumbersome.[24] The estimator of the asymptotic covariance matrix for the maximum likelihood presented by Berndt et al. (1974) is much more convenient. The advantage of this estimator is that it only requires us to compute the first derivatives.[25] For the Box–Cox model,

$$\begin{aligned}\ln f(y_i, \lambda) = (\lambda - 1)\ln y_i &- \frac{1}{2}\ln 2\pi \\ &- \frac{1}{2}\ln \sigma^2 - \frac{1}{2\sigma^2}(y_i^{(\lambda)} - \boldsymbol{\beta}'\mathbf{x}_i^{(\lambda)})^2.\end{aligned} \tag{10-42}$$

Upon using

$$\epsilon_i = y_i^{(\lambda)} - \boldsymbol{\beta}'\mathbf{x}_i^{(\lambda)},$$

the derivatives are

$$\begin{aligned}\frac{\partial \ln f(y_i)}{\partial \boldsymbol{\beta}} &= \frac{\epsilon_i}{\sigma^2}\mathbf{x}_i^{(\lambda)}, \\ \frac{\partial \ln f(y_i)}{\partial \lambda} &= \ln y_i - \frac{\epsilon_i}{\sigma^2}\left[\frac{\partial y_i^{(\lambda)}}{\partial \lambda} - \sum_{k=1}^{K} \beta_k \frac{\partial x_k^{(\lambda)}}{\partial \lambda}\right], \\ \frac{\partial \ln f(y_i)}{\partial \sigma^2} &= \frac{1}{2\sigma^2}\left[\frac{\epsilon_i^2}{\sigma^2} - 1\right].\end{aligned} \tag{10-43}$$

[23] A method of simplifying the search is suggested by Zarembka (1968).

[24] They are presented in full in Fomby et al. (1984, p. 429) and Greene (1995a).

[25] See also Spitzer (1984) and Blackley et al. (1984).

For the second of these,

$$\frac{\partial[z^\lambda - 1]/\lambda}{\partial\lambda} = \frac{\lambda z^\lambda \ln z - (z^\lambda - 1)}{\lambda^2} = \frac{1}{\lambda}(z^\lambda \ln z - z^{(\lambda)}).$$

(See Exercise 7.) The various parts are reasonably simple to compute. If we then let

$$\mathbf{w}_i = \begin{bmatrix} \partial \ln f(y_i)/\partial\boldsymbol{\beta} \\ \partial \ln f(y_i)/\partial\lambda \\ \partial \ln f(y_i)/\partial\sigma^2 \end{bmatrix}, \tag{10-44}$$

the estimator of the asymptotic covariance matrix for the maximum likelihood estimator is

$$\text{Est. Asy. Var}[\hat{\boldsymbol{\theta}}] = \left[\sum_{i=1}^{n} \hat{\mathbf{w}}_i \hat{\mathbf{w}}'\right]^{-1} = (\hat{\mathbf{W}}'\hat{\mathbf{W}})^{-1}, \tag{10-45}$$

where each row of $\hat{\mathbf{W}}$ is an observation $\hat{\mathbf{w}}_i'$ and $\boldsymbol{\theta}$ is the full parameter vector.

Note that the preceding differs from the procedure suggested in (10-34) in the inclusion of a row and a column for σ^2 in the covariance matrix. The difference arises because in the model that transforms y as well as $\mathbf{x}$ [i.e., (10-37) versus (10-33)], the Hessian of the log-likelihood is not block diagonal with respect to λ and σ^2. When y is transformed, the maximum likelihood estimates of λ and σ^2 are positively correlated, as both parameters reflect the scaling of the dependent variable in the model. This may seem a counterintuitive result. Consider the difference in the variance estimators that arises when a linear and a log-linear model are estimated. The variance of $\ln y$ around its mean is obviously different from that of y around its mean. These two models arise with different values of λ. By contrast, consider what happens when only the independent variables are transformed. The slope estimators vary accordingly, but in such a way that the variance of y around its conditional mean will stay constant.[26]

EXAMPLE 10.10 A More General Money Demand Equation (Continued)

The model of Example 10.10 treats y and $\mathbf{x}$ asymmetrically in that there $\theta = 0$, whereas the estimate of λ that was used was 0.45. By using the criterion in (10-36) instead and scanning over the range of -2 to $+2$, we find the maximum likelihood estimate of λ to be -0.35. At this estimate, least squares regression gives the results shown in Table 10.14. The standard errors are computed using the Berndt et al. estimator.[27] For illustration, those computed (incorrectly) by least squares are also shown in parentheses.

---

[26]See Seaks and Layson (1983).

[27]Spitzer (1984) discusses using BHHH versus the Hessian to estimate the asymptotic covariance matrix. His main conclusion (which is, fortunately, incorrect) is that the Hessian is more "accurate." He also neglects to include $\hat{\sigma}^2$ among the estimated parameters.

TABLE 10.14 Estimated Money Demand Equation

	Estimate	*Standard Error*		*t ratio*
Constant	−11.170	3.1515	(0.7830)	−3.177
r	−0.005689	0.021017	(0.0159)	−0.271
Y	5.1437	1.1260	(0.2988)	4.568

In this more general model, the analog to the elasticity computed in Example 10.10 is

$$\frac{d \ln y}{d \ln x} = \beta\left(\frac{x}{y}\right)^{\lambda}. \qquad \textbf{(10-46)}$$

To compute these values, we once again use the mean values of the regressors. For the values of y, we must compute a fitted value at these means. Assuming that $\epsilon = E(\epsilon) = 0$,

$$\mathbf{b}'\overline{\mathbf{x}}^{(\lambda)} = \hat{y}^{(\lambda)} = \frac{\hat{y}^{(\lambda)} - 1}{\lambda},$$

we can then obtain the predicted value by inverting this function:

$$\hat{y} = [\lambda\{\mathbf{b}'\overline{\mathbf{x}}^{(\lambda)}\} + 1]^{1/\lambda}. \qquad \textbf{(10-47)}$$

At the means of the independent variables, the two elasticities are −0.03289 for r and 3.6769 for Y, which, once again, are quite comparable with those obtained with the log-linear model (−0.03157 and 3.65628).

10.4.3. A Test for (Log-) Linearity

Given the unrestricted estimates of $\boldsymbol{\beta}$, λ, and σ^2, a model that is linear ($\lambda = 1$) or log-linear ($\lambda = 0$) is a simple parametric restriction and can be tested with a likelihood ratio statistic. The test statistic, as usual, is

$$\text{chi-squared}(1) = -2[\ln L(\lambda = 1 \text{ or } 0) - \ln L(\lambda = \text{MLE})]. \qquad \textbf{(10-48)}$$

This will have a chi-squared distribution with one degree of freedom and can be referred to the standard table. Using the estimate of λ and its standard error, we could also carry out a t test (actually, a Wald test) of the hypothesis that $\lambda = 0$. An alternative Lagrange multiplier test is derived in Example 10.12.

It is not appropriate to test the linear model as an alternative to the log-linear model in this fashion. The models are not nested and neither estimate (0 or 1) is an MLE. As such, this test is not a likelihood ratio test. (There is nothing to prevent the chi-squared statistic from being negative, which should suggest that there is something amiss with this "test.") It is tempting to use the two log-likelihoods in a heuristic fashion to choose between them, but it should be remembered that except for the classical regression model, maximum likelihood is not a fitting criterion; that is, it does not maximize the fit. As such, choosing between estimators on this basis will not necessarily improve the model.

EXAMPLE 10.11 Test for Linearity

For the money demand data, the three relevant log-likelihood values are

$$\begin{aligned}\ln L(-0.35) &= -116.51,\\ \ln L(0) &= -118.073,\\ \ln L(1) &= -130.133.\end{aligned}$$

With 20 observations, the two chi-squared test statistics are

$$\begin{aligned}\text{linearity:}\quad &-2[-130.133-(-116.51)] = 27.25,\\ \text{log-linearity:}\quad &-2[-118.073-(-116.51)] = 3.13.\end{aligned}$$

Linearity is rejected, but the log-linear model is not rejected at the 5 percent significance level. The critical value from the table is 3.84.

10.5. HYPOTHESIS TESTING AND PARAMETRIC RESTRICTIONS

In most cases, the sorts of hypotheses one would test in this context will involve fairly simple linear restrictions. The tests can be carried out using the usual formulas discussed in Chapter 7 and the asymptotic covariance matrix presented earlier. For more involved hypotheses and for nonlinear restrictions, the procedures are a bit less clear-cut. Three principal testing procedures were discussed in Chapter 4: the Wald, likelihood ratio, and Lagrange multiplier test. For the linear model, we found that all three statistics were transformations of the standard F statistic, so that the tests are essentially identical. In the nonlinear case, they are equivalent only asymptotically. We will work through each of these tests for the general case and then apply them to the example of the previous section.

The hypothesis to be tested is

$$H_0: \mathbf{R}(\boldsymbol{\beta}) = \mathbf{q}. \tag{10-49}$$

These may be any kind of restriction, linear or nonlinear. It is necessary, however, that they be **overidentifying restrictions.** This means, in formal terms, that if the original parameter vector has K free elements, the hypothesis $\mathbf{R}(\boldsymbol{\beta}) = \mathbf{q}$ must impose at least one functional relationship on the parameters. If there is more than one restriction, they must be functionally independent. These two conditions imply that the $J \times K$ matrix

$$\mathbf{C} = \frac{\partial \mathbf{R}(\boldsymbol{\beta})}{\partial \boldsymbol{\beta}'} \tag{10-50}$$

must have full row rank and that J, the number of restrictions, must be strictly less than K. (This is analogous to the linear model, in which $\mathbf{C}$ would be the matrix of coefficients in the restrictions.)

Let $\mathbf{b}$ be the unrestricted, nonlinear least squares estimator, and let $\mathbf{b}_*$ be the estimator obtained when the constraints of the hypothesis are imposed.[28] All the test statistics to be considered here are the same asymptotically. Therefore, which test statistic one uses depends on how difficult the computations are. Unlike the linear model, the various testing procedures vary in complexity. For instance, in our example, the Lagrange multiplier is by far the simplest to compute. Of the four methods we will consider, only this test does not require us to compute a nonlinear regression.

10.5.1. An Asymptotically Valid F Test

The nonlinear analog to the familiar F statistic based on the fit of the regression (i.e., the sum of squared residuals) would be

$$F[J, n - K] = \frac{[S(\mathbf{b}_*) - S(\mathbf{b})]/J}{S(\mathbf{b})/(n - K)}. \qquad \textbf{(10-51)}$$

This has the appearance of our earlier F ratio. In the nonlinear setting, however, neither the numerator nor the denominator has exactly the necessary chi-squared distribution, so the F distribution is only approximate. Note that this F statistic requires that both the restricted and unrestricted models be estimated.

10.5.2. Wald Test

The Wald test is based on the distance between $\mathbf{R}(\mathbf{b})$ and $\mathbf{q}$. If the unrestricted estimates fail to satisfy the restrictions, doubt is cast on the validity of the restrictions. The statistic is

$$\begin{aligned} W &= [\mathbf{R}(\mathbf{b}) - \mathbf{q}]'\{\text{Est. Asy. Var}[\mathbf{R}(\mathbf{b}) - \mathbf{q}]\}^{-1}[\mathbf{R}(\mathbf{b}) - \mathbf{q}] \\ &= [\mathbf{R}(\mathbf{b}) - \mathbf{q}]'\{\mathbf{C}\hat{\mathbf{V}}\mathbf{C}'\}^{-1}[\mathbf{R}(\mathbf{b}) - \mathbf{q}], \end{aligned} \qquad \textbf{(10-52)}$$

where

$$\hat{\mathbf{V}} = \text{Est. Asy. Var}[\mathbf{b}].$$

This is a chi-squared statistic with J degrees of freedom. Under the null hypothesis that the restrictions are correct, the Wald statistic and J times the F statistic are asymptotically equivalent. The Wald statistic can be based on the estimated covariance matrix obtained earlier using the unrestricted estimates. This may provide a large savings in computing effort if the restrictions are nonlinear.

---

[28] This may be an extremely difficult computational problem in its own right, especially if the constraints are nonlinear. We assume that the estimator has been obtained by whatever means is necessary.

The caveat about Wald statistics that applied in the linear case applies here as well. Because it is a pure significance test that does not involve the alternative hypothesis, the Wald statistic is not invariant to how the hypothesis is framed. In cases in which there are more than one equivalent ways to specify $\mathbf{R}(\boldsymbol{\beta}) = \mathbf{q}$, W can give very different answers depending on which is chosen.

10.5.3. Likelihood Ratio Test

The log-likelihood for a sample of n observations, assuming normally distributed disturbances, is

$$\ln L = \text{Jacobian} - \frac{n}{2}\ln(2\pi\sigma^2) - \frac{\epsilon'\epsilon}{2\sigma^2}. \tag{10-53}$$

Letting $\ln L^*$ be the log-likelihood evaluated at the restricted estimates, the likelihood ratio statistic for testing the restrictions is

$$\lambda = -2(\ln L^* - \ln L). \tag{10-54}$$

This statistic is asymptotically distributed as chi-squared with J degrees of freedom. For the present, assume that there is no Jacobian term in L. In each case, the maximum likelihood estimate of σ^2 is $\mathbf{e}'\mathbf{e}/n$, so the log-likelihood computed at the least squares estimates is

$$\ln L = -\frac{n}{2}\left[1 + \ln(2\pi) + \ln\left(\frac{\mathbf{e}'\mathbf{e}}{n}\right)\right] \tag{10-55}$$

and likewise for the restricted estimates. This is easily computed using only the sum of squared residuals. After collecting terms, the likelihood ratio statistic for a classical regression model (linear or nonlinear) is

$$\begin{aligned}\lambda &= n(\ln \hat{\sigma}_*^2 - \ln \hat{\sigma}^2)\\ &= n\ln(\hat{\sigma}_*^2/\hat{\sigma}^2).\end{aligned} \tag{10-56}$$

Like the earlier F statistic, the likelihood ratio statistic requires both restricted and unrestricted estimates.

10.5.4. Lagrange Multiplier Test

The Lagrange multiplier test is based on the decrease in the sum of squared residuals that would result if the restrictions in the restricted model were released. The formalities of the test are given in Section 4.9.3c. For the nonlinear regression model, the test has a particularly appealing form.[29] Let $\mathbf{e}_*$ be the vector of residuals $y_i - h(\mathbf{x}_i, \mathbf{b}_*)$ computed using the restricted estimates. Recall that we defined $\mathbf{X}^0$ as an $n \times K$ matrix of derivatives computed at a particular parameter vector in (10-9). Let $\mathbf{X}_*^0$ be this matrix *computed at the restricted*

[29]This is derived in Judge et al. (1985).

estimates. Then the Lagrange multiplier statistic for the nonlinear regression model is

$$\text{LM} = \frac{\mathbf{e}_*'\mathbf{X}_*^0[\mathbf{X}_*^{0\prime}\mathbf{X}_*^0]^{-1}\mathbf{X}_*^{0\prime}\mathbf{e}_*}{\mathbf{e}_*'\mathbf{e}_*/n}. \qquad \textbf{(10-57)}$$

This is asymptotically distributed as a chi-squared statistic with J degrees of freedom. What is especially appealing about this approach is that it requires only the restricted estimates. This may provide some savings in computing effort if, as in our example, the restrictions result in a linear model. Note, also, that the Lagrange multiplier statistic is n times the uncentered R^2 in the regression of $\mathbf{e}_*$ on $\mathbf{X}_*^0$. Many Lagrange multiplier statistics are computed in this fashion.

EXAMPLE 10.12 Lagrange Multiplier Tests for the Box–Cox Model

For simplicity, we first consider the basic model

$$\begin{aligned} y &= \beta_1 + \beta_2 \frac{x^\lambda - 1}{\lambda} + \epsilon \\ &= f(x, \beta_1, \beta_2, \lambda) + \epsilon. \end{aligned}$$

(For convenience, we have dropped the observation subscript.) We consider a Lagrange multiplier test of the hypothesis that λ equals zero. The pseudoregressors are

$$\begin{aligned} x_1^* &= \frac{\partial f(.)}{\partial \beta_1} = 1, \\ x_2^* &= \frac{\partial f(.)}{\partial \beta_2} = \frac{x^\lambda - 1}{\lambda}, \\ x_3^* &= \frac{\partial f(.)}{\partial \lambda} = \beta_2 \frac{\lambda(\ln x)x^\lambda - x^\lambda + 1}{\lambda^2}. \end{aligned}$$

The test is carried out by first regressing y on a constant and $\ln x$ (i.e., the regressor evaluated at $\lambda = 0$) and then computing nR_*^2 in the regression of the residuals from this first regression on x_1^*, x_2^*, and x_3^*, also evaluated at $\lambda = 0$. The first and second of these are 1 and $\ln x$. To obtain the third, we use the following approach. We require

$$x_{3|\lambda=0}^* = \beta_2 \lim_{\lambda \to 0} \frac{\partial x^{(\lambda)}}{\partial \lambda}.$$

The limit can be obtained thusly:

$$\lim_{\lambda \to 0} \frac{\partial x^{(\lambda)}}{\partial \lambda} = \lim_{\lambda \to 0} \left[\frac{x^\lambda \ln x - x^{(\lambda)}}{\lambda} \right].$$

Now applying L'Hôpital's rule to the right-hand side, differentiate numerator and denominator with respect to λ:

$$\lim_{\lambda\to 0}\frac{\partial x^{(\lambda)}}{\partial\lambda} = \lim_{\lambda\to 0}\left[x^{\lambda}(\ln x)^2 - \frac{\partial x^{(\lambda)}}{\partial\lambda}\right].$$

The limit of the derivative appears on both sides of the equals sign. Collect the two on the left, then divide by 2, to obtain

$$\lim_{\lambda\to 0}\frac{\partial x^{(\lambda)}}{\partial\lambda} = \tfrac{1}{2}\lim_{\lambda\to 0} x^{\lambda}(\ln x)^2 = \tfrac{1}{2}(\ln x)^2.$$[30]

Therefore,

$$\lim_{\lambda\to 0} x_3^* = \beta_2[\tfrac{1}{2}(\ln x)^2].$$

Thus, the Lagrange multiplier test is carried out in two steps. First, we regress $\ln y$ on a constant and $\ln x$ and compute the residuals. Second, we regress these residuals on a constant, $\ln x$, and $b_2(\frac{1}{2}\ln^2 x)$, where b_2 is the coefficient on $\ln x$ in the first regression. The Lagrange multiplier statistic is nR^2 from the second regression. The generalization to several regressors is immediate. In the first regression, we would use the logs of all the regressors. The additional regressor for the second regression would be

$$x_\lambda^* = \sum_{k=1}^{K} b_k(\tfrac{1}{2}\ln^2 x_k),$$

where the sum is taken over all the variables that are transformed in the original model and the b_k's are the least squares coefficients in the first regression.

For an example, consider the Box–Cox model of Example 10.10. The model is

$$\ln M = \alpha + \beta_r r^{(\lambda)} + \beta_Y Y^{(\lambda)} + \epsilon.$$

To carry out the Wald test, we use the square of the ratio of $\hat{\lambda}$ to its estimated standard error as a chi-squared statistic with one degree of freedom. This is $(0.47/0.5467)^2 = 0.7391$. For the likelihood ratio test, we use (10-56). With $\lambda = 0.47$, the sum of squared residuals is 0.1272. With $\lambda = 0$, we obtain the sum of squared residuals in the regression of $\ln M$ on a constant, $\ln r$, and $\ln Y$, which is 0.13196. Therefore, the likelihood ratio statistic is $20\ \ln\{(0.13196/20)/(0.1272/20)\} = 0.7342$. Finally, for the Lagrange multiplier test, we first regress $\ln M$ on a constant, $\ln r$, and $\ln Y$ and compute the residuals, $\mathbf{e}_*$. The R^2 in the regression of $\mathbf{e}_*$ on a constant, $\ln r$, $\ln Y$, and $[b_r(\frac{1}{2}\ln^2 r) + b_Y(\frac{1}{2}\ln^2 Y)]$ is 0.03613, so the Lagrange multiplier test statistic is $20(0.03613) = 0.7226$. None of these is larger than the tabled critical value, so the hypothesis that $\lambda = 0$ is not rejected.

---

[30] See Exercise 7 for an extension to higher derivatives.

By extending this to the model of (10-37), we can devise a bona fide test of log-linearity (against the more general model, not linearity).[31] The log-likelihood for the model

$$\frac{y^\lambda - 1}{\lambda} = \beta_1 + \beta_2 \frac{x^\lambda - 1}{\lambda} + \epsilon$$

is given in (10-39). The first derivatives are obtained in (10-42) to (10-44). Using the Berndt et al. estimator given in (10-45), we can construct the Lagrange multiplier statistic as

$$\text{LM} = \chi^2[1] = \left(\sum_{i=1}^{n} \hat{\mathbf{w}}_i\right)' \left[\sum_{i=1}^{n} \hat{\mathbf{w}}_i \hat{\mathbf{w}}_i'\right]^{-1} \left(\sum_{i=1}^{n} \hat{\mathbf{w}}_i\right),$$

where, for the preceding model, we would compute the various terms at $\lambda = 0$. Thus,

$$\hat{\epsilon}_i = \ln y_i - \hat{\beta}_1 - \hat{\beta}_2 \ln x_i,$$

$\hat{\beta}_1$ and$\hat{\beta}_2$ are computed by the least squares regression of y on a constant and x, and

$$\hat{\sigma}^2 = \frac{1}{n} \sum_{i=1}^{n} \hat{\epsilon}_i^2.$$

Let

$$\hat{\epsilon}_i^* = \tfrac{1}{2} \ln^2 y_i - \hat{\beta}_2 (\tfrac{1}{2} \ln^2 x_i).$$

[See (10-43).] Then

$$\hat{\mathbf{w}}_i = \begin{bmatrix} \hat{\epsilon}_i / \hat{\sigma}^2 \\ (\ln x_i)\hat{\epsilon}_i / \hat{\sigma}^2 \\ \ln y_i - \hat{\epsilon}_i \hat{\epsilon}_i^* / \hat{\sigma}^2 \\ (\hat{\epsilon}_i^2 / \hat{\sigma}^2 - 1)/(2\hat{\sigma}^2) \end{bmatrix}.$$

If there are k regressors in the model, the second component in $\hat{\mathbf{w}}_i$ will be a vector containing the logs of the variables, whereas ϵ_i^* in the third becomes

$$\hat{\epsilon}_i^* = \frac{1}{2} \ln^2 y_i - \sum_{k=1}^{K} \hat{\beta}_k \left(\frac{1}{2} \ln^2 x_{ik}\right).$$

The usefulness of this approach for either of the models we have examined is that in testing the hypothesis, it is not necessary to compute the nonlinear, unrestricted, Box–Cox regression.

EXAMPLE 10.13 Hypotheses Tests in a Nonlinear Regression Model

For a second example, we test the hypothesis $H_0: \gamma = 1$ in the consumption function of Example 10.3.

---

[31]This test was proposed by Davidson and MacKinnon (1985). They also suggested a test of linearity based on the same methodology by using $\lambda = 1$ instead of $\lambda = 0$ in the computations just described.

- **F statistic.** The F statistic is computed in the usual fashion:

$$F[1, 36 - 3] = \frac{(12{,}068 - 8421.95)/1}{8421.95/(36 - 3)} = 14.286.$$

The critical value from the tables is 4.18, so the hypothesis is rejected.

- **Wald statistic.** For our example, this is based on the distance of $\hat{\gamma}$ from 1 and is simply the square of the asymptotic t ratio we computed at the end of the example:

$$W = \frac{(1.1535 - 1)^2}{0.001541} = 15.290.$$

The critical value from the chi-squared table is 3.84.

- **Likelihood ratio.** For the example, $\mathbf{e}'\mathbf{e}$ is 8421.95, whereas $\mathbf{e}_*'\mathbf{e}_*$ is 12,068. With $n = 36$, this yields

$$\lambda = 36(5.8147 - 5.4551) = 12.9456.$$

This is also larger than the tabled critical value. Note, however, that it is noticeably less than the Wald statistic. It is possible that the two different statistics could lead to different inferences. Unfortunately, this is a problem that can arise in a finite sample, and there is no formal result that mandates which is the better to choose.[32]

- **Lagrange multiplier.** For our example, the elements in $\mathbf{x}_i^*$ are

$$\mathbf{x}_i^* = [1, Y^{\gamma}, \beta\gamma Y^{\gamma} \ln Y].$$

To compute this at the restricted estimates, we use the ordinary least squares estimates for α and β and 1 for γ so that

$$\mathbf{x}_i^* = [1, Y, \beta Y \ln Y].$$

The residuals are the least squares residuals computed from the linear regression. Inserting the values given earlier, we have

$$\text{LM} = \frac{3547.3}{12{,}068/36} = 10.582.$$

As expected, this statistic is also larger than the critical value from chi-squared table.

There is a large and growing literature on the use of these tests in econometrics. The emerging results have documented many ways to extend beyond the conventional t and F tests, particularly in the area of nonnested models. The Lagrange multiplier test has been shown to be especially convenient in gathering under a broad umbrella an impressive variety of already familiar tests.[33]

---

[32]There is some evidence, although no prescription, on this problem in Berndt and Savin (1977).

[33]Some useful references are Buse (1982), Pagan and Hall (1983), Engle (1984), Breusch and Pagan (1980), and Godfrey (1988).

EXERCISES

1. Describe how to obtain nonlinear least squares estimates of the parameters of the model
$$y = \alpha x^{\beta} + \epsilon.$$
2. Use MacKinnon et. al's P_E test to determine whether a linear or log-linear production model is more appropriate for the data in Table 7.1. (The test is described in Section 10.2.4 and Example 10.5.)
3. Using the Box–Cox transformation, we may specify an alternative to the Cobb–Douglas model as
$$\ln Y = \alpha + \beta_k \frac{(K^{\lambda} - 1)}{\lambda} + \beta_l \frac{(L^{\lambda} - 1)}{\lambda} + \epsilon.$$
Using Zellner and Revankar's data in Table 10.9, estimate α, β_k, β_l, and λ by using the scanning method suggested in Section 10.4.1. (Do not forget to scale Y, K, and L by the number of establishments.) Use (10-34) to compute the appropriate asymptotic standard errors for your estimates. Compute the two output elasticities, $\partial \ln Y/\partial \ln K$ and $\partial \ln Y/\partial \ln L$, at the sample means of K and L. [Hint: $\partial \ln Y/\partial \ln K = K\partial \ln Y/\partial K$.] How do these estimates compare with the values given in Example 10.8? Finally, compute the estimates of economies of scale for the states shown in Example 10.8 and compare your estimates with the values given there.
4. For the model in Exercise 3, test the hypothesis that $\lambda = 0$ using a Wald test, a likelihood ratio test, and a Lagrange multiplier test. Note that the restricted model is the Cobb–Douglas log-linear model.
5. To extend Zellner and Revankar's model in a fashion similar to theirs, we can use the Box–Cox transformation for the dependent variable as well. Use the method of Section 10.4.2 (with $\theta = \lambda$) to repeat the study of the preceding two exercises. How do your results change?
6. Suppose that we wished to test the specification of Exercise 5 against that of Exercise 3. The models are not nested, so there is no obvious test. Indeed, they both use exactly the same parameters. One possibility is the following: Both models are special cases of (10-37). In Exercise 3, we assume that $\theta = 0$, whereas in Exercise 5, we impose $\theta = \lambda$. Thus, although it might seem otherwise, it is not obvious that Exercise 5 is a less restrictive or preferable model. One way to determine which model is preferable (albeit not a formal test) is to compare the log-likelihoods under the two specifications. This can be done directly, using the results already obtained. Somewhat more evidence can be obtained by estimating the unrestricted model. This requires a two-dimensional search for θ and λ. Estimate the unrestricted model, then carry out an analysis of the sort done in Example 10.11.

7. Verify the following differential equation, which applies to the Box–Cox transformation:

$$\frac{d^i x^{(\lambda)}}{d\lambda^i} = \left(\frac{1}{\lambda}\right)\left[x^{\lambda}(\ln x)^i - \frac{i d^{i-1} x^{(\lambda)}}{d\lambda^{i-1}}\right]. \tag{10-58}$$

Show that the limiting sequence for $\lambda = 0$ is

$$\lim_{\lambda \to 0} \frac{d^i x^{(\lambda)}}{d\lambda^i} = \frac{(\ln x)^{i+1}}{i+1}. \tag{10-59}$$

These results can be used to great advantage in deriving the actual second derivatives of the log-likelihood function for the Box–Cox model. [Hint: See Example 10.12.]

8. How would you estimate the asymptotic standard error of the estimator of the elasticity in (10-46) and (10-47)? If you have access to the necessary software, do this computation for the money demand equation.

CHAPTER 11

Nonspherical Disturbances, Generalized Regression, and GMM Estimation

11.1. INTRODUCTION

In Chapter 10, we extended the classical model introduced in Chapter 6 to allow the conditional mean to be a nonlinear function.[1] But we retained the important assumptions about the disturbances: that they be uncorrelated with each other and that they have a constant variance, conditioned on the independent variables. In this chapter, we extend the multiple regression model to disturbances that violate these classical assumptions. The **generalized linear regression model** is

$$\begin{aligned} \mathbf{y} &= \mathbf{X}\boldsymbol{\beta} + \boldsymbol{\epsilon}, \\ E[\boldsymbol{\epsilon}] &= \mathbf{0}, \\ E[\boldsymbol{\epsilon}\boldsymbol{\epsilon}'] &= \sigma^2\boldsymbol{\Omega}, \end{aligned} \tag{11-1}$$

where $\boldsymbol{\Omega}$ is a positive definite matrix. As we will examine briefly below, the extension of the model to nonlinearity is relatively minor in comparison with the variants considered here. For present purposes, we will retain the linear specification and refer to our model simply as the **generalized regression model.**

Two cases we shall consider in detail are **heteroscedasticity** and **autocorrelation.** Disturbances are heteroscedastic when they have different variances. Heteroscedasticity usually arises in cross-section data where the scale of the dependent variable and the explanatory power of the model tend to vary across observations. Microeconomic data such as expenditure surveys are typical. The disturbances are still assumed to be uncorrelated across observations, so $\sigma^2\boldsymbol{\Omega}$ would be

[1]Recall that our difinition of nonlinearity pertains to the estimation method required to obtain the parameter estimates, not to the way that they enter the regression function.

$$\sigma^2\mathbf{\Omega} = \begin{bmatrix} \sigma_1^2 & 0 & \cdots & 0 \\ 0 & \sigma_2^2 & \cdots & 0 \\ & & \vdots & \\ 0 & 0 & \cdots & \sigma_n^2 \end{bmatrix}.$$

Autocorrelation is usually found in time-series data. Economic time series often display a "memory" in that variation around the regression function is not independent from one period to the next. The seasonally adjusted price and quantity series published by government agencies are examples. The adjustment is done to smooth out unusual movements in the data and, as such, makes the current observation dependent on what was typical in the past. But a series of unusually high or low values will be carried forward to the adjustment of later data points as well. Time-series data are usually homoscedastic, so $\sigma^2\mathbf{\Omega}$ might be

$$\sigma^2\mathbf{\Omega} = \sigma^2\begin{bmatrix} 1 & \rho_1 & \cdots & \rho_{n-1} \\ \rho_1 & 1 & \cdots & \rho_{n-2} \\ & & \vdots & \\ \rho_{n-1} & \rho_{n-2} & \cdots & 1 \end{bmatrix}.$$

The values that appear off the diagonal depend on the model used for the disturbance. In most cases, consistent with the notion of a fading memory, the values decline as we move away from the diagonal.

In recent studies, **panel data** sets, consisting of cross sections observed at several points in time, have exhibited both characteristics. We shall consider them in Chapter 14. This chapter presents some general results for this extended model. The next three chapters examine in detail specific types of generalized regression models.

Our earlier results for the classical model will have to be modified. We first consider the consequences of this more general formula for the least squares estimator. In subsequent sections, we will be interested in both appropriate estimation techniques and procedures for testing for the failure of the classical assumptions. We shall consider their general theoretical aspects in this chapter and then examine each topic in detail in Chapters 12 through 14.

11.2. CONSEQUENCES FOR LEAST SQUARES ESTIMATION

The essential results for the classical model with **spherical** disturbances

$$E[\boldsymbol{\epsilon}] = \mathbf{0}$$

and

$$E[\boldsymbol{\epsilon}\boldsymbol{\epsilon}'] = \sigma^2\mathbf{I} \quad \textbf{(11-2)}$$

are presented in Chapters 6 through 10. To reiterate, we found that the **ordinary least squares (OLS) estimator**

$$\begin{aligned}\mathbf{b} &= (\mathbf{X}'\mathbf{X})^{-1}\mathbf{X}'\mathbf{y} \\ &= \boldsymbol{\beta} + (\mathbf{X}'\mathbf{X})^{-1}\mathbf{X}'\boldsymbol{\epsilon}\end{aligned} \qquad \textbf{(11-3)}$$

is best linear unbiased, consistent and asymptotically normally (CAN) distributed, and if the disturbances are normally distributed, asymptotically efficient among all CAN estimators. We now consider which of these properties continue to hold in the model of (11-1).

To summarize, least squares and the other estimators we have examined retain only some of their desirable properties in this model. Least squares remains unbiased, consistent, and asymptotically normally distributed. It will, however, no longer be efficient—this remains to be verified—and the usual inference procedures are no longer appropriate, however. Nonlinear least squares and instrumental variables likewise remain consistent, but once again, the extension of the model brings about some changes in our earlier results concerning the asymptotic distributions. We will consider these cases in detail.

11.2.1. Finite-Sample Properties of Ordinary Least Squares

By taking expectations on both sides of (11-3), we find that if $E[\boldsymbol{\epsilon}\,|\,\mathbf{X}] = \mathbf{0}$, then

$$E[\mathbf{b}] = E_{\mathbf{X}}[E[\mathbf{b}\,|\,\mathbf{X}]] = \boldsymbol{\beta}. \qquad \textbf{(11-4)}$$

Therefore, we have the following theorem.

Theorem 11.1: Finite Sample Properties of b in the Generalized Regression Model. *If the regressors and disturbances are uncorrelated, then the unbiasedness of least squares is unaffected by violations of assumption (11-2). The least squares estimator is unbiased in the generalized regression model. With nonstochastic regressors, or conditional on* **X**, *the sampling variance of the least squares estimator is*

$$\begin{aligned}\text{Var}[\mathbf{b}\,|\,\mathbf{X}] &= E[(\mathbf{b}-\boldsymbol{\beta})(\mathbf{b}-\boldsymbol{\beta})'\,|\,\mathbf{X}] \\ &= E[(\mathbf{X}'\mathbf{X})^{-1}\mathbf{X}'\boldsymbol{\epsilon}\boldsymbol{\epsilon}'\mathbf{X}(\mathbf{X}'\mathbf{X})^{-1}\,|\,\mathbf{X}] \\ &= (\mathbf{X}'\mathbf{X})^{-1}\mathbf{X}'(\sigma^2\boldsymbol{\Omega})\mathbf{X}(\mathbf{X}'\mathbf{X})^{-1} \\ &= \frac{\sigma^2}{n}\left(\frac{1}{n}\mathbf{X}'\mathbf{X}\right)^{-1}\left(\frac{1}{n}\mathbf{X}'\boldsymbol{\Omega}\mathbf{X}\right)\left(\frac{1}{n}\mathbf{X}'\mathbf{X}\right)^{-1}.\end{aligned} \qquad \textbf{(11-5)}$$

If the regressors are stochastic, as before, the unconditional variance is $E[\text{Var}[\mathbf{b}\,|\,\mathbf{X}]]$. In (11-3), **b** *is a linear function of* $\boldsymbol{\epsilon}$. *Therefore, if* $\boldsymbol{\epsilon}$ *is normally distributed,*

$$\mathbf{b} \sim N[\boldsymbol{\beta}, \sigma^2(\mathbf{X}'\mathbf{X})^{-1}(\mathbf{X}'\boldsymbol{\Omega}\mathbf{X})(\mathbf{X}'\mathbf{X})^{-1}].$$

The end result is that **b** has properties that are similar to those in the classical regression case. Since the variance of the least squares estimator is not $\sigma^2(\mathbf{X}'\mathbf{X})^{-1}$, however, any inference based on $s^2(\mathbf{X}'\mathbf{X})^{-1}$ is likely to be misleading. Not only is this the wrong matrix to be used, but s^2 may be a biased estimator of σ^2. There is usually no way to know whether $\sigma^2(\mathbf{X}'\mathbf{X})^{-1}$ is larger or smaller than the true variance of $\mathbf{b}$, so even with a good estimate of σ^2, the conventional estimator of Var[$\mathbf{b}$] may not be particularly useful. Finally, since we have dispensed with the fundamental underlying assumption, the familiar inference procedures based on the F and t distributions will no longer be appropriate. One issue we will explore at several points below is how badly one is likely to go awry if the result in (11-5) is ignored and if the use of the familiar procedures based on $s^2(\mathbf{X}'\mathbf{X})^{-1}$ is continued.

11.2.2. Asymptotic Properties of Least Squares

If Var[$\mathbf{b}$] converges to zero, $\mathbf{b}$ is consistent. With well-behaved regressors, $(\mathbf{X}'\mathbf{X}/n)^{-1}$ will converge to a constant matrix, and the leading scalar σ^2/n will converge to 0. But $\mathbf{X}'\boldsymbol{\Omega}\mathbf{X}/n$ need not converge at all. If it does, ordinary least squares is consistent as well as unbiased.

Theorem 11.2: Consistency of OLS in the Generalized Regression Model. *If* plim$(\mathbf{X}'\mathbf{X}/n)$ *and* plim$(\mathbf{X}'\boldsymbol{\Omega}\mathbf{X}/n)$ *are both finite positive definite matrices,* $\mathbf{b}$ *is consistent for* $\boldsymbol{\beta}$. *Under the assumed conditions,*

$$\text{plim}\,\mathbf{b} = \boldsymbol{\beta}. \tag{11-6}$$

The conditions in (11-6) depend on both $\mathbf{X}$ and $\boldsymbol{\Omega}$. An alternative formula[2] that separates the two components is as follows. Ordinary least squares is consistent in the generalized regression model if:

1. The smallest characteristic root of $\mathbf{X}'\mathbf{X}$ increases without bound as $n \to \infty$. This implies that plim$(\mathbf{X}'\mathbf{X})^{-1} = \mathbf{0}$. If the regressors satisfy the Grenander conditions **G1** through **G3** of Section 6.7.2, they will meet this requirement.
2. The largest characteristic root of $\boldsymbol{\Omega}$ is finite for all n. For the heteroscedastic model, the variances are the characteristic roots, so this requires them to be finite. For models with autocorrelation, this requires that the elements of $\boldsymbol{\Omega}$ be finite and that the off-diagonal elements not be too large relative to the diagonal elements. We will examine this condition at several points below.

EXAMPLE 11.1 A Model in Which Ordinary Least Squares Is Inconsistent

Suppose that the regression model is $y = \mu + \epsilon$, where ϵ has a zero mean, constant variance, and equal correlation ρ across observations. Then

$$\boldsymbol{\Omega} = \begin{bmatrix} 1 & \rho & \rho & \cdots & \rho \\ \rho & 1 & \rho & \cdots & \rho \\ \rho & \rho & 1 & \cdots & \rho \\ & & & \vdots & \\ \rho & \rho & \rho & \cdots & 1 \end{bmatrix}.$$

[2] Amemiya (1985, p. 184).

The matrix $\mathbf{X}$ is a column of 1s, so the least squares estimator of μ is $\bar{y}$. Inserting this $\boldsymbol{\Omega}$ into (11-5), we obtain

$$\text{Var}[\bar{y}] = \frac{\sigma^2}{n}(1 - \rho + n\rho). \tag{11-7}$$

The limit of this expression is $\rho\sigma^2$, not zero. Although ordinary least squares is unbiased, it is not consistent. For this model, $\mathbf{X}'\boldsymbol{\Omega}\mathbf{X}/n = 1 + \rho(n - 1)$, which does not converge. Using (11-7) instead, $\mathbf{X}$ is a column of 1s, so $\mathbf{X}'\mathbf{X} = n$, a scalar, which satisfies condition 1. But the characteristic roots of $\boldsymbol{\Omega}$ are $(1 - \rho)$ with multiplicity $n - 1$ and $(1 - \rho + n\rho)$, which violates condition 2. The difficulty with the model in this example is essentially that there is too much correlation across observations. In time-series settings, we shall generally require that the timewise correlation of observations fade as the distance between them grows. That condition is not met here. This gives some suggestion of what sort of requirement we shall have to place upon the covariance matrix for autocorrelated disturbances discussed in the introduction to this chapter.

The least squares estimator is asymptotically normally distributed if the limiting distribution of

$$\sqrt{n}(\mathbf{b} - \boldsymbol{\beta}) = \left(\frac{\mathbf{X}'\mathbf{X}}{n}\right)^{-1}\frac{1}{\sqrt{n}}\mathbf{X}'\boldsymbol{\epsilon} \tag{11-8}$$

is normal. If $\text{plim}(\mathbf{X}'\mathbf{X}/n) = \mathbf{Q}$, the limiting distribution of the right-hand side is the same as that of

$$\begin{aligned}\mathbf{v} &= \mathbf{Q}^{-1}\frac{1}{\sqrt{n}}\mathbf{X}'\boldsymbol{\epsilon}\\ &= \mathbf{Q}^{-1}\frac{1}{\sqrt{n}}\sum_{i=1}^{n}\mathbf{x}_i\epsilon_i,\end{aligned} \tag{11-9}$$

where $\mathbf{x}_i'$ is a row of $\mathbf{X}$ (assuming, of course, that the limiting distribution exists at all). The question now is whether a central limit theorem can be applied directly to $\mathbf{v}$. If the disturbances are merely heteroscedastic and still uncorrelated, the answer is generally yes. In fact, we already showed this in Section 6.7.3 when we invoked the Lindberg–Feller central limit theorem. The theorem allows unequal variances in the sum. If $\mathbf{X}$ is nonstochastic, then the exact variance of the sum is

$$\text{Var}\left[\frac{1}{\sqrt{n}}\sum_{i=1}^{n}\mathbf{x}_i\epsilon_i\right] = \frac{1}{n}\sum_{i=1}^{n}\sigma^2\omega_i\mathbf{x}_i\mathbf{x}_i'.$$

If the regressors are stochastic, the counterpart is

$$E_{\mathbf{X}}\left[\text{Var}\left[\frac{1}{\sqrt{n}}\sum_{i=1}^{n}\mathbf{x}_i\epsilon_i\right]\Big|\,\mathbf{x}_i\right] = \frac{1}{n}\sum_{i=1}^{n}\sigma^2\omega_i\mathbf{Q}_i,$$

which, for our purposes, we would require to converge to a positive definite matrix. In our analysis of the classical model, the heterogeneity of the variances arose because of the regressors, but we still achieved the limiting normal distribution in (6-56) through (6-63). All that has changed here is that the variance of ϵ varies across observations *as well.* Therefore, *the proof of asymptotic normality in Section 6.7.3 is general enough to include this model without modification.* As long as $\mathbf{X}$ is well behaved and the diagonal elements of $\mathbf{\Omega}$ are finite and well behaved, the least squares estimator is asymptotically normally distributed, with the covariance matrix given in (11-5). That is:

> *In the heteroscedastic case, if the variances of ϵ_i are finite and are not dominated by any single term, so that the conditions of the Lindberg–Feller central limit theorem apply to* $\mathbf{v}$ *in (11-9), then the least squares estimator is asymptotically normally distributed with covariance matrix*

$$\text{Asy. Var}[\mathbf{b}] = \frac{\sigma^2}{n}\mathbf{Q}^{-1}\text{plim}\left(\frac{1}{n}\mathbf{X}'\mathbf{\Omega}\mathbf{X}\right)\mathbf{Q}^{-1}. \qquad \textbf{(11-10)}$$

For the most general case, asymptotic normality is much more difficult to establish because the sums in (11-9) are not necessarily sums of independent or even uncorrelated random variables. Nonetheless, Amemiya (1985, p. 187) and Anderson (1971) have shown the asymptotic normality of $\mathbf{b}$ in a model of autocorrelated disturbances general enough to include most of the settings we are likely to meet in practice. We can conclude that, except in particularly unfavorable cases, we have the following theorem.

THEOREM 11.3: Asymptotic Distribution of b in the GR Model. *If the regressors are sufficiently well behaved and the off-diagonal terms in* $\mathbf{\Omega}$ *diminish sufficiently rapidly, then the least squares estimator is asymptotically normally distributed with mean* $\boldsymbol{\beta}$ *and covariance matrix given in (11-10).*

There are two cases that remain to be considered, the nonlinear regression model and the instrumental variables estimator.

11.2.3. Asymptotic Properties of Nonlinear Least Squares

If the regression function is nonlinear, then the analysis of this section must be applied to the pseudoregressors $\mathbf{x}_i^0$ rather than the independent variables. Aside from this consideration, no new results are needed. We can just apply this discussion to the linearized regression model. Under most conditions, the results listed above apply to the nonlinear least squares estimator as well as the linear least squares estimator.[3]

[3]Davidson and MacKinnon (1993) consider this case at length.

11.2.4. Asymptotic Properties of the Instrumental Variables Estimator

The second estimator to be considered is the instrumental variables estimator that we considered in Sections 6.7.8 for the linear model and 10.2.5 for the non-linear model. We will confine our attention to the linear model. The nonlinear case can be obtained by applying our results to the linearized regression. To review, we considered cases in which the regressors $\mathbf{X}$ are correlated with the disturbances $\boldsymbol{\epsilon}$. If this is the case, as in the time-series models and the errors in variables models that we examined earlier, then $\mathbf{b}$ is neither unbiased nor consistent.[4] In the classical model, we constructed an estimator around a set of variables $\mathbf{Z}$ that were uncorrelated with $\boldsymbol{\epsilon}$,

$$\begin{aligned}\mathbf{b}_{\text{IV}} &= [\mathbf{X}'\mathbf{Z}(\mathbf{Z}'\mathbf{Z})^{-1}\mathbf{Z}'\mathbf{X}]^{-1}\mathbf{X}'\mathbf{Z}(\mathbf{Z}'\mathbf{Z})^{-1}\mathbf{Z}'\mathbf{y}\\ &= \boldsymbol{\beta} + [\mathbf{X}'\mathbf{Z}(\mathbf{Z}'\mathbf{Z})^{-1}\mathbf{Z}'\mathbf{X}]^{-1}\mathbf{X}'\mathbf{Z}(\mathbf{Z}'\mathbf{Z})^{-1}\mathbf{Z}'\boldsymbol{\epsilon}.\end{aligned}$$

Suppose that $\mathbf{X}$ and $\mathbf{Z}$ are well behaved in the sense discussed in Chapter 6. That is,

$$\text{plim}\,\frac{1}{n}\mathbf{Z}'\mathbf{Z} = \mathbf{Q}_{\mathbf{ZZ}},\ \text{a positive definite matrix,}$$

$$\text{plim}\,\frac{1}{n}\mathbf{Z}'\mathbf{X} = \mathbf{Q}_{\mathbf{ZX}} = \mathbf{Q}'_{\mathbf{XZ}},\text{a nonzero matrix,}$$

$$\text{plim}\,\frac{1}{n}\mathbf{X}'\mathbf{X} = \mathbf{Q}_{\mathbf{XX}},\ \text{a positive definite matrix.}$$

To avoid a string of matrix computations that may well not fit on a single line, for convenience let

$$\begin{aligned}\mathbf{Q}_{\mathbf{XX.Z}} &= [\mathbf{Q}_{\mathbf{XZ}}\mathbf{Q}_{\mathbf{ZZ}}^{-1}\mathbf{Q}_{\mathbf{ZX}}]^{-1}\mathbf{Q}_{\mathbf{XZ}}\mathbf{Q}_{\mathbf{ZZ}}^{-1}\\ &= \text{plim}\left[\left(\frac{1}{n}\mathbf{X}'\mathbf{Z}\right)\left(\frac{1}{n}\mathbf{Z}'\mathbf{Z}\right)^{-1}\left(\frac{1}{n}\mathbf{Z}'\mathbf{X}\right)\right]^{-1}\left(\frac{1}{n}\mathbf{X}'\mathbf{Z}\right)\left(\frac{1}{n}\mathbf{Z}'\mathbf{Z}\right)^{-1}.\end{aligned}$$

Then

$$\begin{aligned}\text{plim}\,\mathbf{b}_{\text{IV}} &= \boldsymbol{\beta} + \mathbf{Q}_{\mathbf{XX.Z}}\,\text{plim}\left(\frac{1}{n}\mathbf{Z}'\boldsymbol{\epsilon}\right)\\ &= \boldsymbol{\beta}\end{aligned}$$

if $\mathbf{Z}$ is a valid set of instrumental variables, that is, if the second term vanishes. This is exactly the result we had before. We might note that at the several points where we have established unbiasedness or consistency of the least squares or instrumental variables estimator, the covariance matrix of the disturbance matrix has played no role; it is a property of the means. As such, this

[4]It may be asymptotically normally distributed, but around a mean that differs from $\boldsymbol{\beta}$.

result should come as no surprise. The large sample behavior of $\mathbf{b}_{\text{IV}}$ depends on the behavior of

$$\mathbf{v}_n = \frac{1}{\sqrt{n}} \sum_{i=1}^{n} \mathbf{z}_i \epsilon_i .$$

This is exactly the result we analyzed in Section 6.7.8. If $\mathbf{v}_n$ converges to a limiting normal distribution, we will be able to construct the asymptotic distribution for $\mathbf{b}_{\text{IV}}$. This is the same set of conditions that was necessary for $\mathbf{X}$ when we considered $\mathbf{b}$ above, with $\mathbf{Z}$ in place of $\mathbf{X}$. We will once again rely on the results of Anderson (1971) or Amemiya (1985) that under very general conditions,

$$\frac{1}{\sqrt{n}} \sum_{i=1}^{n} \mathbf{z}_i \epsilon_i \xrightarrow{d} \sigma^2 \text{plim}\left(\frac{1}{n}\mathbf{Z}'\mathbf{\Omega}\mathbf{Z}\right).$$

With the other results already in hand, we now have the following.

Theorem 11.4: Asymptotic Distribution of the IV Estimator in the GR Model. *If the regressors and the instrumental variables are well behaved in the fashions discussed above, then*

$$\mathbf{b}_{\text{IV}} \xrightarrow{a} N[\boldsymbol{\beta}, \mathbf{V}_{\text{IV}}],$$

where

$$\mathbf{V}_{\text{IV}} = \frac{\sigma^2}{n}(\mathbf{Q}_{\mathbf{XX.Z}})^{-1} \text{plim}\left(\frac{1}{n}\mathbf{Z}'\mathbf{\Omega}\mathbf{Z}\right)(\mathbf{Q}'_{\mathbf{XX.Z}})^{-1}. \tag{11-11}$$

11.2.5. Robust Estimation of Asymptotic Covariance Matrices

There is a remaining question regarding all the preceding. In view of (11-5), is it necessary to discard ordinary least squares as an estimator? Certainly if $\mathbf{\Omega}$ is known, then, as shown in Section 11.3, there is a simple and efficient estimator available based on it, and the answer is yes. If $\mathbf{\Omega}$ is unknown but its structure is known and we can estimate $\mathbf{\Omega}$ using sample information, then the answer is less clear-cut. In many cases, basing estimation of $\boldsymbol{\beta}$ on some alternative procedure that uses an $\hat{\mathbf{\Omega}}$ will be preferable to ordinary least squares. This is the subject of Sections 11.4 and 11.5 and Chapters 12 to 15. The third possibility is that $\mathbf{\Omega}$ is completely unknown, both as to its structure and the specific values of its elements. In this situation, least squares or instrumental variables may be the only estimator available, and as such, the only available strategy is to try to devise an estimator for the appropriate asymptotic covariance matrix of $\mathbf{b}$.

If $\sigma^2\mathbf{\Omega}$ were known, the *estimator* of the asymptotic covariance matrix of $\mathbf{b}$ in (11-10) would be

$$\mathbf{V}_{\text{OLS}} = \frac{1}{n}\left(\frac{1}{n}\mathbf{X}'\mathbf{X}\right)^{-1}\left(\frac{1}{n}\mathbf{X}'[\sigma^2\mathbf{\Omega}]\mathbf{X}\right)\left(\frac{1}{n}\mathbf{X}'\mathbf{X}\right)^{-1}.$$

For the nonlinear least squares estimator, we replace $\mathbf{X}$ with $\mathbf{X}^0$. For the instrumental variables estimator, the left- and right-side matrices are replaced with this sample estimates of $\mathbf{Q}_{\mathbf{XX.Z}}$ and its transpose (using $\mathbf{X}^0$ again for the nonlinear instrumental variables estimator), and $\mathbf{Z}$ replaces $\mathbf{X}$ in the center matrix. In all these cases, the matrices of sums of squares and cross products in the left and right matrices are sample data that are readily estimable, and the problem is the center matrix that involves the unknown $\sigma^2\boldsymbol{\Omega}$. For estimation purposes, note that σ^2 is not a separate unknown parameter. Since $\boldsymbol{\Omega}$ is an unknown matrix, it can be scaled arbitrarily, say by κ, and with σ^2 scaled by $1/\kappa$, the same product remains. In our applications, we will remove the indeterminacy by assuming that $\text{tr}(\boldsymbol{\Omega}) = n$, as it is when $\sigma^2\boldsymbol{\Omega} = \sigma^2\mathbf{I}$ in the classical model. For now, just let

$$\boldsymbol{\Sigma} = \sigma^2\boldsymbol{\Omega}.$$

It might seem that to estimate $\left(\frac{1}{n}\mathbf{X}'\boldsymbol{\Sigma}\mathbf{X}\right)$, an estimator of $\boldsymbol{\Sigma}$, which contains $n(n+1)/2$ unknown parameters, is required. But fortunately (since with n observations, this is going to be hopeless), this is not quite right. What is required is an estimator of the $K(K+1)/2$ unknown elements in the matrix

$$\text{plim}\ \mathbf{Q}_* = \text{plim}\ \frac{1}{n}\sum_{i=1}^{n}\sum_{j=1}^{n}\sigma_{ij}\mathbf{x}_i\mathbf{x}_j'.$$

The point is that $\mathbf{Q}_*$ is a matrix of sums of squares and cross products that involves σ_{ij} *and* the rows of $\mathbf{X}$ (or $\mathbf{Z}$ or $\mathbf{X}^0$). The least squares estimator $\mathbf{b}$ is a consistent estimator of $\boldsymbol{\beta}$. This implies that the least squares residuals e_i are "pointwise" consistent estimators of their population counterparts ϵ_i. The general approach, then, will be to use $\mathbf{X}$ and $\mathbf{e}$ to devise an estimator of $\mathbf{Q}_*$.

Consider the heteroscedasticity case first. We seek an estimator of

$$\mathbf{Q}_* = \frac{1}{n}\sum_{i=1}^{n}\sigma_i^2\mathbf{x}_i\mathbf{x}_i'.$$

White (1980b) has shown that under very general conditions, the estimator

$$\mathbf{S}_0 = \frac{1}{n}\sum_{i=1}^{n}e_i^2\mathbf{x}_i\mathbf{x}_i' \qquad \textbf{(11-12)}$$

has

$$\text{plim}\ \mathbf{S}_0 = \text{plim}\ \mathbf{Q}_*.\text{[5]}$$

We can sketch a proof of this result using the results we obtained in Chapter 6.[6] Note first that $\mathbf{Q}_*$ is not a parameter matrix in itself. It is a weighted sum of the outer products of the rows of $\mathbf{X}$ (or $\mathbf{Z}$ for the instrumental variables case).

[5] See also Eicker (1967), Horn et al. (1975), and MacKinnon and White (1985).

[6] We will give only a broad sketch of the proof. Formal results appear in White (1980b) and (1983).

Thus, we seek not to "estimate" $\mathbf{Q}_*$, but to find a function of the sample data that will be arbitrarily close to this function of the population parameters as the sample size grows large. The distinction is important. We are not estimating the middle matrix in (11-10) or (11-11); we are attempting to construct a matrix from the sample data that will behave the same way that this matrix behaves. In essence, if $\mathbf{Q}_*$ converges to a finite positive matrix, then we would be looking for a function of the sample data that converges to the same matrix. Suppose that the true disturbances ϵ_i could be observed. Then each term in $\mathbf{Q}_*$ would equal $E[\epsilon_i^2 \mathbf{x}_i \mathbf{x}_i' \mid \mathbf{x}_i]$. With some fairly mild assumptions about $\mathbf{x}_i$, then, we could invoke a law of large numbers (see Theorems 6.16 through 6.18) to state that if $\mathbf{Q}_*$ has a probability limit, then

$$\text{plim}\, \frac{1}{n} \sum_{i=1}^{n} \sigma_i^2 \mathbf{x}_i \mathbf{x}_i' = \text{plim}\, \frac{1}{n} \sum_{i=1}^{n} \epsilon_i^2 \mathbf{x}_i \mathbf{x}_i'.$$

The final detail is to justify the transition from ϵ_i to e_i in $\mathbf{S}_0$. The consistency of $\mathbf{b}$ for $\boldsymbol{\beta}$ is sufficient for the argument. (Actually, residuals based on *any* consistent estimator of $\boldsymbol{\beta}$ would suffice for this estimator, but as of now, $\mathbf{b}$ or $\mathbf{b}_{\text{IV}}$ is the only one in hand.) The end result is that the **White heteroscedasticity consistent estimator**

$$\begin{aligned} \text{Est. Asy. Var}[\mathbf{b}] &= \frac{1}{n}\left(\frac{1}{n}\mathbf{X}'\mathbf{X}\right)^{-1}\left(\frac{1}{n}\sum_{i=1}^{n} e_i^2\, \mathbf{x}_i\mathbf{x}_i'\right)\left(\frac{1}{n}\mathbf{X}'\mathbf{X}\right)^{-1} \\ &= n(\mathbf{X}'\mathbf{X})^{-1}\mathbf{S}_0(\mathbf{X}'\mathbf{X})^{-1} \end{aligned} \qquad \textbf{(11-13)}$$

can be used to estimate the asymptotic covariance matrix of $\mathbf{b}$.

This is an extremely important and useful result.[7] It implies that without actually specifying the type of heteroscedasticity, we can still make appropriate inferences based on the results of least squares. This is especially useful if we are unsure of the precise nature of the heteroscedasticity (which is probably most of the time). We will pursue some examples in Chapter 12.

The extension of White's result to the more general case of autocorrelation is much more difficult. The natural counterpart for estimating

$$\mathbf{Q}_* = \frac{1}{n} \sum_{i=1}^{n} \sum_{j=1}^{n} \sigma_{ij} \mathbf{x}_i \mathbf{x}_i' \qquad \textbf{(11-14)}$$

would be

$$\hat{\mathbf{Q}}_* = \frac{1}{n} \sum_{i=1}^{n} \sum_{j=1}^{n} e_i e_j \mathbf{x}_i \mathbf{x}_j'.$$

But there are two problems with this estimator, one theoretical, which applies to $\mathbf{Q}_*$ as well, and one practical, which is specific to the latter.

[7]Further discussion and some refinements may be found in Cragg (1982). Cragg shows how White's observation can be extended to devise an estimator that improves on the efficiency of ordinary least squares.

Unlike the heteroscedasticity case, the matrix in (11-14) is $1/n$ times a sum of n^2 terms, so it is difficult to conclude yet that it will converge to anything at all. Note that this is precisely the result that arose in Example 11.1. This application is most likely to arise in a time series setting. In order to obtain convergence, it is necessary to assume that the terms involving unequal subscripts in (11-14) diminish in importance as n grows. A sufficient condition is that terms with subscript pairs $|i - j|$ grow smaller as the distance between them grows larger. In practical terms, this means that observation pairs are progressively less correlated as their separation in time grows. Intuitively, if one can think of weights with the diagonal elements getting a weight of 1.0, then in the sum, the weights in the sum grow smaller as we move away from the diagonal. If we think of the sum of the weights rather than just the number of terms, then this sum falls off so that as n grows large, the sum is of order n rather than n^2. Thus, we achieve convergence of $\mathbf{Q}_*$ by assuming that the rows of $\mathbf{X}$ are well behaved and that the correlations diminish with increasing separation in time.

The practical problem is that $\hat{\mathbf{Q}}_*$ need not be positive definite. Newey and West (1987a) have devised an estimator that overcomes this difficulty:

$$\hat{\mathbf{Q}}_* = \mathbf{S}_0 + \frac{1}{n}\sum_{l=1}^{L}\sum_{t=l+1}^{n} w_l e_t e_{t-l}(\mathbf{x}_t\mathbf{x}'_{t-l} + \mathbf{x}_{t-l}\mathbf{x}'_t),$$

$$w_l = \frac{l}{(L+1)}.$$

The **Newey–West autocorrelation consistent covariance estimator** is surprisingly simple and relatively easy to implement.[8] There is a final problem to be solved. It must be determined in advance how large L is to be. We will examine some special cases in Chapter 13, but in general, there is little theoretical guidance. Unfortunately, the result is not quite as crisp as that for the heteroscedasticity consistent estimator.

We have the result that $\mathbf{b}$ and $\mathbf{b}_{\text{IV}}$ are asymptotically normally distributed, and we have an appropriate estimator for the asymptotic covariance matrix. We have not specified the distribution of the disturbances, however. This means that for inference purposes, the F statistic is inappropriate. Moreover, for more involved hypotheses, the likelihood ratio and Lagrange multiplier tests are unavailable. That leaves the Wald statistic, including asymptotic "t ratios," as the main tool for statistical inference. We will examine a number of applications in the chapters to follow.

The White and Newey–West estimators are becoming ubiquitous in the econometrics literature and represent major advances in the set of available techniques. We will encounter them at many points in the discussion to follow.

---

[8]Both estimators are now standard features in modern econometrics computer programs.

11.3. EFFICIENT ESTIMATION

Efficient estimation of $\boldsymbol{\beta}$ in the generalized regression model requires knowledge of $\boldsymbol{\Omega}$. To begin, it is useful to consider cases in which $\boldsymbol{\Omega}$ is a known, symmetric, positive definite matrix. This will occasionally be true, but in most models, $\boldsymbol{\Omega}$ will contain unknown parameters that must also be estimated. We shall examine this problem in Section 11.4.

11.3.1. Generalized Least Squares (GLS)

Since $\boldsymbol{\Omega}$ is a positive definite symmetric matrix, it can be factored into

$$\boldsymbol{\Omega} = \mathbf{C}\boldsymbol{\Lambda}\mathbf{C}',$$

where the columns of $\mathbf{C}$ are the characteristic vectors of $\boldsymbol{\Omega}$ and the characteristic roots of $\boldsymbol{\Omega}$ are arrayed in the diagonal matrix $\boldsymbol{\Lambda}$. Let $\boldsymbol{\Lambda}^{1/2}$ be the diagonal matrix with ith diagonal element $\sqrt{\lambda_i}$, and let $\mathbf{T} = \mathbf{C}\boldsymbol{\Lambda}^{1/2}$. Then $\boldsymbol{\Omega} = \mathbf{T}\mathbf{T}'$. Also, let $\mathbf{P}' = \mathbf{C}\boldsymbol{\Lambda}^{-1/2}$, so $\boldsymbol{\Omega}^{-1} = \mathbf{P}'\mathbf{P}$. Premultiply the model in (11-1) by $\mathbf{P}$ to obtain

$$\mathbf{P}\mathbf{y} = \mathbf{P}\mathbf{X}\boldsymbol{\beta} + \mathbf{P}\boldsymbol{\epsilon},$$

or

$$\mathbf{y}_* = \mathbf{X}_*\boldsymbol{\beta} + \boldsymbol{\epsilon}_*. \qquad \textbf{(11-15)}$$

The variance of $\boldsymbol{\epsilon}_*$ is

$$E[\boldsymbol{\epsilon}_*\boldsymbol{\epsilon}_*'] = \mathbf{P}\sigma^2\boldsymbol{\Omega}\mathbf{P}' = \sigma^2\mathbf{I},$$

so the classical regression model of Chapter 6 applies to this transformed model. Since $\boldsymbol{\Omega}$ is known, $\mathbf{y}_*$ and $\mathbf{X}_*$ are observed data. In the classical model, ordinary least squares is efficient; hence

$$\begin{aligned}\hat{\boldsymbol{\beta}} &= (\mathbf{X}_*'\mathbf{X}_*)^{-1}\mathbf{X}_*'\mathbf{y}_* \\ &= (\mathbf{X}'\mathbf{P}'\mathbf{P}\mathbf{X})^{-1}\mathbf{X}'\mathbf{P}'\mathbf{P}\mathbf{y} \\ &= (\mathbf{X}'\boldsymbol{\Omega}^{-1}\mathbf{X})^{-1}\mathbf{X}'\boldsymbol{\Omega}^{-1}\mathbf{y}\end{aligned}$$

is the efficient estimator of $\boldsymbol{\beta}$. This is the **generalized least squares (GLS)** or Aitken (1935) estimator of $\boldsymbol{\beta}$. By appealing to the classical regression model in (11-15), we have the following, which are the generalized regression model analogs to our results of Chapter 6.

THEOREM 11.5: Properties of the Generalized Least Squares Estimator. *If* $E[\boldsymbol{\epsilon}_* | \mathbf{X}_*] = \mathbf{0}$, *then*

$$E[\hat{\boldsymbol{\beta}}] = E[(\mathbf{X}_*'\mathbf{X}_*)^{-1}\mathbf{X}_*'\mathbf{y}_*] = \boldsymbol{\beta} + E[(\mathbf{X}_*'\mathbf{X}_*)^{-1}\mathbf{X}_*'\boldsymbol{\epsilon}_*] = \boldsymbol{\beta}.$$

- *The GLS estimator* $\hat{\boldsymbol{\beta}}$ is unbiased.

This is equivalent to $E[\mathbf{P}\boldsymbol{\epsilon} | \mathbf{P}\mathbf{X}] = \mathbf{0}$, but since $\mathbf{P}$ is a matrix of known constants, we return to the familiar requirement $E[\boldsymbol{\epsilon} | \mathbf{X}] = \mathbf{0}$. The requirement that the regressors and disturbances be uncorrelated is unchanged.

- *The GLS estimator is consistent if* $\operatorname{plim}\left(\frac{1}{n}\mathbf{X}_*'\mathbf{X}_*\right) = \mathbf{Q}_*$, *where* $\mathbf{Q}_*$ *is a finite positive definite matrix.*

Making the substitution, we see that this is

$$\operatorname{plim}\left(\frac{1}{n}\mathbf{X}'\boldsymbol{\Omega}^{-1}\mathbf{X}\right)^{-1} = \mathbf{Q}_*^{-1}. \qquad \textbf{(11-16)}$$

We require the transformed data $\mathbf{X}_* = \mathbf{PX}$, not the original data $\mathbf{X}$, to be well behaved.[9] Under the assumption in (11-1), the following hold.

- *The GLS estimator is asymptotically normally distributed, with mean* $\boldsymbol{\beta}$ *and sampling variance*

$$\operatorname{Var}[\hat{\boldsymbol{\beta}}] = \sigma^2(\mathbf{X}_*'\mathbf{X}_*)^{-1} = \sigma^2(\mathbf{X}'\boldsymbol{\Omega}^{-1}\mathbf{X})^{-1}. \qquad \textbf{(11-17)}$$

- *The GLS estimator* $\hat{\boldsymbol{\beta}}$ *is the minimum variance linear unbiased estimator in the generalized regression model.*

This follows by applying the Gauss–Markov theorem to the model in (11-15). The result in (11-17) is Aitken's (1935) theorem, and $\hat{\boldsymbol{\beta}}$ is sometimes called the *Aitken estimator*. This is a broad result that includes the Gauss–Markov theorem as a special case when $\boldsymbol{\Omega} = \mathbf{I}$.

For testing hypotheses, we can apply the full set of results in Chapter 7 to the transformed model in (11-15). For testing the J linear restrictions, $\mathbf{R}\boldsymbol{\beta} = \mathbf{q}$, the appropriate statistic is

$$\begin{aligned} F[J, n-K] &= \frac{(\mathbf{R}\hat{\boldsymbol{\beta}} - \mathbf{q})'[\mathbf{R}\hat{\sigma}^2(\mathbf{X}_*'\mathbf{X}_*)^{-1}\mathbf{R}']^{-1}(\mathbf{R}\hat{\boldsymbol{\beta}} - \mathbf{q})}{J} \\ &= \frac{(\hat{\boldsymbol{\epsilon}}_c'\hat{\boldsymbol{\epsilon}}_c - \hat{\boldsymbol{\epsilon}}'\hat{\boldsymbol{\epsilon}})/J}{\hat{\sigma}^2}, \end{aligned} \qquad \textbf{(11-18)}$$

where the residual vector is

$$\hat{\boldsymbol{\epsilon}} = \mathbf{y}_* - \mathbf{X}_*\hat{\boldsymbol{\beta}}$$

and

$$\hat{\sigma}^2 = \frac{\hat{\boldsymbol{\epsilon}}'\hat{\boldsymbol{\epsilon}}}{n-K} = \frac{(\mathbf{y} - \mathbf{X}\hat{\boldsymbol{\beta}})'\boldsymbol{\Omega}^{-1}(\mathbf{y} - \mathbf{X}\hat{\boldsymbol{\beta}})}{n-K}.$$

The constrained GLS residuals, $\hat{\boldsymbol{\epsilon}}_c = \mathbf{y}_* - \mathbf{X}_*\hat{\boldsymbol{\beta}}_c$, are based on

$$\hat{\boldsymbol{\beta}}_c = \hat{\boldsymbol{\beta}} - [\mathbf{X}'\boldsymbol{\Omega}^{-1}\mathbf{X}]^{-1}\mathbf{R}'[\mathbf{R}(\mathbf{X}'\boldsymbol{\Omega}^{-1}\mathbf{X})^{-1}\mathbf{R}']^{-1}(\mathbf{R}\hat{\boldsymbol{\beta}} - \mathbf{q}).^{10} \qquad \textbf{(11-19)}$$

To summarize, all the results for the classical model, including the usual inference procedures, apply to the model in (11-15).

There is no precise counterpart to R^2 in the generalized regression model.

[9] Once again, to allow a time trend, we could weaken this assumption a bit.

[10] Note that this is the constrained OLS estimator using the transformed data.

Alternatives have been proposed, but care must be taken when using them. For example, one choice is the R^2 in the transformed regression, (11-15). But this regression need not have a constant term, so the R^2 is not bounded by 0 and 1. Even if there is a constant term, the transformed regression is a computational device, not the model of interest. That a good (or bad) fit is obtained in the "model" in (11-15) may be of no interest; the dependent variable in that model y_* is different from the one in the model as originally specified. The usual R^2 often suggests that the fit of the model is improved by a correction for heteroscedasticity and degraded by a correction for autocorrelation, but both changes can often be attributed to the computation of y_*. A more appealing fit measure might be based on the residuals from the original model once the GLS estimator is in hand, for example,

$$R_G^2 = 1 - \frac{(\mathbf{y} - \mathbf{X}\hat{\boldsymbol\beta})'(\mathbf{y} - \mathbf{X}\hat{\boldsymbol\beta})}{\sum_{i=1}^{n}(y_i - \bar{y})^2}.$$

Like the earlier contender, however, this measure is not bounded in the unit interval. In addition, this measure cannot be reliably used to compare models. The generalized least squares estimator minimizes the generalized sum of squares

$$\boldsymbol\epsilon_*'\boldsymbol\epsilon_* = (\mathbf{y} - \mathbf{X}\boldsymbol\beta)'\boldsymbol\Omega^{-1}(\mathbf{y} - \mathbf{X}\boldsymbol\beta),$$

not $\boldsymbol\epsilon'\boldsymbol\epsilon$. As such, there is no assurance, for example, that dropping a variable from the model will result in a decrease in R_G^2, as it will in R^2. Other goodness-of-fit measures, designed primarily to be a function of the sum of squared residuals (raw or weighted by $\boldsymbol\Omega^{-1}$) and to be bounded by 0 and 1, have been proposed.[11] Unfortunately, they all suffer from at least one of the previously noted shortcomings. The R^2-like measures in this setting are purely descriptive.

11.3.2. Maximum Likelihood Estimation

If the disturbances are multivariate normally distributed, the log-likelihood function for the sample is

$$\ln L = -\frac{n}{2}\ln(2\pi) - \frac{1}{2}\ln|\sigma^2\boldsymbol\Omega| - \frac{1}{2}\boldsymbol\epsilon'(\sigma^2\boldsymbol\Omega)^{-1}\boldsymbol\epsilon.$$

Making the change of variable to $\mathbf{y} - \mathbf{X}\boldsymbol\beta = \boldsymbol\epsilon$, we obtain

$$\begin{aligned}\ln L = {} & -\frac{n}{2}\ln(2\pi) - \frac{n}{2}\ln\sigma^2 \\ & - \frac{1}{2\sigma^2}(\mathbf{y} - \mathbf{X}\boldsymbol\beta)'\boldsymbol\Omega^{-1}(\mathbf{y} - \mathbf{X}\boldsymbol\beta) - \frac{1}{2}\ln|\boldsymbol\Omega|.\end{aligned} \tag{11-20}$$

[11]See, example, Judge et al. (1985, p. 32) and Buse (1973).

Since $\boldsymbol{\Omega}$ is a matrix of known constants, the maximum likelihood estimator of $\boldsymbol{\beta}$ is the vector that minimizes the **generalized sum of squares,**

$$S_*(\boldsymbol{\beta}) = (\mathbf{y} - \mathbf{X}\boldsymbol{\beta})'\boldsymbol{\Omega}^{-1}(\mathbf{y} - \mathbf{X}\boldsymbol{\beta})$$

(hence the name *generalized least squares*). The necessary conditions for maximizing L are

$$\begin{aligned}
\frac{\partial \ln L}{\partial \boldsymbol{\beta}} &= \frac{1}{\sigma^2}\mathbf{X}'\boldsymbol{\Omega}^{-1}(\mathbf{y} - \mathbf{X}\boldsymbol{\beta}) \\
&= \frac{1}{\sigma^2}\mathbf{X}'_*(\mathbf{y}_* - \mathbf{X}_*\boldsymbol{\beta}) = \mathbf{0}, \\
\frac{\partial \ln L}{\partial \sigma^2} &= -\frac{n}{2\sigma^2} + \frac{1}{2\sigma^4}(\mathbf{y} - \mathbf{X}\boldsymbol{\beta})'\boldsymbol{\Omega}^{-1}(\mathbf{y} - \mathbf{X}\boldsymbol{\beta}) \\
&= -\frac{n}{2\sigma^2} + \frac{1}{2\sigma^4}(\mathbf{y}_* - \mathbf{X}_*\boldsymbol{\beta})'(\mathbf{y}_* - \mathbf{X}_*\boldsymbol{\beta}) = 0.
\end{aligned} \tag{11-21}$$

The solutions are the OLS estimators using the transformed data:

$$\hat{\boldsymbol{\beta}}_{\text{ML}} = (\mathbf{X}'_*\mathbf{X}_*)^{-1}\mathbf{X}'_*\mathbf{y}_* = (\mathbf{X}'\boldsymbol{\Omega}^{-1}\mathbf{X})^{-1}\mathbf{X}'\boldsymbol{\Omega}^{-1}\mathbf{y}, \tag{11-22}$$

$$\begin{aligned}
\hat{\sigma}^2_{\text{ML}} &= \frac{1}{n}(\mathbf{y}_* - \mathbf{X}_*\hat{\boldsymbol{\beta}})'(\mathbf{y}_* - \mathbf{X}_*\hat{\boldsymbol{\beta}}) \\
&= \frac{1}{n}(\mathbf{y} - \mathbf{X}\hat{\boldsymbol{\beta}})'\boldsymbol{\Omega}^{-1}(\mathbf{y} - \mathbf{X}\hat{\boldsymbol{\beta}}).
\end{aligned} \tag{11-23}$$

This implies that with normally distributed disturbances, generalized least squares is also maximum likelihood. As in the classical regression model, the maximum likelihood estimator of σ^2 is biased. An unbiased estimator is

$$s^2 = \frac{(\mathbf{y} - \mathbf{X}\hat{\boldsymbol{\beta}})'\boldsymbol{\Omega}^{-1}(\mathbf{y} - \mathbf{X}\hat{\boldsymbol{\beta}})}{n - K}. \tag{11-24}$$

To obtain the asymptotic distribution for the maximum likelihood estimators, we can apply the results of Section 6.8.1 to the transformed model. The asymptotic distribution of $[\hat{\boldsymbol{\beta}}_{\text{ML}}, \hat{\sigma}^2_{\text{ML}}]$ is therefore

$$\begin{bmatrix} \hat{\boldsymbol{\beta}}_{\text{ML}} \\ \hat{\sigma}^2_{\text{ML}} \end{bmatrix} \xrightarrow{a} N\left[\begin{bmatrix} \boldsymbol{\beta} \\ \sigma^2 \end{bmatrix}, \begin{bmatrix} \sigma^2(\mathbf{X}'\boldsymbol{\Omega}^{-1}\mathbf{X})^{-1} & \mathbf{0} \\ \mathbf{0} & 2\sigma^4/n \end{bmatrix}\right]. \tag{11-25}$$

An alternative to (11-18) for testing a hypothesis about $\boldsymbol{\beta}$ is the likelihood ratio statistic. If we insert (11-22) and (11-23) in (11-20), we find, at the maximum likelihood estimators,

$$\ln \hat{L} = -\frac{n}{2}[1 + \ln(2\pi) + \ln \hat{\sigma}^2] - \frac{1}{2}\ln|\boldsymbol{\Omega}|.$$

Therefore, the likelihood ratio test is based on

$$\begin{aligned}\lambda &= -2(\ln \hat{L}_c - \ln \hat{L}) \\ &= n(\ln \hat{\sigma}_c^2 - \ln \hat{\sigma}^2) \\ &= n \ln\left(\frac{\hat{\sigma}_c^2}{\hat{\sigma}^2}\right).\end{aligned} \tag{11-26}$$

The statistic is asymptotically distributed as chi squared with J degrees of freedom, where J is the number of restrictions.

11.4. ESTIMATION WHEN $\boldsymbol{\Omega}$ IS UNKNOWN

To use the results of Section 11.3, $\boldsymbol{\Omega}$ must be known. If $\boldsymbol{\Omega}$ contains unknown parameters that must be estimated, then generalized least squares is not feasible. But with an unrestricted $\boldsymbol{\Omega}$, there are $n(n+1)/2$ additional parameters in $\sigma^2\boldsymbol{\Omega}$. This is far too many to estimate with n observations. Obviously, some structure must be imposed on the model if we are to proceed.

11.4.1. Feasible Generalized Least Squares

The typical problem involves a small set of parameters $\boldsymbol{\theta}$ such that $\boldsymbol{\Omega} = \boldsymbol{\Omega}(\boldsymbol{\theta})$. For example, the $\boldsymbol{\Omega}$ in Example 11.1 has only one unknown parameter, ρ. Another commonly used formula is

$$\boldsymbol{\Omega} = \begin{bmatrix} 1 & \rho & \rho^2 & \rho^3 & \cdots & \rho^{n-1} \\ \rho & 1 & \rho & \rho^2 & \cdots & \rho^{n-2} \\ & & & & \vdots & \\ \rho^{n-1} & \rho^{n-2} & & \cdots & & 1 \end{bmatrix},$$

which also involves only one additional unknown parameter. A model of heteroscedasticity that also has only one new parameter is

$$\sigma_i^2 = \sigma^2 z_i^{\alpha}.$$

Suppose, then, that $\hat{\boldsymbol{\theta}}$ is a consistent estimator of $\boldsymbol{\theta}$. (We consider later how such an estimator might be obtained.) To make GLS estimation feasible, we shall use

$$\hat{\boldsymbol{\Omega}} = \boldsymbol{\Omega}(\hat{\boldsymbol{\theta}})$$

instead of the true $\boldsymbol{\Omega}$. The issue we consider here is whether using $\boldsymbol{\Omega}(\hat{\boldsymbol{\theta}})$ requires us to change any of the results of Section 11.3.

It would seem that if plim $\hat{\boldsymbol{\theta}} = \boldsymbol{\theta}$, using $\hat{\boldsymbol{\Omega}}$ is asymptotically equivalent to using the true $\mathbf{\Omega}$.[12] This need not be the case, however.[13] Let the **feasible generalized least squares (FGLS)** estimator be denoted

$$\hat{\hat{\boldsymbol{\beta}}} = (\mathbf{X}'\hat{\mathbf{\Omega}}^{-1}\mathbf{X})^{-1}\mathbf{X}'\hat{\mathbf{\Omega}}^{-1}\mathbf{y}.$$

Conditions that imply that $\hat{\hat{\boldsymbol{\beta}}}$ is asymptotically equivalent to $\hat{\boldsymbol{\beta}}$ are

$$\text{plim}\left[\left(\frac{1}{n}\mathbf{X}'\hat{\mathbf{\Omega}}^{-1}\mathbf{X}\right) - \left(\frac{1}{n}\mathbf{X}'\mathbf{\Omega}^{-1}\mathbf{X}\right)\right] = \mathbf{0} \tag{11-27}$$

and

$$\text{plim}\left[\left(\frac{1}{\sqrt{n}}\mathbf{X}'\hat{\mathbf{\Omega}}^{-1}\boldsymbol{\epsilon}\right) - \left(\frac{1}{\sqrt{n}}\mathbf{X}'\mathbf{\Omega}^{-1}\boldsymbol{\epsilon}\right)\right] = \mathbf{0}. \tag{11-28}$$

The first of these states that if the weighted sum of squares matrix based on the true $\mathbf{\Omega}$ converges to a positive definite matrix, then the one based on $\hat{\mathbf{\Omega}}$ converges to the same matrix. We are assuming that this is true. In the second condition, if the *transformed* regressors are well behaved, the right-hand side sum will have a limiting normal distribution. This is exactly the condition we used in Chapter 6 to obtain the asymptotic distribution of the least squares estimator; here we are using the same results for $\mathbf{X}_*$ and $\boldsymbol{\epsilon}_*$. Therefore, (11-28) requires the same condition to hold when $\mathbf{\Omega}$ is replaced with $\hat{\mathbf{\Omega}}$.[14]

These are conditions that, in principle, must be verified on a case-by-case basis. Fortunately, in most familiar settings, they are met. If we assume that they are, the FGLS estimator based on $\hat{\boldsymbol{\theta}}$ has the same asymptotic properties as the GLS estimator. This is an extremely useful result. Note, especially, the following theorem.

THEOREM 11.6: Efficiency of the FGLS Estimator. *An asymptotically efficient FGLS estimator does not require that we have an efficient estimator of* $\boldsymbol{\theta}$*; only a consistent one is required to achieve full efficiency for the FGLS estimator.*

Except for the simplest cases, the finite-sample properties and exact distributions of FGLS estimators are unknown.[15] The asymptotic efficiency of

---

[12]This is sometimes denoted plim $\hat{\mathbf{\Omega}} = \mathbf{\Omega}$. Since $\mathbf{\Omega}$ is $n \times n$, it cannot have a probability limit. We use this term to indicate convergence element by element.

[13]Schmidt (1976, p. 69) constructs a counterexample.

[14]The condition actually requires only that if the right-hand sum has *any* limiting distribution, then the left-hand one has the same one. Conceivably, this might not be the normal distribution, but this seems unlikely except in a specially constructed, theoretical case.

[15]The difficult part of most derivations is determining the exact distribution of functions of $\hat{\mathbf{\Omega}}^{-1}$. There is one general, exact result that applies in several settings. If $\hat{\boldsymbol{\theta}}$ is an *even function* of the true disturbances, the FGLS estimator is unbiased. The estimator $\hat{\boldsymbol{\theta}}$ is an even function of $\boldsymbol{\epsilon}$ if the same numerical value would be obtained using $-\boldsymbol{\epsilon}$ instead. Consider, for example, the OLS estimator $\mathbf{e}'\mathbf{e}/(n-K) = \boldsymbol{\epsilon}'\mathbf{M}\boldsymbol{\epsilon}/(n-K) = (-\boldsymbol{\epsilon})'\mathbf{M}(-\boldsymbol{\epsilon})/(n-K)$. The result was first reported by Kakwani (1967) for a multiple equation model. But it is straightforward to broaden the result to encompass the fuller generalized regression model we consider here. See, for example, Schmidt (1976, p. 72). Different conditions for the unbiasedness of the FGLS estimator are presented by Don and Magnus (1980) and Magnus (1978).

FGLS estimators may not carry over to small samples because of the variability introduced by the estimated $\boldsymbol{\Omega}$. Some analyses for the case of heteroscedasticity are given by Taylor (1977). A model of autocorrelation is analyzed by Griliches and Rao (1969). In both studies, the authors find that over a broad range of parameters, FGLS is more efficient than least squares. But if the departure from the classical assumptions is not too severe, least squares may be more efficient than FGLS in a small sample.

11.4.2. Maximum Likelihood Estimation

For the moment, it is useful to treat $\boldsymbol{\Omega}$ as an unrestricted matrix of unknown parameters. We shall impose the restrictions $\boldsymbol{\Omega} = \boldsymbol{\Omega}(\boldsymbol{\theta})$ later. It will also simplify the computations if we estimate $\boldsymbol{\Gamma} = \boldsymbol{\Omega}^{-1}$ instead of $\boldsymbol{\Omega}$. Given the MLE of $\boldsymbol{\Gamma}$, the MLE of $\boldsymbol{\Omega}$ is $\hat{\boldsymbol{\Gamma}}_{\text{ML}}^{-1}$.[16] We shall also use the results

$$\ln|\boldsymbol{\Gamma}| = -\ln|\boldsymbol{\Omega}|,^{17}$$

$$\frac{\partial \ln|\boldsymbol{\Gamma}|}{\partial \boldsymbol{\Gamma}} = \boldsymbol{\Gamma}^{-1},$$

and

$$\frac{\partial \boldsymbol{\epsilon}'\boldsymbol{\Gamma}\boldsymbol{\epsilon}}{\partial \boldsymbol{\Gamma}} = \boldsymbol{\epsilon}\boldsymbol{\epsilon}'.^{18}$$

Substituting $\boldsymbol{\Gamma}$ for $\boldsymbol{\Omega}^{-1}$ in L, we obtain

$$\ln L = -\frac{n}{2}[\ln(2\pi) + \ln\sigma^2] - \frac{1}{2\sigma^2}\boldsymbol{\epsilon}'\boldsymbol{\Gamma}\boldsymbol{\epsilon} + \frac{1}{2}\ln|\boldsymbol{\Gamma}|.$$

Then

$$\frac{\partial \ln L}{\partial \boldsymbol{\beta}} = \frac{1}{\sigma^2}\mathbf{X}'\boldsymbol{\Gamma}(\mathbf{y} - \mathbf{X}\boldsymbol{\beta}), \qquad \textbf{(11-29)}$$

$$\frac{\partial \ln L}{\partial \sigma^2} = -\frac{n}{2\sigma^2} + \frac{1}{2\sigma^4}(\mathbf{y} - \mathbf{X}\boldsymbol{\beta})'\boldsymbol{\Gamma}(\mathbf{y} - \mathbf{X}\boldsymbol{\beta}), \qquad \textbf{(11-30)}$$

$$\frac{\partial \ln L}{\partial \boldsymbol{\Gamma}} = \frac{1}{2}\left[\boldsymbol{\Gamma}^{-1} - \left(\frac{1}{\sigma^2}\right)\boldsymbol{\epsilon}\boldsymbol{\epsilon}'\right] = \frac{1}{2\sigma^2}[\sigma^2\boldsymbol{\Omega} - \boldsymbol{\epsilon}\boldsymbol{\epsilon}']. \qquad \textbf{(11-31)}$$

The following are apparent:

- We would use FGLS to obtain the MLE of $\boldsymbol{\beta}$, using the maximum likelihood estimate of $\boldsymbol{\Omega}$, since (11-29) is the same normal equations we saw earlier.
- Given the MLEs of $\boldsymbol{\beta}$ and $\boldsymbol{\Omega}$, the MLE of σ^2 would be $(1/n)(\mathbf{y} - \mathbf{X}\hat{\boldsymbol{\beta}}_{\text{ML}})'\hat{\boldsymbol{\Omega}}_{\text{ML}}^{-1} \times (\mathbf{y} - \mathbf{X}\hat{\boldsymbol{\beta}}_{\text{ML}})$. This is the solution to (11-30).

[16]The invariance principle is discussed in Section 4.5.1.

[17]The characteristic roots of $\boldsymbol{\Gamma}$ are the reciprocals of those of $\boldsymbol{\Omega}$. The determinants are the products of the characteristic roots, which imply the result.

[18]See Section 2.9.1 for derivations of these results.

The problem of too many parameters can be seen in the likelihood equation for $\mathbf{\Gamma}$. At the solution, we would require the rank one matrix $\hat{\boldsymbol{\epsilon}}\hat{\boldsymbol{\epsilon}}'$ to equal the positive definite matrix $\hat{\sigma}^2\hat{\mathbf{\Omega}}$, which is a contradiction. It might seem that we could simply use $\mathbf{ee}'$ to estimate $\sigma^2\mathbf{\Omega}$, as suggested by (11-31), but this matrix is singular and could not be used in (11-29) or (11-30).

Since $\mathbf{\Omega}$ must be restricted in some way to make the estimation problem tractable, let us assume, once again, that $\mathbf{\Omega} = \mathbf{\Omega}(\boldsymbol{\theta})$, where $\boldsymbol{\theta}$ is a vector of a small number of parameters and *$\boldsymbol{\theta}$ is not a function of any elements of $\boldsymbol{\beta}$*. (The reason for this assumption will be clear shortly.) With this assumption, there are two methods of obtaining estimates of the full set of parameters.

If it is straightforward to obtain estimates of $\boldsymbol{\theta}$ that satisfy (11-31) for a given set of estimates of $\boldsymbol{\beta}$ and σ^2, the iterative two-step method proposed by Oberhofer and Kmenta (1974) will usually be the easiest way to proceed. Since the MLEs of $\boldsymbol{\beta}$ and σ^2 are the GLS estimates using the MLE of $\mathbf{\Omega}$, given an estimate $\hat{\boldsymbol{\theta}}$, we use (11-29) and (11-30) above to estimate $\boldsymbol{\beta}$ and σ^2. With the new estimates of $\boldsymbol{\beta}$ and σ^2, we then reestimate $\boldsymbol{\theta}$. Thereafter we repeat the iteration until satisfactory convergence has been achieved. If the initial $\hat{\boldsymbol{\theta}}$ is a consistent estimator of $\boldsymbol{\theta}$, this estimator will be asymptotically efficient at every step. Under certain additional conditions, however, the values to which $\boldsymbol{\beta}$, σ^2, and $\mathbf{\Omega}$ converge will also be the maximum likelihood estimates.[19] These include the following:

1. The information matrix must be block diagonal. That is, $\mathbf{\Omega}$ must not be a function of $\boldsymbol{\beta}$. (This is the mandate for the assumption.)
2. The initial estimate of $\boldsymbol{\theta}$ must be consistent.
3. At each step, the updated estimate of $\boldsymbol{\theta}$ must be obtained by solving the first-order conditions for maximum likelihood estimates, given the present estimate of $\boldsymbol{\beta}$.

The third condition is important to remember. There are cases, including one that we shall examine in detail in Section 13.7.1, in which there is more than one consistent estimate of $\boldsymbol{\theta}$ given the current estimate of $\boldsymbol{\beta}$.

If the method of Oberhofer and Kmenta is not usable, it may be necessary to maximize the log-likelihood directly using, for example, one of the gradient methods described in Chapter 5. At the solution, regardless of how it is obtained, the MLEs of $\boldsymbol{\beta}$ and σ^2 will be the FGLS estimators. The difficult part of the problem is estimating $\boldsymbol{\theta}$. A complete analysis, including several applications, is presented by Magnus (1978). We shall examine some specific cases in the chapters to follow.

The information matrix for the maximum likelihood estimators of $\boldsymbol{\beta}$, σ^2, and $\boldsymbol{\theta}$ will be block diagonal of the form

[19]Note that the divisor in the estimator of σ^2 must be n, not $n - K$.

$$-E\left[\frac{\partial^2 \ln L}{\partial\begin{pmatrix}\boldsymbol{\beta}\\ \sigma^2\\ \boldsymbol{\theta}\end{pmatrix}\partial(\boldsymbol{\beta}'\quad \sigma^2\quad \boldsymbol{\theta}')}\right] = \left[\begin{array}{c|cc}(1/\sigma^2)\mathbf{X}'\boldsymbol{\Omega}^{-1}\mathbf{X} & \mathbf{0} & \mathbf{0}' \\ \hline \mathbf{0}' & n/(2\sigma^4) & \boldsymbol{\delta} \\ \mathbf{0} & \boldsymbol{\delta}' & \mathbf{C}\end{array}\right]. \tag{11-32}$$

The inverse matrix will be block diagonal as well. Therefore, the asymptotic covariance matrix of the maximum likelihood estimator is

$$\text{Asy. Var}[\hat{\boldsymbol{\beta}}_{\text{ML}}] = \sigma^2(\mathbf{X}'\boldsymbol{\Omega}^{-1}\mathbf{X})^{-1}.$$

This is the same as that of the FGLS estimator. We conclude, therefore, that as long as the information matrix is block diagonal, the GLS, FGLS, and ML estimators of $\boldsymbol{\beta}$ have the same asymptotic distributions. It follows that:

Exact knowledge of $\boldsymbol{\Omega}$ brings no gain in asymptotic efficiency in the estimation of $\boldsymbol{\beta}$ over estimation of $\boldsymbol{\beta}$ with a consistent estimator of $\boldsymbol{\Omega}$.

This is not true if the information matrix is not block diagonal.

It is important to note that in this and many cases we shall examine later, having the same properties as the maximum likelihood estimator does not imply that the FGLS estimator *is* the maximum likelihood estimator. This means that likelihood ratio tests and Lagrange multiplier tests based on the FGLS estimator are only approximate at best. By exploiting the asymptotic normality of the estimator, we can use the usual Wald statistic to test a hypothesis about $\boldsymbol{\beta}$.

EXAMPLE 11.2 Groupwise Heteroscedasticity

A groupwise heteroscedastic regression is based on

$$\begin{aligned} y_i &= \boldsymbol{\beta}'\mathbf{x}_i + \epsilon_i, & i &= 1, \ldots, n, \\ E[\epsilon_i] &= 0, & i &= 1, \ldots, n. \end{aligned}$$

The n observations are grouped into G groups, each with n_g observations. The slope vector is the same in all groups, but within group g:

$$\text{Var}[\epsilon_{ig}] = \sigma_g^2, \quad i = 1, \ldots, n_g.$$

The log-likelihood function is

$$\ln L = -\frac{n}{2}\ln(2\pi) - \frac{1}{2}\sum_{g=1}^{G} n_g \ln \sigma_g^2 - \frac{1}{2}\sum_{g=1}^{G}\sum_{i=1}^{n_g}(\epsilon_{ig}^2/\sigma_g^2).$$

The MLE for $\boldsymbol{\beta}$ is generalized least squares, using the MLEs for σ_g^2. The **weighting matrix** is

$$\sigma^2\boldsymbol{\Omega} = \begin{bmatrix} \sigma_1^2\mathbf{I} & \mathbf{0} & \cdots & \mathbf{0} \\ \mathbf{0} & \sigma_2^2\mathbf{I} & \cdots & \mathbf{0} \\ & & & \vdots \\ \mathbf{0} & \mathbf{0} & \cdots & \sigma_G^2\mathbf{I} \end{bmatrix},$$

so the GLS estimator is

$$\hat{\boldsymbol{\beta}} = \left[\sum_{g=1}^{G} \frac{1}{\sigma_g^2}\mathbf{X}_g'\mathbf{X}_g\right]^{-1}\left[\sum_{g=1}^{G} \frac{1}{\sigma_g^2}\mathbf{X}_g'\mathbf{y}_g\right]. \tag{11-33}$$

For each variance parameter σ_g^2 the likelihood equation is

$$\frac{\partial \ln L}{\partial \sigma_g^2} = -\frac{n_g}{2\sigma_g^2} + \frac{1}{2\sigma_g^4}\sum_{i=1}^{n_g} \epsilon_{ig}^2 = 0,$$

so that given the current value of $\hat{\boldsymbol{\beta}}$,

$$\hat{\sigma}_g^2 = \frac{\mathbf{e}_g'\mathbf{e}_g}{n_g}.$$

To obtain this maximum likelihood estimator, a simple iterative procedure that satisfies the Oberhofer–Kmenta requirements is as follows:

1. Pool the data and estimate $\boldsymbol{\beta}$ by OLS.
2. Estimate the disturbance variances separately with $\mathbf{e}_g'\mathbf{e}_g/n_g$, where $\mathbf{e}_g = \mathbf{y}_g - \mathbf{X}_g\mathbf{b}$.
3. Compute $\hat{\boldsymbol{\beta}}$ according to (11-33).
4. If $\hat{\boldsymbol{\beta}}$ has not converged, go to step 2; otherwise, exit.

The likelihood ratio test of Section 11.3.2 can be used to test a hypothesis about $\boldsymbol{\beta}$ or $\boldsymbol{\Omega}$. Once again, we insert the MLE for σ^2 in (11-23) in the likelihood function. At the maximum, we have

$$\begin{aligned}\ln \hat{L} &= -\frac{n}{2}[1 + \ln(2\pi) + \ln \hat{\sigma}^2] - \frac{1}{2}\ln|\hat{\boldsymbol{\Omega}}| \\ &= -\frac{n}{2}[1 + \ln(2\pi)] - \frac{1}{2}\ln|\hat{\sigma}^2\hat{\boldsymbol{\Omega}}|.\end{aligned}$$

Therefore, for testing constraints on $\boldsymbol{\beta}$ and/or $\boldsymbol{\Omega}$, the likelihood ratio statistic is

$$\lambda = \ln|(\hat{\sigma}^2\hat{\boldsymbol{\Omega}})_c| - \ln|\hat{\sigma}^2\hat{\boldsymbol{\Omega}}|.$$

The degrees of freedom for the chi-squared test is the number of parametric restrictions imposed. For the groupwise heteroscedastic model of Example 11.2, a likelihood ratio test of the hypothesis of homoscedasticity would be based on

$$\lambda = n \ln s^2 - \sum_{g=1}^{G} n_g \ln s_g^2$$

where $n = \Sigma_{g=1}^{G} n_g$; s^2 is the pooled, least squares residual variance, $\mathbf{e}'\mathbf{e}/n$ (not $n - K$); and s_g^2 is defined in Example 11.2.

In general, maximum likelihood estimation of an unknown $\boldsymbol{\Omega}$ greatly complicates the estimation problem. The likelihood equations for the unknown parameters in $\boldsymbol{\Omega}$ are usually extremely involved and difficult to solve. In most cases, the asymptotically equivalent procedure of finding a consistent estimator for $\boldsymbol{\Omega}$ and using FGLS is used instead. (Where it is convenient, analysts often use the Oberhofer–Kmenta procedure.) If $\boldsymbol{\theta}$ contains any of the parameters in $\boldsymbol{\beta}$, neither FGLS nor GLS is efficient. Full maximum likelihood estimation is likely to be extremely difficult in this case, but the maximum likelihood estimator that makes use of the information that $\boldsymbol{\beta}$ enters $\boldsymbol{\Omega}$ as well as the regression will necessarily be more efficient.

11.5. THE GENERALIZED METHOD OF MOMENTS (GMM) ESTIMATOR

A large proportion of the recent empirical work in econometrics, particularly in macroeconomics and finance, has employed what have come to be called GMM estimators. As we shall see, this is a broad class of estimators that, in fact, includes almost all the estimators discussed elsewhere in this book. But recent extensions of the technique have greatly added to the stock to tools available to the applied econometrician.

Before continuing, it will be useful for you to read (or reread) the following sections:

1. Consistent Estimation—The Method of Moments: Section 4.7.
2. Correlation Between $\mathbf{x}_i$ and ϵ_i—Instrumental Variables Estimation: Section 6.7.8.
3. Nonlinear Regression Models: Chapter 10.
4. Optimization: Section 5.5.
5. Robust Estimation of Covariance Asympotic Matrices: Section 11.2.5.
6. The Wald Test: Section 4.9.3b.

The GMM estimation technique is a direct extension of the method of moments technique described in Section 4.6.[20]

11.5.1. Methods of Moments Estimators

Estimation by the method of moments proceeds as follows. The model specified for the random variable y_i implies certain expectations, for example

$$E[y_i] = \mu,$$

where μ is the mean of the distribution of y_i. Estimation of μ then proceeds by forming a sample analog to the "moment condition":

$$E[y_i - \mu] = 0.$$

[20]This section will give a largely heuristic development of the GMM estimator. Formal presentation of the results required for this analysis are given by Hansen (1982), Hansen and Singleton (1988), Chamberlain (1987), Cumby et al. (1983), Newey (1984, 1985a, 1985b), and Davidson and MacKinnon (1993). A useful recent summary of GMM estimation and other developments in econometrics is Pagan and Wickens (1989). An application of some of these techniques that contains useful summaries is Pagan and Vella (1989). Some further discussion can be found in Davidson and MacKinnon (1993).

The sample counterpart to this expectation is

$$\frac{1}{n}\sum_{i=1}^{n}(y_i - \hat{\mu}) = 0.$$

The estimator is the value of $\hat{\mu}$ that satisfies the sample moment condition. The example given is, of course, a trivial one. Example 4.26 gives the much more elaborate case of sampling from a gamma distribution. The moment conditions used for estimation in that example (taken two at a time from a set of four) include

$$E\left[x_i - \frac{P}{\lambda}\right] = 0$$

and

$$E\left[\frac{1}{x_i} - \frac{\lambda}{P-1}\right] = 0.$$

Inserting the sample data into the sample analogs produces the moments equations for estimation.

Now, consider the apparently different case of the ordinary least squares estimator of the parameters in the classical linear regression model. Among the assumptions of the model is

$$E[\mathbf{x}_i\epsilon_i] = \mathbf{0}.$$

The sample analog is

$$\frac{1}{n}\sum_{i=1}^{n}\mathbf{x}_i e_i = \frac{1}{n}\sum_{i=1}^{n}\mathbf{x}_i(\mathbf{y}_i - \mathbf{x}_i'\mathbf{b}) = \frac{1}{n}\mathbf{X}'\mathbf{e} = \mathbf{0}.$$

The estimator of $\boldsymbol{\beta}$ is the one that satisfies these moment equations. This is just the normal equations for the least squares estimator, so we see that the OLS estimator is a method of moments estimator. Indeed, by this construction, nearly all the estimators defined in this book are method of moments estimators. The counterpart for the instrumental variables estimator of Section 6.7.8 was

$$E[\mathbf{z}_i\epsilon_i] = \mathbf{0}.$$

We reconciled the problem of having more moments than parameters by solving

$$\left(\frac{1}{n}\mathbf{X}'\mathbf{Z}\right)\left(\frac{1}{n}\mathbf{Z}'\mathbf{Z}\right)^{-1}\left(\frac{1}{n}\mathbf{Z}'\mathbf{e}\right) = \frac{1}{n}\hat{\mathbf{X}}'\mathbf{e} = \mathbf{0}.$$

The GLS estimator is defined by the normal equations

$$E[\mathbf{X}'\boldsymbol{\Omega}^{-1}\boldsymbol{\epsilon}] = \mathbf{0},$$

which we transformed to

$$E[\mathbf{X}_*'\boldsymbol{\epsilon}_*] = \mathbf{0}$$

or, for one observation,

$$E[\mathbf{x}_{i*}\epsilon_{i*}] = \mathbf{0}.$$

The sample analog that produces the GLS estimator is

$$\frac{1}{n}\sum_{i=1}^{n} \mathbf{x}_{i*}\hat{\epsilon}_{i*} = \frac{1}{n}\mathbf{X}'_{*}\hat{\boldsymbol{\epsilon}}_{*} = \frac{1}{n}\mathbf{X}'\boldsymbol{\Omega}^{-1}\hat{\boldsymbol{\epsilon}} = \mathbf{0}.$$

All the maximum likelihood estimators that we have looked at thus far and will encounter later are obtained by equating the derivatives of a log-likelihood to zero. The operating principle is that

$$\ln L = \sum_{i=1}^{n} \ln f(y_i, \mathbf{x}_i \mid \boldsymbol{\theta}),$$

where $f(\cdot)$ is the density function and $\boldsymbol{\theta}$ is the parameter vector. Underlying the theory of maximum likelihood estimation is the result that for regular problems [see Section 4.5.2 and (4-52)],

$$E\left[\frac{\partial \ln f(y_i, \mathbf{x}_i \mid \boldsymbol{\theta})}{\partial \boldsymbol{\theta}}\right] = \mathbf{0}.$$

The maximum likelihood estimator is obtained by equating the sample analog to zero:

$$\frac{1}{n}\frac{\partial \ln L}{\partial \boldsymbol{\theta}} = \frac{1}{n}\sum_{i=1}^{n}\frac{\partial \ln f(y_i, \mathbf{x}_i \mid \boldsymbol{\theta})}{\partial \boldsymbol{\theta}} = \mathbf{0}.$$

(Dividing by n to make this comparable with our earlier results does not change the solution.) The upshot is that nearly all the estimators we have discussed and will encounter later can be construed as method of moments estimators. [Manski's (1992) treatment of **analog estimation** provides some interesting extensions and methodological discourse.]

11.5.2. Generalizing the Method of Moments

The preceding examples all have a common aspect. In every case listed, there are exactly as many moment equations as there are parameters to be estimated. Thus, each of these are **exactly identified** cases. There will be a single solution to the moment equations, and at the solution, the equations will be exactly satisfied. (That is, of course if there is *any* solution. In the regression model with collinearity, there are K parameters but fewer than K independent moment equations.) But there are cases in which there are more moment equations than parameters, so the system is overdetermined.

EXAMPLE 11.3 (Example 4.26 Continued) The Gamma Distribution

In Example 4.26 we computed four sample moments,

$$\bar{\mathbf{g}} = \frac{1}{n}\sum_{i=1}^{n}\left[x_i, x_i^2, \frac{1}{x_i}, \ln x_i\right]$$

with probability limits P/λ, $P(P+1)/\lambda^2$, $\lambda/(P-1)$, and $\psi(P) - \ln \lambda$, respectively. Any pair could be used to estimate the two parameters, but as shown in the earlier example, the six pairs produce six somewhat different estimates of $\boldsymbol{\theta} = (P, \lambda)$.

In such a case, to use all the information in the sample, it is necessary to devise a way to reconcile the conflicting estimates that will emerge from the overdetermined system. More generally, suppose that the model involves K parameters, $\boldsymbol{\theta} = (\theta_1, \theta_2, \ldots, \theta_K)$, and that it implies a set of $L > K$ moment conditions,

$$E[m_l(y_i, \mathbf{x}_i, \mathbf{z}_i, \boldsymbol{\theta})] = E[m_{il}(\boldsymbol{\theta})] = 0, \quad l = 1, \ldots, L,$$

where y_i, $\mathbf{x}_i$, and $\mathbf{z}_i$ are variables that appear in the model and the subscript i on $m_{il}(\boldsymbol{\theta})$ indicates the dependence on $(y_i, \mathbf{x}_i, \mathbf{z}_i)$. Denote the corresponding sample means as

$$\overline{m}_l(\mathbf{y}, \mathbf{X}, \mathbf{Z}, \boldsymbol{\theta}) = \frac{1}{n}\sum_{i=1}^{n} m_l(y_i, \mathbf{x}_i, \mathbf{z}_i, \boldsymbol{\theta}) = \frac{1}{n}\sum_{i=1}^{n} m_{il}(\boldsymbol{\theta}).$$

Unless the equations are functionally dependent, the system of L equations in K unknown parameters,

$$\overline{m}_l = \frac{1}{n}\sum_{i=1}^{n} m_l(y_i, \mathbf{x}_i, \mathbf{z}_i, \boldsymbol{\theta}) = 0, \quad l = 1, \ldots, L,$$

will not have a unique solution. It will be necessary to reconcile the $\binom{L}{K}$ different sets of estimates that can be produced. One possibility would be to minimize a criterion function, such as the sum of squares,

$$q = \sum_{l=1}^{L} \overline{m}_l^2 = \overline{\mathbf{m}}(\boldsymbol{\theta})'\overline{\mathbf{m}}(\boldsymbol{\theta}).^{21} \tag{11-34}$$

It can be shown [see, e.g., Hansen (1982)] that under the assumptions we have made so far, minimizing q in (11-34) produces a consistent (albeit, as we shall see, inefficient) estimator of $\boldsymbol{\theta}$. We can, in fact, use as the criterion a weighted sum of squares,

$$q = \overline{\mathbf{m}}(\boldsymbol{\theta})'\mathbf{A}\overline{\mathbf{m}}(\boldsymbol{\theta}), \tag{11-35}$$

where $\mathbf{A}$ is *any* positive definite matrix that is not a function of $\boldsymbol{\theta}$, such as $\mathbf{I}$ in (11-34), to produce consistent estimates of $\boldsymbol{\theta}$.[22] For example, we might use a diagonal matrix of weights if some information were available about the importance (by some measure) of the different moments.

Since the moments are sums of the observations, they are, in fact, random variables whose variances are estimable. [See (4-55).] By the same logic that

---

[21]This is one of the approaches that Quandt and Ramsey (1978) suggested for the problem in Example 4.24.

[22]As we have defined the problem, $\mathbf{A}$ must also be of order less than or equal to n.

makes GLS preferable to OLS, it should be beneficial to use a weighted criterion in which the weights are inversely proportional to the variances of the moments. Let **W** be a diagonal matrix whose diagonal elements are

$$w_{ll} = \text{Asy. Var}[\overline{m}_l] = \frac{1}{n}\phi_{ll}.$$

We have written it in this form to emphasize that the right-hand side is the variance of a sample mean and is of order $(1/n)$. Then, a **weighted least squares** procedure would minimize

$$q = \overline{\mathbf{m}}(\boldsymbol{\theta})'\mathbf{W}^{-1}\overline{\mathbf{m}}(\boldsymbol{\theta}). \tag{11-36}$$

In general, the L elements of $\overline{\mathbf{m}}$ are freely correlated. In (11-36), we have used a diagonal **W** that ignores this correlation. To use GLS, we would define

$$\mathbf{W} = \text{Asy. Var}[\overline{\mathbf{m}}]. \tag{11-37}$$

The estimators defined by choosing $\boldsymbol{\theta}$ to minimize

$$q = \overline{\mathbf{m}}(\boldsymbol{\theta})'\mathbf{W}^{-1}\overline{\mathbf{m}}(\boldsymbol{\theta})$$

are **minimum distance estimators.** The general result is that if **W** is a positive definite matrix and if

$$\text{plim}\, \overline{\mathbf{m}}(\boldsymbol{\theta}) = \mathbf{0},$$

then the minimum distance (generalized method of moments, or GMM) estimator of $\boldsymbol{\theta}$ is consistent.[23] Since the OLS criterion in (11-35) uses **I**, this produces a consistent estimator, as does the weighted least squares estimator and the full GLS estimator. What remains to be decided is the best **W** to use. Intuition might suggest (correctly) that the one defined in (11-37) would be optimal, once again based on the logic that motivates generalized least squares. This is the now celebrated result of Hansen (1982). The asymptotic covariance matrix of this **generalized method of moments estimator** is

$$\begin{aligned}\mathbf{V}_{\text{GMM}} &= [\mathbf{G}'\mathbf{W}^{-1}\mathbf{G}]^{-1} \\ &= \frac{1}{n}[\mathbf{G}'\boldsymbol{\Phi}^{-1}\mathbf{G}]^{-1},\end{aligned} \tag{11-38}$$

where **G** is a matrix of derivatives with jth row equal to

$$\mathbf{G}^{jl} = \frac{\partial \overline{m}_l(\boldsymbol{\theta})}{\partial \boldsymbol{\theta}'}$$

and $\boldsymbol{\Phi} = \text{Var}[\sqrt{n}(\overline{\mathbf{m}} - \boldsymbol{\mu})]$. Finally, by virtue of the central limit theorem applied to the sample moments and the Slutsky theorem applied to this manipulation, we can assert the following.

---

[23]In the most general cases, there are a number of other subtle conditions that must be met so as to assert consistency and the other properties we discuss. For our purposes, the conditions given will suffice. Minimum distance estimators are discussed in Malinvaud (1970), Hansen (1982), and Amemiya (1985).

THEOREM 11.7: Asymptotic Distribution of the GMM Estimator. *Under the preceding assumptions,*

$$\hat{\boldsymbol{\theta}}_{\text{GMM}} \xrightarrow{a} N[\boldsymbol{\theta}, \mathbf{V}_{\text{GMM}}], \tag{11-39}$$

where $\mathbf{V}_{\text{GMM}}$ *is defined in (11-38).*

EXAMPLE 11.4 (Example 4.26 Continued) GMM Estimation of a Gamma Distribution

Referring once again to our earlier results, we consider how to use all four of our sample moments to estimate the parameters of the gamma distribution. The four moment equations are

$$E\left[x_i - \frac{P}{\lambda}\right] = 0,$$
$$E\left[x_i^2 - \frac{P(P+1)}{\lambda^2}\right] = 0,$$
$$E[\ln x_i - \Psi(P) + \ln\lambda] = 0,$$
$$E\left[\frac{1}{x_i} - \frac{\lambda}{P-1}\right] = 0.$$

The sample means of these will provide the moment equations for estimation. Let $x_1 = x, x_2 = x^2, x_3 = \ln x$, and $x_4 = 1/x$. Then

$$\begin{aligned}\overline{m}_1(P, \lambda) &= \frac{1}{n}\sum_{i=1}^{n}\left(x_{i1} - \frac{P}{\lambda}\right)\\ &= \frac{1}{n}\sum_{i=1}^{n}(x_{i1} - \mu_1)\\ &= \overline{x}_1 - \mu_1(P, \lambda),\end{aligned}$$

and likewise for $\overline{m}_2(P, \lambda), \overline{m}_3(P, \lambda)$, and $\overline{m}_4(P, \lambda)$.

For our initial set of estimates, we will use ordinary least squares. The optimization problem is

$$\begin{aligned}\text{Minimize}_{P,\lambda} \sum_{l=1}^{4} \overline{m}_l(P, \lambda)^2 &= \sum_{l=1}^{4} [\overline{x}_l - \mu_l(P, \lambda)]^2\\ &= \overline{\mathbf{m}}(P, \lambda)'\overline{\mathbf{m}}(P, \lambda).\end{aligned}$$

This will be the minimum distance estimator with $\mathbf{W} = \mathbf{I}$. This is a nonlinear optimization problem that must be solved iteratively. It turns out that for purposes of the nonlinear optimization procedure, a rescaling of the moment conditions greatly eases convergence. (See Section 5.5 for discussion.) By multiplying the equations by $[\lambda, \lambda^2, 1, (P-1)]$, respectively, we obtain a much more convenient system of equations. Thus, our four moment equations for estimation are

$$\begin{aligned} \lambda\bar{x}_1 - P &= 0, \\ \lambda^2\bar{x}_2 - P(P+1) &= 0, \\ \bar{x}_3 - \Psi(P) + \ln\lambda &= 0, \\ (P-1)\bar{x}_4 - \lambda &= 0. \end{aligned}$$

This is equivalent to minimizing

$$q = \bar{\mathbf{m}}(P,\lambda)'\mathbf{J}'\mathbf{J}\bar{\mathbf{m}}(P,\lambda) = \bar{\mathbf{m}}_*(P,\lambda)'\bar{\mathbf{m}}_*(P,\lambda),$$

where $\mathbf{J} = \text{diag}(\lambda, \lambda^2, 1, P-1)$.[24] As starting values for the iterations, we used the maximum likelihood estimates from Example 4.25, $\hat{P}_{\text{ML}} = 2.4097$ and $\hat{\lambda}_{\text{ML}} = 0.07704137$. The least squares values that result from this procedure are $\hat{P} = 2.1799$ and $\hat{\lambda} = 0.069058$. We can now use these to form our estimate of $\mathbf{W}$. GMM estimation usually requires a first step estimate such as this to obtain a consistent (if not efficient) estimate of $\boldsymbol{\theta}$ to use to compute the weighting matrix $\mathbf{W}$. This application is a bit unusual in that we already had the MLEs and could have used them. At the same time, however, the MLEs were not really necessary as starting values for the iterations used to minimize q; we could have used a grid search or some other method if need be.

With these new estimates in hand, we recomputed the moments and $\mathbf{J}$ and obtained

$$\hat{\mathbf{W}} = \frac{1}{20}\frac{1}{19}\sum_{i=1}^{20}\begin{bmatrix} x_{i1} - \hat{P}/\hat{\lambda} \\ x_{i2} - \hat{P}(\hat{P}+1)/\hat{\lambda}^2 \\ x_{i3} - \Psi(\hat{P}) + \ln\hat{\lambda} \\ x_{i4} - \hat{\lambda}/(\hat{P}-1) \end{bmatrix}\begin{bmatrix} x_{i1} - \hat{P}/\hat{\lambda} \\ x_{i2} - \hat{P}(\hat{P}+1)/\hat{\lambda}^2 \\ x_{i3} - \Psi(\hat{P}) + \ln\hat{\lambda} \\ x_{i4} - \hat{\lambda}/(\hat{P}-1) \end{bmatrix}'.$$

The GMM estimator is now obtained by minimizing

$$q = \bar{\mathbf{m}}(P,\lambda)'\mathbf{J}'[\mathbf{J}\hat{\mathbf{W}}\mathbf{J}']^{-1}\mathbf{J}\bar{\mathbf{m}}(P,\lambda).$$

The two estimates are $\hat{P}_{\text{GMM}} = 2.4820$ and $\hat{\lambda}_{\text{GMM}} = 0.068993$. At these two values, the value of the function is $q = 9.9296$. To obtain an asymptotic covariance matrix for the two estimates, we first obtained

$$\mathbf{R} = \frac{1}{20}\frac{1}{19}\sum_{i=1}^{20}\mathbf{J}\begin{bmatrix} x_{i1} - \hat{\mu}_1 \\ x_{i2} - \hat{\mu}_2 \\ x_{i3} - \hat{\mu}_3 \\ x_{i4} - \hat{\mu}_4 \end{bmatrix}\begin{bmatrix} x_{i1} - \hat{\mu}_1 \\ x_{i2} - \hat{\mu}_2 \\ x_{i3} - \hat{\mu}_3 \\ x_{i4} - \hat{\mu}_4 \end{bmatrix}'$$

$$\mathbf{J}' = \begin{bmatrix} 0.12469 & & & \\ 0.78911 & 5.3231 & & \\ 0.0016847 & 0.030884 & 0.43525 & \\ -0.0031245 & -0.015851 & -0.00099142 & 0.00015174 \end{bmatrix}.$$

[24]At all points, the scales of the four variables were so different that the numerical results computed from the unscaled moments (i.e., not using $\mathbf{J}$) were extremely unstable, even in double precision. Note that using $\mathbf{J}$ in this fashion does not amount to using a weighting matrix that depends on $\boldsymbol{\theta}$. All that we have done is use a different set of moment equations. The weighting matrix is still $\mathbf{I}$.

TABLE 11.1 Estimates of the Parameters of a Gamma Distribution

Parameter	*Maximum Likelihood*	*Generalized Method of Moments*
P	2.4097	2.1799
Standard Error	(0.71556)	(0.45607)
λ	0.077041	0.069058
Standard Error	(0.02541)	(0.015421)

This gives $\mathbf{R} = \mathbf{J} \times \text{Est. Asy. Var}[\overline{\mathbf{m}}(P, \lambda)] \times \mathbf{J}$ (where $\mathbf{J}$ is recomputed with the final estimates). To complete the computation, we will require the derivatives matrix,

$$\mathbf{G}' = \begin{bmatrix} \partial m_1/\partial P & \partial m_2/\partial P & \partial m_3/\partial P & \partial m_4/\partial P \\ \partial m_1/\partial\lambda & \partial m_2/\partial\lambda & \partial m_3/\partial\lambda & \partial m_4/\partial\lambda \end{bmatrix}$$

$$= \begin{bmatrix} -1/\lambda & -(2P+1)/\lambda^2 & -\Psi'(P) & \lambda/(P-1)^2 \\ p/\lambda^2 & 2P(P+1)/\lambda^3 & 1/\lambda & -1/(P-1) \end{bmatrix}.$$

$$\hat{\mathbf{G}} = \begin{bmatrix} -14.494 & -1252.9 & -0.49465 & 0.031413 \\ 521.52 & 52{,}631.0 & 14.494 & -0.67476 \end{bmatrix}.$$

Finally,

$$[\hat{\mathbf{G}}'(\mathbf{J}\mathbf{R}^{-1}\mathbf{J}')\hat{\mathbf{G}}]^{-1} = \begin{bmatrix} 0.20800 & 0.006111 \\ 0.06111 & 0.00023781 \end{bmatrix}$$

gives the estimated asymptotic covariance matrix for the estimates. (Note that the covariance matrix for the moments must be scaled up by $\mathbf{J}$ after inversion because we computed the covariance matrix for the scaled moments.) Recall that in Example 4.26, we obtained maximum likelihood estimates of the same parameters. Table 11.1 summarizes. It appears that there is a considerable payoff to using the additional moments. (The appearance is illusory, as we will see in the next section.)

11.5.3. Computation of q and Using Nonoptimal Weighting Matrices

It is easy to lose sight of the magnitudes involved in computing the GMM estimator and the associated asymptotic covariance matrix. The sample moments are computed as

$$\overline{\mathbf{m}}(\boldsymbol{\theta}) = \frac{1}{n} \sum_{i=1}^{n} \mathbf{m}_i(\boldsymbol{\theta}),$$

where $\mathbf{m}_i$ is a single observation constructed from the moment condition

$$E[\mathbf{m}_i(\boldsymbol{\theta})] = \mathbf{0}$$

and the subscript indicates the dependence on the single observation $(y_i, \mathbf{x}_i, \mathbf{z}_i)$. Therefore, $\overline{\mathbf{m}}(\boldsymbol{\theta})$ is a sample mean that converges to $\mathbf{0}$ stochastically at the rate $1/\sqrt{n}$ if the assumptions of the model are correct or to some other constant if they are not. The variance of $\mathbf{m}_i(\boldsymbol{\theta})$ is

$$E[\mathbf{m}_i(\boldsymbol{\theta})\mathbf{m}_i(\boldsymbol{\theta})'] = \text{Var}[\mathbf{m}_i(\boldsymbol{\theta})] = \boldsymbol{\Phi}, \quad \text{an } L \times L \text{ positive semidefinite matrix.}$$

We would estimate $\boldsymbol{\Phi}$ with

$$\hat{\boldsymbol{\Phi}} = \frac{1}{n-1}\sum_{i=1}^{n} \mathbf{m}_i(\hat{\boldsymbol{\theta}})\mathbf{m}_i(\hat{\boldsymbol{\theta}})',$$

which is also a sample mean. Note, though, that what enters the GMM criterion, q, is not $\hat{\boldsymbol{\Phi}}$, but the estimator of the variance of the mean,

$$\text{Var}[\overline{\mathbf{m}}(\boldsymbol{\theta})] = \frac{1}{n}\boldsymbol{\Phi},$$

which is,

$$\hat{\mathbf{W}} = \frac{1}{n}\hat{\boldsymbol{\Phi}} = \frac{1}{n}\frac{1}{n-1}\sum_{i=1}^{n} \mathbf{m}_i(\hat{\boldsymbol{\theta}})\mathbf{m}_i(\hat{\boldsymbol{\theta}})'.$$

This matrix is $0(1/n)$, which means that it is converging to $\mathbf{0}$. The GMM criterion function

$$q = \overline{\mathbf{m}}(\boldsymbol{\theta})'\hat{\mathbf{W}}^{-1}\overline{\mathbf{m}}(\boldsymbol{\theta})$$

is a quadratic form in a vector that is converging to $\mathbf{0}$ at the rate $(1/\sqrt{n})$ times the inverse of a matrix that is $\mathbf{0}(1/n)$. This is, in fact, a Wald statistic with $E[q] = L - K$ under the hypothesis of the model.

Now, consider the estimator of the variance of the GMM estimator. In the final analysis, the estimator is a function of $\overline{\mathbf{m}}$, so we can approach the derivation as one of finding the variance of a nonlinear function using the delta method. (See Sections 4.4.4 and 6.7.5.) The derivatives matrix is

$$\hat{\mathbf{G}}' = \partial\overline{\mathbf{m}}(\hat{\boldsymbol{\theta}})/\partial\hat{\boldsymbol{\theta}}',$$

which is also a sample mean and thus converges to a constant matrix (by assumption). Then

$$\begin{aligned}\text{Est. Var}[\hat{\boldsymbol{\theta}}] &= [\mathbf{G}(\hat{\boldsymbol{\theta}})'\{\widehat{\text{Var}}[\overline{\mathbf{m}}(\hat{\boldsymbol{\theta}})]\}^{-1}\mathbf{G}(\hat{\boldsymbol{\theta}})]^{-1}\\ &= [\mathbf{G}(\hat{\boldsymbol{\theta}})'\hat{\mathbf{W}}^{-1}\mathbf{G}(\hat{\boldsymbol{\theta}})]^{-1}\\ &= \frac{1}{n}[\mathbf{G}(\hat{\boldsymbol{\theta}})'\{\hat{\boldsymbol{\Phi}}\}^{-1}\mathbf{G}(\hat{\boldsymbol{\theta}})]^{-1},\end{aligned}$$

which is $\mathbf{0}(1/n)$, as expected.

If a matrix other than $\hat{\mathbf{W}}$ is used, we obtain a consistent but inefficient estimator of $\boldsymbol{\theta}$. The asymptotic covariance matrix for the estimator that minimizes

$$q_A = \overline{\mathbf{m}}(\boldsymbol{\theta})'\mathbf{A}\overline{\mathbf{m}}(\boldsymbol{\theta})$$

is

$$\mathbf{V}_A = [\mathbf{G}(\boldsymbol{\theta})'\mathbf{A}\mathbf{G}(\boldsymbol{\theta})]^{-1}\mathbf{G}(\boldsymbol{\theta})'\mathbf{A}\left(\frac{1}{n}\boldsymbol{\Phi}\right)\mathbf{A}\mathbf{G}(\boldsymbol{\theta})[\mathbf{G}(\boldsymbol{\theta})'\mathbf{A}\mathbf{G}(\boldsymbol{\theta})]^{-1}.$$

Two special cases are interesting. If $\mathbf{A}$ equals an estimator of $[(1/n)\boldsymbol{\Phi}]^{-1}$, then we return to the result we had for the GMM estimator. If we use the least squares estimator $\mathbf{A} = \mathbf{I}$, then

$$\mathbf{V}_A = (\mathbf{G}'\mathbf{G})^{-1}\mathbf{G}'\left(\frac{1}{n}\boldsymbol{\Phi}\right)\mathbf{G}(\mathbf{G}'\mathbf{G})^{-1}.$$

As we shall see below, this is exactly (11-5), which returns us to our departure point. This provides a neat symmetry to the GMM principle.

11.5.4. Testing the Validity of the Moment Restrictions

In the exactly identified cases we examined earlier, the criterion for GMM estimation

$$q = \overline{\mathbf{m}}(\boldsymbol{\theta})'\mathbf{W}^{-1}\overline{\mathbf{m}}(\boldsymbol{\theta})$$

would be exactly zero because we can find a set of estimates for which $\overline{\mathbf{m}}(\boldsymbol{\theta})$ is exactly zero. This means, of course, that in the exactly identified case, when there are the same number of moment equations as there are parameters to estimate, the weighting matrix $\mathbf{W}$ is irrelevant. But if the parameters are overidentified by the moment equation, these equations imply substantive restrictions. As such, if the hypothesis of the model that led to the moment equations in the first place is incorrect, at least some of the sample moment restrictions will be systematically violated. This provides the basis for a test of the overidentifying restrictions. By construction,

$$q = \overline{\mathbf{m}}(\hat{\boldsymbol{\theta}})'\{\text{Est. Asy. Var}[\overline{\mathbf{m}}(\hat{\boldsymbol{\theta}})]\}^{-1}\overline{\mathbf{m}}(\hat{\boldsymbol{\theta}}),$$

so q is a Wald statistic. Therefore,

$$q \xrightarrow{d} \chi^2[J - K].$$

(For the exactly identified case, there are zero degrees of freedom and $q = 0$.)

EXAMPLE 11.5 (Example 4.26 Concluded)

In Example 11.4, we found that the value of q for our data was 9.9296. This exceeds the critical value from the chi-squared table of 5.99. As such, the hypothesis that all four moment equations are satisfied is rejected (albeit not decisively). This should have been expected. In point of fact, for random sampling from the gamma distribution, the maximum likelihood estimators are efficient among all consistent estimators. As such, there is surely an inconsistency in the standard errors for the GMM estimators appearing to be smaller than those for the MLE. The conflict is resolved by the hypothesis test, which suggests that the restrictions should be rejected. The implications of this for estimation in this context are, first, that the hypothesis that the data were drawn from an underlying gamma population should be rejected. (They were not; they were chosen at random by the author.) Second, given this, the method used to compute the asymptotic covariance matrix for the MLE is incorrect. Finally, the moment equations themselves should be deemed invalid. You should note that it is not possible to do this sort of analysis based on only two of the moments, regardless of which two are chosen. In an exactly identified case, all the information in the sample is consumed in estimation of the parameters. Only when the restrictions overidentify the parameters can q be used to make inference about the specification of the model.

11.5.5. GMM Estimation of Econometric Models

The preceding has developed the method of moments largely in the context of estimation of the parameters of a distribution using a random sample. The extension to estimation of the parameters of econometric models is fairly straightforward. For purposes of an uncomplicated introduction, we will consider the problem of estimation of the parameters in a single equation, but recent applications have extended the technique to multiple equations models as well. We will examine the extensions in later chapters.

Suppose that the theory specifies a relationship

$$y_i = h(\mathbf{x}_i, \boldsymbol{\beta}) + \epsilon_i,$$

where $\boldsymbol{\beta}$ is a $K \times 1$ parameter vector that we wish to estimate. This might not be a regression relationship, since it is possible that

$$\text{Cov}[\epsilon_i, h(\mathbf{x}_i, \boldsymbol{\beta})] \neq 0,$$

or even

$$\text{Cov}[\epsilon_i, \mathbf{x}_j] \neq \mathbf{0} \quad \text{for all } i \text{ and } j.$$

Consider, for example, a model that contains lagged dependent variables and autocorrelated disturbances. (See Section 13.4.1.) We assume that

$$E[\boldsymbol{\epsilon}] = \mathbf{0}$$

and

$$E[\boldsymbol{\epsilon\epsilon}'] = \boldsymbol{\Sigma},$$

where $\boldsymbol{\Sigma}$ is unrestricted. The disturbances may be heteroscedastic and/or autocorrelated. But for the possibility of correlation between regressors and disturbances, this would be a generalized, possibly nonlinear, regression model. Suppose that at each observation i we observe a vector of L variables, $\mathbf{z}_i$, such that $\mathbf{z}_i$ is uncorrelated with ϵ_i. You will recognize $\mathbf{z}_i$ as a set of **instrumental variables.** The assumptions thus far have implied a set of **orthogonality conditions,**

$$E[\mathbf{z}_i \epsilon_i] = \mathbf{0},$$

which may be sufficient to identify (if $L = K$) or even overidentify (if $L > K$) the parameters of the model.

For convenience, define

$$\mathbf{e}(\mathbf{X}, \hat{\boldsymbol{\beta}}) = y_i - h(\mathbf{x}_i, \hat{\boldsymbol{\beta}}), \quad i = 1, \ldots, n,$$

and

$$\mathbf{Z} = n \times L \text{ matrix whose } i\text{th row is } \mathbf{z}_i'.$$

By a straightforward extension of our earlier results, we can produce a GMM estimator of $\boldsymbol{\beta}$. The sample moments will be

$$\overline{\mathbf{m}}(\boldsymbol{\beta}) = \frac{1}{n}\sum_{i=1}^{n} \mathbf{z}_i e(\mathbf{x}_i, \boldsymbol{\beta}) = \frac{1}{n}\mathbf{Z}'\mathbf{e}(\mathbf{X}, \boldsymbol{\beta}).$$

The minimum distance estimator will be the $\hat{\boldsymbol{\beta}}$ that minimizes

$$\begin{aligned} q &= \mathbf{m}(\hat{\boldsymbol{\beta}})'\mathbf{W}^{-1}\mathbf{m}(\hat{\boldsymbol{\beta}}) \\ &= (1/n^2)[\mathbf{e}(\mathbf{X}, \hat{\boldsymbol{\beta}})'\mathbf{Z}]\mathbf{W}^{-1}[\mathbf{Z}'\mathbf{e}(\mathbf{X}, \hat{\boldsymbol{\beta}})] \end{aligned} \tag{11-40}$$

for some choice of $\mathbf{W}$ that we have yet to determine. The criterion given above produces the **nonlinear instrumental variable estimator.** Indeed, if we use $\mathbf{W} = \mathbf{Z}'\mathbf{Z}$, apart from a scaling of $2/n^2$, this is exactly the estimation criterion we used in Section 10.2.5 where we defined the nonlinear instrumental variables estimator. Apparently (11-40) is more general, since we are not limited to this choice of $\mathbf{W}$. The linear IV estimator is a special case. For any given choice of $\mathbf{W}$, as long as there are enough orthogonality conditions to identify the parameters, estimation by minimizing q is, at least in principle, a straightforward problem in nonlinear optimization. Hansen (1982) showed that the optimal choice of $\mathbf{W}$ for this estimator is

$$\begin{aligned} \mathbf{W}_{\text{GMM}} &= \text{Asy. Var}[\overline{\mathbf{m}}(\boldsymbol{\theta})] \\ &= \text{Asy. Var}\left[\frac{1}{n}\sum_{i=1}^{n}\mathbf{z}_i\epsilon_i\right] \\ &= \text{Asy. Var}\left[\frac{1}{n}\mathbf{Z}'\mathbf{e}(\mathbf{X}, \boldsymbol{\beta})\right]. \end{aligned} \tag{11-41}$$

For our model, this is

$$\begin{aligned} \mathbf{W} &= \frac{1}{n^2}\sum_{i=1}^{n}\sum_{j=1}^{n}\text{Cov}[\mathbf{z}_i\epsilon_i, \mathbf{z}_j\epsilon_j] \\ &= \frac{1}{n^2}\sum_{i=1}^{n}\sum_{j=1}^{n}\sigma_{ij}\mathbf{z}_i\mathbf{z}_j' \\ &= \frac{1}{n^2}\mathbf{Z}'\boldsymbol{\Sigma}\mathbf{Z}. \end{aligned}$$

If we insert this in (11-40), we obtain the criterion for the GMM estimator:

$$q = \left[\left(\frac{1}{n}\right)\mathbf{e}(\mathbf{X}, \hat{\boldsymbol{\beta}})'\mathbf{Z}\right]\left(\frac{1}{n^2}\mathbf{Z}'\boldsymbol{\Sigma}\mathbf{Z}\right)^{-1}\left[\left(\frac{1}{n}\right)\mathbf{Z}'\mathbf{e}(\mathbf{X}, \hat{\boldsymbol{\beta}})\right].$$

There is a possibly difficult detail to be considered. The GMM estimator involves

$$\frac{1}{n^2}\mathbf{Z}'\boldsymbol{\Sigma}\mathbf{Z} = \frac{1}{n^2}\sum_{i=1}^{n}\sum_{j=1}^{n}\mathbf{z}_i\mathbf{z}_j'\text{Cov}[\epsilon_i\epsilon_j]$$
$$= \frac{1}{n^2}\sum_{i=1}^{n}\sum_{j=1}^{n}\mathbf{z}_i\mathbf{z}_j'\text{Cov}[(y_i - h(\mathbf{x}_i, \boldsymbol{\beta}))(y_j - h(\mathbf{x}_j, \boldsymbol{\beta}))].$$

The conditions under which such a double sum might converge to a positive definite matrix are sketched in Section 11.2.5. Assuming that they hold, estimation appears to require that an estimate of $\boldsymbol{\beta}$ be in hand already, even though it is the object of estimation. It may be that a consistent but inefficient estimate of $\boldsymbol{\beta}$ is available. Suppose for the present that one is. If observations are uncorrelated, the cross terms may be omitted, and what is required is

$$\frac{1}{n^2}\mathbf{Z}'\boldsymbol{\Sigma}\mathbf{Z} = \frac{1}{n^2}\sum_{i=1}^{n}\mathbf{z}_i\mathbf{z}_j'\text{Var}[(y_i - h(\mathbf{x}_i, \boldsymbol{\beta}))].$$

We can use the White (1980b) estimator discussed in Section 11.2.5 for this case:

$$\frac{1}{n}\mathbf{S}_0 = \frac{1}{n}\left[\frac{1}{n}\sum_{i=1}^{n}\mathbf{z}_i\mathbf{z}_j'(y_i - h(\mathbf{x}_i, \hat{\boldsymbol{\beta}}))^2\right]. \tag{11-42}$$

If the disturbances are autocorrelated, Newey and West's (1987a) estimator is available:

$$\frac{1}{n}\mathbf{S} = \frac{1}{n}\left[\mathbf{S}_0 + \frac{1}{n}\sum_{\ell=1}^{p}w(\ell)\sum_{i=\ell+1}^{n}e_ie_{i-\ell}(\mathbf{z}_i\mathbf{z}_{i-\ell}' + \mathbf{z}_{i-\ell}\mathbf{z}_i')\right]$$
$$= \frac{1}{n}\sum_{\ell=0}^{p}w(\ell)\mathbf{S}_\ell, \tag{11-43}$$

where

$$w(\ell) = 1 - \ell/(p + 1).$$

The maximum lag length p must be determined in advance. (This will be discussed in Section 13.4.3.) We will require that observations that are far apart in time—that is, for which $|i - \ell|$ is large—must have increasingly smaller covariances for us to establish the convergence results that justify OLS, GLS, and now GMM estimation. The choice of p is a reflection of how far back in time one must go to consider the autocorrelation negligible for purposes of estimating $(1/n^2)\mathbf{Z}'\boldsymbol{\Sigma}\mathbf{Z}$.

This leaves open the question of where the initial consistent estimator should be obtained. One possibility is to obtain an inefficient but consistent GMM estimator by using $\mathbf{W} = \mathbf{I}$ in (11-40). That is, use a nonlinear (or linear, if the equation is linear) instrumental variables estimator. This first step estimator can then be used to construct $\mathbf{W}$, which, in turn, can then be used in the GMM estimator. Another possibility is that $\boldsymbol{\beta}$ may be consistently estimable by some straightforward procedure other than GMM.

Once the GMM estimator has been computed, its asymptotic covariance matrix and asymptotic distribution can be estimated based on (11-38) and (11-39). Recall that

$$\overline{\mathbf{m}}(\boldsymbol{\beta}) = \frac{1}{n}\sum_{i=1}^{n}\mathbf{z}_i\epsilon_i,$$

which is a sum of $L \times 1$ vectors. The derivative, $\partial\overline{\mathbf{m}}(\boldsymbol{\beta})/\partial\boldsymbol{\beta}'$, is a sum of n $K \times \mathrm{L}$ matrices,

$$\mathbf{G}_i(\boldsymbol{\beta}) = \left[\frac{\partial\epsilon_i}{\partial\boldsymbol{\beta}}\right]\mathbf{z}_i',$$

so

$$\mathbf{G}(\boldsymbol{\theta}) = \partial\overline{\mathbf{m}}(\boldsymbol{\beta})/\partial\boldsymbol{\beta} = \frac{1}{n}\sum_{i=1}^{n}\mathbf{G}_i(\boldsymbol{\beta}). \qquad \textbf{(11-44a)}$$

In the model we are considering here,

$$\frac{\partial\epsilon_i}{\partial\boldsymbol{\beta}} = \frac{-\partial h(\mathbf{x}_i, \boldsymbol{\beta})}{\partial\boldsymbol{\beta}}.$$

The derivatives are the pseudoregressors in the linearized regression model that we examined in Section 10.2.1. Using the notation defined there,

$$\frac{\partial\epsilon_i}{\partial\boldsymbol{\beta}} = -\mathbf{x}_i^0,$$

so

$$\mathbf{G}_i(\boldsymbol{\theta}) = -\mathbf{x}_i^0\mathbf{z}_i'.$$

The mean would be

$$\mathbf{G}(\boldsymbol{\beta}) = -\frac{1}{n}\sum_{i=1}^{n}\mathbf{G}_i = -\frac{1}{n}\mathbf{X}^{0\prime}\mathbf{Z}. \qquad \textbf{(11-44b)}$$

With this in hand, the estimated asymptotic covariance matrix for the GMM estimator is

$$\begin{aligned}\text{Est. Asy. Var}[\hat{\boldsymbol{\beta}}] &= \left[\mathbf{G}(\hat{\boldsymbol{\beta}})\left(\frac{1}{n^2}\mathbf{Z}'\hat{\boldsymbol{\Sigma}}\mathbf{Z}\right)^{-1}\mathbf{G}(\hat{\boldsymbol{\theta}})'\right]^{-1} \\ &= [(\mathbf{X}^{0\prime}\mathbf{Z})(\mathbf{Z}'\hat{\boldsymbol{\Sigma}}\mathbf{Z})^{-1}(\mathbf{Z}'\mathbf{X}^0)]^{-1}.\end{aligned} \qquad \textbf{(11-45)}$$

(The two minus signs, a $1/n^2$ and an n^2, all fall out of the result.)

If the $\boldsymbol{\Sigma}$ that appears in (11-45) were $\sigma^2\mathbf{I}$, then (11-45) would be precisely the asymptotic covariance matrix that appears in Theorem 6.15 for linear models and Theorem 10.2 for nonlinear models. But there is an interesting distinction between this estimator and the IV estimators discussed earlier. In the earlier cases, when there were more instrumental variables than parameters, we resolved the overidentification by choosing a subset of the instruments: the K projections of the columns of $\mathbf{X}$ or $\mathbf{X}^0$ into the column space of $\mathbf{Z}$. Here, in contrast, we do not attempt to resolve the overidentification; we simply use all of the instruments and minimize the GMM criterion. Now you should be able to show that when $\boldsymbol{\Sigma} = \sigma^2\mathbf{I}$ *and we use this information*, when all is said and done, these will produce the same parameter estimates. But, if we use a weighting matrix that differs from $\mathbf{I}$, they do not.

EXAMPLE 11.6 Linear Models and GMM

You should be able to prove the following: For the class of linear models,

$$y_i = \mathbf{x}_i'\boldsymbol{\beta} + \epsilon_i,$$

GMM estimation can be based on the orthogonality conditions

$$E[\mathbf{z}_i(y_i - \mathbf{x}_i'\boldsymbol{\beta})].$$

If the disturbances are uncorrelated and homoscedastic and $\mathbf{z} = \mathbf{x}$, this is obviously just the OLS estimator. On the other hand, if we allow for correlation between $\mathbf{x}$ and ϵ, and if $\mathbf{z}$ is a set of K instrumental variables that satisfy the requirements in Section 6.7.8, then the IV estimator in Section 6.7.8 emerges. If $\mathbf{z}$ is $L > K$ instrumental variables but we maintain the assumptions about the disturbances, then the 2SLS estimator in (16-23) is the resulting GMM estimator. (This requires a slight change in notation.) If we continue to assume that $\mathbf{z}$ equals $\mathbf{x}$ but that the disturbances are heteroscedastic, then the GMM estimator will be OLS. But the estimated asymptotic covariance matrix will be the White estimator given in (11-13) and (12-9). If $\mathbf{z} = \mathbf{x}$, but we allow for autocorrelation of the disturbances, the GMM estimator will, once again, be OLS, but the estimated asymptotic covariance matrix will be the Newey–West estimator defined by (12-8), (12-9), (13-24), and (13-25). Finally, if $\mathbf{z} \neq \mathbf{x}$ and we allow for heteroscedasticity, then the GMM estimator is

$$\mathbf{b}_{\text{GMM}} = [\mathbf{X}'\mathbf{Z}\mathbf{S}_0^{-1}\mathbf{Z}'\mathbf{X}]^{-1}[\mathbf{X}'\mathbf{Z}\mathbf{S}_0^{-1}\mathbf{X}'\mathbf{y}],$$

where $\mathbf{S}_0$ must be based on some consistent estimator of $\boldsymbol{\beta}$ (e.g., $\mathbf{b}_{\text{IV}}$).

In two of the cases in Example 11.6, the GMM estimator is inefficient. This is a function of the orthogonality conditions. The GMM estimator is efficient only in the class of instrumental variable estimators *defined by the orthogonality conditions*. One of the cases pointed out in this example merits a second look. In the classical model with heteroscedastic disturbances, this analysis might suggest an improvement on OLS. That is, the GMM estimator would be

$$\mathbf{b}_{\text{GMM}} = [\mathbf{X}'\mathbf{X}\mathbf{S}_0^{-1}\mathbf{X}'\mathbf{X}]^{-1}[\mathbf{X}'\mathbf{X}\mathbf{S}_0^{-1}\mathbf{X}'\mathbf{y}].$$

But $[\mathbf{X}'\mathbf{X}\mathbf{S}_0^{-1}\mathbf{X}'\mathbf{X}]^{-1} = (\mathbf{X}'\mathbf{X})^{-1}\mathbf{S}_0(\mathbf{X}'\mathbf{X})^{-1}$, and after multiplying it out, what remains is the OLS estimator with the familiar White estimator in (11-13) as the estimator of its asymptotic covariance matrix.

11.6. TESTING HYPOTHESES IN THE GMM FRAMEWORK

The estimation framework developed in the previous section provides the basis for a convenient set of statistics for testing hypotheses. We will consider two groups of tests. The first is a trio of tests that correspond to the familiar Wald, LM, and LR tests that we have examined at several points in the preceding chapters. The second is a class of tests based on the theoretical underpinnings of the conditional moments that we used earlier to devise the GMM estimator.

11.6.1. GMM Counterparts to the Wald, LM, and LR Tests

Section 4.8.3 described a trio of testing procedures that can be applied to a hypothesis in the context of maximum likelihood estimation. To reiterate, let the hypothesis to be tested be a set of J possibly nonlinear restrictions on K parameters $\boldsymbol{\theta}$ in the form H_0: $\mathbf{R}(\boldsymbol{\theta}) - \mathbf{r} = \mathbf{0}$, where $\boldsymbol{\theta}$ is the parameter vector being estimated. Let $\mathbf{c}_1$ be the maximum likelihood estimates of $\boldsymbol{\theta}$ estimated without the restrictions, and let $\mathbf{c}_0$ denote the restricted maximum likelihood estimates, that is, the estimates obtained while imposing the null hypothesis. The three statistics, which are asymptotically equivalent, are obtained as follows:

$$\text{LR} = \text{likelihood ratio} = \chi^2[J] = -2(\ln L_0 - \ln L_1), \qquad \textbf{(11-46)}$$

where

$$\ln L_j = \text{log likelihood function evaluated at } \mathbf{c}_j, \quad j = 0, 1.$$

The likelihood ratio statistic requires that both estimates be computed. The Wald statistic is

$$\begin{aligned} W &= \text{Wald} \\ &= \chi^2[J] = [\mathbf{R}(\mathbf{c}_1) - \mathbf{r}]'\{\text{Est. Asy. Var}[\mathbf{R}(\mathbf{c}_1) - \mathbf{r}]\}^{-1}[\mathbf{R}(\mathbf{c}_1) - \mathbf{r}]. \end{aligned} \qquad \textbf{(11-47)}$$

The Wald statistic is the distance measure for the degree to which the unrestricted estimator fails to satisfy the restrictions. The usual estimator for the asymptotic covariance matrix would be

$$\text{Est. Asy. Var}[\mathbf{R}(\mathbf{c}_1) - \mathbf{r}] = \mathbf{A}_1\{\text{Est. Asy. Var}[\mathbf{c}_1]\}\mathbf{A}'_1, \qquad \textbf{(11-48)}$$

where

$$\mathbf{A}_1 = \partial\mathbf{R}(\mathbf{c}_1)/\partial\mathbf{c}'_1 \;\; (\mathbf{A}_1 \text{ is a } J \times K \text{ matrix}).$$

The Wald statistic can be computed using only the unrestricted estimate. The LM statistic is

$$\text{LM} = \text{Lagrange multiplier} = \chi^2[J] = \mathbf{g}'_0\{\text{Est. Asy. Var}[\mathbf{g}_0]\}^{-1}\mathbf{g}_0, \qquad \textbf{(11-49)}$$

where

$$\mathbf{g}_0 = \partial \ln L(\mathbf{c}_0)/\partial \boldsymbol{\theta}_0,$$

that is, the first derivatives of the log-likelihood computed at the restricted estimates. The Est. Asy. Var$[\mathbf{g}_0]$ is the inverse of any of the usual estimators of the asymptotic covariance matrix of the maximum likelihood estimators of the parameters, computed using the restricted estimates. The most convenient choice is often the BHHH estimator. The LM statistic is based on the restricted estimates.

Newey and West (1987b) have devised counterparts to these test statistics for the GMM estimator. The Wald statistic is computed identically, using the results of GMM estimation rather than maximum likelihood. That is, in (11-47), we would use the unrestricted GMM estimator of $\boldsymbol{\beta}$. The appropriate asymptotic covariance matrix is that in (11-45), which might be based on (11-42) or (11-43). Either way, the computation is exactly the same. The counterpart to the LR statistic is the difference in the values of q in (11-40). It is necessary to use the same $\mathbf{W}$ matrix in both restricted and unrestricted estimators. Since the unrestricted estimator is consistent under both H_0 and H_1, a consistent, unrestricted estimator of $\boldsymbol{\theta}$ is used to compute $\mathbf{W}$. Then q is minimized without restrictions to obtain q_1 and subject to the restrictions to obtain q_0. The statistic is then just $(q_0 - q_1)$.[25] Since we are using the same $\mathbf{W}$ in both cases, this is necessarily nonnegative. Finally, the counterpart to the LM statistic would be

$$\text{LM}_{\text{GMM}} = [\mathbf{m}(\mathbf{c}_0)'\mathbf{W}^{-1}\mathbf{A}(\mathbf{c}_0)]\{\text{Est. Asy. Var}[\mathbf{c}_0]\}^{-1}[\mathbf{m}(\mathbf{c}_0)'\mathbf{W}^{-1}\mathbf{A}(\mathbf{c}_0)]'.$$

The logic for this LM statistic is the same as that for the MLE. The derivatives of the criterion q in (11-40) are

$$\boldsymbol{\alpha} = \frac{\partial q}{\partial \boldsymbol{\theta}} = 2\mathbf{G}(\boldsymbol{\theta})'\mathbf{W}^{-1}\overline{\mathbf{m}}(\boldsymbol{\theta}).$$

The LM statistic, LM_{GMM}, is a Wald statistic for testing the hypothesis that this vector equals zero under the restrictions of the null hypothesis. From our earlier results, we would have

$$\text{Var}[\boldsymbol{\alpha}] = 4\mathbf{G}(\boldsymbol{\theta})'\mathbf{W}^{-1}\,\text{Var}[\overline{\mathbf{m}}(\boldsymbol{\theta})]\mathbf{W}^{-1}\mathbf{G}(\boldsymbol{\theta}).$$

The variance of $\overline{\mathbf{m}}(\boldsymbol{\theta})$ is $\mathbf{W}$, so

$$\text{Var}[\boldsymbol{\alpha}] = 4\mathbf{G}(\boldsymbol{\theta})'\mathbf{W}^{-1}\mathbf{G}(\boldsymbol{\theta}).$$

The Wald statistic would be

$$\begin{aligned}\text{Wald} &= \boldsymbol{\alpha}'(\text{Var}[\boldsymbol{\alpha}])^{-1}\boldsymbol{\alpha}.\\ &= \overline{\mathbf{m}}(\boldsymbol{\theta})'\mathbf{W}^{-1}\mathbf{G}[\mathbf{G}'\mathbf{W}^{-1}\mathbf{G}]^{-1}\mathbf{G}'\mathbf{W}^{-1}\overline{\mathbf{m}}(\boldsymbol{\theta}).\end{aligned}$$

[25]Newey and West label this the D test.

If we insert $\mathbf{c}_0$ and interpret the parts as we have earlier, this produces LM_{GMM}.[26]

11.6.2. Conditional Moment Tests

A spate of studies has shown how to use **conditional moment restrictions** for specification testing as well as estimation.[27] The logic of the conditional moment (CM) test is as follows. The model specification implies that certain moment restrictions will hold in the population from which the data were drawn. If the specification is correct, the sample data should mimic the implied relationships. For example, in the classical regression model, the assumption of homoscedasticity implies that the disturbance variance is independent of the regressors. As such,

$$E\{\mathbf{x}_i[(y_i - \boldsymbol{\beta}'\mathbf{x}_i)^2 - \sigma^2]\} = E[\mathbf{x}_i(\epsilon_i^2 - \sigma^2)] = \mathbf{0}.$$

If, on the other hand, the regression is heteroscedastic in a way that depends on $\mathbf{x}_i$, then this covariance will not be zero. If the hypothesis of homoscedasticity is correct, then we would expect the sample counterpart to the moment condition,

$$\mathbf{r} = \frac{1}{n}\sum_{i=1}^{n} \mathbf{x}_i(e_i^2 - s^2),$$

where e_i is the OLS residual, to be close to zero. (This is the basis of Breusch and Pagan's LM test for homoscedasticity. See Section 12.3.3.) The practical problems to be solved are (1) to formulate suitable moment conditions that do correspond to the hypothesis test, which is usually straightforward; (2) to devise the appropriate sample counterpart; and (3) to devise a suitable measure of closeness to zero of the sample moment estimator. The last of these will be in the framework of the Wald statistics that we have examined at various points in this book.[28] So the problem will be to devise the appropriate covariance matrix for the sample moments.

Consider a general case in which the moment condition is written in

---

[26]Throughout this entire discussion, we have suppressed a normalizing constant n. Newey and West's results for these statistics all involve multiplication by n, whereas ours do not. The difference can be traced back to the definition of $\mathbf{V}_T$ in (2.6) on their page 781. Their entire set of derivations is couched in terms of a matrix $\mathbf{V}_T$ that is the asymptotic covariance matrix of $\sqrt{n}\mathbf{m}(\boldsymbol{\theta})$ in our notation. The difference is inconsequential in that they and we reach the identical answers for the test statistics listed above. There is a minor error in their paper that does have implications for our results, however. In the paragraph after their (2.7), they state that $\mathbf{Q}^{-1}$ is the asymptotic covariance matrix of the GMM estimator $\hat{\boldsymbol{\theta}}$. In their terms, it is the asymptotic covariance matrix of $\sqrt{T}(\hat{\boldsymbol{\theta}} - \boldsymbol{\theta})$. The implications for our results would be in the covariance matrix in (11-45). If we adhered strictly to the Newey–West definition, the matrix in (11-45) would be multiplied by n, which would be incorrect. This becomes obvious if $\boldsymbol{\Omega} = \sigma^2\mathbf{I}$ and $\mathbf{X}^0 = \mathbf{Z}$, which would correspond to least squares in the classical regression model.

[27]See, for example, Pagan and Vella (1989).

[28]See Section 4.8.3, especially Section 4.8.3b.

terms of variables in the model $[y_i, \mathbf{x}_i, \mathbf{z}_i]$ and parameters (as in the linear regression model) $\hat{\boldsymbol{\theta}}$. The sample moment can be written

$$\mathbf{r} = \frac{1}{n}\sum_{i=1}^{n} \mathbf{m}_i(y_i, \mathbf{x}_i, \mathbf{z}_i, \hat{\boldsymbol{\theta}}) = \frac{1}{n}\sum_{i=1}^{n} \hat{\mathbf{m}}_i. \tag{11-50}$$

The hypothesis is that based on the true $\boldsymbol{\theta}$, $E[\mathbf{m}_i] = \mathbf{0}$. With random sampling, consistency of the parameter estimates $\hat{\boldsymbol{\theta}}$ yielded $\boldsymbol{\theta}$, and the assumption of the null hypothesis, the central limit theorem (Theorem 4.4), applies, so

$$\sqrt{n}\mathbf{r} \xrightarrow{d} N[\mathbf{0}, \boldsymbol{\Sigma}]$$

for some covariance matrix $\boldsymbol{\Sigma}$ that we have yet to estimate. Given an estimate of $\boldsymbol{\Sigma}$, it follows that the Wald statistic,

$$n\mathbf{r}'\hat{\boldsymbol{\Sigma}}^{-1}\mathbf{r} \xrightarrow{d} \text{chi-squared}(J), \tag{11-51}$$

where the degrees of freedom J is the number of moment restrictions being tested. Thus, the statistic can be referred to the chi-squared table.

It remains to determine the estimator of $\boldsymbol{\Sigma}$. The full derivation of $\boldsymbol{\Sigma}$ is fairly complicated. [See Pagan and Vella (1989, pp. S32–S33).] But when the vector of parameter estimates is a maximum likelihood estimate, as it would be for the least squares estimator with normally distributed disturbances and for most of the other estimates we consider, a surprisingly simple estimator can be used. Suppose that the parameter vector used to compute the moments above is obtained by solving the equations

$$\sum_{i=1}^{n} \mathbf{d}(y_i, \mathbf{x}_i, \mathbf{z}_i, \hat{\boldsymbol{\theta}}) = \sum_{i=1}^{n} \hat{\mathbf{d}}_i = \mathbf{0}, \tag{11-52}$$

where $\hat{\boldsymbol{\theta}}$ is the estimated parameter vector [e.g., $(\hat{\boldsymbol{\beta}}, \hat{\sigma})$ in the linear model]. For the linear regression model, that would be the normal equations

$$\mathbf{X}'\mathbf{e} = \sum_{i=1}^{n} \mathbf{x}_i(y_i - \mathbf{x}_i'\mathbf{b}) = \mathbf{0}.$$

Let the matrix $\mathbf{D}$ be the $n \times K$ matrix with ith row equal to $\hat{\mathbf{d}}_i'$. In a maximum likelihood problem, $\mathbf{D}$ is the matrix of derivatives of the individual terms in the log-likelihood function with respect to the parameters. That is, $\mathbf{D}$ is the $\mathbf{G}$ used to compute the BHHH estimator of the information matrix. [See (4-52)]. Let $\mathbf{M}$ be the $n \times J$ matrix whose ith row is $\hat{\mathbf{m}}_i'$. Pagan and Vella show that for maximum likelihood estimators, $\boldsymbol{\Sigma}$ can be estimated using

$$\mathbf{S} = \frac{1}{n}[\mathbf{M}'\mathbf{M} - \mathbf{M}'\mathbf{D}(\mathbf{D}'\mathbf{D})^{-1}\mathbf{D}'\mathbf{M}].\text{[29]} \tag{11-53}$$

[29]It might be tempting just to use $(1/n)\mathbf{M}'\mathbf{M}$. This would be incorrect, as $\mathbf{S}$ accounts for $\mathbf{M}$ being a function of the estimated parameter vector that is converging to its probability limit at the same rate as the sample moments are converging to theirs.

This looks like an involved matrix computation, but it is simple with any regression program. Each element of **S** is the mean square or cross product of the least squares residuals in a linear regression of a column of **M** on the variables in **D**.[30] Therefore, the operational version of the statistic is

$$C = n\mathbf{r}'\mathbf{S}^{-1}\mathbf{r}, \qquad \textbf{(11-54)}$$

which, once again, is referred to the appropriate critical value in the chi-squared table. This provides a joint test that all the moment conditions are satisfied simultaneously. An individual test of just one of the moment restrictions in isolation can be computed even more easily. For testing one of the L conditions, say the ℓth one, the test can be carried out by a simple t test of whether the constant term is zero in a linear regression of the ℓth column of **M** on a constant term and all the columns of **D**. In fact, the test statistic in (11-54) could also be obtained by stacking the J columns of **M** and treating the L equations as a seemingly unrelated regressions model with (**i**, **D**) as the (identical) regressors in each equation and then testing the joint hypothesis that all the constant terms are zero.

EXAMPLE 11.7 Testing for Heteroscedasticity in the Linear Regression Model

Suppose that the linear model is specified as

$$y_i = \beta_1 + \beta_2 x_i + \beta_3 z_i + \epsilon_i.$$

To test whether

$$E[z_i^2(\epsilon_i^2 - \sigma^2)] = 0,$$

we linearly regress $z_i^2(e_i^2 - s^2)$ on a constant, e_i, $x_i e_i$, and $z_i e_i$. A standard t test of whether the constant term in this regression is zero carries out the test. To test the hypothesis that there is no heteroscedasticity with respect to both x and z, we would regress both x and z on $[1, e_i, x_i e_i, z_i e_i]$ and collect the two columns of residuals in **V**. Then $\mathbf{S} = (1/n)\mathbf{V}'\mathbf{V}$. The moment vector would be

$$\mathbf{r} = \frac{1}{n}\sum_{i=1}^{n}\begin{bmatrix} x_i \\ z_i \end{bmatrix}(e_i^2 - s^2).$$

EXERCISES

1. What is the covariance matrix of the GLS estimator and the difference between it and the OLS estimator?

$$\text{Cov}[\hat{\boldsymbol{\beta}}, \hat{\boldsymbol{\beta}} - \mathbf{b}],$$

[30] If the estimator is not an MLE, estimation of $\boldsymbol{\Sigma}$ is more involved but also straightforward using basic matrix algebra. The advantage of (11-53) is that it involves simple sums of variables that have already been computed to obtain $\hat{\boldsymbol{\theta}}$ and **r**. Note, as well, that if $\boldsymbol{\theta}$ has been estimated by maximum likelihood, the term $(\mathbf{D}'\mathbf{D})^{-1}$ is the BHHH estimator of the asymptotic covariance matrix of $\hat{\boldsymbol{\theta}}$. If it were more convenient, this could be replaced with any other appropriate estimator of Asy. Var$[\hat{\boldsymbol{\theta}}]$.

where

$$\hat{\boldsymbol{\beta}} = (\mathbf{X}'\boldsymbol{\Omega}^{-1}\mathbf{X})^{-1}\mathbf{X}'\boldsymbol{\Omega})^{-1}\mathbf{y}$$

and

$$\mathbf{b} = (\mathbf{X}'\mathbf{X})^{-1}\mathbf{X}'\mathbf{y}.$$

The result plays a pivotal role in the development of specification tests in Hausman (1978).

2. For the Poisson model of Exercise 4 in Chapter 10, show that the maximum likelihood estimator is the GLS estimator. Show that the variances you derived in parts a and b are those in (11-5) and (11-17). (Note that this is an unusual case in that the GLS estimator is fully efficient even though the disturbance variances involve the parameters of the regression.)
3. This and the next two exercises are based on the test statistic usually used to test a set of J linear restrictions in the generalized regression model:

$$F[J, n-K] = \frac{(\mathbf{R}\hat{\boldsymbol{\beta}} - \mathbf{q})'[\mathbf{R}(\mathbf{X}'\boldsymbol{\Omega}^{-1}\mathbf{X})^{-1}\mathbf{R}']^{-1}(\mathbf{R}\hat{\boldsymbol{\beta}} - \mathbf{q})/J}{(\mathbf{y} - \mathbf{X}\hat{\boldsymbol{\beta}})'\boldsymbol{\Omega}^{-1}(\mathbf{y} - \mathbf{X}\hat{\boldsymbol{\beta}})/(n-K)},$$

where $\hat{\boldsymbol{\beta}}$ is the GLS estimator. Show that if $\boldsymbol{\Omega}$ is known and the disturbances are normally distributed, this statistic is exactly distributed as F with J and $n - K$ degrees of freedom. What assumptions about the regressors are needed to reach this conclusion? Need they be nonstochastic?
4. Now suppose that the disturbances are not normally distributed, although $\boldsymbol{\Omega}$ is still known. Proceeding along the lines of the proof in Section 10.3.4, show that the previous statistic is asymptotically distributed as $(1/J)$ times a chi-squared variable with J degrees of freedom. [Hint: The transformed model of (11-12) satisfies the assumptions of the theorem in Chapter 10.] Conclude that in the generalized regression model, the Wald statistic

$$W = (\mathbf{R}\hat{\boldsymbol{\beta}} - \mathbf{q})'\{\mathbf{R}(\text{Est. Var}[\hat{\boldsymbol{\beta}}])\mathbf{R}'\}^{-1}(\mathbf{R}\hat{\boldsymbol{\beta}} - \mathbf{q})$$

tends asymptotically to a chi-squared statistic with J degrees of freedom, regardless of the distribution of the disturbances, as long as the data are otherwise well behaved. Note that in a finite sample, the true distribution may be approximated with an $F[J, n - K]$ distribution. It is a bit ambiguous, however, to interpret this as implying that the statistic is asymptotically distributed as F with J and $n - K$ degrees of freedom, as the limiting distribution used to obtain our result is the chi-squared, not the F. In this instance, the $F[J, n - K]$ is a random variable that tends asymptotically to the chi-squared variate.
5. Finally, suppose that $\boldsymbol{\Omega}$ must be estimated, but that assumptions (11-27) and (11-28) are met by the estimator. What changes are required in the development of the previous problem?
6. An intriguing result is the following:

In the generalized regression model, if the K *columns of* $\mathbf{X}$ *are characteristic vectors of* $\boldsymbol{\Omega}$, *then ordinary least squares and generalized least squares are identical.*

(The result is actually a bit broader; $\mathbf{X}$ may be any linear combination of exactly K characteristic vectors.)

(a) Prove the result directly using matrix algebra.

(b) Prove that if $\mathbf{X}$ contains a constant term and if the remaining columns are in deviation form (so that the column sum is zero), then the model of Example 11.1 is one of these cases. (The seemingly unrelated regressions model with identical regressor matrices, discussed in Chapter 15, is another.)

7. In the generalized regression model, suppose that $\boldsymbol{\Omega}$ is known.

(a) What is the covariance matrix of the OLS and GLS estimators of $\boldsymbol{\beta}$?

(b) What is the covariance matrix of the OLS residual vector $\mathbf{e} = \mathbf{y} - \mathbf{Xb}$?

(c) What is the covariance matrix of the GLS residual vector $\hat{\boldsymbol{\epsilon}} = \mathbf{y} - \mathbf{X}\hat{\boldsymbol{\beta}}$?

(d) What is the covariance matrix of the OLS and GLS residual vectors?

8. Derive a general expression for the expected value of s^2, the OLS estimator of σ^2, in the context of the generalized regression model.

9. Suppose that y has the pdf

$$f(y\,|\,\mathbf{x}) = \left[\frac{1}{\boldsymbol{\beta}'\mathbf{x}}\right] e^{-y/(\boldsymbol{\beta}'\mathbf{x})}, \quad y > 0.$$

Then $E[y\,|\,\mathbf{x}] = \boldsymbol{\beta}'\mathbf{x}$ and $\text{Var}[y\,|\,\mathbf{x}] = (\boldsymbol{\beta}'\mathbf{x})^2$. For this model, prove that GLS and MLE are the same, even though this distribution, like the one in Exercise 2, involves the same parameters in the conditional mean function and the disturbance variance.

10. Consider estimation of σ^2 in the generalized regression model. There is a fundamental ambiguity in regard to this "parameter," as it is merely a scaling of $E[\boldsymbol{\epsilon\epsilon}'] = \sigma^2\boldsymbol{\Omega}$. Since both components are unknown, σ^2 cannot be regarded as an estimable parameter until some scaling of $\boldsymbol{\Omega}$ is assumed to remove the indeterminacy. The most convenient assumption is

$$\text{tr}(\boldsymbol{\Omega}) = n.$$

The classical regression model in which $\boldsymbol{\Omega} = \mathbf{I}$ is one such case, so this provides a useful benchmark. Note that the second example in the introduction to this chapter embodies this assumption. Now consider the estimator $s^2 = \mathbf{e}'\mathbf{e}/(n - \text{K})$, where $\mathbf{e}$ is the vector of least squares residuals.

(a) Prove that the exact expectation of s^2 is

$$E[s^2] = \frac{n\sigma^2}{n - K} - \frac{\sigma^2\text{tr}[\{\mathbf{X}'\mathbf{X}/(n - K)\}^{-1}\{\mathbf{X}'\boldsymbol{\Omega}\mathbf{X}/(n - K)\}]}{n - K},$$

so that s^2 is biased. [Hint: As always, $\mathbf{e} = \mathbf{M}\boldsymbol{\epsilon}$. To obtain the expectation, use the same method as in Chapter 6.]

(b) Prove that if the assumptions in (11-6) hold,

$$\lim_{n \to \infty} E[s^2] = \sigma^2.$$

(c) To consider the issue of consistency, prove that

$$\text{plim } s^2 = \text{plim}\left(\frac{1}{n-K}\right)\sum_i \epsilon_i^2.$$

[Hint: Expand $\mathbf{e}'\mathbf{e}/(n-K) = \boldsymbol{\epsilon}'\mathbf{M}\boldsymbol{\epsilon}/(n-K)$.] What are the exact mean and variance of the statistic on the right-hand side? Under what conditions is plim $s^2 = \sigma^2$?

CHAPTER 12

Heteroscedasticity

12.1. INTRODUCTION

If the disturbance variance is not constant across observations, the regression is **heteroscedastic.** In this case,

$$\text{Var}(\epsilon_i \mid \mathbf{x}_i) = \sigma_i^2, \quad i = 1, \ldots, n.$$

We continue to assume that the disturbances are pairwise uncorrelated. Thus,

$$E[\boldsymbol{\epsilon}\boldsymbol{\epsilon}'] = \sigma^2\boldsymbol{\Omega} = \begin{bmatrix} \sigma_1^2 & 0 & 0 & \cdots & 0 \\ 0 & \sigma_2^2 & 0 & \cdots & 0 \\ & & & \vdots & \\ 0 & 0 & 0 & \cdots & \sigma_n^2 \end{bmatrix}.$$

It will sometimes prove useful to write

$$\sigma_i^2 = \sigma^2 \omega_i.$$

In any case, this is an arbitrary scaling. Thus, we shall use the normalization

$$\text{tr}(\boldsymbol{\Omega}) = \sum_{i=1}^{n} \omega_i = n.$$

This makes the classical regression with homoscedastic disturbances a simple special case with $\omega_i = 1$. Intuitively, one might think of the ω's as weights that are scaled in such a way as to reflect only the variety in the disturbance variances. The scale factor σ^2 then provides the overall scaling for the model of the disturbances process.

Heteroscedasticity arises in numerous applications, primarily in the analysis of cross-section data. For example, even after accounting for differences in firm sizes, we expect to observe greater variation in the profits of large firms than in those of small ones. The variance of profits might also depend on product diversification, research and development expenditure, and industry characteristics and thus might also vary across firms of similar sizes. In analyzing family spending patterns, we find that there is greater variation in expenditure on certain commodity groups among high-income families than low ones due to the greater discretion allowed by higher incomes.[1] Heteroscedasticity is sometimes a consequence of data aggregation. In Section 9.4, we found that the appropriate model for grouped data included a disturbance whose variance was σ^2/n_g, where n_g is the number of data points in the gth group. When we analyze group means, the greater precision of an average based on a larger sample implies that the disturbance variance in the regression model will vary inversely with the group size.

EXAMPLE 12.1 Heteroscedastic Regression

The data in Table 12.1 give per capita expenditure on public schools and per capita income by state in 1979.

Least squares regression of spending on a constant, per capita income and the square of per capita income produces the results given in Table 12.2, with

TABLE 12.1 Spending and Income Data

State	*Expenditure*	*Income*	*State*	*Expenditure*	*Income*	*State*	*Expenditure*	*Income*
Ala.	275	6247	Alaska	821	10851	Ariz.	339	7374
Ark.	275	6183	Cal.	387	8850	Colo.	452	8001
Ct.	531	8914	Del.	424	8604	D.C.	428	10022
Fla.	316	7505	Ga.	265	6700	Hawaii	403	8380
Idaho	304	6813	Ill.	437	8745	Ind.	345	7696
Iowa	431	7873	Kans.	355	8001	Ky.	260	6615
La.	316	6640	Maine	327	6333	Md.	427	8306
Mass.	427	8063	Mich.	466	8442	Minn.	477	7847
Miss.	259	5736	Mo.	274	7342	Mont.	433	7051
Nebr.	294	7391	Nev.	359	9032	N.H.	279	7277
N.J.	423	8818	N. Mex.	388	6505	N.Y.	447	8267
N.C.	335	6607	N. Dak.	311	7478	Ohio	322	7812
Okla.	320	6951	Oreg.	397	7839	Pa.	412	7733
R.I.	342	7526	S.C.	315	6242	S. Dak.	321	6841
Tenn.	268	6489	Texas	315	7697	Utah	417	6622
Vt.	353	6541	Va.	356	7624	Wash.	415	8450
W. Va.	320	6456	Wisc.	missing	7597	Wyo.	500	9096

Source: Data from the U.S. Department of Commerce (1979, p. 157).

[1] Prais and Houthakker (1955).

TABLE 12.2 Ordinary Least Squares Results

	Constant	*Income*	*Income*^{2}
Coefficient	832.91	−1834.2	1587.04
Standard error	(327.3)	(829.0)	(519.1)
t ratio	2.545	−2.213	3.057
$R^2 = 0.65534$			
$s^2 = 3212.46$			

the estimated standard errors given in parentheses. (Income is scaled by 10^{-4} in these and all subsequent calculations.)

Individually, the coefficients appear to be statistically significantly different from zero by the usual t test. The joint test based on $F = [R^2/2]/[(1 - R^2)/47] = 44.68$ suggests that the coefficients are jointly significant as well. (The 1 percent critical value is 5.09.) A plot of the residuals against income for the 15 highest and 15 lowest values of income suggests that the disturbances in this regression are somewhat heteroscedastic (see Figure 12.1). The cluster at the left (with the lower values of income) is a bit tighter than the one at the right, and at the highest values of income, the residuals are quite large.

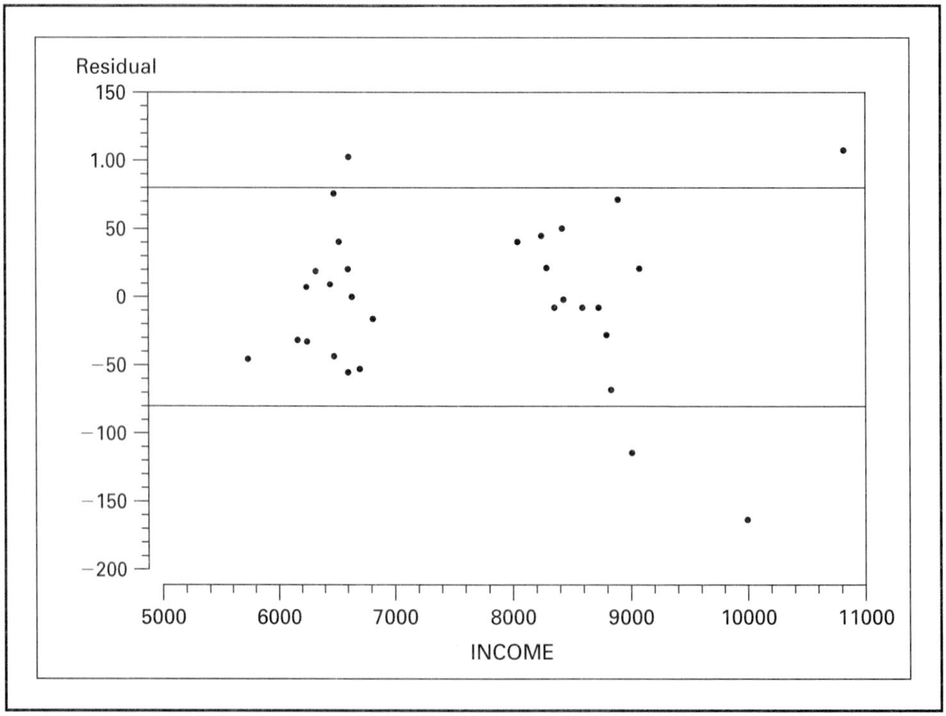

FIGURE 12.1 Plot of Residents Against Income.

12.2. ORDINARY LEAST SQUARES ESTIMATION

We showed in Section 11.2 that in the presence of heteroscedasticity, the least squares estimator $\mathbf{b}$ is still unbiased, consistent, and asymptotically normally distributed. The asymptotic covariance matrix is

$$\text{Asy. Var}[\mathbf{b}] = \frac{\sigma^2}{n}\left(\text{plim}\,\frac{1}{n}\mathbf{X}'\mathbf{X}\right)^{-1}\left(\text{plim}\,\frac{1}{n}\mathbf{X}'\boldsymbol{\Omega}\mathbf{X}\right)\left(\text{plim}\,\frac{1}{n}\mathbf{X}'\mathbf{X}\right)^{-1}.$$

Estimation of the asymptotic covariance matrix would be based on

$$\text{Var}[\mathbf{b}\,|\,\mathbf{X}] = (\mathbf{X}'\mathbf{X})^{-1}\left(\sigma^2\sum_{i=1}^{n}\omega_i\mathbf{x}_i\mathbf{x}_i'\right)(\mathbf{X}'\mathbf{X})^{-1}.$$

[See (11-5).] Assuming, as usual, that the regressors are well behaved, so that $(\mathbf{X}'\mathbf{X}/n)^{-1}$ converges to a positive definite matrix, we find that the mean square consistency of $\mathbf{b}$ depends on the limiting behavior of the matrix:

$$\mathbf{Q}_n^* = \frac{\mathbf{X}'\boldsymbol{\Omega}\mathbf{X}}{n} = \frac{1}{n}\sum_{i=1}^{n}\omega_i\mathbf{x}_i\mathbf{x}_i'. \tag{12-1}$$

If $\mathbf{Q}_n^*$ converges to a positive definite matrix $\mathbf{Q}^*$, as $n \to \infty$, $\mathbf{b}$ will converge to $\boldsymbol{\beta}$ in mean square. Under most circumstances, if ω_i is finite for all i, we would expect this to be true. Note that $\mathbf{Q}_n^*$ is a weighted sum of the squares and cross products of $\mathbf{x}$ with weights ω_i/n, which sum to 1. We have already assumed that another weighted sum $\mathbf{X}'\mathbf{X}/n$, in which the weights are $1/n$, converges to a positive definite matrix $\mathbf{Q}$, so it would be surprising if $\mathbf{Q}_n^*$ did not converge as well. In general, then, we would expect that

$$\mathbf{b} \xrightarrow{a} N\left[\boldsymbol{\beta}, \frac{\sigma^2}{n}\mathbf{Q}^{-1}\mathbf{Q}^*\mathbf{Q}^{-1}\right], \quad \text{with } \mathbf{Q}^* = \text{plim}\ \mathbf{Q}_n^*.$$

A formal proof could be based on Section 6.7.6 with $\mathbf{Q}_i = \omega_i\mathbf{x}_i\mathbf{x}_i'$.

12.2.1. Inefficiency of Least Squares

It follows from our earlier results that $\mathbf{b}$ is inefficient relative to the GLS estimator, although by how much depends on the setting.

EXAMPLE 12.2 Inefficiency of Ordinary Least Squares

Consider a very simple model

$$y_i = \beta x_i + \epsilon_i,$$
$$\text{Var}[\epsilon_i] = \sigma^2 x_i^2,$$

and assume that y and x are measured as deviations from their means. The variances of the OLS and GLS estimators of β are

$$\text{Var}[b] = \sigma^2[\mathbf{X}'\mathbf{X}]^{-1}[\mathbf{X}'\boldsymbol{\Omega}\mathbf{X}][\mathbf{X}'\mathbf{X}]^{-1} = \sigma^2 \frac{\sum_{i=1}^{n} x_i^4}{\left(\sum_{i=1}^{n} x_i^2\right)^2}$$

and

$$\text{Var}[\hat{\beta}] = \sigma[\mathbf{X}'\boldsymbol{\Omega}^{-1}\mathbf{X}]^{-1} = \frac{\sigma^2}{n}.$$

The relative (in)efficiency of OLS is

$$k = \frac{n\sum_{i=1}^{n} x_i^4}{\left(\sum_{i=1}^{n} x_i^2\right)^2} = \frac{\sum_{i=1}^{n} x_i^4/n}{\left(\sum_{i=1}^{n} x_i^2/n\right)^2}. \qquad \textbf{(12-2)}$$

This ratio must be greater than 1. Let z_i equal x_i^2. Then

$$k = \frac{(1/n)\sum_{i=1}^{n} z_i^2}{\left[(1/n)\sum_{i=1}^{n} z_i\right]^2} = \frac{(1/n)\sum_{i=1}^{n} z_i^2}{\bar{z}^2}.$$

But

$$\frac{1}{n}\sum_{i=1}^{n} z_i^2 = \frac{1}{n}\sum_{i=1}^{n} (z_i - \bar{z})^2 + \bar{z}^2,$$

so

$$k = \frac{(1/n)\sum_{i=1}^{n} (z_i - \bar{z})^2}{\bar{z}^2} + 1 > 1.$$

Therefore, in this model, ordinary least squares is never as efficient as generalized least squares.

Suppose that the x's are drawn from a distribution with zero mean and finite fourth moment. Then, by applying the Slutsky theorem and Theorem 4.3 [with (4-20)], we obtain

$$\text{plim } k = \frac{E[x_i^4]}{E[x_i^2]^2} = \frac{\mu_4}{\sigma_x^4}.$$

This is the standardized measure of kurtosis that was discussed in Sections 3.3 and 6.8.6. Its value depends on the distribution of x_i; it is 3 for the normal distribution. Theoretically, k can take any value greater than 1, but for economic data, it is typically between 2 and 4.[2] This example would suggest that the gain

[2]Some examples: The logs of capital and labor in the example used in Section 7.5 have $k = 2.39$ and 2.64; the same variables for the data of Example 11.5 have $k = 2.72$ and 3.15; the kurtosis of the income data in Example 14.1 is 3.40.

in efficiency from GLS over OLS can be substantial. A properly constructed confidence interval based on the OLS estimates would be over 70 percent wider than one based on GLS.

12.2.2. The Estimated Covariance Matrix of b

If the type of heteroscedasticity is known with certainty, the ordinary least squares estimator is undesirable; we should use generalized least squares instead. The precise form of the heteroscedasticity is often unknown, however. In that case, generalized least squares is not usable, and we may need to salvage what we can from the results of ordinary least squares.

The conventionally estimated covariance matrix for the least squares estimator $\sigma^2(\mathbf{X}'\mathbf{X})^{-1}$ is inappropriate; the appropriate matrix is $\sigma^2(\mathbf{X}'\mathbf{X})^{-1}(\mathbf{X}'\boldsymbol{\Omega}\mathbf{X})(\mathbf{X}'\mathbf{X})^{-1}$. It is unlikely that these two would coincide, so the usual estimators of the standard errors are likely to be erroneous. In this section, we consider how erroneous the conventional estimator is likely to be.

As usual,

$$s^2 = \frac{\mathbf{e}'\mathbf{e}}{n-K} = \frac{\boldsymbol{\epsilon}'\mathbf{M}\boldsymbol{\epsilon}}{n-K},$$

where

$$\mathbf{M} = \mathbf{I} - \mathbf{X}(\mathbf{X}'\mathbf{X})^{-1}\mathbf{X}'.$$

Expanding this, we obtain

$$s^2 = \frac{\boldsymbol{\epsilon}'\boldsymbol{\epsilon}}{n-K} - \frac{\boldsymbol{\epsilon}'\mathbf{X}(\mathbf{X}'\mathbf{X})^{-1}\mathbf{X}'\boldsymbol{\epsilon}}{n-K}. \tag{12-3}$$

Taking the two parts separately yields

$$E\left[\frac{\boldsymbol{\epsilon}'\boldsymbol{\epsilon}}{n-K}\right] = \frac{\operatorname{tr} E[\boldsymbol{\epsilon}\boldsymbol{\epsilon}']}{n-K} = \frac{n\sigma^2}{n-K}. \tag{12-4}$$

[We have used the scaling $\operatorname{tr}(\boldsymbol{\Omega}) = n$.] In addition,

$$\begin{aligned} E\left[\frac{\boldsymbol{\epsilon}'\mathbf{X}(\mathbf{X}'\mathbf{X})^{-1}\mathbf{X}'\boldsymbol{\epsilon}}{n-K}\right] &= \frac{\operatorname{tr}[E[(\mathbf{X}'\mathbf{X})^{-1}\mathbf{X}'\boldsymbol{\epsilon}\boldsymbol{\epsilon}'\mathbf{X}]]}{n-K} \\ &= \frac{\operatorname{tr}\left[\sigma^2\left(\frac{\mathbf{X}'\mathbf{X}}{n}\right)^{-1}\left(\frac{\mathbf{X}'\boldsymbol{\Omega}\mathbf{X}}{n}\right)\right]}{n-K} \\ &= \frac{\sigma^2}{n-K}\operatorname{tr}\left[\left(\frac{\mathbf{X}'\mathbf{X}}{n}\right)^{-1}\mathbf{Q}_n^*\right], \end{aligned} \tag{12-5}$$

where $\mathbf{Q}_n^*$ is defined in (12-1). As $n \to \infty$, the term in (12-4) will converge to σ^2. The term in (12-5) will converge to zero if **b** is consistent because both matrices in the product are finite. Therefore:

$$\text{If } \mathbf{b} \text{ is consistent, } \lim_{n\to\infty} E[s^2] = \sigma^2.$$

It can also be shown—we leave it as an exercise—that if the fourth moment of every disturbance is finite and all our other assumptions are met,

$$\lim_{n\to\infty} \text{Var}\left[\frac{\mathbf{e}'\mathbf{e}}{n-K}\right] = \lim_{n\to\infty} \text{Var}\left[\frac{\boldsymbol{\epsilon}'\boldsymbol{\epsilon}}{n-K}\right] = 0.$$

This implies, therefore, that:

$$\text{If plim } \mathbf{b} = \boldsymbol{\beta}, \text{ then plim } s^2 = \sigma^2.$$

Before proceeding, it is useful to pursue this result. The normalization $\text{tr}(\boldsymbol{\Omega}) = n$ implies that

$$\sigma^2 = \overline{\sigma}^2 = \frac{1}{n}\sum_i \sigma_i^2$$

and

$$\omega_i = \frac{\sigma_i^2}{\overline{\sigma}^2}.$$

Therefore, our previous convergence result implies that the least squares estimator s^2 converges to plim $\overline{\sigma}^2$, that is, the probability limit of the average variance of the disturbances, *assuming that this probability limit exists*. Thus, some further assumption about these variances is necessary to obtain the result. For example, note the particular assumption that is needed in Example 12.2. (For another application, see Exercise 5 in Chapter 14.)

The difference between the conventional estimator and the appropriate covariance matrix for **b** is

$$\text{Est. Var}[\mathbf{b}] - \text{Var}[\mathbf{b}] = s^2(\mathbf{X}'\mathbf{X})^{-1} - \sigma^2(\mathbf{X}'\mathbf{X})^{-1}(\mathbf{X}'\boldsymbol{\Omega}\mathbf{X})(\mathbf{X}'\mathbf{X})^{-1}.$$

In a large sample (so that $s^2 \approx \sigma^2$), this is approximately equal to

$$\mathbf{D} = \frac{\sigma^2}{n}\left(\frac{\mathbf{X}'\mathbf{X}}{n}\right)^{-1}\left[\frac{\mathbf{X}'\mathbf{X}}{n} - \frac{\mathbf{X}'\boldsymbol{\Omega}\mathbf{X}}{n}\right]\left(\frac{\mathbf{X}'\mathbf{X}}{n}\right)^{-1}.$$

The difference between the two matrices hinges on

$$\begin{aligned}\boldsymbol{\Delta} &= \frac{\mathbf{X}'\mathbf{X}}{n} - \frac{\mathbf{X}'\boldsymbol{\Omega}\mathbf{X}}{n} \\ &= \sum_{i=1}^{n}\left(\frac{1}{n}\right)\mathbf{x}_i\mathbf{x}_i' - \sum_{i=1}^{n}\left(\frac{\omega_i}{n}\right)\mathbf{x}_i\mathbf{x}_i' \qquad \textbf{(12-6)} \\ &= \frac{1}{n}\sum_{i=1}^{n}(1-\omega_i)\mathbf{x}_i\mathbf{x}_i',\end{aligned}$$

where $\mathbf{x}_i'$ is the ith row of $\mathbf{X}$. These are two weighted averages of the matrices $\mathbf{S}_i = \mathbf{x}_i\mathbf{x}_i'$, using weights 1 for the first term and ω_i for the second. The scaling $\text{tr}(\mathbf{\Omega}) = n$ implies that $\Sigma_i (\omega_i/n) = 1$. Whether the weighted average based on ω_i/n differs much from the one using $1/n$ depends on the weights. If the weights are related to the values in $\mathbf{x}_i$, the difference can be considerable. If the weights are uncorrelated with $\mathbf{x}_i\mathbf{x}_i'$, however, the weighted average will tend to equal the unweighted average.[3]

Therefore, the comparison rests on whether the heteroscedasticity is related to any of x_k or $x_j \cdot x_k$. The conclusion is that, in general:

If the heteroscedasticity is not correlated with the variables in the model, then at least in large samples, the ordinary least squares computations, while not the optimal way to use the data, will not be misleading.

EXAMPLE 12.3 Heteroscedasticity Due to Grouping

In the heteroscedastic regression of Example 11.2, if the observations are grouped in the subsamples in a way that is unrelated to the variables in $\mathbf{X}$, then the usual OLS estimator of Var[$\mathbf{b}$] will, at least in large samples, provide a reliable estimate of the appropriate covariance matrix. It is worth remembering, however, that the least squares estimator will be inefficient, the more so the larger are the differences among the variances of the groups.[4]

The preceding is a useful result, but we should not be overly optimistic. First, it remains true that ordinary least squares is demonstrably inefficient. Second, if the primary assumption of the analysis—that the heteroscedasticity is unrelated to the variables in the model—is incorrect, then the conventional standard errors may be quite far from the appropriate values.

12.2.3. Estimating the Appropriate Covariance Matrix for Ordinary Least Squares

It is clear from the preceding that heteroscedasticity has some potentially serious implications for inferences based on the results of least squares. The application of more appropriate estimation techniques requires a detailed formulation of $\mathbf{\Omega}$, however. It may well be that the form of the heteroscedasticity is unknown. White (1980b) has shown that it is still possible to obtain an appropriate estimator for the variance of the least squares estimator, even if the heteroscedasticity is related to the variables in $\mathbf{X}$.

[3]Suppose, for example, that $\mathbf{X}$ contains a single column and that both $\mathbf{x}_i$ and ω_i are independent and identically distributed random variables. Then $\mathbf{x}'\mathbf{x}/n$ converges to $E[x_i^2]$, whereas $\mathbf{x}'\mathbf{\Omega}\mathbf{x}/n$ converges to $\text{Cov}[\omega_i, x_i^2] + E[\omega_i]E[x_i^2]$. $E[\omega_i] = 1$, so if ω and x^2 are uncorrelated, the sums have the same probability limit. An analogous argument is used earlier.

[4]Some general results, including analysis of the properties of the estimator based on estimated variances, are given in Taylor (1977).

The covariance matrix of $\mathbf{b}$ is $(\mathbf{X}'\mathbf{X})^{-1}[\mathbf{X}'(\sigma^2\mathbf{\Omega})\mathbf{X}](\mathbf{X}'\mathbf{X})^{-1}$. It would appear that to compute an estimate of this matrix, we need an estimate of $\sigma^2\mathbf{\Omega}$, which is unavailable. But what is actually required is an estimate of

$$\mathbf{\Sigma} = \frac{1}{n}\sigma^2\mathbf{X}'\mathbf{\Omega}\mathbf{X} = \frac{1}{n}\sum_{i=1}^{n}\sigma_i^2\mathbf{x}_i\mathbf{x}_i'. \tag{12-7}$$

White (1980b) shows that under very general conditions, the matrix

$$\mathbf{S}_0 = \frac{1}{n}\sum_{i=1}^{n} e_i^2\mathbf{x}_i\mathbf{x}_i', \tag{12-8}$$

where e_i is the ith least squares residual, is a consistent estimator of $\mathbf{\Sigma}$.[5] (See Section 11.2.5.) Therefore, the **White estimator,**

$$\text{Est. Var}[\mathbf{b}] = n(\mathbf{X}'\mathbf{X})^{-1}\mathbf{S}_0(\mathbf{X}'\mathbf{X})^{-1}, \tag{12-9}$$

can be used as an estimate of the true variance of the least squares estimator.

EXAMPLE 12.4 Using the White Estimator

If the disturbances in the regression of Example 12.1 are heteroscedastic, as Figure 12.1 suggests, the ordinary least squares standard errors should be biased. Using the White estimator for the covariance matrix of the least squares estimators produces the results given in Table 12.3. The corrected standard errors are considerably larger than the conventionally computed values. Indeed, neither of the slope coefficients appears to be statistically significant after the correction. The joint test of their significance can no longer be carried out with the F test used in Example 12.1, as it relies on homoscedasticity. We can, however, use a Wald test. The statistic is

$$W = (\mathbf{Rb})'\{\mathbf{R}(\text{Est. Var}[\mathbf{b}])\mathbf{R}'\}^{-1}(\mathbf{Rb}),$$

TABLE 12.3 White Estimator

	Constant	*Income*	*Income*^{2}
Coefficient	832.91	−1834.2	1587.04
OLS standard error	327.3	829.0	519.1
White standard error	460.9	1243.0	830.0
t ratio (using (12 − 9))	1.807	−1.476	1.912
Davidson and MacKinnon standard error (1)	475.4	1282.1	856.1
Davidson and MacKinnon standard error (2)	688.5	1866.4	1250.2

[5]See also Eicker (1967), Horn et al. (1975), and MacKinnon and White (1985).

where

$$\mathbf{R} = \begin{bmatrix} 0 & 1 & 0 \\ 0 & 0 & 1 \end{bmatrix}$$

and the covariance matrix is the White estimator. [See Section 11.5.5 and (11-47).] The statistic is asymptotically distributed as chi-squared with degrees of freedom equal to the number of slopes (here, two). (We use the last two elements of $\mathbf{b}$ and the lower 2×2 submatrix of the estimate of Var[$\mathbf{b}$] for the test.) Using our previous results, we obtain $W = 49.5355$, which is highly significant. The conclusion would be that, as in the cases of multicollinearity, the regressors jointly explain a significant amount of variation in expenditure, but that the individual affects are obscured. Of course, income and income squared cannot vary independently, so this is not surprising.

There have been a number of studies that seek to improve on the White estimator for OLS.[6] The asymptotic properties of the estimator are unambiguous, but its usefulness in small samples is open to question. The possible problems stem from the general result that the squared OLS residuals tend to underestimate the squares of the true disturbances. [That is why we use $1/(n - K)$ rather than $1/n$ in computing s^2.] The end result is that in small samples, at least as suggested by some Monte Carlo studies [e.g., MacKinnon and White (1985)], the White estimator is a bit too optimistic; the matrix is a bit too small, so that asymptotic t ratios are a little too large. Davidson and MacKinnon (1993, p. 554) suggest a number of fixes, which include (1) scaling up the end result by a factor $n/(n - K)$ and (2) using the squared residual scaled by its true variance, $e_i^2 m_{ii}$, instead of e_i^2, where $m_{ii} = 1 - \mathbf{x}_i'(\mathbf{X}'\mathbf{X})^{-1}\mathbf{x}_i$.[7] [See (9-47).] On the basis of their study, Davidson and MacKinnon strongly advocate one or the other correction. The admonition "One should *never* use [the White estimator] since [(2)] *always* performs better" seems a bit strong, but the point is well taken. The use of sharp asymptotic results in small samples can be problematic. The last two rows of Table 12.3 show the recomputed standard errors with these modifications. The second shows that the differences can be substantial.

12.3. TESTING FOR HETEROSCEDASTICITY

Heteroscedasticity poses potentially severe problems for inferences based on least squares. One can rarely be certain that the data are heteroscedastic however, and unfortunately, what form the heteroscedasticity takes if they are. As such, it is useful to be able to test for homoscedasticity and if necessary, modify

---

[6]See, e.g., MacKinnon and White (1985) and Messer and White (1984).

[7]They also suggest a third correction, e_i^2/m_{ii}^2, as an approximation to an estimator based on the "jackknife" technique. But, their advocacy of this estimator is much weaker than that of the other two.

our estimation procedures accordingly.[8] Several types of test have been suggested. They can be roughly grouped in descending order in terms of their generality and, as might be expected, in ascending order in terms of their power.[9]

Most of the tests for heteroscedasticity are based on the following strategy. Ordinary least squares is a consistent estimator of $\boldsymbol{\beta}$ even in the presence of heteroscedasticity. As such, the ordinary least squares residuals will mimic, albeit imperfectly because of sampling variability, the heteroscedasticity of the true disturbances. Therefore, tests designed to detect heteroscedasticity will, in most cases, be applied to the ordinary least squares residuals.

12.3.1. White's General Test

To formulate most of the available tests, it is necessary to specify, at least in rough terms, the nature of the heteroscedasticity. It would be desirable to be able to test a general hypothesis of the form

$$H_0: \sigma_i^2 = \sigma^2 \quad \text{for all } i,$$
$$H_1: \text{Not } H_0.$$

In view of our earlier findings on the difficulty of estimation in a model with n unknown parameters, this is rather ambitious. Nonetheless, such a test has been devised by White (1980b). The correct covariance matrix for the least squares estimator is

$$\text{Var}[\mathbf{b}] = \sigma^2[\mathbf{X}'\mathbf{X}]^{-1}[\mathbf{X}'\boldsymbol{\Omega}\mathbf{X}][\mathbf{X}'\mathbf{X}]^{-1}, \tag{12-10}$$

which, as we have seen, can be estimated by

$$\text{Est. Var}[\mathbf{b}] = [\mathbf{X}'\mathbf{X}]^{-1}\left[\sum_{i=1}^{n} e_i^2\mathbf{x}_i\mathbf{x}_i'\right][\mathbf{X}'\mathbf{X}]^{-1}. \tag{12-11}$$

The conventional estimator is

$$\mathbf{V} = s^2[\mathbf{X}'\mathbf{X}]^{-1}. \tag{12-12}$$

If there is no heteroscedasticity, (12-12) will give a consistent estimator of Var[$\mathbf{b}$], whereas if there is, it will not. White has devised a statistical test based on this observation. A simple operational version of his test is carried out by obtaining nR^2 in the regression of e_i^2 on a constant and all unique variables in $\mathbf{x} \otimes \mathbf{x}$. The statistic is asymptotically distributed as chi-squared with $P - 1$ degrees of freedom, where P is the number of regressors in the regression, not including the constant.

---

[8]In Section 8.5, we considered the problems of pretest estimators. In the current context, the issue is the possibility that a preliminary test for heteroscedasticity will incorrectly lead us to use weighted least squares or fail to alert us to heteroscedasticity and lead us improperly to use ordinary least squares. The situation is rather more favorable here, as both estimators are consistent in both settings. Some limited results for the case of heteroscedasticity are given by Ohtani and Toyoda (1980). Their results suggest that it is best to test first for heteroscedasticity rather than merely to assume that it is present.

[9]A study that examines the power of several tests for heteroscedasticity is Ali and Giacotto (1984).

EXAMPLE 12.5 White's General Test

For the expenditure data of Example 12.1, the regression of the squares of the least squares residuals on a constant, income, and income squared, cubed, and to the fourth power produces an R^2 of 0.42314. The chi-squared statistic is therefore 50(0.42314) = 21.157, which is highly significant. The 95 percent critical value for the chi-squared [3] is 7.81.

The White test is extremely general. To carry it out, we need not make any specific assumptions about the nature of the heteroscedasticity. Although this is a virtue, it is, at the same time, a potentially serious shortcoming. The test may reveal heteroscedasticity, but it may instead simply identify some other specification error (such as the omission of x^2 from a simple regression).[10] Except in the context of a specific problem, little can be said about the power of this test; it may be very low against some alternatives. In addition, unlike some of the other tests we shall discuss, the White test is **nonconstructive.** If we reject the hypothesis of homoscedasticity, the result of the test gives no indication of what to do next.

12.3.2. The Goldfeld–Quandt Test

By narrowing our focus somewhat, we can obtain a more powerful test. Two tests that are relatively general are the Goldfeld–Quandt (1965) test and the Breusch–Pagan (1979) Lagrange multiplier test.

For the Goldfeld–Quandt test, we assume that the observations can be divided into two groups in such a way that under the hypothesis of homoscedasticity, the disturbance variances would be the same in the two groups, while under the alternative, the disturbance variances would differ systematically. The most favorable case for this would be the groupwise heteroscedastic model of Section 12.3.4 and Example 12.9 or a model such as $\sigma_i^2 = \sigma^2 x_i^2$ for some variable x. By ranking the observations based on this x, we can separate the observations into those with high and low variances. The test is applied by dividing the sample into two groups with n_1 and n_2 observations. To obtain statistically independent variance estimators, the regression is then estimated separately with the two sets of observations. The test statistic is

$$F[n_1 - K, n_2 - K] = \frac{\mathbf{e}_1'\mathbf{e}_1/(n_1 - K)}{\mathbf{e}_2'\mathbf{e}_2/(n_2 - K)},$$

where we assume that the disturbance variance is larger in the first sample. (If not, reverse the subscripts.) Under the null hypothesis of homoscedasticity, this has an F distribution with $n_1 - K$ and $n_2 - K$ degrees of freedom. The sample value can be referred to the standard F table to carry out the test, with a large value leading to rejection of the null hypothesis.

[10] Thursby (1982) considers this issue in detail.

To increase the power of the test, Goldfeld and Quandt suggest that a number of observations in the middle of the sample be omitted. The more observations are dropped, however, the smaller the degrees of freedom for estimation in each group will be, which will tend to diminish the power of the test. As a consequence, the choice of how many central observations to drop is largely subjective. Evidence by Harvey and Phillips (1974) suggests that no more than a third of the observations should be dropped. If the disturbances are normally distributed, the Goldfeld–Quandt statistic is exactly distributed as F under the null hypothesis, and the nominal size of the test is correct. If not, the F distribution is inappropriate and some alternative method with known large-sample properties, such as White's test, is called for.

EXAMPLE 12.6 Goldfeld–Quandt Test

We sort the expenditure data of Example 12.1 on the basis of income and then fit separate regressions for observations 1 to 17 and 34 to 51 (omitting the 50th). The sums of squared residuals in the two regressions are 27,096.50 and 52,685.18, so the test statistic is

$$F[14,14] = \frac{52{,}685.18}{27{,}096.50} = 1.944.$$

The 5 percent critical value from the F table is 2.49, so we would not reject the hypothesis of homoscedasticity at this level of significance on the basis of this test. Based on a 25/25 split of the sample, the sums of squares are 44,598.68 and 85,526.35, giving an $F[22, 22]$ of 1.918. The 5 percent critical value is 2.048, so this is insignificant as well.

12.3.3. The Breusch–Pagan/Godfrey Test

The Goldfeld–Quandt test has been found to be reasonably powerful when we are able to identify correctly the variable to use in the sample separation. This requirement does limit its generality, however. For example, several of the models we will consider allow the disturbance variance to vary with a set of regressors. [See (12-18) to (12-23).] Breusch and Pagan[11] have devised a Lagrange multiplier test of the hypothesis that $\sigma_i^2 = \sigma^2 f(\alpha_0 + \boldsymbol{\alpha}'\mathbf{z}_i)$, where $\mathbf{z}_i$ is a vector of independent variables. The model is homoscedastic if $\boldsymbol{\alpha} = \mathbf{0}$. The test can be carried out with a simple regression:

$$\text{LM} = \tfrac{1}{2}\text{ explained sum of squares in the regression of } e_i^2/(\mathbf{e}'\mathbf{e}/n) \text{ on } \mathbf{z}_i. \quad \textbf{(12-13)}$$

For computation purposed, let $\mathbf{Z}$ be the $n \times (P + 1)$ matrix of observations on $(1, \mathbf{z}_i)$, and let $\mathbf{g}$ be the vector of observations of $g_i = e_i^2/(\mathbf{e}'\mathbf{e}/n)$. Then

$$\text{LM} = \tfrac{1}{2}[\mathbf{g}'\mathbf{Z}(\mathbf{Z}'\mathbf{Z})^{-1}\mathbf{Z}'\mathbf{g} - n].$$

[11] Breusch and Pagen (1979).

Under the null hypothesis of homoscedasticity, LM is asymptotically distributed as chi-squared with degrees of freedom equal to the number of variables in $\mathbf{z}_i$. This test can be applied to a variety of models, including, for example, those examined in (12-18) to (12-23).[12]

It has been argued that the Breusch–Pagan Lagrange multiplier test is quite sensitive to the assumption of normality. Koenker (1981) and Koenker and Bassett (1982) suggest that the computation of LM be based on a more robust estimator of the variance of ϵ_i^2,

$$V = \frac{1}{n}\sum_{i=1}^{n}\left[e_i^2 - \frac{\mathbf{e}'\mathbf{e}}{n}\right]^2.$$

The variance of ϵ_i^2 is not necessarily equal to $2\sigma^4$ if ϵ_i is not normally distributed. Let $\mathbf{u}$ equal $(e_1^2, e_2^2, \ldots, e_n^2)$ and $\mathbf{i}$ be an $n \times 1$ column of 1s. Then $\bar{u} = \mathbf{e}'\mathbf{e}/n$. With this change, the computation becomes

$$\text{LM} = \left[\frac{1}{V}\right](\mathbf{u} - \bar{u}\mathbf{i})'\mathbf{Z}(\mathbf{Z}'\mathbf{Z})^{-1}\mathbf{Z}'(\mathbf{u} - \bar{u}\mathbf{i}).$$

Under normality, this modified statistic will have the same asymptotic distribution as the Breusch–Pagan statistic, but absent normality, there is some evidence that it provides a more powerful test. Waldman (1983) has shown that if the variables in $\mathbf{z}_i$ are the same as those used for the White test described earlier, the two tests are algebraically the same.

EXAMPLE 12.7 Breusch and Pagan Test

For the school spending data, the Breusch–Pagan Lagrange multiplier statistic and the corrected version of Koenker and Bassett are 18.904 and 15.384, respectively.[13] These are both statistically significant. The results thus far are mixed. Most of the tests strongly suggest that the disturbance is heteroscedastic, with the Goldfeld–Quandt test standing as an exception.

12.3.4. Testing for Groupwise Heteroscedasticity

The more specific we can be about the form of the heteroscedasticity, the more powerful a test we can devise. For example, for the groupwise heteroscedasticity model of Example 12.9, under normality the likelihood ratio test will be a most powerful consistent test. The log-likelihood function, assuming homoscedasticity, is

$$\ln L_0 = -\frac{n}{2}[\ln(2\pi) + \ln\sigma^2] - \frac{1}{2\sigma^2}\sum_{i=1}^{n}\epsilon_i^2,$$

[12] The model $\sigma_i^2 = \sigma^2 \exp(\boldsymbol{\alpha}'\mathbf{z}_i)$ is one of these cases. In analyzing this model specifically, Harvey (1976) derived the same test statistic.

[13] Waldman's result does not apply here because $\mathbf{z}$ does not contain the third or fourth powers of income.

where $n = \Sigma_g n_g$ is the total number of observations. Under the alternative hypothesis of heteroscedasticity across G groups,

$$\ln L_1 = -\frac{n}{2}\ln(2\pi) - \frac{1}{2}\sum_{g=1}^{G} n_g \ln \sigma_g^2 - \frac{1}{2}\sum_{g=1}^{G}\left(\frac{1}{\sigma_g^2}\sum_{i=1}^{n_g} \epsilon_{ig}^2\right).$$

The maximum likelihood estimators of σ^2 and σ_g^2 are

$$s^2 = \frac{\mathbf{e}'\mathbf{e}}{n} \quad \text{and} \quad s_g^2 = \frac{\mathbf{e}_g'\mathbf{e}_g}{n_g},$$

respectively. The maximum likelihood estimator of $\boldsymbol{\beta}$ in Example 11.2 is to be used for the slope vector.[14] If we evaluate $\ln L_0$ and $\ln L_1$ at these estimates, the likelihood ratio test statistic for homoscedasticity is

$$-2(\ln L_0 - \ln L_1) = n \ln s^2 - \sum_{g=1}^{G} n_g \ln s_g^2.$$

Under the null hypothesis, the statistic is asymptotically distributed as chi-squared with $G - 1$ degrees of freedom.

12.3.5. Tests Based on Regressions — Glesjer's (1969) Test

Section 12.5 considers three specific formulations in the class of models encompassed by the Lagrange multiplier test:

1. $\text{Var}[\epsilon_i] = \sigma^2[\boldsymbol{\alpha}'\mathbf{z}_i]$.
2. $\text{Var}[\epsilon_i] = \sigma^2[\boldsymbol{\alpha}'\mathbf{z}_i]^2$.
3. $\text{Var}[\epsilon_i] = \sigma^2\exp[\boldsymbol{\alpha}'\mathbf{z}_i]$.

In each case, a preliminary regression is computed to estimate $\boldsymbol{\alpha}$ for use in an FGLS estimator of $\boldsymbol{\beta}$. A joint test of the hypothesis that the slopes are all zero in each preceding case would be equivalent to a test of homoscedasticity. In particular, let w_i be e_i^2, $|e_i|$, or $\ln|e_i|$. A Wald statistic can be used in each model to carry out the test. This would be

$$W = \mathbf{a}'\{\text{Var}[\mathbf{a}]\}^{-1}\mathbf{a}.$$

Under the null hypothesis of homoscedasticity, W is asymptotically distributed as chi-squared with P degrees of freedom, where P is the number of variables in $\mathbf{z}_i$, excluding the constant term. The appropriate covariance matrix to use will differ in the three models; an asymptotically valid expedient would be to

[14] It has been suggested that for convenience, we may use the OLS slope vectors within each group instead. If the sample is large enough, this will be valid. But in a small sample, if the information that the slope vector is the same in all groups is not used, the power of the test is likely to be reduced.

use the White estimator in (12-9) (which will now involve the fourth powers of the residuals), however.[15] Each of these tests is likely to be more powerful than an omnibus test such as White's or Breusch–Pagan's *in the specific context of its regression model.*

EXAMPLE 12.8 Glesjer's Tests

The preceding Wald statistics for the three specifications given, based on White's covariance matrix, are 9.692, 5.678, and 11.096. The critical value from the table of chi-squared with two degrees of freedom (for income and income squared) is 5.99.

12.4. GENERALIZED LEAST SQUARES WHEN $\boldsymbol{\Omega}$ IS KNOWN

Having tested for and found evidence of heteroscedasticity, the logical next step is to revise the estimation technique to account for it. The GLS estimator is

$$\hat{\boldsymbol{\beta}} = (\mathbf{X}'\boldsymbol{\Omega}^{-1}\mathbf{X})^{-1}\mathbf{X}'\boldsymbol{\Omega}^{-1}\mathbf{y}.$$

Consider the most general case,

$$\text{Var}[\epsilon_i] = \sigma_i^2 = \sigma^2\omega_i.$$

Then

$$\boldsymbol{\Omega} = \begin{bmatrix} \omega_1 & 0 & 0 & \cdots & 0 \\ 0 & \omega_2 & 0 & \cdots & 0 \\ & & \vdots & & \\ & & \vdots & \cdots & \\ & & \vdots & & \\ 0 & 0 & 0 & \cdots & \omega_n \end{bmatrix},$$

so $\boldsymbol{\Omega}^{-1}$ is a diagonal matrix whose ith diagonal element is $1/\omega_i$. The GLS estimator is obtained by regressing

$$\mathbf{Py} = \begin{bmatrix} y_1/\sqrt{\omega_1} \\ y_2/\sqrt{\omega_2} \\ \vdots \\ y_n/\sqrt{\omega_n} \end{bmatrix} \quad \text{on} \quad \mathbf{PX} = \begin{bmatrix} x_1/\sqrt{\omega_1} \\ x_2/\sqrt{\omega_2} \\ \vdots \\ x_n/\sqrt{\omega_n} \end{bmatrix}.$$

---

[15]See Fomby et al. (1984, pp. 176–187). Harvey (1976) derives an explicit expression for Var[**a**] for the model in Example 12.15.

Applying ordinary least squares to the transformed model, we obtain the **weighted least squares (WLS)** estimator.

$$\hat{\boldsymbol{\beta}} = \left[\sum_{i=1}^{n} w_i \mathbf{x}_i \mathbf{x}_i'\right]^{-1} \left[\sum_{i=1}^{n} w_i \mathbf{x}_i y_i\right],$$

where

$$w_i = \frac{1}{\omega_i}.^{16}$$

The logic of the computation is that observations with smaller variances receive a larger weight in the computations of the sums and therefore have greater influence in the estimates obtained.

EXAMPLE 12.9 Groupwise Heteroscedasticity

Consider again the groupwise heteroscedastic regression model of Example 12.2. Assume that the variances are known. The GLS estimator is

$$\hat{\boldsymbol{\beta}} = \left[\sum_{g=1}^{G} \left(\frac{1}{\sigma_g^2}\right) \mathbf{X}_g' \mathbf{X}_g\right]^{-1} \left[\sum_{g=1}^{G} \left(\frac{1}{\sigma_g^2}\right) \mathbf{X}_g' \mathbf{y}_g\right].$$

Since $\mathbf{X}_g' \mathbf{y}_g = \mathbf{X}_g' \mathbf{X}_g \mathbf{b}_g$, where $\mathbf{b}_g$ is the OLS estimator in the gth subset of observations,

$$\begin{aligned}
\hat{\boldsymbol{\beta}} &= \left[\sum_{g=1}^{G} \left(\frac{1}{\sigma_g^2}\right) \mathbf{X}_g' \mathbf{X}_g\right]^{-1} \left[\sum_{g=1}^{G} \left(\frac{1}{\sigma_g^2}\right) \mathbf{X}_g' \mathbf{X}_g \mathbf{b}_g\right] \\
&= \left[\sum_{g=1}^{G} \mathbf{V}_g\right]^{-1} \left[\sum_{g=1}^{G} \mathbf{V}_g \mathbf{b}_g\right] \\
&= \sum_{g=1}^{G} \mathbf{W}_g \mathbf{b}_g .
\end{aligned}$$

This is a matrix weighted average of the G least squares estimators. The weighting matrices are $\mathbf{W}_g = [\Sigma_g(\text{Var}[\mathbf{b}_g])^{-1}]^{-1}[\text{Var}[\mathbf{b}_g]]^{-1}$. The estimator with the smaller covariance matrix therefore receives the larger weight.

Suppose, in addition, that $\mathbf{X}_g$ is the same in every group. This might occur in repeated sampling of experimental data. With a common $\mathbf{X}$ matrix, the GLS estimator reduces to

$$\hat{\boldsymbol{\beta}} = \sum_{g=1}^{G} w_g \mathbf{b}_g ,$$

[16]The weights are often denoted $w_i = 1/\sigma_i^2$. This expression is consistent with the equivalent $\hat{\boldsymbol{\beta}} = [\mathbf{X}'(\sigma^2\boldsymbol{\Omega})^{-1}\mathbf{X}]^{-1}\mathbf{X}'(\sigma^2\boldsymbol{\Omega})^{-1}\mathbf{y}$. The σ^2's cancel, leaving the expression given previously.

where

$$w_g = \frac{1/\sigma_g^2}{\sum_{g=1}^{G} 1/\sigma_g^2}.$$

Once again, the weights are larger for the estimators with the smaller variances.

A common specification is that the variance is proportional to one of the regressors or its square. Our earlier example of family expenditures is one in which the relevant variable is usually income. Similarly, in studies of firm profits, the dominant variable is typically assumed to be firm size. If

$$\sigma_i^2 = \sigma^2 x_{ik}^2, \qquad \textbf{(12-14)}$$

then the transformed regression model for GLS is

$$\frac{y}{x_k} = \beta_k + \beta_1\left(\frac{x_1}{x_k}\right) + \beta_2\left(\frac{x_2}{x_k}\right) + \cdots + \frac{\epsilon}{x_k}.$$

If the variance is proportional to x_k instead of x_k^2, the weight applied to each observation is $1/\sqrt{x_k}$ instead of $1/x_k$.

EXAMPLE 12.10 Weighted Least Squares

Weighted least squares estimates of the model in (12-14) are given in Table 12.4. Estimated standard errors are shown in parentheses.

In (12-14), the coefficient on x_k becomes the constant term. But if the variance is proportional to any power of x_k other than two, the transformed model will no longer contain a constant, and we encounter the problem of interpreting R^2 mentioned earlier. For example, no conclusion should be drawn if the R^2 in the regression of y/z on $1/z$ and x/z is higher than in the regression of y on a constant and x for any z, including x. The good fit of the weighted regression might be due to the presence of $1/z$ on both sides of the equality.

TABLE 12.4 WLS Results

	Constant	*Income*	*Income*^{2}
Least squares	832.91	−1834.20	1587.04
	(327.3)	(829.0)	(519.1)
Var (ϵ) = σ^2 income	746.36	−1612.25	1447.46
	(328.2)	(844.8)	(537.7)
Var (ϵ) = σ^2 income^2	644.58	−1399.28	1311.35
	(333.6)	(872.1)	(563.7)

12.5. ESTIMATION WHEN $\boldsymbol{\Omega}$ CONTAINS UNKNOWN PARAMETERS

The general form of the heteroscedastic regression model has too many parameters to estimate by ordinary methods. Typically, the model is restricted by formulating $\sigma^2\boldsymbol{\Omega}$ as a function of a few parameters, as in $\sigma_i^2 = \sigma^2 x_i^\alpha$ or $\sigma_i^2 = \sigma^2[\boldsymbol{\alpha}'\mathbf{x}_i]^2$. FGLS based on a consistent estimate of $\boldsymbol{\Omega}$ is asymptotically equivalent to GLS, and FGLS based on a maximum likelihood estimate of $\boldsymbol{\Omega}$ is the maximum likelihood estimator if $\boldsymbol{\Omega}$ does not contain any elements of $\boldsymbol{\beta}$. As in the general case, however, the new problem introduced is that we must first find consistent estimates of the unknown parameters in $\boldsymbol{\Omega}$. Two methods are typically used for models of heteroscedasticity, two-step GLS and maximum likelihood.

12.5.1. Two-Step Estimation

For the heteroscedastic regression model, the GLS estimator is

$$\hat{\boldsymbol{\beta}} = \left[\sum_{i=1}^{n}\left(\frac{1}{\sigma_i^2}\right)\mathbf{x}_i\mathbf{x}_i'\right]^{-1}\left[\sum_{i=1}^{n}\left(\frac{1}{\sigma_i^2}\right)\mathbf{x}_i y_i\right].$$

The two-step estimators are computed by first obtaining estimates $\hat{\sigma}_i^2$, usually by some function of least squares residuals, and then

$$\hat{\hat{\boldsymbol{\beta}}} = \left[\sum_{i=1}^{n}\left(\frac{1}{\hat{\sigma}_i^2}\right)\mathbf{x}_i\mathbf{x}_i'\right]^{-1}\left[\sum_{i=1}^{n}\left(\frac{1}{\hat{\sigma}_i^2}\right)\mathbf{x}_i y_i\right].$$

The OLS estimates of $\boldsymbol{\beta}$, although inefficient, are still consistent. As such, the least squares residuals

$$\begin{aligned} e_i &= y_i - \mathbf{x}_i'\mathbf{b} \\ &= y_i - \mathbf{x}_i'\boldsymbol{\beta} - \mathbf{x}_i'(\mathbf{b} - \boldsymbol{\beta}) \\ &= \epsilon_i + v_i \end{aligned} \tag{12-15}$$

have the same limiting distribution as the true disturbances ϵ_i. For the true ϵ_i's, $E[\epsilon_i^2] = \sigma_i^2$. We can form a regression

$$\epsilon_i^2 = \sigma_i^2 + u_i, \tag{12-16}$$

where u_i is the difference between ϵ_i^2 and its expectation. For the least squares residual,

$$e_i^2 = \epsilon_i^2 + [\mathbf{x}_i'(\mathbf{b} - \boldsymbol{\beta})]^2 - 2\epsilon_i\mathbf{x}_i'(\mathbf{b} - \boldsymbol{\beta}).$$

The latter two terms will be negligible asymptotically, so that, at least approximately,[17]

$$e_i^2 = \sigma_i^2 + v_i. \tag{12-17}$$

[17]Formal analysis may be found in Amemiya (1985).

A general procedure suggested by this is to treat the variance function as a regression model and use the squares of the least squares residuals as the dependent variable to estimate the parameters. If $\text{Var}(\epsilon_i) = \sigma_i^2(\boldsymbol{\alpha}'\mathbf{z}_i)$, the (possibly nonlinear) regression of the squared residuals on $\mathbf{z}$ will provide a consistent estimate of $\boldsymbol{\alpha}$.[18] With estimates of the unknown parameters in $\boldsymbol{\Omega}$ in hand, we then use FGLS.

To take a particularly straightforward case, suppose that

$$\sigma_i^2 = \boldsymbol{\alpha}'\mathbf{z}_i$$[19]

or

$$e_i^2 \simeq \boldsymbol{\alpha}'\mathbf{z}_i + v_i. \tag{12-18}$$

This is not a classical regression model; in a finite sample, v_i has a nonzero mean, is heteroscedastic, and is correlated across observations because each v_i is constructed from the same estimate of $\boldsymbol{\beta}$. As shown by Amemiya, however, the first and third of these difficulties are absent in large samples—v_i has a zero mean and is nonautocorrelated—so we can expect the ordinary least squares estimator of $\boldsymbol{\alpha}$ to be consistent. That is all that is required for the efficient estimation of $\boldsymbol{\beta}$ by FGLS using $\boldsymbol{\Omega}(\hat{\boldsymbol{\alpha}})$.

All the general results obtained earlier apply directly. The small-sample properties of such an estimator are generally unknown. Because v_i is heteroscedastic, the OLS estimator of $\boldsymbol{\alpha}$ is inefficient. A more efficient estimator could be obtained in some cases.[20] The degree to which this would improve the sampling properties of the FGLS estimator remains to be determined. Asymptotically, it makes no difference, but the finite-sample properties remain uncertain.

EXAMPLE 12.11 Two-Step Estimation

In applying the preceding to the school expenditure data of Example 12.1, we find, first, that least squares regression of the squared residuals on a constant, income, and income squared produces the results shown in Table 12.5. The

TABLE 12.5 OLS Regression Using the Squared OLS Residuals

	Constant	*Income*	*Income*^{2}
Coefficient	59,218.80	−161,960	113,663
Standard error	(22,790)	(58,190)	(36,440)
White's SE	(28,170)	(77,000)	(52,225)

[18]Jobson and Fuller (1980) prove a somewhat more general version.

[19]This case is analyzed at length in Amemiya (1985, pp. 203–207, and 1977a).

[20]See Fomby et al. (1984, pp. 177–186) and Amemiya (1985).

TABLE 12.6 Generalized Least Squares Based on $\text{Var}[\epsilon_i] = \sigma^2(\alpha' z_i)$

	Constant	*Income*	*Income*^{2}
Coefficient	709.05	−1506.40	1374.15
Standard error	(451.9)	(1199.0)	(790.8)

large difference between the OLS and White estimators of the standard errors is to be expected, given the heteroscedasticity in v_i. These estimates are then used to compute the elements of $\mathbf{\Omega}$.[21] We then obtain the FGLS estimates in Table 12.6.

The preceding general results have been extended to other functional forms, most commonly

$$\text{Var}[\epsilon_i] = \sigma^2(\boldsymbol{\alpha}'\mathbf{z}_i)^2, \tag{12-19}$$
$$\text{Var}[\epsilon_i] = \sigma^2\exp(\boldsymbol{\alpha}'\mathbf{z}_i), \tag{12-20}$$

where $\mathbf{z}$ is a set of independent variables that may or may not coincide with $\mathbf{x}$.[22] In (12-19), the standard deviation, rather than the variance, is a linear function of the exogenous variables. In this case, a regression of the absolute values of the residuals on $\mathbf{z}$ provides the estimates of $\boldsymbol{\alpha}$ required to compute the FGLS estimator.[23] To estimate $\boldsymbol{\alpha}$ in (12-20), we would regress $\ln(e^2)$ on a constant and $\mathbf{z}$. (See Example 12.15.)

A special case of (12-19) is a model in which the variance is proportional to the square of the mean:

$$\begin{aligned} y_i &= \mathbf{x}_i'\boldsymbol{\beta} + \epsilon_i, \\ \text{Var}[\epsilon_i] &= \sigma^2[\mathbf{x}_i'\boldsymbol{\beta}]^2. \end{aligned} \tag{12-21}$$

This differs from the earlier models in that no secondary regression of the residuals on $\mathbf{x}$ is required to estimate the parameters of the variance. We can use the fitted values from the least squares regression (or, if necessary, their absolute values) as the weights for weighted least squares. For this case, however, FGLS is not fully efficient, as $\boldsymbol{\beta}$ appears in $\mathbf{\Omega}$ as well as the regression.[24]

---

[21]This particular specification, unfortunately, does not preclude negative variances. For these data, none of the predicted variances was negative.

[22]An empirical study employing both of these models is Rutemiller and Bowers (1968).

[23]The estimator was devised by Glesjer (1969). Harvey (1976) shows that this estimator is consistent for $c\boldsymbol{\alpha}$, where c is a constant that depends on the distribution of ϵ_i. This implies that the matrix $\mathbf{\Omega}$ is consistently estimated only up to the scale factor c^2. Since this will fall out of the GLS estimator anyway, the scaling is of no consequence. Additional discussion may be found in Amemiya (1985).

[24]See Theil (1971), Prais and Houthakker (1955), and Amemiya (1973a). Amemiya examines maximum likelihood estimation in a model in which FGLS is efficient despite this complication.

EXAMPLE 12.12 Variance Proportional to the Square of the Mean

Continuing our earlier example, weighted least squares using the absolute values of the fitted values from the first regression produces the results given in Table 12.7.

TABLE 12.7 WLS with the Variance Proportional to the Square of the Mean

	Constant	*Income*	*Income*^{2}
Coefficient	591.08	−1195.15	1172.22
Standard error	(371.0)	(981.2)	(642.7)

In model (12-20), if the variables in **z** are logs, the model is equivalent to

$$\sigma_i^2 = \sigma^2 \prod_{m=1}^{M} z_{im}^{\alpha_m}.$$

A special case, with a single variable, is

$$\sigma_i^2 = \sigma^2 z_i^{\alpha}. \tag{12-22}$$

If $\alpha = 0$, the disturbance is homoscedastic.[25] The models in Example 12.10 are special cases with α equal to 1 and 2. For this model, the regression used to estimate the variance is

$$\ln e_i^2 \simeq \ln \sigma^2 + \boldsymbol{\alpha}'\mathbf{z}_i + v_i. \tag{12-23}$$

EXAMPLE 12.13 Exponential Heteroscedasticity

We use (12-23) to specify the variance of the disturbance in Example 12.1. The regression of the log of the squared residual on a constant, income, and income squared is given in Table 12.8. Then the WLS regression, where the estimated variances are the exponents of the fitted values from the previous regression, is

TABLE 12.8 Regression of ln e^2 on a Constant, Income, and Income^2

	Constant	*Income*	*Income*^{2}
Coefficient	21.858	−44.277	30.863
Standard error	(16.04)	(40.63)	(25.44)

[25] See Park (1966).

TABLE 12.9 WLS Regression Based on $\ln \sigma_i^2 = \ln \sigma^2 + \sum_m \alpha_m z_{im}$

	Constant	*Income*	*Income²*
Coefficient	488.43	−912.69	980.71
Standard error	(529.1)	(1423.0)	(950.3)

shown in Table 12.9. With this specification, the estimated standard errors of the coefficients have become quite large. As before, however, although neither coefficient is statistically significant by the usual test, the Wald statistic for testing their joint significance is 39.291, which far exceeds the tabled critical value of 5.99 for a size of 5 percent.

12.5.2. Maximum Likelihood Estimation

The log-likelihood function for a sample of normally distributed observations would be

$$\ln L = -\frac{n}{2}\ln(2\pi) - \frac{1}{2}\sum_{i=1}^{n}\left[\ln \sigma_i^2 + \frac{1}{\sigma_i^2}(y_i - \mathbf{x}_i'\boldsymbol{\beta})^2\right]. \tag{12-24}$$

This can, in principle, be maximized directly, for example, using one of the methods discussed in Chapter 5. This is likely to be rather involved for most very general models. But if the variance function is relatively uncomplicated, a simple search procedure may simplify things considerably.

EXAMPLE 12.14 MLE for a Heteroscedastic Regression

Consider maximum likelihood estimation of the model in (12-22).[26] In this case, where z_i is income,

$$\sigma_i^2 = \sigma^2 z_i^\alpha$$

involves only a single new parameter whose value will probably fall in a reasonably small range, say, 0 to 3. For this model, let $\epsilon_i = y_i - \mathbf{x}_i'\boldsymbol{\beta}$. Then,

$$\begin{aligned}
\ln L &= -\frac{n}{2}[\ln(2\pi) + \ln \sigma^2] - \frac{\alpha}{2}\sum_{i=1}^{n}\ln z_i - \frac{1}{2\sigma^2}\sum_{i=1}^{n}\frac{\epsilon_i^2}{z_i^\alpha},\\
\frac{\partial \ln L}{\partial \boldsymbol{\beta}} &= \sum_{i=1}^{n}\mathbf{x}_i\frac{\epsilon_i}{\sigma^2 z_i^\alpha},\\
\frac{\partial \ln L}{\partial \sigma^2} &= -\frac{n}{2\sigma^2} + \frac{1}{2\sigma^4}\sum_{i=1}^{n}\frac{\epsilon_i^2}{z_i^\alpha},\\
\frac{\partial \ln L}{\partial \alpha} &= -\frac{1}{2}\sum_{i=1}^{n}\ln z_i + \frac{1}{2\sigma^2}\sum_{i=1}^{n}\frac{\epsilon_i^2 \ln z_i}{z_i^\alpha}.
\end{aligned} \tag{12-25}$$

[26]An empirical study using this model is Lahiri and Egy (1981).

For a given value of α, we estimate $\boldsymbol{\beta}$ and σ^2 by generalized least squares using, as weights, z_i^α. The maximum of the likelihood function can be found by searching over values of α and choosing the one that, with the associated values of $\boldsymbol{\beta}$ and σ^2, maximizes the likelihood function.

For the school spending data, the values of the log likelihood for various values of α are listed in Table 12.10. (Normally, one would do a more precise search or use an iterative technique such as the one discussed in Example 12.15 to estimate α. The maximizer is $\alpha = 3.2948$.) Denoting the full parameter vector by $\boldsymbol{\gamma}$, we use

$$\left(-E\left[\frac{\partial^2 \ln L}{\partial\boldsymbol{\gamma}\partial\boldsymbol{\gamma}'}\right]\right)^{-1} = \begin{bmatrix} \dfrac{1}{\sigma^2}\displaystyle\sum_{i=1}^{n}\mathbf{x}_i\mathbf{x}_i'/z_i^\alpha & \mathbf{0} & \mathbf{0} \\ \mathbf{0}' & \dfrac{n}{2\sigma^4} & \dfrac{1}{2\sigma^2}\displaystyle\sum_{i=1}^{n}\ln z_i \\ \mathbf{0}' & \dfrac{1}{2\sigma^2}\displaystyle\sum_{i=1}^{n}\ln z_i & \dfrac{1}{2}\displaystyle\sum_{i=1}^{n}\ln^2 z_i \end{bmatrix}^{-1}$$

to estimate the asymptotic covariance matrix of the maximum likelihood estimator. The sample estimate is

$$\begin{bmatrix} 112{,}606 & & & & \\ -298{,}867 & 798{,}495 & & & \\ 198{,}404 & -523{,}996 & 346{,}735 & & \\ 0 & 0 & 0 & 9{,}956{,}705 & \\ 0 & 0 & 0 & 4{,}269.91 & 2.24049 \end{bmatrix}.$$

The square roots of the diagonal elements give the estimated asymptotic standard errors. The full set of maximum likelihood estimates is given in Table 12.11.

TABLE 12.10 Log-likelihoods

α	ln L
0.0	−271.2698
0.5	−270.3565
1.0	−269.6020
1.5	−269.0048
2.0	−268.5618
2.5	−268.2684
3.0	−268.1186
3.1	−268.1053
3.2	−268.0974
3.3	−268.0948
3.4	−268.0975
3.5	−268.1055

TABLE 12.11 MLE for Multiplicative Heteroscedasticity

	Estimate	*Standard Error*	*t ratio*
Constant	560.72	335.6	1.67
Income	−1124.18	893.6	−1.26
Income^2	1132.18	588.5	1.92
σ^2	6749.71	3155.9	2.14
α	3.3	1.497	2.20

We now consider more general models of heteroscedasticity. For simplicity, let

$$\sigma_i^2 = \sigma^2 f_i(\boldsymbol{\theta}), \tag{12-26}$$

where $\boldsymbol{\theta}$ is the vector of unknown parameters in $\boldsymbol{\Omega}$ and $f_i(\boldsymbol{\theta})$ is indexed by i to indicate that it is a function of $\mathbf{z}_i$. Assume, as well, that no elements of $\boldsymbol{\beta}$ appear in $\boldsymbol{\theta}$. The log-likelihood function becomes

$$\begin{aligned}\ln L = -\frac{n}{2}[\ln(2\pi) + \ln \sigma^2] - \frac{1}{2}\sum_{i=1}^{n} \ln f_i(\boldsymbol{\theta}) \\ - \frac{1}{2\sigma^2}\sum_{i=1}^{n}\left(\frac{1}{f_i(\boldsymbol{\theta})}\right)(y_i - \mathbf{x}_i'\boldsymbol{\beta})^2.\end{aligned} \tag{12-27}$$

For convenience in what follows, substitute ϵ_i for $(y_i - \mathbf{x}_i'\boldsymbol{\beta})$, denote $f_i(\boldsymbol{\theta})$ as just f_i, and denote the vector of derivatives $\partial f_i(\boldsymbol{\theta})/\partial\boldsymbol{\theta}$ as $\mathbf{g}_i$. Then the derivatives of the log-likelihood function are

$$\begin{aligned}\frac{\partial \ln L}{\partial \boldsymbol{\beta}} &= \sum_{i=1}^{n} \mathbf{x}_i \frac{\epsilon_i}{\sigma^2 f_i}, \\ \frac{\partial \ln L}{\partial \sigma^2} &= -\frac{n}{2\sigma^2} + \frac{1}{2\sigma^4}\sum_{i=1}^{n}\frac{\epsilon_i^2}{f_i}, \\ \frac{\partial \ln L}{\partial \boldsymbol{\theta}} &= -\frac{1}{2}\sum_{i=1}^{n}\mathbf{g}_i\left(\frac{1}{f_i}\right) + \frac{1}{2\sigma^2}\sum_{i=1}^{n}\mathbf{g}_i\left(\frac{\epsilon_i^2}{f_i^2}\right), \\ &= \frac{1}{2}\sum_{i=1}^{n}\left(\frac{\epsilon_i^2}{\sigma^2 f_i} - 1\right)\left(\frac{1}{f_i}\right)\mathbf{g}_i.\end{aligned} \tag{12-28}$$

Since $E[\epsilon_i] = 0$ and $E[\epsilon_i^2] = \sigma^2 f_i$, it is clear that all derivatives have expectation zero, as required. The maximum likelihood estimators are those values of $\boldsymbol{\beta}$, σ^2, and $\boldsymbol{\theta}$ that simultaneously equate these derivatives to zero. The equations are generally highly nonlinear and will often require an iterative solution.

Note that the necessary conditions are identical to those for generalized least squares if $\boldsymbol{\theta}$ is known. Likewise, for a given value of $\boldsymbol{\theta}$, the necessary condition for σ^2 gives the familiar prescription, $1/n$ times the normalized sum of squared residuals. At the same time, conditioned on current values of $\boldsymbol{\beta}$ and σ^2, the third set of first-order conditions is a set of nonlinear equations whose solution will depend on the problem at hand.

Let $\mathbf{G}$ be the $n \times M$ matrix whose ith row is $\partial f_i/\partial\boldsymbol{\theta}'$, and let $\mathbf{i}$ be an $n \times 1$ column vector of 1s. From (12-26), $\boldsymbol{\Omega}$ is a diagonal matrix with ith diagonal element equal to f_i. The asymptotic covariance matrix for the maximum likelihood estimator in this model is

$$\begin{aligned}&\left(-E\left[\frac{\partial^2 \ln L}{\partial\boldsymbol{\gamma}\partial\boldsymbol{\gamma}'}\right]\right)^{-1} \\ &\quad= \begin{bmatrix}(1/\sigma^2)\mathbf{X}'\boldsymbol{\Omega}^{-1}\mathbf{X} & \mathbf{0} & \mathbf{0} \\ \mathbf{0}' & n/(2\sigma^4) & (1/(2\sigma^2))\mathbf{i}'\boldsymbol{\Omega}^{-1}\mathbf{G} \\ \mathbf{0}' & (1/(2\sigma^2))\mathbf{G}'\boldsymbol{\Omega}^{-1}\mathbf{i} & (1/2)\mathbf{G}'\boldsymbol{\Omega}^{-2}\mathbf{G}\end{bmatrix}^{-1},\end{aligned} \tag{12-29}$$

where $\gamma' = [\beta', \sigma^2, \theta']$. (The proof is considered in the exercises.) For computational purposes, the Berndt et al. estimator,[27]

$$\hat{\mathbf{V}} = \left[\sum_{i=1}^{n} \hat{\mathbf{d}}_i \hat{\mathbf{d}}_i'\right]^{-1},$$

where

$$\mathbf{d}_i = \begin{bmatrix} \mathbf{x}_i \dfrac{\epsilon_i}{\sigma^2 f_i} \\ \dfrac{1}{2\sigma^2}\left(\dfrac{\epsilon_i^2}{\sigma^2 f_i} - 1\right) \\ \dfrac{1}{2f_i}\left(\dfrac{\epsilon_i^2}{\sigma^2 f_i} - 1\right)\mathbf{g}_i \end{bmatrix}, \tag{12-30}$$

may be easier to compute than the Hessian. Both estimators are valid asymptotically.

A second method of maximizing the log-likelihood is the procedure proposed by Oberhofer and Kmenta (1974). Solving the full set of likelihood equations simultaneously may be extremely difficult. But as we have seen, for given values of the variance parameters, the solutions for β and σ^2 are the GLS estimators. It may also be possible to solve the first-order conditions for θ for a given set of values for β and σ^2 relatively straightforwardly. In this model, this "zigzag" procedure will be a valid means of finding maximum likelihood estimates.

EXAMPLE 12.15 Multiplicative Heteroscedasticity[28]

Suppose that $\mathbf{q}_i$ is a set of variables and

$$\sigma_i^2 = \sigma^2 \exp(\alpha' \mathbf{q}_i).$$

This is a general model that includes several special cases, including the model in Example 12.14, in which $q_i = \ln z_i$.[29] As Godfrey suggests, there is a useful simplification of the formulation. Let $\mathbf{z}_i = [1, \mathbf{q}_i]$ and $\gamma = [\ln \sigma^2, \alpha]$. Then we can write the model as simply

$$\sigma_i^2 = \exp(\gamma' \mathbf{z}_i). \tag{12-31}$$

Once the full parameter vector is estimated, $\exp(\gamma_1)$ provides the estimator of σ^2.[30]

[27] See Section 4.5.2, (4-52).

[28] This model is examined at length by Harvey (1976).

[29] See Judge et al. (1985, pp. 439–441), Harvey (1976), and Just and Pope (1978).

[30] This uses the invariance result for maximum likelihood estimation. See Section 4.5.1.

The log-likelihood is

$$\ln L = -\frac{n}{2}\ln(2\pi) - \frac{1}{2}\sum_{i=1}^{n}\ln \sigma_i^2 - \frac{1}{2}\sum_{i=1}^{n}\frac{\epsilon_i^2}{\sigma_i^2}$$
$$= -\frac{n}{2}\ln(2\pi) - \frac{1}{2}\sum_{i=1}^{n}\mathbf{z}_i'\boldsymbol{\gamma} - \frac{1}{2}\sum_{i=1}^{n}\frac{\epsilon_i^2}{\exp(\mathbf{z}_i'\boldsymbol{\gamma})}. \tag{12-32}$$

The likelihood equations are

$$\frac{\partial \ln L}{\partial \boldsymbol{\beta}} = \sum_{i=1}^{n}\mathbf{x}_i\frac{\epsilon_i}{\exp(\mathbf{z}_i'\boldsymbol{\gamma})} = \mathbf{X}'\boldsymbol{\Omega}^{-1}\boldsymbol{\epsilon} = \mathbf{0},$$
$$\frac{\partial \ln L}{\partial \boldsymbol{\gamma}} = \frac{1}{2}\sum_{i=1}^{n}\mathbf{z}_i\left(\frac{\epsilon_i^2}{\exp(\mathbf{z}_i'\boldsymbol{\gamma})} - 1\right) = \mathbf{0}. \tag{12-33}$$

For this model, the method of scoring turns out to be a particularly convenient way to maximize the log-likelihood function. The terms in the Hessian are

$$\frac{\partial^2 \ln L}{\partial \boldsymbol{\beta}\,\partial \boldsymbol{\beta}'} = -\sum_{i=1}^{n}\frac{1}{\exp(\mathbf{z}_i'\boldsymbol{\gamma})}\mathbf{x}_i\mathbf{x}_i' = -\mathbf{X}'\boldsymbol{\Omega}^{-1}\mathbf{X},$$
$$\frac{\partial^2 \ln L}{\partial \boldsymbol{\beta}\,\partial \boldsymbol{\gamma}'} = -\sum_{i=1}^{n}\frac{\epsilon_i}{\exp(\mathbf{z}_i'\boldsymbol{\gamma})}\mathbf{x}_i\mathbf{z}_i',$$
$$\frac{\partial^2 \ln L}{\partial \boldsymbol{\gamma}\,\partial \boldsymbol{\gamma}'} = \frac{1}{2}\sum_{i=1}^{n}\frac{\epsilon_i^2}{\exp(\mathbf{z}_i'\boldsymbol{\gamma})}\mathbf{z}_i\mathbf{z}_i'. \tag{12-34}$$

The expected value of $\partial^2 \ln L/\partial\boldsymbol{\beta}\,\partial\boldsymbol{\gamma}'$ is $\mathbf{0}$ since $E[\epsilon_i] = 0$. The expected value of the fraction in $\partial^2 \ln L/\partial\boldsymbol{\gamma}\,\partial\boldsymbol{\gamma}'$ is $E[\epsilon_i^2/\sigma_i^2] = 1$. Let $\boldsymbol{\delta} = [\boldsymbol{\beta}, \boldsymbol{\gamma}]$. Then

$$-E\left(\frac{\partial^2 \ln L}{\partial\boldsymbol{\delta}\,\partial\boldsymbol{\delta}'}\right) = \begin{bmatrix}\mathbf{X}'\boldsymbol{\Omega}^{-1}\mathbf{X} & \mathbf{0}' \\ \mathbf{0} & \frac{1}{2}\mathbf{Z}'\mathbf{Z}\end{bmatrix} = -\mathbf{H}.$$

The scoring method is

$$\boldsymbol{\delta}_{t+1} = \boldsymbol{\delta}_t - \mathbf{H}_t^{-1}\mathbf{g}_t,$$

where $\boldsymbol{\delta}_t$ (i.e., $\boldsymbol{\beta}_t$, $\boldsymbol{\gamma}_t$, and $\boldsymbol{\Omega}_t$) is the estimate at iteration t, $\mathbf{g}_t$ is the two-part vector of first derivatives $[\partial \ln L/\partial\boldsymbol{\beta}_t, \partial \ln L/\partial\boldsymbol{\gamma}_t]$ and $\mathbf{H}_t$ is partitioned likewise. Since $\mathbf{H}_t$ is block diagonal, the iteration can be written as separate equations:

$$\begin{aligned}\boldsymbol{\beta}_{t+1} &= \boldsymbol{\beta}_t + (\mathbf{X}'\boldsymbol{\Omega}_t^{-1}\mathbf{X})^{-1}(\mathbf{X}'\boldsymbol{\Omega}_t^{-1}\boldsymbol{\epsilon}_t)\\ &= \boldsymbol{\beta}_t + (\mathbf{X}'\boldsymbol{\Omega}_t^{-1}\mathbf{X})^{-1}\mathbf{X}'\boldsymbol{\Omega}_t^{-1}(\mathbf{y} - \mathbf{X}\boldsymbol{\beta}_t)\\ &= (\mathbf{X}'\boldsymbol{\Omega}_t^{-1}\mathbf{X})^{-1}\mathbf{X}'\boldsymbol{\Omega}_t^{-1}\mathbf{y} \quad \text{(of course).}\end{aligned}$$

Therefore, the updated coefficient vector $\boldsymbol{\beta}_{t+1}$ is computed by FGLS using the previously computed estimate of $\boldsymbol{\gamma}$ to compute $\boldsymbol{\Omega}$. We use the same approach for $\boldsymbol{\gamma}$:

$$\boldsymbol{\gamma}_{t+1} = \boldsymbol{\gamma}_t + [2(\mathbf{Z}'\mathbf{Z})^{-1}]\left[\frac{1}{2}\sum_{i=1}^{n}\left(\frac{\epsilon_i^2}{\exp(\mathbf{z}_i'\boldsymbol{\gamma})} - 1\right)\right]. \tag{12-35}$$

The 2 and $\frac{1}{2}$ cancel. The updated value of $\boldsymbol{\gamma}$ is computed by updating the old one with the vector of slopes in the least squares regression of $[\epsilon_i^2/\exp(\mathbf{z}_i'\boldsymbol{\gamma}) - 1]$ on $\mathbf{z}$. Note that the correction is $2(\mathbf{Z}'\mathbf{Z})^{-1}\mathbf{Z}'(\partial \ln L/\partial\boldsymbol{\gamma})$, so convergence occurs when the derivative is zero.

The remaining detail is to determine to starting value for the iteration. Since any consistent estimator will do, the simplest procedure is to use OLS for $\boldsymbol{\beta}$ and the slopes in a regression of the logs of the squares of the least squares residuals on $\mathbf{z}_i$ for $\boldsymbol{\gamma}$. Harvey (1976) shows that this will produce an inconsistent estimator of $\gamma_1 = \ln \sigma^2$, but the inconsistency can be corrected just by adding 1.2704 to the value obtained.[31] Thereafter, the iteration is simply:

1. Estimate the disturbance variance σ_i^2 with $\exp(\boldsymbol{\gamma}_t'\mathbf{z}_i)$.
2. Compute $\boldsymbol{\beta}_{t+1}$ by FGLS.[32]
3. Update $\boldsymbol{\gamma}_t$ using the regression shown in (12-35).
4. Compute $\mathbf{d}_{t+1} = [\boldsymbol{\beta}_{t+1}, \boldsymbol{\gamma}_{t+1}] - [\boldsymbol{\beta}_t, \boldsymbol{\gamma}_t]$. If $\mathbf{d}_t$ is large, return to step 1.

If $\mathbf{d}_{t+1}$ at step 4 is sufficiently small, exit the iteration. The asymptotic covariance matrix is simply $-\mathbf{H}^{-1}$, which is block diagonal with blocks

$$\begin{aligned}\text{Asy. Var}[\hat{\boldsymbol{\beta}}_{\text{ML}}] &= (\mathbf{X}'\boldsymbol{\Omega}^{-1}\mathbf{X})^{-1},\\ \text{Asy. Var}[\hat{\boldsymbol{\gamma}}_{\text{ML}}] &= 2(\mathbf{Z}'\mathbf{Z})^{-1}.\end{aligned} \tag{12-36}$$

If desired, $\hat{\sigma}^2 = \exp(\hat{\gamma}_1)$ can be computed. The asymptotic variance would be $[\exp(\gamma_1)]^2(\text{Asy. Var}[\hat{\gamma}_{1,\text{ML}}])$.

12.6. GENERAL CONCLUSIONS

It is rarely possible to be certain about the nature of the heteroscedasticity in a regression model. In one respect, this is only a minor problem. The weighted least squares estimator

$$\hat{\boldsymbol{\beta}} = \left[\sum_{i=1}^{n} w_i\mathbf{x}_i\mathbf{x}_i'\right]^{-1}\left[\sum_{i=1}^{n} w_i\mathbf{x}_i y_i\right]$$

[31] He also presents a correction for the asymptotic covariance matrix for this first step estimator of $\boldsymbol{\gamma}$.

[32] The two-step estimator obtained by stopping here would be fully efficient if the starting value for $\boldsymbol{\gamma}$ were consistent. But it would not be the maximum likelihood estimator.

is consistent regardless of the weights used, as long as the weights are uncorrelated with the disturbances. Note the similarity of the estimates in Table 12.12, which summarizes the estimators discussed earlier. The effect is even more striking in the set of estimates of

$$\gamma = \frac{\partial \text{ spending}}{\partial \text{ income}} = \beta_2 + 2\beta_3 \text{ income},$$

which is computed at the mean income of 7608 for each model.

TABLE 12.12 Weighted Least Squares Estimates

Constant	*Income*	*Income*^{2}	γ
	Ordinary Least Squares		
832.91	−1834.2	1587.4	580.818
(327.3)	(829.0)	(519.1)	
	Weighted Least Squares: $Var[\epsilon_i] = \sigma^2 Income_i$		
560.72	−1124.18	1132.43	598.925
(335.6)	(893.6)	(588.5)	
	Weighted Least Squares: $Var[\epsilon_i] = \sigma^2 Income_i^2$		
644.58	−1399.28	1311.35	596.217
(333.6)	(872.1)	(563.7)	
	Generalized Least Squares: $Var[\epsilon_i] = \alpha' z_i$		
709.05	−1506.40	1374.5	584.661
(451.9)	(1199.0)	(790.8)	
	Generalized Least Squares: $Var[\epsilon_i] = \sigma^2[\beta' x_i]^2$		
591.08	−1195.15	1172.22	588.631
(371.0)	(981.2)	(642.7)	
	Weighted Least Squares: $\ln Var[\epsilon_i] = \ln\sigma^2 + \Sigma_m \alpha_m z_{im}$		
488.43	−912.69	980.71	579.668
(529.1)	(1423.0)	(950.3)	

But using the wrong set of weights has two other consequences that may be less benign. First, the improperly weighted least squares estimator is inefficient. This might be a moot point if the correct weights are unknown, but the GLS standard errors will also be incorrect. The asymptotic covariance matrix of the estimator

$$\hat{\boldsymbol{\beta}} = [\mathbf{X}'\mathbf{V}^{-1}\mathbf{X}]^{-1}\mathbf{X}'\mathbf{V}^{-1}\mathbf{y} \tag{12-37}$$

is

$$\text{Asy. Var}[\hat{\boldsymbol{\beta}}] = [\mathbf{X}'\mathbf{V}^{-1}\mathbf{X}]^{-1}\mathbf{X}'\mathbf{V}^{-1}\boldsymbol{\Omega}\mathbf{V}^{-1}\mathbf{X}[\mathbf{X}'\mathbf{V}^{-1}\mathbf{X}]^{-1}. \tag{12-38}$$

This may or may not resemble the usual estimator, which would be the matrix in brackets. This underscores the usefulness of the White estimator in (12-9).

There is a drift in the literature toward bypassing the sorts of procedures discussed here and simply using OLS with the White estimator or some variant for the asymptotic covariance matrix. One could argue both flaws and virtues in this approach. In its favor, robustness to unknown heteroscedasticity is a compelling virtue. In the clear presence of heteroscedasticity, however, least squares can be extremely inefficient. The question becomes whether using the wrong weights is better than using no weights at all. There are several layers to the question. If we use one of the models discussed earlier—Harvey's, for example, is a versatile and flexible candidate—we may use the wrong set of weights and, in addition, we introduce a new source of variation into the slope estimators for the model. The issue remains to be settled. For better or worse, a heteroscedasticity robust estimator for weighted least squares that appears not to have shown up in the literature previously can be formed by combining (12-38) with the White estimator. For any set of weights $\mathbf{V} = \text{diag}[v_1, v_2, \ldots, v_n]$, the weighted least squares estimator in (12-37) is consistent. Its asymptotic covariance matrix can be estimated consistently with

$$\text{Est. Asy. Var}[\hat{\boldsymbol{\beta}}] = (\mathbf{X}'\mathbf{V}^{-1}\mathbf{X})^{-1}\left[\sum_{i=1}^{n}\left(\frac{e_i^2}{v_i^2}\right)\mathbf{x}_i\mathbf{x}_i'\right](\mathbf{X}'\mathbf{V}^{-1}\mathbf{X})^{-1}. \tag{12-39}$$

Any consistent estimator can be used to form the residuals. The weighted least squares estimator is a natural candidate.

Finally, if the form of the heteroscedasticity is known but involves unknown parameters, it remains uncertain whether FGLS corrections are better than OLS. Asymptotically, the comparison is clear, but in small or moderate-sized samples, the additional variation incorporated by the estimated variance parameters may offset the gains to GLS.

12.7. AUTOREGRESSIVE CONDITIONAL HETEROSCEDASTICITY

Heteroscedasticity is usually associated with cross-sectional data, whereas time series are typically studied in the context of homoscedastic processes. In analyses of macroeconomic data, Engle (1982, 1983) and Cragg (1982) have found evidence that for some phenomena the disturbance variances in time-series models are less stable than usually assumed. More recent studies of financial markets suggest that the phenomenon is very common.

Engle's results suggest that in analyzing models of inflation, large and small forecast errors appear to occur in clusters, suggesting a form of heteroscedasticity in which the variance of the forecast error depends on the size of the preceding disturbance. He has suggested the **A**uto**R**egressive, **C**onditionally **H**eteroscedastic, or **ARCH,** model as an alternative to the usual time-series process. A simple version of his model is

$$\begin{aligned} y_t &= \boldsymbol{\beta}'\mathbf{x}_t + \epsilon_t, \\ \epsilon_t &= u_t[\alpha_0 + \alpha_1\epsilon_{t-1}^2]^{1/2}, \end{aligned} \tag{12-40}$$

where u_t is standard normal.[33] It follows that

$$E[\epsilon_t \mid \epsilon_{t-1}] = 0,$$

so

$$E[\epsilon_t] = 0 \quad \text{and} \quad E[y_t] = \boldsymbol{\beta}'\mathbf{x}_t.$$

Also,

$$\begin{aligned} \text{Var}[\epsilon_t \mid \epsilon_{t-1}] &= E[\epsilon_t^2 \mid \epsilon_{t-1}] \\ &= E[u_t^2][\alpha_0 + \alpha_1\epsilon_{t-1}^2] \\ &= \alpha_0 + \alpha_1\epsilon_{t-1}^2. \end{aligned}$$

Conditional on ϵ_{t-1}, ϵ_t is heteroscedastic. The *unconditional* variance of ϵ_t is[34]

$$\begin{aligned} \text{Var}[\epsilon_t] &= E[\text{Var}[\epsilon_t \mid \epsilon_{t-1}]] \\ &= \alpha_0 + \alpha_1 E[\epsilon_{t-1}^2] \\ &= \alpha_0 + \alpha_1 \text{Var}[\epsilon_{t-1}]. \end{aligned}$$

If the process generating the disturbances is **variance stationary**,[35] the unconditional variance is unchanging over time. Then

$$\begin{aligned} \text{Var}[\epsilon_t] &= \text{Var}[\epsilon_{t-1}] \\ &= \alpha_0 + \alpha_1 \text{Var}[\epsilon_{t-1}] \\ &= \frac{\alpha_0}{1 - \alpha_1}. \end{aligned} \tag{12-41}$$

Therefore, the model obeys the classical assumptions, and ordinary least squares is the most efficient *linear* estimator of $\boldsymbol{\beta}$.

---

[33]The assumption that u_t has unit variance is not a restriction. The scaling implied by any other variance would be absorbed by the other parameters.

[34]We are using the variance decomposition in (3-70). The variance of $E[\epsilon_t \mid \epsilon_{t-1}]$ is zero.

[35]We shall treat this concept in more detail in Chapters 13 and 18.

But there is a more efficient *nonlinear* estimator. The log-likelihood function for this model is given by Engle (1982). Conditioned on starting values y_0 and $\mathbf{x}_0$, the log likelihood for observations $t = 1, \ldots, T$ is

$$\ln L = -\frac{1}{2}\sum_{t=1}^{T}\ln(\alpha_0 + \alpha_1\epsilon_{t-1}^2) - \frac{1}{2}\sum_{t=1}^{T}\frac{\epsilon_t^2}{\alpha_0 + \alpha_1\epsilon_{t-1}^2}, \qquad \textbf{(12-42)}$$

where

$$\epsilon_t = y_t - \boldsymbol{\beta}'\mathbf{x}_t.$$

Maximization of ln L may be done by conventional methods. A simpler, four-step FGLS estimator is available, however.[36] Let the sample consist of y_t and $\mathbf{x}_t$ for $t = 0, 1, \ldots, T$, including the initial values.

1. Regress $\mathbf{y}$ on $\mathbf{X}$, using least squares and all available observations to obtain $\mathbf{b}$ and $\mathbf{e}$.
2. Regress e_t^2 on a constant and e_{t-1}^2 to obtain initial estimates of α_0 and α_1, using the T observations $t = 1, \ldots, T$. Notice that this is the same procedure we have used in several other FGLS procedures to estimate the variance parameters consistently. Denote the 2×1 estimated vector as $[a_0, a_1]' = \mathbf{a}$.
3. Compute $f_t = \alpha_0 + \alpha_1 e_{t-1}^2$ for $t = 1, \ldots, T$. Then compute the asymptotically efficient estimate

$$\hat{\boldsymbol{\alpha}} = \mathbf{a} + \mathbf{d}_\alpha,$$

   where $\mathbf{d}_\alpha$ is the least squares coefficient vector in the regression of $[(e_t^2/f_t) - 1]$ on $(1/f_t)$ and (e_{t-1}^2/f_t). The asymptotic covariance matrix for $\hat{\boldsymbol{\alpha}}$ is $2(\mathbf{Z}'\mathbf{Z})^{-1}$, where $\mathbf{Z}$ is the regressor matrix in this regression.[37]
4. Recompute f_t using $\hat{\boldsymbol{\alpha}}$; then for observations $t = 1, \ldots, T - 1$, compute

$$r_t = \left[\frac{1}{f_t} + 2\left(\frac{\hat{\alpha}_1 e_t}{f_{t+1}}\right)^2\right]^{1/2}$$

   and

$$s_t = \frac{1}{f_t} - \frac{\hat{\alpha}_1}{f_{t+1}}\left(\frac{e_{t+1}^2}{f_{t+1}} - 1\right).$$

   Compute the estimate

$$\hat{\boldsymbol{\beta}} = \mathbf{b} + \mathbf{d}_\beta,$$

   where $\mathbf{d}_\beta$ is the least squares coefficient vector in the regression of $e_t s_t / r_t$ on $\mathbf{x}_t r_t$. The asymptotic covariance matrix for $\hat{\boldsymbol{\beta}}$ is $(\mathbf{W}'\mathbf{W})^{-1}$, where $\mathbf{W}$ is the regressor matrix used in this regression.

[36] See Engle (1982) and Judge et al. (1985, pp. 441–444).

[37] This procedure is based on the method of scoring. Note the similarity of this step to the analogous step in Example 12.15.

This procedure is asymptotically equivalent to maximum likelihood. It is possible to iterate by returning to step 2 with new residuals calculated after step 4, but this brings no gains in efficiency and does not converge to the true maximum likelihood estimate (assuming it converges at all). (Step 2 is not the solution to the likelihood equation for $\boldsymbol{\alpha}$.) One possible refinement of the model would be to add further lags in the ARCH process. The modification of the estimation process is minor; the regression in step 2 and the computation of f_t are extended by adding the additional lags of e^2.[38]

EXAMPLE 12.16 ARCH Process for the Rate of Inflation

The annual percentage rate of increase in the U.S. Consumer Price Index by year from 1940 to 1986 is listed in Table 12.13. We shall use these data and the four-step method outlined earlier to fit the ARCH model:

$$\Delta p_t = \beta_1 + \beta_2 \Delta p_{t-1} + \epsilon_t$$
$$\epsilon_t = u_t[\alpha_0 + \alpha_1 \epsilon_{t-1}^2]^{1/2}.$$

Where appropriate, standard errors are given in parentheses below the estimates.

1. Regression of Δp_t on a constant and Δp_{t-1} for 1941 to 1986:

$$\Delta p_t = \underset{(0.8082)}{2.34625} + \underset{(0.1307)}{0.4968}\ \Delta p_{t-1}.$$

2. Regression of the squared residual on a constant and the lagged squared residual:

$$e_t^2 = 12.0453 - 0.031778 e_{t-1}^2, \qquad R^2 = 0.00104, \qquad T = 45.$$

TABLE 12.13 U.S. Inflation Data

1940	1.0	1950	5.8	1960	1.5	1970	5.5	1980	12.4
1941	9.7	1951	5.9	1961	0.7	1971	3.4	1981	8.9
1942	9.3	1952	0.9	1962	1.2	1972	3.4	1982	3.9
1943	3.2	1953	0.6	1963	1.6	1973	8.8	1983	3.8
1944	2.1	1954	−0.5	1964	1.2	1974	12.2	1984	4.0
1945	2.3	1955	0.4	1965	1.9	1975	7.0	1985	3.8
1946	18.2	1956	2.9	1966	3.4	1976	4.8	1986	1.1
1947	9.0	1957	3.0	1967	3.0	1977	6.8		
1948	2.7	1958	1.8	1968	4.7	1978	9.0		
1949	−1.8	1959	1.5	1969	6.1	1979	13.3		

Source: Data from the *1987 Economic Report of the President,* p. 312.

[38]See Bollerslev (1986) and Chapter 18 for a discussion and some further generalizations.

3. The correction to be applied to the preceding estimates is $\mathbf{d}_\alpha = [-0.02867, 0.0019644]$, which gives $\hat{\boldsymbol{\alpha}}$. Then

$$e_t^2 = \underset{(2.6248)}{12.0166} - \underset{(0.03662)}{0.029814} e_{t-1}^2.$$

4. The correction to the parameters and updated values are $\mathbf{d}_\beta = [-0.105687, -0.031742]$,

$$\Delta p_t = \underset{(0.7923)}{2.45193} + \underset{(0.1248)}{0.46508}\ \Delta p_{t-1}.$$

The change that results from estimating according to the ARCH model is relatively small; compare step 4 with step 1. This was to be expected in view of the insignificant results at step 3.

Engle also presents a Lagrange multiplier test for the ARCH process against the null hypothesis that the disturbance is conditionally homoscedastic. The statistic is T times the R^2 in the regression at step 2. This is asymptotically distributed as chi-squared with one degree of freedom. For the inflation data used in the example, the chi-squared value is 0.0468, which is far from statistically significant.

The recent literature contains a wealth of extensions to Engle's ARCH model. The extension to P lags,

$$\mathrm{Var}[\epsilon_t \mid \epsilon_{t-1}, \epsilon_{t-2}, \ldots, \epsilon_{t-p}] = \sigma_t^2,$$

where

$$\sigma_t^2 = \alpha_0 + \alpha_1 \epsilon_{t-1}^2 + \alpha_2 \epsilon_{t-2}^2 + \cdots + \alpha_P \epsilon_{t-P}^2,$$

requires only a minor change in steps 3 and 4 of the previous method. More recent studies, beginning with Bollerslev (1986), have used the generalized ARCH (or GARCH) model,

$$\sigma_t^2 = \alpha_0 + \alpha_1 \epsilon_{t-1}^2 + \delta \sigma_{t-1}^2.$$

This model is considered in detail in Section 18.7.

EXERCISES

1. Suppose that the regression model is

$$y_i = \mu + \epsilon_i,$$

where

$$E[\epsilon_i \mid x_i] = 0, \qquad \text{but } \mathrm{Var}[\epsilon_i \mid x_i] = \sigma^2 x_i^2, \quad x_i > 0.$$

(a) Given a sample of observations on y_i and x_i, what is the most efficient estimator of μ? What is its variance?

(b) What is the OLS estimator of μ, and what is the variance of the ordinary least squares estimator?
(c) Prove that the estimator in part a is at least as efficient as the estimator in part b.

2. For the model in the previous exercise, what is the probability limit of the following?

$$s^2 = \frac{1}{n}\sum_{i=1}^{n}(y_i - \bar{y})^2$$

Note that this is the least squares estimate of the residual variance. It is also n times the conventional estimator of the variance of the OLS estimator,

$$\text{Est. Var}[\bar{y}] = s^2(\mathbf{X}'\mathbf{X})^{-1} = \frac{s^2}{n}.$$

How does this compare with the true value you found in part b of Exercise 1? Does the conventional estimator produce the correct estimate of the true asymptotic variance of the least squares estimator?

3. Two samples of 50 observations each produce the following moment matrices. (In each case, **X** is a constant and one variable.)

	Sample 1	Sample 2
$\mathbf{X}'\mathbf{X}$	$\begin{bmatrix} 50 & 300 \\ 300 & 2100 \end{bmatrix}$	$\begin{bmatrix} 50 & 300 \\ 300 & 2100 \end{bmatrix}$
$\mathbf{y}'\mathbf{X}$	$[300 \quad 2000]$	$[300 \quad 2200]$
$\mathbf{y}'\mathbf{y}$	2100	2800

(a) Compute the least squares regression coefficients and the residual variances s^2 for each data set. Compute the R^2 for each regression.
(b) Compute the OLS estimate of the coefficient vector assuming that the coefficients and disturbance variance are the same in the two regressions. Also compute the estimate of the asymptotic covariance matrix of the estimate.
(c) Test the hypothesis that the variances in the two regressions are the same without assuming that the coefficients are the same in the two regressions.
(d) Compute the two-step FGLS estimator of the coefficients in the regressions, assuming that the constant and slope are the same in both regressions. Compute the estimate of the covariance matrix and compare it with the result of part b.

4. Using the data in the previous exercise, use the Oberhofer–Kmenta method to compute the maximum likelihood estimate of the common coefficient vector.

5. This exercise is based on the following data set.

50 Observations on Y:

−1.42	2.75	2.10	−5.08	1.49	1.00	0.16	−1.11	1.66
−0.26	−4.87	5.94	2.21	−6.87	0.90	1.61	2.11	−3.82
−0.62	7.01	26.14	7.39	0.79	1.93	1.97	−23.17	−2.52
−1.26	−0.15	3.41	−5.45	1.31	1.52	2.04	3.00	6.31
5.51	−15.22	−1.47	−1.48	6.66	1.78	2.62	−5.16	−4.71
−0.35	−0.48	1.24	0.69	1.91				

50 Observations on X_1:

−1.65	1.48	0.77	0.67	0.68	0.23	−0.40	−1.13	0.15
−0.63	0.34	0.35	0.79	0.77	−1.04	0.28	0.58	−0.41
−1.78	1.25	0.22	1.25	−0.12	0.66	1.06	−0.66	−1.18
−0.80	−1.32	0.16	1.06	−0.60	0.79	0.86	2.04	−0.51
0.02	0.33	−1.99	0.70	−0.17	0.33	0.48	1.90	−0.18
−0.18	−1.62	0.39	0.17	1.02				

50 Observations on X_2:

−0.67	0.70	0.32	2.88	−0.19	−1.28	−2.72	−0.70	−1.55
−0.74	−1.87	1.56	0.37	−2.07	1.20	0.26	−1.34	−2.10
0.61	2.32	4.38	2.16	1.51	0.30	−0.17	7.82	−1.15
1.77	2.92	−1.94	2.09	1.50	−0.46	0.19	−0.39	1.54
1.87	−3.45	−0.88	−1.53	1.42	−2.70	1.77	−1.89	−1.85
2.01	1.26	−2.02	1.91	−2.23				

(a) Compute the ordinary least squares regression of Y on a constant, X_1, and X_2. Be sure to compute the conventional estimator of the asymptotic covariance matrix of the OLS estimator as well.

(b) Compute the White estimator of the appropriate asymptotic covariance matrix for the OLS estimates. [See (12-9).]

(c) Test for the presence of heteroscedasticity using White's general test. Do your results suggest the nature of the heteroscedasticity?

(d) Use the Breusch–Pagan Lagrange multiplier test to test for heteroscedasticity.

(e) Sort the data keying on X_1, and use the Goldfeld-Quandt test to test for heteroscedasticity. Repeat the procedure, using X_2. What do you find?

(f) Use one of Glesjer's tests to test for heteroscedasticity.

6. Using the data of Exercise 5, reestimate the parameters using a two-step FGLS estimator. Try (12-19), (12-20), and (12-21). Which one appears to be most appropriate?

7. For the model in Exercise 1, suppose that ϵ is normally distributed, with mean zero and variance $\sigma^2[1 + (\gamma x)^2]$. Show that σ^2 and γ^2 can be consistently estimated by a regression of the least squares residuals on a constant and x^2. Is this estimator efficient?

8. Derive the log-likelihood function, first-order conditions for maximization, and information matrix for the model

$$y_i = \boldsymbol{\beta}'\mathbf{x}_i + \epsilon_i,$$
$$\epsilon_i \sim N[0, \sigma^2(\boldsymbol{\gamma}'\mathbf{z}_i)^2].$$

9. For the model of (12-26) to (12-29), prove the result in (12-29). [Hints: Remember that the only stochastic components of the derivatives are ϵ and ϵ^2. For all derivatives except $\partial^2 \ln L/\partial\boldsymbol{\theta}/\partial\boldsymbol{\theta}'$, just differentiate and take expected values. Then write sums involving $1/f_i$ in terms of $\boldsymbol{\Omega}^{-1}$. For the remaining term, simplify the expressions by letting $c_i = [\epsilon_i^2/(\sigma^2 f_i) - 1]$ and $\mathbf{r}_i = \mathbf{g}_i/f_i$. $E[c_i] = 0$ and $\mathbf{r}_i$ is nonstochastic. Use $\partial \ln L/\partial\boldsymbol{\theta} = \frac{1}{2}\Sigma_i c_i \mathbf{r}_i$. Now, differentiate, collect terms, and take expected values.]

10. In Example 12.15, it is noted that the initial estimator of γ_1, the constant term in the regression of $\ln e_i^2$ on a constant, and $\mathbf{z}_i$ is inconsistent by the amount 1.2704. Harvey points out that if the purpose of this initial regression is only to obtain starting values for the iterations, then the correction is not necessary. Explain why this would be the case.

CHAPTER 13

Autocorrelated Disturbances

13.1. INTRODUCTION

Heteroscedasticity is most commonly associated with cross-section data. In a time-series setting, the more common problem is autocorrelation, or serial correlation of the disturbances across periods. Consider, for example, the plot of the least squares residuals in the following example.

EXAMPLE 13.1 Investment Equation

The data listed in Table 13.1 are used to fit an investment equation. GNP and gross private domestic investment are in nominal terms in billions of dollars. The price index is the implicit price deflator for GNP. The interest rate is the average yearly discount rate charged by the New York Federal Reserve Bank. Variables used in the regressions reported in the examples to follow are real GNP and real investment obtained by dividing the nominal figures by the price index. An approximation to the real interest rate is obtained by subtracting the rate of change in the price index from the discount rate.

Least squares regression of real investment on real GNP and the real interest rate produces the results given in Table 13.2.

A plot of residuals is shown in Figure 13.1. The pattern in the residuals suggests that knowledge of the sign of a residual in one period is a fair indicator of the sign of the residual in the next period. This suggests that the effect of a given disturbance is carried, at least in part, across periods.

One explanation for autocorrelation is that the factors omitted from the time-series regression, like those included, are correlated across periods. Of course, this may be due to serial correlation in factors that should be in the regression model. Still, even after accounting for this possibility, it is reasonable

TABLE 13.1 Investment Data

Year	*GNP*	*Investment*	*Price Index*	*Interest Rate*
1963	596.7	90.9	0.7167	3.23
1964	637.7	97.4	0.7277	3.55
1965	691.1	113.5	0.7436	4.04
1966	756.0	125.7	0.7676	4.50
1967	799.6	122.8	0.7906	4.19
1968	873.4	133.3	0.8254	5.16
1969	944.0	149.3	0.8679	5.87
1970	992.7	144.2	0.9145	5.95
1971	1077.6	166.4	0.9601	4.88
1972	1185.9	195.0	1.0000	4.50
1973	1326.4	229.8	1.0575	6.44
1974	1434.2	228.7	1.1508	7.83
1975	1549.2	206.1	1.2579	6.25
1976	1718.0	257.9	1.3234	5.50
1977	1918.3	324.1	1.4005	5.46
1978	2163.9	386.6	1.5042	7.46
1979	2417.8	423.0	1.6342	10.28
1980	2631.7	401.9	1.7842	11.77
1981	2954.1	474.9	1.9514	13.42
1982	3073.0	414.5	2.0688	11.02

Source: Data from the *Economic Report of the President,* U.S. Government Printing Office, Washington, D.C., 1984.

to model most time-series data as having some serial correlation. A second source of autocorrelation is the manner in which some published statistics are produced. For example, in seasonally adjusting variables such as the CPI and GNP, government agencies build autocorrelation into series that might otherwise be uncorrelated.

TABLE 13.2 Investment Equation, OLS

Variable	*Coefficient*	*Standard Error*
Constant	−12.5336	24.920
Real interest	−1.00144	2.369
Real GNP	0.16914	0.02057
$R^2 = 0.81406$		

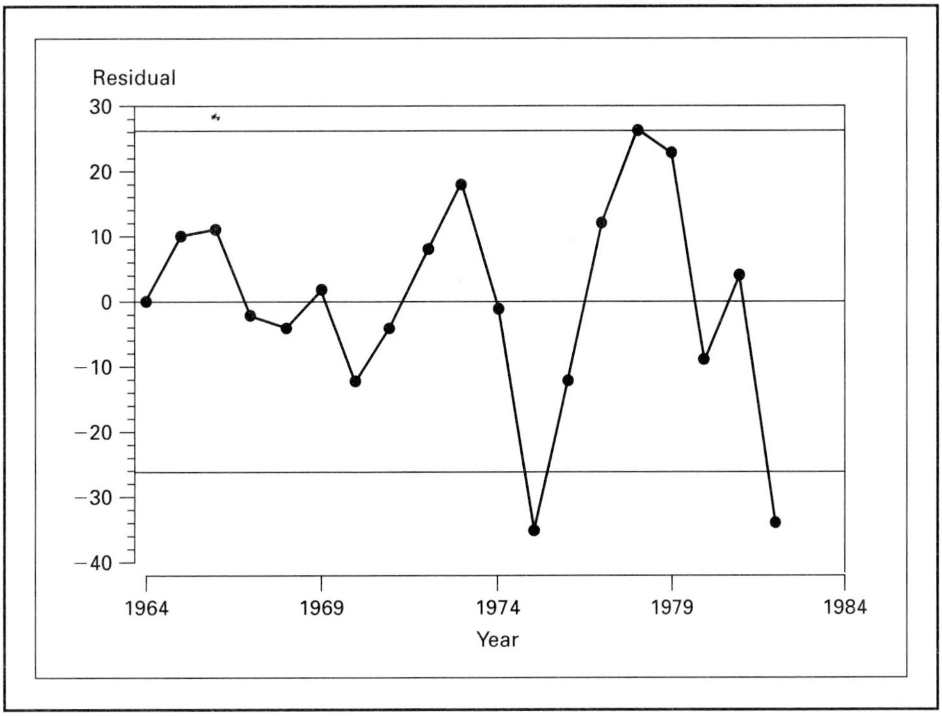

FIGURE 13.1 Plot of Residuals.

EXAMPLE 13.2 Moving-Average Process

Suppose that x_t, $t = 1, \ldots, T$, is a random sample from a distribution with mean zero and variance σ^2.[1] Then $\text{Cov}[x_t, x_s] = 0$ if $t \neq s$. Let z_t be a "seasonally adjusted" series such that

$$z_t = \sum_{s=0}^{11} w_s x_{t-s},$$

where w_s is monthly weight. Then

$$\text{Cov}[z_t, z_{t-s}] = w_0 w_s \sigma^2$$

for $s = 0, 1, \ldots, 11$ and zero for s greater than 11. The original series is uncorrelated, but the adjustment induces autocorrelation of 11 periods' duration.

The problems for estimation and inference caused by autocorrelation are similar to (although, unfortunately, more involved than) those caused by heteroscedasticity. As before, least squares is inefficient, and inference based on the least squares estimates is adversely affected. Depending on the underlying

[1]Since this chapter deals exclusively with time-series data, we shall use the index t for observations and T for the sample size throughout.

process, however, GLS and FGLS estimators can be devised that circumvent these problems. We should emphasize that the models we shall examine here are quite far removed from the classical regression. The exact or small-sample properties of the estimators are rarely known, and only their asymptotic properties have been derived.

13.2. THE ANALYSIS OF TIME-SERIES DATA

The analysis of autocorrelation in disturbances brings us into the realm of time-series analysis. Time-series analysis requires some revision of the interpretation of both data generation and sampling that we have maintained thus far.

A time-series model will typically describe the path of a variable y_t in terms of contemporaneous (and perhaps lagged) factors $\mathbf{x}_t$, disturbances (or innovations in the parlance of the recent work on this subject), ϵ_t, and its own past, $y_{t-1}, \ldots$. For example,

$$y_t = \beta_1 + \beta_2 x_t + \beta_3 y_{t-1} + \epsilon_t.$$

The time series is a single occurrence of a random event. For example, the yearly series on real output in the United States from 1945 to 1990 is a single realization of a process, GNP_t. The entire history over this period constitutes a realization of the process. At least in economics, the process could not be repeated. There is no counterpart to repeated sampling in a cross section. Nonetheless, were circumstances different at the end of World War II, the observed history *could* have been different. In principle, a completely different realization of the entire series might have occurred.

The properties of y_t as a random variable in a cross section are straightforward and are conveniently summarized in a statement about its mean and variance or the probability distribution generating y_t. The statement is less obvious here. It is common to assume that disturbances are generated independently from one period to the next, with the familiar assumptions

$$E[\epsilon_t] = 0,$$
$$\text{Var}[\epsilon_t] = \sigma^2,$$

and

$$\text{Cov}[\epsilon_t, \epsilon_s] = 0 \quad \text{for } t \neq s.$$

In the current context, the distribution of ϵ_t is said to be **covariance stationary** or **weakly stationary.** Thus, although the substantive notion of "random sampling" must be extended for the time series ϵ_t, the mathematical results based on that notion apply here. It can be said that ϵ_t is generated by a process whose mean and variance are not changing over time.[2] As such, by the method we will

---

[2]Stationarity could be extended to "strong stationarity" by asserting that the *distribution* is not changing over time. This would strictly validate results based on a "random sampling" assumption. But the assumption of strong stationarity is not necessary for what we do here, so we will not take this additional step.

discuss in this chapter, we could, at least in principle, obtain sample information and use it to characterize the distribution of ϵ_t. Could the same be said of y_t? There is an obvious difference between the series ϵ_t and y_t; observations on y_t at different points in time are necessarily correlated. Suppose that the y_t series *is* weakly stationary and that x_t is nonstochastic.[3] Then we could say the following:

$$\text{Var}[y_t] = \beta_3^2 \text{Var}[y_{t-1}] + \text{Var}[\epsilon_t]$$

or

$$\gamma_0 = \beta_3^2 \gamma_0 + \sigma^2$$

or

$$\gamma_0 = \frac{\sigma^2}{1 - \beta_3^2}.$$

Thus, γ_0, the variance of y_t, is a fixed characteristic of the process generating y_t. Note how the stationarity assumption, which apparently includes $|\beta_3| < 1$, has been used. The assumption that $|\beta_3| < 1$ is needed to ensure a finite and positive variance.[4]

Alternatively, consider simply repeated substitution of lagged values into the expression for y_t:

$$y_t = \beta_1 + \beta_2 x_t + \beta_3(\beta_1 + \beta_2 x_{t-1} + \beta_3 y_{t-2} + \epsilon_{t-1}) + \epsilon_t \qquad \textbf{(13-1)}$$

and so on. We see that, in fact, the current y_t is an accumulation of the entire history of x_t and ϵ_t. So if we wish to characterize the distribution of y_t, we might do so in terms of sums of random variables. By continuing to substitute for y_{t-2}, then y_{t-3}, . . . in (13-1), we obtain

$$y_t = \sum_{i=0}^{\infty} \beta_3^i(\beta_1 + \beta_2 x_{t-i} + \epsilon_{t-i}).$$

By this construction,

$$\begin{aligned}\text{Var}[y_t] &= \sum_{i=0}^{\infty} (\beta_3^i)^2 \text{Var}[\epsilon_{t-i}] \\ &= \sigma^2 \sum_{i=0}^{\infty} \beta_3^{2i} \\ &= \frac{\sigma^2}{1 - \beta_3^2}.\end{aligned}$$

Once again, the stationarity assumption, $|\beta_3| < 1$, is necessary.

---

[3]Whether $\mathbf{x}_t$ is regarded as stochastic or nonstochastic, as we saw in Chapter 6, is immaterial to large-sample estimation and inference results. The former probably makes more sense. For the present, it is convenient to do the analysis conditionally on $\mathbf{x}_t$, as if it were nonstochastic.

[4]There is an explosion of articles in the current literature in macroeconometrics on cases in which $\beta_3 = 1$ (or counterparts in different models). For example, two surveys of "unit roots" in economic time series are Nerlove and Diebold (1990) and Campbell and Perron (1991). We will return to this subject in Chapter 18.

Do sums that reach back into infinite past make any sense? We might view the process as having begun generating data at some remote, effectively "infinite" past. As long as distant observations become progressively less important, the extension to an infinite past is merely a mathematical convenience. The diminishing importance of past observations is implied by $|\beta_3| < 1$. Notice that, not coincidentally, this is the same requirement as that needed to solve for γ_0 in the preceding paragraphs. A second possibility is to assume that the *observation* of *this* time series begins at some time 0 [with (x_0, ϵ_0) called the **initial conditions**], by which time the underlying process has reached a state such that the mean and variance of y_t are not (or are no longer) changing over time. The mathematics are slightly different, but this leads to the same characterization of the random process generating y_t. In fact, the same weak stationarity assumption ensures both of them.

Except in very special cases, we would expect all the elements in the T component random vector $(y_1, \ldots, y_T)$ to be correlated. In this instance, said correlation is called "autocorrelation." As such, the results pertaining to estimation with independent or uncorrelated observations that we used in the previous chapters are no longer relevant. In point of fact, we have a sample of but one observation on the multivariate random variable $[y_t, t = 1, \ldots, T]$. There is a counterpart to the cross-sectional notion of parameter estimation, but only under assumptions (e.g., weak stationarity) that establish that parameters in the familiar sense even exist. Even with stationarity, it will emerge that for estimation and inference, none of our earlier finite sample results is usable. Consistency and asymptotic normality of estimators are somewhat more difficult to establish in time series settings because results that require independent observations, such as the central limit theorems, are no longer usable. Nonetheless, counterparts to our earlier results have been established for most of the estimation problems we will consider here and in Chapters 16 and 17. Where necessary, we will just invoke them with a minimum of derivation.[5]

13.3. DISTURBANCE PROCESSES

13.3.1. Characteristics of Disturbance Processes

In the usual time-series setting, the disturbances are assumed to be homoscedastic, but correlated across observations, so that

$$E[\boldsymbol{\epsilon\epsilon}'] = \sigma^2\boldsymbol{\Omega},$$

where $\sigma^2\boldsymbol{\Omega}$ is a full, positive definite matrix with a constant $\sigma^2 = \text{Var}[\epsilon_t]$ on the diagonal. As will be clear in the following discussion, we shall also assume that $\boldsymbol{\Omega}_{ts}$ is a function of $|t - s|$, but not of t or s alone. This is a **stationarity** assump-

[5]See section 6.7.10 for a discussion of the results of Mann and Wald (1943).

tion. (See the preceding section.) It implies that the covariance between observations t and s is a function only of $|t - s|$, the distance apart in time of the observations. We define the **autocovariances:**

$$\text{Cov}[\epsilon_t, \epsilon_{t-s}] = \text{Cov}[\epsilon_{t+s}, \epsilon_t] = \gamma_s.$$

Note that $\sigma^2 = \gamma_0$. The correlation between ϵ_t and ϵ_{t-s} is their **autocorrelation,**

$$\text{Corr}[\epsilon_t, \epsilon_{t-s}] = \frac{\text{Cov}[\epsilon_t, \epsilon_{t-s}]}{\sqrt{\text{Var}[\epsilon_t]\text{Var}[\epsilon_{t-s}]}} = \frac{\gamma_s}{\gamma_0} = \rho_s.$$

We can then write

$$E[\boldsymbol{\epsilon\epsilon}'] = \gamma_0\mathbf{R},$$

where $\mathbf{R}$ is an **autocorrelation matrix:**

$$\mathbf{R}_{ts} = \frac{\gamma_{|t-s|}}{\gamma_0}.$$

Different types of processes imply different patterns in $\mathbf{R}$. For example, the most frequently analyzed process is a **first-order autoregression** or AR(1) process,

$$\epsilon_t = \rho\epsilon_{t-1} + u_t,$$

for which we will verify that $\rho_s = \rho^s$. Higher-order **autoregressive processes** of the form

$$\epsilon_t = \theta_1\epsilon_{t-1} + \theta_2\epsilon_{t-2} + \cdots + \theta_p\epsilon_{t-1} + u_t$$

imply more involved patterns, including, for some values of the parameters, cyclical behavior of the autocorrelations.[6] Autoregressions are structured so that the influence of a given disturbance fades as it recedes into the more distant past but vanishes only asymptotically. For example, for the AR(1), $\text{Cov}[\epsilon_t, \epsilon_{t-s}]$ is never zero, but does become negligible if $|\rho|$ is less than 1. *Moving average* processes such as the one in Example 13.2, conversely, have a short memory. For the MA(1) process,

$$\epsilon_t = u_t - \lambda u_{t-1},$$

the memory in the process is only one period:

$$\gamma_0 = \sigma_u^2(1 + \lambda^2),$$
$$\gamma_1 = -\lambda\sigma_u^2,$$

but

$$\gamma_k = 0 \quad \text{if } k > 1.$$

The memory in the MA(11) process of Example 13.2 is 11 periods.

[6]This is considered in more detail in Chapter 18.

13.3.2. AR(1) Disturbances

Time-series processes such as the ones listed here can be characterized by their order, the values of their parameters, and the behavior of their autocorrelations.[7] We shall consider various forms at different points. The received empirical literature is overwhelmingly dominated by the AR(1) model. This is partly a matter of convenience. Processes more involved than this model are usually extremely difficult to analyze.[8] There is, however, a more practical reason. It is very optimistic to expect to know precisely the correct form of the appropriate model for the disturbance in any given situation. The first-order autoregression has withstood the test of time and experimentation as a reasonable *model* for underlying processes that probably, in truth, are impenetrably complex. It is sometimes argued that models can be improved by more elaborate disturbance processes (we shall examine some of these in Chapter 18), but there is often a *je ne sais quoi* flavor to this exercise. The results are often highly sensitive to the specification chosen, and in general, it is the data rather than an underlying theory that lead to the choice of the model, which is risky at best. As such, most researchers choose the simpler expedient of the AR(1) model in most cases.

The first-order autoregressive disturbance, or AR(1) process, is represented in the **autoregressive form** as

$$\epsilon_t = \rho\epsilon_{t-1} + u_t, \tag{13-2}$$

where

$$E[u_t] = 0,$$
$$E[u_t^2] = \sigma_u^2,$$

and

$$\text{Cov}[u_t, u_s] = 0 \quad \text{if } t \neq s.$$

By repeated substitution, we have

$$\epsilon_t = u_t + \rho u_{t-1} + \rho^2 u_{t-2} + \cdots. \tag{13-3}$$

From the preceding **moving average form,** it is evident that each disturbance ϵ_t embodies the entire past history of the u's, with the most recent observations receiving greater weight than those in the distant past. Depending on the sign of ρ, the series will exhibit clusters of positive and then negative observations or, if ρ is negative, regular oscillations of sign.[9]

Since the successive values of u_t are uncorrelated, the variance of ϵ_t is the variance of the right-hand side of (13-3):

$$\text{Var}[\epsilon_t] = \sigma_u^2 + \rho^2\sigma_u^2 + \rho^4\sigma_u^2 + \cdots. \tag{13-4}$$

[7]See Box and Jenkins (1984) for an authoritative study.

[8]The literature on time series and autocorrelation is voluminous and enormously complex. For example, the bibliography in Judge et al. (1985) on the latter subject alone runs to 13 pages.

[9]Unless the data have been first differenced or otherwise manipulated in an unusual fashion, the case of negative autocorrelation is normally not relevant to economic data.

To proceed, a restriction must be placed on ρ,

$$|\rho| < 1, \tag{13-5}$$

because otherwise, the right-hand side of (13-4) must become infinite. This is the stationarity assumption discussed earlier. With (13-5), which implies that $\lim_{s\to\infty} \rho^s = 0$,

$$E[\epsilon_t] = 0$$

and

$$\begin{aligned} \text{Var}[\epsilon_t] &= \frac{\sigma_u^2}{1-\rho^2} \\ &= \sigma_\epsilon^2. \end{aligned} \tag{13-6}$$

With the stationarity assumption, there is an easier way to obtain the variance:

$$\text{Var}[\epsilon_t] = \rho^2\text{Var}[\epsilon_{t-1}] + \sigma_u^2$$

as $\text{Cov}[u_t, \epsilon_s] = 0$ if $t > s$. With stationarity, $\text{Var}[\epsilon_{t-1}] = \text{Var}[\epsilon_t]$, which implies (13-6). Proceeding in the same fashion,

$$\begin{aligned} \text{Cov}[\epsilon_t, \epsilon_{t-1}] &= E[\epsilon_t\epsilon_{t-1}] \\ &= E[\epsilon_{t-1}(\rho\epsilon_{t-1} + u_t)] \\ &= \rho\text{Var}[\epsilon_{t-1}] \\ &= \frac{\rho\sigma_u^2}{1-\rho^2}. \end{aligned} \tag{13-7}$$

By repeated substitution in (13-2), we see that for any s,

$$\epsilon_t = \rho^s\epsilon_{t-s} + \sum_{i=0}^{s-1}\rho^i u_{t-i}$$

(e.g., $\epsilon_t = \rho^3\epsilon_{t-3} + \rho^2 u_{t-2} + \rho u_{t-1} + u_t$). Therefore, since ϵ_s is not correlated with any u_t for which $t > s$ (i.e., any subsequent u_t), it follows that

$$\text{Cov}[\epsilon_t, \epsilon_{t-s}] = E[\epsilon_t\epsilon_{t-s}] = \frac{\rho^s\sigma_u^2}{1-\rho^2}. \tag{13-8}$$

Dividing by $\gamma_0 = \sigma_u^2/(1-\rho^2)$ provides the autocorrelations:

$$\text{Corr}[\epsilon_t, \epsilon_{t-s}] = \rho_s = \rho^s. \tag{13-9}$$

With the stationarity assumption, the autocorrelations fade over time. Depending on the sign of ρ, they will either be declining in geometric progression or alternating in sign if ρ is negative. Collecting terms, we have

$$\sigma^2\mathbf{\Omega} = \frac{\sigma_u^2}{1-\rho^2}\begin{bmatrix} 1 & \rho & \rho^2 & \rho^3 & \cdots & \rho^{T-1} \\ \rho & 1 & \rho & \rho^2 & \cdots & \rho^{T-2} \\ \rho^2 & \rho & 1 & \rho & \cdots & \rho^{T-3} \\ \vdots & \vdots & \vdots & \vdots & \cdots & \rho \\ \rho^{T-1} & \rho^{T-2} & \rho^{T-3} & \cdots & \rho & 1 \end{bmatrix}. \tag{13-10}$$

13.4. LEAST SQUARES ESTIMATION

Since $\mathbf{\Omega}$ is not equal to $\mathbf{I}$, the now familiar problems will apply to least squares estimation. Least squares will continue to be unbiased; the earlier general proof includes autocorrelated disturbances. Whether least squares is consistent or not depends, as before, on the matrix

$$\mathbf{Q}_T^* = \frac{1}{T}\mathbf{X}'\mathbf{\Omega}\mathbf{X}.$$

If this matrix converges to a matrix of finite elements, then by our earlier reasoning, OLS is mean square consistent. We can expand this as

$$\mathbf{Q}_T^* = \frac{1}{T}\sum_{t=1}^{T}\sum_{s=1}^{T} \rho_{|t-s|}\,\mathbf{x}_t\mathbf{x}_s', \tag{13-11}$$

where $\mathbf{x}_t'$ and $\mathbf{x}_s'$ are rows of $\mathbf{X}$ and $\rho_{|t-s|}$ is the autocorrelation between ϵ_t and ϵ_s. Sufficient conditions for this matrix to converge are that the regressors be well behaved and the correlations between disturbances die off reasonably rapidly as the observations become further apart in time. For example, if the disturbances follow the AR(1) process described earlier, $\rho_k = \rho^k$ and $\mathbf{Q}_T^*$ will converge to a positive definite matrix $\mathbf{Q}^*$ as $T \to \infty$.

Asymptotic normality of least squares is extremely difficult to establish for the general model due, once again, to the complexity of (13-11). The results of Amemiya (1985), Mann and Wald (1943), and Anderson (1971) noted in Section 6.7.10 do carry over to most of the familiar types of autocorrelated disturbances, so we shall assume that their analyses include the cases we examine here. We conclude, then, that ordinary least squares continues to be unbiased, consistent, asymptotically normally distributed, and, as before, inefficient.

13.4.1. OLS Estimation with Lagged Dependent Variables

There is an important exception to the results in the preceding paragraph. If the regression contains any lagged values of the dependent variable, least squares will no longer be unbiased or consistent. To take the simplest case, suppose that

$$\begin{aligned} y_t &= \beta y_{t-1} + \epsilon_t, \\ \epsilon_t &= \rho\epsilon_{t-1} + u_t. \end{aligned} \tag{13-12}$$

In this model, the regressor and the disturbance are correlated:

$$\begin{aligned} \text{Cov}[y_{t-1}, \epsilon_t] &= \text{Cov}[y_{t-1}, \rho\epsilon_{t-1} + u_t] \\ &= \rho\,\text{Cov}[y_{t-1}, \epsilon_{t-1}] \\ &= \rho\,\text{Cov}[y_t, \epsilon_t] \end{aligned} \tag{13-13}$$

since the process is stationary and u_t is uncorrelated with everything that precedes it. Continuing,

$$\begin{aligned}\rho \operatorname{Cov}[y_t, \epsilon_t] &= \rho \operatorname{Cov}[\beta y_{t-1} + \epsilon_t, \epsilon_t] \\ &= \rho\{\beta \operatorname{Cov}[y_{t-1}, \epsilon_t] + \operatorname{Cov}[\epsilon_t, \epsilon_t]\} \\ &= \rho\{\beta \operatorname{Cov}[y_{t-1}, \epsilon_t] + \operatorname{Var}[\epsilon_t]\}.\end{aligned}$$

Therefore, by (13-13),

$$\begin{aligned}\operatorname{Cov}[y_{t-1}, \epsilon_t] &= \beta\rho \operatorname{Cov}[y_{t-1}, \epsilon_t] + \rho \operatorname{Var}[\epsilon_t] \\ &= \frac{\rho\sigma_u^2}{(1 - \beta\rho)(1 - \rho^2)}.\end{aligned} \tag{13-14}$$

(Note that this *is* zero if ρ is zero, regardless of β. This result is consistent with the observation that as long as the regressor is asymptotically uncorrelated with the disturbance, ordinary least squares is consistent even if the regressor is stochastic.) For the least squares estimator, we can use the general result

$$\operatorname{plim} b = \beta + \frac{\operatorname{Cov}[y_{t-1}, \epsilon_t]}{\operatorname{Var}[y_t]}.$$

But

$$\operatorname{Var}[y_t] = \beta^2 \operatorname{Var}[y_{t-1}] + \operatorname{Var}[\epsilon_t] + 2\beta \operatorname{Cov}[y_{t-1}, \epsilon_t].$$

Since the process is stationary, $\operatorname{Var}[y_t] = \operatorname{Var}[y_{t-1}]$. $\operatorname{Var}[\epsilon_t]$ is given in (13-6), whereas $\operatorname{Cov}[y_{t-1}, \epsilon_t]$ is given in (13-14). Collecting terms, we have

$$\operatorname{Var}[y_t] = \frac{\sigma_u^2(1 + \beta\rho)}{(1 - \rho^2)(1 - \beta^2)(1 - \beta\rho)},$$

so

$$\operatorname{plim} b = \beta + \frac{\rho(1 - \beta^2)}{1 + \beta\rho}. \tag{13-15}$$

Therefore, least squares is inconsistent unless ρ equals zero. The more general case that includes regressors, $\mathbf{x}_t$, involves more complicated algebra, but gives essentially the same result.

13.4.2. Efficiency of Least Squares

Since the model with autocorrelated disturbances is a generalized regression model, we should expect least squares to be inefficient. There are, however, few general results on how inefficient it is because knowledge of both the disturbance process and the process generating $\mathbf{X}$ is required. A few useful cases have been examined in detail.

First, suppose that the model is

$$\begin{aligned}y_t &= \beta x_t + \epsilon_t, \\ \epsilon_t &= \rho\epsilon_{t-1} + u_t,\end{aligned} \tag{13-16}$$

and suppose that x_t is also generated by an AR(1) process,

$$x_t = \delta x_{t-1} + v_t.$$

For convenience, let

$$\text{Var}[x_t] = \frac{\text{Var}[v_t]}{1 - \delta^2} = \sigma_x^2 \quad \text{and} \quad \text{Var}[\epsilon_t] = \frac{\sigma_u^2}{1 - \rho^2} = \sigma_\epsilon^2.$$

With $\mathbf{\Omega}$ given in (13-10),

$$\frac{1}{T}\mathbf{X}'\mathbf{\Omega}\mathbf{X} = \left(\frac{\sum_{t=1}^{T} x_t^2}{T}\right) + 2\rho\left(\frac{\sum_{t=2}^{T} x_t x_{t-1}}{T}\right) + 2\rho^2\left(\frac{\sum_{t=3}^{T} x_t x_{t-2}}{T}\right) + \cdots + 2\rho^{T-1}\left(\frac{x_1 x_T}{T}\right). \tag{13-17}$$

The autocovariances of x are σ_x^2, $\delta\sigma_x^2$, $\delta^2\sigma_x^2$, and so on. If T is large enough, the leading sums in (13-17) will approximate these, whereas if $|\delta| < 1$, the latter terms will be negligible. So if T is large enough,

$$\begin{aligned}
\frac{1}{T}\mathbf{X}'\mathbf{\Omega}\mathbf{X} &\approx \sigma_x^2 + 2\rho\delta\sigma_x^2 + 2\rho^2\delta^2\sigma_x^2 \\
&= 2\sigma_x^2\left(\sum_{i=0}(\rho\delta)^i\right) - \sigma_x^2 \\
&= \left(\frac{2\sigma_x^2}{1 - \rho\delta}\right) - \sigma_x^2 \\
&= \frac{\sigma_x^2(1 + \rho\delta)}{1 - \rho\delta}.
\end{aligned}$$

Collecting terms, we find that

$$\text{Var}[b] = \frac{\sigma^2}{T}\left[\frac{\mathbf{X}'\mathbf{X}}{T}\right]^{-1}\left[\frac{\mathbf{X}'\mathbf{\Omega}\mathbf{X}}{T}\right]\left[\frac{\mathbf{X}'\mathbf{X}}{T}\right]^{-1}$$

is approximately

$$\text{Var}[b] \approx \frac{\sigma_\epsilon^2(1 + \rho\delta)}{T\sigma_x^2(1 - \rho\delta)}. \tag{13-18}$$

The variance of the GLS estimator is

$$\text{Var}[\hat{\beta}] = \left(\frac{\sigma_\epsilon^2}{T}\right)\left[\frac{\mathbf{X}'\mathbf{\Omega}^{-1}\mathbf{X}}{T}\right]^{-1},$$

for which we require

$$\boldsymbol{\Omega}^{-1} = \begin{bmatrix} 1 & -\rho & 0 & 0 & 0 & \cdots & \cdots & 0 \\ -\rho & 1+\rho^2 & -\rho & 0 & 0 & \cdots & \cdots & 0 \\ 0 & -\rho & 1+\rho^2 & -\rho & 0 & \cdots & \cdots & 0 \\ & & & \vdots & & & & \\ 0 & 0 & 0 & 0 & \cdots & -\rho & 1+\rho^2 & -\rho \\ 0 & 0 & 0 & 0 & \cdots & 0 & -\rho & 1 \end{bmatrix}. \tag{13-19}$$

Then

$$\text{Var}[\hat{\beta}] = \frac{\sigma_\epsilon^2}{T}\left[\frac{1}{1-\rho^2}\left((1+\rho^2)\left(\frac{\sum_{t=1}^{T} x_t^2}{T}\right) - \rho^2\left(\frac{x_1^2 + x_T^2}{T}\right) - 2\rho\left(\frac{\sum_{t=2}^{T} x_t x_{t-1}}{T}\right)\right)\right]^{-1}.$$

If the sample is large, the **end effect,** $(x_1^2 + x_T^2)/T$, will be negligible, so that

$$\text{Var}[\hat{\beta}] \approx \frac{\sigma_\epsilon^2(1-\rho^2)}{T\sigma_x^2(1+\rho^2-2\rho\delta)}. \tag{13-20}$$

The (in)efficiency of least squares relative to GLS is therefore approximately

$$\frac{\text{Var}[b]}{\text{Var}[\hat{\beta}]} = \frac{(1+\rho\delta)/(1-\rho\delta)}{(1-\rho^2)/(1+\rho^2-2\rho\delta)}. \tag{13-21}$$

Values of the ratio are given in Table 13.3. The function is not monotonic in δ, but clearly, the least favorable cases are those with large values of ρ for any given δ. The efficiency of least squares relative to generalized least squares falls to less than 10 percent if ρ is close to 1.

The preceding gives a rather pessimistic conclusion, but it is derived under somewhat narrow assumptions. For models that involve relatively slowly changing variables, such as macroeconomic flows like consumption or out-

TABLE 13.3 Efficiency Ratio: Var[OLS]/Var[GLS]

	ρ						
δ	**−0.9**	**−0.6**	**−0.3**	**0.0**	**0.3**	**0.6**	**0.9**
−0.9	9.53	1.46	1.05	1.00	1.03	1.14	1.90
−0.6	12.86	2.13	1.15	1.00	1.11	1.53	4.54
−0.3	11.63	2.25	1.30	1.00	1.17	1.87	7.11
0.0	9.53	2.12	1.20	1.00	1.20	2.13	9.53
0.3	7.11	1.87	1.17	1.00	1.20	2.25	11.64
0.6	4.54	1.53	1.11	1.00	1.15	2.12	12.86
0.9	1.90	1.14	1.03	1.00	1.05	1.46	9.53

put, the loss of efficiency in using least squares might not be so severe as this result suggests.[10]

13.4.3. Estimating the Variance of the Least Squares Estimator

As usual, $s^2(\mathbf{X}'\mathbf{X})^{-1}$ is an inappropriate estimator of $\sigma^2(\mathbf{X}'\mathbf{X})^{-1}(\mathbf{X}'\boldsymbol{\Omega}\mathbf{X}) \times (\mathbf{X}'\mathbf{X})^{-1}$, both because s^2 is a biased estimator of σ^2 and because the matrix is incorrect. With regard to σ^2, the analysis of Section 12.2.2 concerning heteroscedasticity is in general terms and includes this case as well. It is shown there that s^2 is a biased but consistent estimator of σ^2. Asymptotically, therefore, the difference between the estimated and the true variance of least squares hinges on the two matrices. For the model in (13-16),

$$\frac{(\mathbf{X}'\mathbf{X}/T)^{-1}}{(\mathbf{X}'\mathbf{X}/T)^{-1}(\mathbf{X}'\boldsymbol{\Omega}\mathbf{X}/T)(\mathbf{X}'\mathbf{X}/T)^{-1}} \approx \frac{1-\rho\delta}{1+\rho\delta}. \tag{13-22}$$

If ρ and δ have the same sign, the ratio is less than 1. Since, in most economic time series, the autocorrelation is positive, this would seem to be the norm. As such, the standard errors conventionally *estimated* be least squares are likely to be too small.

In view of this situation, if one is going to use least squares, it is desirable to have an appropriate estimator of the covariance matrix of the least squares estimator. There are two approaches. If the form of the autocorrelation is known, one can estimate the parameters of $\boldsymbol{\Omega}$ directly and compute a consistent estimator. Of course, if so, it would be more sensible to use feasible generalized least squares instead and not waste the sample information on an inefficient estimator. The second approach parallels the use of the White estimator for heteroscedasticity. Suppose that the form of the autocorrelation is unknown. Then, a direct estimator of $\boldsymbol{\Omega}$ or $\boldsymbol{\Omega}(\boldsymbol{\theta})$ is not available. The problem is estimation of

$$\boldsymbol{\Sigma} = \frac{1}{T}\sum_{t=1}^{T}\sum_{s=1}^{T}\rho_{|t-s|}\mathbf{x}_t\mathbf{x}_s'. \tag{13-23}$$

Following White's suggestion for heteroscedasticity,[11] Newey and West's (1987a) robust, consistent estimator for autocorrelated disturbances with an unspecified structure is

$$\mathbf{S}_* = \mathbf{S}_0 + \frac{1}{T}\sum_{j=1}^{L}\sum_{t=j+1}^{T} w(j)e_te_{t-j}[\mathbf{x}_t\mathbf{x}_{t-j}' + \mathbf{x}_{t-j}\mathbf{x}_t'], \tag{13-24}$$

where

$$w(j) = 1 - \frac{j}{L+1}. \tag{13-25}$$

[10]See Judge et al. (1985, p. 280).

[11]See Section 12.2.3.

TABLE 13.4 Robust Covariance Estimation

Variable	*OLS Estimate*	*OLS SE*	*Corrected SE*
Constant	−12.5336	24.92	18.96
Real interest	−1.00144	2.369	3.342
Real GNP	0.16914	0.02057	0.01675

The maximum lag L must be determined in advance to be large enough that autocorrelations at lags longer than L are small enough to ignore. For a moving-average process, this can be expected to be a relatively small number. For autoregressive processes, or mixtures, however, the autocorrelations are never zero, and the researcher must make a judgment as to how far back it is necessary to go.[12]

EXAMPLE 13.3 Autocorrelation Consistent Covariance Estimation

Using the investment data of Example 13.1, we find that the Newey–West estimator of the covariance matrix of least squares based on $L = 4$ yields the results listed in Table 13.4.

13.5. TESTING FOR AUTOCORRELATION

13.5.1. The Durbin–Watson Test

Most of the available tests for autocorrelation are based on the principle that if the true disturbances are autocorrelated, this will be revealed through the autocorrelations of the least squares residuals. By far the most widely used test is the Durbin–Watson test.[13] The test statistic is

$$d = \frac{\sum_{t=2}^{T}(e_t - e_{t-1})^2}{\sum_{t=1}^{T} e_t^2}. \tag{13-26}$$

The statistic is closely related to the sample autocorrelation:

$$d = 2(1 - r) - \frac{e_1^2 + e_T^2}{\sum_{t=1}^{T} e_t^2}.$$

If the sample is reasonably large, the last term will be negligible, leaving

$$d \simeq 2(1 - r). \tag{13-27}$$

[12]Davidson and MacKinnon (1993) give further discussion.

[13]Durbin and Watson (1950, 1951, 1971).

Values of d that differ significantly from two suggest autocorrelation of the disturbances. For testing for positive autocorrelation, the procedure would be to

$$\text{reject } H_0\text{:}\rho = 0 \quad \text{if } d < d*,$$

where $d*$ is the appropriate critical value for the distribution of d under H_0. (A test for negative autocorrelation can be based on $4 - d$.)

A serious shortcoming of the Durbin–Watson test is that the exact distribution of d depends on the data matrix. Durbin and Watson have provided a partial solution to this problem. They show that the true distribution of d lies between that of two other statistics, d_l (the lower bound) and d_u (the upper bound), such that the 5 percent critical value for the true distribution of d must lie to the right of that of d_l and to the left of that of d_u. The usefulness of the result is that the distributions of d_l and d_u depend only on T and K, and their 5 percent and 1 percent critical values have been tabulated.[14] Therefore, the test that may be carried out is

$$\begin{aligned}&\text{do not reject } H_0 \quad \text{if } d > d*_u,\\ &\text{reject } H_0 \quad \text{if } d < d*_l.\end{aligned}$$

No conclusion is drawn if $d*_l \leq d \leq d*_u$. An analogous test has been derived for quarterly data and fourth-order autocorrelation [see (13-39)] by Wallis (1972) based on

$$d_4 = \frac{\sum_{t=5}^{T} (e_t - e_{t-4})^2}{\sum_{t=1}^{T} e_t^2}. \tag{13-28}$$

Tables of the bounding distributions are given by Wallis.

EXAMPLE 13.4 Durbin–Watson Test

The Durbin–Watson statistic for the investment equation is 1.3215. The 5 percent critical values from the Savin–White (1977) tables are 1.074 and 1.536. Since the sample value falls in the inconclusive region, further analysis is called for.

The inconclusive region in the Durbin–Watson tables is a troubling problem. This area can be rather wide. For example, for $T = 19$ and $K = 3$ (i.e., our particular problem), the inconclusive region encompasses values of ρ from 0.218 to 0.463 (using $1 - d/2$). A great deal of research has been devoted to narrowing or eliminating this region. One approach is to deal specifically with certain kinds of regressors. For example, the critical values in the tables assume that the regression contains a constant term. If not, $d*_l$ may be replaced with

[14]See Savin and White (1977) or the appendix at the end of this book.

$d*_m$, where $d*_m$ is greater than $d*_l$.[15] King (1981) presents an alternative set of bounds for regressions with quarterly seasonal dummy variables. Giles and King (1978) present corresponding modifications for the Wallis test.

One could argue, on grounds of conservatism, that $d*_u$ should always be used as the critical value. Failing to account for autocorrelation when it is present is almost surely worse than accounting for it when it is not. If the data are slowly changing, the correct critical value is more likely than not to be close to $d*_u$.[16] It is possible to calculate the correct percentage point for d for the particular data set, but this requires specialized software and is likely to be rather difficult.[17] A number of authors have attempted to derive approximations to the appropriate critical values for the Durbin–Watson test. One that has been found to be quite accurate is also due to Durbin and Watson (1971).

The Durbin–Watson statistic can be written as

$$d = \frac{\mathbf{e}'\mathbf{A}\mathbf{e}}{\mathbf{e}'\mathbf{e}},$$

where

$$\mathbf{A} = \begin{bmatrix} 1 & -1 & 0 & 0 & \cdots & 0 \\ -1 & 2 & -1 & 0 & \cdots & 0 \\ 0 & -1 & 2 & -1 & \cdots & 0 \\ 0 & 0 & \cdots & -1 & 2 & -1 \\ 0 & 0 & 0 & \cdots & -1 & 1 \end{bmatrix}. \tag{13-29}$$

Since $\mathbf{e} = \mathbf{M}\boldsymbol{\epsilon}$, where $\mathbf{M} = \mathbf{I} - \mathbf{X}(\mathbf{X}'\mathbf{X})^{-1}\mathbf{X}'$,

$$d = \frac{(\boldsymbol{\epsilon}/\sigma)'\mathbf{MAM}(\boldsymbol{\epsilon}/\sigma)}{(\boldsymbol{\epsilon}/\sigma)'\mathbf{M}(\boldsymbol{\epsilon}/\sigma)}. \tag{13-30}$$

The exact distribution of this statistic depends on $\mathbf{X}$. The approach is to approximate the true critical value using

$$\hat{d}* = a + bd*_u,$$

where a and b are determined from

$$\begin{aligned} E[d] &= a + bE[d_u], \\ \text{Var}[d] &= b^2\text{Var}[d_u]. \end{aligned} \tag{13-31}$$

The expectations and variances are computed using the characteristic roots of $\mathbf{A}$:

$$\begin{aligned} E[d_u] &= \frac{1}{n}\sum_{j=K+1}^{T} \theta_j = \bar{\theta}, \\ \text{Var}[d_u] &= \frac{2}{n(n+2)}\left[\sum_{j=K+1}^{T} \theta_j^2 - n\bar{\theta}^2\right], \end{aligned} \tag{13-32}$$

---

[15] See Farebrother (1980).

[16] See, for example, Theil and Nagar (1961) and Hannan and Terrell (1966).

[17] It is automated in SHAZAM [White (1993)].

where $n = T - K$. We use the $T - K$ largest roots of $\mathbf{A}$. Then $E[d]$ and $\text{Var}[d]$ are computed in the same manner, using the n nonzero characteristic roots of $\mathbf{MAM}$.[18]

EXAMPLE 13.5 Approximation to the Durbin–Watson Statistic

For our investment data, the characteristic roots λ of $\mathbf{MAM}$ are the following:

3.95633	3.87667	3.74689	3.55003	3.32671	3.08085
2.69580	2.48651	2.10701	1.81835	1.48363	1.18083
0.897094	0.644495	0.398000	0.209969	and three zeros.	

The 18 nonzero characteristic roots θ of $\mathbf{A}$ are the following:

3.97272	3.89163	3.75895	3.57828	3.35456	3.09390
2.80339	2.49097	2.16516	1.83484	1.50903	1.19661
0.906104	0.645437	0.421719	0.241052	0.108366	0.0272774

(The last is always zero.) Inserting these roots in the preceding equations gives $b = 0.9984689$ and $a = -0.0221681$. Therefore, the approximate value for $d*$ is 1.5115. This is consistent with our earlier observation in Example 13.4. Since the Durbin–Watson statistic for the regression is 1.3215, we would reject the hypothesis of no autocorrelation. Note that 1.3215 is squarely in the inconclusive region.

13.5.2. Other Testing Procedures

The Durbin–Watson test has been found to be quite powerful when compared with others for AR(1) processes. The test is not limited to testing for AR(1) disturbances, however. Regardless of the stochastic process,

$$\text{plim } d = 2 - 2\rho_1,$$

where

$$\rho_1 = \text{Corr}[\epsilon_t, \epsilon_{t-1}].$$

Aside from the difficulty of the inconclusive region, however, there are two problems. First, it is strictly correct only when $\mathbf{X}$ is nonstochastic. Second, if the process is not an AR(1), ρ_1 may not be truly indicative of the pattern of autocorrelation.[19] Two alternative tests that are less restrictive have been devised.

[18]The characteristic roots of $\mathbf{A}$ are $\theta_i = 2 - 2\cos[\pi(i-1)/T]$, which can easily be computed. But if T is even moderately large, the calculation of the characteristic roots of $\mathbf{MAM}$, which is a $T \times T$ matrix, is likely to be quite burdensome, assuming that the necessary software is available at all. An alternative calculation based only on $K \times K$ matrices is given in Judge et al. (1982, pp. 468–469).

[19]See Example 13.6.

The Breusch (1978)–Godfrey (1978b) test is a Lagrange multiplier test of

$$H_0\text{:no autocorrelation}$$

versus

$$H_1: \epsilon_t = \text{AR}(P) \quad \text{or} \quad \epsilon_t = \text{MA}(P).$$

The same test is used for either structure. The test can be carried out simply by regressing the ordinary least squares residuals e_t on $\mathbf{x}_t, e_{t-1}, \ldots, e_{t-P}$ (filling in missing values for lagged residuals with zeros) and referring TR^2 to the tabled critical value for the chi-squared distribution with P degrees of freedom. Since $\mathbf{X}'\mathbf{e} = \mathbf{0}$, the test is equivalent to regressing e_t on the part of the lagged residuals that is unexplained by $\mathbf{X}$. There is therefore a compelling logic to it; if any fit is found, it is due to correlation between the current and lagged residuals. The test is a joint test of the first P autocorrelations of ϵ_t, not just the first.

An alternative, although similar, test is due to Box and Pierce (1970). The ***Q* test** is carried out by referring

$$Q = T \sum_{j=1}^{L} r_j^2, \tag{13-33}$$

where

$$r_j = \frac{\sum_{t=j+1}^{T} e_t e_{t-j}}{\sum_{t=1}^{T} e_t^2},$$

to the critical values of the chi-squared table with L degrees of freedom. A refinement suggested by Ljung and Box (1979) is

$$Q' = T(T+2) \sum_{j=1}^{L} \frac{r_j^2}{T-j}. \tag{13-33'}$$

This test has also been found to be reasonably powerful. It and the Breusch–Godfrey test, however, have been criticized for the difficulty with the choice of L. This problem of determining the depth of the lag to consider in these models of autocorrelation has reappeared at various points in our work here and pervades this literature.

EXAMPLE 13.6 Tests of Autocorrelation

The regression of the current residual on a constant, real GNP, the real interest rate, and four lags of the residual (with 0s inserted for the missing values) produces

$$\underset{}{e_t} = \underset{(17.57)}{-0.9840} - \underset{(0.01451)}{0.000273}\,\text{GNP} + \underset{(2.080)}{4.781}i - \underset{(0.308)}{0.387}e_{t-1} - \underset{(0.325)}{0.285}e_{t-2} - \underset{(0.342)}{0.837}e_{t-3} - \underset{(0.372)}{0.640}e_{t-4}$$

$T = 19,\ R^2 = 0.6352$

The Breusch–Godfrey statistic is 12.068. The 5 percent critical value for the chi-squared distribution with four degrees of freedom is 9.488. The 1 percent critical value is 13.277. Therefore, the null hypothesis would be rejected at a significant level of 5 percent. The first four autocorrelations for the least squares residuals are

$$\begin{aligned} r_1 &= 0.2507, \\ r_2 &= -0.2752, \\ r_3 &= -0.6605, \\ r_4 &= -0.3699. \end{aligned}$$

The Box–Pierce Q statistic is 13.5219, whereas the Ljung–Box statistic is 17.6895. Both are statistically significant at the 1 percent level. Both of these tests suggest that the insignificance of the Durbin–Watson test results from a significant autocorrelation appearing at lag 3 but not at lag 1. Unfortunately, there is nothing in the construction of the data that would imply such a pattern of strong negative autocorrelation at lag 3. The small sample size (19 observations) does suggest that these results should be interpreted with caution.

The essential difference between the Godfrey–Breusch and the Box–Pierce tests is the use of partial correlations (controlling for **X** and the other variables) in the former and simple correlations in the latter. Under the hypothesis, there is no autocorrelation in ϵ_t, and no correlation between $\mathbf{x}_t$ and ϵ_s in any event, so the two tests are asymptotically equivalent.

13.5.3. Testing in the Presence of Lagged Dependent Variables

The Durbin–Watson test is not likely to be valid when there is a lagged dependent variable in the equation.[20] The statistic will usually be biased toward a finding of no autocorrelation. Three alternatives have been devised.

The two tests described in the previous section can be used whether or not the regression contains a lagged dependent variable. As an alternative to the standard test, Durbin (1970) has derived a Lagrange multiplier test that is unaffected by the lagged dependent variable. The test may be carried out by referring

$$h = \left(1 - \frac{d}{2}\right)\sqrt{\frac{T}{1 - Ts_c^2}}, \tag{13-34}$$

where s_c^2 is the estimated variance of the least squares regression coefficient on y_{t-1}, to the standard normal tables. Large values of h lead to rejection of H_0. The test has the virtues that it can be used even if the regression contains additional lags of y_t, and it can be computed using the standard results from the ini-

[20]This issue has been studied by Nerlove and Wallis (1966), Durbin (1970), and Dezhbaksh (1990).

tial regression without any further regressions. If $s_c^2 > 1/T$, however, it cannot be computed. An alternative is to regress e_t on $\mathbf{x}_t, y_{t-1}, \ldots, e_{t-1}$, and any additional lags that are appropriate for e_t and then to test the joint significance of the coefficient(s) on the lagged residual(s) with the standard F test. This is a modification of the Breusch–Godfrey test. Under H_0, the coefficients on the remaining variables will be zero, so the tests are the same asymptotically.

13.6. EFFICIENT ESTIMATION WHEN $\boldsymbol{\Omega}$ IS KNOWN

As a prelude to deriving feasible estimators for $\boldsymbol{\beta}$ in this model, we consider full generalized least squares estimation assuming that $\boldsymbol{\Omega}$ is known. In the next section, we will turn to the more realistic case in which $\boldsymbol{\Omega}$ must be estimated as well.

13.6.1. Generalized Least Squares

If the parameters of $\boldsymbol{\Omega}$ are known, the GLS estimator,

$$\hat{\boldsymbol{\beta}} = [\mathbf{X}'\boldsymbol{\Omega}^{-1}\mathbf{X}]^{-1}[\mathbf{X}'\boldsymbol{\Omega}^{-1}\mathbf{y}],$$

and its sampling variance,

$$\text{Var}[\hat{\boldsymbol{\beta}}] = \sigma_\epsilon^2[\mathbf{X}'\boldsymbol{\Omega}^{-1}\mathbf{X}]^{-1},$$

can be computed directly. For the AR(1) process,

$$\mathbf{P} = \begin{bmatrix} \sqrt{1-\rho^2} & 0 & 0 & 0 & \cdots & 0 & 0 \\ -\rho & 1 & 0 & 0 & \cdots & 0 & 0 \\ 0 & -\rho & 1 & 0 & \cdots & 0 & 0 \\ & & & \vdots & & & \\ 0 & 0 & 0 & 0 & \cdots & -\rho & 1 \end{bmatrix}, \tag{13-35}$$

so the data for the transformed model are

$$\mathbf{y}_* = \begin{bmatrix} \sqrt{1-\rho^2}y_1 \\ y_2 - \rho y_1 \\ y_3 - \rho y_2 \\ \vdots \\ y_T - \rho y_{T-1} \end{bmatrix}, \qquad \mathbf{X}_* = \begin{bmatrix} \sqrt{1-\rho^2}\mathbf{x}_1 \\ \mathbf{x}_2 - \rho \mathbf{x}_1 \\ \mathbf{x}_3 - \rho \mathbf{x}_2 \\ \vdots \\ \mathbf{x}_T - \rho \mathbf{x}_{T-1} \end{bmatrix}. \tag{13-36}$$

These transformations are variously labeled **partial differences, quasi differences,** or **pseudodifferences.** Note that in the transformed model, every observation except the first contains a constant term. What was the column of 1s in

$\mathbf{X}$ is transformed to $[(1-\rho^2)^{1/2}, (1-\rho), (1-\rho), \ldots]$. Therefore, if the sample is relatively small, the problems noted earlier with measures of fit will reappear.

The variance of the transformed disturbance is

$$\text{Var}[\epsilon_t - \rho\epsilon_{t-1}] = \text{Var}[u_t] = \sigma_u^2.$$

The variance of the first disturbance is also σ_u^2; see (13-6).

Corresponding results have been derived for higher-order autoregressive processes. For the AR(2) model,

$$\epsilon_t = \theta_1\epsilon_{t-1} + \theta_2\epsilon_{t-2} + u_t, \tag{13-37}$$

the transformed data for generalized least squares are obtained by

$$\begin{aligned} \mathbf{z}*_1 &= \left[\frac{(1+\theta_2)[(1-\theta_2)^2 - \theta_1^2]}{1-\theta_2}\right]^{1/2}\mathbf{z}_1, \\ \mathbf{z}*_2 &= (1-\theta_2^2)^{1/2}\mathbf{z}_2 - \frac{\theta_1(1-\theta_1^2)^{1/2}}{1-\theta_2}\mathbf{z}_1, \\ \mathbf{z}*_t &= \mathbf{z}_t - \theta_1\mathbf{z}_{t-1} - \theta_2\mathbf{z}_{t-2}, \quad t > 2, \end{aligned} \tag{13-38}$$

where $\mathbf{z}_t$ is used for y_t or $\mathbf{x}_t$. The transformation becomes progressively more complex for higher-order processes.[21]

Note that in both the AR(1) and AR(2) models, the transformation to $y*$ and $\mathbf{X}*$ involves "starting values" for the processes that depend only on the first one or two observations. We can view the process as having begun in the infinite past. Since the sample contains only T observations, however, it is convenient to treat the first one or two (or P) observations as shown and consider them as "initial values." Whether we view the process as having begun at time $t = 1$ or in the infinite past is ultimately immaterial in regard to the asymptotic properties of our estimators. As we shall see, however, what we do with the initial values in a finite sample can make a substantial difference.

Higher-order MA processes and mixtures of AR and MA processes can be estimated by approximations to GLS.[22] (Full GLS is not well worked out for very many processes involving MA disturbances.) One would have to ask, however, how such a process might arise in the first place. Nicholls et al. (1975) describe some instances in which MA(1) disturbances might be expected, but as a general rule, they do not arise naturally. In the widely studied case of adjustment models that we examine in Chapter 17, the model does have an MA(1) disturbance, but it also contains a lagged dependent variable. As such, none of the apparatus developed earlier is applicable. The upshot is that MA and

---

[21]See Box and Jenkins (1984) and Fuller (1976).

[22]See, for example, Kmenta (1986, pp. 326–328) and Greenberg and Webster (1983) for moving-average models.

ARMA (mixtures of AR and MA) disturbances in econometric models should be applied with circumspection. A particular type of higher-order AR model has been advocated by Wallis (1972). For quarterly data, he suggests that the model

$$\epsilon_t = \rho\epsilon_{t-4} + u_t \tag{13-39}$$

is more appropriate than, say, an AR(1) model, because random effects are more likely to be correlated with the corresponding previous season than with the immediately preceding season. This process has a distinctive pattern of autocorrelations:

$$\text{Cov}[\epsilon_t, \epsilon_{t-i}] = \begin{cases} \sigma_u^2 \dfrac{\rho^{i/4}}{1-\rho^2}, & i = 0, 4, 8, \ldots \\ 0 & \text{otherwise.} \end{cases}$$

Full GLS for this model is obtained using

$$\mathbf{z}*_t = \begin{cases} \sqrt{1-\rho^2}\mathbf{z}_t & t = 1, 2, 3, 4, \\ \mathbf{z}_t - \rho\mathbf{z}_{t-4}, & t > 4. \end{cases}$$

13.6.2. Maximum Likelihood Estimation

If the parameters of the disturbance process are known, GLS and maximum likelihood estimation for the AR(1) model are equivalent. To obtain the likelihood function for normally distributed disturbances, we make use of

$$f(y_1, y_2, \ldots, y_T) = f(y_1)f(y_2 \mid y_1)f(y_3 \mid y_2) \cdots f(y_T \mid y_T - 1).$$

Based on (13-36), we find that the transformed regression is

$$y_t^* = \boldsymbol{\beta}'\mathbf{x}_t^* + u_t,$$

so that in terms of the original data,

$$y_1 = \mathbf{x}_t'\boldsymbol{\beta} + \frac{u_1}{\sqrt{1-\rho^2}}$$

and

$$y_t \mid y_{t-1} = \rho y_{t-1} + \boldsymbol{\beta}'\mathbf{x}_t - \rho\boldsymbol{\beta}'\mathbf{x}_{t-1} + u_t$$

for $t = 2, \ldots, T$. For the first observation, we use the change of variable formula from Section 3.5 to obtain

$$\begin{aligned} f(y_1) &= \left|\sqrt{1-\rho^2}\right| f_{u_1}[\sqrt{1-\rho^2}(y_1 - \mathbf{x}_1'\boldsymbol{\beta})] \\ &= \sqrt{1-\rho^2}(2\pi\sigma^2)^{-1/2}e^{-[(1-\rho^2)/(2\sigma_u^2)](y_1-\mathbf{x}_1'\boldsymbol{\beta})^2}. \end{aligned}$$

The log-likelihood function is

$$
\begin{aligned}
\ln L &= \ln f(y_1) + \sum_{t=2}^{T} \ln f(y_t \mid y_{t-1}) \\
&= -\frac{1}{2}[\ln(2\pi) + \ln \sigma_u^2 - \ln(1-\rho^2)] - \frac{1-\rho^2}{2\sigma_u^2}(y_1 - \boldsymbol{\beta}'\mathbf{x}_1)^2 \\
&\quad - \frac{T-1}{2}[\ln(2\pi) + \ln \sigma_u^2] \\
&\quad - \frac{1}{2\sigma_u^2}\sum_{t=2}^{T}[(y_t - \rho y_{t-1}) - (\mathbf{x}_t - \rho\mathbf{x}_{t-1})'\boldsymbol{\beta}]^2 \\
&= -\frac{T}{2}[\ln(2\pi) + \ln \sigma_u^2] + \frac{1}{2}\ln(1-\rho^2) \\
&\quad - \frac{1}{2\sigma_u^2}\sum_{t=1}^{T}(y_{*t} - \mathbf{x}'_{*t}\boldsymbol{\beta})^2.
\end{aligned} \tag{13-40}
$$

The sum of squares term is the residual sum of squares from the transformed, classical regression model in (13-36). *If ρ is known, the solution is least squares for $\boldsymbol{\beta}$ and σ^2, as usual, which is the GLS solution given in* (13-36). The derivatives of the log-likelihood for a known $\boldsymbol{\Omega}$ were found earlier and apply here. The information matrix is

$$
\mathbf{I}(\boldsymbol{\beta}, \sigma_u^2) = \begin{bmatrix} (1/\sigma_u^2)(\mathbf{X}'\boldsymbol{\Omega}^{-1}\mathbf{X}) & \mathbf{0} \\ \mathbf{0}' & T/2\sigma_u^4 \end{bmatrix}.
$$

13.7. ESTIMATION WHEN $\boldsymbol{\Omega}$ IS UNKNOWN

13.7.1. AR(1) Disturbances

For an unknown $\boldsymbol{\Omega}$, there is, if anything, an embarrassment of riches of FGLS estimators. All have the same asymptotic properties, as we saw earlier for the general case, as long as the first-round estimators are consistent. But there is considerable variation in their small-sample properties.

Once again, the AR(1) model is the one most widely used and studied. The most common procedure is to begin FGLS with a natural estimator of ρ, the autocorrelation of the residuals. Since **b** is consistent, we can use

$$
r = \frac{\sum_{t=2}^{T} e_t e_{t-1}}{\sum_{t=2}^{T} e_t^2}. \tag{13-41}
$$

Two of the many other modifications that have been suggested are Theil's estimator,[23]

$$r^* = \left[\frac{T-K}{T-1}\right] r,$$

and

$$r^{**} = 1 - \frac{d}{2},$$

where d is the Durbin–Watson statistic for testing the hypothesis that ρ equals zero.[24] The estimator suggested by Durbin (1960) is the coefficient on y_{t-1} in the least squares estimates of

$$y_t = \rho y_{t-1} + \mathbf{x}_t'\boldsymbol{\beta} - \mathbf{x}_{t-1}'(\rho\boldsymbol{\beta}) + u_t. \qquad \textbf{(13-42)}$$

(The coefficients are computed ignoring the constraint.) All these are consistent estimators of ρ. Since ρ must be in the range -1 to 1, another possibility is to search over this range and choose the value of ρ that leads to the smallest sum of squares.[25]

For the second step of FGLS, there are two possibilities:

1. *Full FGLS.* This is the Prais-Winsten (1954) estimator.
2. *FGLS omitting the first observation.* This was first suggested by Cochrane and Orcutt (1949).

In a large sample, the two are likely to be the same. The typical economic time series is not particularly long, however, and which one is chosen may make a great deal of difference. The question is not merely one of different numerical values. The efficiency of the FGLS estimator can be very adversely affected by discarding the initial observation(s) if the sample is relatively small and the regressors have a trend, which is common in economic data.[26]

It is possible to iterate these estimators to convergence. Since the estimator is efficient at every iteration, nothing is gained asymptotically by doing so. Moreover, unlike the heteroscedastic model, iterating when there is autocorrelation does not secure the maximum likelihood estimator. The iterated FGLS estimator does not account for the term $\frac{1}{2}\ln(1-\rho^2)$ in the log-likelihood function [see (13-40)]. None of the estimators discussed thus far satisfies $\partial \ln L/\partial\rho = 0$ for the current estimates of $\boldsymbol{\beta}$ and σ_u^2.

Full maximum likelihood estimators can be obtained by maximizing the log-likelihood in (13-40) with respect to $\boldsymbol{\beta}$, σ^2, and ρ. Apart from the constant term, the log-likelihood function may be written

[23] Theil (1971, p. 254).

[24] See, for example, Johnston (1984, p. 324).

[25] See Hildreth and Lu (1960).

[26] See Maeshiro (1979), Poirier (1978a), and Park and Mitchell (1980).

$$\ln L = -\frac{\sum_{t=1}^{T} u_t^2}{2\sigma_u^2} + \frac{1}{2}\ln(1-\rho^2) - \frac{T}{2}\ln\sigma_u^2, \tag{13-43}$$

where, as before, the first observation is computed differently from the others. The likelihood equations can be derived from (13-40) and (13-43). From (13-43),

$$\frac{\partial \ln L}{\partial \boldsymbol{\beta}} = \frac{1}{\sigma_u^2}\sum_{t=1}^{T} u_t \mathbf{x}_{*t},$$

$$u_1 = \sqrt{1-\rho^2}(y_1 - \mathbf{x}_1'\boldsymbol{\beta}),$$

$$u_t = (y_t - \rho y_{t-1}) - (\mathbf{x}_t - \rho\mathbf{x}_{t-1}) \quad \text{for } t = 2, \ldots, T.$$

Note that $\mathbf{x}_{*1}\sqrt{1-\rho^2}\mathbf{x}_1$ and $\mathbf{x}_{*t} = (\mathbf{x}_t - \rho\mathbf{x}_{t-1})$. Also, from (13-43), we have

$$\frac{\partial \ln L}{\partial \sigma_u^2} = -\frac{T}{2\sigma_u^2} + \frac{1}{2\sigma_u^4}\sum_{t=1}^{T} u_t^2.$$

Turning now to the first part of (13-40), we find that

$$\frac{\partial \ln L}{\partial \rho} = \frac{1}{\sigma_u^2}\sum_{t=2}^{T} u_t\epsilon_{t-1} + \frac{\rho\epsilon_1^2}{\sigma_u^2} - \frac{\rho}{1-\rho^2},$$

where $\epsilon_t = y_t - \mathbf{x}_t'\boldsymbol{\beta}$. For a given value of ρ, the maximum likelihood estimates of $\boldsymbol{\beta}$ and σ_u^2 are the usual ones, GLS and the mean squared residual using the transformed data. The problem is estimation of ρ. One possibility is to search the range $-1 < \rho < 1$ for the value that with the implied estimates of the other parameters maximizes $\ln L$. This is analogous to the Hildreth–Lu estimator.[27] Beach and MacKinnon (1978a) argue that this is a very inefficient way to do the search and have devised a much faster algorithm.

The components of the information matrix are derived from

$$\frac{\partial^2 \ln L}{\partial \boldsymbol{\beta}\,\partial \boldsymbol{\beta}'} = -\frac{1}{\sigma_u^2}\sum_{t=1}^{T}\mathbf{x}_{*t}\mathbf{x}_{*t}' = -\frac{1}{\sigma_u^2}\mathbf{X}'\boldsymbol{\Omega}^{-1}\mathbf{X},$$

$$\frac{\partial^2 \ln L}{\partial \boldsymbol{\beta}\,\partial \sigma_u^2} = -\frac{1}{\sigma_u^4}\sum_{t=1}^{T} u_t\mathbf{x}_{*t},$$

$$\frac{\partial^2 \ln L}{\partial \boldsymbol{\beta}\,\partial \rho} = \frac{1}{\sigma_u^2}\sum_{t=1}^{T} u_t\left[\frac{\partial \mathbf{x}_{*t}}{\partial \rho}\right],$$

$$\frac{\partial^2 \ln L}{\partial (\sigma_u^2)^2} = \frac{T}{2\sigma_u^4} - \frac{1}{\sigma_u^6}\sum_{t=1}^{T} u_t^2,$$

$$\frac{\partial^2 \ln L}{\partial \rho\,\partial \sigma_u^2} = -\frac{1}{\sigma_u^4}\left[\sum_{t=2}^{T} u_t\epsilon_{t-1} + \rho\epsilon_1^2\right],$$

$$\frac{\partial^2 \ln L}{\partial \rho^2} = -\frac{1}{\sigma_u^2}\sum_{t=2}^{T}\epsilon_{t-1}^2 + \frac{\epsilon_1^2}{\sigma_u^2} - \frac{1+\rho^2}{1-\rho^2}$$

[27]An improvement on this is provided by Hildreth and Dent (1974).

using $u_t = \epsilon_t - \rho\epsilon_{t-1}$. Taking the negative of the expected values produces the information matrix

$$\mathbf{I}(\boldsymbol{\beta}, \sigma_u^2, \rho) = \begin{bmatrix} \frac{1}{\sigma_u^2}\mathbf{X}'\Omega\mathbf{X} & \mathbf{0} & \mathbf{0} \\ \mathbf{0}' & \frac{T}{2\sigma_u^4} & \frac{\rho}{\sigma_u^2(1-\rho^2)} \\ \mathbf{0}' & \frac{\rho}{\sigma_u^2(1-\rho^2)} & \frac{T-2}{1-\rho^2} + \frac{1+\rho^2}{(1-\rho^2)^2} \end{bmatrix}.$$

The off-diagonal elements at the lower right result from the treatment of the-first observation. If this observation is omitted, the calculations simplify a bit. Note that the other terms in the block are sums of $T - 1$ observations, so these "end effects" will be negligible asymptotically. Once again, their importance may be greater in a finite sample. Omitting the first observation produces the common approximation

$$\mathbf{I}(\boldsymbol{\beta}, \sigma_u^2, \rho) = \begin{bmatrix} \frac{1}{\sigma_u^2}\mathbf{X}'\Omega^{-1}\mathbf{X} & \mathbf{0} & \mathbf{0} \\ \mathbf{0}' & \frac{T}{2\sigma_u^4} & \mathbf{0} \\ \mathbf{0}' & \mathbf{0}' & \frac{T-1}{1-\rho^2} \end{bmatrix}. \quad \textbf{(13-44)}$$

It is common to drop the first observation from the previous calculations, arguing that it will be negligible asymptotically. Alternatively, one might do the analysis *conditionally* on the first observation (which appears unavoidably in the preceding sums.) From the point of view of the asymptotic properties of the estimators, it is certainly true that the first observation is inconsequential. But it must be remembered that the typical time series is not very long, and the numerical answers one obtains with and without explicit treatment of the first observation may be quite different. In such a case, the evidence suggests that retention is preferable.[28]

All the foregoing estimators have the same asymptotic properties. The available evidence on their small-sample properties comes from Monte Carlo studies and is, unfortunately, only suggestive. Griliches and Rao (1969) find evidence that if the sample is relatively small and ρ is not particularly large, say less than 0.3, least squares is as good as or better than FGLS. The problem is the additional variation introduced into the sampling variance by the variance of r. A second fairly firm conclusion is that it can be far worse to omit the first observation than to keep it.[29] Beyond these, the results are rather mixed. Maxi-

[28]See, for example, Maeshiro (1979) and Poirier (1978a).

[29]See Harvey and McAvinchey (1981).

TABLE 13.5 Estimators of ρ

r	0.3392
$1 - d/2$	0.3393
Theil	0.3015
Theil–Nagar	0.3735[a]
Durbin	0.6385

Source: From Theil and Nagar (1961).
[a] $[T^2(1 - d/2) + K^2]/(T^2 - K^2)$.

mum likelihood seems to perform well in general, but the Prais–Winsten estimator is evidently nearly as efficient.

EXAMPLE 13.7 Estimation of ρ in the AR(1) Model

The various estimators described earlier give rather different results for the investment data of Example 13.1. First, some different estimates of ρ are given in Table 13.5. Estimates of the regression parameters are shown in Table 13.6.

There are some distinctive results in Table 13.6. First, it would appear that the OLS standard errors are considerably biased downward. Second, when comparing the Cochrane–Orcutt estimates with the Prais–Winsten estimates, the loss of efficiency from discarding the initial observation is substantial. Ob-

TABLE 13.6 Parameter Estimates (Standard Errors in Parentheses)

Estimator	*Constant*	*GNP*	*Interest*	ρ
OLS	−12.5336	0.16914	−1.00144	0
	(24.92)	(0.02057)	(2.369)	
Prais–Winsten				
Two-step	−15.6551	0.17073	−0.70394	0.3392
	(33.76)	(0.02791)	(2.816)	
Iterated	−15.673	0.17075	−0.70462	0.3527
(two iterations)	(33.84)	(0.02796)	(2.817)	
Cochrane–Orcutt				
Two-step	−18.3567	0.17286	−0.80775	0.3392
	(44.83)	(0.03633)	(3.102)	
Iterated	−18.3567	0.17286	−0.80775	0.3559
(two iterations)	(44.83)	(0.03633)	(3.102)	
Maximum likelihood	−14.4989	0.17006	−0.82422	0.27996
	(31.56)	(0.02608)	(2.718)	
Durbin	−26.787	0.21351	0.38499	0.6385
	(32.53)	(0.07050)	(3.824)	
Hildreth–Lu	−14.887	0.17029	−0.78936	0.3000
	(32.47)	(0.02681)	(2.754)	

taining the maximum likelihood estimates by the method of Beach and MacKinnon required only three function evaluations, which is only one more than the iterated two-step estimators.

13.7.2. AR(2) Disturbances

Maximum likelihood procedures for most other disturbance processes are exceedingly complex. Beach and MacKinnon (1978b) have derived an algorithm for AR(2) disturbances. For higher-order autoregressive models, maximum likelihood estimation is presently impractical, but the two-step estimators can easily be extended. For models of the form

$$\epsilon_t = \theta_1 \epsilon_{t-1} + \theta_2 \epsilon_{t-2} + \cdots + \theta_p \epsilon_{t-p} + u_t, \tag{13-45}$$

a simple approach for estimation of the autoregressive parameters is to use either of the following methods:

1. An analog of Durbin's method. Regress y_t on $y_{t-1}, \ldots, y_{t-p}, \mathbf{x}_t, \mathbf{x}_{t-1}, \ldots,$ and $\mathbf{x}_{t-p}$. The slopes on the lagged values of y give consistent estimates of the autoregressive parameters. If there are many regressors, this may involve an excessive number of variables.
2. By regressing e_t on $e_{t-1}, \ldots, e_{t-p}$, we also obtain consistent estimates of the autoregressive parameters.

With the estimates of $\theta_1, \ldots, \theta_p$ in hand, the Cochrane–Orcutt estimator can be obtained. If the model is an AR(2), the full FGLS procedure should be used instead.[30] The least squares computations for the transformed data provide (at least asymptotically) the appropriate estimates of σ^2 and the covariance matrix of $\hat{\boldsymbol{\beta}}$. As before, iteration is possible but brings no gains in efficiency.

13.7.3. Estimation with a Lagged Dependent Variable

In Section 13.4.1, we considered the problem of estimation by least squares when the model contains both autocorrelation and lagged dependent variable(s). Since the OLS estimator is inconsistent, the residuals on which an estimator of ρ would be based are likewise inconsistent. Therefore, $\hat{\rho}$ will be inconsistent as well. The consequence is that the FGLS estimators described earlier are not usable in this case. There is, however, an alternative way to proceed, based on the method of instrumental variables.

The method of instrumental variables was introduced in Section 6.7.8. To review, the general problem is that in the model

$$\mathbf{y} = \mathbf{X}\boldsymbol{\beta} + \boldsymbol{\epsilon},$$

if

$$\text{plim}\, \frac{1}{T}\mathbf{X}'\boldsymbol{\epsilon} \neq \mathbf{0},$$

[30] Fuller (1976) gives expressions for general autoregressive processes, but these are rather cumbersome and are not yet in wide use.

the least squares estimator is not consistent. A consistent estimator is

$$\mathbf{b}_{\mathrm{IV}} = (\mathbf{Z}'\mathbf{X})^{-1}(\mathbf{Z}'\mathbf{y}),$$

where $\mathbf{Z}$ is set of K variables chosen such that

$$\text{plim}\,\frac{1}{T}\,\mathbf{Z}'\boldsymbol{\epsilon} = \mathbf{0}$$

but

$$\text{plim}\,\frac{1}{T}\,\mathbf{Z}'\mathbf{X} \neq \mathbf{0}.$$

For the purpose of consistency only, any such set of $\mathbf{z}$'s will suffice. The relevance of that here is that the obstacle to consistent FGLS is, at least for the present, the lack of a consistent estimator of ρ. By using the technique of instrumental variables, we may estimate $\boldsymbol{\beta}$ consistently, then estimate ρ and proceed.

Hatanaka (1974) has devised an efficient two-step estimator based on this principle. To put the estimator in the current context, we consider estimation of the model

$$y_t = \mathbf{x}_t'\boldsymbol{\beta} + \gamma y_{t-1} + \epsilon_t,$$
$$\epsilon_t = \rho\epsilon_{t-1} + u_t.$$

To get to the second step of FGLS, we require consistent estimates of the slope parameters. These can be obtained using an IV estimator, where the column of $\mathbf{Z}$ corresponding to y_{t-1} is the only one that need be different from that of $\mathbf{X}$. An appropriate instrument can be obtained by using the fitted values in the regression of y_t on $\mathbf{x}_t$ and $\mathbf{x}_{t-1}$.[31] The residuals from this regression are then used to construct

$$\hat{\rho} = \frac{\sum_{t=3}^{T} \hat{\epsilon}_t\hat{\epsilon}_{t-1}}{\sum_{t=3}^{T} \hat{\epsilon}_t^2},$$

where

$$\hat{\epsilon}_t = y_t - \mathbf{b}_{\mathrm{IV}}'\mathbf{x}_t - c_{\mathrm{IV}}y_{t-1}.$$

FGLS estimates may now be computed by regressing

$$y*_t = y_t - \hat{\rho}y_{t-1}$$

on

$$\mathbf{x}*_t = \mathbf{x}_t - \hat{\rho}\mathbf{x}_{t-1},$$
$$y*_{t-1} = y_{t-1} - \hat{\rho}y_{t-2},$$

[31]One might use additional lags of $\mathbf{x}$ at this stage, perhaps to improve the small-sample properties of the estimator. Asymptotically, it is immaterial.

and

$$\hat{\epsilon}_{t-1} = y_{t-1} - \mathbf{b}'_{\text{IV}}\mathbf{x}_{t-1} - c_{\text{IV}}y_{t-2}.$$

Let d be the coefficient on $\hat{\epsilon}_{t-1}$ in this regression. The efficient estimator of ρ is

$$\hat{\hat{\rho}} = \hat{\rho} + d.$$

Appropriate asymptotic standard errors for the estimators, including $\hat{\hat{\rho}}$, are obtained from the $s^2[\mathbf{X}'_*\mathbf{X}_*]^{-1}$ computed at the second step. Hatanaka shows that these estimates are asymptotically equivalent to maximum likelihood estimates.

13.8. FORECASTING IN THE PRESENCE OF AUTOCORRELATION

For purposes of forecasting, we refer first to the transformed model,

$$y_{*_t} = \mathbf{x}'_{*_t}\boldsymbol{\beta} + \epsilon_{*_t}.$$

Suppose that the process generating ϵ_t is an AR(1) and that ρ is known. Since this is a classical regression model, the results of Chapter 6 may be used. The optimal forecast of y^0_{*T+1}, given $\mathbf{x}^0_{T+1}$ and $\mathbf{x}_T$ (i.e., $\mathbf{x}^0_{*T+1} = \mathbf{x}^0_{T+1} - \rho\mathbf{x}_T$), is

$$\hat{y}^0_{*T+1} = \mathbf{x}^{0\,\prime}_{*T+1}\hat{\boldsymbol{\beta}}.$$

Disassembling $\hat{y}^0_{*T+1}$, we find

$$\hat{y}^0_{T+1} - \rho y_T = \mathbf{x}^{0\,\prime}_{T+1}\hat{\boldsymbol{\beta}} - \rho\mathbf{x}'_T\hat{\boldsymbol{\beta}}$$

or

$$\begin{aligned}\hat{y}^0_{T+1} &= \mathbf{x}^{0\,\prime}_{T+1}\hat{\boldsymbol{\beta}} + \rho(y_T - \mathbf{x}'_T\hat{\boldsymbol{\beta}}) \\ &= \mathbf{x}^{0\,\prime}_{T+1}\hat{\boldsymbol{\beta}} + \rho e_T.\end{aligned} \tag{13-46}$$

Thus, we carry forward a proportion ρ of the estimated disturbance in the preceding period. This can be justified by reference to

$$E[\epsilon_{T+1} \mid \epsilon_T] = \rho\epsilon_T.$$

It can also be shown that to forecast n periods ahead, we would use

$$\hat{y}^0_{T+n} = \mathbf{x}^{0\,\prime}_{T+n}\hat{\boldsymbol{\beta}} + \rho^n e_T\,. \tag{13-47}$$

The extension to higher-order autoregressions is direct. For a second-order model, for example,

$$\hat{y}^0_{T+n} = \hat{\boldsymbol{\beta}}'\mathbf{x}^0_{T+n} + \theta_1 e_{T+n-1} + \theta_2 e_{T+n-2}. \tag{13-48}$$

For residuals that are outside the sample period, we use the recursion

$$\hat{e}_s = \theta_1\hat{e}_{s-1} + \theta_2\hat{e}_{s-2}, \tag{13-49}$$

beginning with the last two residuals within the sample.

Moving average models are somewhat simpler, as the autocorrelation lasts for only one period. For an MA(1) model, for the first postsample period,

$$\hat{y}^0_{T+1} = \mathbf{x}^{0\,\prime}_{T+1}\hat{\boldsymbol{\beta}} + \hat{\epsilon}_{T+1},$$

where

$$\hat{\epsilon}_{T+1} = \hat{u}_{T+1} - \lambda\hat{u}_T.$$

Therefore, a forecast of ϵ_{T+1} will use all previous residuals. One way to proceed is to accumulate $\hat{\epsilon}_{T+1}$ from the recursion

$$\hat{u}_t = \hat{\epsilon}_t + \lambda\hat{u}_{t-1}$$

with $\hat{u}_{T+1} = \hat{u}_0 = 0$ and $\hat{\epsilon}_t = (y_t - \mathbf{x}_t'\hat{\boldsymbol{\beta}})$. After the first postsample period,

$$\hat{\epsilon}_{T+n} = \hat{u}_{T+n} - \lambda\hat{u}_{T+n-1} = 0.$$

If the parameters of the disturbance process are known, the variances for the forecast errors can be computed using the results of Chapter 6. For an AR(1) disturbance, the estimated variance would be

$$s_f^2 = \hat{\sigma}_\epsilon^2[1 + (\mathbf{x}_t - \rho\mathbf{x}_{t-1})'\{\text{Est. Var}\,[\hat{\boldsymbol{\beta}}]\}(\mathbf{x}_t - \rho\mathbf{x}_{t-1})]. \qquad \textbf{(13-50)}$$

For a higher-order process, it is only necessary to modify the calculation of $\mathbf{x}_{*t}$ accordingly. The forecast variances for an MA(1) process are somewhat more involved. Details may be found in Judge et al. (1985). If the parameters of the disturbance process, ρ, λ, θ_j, and so on, are estimated as well, the forecast variance will be greater. For an AR(1) model, the necessary correction to the forecast variance of the n-period-ahead forecast error is $\hat{\sigma}_\epsilon^2 n^2\rho^{2(n-1)}/T$. [For a one-period-ahead forecast, this merely adds a term, $1/T$, in the brackets in (13-50)]. Higher-order AR and MA processes are analyzed in Baille (1979). Finally, if the regressors are stochastic, the expressions become more complex by another order of magnitude.

If ρ is known, (13-47) provides the best linear unbiased forecast of y_{t+1}.[32] If, however, ρ must be estimated, this assessment must be modified. There is information about ϵ_{t+1} embodied in e_t. Having to estimate ρ, however, implies that some of or all the value of this information is offset by the variation introduced into the forecast by including the stochastic component $\hat{\rho}e_t$.[33] Whether (13-47) is preferable to the obvious expedient $\hat{y}^0_{T+n} = \hat{\boldsymbol{\beta}}'\mathbf{x}^0_{T+n}$ in a small sample when ρ is estimated remains to be settled.

For computational purposes, Pagan and Nicholls (1984) have extended Salkever's augmented regression (Section 6.8.1) to models of autocorrelation. The augmented regression for forecasting T^0 periods ahead, based on $\mathbf{X}^0$, would use

[32]See Goldberger (1962).

[33]See Baille (1979).

$$\tilde{\mathbf{X}} = \begin{bmatrix} \mathbf{X} & \mathbf{0} & & & \\ \mathbf{x}^0_{T+1} & 1 & 0 & 0 & \cdots \\ \mathbf{x}^0_{T+2} & \rho & 1 & 0 & \cdots \\ \mathbf{x}^0_{T+3} & \rho^2 & \rho & 1 & \cdots \end{bmatrix}, \quad \tilde{\mathbf{Y}} = \begin{bmatrix} \mathbf{y} \\ \mathbf{y}^0 \end{bmatrix}.$$
etc.

The authors have obtained general expressions for higher-order models and for mixtures of AR and MA models. There are two drawbacks, however. First, the unknown ρ must be replaced with the sample estimate. This is simple in principle, but it presents a practical difficulty not present in Salkever's computations. The classical regression is done in a single pass, so $\tilde{\mathbf{X}}$ and $\tilde{\mathbf{y}}$ can be constructed before the computations are begun. Pagan and Nicholls's augmented regressors must be constructed *after* the initial least squares regression. Most software does not relinquish control once the estimation of a model with autocorrelated disturbances is begun until all computations are finished. The second difficulty, also not present in Salkever's formulation, is that this augmented regression requires $\mathbf{y}^0$. Therefore, it can be used only for within-sample purposes (or for model validation based on partitioning of the sample).

EXERCISES

1. Does first differencing reduce autocorrelation? Consider the models

$$y_t = \boldsymbol{\beta}'\mathbf{x}_t + \epsilon_t,$$

where

$$\epsilon_t = \rho\epsilon_{t-1} + u_t$$

and

$$\epsilon_t = u_t - \lambda u_{t-1}.$$

Compare the autocorrelation of ϵ_t in the original model with that of ν_t in

$$y_t - y_{t-1} = \boldsymbol{\beta}'(\mathbf{x}_t - \mathbf{x}_{t-1}) + \nu_t,$$

where

$$\nu_t = \epsilon_t - \epsilon_{t-1}.$$

2. Derive the disturbance covariance matrix for the model

$$y_t = \boldsymbol{\beta}'\mathbf{x}_t + \epsilon_t,$$
$$\epsilon_t = \rho\epsilon_{t-1} + u_t - \lambda u_{t-1}.$$

What parameter is estimated by the regression of the OLS residuals on their lagged values?

3. A least squares regression based on 24 observations produces the following results:

$$y_t = \underset{(0.1)}{0.3} + \underset{(0.2)}{1.21}x_t \qquad R^2 = 0.982$$
$$\text{D–W} = 1.31.$$

Test the hypothesis that the disturbances are not autocorrelated.

4. It can be shown that in the regression model

$$y_t = \beta y_{t-1} + \epsilon_t,$$
$$\epsilon_t = \rho\epsilon_{t-1} + u_t,$$
$$\text{plim } r = \frac{\beta\rho(\beta + \rho)}{1 + \beta\rho},$$

where

$$r = \frac{\sum_{t=2}^{T} e_t e_{t-1}}{\sum_{t=2}^{T} e_t^2}.$$

Use this result to show that

$$\text{plim}\,\frac{r}{b} = \beta\rho,$$
$$\text{plim } b + r = \beta + \rho,$$

where b is the OLS estimator of β. If you were given only the ordinary least squares regression results and the Durbin–Watson statistic, could you estimate β and ρ? If so, how? If not, why not?

5. The appendix to Chapter 16 contains data for 1953 to 1984 on gross private domestic investment (I) and corporate profits (P), among other variables. Estimate the efficiency ratio (13-21) for OLS estimation using the model

$$I_t = \alpha + \beta P_t + \epsilon_t,$$

assuming that corporate profits satisfy the assumption made in that derivation.

6. Using the data and model of the previous problem, compute and plot the ordinary least squares residuals. Obtain the first and second autocorrelations of the OLS residuals. Now compute the FGLS estimator, assuming that the disturbances are an AR(1) process. Use the Prais–Winsten estimator and then the Cochrane–Orcutt estimator. What differences do you observe? To estimate ρ, use any of the estimators discussed in the text.

7. The following regression is obtained by ordinary least squares, using 21 ob-

servations. (Estimated asymptotic standard errors are shown in parentheses.)

$$y_t = \underset{(0.3)}{1.3} + \underset{(0.18)}{0.97}y_{t-1} + \underset{(1.04)}{2.31}x_t, \qquad \text{D–W} = 1.21.$$

Test for the presence of autocorrelation in the disturbances.

8. It is commonly asserted that the Durbin–Watson statistic is only appropriate for testing for first-order autoregressive disturbances. What combination of the coefficients of the model is estimated by the Durbin–Watson statistic in each of the following cases: AR(1), AR(2), MA(1)? In each case, assume that the regression model does not contain a lagged dependent variable. Comment on the impact on your results of relaxing this assumption.

CHAPTER 14

Models for Panel Data

14.1. INTRODUCTION

Data sets that combine time series and cross sections are common in economics. For example, the published statistics of the OECD contain numerous series of economic aggregates observed yearly for many countries. Recently constructed **longitudinal** data sets contain observations on thousands of individuals or families, each observed at several points in time. Some empirical studies have analyzed time-series data on several firms, states, or industries simultaneously. These data sets provide a rich source of information about the economy. Modeling in this setting, however, calls for some quite complex stochastic specifications. In this and the next chapter, we will survey the most commonly used techniques for time-series cross-section data analyses. This chapter will describe several techniques that have been applied in single equation models. In Chapter 15, we will consider some different models that also employ time-series cross-section data, but in models that involve sets of equations.

14.2. PANEL DATA MODELS

Many recent studies have analyzed **panel,** or longitudinal, data sets. Two very famous ones are the National Longitudinal Survey of Labor Market Experience (NLS) and the Michigan Panel Study of Income Dynamics (PSID). In these data sets, very large cross sections, consisting of thousands of microunits, are followed through time. But the number of periods is often quite small. The PSID, for example, is a study of roughly 6000 families and 15,000 individuals who have been interviewed periodically from 1968 to the present. Another group of intensively studied panel data sets is those from the negative income tax experiments of the early 1970s in which thousands of families were followed for 8 or 13 quarters. Constructing long, evenly spaced time series in this context would be prohibitively expensive, but for the purposes for which these data are typically used, this is unnecessary. Time effects are often viewed as "transitions" or discrete changes of state. They are typically modeled as specific to the period in which they occur and are not carried across periods within a cross-sectional unit.[1] Panel data sets are more oriented toward cross-section analyses; they are wide but typically short. Heterogeneity across units is an integral part—indeed, often the central focus—of the analysis.

The analysis of panel or longitudinal data is the subject of one of the most active and innovative bodies of literature in econometrics.[2] This is partly because panel data provide such a rich environment for the development of estimation techniques and theoretical results. In more practical terms, however, researchers have been able to use time-series cross-sectional data to examine issues that could not be studied in either cross-sectional or time-series settings alone. Two examples are as follows.

1. In a widely cited study of labor supply, Ben-Porath (1973) observes that at a certain point in time, in a cohort of women, 50 percent may appear to be working. It is ambiguous whether this finding implies that, in this cohort, one-half of the women on average will be working or that the same one-half will be working in every period. These have very different implications for policy and for the interpretation of any statistical results. Cross-sectional data alone will not shed any light on the question.
2. A long-standing problem in the analysis of production functions has been the inability to separate economies of scale and technological change.[3] Cross-sectional data provide information only about the former, whereas time-series data muddle the two effects, with no prospect of separation. It is common, for example, to assume constant returns to scale so as to reveal the technical change.[4] Of course, this assumes away the problem. A study by Greene (1983b) examines the cost of

---

[1]This has not prevented theorists from devising autocorrelation models applicable to panel data sets. See, for example, Lee (1978a). As a practical matter, however, the empirical literature in this field has tended to concentrate on the less intricate models. Time-series modeling of the sort discussed in the previous chapter is somewhat unusual in the analysis of longitudinal data.

[2]The panel data literature rivals the received research on unit roots in econometrics in its rate of growth. A compendium of the earliest literature is Maddala (1993). Book-length surveys on the econometrics of panel data include Hsiao (1986), Dielman (1989), Matyas and Sevestre (1996), Raj and Baltagi (1992), and Baltagi (1995). There are also lengthy surveys devoted to specific topics, such as limited dependent variable models and semiparametric methods. An extensive bibliography is given in Baltagi (1995).

[3]The distinction between these two effects figured prominently in the policy question of whether it was appropriate to break up the AT&T Corporation in the 1980s and, ultimately, to allow competition in the provision of long-distance telephone service.

[4]In a classic study of this issue, Solow (1957) states: "From time series of $\dot{Q}/Q$, w_K, $\dot{K}/K$, w_L and $\dot{L}/L$ or their discrete year-to-year analogues, we could estimate $\dot{A}/A$ and thence $A(t)$ itself. Actually an amusing thing happens here. Nothing has been said so far about returns to scale. But if all factor inputs are classified either as K or L, then the available figures always show w_K and w_L adding up to one. Since we have assumed that factors are paid their marginal products, this amounts to assuming the hypothesis of Euler's theorem. The calculus being what it is, we might just as well assume the conclusion, namely, the F is homogeneous of degree one."

electric power generation for a large number of firms, each observed in each of several years. The basic model, for the ith firm in year t, is

$$\text{cost}_{it} = C(Y_{it}, \mathbf{p}_{it}, t),$$

where Y is output and $\mathbf{p}$ is a vector of factor prices, provides estimates of the rate of technological change

$$\delta_t = \frac{-d \ln C}{dt}$$

and economies of scale

$$\text{e.s.}_{it} = \frac{1}{\left(\dfrac{d \ln C_{it}}{d \ln Y_{it}}\right)} - 1.$$

In principle, the methods of Section 13.3 can be applied to longitudinal data sets. In the typical panel, however, there are a large number of cross-sectional units and only a few periods. Thus, the time-series methods discussed there may be somewhat problematic. Recent work has generally concentrated on models better suited to these short and wide data sets. The techniques are focused on cross-sectional variation, or heterogeneity. In this chapter, we shall examine the two most widely used models, then look briefly at some extensions.

EXAMPLE 14.1 Cost Function

The data in Table 14.1 are taken from the study by Greene described earlier. Output in millions of kilowatt-hours and total generation cost in millions of dollars, consisting of fuel, labor, and capital costs, are observed for six firms in each of 4 years.

TABLE 14.1 Cost and Output Data

		Time			
Firm		*t = 1* *1955*	*t = 2* *1960*	*t = 3* *1965*	*t = 4* *1970*
$i = 1$	Cost	3.154	4.271	4.584	5.849
	Output	214	419	588	1,025
$i = 2$	Cost	3.859	5.535	8.127	10.966
	Output	696	811	1,640	2,506
$i = 3$	Cost	19.035	26.041	32.444	41.180
	Output	3,202	4,802	5,821	9,275
$i = 4$	Cost	35.229	51.111	61.045	77.885
	Output	5,668	7,612	10,206	13,702
$i = 5$	Cost	33.154	40.044	43.125	57.727
	Output	6,000	8,222	8,484	10,004
$i = 6$	Cost	73.050	98.846	138.88	191.56
	Output	11,796	15,551	27,218	30,958

For purposes of the example, we first fit the simple linear regression

$$\ln C_{it} = \alpha + \beta \ln Y_{it} + \epsilon_{it}.$$

Ordinary least squares regression produces

$$\ln C = \underset{(0.2769)}{-4.17478} + \underset{(0.0329)}{0.887987} \ln Y \qquad R^2 = 0.9707, \quad s^2 = 0.04614.$$

The fundamental advantage of a panel data set over a cross section is that it will allow the researcher far greater flexibility in modeling differences in behavior across individuals. The basic framework for this discussion is a regression model of the form

$$y_{it} = \alpha_i + \boldsymbol{\beta}'\mathbf{x}_{it} + \epsilon_{it}. \tag{14-1}$$

There are K regressors in $\mathbf{x}_{it}$, *not including the constant term*. The **individual effect** is α_i, which is taken to be constant over time t and specific to the individual cross-sectional unit i. As it stands, this is a classical regression model. If we take the α_i's to be the same across all units, ordinary least squares provides consistent and efficient estimates of α and β. There are two basic frameworks used to generalize this model. The **fixed** effects approach takes α_i to be a group specific constant term in the regression model. The **random effects** approach specifies that α_i is a group specific disturbance, similar to ϵ_{it} except that for each group, there is but a single draw that enters the regression identically in each period. We will consider these two approaches in turn.

14.3. FIXED EFFECTS

A common formulation of the model assumes that differences across units can be captured in differences in the constant term.[5] Thus, in (14-1), each α_i is an unknown parameter to be estimated. Let $\mathbf{y}_i$ and $\mathbf{X}_i$ be the T observations for the ith unit, and let $\boldsymbol{\epsilon}_i$ be associated $T \times 1$ vector of disturbances. Then we may write (14-1) as

$$\mathbf{y}_i = \mathbf{i}\alpha_i + \mathbf{X}_i\boldsymbol{\beta} + \boldsymbol{\epsilon}_i.$$

Collecting these, we have

$$\begin{bmatrix} \mathbf{y}_1 \\ \mathbf{y}_2 \\ \vdots \\ \mathbf{y}_n \end{bmatrix} = \begin{bmatrix} \mathbf{i} & \mathbf{0} & \cdots & \mathbf{0} \\ \mathbf{0} & \mathbf{i} & \cdots & \mathbf{0} \\ & & \vdots & \\ \mathbf{0} & \mathbf{0} & \cdots & \mathbf{i} \end{bmatrix} \begin{bmatrix} \alpha_1 \\ \alpha_2 \\ \vdots \\ \alpha_n \end{bmatrix} + \begin{bmatrix} \mathbf{X}_1 \\ \mathbf{X}_2 \\ \vdots \\ \mathbf{X}_n \end{bmatrix} \boldsymbol{\beta} + \begin{bmatrix} \boldsymbol{\epsilon}_1 \\ \boldsymbol{\epsilon}_2 \\ \vdots \\ \boldsymbol{\epsilon}_n \end{bmatrix}$$

---

[5]It is also possible to allow the slopes to vary across i, but this introduces some new methodological issues, as well as considerable complexity in the calculations. A study on the topic is Cornwell and Schmidt (1984). Also, the assumption of a fixed T is only for convenience. The more general case in which T_i varies across units is considered below, in the exercises, and in Greene (1995a).

or

$$\mathbf{y} = [\mathbf{d}_1 \quad \mathbf{d}_2 \quad \ldots \quad \mathbf{d}_n \quad \mathbf{X}] \begin{bmatrix} \boldsymbol{\alpha} \\ \boldsymbol{\beta} \end{bmatrix} + \boldsymbol{\epsilon}, \tag{14-2}$$

where $\mathbf{d}_i$ is a dummy variable indicating the ith unit. Let the $nT \times n$ matrix $\mathbf{D} = [\mathbf{d}_1 \quad \mathbf{d}_2 \quad \ldots \quad \mathbf{d}_n]$. Then, assembling all nT rows gives

$$\mathbf{y} = \mathbf{D}\boldsymbol{\alpha} + \mathbf{X}\boldsymbol{\beta} + \boldsymbol{\epsilon}. \tag{14-3}$$

This is usually referred to as the **least squares dummy variable (LSDV) model** (although the "least squares" part of the name refers to the technique usually used to estimate it, not to the model as such).

This is a classical regression model, so no new results are needed to analyze it. If n is small enough, the model can be estimated by ordinary least squares with K regressors in $\mathbf{X}$ and n columns in $\mathbf{D}$, as a multiple regression with n + K parameters. Of course, if n is thousands, as is typical, this is likely to exceed the storage capacity of any computer. But, as we found in Chapter 8, there is an easier way to proceed. Using familiar results for a partitioned regression,[6] we write the OLS estimator of $\boldsymbol{\beta}$ as

$$\mathbf{b} = [\mathbf{X}'\mathbf{M}_d\mathbf{X}]^{-1}[\mathbf{X}'\mathbf{M}_d\mathbf{y}]. \tag{14-4}$$

where

$$\mathbf{M}_d = \mathbf{I} - \mathbf{D}(\mathbf{D}'\mathbf{D})^{-1}\mathbf{D}'.$$

This amounts to a least squares regression using the transformed data $\mathbf{X}* = \mathbf{M}_d\mathbf{X}$ and $\mathbf{y}* = \mathbf{M}_d\mathbf{y}$. The structure of $\mathbf{D}$ is particularly convenient; its columns are orthogonal, so

$$\mathbf{M}_d = \begin{bmatrix} \mathbf{M}^0 & \mathbf{0} & \mathbf{0} & \cdots & \mathbf{0} \\ \mathbf{0} & \mathbf{M}^0 & \mathbf{0} & \cdots & \mathbf{0} \\ & & \vdots & & \\ \mathbf{0} & \mathbf{0} & \mathbf{0} & \cdots & \mathbf{M}^0 \end{bmatrix}.$$

Each matrix on the diagonal is

$$\mathbf{M}^0 = \mathbf{I}_T - \frac{1}{T}\mathbf{i}\mathbf{i}'.$$

Premultiplying any $T \times 1$ *vector* $\mathbf{z}_i$ by $\mathbf{M}^0$ creates $\mathbf{M}^0\mathbf{z}_i = \mathbf{z}_i - \bar{z}\mathbf{i}$. (Note that the mean is taken over only the T observations for unit i.) Therefore, the regression of $\mathbf{M}_d\mathbf{y}$ on $\mathbf{M}_d\mathbf{X}$ is equivalent to the regression of $[y_{it} - \bar{y}_{i.}]$ on $[\mathbf{x}_{it} - \bar{\mathbf{x}}_{i.}]$, where $\bar{\mathbf{x}}_{i.}$ is the $K \times 1$ vector of means of $\mathbf{x}_{it}$ over the T observations. The dummy variable coefficients can be recovered from the other normal equation

[6]See Section 6.4.3.

in the partitioned regression:

$$\mathbf{D}'\mathbf{D}\mathbf{a} + \mathbf{D}'\mathbf{X}\mathbf{b} = \mathbf{D}'\mathbf{y} \tag{14-5}$$

or

$$\mathbf{a} = [\mathbf{D}'\mathbf{D}]^{-1}\mathbf{D}'(\mathbf{y} - \mathbf{X}\mathbf{b}).$$

This implies that for each i,

$$a_i = \text{the mean residual in the } i\text{th group.} \tag{14-6}$$

Alternatively,

$$a_i = \bar{y}_{i.} - \mathbf{b}'\bar{\mathbf{x}}_{i.}.$$

The appropriate estimator of the covariance matrix for $\mathbf{b}$ is

$$\text{Est. Var}[\mathbf{b}] = s^2[\mathbf{X}'\mathbf{M}_d\mathbf{X}]^{-1}, \tag{14-7}$$

which uses the usual second moment matrix with $\mathbf{x}$'s, now expressed as deviations from their respective unit means. The disturbance variance estimator is

$$s^2 = \frac{\sum_{i=1}^{n}\sum_{t=1}^{T}(y_{it} - a_i - \mathbf{x}_{it}'\mathbf{b})^2}{nT - n - K}. \tag{14-8}$$

The ith residual is

$$\begin{aligned} e_{it} &= y_{it} - a_i - \mathbf{x}_{it}'\mathbf{b} \\ &= y_{it} - (\bar{y}_{i.} - \bar{\mathbf{x}}_{i.}'\mathbf{b}) - \mathbf{x}_{it}'\mathbf{b} \\ &= (y_{it} - \bar{y}_{i.}) - (\mathbf{x}_{it} - \bar{\mathbf{x}}_{i.})'\mathbf{b}. \end{aligned}$$

Thus, the numerator in s^2 is exactly the sum of squared residuals from the regression in (14-4). But most computer programs will use $nT - K$ for the denominator in computing s^2, so a correction will be necessary. For the individual effects,

$$\text{Var}[a_i] = \frac{\sigma^2}{T} + \bar{\mathbf{x}}_{i.}'\text{Var}[\mathbf{b}]\bar{\mathbf{x}}_{i.},$$

so a simple estimator based on s^2 can be computed.

14.3.1. Testing the Significance of the Group Effects

The usual t ratio for a_i implies a test of the hypothesis that α_i equals zero. But typically this is not a useful hypothesis to test in a regression context. If we are interested in differences across groups, we can test the hypothesis that the constant terms are all equal with an F test. Under the null hypothesis, the efficient estimator is pooled least squares. The F ratio used for the test is

$$F(n - 1, nT - n - K) = \frac{(R_u^2 - R_p^2)/(n - 1)}{(1 - R_u^2)/(nT - n - K)}, \tag{14-9}$$

where u indicates the unrestricted model and p indicates the pooled or restricted model with only a single overall constant term. (The sums of squared residuals may be used instead if that is more convenient.) It may be more convenient to estimate the model with an overall constant and $n - 1$ dummy variables instead. The other results will be unchanged, and rather than estimate α_i, each dummy variable coefficient will be an estimate of $\alpha_i - \alpha_1$. The F test that the coefficients on the $n - 1$ dummy variables are zero is identical to the one above. It is important to keep in mind that although the statistical results are the same, the interpretation of the dummy variable coefficients in the two formulations is different.[7]

EXAMPLE 14.2 Cost Function with Firm Effects

Least squares estimation of the model in Example 14.1 with individual firm dummy variables produces

$$\ln C = \underset{(0.06113)}{0.674279} \ln Y \qquad R^2 = 0.9924, \quad s^2 = 0.0155$$

$$-\underset{(0.3828)}{2.69353}d_1 - \underset{(0.4396)}{2.9117}d_2 - \underset{(0.5287)}{2.4400}d_3 - \underset{(0.5588)}{2.13449}d_4 - \underset{(0.5532)}{2.3108}d_5 - \underset{(0.6081)}{1.9035}d_6$$

$$F[5, 17] = \frac{(0.9924 - 0.9707)/5}{(1 - 0.9924)/17} = 9.708.$$

The 1 percent critical value from the F table is 4.34, so the hypothesis that the firm effects are the same is rejected at the 1 percent significance level.

14.3.2. The Within and Between Groups Estimators

We could formulate the regression model in three ways. First, the original formulation is

$$y_{it} = \alpha_i + \boldsymbol{\beta}'\mathbf{x}_{it} + \epsilon_{it}. \tag{14-10a}$$

In terms of deviations from the group means,

$$y_{it} - \bar{y}_{i.} = \boldsymbol{\beta}'(\mathbf{x}_{it} - \bar{\mathbf{x}}_{i.}) + \epsilon_{it} - \bar{\epsilon}_{i.}, \tag{14-10b}$$

whereas in terms of the group means,

$$\bar{y}_{i.} = \alpha_i + \boldsymbol{\beta}'\bar{\mathbf{x}}_{i.} + \bar{\epsilon}_{i.}. \tag{14-10c}$$

All three are classical regression models, and in principle, all three could be estimated, at least consistently if not efficiently, by ordinary least squares. [Note that (14-10c) involves only n observations, the group means.] Consider then the matrices of sums of squares and cross products that would be used in each case, where we focus only on estimation of $\boldsymbol{\beta}$. In (14-10a), the moments would be

[7]For a discussion of the differences, see Suits (1984).

about the overall means, $\bar{\bar{y}}$ and $\bar{\bar{\mathbf{x}}}$, and we would use the total sums of squares and cross products,

$$\mathbf{S}_{xx}^{t} = \sum_{i=1}^{n}\sum_{t=1}^{T}(\mathbf{x}_{it} - \bar{\bar{\mathbf{x}}})(\mathbf{x}_{it} - \bar{\bar{\mathbf{x}}})'$$

and

$$\mathbf{S}_{xy}^{t} = \sum_{i=1}^{n}\sum_{t=1}^{T}(\mathbf{x}_{it} - \bar{\bar{\mathbf{x}}})(y_{it} - \bar{\bar{y}}).$$

(The use of the superscript t indicates "total" and is unrelated to the time subscript.) For (14-10b), since the data are in deviations already, the means of $(y_{it} - \bar{y}_{i.})$ and $(\mathbf{x}_{it} - \bar{\mathbf{x}}_{i.})$ are zero. The moment matrices are **within-groups** (i.e., deviations from group means) sums of squares and cross products,

$$\mathbf{S}_{xx}^{w} = \sum_{i=1}^{n}\sum_{t=1}^{T}(\mathbf{x}_{it} - \bar{\mathbf{x}}_{i.})(\mathbf{x}_{it} - \bar{\mathbf{x}}_{i.})'$$

and

$$\mathbf{S}_{xy}^{w} = \sum_{i=1}^{n}\sum_{t=1}^{T}(\mathbf{x}_{it} - \bar{\mathbf{x}}_{i.})(y_{it} - \bar{y}_{i.}).$$

Finally, for (14-10c), the mean of group means is the overall mean. The moment matrices are the **between-groups** sums of squares and cross products,

$$\mathbf{S}_{xx}^{b} = \sum_{i=1}^{n} T(\bar{\mathbf{x}}_{i.} - \bar{\bar{\mathbf{x}}})(\bar{\mathbf{x}}_{i.} - \bar{\bar{\mathbf{x}}})'$$

and

$$\mathbf{S}_{xy}^{b} = \sum_{i=1}^{n} T(\bar{\mathbf{x}}_{i.} - \bar{\bar{\mathbf{x}}})(\bar{y}_{i.} - \bar{\bar{\mathbf{y}}}).$$

It is easy to verify that

$$\mathbf{S}_{xx}^{t} = \mathbf{S}_{xx}^{w} + \mathbf{S}_{xx}^{b}$$

and

$$\mathbf{S}_{xy}^{t} = \mathbf{S}_{xy}^{w} + \mathbf{S}_{xy}^{b}.$$

There are, therefore, three possible least squares estimators of $\boldsymbol{\beta}$ corresponding to the decomposition. The least squares estimator is

$$\mathbf{b}^{t} = [\mathbf{S}_{xx}^{t}]^{-1}\mathbf{S}_{xy}^{t} = [\mathbf{S}_{xx}^{w} + \mathbf{S}_{xx}^{b}]^{-1}[\mathbf{S}_{xy}^{w} + \mathbf{S}_{xy}^{b}]. \qquad \textbf{(14-11)}$$

The **within-groups** estimator is

$$\mathbf{b}^{w} = [\mathbf{S}_{xx}^{w}]^{-1}\mathbf{S}_{xy}^{w}. \qquad \textbf{(14-12)}$$

This is the LSDV estimator computed earlier. [See (14-4).] An alternative estimator would be the **between-groups** estimator,

$$\mathbf{b}^{b} = [\mathbf{S}_{xx}^{b}]^{-1}\mathbf{S}_{xy}^{b} \qquad \textbf{(14-13)}$$

(sometimes called the **group means** estimator). This is the least squares estimator of (14-10c) based on the n sets of groups means. From the preceding expressions (and familiar previous results),

$$\mathbf{S}_{xy}^{w} = \mathbf{S}_{xx}^{w}\mathbf{b}^{w}$$

and

$$\mathbf{S}_{xy}^{b} = \mathbf{S}_{xx}^{b}\mathbf{b}^{b}.$$

Inserting these in (14-11), we see that the OLS estimator is a matrix weighted average of the within- and between-groups estimators:

$$\mathbf{b}^{t} = \mathbf{F}^{w}\mathbf{b}^{w} + \mathbf{F}^{b}\mathbf{b}^{b}, \tag{14-14}$$

where

$$\mathbf{F}^{w} = [\mathbf{S}_{xx}^{w} + \mathbf{S}_{xx}^{b}]^{-1}\mathbf{S}_{xx}^{w} = \mathbf{I} - \mathbf{F}^{b}.$$

EXAMPLE 14.3 Weighted Average of Within and Between Estimators

The OLS (total) estimator for the cost data is given in Example 14.1. The LSDV estimator in Example 14.2 is the within-groups estimator. For the six firms, the group means are as listed in Table 14.2.

The three estimators for the slope are

$$b^{t} = 0.887987,$$
$$b^{w} = 0.674279,$$
$$b^{b} = 0.911073.$$

The weighting for the two estimators can be derived from

$$b^{t} = mb^{w} + (1 - m)b^{b},$$

so

$$m = \frac{b^{t} - b^{b}}{b^{w} - b^{b}} = 0.09749.$$

TABLE 14.2 Firm Means

Firm	*ln Cost*	*ln Output*
1	1.47234	6.17826
2	1.88787	7.11813
3	3.35085	8.58816
4	3.99068	9.08403
5	3.75274	8.99269
6	4.76838	9.89485
Overall	3.20381	8.30935

(This approach only works for the case of one coefficient.) Most of the variation is between groups. The data were chosen to include wide variation in output across firms, so this is not surprising. The steady but undramatic growth of the firms that provides the within-groups variation is small compared to the differences across firms.

14.3.3. Fixed Time and Group Effects

The least squares dummy variable approach can be extended to include a time-specific effect as well. One way to formulate the extended model is simply to add the time effect, as in

$$y_{it} = \alpha_i + \gamma_t + \boldsymbol{\beta}'\mathbf{x}_{it} + \epsilon_{it}. \quad \textbf{(14-15)}$$

This model is obtained from the preceding one by the inclusion of an additional $T - 1$ dummy variables. One of the time effects must be dropped to avoid perfect collinearity. If the number of variables is too large to handle by ordinary regression, this can also be estimated by using the partitioned regression.[8] There is an asymmetry in this formulation, however, since each of the group effects is a group-specific intercept, whereas the time effects are **contrasts,** that is, comparisons to a base period (the one that is excluded). A symmetric form of the model is

$$y_{it} = \mu + \alpha_i + \gamma_t + \boldsymbol{\beta}'\mathbf{x}_{it} + \epsilon_{it}, \quad \textbf{(14-15')}$$

where a full n and T effects are included, but the restrictions

$$\sum_i \alpha_i = \sum_t \gamma_t = 0$$

are imposed. Least squares estimates of the slopes are obtained by regression of

$$y_{*it} = y_{it} - \bar{y}_{i.} - \bar{y}_{.t} + \bar{\bar{y}} \quad \textbf{(14-16)}$$

on

$$\mathbf{x}_{*it} = \mathbf{x}_{it} - \bar{\mathbf{x}}_{i.} - \bar{\mathbf{x}}_{.t} + \bar{\bar{\mathbf{x}}},$$

---

[8]The matrix algebra and the theoretical development of two-way effects in panel data models are quite complex. See, for example, Baltagi (1995). Fortunately, the practical application is much simpler. The number of periods analyzed in most panel data sets is rarely more than a handful. Since modern computer programs, even those written strictly for microcomputers, uniformly allow dozens (or even hundreds) of regressors, almost any application involving a second fixed effect can be handled just by literally including the second effect as a set of actual dummy variables.

where

$$\bar{y}_{.t} = \frac{1}{n}\sum_{i=1}^{n} y_{it},$$
$$\bar{\bar{y}} = \frac{1}{nT}\sum_{i=1}^{n}\sum_{t=1}^{T} y_{it},$$

and likewise for $\bar{\mathbf{x}}_{.t}$ and $\bar{\bar{\mathbf{x}}}$. The overall constant and the dummy variable coefficients can be recovered from the normal equations as

$$\begin{aligned} m &= \bar{\bar{y}} - \mathbf{b}'\bar{\bar{\mathbf{x}}}, \\ a_i &= (\bar{y}_{i.} - \bar{\bar{y}}) - \mathbf{b}'(\bar{\mathbf{x}}_{i.} - \bar{\bar{\mathbf{x}}}), \\ c_t &= (\bar{y}_{.t} - \bar{\bar{y}}) - \mathbf{b}'(\bar{\mathbf{x}}_{.t} - \bar{\bar{\mathbf{x}}}). \end{aligned} \tag{14-17}$$

The estimated covariance matrix for $\mathbf{b}$ is computed using the sums of squares and cross products of $\mathbf{x}*_{it}$ and s^2 computed as usual, $\mathbf{e}'\mathbf{e}/[nT - (n-1) - (T-1) - K - 1]$. If one of n or T is small and the other is large, it will usually be simpler just to treat the smaller set as an ordinary set of variables and apply the previous results to the one-way fixed effects model defined by the larger set. Although more general, this model is rarely used in practice. There are two reasons. First, the cost in terms of degrees of freedom is often not justified. Second, in those instances in which a model of the timewise evolution of the disturbance is desired, a more general model than the dummy variable formulation is usually used.

14.3.4. Unbalanced Panels and Fixed Effects

Missing data are very common in panel data sets. For this reason, or perhaps just because of the way the data were recorded, panels in which the group sizes differ across groups are not unusual. These are called **unbalanced panels.** The preceding analysis assumed equal group sizes and relied on the assumption at several points. A modification to allow unequal group sizes is quite simple.[9] First, the full sample size is $\Sigma_{i=1}^{n} T_i$ instead of nT. This calls for minor modifications in the computations of s^2, Var[$\mathbf{b}$], Var[a_i], and the F statistic. Second, group means must be based on T_i, which varies across groups. The overall means for the regressors are simply

$$\bar{\bar{\mathbf{x}}} = \frac{\sum_{i=1}^{n}\sum_{t=1}^{T_i}\mathbf{x}_{it}}{\sum_{i=1}^{n} T_i} = \frac{\sum_{i=1}^{n} T_i\bar{\mathbf{x}}_{i.}}{\sum_{i=1}^{n} T_i} = \sum_{i=1}^{n} w_i\bar{\mathbf{x}}_{i.},$$

[9]Since most modern econometrics computer packages fully automate the computation, this is presented in the interests of removing the veil over what sometimes appears to be a fairly arcane set of calculations.

where $w_i = T_i / \left(\sum_{i=1}^{n} T_i \right)$. If the group sizes are equal, $w_i = 1/n$. The moment matrix shown in (14-4),

$$\mathbf{S}_{xx}^{w} = \mathbf{X}'\mathbf{M}_d\mathbf{X}$$

is a sum of matrices of sums of squares and cross products, summed across the groups,

$$\sum_{i=1}^{n} \mathbf{X}_i'\mathbf{M}_i^0\mathbf{X}_i = \sum_{i=1}^{n} \left(\sum_{t=1}^{T_i} (\mathbf{x}_{it} - \bar{\mathbf{x}}_{i.})(\mathbf{x}_{it} - \bar{\mathbf{x}}_{i.})' \right).$$

This is called the **within-groups** sum of squares. The other moments, $\mathbf{S}_{xy}^{w}$ and $\mathbf{S}_{yy}^{w}$, are computed likewise. No other changes are necessary for the one factor LSDV estimator. The two-way model can be handled likewise, although with unequal group sizes in both directions, the algebra becomes fairly cumbersome. Once again, however, the practice is much simpler than the theory. The easiest approach for unbalanced panels is just to create the full set of T dummy variables using as T the union of the dates represented in the full data set. One (presumably the last) is dropped, so we revert back to (14-15). Then, within each group, any of the T periods represented is accounted for by using one of the dummy variables. Least squares using the LSDV approach for the group effects will then automatically take care of the messy accounting details.

14.4. RANDOM EFFECTS

The fixed effects model is a reasonable approach when we can be confident that the differences between units can be viewed as parametric shifts of the regression function. This model might be viewed as applying only to the cross-sectional units in the study, not to additional ones outside the sample. For example, an intercountry comparison may well include the full set of countries for which it is reasonable to assume that the model is constant. Likewise, in Greene's study cited earlier, the sample of 114 firms was nearly exhaustive of the investor-owned utilities in the United States. In other settings, it might be more appropriate to view individual specific constant terms as randomly distributed across cross-sectional units. This would be appropriate if we believed that sampled cross-sectional units were drawn from a large population. It would certainly be the case for the longitudinal data sets listed in the introduction to this chapter.[10]

Consider, then, a reformulation of the model

$$y_{it} = \alpha + \boldsymbol{\beta}'\mathbf{x}_{it} + u_i + \epsilon_{it}, \qquad \textbf{(14-18)}$$

where there are K regressors in addition to the constant term. The component u_i is the random disturbance characterizing the ith observation and is constant

[10] This is not a hard and fast distinction; it is purely heuristic. We shall return to this issue later.

through time. In the analysis of families, we can view them as the collection of factors not in the regression that are specific to that family. We assume further that

$$\begin{aligned} E[\epsilon_{it}] &= E[u_i] = 0, \\ E[\epsilon_{it}^2] &= \sigma_\epsilon^2, \\ E[u_i^2] &= \sigma_u^2, \\ E[\epsilon_{it}u_j] &= 0 \quad \text{for all } i, t, \text{ and } j, \\ E[\epsilon_{it}\epsilon_{js}] &= 0 \quad \text{if } t \neq s \text{ or } i \neq j, \\ E[u_iu_j] &= 0 \quad \text{if } i \neq j. \end{aligned} \tag{14-19}$$

As before, it is useful to view the formulation of the model in blocks of T observations for observations i, $\mathbf{y}_i$, $\mathbf{X}_i$, $u_i\mathbf{i}$, and $\boldsymbol{\epsilon}_i$. For these T observations, let

$$w_{it} = \epsilon_{it} + u_i$$

and

$$\mathbf{w}_i = [w_{i1}, w_{i2}, \ldots, w_{iT}]'.$$

Then

$$\begin{aligned} E[w_{it}^2] &= \sigma_\epsilon^2 + \sigma_u^2, \\ E[w_{it}w_{is}] &= \sigma_u^2, \; t \neq s. \end{aligned}$$

For the T observations for unit i, let $\boldsymbol{\Omega} = E[\mathbf{w}_i\mathbf{w}_i']$. Then

$$\boldsymbol{\Omega} = \begin{bmatrix} \sigma_\epsilon^2 + \sigma_u^2 & \sigma_u^2 & \sigma_u^2 & \cdots & \sigma_u^2 \\ \sigma_u^2 & \sigma_\epsilon^2 + \sigma_u^2 & \sigma_u^2 & \cdots & \sigma_u^2 \\ & & \vdots & & \\ \sigma_u^2 & \sigma_u^2 & \sigma_u^2 & & \sigma_\epsilon^2 + \sigma_u^2 \end{bmatrix} = \sigma_\epsilon^2\mathbf{I} + \sigma_u^2\mathbf{ii}', \tag{14-20}$$

where $\mathbf{i}$ is a $T \times 1$ column vector of 1s. Since observations i and j are independent, the disturbance covariance matrix for the full nT observations is

$$\mathbf{V} = \begin{bmatrix} \boldsymbol{\Omega} & \mathbf{0} & \mathbf{0} & \cdots & \mathbf{0} \\ \mathbf{0} & \boldsymbol{\Omega} & \mathbf{0} & \cdots & \mathbf{0} \\ & & & & \vdots \\ \mathbf{0} & \mathbf{0} & \mathbf{0} & \cdots & \boldsymbol{\Omega} \end{bmatrix}. \tag{14-21}$$

This matrix has a particularly simple structure.

14.4.1. Generalized Least Squares

For generalized least squares, we require $\mathbf{V}^{-1/2} = \mathbf{I} \otimes \boldsymbol{\Omega}^{-1/2}$. Therefore, we need only find $\boldsymbol{\Omega}^{-1/2}$, which is

$$\boldsymbol{\Omega}^{-1/2} = \mathbf{I} - \frac{\theta}{T}\mathbf{ii}',$$

where

$$\theta = 1 - \frac{\sigma_\epsilon}{\sqrt{T\sigma_u^2 + \sigma_\epsilon^2}}.$$

The transformation of $\mathbf{y}_i$ and $\mathbf{X}_i$ for GLS is therefore

$$\boldsymbol{\Omega}_i^{-1/2}\mathbf{y}_i = \begin{bmatrix} y_{i1} - \theta\bar{y}_{i.} \\ y_{i2} - \theta\bar{y}_{i.} \\ \vdots \\ y_{iT} - \theta\bar{y}_{i.} \end{bmatrix}, \tag{14-22}$$

and likewise for the rows of $\mathbf{X}_i$.[11] For the data set as a whole, generalized least squares is computed by the regression of these partial deviations of y_{it} on the same transformations of $\mathbf{x}_{it}$. Note the similarity of this procedure to the computation in the LSDV model, which has $\theta = 1$. (One could interpret θ as the effect that would remain if σ_ϵ were zero, as the only effect would then be u_i. In this case, the fixed and random effects models would be indistinguishable, so this result makes sense.)

It can be shown that the GLS estimator is, like the OLS estimator, a matrix weighted average of the within- and between-units estimators:

$$\hat{\boldsymbol{\beta}} = \hat{\mathbf{F}}^w\mathbf{b}^w + (\mathbf{I} - \hat{\mathbf{F}}^w)\mathbf{b}^b,\text{[12]} \tag{14-23}$$

where

$$\hat{\mathbf{F}}^w = [\mathbf{S}_{xx}^w + \lambda\mathbf{S}_{xx}^b]^{-1}\mathbf{S}_{xx}^w,$$

$$\lambda = \frac{\sigma_\epsilon^2}{\sigma_\epsilon^2 + T\sigma_u^2} = (1 - \theta)^2.$$

To the extent that λ differs from one, we see that the inefficiency of least squares will follow from an inefficient weighting of the two least squares estimators. Compared with generalized least squares, ordinary least squares places too much weight on the between-units variation. It includes it all in the variation in $\mathbf{X}$, rather than apportioning some of it to random variation across groups attributable to the variation in u_i across units.

There are some polar cases to consider. If λ equals 1, generalized least squares is ordinary least squares. This would occur if σ_u^2 were zero, in which case a classical regression model would apply. If λ equals zero, the estimator is the dummy variable estimator we used in the fixed effects setting. There are two possibilities. If σ_ϵ^2 were zero, all variation across units would be due to the different u_i's, which, because they are constant across time, would be equivalent to the dummy variables we used in the fixed-effects model. The question of

[11]This is a special case of the more general model treated in Nerlove (1971b).

[12]An alternative form of this expression, in which the weighing matrices are proportional to the covariance matrices of the two estimators, is given by Judge et al. (1985).

whether they were fixed or random would then become moot. They are the only source of variation across units once the regression is accounted for. The other case is $T \to \infty$. We can view it this way: If $T \to \infty$, the unobserved u_i becomes observable. Take the T observations for the ith unit. Our estimator of $[\alpha, \boldsymbol{\beta}]$ is consistent in the dimensions T or n. Therefore,

$$y_{it} - \alpha - \boldsymbol{\beta}'\mathbf{x}_{it} = u_i - \epsilon_{it}$$

is observable. The individual means will provide

$$\bar{y}_{i.} - \alpha - \boldsymbol{\beta}'\bar{\mathbf{x}}_{i.} = u_i + \bar{\epsilon}_{i.}.$$

But $\bar{\epsilon}_{i.}$ converges to zero, which reveals u_i to us. Therefore, if T goes to infinity, u_i becomes the d_i we used earlier. (That it is not 1 is immaterial; it is nonzero only for unit i.)

14.4.2. Feasible Generalized Least Squares When Ω Is Unknown

If the variance components are known, generalized least squares can be computed without much difficulty. Of course, this is not likely, so as usual, we must first estimate the disturbance variances and then use an FGLS procedure. A heuristic approach to estimation of the components is as follows:

$$y_{it} = \alpha + \boldsymbol{\beta}'\mathbf{x}_{it} + \epsilon_{it} + u_i$$

and

$$\bar{y}_{i.} = \alpha + \boldsymbol{\beta}'\bar{\mathbf{x}}_{i.} + \bar{\epsilon}_{i.} + u_i. \tag{14-24}$$

Therefore, taking deviations from the group means removes the heterogeneity:

$$y_{it} - \bar{y}_{i.} = \boldsymbol{\beta}'[\mathbf{x}_{it} - \bar{\mathbf{x}}_{i.}] + [\epsilon_{it} - \bar{\epsilon}_{i.}]. \tag{14-25}$$

Since

$$E\left[\sum_{t=1}^{T}(\epsilon_{it} - \bar{\epsilon}_{i.})^2\right] = (T-1)\sigma_\epsilon^2,$$

if $\boldsymbol{\beta}$ were observed, an unbiased estimator of σ_ϵ^2 based on T observations in group i would be

$$\hat{\sigma}_\epsilon^2(i) = \frac{\sum_{t=1}^{T}(\epsilon_{it} - \bar{\epsilon}_{i.})^2}{T-1}. \tag{14-26}$$

Since $\boldsymbol{\beta}$ must be estimated—we use the LSDV estimator in (14-4)—we make the usual degrees of freedom correction and use

$$s_e^2(i) = \frac{\sum_{t=1}^{T}(e_{it} - \bar{e}_{i.})^2}{T-K-1}. \tag{14-27}$$

We have n such estimators, so we average them to obtain

$$\begin{aligned}\bar{s}_e^2 &= \frac{1}{n}\sum_{i=1}^{n} s_e^2(i)\\ &= \frac{1}{n}\sum_{i=1}^{n}\left[\frac{\sum_{t=1}^{T}(e_{it}-\bar{e}_{i.})^2}{T-K-1}\right]\\ &= \frac{\sum_{i=1}^{n}\sum_{t=1}^{T}(e_{it}-\bar{e}_{i.})^2}{nT-nK-n}.\end{aligned} \tag{14-28}$$

The degrees of freedom correction in $\bar{s}_e^2$ is excessive because it assumes that α and $\boldsymbol{\beta}$ are reestimated for each i. The estimated parameters are the n means $\bar{y}_{i.}$ and the K slopes. Therefore, we propose the unbiased estimator[13]

$$\hat{\sigma}_\epsilon^2 = \frac{\sum_{i=1}^{n}\sum_{t=1}^{T}(e_{it}-\bar{e}_{i.})^2}{nT-n-K}. \tag{14-29}$$

This is the variance estimator in the LSDV model in (14-8), appropriately corrected for degrees of freedom. The n means,

$$\begin{aligned}\epsilon_{**i} &= \bar{y}_{i.} - \alpha - \boldsymbol{\beta}'\bar{\mathbf{x}}_{i.}\\ &= \bar{\epsilon}_{i.} + u_i,\end{aligned} \tag{14-30}$$

are independent and have variance

$$\text{Var}[\epsilon_{**i}] = \sigma_{**}^2 = \frac{\sigma_\epsilon^2}{T} + \sigma_u^2.$$

By incorporating the degrees of freedom correction for the estimate of $\boldsymbol{\beta}$ in the group means least squares regression of (14-24), we can use

$$\hat{\sigma}_{**}^2 = \frac{\mathbf{e}_{**}'\mathbf{e}_{**}}{n-K} = m_{**} \tag{14-31}$$

as an unbiased estimator of $\sigma_\epsilon^2/T + \sigma_u^2$. This suggests the estimator

$$\hat{\sigma}_u^2 = \hat{\sigma}_{**}^2 - \frac{\hat{\sigma}_\epsilon^2}{T}. \tag{14-32}$$

The estimator in (14-32) is unbiased but could be negative in a finite sample. Alternative estimators have been proposed.[14] Since we only require

[13]A formal proof of this proposition may be found in Maddala (1971) or in Judge et al. (1985, p. 551).

[14]See, for example, Wallace and Hussain (1969), Maddala (1971), Fuller and Battese (1974), and Amemiya (1971).

a consistent estimator of σ_u^2, *any* consistent estimate of $\boldsymbol{\beta}$ could be used in (14-31), including the original pooled OLS estimator. Such a finding might cast some doubt on the appropriateness of the model, however, and before proceeding in this fashion, one might do well to reconsider the random effects specification.

There is a remaining complication. If there are any regressors that do not vary within the groups, the LSDV estimator cannot be computed. For example, in a model of family income or labor supply, one of the regressors might be a dummy variable for location, family structure, or living arrangement. Any of these could be perfectly collinear with the fixed effect for that family, which would prevent computation of the LSDV estimator. In this case, it is still possible to estimate the random effects variance components. Once again, let $[a, \mathbf{b}]$ be any consistent estimator of $[\alpha, \boldsymbol{\beta}]$, such as the ordinary least squares estimator. Then, using all nT residuals, $m_{ee} = \mathbf{e}'\mathbf{e}/(nT)$ has

$$\text{plim}\,\frac{\mathbf{e}'\mathbf{e}}{nT} = \sigma_\epsilon^2 + \sigma_u^2.$$

Now, using the n group means, (14-31) is still usable for estimation. This provides two moment equations in the two unknown variance terms,

$$m_{**} = \frac{\sigma_\epsilon^2}{T} + \sigma_u^2,$$
$$m_{ee} = \sigma_\epsilon^2 + \sigma_u^2,$$

which have solutions

$$\hat{\sigma}_\epsilon^2 = \frac{T}{T-1}(m_{ee} - m_{**})$$
$$\hat{\sigma}_u^2 = \frac{T}{T-1}m_{**} - \frac{1}{T-1}m_{ee} = \omega m_{**} + (1-\omega)m_{ee},$$

where $\omega > 1$. As before, this can produce a negative estimate of σ_u^2 that, once again, calls the specification of the model into question.

14.4.3. Testing for Random Effects

Breusch and Pagan (1980) have devised a Lagrange multiplier test for the random effects model based on the OLS residuals. For

$$H_0\colon \sigma_u^2 = 0 \qquad (\text{or } \operatorname{Corr}[w_{it}, w_{is}] = 0),$$
$$H_1\colon \sigma_u^2 \neq 0,$$

the test statistic is

$$\text{LM} = \frac{nT}{2(T-1)}\left[\frac{\sum_{i=1}^{n}\left[\sum_{t=1}^{T} e_{it}\right]^2}{\sum_{i=1}^{n}\sum_{t=1}^{T} e_{it}^2} - 1\right]^2$$

$$= \frac{nT}{2(T-1)}\left[\frac{\sum_{i=1}^{n}(T\bar{e}_{i.})^2}{\sum_{i=1}^{n}\sum_{t=1}^{T} e_{it}^2} - 1\right]^2. \qquad \text{(14-33)}$$

Under the null hypothesis, LM is distributed as chi-squared with one degree of freedom. A useful shortcut for computing LM is as follows. Let **D** be the matrix of dummy variables defined in (14-2), and let **e** be the OLS residual vector. Then

$$\text{LM} = \frac{nT}{2(T-1)}\left[\frac{\mathbf{e}'\mathbf{D}\mathbf{D}'\mathbf{e}}{\mathbf{e}'\mathbf{e}} - 1\right]^2. \qquad \text{(14-34)}$$

EXAMPLE 14.4 Testing for Random Effects

The least squares estimates for the cost data were given in Example 14.1. Based on the OLS residuals, we obtain a Lagrange multiplier test statistic of

$$\frac{6(4)}{2(4-1)}\left[\frac{2.24522}{1.01520} - 1\right]^2 = 5.87185.$$

The 5 percent and 1 percent critical values from the chi-squared distribution with one degree of freedom are 3.842 and 6.635, so the statistic is significant at the 5 percent level of significance but not at the 1 percent level. The evidence in favor of the error components model is present, but not compelling. Once again, given the way the data were selected (not randomly) by the author, this result is not surprising.

With the variance estimators in hand, FGLS can be used to estimate the parameters of the model. All our earlier results for FGLS estimators apply here. It would also be possible to obtain the maximum likelihood estimator.[15] The likelihood function is complicated, but as we have seen repeatedly, the MLE of $\boldsymbol{\beta}$ will be GLS based on the maximum likelihood estimators of the variance components. It can be shown that the MLEs of σ_ϵ^2 and σ_u^2 are the unbiased estimators shown earlier, *without* their degrees of freedom corrections.[16] This model satisfies the requirements for the Oberhofer–Kmenta algorithm, so we could also use the iterated FGLS procedure to obtain the MLEs if desired.

[15]See Hsiao (1986).

[16]See Berzeg (1979).

The initial consistent estimates could be based on least squares residuals. Still other estimators have been proposed. None will have better asymptotic properties than the MLE or FGLS estimators, but they may outperform them in a finite sample.[17]

EXAMPLE 14.5 FGLS Estimation of a Random Effects Model

To compute the FGLS estimator, we require estimates of the variance components. As noted earlier, the unbiased estimator of σ_ϵ^2 is the residual variance estimator in the within-units (LSDV) regression. Thus,

$$\hat{\sigma}_\epsilon^2 = \frac{0.264062}{17} = 0.015531.$$

The group means are given in Example 14.3. The residual sum of squares in the group means regression is 0.135202, so

$$\widehat{\frac{\sigma_\epsilon^2}{T} + \sigma_u^2} = \frac{0.13502}{4} = 0.033801.$$

Therefore,

$$\hat{\sigma}_u^2 = 0.033801 - \frac{0.015531}{4} = 0.0299178.$$

For purposes of FGLS,

$$\hat{\theta} = 1 - \left[\frac{0.015531}{4(0.033801)}\right]^{1/2} = 0.661074.$$

Finally, the FGLS regression produces

$$\ln C_{it} - \hat{\theta}\,\overline{\ln C_{i.}} = \underset{(0.3615)}{-3.41310} + \underset{(0.04256)}{0.796321}\,(\ln Y_{it} - \hat{\theta}\,\overline{\ln Y_{i.}}).$$

It is instructive to compare these with the OLS results we obtained earlier:

$$\ln C = \underset{(0.2769)}{-4.17478} + \underset{(0.0329)}{0.887987}\ln Y.$$

The FGLS constant term is an estimate of $\alpha(1 - \theta)$, so the implied estimate of the constant term would be -10.0703.[18] Recall that we derived the implicit weighing between the within- and between-units estimators for OLS:

$$0.887987 = 0.09749b^w + 0.90251b^b,$$

---

[17]See Maddala and Mount (1973).

[18]The estimate of θ is a function of two moments of the residuals. The constant in the regression is also a sample moment. Therefore, the results of Section 4.7.2 could be used to estimate the standard error of $a/(1 - \hat{\theta})$.

where

$$b^w = 0.674279$$

and

$$b^b = 0.911073.$$

To do likewise for the FGLS estimator, we require the decomposition of the variance of ln Y, which is

$$S^t_{xx} = 42.63166,$$
$$S^b_{xx} = 38.54754,$$
$$S^w_{xx} = 4.15626$$

The weighting to be used would be

$$w_{\text{GLS}} = \frac{S^w_{xx}}{S^w_{xx} + (1 - \hat{\theta})^2 S^b_{xx}} = 0.4846.$$

Therefore, for the FGLS estimator,

$$0.796321 = 0.4846b^w + 0.5154b^b.$$

As expected, the weight attached to the between groups estimator is lower when we use FGLS.

None of the desirable properties of the estimators in the random effects model relies on T going to infinity.[19] Indeed, T is likely to be quite small. The maximum likelihood estimator of σ^2_ϵ is exactly equal to an average of n estimators, each based on the T observations for unit i. [See (14-28).] Each component in this average is, in principle, consistent. That is, its variance is of order $1/T$ or smaller. Since T is small, this may be relatively large; each term provides some information about the parameter, however. The average over the n cross-sectional units has a variance of order $1/(nT)$, which will go to zero if n increases, even if we regard T as fixed. The conclusion to draw is that nothing in this treatment relies on T growing large. Although it can be shown that some consistency results will follow for T increasing, the typical panel data set is based on data sets for which it does not make sense to assume that T increases without bound or, in some cases, at all.[20] As a general proposition, it is necessary to take some care in devising estimators whose properties hinge on whether T is large or not. The widely used conventional ones we have discussed here do not, but we have not exhausted the possibilities.

The LSDV model *does* rely on T increasing for consistency. To see this, we use the partitioned regression. The slopes are

$$\mathbf{b} = [\mathbf{X}'\mathbf{M}_d\mathbf{X}]^{-1}[\mathbf{X}'\mathbf{M}_d\mathbf{y}].$$

---

[19]See Nickell (1981).

[20]In this connection, Chamberlain (1983) has provided some innovative treatments of panel data that, in fact, take T as given in the model and that base consistency results solely on n increasing. Some additional results for dynamic models are given by Bhargava and Sargan (1983).

Since $\mathbf{X}$ is $nT \times K$, as long as the inverted moment matrix converges to a zero matrix, $\mathbf{b}$ is consistent as long as either n or T increases without bound. But the dummy variable coefficients are

$$\begin{aligned} a_i &= \bar{y}_{i.} - \mathbf{b}'\bar{\mathbf{x}}_{i.} \\ &= \frac{1}{T}\sum_{t=1}^{T} e_{it}. \end{aligned}$$

We have already seen that $\mathbf{b}$ is consistent. Suppose, for the present, that $\bar{\mathbf{x}}_{i.} = 0$. Then $\text{Var}[a_i] = \text{Var}[y_{it}]/T$. Therefore, unless $T \rightarrow \infty$, the estimates of the unit-specific effects are not consistent. (They are, however, best linear unbiased.) This is worth bearing in mind when analyzing data sets for which T is fixed and there is no intention to replicate the study, and no logical argument that would justify the claim that it could have been replicated in principle.

The random effects model was developed by Balestra and Nerlove (1966). Their formulation included a time-specific component as well as the individual effect:

$$y_{it} = \alpha + \boldsymbol{\beta}'\mathbf{x}_{it} + \epsilon_{it} + u_i + v_t.$$

The extended formulation is rather complicated analytically. In Balestra and Nerlove's study, it was made even more so by the presence of a lagged dependent variable that causes all the problems discussed earlier in our discussion of autocorrelation. A full set of results for this extended model, including a method for handling the lagged dependent variable, has been developed.[21] The full model is rarely used, however. Most studies limit the model to the individual effects and, if needed, model the time effects in some other fashion.[22]

14.4.4. Hausman's Test for Fixed or Random Effects

At various points, we have made the distinction between fixed and random effects models. An inevitable question is: Which should be used? It has been suggested that the distinction between fixed and random effects models is an erroneous interpretation. Mundlak (1978) argues that we should always treat the individual effects as random. The fixed effects model is simply analyzed conditionally on the effects present in the observed sample. One can argue that certain institutional factors or characteristics of the data argue for one or the other, but unfortunately, this approach does not always provide much guidance. From a purely practical standpoint, the dummy variable approach is costly in terms of degrees of freedom lost, and in a wide, longitudinal data set, the random effects model has some intuitive appeal. On the other hand, the fixed effects approach has one considerable virtue. There is no justification for treating

[21]See Balestra and Nerlove (1966), Fomby et al. (1984), Judge et al. (1985), Hsiao (1986), Anderson and Hsiao (1982), Nerlove (1971a), and Baltagi (1995).

[22]See Macurdy (1982) and Beggs (1986).

the individual effects as uncorrelated with the other regressors, as is assumed in the random effects model. The random effects treatment, therefore, may suffer from the inconsistency due to omitted variables.[23]

It is possible to test for orthogonality of the random effects and the regressors. The specification test devised by Hausman (1978)[24] has the same format as that for the errors in variables model discussed in Section 9.5.5. It is based on the idea that under the hypothesis of no correlation, both OLS in the LSDV model and GLS are consistent, but OLS is inefficient,[25] whereas under the alternative, OLS is consistent, but GLS is not. Therefore, under the null hypothesis, the two estimates should not differ systematically, and a test can be based on the difference. The other essential ingredient for the test is the covariance matrix of the difference vector, $[\mathbf{b} - \hat{\boldsymbol{\beta}}]$:

$$\text{Var}[\mathbf{b} - \hat{\boldsymbol{\beta}}] = \text{Var}[\mathbf{b}] + \text{Var}[\hat{\boldsymbol{\beta}}] - \text{Cov}[\mathbf{b}, \hat{\boldsymbol{\beta}}] - \text{Cov}[\mathbf{b}, \hat{\boldsymbol{\beta}}]'. \qquad \textbf{(14-35)}$$

Hausman's essential result is that *the covariance of an efficient estimator with its difference from an inefficient estimator is zero.* This implies that

$$\text{Cov}[(\mathbf{b} - \hat{\boldsymbol{\beta}}), \hat{\boldsymbol{\beta}}] = \text{Cov}[\mathbf{b}, \hat{\boldsymbol{\beta}}] - \text{Var}[\hat{\boldsymbol{\beta}}] = \mathbf{0}$$

or that

$$\text{Cov}[\mathbf{b}, \hat{\boldsymbol{\beta}}] = \text{Var}[\hat{\boldsymbol{\beta}}].$$

Inserting this in (14-35) produces the required covariance matrix for the test,

$$\text{Var}[\mathbf{b} - \hat{\boldsymbol{\beta}}] = \text{Var}[\mathbf{b}] - \text{Var}[\hat{\boldsymbol{\beta}}] = \boldsymbol{\Sigma}. \qquad \textbf{(14-36)}$$

The chi-squared test is based on the Wald criterion:

$$W = \chi^2[K] = [\mathbf{b} - \hat{\boldsymbol{\beta}}]'\hat{\boldsymbol{\Sigma}}^{-1}[\mathbf{b} - \hat{\boldsymbol{\beta}}]. \qquad \textbf{(14-37)}$$

For $\hat{\boldsymbol{\Sigma}}$, we use the estimated covariance matrices of the slope estimator in the LSDV model and the estimated covariance matrix in the random effects model, excluding the constant term. Under the null hypothesis, W is asymptotically distributed as chi-squared with K degrees of freedom.

EXAMPLE 14.6 Hausman Test

For the cost function example, the test is based on a single coefficient, so it simplifies to

$$W = \frac{(b - \hat{\beta})^2}{\text{Var}[b] - \text{Var}[\hat{\beta}]},$$

which is asymptotically distributed as chi-squared with one degree of freedom. Alternatively, the square root of this statistic may be referred to the standard normal table.

---

[23]See Hausman and Taylor (1981) and Chamberlain (1978).

[24]Related results are given by Baltagi (1986).

[25]Referring to the GLS matrix weighted average given earlier, we see that the efficient weight uses θ, whereas OLS sets $\theta = 1$.

From Examples 14.2 and 14.5, we have

$$W = \frac{(0.674279 - 0.796321)^2}{0.06113^2 - 0.04256^2} = 7.735.$$

The hypothesis that the individual effects are uncorrelated with log Y should be rejected.

14.4.5. Unbalanced Panels and Random Effects

Unbalanced panels add a new layer of difficulty in the random effects model. The first problem can be seen in (14-21). The matrix $\mathbf{V}$ is no longer $\mathbf{I} \otimes \boldsymbol{\Omega}$ because the diagonal blocks in $\mathbf{V}$ are of different sizes. There is also groupwise heteroscedasticity, because the ith diagonal block in $\mathbf{V}^{-1/2}$ is

$$\boldsymbol{\Omega}_i^{-1/2} = \mathbf{I}_{T_i} - \frac{\theta_i}{T_i}\mathbf{ii}',$$

$$\theta_i = 1 - \frac{\sigma_\epsilon}{\sqrt{T_i\sigma_u^2 + \sigma_\epsilon^2}}.$$

In principle, estimation is still straightforward, since the source of the groupwise heteroscedasticity is only the unequal group sizes. Thus, for GLS, or FGLS with estimated variance components, it is necessary only to use the group specific θ_i in the transformation in (14-22).

The problem arises in the estimation of the variance components. The LSDV estimator (properly computed) still provides a consistent estimator of σ_ϵ^2. But we need a second equation to estimate σ_u^2. We used the group means estimator for this in (14-30). In the group means regression (14-30), the disturbances are now heteroscedastic:

$$\text{Var}\left[u_i + \frac{\sum_{t=1}^{T_i} \epsilon_{it}}{T_i}\right] = \sigma_u^2 + \frac{\sigma_\epsilon^2}{T_i} = \kappa_i^2.$$

The unbiasedness result for estimating the variance in this regression no longer holds. The OLS slope estimator for the full sample is still unbiased, however. And, we have seen a similar case in Section 12.2.2. The disturbance variance estimator in a heteroscedastic regression is a consistent estimator of

$$\overline{\kappa}^2 = \text{plim}\,\frac{1}{n}\sum_{i=1}^{n} \kappa_i^2,$$

assuming that the probability limit exists. In fact, the mean squared residual using group means is a consistent estimator of $\overline{\kappa}^2$ based on *any* consistent estimator of $\boldsymbol{\beta}$. Now, in this setting, consistency still applies to n increasing, not T_i. Therefore, the variance estimator in the group means regression is a consistent estimator of

$$\overline{\kappa}^2 = \sigma_u^2 + \sigma_\epsilon^2 \operatorname{plim} \frac{1}{n} \sum_{i=1}^{n} \frac{1}{T_i}$$
$$= \sigma_u^2 + \sigma_\epsilon^2 \operatorname{plim} Q_n,$$

assuming that Q_n has a probability limit (or an ordinary limit). It appears that some assumption about the group sizes is necessary. If T_i were randomly distributed across individuals around a mean of T, then plim $Q_n = 1/T$ (of course). This may be a realistic assumption, but if not, to claim consistency of the variance components, some characterization of the sequence $\{T_i\}$ is needed. If we assume only that the probability limit exists and that we are estimating it consistently, then the feasible counterpart to (14-31) and (14-32) would be

$$\hat{\sigma}_{**}^2 = \frac{\mathbf{e}_{**}'\mathbf{e}_{**}}{n - K},$$
$$\hat{\sigma}_u^2 = \hat{\sigma}_{**}^2 - \hat{\sigma}_\epsilon^2 Q_n.$$

We can now continue with FGLS estimation.

14.5. HETEROSCEDASTICITY AND ROBUST COVARIANCE ESTIMATION

Since the models considered here are extensions of the classical regression model, we can treat heteroscedasticity in the same way that we did in Chapter 12. That is, we can compute the ordinary or feasible generalized least squares estimators and obtain an appropriate robust covariance matrix estimator, or we can impose some structure on the disturbance variances and use generalized least squares. In the panel data settings, there is greater flexibility for the second of these without making strong assumptions about the nature of the heteroscedasticity. We will discuss this model under the heading of "covariance structures" in Section 15.2. In this section, we will consider robust estimation of the asymptotic covariance matrix for least squares.

14.5.1. Robust Estimation of the Fixed Effects Model

In the fixed effects model, the full regressor matrix is $\mathbf{Z} = [\mathbf{D}, \mathbf{X}]$. The White heteroscedasticity consistent covariance matrix for OLS—that is, for the fixed effects estimator—is the lower right block of the partitioned matrix

$$\text{Est. Var}[\mathbf{a}, \mathbf{b}] = (\mathbf{Z}'\mathbf{Z})^{-1}\mathbf{Z}'\mathbf{E}^2\mathbf{Z}(\mathbf{Z}'\mathbf{Z})^{-1},$$

where $\mathbf{E}$ is a diagonal matrix of least squares (fixed effects estimator) residuals. This promises to be a formidable computation, but fortunately, it works out very simply. The White estimator for the slopes is obtained just by using the data in group mean deviation form [see (14-4) and (14-8)] in the familiar computation of $\mathbf{S}_0$ [see (12-7) to (12-9)]. Also, the disturbance variance estimator in (14-8) is the counterpart to the one in (12-3), which we showed that after the appropriate scaling of $\mathbf{\Omega}$ was a consistent estimator of $\sigma^2 = \text{plim}[1/(nT)] \sum_{i=1}^{n} \sum_{t=1}^{T} \sigma_{it}^2$. The implication is that we may still use (14-8) to estimate the variances of the fixed effects.

Arellano (1987) has taken this a step further. If one takes the ith group as a whole, we can treat the observations in

$$\mathbf{y}_i = \alpha_i + \mathbf{X}_i\boldsymbol{\beta} + \boldsymbol{\epsilon}_i$$

as a generalized regression model with disturbance covariance matrix $\mathbf{\Omega}_i$. We saw earlier in Section 11.4 that a model this general, with no structure on $\mathbf{\Omega}$, offered little hope for estimation, robust or otherwise. But the problem is more manageable with a panel data set. As before, let $\mathbf{X}_{i*}$ denote the data in group mean deviation form. The counterpart to $\mathbf{X}'\mathbf{\Omega}\mathbf{X}$ here is

$$\mathbf{X}_*'\mathbf{\Omega}\mathbf{X}_* = \sum_{i=1}^{n} (\mathbf{X}_{i*}'\mathbf{\Omega}_i\mathbf{X}_{i*}).$$

By the same reasoning that we used to construct the White estimator in Chapter 12, we can consider estimating $\mathbf{\Omega}_i$ with the sample of one, $\mathbf{e}_i\mathbf{e}_i'$. As before, it is not consistent estimation of the individual $\mathbf{\Omega}_i$'s that is at issue, but estimation of the sum. If n is large enough, then, we could argue that

$$\begin{aligned}\text{plim}\frac{1}{nT}\mathbf{X}_*'\mathbf{\Omega}\mathbf{X}_* &= \text{plim}\frac{1}{nT}\sum_{i=1}^{n}\mathbf{X}_{i*}'\mathbf{\Omega}\mathbf{X}_{*i}\\ &= \text{plim}\frac{1}{n}\sum_{i=1}^{n}\frac{1}{T}\mathbf{X}_{*i}'\mathbf{e}_i\mathbf{e}_i'\mathbf{X}_{*i}\\ &= \text{plim}\frac{1}{n}\sum_{i=1}^{n}\left(\frac{1}{T}\sum_{t=1}^{T}\sum_{s=1}^{T} e_{it}e_{is}\mathbf{x}_{*it}\mathbf{x}_{*is}'\right).\end{aligned}$$

The result is a combination of the White and Newey–West estimators. But the weights in the latter are 1 rather than $[1 - l/(L + 1)]$. The reason is that there is no correlation across the groups, so the sum is actually just an average of finite matrices.

14.5.2. Heteroscedasticity in the Random Effects Model

Since the random effects model is a generalized regression model with a known structure, robust estimation of the covariance matrix for the OLS estimator in this context is not the best use of the data. If a perfectly general covariance structure is assumed, one can simply use the results in the preceding section with a single overall constant term rather than a set of fixed effects. But within the setting of the random effects model, $v_{it} = \epsilon_{it} + u_i$, allowing the disturbance variance of the group-specific component u_i to vary across groups would be a useful extension. For estimation, we can use the following strategy. In Section 14.4.4, we introduced heteroscedasticity into estimation of the random effects model by allowing the group sizes to vary. But the estimator there (and its feasible counterpart in the next section) would be the same if, instead of $\theta_i = 1 - \sigma_\epsilon/(T_i\sigma_u^2 + \sigma_\epsilon^2)^{1/2}$, we were faced with

$$\theta_i = 1 - \frac{\sigma_\epsilon}{\sqrt{T\sigma_{ui}^2 + \sigma_\epsilon^2}}$$

or even if both T and σ_u^2 varied across groups. Therefore, for computing the appropriate feasible generalized least squares estimator, once again we need only devise an estimator for the variance components and then apply the GLS transformation shown earlier. If

$$\text{Var}[v_{it}] = \sigma_\epsilon^2 + \sigma_{ui}^2,$$

then in (14-29), s^2, the residual variance in the LSDV model, still provides a consistent estimator of σ_ϵ^2. Within each group, we can estimate $\sigma_\epsilon^2 + \sigma_{ui}^2$ with the residual variance based on any consistent estimator of $[\alpha, \boldsymbol{\beta}]$. The ordinary least squares estimator is a natural candidate, so

$$\widehat{\sigma_{ui}^2 + \sigma_\epsilon^2} = \frac{\sum_{t=1}^{T}(e_{it} - \bar{e}_{i.})^2}{T - 1} = s_{i.}^2.$$

Thereafter, an estimator of σ_{ui}^2 is

$$\hat{\sigma}_{ui}^2 = s^2 - s_{i.}^2.$$

We can now compute the FGLS estimator as before.

There is a complication in this method that is likely to be quite common. Nothing in this prescription prevents the variance estimator from being negative. Since T (or T_i) is likely to be quite small, although the full sample is likely to be large, there will be a large amount of sampling variability in $s_{i.}^2$ that is averaged out (over n) of s^2, so the difference is likely to be negative in some applications. Various patches have been suggested for this case. An expedient suggested by Baltagi (see his page 79, Table 5.1) is simply to replace negative values with zeros. This will imply that $\theta_i = 0$, so in the computation of the FGLS estimates, the data for this group will enter the sum of squares or cross products untransformed.

EXAMPLE 14.7 Heteroscedasticity Consistent Estimation

Table 14.3 lists the OLS and fixed effects estimators for the cost equation we have been fitting in this chapter. (These are also reported in Example 14.2.) After inclusion of the fixed effects, the White correction leads to a fairly sizable change in the estimated standard errors of the slopes. Based on the F test—$F[5, 19] = 9.671$—we would strongly reject the hypothesis that the effects are all zero. The critical value is 2.74. The Lagrange multiplier statistic suggests the opposite conclusion, however. LM = 5.87 whereas the critical value with 4 degrees of freedom is 11.14. The Hausman test is consistent with this. The value is 7.73 with a critical value of 3.84. The conclusion would be that the fixed and

TABLE 14.3 Cost Equation Estimates

	α	β
OLS, no effects, $R^2 = 0.97069$, $s^2 = 0.21482^2$		
Estimate	−4.1748	0.88796
Standard Error	0.27689	0.032900
White Standard Error	0.41344	0.046689
Fixed effects model, $R^2 = 0.99238$, $s^2 = 0.12463^2$		
Estimate	—	0.67428
Standard Error	—	0.061131
White Standard Error	—	0.071337
Random effects model, $s_u^2 = 0.24566^2$, $s_\epsilon^2 = 0.13848^2$		
Estimate	−60.291	0.10489
Standard Error	54.167	0.01471

random effects estimators are significantly different. The conclusion seems to be that the fixed effects estimator is preferred both to the random effects estimator and to a model with no effects.

The estimator of σ_ϵ^2 from the LSDV estimator is $s^2 = 0.12467^2$. The two variance components based on the random effects model are $\hat{\sigma}_\epsilon^2 = 0.13848^2$ and $\hat{\sigma}_u^2 = 0.24566^2$. This suggests that adding the fixed effects to the model is reducing the amount of residual variation substantially. The six estimators of the group specific variances $\hat{\sigma}_{ui}^2 + \hat{\sigma}_\epsilon^2$ are $[0.3296^2, 0.1361^2, 0.0822^2, 0.0503^2, 0.0818^2, 0.0899^2]$. Thus, the estimator of σ_{ui}^2 is negative in four of six cases. This is fairly convincing evidence that this heteroscedastic model is not a good specification for the disturbance variance in these data. Of course, estimating a variance parameter with three observations does stretch the notion of asymptotic convergence a bit.

14.6. AUTOCORRELATION

Autocorrelation in the fixed effects model is a minor extension of the model of the preceding chapter. With the LSDV estimator in hand, estimates of the parameters of a disturbance process, and transformations of the data to allow FGLS estimation proceed exactly as before. The extension one might consider is to allow the autocorrelation coefficient(s) to vary across groups. But even if so, treating each group of observations as a sample in itself provides the appropriate framework for estimation.

In the random effects model, as before, there are additional complications. The regression model is

$$y_{it} = \alpha + \boldsymbol{\beta}'\mathbf{x}_{it} + \epsilon_{it} + u_i.$$

If ϵ_{it} is produced by an AR(1) process, $\epsilon_{it} = \rho\epsilon_{i,\,t-1} + v_{it}$, then the familiar partial differencing procedure we used before would produce[26]

$$\begin{aligned} y_{it} - \rho y_{i,t-1} &= \alpha(1-\rho) + \boldsymbol{\beta}'(\mathbf{x}_{it} - \rho\mathbf{x}_{i,t-1}) + \epsilon_{it} - \rho\epsilon_{i,t-1} + u_i(1-\rho) \\ &= \alpha(1-\rho) + \boldsymbol{\beta}'(\mathbf{x}_{it} - \rho\mathbf{x}_{i,t-1}) + v_{it} + u_i(1-\rho) \\ &= \alpha(1-\rho) + \boldsymbol{\beta}'(\mathbf{x}_{it} - \rho\mathbf{x}_{i,t-1}) + v_{it} + w_i. \end{aligned}$$

Therefore, if an estimator of ρ were in hand, one could at least treat partially differenced observations $2 - T$ in each group as the same random effects model that we just examined. Variance estimators would have to be adjusted by a factor of $(1-\rho)^2$. Two issues remain: (1) how is the estimate of ρ obtained? and (2) how does one treat the first observation? For the first of these, the first autocorrelation coefficient of the LSDV residuals (so as to purge the residuals of the individual specific effects, u_i) is a simple expedient. This estimator will be consistent in nT. It is in T alone, but of course, T is likely to be small. The second question is more difficult. Estimation is simple if the first observation is simply dropped. We saw in the previous chapter that omitting the first observation in a time series could lead to a serious loss of efficiency. If the number of cross-section units is small, the same effect might arise here. But if the panel contains many groups (large n), then omitting the first observation is less likely to cause the same kinds of problems. One can apply the Prais–Winsten transformation to the first observation in each group instead [multiply by $(1-\rho^2)^{1/2}$], but then an additional complication arises at the second (FGLS) step when the observations are transformed a second time. On balance, the Cochrane–Orcutt estimator is probably a reasonable middle ground. Baltagi (1995, p. 83) discusses the procedure. He also discusses estimation in higher order AR and MA processes.

In the same manner as in the previous section, we could allow the autocorrelation to differ across groups. An estimate of each ρ_i is computable using the group mean deviation data. This estimator is consistent in T, which is problematic in this setting. In the earlier case, we overcame this difficulty by averaging over n such "weak" estimates and achieving consistency in the dimension of n instead. We lose that advantage when we allow ρ to vary over the groups. This is the same result that arose in our treatment of heteroscedasticity.

For the data we are using in our examples, the estimated autocorrelation is trivial (0.021534) so there is no need to examine this model further with these data.

[26]See Lillard and Willis (1978).

14.7. DYNAMIC MODELS

Panel data are well suited for examining dynamic effects, as in the first-order model,

$$y_{it} = \alpha_i + \mathbf{x}_{it}'\boldsymbol{\beta} + \delta y_{i,t-1} + \epsilon_{it}.$$

Substantial complications arise in estimation of such a model, however, In both the fixed and random effects settings, the difficulty is that the lagged dependent variable is correlated with the disturbance, even if it is assumed that ϵ_{it} is not itself autocorrelated.

For the moment, we can think of the fixed effects model as an ordinary regression with a lagged variable. We considered this case in Section 6.7.10 as a regression with a stochastic regressor that is dependent across observations. In the dynamic regression model, the estimator based on T observations is not unbiased, but it is consistent in T. That was the main result of Section 6.7.10. The inconsistency is of order $1/T$. The same result applies here. But the difference is that whereas before we obtained our large sample results by allowing T to grow large, in this setting, T is assumed to be small, and large-sample results are obtained with respect to n growing large, not T. The fixed effects estimator of $\boldsymbol{\theta} = [\boldsymbol{\beta}, \delta]$ can be viewed as an average of n estimators. For example, if $T \geq K$, then, from (14-4),

$$\begin{aligned}\hat{\boldsymbol{\theta}} &= \left[\sum_{i=1}^{n} \mathbf{X}_i'\mathbf{M}_d\mathbf{X}_i\right]^{-1}\left[\sum_{i=1}^{n} \mathbf{X}_i'\mathbf{M}_d\mathbf{y}_i\right] \\ &= \left[\sum_{i=1}^{n} \mathbf{X}_i'\mathbf{M}_d\mathbf{X}_i\right]^{-1}\left[\sum_{i=1}^{n} \mathbf{X}_i'\mathbf{M}_d\mathbf{X}_i\mathbf{b}_i\right] \\ &= \sum_{i=1}^{n} \mathbf{W}_i\mathbf{b}_i.\end{aligned}$$

The average of n inconsistent estimators will still be inconsistent. (This is only heuristic. If $T < K$, the individual coefficient vectors cannot be computed.[27]) The problem is more transparent in the random effects model. The lagged variable is correlated with the compound disturbance in the model, since u_i (which is α_i) enters the equation for every observation in group i. Neither of these renders the model inestimable, but they do make some technique other than LSDV or FGLS necessary.

The general approach, which has been developed in several stages in the literature,[28] relies on instrumental variables estimators and, most recently [by

[27]Further discussion is given by Nickell (1981), Ridder and Wansbeek (1990), and Kiviet (1993).

[28]See, for example, Anderson and Hsiao (1981), Arellano (1989), Arellano and Bond (1991), Arellano and Bover (1993), and Ahn and Schmidt (1993).

Ahn and Schmidt (1993)] on a GMM estimator. In either the fixed or random effects cases, the heterogeneity can be swept from the model by taking first differences. This produces

$$y_{it} - y_{i,t-1} = (\mathbf{x}_{it} - \mathbf{x}_{i,t-1})'\boldsymbol{\beta} + \delta(y_{i,t-1} - y_{i,t-2}) + (\epsilon_{it} - \epsilon_{i,t-1}).$$

This model is still complicated by correlation between the lagged dependent variable and the disturbance (and by its first-order moving average disturbance). But without the group effects, there is a simple instrumental variables estimator available. Assuming that the time series is long enough, one could use the differences, $(y_{i,t-2} - y_{i,t-3})$, or the lagged levels, $y_{i,t-2}$ and $y_{i,t-3}$, as one or two instrumental variables for $(y_{i,t-1} - y_{i,t-2})$. (The other variables can serve as their own instruments.) By this construction, then, the treatment of this model is a standard application of the instrumental variables technique that we developed in Section 6.7.8. There is a question as to whether one should use differences or levels as instruments. Arellano (1989) gives evidence that the latter is preferable.

Ahn and Schmidt (among others) observed that the IV estimator neglects quite a lot of information and is therefore inefficient. For example, in the first differenced model,

$$E[y_{is}(\epsilon_{it} - \epsilon_{i,t-1})] = 0, \qquad s = 0, \ldots, t-2, t = 2, \ldots, T.$$

That is, the *level* of y is uncorrelated with the differences of disturbances that are at least two periods subsequent. The corresponding moment equations that can enter the construction of a GMM estimator are

$$\frac{1}{n}\sum_{i=1}^{n} y_{is}[(y_{it} - y_{i,t-1}) - (\mathbf{x}_{it} - \mathbf{x}_{i,t-1})'\boldsymbol{\beta} - \delta(y_{i,t-1} - y_{i,t-2})] = 0$$
$$s = 0, \ldots, t-2, \qquad t = 2, \ldots, T.$$

Altogether, Ahn and Schmidt identify $T(T-1)/2 + T - 2$ such equations that involve mixtures of the levels and differences of the variables. The main conclusion that they demonstrate is that in the dynamic model, there is a large amount of information to be culled not only from the familiar relationships among the levels of the variables but also from the implied relationships between the levels and the first differences.

14.8. CONCLUSIONS

The preceding has shown a few of the extensions of the classical model that can be obtained when panel data are available. In principle, any of the models we have examined before this chapter and all those we will consider below, including the multiple equation models, can be extended in the same way. The main advantage, as we noted at the outset, is that with panel data, one can formally model the heterogeneity across groups that is typical in microeconomic data.

We will find in the next chapter that to some extent this model of heterogeneity can be misleading. What might have appeared at one level to be differences in the variances of the disturbances across groups may well be due to heterogeneity of a different sort, associated with the coefficient vectors. We will consider this possibility in the next chapter. We will also examine some additional models for disturbance processes that arise naturally in a multiple equations context but are actually more general cases of some of the models we looked at above, such as the model of groupwise heteroscedasticity.

EXERCISES

1. The following is a panel of data on investment (y) and profit (x) for $n = 3$ firms over $T = 10$ periods.

	$i = 1$		$i = 2$		$i = 3$	
t	y	x	y	x	y	x
1	13.32	12.85	20.30	22.93	8.85	8.65
2	26.30	25.69	17.47	17.96	19.60	16.55
3	2.62	5.48	9.31	9.16	3.87	1.47
4	14.94	13.79	18.01	18.73	24.19	24.91
5	15.80	15.41	7.63	11.31	3.99	5.01
6	12.20	12.59	19.84	21.15	5.73	8.34
7	14.93	16.64	13.76	16.13	26.68	22.70
8	29.82	26.45	10.00	11.61	11.49	8.36
9	20.32	19.64	19.51	19.55	18.49	15.44
10	4.77	5.43	18.32	17.06	20.84	17.87

(a) Pool the data and compute the least squares regression coefficients of the model

$$y_{it} = \alpha + \beta x_{it} + \epsilon_{it}.$$

(b) Estimate the fixed effects model of (14-2), then test the hypothesis that the constant term is the same for all three firms.

(c) Estimate the random effects model of (14-18), then carry out the Lagrange multiplier test of the hypothesis that the classical model without the common effect applies.

(d) Carry out Hausman's specification test for the random versus the fixed model.

2. Suppose that the model of (14-2) is formulated with an overall constant term and $n - 1$ dummy variables (dropping, say, the last one). Investigate the effect that this has on the set of dummy variable coefficients and on the least squares estimates of the slopes.

3. Use the data in Example 15.1 (these are the Grunfeld data) to fit the random and fixed effects models. There are five firms and 20 years of data for each. Use the F, LM, and/or Hausman statistics to determine which model, the fixed or random effects model, is preferable for these data.

4. Derive the log-likelihood function for the model in (14-18), assuming that ϵ_{it} and u_i are normally distributed. [Hints: Write the log-likelihood function as

$$\ln L = \sum_{i=1}^{n} \ln L_i,$$

where $\ln L_i$ is the log-likelihood function for the T observations in group i. These T observations are joint normally distributed, with covariance matrix given in (14-20). The log-likelihood is the sum of the logs of the joint normal densities of the n sets of T observations,

$$\epsilon_{it} + u_i = y_{it} - \alpha - \boldsymbol{\beta}'\mathbf{x}_{it}.$$

This will involve the inverse and determinant of $\boldsymbol{\Omega}$. Use (2-66) to prove that

$$\boldsymbol{\Omega}^{-1} = \frac{1}{\sigma_\epsilon^2}\left[\mathbf{I} - \frac{\sigma_u^2}{\sigma_\epsilon^2 + T\sigma_u^2}\mathbf{ii}'\right].$$

To find the determinant, use the product of the characteristic roots. Note first that

$$|\sigma_\epsilon^2\mathbf{I} + \sigma_u^2\mathbf{ii}'| = (\sigma_\epsilon^2)^T\left|\mathbf{I} + \frac{\sigma_u^2}{\sigma_\epsilon^2}\mathbf{ii}'\right|.$$

The roots are determined by

$$\left[\mathbf{I} + \frac{\sigma_u^2}{\sigma_\epsilon^2}\mathbf{ii}'\right]\mathbf{c} = \lambda\mathbf{c}$$

or

$$\frac{\sigma_\epsilon^2}{\sigma_u^2}\mathbf{ii}'\mathbf{c} = (\lambda - 1)\mathbf{c}.$$

Any vector whose elements sum to zero is a solution. There are $T - 1$ such independent vectors, so $T - 1$ characteristic roots are $(\lambda - 1) = 0$ or $\lambda = 1$. Premultiply the expression by $\mathbf{i}'$ to obtain the remaining characteristic root. (Remember to add 1 to the result.) Now, collect terms to obtain the log-likelihood.]

5. *Unbalanced design for random effects.* Suppose that the random effects model of Section 16.5 is to be estimated with a panel in which the groups have different numbers of observations. Let T_i be the number of observations in group i.

(a) Show that the pooled least squares estimator in (14-11) is unbiased and consistent despite this complication.

(b) Show that the estimator in (14-29) based on the pooled least squares estimator of $\boldsymbol{\beta}$ (or, for that matter, *any* consistent estimator of $\boldsymbol{\beta}$) is a consistent estimator of σ_ϵ^2.

(c) The group mean regression in (14-30) is heteroscedastic. Investigate the properties of the residual variance estimator. [Hints: For large-sample results, rely on $n \to \infty$, not T_i. Take T_i as potentially small and fixed for each i. This set of results will parallel the discussion of Section 14.4.3. What will you require to assert that the estimator based on (14-31) and (14-32),

$$\hat{\sigma}_u^2 = \hat{\sigma}_{**}^2 - Q\hat{\sigma}_\epsilon^2,$$

where

$$Q = \left(\frac{1}{n}\right)\left(\frac{1}{T_1} + \frac{1}{T_2} + \cdots + \frac{1}{T_n}\right),$$

is a consistent estimator of σ_u^2?]

(d) What change is needed in (14-22) to implement an FGLS estimator? [Note: The term $(nT)/(2(T - 1))$ in (14-33) must be replaced with $(\Sigma_{i=1}^n T_i)^2/(2\Sigma_i T_i(T_\text{i} - 1))$.]

6. In estimating the random effects model, if $K + 1$ is greater than n, the group means regression cannot be computed. Comment on the suggestion that in this event, we use a generalized inverse by dropping enough columns (variables) to produce a nonsingular moment matrix and then using the sum of squared residuals from this regression.

7. What are the probability limits of $(1/n)$LM, where LM is defined in (14-33) under the null hypothesis that $\sigma_u^2 = 0$ and under the alternative that $\sigma_u^2 \neq 0$?

8. The text proposes two possible residuals to use in estimation of σ_{**}^2 in (14-31): the least squares coefficient vector, including the constant term in the group means regression, and the full slope vector, including the constant term, in the pooled least squares estimator. Comment on the third alternative, $\bar{e}_{i.} = \bar{y}_{i.} - a_i - \mathbf{b}'\bar{\mathbf{x}}_{i.}$, based on the LSDV estimators.

9. *A two-way fixed effects model.* Suppose that the fixed effects model is modified to include a time-specific dummy variable as well as an individual-specific variable. Then,

$$y_{it} = \alpha_i + \gamma_t + \boldsymbol{\beta}'\mathbf{x}_{it} + \epsilon_{it}.$$

At every observation, the individual- and time-specific dummy variables sum to 1, so there are some redundant coefficients. The discussion in Section 14.4.2 shows that one way to remove the redundancy is to include an overall constant and to drop one of the time specific *and* one of the time-dummy variables. The model is, thus,

$$y_{it} = \mu + (\alpha_i - \alpha_1) + (\gamma_t - \gamma_1) + \boldsymbol{\beta}'\mathbf{x}_{it} + \epsilon_{it}.$$

(Note that the respective time- or individual-specific variable is zero when

t or i equals 1.) Ordinary least squares estimates of $\boldsymbol{\beta}$ are then obtained by regression of

$$y_{it} - \bar{y}_{i.} - \bar{y}_{.t} + \bar{\bar{y}}$$

on

$$\mathbf{x}_{it} - \bar{\mathbf{x}}_{i.} - \bar{\mathbf{x}}_{.t} + \bar{\bar{\mathbf{x}}}.$$

Then, $(\alpha_i - \alpha_1)$ and $(\gamma_t - \gamma_1)$ are estimated using the expressions in (14-16) while $m = \bar{\bar{y}} - \mathbf{b}'\bar{\bar{\mathbf{x}}}$. Using the following data, estimate the full set of coefficients for the least squares dummy variable model:

	t = 1	*t = 2*	*t = 3*	*t = 4*	*t = 5*	*t = 6*	*t = 7*	*t = 8*	*t = 9*	*t = 10*
					i = 1					
y	21.7	10.9	33.5	22.0	17.6	16.1	19.0	18.1	14.9	23.2
x_1	26.4	17.3	23.8	17.6	26.2	21.1	17.5	22.9	22.9	14.9
x_2	5.79	2.60	8.36	5.50	5.26	1.03	3.11	4.87	3.79	7.24
					i = 2					
y	21.8	21.0	33.8	18.0	12.2	30.0	21.7	24.9	21.9	23.6
x_1	19.6	22.8	27.8	14.0	11.4	16.0	28.8	16.8	11.8	18.6
x_2	3.36	1.59	6.19	3.75	1.59	9.87	1.31	5.42	6.32	5.35
					i = 3					
y	25.2	41.9	31.3	27.8	13.2	27.9	33.3	20.5	16.7	20.7
x_1	13.4	29.7	21.6	25.1	14.1	24.1	10.5	22.1	17.0	20.5
x_2	9.57	9.62	6.61	7.24	1.64	5.99	9.00	1.75	1.74	1.82
					i = 4					
y	15.3	25.9	21.9	15.5	16.7	26.1	34.8	22.6	29.0	37.1
x_1	14.2	18.0	29.9	14.1	18.4	20.1	27.6	27.4	28.5	28.6
x_2	4.09	9.56	2.18	5.43	6.33	8.27	9.16	5.24	7.92	9.63

Test the hypotheses that (1) the "period" effects are all zero, (2) the "group" effects are all zero, and (3) both period and group effects are zero. Use an F test in each case.

10. *Two-way random effects model.* We modify the random effects model by the addition of a time specific disturbance. Thus,

$$y_{it} = \alpha + \boldsymbol{\beta}'\mathbf{x}_{it} + \epsilon_{it} + u_i + v_t,$$

where

$$\begin{aligned}
E[\epsilon_{it}] &= E[u_i] = E[v_t] = 0, \\
E[\epsilon_{it}u_j] &= E[\epsilon_{it}v_s] = E[u_i v_t] = 0 \quad \text{for all } i, j, t, s \\
\text{Var}[\epsilon_{it}] &= \sigma_\epsilon^2, \qquad \text{Cov}[\epsilon_{it}, \epsilon_{js}] = 0 \quad \text{for all } i, j, t, s \\
\text{Var}[u_i] &= \sigma_u^2, \qquad \text{Cov}[u_i, u_j] = 0 \quad \text{for all } i, j \\
\text{Var}[v_t] &= \sigma_v^2, \qquad \text{Cov}[v_t, v_s] = 0 \quad \text{for all } t, s.
\end{aligned}$$

Write out the full covariance matrix for a data set with $n = 2$ and $T = 2$.

11. *Estimation of the full random effects model.* Fuller and Battese (1974) have developed a method of FGLS estimation of the two way random effects model.[29] Let

s_1^2 = residual variance in the regression of group means of y_{it} on a constant and the group means of x_{it} (this is n observations),

s_2^2 = residual variance in the regression of period means of y_{it} on a constant and the period means of x_{it} (this is T observations),

s_d^2 = residual variance in the full dummy variable regression with both individual- and time-specific dummies (this can be computed using the method described in Exercise 9).

The following notation is that of Judge et al. (1985, p. 534). Using the three preceding regressions, we can show that

$$\begin{aligned} s_1^2 &\text{ estimates } \sigma_1^2 = \sigma_\epsilon^2 + T\sigma_u^2, \\ s_2^2 &\text{ estimates } \sigma_2^2 = \sigma_\epsilon^2 + n\sigma_v^2, \\ s_d^2 &\text{ estimates } \sigma_\epsilon^2. \end{aligned}$$

Then

$$s_1^2 + s_2^2 - s_d^2 \text{ estimates } \sigma_3^2 = \sigma_\epsilon^2 + T\sigma_u^2 + n\sigma_v^2.$$

Let

$$\begin{aligned} \theta_1 &= 1 - \frac{\sigma_\epsilon}{\sigma_1}, \\ \theta_2 &= 1 - \frac{\sigma_\epsilon}{\sigma_2}, \\ \theta_3 &= \theta_1 + \theta_2 - 1 + \frac{\sigma_\epsilon}{\sigma_3}. \end{aligned}$$

Generalized least squares is equivalent to ordinary least squares regression of

$$y_{it}^* = y_{it} - \theta_1 \bar{y}_{i.} - \theta_2 \bar{y}_{.t} + \theta_3 \bar{\bar{y}}$$

on

$$\mathbf{x}_{it}^* = \mathbf{x}_{it} - \theta_1 \bar{\mathbf{x}}_{i.} - \theta_2 \bar{\mathbf{x}}_{.t} + \theta_3 \bar{\bar{\mathbf{x}}},$$

where $\mathbf{x}_{it}^*$ includes the constant term. This provides efficient estimates of the coefficients of the model. The usual estimator of the asymptotic covariance matrix of the estimated coefficient vector is appropriate. The sample estimates of θ_1, θ_2, and θ_3 are used when their population counterparts are unknown.

(a) Using the data from Exercise 9, estimate the parameters of the two

[29]See also Judge et al. (1985, pp. 530–536).

way random effects model. [Hint: The variance estimators based on the group means lead to negative estimates of the variance components. But (14-31) can be based on any consistent estimator of the slopes. Use the pooled ordinary least squares estimates instead.]

(b) The extension of the Lagrange multiplier statistic of (14-33) to this model is

$$\mathrm{LM} = \frac{nT}{2}\left[\frac{1}{T-1}\left[\frac{\sum_i\left(\sum_t e_{it}\right)^2}{\sum_i\sum_t e_{it}^2} - 1\right]^2 + \frac{1}{n-1}\left[\frac{\sum_t\left(\sum_i e_{it}\right)^2}{\sum_i\sum_t e_{it}^2} - 1\right]^2\right].$$

This statistic is asymptotically distributed as chi-squared with two degrees of freedom. Carry out the Lagrange multiplier test of the two-way random effects model.

CHAPTER 15

Systems of Regression Equations

15.1. INTRODUCTION

There are many settings in which the models of the previous chapters apply to a group of related variables. In these contexts, it makes sense to consider the several models jointly. Some examples follow.

1. In the Grunfeld–Boot and de Witt investment model of Example 15.1 below, we have a set of firms, each of which makes investment decisions based on variables that reflect anticipated profit and replacement of the capital stock. We will specify

   $$I_{it} = \beta_1 + \beta_2 F_{it} + \beta_3 C_{it} + \epsilon_{it}.$$

   Whether the parameter vector should be the same for all firms is a question that we shall study in this chapter. But the disturbances in the investment equations certainly include factors that are common to all the firms, such as the perceived general health of the economy, as well as factors that are specific to the particular firm or industry.

2. The capital asset pricing model of finance specifies that for a given security,

   $$r_{it} - r_{ft} = \alpha_i + \beta_i(r_{mt} - r_{ft}) + \epsilon_{it},$$

   where r_{it} is the return over period t on security i, r_{ft} is the return on a risk-free security, r_{mt} is the market return, and β_i is the security's beta coefficient. The disturbances are obviously correlated across securities. The knowledge that the return on security i exceeds the risk-free rate by a given amount gives some information about the excess return of security j, at least for some j's. It will be useful to estimate the equations jointly rather than to ignore this connection.

3. In a model of production, the optimization conditions of economic theory imply that if a firm faces a set of factor prices $\mathbf{p}$, its set of cost-minimizing factor demands for producing output Y will be a set of equations of the form $x_m = f_m(Y, \mathbf{p})$. The model is

$$
\begin{aligned}
x_1 &= f_1(Y, \mathbf{p}:\boldsymbol{\theta}) + \epsilon_1,\\
x_2 &= f_2(Y, \mathbf{p}:\boldsymbol{\theta}) + \epsilon_2,\\
&\vdots\\
x_M &= f_M(Y, \mathbf{p}:\boldsymbol{\theta}) + \epsilon_M.
\end{aligned}
$$

Once again, the disturbances should be correlated. In addition, the same parameters of the production technology will enter all the demand equations, so the set of equations have cross-equation restrictions. Estimating the equations separately will waste the information that the same set of parameters appears in all the equations.

4. In a cross-country comparison of economic performance over time, Alvarez, Garrett, and Lange (1991) estimated a model of the form

$$y_{it} = f(\text{labor organization}_{it}, \text{political organization}_{it}) + \epsilon_{it}.$$

Beck et al. (1993) found evidence that the substantive conclusions of the study were dependent on the stochastic specification and on the methods used for estimation. One of the interesting issues here concerns a shortage of observations that prevents estimation of the general model that appears to be appropriate for the setting. Even with adequate numbers of observations, in the typical application of this model in political science, such as this one, FGLS upon which we have relied heavily so far may become undesirable in the presence of a proliferation of parameters, not in the regression part of the model, but in the variance parameters.

All these examples have a common multiple equation structure, which we may write as

$$
\begin{aligned}
\mathbf{y}_1 &= \mathbf{X}_1\boldsymbol{\beta}_1 + \boldsymbol{\epsilon}_1,\\
\mathbf{y}_2 &= \mathbf{X}_2\boldsymbol{\beta}_2 + \boldsymbol{\epsilon}_2,\\
&\vdots\\
\mathbf{y}_M &= \mathbf{X}_M\boldsymbol{\beta}_M + \boldsymbol{\epsilon}_M.
\end{aligned}
\tag{15-1}
$$

There are M equations and T observations in the sample of data used to estimate them.[1] The three examples embody different types of constraints across equations and different structures of the disturbances. A basic set of principles will apply to them all, however.

We will examine a number of different model structures in this chapter. In Section 15.2, we will consider **covariance structures.** The models in this section are obtained by assuming that the coefficient vectors in all the equations in (15-1) are the same. The differences across units (i.e., for different i) arise from different variances or from the covariances of the disturbances of the equations. Section 15.3 could be viewed as a hybrid between the restricted model of Section 15.2 and a fully general model that allows every unit to have its own coefficient vector. The **random coefficients** model of Section 15.3 assumes that

[1]The use of T is not necessarily meant to imply any connection to time series. For instance, in Example 3 above, the data might be cross-sectional.

the coefficient vectors of different units are drawn from a multivariate probability distribution with a fixed mean and covariance matrix. Section 15.4 then fully relaxes the constraints on the coefficients—each equation has its own fixed set of parameters—and examines efficient estimation techniques. Production and consumer demand models are a special case of the general model in Section 15.4 in which the equations of the model obey an adding up constraint that has important implications for specification and estimation. Some general results for demand systems are considered in Section 15.5. In Section 15.6, we examine a classic application of the model in Section 15.5 that illustrates a number of the interesting features of the current genre of demand studies in the applied literature. Section 15.7 introduces estimation of nonlinear systems, instrumental variable estimation, and GMM estimation for a system of equations.

EXAMPLE 15.1 Grunfeld's Investment Data

To illustrate the techniques to be developed in this chapter, we will use a panel of data that has for several decades provided a useful tool for examining multiple equation estimators. Table 15.1 lists part of the data used in a classic study

TABLE 15.1 Grunfeld Investment Data

	General Motors			*Chrysler*			*General Electric*			*Westinghouse*			*U.S. Steel*		
Year	I_t	F_t	C_t	I_t	F_t	C_t	I_t	F_t	C_t	I_t	F_t	C_t	I_t	F_t	C_t
1935	317.6	3078.5	2.8	40.29	417.5	10.5	33.1	1170.6	97.8	12.9	191.5	1.8	209.9	1362.4	53.8
1936	391.8	4661.7	52.6	72.76	837.8	10.2	45.0	2015.8	104.4	25.9	516.0	0.8	355.3	1807.1	50.5
1937	410.6	5387.1	156.9	66.26	883.9	34.7	77.2	2803.3	118.0	35.0	729.0	7.4	469.9	2676.3	118.1
1938	257.7	2792.2	209.2	51.60	437.9	51.8	44.6	2039.7	156.2	22.9	560.4	18.1	262.3	1801.9	260.2
1939	330.8	4313.2	203.4	52.41	679.7	64.3	48.1	2256.2	172.6	18.8	519.9	23.5	230.4	1957.3	312.7
1940	461.2	4643.9	207.2	69.41	727.8	67.1	74.4	2132.2	186.6	28.6	628.5	26.5	261.6	2202.9	254.2
1941	512.0	4551.2	255.2	68.35	643.6	75.2	113.0	1834.1	220.9	48.5	537.1	36.2	472.8	2380.5	261.4
1942	448.0	3244.1	303.7	46.80	410.9	71.4	91.9	1588.0	287.8	43.3	561.2	60.8	445.6	2168.6	298.7
1943	499.6	4053.7	264.1	47.40	588.4	67.1	61.3	1749.4	319.9	37.0	617.2	84.4	361.6	1985.1	301.8
1944	547.5	4379.3	201.6	59.57	698.4	60.5	56.8	1687.2	321.3	37.8	626.7	91.2	288.2	1813.9	279.1
1945	561.2	4840.9	265.0	88.78	846.4	54.6	93.6	2007.7	319.6	39.3	737.2	92.4	258.7	1850.2	213.8
1946	688.1	4900.9	402.2	74.12	893.8	84.8	159.9	2208.3	346.0	53.5	760.5	86.0	420.3	2067.7	232.6
1947	568.9	3526.5	761.5	62.68	579.0	96.8	147.2	1656.7	456.4	55.6	581.4	111.1	420.5	1796.7	264.8
1948	529.2	3254.7	922.4	89.36	694.6	110.2	146.3	1604.4	543.4	49.6	662.3	130.6	494.5	1625.8	306.9
1949	555.1	3700.2	1020.1	78.98	590.3	147.4	98.3	1431.8	618.3	32.0	583.8	141.8	405.1	1667.0	351.1
1950	642.9	3755.6	1099.0	100.66	693.5	163.2	93.5	1610.5	647.4	32.2	635.2	136.7	418.8	1677.4	357.8
1951	755.9	4833.0	1207.7	160.62	809.0	203.5	135.2	1819.4	671.3	54.4	723.8	129.7	588.2	2289.5	342.1
1952	891.2	4924.9	1430.5	145.00	727.0	290.6	157.3	2079.7	726.1	71.8	864.1	145.5	645.2	2159.4	444.2
1953	1304.4	6241.7	1777.3	174.93	1001.5	346.1	179.5	2371.6	800.3	90.1	1193.5	174.8	641.0	2031.3	623.6
1954	1486.7	5593.6	2226.3	172.49	703.2	414.9	189.6	2759.9	888.9	68.6	1188.9	213.5	459.3	2115.5	669.7

Notes: I = gross investment, from *Moody's Industrial Manual* and annual reports of corporations; F = value of the firm, from *Bank and Quotation Record* and *Moody's Industrial Manual;* and C = stock of plant and equipment, from *Survey of Current Business.*

of investment demand.[2] The data consist of time series of 20 yearly observations for five firms (of 10 in the original study) and three variables:

I_t = gross investment,
F_t = market value of the firm at the end of the previous year,
C_t = value of the stock of plant and equipment at the end of the previous year.

All figures are in millions of dollars. The variables F_t and I_t reflect anticipated profit and the expected amount of replacement investment required.[3]

The model to be estimated with these data is

$$I_{it} = \beta_{1i} + \beta_{2i}F_{it} + \beta_{3i}C_{it} + \epsilon_{it},$$

where i indexes firms and t indexes years. Different restrictions on the parameters and the variances and covariances of the disturbances will imply different forms of the model.

15.2. COVARIANCE STRUCTURES FOR TIME-SERIES CROSS-SECTION DATA

Many studies have analyzed data observed across countries or firms in which the number of cross-sectional units is relatively small and the number of time periods is (potentially) relatively large. The current literature in political science contains many applications of this sort, such as Example 4 in the introduction to this chapter. The data set in Table 15.1 is an example, with five firms, each observed for 20 years. In this setting, we can emphasize time-series analysis. The data sets are typically "long" enough that we may study the disturbance terms in the context of stochastic processes. Heteroscedasticity is the effect of different processes applying to different cross-sectional units. The "narrow width" (i.e., smallness of the number of cross sections) of some of these data sets is not a serious concern. In the models we shall examine in this section, the data set consists of $M = n$ cross-sectional units, denoted $i = 1, \ldots, n$, observed at each of T time periods, $t = 1, \ldots, T$.[4] We have a total of nT observations. Discussion of asymptotic properties will be couched in terms of $n \rightarrow \infty$ and/or $T \rightarrow \infty$. Which, if either applies, will make a difference in a particular context, and we will have to be specific in each case we examine. Most of the asymptotic results we obtain are with respect to $T \rightarrow \infty$. We assume that n is

[2]Grunfeld (1958) and Grunfeld and Griliches (1960). The data were also used in Boot and deWitt (1960). Although admittedly not quite current, these data are unusually cooperative for illustrating the different aspects of estimating systems of regression equations.

[3]In the original study, the authors used the notation F_{t-1} and C_{t-1}. To avoid possible conflicts with the usual subscripting conventions used here, we have used the preceding notation instead.

[4]The requirement that each unit be observed the same number of periods is not necessary for much of this analysis.

fixed, except where specifically noted otherwise. (Note the contrast to the panel data models of the previous chapter, which save for this consideration, bear a superficial resemblance.)

The basic framework for this analysis is the generalized regression model:

$$y_{it} = \boldsymbol{\beta}'\mathbf{x}_{it} + \epsilon_{it}. \quad \textbf{(15-2)}$$

The essential feature of (15-2) is that we have fixed $\boldsymbol{\beta}_1 = \boldsymbol{\beta}_2 = \cdots = \boldsymbol{\beta}_n$ in (15-1). It is useful to collect the n time series,

$$\mathbf{y}_i = \mathbf{X}_i\boldsymbol{\beta} + \boldsymbol{\epsilon}_i,$$

so that

$$\begin{bmatrix} \mathbf{y}_1 \\ \mathbf{y}_2 \\ \vdots \\ \mathbf{y}_n \end{bmatrix} = \begin{bmatrix} \mathbf{X}_1 \\ \mathbf{X}_2 \\ \vdots \\ \mathbf{X}_n \end{bmatrix}\boldsymbol{\beta} + \begin{bmatrix} \boldsymbol{\epsilon}_1 \\ \boldsymbol{\epsilon}_2 \\ \vdots \\ \boldsymbol{\epsilon}_n \end{bmatrix}. \quad \textbf{(15-3)}$$

Each submatrix or subvector has T observations. In general terms,

$$\mathbf{V} = E[\boldsymbol{\epsilon}\boldsymbol{\epsilon}'] = \begin{bmatrix} \sigma_{11}\boldsymbol{\Omega}_{11} & \sigma_{12}\boldsymbol{\Omega}_{12} & \cdots & \sigma_{1n}\boldsymbol{\Omega}_{1n} \\ \sigma_{21}\boldsymbol{\Omega}_{21} & \sigma_{22}\boldsymbol{\Omega}_{22} & \cdots & \sigma_{2n}\boldsymbol{\Omega}_{2n} \\ & & \vdots & \\ \sigma_{n1}\boldsymbol{\Omega}_{n1} & \sigma_{n2}\boldsymbol{\Omega}_{n2} & \cdots & \sigma_{nn}\boldsymbol{\Omega}_{nn} \end{bmatrix}. \quad \textbf{(15-4)}$$

A variety of models are obtained by varying the structure of $\mathbf{V}$.

The classical regression model specifies that

$$E[\epsilon_{it}] = 0,$$
$$\text{Var}[\epsilon_{it}] = \sigma^2,$$
$$\text{Cov}[\epsilon_{it}, \epsilon_{js}] = 0, \quad \text{if } t \neq s \text{ or } i \neq j.$$

Then

$$\mathbf{V} = \begin{bmatrix} \sigma^2\mathbf{I} & \mathbf{0} & \cdots & \mathbf{0} \\ \mathbf{0} & \sigma^2\mathbf{I} & \cdots & \mathbf{0} \\ & & \vdots & \\ \mathbf{0} & \mathbf{0} & \cdots & \sigma^2\mathbf{I} \end{bmatrix}. \quad \textbf{(15-5)}$$

We can also stack the data in the pooled regression model in

$$\mathbf{y} = \mathbf{X}\boldsymbol{\beta} + \boldsymbol{\epsilon}.$$

For this simple model, the GLS estimator reduces to pooled ordinary least squares.

Some authors [e.g., Beck and Katz (1995)] have suggested that the standard errors for the OLS estimates in this model should be corrected for the possible misspecification in (15-5) that would arise if $\mathbf{V}_{ij}$ were $\sigma_{ij}\mathbf{I}$ instead of $\sigma^2 \times \mathbf{1}(i = j)\mathbf{I}$ as assumed in (15-5). [Note that this is not quite the most general case specified in (15-4), but the additional generality of a model with autocorrelation is often found to be unnecessary.] The appropriate asymptotic covariance matrix for OLS in the general case is, as always,

$$\text{Var}[\mathbf{b}] = (\mathbf{X}'\mathbf{X})^{-1}\mathbf{X}'\mathbf{V}\mathbf{X}(\mathbf{X}'\mathbf{X})^{-1}.$$

For the special case of $\mathbf{V}_{ij} = \sigma_{ij}\mathbf{I}$, this is

$$\text{Var}[\mathbf{b}] = \left(\sum_{i=1}^{n}\mathbf{X}_i'\mathbf{X}_i\right)^{-1}\left(\sum_{i=1}^{n}\sum_{j=1}^{n}\sigma_{ij}\mathbf{X}_i'\mathbf{X}_j\right)\left(\sum_{i=1}^{n}\mathbf{X}_i'\mathbf{X}_i\right)^{-1}. \tag{15-6}$$

This is straightforward to compute with estimates of σ_{ij} in hand. Since the OLS estimates are consistent, a consistent estimator of σ_{ij} is the natural one, $\mathbf{e}_i'\mathbf{e}_j/T$.

EXAMPLE 15.2 Classical Regression and Least Squares

By pooling all 100 observations and estimating the coefficients by ordinary least squares, we obtain

$$\begin{aligned} I_t = &-48.0297 + 0.105085F_t + 0.305366C_t,\\ &(21.16) \quad (0.01121) \quad (0.04285)\\ &(10.81) \quad (0.00818) \quad (0.033043\\ R^2 = 0.77886, \quad &\hat{\sigma}^2 = 15708.84, \quad \text{log-likelihood} = -677.398. \end{aligned}$$

In this and the following examples, estimated standard errors for the parameter estimates are shown in parentheses. To make them comparable with the results below, the variance estimate and estimated standard errors are based on $\mathbf{e}'\mathbf{e}/(nT)$. There is no degrees of freedom correction. The second set of standard errors given above are the (somewhat more) robust standard errors based on Beck and Katz (1995).

15.2.1. Cross-Sectional Heteroscedasticity

The pooled regression model of (15-3) and (15-5) and Example 15.2 implies a number of restrictions on $\mathbf{V}$. Examination of the data in the example suggests that the variance will be quite different in the five time series. If this were a cross-country comparison, we would expect tremendous variation in the scales of all variables in the model. We can relax the classical assumption by allowing σ^2 to vary across i. This results in the groupwise heteroscedastic model of Section 12.3.4:

$$\mathbf{V} = \begin{bmatrix} \sigma_1^2\mathbf{I} & \mathbf{0} & \cdots & \mathbf{0} \\ \mathbf{0} & \sigma_2^2\mathbf{I} & \cdots & \mathbf{0} \\ & \vdots & & \\ \mathbf{0} & \mathbf{0} & \cdots & \sigma_n^2\mathbf{I} \end{bmatrix}.$$

The GLS estimator, as we saw earlier, is

$$\hat{\boldsymbol{\beta}} = [\mathbf{X}'\mathbf{V}^{-1}\mathbf{X}]^{-1}[\mathbf{X}'\mathbf{V}^{-1}\mathbf{y}] = \left[\sum_{i=1}^{n} \frac{1}{\sigma_i^2}\mathbf{X}_i'\mathbf{X}_i\right]^{-1}\left[\sum_{i=1}^{n} \frac{1}{\sigma_i^2}\mathbf{X}_i'\mathbf{y}_i\right].$$

Of course, the disturbance variances, σ_i^2, will rarely be known, so an alternative estimator will be required. The estimation procedure can be either two-step FGLS or, if maximum likelihood estimates are required, iterated two-step estimation.

EXAMPLE 15.3 Testing and Estimation with Groupwise Heteroscedasticity

Using the OLS parameter estimates, we obtain the estimates of σ_i^2 listed in Table 15.2. These estimates suggest that the variance differs substantially across firms. We can use any of three possible tests for heteroscedasticity.

The Lagrange multiplier test is probably the most convenient test, since it does not require another regression after the pooled least squares regression. The log-likelihood function and its derivatives for the sample *without the restrictions of equal variances* are

$$\begin{aligned}
\ln L &= -\frac{nT}{2}\ln(2\pi) - \frac{T}{2}\sum_{i=1}^{n}\ln\sigma_i^2 - \frac{1}{2}\sum_{i=1}^{n}\frac{\boldsymbol{\epsilon}_i'\boldsymbol{\epsilon}_i}{\sigma_i^2},\\
\frac{\partial \ln L}{\partial \boldsymbol{\beta}} &= \sum_{i=1}^{n}\frac{1}{\sigma_i^2}\mathbf{X}_i'(\mathbf{y}_i - \mathbf{X}_i\boldsymbol{\beta}) = \sum_{i=1}^{n}\frac{1}{\sigma_i^2}\mathbf{X}_i'\boldsymbol{\epsilon}_i = \mathbf{X}'\mathbf{V}^{-1}\boldsymbol{\epsilon},\\
\frac{\partial \ln L}{\partial \sigma_i^2} &= -\frac{T}{2\sigma_i^2} + \frac{\boldsymbol{\epsilon}_i'\boldsymbol{\epsilon}_i}{2\sigma_i^4}, \quad i = 1, \ldots, n,\\
\frac{\partial^2 \ln L}{\partial \boldsymbol{\beta}\partial \boldsymbol{\beta}'} &= -\sum_{i=1}^{n}\frac{1}{\sigma_i^2}\mathbf{X}_i'\mathbf{X}_i = -\mathbf{X}'\mathbf{V}^{-1}\mathbf{X},\\
\frac{\partial^2 \ln L}{\partial (\sigma_i^2)^2} &= \frac{T}{2\sigma_i^4} - \frac{\boldsymbol{\epsilon}_i'\boldsymbol{\epsilon}_i}{\sigma_i^6}, \quad i = 1, \ldots, n,\\
\frac{\partial \ln L}{\partial \boldsymbol{\beta}\,\partial \sigma_i^2} &= -\sum_{i=1}^{n}\frac{1}{\sigma_i^4}\mathbf{X}_i'\boldsymbol{\epsilon}_i, \quad i = 1, \ldots, n.
\end{aligned}$$

TABLE 15.2 Residual Variances

General Motors (GM)	9,410.91
Chrysler (CH)	755.85
General Electric (GE)	34,288.89
Westinghouse (WE)	633.42
U.S. Steel (US)	33,455.51
Pooled	15,708.84

Under the null hypothesis of equal variances, the first derivatives are

$$\mathbf{g} = \begin{bmatrix} \dfrac{\partial \ln L}{\partial \boldsymbol{\beta}} \\ \dfrac{\partial \ln L}{\partial \sigma_i^2}, \quad i = 1, \dots, n \end{bmatrix} = \begin{bmatrix} \dfrac{1}{\sigma^2} \sum_{i=1}^{n} \mathbf{X}_i' \boldsymbol{\epsilon}_i \\ -\dfrac{T}{2\sigma^2} + \dfrac{\boldsymbol{\epsilon}_i' \boldsymbol{\epsilon}_i}{2\sigma^4}, \quad i = 1, \dots, n \end{bmatrix},$$

and the negative of the expected second derivatives matrix is

$$\mathbf{H}(\boldsymbol{\beta}, \sigma^2) = \begin{bmatrix} \left(\dfrac{1}{\sigma^2}\right) \mathbf{X}'\mathbf{X} & \mathbf{0} \\ \mathbf{0}' & \left(\dfrac{T}{2\sigma^4}\right) \mathbf{I} \end{bmatrix}.$$

It is convenient to rewrite

$$\frac{\partial \ln L}{\partial \sigma_i^2} = \frac{T}{2\sigma^2} \left[\frac{\hat{\sigma}_i^2}{\sigma^2} - 1 \right],$$

where $\hat{\sigma}_i^2$ is the ith unit-specific estimate of σ^2. The restricted maximum likelihood estimator of $\boldsymbol{\beta}$ is the pooled ordinary least squares estimator. At this restricted estimator, under the null hypothesis, $\partial \ln L/\partial \boldsymbol{\beta} = \mathbf{0}$, as these are the OLS normal equations. The restricted maximum likelihood estimator of the common σ^2 is

$$\begin{aligned} s^2 &= \frac{1}{nT} \mathbf{e}'\mathbf{e} \\ &= \frac{1}{nT} \sum_{i=1}^{n} \mathbf{e}_i' \mathbf{e}_i \\ &= \frac{1}{n} \sum_{i=1}^{n} s_i^2. \end{aligned}$$

It is a simple average of the n consistent estimators. With this in hand, the Lagrange multiplier statistic, $\mathbf{g}'\mathbf{H}^{-1}\mathbf{g}$ (computed at the pooled OLS estimates), reduces to

$$\begin{aligned} \text{LM} &= \sum_{i=1}^{n} \left[\frac{T}{2s^2} \left(\frac{s_i^2}{s^2} - 1 \right) \right]^2 \left(\frac{2s^4}{T} \right) \\ &= \frac{T}{2} \sum_{i=1}^{n} \left[\frac{s_i^2}{s^2} - 1 \right]^2. \end{aligned}$$

The statistic has $n - 1$ degrees of freedom. Based on the preceding least squares results, LM $= 46.63$, which is highly significant.

The Lagrange multiplier statistic is simple to compute and asymptotically equivalent to a likelihood ratio test. It does assume normality. If this is not appropriate, White's general test[5] is an alternative. To use White's test, we regress

[5]See Section 12.3.1.

the squared OLS residual on a constant, F, C, F^2, C^2, and FC. The R^2 in this regression is 0.36854, so the chi-squared statistic is $(nT)R^2 = 36.854$, with five degrees of freedom. The 1 percent critical value from the table is 15.056, so we can reject the hypothesis of homoscedasticity on the basis of this test.

We can also carry out an approximate likelihood ratio test (these are not the maximum likelihood estimators) using the test statistic in Section 12.3.4. The appropriate likelihood ratio statistic is

$$-2 \ln \lambda = (nT)\ln \hat{\sigma}^2 - \sum_{i=1}^{n} T \ln \hat{\sigma}_i^2,$$

where

$$\hat{\sigma}^2 = \frac{1}{nT}\mathbf{e}'\mathbf{e} \quad \text{and} \quad \hat{\sigma}_i^2 = \frac{1}{T}\mathbf{e}_i'\mathbf{e}_i,$$

with all residuals computed using the maximum likelihood estimators. This chi-squared statistic has $n - 1$ degrees of freedom. (Iterated FGLS can be used to compute them.) If only least squares results are available, s^2 and s_i^2 may be used, possibly with some loss of power in small samples. For these data,

$$\chi^2 = 100 \ln s^2 - \sum_{i=1}^{n} 20 \ln s_i^2 = 104.415.$$

This far exceeds the tabled critical value.

We proceed to reestimate the regression, allowing for heteroscedasticity. The two estimators, FGLS and MLE (iterated FGLS), are given in Table 15.3.

The likelihood ratio statistic for a test of homoscedasticity based on the MLEs is 120.914, which is extremely significant. With the unrestricted estimates, as an alternative test procedure, we may use the Wald statistic. If we as-

TABLE 15.3 FGLS and ML Estimates of a Heteroscedastic Model

	FGLS		*ML*	
$\hat{\beta}_1$	−36.2537	(6.1244)	−23.2583	(4.815)
$\hat{\beta}_2$	0.09499	(0.007409)	0.0943499	(0.006283)
$\hat{\beta}_3$	0.337813	(0.030225)	0.333702	(0.02204)
Log-likelihood		—	−616.941	
		Variances $\hat{\sigma}_{ii}$		
GM	8,612.15		8,657.87	
CH	409.19		175.80	
GE	36,563.24		40,211.13	
WE	777.97		1,241.01	
US	32,902.83		29,824.92	

sume normality, the asymptotic variance of each variance estimator is $2\sigma_i^4/T$, and the variances are asymptotically uncorrelated. Therefore, the Wald statistic to test the hypothesis of a common variance σ^2 would be

$$W = \sum_{i=1}^{n} (s_i^2 - \sigma^2)^2 \left(\frac{2\sigma^4}{T} \right)^{-1}.$$

Using s_i^2 to estimate σ_i^2 produces the sample statistic

$$W = \frac{T}{2} \sum_{i=1}^{n} \left(\frac{\sigma^2}{s_i^2} - 1 \right)^2.$$

Note the similarity to the Lagrange multiplier statistic. The estimator of the common variance can be the pooled estimator from the first least squares regression or the total sum of squared GLS residuals divided by nT. Using the FGLS estimates above and the pooled OLS estimator for σ^2, the Wald statistic is 17,676.32. We observe the common occurrence of an extremely large Wald test statistic. (Based on the sum of squared GLS residuals, $\hat{\sigma}^2 = 15{,}853.08$ and $W = 18{,}012.86$.)

If the assumption of normally distributed disturbances is inappropriate, then neither the Lagrange multiplier nor the likelihood ratio tests is usable. Moreover, the Wald statistic defined above is also incorrect, since it is the normality assumption that provides $(2\sigma_i^4/T)$ as $\text{Var}[s_i^2]$. It remains possible to construct a usable Wald statistic as follows: Under the null hypothesis of constant variance, σ^2, the Wald statistic is

$$W = \sum_{i=1}^{n} \frac{(s_i^2 - \sigma^2)^2}{\text{Var}[s_i^2]}.$$

If the hypothesis is correct,

$$W \xrightarrow{d} \chi^2[n].$$

By hypothesis,

$$\text{plim } s^2 = \sigma^2,$$

where s^2 is the disturbance variance estimator from the pooled regression. (For our example, this is 15,708.84. See Example 15.2 and Table 15.2.) The statistic obtained by substituting s^2 for σ^2 in W has the same limiting chi-squared distribution. This is identical to the earlier definition, but we must now reconsider $\text{Var}[s_i^2]$. Since

$$s_i^2 = \frac{1}{T} \sum_{t=1}^{T} e_{it}^2,$$

it is a sample moment, and at the same time, a mean of T observations. As such, we may use the results of Section 4.7.2 to estimate $\text{Var}[s_i^2]$. We can use

$$V_i = \frac{1}{T} \frac{1}{T-1} \sum_{t=1}^{T} (e_{it}^2 - s_i^2)^2.$$

The modified Wald statistic is then

$$W' = \sum_{i=1}^{n} \frac{(s_i^2 - s^2)^2}{V_i}.$$

For our investment data, the values of s_i^2 are given in Table 15.3. The five estimated variances based on residuals computed with the FGLS estimates in Table 15.5 are

$$\mathbf{V} = [8.3931 \times 10^6, 18{,}688., 3.366 \times 10^7, 1.0456 \times 10^5, 4.9012 \times 10^7].$$

The value for W' using these values is 14,681.3, which leads us to the same conclusion.

Returning to the least squares estimators, we should expect the OLS standard errors to be incorrect, given our findings. There are two possible corrections we can use, the White estimator and direct computation of the appropriate asymptotic covariance matrix. (The Beck et al. estimator is a third candidate, but it neglects to use the known restriction that the off-diagonal elements in **V** are zero. The third column given below is their correction with this constraint imposed.) These give the results shown in Table 15.4.

15.2.2. Cross-Sectional Correlation

In the example data, we have two automobile producers, two major suppliers to the electric utility industry, and one major supplier to all four of the others, U.S. Steel. It is very likely that the macroeconomic factors that affect these firms affect them all to varying degrees. For the auto industry, the fates of GM and Chrysler are obviously tied both to the economy as a whole and to factors that are specific to the two firms. As such, it would seem reasonable to allow correlation of the disturbances across firms. The extension of the model for cross-sectional correlation is

$$E[\boldsymbol{\epsilon}_i\boldsymbol{\epsilon}_j'] = \sigma_{ij}\mathbf{I}.$$

We continue to assume that observations are uncorrelated across time. With this generalization, we obtain

TABLE 15.4 Corrected OLS Estimates

Coefficient	*OLS SE*	*White*	*Correct*
−48.0297	21.15	15.02	14.20
0.105085	0.01121	0.009146	0.009065
0.305366	0.04285	0.05911	0.040947

$$\mathbf{V} = \begin{bmatrix} \sigma_{11}\mathbf{I} & \sigma_{12}\mathbf{I} & \cdots & \sigma_{1n}\mathbf{I} \\ \sigma_{21}\mathbf{I} & \sigma_{22}\mathbf{I} & \cdots & \sigma_{2n}\mathbf{I} \\ & \vdots & & \\ \sigma_{n1}\mathbf{I} & \sigma_{n2}\mathbf{I} & \cdots & \sigma_{nn}\mathbf{I} \end{bmatrix}. \tag{15-7}$$

This model can also be estimated either by FGLS or MLE by iterating. As before, at step 1, we use OLS to obtain $\mathbf{b}$ and $\mathbf{e}_i$. A consistent estimate of σ_{ij} can be obtained using the least squares residuals in

$$s_{ij} = \frac{\mathbf{e}_i'\mathbf{e}_j}{T}. \tag{15-8}$$

Some treatments use $T - K$ instead of T in the denominator of s_{ij}.[6] There is no problem created by doing so, but we should note that the resulting estimator is not unbiased regardless. With s_{ij} in hand, FGLS may be computed using

$$\hat{\boldsymbol{\beta}} = [\mathbf{X}'\hat{\mathbf{V}}^{-1}\mathbf{X}]^{-1}[\mathbf{X}'\hat{\mathbf{V}}^{-1}\mathbf{y}],$$

where $\mathbf{X}$ and $\mathbf{y}$ are the stacked data matrices in (15-3).

In practical terms, this is a formidable computation. As before, however, things are simpler than they appear. $\mathbf{V}$ can be written as

$$\mathbf{V} = \boldsymbol{\Sigma}\ \mathbf{I}, \tag{15-9}$$

where $\boldsymbol{\Sigma}$ is an $n \times n$ matrix, so

$$\mathbf{V}^{-1} = \boldsymbol{\Sigma}^{-1}\ \mathbf{I}. \tag{15-10}$$

Let σ^{ij} denote the ijth element of $\boldsymbol{\Sigma}^{-1}$. Then

$$\mathbf{V}^{-1} = \begin{bmatrix} \sigma^{11}\mathbf{I} & \sigma^{12}\mathbf{I} & \cdots & \sigma^{1n}\mathbf{I} \\ \sigma^{21}\mathbf{I} & \sigma^{22}\mathbf{I} & \cdots & \sigma^{2n}\mathbf{I} \\ & \vdots & & \\ \sigma^{n1}\mathbf{I} & \sigma^{n2}\mathbf{I} & \cdots & \sigma^{nn}\mathbf{I} \end{bmatrix}.$$

The usefulness of this is that

$$\mathbf{X}'\mathbf{V}^{-1}\mathbf{X} = \sum_{i=1}^{n}\sum_{j=1}^{n}\sigma^{ij}\mathbf{X}_i'\mathbf{X}_j$$

and

$$\mathbf{X}'\mathbf{V}^{-1}\mathbf{y} = \sum_{i=1}^{n}\sum_{j=1}^{n}\sigma^{ij}\mathbf{X}_i'\mathbf{y}_j,$$

[6] See, for example, Kmenta (1986, p.620). Elsewhere, for example, in Fomby et.al. (1984, p. 327), T is used instead.

so

$$\hat{\boldsymbol{\beta}} = \left[\sum_{i=1}^{n}\sum_{j=1}^{n}\sigma^{ij}\mathbf{X}_i'\mathbf{X}_j\right]^{-1}\left[\sum_{i=1}^{n}\sum_{j=1}^{n}\sigma^{ij}\mathbf{X}_i'\mathbf{y}_j\right]. \tag{15-11}$$

Therefore, to compute the FGLS estimators for this model, we first compute the full set of sample moments, $\mathbf{y}_i'\mathbf{y}_j$, $\mathbf{X}_i'\mathbf{X}_j$, and $\mathbf{X}_i'\mathbf{y}_j$, for all pairs of cross-sectional units. Maximum likelihood estimates can be obtained by iterating to convergence between

$$\hat{\hat{\boldsymbol{\beta}}} = [\mathbf{X}'\hat{\mathbf{V}}^{-1}\mathbf{X}]^{-1}[\mathbf{X}'\hat{\mathbf{V}}^{-1}\mathbf{y}]$$

and

$$s_{ij} = \frac{[\mathbf{y}_i'\mathbf{y}_j + \hat{\hat{\boldsymbol{\beta}}}'\mathbf{X}_i'\mathbf{X}_j\hat{\hat{\boldsymbol{\beta}}} - \hat{\hat{\boldsymbol{\beta}}}'\mathbf{X}_i'\mathbf{y}_j - \hat{\hat{\boldsymbol{\beta}}}'\mathbf{X}_j'\mathbf{y}_i]}{T}. \tag{15-12}$$

The computations are simple, using basic matrix algebra. Hypothesis tests about $\boldsymbol{\beta}$ may be done using the usual results. The appropriate asymptotic covariance matrix is the inverse matrix in brackets in (15-11).[7]

EXAMPLE 15.4 Testing and Estimation with Groupwise Heteroscedasticity and Cross-Sectional Correlation

For the investment data, the FGLS and maximum likelihood estimates are listed in Table 15.5. The estimated covariance matrix for the disturbances based on the FGLS estimates, with correlations placed in parentheses above the diagonal, is given in Table 15.6.[8] Note that the disturbance variances have changed dramatically. This is due in large part to the quite large off-diagonal elements. It is noteworthy that despite the great changes in $\boldsymbol{\Sigma}$, the parameter estimates have not changed much from the earlier ones.

TABLE 15.5 FGLS and ML Estimates

	β_1	β_2	β_3
FGLS	−30.281	0.094127	0.34057
	(5.589)	(0.006836)	(0.02683)
MLE	11.503	0.051921	0.31909
	(2.470)	(0.004274)	(0.01572)
Log-likelihood = −520.27			

[7]For programming purposes, it is useful to note that these are all matrices of small orders, whereas the general formulation involves an $nT \times nT$ matrix.

[8]The estimate of $\boldsymbol{\Sigma}$ computed with the MLEs as well as the implied correlations are somewhat different. The results of the hypothesis tests are the same.

TABLE 15.6 Estimated Covariances and Correlations

	GM	*CH*	*GE*	*WE*	*US*
GM	8,466.464	(−0.216)	(−0.152)	(−0.330)	(0.015)
CH	−323.7408	265.1038	(−0.501)	(−0.152)	(0.578)
GE	−2,755.097	−1,602.251	38,591.00	(0.809)	(−0.819)
WE	−941.3622	−76.33833	4,929.060	961.5490	(−0.552)
US	260.1078	1,665.469	−28,514.58)	−3,029.154	31,365.40

For testing the hypothesis that the off-diagonal elements of $\boldsymbol{\Sigma}$ are zero—that is, that there is no correlation across firms—there are two approaches. If we have obtained maximum likelihood estimates, we can use a likelihood ratio test. This test is based on the statistic

$$\lambda_{\text{LR}} = T\left(\sum_{i=1}^{n} \ln \hat{\sigma}_i^2 - \ln |\hat{\boldsymbol{\Sigma}}|\right), \tag{15-13}$$

where $\hat{\sigma}_i^2$ are the estimates of σ_i^2 obtained from iterating the groupwise heteroscedastic treatment (see Example 15.3) and $\hat{\boldsymbol{\Sigma}}$ is the maximum likelihood estimator in the unrestricted model, that is, this example. The large-sample distribution of the statistic is chi-squared with $n(n-1)/2$ degrees of freedom. The Lagrange multiplier test developed by Breusch and Pagan (1980) provides an alternative. The general form of the statistic is

$$\lambda_{\text{LM}} = T\sum_{i=2}^{n}\sum_{j=1}^{i-1} r_{ij}^2, \tag{15-14}$$

where r_{ij}^2 is the ijth residual correlation coefficient. If every firm had a different parameter vector, then, firm by firm, ordinary least squares would be efficient (and ML), and we would compute r_{ij} from the OLS residuals. Here, however, we are assuming only a single-parameter vector. Therefore, the strictly appropriate basis for computing the correlations is the residuals from the iterated estimator in the groupwise heteroscedastic model, that is, the same residuals used to compute $\hat{\sigma}_i^2$ in Table 15.6. An asymptotically valid approximation to the test can be based on the FGLS residuals instead. The two test statistics based on the results given previously are

$$\lambda_{\text{LR}} = 20(42.264 - 37.838) = 88.52$$

(the MLE of $\boldsymbol{\Sigma}$ is not shown) and

$$\lambda_{\text{LM}} = 51.315$$

based on the FGLS estimates given in Table 15.6. Using the MLEs, $\lambda_{\text{LM}} =$ 43.491. For 10 degrees of freedom, the critical value from the chi-squared table is 23.21, so both results lead to rejection of the hypothesis of a diagonal $\boldsymbol{\Sigma}$. We conclude that the simple heteroscedastic model is not general enough for these data.

Postscript We shall examine the effect of assuming that all five firms have the same parameters in Section 15.4. For now, we note that one of the effects is to inflate the disturbance correlations. When the Lagrange multiplier statistic is recomputed with firm-by-firm separate regressions, the statistic falls to 29.04, which is still significant, but far less than what we found earlier.

15.2.3. Autocorrelation

The preceding discussion dealt with heteroscedasticity and cross-sectional correlation. Through a simple modification of the procedures, it is possible to relax the assumption of nonautocorrelation as well.

Before proceeding, we note that problems are introduced by models that contain lagged dependent variables. These are the same ones we encountered in Chapter 13, and the remedies discussed there will apply here. In addition, because of the Jacobian term in the log-likelihood function pertaining to the initial observation(s), iterated FGLS will no longer give maximum likelihood estimates. Therefore, in what follows, we shall not iterate the FGLS estimators. In many settings, this is likely to be an important consideration, as the typical time series is relatively short. It is possible, however, to scan the admissible range of the autocorrelation parameters for the maximum likelihood estimators. Last, at various points, variance estimators are computed using $\mathbf{e}'\mathbf{e}/T$. One could use the degrees of freedom, $T - K$, instead. Either is appropriate, and the asymptotic properties are the same for both. Because this is not a classical regression model, however, the degrees of freedom correction does not produce an unbiased estimator.

It is simplest to begin with the assumption that

$$\text{Corr}[\epsilon_{it}, \epsilon_{js}] = 0, \quad \text{if } i \neq j.$$

That is, the disturbances between cross-sectional units are uncorrelated. Now we can take the approach of Chapter 13 to allow for autocorrelation within the cross-sectional units. Suppose that for each i,

$$E[\boldsymbol{\epsilon}_i\boldsymbol{\epsilon}_i'] = \sigma_i^2\mathbf{\Omega}_i,$$

where $\mathbf{\Omega}_i$ is an autocorrelation matrix. With our earlier assumption, this produces

$$\mathbf{V} = \begin{bmatrix} \sigma_1^2\mathbf{\Omega}_1 & \mathbf{0} & \cdots & \mathbf{0} \\ \mathbf{0} & \sigma_2^2\mathbf{\Omega} & \cdots & \mathbf{0} \\ & \vdots & & \\ \mathbf{0} & \mathbf{0} & \cdots & \sigma_n^2\mathbf{\Omega}_n \end{bmatrix}. \tag{15-15}$$

The AR(1) model is the simplest to formulate. Generalizations along the lines discussed in Chapter 13 would be cumbersome but straightforward. Consider, in general, the model

$$\epsilon_{it} = \rho_i \epsilon_{i,t-1} + u_{it},$$
$$\text{Var}[\epsilon_{it}] = \sigma_i^2 = \frac{\sigma_{ui}^2}{1 - \rho_i^2}. \tag{15-16}$$

For FGLS estimation of the model, suppose that r_i is a consistent estimate of ρ_i. Then, if we take each time series $[\mathbf{y}_i, \mathbf{X}_i]$ separately, we can transform the data using the Prais–Winsten transformation:

$$\mathbf{y}_{*i} = \begin{bmatrix} \sqrt{1 - r_i^2}\, y_{i1} \\ y_{i2} - r_i\, y_{i1} \\ y_{i3} - r_i\, y_{i2} \\ \vdots \\ y_{iT} - r_i\, y_{i,T-1} \end{bmatrix}, \quad \mathbf{X}_{*i} = \begin{bmatrix} \sqrt{1 - r_i^2}\, \mathbf{x}_{i1} \\ \mathbf{x}_{i2} - r_i\, \mathbf{x}_{i1} \\ \mathbf{x}_{i3} - r_i\, \mathbf{x}_{i2} \\ \vdots \\ \mathbf{x}_{iT} - r_i\, \mathbf{x}_{i,T-1} \end{bmatrix}. \tag{15-17}$$

In terms of the transformed data $\mathbf{y}_{*i}$ and $\mathbf{X}_{*i}$, the model is now only heteroscedastic; the transformation has removed the autocorrelation. As such, the groupwise heteroscedastic model of Section 15.2.1 applies to the transformed data. We may use weighted least squares, as described earlier. This requires a second least squares estimate. The first regression produces initial estimates of ρ_i. The transformed data are then used in a second least squares regression to obtain consistent estimates,

$$\hat{\sigma}_{ui}^2 = \frac{\mathbf{e}_{*i}'\mathbf{e}_{*i}}{T}. \tag{15-18}$$

With these estimates in hand, we may proceed to the calculation of the heteroscedastic regression. At the end of the calculation, the moment matrix used in the last regression gives the correct asymptotic covariance matrix for $\hat{\hat{\boldsymbol{\beta}}}$. If desired, a consistent estimate of $\sigma_{\epsilon i}^2$ is obtained using

$$\hat{\sigma}_{\epsilon i}^2 = \frac{\hat{\sigma}_{ui}^2}{1 - r_i^2}. \tag{15-19}$$

The remaining question is how to obtain the initial estimates r_i. There are two possible structures to consider.

If the disturbances have a common stochastic process with the same ρ_i, $\boldsymbol{\Omega}_i = \boldsymbol{\Omega}$ for all i. Three possible estimators of the common ρ, all of which are consistent, are

$$\bar{r} = \frac{1}{n}\sum_{i=1}^{n} r_i,$$
$$r = \frac{\sum_{i=1}^{n}\sum_{t=2}^{T} e_{it}e_{i,t-1}}{\sum_{i=1}^{n}\sum_{t=2}^{T} e_{it}^2}, \tag{15-20}$$
$$r^* = \text{sample Corr}[e_{i,t-1}, e_{it}].$$

Note that the first is an average of n consistent but inefficient estimates.[9] The components r_i in $\bar{r}$ may be any of the estimators in Section 13.7.1 derived from the individual units. Since asymptotically each estimate has a variance of $(1 - \rho_i^2)/T$, a more efficient weighting would use the reciprocals of the variances, leading to

$$\bar{\bar{r}} = \sum_i w_i r_i,$$
$$w_i = \frac{1/(1 - r_i^2)}{\sum_{i=1}^{n} 1/(1 - r_i^2)}. \tag{15-21}$$

Since FGLS based on any of these estimators is asymptotically efficient, the choice of which to use is arbitrary. The small-sample properties are likely to be different, however.

The assumption of a common ρ is a restriction on the model, but not so severe a restriction as homoscedasticity. In Example 15.5, we shall see that the estimated autocorrelations of the first three firms are quite similar. Also, if the time series are short, this may be a necessary restriction so as to bring enough information to bear on the estimation of ρ to produce a reasonable estimate of $\boldsymbol{\beta}$. Once again, the relevance is to the small-sample properties. If the time series are very short, it may be preferable to impose the restriction of a common ρ, even if it is violated in the population, to improve the small-sample performance of the estimator $\hat{\boldsymbol{\beta}}$.[10]

If the processes are different across observational units, each time series may be analyzed separately. Any of the estimators described in Section 13.7 may be used; once again, the objective is consistency of the estimator. We note, both for this case and the previous one, that if there are lagged dependent variables in the model, the original least squares estimates will not yield consistent estimates of ρ_i. Instrumental variables or the method of Hatanaka may be used instead.

Last, one may wish to allow for cross-sectional correlation across units. Example 15.4 strongly suggests that this is appropriate for our investment data. The preceding has a natural generalization. If we assume that

$$\text{Cov}[u_{it}, u_{jt}] = \sigma_{uij},$$

we obtain the model of Section 15.2.2 in which the off-diagonal blocks of $\mathbf{V}$, $\sigma_{ij}\mathbf{I}$, are replaced by

[9]The consistency of $\bar{r}$ follows from the consistency of r_i in the dimension T, not from convergence in the dimension of n. An average of a fixed number of consistent estimators will be consistent, even if they are correlated. We continue to take n as fixed in this section.

[10]This is a point at which increasing n can play a role in the asymptotic properties of the estimates. Suppose that T is fixed and relatively small. Then, if $n \to +\infty$, all the estimators of ρ will still be consistent.

$$\sigma_{ij}\boldsymbol{\Omega}_{ij} = \frac{\sigma_{uij}}{1-\rho_i\rho_j}\begin{bmatrix} 1 & \rho_j & \rho_j^2 & \cdots & \rho_j^{T-1} \\ \rho_i & 1 & \rho_j & \cdots & \rho_j^{T-2} \\ \rho_i^2 & \rho_i & 1 & \cdots & \rho_j^{T-3} \\ & & \vdots & & \\ \rho_i^{T-1} & \rho_i^{T-2} & \rho_i^{T-3} & \cdots & 1 \end{bmatrix}. \tag{15-22}$$

For estimation of this model, the technique of the preceding section needs only to be extended to the model of cross-sectional correlation in an obvious fashion. Initial estimates of ρ_i are required, as before. The Prais–Winsten transformation renders all of the blocks in $\mathbf{V}$ diagonal. Therefore, the model of cross-sectional correlation in Section 15.2.2 applies to the transformed data. The method of estimation described there may be used directly. Once again, the GLS moment matrix obtained at the last iteration (or the first, if no iterations are performed) provides the asymptotic covariance matrix for $\hat{\hat{\boldsymbol{\beta}}}$. Estimates of $\sigma_{\epsilon ij}$ can be obtained from the least squares residual covariances obtained from the transformed data:

$$\hat{\sigma}_{\epsilon ij} = \frac{\hat{\sigma}_{uij}}{1-r_ir_j}, \tag{15-23}$$

where

$$\hat{\sigma}_{uij} = \frac{\mathbf{e}_{*i}'\mathbf{e}_{*j}}{T}.$$

EXAMPLE 15.5 Models with Autocorrelation

We now allow for different AR(1) processes for each firm. From the initial least squares estimates, the firm-specific autocorrelations and estimated variances of u_{it} and ϵ_{it} based on the transformed data are given in Table 15.7. The FGLS parameter estimates based on the transformed data are as shown in Table 15.8. Finally, the estimates are recomputed using the full model with cross-sectional covariances, giving the results in the lower part of Table 15.8. The estimated variances using these estimates follow in Table 15.9.

TABLE 15.7 Estimated Autocorrelations and Disturbance Variances

			Firm		
Estimate	***GM***	***CH***	***GE***	***WE***	***US***
r	0.47792	0.79364	0.90456	0.60208	0.86840
s_{ui}^2	5792.1	453.57	11,330.0	381.59	12,444.51
$s_{\epsilon i}^2$	7506.68	1225.45	62,330.4	598.58	50,611.8

TABLE 15.8 Models Estimated with Autocorrelation

β_1	β_2	β_3
Groupwise Heteroscedasticity		
−37.447	0.09128	0.35000
(7.393)	(0.007721)	(0.03283)
Cross Sectional Correlation and Groupwise Heteroscedasticity		
−35.523	0.09064	0.34777
(7.288)	(0.007724)	(0.03184)

TABLE 15.9 Estimated Variances and Correlations

	Firm				
Estimate	*GM*	*CH*	*GE*	*WE*	*US*
s^2_{ui}	6166.08	368.182	10,908.4	399.729	12,851.18
$s^2_{\epsilon i}$	7991.3	994.74	60,011.0	627.03	52,266.0
r_{uiuj} (cross-sectional correlations)					
CH	0.065	—	—	—	—
GE	−0.160	−0.321	—	—	—
WE	−0.378	−0.057	0.518	—	—
US	0.041	0.198	−0.646	−0.202	—

15.2.4. Summary

The preceding sections have suggested a variety of different specifications of the generalized regression model. Which ones apply in a given situation depends on the setting. Homoscedasticity will depend on the nature of the data and will often be directly observable at the outset. Uncorrelatedness across the cross-sectional units is a strong assumption, particularly because the model assigns the same parameter vector to all units. Autocorrelation is a qualitatively different property. Although it does appear to arise naturally in time-series data, one would want to look carefully at the data before assuming that it is present. The properties of all these estimators depend on an increase in T, so they are generally not well suited to types of data sets described in the previous chapter.

Our sample estimates of the various models, in increasing order of their generality, are shown in Table 15.10. Moving down the columns, we see that the

TABLE 15.10 Summary of FGLS Estimates

Model	β_1	β_2	β_3
Classical regression	−48.030 (21.16)	0.10508 (0.01121)	0.30534 (0.04285)
Groupwise heteroscedastic	−36.254 (6.124)	0.09499 (0.0074)	0.33781 (0.0302)
Groupwise heteroscedastic and cross-sectionally correlated	−30.281 (5.589)	0.09412 (0.0068)	0.34057 (0.0268)
Groupwise heteroscedastic, cross-sectionally correlated, and within-group autocorrelated	−37.447 (7.393)	0.09128 (0.0077)	0.35000 (0.0328)
Groupwise heteroscedastic, cross-sectionally correlated, within- and between-group autocorrelated	−35.523 (7.288)	0.09064 (0.0077)	0.34777 (0.0318)

gains in efficiency that result from relaxing the constraints in **V** are clearly visible in the first three models. Not surprisingly, the standard errors rise noticeably with the introduction of autocorrelation in the fourth model. The disturbance variance that previously contained only contemporaneous variation now reflects the retention of lagged effects and their attendant variation in the current disturbance. This suggests that one might want to exercise some caution in extending a model to this level of generality. Nonautocorrelation is a testable restriction, and it is clear that there is some benefit to be gained if it is not present. (Of course, neglecting it when it *is* present is probably even worse.) The reduction in the standard errors of the estimates from the fourth to the fifth models reflects the same gain present in the difference between the second and third models. Allowing the off-diagonal elements of the contemporaneous disturbance covariance matrix to be nonzero introduces a large amount of new information into the estimator.

Beck et al. (1993) suggest several problems that might arise when using this model in small samples. If $T < N$, then with or without a correction for autocorrelation, the matrix

$$\hat{\Sigma} = \frac{1}{T}\sum_{t=1}^{T} \mathbf{e}_t \mathbf{e}_t'$$

is an $N \times \text{N}$ matrix of rank T (or less) and is thus singular. This precludes FGLS estimation. A preferable approach then might be to use pooled OLS and make the appropriate correction to the asymptotic covariance matrix. [See (15-6) and Example 15.2.] But in this situation, there remains the possibility of accommodating cross unit heteroscedasticity. One could use the groupwise heteroscedasticity model of Section 15.2.1. The estimates will be consistent and more efficient than OLS, although the standard errors will be inappropriate if there is cross-sectional correlation. In the same spirit as in (15-6), an appropriate estimator that extends (12-39) would be

$$\begin{aligned}\text{Est. Var}[\mathbf{b}] &= [\mathbf{X}'\hat{\mathbf{V}}^{-1}\mathbf{X}]^{-1}[\mathbf{X}'\hat{\mathbf{V}}^{-1}\hat{\boldsymbol{\Omega}}\hat{\mathbf{V}}^{-1}\mathbf{X}][\mathbf{X}'\hat{\mathbf{V}}^{-1}\mathbf{X}]^{-1}\\ &= \left[\sum_{i=1}^{n}\left(\frac{1}{s_{ii}}\right)\mathbf{X}_i'\mathbf{X}_i\right]^{-1}\left[\sum_{i=1}^{n}\sum_{j=1}^{n}\left(\frac{s_{ij}}{s_{ii}s_{jj}}\right)\mathbf{X}_i'\mathbf{X}_j\right]\left[\sum_{i=1}^{n}\left(\frac{1}{s_{ii}}\right)\mathbf{X}_i'\mathbf{X}_i\right]^{-1}\\ &= \left[\sum_{i=1}^{n}\left(\frac{1}{s_{i}}\right)\mathbf{X}_i'\mathbf{X}_i\right]^{-1}\left[\sum_{i=1}^{n}\sum_{j=1}^{n}\left(\frac{r_{ij}^2}{s_{ij}}\right)\mathbf{X}_i'\mathbf{X}_j\right]\left[\sum_{i=1}^{n}\left(\frac{1}{s_{ii}}\right)\mathbf{X}_i'\mathbf{X}_i\right]^{-1}.\end{aligned}$$

(Note that this bases the estimates on the model of groupwise heteroscedasticity, but it is "robust" to the possibility of cross-sectional correlation. When N is large relative to T, the number of estimated parameters in the autocorrelation model becomes very large relative to the number of observations. Beck and Katz (1995) found that as a consequence, the estimated asymptotic covariance matrix for the FGLS slopes tends to underestimate the true variability of the estimator. Two compromises they suggest are first, using OLS and the appropriate covariance matrix and second, imposing the restriction of equal autocorrelation coefficients across groups.

Figure 15.1 is a plot of the residuals from the FGLS regression based on the least restrictive specification (the last one in Table 15.10). The figure is particularly revealing. Not only does it show quite clearly the groupwise het-

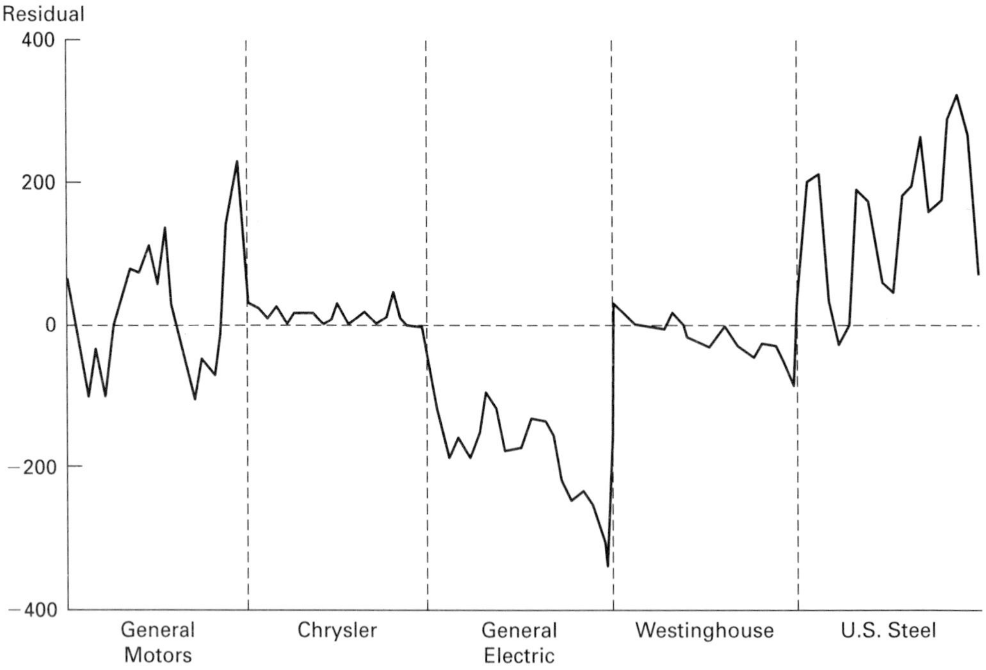

FIGURE 15.1 FGLS Residuals.

eroscedasticity induced by this model, but the autocorrelation of the residuals is also clearly visible. It is also clear that assuming that the same coefficient vector applies to all firms induces quite a serious misspecification for GE and U.S. Steel. We will return to this issue in Section 15.4.

15.3. A RANDOM COEFFICIENTS MODEL

Thus far, the model $\mathbf{y}_i = \mathbf{X}_i\boldsymbol{\beta} + \boldsymbol{\epsilon}_i$ has been analyzed within the familiar limits of heteroscedasticity and autocorrelation. Although the models in Sections 15.2.2 and 15.2.3 allow considerable flexibility, they do entail the not entirely plausible assumption that there is no parameter variation across firms (i.e., across the cross-sectional units). A fully general approach would combine all the machinery of the previous sections with a model that allows $\boldsymbol{\beta}$ to vary across firms. We shall examine such a model in Section 15.4.

A number of authors have suggested that parameter heterogeneity can be reasonably viewed as due to stochastic variation.[11] Suppose that we write

$$\mathbf{y}_i = \mathbf{X}_i\boldsymbol{\beta}_i + \boldsymbol{\epsilon}_i,$$

where

$$\begin{aligned}\boldsymbol{\beta}_i &= \boldsymbol{\beta} + \mathbf{v}_i,\\ E[\mathbf{v}_i] &= \mathbf{0},\end{aligned}$$

and

$$E[\mathbf{v}_i\mathbf{v}_i'] = \boldsymbol{\Gamma}.$$

Assume for now that there is no autocorrelation or cross-sectional correlation of the sort examined in the previous section. Then the $\boldsymbol{\beta}_i$ that applies to a particular cross-sectional unit is the outcome of a random process with mean vector $\boldsymbol{\beta}$ and covariance matrix $\boldsymbol{\Gamma}$. Combining terms, we obtain the model

$$\begin{aligned}\mathbf{y}_i &= \mathbf{X}_i\boldsymbol{\beta} + (\boldsymbol{\epsilon}_i + \mathbf{X}_i\mathbf{v}_i)\\ &= \mathbf{X}_i\boldsymbol{\beta} + \mathbf{w}_i,\end{aligned} \qquad \textbf{(15-24)}$$

where

$$E[\mathbf{w}_i] = \mathbf{0}$$

and

$$\begin{aligned}E[\mathbf{w}_i\mathbf{w}_i'] &= \sigma_i^2\mathbf{I} + \mathbf{X}_i\boldsymbol{\Gamma}\mathbf{X}_i'\\ &= \boldsymbol{\Pi}_i.\end{aligned}$$

[11] The most widely cited studies are Hildreth and Houck (1968), Swamy (1970, 1971, 1974), and Hsiao (1975). The model bears some resemblance to the Bayesian approach of Section 6.9, but the similarity is only superficial. We maintain our classical approach to estimation.

This model fits into our earlier framework of groupwise heteroscedasticity (although the matrix algebra is a bit more weighty). For the full sample of observations,

$$\mathbf{V} = \begin{bmatrix} \mathbf{\Pi}_1 & \mathbf{0} & \mathbf{0} & \cdots & \mathbf{0} \\ \mathbf{0} & \mathbf{\Pi}_2 & \mathbf{0} & \cdots & \mathbf{0} \\ & & \vdots & & \\ \mathbf{0} & \mathbf{0} & \mathbf{0} & \cdots & \mathbf{\Pi}_n \end{bmatrix}.$$

For purposes of estimation, let $\mathbf{b}_i$ be the ith ordinary least squares coefficient vector, and let

$$\mathbf{V}_i + \mathbf{\Gamma} = (\mathbf{X}_i'\mathbf{X}_i)^{-1}\mathbf{X}_i'\mathbf{\Pi}_i\mathbf{X}_i(\mathbf{X}_i'\mathbf{X}_i)^{-1} \qquad \textbf{(15-25)}$$

be the covariance matrix of $\mathbf{b}_i$ [see (11-5)], where

$$\mathbf{V}_i = \sigma_i^2(\mathbf{X}_i'\mathbf{X}_i)^{-1}. \qquad \textbf{(15-26)}$$

It can be shown[12] that the GLS estimator in this groupwise heteroscedastic model may be written

$$\hat{\boldsymbol{\beta}} = \sum_{i=1}^{n} \mathbf{W}_i\mathbf{b}_i, \qquad \textbf{(15-27)}$$

where

$$\mathbf{W}_i = \left[\sum_{i=1}^{n} (\mathbf{\Gamma} + \mathbf{V}_i)^{-1}\right]^{-1} (\mathbf{\Gamma} + \mathbf{V}_i)^{-1}.$$

This result shows (once again) the intuitive property that the GLS estimator is a matrix weighted average of the OLS estimators. (As in all such cases, $\Sigma_{i=1}^{n}\mathbf{W}_i = \mathbf{I}$.) The asymptotic covariance matrix for $\hat{\boldsymbol{\beta}}$ is the inverse matrix in brackets in the previous expression.

The obstacle to the application of (15-27) is the unknown parameters in $\mathbf{\Gamma}$ and $\mathbf{V}_i$. Swamy (1971) has suggested a two-step approach. As always, it begins with ordinary least squares. Let $\mathbf{b}_i$ be the group specific OLS coefficient vector, and let $\hat{\mathbf{V}}_i$ be the sample covariance matrix, $s_i^2(\mathbf{X}_i'\mathbf{X}_i)^{-1}$, where $s_i^2 = \mathbf{e}_i'\mathbf{e}_i/(T - K)$. Let

$$\bar{\mathbf{b}} = \frac{1}{n}\sum_{i=1}^{n} \mathbf{b}_i. \qquad \textbf{(15-28)}$$

Then

$$\hat{\mathbf{\Gamma}} = \mathbf{G} = \frac{1}{n-1}\left(\sum_{i=1}^{n} \mathbf{b}_i\mathbf{b}_i' - n\bar{\mathbf{b}}\,\bar{\mathbf{b}}'\right) - \frac{1}{n}\sum_{i=1}^{n}\hat{\mathbf{V}}_i. \qquad \textbf{(15-29)}$$

A potential problem (which appears in our data) is that $\mathbf{G}$ may not be positive definite. The two matrices in $\mathbf{G}$ are of order 1 and $1/(nT)$. Therefore, in terms of

[12]This uses a result due to Rao (1973, p. 29).

the large-sample behavior of **G**, the second matrix will be negligible, but in a small or moderately sized sample, **G** could be dominated by the second (negative) term. Swamy suggests various fix-ups for a nonpositive definite **G**, but a simple and asymptotically valid expedient is simply to drop the second part.[13]

EXAMPLE 15.6 A Random Coefficients Model for Investment

For our investment data, least squares for the five firms produces the estimates given in Table 15.11. (The estimate $\tilde{\mathbf{b}}$ is an alternative weighted average of the OLS estimates that is discussed in Examples 15.7 and 15.8.) As noted, $\hat{\mathbf{\Gamma}}$ in (15-29) is not positive definite. Using the simpler version, we obtain the FGLS random coefficients estimator given in Table 15.11 as $\hat{\boldsymbol{\beta}}_r$.

Finally, for comparison, the FGLS estimates from the least restrictive model of the previous section are given in the last row of the table. The standard errors of the random coefficient estimators are quite a bit larger than those of the FGLS estimator. This is to be expected. The variation of the estimates across firms is explicitly accounted for in the variance of the random coefficients model, whereas it is not in the generalized regression. Finally, the random coefficients model undoes some of the alleged efficiencies of the previous models by apportioning some of the cross-unit variation to the parameters instead of putting it all in the disturbances.

The FGLS procedure estimates the mean vector of the random process generating $\boldsymbol{\beta}_i$. It may be useful to produce predictions of the individual parameter vectors as well. A best linear predictor for $\boldsymbol{\beta}_i$ would be

TABLE 15.11 Individual Least Squares and FGLS Estimates

	β_1		β_2		β_3	
			Individual Group Estimates			
GM	−149.782	(105.8)	0.11928	(0.02583)	0.37145	(0.03707)
CH	−6.18995	(13.51)	0.07795	(0.01997)	0.31572	(0.0288)
GE	−9.9563	(31.37)	0.02655	(0.01557)	0.15169	(0.02570)
WE	−0.50938	(8.015)	0.05289	(0.01571)	0.09241	(0.05610)
US	−30.3685	(157.0)	0.15657	(0.07889)	0.42386	(0.1552)
			Average and FGLS Estimates			
$\hat{\boldsymbol{\beta}}_r$	−18.5201	(34.42)	0.080011	(0.01979)	0.268353	(0.03196)
$\bar{\mathbf{b}}$	−39.3613		0.086649		0.271026	
$\tilde{\mathbf{b}}$	−2.0571		0.05372		0.21136	
$\hat{\boldsymbol{\beta}}$	−35.523	(7.288)	0.09064	(0.00724)	0.34777	(0.03184)

[13]We should note that **G** is not a matrix that converges to **0** asymptotically. It is the estimator of the variance of the process generating $\boldsymbol{\beta}_i$, not of a sampling distribution of an estimator.

$$\hat{\boldsymbol{\beta}}_i = [\boldsymbol{\Gamma}^{-1} + \mathbf{V}_i^{-1}]^{-1}[\boldsymbol{\Gamma}^{-1}\hat{\boldsymbol{\beta}} + \mathbf{V}_i^{-1}\mathbf{b}_i] = \mathbf{A}_i\hat{\boldsymbol{\beta}} + [\mathbf{I} - \mathbf{A}_i]\mathbf{b}_i, \quad \textbf{(15-30)}$$

once again, a matrix weighted average.[14] In this case, the weights are the inverses of the variance matrices of $\hat{\boldsymbol{\beta}}_i$ and $\mathbf{b}_i$. The forecast is made feasible by inserting our estimates $\mathbf{G}$ and $\hat{\mathbf{V}}_i$. For standard errors and confidence bounds,

$$\text{Var}[\hat{\boldsymbol{\beta}}_i] = \begin{bmatrix} \mathbf{A}_i \\ \mathbf{I} - \mathbf{A}_i \end{bmatrix}' \begin{bmatrix} \sum_{i=1}^{n} \mathbf{W}_i(\boldsymbol{\Gamma} + \mathbf{V}_i)\mathbf{W}_i' & \mathbf{W}_i(\boldsymbol{\Gamma} + \mathbf{V}_i) \\ (\boldsymbol{\Gamma} + \mathbf{V}_i)\mathbf{W}_i' & (\boldsymbol{\Gamma} + \mathbf{V}_i) \end{bmatrix} \begin{bmatrix} \mathbf{A}_i \\ \mathbf{I} - \mathbf{A}_i \end{bmatrix}$$

$$\mathbf{A}_i = (\boldsymbol{\Gamma}^{-1} + \mathbf{V}_i^{-1})\boldsymbol{\Gamma}^{-1},$$

where $\mathbf{V}_i = \sigma_i^2(\mathbf{X}_i'\mathbf{X}_i)^{-1}$, $\mathbf{W}_i$ is defined in (15-27), and $\mathbf{G} = \hat{\boldsymbol{\Gamma}}$ is defined in (15-29). For computation, one would compute $(\mathbf{b}_i, \mathbf{V}_i)$, for $i = 1, \ldots, n$, then $\boldsymbol{\Gamma}, \mathbf{D}_i = \boldsymbol{\Gamma} + \mathbf{V}_i$, and $\mathbf{W}_i$, then the various estimators.

Computation of the asymptotic covariance matrices for the predictions involves a large amount of matrix manipulation. The calculation is greatly simplified, however, by a useful result from Hausman (1980):

> *The covariance matrix of an efficient estimator of a parameter vector and its difference from an inefficient estimator of the same parameter vector is zero.*

The GLS and ith OLS estimators satisfy the condition of the theorem, so, Asy. Cov$[\hat{\boldsymbol{\beta}}, \hat{\boldsymbol{\beta}} - \mathbf{b}_i] = \mathbf{0}$, or Asy. Cov$[\hat{\boldsymbol{\beta}}, \mathbf{b}_i]$ = Asy. Var$[\hat{\boldsymbol{\beta}}]$. With this simplification, Asy. Var$[\hat{\boldsymbol{\beta}}_i]$ = Asy. Var$\{\mathbf{A}_i\hat{\boldsymbol{\beta}} + [\mathbf{I} - \mathbf{A}_i]\mathbf{b}_i\}$ can be written

$$\text{Asy. Var}[\hat{\boldsymbol{\beta}}_i] = \text{Asy. Var}[\hat{\boldsymbol{\beta}}] + (\mathbf{I} - \mathbf{A}_i)\{\text{Asy. Var}[\mathbf{b}_i] - \text{Asy. Var}[\hat{\boldsymbol{\beta}}]\}(\mathbf{I} - \mathbf{A}_i)'.$$

The asymptotic covariance matrices are defined in (15-25) and (15-27), and $\mathbf{A}_i$ is defined above.

EXAMPLE 15.7 Predictions for Random Coefficients Estimates

The forecasts and associated standard errors for the individual firms and for the population mean are listed in Table 15.12. The standard errors for the individual predictions are much larger than those for the FGLS estimator of the mean. This is to be expected, since the individual estimates will be largely dominated by the individual, inefficient, least squares estimates, whereas the overall estimator uses GLS to weight the five terms efficiently.

It has been suggested that a test of the random coefficients model can be based on the differences between the OLS estimates equation by equation and a weighted average of the OLS estimates. The test statistic suggested by Swamy (1971) is

[14] See Lee and Griffiths (1979).

TABLE 15.12 Individual Firm Predicted Coefficients

	β_1		β_2		β_3	
GM	−71.074	(52.989)	0.10256	(0.05524)	0.36854	(0.15482)
CH	−9.751	(63.309)	0.08408	(0.05469)	0.30958	(0.15435)
GE	−12.111	(61.407)	0.02805	(0.05509)	0.15041	(0.15447)
WE	3.275	(63.399)	0.04126	(0.05521)	0.13945	(0.15319)
US	−29.975	(45.608)	0.14821	(0.05286)	0.45787	(0.14422)
Overall	−18.520	(33.418)	0.08001	(0.01979)	0.26835	(0.03196)

$$\chi^2 = \sum_{i=1}^{n} [\mathbf{b}_i - \tilde{\mathbf{b}}]'\hat{\mathbf{V}}_i^{-1}[\mathbf{b}_i - \tilde{\mathbf{b}}], \tag{15-31}$$

where

$$\mathbf{b} = \left[\sum_{i=1}^{n} \hat{\mathbf{V}}_i^{-1}\right]^{-1} \sum_{i=1}^{n} \hat{\mathbf{V}}_i^{-1}\mathbf{b}_i.$$

The statistic is asymptotically distributed as chi-squared with $K(n - 1)$ degrees of freedom under the null hypothesis of parameter constancy. It can be shown[15] that the statistic is algebraically the same as the standard F statistic for testing

$$H_0 : \boldsymbol{\beta}_1 = \boldsymbol{\beta}_2 = \cdots = \boldsymbol{\beta}_n$$

in the generalized model

$$\begin{bmatrix} \mathbf{y}_1 \\ \mathbf{y}_2 \\ \vdots \\ \mathbf{y}_n \end{bmatrix} = \begin{bmatrix} \mathbf{X}_1 & \mathbf{0} & \cdots & \mathbf{0} \\ \mathbf{0} & \mathbf{X}_2 & \cdots & \mathbf{0} \\ & & \vdots & \\ \mathbf{0} & \mathbf{0} & \cdots & \mathbf{X}_n \end{bmatrix} \begin{bmatrix} \boldsymbol{\beta}_1 \\ \boldsymbol{\beta}_2 \\ \vdots \\ \boldsymbol{\beta}_n \end{bmatrix} + \begin{bmatrix} \boldsymbol{\epsilon}_1 \\ \boldsymbol{\epsilon}_2 \\ \vdots \\ \boldsymbol{\epsilon}_n \end{bmatrix}$$

$$E[\boldsymbol{\epsilon}_i\boldsymbol{\epsilon}_j'] = \sigma_i^2\mathbf{I} \quad \text{if } i = j \text{ and } [\mathbf{0}] \text{ if not.}$$

Which method is more convenient will depend on the format of the data and the available software.

EXAMPLE 15.8 Testing for Random Coefficients

For the investment data, the weighted average estimator $\tilde{\mathbf{b}}$ is given in Table 15.11. The chi-squared test statistic, with 12 degrees of freedom, is 603.99. This is statistically significant by any measure. Consequently, we would reject the hypothesis of parameter homogeneity (again).

[15] See Johnston (1984, p. 415).

This test is not strictly a test for the random coefficients model. It can be construed as such, but also simply as a test of constancy of the parameter vector across classical regression models. This raises an interesting question that reappears at various points in this literature. If the coefficients are found to differ across units, should we attribute this to random variation or to fixed parameters that simply are different? Unfortunately, the same data are consistent with both hypotheses. Conditioned on the data we have actually observed, in this model, it is little more than a matter of interpretation whether we attribute heterogeneity to random or fixed effects.

15.4. THE SEEMINGLY UNRELATED REGRESSIONS MODEL

An unrestricted form of the model in (15-3) is

$$\mathbf{y}_i = \mathbf{X}_i\boldsymbol{\beta}_i + \boldsymbol{\epsilon}_i, \quad i = 1, \ldots, M, \tag{15-32}$$

where

$$\boldsymbol{\epsilon} = [\boldsymbol{\epsilon}_1', \boldsymbol{\epsilon}_2', \ldots, \boldsymbol{\epsilon}_M']'$$

and

$$E[\boldsymbol{\epsilon}] = \mathbf{0},$$
$$E[\boldsymbol{\epsilon}\boldsymbol{\epsilon}'] = \mathbf{V}.$$

We assume that a total of T observations are used in estimating the parameters of the M equations.[16] Each equation involves K_m regressors, for a total of $K = \Sigma_{i=1}^{n} K_i$. The data are assumed to be well behaved, as described in Chapter 6, and we shall not treat the issue separately here. For the present, we also assume that disturbances are uncorrelated across observations. Therefore,

$$E[\epsilon_{it}\epsilon_{js}] = \sigma_{ij}, \quad \text{if } t = s \text{ and 0 otherwise.}$$

[See Section 15.2.2 and (15-7).] The disturbance formulation is therefore

$$E[\boldsymbol{\epsilon}_i\boldsymbol{\epsilon}_j'] = \sigma_{ij}\mathbf{I}_T$$

or

$$E[\boldsymbol{\epsilon}\boldsymbol{\epsilon}'] = \mathbf{V} = \begin{bmatrix} \sigma_{11}\mathbf{I} & \sigma_{12}\mathbf{I} & \cdots & \sigma_{1M}\mathbf{I} \\ \sigma_{21}\mathbf{I} & \sigma_{22}\mathbf{I} & \cdots & \sigma_{2M}\mathbf{I} \\ & \vdots & & \\ \sigma_{M1}\mathbf{I} & \sigma_{M2}\mathbf{I} & \cdots & \sigma_{MM}\mathbf{I} \end{bmatrix}. \tag{15-33}$$

[16]There are a few results for unequal numbers of observations, such as Schmidt (1977) and Im (1994). But generally, the case of fixed T is the norm in practice.

15.4.1. Generalized Least Squares

Each equation is, by itself, a classical regression. Therefore, the parameters could be estimated consistently, if not efficiently, by ordinary least squares. The generalized regression model applies to the stacked model,

$$\begin{bmatrix} \mathbf{y}_1 \\ \mathbf{y}_2 \\ \vdots \\ \mathbf{y}_M \end{bmatrix} = \begin{bmatrix} \mathbf{X}_1 & \mathbf{0} & \cdots & \mathbf{0} \\ \mathbf{0} & \mathbf{X}_2 & \cdots & \mathbf{0} \\ & & \vdots & \\ \mathbf{0} & \mathbf{0} & \cdots & \mathbf{X}_M \end{bmatrix} \begin{bmatrix} \boldsymbol{\beta}_1 \\ \boldsymbol{\beta}_2 \\ \vdots \\ \boldsymbol{\beta}_M \end{bmatrix} + \begin{bmatrix} \boldsymbol{\epsilon}_1 \\ \boldsymbol{\epsilon}_2 \\ \vdots \\ \boldsymbol{\epsilon}_M \end{bmatrix} \tag{15-34}$$

$$= \mathbf{X}\boldsymbol{\beta} + \boldsymbol{\epsilon}.$$

Therefore, the efficient estimator is generalized least squares.[17] The model has a particularly convenient form. For the tth observation, the $M \times M$ covariance matrix of the disturbances is

$$\boldsymbol{\Sigma} = \begin{bmatrix} \sigma_{11} & \sigma_{12} & \cdots & \sigma_{1M} \\ \sigma_{21} & \sigma_{22} & \cdots & \sigma_{2M} \\ & \vdots & & \\ \sigma_{M1} & \sigma_{M2} & \cdots & \sigma_{MM} \end{bmatrix}, \tag{15-35}$$

so, in (15-33),

$$\mathbf{V} = \boldsymbol{\Sigma} \otimes \mathbf{I} \tag{15-36}$$

and

$$\mathbf{V}^{-1} = \boldsymbol{\Sigma}^{-1} \otimes \mathbf{I}. \tag{15-37}$$

Denoting the ijth element of $\boldsymbol{\Sigma}^{-1}$ by σ^{ij}, we find that the GLS estimator is

$$\begin{aligned} \hat{\boldsymbol{\beta}} &= [\mathbf{X}'\mathbf{V}^{-1}\mathbf{X}]^{-1}\mathbf{X}'\mathbf{V}^{-1}\mathbf{y} \\ &= [\mathbf{X}'(\boldsymbol{\Sigma}^{-1} \otimes \mathbf{I})\mathbf{X}]^{-1}\mathbf{X}'(\boldsymbol{\Sigma}^{-1} \otimes \mathbf{I})\mathbf{y} \end{aligned}$$

$$= \begin{bmatrix} \sigma^{11}\mathbf{X}_1'\mathbf{X}_1 & \sigma^{12}\mathbf{X}_1'\mathbf{X}_2 & \cdots & \sigma^{1M}\mathbf{X}_1'\mathbf{X}_M \\ \sigma^{21}\mathbf{X}_2'\mathbf{X}_1 & \sigma^{22}\mathbf{X}_2'\mathbf{X}_2 & \cdots & \sigma^{2M}\mathbf{X}_2'\mathbf{X}_M \\ & & \vdots & \\ \sigma^{M1}\mathbf{X}_M'\mathbf{X}_1 & \sigma^{M2}\mathbf{X}_M'\mathbf{X}_2 & \cdots & \sigma^{MM}\mathbf{X}_M'\mathbf{X}_M \end{bmatrix}^{-1} \begin{bmatrix} \sum_{j=1}^{M} \sigma^{1j}\mathbf{X}_1'\mathbf{y}_j \\ \sum_{j=1}^{M} \sigma^{2j}\mathbf{X}_2'\mathbf{y}_j \\ \vdots \\ \sum_{j=1}^{M} \sigma^{Mj}\mathbf{X}_M'\mathbf{y}_j \end{bmatrix}. \tag{15-38}$$

[17]See Zellner (1962).

The asymptotic covariance matrix for the GLS estimator is the inverse matrix in (15-38). All the results of Chapter 11 for the generalized regression model extend to this model.

This is obviously different from ordinary least squares. At this point, however, the equations are linked only by their disturbances—hence the name *seemingly unrelated regressions model*—so it is interesting to ask just how much efficiency is gained by using generalized least squares instead of ordinary least squares. Zellner (1962) and Dwivedi and Srivastava (1978) have analyzed some special cases in detail.

1. If the equations are actually unrelated—that is, if $\sigma_{ij} = 0$—there is obviously no payoff to GLS. Indeed, GLS is OLS.
2. If the equations have identical explanatory variables—that is, if $\mathbf{X}_i = \mathbf{X}_j$—it can be shown (we leave it as an exercise) that OLS and GLS are identical.[18]
3. If the regressors in one block of equations are a subset of those in another, GLS brings no efficiency gain in estimation of the smaller equations.[19]

In the more general case, with unrestricted correlation of the disturbances and different regressors in the equations, the results are complicated and dependent on the data. Two propositions that apply generally are as follows:

1. The greater the correlation of the disturbances, the greater the efficiency gain accruing to GLS.
2. The less correlation there is between the $\mathbf{X}$ matrices, the greater the gain in using GLS.

15.4.2. Feasible Generalized Least Squares

The preceding discussion assumes that $\mathbf{\Sigma}$ is known, which, as usual, is rarely the case. FGLS estimators have been devised, however.[20] The least squares residuals may be used (of course) to estimate consistently the elements of $\mathbf{\Sigma}$ with

$$\hat{\sigma}_{ij} = s_{ij} = \frac{\mathbf{e}_i'\mathbf{e}_j}{T}. \tag{15-39}$$

The consistency of s_{ij} follows from that of $\mathbf{b}_i$ and $\mathbf{b}_j$. A degrees of freedom correction in the divisor is occasionally suggested.[21] Two possibilities are

$$s_{ij}^* = \frac{\mathbf{e}_i'\mathbf{e}_j}{[(T - K_i)(T - K_j)]^{1/2}}$$

and

---

[18]An intriguing result, albeit probably of negligible practical significance, is that the result also applies if the $\mathbf{X}$'s are all nonsingular, and not necessarily identical, linear combinations of the same set of variables.

[19]We shall examine one such model in detail later. The result was analyzed by Goldberger (1970) and later by Revankar (1974) and Conniffe (1982a).

[20]See Zellner (1962) and Zellner and Huang (1962).

[21]See, for example, Theil (1971, p. 321) and Judge et al. (1985, p. 469).

$$s_{ij}^{**} = \frac{\mathbf{e}_i'\mathbf{e}_j}{T - \max(K_i, K_j)}.$$

The second is unbiased only if i equals j or K_i equals K_j, whereas the first is unbiased only if i equals j. Whether unbiasedness of the estimate of $\boldsymbol{\Sigma}$ used for FGLS is a virtue here is uncertain.[22] The asymptotic properties of $\hat{\hat{\boldsymbol{\beta}}}$ do not rely on an unbiased estimator of $\boldsymbol{\Sigma}$; all our results from Chapter 13 for FGLS estimators carry over to this model, with no modification. It is worth noting that the matrix $\boldsymbol{\Sigma}$ based on the second correction is not necessarily positive definite. If the sample is large, it will be, but then the degrees of freedom correction is moot anyway. How the different estimators will behave in small samples is another question. Precise results are available only for some special cases, although suggestive results have been obtained in Monte Carlo studies.[23] We shall use (15-39) in what follows. With

$$\mathbf{S} = \begin{bmatrix} s_{11} & s_{12} & \cdots & s_{1M} \\ s_{21} & s_{22} & \cdots & s_{2M} \\ & \vdots & & \\ s_{M1} & s_{M2} & \cdots & s_{MM} \end{bmatrix} \tag{15-40}$$

in hand, FGLS can proceed as usual. Iterated FGLS will be maximum likelihood if it is based on (15-39).

Goodness-of-fit measures for the system have been devised. For instance, McElroy (1977) suggested the systemwide measure

$$R_*^2 = 1 - \frac{\hat{\boldsymbol{\epsilon}}'\hat{\mathbf{V}}^{-1}\hat{\boldsymbol{\epsilon}}}{\sum_{i=1}^{M}\sum_{j=1}^{M}\hat{\sigma}^{ij}\left[\sum_{t=1}^{T}(y_{it} - \bar{y}_i)(y_{jt} - \bar{y}_j)\right]}, \tag{15-41}$$

where ˆ indicates the FGLS estimate. The measure is bounded by 0 and 1 and is related to the F statistic used to test the hypothesis that all the slopes in the model are zero. Fit measures in this context have all the shortcomings discussed in Chapter 11. An additional problem for this model is that overall fit measures such as (15-41) will obscure the variation in fit across equations. For the investment example, using the FGLS residuals for the model in Table 15.8, McElroy's measure gives a value of $1 - 100/648.94$, or 0.846. But a look at Figure 15.1 shows that this apparently good overall fit is an aggregate of mediocre fits for Chrysler and Westinghouse and obviously terrible fits for GM, GE, and U.S. Steel. Indeed, the conventional measure $1 - \mathbf{e}'\mathbf{e}/\mathbf{y}'\mathbf{M}^0\mathbf{y}$ for GE based on the same FGLS residuals is -16.7!

[22] Kakwani's (1967) result applies to all three; the FGLS estimator of $\boldsymbol{\beta}$ is unbiased regardless of which divisor is used.

[23] Zellner (1963), Kmenta and Gilbert (1968), Conniffe (1982b), and Revankar (1974).

It might be desirable to compare the fit of the unrestricted model, with separate coefficient vectors by firm, with the restricted one in Section 15.2. The computation in (15-41) with the FGLS residuals based on the seemingly unrelated regression estimates in Table 15.13 on page 680 gives a value of 0.871, which appears to be an unimpressive improvement in the fit of the model. But a comparison of the residual plot in Figure 15.2 with that in Figure 15.1 shows that, on the contrary, the fit of the model has improved dramatically. The upshot is that although a fit measure for the system might have some virtue as a descriptive measure, it should be used with care.

The value of exactly $MT = 100$ for the numerator for R_*^2 might seem odd. But combining (15-37) and (15-39), we see that since the matrix $\hat{\mathbf{V}}$ in (15-41) is computed using $\hat{\boldsymbol{\epsilon}}$, the quantity in the numerator is nothing more than

$$T\sum_{i=1}^{M}\sum_{j=1}^{M}\hat{\sigma}^{ij}\hat{\sigma}_{ij} = T \times \text{tr}(\hat{\boldsymbol{\Sigma}}^{-1}\hat{\boldsymbol{\Sigma}}) = T \times \text{tr}(\mathbf{I}_M) = MT.$$

(Further discussion of this result appears in Section 15.4.3b.) The denominator can also be simplified in a way that facilitates the computation. By the same logic as above, the double sum in the denominator is

$$T\sum_{i=1}^{M}\sum_{j=1}^{M}\hat{\sigma}^{ij}s_{yy,ij} = T \times \text{tr}(\hat{\boldsymbol{\Sigma}}^{-1}\mathbf{S}_{yy}),$$

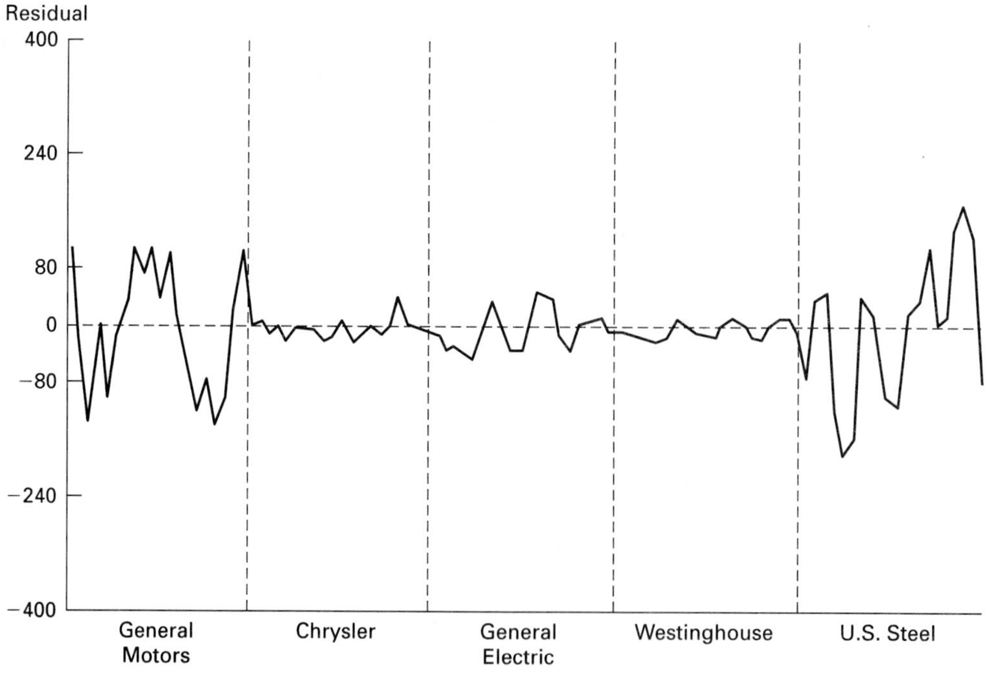

FIGURE 15.2 SUR Residuals.

where

$$[\mathbf{S}_{yy}]_{mn} = \frac{1}{T}\sum_{t=1}^{T}(y_{it} - \bar{y}_i)(y_{jt} - \bar{y}_j).$$

Combining all these, we get

$$R_*^2 = 1 - \frac{M}{\operatorname{tr}(\hat{\boldsymbol{\Sigma}}^{-1}\mathbf{S}_{yy})}.$$

The advantage of this formulation is that it involves $M \times M$ matrices, which are typically quite small, whereas $\hat{\mathbf{V}}$ in (15-41) is $MT \times MT$. In our case, M equals 5, but MT equals 100.

For testing a hypothesis about $\boldsymbol{\beta}$, a statistic analogous to the F ratio in multiple regression analysis is

$$F[J, MT - K] = \frac{(\mathbf{R}\hat{\boldsymbol{\beta}} - \mathbf{q})'[\mathbf{R}(\mathbf{X}'\mathbf{V}^{-1}\mathbf{X})^{-1}\mathbf{R}']^{-1}(\mathbf{R}\hat{\boldsymbol{\beta}} - \mathbf{q})/J}{\hat{\boldsymbol{\epsilon}}'\hat{\mathbf{V}}^{-1}\hat{\boldsymbol{\epsilon}}/(MT - K)}. \quad \textbf{(15-42)}$$

The computation requires the unknown $\mathbf{V}$. If we insert the FGLS estimate $\hat{\mathbf{V}}$ based on (15-39) and use the result that the denominator converges to 1, the statistic will behave the same as

$$\hat{F} = \frac{1}{J}(\mathbf{R}\hat{\hat{\boldsymbol{\beta}}} - \mathbf{q})'[\mathbf{R}\,\widehat{\text{Var}}[\hat{\hat{\boldsymbol{\beta}}}]\mathbf{R}']^{-1}(\mathbf{R}\hat{\hat{\boldsymbol{\beta}}} - \mathbf{q}). \quad \textbf{(15-43)}$$

This can be referred to the standard F table. Because it uses the estimated $\boldsymbol{\Sigma}$, even with normally distributed disturbances, the F distribution is only valid approximately. In general, the statistic $F[J, n]$ converges to $1/J$ times a chi-squared $[J]$ as $n \to \infty$. Therefore, an alternative test statistic that is asymptotically distributed as chi-squared with J degrees of freedom is

$$J\hat{F} = (\mathbf{R}\hat{\hat{\boldsymbol{\beta}}} - \mathbf{q})'[\mathbf{R}\,\widehat{\text{Var}}[\hat{\hat{\boldsymbol{\beta}}}]\mathbf{R}']^{-1}(\mathbf{R}\hat{\hat{\boldsymbol{\beta}}} - \mathbf{q}). \quad \textbf{(15-44)}$$

This can be recognized as a Wald statistic that measures the distance between $\mathbf{R}\hat{\hat{\boldsymbol{\beta}}}$ and $\mathbf{q}$. Both statistics are valid asymptotically, but (15-43) may perform better in a small or moderately sized sample.[24] Once again, the divisor used in computing $\hat{\sigma}_{ij}$ will make a difference, and there is no general rule.

EXAMPLE 15.9 FGLS Estimates of a Seemingly Unrelated Regressions Model

By relaxing the constraint that all five firms have the same parameter vector in Example 15.4, we obtain a five-equation seemingly unrelated regression model. The FGLS estimates for the system are given in Table 15.13, where we have included the equality constrained estimator of Example 15.4 for comparison, as well as the ordinary least squares estimates of the GM equation. The variables are the constant terms, F and C, respectively. It is also interesting to compare these with the predictions from the random coefficients model in Table 15.12.

[24]See Judge et al. (1985, p. 476).

Save for the constant terms, the estimates are quite similar. This makes sense; in the final analysis, these are different weighted averages of the least squares estimates.

The correlations of the GLS residuals are given above the diagonal in Table 15.13. The assumption of equal-parameter vectors appears to have seriously distorted the correlations computed earlier. A comparison with Table 15.6 shows that the elements in $\hat{\Sigma}$ are drastically inflated by the imposition of the constraint, as are the correlations across equations.

The F statistic for testing the hypothesis of equal-parameter vectors in all five equations is 1550.03 with 12 and $(100 - 15)$ degrees of freedom. This is obviously larger than the tabled critical value, so the hypothesis of parameter homogeneity should be rejected. We might have expected this result in view of the dramatic reduction in the diagonal elements of $\hat{\Sigma}$ compared with those of Example 16.4.

It may also be of interest to test whether Σ is a diagonal matrix. Two possible approaches were described in Example 15.4 [see (15-13) and (15-14)]. The unrestricted model is the one we are using here, whereas the restricted model is the groupwise heteroscedastic model of Example 15.3, without the restriction of equal-parameter vectors. As such, the restricted model reduces to separate

TABLE 15.13 **Parameter Estimates (Standard Errors in Parentheses)**

	GM	CH	GE	WE	US	Pooled	GM by OLS
			Seemingly Unrelated Regressions				
β_0	−162.36 (89.46)	0.5043 (11.51)	−22.439 (25.52)	1.0889 (6.2959)	85.423 (111.9)	−30.281 (5.589)	−149.78 (105.8)
β_1	0.12049 (0.0216)	0.06955 (0.0169)	0.03729 (0.0123)	0.05701 (0.0114)	0.1015 (0.0547)	0.09413 (0.00684)	0.11928 (0.0258)
β_2	0.38275 (0.0328)	0.3086 (0.0259)	0.13078 (0.0221)	0.0415 (0.0412)	0.3999 (0.1278)	0.3406 (0.0268)	0.37145 (0.0371)

Residual Covariance Matrix $\quad\Sigma$

	GM	CH	GE	WE	US
GM	7216.04	(−0.299)	(0.269)	(0.257)	(−0.330)
CH	−313.70	152.85	(0.006)	(0.238)	(0.384)
GE	605.34	2.0474	700.46	(0.777)	(0.482)
WE	129.89	16.661	200.32	94.912	(0.699)
US	−2686.5	455.09	1224.4	652.72	9188.2

regression models, estimable by ordinary least squares. The likelihood ratio statistic would be

$$\lambda_{LR} = T\left[\sum_{i=1}^{M} \ln s_i^2 - \ln|\hat{\Sigma}|\right], \tag{15-45}$$

where s_i^2 is $\mathbf{e}_i'\mathbf{e}_m/T$ from the individual least squares regressions and $\hat{\Sigma}$ is the maximum likelihood estimate of Σ. This statistic is asymptotically distributed as chi-squared with $M(M-1)/2$ degrees of freedom. The alternative suggested by Breusch and Pagan (1980) is the Lagrange multiplier statistic,

$$\lambda_{LM} = T\sum_{i=2}^{M}\sum_{j=1}^{i-1} r_{ij}^2, \tag{15-46}$$

where r_{ij} is the estimated correlation $s_{ij}/[s_{ii}s_{jj}]^{1/2}$. Note the similarity of this to the Box–Pierce statistic we encountered in Chapter 13. Asymptotically, this statistic is also distributed as chi-squared with $M(M-1)/2$ degrees of freedom. This test has the advantage that it does not require computation of the maximum likelihood estimator of Σ, since it is based on the OLS residuals.

EXAMPLE 15.10 FGLS Versus SUR Residuals

The sample correlations of the ordinary least squares residuals are shown below the diagonal in Table 15.14. For comparison, the estimates of the correlations using the FGLS estimator of $\boldsymbol{\beta}$ are shown above the diagonal. Based on the OLS results, the Lagrange multiplier statistic is 29.046, with 10 degrees of freedom. The 1 percent critical value is 23.209, so the hypothesis that Σ is diagonal can be rejected.

15.4.3. Maximum Likelihood Estimation

15.4.3a. Iterated FGLS. The Oberhofer–Kmenta (1974) conditions are met for the seemingly unrelated regressions model, so maximum likelihood

TABLE 15.14 Residual Correlations

	GM	*GE*	*US*	*CH*	*WE*
GM	—	0.269	−0.329	−0.298	0.157
US	0.279	—	0.483	0.0006	0.777
GE	−0.278	0.373	—	0.384	0.699
CH	−0.273	−0.068	0.362	—	0.138
WE	0.158	0.729	0.615	0.115	—

estimates can be obtained by iterating the FGLS procedure. We note, once again, that this presumes the use of (15-39) for estimation of σ_{ij} at each iteration. It is worth noting that maximum likelihood enjoys no advantages over FGLS in its asymptotic properties. Whether it would be preferable in a small sample is an open question whose answer will depend on the particular data set.

EXAMPLE 15.11 ML Estimates of a SUR Model

The maximum likelihood estimates of the parameters estimated by FGLS in Example 15.9 are given in Table 15.15. As might be expected, the differences are not substantial. The estimates are, in fact, not radically different from the ordinary least squares estimates, but they are very different from the values in Table 15.5.

15.4.3b. Direct Maximum Likelihood Estimation. By simply inserting the special form of $\mathbf{V}$ in the log-likelihood function for the generalized regression model in (11-20), we can consider direct maximization instead of iterated FGLS. It is useful, however, to reexamine the model in a somewhat different formulation. This alternative construction of the likelihood function appears in many other related models in a number of literatures.

Consider one observation on each of the M dependent variables and their

TABLE 15.15 Maximum Likelihood Estimates

	GM	*CH*	*GE*	*WE*	*US*
Constant	−173.218	2.39111	−16.6623	4.37312	136.969
	(84.30)	(11.63)	(24.96)	(6.018)	(94.8)
F	0.122040	0.06741	0.0371	0.05397	0.08865
	(0.02025)	(0.01709)	(0.01177)	(0.0103)	(0.04542)
C	0.38914	0.30520	0.11723	0.026930	0.31246
	(0.03185)	(0.02606)	(0.02173)	(0.03708)	(0.118)

Residual Covariance Matrix

	GM	*CH*	*GE*	*WE*	*US*
GM	7307.30				
CH	−330.55	155.08			
GE	550.27	11.429	741.22		
WE	118.83	18.376	220.33	103.13	
US	−2879.10	463.21	1408.11	734.83	9671.4

associated regressors. We wish to arrange this observation horizontally instead of vertically. The model for this observation can be written

$$[y_1 \ y_2 \ \ldots \ y_M]_t = [\mathbf{x}_t^*]'[\boldsymbol{\pi}_1 \ \boldsymbol{\pi}_2 \ \ldots \ \boldsymbol{\pi}_M] + [\epsilon_1 \ \epsilon_2 \ \ldots \ \epsilon_M]_t, \quad \textbf{(15-47)}$$

where $\mathbf{x}_t^*$ is the full set of all K *different* independent variables that appear in the model. The parameter matrix then has one column for each equation, but the columns are not the same as $\boldsymbol{\beta}_i$ in (15-32) unless every variable happens to appear in every equation. Otherwise, in the ith equation, $\boldsymbol{\pi}_i$ will have a number of zeros in it, imposing an **exclusion restriction.**

EXAMPLE 15.12 Specification of a Cobb–Douglas Model

Consider the GM and GE equations from the Boot–de Witt data we have used in the previous examples. The tth observation would be

$$[I_g \ \ I_e] = [1 \ \ F_g \ \ C_g \ \ F_e \ \ C_e]\begin{bmatrix} \alpha_g & \alpha_e \\ \beta_{1g} & 0 \\ \beta_{2g} & 0 \\ 0 & \beta_{1e} \\ 0 & \beta_{2e} \end{bmatrix} + [\epsilon_g \ \ \epsilon_e].$$

This is one observation. Let $\boldsymbol{\epsilon}_t$ be the vector of M disturbances for this observation arranged, for now, in a column. Then $E[\boldsymbol{\epsilon}_t\boldsymbol{\epsilon}_t'] = \boldsymbol{\Sigma}$. The log of the joint normal density of these M disturbances is

$$\ln L_t = -\frac{M}{2}\ln(2\pi) - \frac{1}{2}\ln|\boldsymbol{\Sigma}| - \frac{1}{2}\boldsymbol{\epsilon}_t'\boldsymbol{\Sigma}^{-1}\boldsymbol{\epsilon}_t. \quad \textbf{(15-48)}$$

The log-likelihood for a sample of T joint observations is the sum of these over t:

$$\begin{aligned} \ln L &= \sum_{t=1}^{T} \ln L_t \\ &= -\frac{MT}{2}\ln(2\pi) - \frac{T}{2}\ln|\boldsymbol{\Sigma}| - \frac{1}{2}\sum_{t=1}^{T}\boldsymbol{\epsilon}_t'\boldsymbol{\Sigma}^{-1}\boldsymbol{\epsilon}_t. \end{aligned} \quad \textbf{(15-49)}$$

Denote the ijth element of $\boldsymbol{\Sigma}^{-1}$ as σ^{ij}. Then

$$\boldsymbol{\epsilon}_t'\boldsymbol{\Sigma}^{-1}\boldsymbol{\epsilon}_t = \sum_{i=1}^{M}\sum_{j=1}^{M}\epsilon_{ti}\epsilon_{tj}\sigma^{ij}.$$

Summing these over T observations, we have

$$\sum_{t=1}^{T}\boldsymbol{\epsilon}_t'\boldsymbol{\Sigma}^{-1}\boldsymbol{\epsilon}_t = \sum_{t=1}^{T}\sum_{i=1}^{M}\sum_{j=1}^{M}\epsilon_{ti}\epsilon_{tj}\sigma^{ij}.$$

Now reverse the order of summation and move σ^{mn} outside to obtain

$$\sum_{t=1}^{T} \boldsymbol{\epsilon}_t' \boldsymbol{\Sigma}^{-1} \boldsymbol{\epsilon}_t = \sum_{i=1}^{M} \sum_{j=1}^{M} \sigma^{ij} \sum_{t=1}^{T} \epsilon_{ti}\epsilon_{tj}.$$

The innermost sum, $\Sigma_{t=1}^{T} \epsilon_{ti}\epsilon_{tj}$, is T times the ijth element of $\mathbf{W}$, where

$$\mathbf{W}_{ij} = \frac{1}{T} \sum_{t=1}^{T} \epsilon_{ti}\epsilon_{tj}.$$

Since this uses actual disturbances, $E[\mathbf{W}_{ij}] = \sigma_{ij}$; $\mathbf{W}$ is the $M \times M$ matrix we would use to estimate $\boldsymbol{\Sigma}$ if the ϵ's were actually observed. Returning to the derivation, we have, therefore,

$$\sum_{t=1}^{T} \boldsymbol{\epsilon}_t' \boldsymbol{\Sigma}^{-1} \boldsymbol{\epsilon}_t = T \sum_{i=1}^{M} \sum_{j=1}^{M} \sigma^{ij} \mathbf{W}_{ij}.$$

Finally, the ith diagonal element of the matrix product $\boldsymbol{\Sigma}^{-1}\mathbf{W}$ is $\Sigma_j \sigma^{ij}\mathbf{W}_{ij}$. The preceding sum is T times the sum of these, which is T times the trace of the product. Therefore,

$$\sum_{t=1}^{T} \boldsymbol{\epsilon}_t' \boldsymbol{\Sigma}^{-1} \boldsymbol{\epsilon}_t = T \operatorname{tr}(\boldsymbol{\Sigma}^{-1}\mathbf{W}). \tag{15-50}$$

Inserting this in the log-likelihood, we have

$$\ln L = -\frac{T}{2}[M \ln(2\pi) + \ln|\boldsymbol{\Sigma}| + \operatorname{tr}(\boldsymbol{\Sigma}^{-1}\mathbf{W})]. \tag{15-51}$$

Recall that $\mathbf{W}$ is the matrix of residual sums of squares and cross products. We now consider maximum likelihood estimation of parameters of a model.

It has been shown[25] that

$$\frac{\partial \ln L}{\partial \boldsymbol{\Sigma}} = -\frac{T}{2} \boldsymbol{\Sigma}^{-1}(\boldsymbol{\Sigma} - \mathbf{W})\boldsymbol{\Sigma}^{-1}. \tag{15-52}$$

Equating this to a zero matrix, we see that given the maximum likelihood estimates of the slope parameters, the maximum likelihood estimator of $\boldsymbol{\Sigma}$ is $\mathbf{W}$, the matrix of mean residual sums of squares and cross products, that is, the matrix we have used for FGLS. [Notice that there is no correction for degrees of freedom; $\partial \ln L/\partial \boldsymbol{\Sigma} = \mathbf{0}$ implies (15-39).]

We also know that because this is a generalized regression model, the maximum likelihood estimator of the parameter matrix $[\boldsymbol{\beta}]$ must be equivalent to the FGLS estimator we discussed earlier.[26] It is useful to go a step further. If

[25] See, for example, Joreskog (1973).

[26] This establishes the Oberhofer–Kmenta conditions.

we insert our solution for $\boldsymbol{\Sigma}$ in the likelihood function, we obtain the **concentrated log likelihood,**

$$\ln L_c = -\frac{T}{2}[M(1 + \ln(2\pi)) + \ln|\mathbf{W}|]. \quad \textbf{(15-53)}$$

We have shown, therefore, that the criterion for choosing the maximum likelihood estimator of $\boldsymbol{\beta}$ is

$$\hat{\boldsymbol{\beta}}_{\text{ML}} = \text{Min}_{\beta} 1/2 \ln|\mathbf{W}|, \quad \textbf{(15-54)}$$

subject to the exclusion restrictions. This is an important result that reappears in many other models and settings. This minimization must be done subject to the constraints in the parameter matrix. In our two-equation example, there are two blocks of zeros in the parameter matrix. These must be present in the MLE as well.[27]

This maximization problem is particularly simple to solve using Newton's method. To construct the gradient of the log-likelihood, let

$$\boldsymbol{\Pi} = [\boldsymbol{\pi}_1 \quad \boldsymbol{\pi}_2 \quad \cdots \quad \boldsymbol{\pi}_M].$$

So $\boldsymbol{\Pi}$ is a $K \times M$ parameter matrix (which usually contains many zeros). Then

$$\ln L_c = -\frac{MT}{2}[1 + \ln(2\pi)] - \frac{T}{2}\ln|\mathbf{W}|,$$

where

$$\mathbf{W} = \frac{1}{T}(\mathbf{Y} - \mathbf{X}\boldsymbol{\Pi})'(\mathbf{Y} - \mathbf{X}\boldsymbol{\Pi}).$$

The matrix of derivatives is

$$\frac{\partial \ln L_c}{\partial \boldsymbol{\Pi}} = \mathbf{X}'(\mathbf{Y} - \mathbf{X}\boldsymbol{\Pi})\mathbf{W}^{-1}.$$

To construct the appropriate vector, just extract the elements that correspond to nonzero elements of $\boldsymbol{\Pi}$, columnwise, and arrange them in a column vector. The Hessian is

$$\frac{\partial^2 \ln L_c}{\partial \pi_{ki}\, \partial \pi_{lj}} = -\mathbf{W}^{ij}(\mathbf{X}'\mathbf{X})_{kl}.$$

These are then arranged in a matrix that corresponds to the column vector of derivatives. Then Newton's method can be used to maximize the log-likelihood. As we saw earlier, iterated FGLS can also be used to compute the MLE. One advantage of this method is that it is particularly fast. The first and second derivatives are, after a small amount of manipulation, functions only of $\mathbf{Y}'\mathbf{Y}/T$,

[27]The estimate of $\boldsymbol{\beta}$ is the set of nonzero elements in the parameter matrix in (15-47).

$\mathbf{X}'\mathbf{X}/T$, and $\mathbf{X}'\mathbf{Y}/T$. This means that the amount of computation needed is independent of the sample size once the moments are computed. Second, the log-likelihood function is globally concave, so this method normally converges after only a few iterations. Finally, it is particularly simple to impose the sort of cross-equation equality constraints that arise in demand systems with this method. Joreskog (1973) provides details.

The results of Chapter 11 apply here, so we need not rederive the information matrix to obtain the correct asymptotic covariance matrix for the maximum likelihood estimates. They are the ones given earlier for GLS. It would rarely be used, but if needed, the asymptotic covariance matrix for the maximum likelihood estimator of $\boldsymbol{\Sigma}$ is (with the elements stacked in an $M^2 \times 1$ vector)

$$\text{Asy. Var}[\hat{\boldsymbol{\Sigma}}_{\text{ML}}] = \frac{2}{T}\boldsymbol{\Sigma} \otimes \boldsymbol{\Sigma}. \tag{15-55}$$

This can be estimated with $(2/T)\mathbf{W} \otimes \mathbf{W}$. It can be used, for example, to test the hypothesis that $\boldsymbol{\Sigma}$ is diagonal.

The likelihood ratio statistic is an alternative to the F statistic discussed earlier for testing hypotheses about $\boldsymbol{\beta}$. The likelihood ratio statistic is

$$\lambda = -2(\ln L_r - \ln L_u) = T(\ln|\mathbf{W}_r| - \ln|\mathbf{W}_u|), \tag{15-56}$$

where $\mathbf{W}_r$ and $\mathbf{W}_u$ are the residual sums of squares and cross-product matrices using the constrained and unconstrained estimators, respectively. The likelihood ratio statistic is asymptotically distributed as chi-squared with degrees of freedom equal to the number of restrictions.

EXAMPLE 15.13 Likelihood Ratio Test in a SUR Model

The log determinant of the unrestricted maximum likelihood estimator of $\boldsymbol{\Sigma}$ given in Example 15.11 is 31.71986. The log-likelihood is therefore

$$\begin{aligned} L_u &= -\frac{20(5)}{2}[\ln(2\pi) + 1] - \frac{20}{2}31.71986 \\ &= -459.0925. \end{aligned}$$

The restricted model with equal-parameter vectors and correlation across equations is discussed in Section 15.2.2, and the restricted MLEs are given in Example 15.4. (The MLE of $\boldsymbol{\Sigma}$ is not shown there.) The log determinant for the constrained model is 37.838. The log-likelihood for the constrained model is therefore -520.27. The likelihood ratio test statistic is 122.36. The 1 percent critical value from the chi-squared distribution with 12 degrees of freedom is 26.217, so the hypothesis that the parameters in all five equations are equal is (once again) rejected.

15.4.4. Autocorrelation

The seemingly unrelated regressions model can be extended to allow for autocorrelation in the same fashion as in Section 15.2.3. To reiterate, suppose that

$$\mathbf{y}_i = \mathbf{X}_i\boldsymbol{\beta}_i + \boldsymbol{\epsilon}_i,$$
$$\epsilon_{it} = \rho_i\epsilon_{i,t-1} + u_{it},$$

where u_{it} is uncorrelated across observations. This will imply that the blocks in $\mathbf{V}$, instead of $\sigma_{ij}\mathbf{I}$, are $\sigma_{ij}\boldsymbol{\Omega}_{ij}$, where $\boldsymbol{\Omega}_{ij}$ is given in (15-22).

The treatment shown by Park (1967) is the one we used earlier.[28] This calls for a three-step approach:

1. Estimate each equation in the system by ordinary least squares. Use any of the consistent estimators of ρ described in Chapter 13. For that equation, transform the data by the Prais–Winsten transformation to remove the autocorrelation.[29] Note that there will not be a constant term in the transformed data because there will be a column with $(1 - r_i^2)^{1/2}$ as the first observation and $(1 - r_i)$ for the remainder.
2. Using the transformed data, use ordinary least squares once more to estimate $\boldsymbol{\Sigma}$.
3. Use FGLS based on the estimated $\boldsymbol{\Sigma}$ and the transformed data.

There is no benefit to iteration. The estimator is efficient at every step, and iteration does not produce a maximum likelihood estimator. After the last step, $\boldsymbol{\Sigma}$ should be reestimated with the GLS estimates. The estimated covariance matrix for $\boldsymbol{\epsilon}$ can then be reconstructed using

$$\hat{\sigma}_{mn}(\boldsymbol{\epsilon}) = \frac{\hat{\sigma}_{mn}}{1 - r_m r_n}. \qquad \textbf{(15-57)}$$

EXAMPLE 15.14 Autocorrelation in a SUR Model

Table 15.16 is a list of the autocorrelation-corrected estimates of the model of Example 15.8. The Durbin–Watson statistics for the five data sets given here, with the exception of Chrysler, strongly suggest that there is, indeed, autocorrelation in the disturbances. The differences between these and the uncorrected estimates given earlier are sometimes relatively large, as might be expected, given the fairly high autocorrelation and small sample size. The smaller diagonal elements in the disturbance covariance matrix compared with those of Ex-

[28] Guilkey (1974) and Guilkey and Schmidt (1973) present an alternative treatment based on $\boldsymbol{\epsilon}_t = \mathbf{R}\boldsymbol{\epsilon}_{t-1} + \mathbf{u}_t$, where $\boldsymbol{\epsilon}_t$ is the $M \times 1$ vector of disturbances at time t and $\mathbf{R}$ is a correlation matrix.

[29] There is a complication with the first observation that is not treated quite correctly by this procedure. For details, see Judge et al. (1985, pp. 486–489). The strictly correct (and quite cumbersome) results are for the true GLS estimator, which assumes a known $\boldsymbol{\Omega}$. It is unlikely that in a finite sample, anything is lost by using the Prais–Winsten procedure with the estimated $\boldsymbol{\Omega}$. One suggestion has been to use the Cochrane–Orcutt procedure and drop the first observation. But in a small sample, the cost of discarding the first observation is almost surely greater than that of neglecting to account properly for the correlation of the first disturbance with the other first disturbances. It is an issue that merits further study.

TABLE 15.16 Autocorrelation Coefficients

	GM	*CH*	*GE*	*WE*	*US*
Durbin–Watson	0.9375	1.984	1.0721	1.413	0.9091
Autocorrelation	0.531	0.008	0.463	0.294	0.545
Residual Covariance Matrix $[\hat{\sigma}_{ij}/(1 - r_i r_j)]$					
GM	6679.5				
CH	−220.97	151.96			
GE	483.79	43.7891	684.59		
WE	88.373	19.964	190.37	92.788	
US	−1381.6	342.89	1484.10	676.88	8638.1
Parameter Estimates (Standard Errors in Parentheses)					
β_1	−51.337	−0.4536	−24.913	4.7091	14.0207
	(80.62)	(11.86)	(25.67)	(6.510)	(96.49)
β_2	0.094038	0.06847	0.04271	0.05091	0.16415
	(0.01733)	(0.0174)	(0.01134)	(0.01060)	(0.0386)
β_3	0.040723	0.32041	0.10954	0.04284	0.2006
	(0.04216)	(0.0258)	(0.03012)	(0.04127)	(0.1428)

ample 15.9 reflect the improved fit brought about by introducing the lagged variables into the equation.

15.5. SYSTEMS OF DEMAND EQUATIONS – SINGULAR SYSTEMS

Most of the recent applications of the multivariate regression model[30] have been in the context of systems of demand equations, either commodity demands or factor demands in studies of production.

EXAMPLE 15.15 Stone's Expenditure System

Stone's expenditure system[31] based on a set of logarithmic commodity demand equations, income Y, and commodity prices p_n is

$$\ln q_i = \alpha_i + \eta_i \ln\left(\frac{Y}{P}\right) + \sum_{j=1}^{M} \eta_{ij}^* \ln\left(\frac{p_j}{P}\right),$$

[30]Note the distinction between the multi*variate* or multiple-equation model discussed here and the *multiple* regression model introduced in Chapter 6.

[31]A very readable survey of the estimation of systems of commodity demands is Deaton and Muellbauer (1980b). The example discussed here is taken from their Chapter 3 and the references to Stone's (1954a,b) work cited therein. A counterpart for production function modeling is Chambers (1988).

where P is a generalized (share-weighted) price index, η_i is an income elasticity, and η^*_{in} is a compensated price elasticity. We can interpret this as the demand equation in real expenditure and real prices. The resulting set of equations constitutes an econometric model in the form of a set of seemingly unrelated regressions. In estimation, we must account for a number of restrictions including homogeneity of degree one in income, $\Sigma_i \eta_i = 1$, and symmetry of the matrix of compensated price elasticities, $\eta^*_{ij} = \eta^*_{ji}$.

Other examples include the system of factor demands and factor cost shares from production, which we shall consider again later. In principle, each of these is merely a particular application of the model of the previous section. But some special problems arise in these settings. First, the parameters of the systems are generally constrained across equations. That is, the unconstrained model is inconsistent with the underlying theory.[32] The numerous constraints in the system of demand equations presented earlier give an example. A second intrinsic feature of many of these models is that the disturbance covariance matrix $\boldsymbol{\Sigma}$ is singular.

EXAMPLE 15.16 Cobb–Douglas Cost Function

Consider a Cobb–Douglas production function,

$$Y = \alpha_0 \prod_{i=1}^{M} x_i^{\alpha_i}. \tag{15-58}$$

Profit maximization calls for the firm to maximize output for a given cost level C (or minimize costs for a given output Y). The Lagrangean for the maximization problem is

$$\Lambda = \alpha_0 \prod_{i=1}^{M} x_i^{\alpha_i} + \lambda(C - \mathbf{p}'\mathbf{x})$$

where $\mathbf{p}$ is the vector of M factor prices. The necessary conditions for maximizing this are

$$\frac{\partial \Lambda}{\partial x_i} = \frac{\alpha_i Y}{x_i} - \lambda p_i = 0,$$
$$\frac{\partial \Lambda}{\partial \lambda} = C - \mathbf{p}'\mathbf{x} = 0.$$

---

[32]This does not imply that the theoretical restrictions are not testable or that the unrestricted model cannot be estimated. Sometimes the meaning of the model is ambiguous without the restrictions, however. Statistically rejecting the restrictions implied by the theory, which were used to derive the econometric model in the first place, can put us in a rather uncomfortable position. For example, in a study of utility functions, Christensen et al. (1975), after rejecting the cross-equation symmetry of a set of commodity demands, stated, "With this conclusion we can terminate the test sequence, since these results invalidate the theory of demand" (p. 380).

The joint solution provides $x_i(Y, \mathbf{p})$ and $\lambda(Y, \mathbf{p})$. The total cost of production is

$$\sum_{i=1}^{M} p_i x_i = \sum_{i=1}^{M} \frac{\alpha_i Y}{\lambda}.$$

The cost share allocated to the ith factor is

$$\frac{p_i x_i}{\sum_{i=1}^{M} p_i x_i} = \frac{\alpha_i}{\sum_{i=1}^{M} \alpha_i} = \beta_i. \tag{15-59}$$

This provides the basis for a multivariate regression model. The full model is[33]

$$\begin{aligned} \ln C &= \beta_0 + \beta_y \ln Y + \sum_{i=1}^{M} \beta_i \ln p_i + \epsilon_c, \\ s_1 &= \beta_1 + \epsilon_1, \\ s_2 &= \beta_2 + \epsilon_2, \\ &\vdots \\ s_M &= \beta_M + \epsilon_M. \end{aligned} \tag{15-60}$$

By construction,

$$\sum_{i=1}^{M} \beta_i = 1 \tag{15-61}$$

and

$$\sum_{i=1}^{M} s_i = 1.$$

The cost shares will also sum identically to one in the data. It follows, therefore, that

$$\sum_{i=1}^{M} \epsilon_M = 0.$$

at every data point, so the system is singular. For the moment, ignore the cost function. Let the $M \times 1$ disturbance vector from the shares be

$$\boldsymbol{\epsilon} = [\epsilon_1, \epsilon_2, \ldots, \epsilon_M]'.$$

Since

$$\boldsymbol{\epsilon}'\mathbf{i} = 0, \quad \text{where } \mathbf{i} \text{ is a column of 1s,}$$

it follows that

$$E[\boldsymbol{\epsilon\epsilon}'\mathbf{i}] = \boldsymbol{\Sigma}\mathbf{i} = \mathbf{0}.$$

[33]We leave as an exercise the derivation of β_0, which is a mixture of all the parameters and β_y, which equals $1/\Sigma_m \alpha_m$.

This implies that $\mathbf{\Sigma}$ is singular. Therefore, the methods of the previous sections cannot be used here. (You should verify that the *sample* covariance matrix of the OLS residuals will also be singular.)

The solution to the singularity problem appears to be to drop one of the equations, estimate the remainder, and solve for the last parameter from the other $M - 1$. The constraint in (15-61) is that the cost function must be homogeneous of degree one in the prices, a theoretical necessity. If we impose the constraint

$$\beta_M = 1 - \beta_1 - \beta_2 - \cdots - \beta_{M-1}, \tag{15-62}$$

the system is reduced to a nonsingular one:

$$\begin{aligned}
\ln\left(\frac{C}{p_M}\right) &= \beta_0 + \beta_y \ln Y + \sum_{i=1}^{M-1} \beta_i \ln\left(\frac{p_i}{p_M}\right) + \epsilon_c, \\
s_1 &= \beta_1 + \epsilon_1, \\
s_2 &= \beta_2 + \epsilon_2, \\
&\vdots \\
s_{M-1} &= \beta_{M-1} + \epsilon_{M-1}.
\end{aligned}$$

This system provides estimates of β_0, β_y, and $\beta_1, \ldots, \beta_{M-1}$. The last parameter is estimated using (15-62).

In principle, it is immaterial which factor is chosen as the numeraire. Unfortunately, the FGLS parameter estimates in the now nonsingular system will depend on which one is chosen. Invariance is achieved by using maximum likelihood estimates instead of FGLS.[34] These can be obtained by iterating FGLS or by direct maximum likelihood estimation.[35]

EXAMPLE 15.17 SUR Estimates of a Cost Function

Nerlove's (1963) study of the electric power industry described in Example 8.3 provides an example of the preceding Cobb–Douglas cost function model. His ordinary least squares estimates of the parameters were listed in the earlier example. Among the results are (unfortunately) a negative capital coefficient in three of the six regressions. Nerlove also found that the simple Cobb–Douglas model did not adequately account for the relationship between output and average cost. Christensen and Greene (1976) further analyzed the Nerlove data and augmented the data set with cost share data to estimate the complete demand system. Table 15.17 lists 20 of Nerlove's 145 observations with Christensen and Greene's cost share data. Cost is the total cost of generation in millions of dollars, output is in millions of kilowatt-hours, the capital price is an index of construction costs, the wage rate is in dollars per hour for production and maintenance, the fuel price is an index of the cost per Btu of fuel pur-

[34]The invariance result is proved in Barten (1969).

[35]Some additional results on the method are given by Revankar (1976).

TABLE 15.17 Cost Function Data

Firm	*Cost*	*Output*	*Pk*	*Pl*	*Pf*	*Sk*	*Sl*	*Sf*
1	0.423	39	164	2.30	23.6	0.4137	0.1702	0.4161
2	1.130	130	176	1.82	38.9	0.2779	0.1712	0.6049
3	1.565	197	183	2.19	29.1	0.4151	0.0692	0.5157
4	2.382	338	163	1.85	24.6	0.4799	0.0616	0.4585
5	4.580	484	176	1.75	42.8	0.2828	0.1009	0.6162
6	5.535	719	174	1.70	26.9	0.4946	0.0703	0.4351
7	6.754	984	158	1.76	26.9	0.2435	0.1083	0.6482
8	7.743	1,122	162	2.19	29.1	0.3744	0.0977	0.5279
9	8.488	1,215	164	2.19	29.1	0.4390	0.0695	0.4915
10	10.879	1,649	177	2.32	31.9	0.3991	0.0974	0.5035
11	15.437	2,023	163	2.11	24.4	0.3989	0.0808	0.5203
12	12.905	2,341	183	2.04	20.7	0.4165	0.0945	0.4890
13	11.320	2,870	167	1.76	10.3	0.5822	0.1333	0.2845
14	19.035	3,202	170	2.30	23.6	0.4974	0.0983	0.4043
15	29.845	4,764	195	2.19	29.1	0.3530	0.1328	0.5142
16	21.988	5,283	159	2.04	20.7	0.4491	0.0630	0.4879
17	40.594	7,193	162	2.12	28.6	0.3550	0.0729	0.5721
18	33.354	7,886	178	1.61	17.8	0.5835	0.0587	0.3578
19	67.120	11,477	151	2.24	26.5	0.3458	0.0670	0.5872
20	119.939	16,719	162	2.30	23.6	0.4340	0.0906	0.4754

chased by the firms, and the data reflect the 1955 costs of production. The regression estimates are given in Table 15.18.

Least squares estimates of the Cobb–Douglas cost function are given in the first column.[36] As expected, the coefficient on capital is negative. Because

TABLE 15.18 Regression Estimates (Standard Errors in Parentheses)

	Ordinary Least Squares				*Multivariate Regression*			
β_0	−6.512	(1.03)	−6.380	(1.01)	−8.192	(0.148)	−7.114	(0.444)
β_y	0.9044	(0.021)	0.6959	(0.156)	0.9173	(0.019)	0.5975	(0.131)
β_{yy}	—		0.01543	(0.011)	—		0.02250	(0.0095)
β_k	−0.08659	(0.229)	−0.1911	(0.237)	0.4108	(0.019)	0.4118	(0.0194)
β_l	0.4802	(0.231)	0.3492	(0.245)	0.0958	(0.007)	0.0957	(0.007)
β_f	0.4332	(0.117)	0.4597	(0.116)	0.4934	(0.019)	0.4926	(0.018)
R^2	0.9931		0.9939		—	—		
Log |W|	—		—		−15.874		−16.049	

[36] Results based on Nerlove's full data set are given in Example 8.3.

$\beta_i = \beta_y\, \partial \ln Y/\partial \ln x_i$—that is, a positive multiple of the output elasticity of the ith factor—this is a troubling finding. The third column gives the maximum likelihood estimates obtained in the constrained system. Two things to note are the dramatically smaller standard errors and the now positive (and reasonable) estimate of the capital coefficient. The estimates of economies of scale in the basic Cobb–Douglas model are $1/\beta_y = 1.11$ (column 1) and 1.05 (column 3), which suggests some increasing returns to scale. Nerlove, however, had found evidence that at extremely large firm sizes, economies of scale diminished and eventually disappeared. To account for this (essentially a classical U-shaped average cost curve), he appended a quadratic term in log output in the cost function. The single equation and maximum likelihood multivariate regression estimates are given in the second and fourth columns.

15.6. FLEXIBLE FUNCTIONAL FORMS – THE TRANSLOG COST FUNCTION

The literatures on production and cost and on utility and demand have evolved in several directions. In the area of models of producer behavior, the classic paper by Arrow et al. (1961) called into question the inherent restriction of the Cobb–Douglas model that all elasticities of factor substitution are equal to 1. Researchers have since developed numerous flexible functions that allow substitution to be unrestricted (i.e., not even constant).[37] Similar strands of literature have appeared in the analysis of commodity demands.[38] In this section, we examine in detail a model of production.

Suppose that production is characterized by a production function,

$$Y = f(\mathbf{x}).$$

The solution to the problem of minimizing the cost of producing a specified output rate given a set of factor prices produces the cost-minimizing set of factor demands

$$x_i = x_i(Y, \mathbf{p}).$$

The total cost of production is given by the cost function,

$$C = \sum_{i=1}^{M} p_i x_i(Y, \mathbf{p}) = C(Y, \mathbf{p}). \tag{15-63}$$

If there are constant returns to scale, it can be shown that

$$C = Yc(\mathbf{p}) \tag{15-64}$$

[37]See, in particular, Berndt and Christensen (1973). Two useful surveys of the topic are Jorgenson (1983) and Diewert (1974).

[38]See, for example, Christensen et al. (1975) and two surveys, Deaton and Muellbauer (1980b) and Deaton (1983). Berndt (1990) contains many useful results.

or

$$\frac{C}{Y} = c(\mathbf{p}),$$

where $c(\mathbf{p})$ is the unit or average cost function.[39] The cost-minimizing factor demands are obtained by applying Shephard's (1970) lemma, which states that if $C(Y, \mathbf{p})$ gives the minimum total cost of production, then the cost-minimizing set of factor demands is given by

$$\begin{aligned} x_i^* &= \frac{\partial C(Y, \mathbf{p})}{\partial p_i} \\ &= \frac{Y\,\partial c(\mathbf{p})}{\partial p_i}. \end{aligned} \tag{15-65}$$

Alternatively, by differentiating logarithmically, we obtain the cost-minimizing factor cost shares:

$$\begin{aligned} s_i &= \frac{\partial \ln C(Y, \mathbf{p})}{\partial \ln p_i} \\ &= \frac{p_i x_i}{C}. \end{aligned} \tag{15-66}$$

With constant returns to scale, $\ln C(Y, \mathbf{p}) = \ln Y + \ln c(\mathbf{p})$, so

$$s_i = \frac{\partial \ln c(\mathbf{p})}{\partial \ln p_i}. \tag{15-67}$$

In many empirical studies, the objects of estimation are the elasticities of factor substitution and the own price elasticities of demand. These are given by

$$\theta_{ij} = \frac{c(\partial^2 c/\partial p_i \partial p_j)}{(\partial c/\partial p_i)(\partial c/\partial p_j)}$$

and

$$\eta_{ii} = s_i \theta_{ii}.$$

By suitably parameterizing the cost function (15-64) and the cost shares (15-67), we obtain an M or $M + 1$ equation econometric model that can be used to estimate these quantities.[40]

The translog function is the most frequently used flexible function in em-

---

[39]The Cobb–Douglas function of the previous section gives an illustration. The restriction of constant returns to scale is $\beta_y = 1$, which is equivalent to $C = Yc(\mathbf{p})$. Nerlove's more general version of the cost function allows nonconstant returns to scale. See Christensen and Greene (1976) and Diewert (1974) for some of the formalities of the cost function and its relationship to the structure of production.

[40]The cost function is only one of several approaches to this study. See Jorgenson (1983) for a discussion.

pirical work.[41] By expanding $\ln c(\mathbf{p})$ in a second-order Taylor series about the point $\ln \mathbf{p} = \mathbf{0}$, we obtain

$$\ln c \approx \beta_0 + \sum_{i=1}^{M} \left(\frac{\partial \ln c}{\partial \ln p_i} \right) \ln p_i$$

Shares 1st derivative

$$+ \frac{1}{2} \sum_{i=1}^{M} \sum_{j=1}^{M} \left(\frac{\partial^2 \ln c}{\partial \ln p_i \, \partial \ln p_j} \right) \ln p_i \ln p_j,$$

(15-68)

Shares 2nd derivative

where all derivatives are evaluated at the expansion point. If we identify these derivatives as coefficients and impose the symmetry of the cross-price derivatives, the cost function becomes

$$\ln c = \beta_0 + \beta_1 \ln p_1 + \cdots + \beta_M \ln p_M + \delta_{11}(\tfrac{1}{2}\ln^2 p_1) + \delta_{12}\ln p_1 \ln p_2$$
$$+ \delta_{22}(\tfrac{1}{2}\ln^2 p_2) + \cdots + \delta_{MM}(\tfrac{1}{2}\ln^2 p_M).$$

(15-69)

if $\delta_{ij} = 0$ CD

This is the transcendental logarithmic, or translog, cost function. If δ_{ij} equals zero, it reduces to the Cobb–Douglas function we looked at earlier. The cost shares are given by

$$s_1 = \frac{\partial \ln c}{\partial \ln p_1} = \beta_1 + \delta_{11}\ln p_1 + \delta_{12}\ln p_2 + \cdots + \delta_{1M}\ln p_M,$$

$$s_2 = \frac{\partial \ln c}{\partial \ln p_2} = \beta_2 + \delta_{12}\ln p_1 + \delta_{22}\ln p_2 + \cdots + \delta_{2M}\ln p_M,$$

(15-70)

cost shares
$s_1 + s_2 + \cdots = 1$

$$s_M = \frac{\partial \ln c}{\partial \ln p_M} = \beta_M + \delta_{1M}\ln p_1 + \delta_{2M}\ln p_2 + \cdots + \delta_{MM}\ln p_M.$$

The cost shares must sum to 1, which requires, in addition to the symmetry restrictions already imposed,

$$\beta_1 + \beta_2 + \cdots + \beta_M = 1,$$

$\beta_1 + \beta_2 + \cdots = 1$

$$\sum_{i=1}^{M} \delta_{ij} = 0 \quad \text{(column sums equal zero)},$$

$\delta_{ij} = 0$

(15-71)

$$\sum_{j=1}^{M} \delta_{ij} = 0 \quad \text{(row sums equal zero)}.$$

---

[41]The function was developed by Kmenta (1967) as a means of approximating the CES production function and was introduced formally in a series of papers by Berndt, Christensen, Jorgenson, and Lau, including Berndt and Christensen (1973) and Christensen et al. (1973). The literature has produced something of a competition in the development of exotic functional forms. The translog function has remained the most popular, however, and by one account, Guilkey et al. (1983) is the most reliable of several available alternatives. See also Example 6.4.

The system of share equations provides a seemingly unrelated regressions model that can be used to estimate the parameters of the model.[42] To make the model operational, we must impose the restrictions in (15-71) and solve the problem of singularity of the disturbance covariance matrix of the share equations. The first is accomplished by dividing the first $M - 1$ prices by the Mth, thus eliminating the last term in each row and column of the parameter matrix. As in the Cobb–Douglas model, we obtain a nonsingular system by dropping the Mth share equation. We compute maximum likelihood estimates of the parameters to ensure invariance with respect to the choice of which share equation we drop. For the translog cost function, the elasticities of substitution are particularly simple to compute once the parameters have been estimated:

$$\theta_{mn} = \frac{\delta_{ij} + s_i s_j}{s_i s_j}, \qquad \theta_{mm} = \frac{\delta_{ii} + s_i(s_i - 1)}{s_i^2}. \tag{15-72}$$

These will differ at every data point. It is common to compute them at some central point such as the means of the data.[43]

EXAMPLE 15.18 A Cost Function for U.S. Manufacturing

A number of recent studies using the translog methodology have used a four-factor model, with capital K, labor L, energy E, and materials M, the factors of production. Berndt and Wood (1975) have estimated a translog cost function for the U.S. manufacturing sector. The three factor shares used to estimate the model are

$$s_K = \beta_K + \delta_{KK}\ln\left(\frac{p_K}{p_M}\right) + \delta_{KL}\ln\left(\frac{p_L}{p_M}\right) + \delta_{KE}\ln\left(\frac{p_E}{p_M}\right),$$

$$s_L = \beta_L + \delta_{KL}\ln\left(\frac{p_K}{p_M}\right) + \delta_{LL}\ln\left(\frac{p_L}{p_M}\right) + \delta_{LE}\ln\left(\frac{p_E}{p_M}\right),$$

$$s_E = \beta_E + \delta_{KE}\ln\left(\frac{p_K}{p_M}\right) + \delta_{LE}\ln\left(\frac{p_L}{p_M}\right) + \delta_{EE}\ln\left(\frac{p_E}{p_M}\right).$$

Berndt and Wood's data are reproduced in Table 15.19. Maximum likelihood estimates of the full set of parameters are given in Table 15.20.[44]

---

[42]The cost function may be included if desired. This will provide an estimate of β_0 but is otherwise inessential. Absent the assumption of constant returns to scale, however, the cost function will contain parameters of interest that do not appear in the share equations. As such, one would want to include it in the model. See Christensen and Greene (1976) for an example.

[43]They will also be highly nonlinear functions of the parameters and the data. A method of computing asymptotic standard errors for the estimated elasticities is presented in Anderson and Thursby (1986).

[44]These are not the same as those reported by Berndt and Wood. To purge their data of possible correlation with the disturbances, they first regressed the prices on 10 exogenous macroeconomic variables, such as U.S. population, government purchases of labor services, real exports of durable goods, and U.S. tangible capital stock, and then based their analysis on the fitted values. The estimates given here are, in general, quite close to those given by Berndt and Wood. For example, their estimates of the first five parameters are 0.0564, 0.2539, 0.0442, 0.6455, and 0.0254.

TABLE 15.19 Manufacturing Cost Data, U.S. Economy 1947–1971

Year	Total Input Cost[a]	Cost Shares				Input Prices			
		K	L	E	M	P_k	P_l	P_e	P_m
1947	182.373	0.05107	0.24727	0.04253	0.65913	1.00000	1.00000	1.00000	1.00000
1948	183.161	0.05817	0.27716	0.05127	0.61340	1.00270	1.15457	1.30258	1.05525
1949	186.533	0.04602	0.25911	0.05075	0.64411	0.74371	1.15584	1.19663	1.06225
1950	221.710	0.04991	0.24794	0.04606	0.65609	0.92497	1.23535	1.21442	1.12430
1951	255.945	0.05039	0.25487	0.04482	0.64992	1.04877	1.33784	1.25179	1.21694
1952	264.699	0.04916	0.26655	0.04460	0.63969	0.99744	1.37949	1.27919	1.19961
1953	291.160	0.04728	0.26832	0.04369	0.64071	1.00653	1.43458	1.27505	1.19044
1954	274.457	0.05635	0.27167	0.04787	0.62411	1.08757	1.45362	1.30356	1.20612
1955	308.908	0.05258	0.26465	0.04517	0.63760	1.10315	1.51120	1.34277	1.23835
1956	328.286	0.04604	0.26880	0.04576	0.63940	0.99606	1.58186	1.37154	1.29336
1957	338.633	0.05033	0.27184	0.04820	0.62962	1.06321	1.64641	1.38010	1.30703
1958	323.318	0.06015	0.27283	0.04836	0.61866	1.15619	1.67389	1.39338	1.32699
1959	358.435	0.06185	0.27303	0.04563	0.61948	1.30758	1.73430	1.36756	1.30774
1960	366.251	0.05788	0.27738	0.04585	0.61889	1.25413	1.78280	1.38025	1.33946
1961	366.162	0.05903	0.27839	0.04640	0.61617	1.26328	1.81977	1.37630	1.34319
1962	390.668	0.05578	0.28280	0.04530	0.61613	1.26525	1.88531	1.37689	1.34745
1963	412.188	0.05601	0.27986	0.04470	0.61962	1.32294	1.93379	1.34737	1.33143
1964	433.768	0.05452	0.28343	0.04392	0.61814	1.32798	2.00998	1.38969	1.35197
1965	474.969	0.05467	0.27996	0.04114	0.62423	1.40659	2.05539	1.38635	1.37542
1966	521.291	0.05460	0.28363	0.04014	0.62163	1.45100	2.13441	1.40102	1.41878
1967	540.941	0.05443	0.28646	0.04074	0.61837	1.38617	2.20616	1.39197	1.42428
1968	585.447	0.05758	0.28883	0.03971	0.61388	1.49901	2.33869	1.43388	1.42481
1969	630.450	0.05410	0.29031	0.03963	0.61597	1.44957	2.46412	1.46481	1.53356
1970	623.466	0.05255	0.29755	0.04348	0.60642	1.32464	2.60532	1.45907	1.54758
1971	658.235	0.04675	0.28905	0.04479	0.61940	1.20177	2.76025	1.64689	1.54978

Source: E. Berndt and D. Wood, "Technology, Prices, and the Derived Demand for Energy," *Review of Economics and Statistics,* 57, 1975, p. 381.

[a]Billions of current dollars.

TABLE 15.20 Parameter Estimates (Standard Errors in Parentheses)

β_K	0.05694	(0.00134)	δ_{KM}	−0.1911	(0.00970)
β_L	0.2535	(0.00218)	δ_{LL}	0.07536	(0.00676)
β_E	0.0444	(0.00085)	δ_{LE}	−0.00479	(0.00234)
β_M	0.6542	(0.00330)	δ_{LM}	−0.07042	(0.01059)
δ_{KK}	0.02974	(0.00579)	δ_{EE}	0.01848	(0.00499)
δ_{KL}	−0.000143	(0.00384)	δ_{EM}	−0.00320	(0.00799)
δ_{KE}	−0.01048	(0.00339)	δ_{MM}	0.09274	(0.02244)

TABLE 15.21 Estimated Elasticities

	Capital	*Labor*	*Energy*	*Materials*
		Cost Shares for 1959		
Fitted share	0.05643	0.27451	0.04391	0.62515
Actual share	0.06185	0.27303	0.04563	0.61948
		Implied Elasticities of Substitution		
Capital	−7.783			
Labor	0.9908	−1.643		
Energy	−3.230	0.6021	−12.19	
Materials	0.4581	0.5896	0.8834	−0.3623
		Implied Own Price Elasticities		
	−0.4166	−0.4510	−0.5353	−0.2265

The implied estimates of the elasticities of substitution and demand for 1959 (the central year in the data) are derived in Table 15.21 using the fitted cost shares. The departure from the Cobb–Douglas model with unit elasticities is substantial. For example, the results suggest almost no substitutability between energy and labor[45] and some complementarity between capital and energy.

15.7. NONLINEAR SYSTEMS AND GMM ESTIMATION

We now consider estimation of nonlinear systems of equations. The underlying theory is essentially the same as that for linear systems. We will briefly consider two cases in this section, maximum likelihood (or FGLS) estimation and GMM estimation. Since the theory *is* essentially that of Section 15.4.3b, most of the following will describe practical aspects of estimation.

Consider estimation of the parameters of the equation system

$$\begin{aligned} \mathbf{y}_1 &= \mathbf{h}_1(\boldsymbol{\beta}, \mathbf{X}) + \boldsymbol{\epsilon}_2, \\ \mathbf{y}_2 &= \mathbf{h}_2(\boldsymbol{\beta}, \mathbf{X}) + \boldsymbol{\epsilon}_2, \\ &\vdots \\ \mathbf{y}_M &= \mathbf{h}_M(\boldsymbol{\beta}, \mathbf{X}) + \boldsymbol{\epsilon}_M. \end{aligned} \qquad \textbf{(15-73)}$$

[45]Berndt and Wood's estimate of θ_{EL} for 1959 is 0.64.

There are M equations in total, to be estimated with $t = 1, \ldots, T$ observations. There are K parameters in the model. No assumption is made that each equation has "its own" parameter vector; we simply use some of or all the K elements in $\boldsymbol{\beta}$ in each equation. Likewise, there is a set of T observations on each of P independent variables $\mathbf{x}_p$, $p = 1, \ldots, P$, some of or all that appear in each equation. For convenience, the equations are written generically in terms of the full $\boldsymbol{\beta}$ and $\mathbf{X}$. The disturbances are assumed to have zero means and contemporaneous covariance matrix $\boldsymbol{\Sigma}$. We will leave the extension to autocorrelation for more advanced treatments.

EXAMPLE 15.19 Nonlinear Demand System

One variant of Christensen et al.'s (1975) demand system derived from a translog indirect utility function is the set of M budget share equations for total expenditure E:

$$s_i = \frac{\alpha_i + \sum_{j=1}^{M} \gamma_{ij} \ln\left(\frac{p_j}{E}\right)}{\alpha_E + \sum_{j=1}^{M} \gamma_{Ej} \ln\left(\frac{p_j}{E}\right)} + \epsilon_i, \quad i = 1, \ldots, M. \tag{15-74}$$

The budget shares sum to 1, so there are a number of constraints on the parameters of the model:

$$\sum_{i=1}^{M} \alpha_i = \alpha_E, \qquad \sum_{i=1}^{M} \gamma_{ij} = \gamma_{Ej}. \tag{15-75}$$

Symmetry requires $\gamma_{ij} = \gamma_{ji}$, so $\Sigma_{i=1}^{M} \gamma_{ji} = \gamma_{Ej}$. The system is homogeneous of degree zero in the full parameter vector; the budget shares in the model are unchanged if every parameter is multiplied by the same constant. This indeterminacy is removed by the normalization $\alpha_E = 1$. Finally, since the disturbances must sum to zero, their contemporaneous covariance matrix is singular. To achieve invariance of the estimates to the equation dropped, the parameters are estimated by maximum likelihood.

15.7.1. GLS Estimation

In the multivariate regression model, if $\boldsymbol{\Sigma}$ is known, the generalized least squares estimator of $\boldsymbol{\beta}$ is the vector that minimizes the generalized sum of squares

$$\boldsymbol{\epsilon}(\boldsymbol{\beta})'\boldsymbol{\Omega}^{-1}\boldsymbol{\epsilon}(\boldsymbol{\beta}) = \sum_{i=1}^{M} \sum_{j=1}^{M} \sigma^{ij}[\mathbf{y}_i - \mathbf{h}_i(\boldsymbol{\beta}, \mathbf{X})]'[\mathbf{y}_j - \mathbf{h}_j(\boldsymbol{\beta}, \mathbf{X})], \tag{15-76}$$

where $\boldsymbol{\epsilon}(\boldsymbol{\beta})$ is an $MT \times 1$ vector of disturbances obtained by stacking the equations and $\boldsymbol{\Omega} = \boldsymbol{\Sigma} \otimes \mathbf{I}$. [See (15-3).] As we did in Chapter 10, define the pseudoregressors as the derivatives of the $\mathbf{h}(\boldsymbol{\beta}, \mathbf{X})$ functions with respect to $\boldsymbol{\beta}$. That is, linearize each of the equations. Then, the first-order condition for minimizing this sum of squares is

$$\frac{\partial \boldsymbol{\epsilon}(\boldsymbol{\beta})'\boldsymbol{\Omega}^{-1}\boldsymbol{\epsilon}(\boldsymbol{\beta})}{\partial \boldsymbol{\beta}} = \sum_{i=1}^{M}\sum_{j=1}^{M} \sigma^{ij}(2\mathbf{X}_i^{0\prime}(\boldsymbol{\beta})\boldsymbol{\epsilon}_j(\boldsymbol{\beta})) = \mathbf{0}, \tag{15-77}$$

where σ^{ij} is the ijth element of $\boldsymbol{\Sigma}^{-1}$ and $\mathbf{X}_i^0(\boldsymbol{\beta})$ is a $T \times K$ matrix of pseudoregressors from the linearization of the ith equation. (See Section 10.2.) If any of the parameters in $\boldsymbol{\beta}$ do not appear in the ith equation, the corresponding column of $\mathbf{X}_i^0(\boldsymbol{\beta})$ will be a column of zeros.

This is a doubly complex problem of estimation. In almost any circumstance, solution will require an iteration using one of the methods discussed in Chapter 5. Second, of course, is that $\boldsymbol{\Sigma}$ is not known and must be estimated. Remember that efficient estimation in the multivariate regression model does not require an efficient estimate of $\boldsymbol{\Sigma}$, only a consistent one. Therefore, one approach would be to estimate the parameters of each equation separately using nonlinear least squares. This will be inefficient if any of the equations share parameters, since that information will be ignored. But at this step, consistency is the objective, not efficiency. The resulting residuals can then be used to compute

$$\mathbf{S} = \frac{1}{T}\mathbf{E}'\mathbf{E}. \tag{15-78}$$

The second step of FGLS is the solution of (15-77). This will require an iterative procedure once again and can be based on $\mathbf{S}$ instead of $\boldsymbol{\Sigma}$. With well-behaved pseudoregressors, this second-step estimator is fully efficient. Once again, the same theory used for FGLS in the linear, single-equation case applies here.[46] Once the FGLS estimator is obtained, the appropriate asymptotic covariance matrix is estimated with

$$\text{Est. Asy. Var}[\hat{\boldsymbol{\beta}}] = \left[\sum_{i=1}^{M}\sum_{j=1}^{M} s^{ij}\mathbf{X}_i^0(\boldsymbol{\beta})'\mathbf{X}_j^0(\boldsymbol{\beta})\right]^{-1}. \tag{15-79}$$

There is a possible flaw in the strategy outlined above. It may not be possible to fit all the equations individually by nonlinear least squares. It is conceivable that identification of some of the parameters requires joint estimation of more than one equation. But as long as the full system identifies all parameters, there is a simple way out of this problem. Recall that all we need for our first step is a consistent set of estimates of the elements of $\boldsymbol{\beta}$. It is easy to show

[46]Neither the nonlinearity nor the multiple equation aspect of this model brings any new statistical issues to the fore. By stacking the equations, we see that this model is simply a variant of the nonlinear regression model that we treated in Chapter 10 with the added complication of a nonscalar disturbance covariance matrix, which we analyzed in Chapter 11. The new complications are primarily practical.

that the preceding defines a GMM estimator (see Section 11.5.) We can use this result to devise an alternative, simple strategy. The weighting of the sums of squares and cross products in (15-76) by σ^{ij} produces an efficient estimate of $\boldsymbol{\beta}$. Any other weighting based on some positive definite $\mathbf{A}$ would produce consistent, although inefficient, estimates. At this step, though, efficiency is secondary, so the choice of $\mathbf{A} = \mathbf{I}$ is a convenient candidate. Thus, for our first step, we can find $\boldsymbol{\beta}$ to minimize

$$\begin{aligned}\boldsymbol{\epsilon}(\boldsymbol{\beta})'\boldsymbol{\epsilon}(\boldsymbol{\beta}) &= \sum_{i=1}^{M} [\mathbf{y}_i - \mathbf{h}_i(\boldsymbol{\beta}, \mathbf{X})]'[\mathbf{y}_i - \mathbf{h}_i(\boldsymbol{\beta}, \mathbf{X})] \\ &= \sum_{i=1}^{M}\sum_{t=1}^{T} [y_{it} - h_i(\boldsymbol{\beta}, \mathbf{x}_{it})]^2.\end{aligned} \tag{15-80}$$

(This is just pooled nonlinear least squares, where the regression function varies across the sets of observations.) This will produce the $\hat{\boldsymbol{\beta}}$ we need to compute $\mathbf{S}$.

15.7.2. Maximum Likelihood Estimation

With normally distributed disturbances, the log-likelihood function for this model is still given by (15-49). Therefore, estimation of $\boldsymbol{\Sigma}$ is done exactly as before, using the $\mathbf{S}$ in (15-78). Likewise, the concentrated log-likelihood in (15-53) and the criterion function in (15-54) are unchanged. Therefore, one approach to maximum likelihood estimation is iterated FGLS, based on the results in Section 15.4. This will require two levels of iteration, however, since for each estimated $\boldsymbol{\Sigma}(\boldsymbol{\beta}_l)$, written as a function of the estimates of $\boldsymbol{\beta}$ obtained at iteration l, a nonlinear, iterative solution is required to obtain $\boldsymbol{\beta}_{l+1}$. The iteration then returns to $\mathbf{S}$. Convergence is based either on $\mathbf{S}$ or $\hat{\boldsymbol{\beta}}$; if one stabilizes, the other will also.

The advantage of direct maximum likelihood estimation that was discussed in Section 15.4.3b is lost here because of the nonlinearity of the regressions; there is no convenient arrangement of parameters into a matrix $\boldsymbol{\Pi}$. But a few practical aspects to formulating the criterion function and its derivatives that may be useful do remain. Estimation of the model in (15-73) might be slightly more convenient if each equation did have its own coefficient vector. Suppose then that there is one underlying parameter vector $\boldsymbol{\beta}$ and that we formulate each equation as

$$h_{it} = h_i[\boldsymbol{\gamma}_i(\boldsymbol{\beta}), \mathbf{x}_{it}] + \epsilon_{it}. \tag{15-81}$$

Then the derivatives of the log-likelihood function are built up from

$$\frac{\partial \ln|\mathbf{S}(\boldsymbol{\gamma})|}{\partial \boldsymbol{\gamma}_i} = \mathbf{d}_i = -\frac{1}{T}\sum_{t=1}^{T}\left(\sum_{j=1}^{M} s^{ij}\mathbf{x}_{it}^{0}(\boldsymbol{\gamma}_i)e_{jt}(\boldsymbol{\gamma}_j)\right), \quad i = 1, \ldots, M. \tag{15-82}$$

It remains to impose the equality constraints that have been built into the model. Since each $\boldsymbol{\gamma}_i$ is built up just by extracting elements from $\boldsymbol{\beta}$, the relevant derivative with respect to $\boldsymbol{\beta}$ is just a sum of those with respect to $\boldsymbol{\gamma}$:

$$\frac{\partial \ln L_c}{\partial \beta_k} = \sum_{i=1}^{n}\left(\sum_{g=1}^{K_i} \frac{\partial \ln L_c}{\partial \gamma_{ig}} \mathbf{1}(\gamma_{ig} = \beta_k)\right), \tag{15-83}$$

where $\mathbf{1}(\gamma_{ig} = \beta_k)$ equals 1 if γ_{ig} equals β_k and 0 if not. This can be formulated fairly simply as follows. There are a total of $G = \Sigma_{i=1}^{n} K_i$ parameters in $\boldsymbol{\gamma}$, but only $K < G$ underlying parameters in $\boldsymbol{\beta}$. Define the matrix $\mathbf{F}$ with G rows and K columns. Then let $\mathbf{F}_{gj} = 1$ if $\gamma_g = \beta_j$ and 0 otherwise. Thus, there is exactly one 1 and $K - 1$ 0s in each row of $\mathbf{F}$. Let $\mathbf{d}$ be the $G \times 1$ vector of derivatives obtained by stacking $\mathbf{d}_i$ from (15-82). Then

$$\frac{\partial \ln L_c}{\partial \boldsymbol{\beta}} = \mathbf{F}'\mathbf{d}. \tag{15-84}$$

The Hessian is likewise computed as a simple sum of terms. We can construct it in blocks using

$$\mathbf{H}_{ij} = \frac{\partial^2 \ln L_c}{\partial \boldsymbol{\gamma}_i \, \partial \boldsymbol{\gamma}_j'} = -\sum_{t=1}^{T} s^{ij} \mathbf{x}_{it}^0(\boldsymbol{\gamma}_i)\mathbf{x}_{jt}^0(\boldsymbol{\gamma}_j)'. \tag{15-85}$$

The asymptotic covariance matrix for $\hat{\boldsymbol{\beta}}$ is once again a sum of terms:

$$\text{Est. Asy. Var}[\hat{\boldsymbol{\beta}}] = \mathbf{V} = [-\mathbf{F}'\hat{\mathbf{H}}\mathbf{F}]^{-1}.$$

15.7.3. GMM Estimation

All the preceding estimation techniques (including the linear models in the earlier sections of this chapter) can be obtained as GMM estimators. Suppose that in the general formulation of the model in (15-73), we allow for nonzero correlation between $\mathbf{x}_{it}^0$ and ϵ_{is}. (It will not always be present, but we generalize the model to allow this as a possibility). Suppose, as well, that there are a set of instrumental variables $\mathbf{z}_t$ such that

$$E[\mathbf{z}_t \epsilon_{it}] = \mathbf{0}, \quad t = 1, \ldots, T, \text{ and } i = 1, \ldots, M. \tag{15-86}$$

(We could allow a separate set of instrumental variables for each equation, but this would needlessly complicate the presentation and is generally not the case in practice in any event.)

Under these assumptions, the nonlinear FGLS and ML estimators above will be inconsistent. But a relatively minor extension of the instrumental variables technique developed for the single equation case in Section 11.5.5 can be used instead. The sample analog to (15-86) is

$$\frac{1}{T}\sum_{t=1}^{T} \mathbf{z}_t[y_{it} - h_i(\boldsymbol{\beta}, \mathbf{x}_t)] = \mathbf{0}, \quad i = 1, \ldots, \boldsymbol{M}. \tag{15-87}$$

If we use this result for each equation in the system, one at a time, we obtain exactly the GMM estimator discussed in Section 11.5.5. But in addition to the efficiency loss that results from not imposing the cross-equation constraints in $\boldsymbol{\gamma}_i$, we would also neglect the correlation between the disturbances. Let

$$\frac{1}{T}\mathbf{Z}'\boldsymbol{\Omega}_{ij}\mathbf{Z} = E[\mathbf{Z}'\boldsymbol{\epsilon}_i\boldsymbol{\epsilon}_j'\mathbf{Z}]. \tag{15-88}$$

The GMM criterion for estimation in this setting is

$$\begin{aligned} q &= \sum_{i=1}^{M}\sum_{j=1}^{M}[(\mathbf{y}_i - \mathbf{h}_i(\boldsymbol{\beta}, \mathbf{X}))'\mathbf{Z}][\mathbf{Z}'\boldsymbol{\Omega}_{ij}\mathbf{Z}]^{ij}[\mathbf{Z}'(\mathbf{y}_j - \mathbf{h}_j(\boldsymbol{\beta}, \mathbf{X}))] \\ &= \sum_{i=1}^{M}\sum_{j=1}^{M}[\boldsymbol{\epsilon}_i(\boldsymbol{\beta})'\mathbf{Z}][\mathbf{Z}'\boldsymbol{\Omega}_{ij}\mathbf{Z}]^{ij}[\mathbf{Z}'\boldsymbol{\epsilon}_j(\boldsymbol{\beta})], \end{aligned} \tag{15-89}$$

where $[\mathbf{Z}'\boldsymbol{\Omega}_{ij}\mathbf{Z}]^{ij}$ denotes the ijth block of the inverse of the matrix with ijth block equal to $\mathbf{Z}'\boldsymbol{\Omega}_{ij}\mathbf{Z}$. (This matrix is laid out in full in Section 16.6.3.)

GMM estimation would proceed in several passes. To compute any of the variance parameters, we will require an initial set of consistent estimates of $\boldsymbol{\beta}$. This can be done with equation by equation nonlinear instrumental variables—see Section 10.2.5—although if equations have parameters in common, a choice must be made as to which to use. At the next step, the familiar White or Newey–West technique is used to compute, block by block, the matrix in (15-88). Since it is based on a consistent estimator of $\boldsymbol{\beta}$ (we assume), this matrix need not be recomputed. Now, with this in hand, an iterative solution to the maximization problem in (15-89) can be sought, for example, using the methods of Chapter 5. The first-order conditions are

$$\frac{\partial q}{\partial \boldsymbol{\beta}} = \sum_{i=1}^{M}\sum_{j=1}^{M}[\mathbf{X}_i^0(\boldsymbol{\beta})'\mathbf{Z}][\mathbf{Z}'\mathbf{W}_{ij}\mathbf{Z}]^{ij}[\mathbf{Z}'\boldsymbol{\epsilon}_j(\boldsymbol{\beta})] = 0. \tag{15-90}$$

Note again that the blocks of the inverse matrix in the center are extracted from the larger constructed matrix *after inversion*. [This brief discussion might understate the complexity of the optimization problem in (15-90), but that is inherent in the procedure.] At completion, the asymptotic covariance matrix for the GMM estimator is estimated with

$$\mathbf{V}_{\text{GMM}} = \left[\sum_{i=1}^{M}\sum_{j=1}^{M}(\mathbf{X}_i^0(\boldsymbol{\beta})'\mathbf{Z})(\mathbf{Z}'\mathbf{W}_{ij}\mathbf{Z})^{ij}(\mathbf{Z}'\mathbf{X}_j^0(\boldsymbol{\beta}))\right]^{-1}. \tag{15-91}$$

EXERCISES

1. The model

$$\begin{bmatrix}\mathbf{y}_1 \\ \mathbf{y}_2\end{bmatrix} = \begin{bmatrix}\mathbf{x}_1 \\ \mathbf{x}_2\end{bmatrix}\beta + \begin{bmatrix}\epsilon_1 \\ \epsilon_2\end{bmatrix}$$

satisfies the groupwise heteroscedastic regression model of Section 15.2.1.

All variables have zero means. The following sample second-moment matrix is obtained from a sample of 20 observations:

$$\begin{array}{c} \\ y_1 \\ y_2 \\ x_1 \\ x_2 \end{array}\begin{array}{c} \begin{array}{cccc} y_1 & y_2 & x_1 & x_2 \end{array} \\ \begin{bmatrix} 20 & 6 & 4 & 3 \\ 6 & 10 & 3 & 6 \\ 4 & 3 & 5 & 2 \\ 3 & 6 & 2 & 10 \end{bmatrix} \end{array}.$$

(a) Compute the two separate OLS estimates of β, their sampling variances, the estimates of σ_1^2 and σ_2^2, and the R^2's in the two regressions.
(b) Carry out the Lagrange multiplier test of the hypothesis that $\sigma_1^2 = \sigma_2^2$.
(c) Compute the two-step FGLS estimate of β and an estimate of its sampling variance. Test the hypothesis that β equals 1.
(d) Carry out the Wald test of equal disturbance variances.
(e) Compute the maximum likelihood estimates of β, σ_1^2, and σ_2^2 by iterating the FGLS estimates to convergence.
(f) Carry out a likelihood ratio test of equal disturbance variances.
(g) Compute the two-step FGLS estimate of β, assuming that the model in (15-7) applies. [That is, allow for cross-sectional correlation.] Compare your results with those of part c.

2. Suppose that in the model of Section 15.2.1, $\mathbf{X}_i$ is the same for all i. What is the generalized least squares estimator of $\boldsymbol{\beta}$? How would you compute the estimator if it were necessary to estimate σ_i^2?

3. Repeat Exercise 2 for the model of Section 15.2.2.

4. The following table presents a hypothetical panel of data:

	i = *1*		*i* = 2		*i* = 3	
t	*y*	*x*	*y*	*x*	*y*	*x*
1	30.27	24.31	38.71	28.35	37.03	21.16
2	35.59	28.47	29.74	27.38	43.82	26.76
3	17.90	23.74	11.29	12.74	37.12	22.21
4	44.90	25.44	26.17	21.08	24.34	19.02
5	37.58	20.80	5.85	14.02	26.15	18.64
6	23.15	10.55	29.01	20.43	26.01	18.97
7	30.53	18.40	30.38	28.13	29.64	21.35
8	39.90	25.40	36.03	21.78	30.25	21.34
9	20.44	13.57	37.90	25.65	25.41	15.86
10	36.85	25.60	33.90	11.66	26.04	13.28

(a) Estimate the groupwise heteroscedastic model of Section 15.2.1. Include an estimate of the asymptotic variance of the slope estimator.

Use a two-step procedure, basing the FGLS estimator at the second step on residuals from the pooled least squares regression.

(b) Carry out the Wald, Lagrange multiplier, and likelihood ratio tests of the hypothesis that the variances are all equal. For the likelihood ratio test, use the FGLS estimates.

(c) Carry out a Lagrange multiplier test of the hypothesis that the disturbances are uncorrelated across individuals.

5. A sample of 100 observations produces the following sample data:

$$\begin{aligned}\bar{y}_1 &= 1, \qquad \bar{y}_2 = 2,\\ \mathbf{y}_1'\mathbf{y}_1 &= 150,\\ \mathbf{y}_2'\mathbf{y}_2 &= 550,\\ \mathbf{y}_1'\mathbf{y}_2 &= 260.\end{aligned}$$

The underlying bivariate regression model is

$$\begin{aligned}y_1 &= \mu + \epsilon_1,\\ y_2 &= \mu + \epsilon_2.\end{aligned}$$

(a) Compute the OLS estimate of μ, and estimate the sampling variance of this estimator.

(b) Compute the FGLS estimate of μ and the sampling variance of your estimator.

6. Consider estimation of the following two equation models:

$$\begin{aligned}y_1 &= \beta_1 + \epsilon_1,\\ y_2 &= \beta_2 x + \epsilon_2.\end{aligned}$$

A sample of 50 observations produces the following moment matrix:

$$\begin{array}{c} \\ 1 \\ y_1 \\ y_2 \\ x \end{array}\begin{array}{c} \begin{array}{cccc} 1 & y_1 & y_2 & x \end{array} \\ \begin{bmatrix} 50 & & & \\ 150 & 500 & & \\ 50 & 40 & 90 & 100 \\ 100 & 60 & 50 & \end{bmatrix} \end{array}.$$

(a) Write the explicit formula for the GLS estimator of $[\beta_1, \beta_2]$. What is the asymptotic covariance matrix of the estimator?

(b) Derive the OLS estimator and its sampling variance in this model.

(c) Obtain the OLS estimates of β_1 and β_2, and estimate the sampling covariance matrix of the two estimates. Use n instead of $(n - 1)$ as the divisor to compute the estimates of the disturbance variances.

(d) Compute the FGLS estimates of β_1 and β_2 and the estimated sampling covariance matrix.

(e) Test the hypothesis that $\beta_2 = 1$.

7. The model

$$y_1 = \beta_1 x_1 + \epsilon_1,$$
$$y_2 = \beta_2 x_2 + \epsilon_2$$

satisfies all the assumptions of the classical multivariate regression model. All variables have zero means. Using the data in Exercise 1:

(a) Compute the FGLS estimates of β_1 and β_2.
(b) Test the hypothesis that $\beta_1 = \beta_2$.
(c) Compute the maximum likelihood estimates of the model parameters.
(d) Use the likelihood ratio test to test the hypothesis in part b.

8. Prove that in the model

$$\mathbf{y}_1 = \mathbf{X}_1\boldsymbol{\beta}_1 + \boldsymbol{\epsilon}_1,$$
$$\mathbf{y}_2 = \mathbf{X}_2\boldsymbol{\beta}_2 + \boldsymbol{\epsilon}_2,$$

generalized least squares is equivalent to equation-by-equation ordinary least squares if $\mathbf{X}_1 = \mathbf{X}_2$. Does your result hold if it is also known that $\boldsymbol{\beta}_1 = \boldsymbol{\beta}_2$?

9. Consider the two-equation system

$$y_1 = \beta_1 x_1 \qquad\qquad\qquad + \epsilon_1,$$
$$y_2 = \qquad \beta_2 x_2 + \beta_3 x_3 + \epsilon_2.$$

Assume that the disturbance variances and covariance are known. Now suppose that the analyst of this model applies GLS, but erroneously omits x_3 from the second equation. What effect does this specification error have on the consistency of the estimator of β_1?

10. Consider the system

$$y_1 = \alpha_1 + \beta x + \epsilon_1,$$
$$y_2 = \alpha_2 \qquad\quad + \epsilon_2.$$

The disturbances are freely correlated. Prove that GLS applied to the system leads to the OLS estimates of α_1 and α_2 but to a mixture of the least squares slopes in the regressions of y_1 and y_2 on x as the estimator of β. What is the mixture? To simplify the algebra, assume (with no loss of generality) that $\bar{x} = 0$.

11. For the model

$$y_1 = \alpha_1 + \beta x + \epsilon_1,$$
$$y_2 = \alpha_2 \qquad\quad + \epsilon_2,$$
$$y_3 = \alpha_3 \qquad\quad + \epsilon_3,$$

assume that $y_{i2} + y_{i3} = 1$ at every observation. Prove that the sample covariance matrix of the least squares residuals from the three equations will be singular, thereby precluding computation of the FGLS estimator. How could you proceed in this case?

12. Continuing the analysis of Section 15.6, we find that a translog cost function for one output and three factor inputs that does not impose constant returns to scale is

$$\begin{aligned}\ln C = \alpha &+ \beta_1 \ln p_1 + \beta_2 \ln p_2 + \beta_3 \ln p_3 + \delta_{11}\tfrac{1}{2}\ln^2 p_1 + \delta_{12}\ln p_1 \ln p_2 \\ &+ \delta_{13}\ln p_1 \ln p_3 + \delta_{22}\tfrac{1}{2}\ln^2 p_2 + \delta_{23}\ln p_2 \ln p_3 + \delta_{33}\tfrac{1}{2}\ln^2 p_3 \\ &+ \gamma_{y1}\ln Y \ln p_1 + \gamma_{y2}\ln p_2 + \gamma_{y3}\ln Y \ln p_3 \\ &+ \beta_y \ln Y + \beta_{yy}\tfrac{1}{2}\ln^2 Y + \epsilon_c.\end{aligned}$$

The factor share equations are

$$\begin{aligned}S_1 &= \beta_1 + \delta_{11}\ln p_1 + \delta_{12}\ln p_2 + \delta_{13}\ln p_3 + \gamma_{y1}\ln Y + \epsilon_1,\\ S_2 &= \beta_2 + \delta_{12}\ln p_1 + \delta_{22}\ln p_2 + \delta_{23}\ln p_3 + \gamma_{y2}\ln Y + \epsilon_2,\\ S_3 &= \beta_3 + \delta_{13}\ln p_1 + \delta_{23}\ln p_2 + \delta_{33}\ln p_3 + \gamma_{y3}\ln Y + \epsilon_3.\end{aligned}$$

[See Christensen and Greene (1976) for analysis of this model.]

(a) The three factor shares must add identically to 1. What restrictions does this place on the model parameters?

(b) Show that the adding-up condition in (15-71) can be imposed directly on the model by specifying the translog model in (C/p_3), (p_1/p_3), and (p_2/p_3) and dropping the third share equation. (See Example 15.18.) Notice that this reduces the number of free parameters in the model to 10.

(c) Continuing part b, the model as specified with the symmetry and equality restrictions has 15 parameters. By imposing the constraints, you reduce this number to 10 in the estimating equations. How would you obtain estimates of the parameters not estimated directly?

The remaining parts of this exercise will require specialized software. The **TSP**, **LIMDEP**, **Shazam**, or **ET** programs noted in the preface are four that could be used. All estimation is to be done using the data in Example 15.17.

(d) Estimate each of the three equations you obtained in part b by ordinary least squares. Do the estimates appear to satisfy the cross-equation equality and symmetry restrictions implied by the theory?

(e) Using the data in Example 15.17, estimate the full system of three equations (cost and the two independent shares), imposing the symmetry and cross-equation equality constraints.

(f) Using your parameter estimates, compute the estimates of the elasticities in (15-72) at the means of the variables.

(g) Use a likelihood ratio statistic to test the joint hypothesis that $\gamma_{yi} = 0$, $i = 1, 2, 3$. [Hint: Just drop the relevant variables from the model.]

CHAPTER 16

Simultaneous Equations Models

16.1. INTRODUCTION

Most of our work thus far has been in the context of single-equation models. But even a cursory look through almost any economics textbook shows that much of the theory is built on sets, or *systems,* of relationships. Familiar examples include market equilibrium, models of the macroeconomy, and sets of factor or commodity demand equations. Whether one's interest is only in a particular part of the system or in the system as a whole, the interaction of the variables in the model will have important implications for both interpretation and estimation of the model's equations. The implications of simultaneity for econometric estimation were recognized long before the apparatus discussed in this chapter was developed.[1] The subsequent research in the subject, continuing to the present, is among the most extensive in econometrics.[2]

This chapter considers the issues that arise in interpreting and estimating multiple-equations models. Section 16.2 describes the general framework used for analyzing systems of simultaneous equations and presents some examples. Most of the discussion of these models centers on problems of estimation. But before estimation can even be considered, the fundamental question of whether the parameters of interest in the model are even estimable must be resolved. This problem of identification is discussed in Section 16.3. Sections 16.4

[1]See, for example, Working (1926) and Haavelmo (1943).

[2]The literature on simultaneous-equations models is enormous and continually expanding. Even constructing a complete and current bibliography is a considerable undertaking. Three surveys in the *Handbook of Econometrics*, vol. 1 (Griliches and Intrilligator, 1983) by C. Hsiao on identification, J. Hausman on specification and estimation, and P. Phillips on small-sample properties of estimators provide a good overview of the literature. Other extensive sources include Judge et al. (1985) and Fomby et al. (1984). The latter half of Schmidt (1976) contains many useful theorems and results.

to 16.7 then discuss methods of estimation. Section 16.8 is concerned with specification tests. In Section 16.9, the special characteristics of dynamic models are examined.

16.2. FUNDAMENTAL ISSUES IN SIMULTANEOUS EQUATIONS MODELS

In this section, we describe the basic terminology and statistical issues in the analysis of simultaneous-equations models. We begin with some simple examples and then present a general framework.

16.2.1. Illustrative Systems of Equations

A familiar example of a system of simultaneous equations is a model of market equilibrium, consisting of the following:

$$\begin{aligned} &\textbf{demand equation:} \quad && q_d = \alpha_1 p + \alpha_2 y + \epsilon_d, \\ &\textbf{supply equation:} \quad && q_s = \beta_1 p \qquad\quad + \epsilon_s, \\ &\textbf{equilibrium condition:} \quad && q_d = q_s = q. \end{aligned}$$

These are **structural equations** in that they are derived from theory and each purports to describe a particular aspect of the economy.[3] Since the model is one of the joint determination of price and quantity, they are labeled **jointly dependent** or **endogenous** variables. Income y is assumed to be determined outside of the model, which makes it **exogenous.** The disturbances are added to the usual textbook description to obtain an **econometric model.** All three equations are needed to determine the equilibrium price and quantity, so the system is **interdependent.** Finally, since an equilibrium solution for price and quantity in terms of income and the disturbances is, indeed, implied (unless α_1 equals β_1), the system is said to be a **complete system of equations.** *The completeness of the system requires that the number of equations equal the number of endogenous variables.* As a general rule, it is not possible to estimate the parameters of incomplete systems.

Suppose that interest centers on estimating the demand elasticity α_1. For simplicity, assume that ϵ_d and ϵ_s are well-behaved, classical disturbances with

$$\begin{aligned} &E[\epsilon_{dt}] = E[\epsilon_{st}] = 0, \\ &E[\epsilon_{dt}^2] = \sigma_d^2, \quad E[\epsilon_{st}^2] = \sigma_s^2, \qquad E[\epsilon_{dt}\epsilon_{st}] = 0, \end{aligned}$$

and

$$E[\epsilon_{dt}y_t] = E[\epsilon_{st}y_t] = 0.$$

[3]The distinction between **structural** and **nonstructural** models is sometimes drawn on this basis. See, for example, Cooley and LeRoy (1985).

All variables are mutually uncorrelated with observations at different time periods. Price, quantity, and income are measured in logarithms in deviations from their sample means. Solving the equations for p and q in terms of y, and ϵ_d, and ϵ_s produces the **reduced form** of the model

$$\begin{aligned} p &= \frac{\alpha_2 y}{\beta_1 - \alpha_1} + \frac{\epsilon_d - \epsilon_s}{\beta_1 - \alpha_1} = \pi_1 y + v_1, \\ q &= \frac{\beta_1 \alpha_2 y}{\beta_1 - \alpha_1} + \frac{\beta_1 \epsilon_d - \alpha_1 \epsilon_s}{\beta_1 - \alpha_1} = \pi_2 y + v_2. \end{aligned} \qquad \textbf{(16-1)}$$

(Note the "completeness" requirement that α_1 not equal β_1.)

It follows that $\text{Cov}[p, \epsilon_d] = \sigma_d^2/(\beta_1 - \alpha_1)$, so the demand equation does not satisfy the assumptions of the classical regression model. The price elasticity cannot be consistently estimated by least squares regression of q on y and p. This result is characteristic of simultaneous-equations models. Because the endogenous variables are all correlated with the disturbances, least squares estimates of the parameters of equations with endogenous variables on the right-hand side are inconsistent.[4]

Suppose that we have a sample of T observations on p, q, and y such that

$$\text{plim} \frac{1}{T} \mathbf{y}'\mathbf{y} = \sigma_y^2.$$

Since least squares is inconsistent, we might instead use an **instrumental variable estimator.**[5] The only variable in the system that is not correlated with the disturbances is y. Consider, then, the IV estimator, $\hat{\beta}_1 = \mathbf{q}'\mathbf{y}/\mathbf{p}'\mathbf{y}$. This estimator has

$$\text{plim } \hat{\beta}_1 = \text{plim} \frac{\mathbf{q}'\mathbf{y}/T}{\mathbf{p}'\mathbf{y}/T} = \frac{\beta_1 \alpha_2/(\beta_1 - \alpha_1)}{\alpha_2/(\beta_1 - \alpha_1)} = \beta_1.$$

Evidently, the parameter of the supply curve can be estimated by using an instrumental variable estimator. There are two useful arrangements of this result. First, from (16-1), we see that

$$\hat{\beta}_1 = \frac{p_{11}}{p_{12}} = \frac{\text{slope in the regression of } q \text{ on } y}{\text{slope in the regression of } p \text{ on } y}.$$

Thus, the estimator is the ratio of the OLS estimates of π_1 and π_2. This technique is labeled **indirect least squares.** Second, in the least squares regression of $\mathbf{p}$ on $\mathbf{y}$, the predicted values are

$$\hat{\mathbf{p}} = \left(\frac{\mathbf{p}'\mathbf{y}}{\mathbf{y}'\mathbf{y}}\right)\mathbf{y}.$$

[4] This failure of least squares is sometimes labeled **simultaneous-equations bias.**

[5] See Section 6.7.8.

It follows that in the instrumental variable regression the instrument is $\hat{\mathbf{p}}$. That is,

$$\hat{\beta}_1 = \frac{\hat{\mathbf{p}}'\mathbf{q}}{\hat{\mathbf{p}}'\mathbf{p}}.$$

Finally, since $\hat{\mathbf{p}}'\mathbf{p} = \hat{\mathbf{p}}'\hat{\mathbf{p}}$, $\hat{\beta}_1$ is also the slope in a regression of q on these predicted values. This interpretation defines the **two-stage least squares estimator.**

EXAMPLE 16.1 Supply Equation for Agricultural Goods

Yearly data on price and quantity for the U.S. agricultural sector and real per capita disposable income for U.S. consumers for the years 1960 to 1986 are listed in the appendix to this chapter. Ordinary least squares regression of Q on P produces

$$\hat{Q} = 54.13 + 0.4195P.$$

The instrumental variable estimator suggested earlier produces

$$\hat{Q} = 46.93 + 0.5038P,$$

a 20.1 percent difference in the estimated slope.

It would be desirable to use a similar device to estimate the parameters of the demand equation. But unfortunately, we have exhausted the information in the sample. Not only does least squares fail to estimate the demand equation but, without some further assumptions, the sample contains no other information that can be used. This example illustrates the **problem of identification** alluded to in the introduction to this chapter.

A second example is the following simple model of income determination.

EXAMPLE 16.2 A Small Macroeconomic Model

In this model,

$$\begin{aligned}
\text{consumption:}\quad & c_t = \alpha_0 + \alpha_1 y_t + \alpha_2 c_{t-1} + \epsilon_{t1},\\
\text{investment:}\quad & i_t = \beta_0 + \beta_1 r_t + \beta_2(y_t - y_{t-1}) + \epsilon_{t2},\\
\text{demand:}\quad & y_t = c_t + i_t + g_t.
\end{aligned}$$

The model contains an autoregressive consumption function, an investment equation based on interest and the growth in output, and an equilibrium condition. The model determines the values of the three endogenous variables c_t, i_t, and y_t. This is a **dynamic model.** In addition to the exogenous variables r_t and g_t, it contains two **predetermined variables,** c_{t-1} and y_{t-1}. These are obviously not exogenous, but as regards the current values of the endogenous variables, may be regarded as having already been determined. The deciding factor is whether or not they are uncorrelated with the current disturbances, which we might assume. The reduced form of this model is

$$\begin{aligned}
Ac_t &= \alpha_0(1-\beta_2) + \beta_0\alpha_1 + \alpha_1\beta_1 r_t + \alpha_1 g_t + \alpha_2(1-\beta_2)c_{t-1} - \alpha_1\beta_2 y_{t-1} \\
&\quad + (1-\beta_2)\epsilon_{t1} + \alpha_1\epsilon_{t2}, \\
Ai_t &= \alpha_0\beta_2 + \beta_0(1-\alpha_1) + \beta_1(1-\alpha_1)r_t + \beta_2 g_t + \alpha_2\beta_2 c_{t-1} \\
&\quad - \beta_2(1-\alpha_1)y_{t-1} + \beta_2\epsilon_{t1} + (1-\alpha_1)\epsilon_{t2}, \\
Ay_t &= \alpha_0 + \beta_0 + \beta_1 r_t + g_t + \alpha_2 c_{t-1} - \beta_2 y_{t-1} + \epsilon_{t1} + \epsilon_{t2},
\end{aligned}$$

where $A = 1 - \alpha_1 - \beta_2$. Note that the reduced form preserves the equilibrium condition.

The preceding two models illustrate systems in which there are **behavioral equations** and **equilibrium conditions.** The latter are distinct in that even in an econometric model, they have no disturbances. Another model, which illustrates nearly all of the concepts to be discussed in this chapter, is shown in the next example.

EXAMPLE 16.3 Klein's Model I

A widely used example of a simultaneous equations model of the economy is Klein's (1950) *Model I*. The model may be written

$$\begin{aligned}
C_t &= \alpha_0 + \alpha_1 P_t + \alpha_2 P_{t-1} + \alpha_3(W_t^p + W_t^g) + \epsilon_{1t} && \text{(consumption)}, \\
I_t &= \beta_0 + \beta_1 P_t + \beta_2 P_{t-1} + \beta_3 K_{t-1} + \epsilon_{2t} && \text{(investment)}, \\
W_t^p &= \gamma_0 + \gamma_1 X_t + \gamma_2 X_{t-1} + \gamma_3 A_t + \epsilon_3 t && \text{(private wages)}, \\
X_t &= C_t + I_t + G_t && \text{(equilibrium demand)}, \\
P_t &= X_t - T_t - W_t^p && \text{(private profits)}, \\
K_t &= K_{t-1} + I_t && \text{(capital stock)}.
\end{aligned}$$

The endogenous variables are each on the left-hand side of an equation and labeled on the right. The exogenous variables are G = government nonwage spending, T = indirect business taxes plus net exports, W^g = government wage bill, A = time trend measured as years from 1931, and the constant term. There are also three predetermined variables: the lagged values of the capital stock, private profits, and total demand. The model contains three behavioral equations, an equilibrium condition and two accounting identities. This model provides an excellent example of a small, dynamic model of the economy. It has also been widely used as a test ground for simultaneous-equations estimators. Klein estimated the parameters using data for 1921 to 1941. The data are listed in the appendix to this chapter.

16.2.2. Endogeneity and Causality

The distinction between "exogenous" and "endogenous" variables in a model is a subtle and sometimes controversial complication. It is the subject of a long literature.[6] We have drawn the distinction in a useful economic fashion at a few points in terms of whether a variable in the model could reasonably be ex-

[6] See, for example, Zellner (1979), Sims (1977), Granger (1969), and especially Engle et al. (1983).

pected to vary "autonomously," independently of the other variables in the model. Thus, in a model of supply and demand, the weather variable in a supply equation seems obviously to be exogenous in a pure sense to the determination of price and quantity, whereas the current price clearly is "endogenous" by any reasonable construction. Unfortunately, this neat classification is of fairly limited use in macroeconomics, where almost no variable can be said to be truly exogenous in the fashion that most observers would understand the term. To take a common example, the estimation of consumption functions by least squares, as we did in some earlier examples, is usually treated as a respectable enterprise, even though most macroeconomic models (including the examples given here) depart from a consumption function in which income is endogenous. This has led analysts, for better or worse, to draw the distinction we seek largely on statistical grounds.

In the context of a model, there is a temptation to characterize endogeneity in terms of correlation with the disturbances in the equations. But as we shall readily show, this is a false distinction. Consider the simple model

$$y_1 = \alpha x + \gamma_1 y_2 + \epsilon_1,$$
$$y_2 = \beta z + \gamma_2 y_1 + \epsilon_2,$$

where (y_1, y_2) are "endogenous" by the description we gave earlier and (x, z) are exogenous. Or are they? Suppose that $(x, z, \epsilon_1, \epsilon_2)$ are joint normally distributed. The "reduced form" (see Section 16.2.1) can be written

$$\left.\begin{aligned} y_1 &= a_1 x + b_1 z + d_{11}\epsilon_1 + d_{12}\epsilon_2 \\ y_2 &= a_2 x + b_2 z + d_{21}\epsilon_1 + d_{22}\epsilon_2 \end{aligned}\right\} \quad \text{or} \quad \mathbf{y} = \mathbf{A}[x, z, \epsilon_1, \epsilon_2]'$$

so that $[\mathbf{y}, x, z, \epsilon_1, \epsilon_2]$ have a six-variate joint normal distribution. We know from Chapter 3's results that in a multivariate normal distribution, the conditional distributions are normal as well, with conditional means that are linear in the conditioning variables. Thus, based on the preceding, we could write $E[y_1 | x, y_2] = \delta x + \theta y_2$, where δ and θ are functions of $(\alpha, \beta, \gamma_1, \gamma_2)$, or

$$y_1 = \delta x + \theta y_2 + u_1,$$

where y_2 and u_1 are uncorrelated (indeed, independent) by construction. (As an exercise, you might derive these functions.) The upshot is that from this standpoint, endogeneity is a function of how the model is written. The regression form is no less "the model" than is the structure. We could fit the regressions by least squares and solve for the structure.

The methodological development in the literature has produced some consensus on this subject. In the final analysis, as we shall see, the definitions formalize the economic characterization we drew earlier. We will loosely sketch a few results here for purposes of our derivations to follow. The interested reader is referred to the literature (and forewarned of some challenging reading).

Engle et al. (1983) define a set of variables $\mathbf{x}_t$ in a parameterized model to be **weakly exogenous** if the full model can be written in terms of a marginal probability distribution for $\mathbf{x}_t$ and a conditional distribution for $\mathbf{y}_t|\mathbf{x}_t$ such that estimation of the parameters of the conditional distribution is no less efficient than estimation of the full set of parameters of the joint distribution. This will be the case if none of the parameters in the conditional distribution appears in the marginal distribution for $\mathbf{x}_t$. You might note how we used this notion in our treatment of stochastic regressors in the regression model in Section 6.8.2. In the present context, we will need this sort of construction in order to derive reduced forms the way we did previously.

With reference to time series applications (although the notion extends to cross sections as well), variables $\mathbf{x}_t$ are said to be **predetermined** in the model if $\mathbf{x}_t$ is independent of all *subsequent* structural disturbances ϵ_{t+s} for $s > 0$. Variables that are predetermined in a model can be treated, at least asymptotically, as if they were exogenous in the sense that consistent estimates can be obtained when they appear as regressors. We used this result in Chapter 6 as well, when we derived the properties of regressions containing lagged values of the dependent variable.

A related concept is **Granger causality.** Granger causality (a kind of statistical feedback) is absent when $f(\mathbf{x}_t|\mathbf{x}_{t-1}, \mathbf{y}_{t-1})$ equals $f(\mathbf{x}_t|\mathbf{x}_{t-1})$. The definition states that in the conditional distribution, lagged values of $\mathbf{y}_t$ add no information to explanation of movements of $\mathbf{x}_t$ beyond that provided by lagged values of $\mathbf{x}_t$, itself. This concept is useful in the construction of forecasting models.

Finally, if $\mathbf{x}_t$ is weakly exogenous and if $\mathbf{y}_{t-1}$ does not Granger cause $\mathbf{x}_t$, then $\mathbf{x}_t$ is **strongly exogenous.**

We have done little more than define some terms in this discussion of exogeneity. The literature, particularly that in time-series analysis, is extensive. Our need for these results arises only from our a priori distinction between current endogenous and exogenous and predetermined variables in the simultaneous equations discussed in the next section. The terms will reappear, however, in the discussion of models for time series in Chapters 17 and 18.

16.2.3. A General Notation for Linear Simultaneous Equations Models

The **structural form** of the model is[7]

$$\begin{aligned}
\gamma_{11}y_{t1} + \gamma_{21}y_{t2} + \cdots + \gamma_{M1}y_{tM} + \beta_{11}x_{t1} + \cdots + \beta_{K1}x_{tK} &= \epsilon_{t1},\\
\gamma_{12}y_{t1} + \gamma_{22}y_{t2} + \cdots + \gamma_{M2}y_{tM} + \beta_{12}x_{t1} + \cdots + \beta_{K2}x_{tK} &= \epsilon_{t2},\\
&\vdots\\
\gamma_{1M}y_{t1} + \gamma_{2M}y_{t2} + \cdots + \gamma_{MM}y_{tM} + \beta_{1M}x_{t1} + \cdots + \beta_{KM}x_{tK} &= \epsilon_{tM}.
\end{aligned} \tag{16-2}$$

[7]For the present, it is convenient to ignore the special nature of lagged endogenous variables and treat them the same as the strictly exogenous variables.

There are M equations and M endogenous variables, denoted $y_1, \ldots, y_M$. There are K exogenous variables, $x_1, \ldots, x_K$, which may include predetermined values of $y_1, \ldots, y_M$ as well. The first element of $\mathbf{x}_t$ will usually be the constant, 1. Finally, $\epsilon_{t1}, \ldots, \epsilon_{tM}$ are the **structural disturbances.** The subscript t will be used to index observations, $t = 1, \ldots, T$.

In matrix terms, the system may be written

$$[y_1 \quad y_2 \quad \cdots \quad y_M]_t \begin{bmatrix} \gamma_{11} & \gamma_{12} & \cdots & \gamma_{1M} \\ \gamma_{21} & \gamma_{22} & \cdots & \gamma_{2M} \\ & & \vdots & \\ \gamma_{M1} & \gamma_{M2} & \cdots & \gamma_{MM} \end{bmatrix}$$

$$+ [x_1 \quad x_2 \quad \cdots \quad x_K]_t \begin{bmatrix} \beta_{11} & \beta_{12} & \cdots & \beta_{1M} \\ \beta_{21} & \beta_{22} & \cdots & \beta_{2M} \\ & & \vdots & \\ \beta_{K1} & \beta_{K2} & \cdots & \beta_{KM} \end{bmatrix} = [\epsilon_1 \quad \epsilon_2 \quad \cdots \quad \epsilon_M]_t$$

or

$$\mathbf{y}_t'\mathbf{\Gamma} + \mathbf{x}_t'\mathbf{B} = \boldsymbol{\epsilon}_t'.$$

Each column of the parameter matrices is the vector of coefficients in a particular equation, whereas each row applies to a specific variable.

The underlying theory will imply a number of restrictions on $\mathbf{\Gamma}$ and $\mathbf{B}$. One of the variables in each equation is labeled the *dependent* variable so that its coefficient in the model will be 1. Thus, there will be at least one "1" in each column of $\mathbf{\Gamma}$. This **normalization** is not a substantive restriction. The relationship defined for a given equation will be unchanged if every coefficient in the equation is multiplied by the same constant. Choosing a "dependent variable" simply removes this indeterminacy. If there are any identities, the corresponding columns of $\mathbf{\Gamma}$ and $\mathbf{B}$ will be completely known, and there will be no disturbance for that equation. Since not all variables appear in all equations, some of the parameters will be zero. The theory may also impose other types of restrictions on the parameter matrices.

A special case of the preceding is worth noting before we proceed. If $\mathbf{\Gamma}$ is an upper triangular matrix, the system is said to be **triangular.** In this case, the model is of the form

$$\begin{aligned} y_{t1} &= f_1(\mathbf{x}_t) + \epsilon_{t1}, \\ y_{t2} &= f_2(y_{t1}, \mathbf{x}_t) + \epsilon_{t2}, \\ &\vdots \\ y_{tM} &= f_M(y_{t1}, y_{t2}, \ldots, y_{t,M-1}, \mathbf{x}_t) + \epsilon_{tM}. \end{aligned}$$

The joint determination of the variables in this model is **recursive.** The first is completely determined by the exogenous factors. Then, given the first, the second is likewise determined, and so on. The temporal aspects of some processes in the economy suggest this form of model.

EXAMPLE 16.4 Cobweb Model

The cobweb model of market equilibrium may be written

$$\begin{aligned} Q_t &= \alpha_0 + \alpha_1 P_{t-1} + \epsilon_{1t} \quad \text{(supply)}, \\ P_t &= \beta_0 + \beta_1 Q_t + \epsilon_{2t} \quad \text{(inverse demand)}. \end{aligned}$$

The quantity supplied to the market is determined by last year's price, a bygone. Supply in the current period is perfectly inelastic. Demand responds to the usual forces and determines an equilibrium price, which feeds into next year's supply.

In essence, the endogenous variables are determined in turn, each one depending on the values of the logically preceding ones. Users of spreadsheet programs and those who fill out their own tax returns will recognize other familiar examples of recursive systems.

The solution of the system of equations determining $\mathbf{y}_t$ in terms of $\mathbf{x}_t$ and $\boldsymbol{\epsilon}_t$ is the **reduced form** of the model,

$$\begin{aligned} \mathbf{y}_t' &= -\mathbf{x}_t'\mathbf{B}\boldsymbol{\Gamma}^{-1} + \boldsymbol{\epsilon}_t'\boldsymbol{\Gamma}^{-1} \\ &= \mathbf{x}_t'\boldsymbol{\Pi} + \mathbf{v}_t' \\ &= [x_1 \quad x_2 \quad \cdots \quad x_K]_t \begin{bmatrix} \pi_{11} & \pi_{12} & \cdots & \pi_{1M} \\ \pi_{21} & \pi_{22} & \cdots & \pi_{2M} \\ & & \vdots & \\ \pi_{K1} & \pi_{K2} & \cdots & \pi_{KM} \end{bmatrix} + [\nu_1 \quad \cdots \quad \nu_M]_t, \end{aligned}$$

where

$$\boldsymbol{\Pi} = -\mathbf{B}\boldsymbol{\Gamma}^{-1}$$

and

$$\mathbf{v}_t' = \boldsymbol{\epsilon}_t'\boldsymbol{\Gamma}^{-1}.$$

For this solution to exist, the model must satisfy the

completeness condition: $\boldsymbol{\Gamma}$ is nonsingular.

EXAMPLE 16.5 Structure and Reduced Form

For the small model in Example 16.2, $\mathbf{y}' = [c, i, y]$, $\mathbf{x}' = [1, r, g, c_{-1}, y_{-1}]$, and

$$\boldsymbol{\Gamma} = \begin{bmatrix} 1 & 0 & -1 \\ 0 & 1 & -1 \\ -\alpha_1 & \beta_2 & 1 \end{bmatrix}, \qquad \mathbf{B} = \begin{bmatrix} -\alpha_0 & -\beta_0 & 0 \\ 0 & -\beta_1 & 0 \\ 0 & 0 & -1 \\ -\alpha_2 & 0 & 0 \\ 0 & \beta_2 & 0 \end{bmatrix},$$

$$\mathbf{\Gamma}^{-1} = \frac{1}{1 - \alpha_1 - \beta_2}\begin{bmatrix} 1 - \beta_2 & \beta_2 & 1 \\ \alpha_1 & 1 - \alpha_1 & 1 \\ \alpha_1 & \beta_2 & 1 \end{bmatrix},$$

$$\mathbf{\Pi}' = \frac{1}{1 - \alpha_1 - \beta_2}$$

$$\begin{bmatrix} \alpha_0(1 - \beta_2 + \beta_0\alpha_1) & \alpha_1\beta_1 & \alpha_1 & \alpha_2(1 - \beta_2) & -\beta_2\alpha_1 \\ \alpha_0\beta_2 + \beta_0(1 - \alpha_1) & \beta_1(1 - \alpha_1) & \beta_2 & \alpha_2\beta_2 & -\beta_2(1 - \alpha_1) \\ \alpha_0 + \beta_0 & \beta_1 & 1 & \alpha_2 & -\beta_2 \end{bmatrix}.$$

The completeness condition is that α_1 and β_2 do not sum to one.

The structural disturbances are assumed to be randomly drawn from an M-variate distribution with

$$E[\boldsymbol{\epsilon}_t] = \mathbf{0} \quad \text{and} \quad E[\boldsymbol{\epsilon}_t\boldsymbol{\epsilon}_t'] = \mathbf{\Sigma}.$$

For the present, we assume that

$$E[\boldsymbol{\epsilon}_t\boldsymbol{\epsilon}_s'] = \mathbf{0} \quad \text{for all } t \neq s.$$

Later, we will drop this assumption to allow for heteroscedasticity and autocorrelation. It will occasionally be useful to assume that ϵ_t has a multivariate normal distribution, but we shall postpone this assumption until it becomes necessary. It may be convenient to retain the identities without disturbances as separate equations. If so, one way to proceed with the stochastic specification is to place rows and columns of zeros in the appropriate places in $\mathbf{\Sigma}$.

It follows that the **reduced-form disturbances**

$$\mathbf{v}_t' = \boldsymbol{\epsilon}_t'\mathbf{\Gamma}^{-1}$$

have

$$E[\mathbf{v}_t] = (\mathbf{\Gamma}^{-1})'\mathbf{0} = \mathbf{0},$$
$$E[\mathbf{v}_t\mathbf{v}_t'] = (\mathbf{\Gamma}^{-1})'\mathbf{\Sigma}\mathbf{\Gamma}^{-1} = \mathbf{\Omega}.$$

This implies that

$$\mathbf{\Sigma} = \mathbf{\Gamma}'\mathbf{\Omega}\mathbf{\Gamma}.$$

The preceding formulation describes the model as it applies to an observation $[\mathbf{y}', \mathbf{x}', \boldsymbol{\epsilon}']_t$ at a particular point in time or in a cross section. In a sample of data, each joint observation will be one row in a data matrix,

$$[\mathbf{Y} \quad \mathbf{X} \quad \mathbf{E}] = \begin{bmatrix} \mathbf{y}_1' & \mathbf{x}_1' & \boldsymbol{\epsilon}_1' \\ \mathbf{y}_2' & \mathbf{x}_2' & \boldsymbol{\epsilon}_2' \\ & \vdots & \\ \mathbf{y}_T' & \mathbf{x}_T' & \boldsymbol{\epsilon}_T' \end{bmatrix}.$$

In terms of the full set of T observations, the structure is

$$\mathbf{Y\Gamma} + \mathbf{XB} = \mathbf{E},$$

with

$$E[\mathbf{E}] = \mathbf{0} \quad \text{and} \quad E\left[\frac{1}{T}\mathbf{E}'\mathbf{E}\right] = \mathbf{\Sigma}.$$

Under general conditions, we can strengthen this to

$$\text{plim } E\left[\frac{1}{T}\mathbf{E}'\mathbf{E}\right] = \mathbf{\Sigma}.$$

An important assumption, comparable with the one made in Chapter 6 for the classical regression model, is

$$\text{plim}\frac{1}{T}\mathbf{X}'\mathbf{X} = \mathbf{Q}, \quad \text{a finite positive definite matrix.}^{8} \tag{16-3}$$

We also assume that

$$\text{plim }\frac{1}{T}\mathbf{X}'\mathbf{E} = \mathbf{0}. \tag{16-4}$$

This is what distinguishes the predetermined variables from the endogenous variables.

The reduced form is

$$\mathbf{Y} = \mathbf{X\Pi} + \mathbf{V},$$

where

$$\mathbf{V} = \mathbf{E\Gamma}^{-1}.$$

With the earlier assumptions, we also have

$$\begin{aligned}
\text{plim }\frac{1}{T}\mathbf{V}'\mathbf{V} &= (\mathbf{\Gamma}^{-1})'\mathbf{\Sigma\Gamma}^{-1} = \mathbf{\Omega},\\
\text{plim}\frac{1}{T}\mathbf{Y}'\mathbf{Y} &= \mathbf{\Pi}'\mathbf{Q\Pi} + \mathbf{\Omega},\\
\text{plim}\frac{1}{T}\mathbf{X}'\mathbf{V} &= \mathbf{0},\\
\text{plim}\frac{1}{T}\mathbf{X}'\mathbf{Y} &= \mathbf{Q\Pi}.
\end{aligned} \tag{16-5}$$

[8]The time trend is, once again, an important exception. The conditions required for **X** to be well behaved are discussed in Section 6.7.2. If **X** contains lagged dependent variables, the results of Mann and Wald (1943) will be required. Schmidt (1976) gives some additional results.

16.2.4. Nonlinear Systems of Equations

At various points in the preceding chapters, we have found that the extension of the model to nonlinear equations was relatively straightforward and required only minor changes in the analysis. In most instances, the analysis at hand was simply applied to the linearized regression model. Unfortunately, this simplicity does not reappear here except in a few special cases. If the nonlinearity in a system of equations arises because of nonlinearities in the exogenous variables or nonlinearities in the parameters that arise, say, because of restrictions, then, by a suitable redefinition of the components, the linear model can be reproduced. So these possibilities do not raise any new issues. The major complication arises in models in which the endogenous variables enter the equations nonlinearly. In the general system of equations,

$$\begin{aligned} h_1[(\mathbf{y}, \mathbf{x}, \boldsymbol{\epsilon})_t] &= 0, \\ h_2[(\mathbf{y}, \mathbf{x}, \boldsymbol{\epsilon})_t] &= 0, \\ &\vdots \\ h_M[(\mathbf{y}, \mathbf{x}, \boldsymbol{\epsilon})_t] &= 0, \end{aligned}$$

there is no assurance that a reduced form, $y_{mt} = g_m[(\mathbf{x}, \boldsymbol{\epsilon})_t]$, $m = 1, \ldots, M$, exists for all values of $\mathbf{x}$ and $\boldsymbol{\epsilon}$, but by construction, even if it does, it will be a nonlinear function of the exogenous variables and disturbances. The practical difficulty this raises is that there may be no feasible way to construct a consistent estimator of the parameters based on instrumental variables that exist *within the structure of the model.*[9] Gallant (1987), Gallant and Holley (1980), Gallant and White (1988), and Davidson and MacKinnon (1993) provide further discussion.

16.3. THE PROBLEM OF IDENTIFICATION

Solving the problem to be considered here, the identification problem, logically precedes estimation. We ask at this point whether there is *any* way to obtain estimates of the parameters of the model. We have in hand a certain amount of information upon which to base any inference about its underlying structure. If

[9]There is a philosophical problem induced by this construction as well. As shown in a simple example in Davidson and MacKinnon, the reduced form solution that does exist may not make economic sense. For example, nonlinear dynamic models habitually become wildly unstable and oscillatory in response to only minor changes in the stimuli—see the recent work on "chaos" such as Gleick's (1987) layperson's introduction—although such behavior is extremely rare in the modern world. In Davidson and MacKinnon's example, the reduced-form solutions to the two equations need be neither real nor unique. The idea of positing a model of a real economy whose only predictions are "imaginary" does raise some intriguing questions. In the end, the linear model as an approximation to some underlying real, physical economic counterpart may have substantial virtue here.

more than one theory is consistent with the same "data," they are said to be **observationally equivalent,** and there is no way of distinguishing them. The structure is said to be *unidentified*.[10]

EXAMPLE 16.6 Observational Equivalence

The *observed* data consist of the market outcomes shown in Figure 16.1a. We have no knowledge of the conditions of supply and demand beyond our belief that the data represent *equilibria*. Unfortunately, Figures 16.1b and c both show *structures*, that is, true underlying supply and demand curves, which are consistent with the data in Figure 16.1a. With only the data in Figure 16.1a, we have no way of determining which of theories 16.1b or c is the right one. Thus, the structure underlying the data in Figure 16.1a is unidentified.[11] To suggest where our discussion is headed, suppose that we add to the preceding the known fact that the conditions of supply were unchanged during the period over which the data were drawn. This rules out 16.1c and identifies 16.1b as the correct structure. Note how this scenario relates to the first example in Section 16.2.1 and to the discussion following Example 16.1.

The identification problem is not one of sampling properties or the size of the sample. To focus ideas, it is even useful to suppose that we have at hand an infinite-sized sample of observations on the variables in the model. Now, with this and our prior theory, what information do we have?

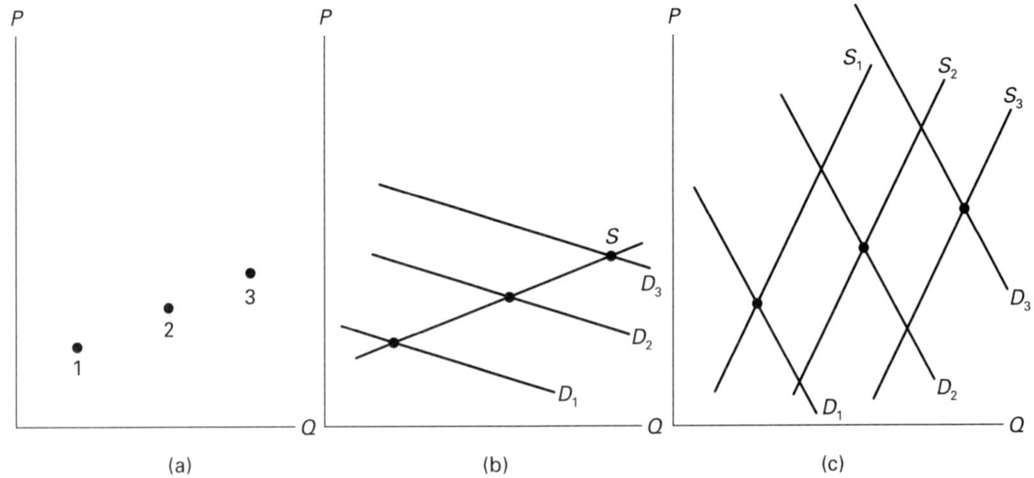

FIGURE 16.1 Market Equilibria.

[10]A useful survey of this issue is Hsiao (1983).

[11]This example paraphrases the classic argument of Working (1926).

In the reduced form,

$$\mathbf{y}_t' = \mathbf{x}_t'\mathbf{\Pi} + \mathbf{v}_t', \; E[\mathbf{v}_t\mathbf{v}_t'] = \mathbf{\Omega},$$

the predetermined variables are uncorrelated with the disturbances. Thus, we can "observe"

$$\text{plim}\,\frac{1}{T}\mathbf{X}'\mathbf{X} = \mathbf{Q} \quad \text{[assumed; see (16-3)]},$$

$$\text{plim}\,\frac{1}{T}\mathbf{X}'\mathbf{Y} = \text{plim}\,\frac{1}{T}\mathbf{X}'(\mathbf{X\Pi} + \mathbf{V}) = \mathbf{Q\Pi},$$

$$\text{plim}\,\frac{1}{T}\mathbf{Y}'\mathbf{Y} = \text{plim}\,\frac{1}{T}'(\mathbf{\Pi}'\mathbf{X}' + \mathbf{V}')(\mathbf{X\Pi} + \mathbf{V}) = \mathbf{\Pi}'\mathbf{Q\Pi} + \mathbf{\Omega}.$$

Therefore, $\mathbf{\Pi}$, the matrix of reduced-form coefficients, is observable:

$$\mathbf{\Pi} = \left[\text{plim}\left(\frac{\mathbf{X}'\mathbf{X}}{T}\right)\right]^{-1}\left[\text{plim}\left(\frac{\mathbf{X}'\mathbf{Y}}{T}\right)\right].$$

This is simply the equation-by-equation least squares regression of $\mathbf{Y}$ on $\mathbf{X}$. Since $\mathbf{\Pi}$ is observable, $\mathbf{\Omega}$ is also:

$$\mathbf{\Omega} = \text{plim}\,\frac{\mathbf{Y}'\mathbf{Y}}{T} - \text{plim}\left[\frac{\mathbf{Y}'\mathbf{X}}{T}\right]\left[\frac{\mathbf{X}'\mathbf{X}}{T}\right]^{-1}\left[\frac{\mathbf{X}'\mathbf{Y}}{T}\right].$$

This should be recognized as the matrix of least squares residual variances and covariances. Therefore,

> $\mathbf{\Pi}$ *and* $\mathbf{\Omega}$ *can be estimated consistently by ordinary least squares regression of* $\mathbf{Y}$ *on* $\mathbf{X}$.

The information in hand, therefore, consists of $\mathbf{\Pi}$, $\mathbf{\Omega}$, and whatever other nonsample information we have about the structure.[12] Now, can we deduce the structural parameters from the reduced form? Consider the following example.

EXAMPLE 16.7 Identification

Consider a market in which q is quantity of Q, p is price, and z is the price of Z, a related good. We assume that z enters both the supply and demand equations. For example, Z might be a crop that is purchased by consumers and that will be grown by farmers instead of Q if its price rises enough relative to p. Thus, we would expect $\alpha_2 > 0$ and $\beta_2 < 0$. So,

$$\begin{aligned} q_d &= \alpha_0 + \alpha_1 p + \alpha_2 z + \epsilon_1 && \text{(demand)},\\ q_s &= \beta_0 + \beta_1 p + \beta_2 z + \epsilon_2 && \text{(supply)},\\ q_d &= q_s = q && \text{(equilibrium)}.\end{aligned}$$

---

[12]We have not necessarily shown that this is *all* the information in the sample. In general, we observe the conditional distribution $f(\mathbf{y}_t|\mathbf{x}_t)$, which constitutes the likelihood for the reduced form. With normally distributed disturbances, this is a function of $\mathbf{\Pi}$, $\mathbf{\Omega}$. (See Section 16.6.2.) With other distributions, other or higher moments of the variables might provide additional information. See, for example, Goldberger (1964, p. 311), Hausman (1983, pp. 402–403), and especially Riersøl (1950).

The reduced form is

$$q = \frac{\alpha_1\beta_0 - \alpha_0\beta_1}{\alpha_1 - \beta_1} + \frac{\alpha_1\beta_2 - \alpha_2\beta_1}{\alpha_1 - \beta_1}z + \frac{\alpha_1\epsilon_2 - \alpha_2\epsilon_1}{\alpha_1 - \beta_1}$$
$$= \pi_{11} + \pi_{21}z + \nu_q,$$
$$p = \frac{\beta_0 - \alpha_0}{\alpha_1 - \beta_1} + \frac{\beta_2 - \alpha_2}{\alpha_1 - \beta_1}z + \frac{\epsilon_2 - \epsilon_1}{\alpha_1 - \beta_1}$$
$$= \pi_{12} + \pi_{22}z + \nu_p.$$

With only four reduced form coefficients and six structural parameters, it is obvious that there will not be a solution. Suppose, though, that it is known that $\beta_2 = 0$ (farmers do not substitute the alternative crop for this one). Then the solution for β_1 is π_{22}/π_{21}. After a bit of manipulation, we also obtain $\beta_0 = \pi_{11} - \pi_{12}\pi_{22}/\pi_{21}$. The restriction identifies the supply parameters. But this is as far as we can go.

The correspondence between the structural and reduced-form parameters is the relationships

$$\mathbf{\Pi} = -\mathbf{B\Gamma}^{-1} \quad \text{and} \quad \mathbf{\Omega} = E[\mathbf{vv}'] = (\mathbf{\Gamma}^{-1})'\mathbf{\Sigma\Gamma}^{-1}.$$

If $\mathbf{\Gamma}$ were known, we could deduce $\mathbf{B}$ as $-\mathbf{\Pi\Gamma}$ and $\mathbf{\Sigma}$ and $\mathbf{\Gamma}'\mathbf{\Omega\Gamma}$. It would appear, therefore, that our problem boils down to obtaining $\mathbf{\Gamma}$. This makes sense. If $\mathbf{\Gamma}$ were known, we could rewrite (16-2), collecting the endogenous variables times their respective coefficients on the left-hand side of a regression, and estimate the remaining unknown coefficients on the predetermined variables by ordinary least squares.[13]

Suppose that the true structure is $[\mathbf{\Gamma}, \mathbf{B}, \mathbf{\Sigma}]$. Now consider an imposter,

$$\mathbf{y}'\tilde{\mathbf{\Gamma}} + \mathbf{x}'\tilde{\mathbf{B}} = \tilde{\boldsymbol{\epsilon}}',$$

that is obtained by postmultiplying the first structure by some nonsingular matrix $\mathbf{F}$. Thus,

$$\tilde{\mathbf{\Gamma}} = \mathbf{\Gamma F}, \qquad \tilde{\mathbf{B}} = \mathbf{BF}, \qquad \tilde{\boldsymbol{\epsilon}}' = \boldsymbol{\epsilon}'\mathbf{F}.$$

The reduced form that corresponds to this structure is

$$\tilde{\mathbf{\Pi}} = -\tilde{\mathbf{B}}\tilde{\mathbf{\Gamma}}^{-1} = \mathbf{BFF}^{-1}\mathbf{\Gamma}^{-1} = \mathbf{\Pi},$$

and, in the same fashion, $\tilde{\mathbf{\Omega}} = \mathbf{\Omega}$. The false structure looks just like the true one, at least in terms of the information we have. Statistically, there is no way we can tell them apart. The structures are observationally equivalent.

Since $\mathbf{F}$ was chosen arbitrarily, we conclude that *any* nonsingular transformation of the original structure has the same reduced form. Any reason for optimism that we might have had should be abandoned. As the model stands, there is no means by which the structural parameters can be deduced from the reduced form. The practical implication is that if the only information that we

[13]This is precisely the approach of the LIML estimator. See Section 16.5.2d.

have is the reduced-form parameters, then the model is not estimable. So how were we able to identify the models in the earlier examples? The answer is: by bringing to bear our nonsample information, namely our theoretical restrictions. Look once again at Example 16.7. Before formalizing the notion, it is useful to consider another example.

EXAMPLE 16.8 An Identified Model

Suppose that in the earlier example income y, rather than z, appears in the demand equation. The revised model is

$$q = \alpha_0 + \alpha_1 p + \alpha_2 y + \epsilon_1,$$
$$q = \beta_0 + \beta_1 p + \beta_2 z + \epsilon_2.$$

The structure is now

$$[q \quad p]\begin{bmatrix} 1 & 1 \\ -\alpha_1 & -\beta_1 \end{bmatrix} + [1 \quad y \quad z]\begin{bmatrix} -\alpha_0 & -\beta_0 \\ -\alpha_2 & 0 \\ 0 & -\beta_2 \end{bmatrix} = [\epsilon_1 \quad \epsilon_2].$$

The reduced form is

$$[q \quad p] = [1 \quad y \quad z]\begin{bmatrix} (\alpha_1\beta_0 - \alpha_0\beta_1)/\Delta & (\beta_0 - \alpha_0)/\Delta \\ -\alpha_2\beta_1/\Delta & -\alpha_2/\Delta \\ \alpha_1\beta_2/\Delta & \beta_2/\Delta \end{bmatrix} + [\nu_1 \quad \nu_2],$$

where

$$\Delta = (\alpha_1 - \beta_1).$$

Every false structure has the same reduced form. But in the coefficient matrix,

$$\tilde{\mathbf{B}} = \mathbf{BF} = \begin{bmatrix} \alpha_0 f_{11} + \beta_0 f_{12} & \alpha_0 f_{12} + \beta_0 f_{22} \\ \alpha_3 f_{11} & \alpha_3 f_{12} \\ \beta_2 f_{21} & \beta_2 f_{22} \end{bmatrix},$$

if f_{12} is not zero, the imposter will have income appearing in the supply equation, which our theory has ruled out. Likewise, if f_{21} is not zero, z will appear in the demand equation, which is also ruled out by our theory. Thus, although all false structures have the same reduced form as the true one, the only one that is consistent with our theory (i.e., is **admissible**) and has coefficients of 1 on q in both equations (examine $\mathbf{\Gamma F}$) is $\mathbf{F} = \mathbf{I}$. This just produces the original structure.

The unique solutions for the structural parameters in terms of the reduced form parameters are

$$\alpha_0 = \pi_{11} - \pi_{12}\left(\frac{\pi_{31}}{\pi_{32}}\right), \qquad \beta_0 = \pi_{11} - \pi_{12}\left(\frac{\pi_{21}}{\pi_{22}}\right),$$

$$\alpha_1 = \frac{\pi_{31}}{\pi_{32}}, \qquad \beta_1 = \frac{\pi_{21}}{\pi_{22}},$$

$$\alpha_2 = \pi_{22}\left(\frac{\pi_{21}}{\pi_{22}} - \frac{\pi_{31}}{\pi_{32}}\right), \qquad \beta_2 = \pi_{32}\left(\frac{\pi_{31}}{\pi_{32}} - \frac{\pi_{21}}{\pi_{22}}\right).$$

The preceding discussion has considered two equivalent methods of establishing identifiability. If it is possible to deduce the structural parameters from the known reduced form parameters, the model is identified. Alternatively, if it can be shown that no false structure is admissible—that is, satisfies the theoretical restrictions—then the model is identified.[14]

16.3.1. The Rank and Order Conditions for Identification

It is useful to summarize what we have determined thus far. The unknown structural parameters consist of

$$\begin{aligned}\mathbf{\Gamma} &= \text{an } M \times M \text{ nonsingular matrix,}\\ \mathbf{B} &= \text{a } K \times M \text{ parameter matrix,}\\ \mathbf{\Sigma} &= \text{an } M \times M \text{ symmetric positive definite matrix.}\end{aligned}$$

The known, reduced-form parameters are

$$\begin{aligned}\mathbf{\Pi} &= \text{a } K \times M \text{ reduced-form coefficients,}\\ \mathbf{\Omega} &= \text{an } M \times M \text{ reduced-form covariance matrix.}\end{aligned}$$

Simply counting parameters in the structure and reduced forms yields an excess of

$$l = M^2 + KM + \tfrac{1}{2}M(M+1) - KM - \tfrac{1}{2}M(M+1) = M^2,$$

which is, as might be expected from the earlier results, the number of unknown elements in $\mathbf{\Gamma}$. Without further information, identification is clearly impossible. The additional information comes in several forms.

1. *Normalizations*. In each equation, one variable has a coefficient of 1. This normalization is a necessary scaling of the equation that is logically equivalent to putting one variable on the left-hand side of a regression. For purposes of identification (and some estimation methods), the choice among the endogenous variables is arbitrary. But at the time the model is formulated, each equation will usually have some natural dependent variable. The normalization does not identify the dependent variable in any formal or causal sense. For example, in a model of supply and demand, both the "demand" equation, $Q = f(P, \mathbf{x})$, and the "inverse demand" equation, $P = g(Q, \mathbf{x})$, are appropriate specifications of the relationship between price and quantity. We note, though, the following:

   With the normalizations, there are $M(M-1)$, not M^2, undetermined values in $\mathbf{\Gamma}$ and this many indeterminacies in the model to be resolved through nonsample information.

2. *Identities*. In some models, variable definitions or equilibrium conditions imply that all the coefficients in a particular equation are known. In the preceding market example, there are three equations, but the third is the equilibrium condition $Q_d = Q_s$. Klein's Model I (Example 16.3) contains six equations, including two

[14] For other interpretations, see Amemiya (1985, p. 230) and Gabrielsen (1978).

accounting identities and the equilibrium condition. There is no question of identification with respect to identities. They may be carried as additional equations in the model, as we do with Klein's Model I in several later examples, or built into the model a priori, as is typical in models of supply and demand.

The substantive nonsample information that will be used in identifying the model will consist of the following:

3. *Exclusions*. The omission of variables from an equation places zeros in $\mathbf{B}$ and $\mathbf{\Gamma}$. In the previous example, the exclusion of income from the supply equation served to identify its parameters.
4. *Linear restrictions*. Restrictions on the structural parameters may also serve to rule out false structures. For example, a long-standing problem in the estimation of production models using time-series data is the inability to disentangle the effects of economies of scale from those of technological change. In some treatments, the solution is to assume that there are constant returns to scale, thereby identifying the effects due to technological change.[15]
5. *Restrictions on the disturbance covariance matrix*. In the identification of a model, these are similar to restrictions on the slope parameters. For example, if the previous market model were to apply to a microeconomic setting, it would probably be reasonable to assume that the structural disturbances in these supply and demand equations are uncorrelated. Example 16.12 shows a case in which a covariance restriction identifies an otherwise unidentified model.
6. *Nonlinearities*. In many models, the variables and/or the parameters enter nonlinearly. For example, a variable may appear in both levels and logarithms. Or there may be nonlinear restrictions on the coefficients. Although this will usually greatly complicate the analysis, nonlinearities can aid in identification. Exercise 4 considers such a case.

To formalize the identification criteria, we require a notation for a single equation. The coefficients of the jth equation are contained in the jth columns of $\mathbf{\Gamma}$ and $\mathbf{B}$. The jth equation is

$$\mathbf{y}'\mathbf{\Gamma}_j + \mathbf{x}'\mathbf{B}_j = \epsilon_j. \tag{16-6}$$

(For convenience, we have dropped the observation subscript.) In this equation, we know that (1) one of the elements in $\mathbf{\Gamma}_j$ is 1 and (2) some variables that appear elsewhere in the model are excluded from this equation. Table 16.1 defines the notation used to incorporate these restrictions in (16-6).

Equation j may be written

$$\mathbf{y}_j = \mathbf{Y}_j'\boldsymbol{\gamma}_j + \mathbf{Y}_j^{*\prime}\boldsymbol{\gamma}_j^* + \mathbf{x}_j'\boldsymbol{\beta}_j + \mathbf{x}_j^{*\prime}\boldsymbol{\beta}_j^* + \epsilon_j.$$

The exclusions imply that $\boldsymbol{\gamma}_j^* = \mathbf{0}$ and $\boldsymbol{\beta}_j^* = \mathbf{0}$. Thus,

$$\mathbf{\Gamma}_j' = [1 \quad -\boldsymbol{\gamma}_j' \quad \mathbf{0}'] \quad \text{and} \quad \mathbf{B}_j' = [-\boldsymbol{\beta}_j' \quad \mathbf{0}'].$$

[15]See footnote 4 in Chapter 14.

TABLE 16.1 Components of Equation j (Dependent Variable $= y_j$)

	Endogenous Variables	*Exogenous Variables*
Included	$\mathbf{Y}_j = M_j$ variables	$\mathbf{x}_j = K_j$ variables
Excluded	$\mathbf{Y}_j^* = M_j^*$ variables	$\mathbf{x}_j^* = K_j^*$ variables

The number of equations is $M_j + M_j^* + 1 = M$.
The number of exogenous variables is $K_j + K_j^* = K$.
The coefficient on y_j in equation j is one.
*s will always be associated with excluded variables.

(Note the sign convention.) For this equation, we partition the reduced-form coefficient matrix in the same fashion:

$$[\mathbf{y}_j \quad \mathbf{Y}_j' \quad \mathbf{Y}_j^{*\prime}] = [\mathbf{x}_j' \quad \mathbf{x}_j^{*\prime}] \overset{\begin{matrix}(1) & (M_j) & (M_j^*)\end{matrix}}{\begin{bmatrix} \boldsymbol{\pi}_j & \underline{\mathbf{\Pi}}_j & \overline{\mathbf{\Pi}}_j \\ \boldsymbol{\pi}_j^* & \underline{\mathbf{\Pi}}_j^* & \overline{\mathbf{\Pi}}_j^* \end{bmatrix}} + [\mathbf{v}_j \quad \mathbf{V}_j \quad \mathbf{V}_j^*] \quad \begin{matrix}[K_j \text{ rows}] \\ [K_j^* \text{ rows}].\end{matrix} \tag{16-7}$$

The reduced-form coefficient matrix is

$$\mathbf{\Pi} = -\mathbf{B}\mathbf{\Gamma}^{-1},$$

which implies that

$$\mathbf{\Pi}\mathbf{\Gamma} = -\mathbf{B}.$$

The jth column of this matrix equation applies to the jth equation,

$$\mathbf{\Pi}\mathbf{\Gamma}_j = -\mathbf{B}_j.$$

Inserting the parts from Table 16.1 yields

$$\begin{bmatrix} \boldsymbol{\pi}_j & \underline{\mathbf{\Pi}}_j & \overline{\mathbf{\Pi}}_j \\ \boldsymbol{\pi}_j^* & \underline{\mathbf{\Pi}}_j^* & \overline{\mathbf{\Pi}}_j^* \end{bmatrix} \begin{bmatrix} 1 \\ -\boldsymbol{\gamma}_j \\ \mathbf{0} \end{bmatrix} = \begin{bmatrix} \boldsymbol{\beta}_j \\ \mathbf{0} \end{bmatrix}.$$

Now extract the two subequations,

$$\boldsymbol{\pi}_j - \underline{\mathbf{\Pi}}_j \boldsymbol{\gamma}_j = \boldsymbol{\beta}_j \quad (K_j \text{ equations}), \tag{16-8}$$

$$\boldsymbol{\pi}_j^* - \underline{\mathbf{\Pi}}_j^* \boldsymbol{\gamma}_j = \mathbf{0} \quad (K_j^* \text{ equations}), \tag{16-9}$$

$$(1) \qquad (M_j).$$

The solution for $\mathbf{B}$ in terms of $\mathbf{\Gamma}$ that we observed at the beginning of this discussion is in (16-8). Equation (16-9) may be written

$$\underline{\mathbf{\Pi}}_j^* \boldsymbol{\gamma}_j = \boldsymbol{\pi}_j^*. \tag{16-10}$$

This is K_j^* equations in M_j unknowns. If they can be solved for $\boldsymbol{\gamma}_j$, (16-8) gives the solution for $\boldsymbol{\beta}_j$ and the equation is identified. For there to be a solution, there must be at least as many equations as unknowns, which leads to the following condition.

Order Condition for Identification of Equation j.

$$K_j^* \geq M_j. \tag{16-11}$$

The number of exogenous variables excluded from equation j must be at least as large as the number of endogenous variables included in equation j.

The order condition is only a counting rule. It is a necessary, but not sufficient condition for identification. It ensures that (16-10) has at least one solution, but it does not ensure that it has only one solution. The sufficient condition for uniqueness follows.

Rank Condition for Identification.

$$\text{rank}[\boldsymbol{\pi}_j^*, \boldsymbol{\Pi}_j^*] = \text{rank}[\boldsymbol{\Pi}_j^*] = M_j.$$

This condition imposes a restriction on a submatrix of the reduced-form coefficient matrix.

The rank condition ensures that there is exactly one solution for the structural parameters given the reduced-form parameters. Our alternative approach to the identification problem was to use the prior restrictions on $[\boldsymbol{\Gamma}, \mathbf{B}]$ to eliminate all false structures. An equivalent condition based on this approach is simpler to apply and has more intuitive appeal. We first rearrange the structural coefficients in the matrix

$$\mathbf{A} = \begin{bmatrix} \boldsymbol{\Gamma} \\ \mathbf{B} \end{bmatrix} = \begin{bmatrix} 1 & \mathbf{A}_1 \\ -\boldsymbol{\gamma}_j & \mathbf{A}_2 \\ \mathbf{0} & \mathbf{A}_3 \\ -\boldsymbol{\beta}_j & \mathbf{A}_4 \\ \mathbf{0} & \mathbf{A}_5 \end{bmatrix} = [\mathbf{a}_j \quad \mathbf{A}_j]. \tag{16-12}$$

The jth column in a false structure $[\boldsymbol{\Gamma}\mathbf{F}, \ \mathbf{B}\mathbf{F}]$ (i.e., the imposter for our equation j) would be $[\boldsymbol{\Gamma}\mathbf{f}_j, \quad \mathbf{B}\mathbf{f}_j]$, where $\mathbf{f}_j$ is the jth column of $\mathbf{F}$. This new jth equation is to be built up as a linear combination of the old one and the other equations in the model. Thus, partitioning as previously,

$$\tilde{\mathbf{a}}_j = \begin{bmatrix} 1 & \mathbf{A}_1 \\ -\boldsymbol{\gamma}_j & \mathbf{A}_2 \\ \mathbf{0} & \mathbf{A}_3 \\ -\boldsymbol{\beta}_j & \mathbf{A}_4 \\ \mathbf{0} & \mathbf{A}_5 \end{bmatrix} \begin{bmatrix} f^0 \\ \mathbf{f}^1 \end{bmatrix} = \begin{bmatrix} 1 \\ \tilde{\boldsymbol{\gamma}}_j \\ \mathbf{0} \\ \tilde{\boldsymbol{\beta}}_j \\ \mathbf{0} \end{bmatrix}.$$

If this hybrid is to have the same variables as the original, it must have nonzero elements in the same places, which can be ensured by taking $f^0 = 1$, and zeros in the same positions as the original $\mathbf{a}_j$. Extracting the third and fifth rows, if $\tilde{\mathbf{a}}_j$ is to be admissible, it must meet the requirement

$$\begin{bmatrix}\mathbf{A}_3\\ \mathbf{A}_5\end{bmatrix}\mathbf{f}^1 = \mathbf{0}.$$

This is not possible if the $(M_j^* + K_j^*) \times (M - 1)$ matrix in brackets has full column rank, so we have the equivalent rank condition,

$$\text{rank}\begin{bmatrix}\mathbf{A}_3\\ \mathbf{A}_5\end{bmatrix} = M - 1.$$

The corresponding order condition is that the matrix in brackets must have at least as many rows as columns. Thus, $M_j^* + K_j^* \geq M - 1$. But since $M = M_j + M_j^* + 1$, this is the same as the order condition in (16-11). The equivalence of the two rank conditions is pursued in the exercises.

The preceding provides a simple method for checking the rank and order conditions. We need only arrange the structural parameters in a tableau and examine the relevant submatrices one at a time; $\mathbf{A}_3$ and $\mathbf{A}_5$ are the structural coefficients in the other equations on the variables that are excluded from equation *j*.

EXAMPLE 16.9 Rank and Order Conditions

The structural coefficients in the model of Example 16.7 may be written in the preceding form as

	q	*p*	*1*	*z*
Demand	1	$-\alpha_1$	$-\alpha_0$	$-\alpha_2$
Supply	1	$-\beta_1$	$-\beta_0$	$-\beta_2$

Neither $\mathbf{A}_3$ nor $\mathbf{A}_5$ has any rows, so $[\mathbf{A}_3' \ \mathbf{A}_5']$ cannot have rank $M - 1 = 1$. Neither equation is identified. The alternative in Example 16.8 is

	q	*p*	*1*	*y*	*z*
Demand	1	$-\alpha_1$	$-\alpha_0$	$-\alpha_2$	0
Supply	1	$-\beta_1$	$-\beta_0$	0	$-\beta_2$

For the demand equation, $[\mathbf{A}_3' \ \mathbf{A}_5'] = -\beta_2$, which has rank $M - 1 = 1$ unless $\beta_2 = 0$. The supply equation is also identified unless $\alpha_2 = 0$. Now suppose that *z* appears in the demand equation but not in the supply equation. Then the structure is

	q	*p*	*1*	*y*	*z*
Demand	1	$-\alpha_1$	$-\alpha_0$	$-\alpha_2$	$-\alpha_3$
Supply	1	$-\beta_1$	$-\beta_0$	0	0

For the demand equation, $[\mathbf{A}_3' \ \mathbf{A}_5']$ has no rows, so the equation is not identified. But for the supply equation, $[\mathbf{A}_3' \ \mathbf{A}_5'] = [-\alpha_2 \ -\alpha_3]$, which has rank one, so the supply equation is identified. This example illustrates the possibility that a model may be **partially identified.**

There is a rule of thumb that is sometimes useful in checking the rank and order conditions of a model: If every equation has its own predetermined variable, the entire model is identified. The proof is simple and is left as an exercise. For a final example, we consider a somewhat larger model.

EXAMPLE 16.10 Identification of Klein's Model I

The structural coefficients in the consumption function of Klein's Model I (transposed and multiplied by minus one for convenience) are listed in Table 16.2.

TABLE 16.2 Klein's Model I, Structural Coefficients

	C	*I*	W^p	*X*	*P*	*K*	1	W^g	*G*	*T*	*A*	P_{-1}	K_{-1}	X_{-1}
C	−1	0	α_3	0	α_1	0	α_0	α_3	0	0	0	α_2	0	0
I	0	−1	0	0	β_1	0	β_0	0	0	0	0	β_2	β_3	0
W^p	0	0	−1	γ_1	0	0	γ_0	0	0	0	γ_3	0	0	γ_2
X	1	1	0	−1	0	0	0	0	1	0	0	0	0	0
P	0	0	−1	1	−1	0	0	0	0	−1	0	0	0	0
K	0	1	0	0	0	−1	0	0	0	0	0	0	1	0

Identification requires that the matrix shown in Table 16.3 have rank five. None of the columns marked by *x*'s can be formed as linear combinations of the others, so the rank condition is met. Verification of the rank and order conditions for the other two equations is left as an exercise.

TABLE 16.3 Identification of the Consumption Function

Eq.		A_3'				A_5'		
	I	*X*	*K*	*G*	*T*	*A*	K_{-1}	X_{-1}
I	−1	0	0	0	0	0	β_3	0
W_p	0	γ_1	0	0	0	γ_3	0	γ_2
X	1	−1	0	1	−1	0	0	0
P	0	1	0	0	0	0	0	0
X	1	0	−1	0	0	0	1	0
		x	*x*		*x*	*x*	*x*	

It is unusual for a model to pass the order but not the rank condition. (But see Example 16.13 for a case in the literature.) Generally, either the conditions are obvious or the model is so large and has so many predetermined variables that the conditions are met trivially. In practice, for a small model it is simple to check both conditions. For a large model, frequently only the order condition is verified. We distinguish three cases:

1. *Underidentified.* $K_j^* < M_j$ or rank condition fails.
2. *Exactly identified.* $K_j^* = M_j$ and rank condition is met.
3. *Overidentified.* $K_j^* > M_j$ and rank condition is met.

16.3.2. Identification Through Nonsample Information

The rank and order conditions given in the preceding section apply to identification of an equation through **exclusion restrictions.** Intuition might suggest that other types of nonsample information should be equally useful in securing identification. To take a specific example, suppose that in Example 16.7, it is known that β_2 equals 2, not 0. The second equation could then be written as

$$\mathbf{q}_d - 2\mathbf{z} = \mathbf{q}_d^* = \beta_0 + \beta_1\mathbf{p} + \beta_j^*\mathbf{z} + \epsilon_2.$$

But we know that $\beta_j^* = 0$, so the supply equation is identified by this restriction. (This is exactly the case examined at the end of that example.) As this example suggests, a linear restriction on the parameters *within* an equation is, for identification purposes, essentially the same as an exclusion.[16] By an appropriate manipulation—that is, by "solving out" the restriction—we can turn the restriction into one more exclusion. A general formulation for identification of an equation that treats exclusions the same as any other type of linear restriction on the parameters is as follows:[17] Let

$\mathbf{\Phi}_j =$ matrix with one row for each restriction and one column for each parameter in the equation.

That is, $\mathbf{\Phi}_j$ has the same number of columns, $M + K$, as $\mathbf{A}$ in (16-12) has rows. Each row in $\mathbf{\Phi}_j$ is the coefficient in a linear restriction, and the restrictions that apply to equation j are

$$\mathbf{\Phi}_j\begin{bmatrix}\mathbf{\Gamma}_j \\ \mathbf{B}_j\end{bmatrix} = \mathbf{c}_j, \quad \text{a vector of constants.}$$

Then the rank condition for identification with restrictions is

$$\text{rank}(\mathbf{\Phi}_j\mathbf{A}_j) = M - 1,$$

[16]The analysis is more complicated if the restrictions are *across* equations, that is, involve the parameters in more than one equation. Kelly (1975) contains a number of results and examples.

[17]See Fisher (1976).

where $\mathbf{A}_j$ is defined in (16-12). The order condition that emerges is

$$n_j \geq M - 1,$$

where n_j is the total number of restrictions. Since $M - 1 = M_j + M_j^*$ and n_j is the number of exclusions plus r_j, the number of additional restrictions, this condition is equivalent to

$$r_j + K_j^* + M_j^* \geq M_j + M_j^*$$

or

$$r_j + K_j^* \geq M_j.$$

This is the same as (16-11) save for the addition of the number of restrictions, which is the result suggested previously.

The rows of $\mathbf{\Phi}_j$ that correspond to simple exclusions just have a 1 in the position corresponding to the appropriate coefficient. By multiplying it out, you can see that if the only restrictions are exclusions, then

$$\mathbf{\Phi}_j = \begin{matrix} 1 & M_j & M_j^* & K_j & K_j^* & \\ \left[\mathbf{0}\right. & \mathbf{0} & \mathbf{I} & \mathbf{0} & \left.\mathbf{0}\right] & M_j^* \\ \left[\mathbf{0}\right. & \mathbf{0} & \mathbf{0} & \mathbf{0} & \left.\mathbf{I}\right] & K_j^* \end{matrix},$$

and we get exactly the same result as before.

EXAMPLE 16.11 Identification with Linear Restrictions

We verified in Example 16.10 that the consumption function in Klein's Model I is identified using only the exclusion restrictions. But there is also a linear restriction in the equation. The coefficients on W^p and W^g are equal. Using the ordering of the variables in Example 16.10, this would add a row $\boldsymbol{\phi}_9 = [0, 0, 1, 0, 0, 0, 0, -1, 0, 0, 0, 0, 0, 0]$. The resulting tableau in Table 16.3 would have another column, $[0, -1, 0, -1, 0]'$. Of course, since the equation is already identified, the restriction is superfluous.

The observant reader will have noticed that no mention of $\mathbf{\Sigma}$ is made in the preceding discussion. To this point, this is because all of the information provided by $\mathbf{\Omega}$ is used in the estimation of $\mathbf{\Sigma}$; for given $\mathbf{\Gamma}$, the relationship between $\mathbf{\Omega}$ and $\mathbf{\Sigma}$ is one-to-one. Recall that $\mathbf{\Sigma} = \mathbf{\Gamma}'\mathbf{\Omega}\mathbf{\Gamma}$. But if restrictions are placed on $\mathbf{\Sigma}$, there is more information in $\mathbf{\Omega}$ than is needed for estimation of $\mathbf{\Sigma}$. This is useful because the excess information can be used instead to help infer the elements in $\mathbf{\Gamma}$. A useful case is that of zero covariances across the disturbances.[18] Once again, it is most convenient to consider this case in terms of a false structure. If the structure is $[\mathbf{\Gamma}, \mathbf{B}, \mathbf{\Sigma}]$, a false structure would have parameters

$$[\tilde{\mathbf{\Gamma}}, \tilde{\mathbf{B}}, \tilde{\mathbf{\Sigma}}] = [\mathbf{\Gamma F}, \mathbf{BF}, \mathbf{F}'\mathbf{\Sigma F}].$$

[18]More general cases are discussed in Hausman (1983) and Judge et al. (1985).

If any of the elements in $\boldsymbol{\Sigma}$ are zero, the false structure must preserve those restrictions to be admissible. For example, suppose that we specify that $\sigma_{12} = 0$. Then it must also be true that $\tilde{\sigma}_{12} = \mathbf{f}_1'\boldsymbol{\Sigma}\mathbf{f}_2 = 0$, where $\mathbf{f}_1$ and $\mathbf{f}_2$ are columns of $\mathbf{F}$. As such, there is a restriction on $\mathbf{F}$ that may identify the model.

EXAMPLE 16.12 The Fully Recursive Model

The fully recursive model is an important special case of the preceding result. A triangular model is

$$\begin{aligned} y_1 &= \boldsymbol{\beta}_1'\mathbf{x} + \epsilon_1, \\ y_2 &= \gamma_{12}y_1 + \boldsymbol{\beta}_2'\mathbf{x} + \epsilon_2, \\ &\vdots \\ y_M &= \gamma_{1M}y_1 + \gamma_{2M}y_2 + \cdots + \gamma_{M-1,M}y_{M-1} + \boldsymbol{\beta}_M'\mathbf{x} + \epsilon_M. \end{aligned}$$

We place no restrictions on $\mathbf{B}$. The first equation is identified, since it is already in reduced form. But for any of the others, linear combinations of it and the ones above it involve the same variables. Thus, we conclude that *without some identifying restrictions, only the parameters of the first equation in a triangular system are identified*. But suppose that $\boldsymbol{\Sigma}$ is diagonal. Then the entire model is identified, as we now prove. As usual, we attempt to find a false structure that satisfies the restrictions of the model.

The jth column of $\mathbf{F}$, $\mathbf{f}_j$, is the coefficients in a linear combination of the equations that will be an imposter for equation j. Many $\mathbf{f}_j$'s are already precluded.

1. $\mathbf{f}_1$ must be the first column of an identity matrix. The first equation is identified and normalized on y_1.
2. In all remaining columns of $\mathbf{F}$, all elements below the diagonal must be zero, since an equation can only involve the y's in it or in the equations above it.

Without further restrictions, any upper triangular $\mathbf{F}$ is an admissible transformation. But with a diagonal $\boldsymbol{\Sigma}$, we have more information. Consider the second column. Since $\tilde{\boldsymbol{\Sigma}}$ must be diagonal, $\mathbf{f}_1'\boldsymbol{\Sigma}\mathbf{f}_2 = 0$. But given $\mathbf{f}_1$ in 1 above,

$$\mathbf{f}_1'\boldsymbol{\Sigma}\mathbf{f}_2 = \sigma_{11}f_{12} = 0,$$

so $f_{12} = 0$. The second column of $\mathbf{F}$ is now complete and is equal to the second column of $\mathbf{I}$. Continuing in the same manner, we find that

$$\mathbf{f}_1'\boldsymbol{\Sigma}\mathbf{f}_3 = 0 \quad \text{and} \quad \mathbf{f}_2'\boldsymbol{\Sigma}\mathbf{f}_3 = 0$$

will suffice to establish that $\mathbf{f}_3$ is the third column of $\mathbf{I}$. In this fashion, it can be shown that the only admissible $\mathbf{F}$ is $\mathbf{F} = \mathbf{I}$, which was to be shown.

With $\boldsymbol{\Gamma}$ upper triangular, $M(M-1)/2$ unknown parameters remained. That is exactly the number of restrictions placed on $\boldsymbol{\Sigma}$ when it was assumed to be diagonal.

Another even more complex problem arises in models that are nonlinear in the endogenous variables. They arise fairly frequently, for example, in models in which variables appear both in levels and in logarithms, and in macroeconomic models in which the price level and real and nominal variables all appear. For some reasonably general cases, a number of results have been obtained.[19] A very useful, simple result has been obtained for the common case in which the model involves the endogenous variables and nonlinear functions of them that each involve a single variable.[20] For these models, the fundamental rank condition,

$$\text{rank}[\mathbf{\Phi A}] = M - 1,$$

is extended by simply adding the nonlinear functions to the system as additional endogenous variables (but without increasing the number of equations). The following example illustrates the use of this criterion.

EXAMPLE 16.13 A Model of Industry Structure

The following model of industry structure and performance was estimated by Strickland and Weiss (1976). Note that the square of the endogenous variable, C, appears in the first equation.

$$\frac{A}{S} = \alpha_0 + \alpha_1 M + \alpha_2\left(\frac{Cd}{S}\right) + \alpha_3 C + \alpha_4 C^2 + \alpha_5 Gr + \alpha_6 D + \epsilon_1,$$

$$C = \beta_0 + \beta_1\left(\frac{A}{S}\right) + \beta_2\left(\frac{MES}{S}\right) + \epsilon_2,$$

$$M = \gamma_0 + \gamma_1\left(\frac{K}{S}\right) + \gamma_2 Gr + \gamma_3 C + \gamma_4 Gd + \gamma_5\left(\frac{A}{S}\right) + \gamma_6\left(\frac{MES}{S}\right) + \epsilon_3.$$

A = advertising,	M = price cost margin,
S = industry sales,	D = durable goods industry (0/1),
C = concentration,	Gr = industry growth rate,
Cd = consumer demand,	K = capital stock,
MES = efficient scale,	Gd = geographic dispersion.

Since the only restrictions are exclusions, we may use the rule rank $[\mathbf{A}_3', \mathbf{A}_5'] = M - 1$ discussed in the first part of this section. The augmented coefficient matrix (with all signs reversed) is shown in Table 16.4. Identification of the first equation requires

$$[\mathbf{A}_3', \mathbf{A}_5'] = \begin{bmatrix} \beta_2 & 0 & 0 \\ \gamma_6 & \gamma_1 & \gamma_4 \end{bmatrix}$$

[19]See Brown (1983).

[20]See Fisher (1976, pp. 127–167, especially pp. 147–148).

TABLE 16.4 Structural Coefficients in Strickland and Weiss' Model

	Γ					$\mathbf{B}$					
	A/S	*C*	C^2	*M*	*1*	*Cd/S*	*Gr*	*D*	*MES/S*	*K/S*	*Gd*
Advertising	-1	α_3	α_4	α_1	α_0	α_2	α_5	α_6	0	0	0
Concentration	β_1	-1	0	0	β_0	0	0	0	β_2	0	0
Margin	γ_5	γ_3	0	-1	γ_0	0	γ_2	0	γ_6	γ_1	γ_4

to have rank two, which it does unless $\beta_2 = 0$. Thus, the first equation is identified by the presence of the scale variable in the second equation. It is easily seen that the second equation is overidentified. But for the third,

$$[\mathbf{A}_3' \ \mathbf{A}_5'] = \begin{bmatrix} \alpha_4 & \alpha_2 & \alpha_6 \\ 0 & 0 & 0 \end{bmatrix} (!),$$

which has rank one, not two. The third equation is not identified. It passes the order condition but fails the rank condition.[21]

16.4. METHODS OF ESTIMATION

It is possible to estimate the reduced-form parameters, $\mathbf{\Pi}$ and $\mathbf{\Omega}$, consistently by ordinary least squares. But except for forecasting $\mathbf{y}$ given $\mathbf{x}$, these are generally not the parameters of interest; $\mathbf{\Gamma}$, $\mathbf{B}$, and $\mathbf{\Sigma}$ are. Ordinary least squares (OLS) estimates of the structural parameters are inconsistent, ostensibly because the included endogenous variables in each equation are correlated with the disturbances. Still, it is at least of passing interest to examine what is estimated by ordinary least squares, particularly in view of its widespread use (despite its inconsistency). Since the proof of identification was based on solving for $\mathbf{\Gamma}$, $\mathbf{B}$, and $\mathbf{\Sigma}$ from $\mathbf{\Pi}$ and $\mathbf{\Omega}$, one way to proceed is to apply our finding to the sample estimates, $\mathbf{P}$ and $\mathbf{W}$. This **indirect least squares approach** is feasible but inefficient. Worse, there will usually be more than one possible estimator and no obvious means of choosing among them. There are two approaches for direct estimation, both based on the principle of instrumental variables. It is possible to estimate each equation separately using a **limited information** estimator. But the same principle that suggests that joint estimation brings efficiency gains in the seemingly unrelated regressions setting is at work here, so we shall also consider **full information** or system methods of estimation.

[21]The failure of the third equation is obvious on inspection. There is no variable in the second equation that is not in the third. The reader who has already studied this topic may wonder at this point how the authors were able to obtain their two-stage least squares estimates of this equation. This question is considered in Section 16.5.2f.

16.5. SINGLE EQUATION – LIMITED INFORMATION METHODS

Estimation of the system one equation at a time has the benefit of computational simplicity. But because these methods neglect information contained in the other equations, they are labeled **limited information methods.**

16.5.1. Ordinary Least Squares

For all T observations, the nonzero terms in the jth equation are

$$\begin{aligned}\mathbf{y}_j &= \mathbf{Y}_j\boldsymbol{\gamma}_j + \mathbf{X}_j\boldsymbol{\beta}_j + \boldsymbol{\epsilon}_j \\ &= \mathbf{Z}_j\boldsymbol{\delta}_j + \boldsymbol{\epsilon}_j.\end{aligned}$$

The M reduced-form equations are

$$\mathbf{Y} = \mathbf{X\Pi} + \mathbf{V}.$$

For the included endogenous variables $\mathbf{Y}_j$, the reduced forms are the M_j appropriate columns of $\mathbf{\Pi}$ and $\mathbf{V}$, written

$$\mathbf{Y}_j = \mathbf{X\Pi}_j + \mathbf{V}_j. \quad \textbf{(16-13)}$$

[Note that $\mathbf{\Pi}_j$ is the middle part of $\mathbf{\Pi}$ shown in (16-7).] Likewise, $\mathbf{V}_j$ is M_j columns of $\mathbf{V} = \mathbf{E\Gamma}^{-1}$. This least squares estimator is

$$\begin{aligned}\mathbf{d}_j &= [\mathbf{Z}_j'\mathbf{Z}_j]^{-1}\mathbf{Z}_j'\mathbf{Y}_j \\ &= \boldsymbol{\delta}_j + \begin{bmatrix}\mathbf{Y}_j'\mathbf{Y}_j & \mathbf{Y}_j'\mathbf{X}_j \\ \mathbf{X}_j'\mathbf{Y}_j & \mathbf{X}_j'\mathbf{X}_j\end{bmatrix}^{-1}\begin{bmatrix}\mathbf{Y}_j'\boldsymbol{\epsilon}_j \\ \mathbf{X}_j'\boldsymbol{\epsilon}_j\end{bmatrix}.\end{aligned}$$

None of the terms in the inverse matrix converges to $\mathbf{0}$. Although $\text{plim}(1/T)\mathbf{X}_j'\boldsymbol{\epsilon}_j = \mathbf{0}$,

$$\text{plim}\frac{1}{T}\mathbf{Y}_j'\boldsymbol{\epsilon}_j = \underline{\boldsymbol{\omega}}_j - \mathbf{\Omega}_{jj}\boldsymbol{\gamma}_j,$$

where $\underline{\boldsymbol{\omega}}_j$ and $\mathbf{\Omega}_{jj}$ are parts of $\mathbf{\Omega}$. [See the equation before (16-24).]

To show this, first note that since $\mathbf{V} = \mathbf{E\Gamma}^{-1}$, $\mathbf{E} = \mathbf{V\Gamma}$. Thus, $\boldsymbol{\epsilon}_j = \mathbf{V\Gamma}_j$, where $\mathbf{\Gamma}_j$ is the jth column of $\mathbf{\Gamma}$. This is $(1, -\boldsymbol{\gamma}_j', \mathbf{0}')'$. [See the equation preceding (16-8).] Thus, $\text{plim}(\mathbf{Y}_j'\boldsymbol{\epsilon}_i/T) = \text{plim}(\mathbf{V}_j'\mathbf{V\Gamma}_j/T) = \text{plim}(\mathbf{V}_j'\mathbf{V}/T)\mathbf{\Gamma}_j$. The first matrix is the second row of the partitioning of $\mathbf{\Omega}$ which is given in the equation preceding (16-24). Then, $[\underline{\boldsymbol{\omega}}_j\mathbf{\Omega}_{jj}](1, -\boldsymbol{\gamma}_j', \mathbf{0}')' = \underline{\boldsymbol{\omega}}_j - \mathbf{\Omega}_{jj}\boldsymbol{\gamma}_j$, which is the result given above. Therefore, both parts of $\mathbf{d}_j$ are inconsistent.

Although we can say with certainty that $\mathbf{d}_j$ is inconsistent, we cannot state how serious this problem is. OLS does have the virtue of computational simplicity, though with modern software, this is an extremely modest virtue. For better or worse, OLS is a very commonly used estimator in this context. We will return to this issue later in a comparison of several estimators.

EXAMPLE 16.14 Regression Function

The model of Example 16.7 is

$$q = \alpha_1 p + \alpha_2 z + \epsilon_1 \quad \text{(demand)},$$
$$q = \beta_1 p + \beta_2 z + \epsilon_2 \quad \text{(supply)}.$$

The reduced form is

$$q = \frac{\alpha_1\beta_2 - \alpha_2\beta_1}{\alpha_1 - \beta_1} z + \nu_1 = \pi_1 z + \nu_1,$$
$$p = \frac{\beta_2 - \alpha_2}{\alpha_1 - \beta_1} z + \nu_2 = \pi_2 z + \nu_2.$$

It is convenient to assume that $\text{Var}(z) = \Sigma_{zz} = 1$. Based on this, we may derive the quantities

$$\begin{aligned} \text{Var}[q] &= \pi_1^2 + \omega_{11}, & \text{Cov}[q, z] &= \pi_1, \\ \text{Var}[p] &= \pi_2^2 + \omega_{22}, & \text{Cov}[p, z] &= \pi_2, \\ \text{Cov}[q, p] &= \pi_1\pi_2 + \omega_{12}. \end{aligned}$$

If we compute the OLS regression of q on p and z, using a sample of observations, the slope vector, **d** will estimate

$$\text{plim}\begin{bmatrix} \mathbf{p}'\mathbf{p}/T & \mathbf{p}'\mathbf{z}/T \\ \mathbf{z}'\mathbf{p}/T & \mathbf{z}'\mathbf{z}/T \end{bmatrix}^{-1} \begin{bmatrix} \mathbf{p}'\mathbf{q}/T \\ \mathbf{z}'\mathbf{q}/T \end{bmatrix} = \begin{bmatrix} \text{Var}[p] & \text{Cov}[p, z] \\ \text{Cov}[z, p] & \text{Var}[z] \end{bmatrix}^{-1} \begin{bmatrix} \text{Cov}[p, q] \\ \text{Cov}[z, q] \end{bmatrix}.$$

After some tedious algebra (including the computation of $\mathbf{\Omega} = (\mathbf{\Gamma}^{-1})'\mathbf{\Sigma}\mathbf{\Gamma}^{-1}$), this reduces to

$$\text{plim}\ \mathbf{d} = \theta\begin{bmatrix} \alpha_1 \\ \alpha_2 \end{bmatrix} + (1 - \theta)\begin{bmatrix} \beta_1 \\ \beta_2 \end{bmatrix},$$

where

$$\theta = \frac{\sigma_{11} - \sigma_{12}}{\sigma_{11} + \sigma_{22} - 2\sigma_{12}}.$$

Therefore, least squares estimates a mixture of the supply and demand curves, where the weights are proportional to the sources of variation.

16.5.1a. Least Squares Estimation of Triangular Systems. The preceding example illustrates a general result. The least squares estimates are inconsistent estimates of a structural equation precisely because they are consistent estimates of a mixture of all of the equations in the model.[22]

[22]The distinction between structures and regressions, or conditional mean functions that we have explored here, is the subject of some interesting commentary in the literature. See, for example, Working (1926), Haavelmo (1943), and Waugh (1961). Waugh argued for the use of least squares, offering as justification the example in which hog farmers would be interested in knowing the expected price given a year's output.

An intuitively appealing form of simultaneous equations model is the **triangular system,**

$$
\begin{aligned}
(1)\ y_1 &= \mathbf{x}'\boldsymbol{\beta}_1 && && + \epsilon_1,\\
(2)\ y_2 &= \mathbf{x}'\boldsymbol{\beta}_2 + \gamma_{12}y_1 && && + \epsilon_2,\\
(3)\ y_3 &= \mathbf{x}'\boldsymbol{\beta}_3 + \gamma_{13}y_1 + \gamma_{23}y_2 && && + \epsilon_3,
\end{aligned}
$$

and so on. If $\boldsymbol{\Gamma}$ is upper triangular and $\boldsymbol{\Sigma}$ is diagonal, so that the disturbances are uncorrelated, the system is a **fully recursive model.** (No restrictions are placed on $\mathbf{B}$.) It is easy to see that in this case the entire system may be estimated consistently (and, as we shall show later, efficiently) by ordinary least squares. The first equation is a classical regression model. In the second equation, $\text{Cov}(y_1, \epsilon_2) = \text{Cov}(\mathbf{x}'\boldsymbol{\beta}_1 + \epsilon_1, \epsilon_2) = 0$, so it too may be estimated by ordinary least squares. Proceeding in the same fashion to (3), it is clear that y_1 and ϵ_3 are uncorrelated. Likewise, if we substitute (1) in (2) and then the result for y_2 in (3), we find that y_2 is also uncorrelated with ϵ_3. Continuing in this way, we find that in every equation the full set of right-hand variables is uncorrelated with the respective disturbance. The result is that *the fully recursive model may be consistently estimated using equation-by-equation ordinary least squares.*

In the more general case, in which $\boldsymbol{\Sigma}$ is not diagonal, the preceding argument does not apply. Consistent and efficient estimates can be obtained using the methods to be discussed next. This model does have an interesting feature, however. Although *ordinary* least squares is inconsistent, *generalized* least squares estimation of the entire system, in the manner of the seemingly unrelated regressions model, *ignoring the simultaneity*, produces both consistent and efficient estimates.[23] If $\boldsymbol{\Sigma}$ must be estimated, which will almost always be the case, Lahiri and Schmidt find that full efficiency in estimation requires an *efficient* estimate of $\boldsymbol{\Sigma}$. This is in contrast to the seemingly unrelated regressions model, which requires only a consistent estimate of $\boldsymbol{\Sigma}$. (See Section 15.4.2.) Iterating via the Oberhofer and Kmenta (1974) method produces the desired estimates. (See Section 15.4.3a.)

16.5.1b. Indirect Least Squares. In obtaining the rank and order conditions for identification, we implicitly defined an estimator for the structural parameters. For the jth equation,

$$
\begin{aligned}
\boldsymbol{\pi}_j - \underline{\boldsymbol{\Pi}}_j\boldsymbol{\gamma}_j &= \boldsymbol{\beta}_j \quad (K_j \text{ equations}),\\
\boldsymbol{\pi}_j^* - \boldsymbol{\Pi}_j^*\boldsymbol{\gamma}_j &= \mathbf{0} \quad (K_j^* \text{ equations}).
\end{aligned}
\tag{16-14}
$$

By analogy, then, if $\mathbf{P}$ is the OLS estimate of $\boldsymbol{\Pi}$, the ILS estimator of $\boldsymbol{\beta}_j$ would be

$$\mathbf{b}_j = \mathbf{p}_j - \underline{\mathbf{P}}_j\mathbf{c}_j.$$

[23]This intriguing result is due to Lahiri and Schmidt (1978).

It remains to find $\mathbf{c}_j$, the indirect least squares (ILS) estimator of $\boldsymbol{\gamma}_j$. In the second equation, there are K_j^* equations and M_j unknown parameters to be determined. There are three possibilities:

1. $K_j^* < M_j$. Then the equation is unidentified, and no solution can be obtained.
2. $K_j^* = M_j$. The equation is exactly identified. In this case, we may compute

$$\mathbf{c}_j = [\mathbf{P}_j^*]^{-1}\mathbf{p}_j^*.$$

3. $K_j^* > M_j$. The equation is overidentified. There is more than one solution. One candidate that would reconcile the several choices uses a generalized inverse,

$$\mathbf{c}_j = (\mathbf{P}_j^{*\prime}\mathbf{P}_j^*)^{-1}\mathbf{P}_j^*\mathbf{p}_j^*.$$

16.5.2. Estimation by Instrumental Variables and GMM

In the next several sections, we will discuss various methods of consistent and efficient estimation. As will be evident quite soon, there is a surprisingly long menu of choices. It is a useful result that all of the methods in general use can be placed under the umbrella of **instrumental variable (IV) estimators.**

Returning to the structural form, we first consider direct estimation of the jth equation,

$$\begin{aligned}\mathbf{y}_j &= \mathbf{Y}_j\boldsymbol{\gamma}_j + \mathbf{X}_j\boldsymbol{\beta}_j + \boldsymbol{\epsilon}_j\\ &= \mathbf{Z}_j\boldsymbol{\delta}_j + \boldsymbol{\epsilon}_j.\end{aligned}$$

As we saw previously, OLS estimates of $\boldsymbol{\delta}_j$ are inconsistent because of the correlation of $\mathbf{Z}_j$ and $\boldsymbol{\epsilon}_j$. A general method of obtaining consistent estimates is the method of instrumental variables. (See Section 6.7.8.) Let $\mathbf{W}_j$ be a $T \times (M_j + K_j)$ matrix that satisfies the requirements for an IV estimator,

$$\text{plim}\,\frac{1}{T}\mathbf{W}_j'\mathbf{Z}_j = \boldsymbol{\Sigma}_{wz} = \text{a finite nonsingular matrix,} \qquad \textbf{(16-15a)}$$

$$\text{plim}\,\frac{1}{T}\mathbf{W}_j'\boldsymbol{\epsilon}_j = \mathbf{0}, \qquad \textbf{(16-15b)}$$

$$\text{plim}\,\frac{1}{T}\mathbf{W}_j'\mathbf{W}_j = \boldsymbol{\Sigma}_{ww} = \text{a positive definite matrix.} \qquad \textbf{(16-15c)}$$

Then the IV estimator,

$$\hat{\boldsymbol{\delta}}_{j,\text{IV}} = [\mathbf{W}_j'\mathbf{Z}_j]^{-1}\mathbf{W}_j'\mathbf{y}_j,$$

will be consistent and have asymptotic covariance matrix

$$\begin{aligned}\text{Asy. Var}[\hat{\boldsymbol{\delta}}_{j,\text{IV}}] &= \frac{\sigma_{jj}}{T}\,\text{plim}\left[\frac{1}{T}\mathbf{W}_j'\mathbf{Z}_j\right]^{-1}\left[\frac{1}{T}\mathbf{W}_j'\mathbf{W}_j\right]\left[\frac{1}{T}\mathbf{Z}_j'\mathbf{W}_j\right]^{-1} \qquad \textbf{(16-16)}\\ &= \frac{\sigma_{jj}}{T}[\boldsymbol{\Sigma}_{wz}^{-1}\boldsymbol{\Sigma}_{ww}\boldsymbol{\Sigma}_{zw}^{-1}].\end{aligned}$$

A consistent estimate of σ_{jj} is obtained using

$$\hat{\sigma}_{jj} = \frac{(\mathbf{y}_j - \mathbf{Z}_j\hat{\boldsymbol{\delta}}_{j,\text{IV}})'(\mathbf{y}_j - \mathbf{Z}_j\hat{\boldsymbol{\delta}}_{j,\text{IV}})}{T}. \tag{16-17}$$

This is the familiar sum of squares of the estimated disturbances. A degrees of freedom correction for the denominator, $T - M_j - K_j$, is sometimes suggested. Asymptotically, the correction is immaterial. Whether it is beneficial in a small sample remains to be settled. The resulting estimator is not unbiased in any event, as it would be in the classical regression model. (Only) in the interest of simplicity, we shall omit the degrees of freedom correction in what follows.

The various estimators that have been developed for simultaneous-equations models are all IV estimators. They differ in the choice of instruments and in whether the equations are estimated one at a time or jointly. We divide them into two classes, **limited information** or **full information,** on this basis.

16.5.2a. Estimating an Exactly Identified Equation. A useful departure point is an exactly identified equation. Identification of equation j requires that K_j^*, the number of excluded exogenous variables, be at least as large as M_j, the number of included endogenous variables in $\mathbf{Y}_j$. If the equation is exactly identified, $K_j^* = M_j$. Consider, then, the IV estimator based on

$$\mathbf{W}_j = [\mathbf{X}_j^* \; \mathbf{X}_j] = \mathbf{X}.$$

There is an excluded exogenous variable available to serve as an instrument for each included endogenous variable. The estimator is

$$\hat{\boldsymbol{\delta}}_{j,\text{ILS}} = [\mathbf{X}'\mathbf{Z}_j]^{-1}\mathbf{X}'\mathbf{y}_j = \begin{bmatrix}\mathbf{c}_j \\ \mathbf{b}_j\end{bmatrix}. \tag{16-18}$$

This is the ILS estimator. The estimated reduced form is

$$\mathbf{P} = (\mathbf{X}'\mathbf{X})^{-1}\mathbf{X}'[\mathbf{y}_j \; \mathbf{Y}_j \; \mathbf{Y}_j^*].$$

We do not require the last M_j^* columns. For the remainder, after premultiplying by $\mathbf{X}'\mathbf{X}$ and partitioning $\mathbf{X}$ as $\mathbf{W}_j$ as shown previously, we have

$$\begin{bmatrix}\mathbf{X}_j^{*\prime}\mathbf{X}_j^* & \mathbf{X}_j^{*\prime}\mathbf{X}_j \\ \mathbf{X}_j'\mathbf{X}_j^* & \mathbf{X}_j'\mathbf{X}_j\end{bmatrix}\begin{bmatrix}\mathbf{p}_j^* & \mathbf{P}_j^* \\ \mathbf{p}_j & \underline{\mathbf{P}}_j\end{bmatrix} = \begin{bmatrix}\mathbf{X}_j^{*\prime}\mathbf{y}_j & \mathbf{X}_j^{*\prime}\mathbf{Y}_j \\ \mathbf{X}_j'\mathbf{y}_j & \mathbf{X}_j'\mathbf{Y}_j\end{bmatrix}. \tag{16-19}$$

Recall the equations that defined the ILS estimator (16-14). Using $\mathbf{P}$ instead,

$$\begin{bmatrix}\mathbf{p}_j^* & \mathbf{P}_j^* \\ \mathbf{p}_j & \underline{\mathbf{P}}_j\end{bmatrix}\begin{bmatrix}1 \\ -\mathbf{c}_j\end{bmatrix} = \begin{bmatrix}\mathbf{0} \\ \mathbf{b}_j\end{bmatrix}.$$

Postmultiplying both sides of (16-19) by $[1 \; -\mathbf{c}_j']'$ produces

$$\begin{bmatrix}\mathbf{X}_j^{*\prime}\mathbf{X}_j^* & \mathbf{X}_j^{*\prime}\mathbf{X}_j \\ \mathbf{X}_j'\mathbf{X}_j^* & \mathbf{X}_j'\mathbf{X}_j\end{bmatrix}\begin{bmatrix}\mathbf{0} \\ \mathbf{b}_j\end{bmatrix} = \begin{bmatrix}\mathbf{X}_j^{*\prime}\mathbf{y}_j & \mathbf{X}_j^{*\prime}\mathbf{Y}_j \\ \mathbf{X}_j'\mathbf{y}_j & \mathbf{X}_j'\mathbf{Y}_j\end{bmatrix}\begin{bmatrix}1 \\ -\mathbf{c}_j\end{bmatrix}.$$

Upon collecting terms, this defines the ILS estimator according to the equations

$$\begin{bmatrix} \mathbf{X}_j^{*\prime}\mathbf{X}_j & \mathbf{X}_j^{*\prime}\mathbf{Y}_j \\ \mathbf{X}_j'\mathbf{X}_j & \mathbf{X}_j'\mathbf{Y}_j \end{bmatrix} \begin{bmatrix} \mathbf{b}_j \\ \mathbf{c}_j \end{bmatrix} = \begin{bmatrix} \mathbf{X}_j^{*\prime}\mathbf{y}_j \\ \mathbf{X}_j'\mathbf{y}_j \end{bmatrix}.$$

By premultiplying (16-18) by $\mathbf{X}'\mathbf{Z}_j$, we obtain exactly this expression, so the two are equivalent. To reiterate the result, for an exactly identified equation, we may obtain consistent estimates by using the excluded exogenous variables as instruments for the included endogenous variables. The appropriate asymptotic covariance matrix can be computed using (16-16) and (16-17).

16.5.2b. Two-Stage Least Squares. For the exactly identified equation, ILS provides a consistent (and, we shall show, efficient) estimate. In the usual case, however, the equation to be estimated will be overidentified, so $\mathbf{X}'\mathbf{Z}_j$ will have more rows than columns and cannot be inverted. As such, the ILS/IV estimator cannot be used. The method of two-stage least squares is the usual alternative.[24] We developed the full set of results for this estimator in Section 6.7.8. By merely changing notation slightly, the results of Section 6.7.8 are exactly the derivation of the estimator we will describe here. Thus, you might want to review this section before continuing.

Since we have an excess of exogenous variables in $\mathbf{X}_j^*$ to choose from, it might make sense just to choose M_j from the set. Indeed, you can easily show that we could just use any M_j independent linear combinations of them,

$$\hat{\mathbf{Y}}_j = \mathbf{X}_j^*\mathbf{D}, \qquad \textbf{(16-20)}$$

for some matrix **D** with full column rank. A natural candidate would be the predicted values from a set of regressions of the variables in $\mathbf{Y}_j$ on $\mathbf{X}_j^*$. We leave as an exercise the proof that this would provide a consistent estimator. It would not be efficient, however. In our discussion of IV estimators in Section 6.7.8, we obtained the qualitative result that the greater the correlation of the instruments with the included variables, the smaller the asymptotic variance matrix. Now from the reduced form (16-13), we know that $\mathbf{Y}_j = \mathbf{X}\mathbf{\Pi}_j + \mathbf{V}_j$, so by regressing $\mathbf{Y}_j$ only on a subset of the x's, we neglect the information about $\mathbf{Y}_j$ contained in the remainder. The **two-stage least squares (2SLS)** method consists of using as the instruments for $\mathbf{Y}_j$ the predicted values in a regression of $\mathbf{Y}_j$ on *all* the x's:

$$\hat{\mathbf{Y}}_j = \mathbf{X}[(\mathbf{X}'\mathbf{X})^{-1}\mathbf{X}'\mathbf{Y}_j] = \mathbf{X}\mathbf{P}_j.$$

(It can be shown that this is the most efficient IV estimator that can be formed using only the columns of **X**.) Note the emulation of $E[\mathbf{Y}_j] = \mathbf{X}\mathbf{\Pi}_j$ in the result. The 2SLS estimator is, thus,

[24]Since this method leads to indirect least squares if the equation is exactly identified, the two cases need not be considered separately.

$$\hat{\boldsymbol{\delta}}_{j,2SLS} = \begin{bmatrix} \hat{\mathbf{Y}}_j'\mathbf{Y}_j & \hat{\mathbf{Y}}_j'\mathbf{X}_j \\ \mathbf{X}_j'\mathbf{Y}_j & \mathbf{X}_j'\mathbf{X}_j \end{bmatrix}^{-1} \begin{bmatrix} \hat{\mathbf{Y}}_j'\mathbf{y}_j \\ \mathbf{X}_j'\mathbf{y}_j \end{bmatrix}. \quad \textbf{(16-21)}$$

Before proceeding, it is important to emphasize the role of the identification condition in this result. In the matrix $[\hat{\mathbf{Y}}_j \;\; \mathbf{X}_j]$, which has $M_j + K_j$ columns, all columns are linear functions of the K columns of $\mathbf{X}$. There exist, at most, K linearly independent combinations of the columns of $\mathbf{X}$. If the equation is not identified, $M_j + K_j$ is greater than K, and $[\hat{\mathbf{Y}}_j \;\; \mathbf{X}_j]$ will not have full column rank. In this case, the 2SLS estimator cannot be computed. If, however, the order condition but not the rank condition is met, then although the 2SLS estimator can be computed, it is not a consistent estimator. See Example 16.13 for a case in point.

There are a few useful simplifications. First, since

$$\mathbf{X}(\mathbf{X}'\mathbf{X})^{-1}\mathbf{X}' = (\mathbf{I} - \mathbf{M})$$

is idempotent, $\hat{\mathbf{Y}}_j'\mathbf{Y}_j = \hat{\mathbf{Y}}_j'\hat{\mathbf{Y}}_j$. Second,

$$\mathbf{X}_j'\mathbf{X}(\mathbf{X}'\mathbf{X})^{-1}\mathbf{X}' = \mathbf{X}_j'$$

implies that

$$\mathbf{X}_j'\mathbf{Y}_j = \mathbf{X}_j'\hat{\mathbf{Y}}_j.$$

Thus, (16-21) can also be written

$$\hat{\boldsymbol{\delta}}_{j,2SLS} = \begin{bmatrix} \hat{\mathbf{Y}}_j'\hat{\mathbf{Y}}_j & \hat{\mathbf{Y}}_j'\mathbf{X}_j \\ \mathbf{X}_j'\hat{\mathbf{Y}}_j & \mathbf{X}_j'\mathbf{X}_j \end{bmatrix}^{-1} \begin{bmatrix} \hat{\mathbf{Y}}_j'\mathbf{y}_j \\ \mathbf{X}_j'\mathbf{y}_j \end{bmatrix}. \quad \textbf{(16-22)}$$

The 2SLS estimator is obtained by ordinary least squares regression of $\mathbf{y}_j$ on $\hat{\mathbf{Y}}_j$ and $\mathbf{X}_j$. Thus, the name stems from the two regressions in the procedure:

1. *Stage 1.* Obtain the ordinary least squares predictions from regression of $\mathbf{Y}_j$ on $\mathbf{X}$.
2. *Stage 2.* Estimate $\boldsymbol{\delta}_j$ by ordinary least squares regression of $\mathbf{y}_j$ on $\hat{\mathbf{Y}}_j$ and $\mathbf{X}_j$.

A direct proof of the consistency of the 2SLS estimator requires only that we establish that it is a valid IV estimator. For (16-15a) we require

$$\text{plim}\begin{bmatrix} \hat{\mathbf{Y}}_j'\mathbf{Y}_j/T & \hat{\mathbf{Y}}_j'\mathbf{X}_j/T \\ \mathbf{X}_j'\mathbf{Y}_j/T & \mathbf{X}_j'\mathbf{X}_j/T \end{bmatrix} = \text{plim}\begin{bmatrix} \mathbf{P}_j'\mathbf{X}'(\mathbf{X}\boldsymbol{\Pi}_j + \mathbf{V}_j)/T & \mathbf{P}_j'\mathbf{X}'\mathbf{X}_j/T \\ \mathbf{X}_j'(\mathbf{X}\boldsymbol{\Pi}_j + \mathbf{V}_j)/T & \mathbf{X}_j'\mathbf{X}_j/T \end{bmatrix}$$

to be a finite nonsingular matrix. We have used (16-13) for $\mathbf{Y}_j$. This is a continuous function of $\mathbf{P}_j$, which has plim $\mathbf{P}_j = \boldsymbol{\Pi}_j$. The Slutsky theorem thus allows us to substitute $\boldsymbol{\Pi}_j$ for $\mathbf{P}_j$ in the probability limit. That the parts converge to a finite matrix follows from (16-3) and (16-5). It will be nonsingular if $\boldsymbol{\Pi}_j$ has full column rank, which, in turn, will be true if the equation is identified.[25] For (16-15b), we require

$$\text{plim}\frac{1}{T}\begin{bmatrix} \hat{\mathbf{Y}}_j'\boldsymbol{\epsilon}_j \\ \mathbf{X}_j'\boldsymbol{\epsilon}_j \end{bmatrix} = \begin{bmatrix} \mathbf{0} \\ \mathbf{0} \end{bmatrix}.$$

[25] Schmidt (1976, pp. 150–151) provides a proof of this result.

The second part is assumed in (16-4). For the first, by direct substitution,

$$\text{plim}\,\frac{1}{T}\hat{\mathbf{Y}}_j'\mathbf{X}(\mathbf{X}'\mathbf{X})^{-1}\mathbf{X}'\boldsymbol{\epsilon}_j = \text{plim}\left(\frac{\mathbf{Y}_j'\mathbf{X}}{T}\right)\left(\frac{\mathbf{X}'\mathbf{X}}{T}\right)^{-1}\left(\frac{\mathbf{X}'\boldsymbol{\epsilon}_j}{T}\right).$$

The third part on the right converges to zero, whereas the other two converge to finite matrices, which confirms the result. Since $\hat{\boldsymbol{\delta}}_{j,2SLS}$ is an IV estimator, we can just invoke Theorem 6.15 for the asymptotic distribution. A proof of asymptotic efficiency requires the establishment of the benchmark, which we shall do in the discussion of the MLE. Finally, by a (rather involved) application of the central limit theorem, it can be shown that if the data are well behaved, the two-stage least squares estimator is asymptotically normally distributed. (Once again, see the discussion in Section 6.7.8.)

As a final shortcut that is useful for programming purposes, we note that if $\mathbf{X}_j$ is regressed on $\mathbf{X}$, a perfect fit is obtained, so $\hat{\mathbf{X}}_j = \mathbf{X}_j$. Using the idempotent matrix $(\mathbf{I} - \mathbf{M})$, (16-22) becomes

$$\hat{\boldsymbol{\delta}}_{j,2SLS} = \begin{bmatrix} \mathbf{Y}_j'(\mathbf{I}-\mathbf{M})\mathbf{Y}_j & \mathbf{Y}_j'(\mathbf{I}-\mathbf{M})\mathbf{X}_j \\ \mathbf{X}_j'(\mathbf{I}-\mathbf{M})\mathbf{Y}_j & \mathbf{X}_j'(\mathbf{I}-\mathbf{M})\mathbf{X}_j \end{bmatrix}^{-1} \begin{bmatrix} \mathbf{Y}_j'(\mathbf{I}-\mathbf{M})\mathbf{y}_j \\ \mathbf{X}_j'(\mathbf{I}-\mathbf{M})\mathbf{y}_j \end{bmatrix}.$$

Thus

$$\begin{aligned} \hat{\boldsymbol{\delta}}_{j,2SLS} &= [\hat{\mathbf{Z}}_j'\hat{\mathbf{Z}}_j]^{-1}\hat{\mathbf{Z}}_j'\mathbf{y}_j \\ &= [(\mathbf{Z}_j'\mathbf{X})(\mathbf{X}'\mathbf{X})^{-1}(\mathbf{X}'\mathbf{Z}_j)]^{-1}(\mathbf{Z}_j'\mathbf{X})(\mathbf{X}'\mathbf{X})^{-1}\mathbf{X}'\mathbf{y}_j, \end{aligned} \tag{16-23}$$

where all columns of $\hat{\mathbf{Z}}_j'$ are obtained as predictions in a regression of the corresponding column of $\mathbf{Z}_j$ on $\mathbf{X}$. This also results in a useful simplification of the estimated asymptotic covariance matrix,

$$\text{Est. Asy. Var}[\hat{\boldsymbol{\delta}}_{j,2SLS}] = \hat{\sigma}_{jj}[\hat{\mathbf{Z}}_j'\hat{\mathbf{Z}}_j]^{-1}.$$

It is important to note that σ_{jj} is estimated by

$$\hat{\sigma}_{jj} = \frac{(\mathbf{y}_j - \mathbf{Z}_j\hat{\boldsymbol{\delta}}_j)'(\mathbf{y}_j - \mathbf{Z}_j\hat{\boldsymbol{\delta}}_j)}{T},$$

using the original data, not $\hat{\mathbf{Z}}_j$.

It can also be shown that 2SLS applied to an exactly identified equation is the same as ILS. If the equation is exactly identified, $\mathbf{Z}_j'\mathbf{X}$ is square and has an inverse. Thus, the inverse in brackets in (16-23) may be expanded to obtain

$$\hat{\boldsymbol{\delta}}_{j,2SLS} = (\mathbf{X}'\mathbf{Z}_j)^{-1}(\mathbf{X}'\mathbf{X})(\mathbf{Z}_j'\mathbf{X})^{-1}(\mathbf{Z}_j'\mathbf{X})(\mathbf{X}'\mathbf{X})^{-1}\mathbf{X}'\mathbf{y}_j.$$

Eliminating the products of inverses leaves (*for the exactly identified case only*)

$$\hat{\boldsymbol{\delta}}_{j,2SLS} = (\mathbf{X}'\mathbf{Z}_j)^{-1}\mathbf{X}'\mathbf{y}_j,$$

which is (16-18).

16.5.2c. GMM Estimation. The GMM estimator described in Section 11.5.5 is, with a minor change of notation, precisely the set of procedures we have been using here. Using this method, however, will allow us to generalize the covariance structure for the disturbances. That is, we assume that

$$y_{jt} = \mathbf{z}'_{jt}\boldsymbol{\delta}_j + \epsilon_{jt},$$

where $\mathbf{z}_{jt} = [\mathbf{Y}_{jt}, \mathbf{x}_{jt}]$ (we use the capital $\mathbf{Y}_{jt}$ to denote the L_j included endogenous variables). Thus far, we have assumed that ϵ_{jt} is neither heteroscedastic nor autocorrelated in the jth equation. There is no need to impose those assumptions at this point. Autocorrelation in the context of a simultaneous equations model is a substantial complication, however. We will take up the issue next. For the present, we will consider the heteroscedastic case only.

The assumptions of the model provide the orthogonality conditions,

$$E[\mathbf{x}_t\epsilon_{jt}] = E[\mathbf{x}_t(y_{jt} - \mathbf{z}'_{jt}\boldsymbol{\delta}_j)] = \mathbf{0}.$$

If $\mathbf{x}_t$ is taken to be the full set of exogenous variables in the model, we obtain the criterion for the GMM estimator,

$$\begin{aligned} q &= \mathbf{e}(\mathbf{z}_t, \boldsymbol{\delta}_j)'\mathbf{X}\mathbf{W}_{jj}^{-1}\mathbf{X}'\mathbf{e}(\mathbf{z}_t, \boldsymbol{\delta}_j) \\ &= \mathbf{m}(\boldsymbol{\delta}_j)'\mathbf{W}_{jj}^{-1}\mathbf{m}(\boldsymbol{\delta}_j), \end{aligned}$$

where

$$\mathbf{m}(\boldsymbol{\delta}_j) = \frac{1}{T}\sum_{t=1}^{T}\mathbf{x}_t(y_{jt} - \mathbf{z}'_{jt}\boldsymbol{\delta}_j)$$

and

$$\mathbf{W}_{jj} = \text{the weighting matrix.}$$

Once again, this is precisely the estimator defined in Section 11.5.5. If the disturbances are assumed to be homoscedastic and nonautocorrelated, then the optimal weighting matrix will be an estimator of

$$\begin{aligned} \boldsymbol{\Sigma}_{jj} &= E[\mathbf{m}(\boldsymbol{\delta}_j)\mathbf{m}(\boldsymbol{\delta}_j)'] \\ &= \frac{1}{T}E\left[\sum_{t=1}^{T}\mathbf{x}_t\mathbf{x}'_t(y_{jt} - \mathbf{z}'_{jt}\boldsymbol{\delta}_j)^2\right] \\ &= \frac{1}{T}\sum_{t=1}^{T}\sigma_{jj}\mathbf{x}_t\mathbf{x}'_t \\ &= \frac{1}{T}\sigma_{jj}(\mathbf{X}'\mathbf{X}). \end{aligned}$$

The constant σ_{jj} is irrelevant to the solution. If we use $(\mathbf{X}'\mathbf{X})^{-1}$ as the weighting matrix, then the GMM estimator that minimizes q is, once again, the 2SLS estimator. [We found this result earlier after (11-40).]

The extension that we can obtain here is to allow for heteroscedasticity of unknown form. There is no need to rederive the earlier result. If the disturbances are heteroscedastic, then

$$\boldsymbol{\Sigma}_{jj} = \frac{1}{T}\sum_{t=1}^{T} \omega_{jj,t}\,\mathbf{x}_t\mathbf{x}_t'$$
$$= \frac{1}{T}\mathbf{X}'\boldsymbol{\Omega}_{jj}\mathbf{X}.$$

The weighting matrix can be estimated with White's consistent estimator—see (11-13)—if a consistent estimator of $\boldsymbol{\delta}_j$ is in hand with which to compute the residuals. Of course, one is, since 2SLS ignoring the heteroscedasticity is consistent, albeit inefficient. The conclusion then is that under these assumptions, there is a way to improve on 2SLS by adding another step. The name 3SLS is reserved for the systems estimator of this sort, so choosing between 2.5 stage least squares and Davidson and MacKinnon's suggested "heteroscedastic 2SLS, or **H2SLS**," we will opt for the latter. The estimator is based on the initial two-stage least squares procedure.

$$\hat{\boldsymbol{\delta}}_{j,\text{H2SLS}} = [\mathbf{Z}_j'\mathbf{X}(\mathbf{S}_{0,jj})^{-1}\mathbf{X}'\mathbf{Z}_j]^{-1}[\mathbf{Z}_j'\mathbf{X}(\mathbf{S}_{0,jj})^{-1}\mathbf{X}'\mathbf{y}_j],$$

where

$$\mathbf{S}_{0,jj} = \sum_{t=1}^{T}\mathbf{x}_t\mathbf{x}_t'(y_{jt} - \mathbf{z}_{jt}'\hat{\boldsymbol{\delta}}_{j,\text{2SLS}})^2.$$

The asymptotic covariance matrix is estimated with

$$\text{Est. Asy. Var}[\hat{\boldsymbol{\delta}}_{j,\text{H2SLS}}] = [\mathbf{Z}_j'\mathbf{X}(\mathbf{S}_{0,jj})^{-1}\mathbf{X}'\mathbf{Z}_j]^{-1}.$$

Extensions of this estimator were suggested by Cragg (1983) and Cumby et al. (1983).

16.5.2d. Limited Information Maximum Likelihood and the *k* Class of Estimators. The **limited information maximum likelihood (LIML) estimator** is based on a single equation. With normally distributed disturbances, LIML is efficient among single-equation estimators. To construct the log-likelihood function for the *j*th equation, we consider the joint distribution of the endogenous variables, $\mathbf{y}_j$ and $\mathbf{Y}_j$. The reduced form for these $M_j + 1$ variables is

$$[\mathbf{y}_j \quad \mathbf{Y}_j] = [\mathbf{X}_j \quad \mathbf{X}_j^*]\begin{bmatrix} \boldsymbol{\pi}_j & \underline{\boldsymbol{\Pi}}_j \\ \boldsymbol{\pi}_j^* & \underline{\boldsymbol{\Pi}}_j^* \end{bmatrix} + [\mathbf{v}_j \quad \mathbf{V}_j]$$

or

$$\mathbf{Y}_j^0 = \mathbf{X}\boldsymbol{\Pi}_j^0 + \mathbf{V}_j^0.$$

The $(M_j + 1) \times (M_j + 1)$ reduced-form covariance matrix is

$$\boldsymbol{\Omega}_j^0 = \begin{bmatrix} \omega_{jj} & \underline{\boldsymbol{\omega}}_j' \\ \underline{\boldsymbol{\omega}}_j & \boldsymbol{\Omega}_{jj} \end{bmatrix}.$$

The log of the joint density is therefore

$$\ln L_j^0 = -\frac{T}{2}[(M_j + 1)\ln(2\pi) + \ln|\boldsymbol{\Omega}_j^0|] \\ - \frac{1}{2}\sum_{t=1}^{T}[\mathbf{Y}_{jt}^0 - \mathbf{x}_t'\boldsymbol{\Pi}_j^0]'(\boldsymbol{\Omega}_j^0)^{-1}[\mathbf{Y}_{jt}^0 - \mathbf{x}_t'\boldsymbol{\Pi}_j^0]. \tag{16-24}$$

The LIML estimator maximizes this log-likelihood, subject to the constraints that relate the structure to the reduced form,

$$\boldsymbol{\pi}_j - \underline{\boldsymbol{\Pi}}_j\boldsymbol{\gamma}_j = \boldsymbol{\beta}_j, \\ \boldsymbol{\pi}_j^* - \boldsymbol{\Pi}_j^*\boldsymbol{\gamma}_j = \mathbf{0}. \tag{16-25}$$

The first of these just shows how to obtain $\boldsymbol{\beta}_j$ given $\boldsymbol{\gamma}_j$. The second shows the restrictions on $\boldsymbol{\Pi}$. There are three cases to consider:

1. The equation is unidentified. No estimation is possible.
2. The equation is exactly identified. There are no restrictions: $\boldsymbol{\gamma}_j = (\boldsymbol{\Pi}_j^*)^{-1}\boldsymbol{\pi}_j^*$.
3. The equation is overidentified. The restrictions in (16-25) are substantive.

Absent any restrictions, (16-24) is the log-likelihood function for the seemingly unrelated regressions model analyzed in Chapter 15. As such, since all equations have the same regressors, ordinary least squares, equation by equation, is consistent and efficient. Before proceeding, therefore, we obtain the following useful result:

If the equation is exactly identified, the LIML estimator is the ILS estimator. Moreover, it is also equal to the 2SLS, as was proved earlier.

If the equation is overidentified, the likelihood function is to be maximized with respect to all its unknown parameters. The analytical solution to the resulting problem is extremely lengthy and involved. But this is one of those unusual cases in which the practical application is far simpler than the formal solution.[26]

The LIML, or **least variance ratio** estimator, can be computed as follows. Let

$$\mathbf{W}_j^0 = \mathbf{E}_j^{0\prime}\mathbf{E}_j^0$$

where

$$\mathbf{E}_j^0 = \mathbf{M}_j\mathbf{Y}_j^0 = [\mathbf{I} - \mathbf{X}_j(\mathbf{X}_j'\mathbf{X}_j)^{-1}\mathbf{X}_j']\mathbf{Y}_j^0.$$

Each column of $\mathbf{E}_j^0$ is a set of least squares residuals in the regression of the corresponding column of $\mathbf{Y}_j^0$ on $\mathbf{X}_j$, that is, the exogenous variables that appear in the jth equation. Thus, $\mathbf{W}_j^0$ is the matrix of sums of squares and cross products of these residuals. Define

$$\mathbf{W}_j^1 = \mathbf{E}_j^{1\prime}\mathbf{E}_j^1 = \mathbf{Y}_j^{0\prime}[\mathbf{I} - \mathbf{X}(\mathbf{X}'\mathbf{X})^{-1}\mathbf{X}']\mathbf{Y}_j^0. \tag{16-26}$$

[26] See Theil (1971, Appendix). The least variance ratio estimator is derived in Johnston (1984). The LIML estimator was derived by Anderson and Rubin (1949, 1950).

That is, $\mathbf{W}_j^1$ is defined like $\mathbf{W}_j^0$ except that the regressions are on all of the x's in the model, not just the ones in the jth equation. Let

$$\lambda_1 = \text{smallest characteristic root of } (\mathbf{W}_j^1)^{-1}\mathbf{W}_j^0. \tag{16-27}$$

This is an asymmetric matrix, but all of the roots are real and greater than or equal to 1.[27] Depending on the available software, it may be more convenient to obtain the identical smallest root of the symmetric matrix

$$\mathbf{D} = (\mathbf{W}_j^1)^{-1/2}\mathbf{W}_j^0(\mathbf{W}_j^1)^{-1/2}.$$

Now partition $\mathbf{W}_j^0$:

$$\mathbf{W}_j^0 = \begin{bmatrix} w_{jj}^0 & \mathbf{w}_j^{0\prime} \\ \underline{\mathbf{w}}_j^0 & \mathbf{W}_{jj}^0 \end{bmatrix}$$

corresponding to $[\mathbf{y}_j, \mathbf{Y}_j]$, and partition $\mathbf{W}_j^1$ likewise. Then, with these parts in hand,

$$\hat{\boldsymbol{\gamma}}_{j,\text{LIML}} = [\mathbf{W}_{jj}^0 - \lambda_1\mathbf{W}_{jj}^1]^{-1}(\mathbf{w}_j^0 - \lambda_1\mathbf{w}_j^1) \tag{16-28}$$

and

$$\hat{\boldsymbol{\beta}}_{j,\text{LIML}} = [\mathbf{X}_j'\mathbf{X}_j]^{-1}\mathbf{X}_j'(\mathbf{y}_j - \mathbf{Y}_j\hat{\boldsymbol{\gamma}}_{j,\text{LIML}}).$$

Note that $\boldsymbol{\beta}_j$ is estimated by a simple least squares regression. The asymptotic covariance matrix for the LIML estimator is identical to that for the 2SLS estimator.[28] The implication is that with normally distributed disturbances, 2SLS is fully efficient. If the equation is exactly identified, it can be shown that $\lambda_1 = 1$, which leads to the ILS estimator.

Note, finally, that the LIML estimator is a method of moments estimator and a function of sufficient statistics. (See Section 4.7.)

EXAMPLE 16.15 Limited Information Estimation of Klein's Consumption Function

The following will apply the single equation estimators that we have discussed to estimation of the consumption function in Klein's Model I. We will derive the LIML estimates first. The included and full set of exogenous and predetermined variables are

$$\mathbf{X}_c = [1, P_{-1}] \quad \text{and} \quad \mathbf{X} = [1, G, T, A, W^g, P_{-1}, K_{-1}, X_{-1}],$$

respectively. The included endogenous variables are

$$\mathbf{Y}_c^0 = [C \quad P \quad (W^p + W^g)].$$

[27] A proof appears in Schmidt (1976, pp. 173–174).

[28] This is proved by showing that both estimators are members of the "k class" of estimators, all of which have the same asymptotic covariance matrix. Details are given in Theil (1971) and Schmidt (1976).

The residual sums of squares and cross-product matrices in the regressions of $\mathbf{Y}_c^0$ on $\mathbf{X}_c$ and $\mathbf{X}$ are

$$\mathbf{W}_c^0 = \begin{bmatrix} 541.16 & & \\ 123.82 & 145.49 & \\ 672.21 & 120.26 & 758.59 \end{bmatrix}, \qquad \mathbf{W}_c^1 = \begin{bmatrix} 58.099 & & \\ 58.628 & 61.950 & \\ 43.661 & 41.576 & 40.072 \end{bmatrix}.$$

Using (2-105), we obtain

$$(\mathbf{W}_c^1)^{-1/2} = \begin{bmatrix} 0.785645 & & \\ -0.490974 & 0.523609 & \\ -0.266918 & 0.053884 & 0.355695 \end{bmatrix}.$$

The characteristic roots of $(\mathbf{W}_c^1)^{-1/2}\mathbf{W}_c^0(\mathbf{W}_c^1)^{-1/2}$ are 186.161, 7.61756, and 1.49874. Using (16-28), we obtain

$$\hat{\gamma}_c = [-.2225, 0.8226].$$

Finally, the least squares regression of

$$y_c^0 = C + 0.2225P - 0.8226(W^p + W^g)$$

on 1 and P_{-1} produces estimates of 17.477 and 0.396027. (Note that the coefficient on P has the wrong sign. The full information maximum likelihood estimator does also.)

Table 16.5 lists the OLS, 2SLS, LIML, and H2SLS estimates for this equation with the estimated asymptotic standard errors. The large difference between the inconsistent OLS and the other estimates suggests the bias discussed earlier. The 2SLS and LIML estimates are asymptotically equivalent, so the difference between them, which is substantial, can be attributed to small sample variation. The GMM estimator is striking. The estimated standard errors are noticeably smaller for all of the coefficients. It should be noted, however, that this estimator is based on a presumption of heteroscedasticity, when, in this time series, there is little evidence of its presence. Nonetheless, the results are broadly suggestive. But we should note that the appearance of having achieved something for nothing here is deceiving. Our earlier results on the efficiency of 2SLS have not been negated. If there is heteroscedasticity, then 2SLS is no longer fully efficient, but then, again, neither is H2SLS. The latter is more efficient than the former in the presence of heteroscedasticity, but it is equivalent to 2SLS in its absence.

TABLE 16.5 Single-Equation Estimates of Klein's Consumption Function

	OLS	*2SLS*	*GMM (H2SLS)*	*LIML*
Constant	16.2 (1.30)	16.6 (1.32)	14.7 (1.16)	17.5 (1.93)
P	0.193 (0.091)	0.017 (0.118)	0.076 (0.094)	−0.222 (0.212)
P_{-1}	0.090 (0.091)	0.216 (0.107)	0.166 (0.082)	0.396 (0.182)
$\mathbf{W}^p + \mathbf{W}^g$	0.796 (0.040)	0.810 (0.040)	0.849 (0.036)	0.823 (0.058)

There is another approach to the computation of the LIML estimator. For the endogenous variables in equation j, we have $M_j + 1$ equations

$$\begin{aligned}\mathbf{y}_j &= \mathbf{Y}_j\boldsymbol{\gamma}_j + \mathbf{X}_j\boldsymbol{\beta}_j + \boldsymbol{\epsilon}_j,\\ \mathbf{Y}_j &= \mathbf{X}\boldsymbol{\Pi}_j^0 + \mathbf{V}_j.\end{aligned}$$

Pagan (1979) has shown that the LIML estimator may be computed by treating the preceding as a seemingly unrelated regressions model, ignoring both the constraints on the reduced form and the correlation between $\mathbf{Y}_j$ and $\boldsymbol{\epsilon}_j$, and using the iterative GLS method discussed in Chapter 15.[29]

The "k class" of estimators is defined by the following form

$$\hat{\boldsymbol{\delta}}_{j,k} = \begin{bmatrix}\mathbf{Y}_j'\mathbf{Y}_j - k\mathbf{V}_j'\mathbf{V}_j & \mathbf{Y}_j'\mathbf{X}_j\\ \mathbf{X}_j'\mathbf{Y}_j & \mathbf{X}_j'\mathbf{X}_j\end{bmatrix}^{-1}\begin{bmatrix}\mathbf{Y}_j'\mathbf{y}_j - k\mathbf{V}_j'\mathbf{v}_j\\ \mathbf{X}_j'\mathbf{y}_j\end{bmatrix}.$$

We have considered three members of the class, OLS with $k = 0$, 2SLS with $k = 1$, and, it can be shown, LIML with $k = \lambda_1$. [This follows from (16-28). Schmidt (1976) gives further details.] There have been many other k-class estimators derived; Davidson and MacKinnon (1993, pages 649–651) give discussion. It has been shown that all members of the k class for which k converges to 1 at a rate faster than $1/\sqrt{n}$ have the same asymptotic distribution, that of the 2SLS estimator that we examined earlier. These are largely of theoretical interest, given the pervasive use of 2SLS or OLS, save for an important consideration. The large sample properties of all k-class estimator estimators are the same, but the finite sample properties are possibly very different. Davidson and MacKinnon (1993) and Mariano (1982) suggest that some evidence favors LIML when the sample size is not large and the number of overidentifying restrictions is.

16.5.2e. Two-Stage Least Squares with Autocorrelation. If the equation being estimated does not contain any lagged endogenous variables, the treatment of autocorrelation is a simple extension of the methods of Chapter 15. Suppose that the autocorrelation is a first-order autoregression

$$\epsilon_{t,j} = \rho_j\epsilon_{t-1,j} + u_{t,j}.$$

In the absence of lagged endogenous variables, the problems caused by autocorrelation concern efficiency and the inappropriateness of the usual estimators of the standard errors of the estimates, not consistency. Making the usual transformation, we have

$$y_{t,j} - \rho_j y_{t-1,j} = (\mathbf{Y}_{t,j}' - \rho_j\mathbf{Y}_{t-1,j}')\boldsymbol{\gamma}_j + (\mathbf{x}_{t,j}' - \rho_j\mathbf{x}_{t-1,j}')\boldsymbol{\beta}_j + u_{t,j}. \qquad \textbf{(16-29)}$$

If ρ_j were known, the simultaneous-equations estimation problem would carry

[29]For Klein's Model I, this procedure took over 80 iterations to converge for the consumption function and over 100 for the investment equation. In view of the rather small number of computations that succeed the extraction of the smallest root, the iterative SURE procedure is rather inefficient. See Hausman (1983, p. 426) as well.

over in the familiar fashion to this modified equation. A consistent estimate of ρ_j can be obtained by using

$$\hat{\rho}_j = \frac{\sum_{t=2}^{T} \hat{\epsilon}_{t,j}\hat{\epsilon}_{t-1,j}}{\sum_{t=2}^{T} \hat{\epsilon}^2_{t,j}}, \qquad \textbf{(16-30)}$$

where $\hat{\epsilon}_{t,j}$ is an estimated disturbance based on consistent estimate of $\boldsymbol{\delta}_j$. The obvious choice is the 2SLS estimator. With $\hat{\rho}_j$ in hand, (16-29) can be estimated by an IV estimator. The asymptotic properties of the resulting estimator are the same as if the true ρ_j were used, so the only issue remaining concerns the choice of the instrumental variables. Since only $\mathbf{Y}_{t,j}$ is correlated with $u_{t,j}$, a consistent estimator is obtained by using $\hat{\mathbf{Y}}_j = \mathbf{XP}_j$ as usual.[30] The model may be estimated by a three-step procedure:

1. Estimate $\boldsymbol{\Pi}$ with $(\mathbf{X}'\mathbf{X})^{-1}\mathbf{X}'\mathbf{Y}$ and compute $\hat{\mathbf{Y}}_j = \mathbf{XP}_j$.
2. Compute $\hat{\boldsymbol{\delta}}_j$ using 2SLS; then estimate ρ_j as shown earlier.
3. Using $\hat{\mathbf{Y}}_{t,j}$ based on $\mathbf{x}_t$, compute FGLS estimates on the modified structural equation (16-29).

It is also possible to iterate step 3, but the benefit of doing so remains to be verified. Asymptotically, it makes no difference, since the estimator is efficient at the first repetition.

If the equation contains lagged endogenous variables, neither the reduced-form estimates at the first step nor $\hat{\rho}_j$ at the second will be consistent. By repeating the transformation of (16-29), we see that in terms of temporally uncorrelated disturbances, the full reduced form includes $\mathbf{x}_t$, $\mathbf{x}_{t-1}$, $\mathbf{Y}_{t-1}$, and $\mathbf{Y}_{t-2}$, which is likely to be an inordinately large number of variables.[31] With a moderately sized sample, it may even be impossible to compute the estimated reduced form. But at the first step, we only require a consistent estimate of ρ, not an efficient one. A simple expedient is to treat the lagged endogenous variables as if they were current endogenous variables and include only the current and lagged values of the strictly exogenous variables among the predetermined variables at step 1. The regression at step 2, then is consistent but not efficient. A consistent set of residuals is produced that can be used in (16-30) to compute $\hat{\rho}$. FGLS estimates based on this $\hat{\rho}$ and the "purged" endogenous variables, $\mathbf{Y}_j$ and $\mathbf{Y}_{-1,j}$, are then computed at step 3.

Step 3 almost surely brings gains in asymptotic efficiency, although, as always, the issue as regards a small sample is less clear. We should note, though, that even with normally distributed disturbances, the estimator is not fully effi-

[30] The restricted set of instruments is a practical simplification. As suggested by (16-29), full efficiency requires the full set of instruments, $\mathbf{y}_{t-1}$, $\mathbf{x}_t$, and $\mathbf{x}_{t-1}$. See Sargan (1961) and Fair (1972). Fair also considers higher-order autocorrelation. Fomby et al. (1984, pp. 582–583) and our first edition incorrectly claim full efficiency for the IV estimator based on $\mathbf{XP}_j$.

[31] Fair (1970).

cient for two reasons. First, as suggested by Sargan (1961), full efficiency would require an estimate of the full reduced form.[32] Second, unlike the previous case, this estimator requires an efficient estimator of ρ. This can be achieved by iterating over ρ at step 3. Another approach that is also fully efficient involves an extension of Hatanaka's method.[33]

16.5.2f. Two-Stage Least Squares in Models that Are Nonlinear in Variables. The analysis of simultaneous equations becomes considerably more complicated when the equations are nonlinear. Amemiya presents a general treatment of nonlinear models.[34] A case that is broad enough to include many practical applications is the one analyzed by Kelejian (1971),

$$\mathbf{y}_j = \gamma_{1j}\mathbf{f}_{1j}(\mathbf{y}, \mathbf{x}) + \gamma_{2j}\mathbf{f}_{2j}(\mathbf{y}, \mathbf{x}) + \cdots + \mathbf{X}_j\boldsymbol{\beta}_j + \boldsymbol{\epsilon}_j^{35}$$

This is the direct extension of (8-4). Ordinary least squares will be inconsistent for the same reasons as before, but an IV estimator, if one can be devised, should have the usual properties. Because of the nonlinearity, it may not be possible to solve for the reduced-form equations (assuming that they exist), $h_{ij}(\mathbf{x}) = E[f_{ij} \mid \mathbf{x}]$. Kelejian shows that 2SLS based on a Taylor series approximation to h_{ij}, using the linear terms, higher powers, and cross-products of the variables in $\mathbf{x}$, will be consistent. The analysis of 2SLS presented earlier then applies to the $\hat{\mathbf{Z}}_j$ consisting of $[\hat{\mathbf{f}}_{1j}, \hat{\mathbf{f}}_{2j}, \ldots, \mathbf{X}_j]$.[36]

EXAMPLE 16.16 Nonlinear Two-Stage Least Squares

The model of Example 16.13 contains three endogenous variables, *A/S*, *C*, and *M*. The first equation also involves C^2. Fitted values for 2SLS were obtained by regressing all four endogenous functions on a constant, the exogenous variables and their squares, and all distinct cross products. A much larger nonlinear model (42 equations in total, including 16 behavioral equations) was estimated by Rice and Smith (1977). They used linear approximations for the reduced forms.

In a linear model, if an equation fails the order condition, it cannot be estimated by 2SLS. This is not true of Kelejian's approach, however, since taking higher powers of the regressors creates many more linearly independent instrumental variables. If an equation in a linear model fails the rank condition but not the order condition, the 2SLS estimates can be computed in a finite sample but will fail to exist asymptotically because $\mathbf{X\Pi}_j$ will have short rank.

[32] See, as well, Fair (1972).

[33] See Section 13.7.3 and Hatanaka (1976).

[34] Amemiya (1985, pp. 245–265).

[35] 2SLS for models which are nonlinear in the parameters is discussed in Chapters 10 and 11 in connection with GMM estimators.

[36] The alternative approach of directly computing fitted values for $\mathbf{y}$ appears to be inconsistent. See Kelejian (1971) and Goldfeld and Quandt (1968).

Unfortunately, to the extent that Kelejian's approximation never exactly equals the true reduced form unless it happens to be the polynomial in $\mathbf{x}$ (unlikely), this built-in control need not be present, even asymptotically. As such, there is an interesting (and open) question of just what is estimated by the estimator if the model is not identified. Thus, as we saw earlier, although the model in Example 16.13 is unidentified, computation of Kelejian's 2SLS estimator appears to be routine. The upshot, of course, is that one should ensure that the model is identified before embarking on the estimation step.

16.6. SYSTEM METHODS OF ESTIMATION

We may formulate the full system of equations as

$$\begin{bmatrix} \mathbf{y}_1 \\ \mathbf{y}_2 \\ \vdots \\ \mathbf{y}_M \end{bmatrix} = \begin{bmatrix} \mathbf{Z}_1 & \mathbf{0} & \cdots & \mathbf{0} \\ \mathbf{0} & \mathbf{Z}_2 & \cdots & \mathbf{0} \\ \vdots & \vdots & \vdots & \vdots \\ \mathbf{0} & \mathbf{0} & \cdots & \mathbf{Z}_M \end{bmatrix} \begin{bmatrix} \boldsymbol{\delta}_1 \\ \boldsymbol{\delta}_2 \\ \vdots \\ \boldsymbol{\delta}_M \end{bmatrix} + \begin{bmatrix} \boldsymbol{\epsilon}_1 \\ \boldsymbol{\epsilon}_2 \\ \vdots \\ \boldsymbol{\epsilon}_M \end{bmatrix}$$

or

$$\mathbf{y} = \mathbf{Z}\boldsymbol{\delta} + \boldsymbol{\epsilon},$$

where

$$E[\boldsymbol{\epsilon}] = \mathbf{0}$$

and

$$E[\boldsymbol{\epsilon}\boldsymbol{\epsilon}'] = \overline{\boldsymbol{\Sigma}} = \begin{bmatrix} \sigma_{11}\mathbf{I} & \sigma_{12}\mathbf{I} & \cdots & \sigma_{1M}\mathbf{I} \\ \sigma_{21}\mathbf{I} & \sigma_{22}\mathbf{I} & \cdots & \sigma_{2M}\mathbf{I} \\ \vdots & \vdots & \vdots & \vdots \\ \sigma_{M1}\mathbf{I} & \sigma_{M2}\mathbf{I} & \cdots & \sigma_{MM}\mathbf{I} \end{bmatrix} = \boldsymbol{\Sigma} \otimes \mathbf{I}.$$

The least squares estimator

$$\mathbf{d} = [\mathbf{Z}'\mathbf{Z}]^{-1}\mathbf{Z}'\mathbf{y}$$

is equation-by-equation ordinary least squares and is inconsistent. But even if ordinary least squares were consistent, we know from our results for the seemingly unrelated regressions model that it would be inefficient compared with an estimator that makes use of the cross-equation correlations of the disturbances. For the first issue, we turn once again to an IV estimator. For the second, as we did in Chapter 15, we use a generalized least squares approach. Thus, assuming that $\overline{\mathbf{W}}$ satisfies the requirements for an IV estimator, a consistent though inefficient estimator would be

$$\hat{\boldsymbol{\delta}}_{\text{IV}} = [\overline{\mathbf{W}}'\mathbf{Z}]^{-1}\overline{\mathbf{W}}'\mathbf{y}.$$

Analogous to the seemingly unrelated regressions model, a more efficient estimator would be based on the generalized least squares principle,

$$\hat{\boldsymbol{\delta}}_{\text{IV,GLS}} = [\overline{\mathbf{W}}'(\boldsymbol{\Sigma}^{-1} \otimes \mathbf{I})\mathbf{Z}]^{-1}\overline{\mathbf{W}}'(\boldsymbol{\Sigma}^{-1} \otimes \mathbf{I})\mathbf{y}$$

or

$$\hat{\boldsymbol{\delta}}_{\text{IV,GLS}} = \begin{bmatrix} \sigma^{11}\mathbf{W}_1'\mathbf{Z}_1 & \sigma^{12}\mathbf{W}_1'\mathbf{Z}_2 & \cdots & \sigma^{1M}\mathbf{W}_1'\mathbf{Z}_M \\ \sigma^{21}\mathbf{W}_2'\mathbf{Z}_1 & \sigma^{22}\mathbf{W}_2'\mathbf{Z}_2 & \cdots & \sigma^{2M}\mathbf{W}_2'\mathbf{Z}_M \\ & & \vdots & \\ \sigma^{M1}\mathbf{W}_M'\mathbf{Z}_1 & \sigma^{M2}\mathbf{W}_M'\mathbf{Z}_2 & \cdots & \sigma^{MM}\mathbf{W}_M'\mathbf{Z}_M \end{bmatrix}^{-1} \begin{bmatrix} \sum_{j=1}^{M} \sigma^{1j}\mathbf{W}_1'\mathbf{y}_j \\ \sum_{j=1}^{M} \sigma^{2j}\mathbf{W}_2'\mathbf{y}_j \\ \vdots \\ \sum_{j=1}^{M} \sigma^{Mj}\mathbf{W}_M'\mathbf{y}_j \end{bmatrix}.$$

Three techniques are generally used for joint estimation of the entire system of equations: three-stage least squares, GMM, and maximum likelihood.

16.6.1. Three-Stage Least Squares

Consider the IV estimator formed from

$$\overline{\mathbf{W}} = \hat{\mathbf{Z}} = \begin{bmatrix} \mathbf{X}(\mathbf{X}'\mathbf{X})^{-1}\mathbf{X}'\mathbf{Z}_1 & \mathbf{0} & \cdots & \mathbf{0} \\ \mathbf{0} & \mathbf{X}(\mathbf{X}'\mathbf{X})^{-1}\mathbf{X}'\mathbf{Z}_2 & \cdots & \mathbf{0} \\ \vdots & \vdots & \vdots & \vdots \\ \mathbf{0} & \mathbf{0} & \cdots & \mathbf{X}(\mathbf{X}'\mathbf{X})^{-1}\mathbf{X}'\mathbf{Z}_M \end{bmatrix}$$

$$= \begin{bmatrix} \hat{\mathbf{Z}}_1 & \mathbf{0} & \cdots & \mathbf{0} \\ \mathbf{0} & \hat{\mathbf{Z}}_2 & \cdots & \mathbf{0} \\ \vdots & \vdots & \vdots & \vdots \\ \mathbf{0} & \mathbf{0} & \cdots & \hat{\mathbf{Z}}_M \end{bmatrix}.$$

The IV estimator

$$\hat{\boldsymbol{\delta}}_{\text{IV}} = [\hat{\mathbf{Z}}'\mathbf{Z}]^{-1}\hat{\mathbf{Z}}'\mathbf{y}$$

is nothing more than equation-by-equation 2SLS. We have already established the consistency of 2SLS. By analogy with the seemingly unrelated regressions model of Chapter 15, however, we would expect this estimator to be less efficient than a GLS estimator. A natural candidate would be

$$\hat{\boldsymbol{\delta}}_{\text{3SLS}} = [\hat{\mathbf{Z}}'(\boldsymbol{\Sigma}^{-1} \otimes \mathbf{I})\mathbf{Z}]^{-1}\hat{\mathbf{Z}}'(\boldsymbol{\Sigma}^{-1} \otimes \mathbf{I})\mathbf{y}.$$

For this to be a valid IV estimator, we must establish that

$$\operatorname{plim} \frac{1}{T}\hat{\mathbf{Z}}'(\boldsymbol{\Sigma}^{-1} \otimes \mathbf{I})\boldsymbol{\epsilon} = \mathbf{0}.$$

This is M sets of equations of the form

$$\text{plim}\,\frac{1}{T}\sum_{j=1}^{M}\sigma^{ij}\hat{\mathbf{Z}}_j'\boldsymbol{\epsilon}_j = \mathbf{0}.$$

Each is the sum of vectors all of which converge to zero, as we saw in the development of the 2SLS estimator. The second requirement, that

$$\text{plim}\,\frac{1}{T}\,\hat{\mathbf{Z}}'(\boldsymbol{\Sigma}^{-1}\otimes\mathbf{I})\mathbf{Z} \neq \mathbf{0},$$

and that the matrix be nonsingular, can be established along the lines of its counterpart for 2SLS. Identification of every equation by the rank condition is sufficient.[37]

Once again using the idempotency of $\mathbf{I}-\mathbf{M}$, we may also interpret this as a GLS estimator of the form

$$\hat{\boldsymbol{\delta}}_{3\text{SLS}} = [\hat{\mathbf{Z}}'(\boldsymbol{\Sigma}^{-1}\otimes\mathbf{I})\hat{\mathbf{Z}}]^{-1}\hat{\mathbf{Z}}'(\boldsymbol{\Sigma}^{-1}\otimes\mathbf{I})\mathbf{y}. \qquad \textbf{(16-31)}$$

The appropriate asymptotic covariance matrix for the estimator is

$$\text{Asy. Var}[\hat{\boldsymbol{\delta}}_{3\text{SLS}}] = [\overline{\mathbf{Z}}'(\boldsymbol{\Sigma}^{-1}\otimes\mathbf{I})\overline{\mathbf{Z}}]^{-1},$$

where $\overline{\mathbf{Z}} = \text{diag}[\mathbf{X}\boldsymbol{\Pi}_j, \mathbf{X}_j]$. This would be estimated with the inverse matrix in (16-31).

Using sample data, we find that $\overline{\mathbf{Z}}$ may be estimated with $\hat{\mathbf{Z}}$. The remaining difficulty is to obtain an estimate of $\boldsymbol{\Sigma}$. In estimation of the multivariate regression model, for efficient estimation (that remains to be shown), any consistent estimate of $\boldsymbol{\Sigma}$ will do. The designers of the 3SLS method, Zellner and Theil (1962), suggest the natural choice arising out of the two-stage least estimates. The **three-stage least squares (3SLS) estimator** is thus defined as follows:

1. Estimate $\boldsymbol{\Pi}$ by ordinary least squares and compute $\hat{\mathbf{Y}}_j$ for each equation.
2. Compute $\hat{\boldsymbol{\delta}}_{j,2\text{SLS}}$ for each equation; then

$$\hat{\sigma}_{ij} = \frac{(\mathbf{y}_i - \mathbf{Z}_i\hat{\boldsymbol{\delta}}_i)'(\mathbf{y}_j - \mathbf{Z}_j\hat{\boldsymbol{\delta}}_j)}{T}. \qquad \textbf{(16-32)}$$

3. Compute the GLS estimator according to (16-31) and an estimate of the asymptotic covariance matrix according to (16-32) using $\hat{\mathbf{Z}}$ and $\hat{\boldsymbol{\Sigma}}$.

It is also possible to iterate the 3SLS computation. Unlike the seemingly unrelated regressions estimator, however, this does not provide the maximum likelihood estimator, nor does it improve the asymptotic efficiency.

By showing that the 3SLS estimator satisfies the requirements for an IV estimator, we have established its consistency. The question of asymptotic efficiency remains. Now it can be shown that among all IV estimators that use only the sample information embodied in the system, 3SLS is asymptotically effi-

[37] A formal proof is given by Schmidt (1976, pp. 205–207).

cient.[38] For normally distributed disturbances, it can also be shown that 3SLS has the same asymptotic distribution as the full-information maximum likelihood estimator, which is asymptotically efficient among all estimators. A direct proof based on the information matrix is possible, but we shall take a much simpler route by simply exploiting a handy result due to Hausman in the next section.

16.6.2. Full-Information Maximum Likelihood

Because of their simplicity and asymptotic efficiency, 2SLS and 3SLS are used almost exclusively (when ordinary least squares is not used) for the estimation of simultaneous-equations models. Nonetheless, it is occasionally useful to obtain maximum likelihood estimates directly. The **full-information maximum likelihood (FIML) estimator** is based on the entire system of equations. With normally distributed disturbances, FIML is efficient among all estimators.

The FIML estimator treats all equations and all parameters jointly. To formulate the appropriate log-likelihood function, we begin with the reduced form,

$$\mathbf{Y} = \mathbf{X}\boldsymbol{\Pi} + \mathbf{V},$$

where each row of $\mathbf{V}$ is assumed to be multivariate normally distributed, with mean $\mathbf{0}$ and covariance matrix, $E[\mathbf{v}_t\mathbf{v}_t'] = \boldsymbol{\Omega}$. The log-likelihood for this model is precisely that of the seemingly unrelated regressions model of Chapter 15. For the moment, we can ignore the relationship between the structural and reduced-form parameters. Thus, from (15-51),

$$\ln L = -\frac{T}{2}[M\ln(2\pi) + \ln|\boldsymbol{\Omega}| + \operatorname{tr}(\boldsymbol{\Omega}^{-1}\mathbf{W})], \tag{16-33}$$

where

$$\mathbf{W}_{ij} = \frac{1}{T}(\mathbf{y} - \mathbf{X}\boldsymbol{\pi}_i^0)'(\mathbf{y} - \mathbf{X}\boldsymbol{\pi}_j^0)$$

and

$$\boldsymbol{\pi}_j^0 = j\text{th column of } \boldsymbol{\Pi}.$$

This is to be maximized subject to all the restrictions imposed by the structure. Make the substitutions

$$\boldsymbol{\Pi} = -\mathbf{B}\boldsymbol{\Gamma}^{-1} \quad \text{and} \quad \boldsymbol{\Omega} = (\boldsymbol{\Gamma}^{-1})'\boldsymbol{\Sigma}\boldsymbol{\Gamma}^{-1}$$

so that

$$\boldsymbol{\Omega}^{-1} = \boldsymbol{\Gamma}\boldsymbol{\Sigma}^{-1}\boldsymbol{\Gamma}'.$$

[38] See Schmidt (1976) for a proof of its efficiency relative to 2SLS.

Thus,

$$\ln L = -\frac{MT}{2}\ln(2\pi) - \frac{T}{2}\ln|(\mathbf{\Gamma}^{-1})'\mathbf{\Sigma}\mathbf{\Gamma}^{-1}| - \frac{T}{2}\text{tr}\left[\frac{1}{T}(\mathbf{\Gamma}\mathbf{\Sigma}^{-1}\mathbf{\Gamma}'(\mathbf{Y} + \mathbf{X}\mathbf{B}\mathbf{\Gamma}^{-1})'(\mathbf{Y} + \mathbf{X}\mathbf{B}\mathbf{\Gamma}^{-1}))\right].$$

This can be simplified. First,

$$-\frac{T}{2}\ln|(\mathbf{\Gamma}^{-1})'\mathbf{\Sigma}\mathbf{\Gamma}^{-1}| = -\frac{T}{2}\ln|\mathbf{\Sigma}| + T\ln|\mathbf{\Gamma}|.$$

Second, $\mathbf{\Gamma}'(\mathbf{Y} + \mathbf{X}\mathbf{B}\mathbf{\Gamma}^{-1})' = \mathbf{\Gamma}'\mathbf{Y}' + \mathbf{B}'\mathbf{X}'$. By permuting $\mathbf{\Gamma}$ from the beginning to the end of the trace and collecting terms,

$$\text{tr}(\mathbf{\Omega}^{-1}\mathbf{W}) = \text{tr}\left[\frac{\mathbf{\Sigma}^{-1}(\mathbf{Y}\mathbf{\Gamma} + \mathbf{X}\mathbf{B})'(\mathbf{Y}\mathbf{\Gamma} + \mathbf{X}\mathbf{B})}{T}\right].$$

Therefore, the log-likelihood is

$$\ln L = -\frac{MT}{2}\ln(2\pi) + T\ln|\mathbf{\Gamma}| - \frac{T}{2}\text{tr}(\mathbf{\Sigma}^{-1}\mathbf{S}),$$

where

$$s_{ij} = \frac{1}{T}(\mathbf{Y}\mathbf{\Gamma}_i + \mathbf{X}\mathbf{B}_i)'(\mathbf{Y}\mathbf{\Gamma}_j + \mathbf{X}\mathbf{B}_j).$$

[In terms of nonzero parameters, s_{ij} is $\hat{\sigma}_{ij}$ of (16-32).]

In maximizing $\ln L$, it is necessary to impose all the additional restrictions on the structure. It is useful, therefore, to note that the trace may be written in the form

$$\text{tr}(\mathbf{\Sigma}^{-1}\mathbf{S}) = \frac{\sum_{i=1}^{M}\sum_{j=1}^{M}\sigma^{ij}(\mathbf{y}_i - \mathbf{Y}_i\boldsymbol{\gamma}_i - \mathbf{X}_i\boldsymbol{\beta}_i)'(\mathbf{y}_j - \mathbf{Y}_j\boldsymbol{\gamma}_j - \mathbf{X}_j\boldsymbol{\beta}_j)}{T}. \quad \textbf{(16-34)}$$

Maximizing $\ln L$ subject to the exclusions in (16-34) and any other restrictions, if necessary, produces the FIML estimator. This has all the desirable asymptotic properties of maximum likelihood estimators and, therefore, is asymptotically efficient among estimators of the simultaneous-equations model. The asymptotic covariance matrix for the FIML estimator is the same as that for the 3SLS estimator.

A useful interpretation of the FIML estimator is provided by Hausman (1975, 1983). He shows that the FIML estimator of $\boldsymbol{\delta}$ is a fixed point in the equation

$$\hat{\boldsymbol{\delta}}_{\text{FIML}} = [\hat{\mathbf{Z}}(\hat{\boldsymbol{\delta}})'(\hat{\mathbf{\Sigma}}^{-1} \otimes \mathbf{I})\mathbf{Z}]^{-1}[\hat{\mathbf{Z}}(\hat{\boldsymbol{\delta}})'(\hat{\mathbf{\Sigma}}^{-1} \otimes \mathbf{I})\mathbf{y}] = [\hat{\hat{\mathbf{Z}}}'\mathbf{Z}]^{-1}\hat{\hat{\mathbf{Z}}}'\mathbf{y},$$

where

$$\hat{\mathbf{Z}}(\hat{\boldsymbol{\delta}})'(\hat{\boldsymbol{\Sigma}}^{-1}\otimes\mathbf{I}) = \begin{bmatrix} \hat{\sigma}^{11}\hat{\mathbf{Z}}_1 & \hat{\sigma}^{12}\hat{\mathbf{Z}}_1 & \cdots & \hat{\sigma}^{1M}\hat{\mathbf{Z}}_1 \\ \hat{\sigma}^{12}\hat{\mathbf{Z}}_2 & \hat{\sigma}^{22}\hat{\mathbf{Z}}_2 & \cdots & \hat{\sigma}^{2M}\hat{\mathbf{Z}}_2 \\ \vdots & \vdots & \cdots & \vdots \\ \hat{\sigma}^{1M}\hat{\mathbf{Z}}_M & \hat{\sigma}^{2M}\hat{\mathbf{Z}}_M & \cdots & \hat{\sigma}^{MM}\hat{\mathbf{Z}}_M \end{bmatrix} = \hat{\hat{\mathbf{Z}}}'$$

and

$$\hat{\mathbf{Z}}_j = [\mathbf{X}\hat{\boldsymbol{\Pi}}_j \quad \mathbf{X}_j].$$

$\hat{\boldsymbol{\Pi}}$ is computed from the structural estimates:

$$\hat{\boldsymbol{\Pi}}_j = M_j \text{ columns of } -\hat{\mathbf{B}}\hat{\boldsymbol{\Gamma}}^{-1}$$

and

$$\hat{\sigma}_{ij} = \frac{1}{T}(\mathbf{y}_i - \mathbf{Z}_i\hat{\boldsymbol{\delta}}_i)'(\mathbf{y}_j - \mathbf{Z}_j\hat{\boldsymbol{\delta}}_j),$$

$$\hat{\sigma}^{ij} = (\hat{\boldsymbol{\Sigma}}^{-1})_{ij}.$$

This result implies that the FIML estimator is also an IV estimator. The asymptotic covariance matrix for the FIML estimator follows directly from its form as an IV estimator. Since this is the same as that of the 3SLS estimator, we conclude that with normally distributed disturbances, 3SLS has the same asymptotic distribution as maximum likelihood. The practical usefulness of this important result has not gone unnoticed by practitioners. The 3SLS estimator is far easier to compute than the FIML estimator. The benefit in computational cost comes at no cost in asymptotic efficiency. As always, the small sample properties remain ambiguous, but by and large, where a systems estimator is used, 3SLS dominates FIML nonetheless.[39]

Finally, there are two special cases worth noting. First, for the fully recursive model,

1. $\boldsymbol{\Gamma}$ is upper triangular, with ones on the diagonal. Therefore, $|\boldsymbol{\Gamma}| = 1$ and $\ln|\boldsymbol{\Gamma}| = 0$.
2. $\boldsymbol{\Sigma}$ is diagonal, so $\ln|\boldsymbol{\Sigma}| = \Sigma_{j=1}^{M} \ln \sigma_{jj}$ and the trace in the exponent becomes

$$\text{tr}(\boldsymbol{\Sigma}^{-1}\mathbf{S}) = \sum_{j=1}^{M} \frac{1}{\sigma_{jj}} \frac{1}{T}(\mathbf{y}_j - \mathbf{Y}_j\boldsymbol{\gamma}_j - \mathbf{X}_j\boldsymbol{\beta}_j)'(\mathbf{y}_j - \mathbf{Y}_j\boldsymbol{\gamma}_j - \mathbf{X}_j\boldsymbol{\beta}_j).$$

The log-likelihood reduces to $\ln L = \Sigma_{j=1}^{M} \ln L_j$, where

$$\ln L_j = -\frac{T}{2}[\ln(2\pi) + \ln \sigma_{jj}] - \frac{1}{2\sigma_{jj}}(\mathbf{y}_j - \mathbf{Y}_j\boldsymbol{\gamma}_j - \mathbf{X}_j\boldsymbol{\beta}_j)'(\mathbf{y}_j - \mathbf{Y}_j\boldsymbol{\gamma}_j - \mathbf{X}_j\boldsymbol{\beta}_j).$$

Therefore, the FIML estimator for this model is just equation-by-equation least

[39]There are relatively fewer computer programs available for FIML than for 3SLS. PC-GIVE(8) and TSP(4.2) are two that are widely used.

squares. We found earlier that ordinary least squares was consistent in this setting. We now find that it is asymptotically efficient as well.

The second case is that of the exactly identified model. If every equation is exactly identified, there is a one-to-one correspondence between $[\boldsymbol{\Gamma}, \mathbf{B}]$ and $[\boldsymbol{\Pi}]$. Since $\boldsymbol{\Pi}$ is unrestricted in the exactly identified case, FIML is obtained by estimating $\boldsymbol{\Pi}$ by OLS. Without going further, we may simply appeal to the general invariance result of MLEs. In an exactly identified model, ILS is also the FIML estimator.

16.6.3. GMM Estimation

The GMM estimator for a system of equations is described in Section 15.7.3. As in the single equation case, a minor change in notation produces the estimators of this chapter.

As before, we will consider the case of unknown heteroscedasticity only. The extension to autocorrelation is quite complicated. [See Cumby et al. (1983).] The orthogonality conditions defined in Section 16.5.2c are

$$E[\mathbf{x}_t\epsilon_{jt}] = E[\mathbf{x}_t(\mathbf{y}_{jt} - \mathbf{z}_{jt}'\boldsymbol{\delta}_j)] = \mathbf{0}.$$

If we consider all of the equations jointly, we obtain the criterion for estimation of all the model's parameters,

$$\begin{aligned} q &= \sum_{j=1}^{M}\sum_{l=1}^{M} \mathbf{e}(\mathbf{z}_t, \boldsymbol{\delta}_j)'\mathbf{X}[\mathbf{W}]^{jl}\mathbf{X}'\mathbf{e}(\mathbf{z}_t, \boldsymbol{\delta}_l) \\ &= \sum_{j=1}^{M}\sum_{l=1}^{M} \mathbf{m}(\boldsymbol{\delta}_j)'[\mathbf{W}]^{jl}\mathbf{m}(\boldsymbol{\delta}_l) \end{aligned}$$

where

$$\mathbf{m}(\boldsymbol{\delta}_j) = \frac{1}{T}\sum_{t=1}^{T} \mathbf{x}_t(y_{jt} - \mathbf{z}_{jt}'\boldsymbol{\delta}_j)$$

and

$$[\mathbf{W}]^{jl} = \text{block } jl \text{ of the weighting matrix, } \mathbf{W}^{-1}.$$

As before, we consider the optimal weighting matrix obtained as the covariance matrix of the empirical moments,

$$\mathbf{m}_j(\boldsymbol{\delta}_j) = \frac{1}{T}\sum_{t=1}^{T} \mathbf{x}_t(y_{jt} - \mathbf{z}_{jt}'\boldsymbol{\delta}_j).$$

These are stacked in a single vector $\mathbf{m}(\boldsymbol{\delta})$. Then, the jlth block of $E[\mathbf{m}(\boldsymbol{\delta})\mathbf{m}(\boldsymbol{\delta})']$ is

$$\begin{aligned} \boldsymbol{\Sigma}_{jl} &= \frac{1}{T}\sum_{t=1}^{T} E[\mathbf{x}_t'\mathbf{x}_t(y_{jt} - \mathbf{z}_{jt}'\boldsymbol{\delta}_j)(y_{lt} - \mathbf{z}_{lt}'\boldsymbol{\delta}_l)] \\ &= \frac{1}{T}\sum_{t=1}^{T} \omega_{jl,t}\mathbf{x}_t'\mathbf{x}_t. \end{aligned}$$

If the disturbances are homoscedastic, this produces $\boldsymbol{\Sigma}_{jl} = \sigma_{jl}(\mathbf{X}'\mathbf{X})$. Otherwise, we obtain a matrix of the form

$$\boldsymbol{\Sigma}_{jl} = \mathbf{X}'\boldsymbol{\Omega}_{jl}\mathbf{X}.$$

Collecting terms, then, the criterion function for GMM estimation is

$$q = \begin{bmatrix} (\mathbf{y}_1 - \mathbf{Z}_1\boldsymbol{\delta}_1)'\mathbf{X} \\ (\mathbf{y}_2 - \mathbf{Z}_2\boldsymbol{\delta}_2)'\mathbf{X} \\ \vdots \\ (\mathbf{y}_M - \mathbf{Z}_M\boldsymbol{\delta}_M)'\mathbf{X} \end{bmatrix}' \begin{bmatrix} \mathbf{X}'\boldsymbol{\Omega}_{11}\mathbf{X} & \mathbf{X}'\boldsymbol{\Omega}_{12}\mathbf{X} & \cdots & \mathbf{X}'\boldsymbol{\Omega}_{1M}\mathbf{X} \\ \mathbf{X}'\boldsymbol{\Omega}_{21}\mathbf{X} & \mathbf{X}'\boldsymbol{\Omega}_{22}\mathbf{X} & \cdots & \mathbf{X}'\boldsymbol{\Omega}_{2M}\mathbf{X} \\ \vdots & \vdots & \cdots & \vdots \\ \mathbf{X}'\boldsymbol{\Omega}_{M1}\mathbf{X} & \mathbf{X}'\boldsymbol{\Omega}_{M2}\mathbf{X} & \cdots & \mathbf{X}'\boldsymbol{\Omega}_{MM}\mathbf{X} \end{bmatrix}^{-1} \begin{bmatrix} \mathbf{X}'(\mathbf{y}_1 - \mathbf{Z}_1\boldsymbol{\delta}_1) \\ \mathbf{X}'(\mathbf{y}_2 - \mathbf{Z}_2\boldsymbol{\delta}_2) \\ \vdots \\ \mathbf{X}'(\mathbf{y}_M - \mathbf{Z}_M\boldsymbol{\delta}_M) \end{bmatrix}.$$

For the general case, $\boldsymbol{\Sigma}_{jl}$ can be estimated with

$$\mathbf{S}_{jl} = \frac{1}{T}\sum_{t=1}^{T} \mathbf{x}_t\mathbf{x}_t'(y_{jt} - \mathbf{z}_{jt}'\mathbf{d}_j)(y_{lt} - \mathbf{z}_{lt}'\mathbf{d}_l),$$

where $\mathbf{d}_j$ is a consistent estimator of $\boldsymbol{\delta}_j$. The two stage least squares estimator is a natural choice. For the diagonal blocks, this is the White estimator as usual. For the off-diagonal blocks, it is a simple extension. With this in hand, the first order conditions for GMM estimation are

$$\frac{\partial \hat{q}}{\partial \boldsymbol{\delta}_j} = \sum_{l=1}^{M} \mathbf{Z}_j'\mathbf{X}(\mathbf{X}'\mathbf{S}_{jl}\mathbf{X})^{-1}\mathbf{X}'(\mathbf{y}_l - \mathbf{Z}_l\boldsymbol{\delta}_l).$$

The solution is

$$\begin{bmatrix} \hat{\boldsymbol{\delta}}_{1,\text{GMM}} \\ \hat{\boldsymbol{\delta}}_{2,\text{GMM}} \\ \vdots \\ \hat{\boldsymbol{\delta}}_{M,\text{GMM}} \end{bmatrix} = \begin{bmatrix} \mathbf{Z}_1'\mathbf{X}(\mathbf{X}'\mathbf{S}_{11}\mathbf{X})^{-1}\mathbf{X}'\mathbf{Z}_1 & \mathbf{Z}_1'\mathbf{X}(\mathbf{X}'\mathbf{S}_{12}\mathbf{X})^{-1}\mathbf{X}'\mathbf{Z}_2 & \cdots & \mathbf{Z}_1'\mathbf{X}(\mathbf{X}'\mathbf{S}_{1M}\mathbf{X})^{-1}\mathbf{X}'\mathbf{Z}_M \\ \mathbf{Z}_2'\mathbf{X}(\mathbf{X}'\mathbf{S}_{21}\mathbf{X})^{-1}\mathbf{X}'\mathbf{Z}_1 & \mathbf{Z}_2'\mathbf{X}(\mathbf{X}'\mathbf{S}_{22}\mathbf{X})^{-1}\mathbf{X}'\mathbf{Z}_2 & \cdots & \mathbf{Z}_2'\mathbf{X}(\mathbf{X}'\mathbf{S}_{2M}\mathbf{X})^{-1}\mathbf{X}'\mathbf{Z}_M \\ \vdots & \vdots & \cdots & \vdots \\ \mathbf{Z}_M'\mathbf{X}(\mathbf{X}'\mathbf{S}_{M1}\mathbf{X})^{-1}\mathbf{X}'\mathbf{Z}_1 & \mathbf{Z}_M'\mathbf{X}(\mathbf{X}'\mathbf{S}_{M2}\mathbf{X})^{-1}\mathbf{X}'\mathbf{Z}_2 & \cdots & \mathbf{Z}_M'\mathbf{X}(\mathbf{X}'\mathbf{S}_{MM}\mathbf{X})^{-1}\mathbf{X}'\mathbf{Z}_M \end{bmatrix}^{-1}$$

$$\times \begin{bmatrix} \sum_{j=1}^{M} \mathbf{Z}_1'\mathbf{X}(\mathbf{X}'\mathbf{S}_{1j}\mathbf{X})^{-1}(\mathbf{y}_j - \mathbf{Z}_j\boldsymbol{\delta}_j) \\ \sum_{j=1}^{M} \mathbf{Z}_2'\mathbf{X}(\mathbf{X}'\mathbf{S}_{2j}\mathbf{X})^{-1}(\mathbf{y}_j - \mathbf{Z}_j\boldsymbol{\delta}_j) \\ \vdots \\ \sum_{j=1}^{M} \mathbf{Z}_M'\mathbf{X}(\mathbf{X}'\mathbf{S}_{Mj}\mathbf{X})^{-1}(\mathbf{y}_j - \mathbf{Z}_j\boldsymbol{\delta}_j) \end{bmatrix}.$$

The asymptotic covariance matrix for the estimator would be estimated with the inverse of large matrix in brackets.

Several of the estimators we have already considered are special cases:

- If $\mathbf{S}_{jj} = \hat{\sigma}_{jj}(\mathbf{X}'\mathbf{X})$ and $\mathbf{S}_{jl} = \mathbf{0}$ for $j \neq l$, $\hat{\boldsymbol{\delta}}_j$ is 2SLS.

- If $\mathbf{S}_{jl} = \hat{\sigma}_{jl}(\mathbf{X}'\mathbf{X})$, $\hat{\boldsymbol{\delta}}_j$ is 3SLS.
- If $\mathbf{S}_{jl} = \mathbf{0}$ for $j \neq l$, $\hat{\boldsymbol{\delta}}_j$ is H2SLS, the single-equation GMM estimator.

As before, the GMM estimator brings efficiency gains in the presence of heteroscedasticity. If the disturbances are homoscedastic, it is asymptotically the same as 3SLS, [although in a finite sample, it will differ numerically because $\mathbf{S}_{jl}$ will not be identical to $\hat{\sigma}_{jl}(\mathbf{X}'\mathbf{X})$].

16.7. COMPARISON OF METHODS

EXAMPLE 16.17 Estimates of Klein's Model I

The preceding has described a large number of estimators for simultaneous-equations models. As an example, Table 16.6 presents limited- and full-information estimates for Klein's Model I based on the original data for 1921 and 1941. The H3SLS estimates for the system were computed in two pairs, (C, I) and (C, W^p), as there were insufficient observations to fit the system as a whole. The first of these are reported for the C equation. (For those who wish to update these results, the appendix to this chapter contains yearly data from 1953 to 1984 on the variables in Klein's Model I, as well as several other macroeconomic variables.)

It might seem, in light of the entire discussion, that one of the structural estimators described previously should always be preferred to ordinary least squares, which, alone among the estimators considered here, is inconsistent. Unfortunately, the issue is not so clear. First, it is often found that the OLS estimator is surprisingly close to the structural estimator. It can be shown that at least in some cases, OLS has a smaller variance about its mean than does 2SLS about its mean, leading to the possibility that OLS might be more precise in a mean-squared-error sense.[40] But this result must be tempered by the finding that the OLS standard errors are, in all likelihood, not useful for inference purposes.[41] Nonetheless, OLS appears to be the most frequently used estimator. Obviously this discussion is relevant only to finite samples. Asymptotically, 2SLS must dominate OLS, and in a correctly specified model, any full-information estimator must dominate any limited-information one. The finite-sample properties are of crucial importance. Most of what we know is asymptotic properties, but nearly all applications are based on rather small or moderately sized samples.

Intuition would surely suggest that systems methods, 3SLS, GMM, and FIML, are to be preferred to single-equation methods, 2SLS and LIML. Indeed, since the advantage is so transparent, why would one ever choose a single-equation estimator? The proper analogy is to the use of single-equation

[40]See Goldberger (1964, pp. 359–360).

[41]Cragg (1967).

TABLE 16.6 Estimates of Klein's Model I (Estimated Asymptotic Standard Errors in Parentheses)

	Limited-Information Estimates				*Full-Information Estimates*			
	2SLS				**3SLS**			
C	16.6	0.017	0.216	0.810	16.4	0.125	0.163	0.790
	(1.32)	(0.118)	(0.107)	(0.040)	(1.30)	(0.108)	(0.100)	(0.033)
I	20.3	0.150	0.616	−0.158	28.2	−0.013	0.756	−0.195
	(7.54)	(0.173)	(0.162)	(0.036)	(6.79)	(0.162)	(0.153)	(0.038)
W^p	1.50	0.439	0.147	0.130	1.80	0.400	0.181	0.150
	(1.15)	(0.036)	(0.039)	(0.029)	(1.12)	(0.032)	(0.034)	(0.028)
	LIML				**FIML**			
C	17.5	−0.222	0.396	0.823	17.8	−0.214	0.351	0.853
	(1.93)	(0.212)	(0.182)	(0.058)	(2.12)	(0.096)	(0.101)	(0.047)
I	22.6	0.075	0.680	−0.168	17.2	0.130	0.613	−0.136
	(6.89)	(0.275)	(0.205)	(0.049)	(6.47)	(0.137)	(0.140)	(0.038)
W^p	1.53	0.434	0.151	0.132	1.41	0.498	0.087	0.403
	(1.08)	(0.057)	(0.141)	(0.169)	(0.943)	(0.018)	(0.015)	(0.021)
	GMM (H2SLS)				**GMM (H3SLS)**			
C	14.7	0.076	0.166	0.849	15.7	0.068	0.167	0.829
	(1.16)	(0.094)	(0.082)	(0.036)	(0.951)	(0.091)	(0.080)	(0.033)
I	21.4	0.186	0.551	−0.161	20.6	0.213	−0.520	−0.157
	(6.33)	(0.129)	(0.125)	(0.030)	(4.89)	(0.087)	(0.099)	(0.025)
W^p	2.67	0.456	0.111	0.131	2.09	0.446	0.131	0.112
	(0.79)	(0.030)	(0.032)	(0.024)	(0.510)	(0.019)	(0.021)	(0.021)
	OLS				**I3SLS**			
C	16.2	0.193	0.090	0.796	16.6	0.165	0.177	0.766
	(1.30)	(0.091)	(0.091)	(0.040)	(1.22)	(0.096)	(0.090)	(0.035)
I	10.1	0.480	0.333	−0.112	42.9	−0.356	1.01	−0.260
	(5.47)	(0.097)	(0.101)	(0.027)	(10.6)	(0.260)	(0.249)	(0.051)
W^p	1.48	0.439	0.146	0.130	2.62	0.375	0.194	0.168
	(1.27)	(0.032)	(0.037)	(0.032)	(1.20)	(0.031)	(0.032)	(0.029)

OLS versus GLS in the SURE model of Chapter 15. An obvious practical consideration is the computational simplicity of the single-equation methods. But the current state of available software has all but eliminated this advantage. Several related aspects make the choice less clear-cut, however.

Although the systems methods are asymptotically better, they have two problems. First, any specification error in the structure of the model will be propagated throughout the system by 3SLS or FIML. The limited-information estimators will, by and large, confine a problem to the particular equation in which it appears. Second, in the same fashion as the SURE model, the finite-sample variation of the estimated covariance matrix is transmitted throughout the system. Thus, the finite-sample variance of 3SLS may well be as large as or larger than that of 2SLS. Although they are only estimates, the previous results for Klein's Model I give a striking example. The upshot would appear to be that the advantage of the systems estimators in finite samples may be more modest than the asymptotic results would suggest. Monte Carlo studies of the issue have tended to reach the same conclusion.[42]

Since asymptotic comparisons are unambiguous, the remaining considerations are based primarily on small-sample behavior. Unfortunately, there are few usable general results. What results there are come from two sources: extensive analysis of very small models and Monte Carlo studies.[43] In the main, these studies tend to reinforce what intuition would suggest.

16.8. SPECIFICATION TESTS

In a strident criticism of structural estimation, Liu (1960) argued that all simultaneous-equations models of the economy were truly unidentified and that only reduced forms could be estimated. Although his criticisms may have been exaggerated (and never gained wide acceptance), modelers have been interested in testing the restrictions that overidentify an econometric model.

The first procedure for testing the overidentifying restrictions in a model was developed by Anderson and Rubin (1950). Their likelihood ratio test statistic is a by-product of LIML estimation:

$$\text{LR} = \chi^2[K_j^* - M_j] = T(\lambda_j - 1),$$

where λ_j is the root used to find the LIML estimator. [See (16-27).] The statistic is asymptotically distributed as chi-squared with degrees of freedom equal to the number of overidentifying restrictions. A large value is taken as evidence that there are exogenous variables in the model that have been inappropriately omitted from the equation being examined. If the equation is exactly identified, $K_j^* - M_j = 0$, but at the same time, the root will be 1. In later work, Basmann (1960) found that Anderson–Rubin statistic rejected the null hypothesis too often. He suggested two alternatives. First,

$$F'[K_j^* - M_j, T - K] = \frac{T - K}{K_j^* - M_j}(\lambda_j' - 1),$$

where

$$\lambda_j' = \frac{\hat{\boldsymbol{\gamma}}_{j,2SLS}^{0\prime}\mathbf{W}_j^0\hat{\boldsymbol{\gamma}}_{j,2SLS}^0}{\hat{\boldsymbol{\gamma}}_{j,2SLS}^{0\prime}\mathbf{W}_j^1\hat{\boldsymbol{\gamma}}_{j,2SLS}^0},$$

$$\hat{\boldsymbol{\gamma}}_{j,2SLS}^{0\prime} = [1, -\hat{\boldsymbol{\gamma}}_{j,2SLS}'].$$

[42]See Cragg (1967) and the many related studies listed by Judge et al. (1985, pp. 646–653).

[43]See, for example, Greenberg and Webster (1983, pp. 243–280) and Phillips (1983).

[If the LIML estimator is used instead of 2SLS, this gives the $\boldsymbol{\lambda}_j$ in (16-27).] The matrices $\mathbf{W}_j^0$ and $\mathbf{W}_j^1$ are defined in (16-26). Second, he suggested computing F' at the LIML estimator. Both are approximately distributed as $F[K_j^* - M_j, T - K]$ under the null hypothesis of exact identification. An alternative based on the Lagrange multiplier principle was proposed by Hausman (1983, p. 433). Operationally, the test requires only the calculation of TR^2, where the R^2 is the uncentered R^2 in the regression of

$$\hat{\boldsymbol{\epsilon}}_j = \mathbf{y}_j - \mathbf{Z}_j\hat{\boldsymbol{\delta}}_j$$

on all the predetermined variables in the model. The estimated parameters may be computed using 2SLS, LIML, or any other *efficient* limited-information estimator. The statistic is asymptotically distributed as chi-squared with $K_j^* - M_j$ degrees of freedom.

Finally, a systemwide statistic may be based on the restrictions imposed on $\boldsymbol{\Pi}$ by the structure. If the entire system is exactly identified, the reduced form estimated by OLS is fully efficient. If not, an efficient estimate of $\boldsymbol{\Pi}$ that embodies the restrictions is $\hat{\boldsymbol{\Pi}} = -\hat{\mathbf{B}}\hat{\boldsymbol{\Gamma}}^{-1}$, where the latter are *any efficient full-information estimators* (say, 3SLS or FIML). The log-likelihood for the reduced form is given in (16-33). By concentrating over $\boldsymbol{\Omega}$, we obtain, at the maximum,

$$\ln L = -\frac{MT}{2}(1 + \ln 2\pi) - \frac{T}{2}\ln|\mathbf{W}|,$$

where

$$\mathbf{W} = \frac{1}{T}(\mathbf{Y} - \mathbf{X}\hat{\boldsymbol{\Pi}})'(\mathbf{Y} - \mathbf{X}\hat{\boldsymbol{\Pi}}).^{44}$$

Therefore, the likelihood ratio statistic based on the two estimators of $\boldsymbol{\Pi}$ is simply

$$\text{LR} = -2(\ln L_r - \ln L_u) = T(\ln|\mathbf{W}_{\text{FI}}| - \ln|\mathbf{W}_{\text{OLS}}|).$$

This statistic is asymptotically distributed as chi-squared with degrees of freedom equal to the total number of overidentifying restrictions:

$$d = \sum_j (K_j^* - M_j).$$

EXAMPLE 16.18 Testing Overidentifying Restrictions

For Klein's Model I, the test statistics for the overidentifying restrictions for the three equations are given in Table 16.7. The likelihood ratio statistic for the entire system is 77.441. Critical values for the chi-squared and F distributions are listed in Table 16.7. There are 21 observations used to estimate the model and eight predetermined variables. The overidentifying restrictions for the

[44]For a system containing identities, $\mathbf{W}$ is computed by assembling $\hat{\boldsymbol{\Pi}}$ for the full system first and then discarding columns corresponding to the identities. Doing the same for $\mathbf{Y}$, we then compute $\mathbf{W} = (\mathbf{Y}'\mathbf{Y} - \mathbf{Y}'\mathbf{X}\hat{\boldsymbol{\Pi}} - \hat{\boldsymbol{\Pi}}'\mathbf{X}'\mathbf{Y} + \hat{\boldsymbol{\Pi}}'\mathbf{X}'\mathbf{X}\hat{\boldsymbol{\Pi}})/T$.

TABLE 16.7 Test Statistics and Critical Values

	λ	λ'	LR	TR^2	F	F'	$K_j^* - M_j$
Consumption	1.499	1.716	9.98	8.77	1.08	1.55	2
Investment	1.086	1.095	1.72	1.81	0.223	0.247	3
Wages	2.466	2.469	29.3	12.49	3.81	3.82	3

Critical Values

	$F[2, 13]$	$F[3, 13]$	$\chi^2[2]$	$\chi^2[3]$	$\chi^2[8]$
5%	3.81	3.41	5.99	7.82	15.51
1%	6.70	5.74	9.21	11.34	22.09

wage equation are rejected by all single-equation tests. There are two possibilities. The equation may well be misspecified. Or, as Liu suggests, in a dynamic model, if there is autocorrelation of the disturbances, the treatment of lagged endogenous variables as if they were exogenous is a specification error.

Another specification error occurs if the variables assumed to be exogenous in the system are not, in fact, uncorrelated with the structural disturbances. Since all the asymptotic properties claimed earlier rest on this assumption, this specification error would be quite serious. Several authors have studied this issue.[45] The specification test devised by Hausman that we used in Section 9.5.5 in the errors in variables model and Section 14.4.4 in analyzing cross-section/time-series models provides a method of testing for exogeneity in a simultaneous-equations model. Suppose that the variable x^* is in question. The test is based on the existence of two estimators, say $\hat{\boldsymbol{\delta}}$ and $\hat{\boldsymbol{\delta}}^*$, such that

under H_0: (x^* is exogenous), both $\hat{\boldsymbol{\delta}}$ and $\hat{\boldsymbol{\delta}}^*$ are consistent and $\hat{\boldsymbol{\delta}}^*$ is asymptotically efficient,

under H_1: (x^* is endogenous), $\hat{\boldsymbol{\delta}}$ is consistent, but $\hat{\boldsymbol{\delta}}^*$ is inconsistent.

Hausman bases his version of the test on $\hat{\boldsymbol{\delta}}$ being the 2SLS estimator and $\hat{\boldsymbol{\delta}}^*$ being the 3SLS estimator. A shortcoming of the procedure is that it requires an arbitrary choice of some equation that does not contain x^* for the test. For instance, in the next example, to pursue the finding of Example 16.18, we consider the exogeneity of X_{-1} in the third equation of Klein's Model I. To apply this test, we must use one of the other two equations.

A single-equation version of the test has been devised by Spencer and Berk (1981). We now suppose that x^* appears in equation j, so that

$$\begin{aligned}\mathbf{y}_j &= \mathbf{Y}_j\boldsymbol{\gamma}_j + \mathbf{X}_j\boldsymbol{\beta}_j + x^*\theta + \boldsymbol{\epsilon}_j \\ &= [\mathbf{Y}_j\mathbf{X}_j\mathbf{x}^*]\boldsymbol{\delta}_j + \boldsymbol{\epsilon}_j.\end{aligned}$$

[45] Wu (1973), Durbin (1954), Hausman (1978), and Nakamura and Nakamura (1981).

Then $\hat{\boldsymbol{\delta}}^*$ is the 3SLS estimator, treating x^* as an exogenous variable in the system, whereas $\hat{\boldsymbol{\delta}}$ is the IV estimator based on regressing $\mathbf{y}_j$ on $\mathbf{Y}_j$, $\mathbf{X}_j$, $\hat{x}^*$, where the least squares fitted values are based on all of the remaining exogenous variables, excluding x^*. The test statistic is then

$$w = (\hat{\boldsymbol{\delta}}^* - \hat{\boldsymbol{\delta}})'\{\text{Est. Var}[\hat{\boldsymbol{\delta}}] - \text{Est. Var}[\hat{\boldsymbol{\delta}}^*]\}^{-1}(\hat{\boldsymbol{\delta}}^* - \hat{\boldsymbol{\delta}}). \qquad \textbf{(16-35)}$$

This is the Wald statistic based on the difference of the two estimators. The statistic has one degree of freedom. (The extension to a set of variables is direct.)

EXAMPLE 16.19 Exogeneity Test

The previous example suggested a specification problem in the third equation of Klein's Model I. To pursue that finding, we now apply the preceding to test the exogeneity of X_{-1}. This is roughly equivalent to a test of autocorrelation, albeit a bit indirect (and probably not too powerful), since if the disturbances are autocorrelated, lagged endogenous variables may no longer be treated as predetermined. The two estimated parameter vectors are

$$\boldsymbol{\delta}^* = [1.5003, 0.43886, 0.14667, 0.13040] \quad \text{(i.e.. 2SLS)}$$

and

$$\hat{\boldsymbol{\delta}} = [1.2524, 0.42277, 0.167614, 0.13062].$$

Using the Wald criterion, the chi-squared statistic is 1.3977. Thus, the hypothesis (such as it is) is not rejected.

16.9. PROPERTIES OF DYNAMIC MODELS

In models with lagged endogenous variables, the entire previous time path of the exogenous variables and disturbances, not just their current values, determines the current value of the dependent variables. The intrinsic dynamic properties of the autoregressive model, such as stability and the existence of an equilibrium value, are embodied in their autoregressive parameters. In this section, we are interested in long- and short-run multipliers, stability properties, and simulated time paths of the dependent variables.

16.9.1. Dynamic Models and Their Multipliers

The structural form of a dynamic model is

$$\mathbf{y}_t'\boldsymbol{\Gamma} + \mathbf{x}_t'\mathbf{B} + \mathbf{y}_{t-1}'\boldsymbol{\Phi} = \boldsymbol{\epsilon}_t'. \qquad \textbf{(16-36)}$$

If the model contains additional lags, we can add additional equations to the system of the form

$$y_{t-1} = y_{t-1},$$
$$y_{t-2} = y_{t-2},$$

and so on, then add additional rows and columns to $\boldsymbol{\Phi}$ as necessary to produce a model with only a single lag. (That is, we obtain the correct representations if we treat lags of two periods as one period lags of variables lagged one period.) The reduced form is

$$\mathbf{y}_t' = \mathbf{x}_t'\mathbf{\Pi} + \mathbf{y}_{t-1}'\mathbf{\Delta} + \mathbf{v}_t',$$

where

$$\mathbf{\Pi} = -\mathbf{B\Gamma}^{-1}$$

and

$$\mathbf{\Delta} = -\mathbf{\Phi\Gamma}^{-1}.$$

EXAMPLE 16.20 Dynamic Model

The 2SLS estimates of the structure and reduced form of Klein's Model I are given in Table 16.8. (Only the nonzero rows of $\hat{\mathbf{\Phi}}$ and $\hat{\mathbf{\Delta}}$ are shown.)

TABLE 16.8 2SLS Estimates of Coefficient Matrices in Klein's Model I

		Equation					
Variable		***C***	***I***	***W^p***	***X***	***P***	***K***
	C	1	0	0	−1	0	0
	I	0	1	0	−1	0	−1
	W^p	−0.810	0	1	0	1	0
$\hat{\Gamma}$ =	X	0	0	−0.439	1	−1	0
	P	−0.017	−0.15	0	0	1	0
	K	0	0	0	0	0	1
	1	−16.555	−20.278	−1.5	0	0	0
	W^g	−0.810	0	0	0	0	0
$\hat{B}$ =	T	0	0	0	0	1	0
	G	0	0	0	−1	0	0
	t	0	0	−0.13	0	0	0
	X_{-1}	0	0	−0.147	0	0	0
$\hat{\Phi}$ =	P_{-1}	−0.216	−0.6160	0	0	0	0
	K_{-1}	0	0.158	0	0	0	−1
	1	42.80	25.83	31.63	68.63	37.00	25.83
	W^g	1.35	0.124	0.646	1.47	0.825	0.125
$\hat{\Pi}$ =	T	−0.128	−0.176	−0.133	−0.303	−1.17	−0.176
	G	0.663	0.153	0.797	1.82	1.02	0.153
	t	0.159	−0.007	0.197	0.152	−0.045	−0.007
	X_{-1}	0.179	−0.008	0.222	0.172	−0.051	−0.008
$\hat{\Delta}$ =	P_{-1}	0.767	0.743	0.663	1.51	0.848	0.743
	K_{-1}	−0.105	−0.182	−0.125	−0.287	−0.161	0.818

From the reduced form,

$$\frac{\partial y_{t,m}}{\partial x_{t,k}} = \mathbf{\Pi}_{km}.$$

The short-run effects are the coefficients on the current x's, so $\mathbf{\Pi}$ is the matrix of **impact multipliers.** By substituting for $\mathbf{y}_{t-1}$ in (16-36), we obtain

$$\mathbf{y}_t' = \mathbf{x}_t'\mathbf{\Pi} + \mathbf{x}_{t-1}'\mathbf{\Pi\Delta} + \mathbf{y}_{t-2}'\mathbf{\Delta}^2 + (\mathbf{v}_t' + \mathbf{v}_{t-1}'\mathbf{\Delta}^2).$$

Continuing this for the full t periods, we obtain

$$\mathbf{y}_t' = \sum_{s=0}^{t-1} [\mathbf{x}_{t-s}'\mathbf{\Pi\Delta}^s] + \mathbf{y}_0'\mathbf{\Delta}^t + \sum_{s=0}^{t-1} \mathbf{v}_{t-s}'\mathbf{\Delta}^s. \quad \textbf{(16-37)}$$

This shows how the **initial conditions** $\mathbf{y}_0$ and the subsequent time path of the exogenous variables and disturbances completely determine the current values of the endogenous variables. The coefficient matrices in the bracketed sum are the **dynamic multipliers,**

$$\frac{\partial y_{t,m}}{\partial x_{t-s,k}} = (\mathbf{\Pi\Delta}^s)_{km}.$$

The **cumulated multipliers** are obtained by adding the matrices of dynamic multipliers. If we let s go to infinity in (16-37), we obtain the **final form** of the model,[46]

$$\mathbf{y}_t' = \sum_{s=0}^{\infty} [\mathbf{x}_{t-s}'\mathbf{\Pi\Delta}^s] + \sum_{s=0}^{\infty} [\mathbf{v}_{t-s}'\mathbf{\Delta}^s].$$

Assume for the present that $\lim_{t\to\infty} \mathbf{\Delta}^t = \mathbf{0}$. Then the matrix of cumulated multipliers in the final form is

$$\mathbf{\Pi}[\mathbf{I} + \mathbf{\Delta} + \mathbf{\Delta}^2 + \cdots] = \mathbf{\Pi}[\mathbf{I} - \mathbf{\Delta}]^{-1}.$$

These coefficient matrices are the long-run or **equilibrium multipliers.** Analogous to our single-equation case, we can also obtain the cumulated multipliers for s periods as

$$\text{cumulated multipliers} = \mathbf{\Pi}[\mathbf{I} - \mathbf{\Delta}]^{-1}[\mathbf{I} - \mathbf{\Delta}^s].$$

Suppose that the values of $\mathbf{x}$ were permanently fixed at $\bar{\mathbf{x}}$. Then the final form shows that if there are no disturbances, the equilibrium value of $\mathbf{y}_t$ would be

[46]In some treatments, (16-37) is labeled the final form instead. Both forms eliminate the lagged values of the dependent variables from the current value. The dependence of the first form on the initial values may be simpler to interpret.

$$\begin{aligned}\bar{\mathbf{y}}' &= \sum_{s=0}^{\infty}[\bar{\mathbf{x}}'\mathbf{\Pi}\mathbf{\Delta}^s] \\ &= \bar{\mathbf{x}}'\sum_{s=0}^{\infty}\mathbf{\Pi}\mathbf{\Delta}^s = \bar{\mathbf{x}}'\mathbf{\Pi}[\mathbf{I} - \mathbf{\Delta}]^{-1}.\end{aligned} \quad \textbf{(16-38)}$$

Therefore, the equilibrium multipliers are

$$\frac{\partial \bar{y}_m}{\partial \bar{x}_k} = [\mathbf{\Pi}(\mathbf{I} - \mathbf{\Delta})^{-1}]_{km}.$$

Some examples will now be shown for Klein's Model I.

EXAMPLE 16.21 Dynamic Multipliers

For a particular variable or group of variables, the various multipliers are submatrices of the multiplier matrices. The dynamic multipliers for the fiscal policy variables, T and G, corresponding to the estimates in Example 16.20 are given in Table 16.9 for several lags.[47]

A plot of the period multipliers against the lag length is called the **impulse response function.** The policy effects on output are shown in Figure 16.2. The damped sine wave pattern is characteristic of a dynamic system with imaginary roots. (See the next example.) Another model based on an equation with real roots appears in Example 17.8. When the roots are real, the impulse response function is a monotonically declining function, instead.

The model has the interesting feature that the long-run multipliers of both policy variables for investment are zero. This is intrinsic to the model. We shall return to this point in the later discussion of equilibrium. The estimated long-run *balanced-budget multiplier* for equal increases in spending and taxes (an anachronism?) is $2.10 + (-1.48) = 0.62$.

16.9.2. Stability

It remains to be shown that the matrix of multipliers in the final form converges. For the analysis to proceed, it is necessary for the matrix $\mathbf{\Delta}^t$ to converge to a zero matrix. Although $\mathbf{\Delta}$ is not a symmetric matrix, it will still have a spectral decomposition of the form

$$\mathbf{\Delta} = \mathbf{C}\mathbf{\Lambda}\mathbf{C}^{-1}, \quad \textbf{(16-39)}$$

where $\mathbf{\Lambda}$ is a diagonal matrix containing the characteristic roots of $\mathbf{\Delta}$ and each column of $\mathbf{C}$ is a right characteristic vector,

$$\mathbf{\Delta}\mathbf{c}_m = \lambda_m\mathbf{c}_m. \quad \textbf{(16-40)}$$

[47]A method of computing asymptotic standard errors for the estimates of the dynamic multipliers is given by Schmidt (1973).

TABLE 16.9 Dynamic Multipliers

	Taxes				*Spending*			
	Investment		*Output*		*Investment*		*Output*	
Lag	*Period*	*Cumulative*	*Period*	*Cumulative*	*Period*	*Cumulative*	*Period*	*Cumulative*
0	−0.760	−0.760	−1.30	−1.30	0.153	0.153	1.82	1.82
1	−0.834	−1.59	−1.74	−3.04	0.715	0.868	1.46	3.28
2	−0.507	−2.10	−1.27	−4.31	0.383	1.25	1.01	4.29
3	−0.122	−2.22	−0.502	−4.81	0.061	1.31	0.334	4.62
4	0.192	−2.03	0.198	−4.61	−0.184	1.13	−0.225	4.40
5	0.388	−1.64	0.682	−3.93	−0.328	0.800	−0.590	3.81
6	0.462	−1.18	0.914	−3.02	−0.374	0.426	−0.748	3.06
7	0.434	−0.749	0.921	−2.10	−0.342	0.084	−0.731	2.33
8	0.338	−0.411	0.764	−1.33	−0.258	−0.174	−0.591	1.74
9	0.210	−0.201	0.519	−0.814	−0.154	−0.328	−0.387	1.352
10	0.082	−0.119	0.253	−0.561	−0.052	−0.380	−0.173	1.179
11	−0.023	−0.142	0.019	−0.542	0.030	−0.350	0.009	1.188
12	−0.095	−0.237	−0.152	−0.694	0.083	−0.267	0.138	1.326
13	−0.129	−0.366	−0.247	−0.941	0.106	−0.161	0.206	1.532
14	−0.131	−0.497	−0.271	−1.21	0.104	−0.057	0.218	1.75
15	−0.109	−0.606	−0.241	−1.45	0.085	0.028	0.189	1.94
16	−0.075	−0.681	−0.178	−1.63	0.056	0.084	0.134	2.07
17	−0.037	−0.718	−0.101	−1.73	0.025	0.109	0.072	2.15
18	−0.003	−0.721	−0.023	−1.76	−0.007	0.102	0.015	2.16
19	0.021	−0.700	0.028	−1.73	−0.019	0.083	−0.028	2.13
20	0.035	−0.665	0.064	−1.67	−0.029	0.054	−0.054	2.078
∞	0	0	0	−1.48	0	0	0	2.10

Since $\boldsymbol{\Delta}$ is not symmetric, the elements of $\boldsymbol{\Lambda}$ (and $\mathbf{C}$) may be complex. Nonetheless, (2-105) continues to hold:

$$\boldsymbol{\Delta}^2 = \mathbf{C}\boldsymbol{\Lambda}\mathbf{C}^{-1}\mathbf{C}\boldsymbol{\Lambda}\mathbf{C}^{-1} = \mathbf{C}\boldsymbol{\Lambda}^2\mathbf{C}^{-1}$$

and

$$\boldsymbol{\Delta}^t = \mathbf{C}\boldsymbol{\Lambda}^t\mathbf{C}^{-1}. \tag{16-41}$$

It is apparent that whether or not $\boldsymbol{\Delta}^t$ vanishes as $t \rightarrow \infty$ depends on its characteristic roots. The condition is $|\lambda_m| < 1$. For the case of a complex root,

$$|\lambda_m| = |a + bi| = a^2 + b^2.$$

For a given model, the stability may be established by examining the largest or **dominant root.** Since it is ultimately a function of the sample estimates of the

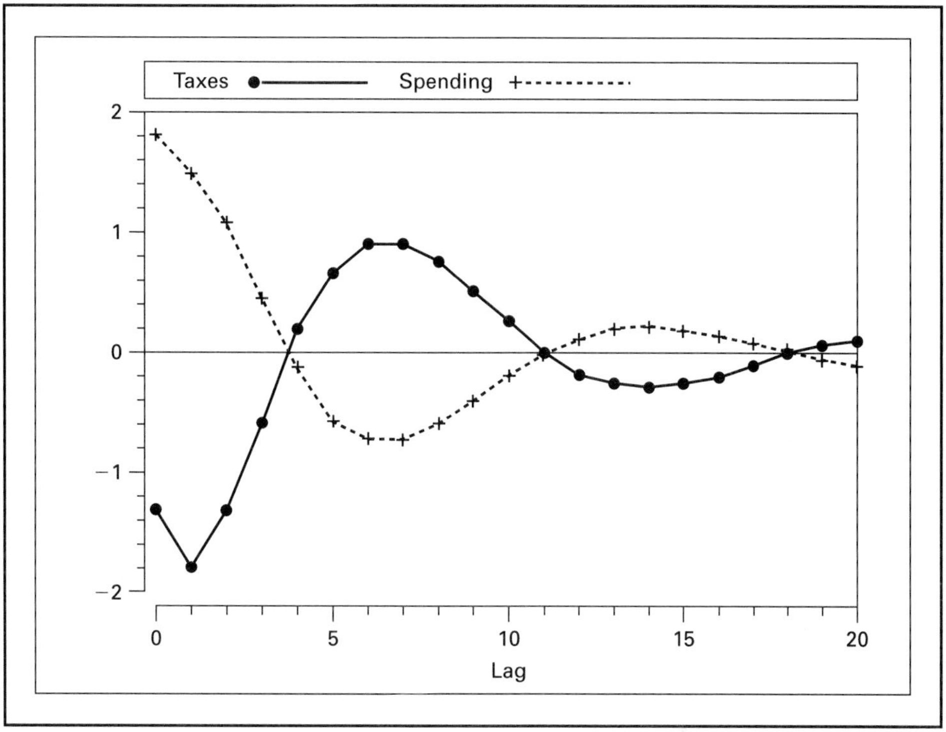

FIGURE 16.2 Policy Multipliers.

parameters, the estimate of the dominant root of the model is a sample statistic for which an estimate of its asymptotic sampling variance can be computed.[48]

With many endogenous variables in the model but only a few lagged variables, $\boldsymbol{\Delta}$ is a large but sparse matrix. Finding the characteristic roots of large, asymmetric matrices is a rather complex computation problem (although there exists specialized software for doing so). There is a way to make the problem a bit more compact. To put this in the context of an example, in Klein's Model I, $\boldsymbol{\Delta}$ is 6×6, but with three rows of zeros, it has only rank three and three nonzero roots. The following partitioning is useful. Let $\mathbf{y}_{t1}$ be the set of endogenous variables that appear in both current and lagged form, and let $\mathbf{y}_{t2}$ be those that appear only in current form. Then the model may be written

$$[\mathbf{y}_{t1}' \quad \mathbf{y}_{t2}'] = \mathbf{x}_t'[\boldsymbol{\Pi}_1 \quad \boldsymbol{\Pi}_2] + [\mathbf{y}_{t-1,1}' \quad \mathbf{y}_{t-1,2}'] \begin{bmatrix} \boldsymbol{\Delta}_1 & \boldsymbol{\Delta}_2 \\ \mathbf{0} & \mathbf{0} \end{bmatrix} + [\mathbf{v}_{t1}' \quad \mathbf{v}_{t2}']. \qquad \textbf{(16-42)}$$

[48]The computations are detailed in Theil and Boot (1962). An alternative approach is given by Kmenta and Oberhofer (1973). Schmidt (1974d) shows that (as might be expected) the Theil–Boot formula based on the reduced form and the Oberhofer–Kmenta formula based on the structural form give the same result.

The characteristic roots of $\mathbf{\Delta}$ are defined by the characteristic polynomial, $|\mathbf{\Delta} - \lambda\mathbf{I}| = 0$. For the partitioned model, this is

$$\begin{vmatrix} \mathbf{\Delta}_1 - \lambda\mathbf{I} & \mathbf{\Delta}_2 \\ \mathbf{0} & -\lambda\mathbf{I} \end{vmatrix} = 0.$$

We may use (2-72) to obtain

$$|\mathbf{\Delta} - \lambda\mathbf{I}| = (-\lambda)^{M_2}|\mathbf{\Delta}_1 - \lambda\mathbf{I}| = 0,$$

where M_2 is the number of variables in $\mathbf{y}_2$. Consequently, we need only concern ourselves with the submatrix of $\mathbf{\Delta}$ that defines explicit autoregressions. The part of the reduced form defined by

$$\mathbf{y}'_{t2} = \mathbf{x}'_t\mathbf{\Pi}_2 + \mathbf{y}'_{t-1,1}\mathbf{\Delta}_2$$

is not directly relevant.

EXAMPLE 16.22 Model Stability

For the 2SLS estimates of Klein's Model I, the relevant submatrix of $\hat{\mathbf{\Delta}}$ is

$$\begin{matrix} & K & P & K & \\ \hat{\mathbf{\Delta}}_1 = & \left[\begin{matrix} 0.172 & -0.051 & -0.008 \\ 1.511 & 0.0848 & 0.743 \\ -0.287 & -0.161 & 0.818 \end{matrix}\right] & & & \begin{matrix} X_{-1} \\ P_{-1}\,. \\ K_{-1} \end{matrix} \end{matrix}$$

The characteristic roots of this matrix are 0.2995 and the complex pair $0.7692 \pm 0.3494i$. The moduli of the complex roots are 0.8448, so we conclude that the model is stable.

16.9.3. Adjustment to Equilibrium

The adjustment of a dynamic model to an equilibrium involves the following conceptual experiment. We assume that the exogenous variables $\mathbf{x}_t$ have been fixed at a level $\bar{\mathbf{x}}$ for a long enough time that the endogenous variables have fully adjusted to their equilibrium $\bar{\mathbf{y}}$ [defined in (16-38)]. In some arbitrarily chosen period, labeled period 0, an exogenous one-time shock hits the system, so that in period $t = 0$, $\mathbf{x}_t = \mathbf{x}_0 \neq \bar{\mathbf{x}}$. Thereafter, $\mathbf{x}_t$ returns to its former value $\bar{\mathbf{x}}$, and $\mathbf{x}_t = \bar{\mathbf{x}}$ for all $t > 0$. We know from the expression for the final form that, if disturbed, $\mathbf{y}_t$ will ultimately return to the equilibrium. That is ensured by the stability condition. Here we consider the time path of the adjustment. Since our only concern at this point is with the exogenous shock, we will ignore the disturbances in the analysis.

At time 0,

$$\mathbf{y}'_0 = \mathbf{x}'_0\mathbf{\Pi} + \mathbf{y}'_{-1}\mathbf{\Delta}.$$

But prior to time 0, the system was in equilibrium, so

$$\mathbf{y}'_0 = \mathbf{x}'_0\mathbf{\Pi} + \bar{\mathbf{y}}'\mathbf{\Delta}.$$

The initial displacement due to the shock to $\bar{\mathbf{x}}$ is

$$\mathbf{y}_0' - \bar{\mathbf{y}}' = \mathbf{x}_0'\mathbf{\Pi} - \bar{\mathbf{y}}'(\mathbf{I} - \mathbf{\Delta}).$$

Substituting $\bar{\mathbf{x}}'\mathbf{\Pi} = \bar{\mathbf{y}}'(\mathbf{I} - \mathbf{\Delta})$ produces

$$\mathbf{y}_0' - \bar{\mathbf{y}}' = (\mathbf{x}_0' - \bar{\mathbf{x}}')\mathbf{\Pi}. \qquad \textbf{(16-43)}$$

As might be expected, the initial displacement is determined entirely by the exogenous shock occurring in that period. Since $\mathbf{x}_t = \bar{\mathbf{x}}$ after period 0, (16-37) implies that

$$\begin{aligned}\mathbf{y}_t' &= \sum_{s=0}^{t-1} \bar{\mathbf{x}}'\mathbf{\Pi}\mathbf{\Delta}^s + \mathbf{y}_0'\mathbf{\Delta}^t \\ &= \bar{\mathbf{x}}'\,\mathbf{\Pi}(\mathbf{I} - \mathbf{\Delta})^{-1}(\mathbf{I} - \mathbf{\Delta}^t) + \mathbf{y}_0'\mathbf{\Delta}^t \\ &= \bar{\mathbf{y}}' - \bar{\mathbf{y}}'\,\mathbf{\Delta}^t + \mathbf{y}_0'\mathbf{\Delta}^t \\ &= \bar{\mathbf{y}}' + (\mathbf{y}_0' - \bar{\mathbf{y}}')\mathbf{\Delta}^t.\end{aligned}$$

Thus, the entire time path is a function of the initial displacement. By inserting (16-43), we see that

$$\mathbf{y}_t' = \bar{\mathbf{y}}' + (\mathbf{x}_0' - \bar{\mathbf{x}}')\mathbf{\Pi}\mathbf{\Delta}^t. \qquad \textbf{(16-44)}$$

Since $\lim_{t\to\infty} \mathbf{\Delta}^t = \mathbf{0}$, this defines the path back to the equilibrium subsequent to the exogenous shock $(\mathbf{x}_0 - \bar{\mathbf{x}})$. The stability condition imposed on $\mathbf{\Delta}$ ensures that if the system is disturbed at some point by a one-time shock, barring further shocks or disturbances, it will return to its equilibrium. Since $\mathbf{y}_0$, $\bar{\mathbf{x}}$, $\mathbf{x}_0$, and $\mathbf{\Pi}$ are fixed for all time, the shape of the path is completely determined by the behavior of $\mathbf{\Delta}^t$, which we now examine.

In the preceding section, in (16-39) to (16-42), we used the characteristic roots of $\mathbf{\Delta}$ to infer the (lack of) stability of the model. The spectral decomposition of $\mathbf{\Delta}^t$ given in (16-41) may be written

$$\mathbf{\Delta}^t = \sum_{m=1}^{M} \lambda_m^t \mathbf{c}_m \mathbf{d}_m',$$

where $\mathbf{c}_m$ is the mth column of $\mathbf{C}$ and $\mathbf{d}_m'$ is the mth row of $\mathbf{C}^{-1}$.[49] Inserting this in (16-44), we have

$$\begin{aligned}(\mathbf{y}_t - \bar{\mathbf{y}})' &= [(\mathbf{x}_0 - \bar{\mathbf{x}})'\mathbf{\Pi}] \sum_{m=1}^{M} \lambda_m^t \mathbf{c}_m \mathbf{d}_m' \\ &= \sum_{m=1}^{M} \lambda_m^t [(\mathbf{x}_0 - \bar{\mathbf{x}})'\mathbf{\Pi}\mathbf{c}_m\mathbf{d}_m'] = \sum_{m=1}^{M} \lambda_m^t \mathbf{g}_m'.\end{aligned}$$

(Note that this may involve fewer than M terms, since some of the roots may be zero. For Klein's Model I, $M = 6$, but there are only three nonzero roots.)

[49]See Section 2.7.9.

Since $\mathbf{g}_m$ depends only on the initial conditions and the parameters of the model, the behavior of the time path of $(\mathbf{y}_t - \bar{\mathbf{y}})$ is completely determined by λ_m^t. In each period, the deviation from the equilibrium is a sum of M terms of powers of λ_m times a constant. (Each variable has its own set of constants.) The terms in the sum behave as follows:

$$\begin{aligned} &\lambda_m \text{ real} > 0, && \lambda_m^t \text{ adds a damped exponential term,}\\ &\lambda_m \text{ real} < 0, && \lambda_m^t \text{ adds a damped sawtooth term,}\\ &\lambda_m \text{ complex,} && \lambda_m^t \text{ adds a damped sinusoidal term.} \end{aligned}$$

If we write the complex root $\lambda_m = a + bi$ in polar form,

$$\lambda = A[\cos B + i \sin B],$$

where

$$A = [a^2 + b^2]^{1/2}$$

and

$$B = \arccos \frac{a}{A} \text{ (in radians),}$$

the sinusoidal components each have amplitude A^t and period $2\pi/B$.[50]

EXAMPLE 16.23 Adjustment of Klein's Model I

We start the model at the conditions of the last data point, 1941. The initial and equilibrium values for the six endogenous variables are given in Table 16.10. The equilibrium is based on $W^g = 8.5$, $G = 13.8$, $T = 11.6$, and $A = 10$. The equilibrium of zero for investment might seem a bit peculiar. But note that the model imposes $K_t - K_{t-1} = I_t$, and both K and I are endogenous. If K_t is in equilibrium, there is no investment. The path to the new equilibrium for the six endogenous variables is shown in Table 16.11. Note the cyclical behavior shown. The complex roots are 0.8448 [cos 0.4263 $\pm$ i sin 0.4263]. The period for the oscillations is, thus, $2\pi/0.4263 = 14.73$.

TABLE 16.10 Initial and Equilibrium Values for Klein's Model I

	C	I	W^p	X	P	K
Initial	69.7	4.9	53.3	88.4	23.5	209.4
Equilibrium	70.5	0	52.2	84.3	20.5	227.7

[50]Goldberger (1964, p. 378).

TABLE 16.11 Deviations from Equilibrium

Year	C	I	W_p	X	P	K
1941	−0.5	4.9	1.1	4.1	3.0	−18.3
1942	5.0	5.5	5.2	10.5	5.3	−12.8
1943	7.3	6.2	7.4	13.5	6.0	−6.6
1944	7.7	5.6	7.8	13.3	5.5	−1.0
1945	6.7	4.2	6.7	10.8	4.1	3.1
1946	4.8	2.4	4.8	7.2	2.5	5.5
1947	2.6	0.8	2.5	3.4	0.8	6.3
1948	0.6	−0.6	0.5	0.0	−0.5	5.7
1949	−1.0	−1.4	−1.0	−2.4	−1.3	4.3
1950	−1.9	−1.8	−2.0	−3.7	−1.7	2.6
1951	−2.2	−1.7	−2.3	−3.9	−1.7	0.9
1952	−2.1	−1.4	−2.1	−3.4	−1.4	−0.5
1953	−1.6	−0.9	−1.6	−2.5	−0.9	−1.4
1954	−1.0	−0.4	−1.0	−1.4	−0.4	−1.8
1955	−0.4	0.0	−0.3	−0.3	0.0	−1.8
1956	0.1	0.3	0.2	0.5	0.3	−1.4
1957	0.5	0.5	0.5	1.0	0.5	−0.9
1958	0.6	0.5	0.6	1.1	0.5	−0.4
1959	0.6	0.4	0.6	1.1	0.4	0.0
1960	0.5	0.3	0.5	0.8	0.3	0.3
1961	0.4	0.2	0.3	0.5	0.2	0.5
1962	0.2	0.0	0.2	0.2	0.0	0.5
1963	0.0	0.0	0.0	0.0	−0.0	0.5
1964	−0.1	−0.1	−0.1	−0.2	−0.1	0.3
1965	−0.2	−0.1	−0.2	−0.3	−0.1	0.2
1966	−0.2	−0.1	−0.2	−0.3	−0.1	0.0
1967	−0.2	−0.1	−0.2	−0.3	−0.1	−0.0
1968	−0.1	−0.0	−0.1	−0.2	0.0	−0.1
1969	0.0	0.0	0.0	0.0	0.0	−0.2
1970	0.0	0.0	0.0	0.0	0.0	−0.1
1971	0.0	0.0	0.0	0.0	0.0	−0.1
1972	0.0	0.0	0.0	0.0	0.0	0.0

EXERCISES

1. Consider the following two-equation model:

$$y_1 = \gamma_1 y_2 + \beta_{11}x_1 + \beta_{21}x_2 + \beta_{31}x_3 + \epsilon_1,$$
$$y_2 = \gamma_2 y_1 + \beta_{12}x_1 + \beta_{22}x_2 + \beta_{32}x_3 + \epsilon_1.$$

(a) Verify that, as stated, neither equation is identified.

(b) Establish whether or not the following restrictions are sufficient to identify (or partially identify) the model:

(1) $\beta_{21} = \beta_{32} = 0$,
(2) $\beta_{12} = \beta_{22} = 0$,
(3) $\gamma_1 = 0$,
(4) $\gamma_1 = \gamma_2$ and $\beta_{32} = 0$,
(5) $\sigma_{12} = 0$ and $\beta_{31} = 0$,
(6) $\gamma_1 = 0$ and $\sigma_{12} = 0$,
(7) $\beta_{21} + \beta_{22} = 1$,
(8) $\sigma_{12} = 0, \beta_{21} = \beta_{22} = \beta_{31} = \beta_{32} = 0$,
(9) $\sigma_{12} = 0, \beta_{11} = \beta_{21} = \beta_{22} = \beta_{31} = \beta_{32} = 0$.

2. Verify the rank and order conditions for identification of the second and third behavioral equations in Klein's Model I. [Hint: See Example 16.10.]

3. Check the identifiability of the parameters of the following model:

$$[y_1 \quad y_2 \quad y_3 \quad y_4]\begin{bmatrix} 1 & \gamma_{12} & 0 & 0 \\ \gamma_{21} & 1 & \gamma_{23} & \gamma_{24} \\ 0 & \gamma_{32} & 1 & \gamma_{34} \\ \gamma_{41} & \gamma_{42} & 0 & 1 \end{bmatrix}$$

$$+ [x_1 \quad x_2 \quad x_3 \quad x_4 \quad x_5]\begin{bmatrix} 0 & \beta_{12} & \beta_{13} & \beta_{14} \\ \beta_{21} & 1 & 0 & \beta_{24} \\ \beta_{31} & \beta_{32} & \beta_{33} & 0 \\ 0 & 0 & \beta_{43} & \beta_{44} \\ 0 & \beta_{52} & 0 & 0 \end{bmatrix} + [\epsilon_1 \quad \epsilon_2 \quad \epsilon_3 \quad \epsilon_4].$$

4. Examine the identifiability of the following supply and demand model:

$$\ln Q = \beta_0 + \beta_1 \ln P + \beta_2 \ln \text{income} + \epsilon_1 \quad \text{(demand)},$$
$$Q = \gamma_0 + \gamma_1 P + \gamma_2 \text{input cost} + \epsilon_2 \quad \text{(supply)}.$$

5. Obtain the reduced form for the model in Exercise 1 under each of the assumptions made in parts a and in parts b1, and b9.

6. The following model is specified:

$$y_1 = \gamma_1 y_2 + \beta_{11} x_1 + \epsilon_1,$$
$$y_2 = \gamma_2 y_1 + \beta_{22} x_2 + \beta_{32} x_3 + \epsilon_2.$$

All variables are measured as deviations from their means. The sample of 25 observations produces the following matrix of sums of squares and cross-products:

	y_1	y_2	x_1	x_2	x_3
y_1	20	6	4	3	5
y_2	6	10	3	6	7
x_1	4	3	5	2	3
x_2	3	6	2	10	8
x_3	5	7	3	8	15

(a) Estimate the two equations by OLS.
(b) Estimate the parameters of the two equations by 2SLS. Also estimate the asymptotic covariance matrix of the 2SLS estimates.
(c) Obtain the LIML estimates of the parameters of the first equation.
(d) Estimate the two equations by 3SLS.
(e) Estimate the reduced-form coefficient matrix by OLS and indirectly by using your structural estimates from part b.

7. For the model

$$\begin{aligned} y_1 &= \gamma_1 y_2 + \beta_{11}x_1 + \beta_{21}x_2 + \epsilon_1, \\ y_2 &= \gamma_2 y_1 + \beta_{32}x_3 + \beta_{42}x_4 + \epsilon_2, \end{aligned}$$

show that there are two restrictions on the reduced-form coefficients. Describe a procedure for estimating the model while incorporating the restrictions.

8. Show that (16-20) produces a consistent estimate for any $\mathbf{D}$ with rank M_j.

9. An updated version of Klein's Model I was estimated with the data in the appendix to this chapter. Using the 2SLS estimates, the relevant submatrix of $\boldsymbol{\Delta}$ [see (16-42)] is

$$\boldsymbol{\Delta}_1 = \begin{bmatrix} -0.1899 & -0.9471 & -0.8991 \\ 0 & 1.0287 & 0 \\ -0.0656 & -0.0791 & 0.0952 \end{bmatrix}.$$

Is the model stable?

10. Prove that

$$\operatorname{plim} \frac{\mathbf{Y}_j'\boldsymbol{\epsilon}_j}{T} = \underline{\boldsymbol{\omega}}_j - \boldsymbol{\Omega}_{jj}\boldsymbol{\gamma}_j.$$

11. Prove that an underidentified equation cannot be estimated by 2SLS.

12. The full set of data necessary for updating Klein's Model I is given in Table 16.12 in the appendix to this chapter.
(a) Reestimate the three structural equations of Klein's Model I, using 2SLS and the 1953 to 1984 data.
(b) Reestimate the system, using 3SLS.
(c) Compare your results with those obtained in the text for the earlier period.

APPENDIX: YEARLY DATA ON THE U.S. ECONOMY

The data used to estimate Klein's Model I are listed in Table 16.12. Variable definitions are given in Example 16.3. All estimates are computed using the 1921 to 1941 data because of the lagged values of P and X.

The data used for the updated version of Klein's Model I are listed in Tables 16.13 to 16.16. Several other variables are also listed for those who wish

TABLE 16.12 Data for Klein's Model I

Year	*C*	*P*	W^p	*I*	K_{-1}	*X*	W^g	*G*	*T*
1920	39.5	12.7	28.8	2.7	180.1	44.9	2.2	2.4	3.4
1921	41.9	12.4	25.5	−0.2	182.8	45.6	2.7	3.9	7.7
1922	45.0	16.9	29.3	1.9	182.6	50.1	2.9	3.2	3.9
1923	49.2	18.4	34.1	5.2	184.5	57.2	2.9	2.8	4.7
1924	50.6	19.4	33.9	3.0	189.7	57.1	3.1	3.5	3.8
1925	52.6	20.1	35.4	5.1	192.7	61.0	3.2	3.3	5.5
1926	55.1	19.6	37.4	5.6	197.8	64.0	3.3	3.3	7.0
1927	56.2	19.8	37.9	4.2	203.4	64.4	3.6	4.0	6.7
1928	57.3	21.1	39.2	3.0	207.6	64.5	3.7	4.2	4.2
1929	57.8	21.7	41.3	5.1	210.6	67.0	4.0	4.1	4.0
1930	55.0	15.6	37.9	1.0	215.7	61.2	4.2	5.2	7.7
1931	50.9	11.4	34.5	−3.4	216.7	53.4	4.8	5.9	7.5
1932	45.6	7.0	29.0	−6.2	213.3	44.3	5.3	4.9	8.3
1933	45.5	11.2	28.5	−5.1	207.1	45.1	5.6	3.7	5.4
1934	48.7	12.3	30.6	−3.0	202.0	49.7	6.0	4.0	6.8
1935	51.3	14.0	33.2	−1.3	199.0	54.4	6.1	4.4	7.2
1936	57.7	17.6	36.8	2.1	197.7	62.7	7.4	2.9	8.3
1937	58.7	17.3	41.0	2.0	199.8	65.0	6.7	4.3	6.7
1938	57.5	15.3	38.2	−1.9	201.8	60.9	7.7	5.3	7.4
1939	61.6	19.0	41.6	1.3	199.9	69.5	7.8	6.6	8.9
1940	65.0	21.1	45.0	3.3	201.2	75.7	8.0	7.4	9.6
1941	69.7	23.5	53.3	4.9	204.5	88.4	8.5	13.8	11.6

to estimate different specifications of alternative models. For constructing more extensive data sets, the data sources also contain quarterly data on these and numerous other variables.[51] All flow variables (e.g., consumption, investment, imports) are seasonally adjusted annual rates in constant (1972) dollars. The variables in the table are as follows:

P^c = implicit price deflator for personal consumption (1972 = 100),
P^g = implicit price deflator for GNP (1972 = 100),
C = personal consumption, total,
Y^d = disposable personal income,
GNP = gross national product,
G = federal government nonwage spending,
T = indirect business taxes,
$M1$ = money stock,
I = gross private domestic investment,

[51]A pitfall to avoid: The data in the national income and product accounts are annual rates. Thus, direct application of $K_t = K_{t-1} + I_t$ overestimates the capital stock by a factor of almost four. The investment series must be converted to a quarterly rate.

TABLE 16.13 Macroeconomic Data for the U.S. Economy

	P^c	P^x	C	Y^d	GNP	G	T
1953	63.2	58.8	363.4	399.1	623.6	114.7	19.0
1954	63.7	59.6	370.0	403.6	616.1	96.1	17.0
1955	64.4	60.8	394.1	427.0	657.5	88.2	18.1
1956	65.6	62.8	405.4	446.5	671.6	86.8	18.5
1957	67.8	64.9	413.8	455.2	683.8	90.6	18.8
1958	69.2	66.0	418.0	461.0	680.9	93.4	18.0
1959	70.6	67.6	440.4	479.3	721.7	91.4	18.6
1960	71.9	68.7	452.0	489.6	737.2	90.4	20.1
1961	72.6	69.3	461.4	503.9	756.6	95.3	20.2
1962	73.7	70.6	482.0	524.8	800.3	102.8	21.5
1963	74.8	71.7	500.5	542.7	832.5	101.8	22.6
1964	75.9	72.8	528.0	580.5	876.4	100.2	22.5
1965	77.2	74.4	557.5	616.3	929.3	100.3	22.5
1966	79.4	76.7	585.7	647.0	984.8	112.6	20.7
1967	81.4	79.1	602.7	673.1	1011.4	125.1	21.0
1968	84.6	82.5	634.4	701.4	1058.1	128.1	21.8
1969	88.4	86.8	657.9	722.7	1087.6	121.8	21.7
1970	92.5	91.5	672.1	751.7	1085.6	110.6	21.1
1971	96.5	96.0	696.8	779.1	1122.4	103.7	21.1
1972	100.0	100.0	737.1	810.3	1185.9	101.7	19.9
1973	105.7	105.8	767.9	865.2	1254.3	95.9	19.9
1974	116.4	115.1	762.8	857.7	1246.3	96.6	18.9
1975	125.3	125.8	779.4	874.8	1231.6	97.4	11.3
1976	131.7	132.3	823.1	906.9	1298.2	96.8	17.7
1977	139.3	140.0	864.3	943.3	1369.7	100.4	17.8
1978	149.1	150.4	903.2	988.6	1438.6	100.3	18.7
1979	162.5	163.4	927.6	1015.5	1479.4	102.1	18.4
1980	179.0	178.4	931.8	1021.7	1475.0	106.4	22.8
1981	194.5	195.6	950.5	1049.7	1512.2	110.3	31.3
1982	206.0	207.8	963.3	1058.5	1480.0	117.0	24.1
1983	213.6	215.3	1009.2	1095.5	1534.7	116.2	24.3
1984	220.4	223.4	1062.4	1169.1	1639.3	122.5	24.8

Source: With two exceptions, all data have been obtained from the U.S. Department of Commerce, Bureau of Economic Analysis, *Business Statistics 1984* and Supplement to the *Survey of Current Business.* The exceptions are $M1$, K_{1952}, and r, which were obtained from Gordon (1986), and T, which was obtained from various issues of the *Survey of Current Business.*

TABLE 16.14 Macroeconomic Data for the U.S. Economy

	M1	*K*	*I*	*P*	*E*	*M*	*r*
1953	125.99	655.7	85.3	70.0	26.6	21.8	2.52
1954	127.95	738.8	83.1	65.0	27.8	20.9	1.59
1955	132.00	842.6	103.8	80.9	30.7	23.4	2.19
1956	133.51	945.2	102.6	79.0	35.3	25.2	3.31
1957	134.10	1042.2	97.0	74.1	38.0	26.1	3.82
1958	136.02	1129.7	87.5	63.4	33.2	27.6	2.47
1959	141.38	1237.7	108.0	77.8	33.8	31.1	3.96
1960	141.41	1342.4	104.7	72.5	38.4	30.7	3.85
1961	144.45	1446.3	103.9	71.7	39.3	30.9	2.96
1962	147.99	1563.9	117.6	77.9	41.8	34.3	3.26
1963	152.64	1689.0	125.1	83.2	44.8	35.4	3.56
1964	158.61	1822.0	133.0	91.4	50.3	37.5	3.96
1965	165.49	1973.9	151.9	103.8	51.7	41.6	4.38
1966	172.76	2136.9	163.0	108.1	54.4	47.9	5.55
1967	180.00	2291.8	154.9	100.8	56.7	51.3	5.11
1968	192.66	2453.4	161.6	107.2	61.2	59.3	5.90
1969	203.79	2624.8	171.4	99.9	65.0	64.1	7.83
1970	211.63	2783.3	158.5	82.4	70.5	66.6	7.71
1971	226.17	2957.2	173.9	90.4	71.0	69.3	5.11
1972	242.56	3152.2	195.0	100.6	77.5	76.7	4.73
1973	259.73	3369.7	217.5	118.8	97.3	81.8	8.15
1974	272.61	3565.2	195.5	118.8	108.5	80.7	9.84
1975	285.39	3720.0	154.8	105.0	103.5	71.4	6.32
1976	301.85	3904.5	184.5	125.7	110.1	84.7	5.34
1977	325.19	4118.7	214.2	139.0	112.9	90.9	5.61
1978	351.66	4355.4	236.7	152.3	126.7	102.7	7.99
1979	379.03	4591.7	236.3	154.6	146.2	109.0	10.91
1980	401.48	4800.2	208.5	131.5	159.1	108.8	12.29
1981	430.08	5031.1	230.9	113.1	160.2	116.4	14.76
1982	458.50	5225.4	194.3	79.6	147.6	118.0	11.89
1983	509.18	5446.4	221.0	94.4	139.5	126.9	8.81
1984	547.30	5736.3	289.9	105.5	146.0	161.1	10.16

K = capital stock = $K_{-1} + I$, $K_{1952} = 655.7$,
P = corporate profits,
E = exports,
M = imports,
r = 6-month commercial paper rate,

TABLE 16.15 Macroeconomic Data for the U.S. Economy

	W^g	W^p	W	X	U
1953	49.6	429.5	479.1	578.2	3.9
1954	47.2	427.0	474.1	556.1	4.1
1955	45.9	448.6	494.4	593.4	4.0
1956	45.6	461.8	507.4	604.9	4.1
1957	45.8	474.6	520.4	613.3	4.3
1958	44.5	478.5	523.0	604.5	6.9
1959	44.5	501.5	546.0	642.5	5.5
1960	45.2	517.0	562.2	654.8	5.5
1961	46.2	530.9	577.1	669.0	6.7
1962	48.3	562.2	610.5	699.9	5.5
1963	48.2	582.8	631.0	736.8	5.7
1964	48.5	611.6	660.1	774.0	5.2
1965	48.7	644.8	693.5	819.8	4.5
1966	53.0	686.0	739.0	867.8	3.8
1967	57.2	709.1	766.3	888.1	3.8
1968	58.0	739.0	797.0	926.0	3.6
1969	58.2	772.2	830.4	954.0	3.5
1970	55.2	786.3	841.5	965.1	4.9
1971	52.5	812.0	864.5	976.1	5.9
1972	50.1	864.0	914.1	1034.6	5.6
1973	48.2	910.0	958.2	1096.8	4.9
1974	48.5	896.6	945.1	1082.7	5.6
1975	48.4	899.0	947.4	1063.7	8.5
1976	48.5	938.0	986.5	1129.8	7.7
1977	48.6	995.4	1044.0	1200.8	7.1
1978	49.3	1043.9	1093.2	1264.2	6.1
1979	49.0	1081.2	1130.2	1303.2	5.8
1980	49.6	1093.2	1142.8	1297.0	7.1
1981	50.0	1141.1	1191.1	1335.5	7.6
1982	50.5	1150.0	1200.5	1304.2	9.7
1983	51.3	1189.0	1240.3	1359.0	9.6
1984	51.9	1277.5	1329.4	1459.7	7.5

X = total product = $C + I + G + X - M$,
W^g = federal government compensation of employees,
W^p = private wages = $X - P - W^g$,
W = total wages = $W^p + W^g$,
U = civilian rate of unemployment.

TABLE 16.16 Yearly Data on U.S. Agriculture

Year	*Output*	*Price Index*	*Land Value*	*Input Cost*	*CPI*	*Income*
1960	72	51	24	46	88.7	6,036
1961	70	52	25	46	89.6	6,113
1962	71	54	26	47	90.6	6,271
1963	74	55	27	47	91.7	6,378
1964	72	55	29	47	92.9	6,727
1965	76	53	31	48	94.5	7,027
1966	73	55	33	50	97.2	7,280
1967	77	52	35	50	100.0	7,513
1968	79	52	38	50	104.2	7,728
1969	80	50	40	52	109.8	7,891
1970	77	52	42	54	116.3	8,134
1971	86	56	43	57	121.3	8,322
1972	87	60	47	61	125.3	8,562
1973	92	91	53	73	133.1	9,042
1974	84	117	66	83	147.7	8,867
1975	93	105	75	91	161.2	8,944
1976	92	102	86	97	170.5	9,175
1977	100	100	100	100	181.5	9,381
1978	102	105	109	108	195.4	9,735
1979	113	116	125	125	217.4	9,829
1980	101	125	145	138	246.8	9,722
1981	117	134	158	148	272.4	9,769
1982	117	121	157	150	289.1	9,725
1983	88	128	148	153	298.4	9,930
1984	111	139	146	155	311.1	10,421
1985	117	120	128	151	322.2	10,563
1986	108	106	112	146	328.4	10,780

Source: Economic Report of the President, 1987.

The data used for estimating the model of the agricultural sector are listed in Table 16.16. Output, the agricultural price, land values, input costs, and the consumer price index are all index numbers. Income is real (1982) per capita disposable income. Some variables not used in the text are listed for readers who are interested in estimating different forms of the model.

CHAPTER 17

Regressions with Lagged Variables

17.1. INTRODUCTION

With the exceptions of autocorrelation and the possibly deleterious effects of lagged dependent variables on ordinary least squares, most of the models we have considered thus far have given only a very limited role to time as an influencing factor. But in Section 16.9, we found that lagged endogenous variables in simultaneous equations models created some new problems in estimation, but also brought some interesting features to the equations of the model. In this and the next chapter, we consider a number of additional models and topics in which time and relationships through time play an explicit part in the formulation. We begin with a discussion of **distributed lag models.** These are models that specifically include as independent variables earlier as well as contemporaneous values of the regressors. It is also in this context that lagged values of the dependent variable appear as a consequence of the theoretical basis of the model rather than as a computational means of removing autocorrelation. In Sections 17.2.3 to 17.2.5, we discuss in detail three types of distributed lag models: unrestricted finite lag models, polynomial lag models, and the geometric lag model. These do not nearly exhaust the list of available models. But this discussion will present the elements that are common to estimation of most types of distributed lag models. In Section 17.3, we describe a very general dynamic model that encompasses many types of distributed lag models, as well as many of the extensions and more formal macroeconomic models for time-series data that are presented in Chapter 18.[1] Section 17.4 considers sys-

[1]Basic sources to consider on the subject of distributed lag models are Griliches (1967), Dhrymes (1971), Nerlove (1972), Hendry et al. (1984), and Harvey (1990).

tems of dynamic equations. These are largely extensions of the models that we examined at the end of the previous chapter. But the interpretation is a bit different here.

This chapter begins our brief but formal introduction to the analysis of economic time series. By most views, this field has become almost synonymous with empirical macroeconomics. The literature in this area has grown at an impressive rate, and, more so than in any other area, it has become impossible to provide comprehensive surveys in general textbooks such as this one. Fortunately, specialized volumes have been produced that can fill this need. Harvey (1990) has been in wide use for some time. Among the many other books that have been written in the past decade, two very useful recent works are Enders (1995), which presents the basics of time series analysis at an introductory level with several very detailed applications, and Hamilton (1994), which gives a relatively technical but quite comprehensive survey of the field. Hamilton also surveys a number of the applications in the contemporary literature.

17.2. DISTRIBUTED LAG MODELS

Many events have effects that persist over time, and an appropriate model will include lagged variables.

EXAMPLE 17.1 The Demand for Energy

In the typical household, electricity, heating fuels, and gasoline are demanded not for their own sake but for use in appliances, furnaces, and cars. The household's accumulated energy using "capital stock" is determined by income, habits, and past prices of fuels. Consequently, in any period, the household's demand for energy Q_t is a function of the current price P_t, which influences how intensively the stock of equipment K_t is used, and of income Y_t and past prices, which have influenced the size and composition of the stock. A simple structural model of these effects might be

$$\begin{aligned}
&\text{demand:} && Q_t = \alpha + \beta P_t + \gamma K_t + u_t,\\
&\text{equipment:} && K_t = \delta Y_t + \theta_0 + \theta_1 P_{t-1} + \theta_2 P_{t-2} + \cdots + v_t.
\end{aligned}$$

Inserting the second equation in the first produces a **distributed lag model,**

$$\begin{aligned}
Q_t &= \alpha + \beta P_t + \gamma(\delta Y_t + \theta_0 + \theta_1 P_{t-1} + \theta_2 P_{t-2} + \cdots) + u_t + \gamma v_t\\
&= \alpha_0 + \alpha_1 Y_t + \beta_0 P_t + \beta_1 P_{t-1} + \beta_2 P_{t-2} + \cdots + \epsilon_t.
\end{aligned}$$

When the price of energy changes, its immediate impact will be to cause households to use their equipment less intensively. But it takes time to replace that equipment, so the full effect of a price change will not be felt for some time thereafter.

17.2.1. Lagged Effects in a Regression Model

A general form of distributed lag model is

$$y_t = \alpha + \sum_{i=0}^{\infty} \beta_i x_{t-i} + \epsilon_t. \tag{17-1}$$

In this model, a one-time change in x_t at any point in time will affect $E[y_s]$ in every period thereafter. When it is believed that the duration of the lagged effects is extremely long—for example, in the analysis of monetary policy—**infinite lag** models that have effects that gradually fade over time are quite common. But models are often constructed in which changes in x cease to have any influence after a fairly small number of periods. We shall consider these **finite lag** models first.[2]

Marginal effects in the classical regression model are one-time events. The response of y to a change in x is assumed to be immediate and to be complete at the end of the period of measurement. In a distributed lag model, the counterpart to a marginal effect is the effect of a one-time change in x_t on the equilibrium of y_t. If the level of x_t has been unchanged for many periods prior to t, the equilibrium value of $E[y_t]$ (assuming that it exists) will be

$$\begin{aligned}\bar{y} &= \alpha + \sum_{i=0}^{\infty} \beta_i \bar{x} \\ &= \alpha + \bar{x} \sum_{i=0}^{\infty} \beta_i,\end{aligned} \tag{17-2}$$

where $\bar{x}$ is the permanent value of x_t. For this to be finite, we require that

$$\left| \sum_{i=0}^{\infty} \beta_i \right| < \infty.$$

Consider the effect of a unit change in $\bar{x}$ occurring in period s. To focus ideas, consider the earlier example of consumers' demand for electricity and suppose that x_t is the unit price. Prior to the oil shock, demand had reached an equilibrium consistent with accumulated habits, experience with stable real prices, and the accumulated stocks of appliances. Now suppose that the price, x rises from $\bar{x}$ to $\bar{x} + 1$ in period s. The path to the new equilibrium might appear as shown in Figure 17.1. The short-run effect is the one that occurs in the same period as the change in x. This is β_0 in the figure.

DEFINITION 17.1: Impact Multiplier. β_0 = **impact multiplier = short-run multiplier**.

The difference between the old equilibrium D_0 and the new one D_1 is the sum of the individual period effects. The **long-run multiplier** is this total effect.

---

[2]As in Section 13.2, the formulation of a model with infinite lags is not meant to imply that lagged effects from the infinite past are necessarily of substance in the current period. This is just a convenient representation of a model in which lagged effects are very persistent and fade only gradually over time.

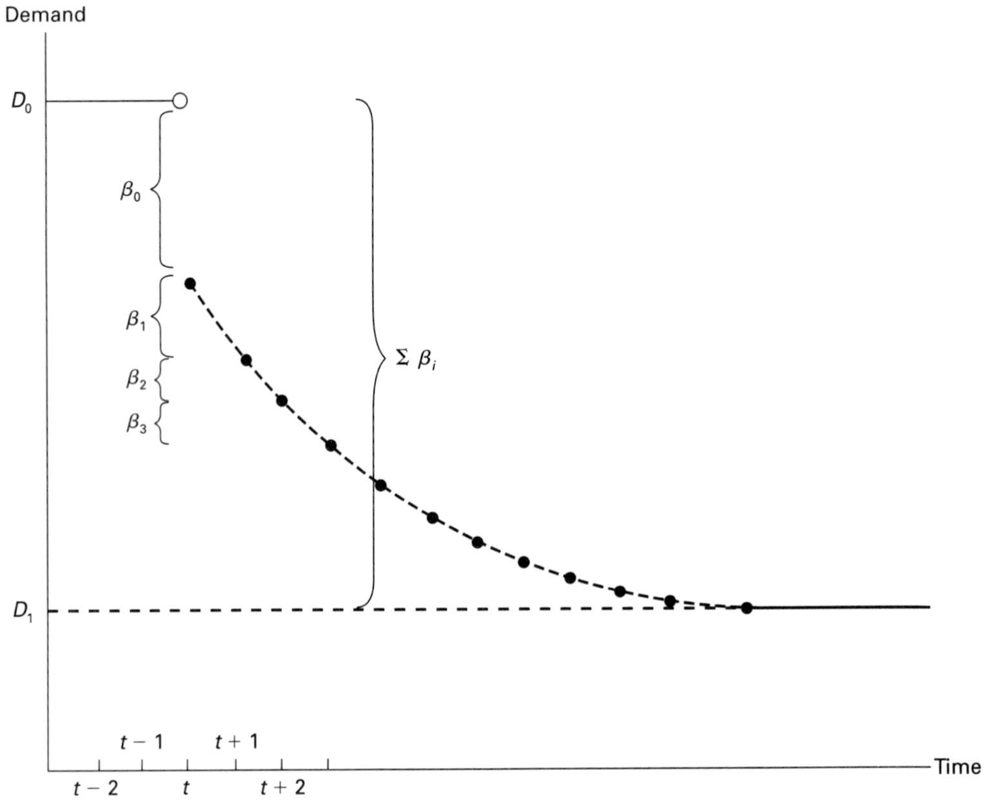

FIGURE 17.1 Lagged Adjustment.

DEFINITION 17.2: Equilibrium Multiplier. $\beta = \Sigma_{i=0}^{\infty} \beta_i$ = **equilibrium multiplier.**

Since the lag coefficients are regression coefficients, their scale is determined by the scales of the variables in the model. As such, it is often useful to define the

$$\textbf{lag weights: } w_i = \frac{\beta_i}{\sum_{i=0}^{\infty} \beta_i} \tag{17-3}$$

so that $\Sigma_{i=0}^{\infty} w_i = 1$ and to rewrite the model as

$$y_t = \alpha + \beta \sum_{i=0}^{\infty} w_i x_{t-i} + \epsilon_t. \tag{17-4}$$

Two useful statistics, based on the lag weights, that characterize the period of adjustment to a new equilibrium are the

$$\textbf{median lag} = q^* \quad \text{such that } \sum_{i=0}^{q^*-1} w_i = 0.5 \tag{17-5}$$

and the

$$\textbf{mean lag} = \sum_{i=0}^{\infty} iw_i.^3 \quad \textbf{(17-6)}$$

17.2.2. The Lag and Difference Operators

A convenient device for manipulating lagged variables is the lag operator,

$$Lx_t = x_{t-1}.$$

Some basic results are $La = a$ if a is a constant and $L(Lx_t) = L^2x_t = x_{t-2}$. Thus, $L^px_t = x_{t-p}$, $L^q(L^px_t) = L^{p+q}x_t = x_{t-p-q}$, and $(L^p + L^q)x_t = x_{t-p} + x_{t-q}$. By convention, $L^0x_t = 1x_t = x_t$. A related operation is the first difference,

$$\Delta x_t = x_t - x_{t-1}.$$

Obviously, $\Delta x_t = (1 - L)x_t$. These two operations can be usefully combined, for example, as in

$$\Delta^2 x_t = (1 - L)^2 x_t = (1 - 2L + L^2)x_t = x_t - 2x_{t-1} + x_{t-2}.$$

Note that

$$(1 - L)^2 x_t = (1 - L)(1 - L)x_t = (1 - L)(x_t - x_{t-1}) = (x_t - x_{t-1}) - (x_{t-1} - x_{t-2}).$$

The distributed lag model can be written

$$\begin{aligned} y_t &= \alpha + \sum_{i=0}^{\infty} \beta_i L^i x_t + \epsilon_t \\ &= \alpha + B(L)x_t + \epsilon_t, \end{aligned} \quad \textbf{(17-7)}$$

where $B(L)$ is a polynomial in L, $B(L) = \beta_0 + \beta_1 L + \beta_2 L^2 + \cdots$. A polynomial in the lag operator which reappears in many contexts is

$$A(L) = 1 + aL + (aL)^2 + (aL)^3 + \cdots = \sum_{i=0}^{\infty} (aL)^i.$$

If $|a| < 1$,

$$A(L) = \frac{1}{1 - aL}.$$

A distributed lag model in the form

$$y_t = \alpha + \beta \sum_{i=0}^{\infty} \gamma^i L^i x_t$$

---

[3]If the lag coefficients do not all have the same sign, these results may not be meaningful. In some contexts, lag coefficients with different signs may be taken as an indication that there is a flaw in the specification of the model.

can be written

$$y_t = \alpha + \beta x_t/(1 - \gamma L),$$

if $|\gamma| < 1$. This is called the **moving-average form** or **distributed lag form.** If we multiply through by $(1 - \gamma L)$ and collect terms, we obtain the **autoregressive form,**

$$y_t = \alpha(1 - \gamma) + \beta x_t + \gamma y_{t-1}.$$

Two useful results are

$$B(1) = \beta_0 1^0 + \beta_1 1^1 + \beta_2 1^2 + \cdots = \text{long-run multiplier} \quad \textbf{(17-8)}$$

and $B'(1) = [dB(L)/dL]_{|L=1} = \sum_{i=0}^{\infty} i\beta_i$. It follows that

$$B'(1)/B(1) = \text{mean lag}. \quad \textbf{(17-9)}$$

17.2.3. Unrestricted Finite Distributed Lag Models

An unrestricted finite distributed lag model would be specified as

$$y_t = \alpha + \sum_{i=0}^{q} \beta_i x_{t-i} + \epsilon_t. \quad \textbf{(17-10)}$$

For the present, we assume that x_t satisfies the conditions discussed in Section 6.7. The assumption that there are no other regressors is just a convenience. We also assume that ϵ_t is distributed with mean zero and variance σ_ϵ^2. Unstructured models such as this, with long but finite lags, have been used in many macroeconomic analyses.[4]

If the lag length q is known, (17-10) is a classical regression model. Aside from questions about the properties of the independent variables, the usual estimation results apply.[5] But the appropriate length of the lag is rarely, if ever, known, so one must undertake a specification search, with all its pitfalls. Worse yet, least squares is likely to be rather ineffective because (1) the typical time series is fairly short, so (17-10) will consume an excessive number of degrees of freedom; (2) ϵ_t will usually be serially correlated; and (3) multicollinearity is likely to be quite severe.

Various procedures have been suggested for determining the appropriate

---

[4]See, for example, Sims (1972) and the spate of subsequent related studies.

[5]The question of whether the regressors are well behaved or not becomes particularly pertinent in this setting, especially if one or more of them happen to be lagged values of the dependent variable. In what follows, we shall assume that the Grenander conditions discussed in Section 6.7 are met. We thus assume that the usual asymptotic results for the classical or generalized regression model will hold.

lag length. The adjusted R^2, $\overline{R}^2$ [see (6-40)], is one possibility. Another commonly used fit measure is **Akaike's** (1973) **information criterion (AIC),**

$$\text{AIC}(q) = \ln\frac{\mathbf{e}'\mathbf{e}}{T} + \frac{2q}{T}. \qquad \textbf{(17-11)}$$

If some maximum Q is known, $q \leq Q$ can be chosen to minimize AIC(q). AIC(q) is similar in spirit to $\overline{R}^2$ in that it rewards good fit but penalizes the loss of degrees of freedom.[6] An alternative approach, also based on a known Q, is to do sequential F tests on the last $Q - q$ coefficients, stopping when the test rejects the hypothesis that the coefficients are jointly zero. Each of these criteria has flaws and virtues. The AIC criterion, for example, retains a positive probability of leading to overfitting even as $T \to \infty$. It does, however, avoid the inference problems of sequential estimators. The sequential F tests requires successive revision of the significance levels to be appropriate, but do have a statistical underpinning.[7]

EXAMPLE 17.2 Finite Unstructured Distributed Lag Models

"Does money matter?" The received literature is ambivalent on whether the evidence suggests that a change in the money stock ultimately leads to a change in output.[8] In this example, we estimate a distributed lag model for changes in real $M1$ and changes in real GNP. Table 17.1 presents quarterly data on $M1$, nominal GNP, and the implicit price deflator for GNP from 1950 to 1983.

The estimated model is

$$\Delta \ln\left(\frac{Y_t}{P_t}\right) = \alpha + \sum_{i=0}^{g} \beta_i \Delta \ln\left(\frac{M_{t-i}}{P_{t-i}}\right) + \epsilon_t.$$

(What is the implication of the nonzero constant term in this model?) Results for various lag lengths are given in Table 17.2. Observations for 1952.III through 1983.IV are used in all regressions. Absolute values of t ratios for the estimates are given in parentheses below the estimated coefficients.

There is no obvious interpretation of the persistent negative weights at lags of four, five, and six quarters. It is intriguing to note that in their much more extensive study, which included several other variables in the regression, used levels instead of logarithms, and used data from a different period, Schmidt and Waud (1973) found negative weights at lags of five and six quarters in regressions of nominal GNP on money. The results suggest that there is

[6]For further discussion and some alternative measures, see Geweke and Meese (1981), Amemiya (1985, pp. 146–147), and Judge et al. (1985, pp. 353–355).

[7]See Pagano and Hartley (1981) and Trivedi and Pagan (1979).

[8]See, for example, the survey by Blanchard (1987). An interesting empirical study is Schmidt and Waud (1973).

TABLE 17.1 Money, Output, and Price Deflator Data

	Nominal GNP				*M1*				*Implicit Price Deflator*			
Year	***I***	***II***	***III***	***IV***	***I***	***II***	***III***	***IV***	***I***	***II***	***III***	***IV***
1950	267.6	277.1	294.8	306.3	110.20	111.75	112.95	113.93	56.04	56.21	56.41	56.67
1951	320.4	328.3	335.0	339.2	115.08	116.19	117.76	119.89	56.77	57.01	56.99	57.58
1952	341.9	342.1	347.8	360.0	121.31	122.37	123.64	124.72	57.58	57.57	57.92	58.58
1953	366.1	369.4	368.4	363.1	125.33	126.05	126.22	126.37	58.76	58.80	59.00	58.74
1954	362.5	362.3	366.7	375.6	126.54	127.18	128.38	129.72	59.38	59.58	59.45	59.77
1955	388.2	396.2	404.8	411.0	131.07	131.88	132.40	132.64	60.27	60.65	61.03	61.40
1956	412.8	418.4	423.5	432.1	133.11	133.38	133.48	134.09	61.91	62.43	63.13	63.69
1957	440.2	442.3	449.4	444.0	134.29	134.36	134.26	133.48	64.40	64.65	65.28	65.37
1958	436.8	440.7	453.9	467.0	133.72	135.22	136.64	138.48	65.63	65.79	66.17	66.47
1959	477.0	490.6	489.0	495.0	140.35	141.75	142.23	141.20	67.04	67.55	67.81	68.00
1960	506.9	506.3	508.0	504.8	140.83	140.83	142.00	141.98	68.44	68.56	68.86	68.96
1961	508.2	519.2	528.2	542.6	142.85	143.88	144.90	146.18	68.88	69.22	69.54	69.65
1962	554.2	562.7	568.9	574.3	147.18	147.95	147.90	148.93	70.23	70.48	70.62	71.08
1963	582.0	590.7	601.8	612.4	150.45	151.93	153.38	154.80	71.41	71.46	71.66	72.17
1964	625.3	634.0	642.8	648.8	155.85	157.20	159.75	161.63	72.36	72.57	72.97	73.16
1965	668.8	681.7	696.4	717.2	162.90	163.90	166.05	169.10	73.77	74.13	74.56	74.96
1966	738.5	750.0	760.6	774.9	171.95	172.98	172.80	173.33	75.71	76.58	76.99	77.75
1967	780.7	788.6	805.7	823.3	175.25	178.10	181.93	184.73	78.27	78.53	79.28	80.13
1968	841.2	867.2	884.9	900.3	187.15	190.63	194.30	198.55	81.15	82.14	82.84	83.99
1969	921.2	937.4	955.3	962.0	201.73	203.18	204.18	206.10	84.97	86.10	87.49	88.62
1970	972.0	986.3	1003.6	1009.0	207.90	209.78	212.78	216.08	89.89	91.07	91.79	93.03
1971	1049.3	1068.9	1086.6	1105.8	220.28	225.25	228.45	230.70	94.40	95.70	96.52	97.39
1972	1142.4	1171.7	1196.1	1233.5	235.60	239.38	244.55	250.70	98.72	99.42	100.25	101.54
1973	1283.5	1307.6	1337.7	1376.7	254.80	258.40	261.03	264.68	102.95	104.75	106.53	108.74
1974	1387.7	1423.8	1451.6	1473.8	268.77	271.23	273.73	276.73	110.72	113.48	116.42	119.79
1975	1479.8	1516.7	1578.5	1621.8	278.75	283.80	288.13	290.88	122.88	124.44	126.68	128.99
1976	1672.0	1698.6	1729.0	1772.5	295.18	299.53	303.35	309.35	130.12	131.30	132.89	134.99
1977	1834.8	1895.1	1954.4	1988.9	316.55	321.80	327.60	334.80	136.80	139.01	141.03	143.24
1978	2031.7	2139.5	2202.5	2281.6	341.13	348.70	335.45	361.38	145.12	148.89	152.02	155.38
1979	2335.5	2377.9	2454.8	2502.9	367.08	376.10	384.58	388.38	158.60	161.85	165.12	168.05
1980	2572.9	2578.8	2639.1	2736.0	394.30	390.00	405.50	416.10	171.94	176.46	180.24	185.13
1981	2875.8	2918.0	3009.3	3027.9	420.90	429.30	432.60	437.50	190.01	193.03	197.70	201.69
1982	3026.0	3061.2	3080.1	3109.6	448.80	451.30	458.20	475.70	203.98	206.77	208.53	210.27
1983	3173.8	3267.0	3346.6	3431.7	490.90	505.20	517.20	523.40	212.87	214.25	215.89	218.21

Source: Data from Gordon (1986, Appendix), compiled by R. Gordon and N. Balke.

a long-run response of the growth of real output to changes in the growth of the money stock. The estimated long-run elasticity suggested by these results is about 0.8. The Wald statistics given in Table 17.2 are quite large, which suggests that this estimate is significantly different from zero.

TABLE 17.2 Unrestricted Distributed Lags

Lag	*8*	*7*	*6*	*5*	*4*	*3*	*2*	*1*	*0*
R^2	0.2861	0.2854	0.2812	0.2699	0.2693	0.2692	0.2548	0.1982	0.1069
$\overline{R}^2$	0.2312	0.2369	0.2389	0.2333	0.2391	0.2453	0.2366	0.1852	0.0997
D-W[a]	1.426	1.425	1.434	1.462	1.425	1.455	1.4666	1.428	1.327
Sum	0.741	0.766	0.717	0.812	0.833	0.837	0.756	0.574	0.307
Wald[b]	14.64	18.18	17.91	24.47	34.88	43.27	41.98	30.64	14.96
$t-0$	0.221	0.225	0.231	0.242	0.241	0.241	0.258	0.291	0.307
	(2.86)	(2.97)	(3.07)	(3.22)	(3.22)	(3.25)	(3.48)	(3.86)	(3.86)
$t-1$	0.267	0.264	0.257	0.253	0.255	0.254	0.272	0.283	
	(3.51)	(3.50)	(3.44)	(3.37)	(3.42)	(3.46)	(3.72)	(3.76)	
$t-2$	0.218	0.220	0.223	0.229	0.226	0.225	0.226		
	(2.85)	(2.91)	(2.94)	(3.02)	(3.02)	(3.05)	(3.06)		
$t-3$	0.139	0.138	0.134	0.119	0.117	0.117			
	(1.80)	(1.79)	(1.75)	(1.57)	(1.55)	(1.55)			
$t-4$	−0.0072	−0.0050	0.0056	−0.0058	−0.0054				
	(0.09)	(0.06)	(0.07)	(0.08)	(0.07)				
$t-5$	−0.031	−0.035	−0.027	−0.025					
	(0.39)	(0.45)	(0.34)	(0.32)					
$t-6$	−0.104	−0.107	−0.107						
	(1.31)	(1.36)	(1.37)						
$t-7$	0.067	0.066							
	(0.84)	(0.83)							
$t-8$	−0.029								
	(0.35)								

[a]Durbin-Watson statistic.
[b]Wald = sum^2/Est. Var[Sum]. The 5 percent critical value is 3.84.

17.2.4. Polynomial Distributed Lag Models

In some settings, the necessary lag length may be extremely long. In principle, this merely extends (17-10), but the problem of multicollinearity is likely to become quite severe, especially in macroeconomic data. In such cases, it is common to impose some structure on the lag distribution, or in effect, to reduce the number of parameters in the model. A model that is quite popular is the **polynomial distributed lag,** or *Almon* (1965) *lag*. The polynomial lag model is based on an assumption that the true distribution of lag coefficients can be well approximated by a polynomial of fairly low order,

$$\beta_i = \alpha_0 + \alpha_1 i + \alpha_2 i^2 + \cdots + \alpha_p i^p, \quad i = 0, \ldots, q > p.^9 \qquad \textbf{(17-12)}$$

[9]The original formulation in terms of Lagrangean polynomials is considerably more complex but produces the same results.

Figure 17.2 shows the principle. The order of the polynomial p is usually taken to be quite low, rarely exceeding three or four.[10]

In addition to the $p + 1$ parameters of the polynomial, there are two unknowns to be determined: the length of the lag structure q and the degree of the polynomial p. We shall return to these later and, for the present, take them as given. After substituting (17-12) in (17-10) and collecting terms, the model can be written

$$\begin{aligned} y_t = \alpha &+ \alpha_0(x_t + x_{t-1} + x_{t-2} + x_{t-3} + \cdots + x_{t-q}) \\ &+ \alpha_1(x_{t-1} + 2x_{t-2} + 3x_{t-3} + \cdots + qx_{t-q}) \\ &+ \alpha_2(x_{t-1} + 4x_{t-2} + 9x_{t-3} + \cdots + q^2x_{t-q}) \\ &+ \quad \vdots \\ &+ \alpha_p(x_{t-1} + 2^px_{t-2} + 3^px_{t-3} + \cdots + q^px_{t-q}) \\ &+ \epsilon_t \\ = \alpha &+ \alpha_0 z_{t0} + \alpha_1 z_{t1} + \alpha_2 z_{t2} + \cdots + \alpha_p z_{tp} + \epsilon_t. \end{aligned} \tag{17-13}$$

Each z_{tj} is a linear combination of x_t and the q lagged variables. We can collect the relationships in (17-13) in $\boldsymbol{\beta} = \mathbf{H}\boldsymbol{\alpha}$, where

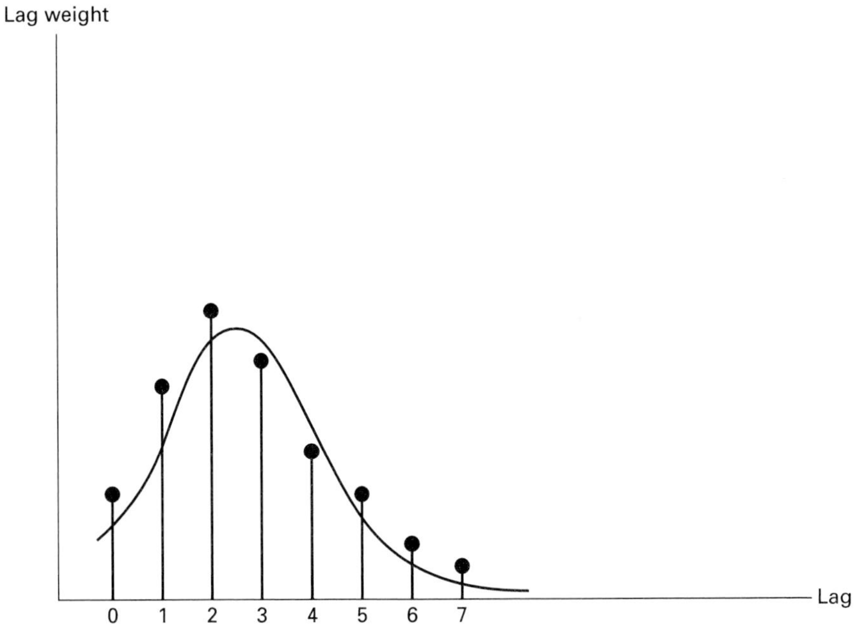

FIGURE 17.2 Polynomial Approximation.

[10]See Amemiya and Morimune (1974).

$$\mathbf{H} = \begin{bmatrix} 1 & 0 & 0 & \cdots & 0 \\ 1 & 1 & 1 & \cdots & 1 \\ 1 & 2 & 4 & \cdots & 2^p \\ 1 & 3 & 9 & & 3^p \\ & & \vdots & & \\ 1 & q & q^2 & \cdots & q^p \end{bmatrix}, \tag{17-14}$$

and write the full model as

$$\begin{aligned} \mathbf{y} &= \mathbf{XH}\boldsymbol{\alpha} + \boldsymbol{\epsilon} \\ &= \mathbf{Z}\boldsymbol{\alpha} + \boldsymbol{\epsilon}. \end{aligned} \tag{17-15}$$

In this formulation, the model can be estimated by OLS or FGLS if the disturbances are autocorrelated. Once again, this is a classical regression model, so no new tools are required. After

$$\hat{\boldsymbol{\alpha}} = [\mathbf{Z}'\mathbf{Z}]^{-1}\mathbf{Z}'\mathbf{y} \tag{17-16}$$

has been computed, estimates of the distributed lag coefficients may be recovered using

$$\hat{\boldsymbol{\beta}} = \mathbf{H}\hat{\boldsymbol{\alpha}}. \tag{17-17}$$

Asymptotic standard errors may be obtained using

$$\text{Est. Asy. Var}[\hat{\boldsymbol{\beta}}] = \mathbf{H}\{\hat{\text{Var}}[\hat{\boldsymbol{\alpha}}]\}\mathbf{H}' = s^2\mathbf{H}[\mathbf{Z}'\mathbf{Z}]^{-1}\mathbf{H}'. \tag{17-18}$$

It is suggested occasionally that the lag distribution should be "tied down" at its endpoints by imposing $\beta_{-1} = 0$ and $\beta_{q+1} = 0$.[11] Normally, it is inadvisable to impose these restrictions. The model does not pertain to the coefficients outside the interval $[0, \ldots, q]$, so the restrictions are not justifiable on theoretical grounds. But more important, the endpoint restrictions will constrain all the coefficients in the model, not just the head and tail, in ways that might not be desirable.[12]

EXAMPLE 17.3 Polynomial Distributed Lag Models

In her pioneering study, Almon (1965) estimated a polynomial lag model for the relationship between appropriations and capital expenditure for "all manufacturing" and a large number of specific industries. The aggregate quarterly data used for this study are listed in Table 17.3.[13]

[11]The implied restrictions are $\beta_{-1} = \alpha_0 - \alpha_1 + \alpha_2 - \cdots = 0$ and $\beta_{q+1} = \alpha_0 + \alpha_1(q+1) + \alpha_2(q+1)^2 + \cdots = 0$.

[12]See Schmidt and Waud (1973).

[13]The original study used quarterly data for 1953 to 1961. Longer series for the same variables may be found in Maddala (1977a, p. 370, through 1967) and Judge et al. (1982, p. 734, through 1974). Those wishing to extend these results to more recent data sets might consider these sources and the original, National Industrial Conference Board, "Survey of Capital Appropriations," *Conference Board Business Record*, various years.

TABLE 17.3 Capital Appropriations Data (Millions of Dollars)

	Expenditures				*Appropriations*			
Year	***I***	***II***	***III***	***IV***	***I***	***II***	***III***	***IV***
1953	2072	2077	2078	2043	1660	1926	2181	1897
1954	2062	2067	1964	1981	1695	1705	1731	2151
1955	1914	1991	2129	2309	2556	3152	3763	3903
1956	2614	2896	3058	3309	3912	3571	3199	3262
1957	3446	3466	3435	3183	3476	2993	2262	2011
1958	2697	2338	2140	2012	1511	1631	1990	1993
1959	2071	2192	2240	2421	2520	2804	2919	3024
1960	2639	2733	2721	2640	2725	2321	2131	2552
1961	2513	2448	2429	2516	2234	2282	2533	2517

TABLE 17.4 Polynomial Distributed Lag Models

	Unrestricted Model		*Polynomial Lag*		*Polynomial Lag with $\beta_{-1} = \beta_8 = 0$*	
	OLS	***MLE***	***OLS***	***MLE***	***OLS***	***MLE***
			Quarterly Dummy Variables			
Quarter I	−2.97	1.01	−6.98	−5.95	−13.30	−7.96
Quarter II	−5.54	−.51	−8.76	−3.00	−7.02	−3.36
Quarter III	−23.31	−14.81	−15.70	−6.41	−7.63	−4.16
Quarter IV	31.84	14.31	31.44	15.36	27.95	15.48
			Distributed Lag			
$t - 0$	0.040	0.065	0.027	0.059	0.087	0.090
$t - 1$	0.110	0.090	0.144	0.131	0.123	0.133
$t - 2$	0.189	0.199	0.182	0.169	0.134	0.147
$t - 3$	0.223	0.218	0.165	0.170	0.137	0.148
$t - 4$	0.070	0.092	0.122	0.141	0.139	0.143
$t - 5$	0.064	0.074	0.085	0.102	0.139	0.134
$t - 6$	0.139	0.140	0.088	0.085	0.129	0.115
$t - 7$	0.146	0.113	0.168	0.133	0.092	0.076
Sum	0.981	0.991	0.981	0.990	0.980	0.986
R^2	0.919	—	0.9177	—	0.9142	—
$F[q - p, 27]$			0.1331		0.3129	
D–W	0.406	—	0.445	—	0.445	—
ln L	—	−168.22	—	−169.49	—	−169.87

Almon's regressions were computed using a fourth-order polynomial and lags extending back for seven periods. She also included seasonal dummy variables whose four coefficients were constrained to sum to zero and imposed both endpoint restrictions noted earlier. The results of several regressions are reported in Table 17.4.[14] The maximum likelihood estimates were obtained

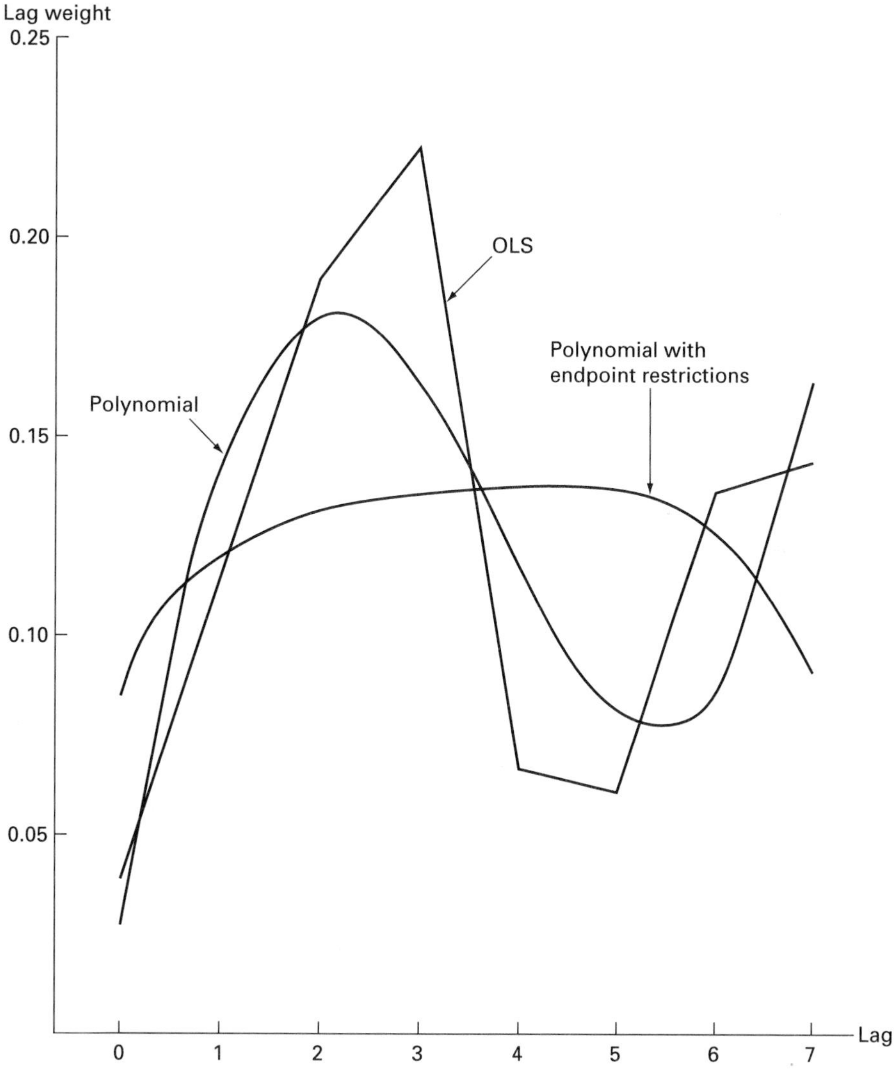

FIGURE 17.3 Polynomial Lags for Investment.

[14]The OLS results for the polynomial lag with $\beta_{-1} = \beta_8 = 0$ do not match those reported by Almon. It was not possible to reproduce her results with these data.

using Beach and MacKinnon's (1978a) method for AR(1) disturbances. For brevity, only the overall test statistics are reported.

Note the similarity of the polynomial lag coefficients to the unrestricted least squares estimates. The F test of the restrictions implied by the polynomial model is far from significant by any standard. (There are three restrictions in the lag model and two additional restrictions for the endpoint constraints.) Figure 17.3 shows the three lag distributions estimated by least squares. In principle, the sum of the lag coefficients should be 1 if all appropriations ultimately become expenditures within the length of time of the longest lag. Our results come quite close to this. (Almon's estimate of the long-run multiplier for this model was 0.922. She attributed the discrepancy to cancellations of past appropriations.)

17.2.4a. Estimation by Restricted Least Squares. If there are q lags in the model, the polynomial lag model imposes $q - p$ constraints on the parameters. A pth-order polynomial lag structure implies the constraints

$$(1 - L)^{p+1}\beta_i = 0.$$[15]

For example, for a third-order polynomial, the restrictions would be

$$\beta_0 - 4\beta_1 + 6\beta_2 - 4\beta_3 + \beta_4 = 0,$$
$$\beta_1 - 4\beta_2 + 6\beta_3 - 4\beta_4 + \beta_5 = 0,$$

and so on, with a total of $q - p$ restrictions. Thus the polynomial distributed lag model can also be estimated using constrained least squares. Ignoring for the moment any other parameters (such as the constant term) that might appear in the model, the restrictions of the polynomial lag model may be written in the form $\mathbf{R}\boldsymbol{\beta} = \mathbf{0}$. The elements in $\mathbf{R}$ are the coefficients in the binomial expansion, alternating in sign.

There are two practical advantages to this approach. First, if the maximum lag length is known, the entire analysis of the polynomial lags may be based on the single unrestricted regression involving the full set of lagged variables. Second, considerable rounding error can accumulate in calculation of the "scrambled variables" in (17-13), whereas the restricted regression is computed with the full precision of the initial least squares. In a relatively low-order polynomial, the problem will be insignificant. But for higher-order models, particularly if the data are highly collinear, the differences can be quite large.[16]

17.2.4b. Determining the Degree of the Polynomial. If the appropriate lag length q is known, determining the right degree for the polynomial becomes a problem of testing nested hypotheses. If we use a q-degree polynomial when the maximum lag is q, then $\mathbf{H}$ is square and we simply have $\boldsymbol{\alpha} = \mathbf{H}^{-1}\boldsymbol{\beta}$. As a

---

[15] See, for example, Fomby et al. (1984, pp. 375–377).

[16] See Cooper (1972).

consequence, the $q + 1$ OLS estimates (including the coefficient on x_t) will fit exactly on the qth-order polynomial. The polynomial lag model thus places no restrictions on the coefficients. Successively lower-order polynomials do impose restrictions. A sequential testing procedure may be used by beginning with a high-order polynomial, say p^*—absent any knowledge about p^*, we might use $p^* = q$—and reducing its degree by one in successive regressions.[17] At each step, the F statistic for testing a polynomial of degree p against one of the degree p^* is

$$F[p^* - p, T - p^* - 1] = \frac{[(\mathbf{e}'\mathbf{e}\,|\,p) - (\mathbf{e}'\mathbf{e}\,|\,p^*)]/(p^* - p)}{(\mathbf{e}'\mathbf{e}\,|\,p^*)/(T - p^* - 1)}. \tag{17-19}$$

The denominator degrees of freedom is reduced if there are other coefficients, such as a constant term, in the model. The appropriate degree of the polynomial is assumed to be the lowest p for which the statistic in (17-19) is less than the appropriate critical value from the F table. It must be remembered, though, that at each step except the first, the true significance level differs from the nominal one because of the probability of a type 2 error at the previous step. Trivedi and Pagan (1979) suggest that the appropriate significance level at the jth step is

$$\alpha_j' = 1 - (1 - \alpha_1)(1 - \alpha_2) \cdots (1 - \alpha_j). \tag{17-20}$$

If, as would be common, the same nominal significance level is used at each step, the true significance level would be

$$\alpha_j' = 1 - (1 - \alpha)^j.$$

For example, at the usual 5 percent significance level, we would have 5 percent, 9.75 percent, 14.26 percent, and so on for the sequential tests. The practical implication is that at successively lower levels, we should require progressively higher F statistics to reject the restrictions at the same true significance level.

17.2.4c. Determining the Lag Length. If the lag length is unknown, the problem of inference is compounded.[18] One possible procedure would be first to determine the lag length using the OLS or GLS estimates and the procedures described in the preceding section. Once the maximum lag is determined, we may then employ the method just described to determine the appropriate degree of the polynomial. Unfortunately, unless the test statistics are overwhelming, a large amount of caution must be exercised. The true significance levels in these tests remains to be derived, and the true distribution of the resulting estimator is unknown.

There has been extensive analysis of the consequences of misspecifying the lag length and order of the polynomial in the polynomial lag model. The

[17] See Godfrey and Poskitt (1975).

[18] Frost (1975).

generalities are what intuition would suggest. Assuming that there is a true polynomial and lag length, fitting a polynomial of insufficient order is equivalent to imposing invalid restrictions.[19] Overfitting the polynomial would lead only to inefficiency, since if the lag coefficients lie on a polynomial of order p, they will also lie on one of order $p + 1, p + 2$, and so on. The consequences of misspecifying the lag length are somewhat more complicated. Underestimating the lag length leads to the familiar results. Overfitting the lag may not be so harmless here, however. In an unrestricted model, the zero coefficients on superfluous variables would be consistently estimated by least squares. If we force the coefficients to lie on a polynomial, however, the restriction may force a coefficient that is truly zero to be nonzero in the model.[20]

17.2.5. The Geometric Lag Model — A Lagged Dependent Variable

Estimation of the unrestricted model of (17-10) will be difficult at best. The polynomial lag model reduces the problem, but it has some troubling limitations. Finding the right degree for the polynomial and the appropriate lag length presents difficult inference problems. The infinite lag model is often preferable, but obviously, some restrictions have to be placed on the parameters to make it estimable. These considerations have led researchers to formulate compact parametric models that allow infinite lags, but require only a small number of parameters. The geometric lag model is a common choice.[21]

The geometric lag model is

$$y_t = \alpha + \beta \sum_{i=0}^{\infty} (1 - \lambda)\lambda^i x_{t-i} + \epsilon_t, \quad |\lambda| < 1. \tag{17-21}$$

The lag coefficients are

$$\beta_i = \beta(1 - \lambda)\lambda^i. \tag{17-22}$$

This model incorporates infinite lags but assigns arbitrarily small weights to the distant past,

$$w_i = (1 - \lambda)\lambda^i, \quad 0 \leq \lambda < 1. \tag{17-23}$$

The polynomial in the lag operator in $y_t = \alpha + \beta B(L)x_t + \epsilon_t$ is

$$B(L) = (1 - \lambda)(1 + \lambda L + \lambda^2 L^2 + \lambda^3 L^3 + \cdots) = \frac{1 - \lambda}{1 - \lambda L},$$

[19] This assumption may be a bit optimistic. See Schmidt and Sickles (1975).

[20] See, for example, Schmidt and Waud (1973), Trivedi and Pagan (1979), Hendry et al. (1984), and Schmidt and Sickles (1975) for extensive discussion.

[21] The model was first associated with Koyck's (1954) study of investment.

which converges if $|\lambda| < 1$, which we have assumed. The lag mean is

$$\overline{w} = \frac{B'(1)}{B(1)} = \frac{\lambda}{1-\lambda}.$$

The median lag is q^* such that $\Sigma_{i=0}^{q^*-1} w_i = 0.5$. We can solve for q^* by using the result that

$$\sum_{i=0}^{q} \lambda^i = \frac{1-\lambda^{q+1}}{1-\lambda}.$$

Thus

$$q^* = \frac{\ln 0.5}{\ln \lambda}.$$

The impact multiplier is $\beta(1-\lambda)$. The long-run multiplier is

$$\beta(1-\lambda)\sum_{i=0}^{\infty} \lambda^i = \beta.$$

As in (17-2), the equilibrium value of y_t would be obtained by fixing x_t at $\overline{x}$ and ϵ_t at zero in (17-21). Thus,

$$\overline{y} = \alpha + \beta\overline{x}. \qquad \textbf{(17-24)}$$

17.2.5a. Economic Models with Geometric Lags. There are cases in which the distributed lag is a model of the accumulation of information. The formation of expectations is an example. In these instances, intuition suggests that the most recent past will receive the greatest weight in the process, and the influence of past observations will fade uniformly with the passage of time. The geometric lag model is a commonly used tool for these settings. It arises naturally in two familiar economic frameworks: models of expectations and models of partial adjustment.

The **adaptive expectations** model consists of a regression equation,

$$y_t = \alpha + \beta x_t^* + \epsilon_t \qquad \textbf{(17-25)}$$

in the expectations variable x_t^* and a mechanism for the formation of the expectation based on the current observation x_t:

$$x_t^* - x_{t-1}^* = (1-\lambda)(x_t - x_{t-1}^*). \qquad \textbf{(17-26)}$$

One example is a demand equation based on an expected price. The expectation would be revised after observing the current outcome. A more intuitively appealing, equivalent form might be

$$x_t^* = \lambda x_{t-1}^* + (1-\lambda)x_t. \qquad \textbf{(17-27)}$$

Thus, the currently formed expectation is a weighted average of the previous expectation and the most recent observation. The parameter λ is the adjustment coefficient. If λ equals 1, the current datum is ignored and expectations are never revised. A value of zero characterizes a strict pragmatist. The model can be "solved" by writing (17-27) as

$$x_t^* = \lambda L x_t^* + (1 - \lambda)x_t$$

or

$$\begin{aligned} x_t^* &= \frac{1-\lambda}{1-\lambda L}x_t \\ &= (1-\lambda)[x_t + \lambda x_{t-1} + \lambda^2 x_{t-2} + \cdots]. \end{aligned} \qquad \textbf{(17-28)}$$

Inserting (17-28) in (17-25) leads to a regression with geometrically declining weights:

$$y_t = \alpha + \beta(1-\lambda)[x_t + \lambda x_{t-1} + \lambda^2 x_{t-2} + \cdots] + \epsilon_t. \qquad \textbf{(17-29)}$$

The model in (17-29) is called the **moving-average (MA),** or **distributed lag** form. Estimation in this form can be done with nonlinear least squares; see Zellner and Geisel (1970), for example. But the **autoregressive (AR)** form is usually used in applications. Insert (17-28) in (17-25) to obtain

$$y_t = \alpha + \beta\left[\frac{1-\lambda}{1-\lambda L}\right]x_t + \epsilon_t.$$

Now multiply through by $(1 - \lambda L)$ and collect terms in

$$y_t = \alpha(1-\lambda) + \lambda y_{t-1} + \beta(1-\lambda)x_t + (\epsilon_t - \lambda\epsilon_{t-1}). \qquad \textbf{(17-30)}$$

The autoregressive form is often used in demand equations. If the variables are in logarithms, the short-run elasticity is $\beta(1 - \lambda)$ and the long-run elasticity is β. But for the (serious) complication of a lagged dependent variable appearing with an autocorrelated disturbance, the parameters could be estimated by OLS or two-step GLS. Unfortunately, without some special assumptions, neither of these methods will provide consistent estimates. We will consider estimation by instrumental variables below.

The primary equation of the **partial adjustment** model describes the *desired* level of y_t:

$$y_t^* = \alpha + \beta x_t. \qquad \textbf{(17-31)}$$

For example, this might describe a rule for the optimal inventory level as a function of sales. The adjustment of the actual level is a proportion of the difference between this period's desired level and last period's actual level:

$$y_t - y_{t-1} = (1-\lambda)(y_t^* - y_{t-1}) + \epsilon_t. \qquad \textbf{(17-32)}$$

In the alternative form,

$$y_t = (1-\lambda)y_t^* + \lambda y_{t-1} + \epsilon_t,$$

the actual current level is a weighted average of the desired level and last period's actual level. The adjustment parameter reflects the degree to which the input variable x_t will be incorporated in y_t. To continue the example, $\lambda = 0$ would reflect a fixed-inventory policy, whereas $\lambda = 1$ would make desired inventory a function only of current sales. Inserting (17-31) into (17-32) and rearranging terms produces the autoregressive model,

$$y_t = \alpha(1 - \lambda) + \lambda y_{t-1} + \beta(1 - \lambda)x_t + \epsilon_t. \tag{17-33}$$

17.2.5b. Estimating the Autoregressive Form of the Geometric Lag Model. The lagged dependent variable removes the autoregressive model from the classical regression framework. Depending on the formulation of u_t, the estimation may be further complicated by autocorrelation. For example, in the adaptive expectations model, the disturbance is $u_t = \epsilon_t - \lambda\epsilon_{t-1}$, where the same regression parameter λ enters the disturbance process. As we saw in Section 13.4.1, autocorrelation in the presence of a lagged dependent variable renders the usual two-step procedures ineffective because the estimates at the first step are inconsistent.[22] In the partial adjustment model, ϵ_t might be a classical disturbance, but in time-series data, autocorrelation is likely to be a problem anyway.

17.2.5c. Uncorrelated Disturbances. Even if ϵ_t is not serially correlated, the classical assumption that ϵ_t is uncorrelated with $z_s = [1, x_s, y_{s-1}]$ *for all t and s* is violated. Since y_t embodies all *previous* values y_s, it follows that every ϵ_t is correlated with every *subsequent* y_s. The correlation does fade with increasing separation in time, however, with the consequence that despite this complication and its stochastic regressor, (17-33) may be treated as a classical regression, at least asymptotically. The requirements that

$$|\lambda| < 1$$

and

$$\text{plim}\,\frac{1}{T}\sum_{t=1}^{T}\begin{bmatrix}1\\ x_t\\ y_{t-1}\end{bmatrix}[1, x_t, y_{t-1}] = \mathbf{Q},$$

where $\mathbf{Q}$ is a positive definite matrix, are sufficient to ensure that the OLS estimates retain their desirable *asymptotic* properties. The exact finite-sample properties are largely unknown.[23] We can show that OLS is the asymptotically efficient estimator for the partial adjustment model, assuming that the disturbance in (17-33) is not autocorrelated.

[22]For some overviews, see, for example, Grether and Maddala (1973) and Dhrymes (1969 and 1971).

[23]Doran and Griffiths (1978). See also Schmidt (1976, pp. 96–101).

17.2.5d. Autocorrelated Disturbances—Instrumental Variables. If ϵ_t is autocorrelated, OLS estimates based on (17-33) are biased and inconsistent. (See Section 13.4.1 for a derivation of the precise result when there is no regressor.[24]) There are, however, several ways to obtain consistent estimates.

The method of instrumental variables was introduced in Section 6.7.8 and used in Section 13.7.3 for precisely the problem facing us here. To reiterate, let $\mathbf{X} = [\mathbf{i}, \mathbf{x}, \mathbf{y}_{-1}]$. The problem is that

$$\text{plim}\,\frac{1}{T}\mathbf{X}'\boldsymbol{\epsilon} \neq \mathbf{0}.$$

The instrumental variable estimator of the parameter vector $\boldsymbol{\theta}$,

$$\hat{\boldsymbol{\theta}}_{\text{IV}} = (\mathbf{Z}'\mathbf{X})^{-1}\mathbf{Z}'\mathbf{y},$$

will be consistent and asymptotically normally distributed as

$$\hat{\boldsymbol{\theta}}_{\text{IV}} \xrightarrow{a} N[\boldsymbol{\theta}, \sigma_\epsilon^2(\mathbf{Z}'\mathbf{X})^{-1}(\mathbf{Z}'\mathbf{Z})(\mathbf{X}'\mathbf{Z})^{-1}], \qquad \textbf{(17-34)}$$

provided that the matrix of instrumental variables satisfies the two requirements

$$\text{plim}\,\frac{1}{T}\mathbf{Z}'\boldsymbol{\epsilon} = \mathbf{0} \quad \text{and} \quad \text{plim}\,\frac{1}{T}\mathbf{Z}'\mathbf{X} \neq \mathbf{0}. \qquad \textbf{(17-35)}$$

The constant and $\mathbf{x}$ can serve as their own instruments. A frequent choice for the instrumental variable for y_{t-1} is x_{t-1}, leading to $\mathbf{Z} = [\mathbf{i}, \mathbf{x}, \mathbf{x}_{-1}]$.[25] It is useful to note at this point that if the instrumental variables satisfy (17-35), $\hat{\boldsymbol{\theta}}_{\text{IV}}$ is consistent *regardless of the type of autocorrelation in* ϵ. Thus, that the adaptive expectations model contains an MA(1) disturbance rather than the familiar AR(1) does not affect the result.

17.2.5e. Autoregressive Disturbances—Hatanaka's Estimator and the Maximum Likelihood Estimator. Although the IV estimator is consistent, it is generally inefficient. Hatanaka (1976) showed that a second-round estimator using the IV estimator at the first step would have the same asymptotic properties as the maximum likelihood estimator for normally distributed AR(1) disturbances. (However, he did raise some questions about the small sample performance of the estimator.) The procedure, detailed in Section 13.7.3, is as follows.

[24]For an extensive analysis of the finite-sample properties of OLS in this model, see Maeshiro (1996).

[25]Liviatan (1963).

1. Use the IV estimator to estimate the parameters, then compute $\hat{\rho}$ using the residuals.
2. Regress $y_t - \hat{\rho}y_{t-1}$ on a constant, $x_t - \hat{\rho}x_{t-1}, y_{t-1} - \hat{\rho}y_{t-2}$, and $\hat{u}_{t-1}$.

The appropriate asymptotic covariance matrix is the conventional estimator computed at step 2.

For normally distributed disturbances, we may also compute a maximum likelihood estimator. If $\epsilon_t = \rho\epsilon_{t-1} + u_t$, then

$$u_t = (y_t - \rho y_{t-1}) - \alpha(1-\lambda)(1-\rho) - \beta(1-\lambda)(x_t - \rho x_{t-1}) - \lambda(y_{t-1} - \rho y_{t-2}). \quad \textbf{(17-36)}$$

Conditioned on the initial observations, the estimates that minimize the sum of squares provide the maximum likelihood estimates. For a given value of ρ, this requires only a linear regression of δy_t on a constant δx_t and δy_{t-1}, where $\delta x_t = x_t - \rho x_{t-1}$. Since the OLS estimates are inconsistent, the Cochrane–Orcutt method will not necessarily produce a consistent estimate, even if it is iterated.[26] A simple expedient is to scan the range of $-1 < \rho < 1$ for the value that produces the global minimum of $\Sigma_{t=1}^T u_t^2$. Alternatively, if the process is begun with a consistent estimator of ρ, such as the IV estimator, the second-step (and subsequent) estimators will have the desirable properties of maximum likelihood estimators. Standard errors for the maximum likelihood estimates of $[\alpha(1-\lambda), \beta(1-\lambda), \lambda, \rho, \sigma_u^2]$ may be obtained from the inverse of the estimate of the information matrix,

$$\mathbf{I}\begin{bmatrix}\gamma\\ \theta\\ \lambda\\ \rho\\ \sigma_u^2\end{bmatrix} = \frac{1}{\sigma_u^2}\begin{bmatrix} T(1-\rho)^2 & & & & \\ (1-\rho)\sum_{t=2}^{T}\delta x_t & \sum_{t=2}^{T}(\delta x_t)^2 & & & \\ (1-\rho)\sum_{t=2}^{T}\delta y_{t-1} & \sum_{t=2}^{T}\delta x_t\delta y_{t-1} & \sum_{t=2}^{T}(\delta y_{t-1})^2 & & \\ 0 & 0 & T\sigma_u^2/(1-\lambda) & T\sigma_u^2/(1-\rho^2) & \\ 0 & 0 & 0 & 0 & T/(2\sigma_u^4)\end{bmatrix}, \quad \textbf{(17-37)}$$

where $\gamma = \alpha(1-\lambda)$ and $\theta = \beta(1-\lambda)$.[27] Standard errors for the individual estimates of α and β can be computed using the delta method for the variance of a nonlinear function.

---

[26]Betancourt and Kelejian (1981) and Fomby and Guilkey (1983).

[27]The counterpart to the 4,3 element in Johnston (1984, p. 367) is in error. It is obtained here as $TE[(-\partial u_t/\partial\lambda)(-\partial u_t/\partial\rho)]$. We use (17-36) to find $-\partial u_t/\partial\lambda = y_{t-1} - \rho y_{t-2}$ and $u_t = \epsilon_t - \rho\epsilon_{t-1}$ to obtain $-\partial u_t/\partial\rho = \epsilon_{t-1}$. Now write (17-33) as $y_s = \alpha + \beta(1-\lambda)x_s/(1-\lambda L)$ for $s = t-1$ and $t-2$. Therefore, $E[\epsilon_{t-1}y_{t-1}] = \sigma_\epsilon^2/(1-\lambda)$ and $\rho E[\epsilon_{t-1}y_{t-2}] = \rho^2\sigma_\epsilon^2/(1-\lambda)$. Combining terms and imposing $\sigma_\epsilon^2 = \sigma_u^2/(1-\rho^2)$ leads to the previous result. For $\partial u_t/\partial\lambda$, note that $\alpha(1-\lambda)$ and $\beta(1-\lambda)$ are free parameters, δ and θ.

TABLE 17.5 Consumption and Income Data

	Consumption				*Disposable Income*			
Year	***I***	***II***	***III***	***IV***	***I***	***II***	***III***	***IV***
1953	362.8	364.6	363.6	362.6	395.5	401.0	399.7	400.2
1954	363.5	366.2	371.8	378.6	399.7	397.3	403.8	411.8
1955	385.2	392.2	396.4	402.6	414.7	423.8	430.8	437.6
1956	403.2	403.9	405.1	409.3	441.2	444.7	446.6	452.7
1957	411.7	412.4	415.2	416.0	452.6	455.4	457.9	456.0
1958	411.0	414.7	420.9	425.2	452.1	455.1	464.6	471.3
1959	424.1	439.7	443.3	444.6	474.5	482.2	479.0	483.1
1960	448.1	454.1	452.7	453.2	487.8	490.7	491.0	488.8
1961	454.0	459.9	461.4	470.3	493.4	500.7	505.5	514.8
1962	474.5	479.8	483.7	490.0	519.5	523.9	526.7	529.0
1963	493.1	497.4	503.9	507.5	533.3	538.9	544.4	552.5
1964	516.6	525.6	534.3	535.3	563.6	579.4	586.4	593.0
1965	546.0	550.7	559.2	573.9	599.7	607.8	623.6	634.6
1966	581.2	582.3	588.6	590.5	639.7	642.0	649.2	700.7
1967	594.8	602.4	605.2	608.2	665.0	671.3	676.5	682.0
1968	620.7	629.9	642.3	644.7	690.4	701.9	703.6	708.7
1969	651.9	656.2	659.6	663.9	710.4	717.0	730.1	733.2
1970	667.4	670.5	676.5	673.9	737.1	752.6	759.7	756.1
1971	687.0	693.3	698.2	708.6	771.3	779.7	781.0	785.5
1972	718.6	731.1	741.3	757.1	791.7	798.5	842.2	838.1
1973	768.8	766.3	769.7	766.7	855.0	862.1	868.0	873.4
1974	761.2	764.1	769.4	756.5	859.9	859.7	859.7	851.1
1975	763.3	775.6	785.4	793.3	845.1	891.3	878.4	884.9
1976	809.9	817.1	826.5	838.9	899.3	904.1	908.8	914.9
1977	851.7	858.0	867.3	880.4	919.6	934.1	951.9	965.9
1978	883.8	901.1	908.6	919.2	973.5	982.6	994.2	1005.0
1979	921.2	919.5	930.9	938.6	1011.1	1011.8	1019.7	1020.2
1980	938.3	919.6	929.4	940.0	1025.9	1011.8	1019.3	1030.2
1981	950.2	949.1	955.7	946.8	1044.0	1041.0	1058.4	1056.0
1982	953.7	958.9	964.2	976.3	1052.8	1054.7	1057.7	1067.5
1983	982.5	1006.2	1015.6	1032.4	1073.3	1082.2	1102.1	1124.4
1984	1044.1	1064.2	1065.9	1075.4	1147.8	1165.3	1176.7	1186.9

Source: Data from the National Income and Product Accounts, U.S. Department of Commerce, Bureau of Economic Analysis, *Survey of Current Business: Business Statistics, 1984,* Washington, D.C., 1984, pp. 205, 212, and 221. The data are normalized to 1972 dollars, using the implicit price deflator for personal consumption.

EXAMPLE 17.4 Consumption Function

In a widely cited study, Zellner and Geisel (1970) applied the foregoing results to estimation of a consumption function

$$C_t = \beta Y_t^* + \epsilon_t,$$

where C_t is consumption and Y_t^* is normal real income. Normal income satisfies the adjustment model:

$$Y_t^* = (1 - \lambda)Y_t + \lambda Y_{t-1}^*.$$

Then

$$Y_t^* = \frac{1 - \lambda}{1 - \lambda L} Y_t,$$

so

$$C_t = \beta \frac{1 - \lambda}{1 - \lambda L} Y_t + \epsilon_t.$$

The autoregressive model is then

$$C_t = \lambda C_{t-1} + \beta(1 - \lambda)Y_t + \epsilon_t - \lambda\epsilon_{t-1}.$$

The authors estimated the model using quarterly data on U.S. consumption and disposable personal income for the years 1947 to 1960.[28] In this example, we reestimate the model using more recent data and then compare our results with those of Zellner and Geisel. Table 17.5 lists quarterly data for real consumption and real disposable income for the years 1953 to 1984. Using the

TABLE 17.6 Estimates of a Geometric Lag Model for Consumption

	Least Squares	*Instrumental Variables*	*Hatanaka Two-Step*	*AR(1) with Grid Search*	*Zellner–Geisel*
$\beta(1 - \lambda)$	0.1767	0.4651	0.2863	0.2423	0.321
	(0.0451)	(0.1115)	(0.0560)	(0.0498)	—
λ	0.8119	0.4913	0.6901	0.7386	0.66
	(0.0502)	(0.1240)	(0.0623)	(0.0555)	(0.085)
β	0.9394	0.9142	0.9238	0.9269	0.94
	(0.0148)	(0.0122)	(0.0078)	(0.0067)	(0.46)
$\frac{\lambda}{1-\lambda}$	4.32	0.966	2.27	2.83	1.94
	(1.419)	(0.4791)	(0.6487)	(0.8122)	(0.74)
ρ	0	0	0.3869	0.27	0.69
	—	—	(0.0805)	(0.0861)	(0.076)
$\frac{\mathbf{e}'\mathbf{e}}{T}$	29.26	31.41	28.38	27.78	—

[28]Their data are listed in Griliches et al. (1962).

techniques described earlier, we obtain the estimates in Table 17.6 for the autoregressive form of the consumption function. Estimated asymptotic standard errors are given in parentheses. The grid search produced a single minimum of the sum of squared deviations. The sum of squares declined monotonically from 5384 at $\rho = -0.5$ to the minimum of 3500.04 at $\rho = 0.27$, then increased monotonically to 4735 at $\rho = 0.9$.

17.3. DYNAMIC REGRESSION MODELS

The polynomial lag model has the attractive feature that it allows a great deal of flexibility in the shape of the lag distribution. In contrast, the geometric lag model imposes a declining pattern of the lag weights that might be inconsistent with the data. Unlike the geometric lag model, however, the polynomial model truncates the distribution at an arbitrarily chosen point and requires an estimate of the degree of the polynomial. Many alternatives to these two popular functional forms have been devised that combine the desirable features of both models.[29] A very general specification that has proved useful in recent applications is Jorgenson's (1966) **rational lag model,** or in most recent literature, the **autoregressive distributed lag (ARDL)** model,

$$y_t = \mu + \frac{B(L)}{C(L)}x_t + \epsilon_t. \tag{17-38}$$

$B(L)$ and $C(L)$ are polynomials in the lag operator.[30] The ratio of two polynomials in the lag operator can produce essentially any desired shape of the lag distribution with relatively few parameters. The autoregressive form is

$$C(L)y_t = \alpha + B(L)x_t + C(L)\epsilon_t. \tag{17-39}$$

In this form, the model has lagged dependent and independent variables and a moving-average (MA) disturbance. For example, if both $B(L)$ and $C(L)$ are quadratic, then

$$y_t = \mu + \frac{\beta_0 + \beta_1 L + \beta_2 L^2}{1 - \gamma_1 L - \gamma_2 L^2}x_t + \epsilon_t,$$

or

[29]The sources mentioned in the introduction to this chapter provide extensive summaries. Maddala (1977a) also provides a concise catalog with many useful observations on the mechanics of estimation. There is a bit of gadgetry in some of the proposed lag distributions, but unfortunately, economic theory is usually silent on what a lag distribution should look like. The data themselves and the resourcefulness of the analyst often provide most of the guidance.

[30]We could add additional independent variables, each with its own lag structure. But that would add notation without changing the essential character of the model. Our assumption of only a single regressor is purely for convenience.

$$y_t = \mu(1 - \gamma_1 - \gamma_2) + \beta_0 x_t + \beta_1 x_{t-1} + \beta_2 x_{t-2} + \gamma_1 y_{t-1} + \gamma_2 y_{t-2} + \epsilon_t - \gamma_1 \epsilon_{t-1} - \gamma_2 \epsilon_{t-2}.$$[31]

In (17-39), the same lag structure is applied to ϵ_t and y_t. This is an unnecessary and sometimes undesirable restriction on the model. A much more general, flexible model is obtained by allowing the disturbance to have a dynamic structure of its own. The resulting model is

$$C(L)y_t = \alpha + B(L)x_t + D(L)\epsilon_t, \tag{17-40}$$

where $\alpha = \mu C(1)$. This is known as an ARMAX model.[32] An important special case is the ARMA model, which is an ARMAX model with no regressor:

$$y_t = \alpha + \gamma_1 y_{t-1} + \gamma_2 y_{t-2} + \cdots + \gamma_p y_{t-p} + \epsilon_t - \theta_1 \epsilon_{t-1} - \cdots - \theta_q \epsilon_{t-q}. \tag{17-41}$$

The conventional notation ARMA(p, q) or ARMAX(p, q) indicates the number of lagged terms in the AR part, $C(L)y_t$, and MA part, $D(L)\epsilon_t$, respectively. The example given earlier is an ARMAX(2, 2) model. ARMAX and ARMA models are pervasive in the analysis of time series. For the present, we will continue to analyze them in the context of dynamic regression models. Alternative uses and interpretations are considered in Chapter 18.

The disturbance ϵ_t in (17-40) is taken to be a serially uncorrelated, constant variance random variable. That is, we have not allowed for the possibility of autoregressive disturbances of the sort that have appeared repeatedly in previous models. In fact, no generality had been lost, since we may assume that if the original disturbance were subject to autoregression, (17-40) is the result of partial differencing that has removed that part of the disturbance process. Second, even allowing for more than one exogenous variable, as long as $B(L)$ has a finite number of terms for each, the exogenous part of the model could simply be written as

$$\sum_i B_i(L)x_{ti} = \boldsymbol{\beta}'\mathbf{x}_t$$

for some set of unknown coefficients and contemporaneous and lagged values x_{si}. Finally, the variables in the model, y_t and x_t, could themselves have been

---

[31]Note that the leading coefficient in $C(L)$ is normalized to 1. This is necessary because the two polynomials could each be multiplied by the same constant without changing the dynamic model. To remove the indeterminacy, γ_0 is set to equal to 1. The result is nothing more than to eliminate an unknown coefficient on the dependent variable in the regression.

[32]It is also known as a transfer function. Functions of this sort have been used extensively in engineering applications. In that context, x_t represents the **impulse** and what we have identified as the distributed lag coefficients are the **impulse response characteristics.** Harvey (1990) contains extensive discussion and numerous examples of transfer functions and ARMAX models. An application appears in Example 16.21.

differenced one or more times.[33] (See Example 17.5 below.) As such, a quite general formulation of the ARMAX model is

$$y_t = \mu + \gamma_1 y_{t-1} + \cdots + \gamma_p y_{t-p} + \boldsymbol{\beta}'\mathbf{x}_t + \epsilon_t - \theta_1\epsilon_{t-1} - \cdots - \theta_q\epsilon_{t-q}. \quad \textbf{(17-42)}$$

What appears to be a simple modification of the basic ARMA model produces a dynamic model of considerable generality.[34]

17.3.1. Nonlinear Least Squares Estimation of ARMA and ARMAX Models

If there are no moving average terms in (17-42), it is a linear regression model with stochastic regressors. The results of Mann and Wald (1943) and the discussion of Section 6.7.10 apply. The parameter vector

$$\boldsymbol{\phi} = [\mu, \gamma_1, \ldots, \gamma_p, \beta_1, \ldots, \beta_K]'$$

may be estimated consistently by ordinary least squares regression of y_t on

$$\mathbf{z}_t = [1, y_{t-1}, y_{t-2}, \ldots, y_{t-p}, \mathbf{x}_t']'.$$

(Recall that $\mathbf{x}_t$ may also contain lagged values of exogenous variables.) The OLS estimator in this setting would be asymptotically normally distributed with asymptotic covariance matrix

$$\text{Asy. Var}[\hat{\boldsymbol{\phi}}] = \frac{1}{T-p}\,\text{plim}\,\sigma_\epsilon^2\left(\frac{\mathbf{Z}'\mathbf{Z}}{T-p}\right)^{-1}.$$

The disturbance variance σ_ϵ^2 may be estimated residually as usual, since

$$\text{plim}\frac{1}{T-p}\sum_{t=p+1}^{T}\hat{\epsilon}_t^2 = \sigma_\epsilon^2.$$

Under the Mann and Wald conditions, ordinary, linear least squares estimation and inference procedures are valid asymptotically. Henceforth, we assume that this is the case.

When there are moving average disturbances, the model becomes nonlinear. In this case, the nonlinear least squares estimator will be consistent and asymptotically normally distributed. If ϵ_t is assumed to be normally distributed, nonlinear least squares, conditioned on the initial observations, will also be maximum likelihood. As such, least squares will also be efficient. But ordinary, linear least squares applied to (17-42) will not even be consistent. The model

[33]This produces an *ARIMA model,* which is developed further in Chapter 18.

[34]Extensive analysis of the many special cases appears in Granger and Watson (1984), Hendry et al. (1984), and Harvey (1990).

contains both lagged dependent variables and autocorrelation.[35] The sum of squares to be minimized is

$$S(\mu, \boldsymbol{\gamma}, \boldsymbol{\beta}, \boldsymbol{\theta}) = S(\boldsymbol{\phi}) = \sum_{t=1}^{T} \epsilon_t^2 .$$

Nonlinear least squares estimates of the dynamic regression model can be obtained as follows. The iteration is based on the Gauss–Newton method.[36] The iteration is

$$\hat{\boldsymbol{\phi}}^{s+1} = \hat{\boldsymbol{\phi}}^{s} - [\mathbf{G}_s'\mathbf{G}_s]^{-1}\mathbf{G}_s'\hat{\boldsymbol{\epsilon}}_s,$$

where $\mathbf{G}_s$ is a $(T - p - q) \times (1 + p + K + q)$ matrix of derivatives of the residuals with respect to the parameters. The derivatives are computed as follows:

$$\frac{\partial \epsilon_t}{\partial \mu} = 1 - \theta_1\left(\frac{\partial \epsilon_{t-1}}{\partial \mu}\right) - \cdots - \theta_q\left(\frac{\partial \epsilon_{t-q}}{\partial \mu}\right),$$

$$\frac{\partial \epsilon_t}{\partial \gamma_i} = y_{t-i} - \theta_1\left(\frac{\partial \epsilon_{t-1}}{\partial \gamma_i}\right) - \cdots - \theta_q\left(\frac{\partial \epsilon_{t-q}}{\partial \gamma_i}\right), \quad i = 1, \ldots, p,$$

$$\frac{\partial \epsilon_t}{\partial \beta_k} = x_{tk} - \theta_1\left(\frac{\partial \epsilon_{t-1}}{\partial \beta_k}\right) - \cdots - \theta_q\left(\frac{\partial \epsilon_{t-q}}{\partial \beta_k}\right), \quad k = 1, \ldots, K,$$

$$\frac{\partial \epsilon_t}{\partial \theta_j} = \epsilon_{t-j} - \theta_1\left(\frac{\partial \epsilon_{t-1}}{\partial \theta_j}\right) - \cdots - \theta_q\left(\frac{\partial \epsilon_{t-q}}{\partial \theta_j}\right), \quad j = 1, \ldots, q.$$

These are difference equations that can be computed recursively after initializing ϵ_t and the derivatives with q zeros. In a matrix format, we would have

$$\mathbf{G}_{\mu,t} = \left[\frac{\partial \epsilon_{t-s}}{\partial \mu}\right], \quad s = 1, \ldots, q(1 \times q),$$

$$\mathbf{G}_{\gamma,t} = \left[\frac{\partial \epsilon_{t-s}}{\partial \boldsymbol{\gamma}}\right], \quad s = 1, \ldots, q(p \times q),$$

$$\mathbf{G}_{\beta,t} = \left[\frac{\partial \epsilon_{t-s}}{\partial \boldsymbol{\beta}}\right], \quad s = 1, \ldots, q(K \times q),$$

$$\mathbf{G}_{\theta,t} = \left[\frac{\partial \epsilon_{t-s}}{\partial \boldsymbol{\theta}}\right], \quad s = 1, \ldots, q(q \times q).$$

Then the tth row of $\mathbf{G}_s$ is

$$\mathbf{g}_s^{(t)} = \left[\left(\frac{\partial \epsilon_t}{\partial \mu}\right), \left(\frac{\partial \epsilon_t}{\partial \boldsymbol{\gamma}'}\right), \left(\frac{\partial \epsilon_t}{\partial \boldsymbol{\beta}'}\right), \left(\frac{\partial \epsilon_t}{\partial \boldsymbol{\theta}'}\right)\right],$$

[35] See Section 13.4.1.

[36] See Section 10.2.3. Note that the ARMA model is a special case in which there is no exogenous variable. Thus, there is no need to consider ARMA models separately from ARMAX models.

where

$$\frac{\partial \epsilon_t}{\partial \mu} = 1 - \mathbf{G}_{\mu,t}\boldsymbol{\theta},$$
$$\frac{\partial \epsilon_t}{\partial \boldsymbol{\gamma}} = \mathbf{y}_{\text{lags}} - \mathbf{G}_{\gamma,t}\boldsymbol{\theta},$$
$$\frac{\partial \epsilon_t}{\partial \boldsymbol{\beta}} = \mathbf{x}_t - \mathbf{G}_{\beta,t}\boldsymbol{\theta},$$
$$\frac{\partial \epsilon_t}{\partial \boldsymbol{\theta}} = \boldsymbol{\epsilon}_{\text{lags}} - \mathbf{G}_{\theta,t}\boldsymbol{\theta}.$$

An instrumental variables estimator can be used to obtain starting values. We can use lagged values of the exogenous variables $\mathbf{x}_t$ as instruments for $[y_{t-1}, \ldots, y_{t-p}]$. Constructing initial values for $[\theta_1, \ldots, \theta_q]$ is a bit involved. Box and Jenkins (1984) suggest the following method of moments estimation procedure, which can be based on the residuals from the instrumental variable estimator.

1. Let $c_i, i = 0, 1, \ldots, q$, be the sample covariances of e_t and e_{t-i}. (These are *autocovariances*.) Start with $\boldsymbol{\theta} = 0$.
2. Compute $s^2 = c_0/(1 + \boldsymbol{\theta}'\boldsymbol{\theta})$.
3. For $i = q, q-1, \ldots, 1$ (working backward), compute $\theta_i = c_i/s^2 - \Sigma_{j=1}^{q-i}\theta_j\theta_{j+i}$.
4. Check for convergence based on the change from the last iteration. If so, exit; otherwise, return to step 2.

This method may not converge. The estimates may diverge, in which case the specification of the model becomes suspect. Overfitting—that is, specifying too many moving average terms—can lead to this condition. After the parameters have been estimated, the variance estimator is

$$\hat{\sigma}_\epsilon^2 = \frac{1}{T-p-1-K-q}\sum_{t=p+q+1}^{T}\hat{\epsilon}_t^2,$$

where

$$\hat{\epsilon}_t = y_t - \hat{\gamma}_1 y_{t-1} - \cdots - \hat{\gamma}_p y_{t-p} - \hat{\mu} - \hat{\boldsymbol{\beta}}'\mathbf{x}_t + \hat{\theta}_1\hat{\epsilon}_{t-1} + \cdots + \hat{\theta}_q\hat{\epsilon}_{t-q}. \quad \textbf{(17-43)}$$

The estimated asymptotic covariance matrix for the parameter estimates is

$$\text{Est. Asy. Var}[\hat{\boldsymbol{\phi}}] = \hat{\sigma}_\epsilon^2(\hat{\mathbf{G}}'\hat{\mathbf{G}})^{-1},$$

where $\mathbf{G}$ is the $(T-p-q) \times (1+K+p+q)$ matrix of derivatives of the residuals with respect to the parameters. [This is (10-13).] The matrix is the sum of squares and cross products computed at the last iteration.[37]

[37]Harvey (1990, pp. 207–210) provides further discussion of the estimation problem for this model. With normally distributed disturbances, the estimator described here is an "approximate MLE," conditioned on the initial observations. Normality may be a bit much to ask for, but asymptotic properties of nonlinear least squares may be claimed in any event.

EXAMPLE 17.5 ARMAX Model

To continue Example 17.2, we will analyze the ARMAX model

$$\Delta \ln\left(\frac{Y_t}{P_t}\right) = \mu + \beta_0\Delta \ln\left(\frac{M_t}{P_t}\right) + \beta_1\Delta \ln\left(\frac{M_{t-1}}{P_{t-1}}\right)$$
$$+ \beta_2\Delta \ln\left(\frac{M_{t-2}}{P_{t-2}}\right) + \gamma_1\Delta \ln\left(\frac{Y_{t-1}}{P_{t-1}}\right) + \beta_2\Delta \ln\left(\frac{Y_{t-2}}{P_{t-2}}\right) + \epsilon_t - \theta\epsilon_{t-1}.$$

We will use this model to analyze the effect of changes in the rate of growth of M1 on the growth of real output. Nonlinear least squares estimates of the parameter are given in Table 17.7.

Using a likelihood ratio statistic, we find that the two lagged values of the output variable are not significant with the moving-average term present,

$$\text{LR}_{\text{MA}} = 132 \ln\frac{0.008785^2}{0.008676^2} = 3.1712$$

but they are when it is omitted:

$$\text{LR} = 132 \ln\frac{0.008930^2}{0.008676^2} = 17.094.$$

The 5 percent critical value from the chi-squared distribution is 5.99. The corresponding F statistics defined in (10-51) are 1.537 and 7.049, and the critical

TABLE 17.7 Estimated ARMAX Models (Estimated Standard Errors in Parentheses)

	ARMAX	*Distributed Lag/MA*	*Distributed Lag*	*ARDL*
	0.003122	0.006952	0.006871	0.005027
	(0.002482)	(0.000577)	(0.000832)	(0.001066)
β_0	0.25449	0.29027	0.25756	0.27304
	(0.07064)	(0.07068)	(0.07392)	(0.07159)
β_1	0.080251	0.27887	0.27152	0.18488
	(0.14841)	(0.07270)	(0.07292)	(0.07501)
β_2	0.080062	0.19309	0.22649	0.15180
	(0.09204)	(0.07102)	(0.074079)	(0.07679)
γ_1	0.70340	—	—	0.29705
	(0.46196)			(0.08976)
γ_2	−0.15389	—	—	−0.03488
	(0.017993)			(0.08519)
θ_1	−0.43921	0.27191	—	—
	(0.48094)	(0.86066)		
σ_ϵ	0.008676	0.008785	0.009280	0.008930
e′e	0.009484	0.009725	0.010589	0.009659

Data: Quarterly, 1952.III to 1983.IV. $T = 126$.

value from the table is 3.09. The moving-average term is not significant; the asymptotic t ratio is only -0.913 with the lagged dependent variables and 0.438 without them. The autoregressive terms are not significant in the presence of the moving-average term, whereas they are when it is absent. This suggests that perhaps the full model with both AR and MA terms might be overparameterized. It remains to be seen whether this model suggests that changes in the growth rate of $M1$ ultimately translate into changes in the growth of output. We pursue that in the examples to follow.

17.3.2. Computation of the Lag Weights in the ARMAX Model

The lag coefficients on $x_t, x_{t-1}, \ldots$ in the model in (17-38) are the individual terms in the ratio of polynomials. We denote these as

$$\alpha_0, \alpha_1, \alpha_2, \ldots = \text{the coefficient on } 1, L, L^2, \ldots \text{ in } B(L)/C(L). \qquad \textbf{(17-44)}$$

A convenient way to compute these lag coefficients is to write the left-hand side of (17-44) as $A(L)$ and note that (17-44) implies that $A(L)C(L) = B(L)$. So we can just equate coefficients. Example 17.6 demonstrates the procedure.

EXAMPLE 17.6 Lag Weights in a Rational Lag Model

The systematic part of the model in Example 17.5 is

$$y_t = \mu + \gamma_1 y_{t-1} + \gamma_2 y_{t-2} + \beta_0 x_t + \beta_1 x_{t-1} + \beta_2 x_{t-2}.$$ [38]

The lag coefficients are given by the equality

$$(\alpha_0 + \alpha_1 L + \alpha_2 L^2 + \cdots)(1 - \gamma_1 L - \gamma_2 L^2) = (\beta_0 + \beta_1 L + \beta_2 L^2).$$

Note that $A(L)$ is an infinite polynomial. Thus, the lag coefficients are

$$\begin{aligned}
1:&\quad \alpha_0 &&= \beta_0 \text{ (this will always be the case)},\\
L:&\quad -\alpha_0\gamma_1 + \alpha_1 &&= \beta_1 \text{ or } \alpha_1 = \beta_1 + \alpha_0\gamma_1,\\
L:&\quad -\alpha_0\gamma_2 - \alpha_1\gamma_1 + \alpha_2 &&= \beta_2 \text{ or } \alpha_2 = \beta_2 + \alpha_0\gamma_2 + \alpha_1\gamma_1,\\
L:&\quad -\alpha_1\gamma_2 - \alpha_2\gamma_1 + \alpha_3 &&= 0 \text{ or } \alpha_3 = \alpha_2\gamma_1 + \alpha_1\gamma_2,\\
L:&\quad -\alpha_2\gamma_2 - \alpha_3\gamma_1 + \alpha_4 &&= 0,
\end{aligned}$$

and so on. Notice that from the fourth term onward, the series follows the recursion

$$\alpha_k = \gamma_1\alpha_{k-1} + \gamma_2\alpha_{k-2}. \qquad \textbf{(17-45)}$$

The general result is that after a few initial terms that involve the lag coefficients in $B(L)$, the series of lag weights will follow the same difference

---

[38]The dynamic characteristics of the systematic part of the equation are unrelated to ϵ_t or any moving-average terms, so we have omitted that part of the model.

equation that the lagged values of y_t follow in the autoregressive part of the model. Thus, the lag coefficients are calculated using a simple recursion. For the most general model in Table 17.7, the first nine terms are

$$\boldsymbol{\alpha} = [0.2544, 0.2593, 0.2233, 0.1171, 0.0481, 0.0158, 0.0037, 0.0002, -0.0005].$$

The coefficients replicate the unrestricted lag model in Table 17.2 surprisingly well.

The long-run effect in a rational lag model is $\Sigma_{i=0}^{\infty}\alpha_i$. This is easy to compute, since it is simply

$$\sum_{i=0}^{\infty} \alpha_i = \frac{B(1)}{C(1)}. \tag{17-46}$$

For the four models listed in Table 17.7, (17-46) gives 0.92078, 0.76223, 0.75557, and 0.82637, respectively.

The results obtained with this model are similar to those in Table 17.3. The two lag distributions are shown in Figure 17.4. The solid curve is the unrestricted model, the dashed one is the ARMAX model.

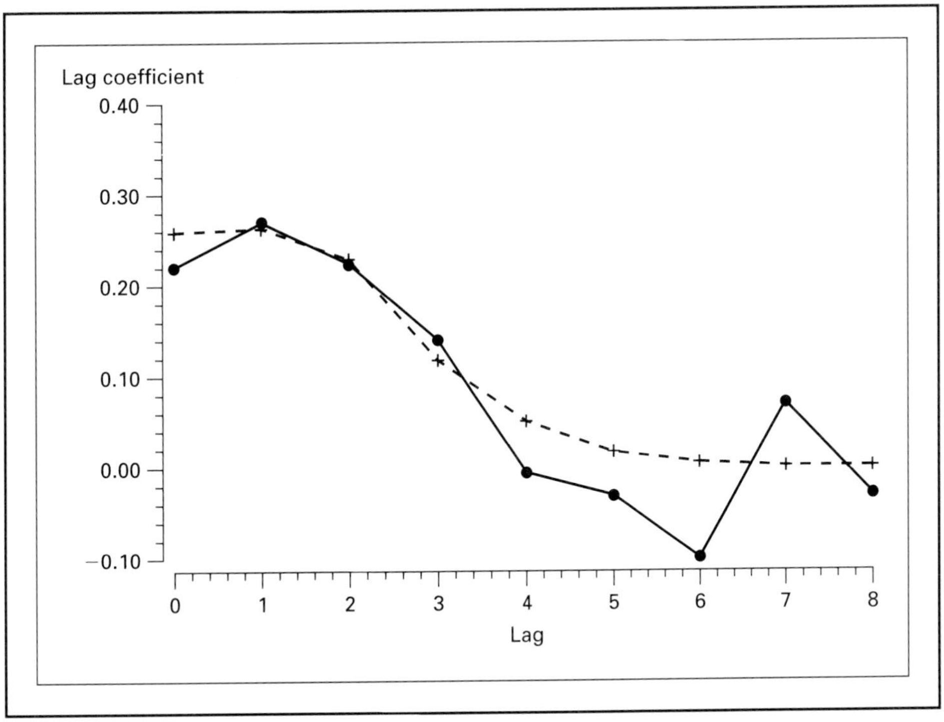

FIGURE 17.4 Estimated Distributed Lags.

17.3.3. Stability of a Dynamic Equation

In the geometric lag model, we found that a stability condition $|\lambda| < 1$ was necessary for the model to be well behaved. Similarly, in the AR(1) model, the autocorrelation parameter ρ must be restricted to $|\rho| < 1$ for the same reason. The dynamic model in (17-41) must also be restricted, but in ways that are less obvious. Consider once again the question of whether there exists an equilibrium value of y_t.

In (17-39), suppose that x_t is fixed at some value $\bar{x}$ and that the disturbances ϵ_t are fixed at their expectation of zero. Would y_t converge to an equilibrium? The relevant dynamic equation is

$$y_t = \bar{\alpha} + \gamma_1 y_{t-1} + \gamma_2 y_{t-1} + \cdots + \gamma_p y_{t-p},$$

where $\bar{\alpha} = \mu + B(1)\bar{x}$. Whether this converges or explodes depends on the coefficients. If so, the equilibrium is

$$\bar{y} = \frac{\mu + B(1)\bar{x}}{C(1)} = \frac{\bar{\alpha}}{C(1)}.$$

Note that this exactly is what appears in (17-2), where $C(L) = 1$, and in (17-24), where $B(L) = \beta$ and $C(L) = 1 - \lambda L$. Stability of a dynamic equation hinges on the **characteristic equation** for the autoregressive part of the model. The roots of the characteristic equation,

$$C(z) = 1 - \gamma_1 z - \gamma_2 z^2 - \cdots - \gamma_p z^p = 0,$$

must be greater than 1 in absolute value for the model to be stable. To take a simple example, the characteristic equation for the first-order models we have examined thus far is

$$C(z) = 1 - \lambda z = 0.$$

This single root of this equation is $z = 1/\lambda$, which is greater than 1 in absolute value if $|\lambda|$ is less than 1. The roots of a more general characteristic equation are the reciprocals of the characteristic roots of the matrix

$$\mathbf{C} = \begin{bmatrix} \gamma_1 & \gamma_2 & \gamma_3 & \cdots & \gamma_{p-1} & \gamma_p \\ 1 & 0 & 0 & \cdots & 0 & 0 \\ 0 & 1 & 0 & \cdots & 0 & 0 \\ 0 & 0 & 1 & \cdots & 0 & 0 \\ & & & \vdots & & \\ 0 & 0 & 0 & \cdots & 1 & 0 \end{bmatrix}.$$

Since the matrix is asymmetric, its roots may include complex pairs. The reciprocal of the complex number $a + bi$ is $a/M - (b/M)i$, where $M = a^2 + b^2$ and $i^2 = -1$. We thus require that M be less than 1.

It is useful to examine the role of the matrix **C** in a dynamic equation. The **univariate autoregression,**

$$y_t = \mu + \gamma_1 y_{t-1} + \gamma_2 y_{t-2} + \cdots + \gamma_p y_{t-p},$$

can be augmented with the $p - 1$ equations

$$y_{t-1} = y_{t-1},$$
$$y_{t-2} = y_{t-2},$$

and so on to give a **vector autoregression, VAR** (to be considered in the next section):

$$\mathbf{y}_t = \boldsymbol{\mu} + \mathbf{C}\mathbf{y}_{t-1},$$

where $\mathbf{y}_t$ has p elements and $\boldsymbol{\mu} = (\mu, 0, 0, \ldots)'$. Now, by successive substitution, we obtain

$$\mathbf{y}_t = \boldsymbol{\mu} + \mathbf{C}\boldsymbol{\mu} + \mathbf{C}^2\boldsymbol{\mu} + \cdots,$$

which may or may not converge. Write **C** in the spectral form $\mathbf{C} = \mathbf{P}\boldsymbol{\Lambda}\mathbf{Q}$, where $\mathbf{QP} = \mathbf{I}$ and $\boldsymbol{\Lambda}$ is a diagonal matrix of the characteristic roots. (Note that the characteristic vectors in **P** are also complex.) We then obtain

$$\mathbf{y}_t = \left[\sum_{i=0}^{\infty} \mathbf{P}\boldsymbol{\Lambda}^i\mathbf{Q}\right]\boldsymbol{\mu}.$$

If all the roots of **C** are finite, this will converge to the equilibrium

$$\mathbf{y}_\infty = (\mathbf{I} - \mathbf{C})^{-1}\boldsymbol{\mu}.$$

Nonexplosion of the powers of the roots of **C** is equivalent to $|\lambda_p| < 1$, or $|1/\lambda_p| > 1$, which was our original requirement. Note finally that since $\boldsymbol{\mu}$ is a multiple of the first column of $\mathbf{I}_p$, it must be the case that each element in the first column of $(\mathbf{I} - \mathbf{C})^{-1}$ is the same. At equilibrium, we must have $y_t = y_{t-1} = \cdots = y_\infty$.

EXAMPLE 17.7 Characteristic Roots of a Dynamic Equation

For the first model given in Table 17.7, the roots of the characteristic equation are a complex pair, $[0.3517 \pm 0.17377i]$. The modulus is 0.1539, so the model is stable. The roots also give information about the path of y_t to its equilibrium. See Section 16.9 for details.

17.3.4. Forecasting

Thus far, we have treated the ARMAX model essentially as an extension of the rational lag model. In that context, primary interest centers on the lag weights in the ARDL model.[39] Another use of the model is for forecasting.[40]

[39] See Harvey (1990, Chapter 7).

[40] Extensive analysis may be found in Harvey (1990) and Mills (1990).

Conditioned on the full set of information available up to time T and on forecasts of the exogenous variables $\mathbf{x}$, the l-period-ahead forecast of y_t would be

$$\hat{y}_{T+l|T} = \mu + \boldsymbol{\beta}'\mathbf{x}_{T+l} + \gamma_1\hat{y}_{T+l-1|T} + \gamma_2\hat{y}_{T+l-2|T} + \cdots + \hat{\epsilon}_{T+l|T} - \theta_1\hat{\epsilon}_{T+l-1|T} - \cdots.$$

Disturbances past the sample period $\epsilon_{T+1}, \ldots$ are replaced with their expectation of zero. The sequence of within-sample disturbances can be generated recursively using (17-43) and q initial value of zero. The forecasts will require $(q - l + 1)$ forecasted disturbances at the end of the sample period for $\hat{y}_{T+1|T}$. The forecasts themselves are based on observed values of y_t for the last p values in the sample and the forecasted lagged values when $T + l$ extends beyond $T + p$.

If the data have been differenced before estimation, the series must be reintegrated to produce a forecast of y_{T+1}. For example, if the first difference has been taken, then

$$\hat{y}_{T+l|T} = \hat{y}_{T+l-1|T} + \Delta\hat{y}_{T+l|T}\,.$$

For second and higher differences, the operation must be repeated.

The expected squared forecast error can be derived by reverting back to the moving-average form of the model. Thus,

$$y_{T+l|T} = \frac{\mu + \boldsymbol{\beta}'\mathbf{x}_{T+l|T}}{C(L)} + \frac{D(L)}{C(L)}\epsilon_t.$$

We may proceed in the same fashion as in Example 17.6 to derive Ψ_j, the coefficients on L^j in $[D(L)/C(L)]\epsilon_t$;

$$(1 + \Psi_1 L + \Psi_2 L^2 + \cdots)(1 - \gamma_1 L - \gamma_2 L^2 - \cdots - \gamma_p L^p) = (1 - \theta_1 L - \theta_2 L^2 - \cdots - \theta_q L^q).$$

Then the expected square forecast error is

$$\text{MSE}(\hat{y}_{T+l|T}) = \sigma_\epsilon^2(1 + \Psi_1^2 + \cdots + \Psi_{l-1}^2). \qquad \textbf{(17-47)}$$

The number of nonzero terms increases with the number of periods ahead for which the forecast is made.

The preceding takes the parameters as known. Obviously, this is not going to hold in practice. Unfortunately, except in the simplest cases, the precise form of the MSE that accounts for the sampling variability of the parameter estimates remains to be derived. Harvey (1990, pages 215–216 and 254) suggests that the contribution of the parameter estimates to the forecast variance is $O(1)$. Thus, if T is relatively large, the variance of the parameter estimates could be ignored. Of course, the typical time-series setting involves a relatively small T, so this advice may be a bit optimistic. One possibility could be to revert back to the ARDL form of the model and use the familiar form of the forecast variance given in (7-40):

$$\text{MSE}(\hat{y}_{T+l|T}) = \sigma_\epsilon^2(1 + \Psi_1^2 + \cdots + \Psi_{l-1}^2) + \mathbf{z}^{0\prime}\{\text{Est. Var}[\hat{\mu}, \hat{\boldsymbol{\gamma}}, \hat{\boldsymbol{\beta}}]\}\mathbf{z}^0$$

and

$$\mathbf{z}^0 = [1, \hat{y}_{T+l-1|T}, \ldots, \mathbf{x}_{T+l}].$$

Since the disturbance and the regressors in this model are correlated, the decomposition above neglects a covariance term that might be substantial. It is not obvious whether ignoring the parameter variation or using what might be an erroneous approximation is the poorer option in this setting. On the other hand, it is unambiguous that the correct variance to use would be understated by (17-47).

17.4. VECTOR AUTOREGRESSIONS

The preceding can be extended to sets of variables. In the most general case, we would have

$$\mathbf{y}_t = \boldsymbol{\mu} + \boldsymbol{\Delta}_1\mathbf{y}_{t-1} + \cdots + \boldsymbol{\Delta}_p\mathbf{y}_{t-p} + \mathbf{v}_t + \boldsymbol{\Theta}_1\mathbf{v}_{t-1} + \cdots + \boldsymbol{\Theta}_q\mathbf{v}_{t-q},$$

where $\mathbf{y}_t$ and $\mathbf{v}_t$ are $M \times 1$ vectors of random variables, $\boldsymbol{\mu}$ is the mean vector, and $\boldsymbol{\Delta}_1, \ldots, \boldsymbol{\Delta}_p, \boldsymbol{\Theta}_1, \ldots, \boldsymbol{\Theta}_q$, and $\boldsymbol{\Omega} = [\mathbf{v}_t\mathbf{v}_t']$ are $M \times M$ parameter matrices. In principle, $\boldsymbol{\Theta}_1, \ldots, \boldsymbol{\Theta}_q$ are unrestricted. This produces a **vector ARMA** model.[41] Applications in econometrics have typically been based on simpler models without moving-average terms. The resulting model,

$$\mathbf{y}_t = \boldsymbol{\mu} + \boldsymbol{\Delta}_1\mathbf{y}_{t-1} + \cdots + \boldsymbol{\Delta}_p\mathbf{y}_{t-p} + \mathbf{v}_t, \qquad \textbf{(17-48)}$$

is a **vector autoregression,** or **VAR.** The individual equations are

$$y_{mt} = \mu_m + \sum_{j=1}^{p}(\boldsymbol{\Delta}_j)_{m1}y_{1,t-j} + \sum_{j=1}^{p}(\boldsymbol{\Delta}_j)_{m2}y_{2,t-j} + \cdots + \sum_{j=1}^{p}(\boldsymbol{\Delta}_j)_{mM}y_{M,t-j} + \epsilon_{mt},$$

where $(\boldsymbol{\Delta}_j)_{lm}$ indicates the lmth element of $\boldsymbol{\Delta}_j$.

VARs have been used primarily in macroeconomics. It was argued by some authors[42] that unrestricted VARs would do a better job of forecasting than structural multiple equations models. This view would have to be purely empirical, however. One could argue that as long as $\boldsymbol{\mu}$ includes the current observations on the (truly) relevant exogenous variables, the VAR is simply an overfit reduced form of some simultaneous equations model. The overfitting results from the possible inclusion of more lags than would be appropriate in the original model. (See Section 16.9 for a detailed examination of one such model.) On the other hand, one of the virtues of the VAR (it is argued) is that it obviates a decision as to what contemporaneous variables are exogenous; it

---

[41]See Box and Tiao (1981).

[42]See, for example, Litterman (1979, 1986).

has only lagged variables on the right-hand side. In addition to forecasting, VARs have been used for two primary functions, testing Granger causality and studying impulse response characteristics.

In the form of (17-48), that is, without autocorrelation of the disturbances, VARs are particularly simple to estimate. Although the equation system can be exceedingly large, it is, in fact, a seemingly unrelated regressions model with identical regressors. As such, the equations should be estimated separately by ordinary least squares.[43] The disturbance covariance matrix can then be estimated with average sums of squares or cross products of the least squares residuals. The proliferation of parameters in VARs is often cited as a major disadvantage of their use. Consider, for example, a VAR involving five variables and five lags. Each $\boldsymbol{\Delta}$ has 25 unconstrained elements, and there are five of them, for 125 free parameters, plus any others in $\boldsymbol{\mu}$, plus $5(6)/2 = 15$ free parameters in $\boldsymbol{\Omega}$. On the other hand, each single equation has only 25 parameters, and at least given sufficient degrees of freedom—there's the rub—a linear regression with 25 parameters is simple work even for a PC. Moreover, applications rarely involve even as many as four variables, so the model-size issue may well be exaggerated.

17.4.1. Testing for Granger Causality

Causality in the sense defined by Granger (1969) and Sims (1980) is inferred when lagged values of a variable, say x_t, have explanatory power in a regression of a variable y_t on lagged values of y_t and x_t. (See Section 16.2.2.) The VAR can be used to test the hypothesis.[44] Tests of the restrictions can be based on simple F tests in the single equations of the VAR model. That the unrestricted equations have identical regressors means that these tests can be based on the results of simple OLS estimates. The notion can be extended in a system of equations to attempt to ascertain if a given variable is weakly exogenous to the system. If lagged values of a variable x_t have no explanatory for *any* of the variables in a system, we would view x as weakly exogenous to the system. Once again, this can be tested with a likelihood ratio test as described below—the restriction will be to put "holes" in one or more $\boldsymbol{\Delta}$ matrices—or with a form of F test constructed by stacking the equations.

There is a complication in these causality tests. The VAR is an article of faith. There is no theory behind the formulation. As such, the causality tests are predicated on a model that may, in fact, be missing either intervening variables or additional lagged effects that should be present but are not. For the first of these, the problem is that a finding of causal effects might equally well result

[43]See Section 15.2.1.

[44]See Geweke et al. (1984) as well as Sims (1980).

from the omission of a variable that is correlated with both of (or all) the left-hand-side variables. The second shortcoming is more tractable if one is willing to assume normality for the disturbances. Let $\mathbf{W}$ be the $M \times M$ residual covariance matrix based on a lag length of p, and let $\mathbf{W}^*$ be its counterpart when there are $p + 1$ lags. Then the likelihood ratio statistic,

$$\lambda = T(\ln|\mathbf{W}| - \ln|\mathbf{W}^*|),$$

can be used to test the hypothesis that $\boldsymbol{\Delta}_{p+1} = \mathbf{0}$. The statistic would have a limiting chi-squared distribution with M^2 degrees of freedom. In principle, one might base a specification search for the right lag length on this calculation. The procedure would be to test up from $p = 1$ until addition of the last parameter matrix does not lead to a significant improvement in the fit. The same caution that underlies (17-20) would apply here; one would have to adjust the significance level at each step.

17.4.2. Impulse Response Functions

Any VAR can be written as a first order model by augmenting it, if necessary, with additional identity equations. For example, the model

$$\mathbf{y}_t = \boldsymbol{\mu} + \boldsymbol{\Delta}_1\mathbf{y}_{t-1} + \boldsymbol{\Delta}_2\mathbf{y}_{t-2} + \mathbf{v}_t$$

can be written

$$\begin{bmatrix} \mathbf{y}_t \\ \mathbf{y}_{t-1} \end{bmatrix} = \begin{bmatrix} \boldsymbol{\mu} \\ \mathbf{0} \end{bmatrix} + \begin{bmatrix} \boldsymbol{\Delta}_1 & \boldsymbol{\Delta}_2 \\ \mathbf{I} & \mathbf{0} \end{bmatrix} \begin{bmatrix} \mathbf{y}_{t-1} \\ \mathbf{y}_{t-2} \end{bmatrix} + \begin{bmatrix} \mathbf{v}_t \\ \mathbf{0} \end{bmatrix},$$

which is a first-order model. We can study the dynamic characteristics of the model in either form, but the second is more convenient, as will soon be apparent.

As we analyzed earlier, in the model

$$\mathbf{y}_t = \boldsymbol{\mu} + \boldsymbol{\Delta}\mathbf{y}_{t-1} + \mathbf{v}_t,$$

dynamic stability is achieved if the characteristic roots of $\boldsymbol{\Delta}$ have modulus less than one. (The roots may be complex, as $\boldsymbol{\Delta}$ need not be symmetric. See Section 17.3.4 for the case of a single equation and Section 16.9 for analysis of essentially this model in a simultaneous equations context.) Assuming that the equation is stable, the equilibrium is found by obtaining the final form of the system. We can do this by repeated substitution, or more simply by using the lag operator to write

$$\mathbf{y}_t = \boldsymbol{\mu} + \boldsymbol{\Delta}(L)\mathbf{y}_t + \mathbf{v}_t$$

or

$$[\mathbf{I} - \boldsymbol{\Delta}(L)]\mathbf{y}_t = \boldsymbol{\mu} + \mathbf{v}_t.$$

With the stability condition, we have

$$\begin{aligned}\bar{\mathbf{y}} &= [\mathbf{I} - \boldsymbol{\Delta}(L)]^{-1}(\boldsymbol{\mu} + \mathbf{v}_t)\\ &= (\mathbf{I} - \boldsymbol{\Delta})^{-1}\boldsymbol{\mu} + \sum_{i=0}^{\infty} \boldsymbol{\Delta}^i \mathbf{v}_{t-i}\\ &= \bar{\boldsymbol{\mu}} + \sum_{i=0}^{\infty} \boldsymbol{\Delta}^i \mathbf{v}_{t-i}\\ &= \bar{\boldsymbol{\mu}} + \mathbf{v}_t + \boldsymbol{\Delta}\mathbf{v}_{t-1} + \boldsymbol{\Delta}^2\mathbf{v}_{t-2} + \cdots .\end{aligned} \qquad \textbf{(17-49)}$$

The coefficients in the powers of $\boldsymbol{\Delta}$ are the multipliers in the system. In fact, by renaming things slightly, this is precisely the set results we examined in Section 16.9 in our discussion of dynamic simultaneous equations models. We will change the interpretation slightly here, however. As we did in Section 16.9, we consider the conceptual experiment of disturbing a system at equilibrium. Suppose that $\mathbf{v}$ has equaled $\mathbf{0}$ for long enough that $\mathbf{y}$ reached equilibrium, $\bar{\mathbf{y}}$. Now, we consider injecting a shock to the system by changing one of the v's, for one period, then returning it to zero thereafter. As we saw earlier, y_{mt} will move away from, then return to, its equilibrium. The path whereby the variables return to the equilibrium is called the **impulse response** of the VAR.[45]

In the autoregressive form of the model, we can identify each **innovation,** v_{mt}, with a particular variable in $\mathbf{y}_t$, say y_{mt}. Consider, then, the effect of a one time shock to the system, dv_{mt}. As compared with the equilibrium, we will have, in the current period,

$$y_{mt} - \bar{y}_m = dv_{mt} = \phi_{mm}(0)\, dv_t.$$

One period later, we will have

$$y_{m,t+1} - \bar{y}_m = (\boldsymbol{\Delta})_{mm} dv_{mt} = \phi_{mm}(1)\, dv_t,$$

Two periods later,

$$y_{m,t+2} - \bar{y}_m = (\boldsymbol{\Delta}^2)_{mm} dv_{mt} = \phi_{mm}(2)\, dv_t$$

and so on. The function, $\phi_{mm}(i)$ gives the impulse response characteristics of variable y_m to innovations in v_m. A useful way to characterize the system is to plot the impulse response functions. The preceding traces through the effect on variable m of a one time innovation in v_m. We could also examine the effect of a one-time innovation of v_l on variable m. The impulse response function would be

$$\phi_{ml}(i) = \text{element } m, l \text{ in } \boldsymbol{\Delta}^i.$$

[45]See Hamilton (1994, pp. 318–323 and 336–350) for discussion and a number of related results.

EXAMPLE 17.8 Impulse Response Functions

Least squares estimates of the simple VAR

$$\Delta \ln\left(\frac{Y_t}{P_t}\right) = \mu_y + \delta_{11}\Delta \ln\left(\frac{Y_{t-1}}{P_{t-1}}\right) + \delta_{12}\Delta \ln\left(\frac{M_{t-1}}{P_{t-1}}\right) + \nu_{yt},$$

$$\Delta \ln\left(\frac{M_t}{P_t}\right) = \mu_m + \delta_{21}\Delta \ln\left(\frac{Y_{t-1}}{P_{t-1}}\right) + \delta_{22}\Delta \ln\left(\frac{M_{t-1}}{P_{t-1}}\right) + \nu_{mt}$$

produce

$$\boldsymbol{\Delta} = \begin{bmatrix} 0.56694 & 0.15293 \\ -0.029546 & 0.053978 \end{bmatrix}.$$

The characteristic roots are real, 0.56606 and 0.054859, so the system is stable. A plot of $\phi_{11}(i)$ and $\phi_{12}(i)$, the effects of the shocks on the rate of growth of real output, is given in Figure 17.5. The behavior is to be expected because the roots are real. We note, in passing, that the t ratio on d_{12} in the first equation is 1.798 whereas that on d_{21} in the second is -0.029. Thus, on the basis of this admittedly meager evidence, we would conclude that neither of these two variables Granger causes the other.

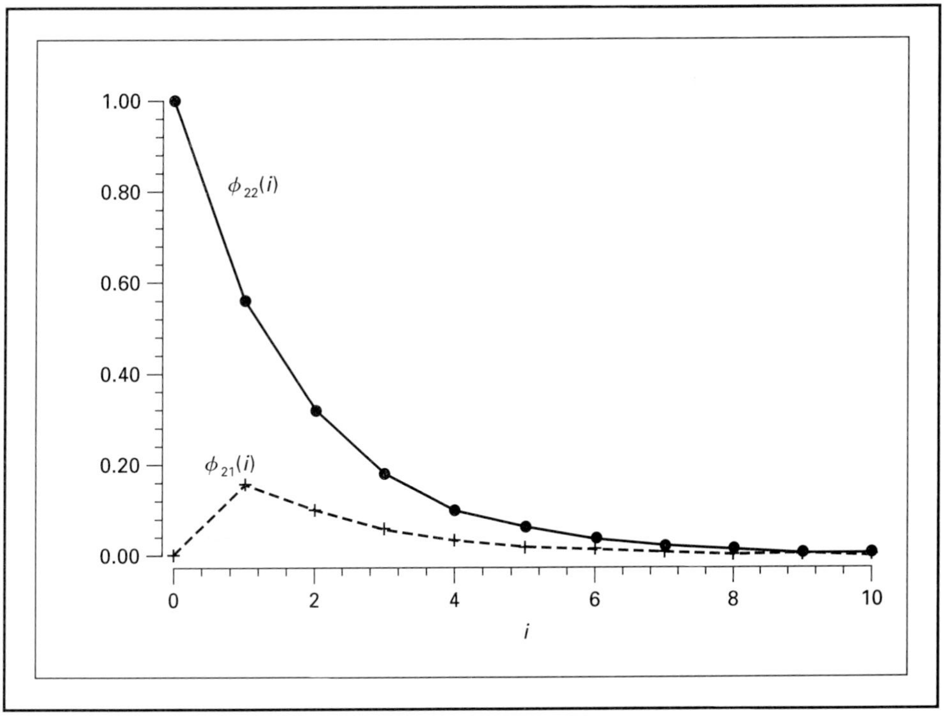

FIGURE 17.5 Impulse Response Functions.

17.4.3. Structural VARs

The VAR approach to modeling dynamic behavior of economic variables has provided some interesting insights and appears [see Litterman (1986)] to bring some real benefits for forecasting. The approach has received some strident criticism for its atheoretical approach, however. The "unrestricted" nature of the lag structure in (17-48) could be synonymous with "unstructured." With no theoretical input to the model, it is difficult to claim that its output provides much of a theoretically justified result. For example, how are we to interpret the impulse response functions derived in the previous section? What lies behind much of this discussion is the idea that there is, in fact, a structure underlying the model, and the VAR that we have specified is a mere hodgepodge of all its components. Of course, that is exactly what reduced forms are. As such, to respond to this sort of criticism, analysts have begun to cast VARs formally as reduced forms and thereby attempt to deduce the structure that they had in mind all along.

A VAR model $\mathbf{y}_t = \boldsymbol{\mu} + \boldsymbol{\Delta}\mathbf{y}_{t-1} + \mathbf{v}_t$ could, in principle, be viewed as the reduced form of the dynamic structural model

$$\boldsymbol{\Gamma}\mathbf{y}_t = \boldsymbol{\alpha} + \boldsymbol{\Phi}\mathbf{y}_{t-1} + \boldsymbol{\epsilon}_t,$$

where we have embedded any exogenous variables $\mathbf{x}_t$ in the vector of constants $\boldsymbol{\alpha}$. Thus, $\boldsymbol{\Delta} = \boldsymbol{\Gamma}^{-1}\boldsymbol{\Phi}$, $\boldsymbol{\mu} = \boldsymbol{\Gamma}^{-1}\boldsymbol{\alpha}$, $\mathbf{v} = \boldsymbol{\Gamma}^{-1}\boldsymbol{\epsilon}$, and $\boldsymbol{\Omega} = \boldsymbol{\Gamma}^{-1}\boldsymbol{\Sigma}(\boldsymbol{\Gamma}^{-1})'$. Perhaps it is the structure, specified by an underlying theory, that is of interest. For example, we can discuss the impulse response characteristics of this system. For particular configurations of $\boldsymbol{\Gamma}$, such as a triangular matrix, we can meaningfully interpret innovations, $\boldsymbol{\epsilon}$. As we explored at great length in the previous chapter, however, as this model stands, there is not sufficient information contained in the reduced form as just stated to deduce the structural parameters. A possibly large number of restrictions must be imposed on $\boldsymbol{\Gamma}$, $\boldsymbol{\Phi}$, and $\boldsymbol{\Sigma}$ to enable us to deduce structural forms from reduced form estimates, which are always obtainable. The recent work on "structural VARs" centers on the types of restrictions and forms of the theory which can be brought to bear to allow this analysis to proceed. See, for example, the survey in Hamilton (1994, Chapter 11). At this point, the literature on this subject has come full circle as the contemporary development of "unstructured VARs" becomes very much the analysis of quite conventional dynamic structural simultaneous equations models.

17.4.4. VARs in Microeconomics

VARs have recently appeared in the microeconometrics literature as well. Chamberlain (1983) suggested that a useful approach to the analysis of panel data would be to treat each period's observation as a separate equation. For the case of $T = 2$, we would have

$$\begin{aligned} y_{i1} &= \alpha_i + \boldsymbol{\beta}'\mathbf{x}_{i1} + \epsilon_{i1}, \\ y_{i2} &= \alpha_i + \boldsymbol{\beta}'\mathbf{x}_{i2} + \epsilon_{i2}, \end{aligned}$$

where i indexes individuals and α_i are unobserved individual effects. This produces a multivariate regression, to which Chamberlain added restrictions related to the individual effects. Holtz–Eakin et al.'s (1988) approach is to specify the equation as

$$y_{it} = \alpha_{0t} + \sum_{l=1}^{m} \alpha_{lt} y_{i,t-1} + \sum_{l=1}^{m} \delta_{lt} x_{i,t-1} + \boldsymbol{\Psi}_t f_i + \mu_{it}.$$

In their study, y_{it} is hours worked by individual i in period t and x_{it} is the individual's wage in that period. A second equation for earnings is specified with lagged values of hours and earnings on the right-hand side. The individual, unobserved effects are f_i. This model is similar to the VAR in (17-48), but differs in several ways as well. The number of periods is quite small (14 yearly observations for each individual), but there are nearly 1000 individuals. The dynamic equation is specified for a specific period, however, so the relevant sample size in each case is n, not T. Also, the number of lags in the model used is relatively small; the authors fixed it at three. They thus have a two-equation VAR containing 12 unknown parameters, six in each equation. The authors used the model to analyze causality, measurement error, and parameter stability, that is, constancy of α_{it} and δ_{lt} across time.

EXERCISES

1. Obtain the mean lag and the long- and short-run multipliers for the following distributed lag models:

(a) $y_t = 0.55(0.02x_t + 0.15x_{t-1} + 0.43x_{t-2} + 0.23x_{t-3} + 0.17x_{t-4}) + \epsilon_t$.

(b) The model in Exercise 5.

(c) The model in Exercise 7. (Do for either x or z.)

2. Explain how to estimate the parameters of the following model:

$$y_t = \alpha + \beta x_t + \gamma y_{t-1} + \delta y_{t-2} + \epsilon_t,$$
$$\epsilon_t = \rho \epsilon_{t-1} + u_t.$$

Is there any problem with ordinary least squares? Using the method you have described, fit the previous model to the data in Table 17.5. Report your results.

3. Show how to estimate a polynomial distributed lag model with lags of six periods and a third-order polynomial.

4. Using the data in the appendix to Chapter 16, fit a polynomial distributed lag model of the form

$$\text{investment} = \alpha + \sum_{i=0}^{p} \delta_i \, \text{profit}_{t-i} + \epsilon_t.$$

Attempt to determine the appropriate lag length and polynomial degree using the methods discussed in the text.

5. Expand the rational lag model $y_t = [(0.6 + 2L)/(1 - 0.6L + 0.5L^2)]x_t + \epsilon_t$. What are the coefficients on $x_t, x_{t-1}, x_{t-2}, x_{t-3}$, and x_{t-4}?
6. Suppose that the model of Exercise 5 were specified as

$$y_t = \alpha + \frac{\beta + \gamma L}{1 - \delta_1 L - \delta_2 L^2} x_t + \epsilon_t.$$

Describe a method of estimating the parameters. Is ordinary least squares consistent?

7. Describe how to estimate the parameters of the model

$$y_t = \alpha + \beta \frac{x_t}{1 - \gamma L} + \delta \frac{z_t}{1 - \phi L} + \epsilon_t,$$

where ϵ_t is a serially uncorrelated, homoscedastic, classical disturbance.

CHAPTER 18

Time-Series Models

18.1. INTRODUCTION

For forecasting purposes, a simple model that *describes* the behavior of a variable (or a set of variables) in terms of past values, without the benefit of a well developed theory, may well prove quite satisfactory. Researchers have observed that the large simultaneous equations macroeconomic models constructed in the 1960s frequently have poorer forecasting performance than fairly simple, univariate time-series models based on just a few parameters and compact specifications. It is just this observation that has raised to prominence the univariate time-series forecasting models pioneered by Box and Jenkins (1984).

In this chapter, we will introduce some of the tools employed in the analysis of time-series data.[1] Section 18.2 describes stationary stochastic processes. We encountered this body of theory in Chapters 13, 16, and 17, where we discovered that certain assumptions were required to ascribe familiar properties to a time-series of data. We continue that discussion by defining several characteristics of a stationary time-series. The recent literature in macroeconometrics

---

[1]Each of the topics discussed here is the subject of a vast literature with articles and book-length treatments at all levels. For example, two survey papers on the subject of unit roots in economic time-series data, Nerlove and Diebold (1990) and Campbell and Perron (1991), cite between them over 200 basic sources on the subject. The literature on unit roots and cointegration is almost surely the most rapidly moving target in econometrics. Stock's (1994) survey adds hundreds of references to those in the aforementioned surveys and brings the literature up to date as of then. Useful basic references on the subjects of this chapter are Box and Jenkins (1984), Judge et al. (1985), Mills (1990), Granger and Newbold (1977), Granger and Watson (1984), Hendry et al. (1984), Geweke (1984), and especially Harvey (1989, 1990), Enders (1995), and Hamilton (1994). There are also many survey style and pedagogical articles on these subjects. The aforementioned paper by Diebold and Nerlove is a useful tour guide through some of the most recent literature. We recommend Dickey et al. (1986) and Dickey et al. (1991) as well. The latter is an especially clear introduction at a very basic level of the fundamental tools for empirical researchers.

has seen an explosion of studies of nonstationary time series. Nonstationarity mandates a revision of the standard inference tools we have used thus far. In Section 18.3, on nonstationarity and unit roots, we discuss some of these tools. Section 18.4 on cointegration discusses some extensions of regression models that are made necessary when strongly trended, nonstationary variables appear in them. Finally, Section 18.5 on GARCH models extends the time-series models of Section 18.2 to the regression variance.

Some of the concepts to be discussed here were introduced in Section 13.2. This section also contains a cursory introduction to the nature of time-series processes. It will be useful to review that material before proceeding with the rest of this chapter. In addition, Section 6.7, in which we discuss regressions with stochastic regressors and the important theorem of Mann and Wald, is directly relevant to the material of this chapter. Finally, Sections 16.9.1 on estimation and 16.9.3 on stability of dynamic models will be especially useful for the latter sections of this chapter.

18.2. STATIONARY STOCHASTIC PROCESSES

The essential building block for the models to be discussed in this chapter is the **white noise** time series,

$$\{\epsilon_t\}, t = -\infty, +\infty,$$

where each element in the sequence has $E[\epsilon_t] = 0$, $E[\epsilon_t^2] = \sigma_\epsilon^2$, and $\text{Cov}[\epsilon_t, \epsilon_s] = 0$ for all $s \neq t$. Each element in the series is a random draw from a population with zero mean and constant variance. It is occasionally assumed that the draws are independent or normally distributed, although for most of our analysis, neither assumption will be essential.

A univariate time-series model describes the behavior of a variable in terms of its own past values. Consider, for example, the autoregressive disturbance models introduced in Chapter 13,

$$u_t = \rho u_{t-1} + \epsilon_t. \tag{18-1}$$

Autoregressive disturbances are generally the residual variation in a regression model built up from what may be an elaborate underlying theory, $y_t = \boldsymbol{\beta}'\mathbf{x}_t + u_t$. The theory usually stops short of stating what enters the disturbance. But the presumption that some time-series process generates $\mathbf{x}_t$ should extend equally to u_t. Note, for example, the symmetric approach to modeling x_t and u_t (denoted ϵ_t there) in Section 13.4.2. As we saw earlier, there are two ways to interpret this simple series. As stated above, u_t equals the previous value of u_t plus an "innovation," ϵ_t. Alternatively, by manipulating the series, we showed that u_t could be interpreted as an aggregation of the entire history of the ϵ_t's.

Occasionally, statistical evidence is convincing that a more intricate process is at work in the disturbance. Perhaps a second-order autoregression,

$$u_t = \rho_1 u_{t-1} + \rho_2 u_{t-2} + \epsilon_t, \tag{18-2}$$

better explains the movement of the disturbances in the regression. The model may not arise naturally from an underlying behavioral theory. But in the face of certain kinds of statistical evidence, one might conclude that the more elaborate model would be preferable.[2] This section will describe several alternatives to the AR(1) model that we have relied on in most of the preceding applications.

18.2.1. Autoregressive Moving-Average Processes

The variable y_t in the model

$$y_t = \mu + \gamma y_{t-1} + \epsilon_t \tag{18-3}$$

is said to be **autoregressive** (or self-regressive) because under certain assumptions,

$$E[y_t \mid y_{t-1}] = \mu + \gamma y_{t-1}.$$

A more general pth-order autoregression or AR(p) process would be written

$$y_t = \mu + \gamma_1 y_{t-1} + \gamma_2 y_{t-2} + \cdots + \gamma_p y_{t-p} + \epsilon_t. \tag{18-4}$$

The analogy to the classical regression is clear. Now consider the MA(1) specification

$$y_t = \mu + \epsilon_t - \theta\epsilon_{t-1}. \tag{18-5}$$

By writing

$$y_t = \mu + (1 - \theta L)\epsilon_t$$

or

$$\frac{y_t}{1 - \theta L} = \frac{\mu}{1 - \theta} + \epsilon_t,^{3}$$

we find that

$$y_t = \frac{\mu}{1 - \theta} - \theta y_{t-1} - \theta^2 y_{t-2} - \cdots + \epsilon_t.$$

Once again, the effect is to represent y_t as a function of its own past values.

An extremely general model that encompasses (18-4) and (18-5) is the **autoregressive moving average,** or ARMA(p, q), model:

$$y_t = \mu + \gamma_1 y_{t-1} + \gamma_2 y_{t-2} + \cdots + \gamma_p y_{t-p} + \epsilon_t - \theta_1\epsilon_{t-1} - \cdots - \theta_q\epsilon_{t-q}. \tag{18-6}$$

[2]For example, the estimates of u_t computed after a correction for first-order autocorrelation may fail tests of randomness such as the Durbin–Watson test.

[3]The lag operator is discussed in Section 17.2.2. Since μ is a constant, $\mu/(1 - \theta L) = \mu + \theta\mu + \theta^2\mu + \cdots = \mu/(1 - \theta)$. The lag operator may be set equal to 1 when it operates on a constant.

Note the convention that the ARMA(p, q) process has p autoregressive (lagged dependent-variable) terms and q lagged moving-average terms. Researchers have found that models of this sort with relatively small values of p and q have proved quite effective as forecasting models.

The disturbances ϵ_t are labeled the **innovations** in the model. The term is fitting because the only new information that enters the processes in period t is this innovation. Consider, then, the AR(1) process

$$y_t = \mu + \gamma y_{t-1} + \epsilon_t. \tag{18-7}$$

Either by successive substitution or by just using the lag operator, we obtain

$$y_t(1 - \gamma L) = \mu + \epsilon_t$$

or

$$y_t = \frac{\mu}{1 - \gamma} + \sum_{i=0}^{\infty} \gamma^i \epsilon_{t-i}.[4] \tag{18-8}$$

The observed series is a particular type of aggregation of the history of the innovations. The moving average, MA(q) model,

$$y_t = \mu + \epsilon_t - \theta_1 \epsilon_{t-1} - \cdots - \theta_q \epsilon_{t-q} = \mu + D(L)\epsilon_t, \tag{18-9}$$

is yet another, particularly simple form of aggregation in that only information from the q most recent periods is retained. (See, for example, Example 13.2.) The general result is that many time-series processes can be viewed either as regressions on lagged values with additive disturbances or as aggregations of a history of innovations. They differ from one to the next in the form of that aggregation.

More involved processes can be similarly represented in either an autoregressive or moving average form. (We will turn to the mathematical requirements below.) Consider, for example, the ARMA(2, 1) process

$$y_t = \mu + \gamma_1 y_{t-1} + \gamma_2 y_{t-2} + \epsilon_t - \theta \epsilon_{t-1}.$$

We can write this as

$$\epsilon_t(1 - \theta L) = y_t - \mu - \gamma_1 y_{t-1} - \gamma_2 y_{t-2}.$$

If $|\theta| < 1$, we can divide both sides of the equation by $(1 - \theta L)$ and obtain

$$\epsilon_t = \sum_{i=0}^{\infty} \theta^i (y_{t-i} - \mu - \gamma_1 y_{t-i-1} - \gamma_2 y_{t-i-2}).$$

After some tedious manipulation, this produces the autoregressive form,

$$y_t = \frac{-\mu}{1 - \theta} + \sum_{i=1}^{\infty} \pi_i y_{t-i} + \epsilon_t,$$

[4]See Section 13.2 for discussion of models with infinite lag structures.

where

$$\pi_1 = \gamma_1 - \theta \quad \text{and} \quad \pi_j = -(\theta^j - \gamma_1\theta^{j-1} - \gamma_2\theta^{j-2}), \quad j = 2, 3, \ldots. \tag{18-10}$$

Alternatively, by similar (yet more tedious) manipulation, we would be able to write

$$\begin{aligned} y_t &= \frac{\mu}{1 - \gamma_1 - \gamma_2} + \left[\frac{1 - \theta L}{1 - \gamma_1 L - \gamma_2 L^2}\right]\epsilon_t \\ &= \frac{\mu}{1 - \gamma_1 - \gamma_2} + \sum_{i=0}^{\infty} \delta_i \epsilon_{t-i}. \end{aligned} \tag{18-11}$$

In each case, the weights, π_i in the **autoregressive form** and δ_i in the **moving-average form,** are complicated functions of the original parameters. But nonetheless, each is just an alternative representation of the same time-series process that produces the current value of y_t. This is a fundamental property of certain time series. We will return to the issue after we define formally the assumption that we have used at several steps above that allows these transformations.

18.2.2. Stationarity and Invertibility

At several points in the preceding, we have alluded to the notion of **stationarity,** either directly or indirectly by making certain assumptions about the parameters in the model. In Section 13.2, we characterized an AR(1) disturbance process

$$u_t = \rho u_{t-1} + \epsilon_t,$$

as stationary if $|\rho| < 1$ and ϵ_t is white noise. Then

$$\begin{aligned} E[u_t] &= 0 \quad \text{for all } t, \\ \text{Var}[u_t] &= \frac{\sigma_\epsilon^2}{1 - \rho^2}, \\ \text{Cov}[u_t, u_s] &= \frac{\rho^{|t-s|}\sigma_\epsilon^2}{1 - \rho^2}. \end{aligned} \tag{18-12}$$

If $|\rho| \geq 1$, the variance and covariances are undefined.

In the following, we use ϵ_t to denote the white noise innovations in the process. The ARMA(p, q) process will be denoted as in (18-6).

DEFINITION 18.1: Covariance Stationarity. *A stochastic process y_t is* ***weakly stationary*** *or* ***covariance stationary*** *if it satisfies the following requirements:*[5]

[5]*Strong* stationarity requires that the joint distribution of all sets of observations $(y_t, y_{t-1}, \ldots)$ be invariant to when the observations are made. For practical purposes in econometrics, this is a theoretical fine point. Although weak stationary suffices for our applications, we would not normally analyze weakly stationary time series that were not strongly stationary as well. Indeed, we often go even one step beyond this and assume joint normality.

1. $E[y_t]$ is independent of t. ✓
2. $Var[y_t]$ is a constant, independent of t. ✓
3. $Cov[y_t, y_s]$ is a function of $t - s$, but not of t or s. ✓

The third requirement is that the covariance between observations in the series is a function only of how far apart they are in time, not the time at which they occur. These properties clearly hold for the AR(1) process immediately above. Whether they apply for the other models we have examined remains to be seen.

We define the **autocovariance at lag k** as

$$\lambda_k = \mathrm{Cov}[y_t, y_{t-k}].$$

Note that

$$\lambda_{-k} = \mathrm{Cov}[y_t, y_{t+k}] = \lambda_k.$$

Stationarity implies that autocovariances are a function of k, but not of t. For example, in (18-12), we see that the autocovariances of the AR(1) process $y_t = \mu + \gamma y_{t-1} + \epsilon_t$ are

$$\mathrm{Cov}[y_t, y_{t-k}] = \frac{\gamma^k \sigma_\epsilon^2}{1 - \gamma^2}, \quad k = 0, 1 \ldots. \tag{18-13}$$

If $|\gamma| < 1$, this process is stationary. For any MA(q) series,

$$
\begin{aligned}
y_t &= \mu + \epsilon_t - \theta_1 \epsilon_{t-1} - \cdots - \theta_q \epsilon_{t-q}, \\
E[y_t] &= \mu + E[\epsilon_t] + \theta_1 E[\epsilon_{t-1}] + \cdots + \theta_q E[\epsilon_{t-q}] = \mu, \\
\mathrm{Var}[y_t] &= (1 + \theta_1^2 + \cdots + \theta_q^2)\sigma_\epsilon^2, \\
\mathrm{Cov}[y_t, y_{t-1}] &= (-\theta_1 + \theta_1 \theta_2 + \theta_2 \theta_3 + \cdots + \theta_{q-1}\theta_q)\sigma_\epsilon^2,
\end{aligned}
\tag{18-14}
$$

and so on until

$$
\begin{aligned}
\mathrm{Cov}[y_t, y_{t-q-1}] &= \theta_{q-1}\theta_q \sigma_\epsilon^2, \\
\mathrm{Cov}[y_t, y_{t-q}] &= -\theta_q \sigma_\epsilon^2,
\end{aligned}
$$

and, for lags greater than q, the autocovariances are zero. It follows, therefore, that finite moving-average processes are stationary regardless of the values of the parameters. The MA(1) process $y_t = \epsilon_t - \theta \epsilon_{t-1}$ is an important special case that has $\mathrm{Var}[y_t] = (1 + \theta^2)\sigma_\epsilon^2$, $\lambda_1 = -\theta\sigma_\epsilon^2$, and $\lambda_k = 0$ for $|k| > 1$.

For the AR(1) process, the stationarity requirement is that $|\gamma| < 1$. This, in turn, implies that the variance of the moving average representation in (18-8) is finite. Consider the AR(2) process

$$y_t = \mu + \gamma_1 y_{t-1} + \gamma_2 y_{t-2} + \epsilon_t.$$

Write this as

$$C(L)y_t = \mu + \epsilon_t,$$

where

$$C(L) = 1 - \gamma_1 L - \gamma_2 L^2.$$

Then, if it is possible, we invert this to produce

$$y_t = [C(L)]^{-1}(\mu + \epsilon_t).$$

Whether the inversion of the polynomial in the lag operator leads to a convergent series depends on the values of γ_1 and γ_2. If so, the moving average representation will be

$$y_t = \sum_{i=0}^{\infty} \delta_i(\mu + \epsilon_{t-i})$$

so that

$$\text{Var}[y_t] = \sum_{i=0}^{\infty} \delta_i^2 \sigma_\epsilon^2.$$

Whether this is finite or not depends on whether the series of $\delta_i s$ is exploding or converging. For the AR(2) case, the series converges if $|\gamma_2| < 1$, $\gamma_1 + \gamma_2 < 1$, and $\gamma_2 - \gamma_1 < 1$.[6]

For the more general case, the autoregressive process is stationary if the roots of the **characteristic equation,**

$$C(z) = 1 - \gamma_1 z - \gamma_2 z^2 - \cdots - \gamma_p z^p = 0,$$

have modulus greater than 1, or "lie outside the unit circle."[7] It follows that if a stochastic process is stationary, it has an infinite moving average representation (and, if not, it does not). The AR(1) process is the simplest case. The characteristic equation is

$$C(z) = 1 - \gamma z = 0,$$

and its single root is $1/\gamma$. This lies outside the unit circle if $|\gamma| < 1$, which we saw earlier.

Finally, consider the inversion of the moving-average process in (18-9) and (18-10). Whether this is possible depends on the coefficients in $D(L)$ in the same fashion that stationarity hinges on the coefficients in $C(L)$. This counterpart to stationarity of an autoregressive process is called **invertibility.** For it to be possible to invert a moving-average process to produce an autoregressive representation, the roots of $D(L) = 0$ must be outside the unit circle. Notice, for example, that in (18-5), the inversion of the moving-average process is possible only if $|\theta| < 1$. Since the characteristic equation for the MA(1) process is $1 - \theta L = 0$, the root is $1/\theta$, which must be larger than 1.

If the roots of the characteristic equation of a moving-average process all lie outside the unit circle, the series is said to be invertible. Note that invertibil-

---

[6]This restricts (γ_1, γ_2) to a triangle with points at $(-1, 2)$, $(-1, -2)$, and $(1, 0)$.

[7]The roots may be complex. (See Sections 16.9.2 and 17.3.4.) They are of the form $a \pm bi$, where $i = \sqrt{-1}$. The unit circle refers to the two-dimensional set of values of a and b defined by $a^2 + b^2 = 1$, which defines a circle centered at the origin with radius 1.

ity has no bearing on the stationarity of a process. All moving average processes with finite coefficients are stationary. Whether an ARMA process is stationary or not depends only on the AR part of the model.

18.2.3. Autocorrelations of a Stationary Stochastic Process

The function

$$\lambda_k = \text{Cov}[y_t, y_{t-k}]$$

is called the **autocovariance function** of the process y_t. The **autocorrelation function,** or **ACF,** is obtained by dividing by the variance λ_0 to obtain

$$\rho_k = \frac{\lambda_k}{\lambda_0}, \ -1 \le \rho_k \le 1.$$

For a stationary process, the ACF will be a function of k and the parameters of the process. The ACF is a useful device for describing a time-series process, in much the way that the moments are used to describe the distribution of a random variable. One of the characteristics of a stationary stochastic process is an autocorrelation function that eventually tapers off to zero. The AR(1) process provides the simplest example, since

$$\rho_k = \gamma^k.$$

This is a geometric series that either declines monotonically from $\rho_0 = 1$ if γ is positive or with a sawtooth pattern if γ is negative. Note, as well, that for the process $y_t = \gamma y_{t-1} + \epsilon_t$,

$$\rho_k = \gamma \rho_{k-1}, \quad k \ge 1,$$

which bears a noteworthy resemblance to the process itself.

For higher-order autoregressive series, the autocorrelations may decline monotonically or may progress in the fashion of a damped sine wave.[8] Consider, for example, the second-order autoregression, where we assume without loss of generality that $\mu = 0$ (since we are examining second moments in deviations from the mean):

$$y_t = \gamma_1 y_{t-1} + \gamma_2 y_{t-2} + \epsilon_t.$$

If the process is stationary, then $\text{Var}[y_t] = \text{Var}[y_{t-1}]$ and so on. Also, $\text{Var}[y_t] = \text{Cov}[y_t, y_t]$ and so on, and $\text{Cov}[\epsilon_t, y_{t-s}] = 0$ if $s > 0$. These relationships imply, first, that

$$\lambda_0 = \gamma_1 \lambda_1 + \gamma_2 \lambda_2 + \sigma_\epsilon^2.$$

[8]The behavior is a function of the roots of the characteristic equation. This aspect is discussed further in Section 16.9 and especially 16.9.3.

Now, using additional lags, we find

$$\lambda_1 = \gamma_1\lambda_0 + \gamma_2\lambda_1$$

and **(18-15)**

$$\lambda_2 = \gamma_1\lambda_1 + \gamma_2\lambda_0.$$

These three equations provide the solution

$$\lambda_0 = \frac{\sigma_\epsilon^2}{1 - \gamma_1^2/(1 - \gamma_2) + \gamma_2}.$$

The variance is unchanging, so we can divide throughout by λ_0 to obtain the relationships for the autocorrelations,

$$\rho_1 = \gamma_1\rho_0 + \gamma_2\rho_1.$$

Since $\rho_0 = 1, \rho_1 = \gamma_1/(1 - \gamma_2)$. Using the same procedure for additional lags, we find

$$\rho_2 = \gamma_1\rho_1 + \gamma_2,$$

so $\rho_2 = \gamma_1^2/(1 - \gamma_2) + \gamma_2$. Generally, then, for lags of two or more,

$$\rho_k = \gamma_1\rho_{k-1} + \gamma_2\rho_{k-2}.$$

Once again, the autocorrelations follow the same difference equation as the series itself. The behavior of this function depends on γ_1, γ_2, and k, although not in an obvious way. The inherent behavior of the autocorrelation function can be deduced from the characteristic equation.[9] For the second order process we are examining the autocorrelations are of the form

$$\rho_k = \phi_1(1/z_1)^k + \phi_2(1/z_2)^k,$$

where the two roots are[10]

$$z = \tfrac{1}{2}[\gamma_1 \pm \sqrt{\gamma_1^2 + 4\gamma_2}].$$

If the two roots are real, we know that their reciprocals will be less than 1 in absolute value, so that ρ_k will be the sum of two terms that are decaying to zero. If the two roots are complex, then ρ_k will be the sum of two terms that are oscillating in the form of a damped sine wave.

Applications that involve autoregressions of order greater than two are

[9]The set of results that we would use to derive this result are exactly those we used in Section 16.9.2 to analyze the stability of a dynamic equation. This makes sense, of course, since the equation linking the autocorrelations is a simple difference equation.

[10]We used the device in Section 17.3.4 to find the characteristic roots. For a second-order equation, the quadratic is easy to manipulate.

relatively unusual. Nonetheless, higher-order models can be handled in the same fashion. For the AR(p) process

$$y_t = \gamma_1 y_{t-1} + \gamma_2 y_{t-2} + \cdots + \gamma_p y_{t-p} + \epsilon_t,$$

the autocovariances will obey the **Yule–Walker equations**

$$\lambda_0 = \gamma_1\lambda_1 + \gamma_2\lambda_2 + \cdots + \gamma_p\lambda_p + \sigma_\epsilon^2,$$
$$\lambda_1 = \gamma_1\lambda_0 + \gamma_2\lambda_1 + \cdots + \gamma_p\lambda_{p-1},$$

and so on. The autocorrelations will once again follow the same difference equation as the original series,

$$\rho_k = \gamma_1\rho_{k-1} + \gamma_2\rho_{k-2} + \cdots + \gamma_p\rho_{k-p}.$$

The ACF for a moving average process is very simple to obtain. For the first-order process,

$$y_t = \epsilon_t - \theta\epsilon_{t-1},$$
$$\lambda_0 = (1 + \theta^2)\sigma_\epsilon^2,$$
$$\lambda_1 = -\theta\sigma_\epsilon^2,$$

then $\lambda_k = 0$ for $k > 1$. Higher-order processes appear similarly. For the MA(2) process, by multiplying out the terms and taking expectations, we find that

$$\lambda_0 = (1 + \theta_1^2 + \theta_2^2)\sigma_\epsilon^2,$$
$$\lambda_1 = (-\theta_1 + \theta_1\theta_2)\sigma_\epsilon^2,$$
$$\lambda_2 = -\theta_1\sigma_\epsilon^2,$$
$$\lambda_k = 0, k > 2.$$

The pattern for the general MA(q) process $y_t = \epsilon_t - \theta_1\epsilon_{t-1} - \theta_2\epsilon_{t-1} - \cdots - \theta_q\epsilon_{t-q}$ is analogous. The signature of a moving-average process is an autocorrelation function that abruptly drops to zero at one lag past the order of the process. As we will explore below, this sharp distinction provides a statistical tool that will help us distinguish between these two types of processes empirically.

The mixed process, ARMA(p, q), is more complicated since it is a mixture of the two forms. For the ARMA(1, 1) process

$$y_t = \gamma y_{t-1} + \epsilon_t - \theta\epsilon_{t-1},$$

the Yule–Walker equations are

$$\lambda_0 = E[y_t(\gamma y_{t-1} + \epsilon_t - \theta\epsilon_{t-1})] = \gamma\lambda_1 + \sigma_\epsilon^2 - \sigma_\epsilon^2(\theta\gamma - \theta^2),$$
$$\lambda_1 = \gamma\lambda_0 - \theta\sigma_\epsilon^2,$$

then

$$\lambda_k = \gamma\lambda_{k-1}, \quad k > 1.$$

The general characteristic of ARMA processes is that when the moving-average component is of order q, then in the series of autocorrelations, there will be an initial q terms that are complicated functions of both the AR and MA parameters, but after q periods,

$$\rho_k = \gamma_1\rho_{k-1} + \gamma_2\rho_{k-1} + \cdots + \gamma_p\rho_{k-p}, \quad k > q.$$

18.2.4. Partial Autocorrelations of a Stationary Stochastic Process

The autocorrelation function ACF(k) gives the gross correlation between y_t and y_{t-k}. But as we saw in our analysis of the classical regression model in Section 6.4.4, a gross correlation such as this can mask a completely different underlying relationship. In this setting, we observe, for example, that a correlation between y_t and y_{t-2} could arise primarily because both variables are correlated with y_{t-1}. Consider the AR(1) process $y_t = \gamma y_{t-1} + \epsilon_t$. The second gross autocorrelation is $\rho_2 = \gamma^2$. But in the same spirit, we might ask what is the correlation between y_t and y_{t-2} *net of the intervening effect of* y_{t-1}? In this model, if we remove the effect of y_{t-1} from y_t, only ϵ_t remains, and this is uncorrelated with y_{t-2}. We would conclude that the **partial autocorrelation** between y_t and y_{t-2} in this model is zero.

DEFINITION 18.2: Partial Autocorrelation Coefficient. *The partial correlation between y_t and y_{t-k} is the simple correlation between y_{t-k} and y_t minus that part explained linearly by the intervening lags. That is,*

$$\rho_k^* = \text{Corr}[y_t - E^*(y_t \mid y_{t-1}, \ldots, y_{t-k+1}), y_{t-k}],$$

where

$$E^*(y_t \mid y_{t-1}, \ldots, y_{t-k+1}) = \textit{the best linear prediction of } y_t \textit{ by } y_{t-1}, \ldots, y_{t-k+1}.$$

The function $E^*(.)$ might be the linear regression if the conditional mean happened to linear, but it might not. The optimal *linear* predictor *is* the linear regression, however, so what we have is

$$\rho_k^* = \text{Corr}[y_t - \beta_1 y_{t-1} - \beta_2 y_{t-2} - \cdots - \beta_{k-1} y_{t-k+1}, y_{t-k}],$$

where $\boldsymbol{\beta} = [\beta_1, \ \beta_2, \ \ldots, \ \beta_{k-1}] = \{\text{Var}[y_{t-1}, \ y_{t-2}, \ \ldots, \ y_{t-k+1}]\}^{-1} \times \text{Cov}[y_t, (y_{t-1}, y_{t-2}, \ldots, y_{t-k+1})]'$. This will be recognized as a vector of regression coefficients. As such, what we are computing here (of course) is the correlation between a vector of residuals and y_{t-k}. There are various ways to formalize this computation [see, e.g., Enders (pp. 82-85)]. One intuitively appealing approach is suggested by the equivalent definition (which is also a prescription for computing it), as follows.

Definition 18.3: Partial Autocorrelation Coefficient. *The partial correlation between* y_t and y_{t-k} *is the last coefficient in the linear projection of* y_t *on* $[y_{t-1}, y_{t-2}, \dots, y_{t-k}]$,

$$\begin{bmatrix} \beta_1 \\ \beta_2 \\ \vdots \\ \beta_{k-1} \\ \rho_k^* \end{bmatrix} = \begin{bmatrix} \lambda_0 & \lambda_1 & \cdots & \lambda_{k-2} & \lambda_{k-1} \\ \lambda_1 & \lambda_0 & \cdots & \lambda_{k-3} & \lambda_{k-2} \\ & \cdots & \vdots & \cdots & \\ \lambda_{k-1} & \lambda_{k-2} & \cdots & \lambda_1 & \lambda_0 \end{bmatrix}^{-1} \begin{bmatrix} \lambda_1 \\ \lambda_2 \\ \vdots \\ \lambda_k \end{bmatrix}.$$

As before, there are some distinctive patterns for particular time series processes. Consider first the autoregressive processes,

$$y_t = \gamma_1 y_{t-1} + \gamma_2 y_{t-2} + \cdots + \gamma_p y_{t-p} + \epsilon_t.$$

We are interested in the last coefficient in the projection of y_t on y_{t-1}, then on $[y_{t-1}, y_{t-2}]$, and so on. The first of these is the simple regression coefficient of y_t on y_{t-1}, so

$$\rho_1^* = \frac{\text{Cov}[y_t, y_{t-1}]}{\text{Var}[y_{t-1}]} = \frac{\lambda_1}{\lambda_0} = \rho_1.$$

The first partial autocorrelation coefficient for any process equals the first autocorrelation coefficient.

Without doing the messy algebra, we observe as well that for the AR(p) process, ρ_1^* is a mixture of all the γ coefficients. Of course, if p equals 1, then $\rho_1^* = \rho_1 = \gamma$. For the higher-order processes, the autocorrelations are likewise mixtures of the autoregressive coefficients until we reach ρ_p^*. In view of the form of the AR(p) model, the last coefficient in the linear projection on p lagged values is γ_p. Also, we can see the signature pattern of the AR(p) process, any additional partial autocorrelations must be zero, as they will be simply $\rho_k^* = \text{Corr}[\epsilon_t, y_{t-k}] = 0$ if $k > p$.

Combining results thus far, we have the characteristic pattern for an autoregressive process. The ACF, ρ_k, will gradually decay to zero, either monotonically if the characteristic roots are real or in a sinusoidal pattern if they are complex. The PACF, ρ_k^*, will be irregular out to lag p, when they abruptly drop to zero and remain there.

The moving-average process is the mirror image of this. We have already examined the ACF for the MA(q) process; it has q irregular spikes then falls to zero and stays there. For the PACF, write the model as

$$y_t = (1 - \theta_1 L - \theta_2 L^2 - \cdots - \theta_q L^q)\epsilon_t.$$

If the series is invertible, which we will assume throughout, then we have

$$\frac{y_t}{1 - \theta_1 L - \cdots - \theta_q L^q} = \epsilon_t,$$

or

$$y_t = \pi_1 y_{t-1} + \pi_2 y_{t-1} + \cdots + \epsilon_t$$
$$= \sum_{i=1}^{\infty} \pi_i y_{t-i} + \epsilon_t.$$

The autoregressive form of the MA(q) process has an infinite number of terms, which means that the PACF will not fall off to zero the way that the PACF of the AR process does. Rather the PACF of an MA process will resemble the ACF of an AR process. For example, for the MA(1) process $y_t = \epsilon_t - \theta\epsilon_{t-1}$, the AR representation is

$$y_t = \theta y_{t-1} + \theta^2 y_{t-2} + \cdots + \epsilon_t,$$

which is the familiar form of an AR(1) process. Thus, the PACF of an MA(1) is identical to the ACF of an AR(1) process, $\rho_k^* = \theta^k$.

The ARMA (p, q) is a mixture of the two types of processes, so its ACF and PACF are likewise mixtures of the two forms discussed above. Generalities are difficult to draw, but normally, the ACF of an ARMA process will have a few distinctive spikes in the early lags corresponding to the number of MA terms, followed by the characteristic smooth pattern of the AR part of the model. High-order MA processes are relatively uncommon in general, and high-order AR processes (greater than two) seem primarily to arise in the form of the nonstationary processes described in the next section. For a stationary process, the workhorses of the applied literature are the (2, 0) and (1, 1) processes. For the ARMA (1, 1) process, both the ACF and the PACF will display a distinctive spike at lag 1 followed by an exponentially decaying pattern thereafter.

18.2.5. Modeling Univariate Time Series

The preceding is largely descriptive. There is no underlying theory that states *why* a compact ARMA (p, q) representation should adequately describe the movement of a given economic time series. Nonetheless, as a methodology for building forecasting models, this set of tools and its empirical counterpart have proved as good as and even superior to much more elaborate specifications (perhaps to the consternation of the builders of large macroeconomic models).[11] Box and Jenkins (1984) have pioneered a forecasting framework based on the preceding that has been used in a great many fields and that has, certainly in terms of numbers, largely supplanted the use of large integrated econometric models.

Box and Jenkins's approach to modeling a stochastic process can be motivated by the following.

[11]This observation can be overstated. Even the most committed advocate of the Box–Jenkins methods would concede that an ARMA model of, for example, housing starts, will do little to reveal the link between the interest rate policies of the Federal Reserve and their variable of interest. That is, the *covariation* of economic variables remains as interesting as ever.

THEOREM 18.1: Wold's Decomposition Theorem. *Every zero mean covariance stationary stochastic process can be represented in the form*

$$y_t = E^*[y_t \mid y_{t-1}, y_{t-2}, \cdots, y_{t-p}] + \sum_{i=0}^{\infty} \pi_i \epsilon_{t-i},$$

where ϵ_t is white noise, $\pi_0 = 1$, and the weights are ***absolutely summable***—*that is,*

$$\sum_{i=1}^{\infty} |\pi_i| < \infty$$

—$E^*[y_t \mid y_{t-1}, y_{t-2}, \ldots, y_{t-p}]$ is the optimal linear predictor of y_t based on the lagged values, and the predictor E_t^* is uncorrelated with ϵ_{t-i}.

Thus, the theorem decomposes the process generating y_t into

$E_t^* = E^*[y_t \mid y_{t-1}, y_{t-2}, \cdots, y_{t-p}] =$ the **linearly deterministic component**

and

$\sum_{i=0}^{\infty} \pi_i \epsilon_{t-i} =$ the **linearly indeterministic component.**

The theorem states that for any stationary stochastic process, for a given choice of p, there is a Wold representation of the stationary series

$$y_t = \sum_{i=1}^{p} \gamma_i y_{t-i} + \sum_{i=0}^{\infty} \pi_i \epsilon_{t-i}.$$

Note that for a specific ARMA (P, Q) process, if $p \geq P$, then $\pi_i = 0$ for $i > Q$. For practical purposes, the problem with the Wold representation is that we cannot estimate the infinite number of parameters needed to produce the full right-hand side, and, of course, P and Q are unknown. The compromise, then, is to base an estimate of the representation on a model with a finite number of moving-average terms. We can seek the one that best fits the data in hand.

It is important to note that neither the ARMA representation of a process nor the Wold representation are unique. In general terms, suppose that the process generating y_t is

$$\Gamma(L) y_t = \Theta(L) \epsilon_t.$$

We assume that $\Gamma(L)$ is finite, but, $\Theta(L)$ need not be. Let $\Phi(L)$ be some other polynomial in the lag operator with roots that are outside the unit circle. Then

$$\left[\frac{\Phi(L)}{\Gamma(L)}\right] \Gamma(L) y_t = \left[\frac{\Phi(L)}{\Gamma(L)}\right] \Theta(L) \epsilon_t$$

or

$$\Phi(L) y_t = \Pi(L) \epsilon_t.$$

The new representation is fully equivalent to the old one, but might have a different number of autoregressive parameters, which is exactly the point of the Wold decomposition. The implication is that part of the model-building process will be to determine the lag structures. Further discussion on the methodology is given by Box and Jenkins (1984).

The Box–Jenkins approach to modeling stochastic processes consists of the following steps:

1. Satisfactorily transform the data so as to obtain a stationary series. This will usually mean taking first differences, logs, or both to obtain a series whose autocorrelation function eventually displays the characteristic exponential decay of a stationary series.
2. Estimate the parameters of the resulting ARMA model, generally by nonlinear least squares.
3. Generate the set of residuals from the estimated model and verify that they satisfactorily resemble a white noise series. If not, respecify the model and return to step 2.
4. The model can now be used for forecasting purposes.

Space limitations prevent us from giving a full presentation of the set of techniques. Since this methodology has spawned a mini-industry of its own, however, there is no shortage of book length analyses and prescriptions to which the reader may refer. Three to consider are the canonical source, Box and Jenkins (1984), Mills (1990), and Enders (1995). Some of the aspects of the estimation and analysis steps do have broader relevance for our work here, so we will continue to examine them in some detail.

18.2.6. Estimation of the Parameters of a Univariate Time Series

We first encountered the problem of estimation with time-series data in Chapter 6, in our discussions of stochastic regressors. The broad problem, which carries through to all the discussions of this chapter, is that the consistency and asymptotic normality results that we derived based on random sampling will no longer apply. For example, for a stationary series, we have assumed that $\text{Var}[y_t] = \lambda_0$ regardless of t. But we have yet to establish that an *estimated* variance,

$$c_0 = \frac{1}{T-1}\sum_{t=1}^{T}(y_t - \bar{y})^2$$

will converge to λ_0, or anything else, for that matter. A process is said to be **ergodic** if moments such as $\bar{y}$ and c_0 converge to their population counterparts μ and λ_0.[12] In most cases, stationarity is sufficient. The essential component of the condition is one that we have met at many points in this discussion, that autocovariances must decline sufficiently rapidly as the separation in time increases. It is possible to construct theoretical examples of processes that are stationary but not ergodic, but for practical purposes, a stationarity assumption

[12] The formal conditions for ergodicity are quite involved; see Davidson and MacKinnon (1993) or Hamilton (1994, Chapter 7).

will be sufficient for us to proceed with estimation. For example, in our models of stationary processes, if we assume that $\epsilon_t \sim N[0, \sigma^2]$, which is common, then the stationary processes are ergodic as well.

Estimation of the parameters of a time-series process must begin with a determination of the type of process that we have in hand. (Box and Jenkins label this the **identification** step. But identification is a term of art in econometrics, so we will steer around that admittedly standard name.) For this purpose, the empirical estimates of the autocorrelation and partial autocorrelation functions are useful tools.

The sample counterpart to the ACF is the **correlogram,**

$$r_k = \frac{\sum_{t=k+1}^{T} (y_t - \bar{y})(y_{t-k} - \bar{y})}{\sum_{t=1}^{T} (y_t - \bar{y})^2}.$$

A plot of r_k against k provides a description of a process and can be used to help discern what type of process is generating the data. The sample PACF is the counterpart to the ACF, but net of the intervening lags; that is,

$$r_k^* = \frac{\sum_{t=k+1}^{T} y_t^* y_{t-k}^*}{\sum_{t=k+1}^{T} (y_{t-k}^*)^2},$$

where y_t^* and y_{t-k}^* are residuals from the regressions of y_t and y_{t-k} on $[1, y_{t-1}, y_{t-2}, \ldots, y_{t-k+1}]$. We have seen this at many points before; r_k^* is simply the last linear least squares regression coefficient in the regression of y_t on $[1, y_{t-1}, y_{t-2}, \ldots, y_{t-k+1}, y_{t-k}]$. Plots of the ACF and PACF of a series are usually presented together. Since the sample estimates of the autocorrelations and partial autocorrelations are not likely to be identically zero even when the population values are, we use diagnostic tests to discern whether a time series appears to be nonautocorrelated.[13] Individual sample autocorrelations will be approximately distributed with mean zero and variance $1/T$ under the hypothesis that the series is white noise. The Box–Pierce (1970) statistic

$$Q = T \sum_{k=1}^{p} r_k^2$$

is commonly used to test whether a series is white noise. Under the null hypothesis that the series is white noise, Q is asymptotically distributed as chi-squared with p degrees of freedom. A refinement that appears to have better finite-sample properties is the Ljung–Box (1978a) statistic,

[13]The Durbin–Watson test discussed in Section 13.5.1 is one of these.

$$Q' = T(T+2)\sum_{k=1}^{p}\frac{r_k^2}{T-k}.$$

The asymptotic distribution of Q' is the same as that of Q.[14]

The process of finding the appropriate specification is essentially trial and error. An initial specification based on the sample ACF and PACF can be found. The parameters of the model can then be estimated by least squares. For pure AR(p) processes, the estimation step is simple. The parameters can be estimated by linear least squares. If there are moving-average terms, linear least squares is inconsistent, but the parameters of the model can be fit by nonlinear least squares as shown in Section 17.3.2. Once the model has been estimated, a set of residuals is computed to assess the adequacy of the specification. In an AR model, the residuals are just the deviations from the regression line. In the presence of MA terms, residuals must be computed recursively—see (17-43).

The adequacy of the specification can be examined by applying the foregoing techniques to the estimated residuals. If they appear to satisfactorily mimic a white noise process, then analysis can proceed to the forecasting step. If not, a new specification should be considered.

EXAMPLE 18.1 ACF and PACF for a Series of Bond Yields

Table 18.1 lists five years of monthly averages of the yield on a Moody's Aaa rated corporate bond. The series is plotted in Figure 18.1. From the figure, it

TABLE 18.1 Bond Yield on a Moody's Aaa Rated Corporate Bond (percent/year)

Month	*1990*	*1991*	*1992*	*1993*	*1994*
Jan.	8.99	9.04	8.20	7.91	6.92
Feb.	9.72	8.83	8.29	7.71	7.08
Mar.	9.37	8.93	8.35	7.58	7.48
Apr.	9.46	8.86	8.33	7.46	7.88
May	9.47	8.86	8.28	7.43	7.99
Jun.	9.26	9.01	8.22	7.33	7.97
Jul.	9.24	9.00	8.07	7.17	8.11
Aug.	9.41	8.75	7.95	6.85	8.07
Sep.	9.56	8.61	7.92	6.66	8.34
Oct.	9.53	8.55	7.99	6.67	8.57
Nov.	9.30	8.48	8.10	6.93	8.68
Dec.	9.05	8.31	7.98	6.93	8.46

Source: Economic Report of the President, U.S. Government Printing Office, 1995, p. 359.

[14]There is some disagreement about the appropriateness of Q and Q' for testing model adequacy in this context. [See Maddala (1992, pp. 540–542).] The argument is essentially the same as that against using the Durbin–Watson statistic in the presence of lagged dependent variables. See Section 13.5.3.

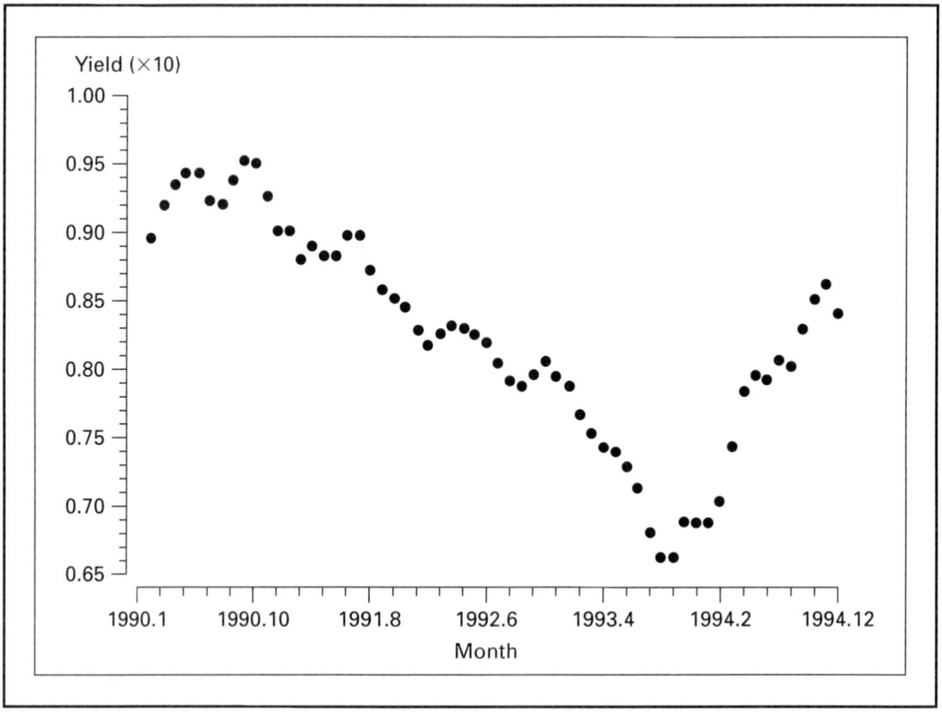

FIGURE 18.1 Monthly Data on Bond Yields.

TABLE 18.2 ACF and PACF for Bond Yields

Time-series identification for YIELD

Box–Pierce statistic = 323.0587		Box–Ljung Statistic = 317.4389	
Degrees of freedom = 14		Degrees of freedom = 14	
Significance level = 0.0000		Significance level = 0.0000	

♦ → |coefficient| > 2/sqrt(N) or > 95% significant

Lag	*Autocorrelation Function*	−1 0 +1	*Box–Pierce*	*Partial Autocorrelations*	−1 0 +1
1	0.970♦		56.42♦	0.970♦	
2	0.908♦		105.93♦	−0.573♦	
3	0.840♦		148.29♦	0.157	
4	0.775♦		184.29♦	−0.043	
5	0.708♦		214.35♦	−0.309♦	
6	0.636♦		238.65♦	−0.024	
7	0.567♦		257.93♦	−0.037	
8	0.501♦		272.97♦	0.059	
9	0.439♦		284.51♦	−0.068	
10	0.395♦		293.85♦	0.216	
11	0.370♦		302.08♦	−0.180	
12	0.354♦		309.58♦	0.048	
13	0.339♦		316.48♦	0.162	
14	0.331♦		323.06♦	0.171	

TABLE 18.3 ACF and PACF for Residuals

Time-series identification for U

Box–Pierce statistic = 13.7712	Box–Ljung statistic = 16.1336
Significance level = 0.4669	Significance level = 0.3053

♦ → |coefficient| > 2/sqrt(N) or > 95% significant

Lag	*Autocorrelation Function*	*−1 0 +1*	*Box–Pierce*	*Partial Autocorrelations*	*−1 0 +1*
1	0.154		1.38	0.154	
2	−0.147		2.64	−0.170	
3	−0.207		5.13	−0.179	
4	0.161		6.64	0.183	
5	0.117		7.43	0.068	
6	0.114		8.18	0.094	
7	−0.110		8.89	−0.066	
8	0.041		8.99	0.125	
9	−0.168		10.63	−0.258	
10	0.014		10.64	0.035	
11	−0.016		10.66	0.015	
12	−0.009		10.66	−0.089	
13	−0.195		12.87	−0.166	
14	−0.125		13.77	−0.132	

would appear that stationarity may not be a reasonable assumption. We will return to this question below. The ACF and PACF for the original series are shown in Table 18.2 (page 840), with the diagnostic statistics discussed earlier.

The plots appear to be consistent with an AR(2) process, although the ACF at longer lags seems a bit more persistent than might have been expected. Once again, this may indicate that the series is not stationary. Maintaining that assumption for the present, we computed the residuals from the AR(2) model and subjected them to the same tests as the original series. Despite the earlier suggestions, the residuals do appear to resemble a white noise series (Table 18.3).

18.3. NONSTATIONARY PROCESSES AND UNIT ROOTS

Most economic variables that exhibit strong trends, such as GNP, consumption, or the price level, are not stationary and are thus not amenable to the analysis of the previous section. In many cases, stationarity can be achieved by simple differencing or some other transformation. But new statistical issues arise in analyzing nonstationary series that are understated by this superficial observation.

18.3.1. Integrated Processes and Differencing

A process that figures prominently in recent work is the **random walk,**

$$y_t = \mu + y_{t-1} + \epsilon_t.$$

By direct substitution,

$$y_t = \sum_{i=0}^{\infty} (\mu + \epsilon_{t-i}).$$

That is, y_t is the simple sum of what will eventually be an infinite number of random variables, possibly with nonzero mean. If the innovations are being generated by the same zero-mean, constant-variance distribution, the variance of y_t would obviously be infinite. As such, the random walk is clearly a nonstationary process, even if μ equals zero. On the other hand, the first difference of y_t,

$$z_t = y_t - y_{t-1} = \mu + \epsilon_t,$$

is simply the innovation plus the mean, which we have already assumed is stationary.

The series y_t is said to be **integrated of order one,** denoted $I(1)$, because taking a first difference produces a stationary process. A nonstationary series is integrated of order d, denoted $I(d)$, if it becomes stationary after being first differenced d times. A further generalization of the ARMA model discussed in Section 18.2.1 would be the series

$$z_t = (1 - L)^d y_t = \Delta^d y_t.$$

The resulting model is denoted an **autoregressive integrated moving-average** model, or ARIMA (p, d, q).[15] In full, the model would be

$$\Delta^d y_t = \mu + \gamma_1 \Delta^d y_{t-1} + \gamma_2 \Delta^d y_{t-2} + \cdots + \gamma_p \Delta^d y_{t-p} + \epsilon_t - \theta_1 \epsilon_{t-1} - \cdots - \theta_q \epsilon_{t-q},$$

where

$$\Delta y_t = y_t - y_{t-1} = (1 - L) y_t. \tag{18-16}$$

This may be written compactly as

$$C(L)[(1 - L)^d y_t] = \mu + D(L)\epsilon_t, \tag{18-17}$$

where $C(L)$ and $D(L)$ are the polynomials in the lag operator and $(1 - L)^d y_t = \Delta^d y_t$ is the dth difference of y_t.

[15]There are yet further refinements one might consider, for example, removing seasonal effects from z_t by differencing by quarter or month. See Harvey (1990) and Davidson and MacKinnon (1993). Some recent work has relaxed the assumption that d is an integer. The **fractionally** integrated series, or ARFIMA has been used to model series in which the very long run multipliers decay more slowly than would be predicted otherwise. See Hamilton (1994, pp. 448–450) for discussion. These refinements are beyond the scope of our work in this text.

An $I(1)$ series in its raw (undifferenced) form is constantly growing. Most macroeconomic flows and stocks that relate to population size, such as output or employment, are $I(1)$. The nominal GNP series in Table 17.1 is an example. An $I(2)$ series is growing at an ever-increasing rate. The price-level data in Table 17.1 and shown below appear to be $I(2)$. Series that are $I(3)$ or greater are extremely unusual, but do exist. Among the few manifestly $I(3)$ series that could be listed, one would find, for example, the money stocks or price levels in hyperinflationary economies such as interwar Germany or Hungary after World War II.

EXAMPLE 18.2 A Nonstationary Series

The variables in Tables 17.1 and 17.5 are strongly trended, so the mean is changing over time. Figures 18.2, 18.3, and 18.4 plot the log of the GNP deflator series in Table 17.1 and its first and second differences. The original series and first differences are obviously nonstationary, but the second differencing appears to have rendered the series stationary.

The first 10 autocorrelations of the log of the GNP deflator series are shown in Table 18.4. The autocorrelations of the original series show the signa-

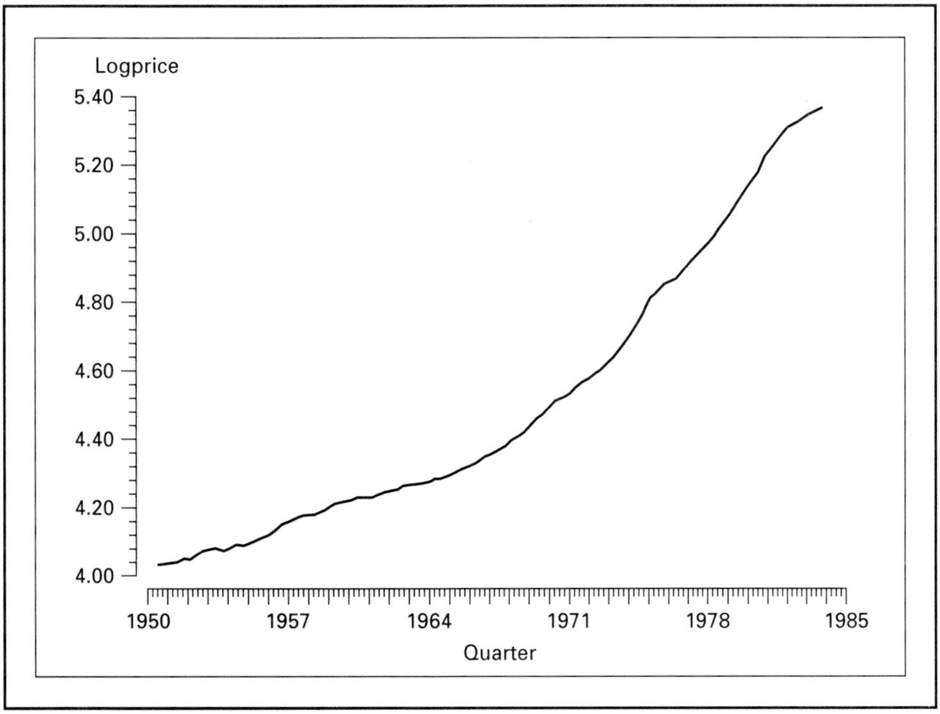

FIGURE 18.2 Quarterly Data on ln GNP Deflator.

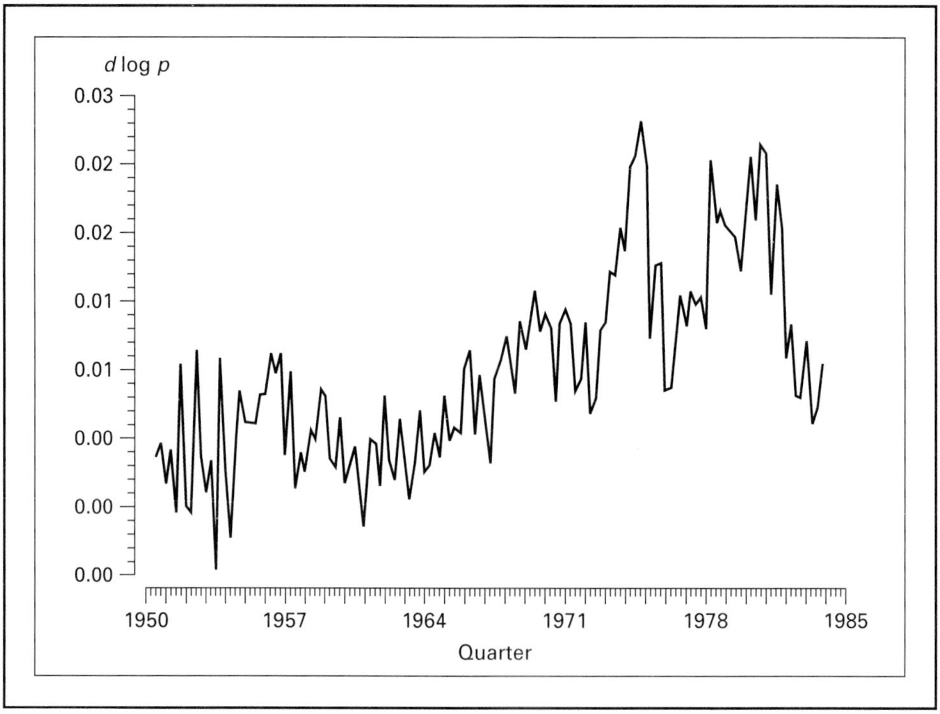

FIGURE 18.3 First Difference of ln GNP Deflator.

ture of a strongly trended, nonstationary series. The first difference also exhibits nonstationarity, as the autocorrelations are still very large after a lag of 10 periods. The second difference appears to be stationary, with mild negative autocorrelation at the first lag, but essentially none after that. Intuition might suggest that further differencing would reduce the autocorrelation further, but this would be incorrect. We leave as an exercise to show that, in fact, for values of γ less than about 0.5, first differencing of an AR(1) process actually increases autocorrelation.

18.3.2. Random Walks, Trends, and Spurious Regressions

In a seminal paper, Granger and Newbold (1974) argued that researchers had not paid sufficient attention to the warning of a very high autocorrelation in the residuals from conventional regression models. Among their conclusions were that macroeconomic data, as a rule, were integrated and that in regressions involving the levels of such data, the standard significance tests were usually misleading. The conventional t and F test would tend to reject the hypothesis of no relationship when, in fact, there might be none. The general result at

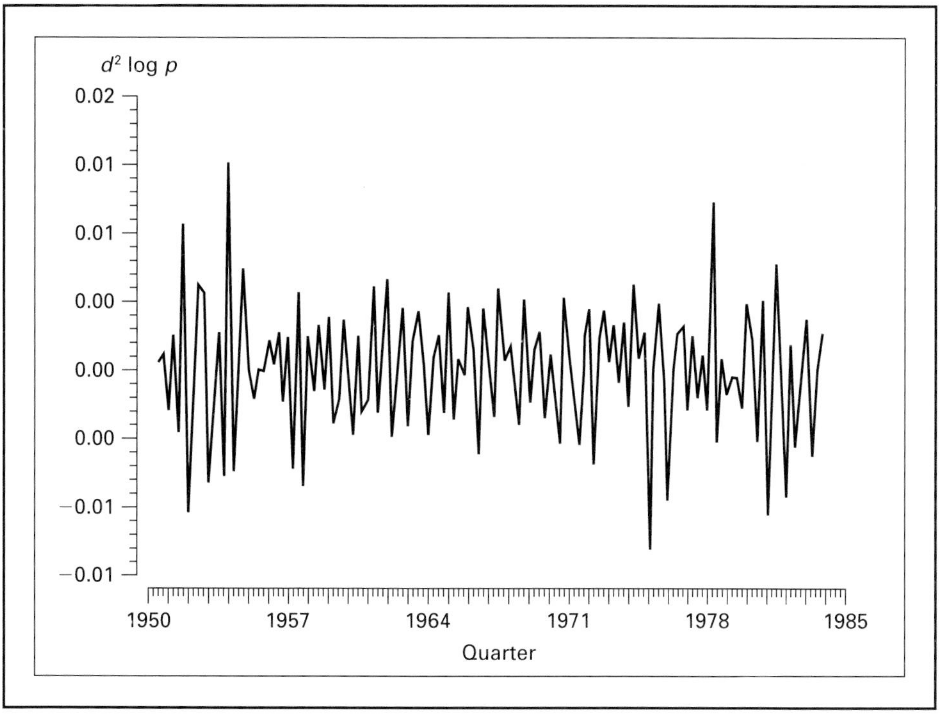

FIGURE 18.4   Second Difference of ln GNP Deflator.

TABLE 18.4   Autocorrelations for ln GNP Deflator

Lag	*Autocorrelation Function Original Series, ln Price*			*Autocorrelation Function First Difference of ln Price*			*Autocorrelation Function Second Difference of ln Price*		
1	1.000		▬▬	0.812		▬▬	−0.395	▮	
2	1.000		▬▬	0.765		▬▬	−0.112	▪	
3	0.999		▬▬	0.776		▬▬	0.258		▮
4	0.999		▬▬	0.682		▬▬	−0.101	▪	
5	0.999		▬▬	0.631		▬▬	−0.022	▪	
6	0.998		▬▬	0.592		▬▬	0.076		▪
7	0.998		▬▬	0.523		▬▬	−0.163	▮	
8	0.997		▬▬	0.513		▬▬	0.052		▪
9	0.997		▬▬	0.488		▬	−0.054	▪	
10	0.997		▬▬	0.491		▬	0.062		▪

the center of these findings is that the regression of one random walk on another is virtually certain to produce a significant relationship, even if the two are, in fact, independent. Among their extreme conclusions, Granger and Newbold suggested that researchers use a critical t value of 11.2 rather than the standard normal value of 1.96 to assess the significance of a coefficient estimate. Phillips (1986) takes strong issue with this conclusion. Based on a more general model and on an analytical rather than a Monte Carlo approach, he suggests that the normalized statistic $t_\beta/\sqrt{T}$ be used for testing purposes rather than t_β itself. For the 50 observations used by Granger and Newbold, the appropriate critical value would be close to 15! If anything, Granger and Newbold were too optimistic.

The **random walk with drift,**

$$z_t = \mu + z_{t-1} + u_t, \tag{18-18}$$

and the **trend stationary process,**

$$z_t = \mu + \beta t + u_t, \tag{18-19}$$

where, in both cases, u_t is a white noise process, appear to be reasonable characterizations of many macroeconomic time series.[16] Clearly both of these will produce strongly trended, nonstationary series,[17] so it is not surprising that regressions involving such variables almost always produce significant relationships. The strong correlation would seem to be a consequence of the underlying trend, whether or not there really is any regression at work. But Granger and Newbold went a step further. The intuition is less clear if there is a pure **random walk** at work,

$$z_t = z_{t-1} + u_t, \tag{18-20}$$

but even here, they found that regression "relationships" appear to persist even in unrelated series.

Each of these three series is characterized by a **unit root.** In each case, the **data-generating process (DGP)** can be written

$$(1 - L)z_t = \alpha + \nu_t, \tag{18-21}$$

where $\alpha = \mu$, β, and 0, respectively, and ν_t is a stationary process. Thus, the characteristic equation has a single root equal to 1; hence the name. The upshot of Granger and Newbold's and Phillips's findings is that the use of data characterized by unit roots has the potential to lead to serious errors in inferences.

---

[16]The analysis to follow has been extended to more general disturbance processes, but that complicates matters substantially. In this case, in fact, our assumption does cost considerable generality, but the extension is beyond the scope of our work. Some references on the subject are Phillips and Perron (1988) and Davidson and MacKinnon (1993).

[17]The constant term μ produces the trend in the random walk with drift. For convenience, suppose that the process starts at time zero. Then $z_t = \Sigma_{s=0}^{t}(\mu + \epsilon_s) = \mu t + \Sigma_{s=0}^{t}\epsilon_s$. Thus, z_t consists of a trend plus the sum of the innovations. The result is a variable with increasing variance around a linear trend.

In all three settings, the case for first differencing or detrending is compelling. On the other hand, it is not going to be immediately obvious which is the correct way to proceed—the data are strongly trended in all three cases—and taking the incorrect approach will not necessarily improve matters. For example, first differencing in (18-18) or (18-20) produces a white noise series, but first differencing in (18-19) trades the trend for autocorrelation in the form of an MA(1) process. On the other hand, detrending—that is, computing the residuals from a regression on time—is obviously counterproductive in (18-18) and (18-20), even though the regression of z_t on a trend will appear to be significant for the reasons we have been discussing, whereas detrending in (18-19) appears to be the right approach.[18] Since none of these approaches is likely to be obviously preferable at the outset, some means of choosing is necessary. Consider nesting all three models in a single equation,

$$z_t = \mu + \beta t + z_{t-1} + u_t.$$

Now subtract z_{t-1} from both sides of the equation and introduce the artificial parameter γ:

$$\begin{aligned} z_t - z_{t-1} &= \mu\gamma + \beta(1-\gamma)t + (\gamma - 1)z_{t-1} + u_t \\ &= \alpha_0 + \alpha_1 t + (\gamma - 1)z_{t-1}. \end{aligned} \tag{18-22}$$

where, by hypothesis, $\gamma = 1$. Equation (18-22) provides the basis for a variety of tests for unit roots in economic data. In principle, a test of the hypothesis that $\gamma - 1$ equals zero gives confirmation of the random walk with drift, since if γ equals 1 (and α_1 equals zero), (18-18) results. If $\gamma - 1$ is less than zero, the evidence favors the trend stationary (or some other) model, and detrending (or some alternative) is the preferable approach. The practical difficulty is that standard inference procedures based on least squares and the familiar test statistics are not valid in this setting. The issue is discussed in the next section.

18.3.3. Tests for Unit Roots in Economic Data

The implications of unit roots in macroeconomic data are, at least potentially, profound. If a structural variable, such as real output, is truly $I(1)$, shocks to it will have permanent effects. If confirmed, this observation would mandate some rather serious reconsideration of the analysis of macroeconomic policy. For example, the argument that a change in monetary policy could have a transitory effect on real output (which seems to be consistent with our regressions in Chapter 17) would vanish.[19] The literature is not without its skeptics, however. This result rests on a razor's edge. Although the literature is thick with

[18]See Nelson and Kang (1984).

[19]The observation seems to have touched off a bit of a feeding frenzy in the literature, as the 1980s saw the appearance of literally hundreds of studies, both theoretical and applied, of unit roots in economic data. An important example is the seminal paper by Nelson and Plosser (1982). In point of fact, there is little question but that this is an early part of the radical paradigm shift that has occurred in empirical macroeconomics.

tests that have failed to reject the hypothesis that $\gamma = 1$, many have also not rejected the hypothesis that $\gamma \geq 0.95$, and at 0.95 (or even at 0.99), the entire issue becomes moot.[20]

Consider the simple AR(1) model with zero-mean, white noise innovations,

$$y_t = \gamma y_{t-1} + \epsilon_t.$$

The downward bias of the least squares estimator when γ approaches 1 has been widely documented.[21] For $|\gamma| < 1$, however, the least squares estimator

$$c = \frac{\sum_{t=2}^{T} y_t y_{t-1}}{\sum_{t=2}^{T} y_{t-1}^2}$$

does have

$$\text{plim } c = \gamma$$

and

$$\sqrt{T}(c - \gamma) \xrightarrow{d} N[0, 1 - \gamma^2].$$

Does the result hold up if $\gamma = 1$? The case is called the unit root case, since in the ARMA representation $C(L)y_t = \epsilon_t$, the characteristic equation $1 - \gamma z = 0$ has one root equal to 1. That the asymptotic variance appears to go to zero should raise suspicions. The literature on the questions dates back to Mann and Wald (1943) and Rubin (1950). But for econometric purposes, the literature has a focal point at the celebrated papers of Dickey and Fuller (1979, 1981). They showed that if γ equals 1, then

$$T(c - \gamma) \xrightarrow{d} v,$$

where v is a random variable with finite variance, and in finite samples, $E[c] < 1$.

There are two important implications in the Dickey–Fuller results. First, the estimator of γ is biased downward if γ equals 1. Second, the OLS estimate of c converges to its probability limit more rapidly than the estimators to which we are accustomed. That is, the variance of c under the null hypothesis is $O(1/T^2)$, not $O(1/T)$. It turns out that the implications of this finding for the regressions with trended data are considerable.

We have already observed that in some cases, differencing or detrending is required to achieve stationarity of a series. Suppose, though, that the AR(1) model above is fit to an $I(1)$ series, despite that fact. The upshot of the preceding is that the conventional measures will tend to hide the true value of γ; the

[20]A large number of issues are raised in Maddala (1992, pp. 582–588).

[21]See, for example, Evans and Savin (1981, 1984).

sample estimate is biased downward, and by dint of the very small *true* sampling variance, the conventional t test will tend, incorrectly, to reject the hypothesis that $\gamma = 1$. The practical solution to this problem devised by Dickey and Fuller was to derive, through Monte Carlo methods, an appropriate set of critical values for testing the hypothesis that γ equals 1 in an AR(1) regression when there truly is a unit root. The hypothesis may be carried out with a conventional t test, but with a revised set of critical values. A few of the values from the Dickey–Fuller tables are reproduced in Table 18.5.

They also present values for testing for a unit root in the modified regressions:

$$y_t = \mu + \gamma y_{t-1} + \epsilon_t$$

and

$$y_t = \mu + \beta t + \gamma y_{t-1} + \epsilon_t.$$

A convenient reformulation of the $I(1)$ model is

$$\Delta y_t = \mu + \gamma^* y_{t-1} + \epsilon_t,$$

TABLE 18.5 Critical Values for the Dickey–Fuller Test

	Sample Size			
	25	***50***	***100***	∞
F ratio (D–F)[a]	7.24	6.73	6.49	6.25
F ratio (standard)	3.42	3.20	3.10	3.00
AR model[b]				
0.01	−2.66	−2.62	−2.60	−2.58
0.025	−2.26	−2.25	−2.24	−2.23
0.975	1.70	1.66	1.64	1.62
0.99	2.16	2.08	2.03	2.00
AR model with constant				
0.01	−3.75	−3.58	−3.51	−3.43
0.025	−3.333	−3.22	−3.17	−3.12
0.975	0.34	0.29	0.26	0.23
0.99	0.72	0.66	0.63	0.60
AR model with constant and time trend				
0.01	−4.38	−4.15	−4.04	−3.96
0.025	−3.95	−3.80	−3.69	−3.66
0.975	−0.50	−0.58	−0.62	−0.66
0.99	−0.15	−0.15	−0.28	−0.33

[a]From Dickey and Fuller (1981, p. 1063). Degrees of freedom are 2 and $T - p - 3$.

[b]From Fuller (1976, p. 373).

where

$$\gamma^* = \gamma - 1.$$

With this formulation, the Dickey–Fuller test for a unit root is carried out by testing the hypothesis that γ^* equals zero. The standard t statistic

$$\frac{c^*}{\{\text{Est. Var}[c^*]\}^{1/2}}$$

is then referred to the Dickey–Fuller tables. The **augmented Dickey–Fuller test** is the same one as above, carried out in the context of the model

$$\Delta y_t = \mu + \gamma^* y_{t-1} + \sum_{j=1}^{p-1} \phi_j \Delta y_{t-j} + \epsilon_t,$$

where

$$\phi_j = -\sum_{k=j+1}^{p} \gamma_k$$

and

$$\gamma^* = \left(\sum_{i=1}^{p} \gamma_i\right) - 1.$$

The advantage of this formulation is that it can accommodate higher-order autoregressive moving-average processes in ϵ_t. The unit root test is carried out as before against $\gamma^* = 0$.[22] The failure to reject the unit root produces the AR$(p - 1)$ model in the first differences. For a model with a time trend,

$$\Delta y_t = \mu + \beta t + \gamma^* y_{t-1} + \sum_{j=1}^{p-1} \phi_j \Delta y_{t-j} + \epsilon_t,$$

the test is carried out by testing the joint hypothesis that $\beta = \gamma^* = 0$. Dickey and Fuller (1981) present counterparts to the critical F statistics for testing the hypothesis.

EXAMPLE 18.3 Test for a Unit Root

In their 1981 paper, Dickey and Fuller apply their methodology to a model for the log of a quarterly series on output, the Federal Reserve Board Production Index. The model used is

$$y_t = \mu + \beta t + \gamma y_{t-1} + \phi(y_{t-1} - y_{t-2}) + \epsilon_t.$$

The test is carried out by testing the joint hypothesis that both β and γ^* are zero in the model

$$y_t - y_{t-1} = \mu + \beta t + \gamma^* y_{t-1} + \phi(y_{t-1} - y_{t-2}) + \epsilon_t.$$

---

[22]It is easily verified that one of the roots of the characteristic polynomial is $1/(\gamma_1 + \gamma_2 + \cdots + \gamma_p)$.

We will replicate the study with our data on real GNP from Table 17.1 using observations 1950III to 1983IV for all regressions. Recall, for our examples, $y_t = \ln(\text{GNP}_t/P_t)$. To begin, the simple AR(1) regression produces

$$\underset{}{y_t - y_{t-1}} = \underset{(3.605)}{0.025579} - \underset{(-2.401)}{0.0075059}y_{t-1}.$$

Asymptotic t ratios are given in parentheses. Based on the conventional critical point of -1.96, we would reject the hypothesis of a unit root. But the value from Table 18.5 for 134 observations would be roughly -3.17. So the hypothesis of a unit root is decidedly not rejected. The augmented regressions produce

$$y_t - y_{t-1} = \underset{(3.629)}{0.14331} + \underset{(3.329)}{0.00065504}t - \underset{(-3.478)}{0.08126}y_{t-1} + \underset{(6.721)}{0.49263}(y_{t-1} - y_{t-2}), \qquad R^2 = 0.33089$$

and

$$y_t - y_{t-1} = \underset{(3.904)}{0.0043356} + \underset{(6.303)}{0.49180}(y_{t-1} - y_{t-2}), \qquad R^2 = 0.024829.$$

The sample is observations 1950.3 to 1983.4:

$$F = \frac{(0.33089 - 0.24829)/2}{(1 - 0.33089)/(134 - 4)} = 8.024.$$

The F statistic is larger than the Dickey–Fuller value of 6.49. Therefore, we now reject the hypothesis of a unit root in the process generating the log of real GNP.

Recent literature on this subject has produced a hunt for unit roots in published data [e.g., Nelson and Plosser (1982)][23] and numerous extensions of the methodology. Convenient summaries are Nerlove and Diebold (1990) and Campbell and Perron (1991). The extensions include regressions with polynomials in time (Ouliaris et al., 1989) and splines in time (Perron, 1990). The extension to models with regressors of a general nature is complicated because the distribution of the standard test statistics is a function of the right-hand-side variables. Some useful results on the subject are in Phillips (1986).

18.4. COINTEGRATION

Studies in empirical macroeconomics almost always involve nonstationary and/or trending variables, such as income, consumption, money demand, the price level, trade flows, and exchange rates. Accumulated wisdom and the re-

[23]For the bond yield data examined in Example 18.1, the coefficient on y_{t-1} in the regression of Δy_t on a constant and y_{t-1} is -0.0313, with a t-ratio of -1.206. The hypothesis that there is a unit root in the bond yield data cannot be rejected on the basis of the Dickey–Fuller test. Given the appearance of the original series, this is hardly surprising.

sults of the previous sections suggest that the appropriate way to manipulate such series is to use differencing and other transformations (such as seasonal adjustment) to reduce them to stationarity and then to analyze the resulting series as VARs or with the methods of Box and Jenkins. But recent research and a growing literature has shown that there are more interesting, appropriate ways to analyze trending variables.

In the *fully specified* regression model

$$y_t = \beta x_t + \epsilon_t,$$

there is a presumption that the disturbances ϵ_t are a stationary, white noise series.[24] But this is unlikely to be true if y_t and x_t are integrated series. Generally, if two series are integrated to different orders, linear combinations of them will be integrated to the higher of the two orders. Thus, if y_t and x_t are $I(1)$—that is, if both are trending variables—then we would normally expect $y_t - \beta x_t$ to be $I(1)$ regardless of the value of β, not $I(0)$ (i.e., not stationary). If y_t and x_t are each drifting upward with their own trend, then unless there is some relationship between those trends, the difference between them should also be growing, with yet another trend. There must be some kind of inconsistency in the model. On the other hand, if the two series are both $I(1)$, there *may* be a β such that

$$\epsilon_t = y_t - \beta x_t$$

is $I(0)$. Intuitively, if the two series are both $I(1)$, this difference between them might be stable around a fixed mean. The implication would be that the series are drifting upward together at roughly the same rate. Two series that satisfy this requirement are said to be **cointegrated,** and the vector $[1, -\beta]$ (or any multiple of it) is a **cointegrating vector.** In such a case, we can distinguish between a long-run relationship between y_t and x_t, that is, the manner in which the two variables drift upward together, and the short-run dynamics, that is, the relationship between deviations of y_t from its long-run trend and deviations of x_t from its long-run trend. If this is the case, differencing of the data would be counterproductive, since it would obscure the long-run relationship between y_t and x_t. Studies of cointegration and a related technique, **error correction,** are concerned with methods of estimation that preserve the information about both forms of covariation.[25]

EXAMPLE 18.4 Cointegrated Series

The theory of purchasing power parity specifies that in long-run equilibrium, exchange rates will adjust to erase differences in purchasing power across different economies. Thus, if p_1 and p_0 are the price levels in two countries and E

---

[24]If there is autocorrelation in the model, it has been removed through an appropriate transformation.

[25]See, for example, Engle and Granger (1987) and the lengthy literature cited in Hamilton (1994). A survey paper on VARs and cointegration is Watson (1994).

is the exchange rate between the two currencies, then in equilibrium,

$$\nu_t = E_t \frac{p_{1t}}{p_{0t}} = \mu, \text{ a constant.}$$

$q_t = E_t \frac{p_{1t}}{p_{0t}}$

The price levels in any two countries are likely to be strongly trended. But allowing for short-term deviations from equilibrium, the theory suggests that for a particular $\boldsymbol{\beta} = (\ln \mu, -1, 1)$, in the model

$$\ln E_t = \beta_1 + \beta_2 \ln p_{1t} + \beta_3 \ln p_{0t} + \epsilon_t,$$

$\epsilon_t = \ln \nu_t$ would be a stationary series. This would imply that the logs of the three variables in the model are cointegrated.

We suppose that the model involves M variables, $\mathbf{y}_t = [y_1, \ldots, y_M]$, which individually may be $I(0)$ or $I(1)$, and a long-run equilibrium relationship,

$$\mathbf{y}_t'\boldsymbol{\gamma} - \mathbf{x}_t'\boldsymbol{\beta} = 0.$$

The "regressors" may include a constant, exogenous variables, assumed to be $I(0)$, and/or a time trend. The vector of parameters $\boldsymbol{\gamma}$ is the cointegrating vector. In the short run, the system may deviate from its equilibrium, so the relationship is rewritten as

$$\mathbf{y}_t'\boldsymbol{\gamma} - \mathbf{x}_t'\boldsymbol{\beta} = \epsilon_t,$$

where the **equilibrium error** ϵ_t must be a stationary series. In fact, since there are M variables in the system, at least in principle, there could be more than one cointegrating vector. In a system of M variables, there can only be up to $M - 1$ linearly independent cointegrating vectors. A proof of this proposition is very simple, but useful at this point.

> ***Proof:*** Suppose that $\boldsymbol{\gamma}_i$ is a cointegrating vector and that there are M linearly independent cointegrating vectors. Then, neglecting $\mathbf{x}_t'\boldsymbol{\beta}$ for the moment, for every $\boldsymbol{\gamma}_i$, $\mathbf{y}_t'\boldsymbol{\gamma}_i$ is a stationary series ν_{ti}. Any linear combination of a set of stationary series is stationary, so it follows that every linear combination of the cointegrating vectors is also a cointegrating vector. If there are M such $M \times 1$ linearly independent vectors, then they form a basis for the M-dimensional space, so any $M \times 1$ vector can be formed from these cointegrating vectors, including the columns of an $M \times M$ identity matrix. That means that the first column of an identity matrix would be a cointegrating vector, or that y_{t1} is $I(0)$. This is a contradiction, since we are allowing y_1 to be $I(1)$. It follows that there can be at most $M - 1$ cointegrating vectors.

The number of linearly independent cointegrating vectors that exist in the equilibrium system is called its **cointegrating rank.** The cointegrating rank may range from 1 to $M - 1$. If it exceeds 1, then we will encounter an interesting identification problem. As a consequence of the observation in the preceding proof, we have the unfortunate result that, in general, *if the cointegrating rank of a system exceeds 1*, then without out-of-sample, *exact* information, it is not possible to estimate behavioral relationships as cointegrating vectors. Enders (1995) provides a useful example.

EXAMPLE 18.5 Multiple Cointegrating Vectors

We consider the logs of four variables, money demand m, the price level p, real income y, and an interest rate r. The basic relationship is

$$m = \gamma_0 + \gamma_1 p + \gamma_2 y + \gamma_3 r + \epsilon.$$

The price level and real income are assumed to be $I(1)$ (but see Example 18.2). The existence of long-run equilibrium in the money market implies a cointegrating vector $\boldsymbol{\gamma}_1$. If the Fed follows a certain feedback rule increasing the money stock when *nominal* income $(y + p)$ is low and decreasing it when nominal income is high—these might make more sense in terms of rates of growth—then there is a second cointegrating vector in which $\gamma_1 = \gamma_2$ and $\gamma_3 = 0$. Suppose that we label this $\boldsymbol{\gamma}_2$. The parameters in the money demand equation, notably the interest elasticity, are interesting quantities, and we might seek to estimate $\boldsymbol{\gamma}_1$ to learn the value of this quantity. But since every linear combination of $\boldsymbol{\gamma}_1$ and $\boldsymbol{\gamma}_2$ is a cointegrating vector, to this point we are only able to estimate a hash of the two cointegrating vectors.

In fact, the parameters of this model *are* identifiable from sample information (in principle). We have specified two cointegrating vectors,

$$\boldsymbol{\gamma}_1 = 1, \; -\gamma_{10} \; -\gamma_{11}, \; -\gamma_{12}, \; -\gamma_{13}$$

and

$$\boldsymbol{\gamma}_2 = 1, \; -\gamma_{20} \; \gamma_{21}, \; \gamma_{21}, \; 0.$$

Although it is true that every linear combination of $\boldsymbol{\gamma}_1$ and $\boldsymbol{\gamma}_2$ is a cointegrating vector, only the original two vectors, as they are, have 1s in the first position of both and a 0 in the last position of the second. (The equality restriction actually overidentifies the parameter matrix.) This is, of course, exactly the sort of analysis that we used in establishing the identifiability of a simultaneous equation system.

18.4.1. Common Trends

If two $I(1)$ variables are cointegrated, then a linear combination of them is $I(0)$. Intuition should suggest that the linear combination does not mysteriously create a well behaved new variable; rather, something present in the original variables must be missing from the aggregated one. Consider an example. Suppose that the two $I(1)$ variables have a linear trend,

$$y_{1t} = \alpha + \beta t + u_t,$$
$$y_{2t} = \gamma + \delta t + v_t,$$

where u_t and v_t are white noise. A linear combination of y_{1t} and y_{2t} with vector $(1, \theta)$ produces the new variable,

$$z_t = (\alpha + \theta\gamma) + (\beta + \theta\delta)t + u_t + \theta v_t,$$

which, in general, is still $I(1)$. In fact, the only way the z_t series can be made stationary is if $\theta = -\beta/\delta$. If so, then the effect of combining the two variables linearly is *to remove the common linear trend.* This is the basis of Stock and Watson's (1988) analysis of the problem. But their observation goes an important step beyond this. *The only way that y_{1t} and y_{2t} can be cointegrated to begin with is if they have a common trend of some sort.* To continue this, suppose that instead of the linear trend t, the terms on the right-hand side, y_1 and y_2, are functions of a random walk, $w_t = w_{t-1} + \eta_t$, where η_t is white noise. The analysis is identical. But, now suppose that each variable y_{it} has its own random walk component w_{it}, $i = 1, 2$. Any linear combination of y_{1t} and y_{2t} must involve *both* random walks. It is clear that they cannot be cointegrated unless, in fact, $w_{1t} = w_{2t}$. That is, once again, they must have a **common trend.** Finally, suppose that y_{1t} and y_{2t} share two common trends,

$$y_{1t} = \alpha + \beta t + \lambda w_t + u_t,$$
$$y_{2t} = \gamma + \delta t + \pi w_t + v_t.$$

We place no restriction on λ and π. Then, a bit of manipulation will show that it is not possible to find a linear combination of y_{1t} and y_{2t} that is cointegrated, even though they share common trends. The end result for this example is that if y_{1t} and y_{2t} are cointegrated, they must share exactly one common trend.

As Stock and Watson determined, the preceding is the crux of the cointegration of economic variables. A set of M variables which are cointegrated can be written as a stationary component plus linear combinations of a smaller set of common trends. If the cointegrating rank of the system is r, then there can be up to $M - r$ linear trends and $M - r$ common random walks. [See Hamilton (1994, p. 578).] (The two-variable case is special. In a two-variable system, there can be only one common trend in total.) The effect of the cointegration is to purge these common trends from the resultant variables.

18.4.2. Error Correction and VAR Representations

Suppose that the two $I(1)$ variables y_t and z_t are cointegrated and that the cointegrating vector is $[1, -\theta]$. Then all three variables $\Delta y_t = y_t - y_{t-1}$, Δz_t, and $(y_t - \theta z_t)$ are $I(0)$. The **error correction model**

$$\Delta y_t = \boldsymbol{\beta}'\mathbf{x}_t + \gamma(\Delta z_t) + \lambda(y_t - \theta z_t) + \epsilon_t$$

describes the variation in y_t around its long run trend in terms of a set of $I(0)$ exogenous factors $\mathbf{x}_t$, the variation of z_t around its long-run trend, and the error correction $(y_t - \theta z_t)$, which is the equilibrium error in the model of cointegration. There is a tight connection between models of cointegration and models of error correction. The model in this form is reasonable as it stands, but in fact, it is only internally consistent if the two variables are cointegrated. If not, then the third term, and hence the right-hand side, cannot be $I(0)$, even though the left-hand side must be. The upshot is that the same assumption that we make to produce the cointegration implies (and is implied by) the existence of an error correction model.[26] As we will examine in the next section, the utility of this representation is that it suggests a way to build an elaborate model of the long-run variation in y_t as well as a test for cointegration. Looking ahead, the preceding suggests that residuals from an estimated cointegration model—that is, estimated equilibrium errors—can be included in an elaborate model of the long-run covariation of y_t and z_t. Once again, this is the foundation of Engel and Granger's approach to analyzing cointegration.

Consider the VAR representation of the model

$$\mathbf{y}_t = \mathbf{\Gamma}\mathbf{y}_{t-1} + \epsilon_t.$$

Now take first differences to obtain

$$\mathbf{y}_t - \mathbf{y}_{t-1} = (\mathbf{\Gamma} - \mathbf{I})\mathbf{y}_{t-1} + \boldsymbol{\epsilon}_t$$

or

$$\Delta\mathbf{y}_t = \mathbf{\Pi}\mathbf{y}_{t-1} + \boldsymbol{\epsilon}_t.$$

If all variables are $I(1)$, then all M variables on the left-hand side are $I(0)$. Whether those on the right-hand side are remains to be seen. The matrix $\mathbf{\Pi}$ produces linear combinations of the variables in $\mathbf{y}_t$. But as we have seen, not all linear combinations can be cointegrated. The number of such independent linear combinations is $r < M$. Therefore, although there must be a VAR representation of the model, cointegration implies a restriction on the rank of $\mathbf{\Pi}$. It cannot have full rank; its rank is r. From another viewpoint, this suggests a different approach to discerning cointegration. Suppose that we estimate this model as an unrestricted VAR. The resultant coefficient matrix should be short ranked. The implication is that if we fit the VAR model and impose short rank on the coefficient matrix as a restriction—how we could do that remains to be seen—then if the variables really are cointegrated, this restriction should not lead to a loss of fit. This is the basis of Johansen's (1988) and Stock and Watson's (1988) analysis of cointegration.

18.4.3. Testing for Cointegration

A natural first step in the analysis of cointegration is to establish that it is, indeed, a characteristic of the data. Two broad approaches for testing for cointegration have been developed. The Engle and Granger (1987) method is based on assessing whether single equation estimates of the equilibrium errors appear to be stationary. The second approach, due to Johansen (1988) and Stock

---

[26]The result in its general form is known as the Granger representation theorem. See Hamilton (1994, p. 582).

and Watson (1988), is based on the VAR approach. As noted earlier, if a set of variables is truly cointegrated, then we should be able to detect the implied restrictions in an otherwise unrestricted VAR. We will examine these two methods in turn.

Let $\mathbf{y}_t$ denote the set of M variables that are believed to be cointegrated. Step one of either analysis is to establish that the variables are indeed integrated to the same order. The Dickey–Fuller tests discussed in Section 18.3.3 can be used for this purpose. If the evidence suggests that the variables are integrated to different orders, or not at all, then the specification of the model should be reconsidered.

If the cointegration rank of the system is r, then there are r independent vectors, $\boldsymbol{\gamma}_i = [1, -\boldsymbol{\theta}_i]$, where each vector is distinguished by being normalized on a different variable. If we suppose that there are also a set of $I(0)$ exogenous variables, including a constant, in the model, then each cointegrating vector produces the equilibrium relationship:

$$\mathbf{y}_t'\boldsymbol{\gamma}_i = \mathbf{x}_t'\boldsymbol{\beta} + \epsilon_t,$$

which we may rewrite as

$$y_{it} = \mathbf{Y}_{it}'\boldsymbol{\theta}_i + \mathbf{x}_t'\boldsymbol{\beta} + \epsilon_t.$$

We can obtain estimates of $\boldsymbol{\theta}_i$ by least squares regression. If the theory is correct, *and* if this OLS estimate is consistent, then residuals from this regression should estimate the equilibrium errors. There are two obstacles to consistency. First, since both sides of the equation contain $I(1)$ variables, the problem of spurious regressions appears. Second, a moment's thought should suggest that what we have done is extract an equation from an otherwise ordinary simultaneous equations model and propose to estimate its parameters by ordinary least squares. As we examined in Chapter 16, consistency is unlikely in that case. It is one of the extraordinary results of this body of theory that in this setting, neither of these considerations is a problem. In fact, as shown by a number of authors [see, e.g., Davidson and MacKinnon (1993)], not only is $\mathbf{c}_i$, the OLS estimate of $\boldsymbol{\theta}_i$, consistent, it is **superconsistent** in that its asymptotic variance is $O(1/T^2)$ rather than $O(1/T)$ as in the usual case. Consequently, the problem of spurious regressions disappears as well. Therefore, the next step is to estimate the cointegrating vector(s), by OLS. Under all the assumptions thus far, the residuals from these regressions, e_{it}, are estimates of the equilibrium errors, ϵ_{it}. As such, they should be $I(0)$. The natural approach would be to apply the familiar Dickey–Fuller tests to these residuals. The logic is sound, but the Dickey–Fuller tables are inappropriate for these estimated errors. Estimates of the appropriate critical values for the tests are given by Engle and Granger (1987), Engle and Yoo (1987), Phillips and Ouliaris (1990), and Davidson and MacKinnon (1993). If autocorrelation in the equilibrium errors is suspected, an augmented Engle and Granger test can be based on the template

$$\Delta e_{it} = \delta e_{i,t-1} + \phi_1(\Delta e_{i,t-1}) + \cdots + u_t.$$

If the null hypothesis that $\delta = 0$ cannot be rejected (against the alternative $\delta < 0$), then we conclude that the variables are not cointegrated. (Cointegration can be rejected by this method. Failing to reject does not confirm it, of course. But having failed to reject the presence of cointegration, we will proceed as if our finding had been affirmative.)

The Johansen (1988) and Stock and Watson (1988) methods are similar, so we will describe only the first one. The theory is beyond the scope of this text, although the operational details are suggestive. To carry out the Johansen test, we first formulate the VAR

$$\mathbf{y}_t = \mathbf{\Gamma}_1\mathbf{y}_{t-1} + \mathbf{\Gamma}_2\mathbf{y}_{t-2} + \cdots + \mathbf{\Gamma}_p\mathbf{y}_{t-p} + \boldsymbol{\epsilon}_{t-p}.$$

The order of the model p must be determined in advance. Now, let $\mathbf{z}_t$ denote the vector of $M(p-1)$ variables,

$$\mathbf{z}_t = \Delta\mathbf{y}_{t-1}, \Delta\mathbf{y}_{t-2}, \ldots, \Delta\mathbf{y}_{t-p+1}.$$

That is, $\mathbf{z}_t$ contains the lags 1 to $p-1$ of the first differences of all M variables. Now, using the T available observations, we obtain two $T \times M$ matrices of least squares residuals:

$$\mathbf{D} = \text{the residuals in the regressions of } \Delta\mathbf{y}_t \text{ on } \mathbf{z}_t,$$
$$\mathbf{E} = \text{the residuals in the regressions of } \mathbf{y}_{t-p} \text{ on } \mathbf{z}_t.$$

We now require the M squared **canonical correlations** between the columns in $\mathbf{D}$ and those in $\mathbf{E}$. To continue, we will digress briefly to define the canonical correlations. Let $\mathbf{d}_1^*$ denote a linear combination of the columns of $\mathbf{D}$, and let $\mathbf{e}_1^*$denote the same from $\mathbf{E}$. We wish to choose these two linear combinations so as to maximize the correlation between them. This pair of variables are the first canonical variates, and their correlation r_1^* is the first canonical correlation. In the setting of cointegration, this computation has some intuitive appeal. Now, with $\mathbf{d}_1^*$ and $\mathbf{e}_1^*$ in hand, we seek a second pair of variables $\mathbf{d}_2^*$ and $\mathbf{e}_2^*$ to maximize *their* correlation, subject to the constraint that this second variable in each pair be orthogonal to the first. This continues for all M pairs of variables. It turns out that the computation of all these is quite simple. We will not need to compute the coefficient vectors for the linear combinations. The squared canonical correlations are simply the ordered characteristic roots of the matrix

$$\mathbf{R}^* = \mathbf{R}_{DD}^{-1/2}\mathbf{R}_{DE}\mathbf{R}_{EE}^{-1}\mathbf{R}_{ED}\mathbf{R}_{DD}^{-1/2},$$

where $\mathbf{R}_{ij}$ is the (cross-) correlation matrix between variables in set i and set j, for $i, j = D, E$.

Finally, the null hypothesis that there are r or fewer cointegrating vectors is tested using the test statistic

$$\text{TRACE TEST} = -T\sum_{i=r+1}^{M}\ln[1 - (r_i^*)^2].$$

If the correlations based on actual disturbances had been observed instead of estimated, we would refer this statistic to the chi-squared distribution with $M - r$ degrees of freedom. An alternative set of appropriate tables is given by Johansen and Juselius (1990). Large values give evidence against the hypothesis of cointegration.

18.4.4. Estimating Cointegration Relationships

Both of the testing procedures discussed above involve actually estimating the cointegrating vectors, so this additional section is actually superfluous. In the Engle and Granger framework, at a second step after the cointegration test, we can use the residuals from the static regression as an error correction term in a dynamic, first-difference regression, as shown in Section 18.4.2. One can then "test down" to find a satisfactory structure. In the Johansen test shown earlier, the characteristic vectors corresponding to the canonical correlations are the sample estimates of the cointegrating vectors. Once again, computation of an error correction model based on these first step results is a natural next step.

18.5. GENERALIZED AUTOREGRESSIVE CONDITIONAL HETEROSCEDASTICITY

The ARCH model discussed in Section 12.7 has proven to be useful in studying a variety of macroeconomic phenomena, including the volatility of inflation (Coulson and Robins, 1985), the term structure of interest rates (Engle et al., 1985), and foreign exchange markets (Domowitz and Hakkio, 1985), to name a few.[27] The common element in these studies is the observation of clusters of small and large regression residuals, which cannot be described adequately by conventional regression models. The ARCH (1) model is

$$\begin{aligned} y_t &= \boldsymbol{\beta}'\mathbf{x}_t + \epsilon_t, \\ \epsilon_t \mid \epsilon_{t-1} &\sim N[0, \sigma_t^2], \\ \sigma_t^2 &= \alpha_0 + \alpha_1 \epsilon_{t-1}^2. \end{aligned} \tag{18-23}$$

If $|\alpha_1| < 1$, then unconditionally,

$$\epsilon_t \sim N\left[0, \frac{\alpha_0}{1 - \alpha_1}\right].$$

OLS is still the best *linear* unbiased estimator, but the *nonlinear* GLS estimator discussed in Section 12.7 is more efficient. Later empirical studies—for example, Engle and Kraft (1983)—have used the more general ARCH(q) model,

$$\sigma_t^2 = \alpha_0 + \alpha_1 \epsilon_{t-1}^2 + \alpha_2 \epsilon_{t-2}^2 + \cdots + \alpha_q \epsilon_{t-q}^2. \tag{18-24}$$

The ARCH(q) process in (18-23) is an MA process as discussed in Section

[27]Engle and Rothschild (1992) give an up-to-date survey of this literature.

18.2.1, and much of the analysis of the model parallels that set of results. [Once again, see Engle (1982).] This section will generalize the ARCH(q) model, as suggested by Bollerslev (1986), in the direction of the ARMA models of Section 18.2.1. The discussion will parallel his development, although many details are omitted for brevity. The reader is referred to his paper for the background and some of the less critical details. In addition, the discussion to follow will draw heavily on Example 12.16, so it may be helpful to review that example and Section 12.7 before proceeding.[28]

The model of generalized autoregressive conditional heteroscedasticity (GARCH) is defined as follows. The underlying regression is the usual one in (18-23). *Conditioned on an information set at time t*, denoted ψ_t, the distribution of the disturbance is assumed to be

$$\epsilon_t \mid \psi_t \sim N[0, \sigma_t^2],$$

where the conditional variance is

$$\sigma_t^2 = \alpha_0 + \delta_1 \sigma_{t-1}^2 + \delta_2 \sigma_{t-2}^2 + \cdots + \delta_p \sigma_{t-p}^2 + \alpha_1 \epsilon_{t-1}^2 + \alpha_2 \epsilon_{t-2}^2 + \cdots + \alpha_q \epsilon_{t-q}^2.^{29} \tag{18-25}$$

Define

$$\mathbf{z}_t = [1, \sigma_{t-1}^2, \sigma_{t-2}^2, \ldots, \sigma_{t-p}^2, \epsilon_{t-1}^2, \epsilon_{t-2}^2, \ldots, \epsilon_{t-q}^2]'$$

and

$$\boldsymbol{\gamma} = [\alpha_0, \delta_1, \delta_2, \ldots, \delta_p, \alpha_1, \ldots, \alpha_q]' = [\alpha_0, \boldsymbol{\delta}', \boldsymbol{\alpha}']'.$$

Then

$$\sigma_t^2 = \boldsymbol{\gamma}'\mathbf{z}_t.$$

Notice that the conditional variance is defined by an ARMA (p, q) process in the innovations ϵ_t^2, exactly as in Section 18.2.1. The difference here is that the *mean* of the random variable of interest y_t is described completely by a heteroscedastic, but otherwise ordinary, regression model. The *conditional variance*, however, evolves over time in what might be a very complicated manner, depending on the parameter values and on p and q. The model in (18-25) is a GARCH(p, q) model, where p refers, as before, to the order of the autoregressive part. As Bollerslev demonstrates with an example, the virtue of this approach is that a GARCH model with a small number of terms appears to perform as well as or better than an ARCH model with many.

[28] As have most areas in time-series econometrics, the line of literature on GARCH models has progressed rapidly in recent years and will surely continue to do so. We have presented Bollerslev's model in some detail, despite many recent extensions, not only to introduce the topic as a bridge to the literature, but also because it provides a convenient and interesting setting in which to discuss several related topics such as double-length regression and pseudo–maximum likelihood estimation.

[29] We have changed Bollerslev's notation slightly so as not to conflict with our previous presentation. He used $\boldsymbol{\beta}$ instead of our $\boldsymbol{\delta}$ in (18-25) and $\mathbf{b}$ instead of our $\boldsymbol{\beta}$ in (18-23).

The stationarity conditions discussed in Section 18.2.2 are important in this context to ensure that the moments of the normal distribution are finite. The reason is that higher moments of the normal distribution are finite powers of the variance. A normal distribution with variance σ_t^2 has fourth moment $3\sigma_t^4$, sixth moment $15\sigma_t^6$, and so on. (The precise relationship of the even moments of the normal distribution to the variance is given in Exercise 14 of Chapter 4.) Simply ensuring that σ_t^2 is stable does not ensure that higher powers are as well.[30] Bollerslev presents a useful figure that shows the conditions needed to ensure stability for moments up to order 12 for a GARCH(1, 1) model and gives some additional discussion. For example, for a GARCH(1, 1) process, for the fourth moment to exist, $3\alpha_1^2 + 2\alpha_1\delta_1 + \delta_1^2$ must be less than 1.

It is convenient to write (18-25) in terms of polynomials in the lag operator in the format of (18-7):

$$\sigma_t^2 = \alpha_0 + D(L)\sigma_t^2 + A(L)\epsilon_t^2.$$

As we saw in Section 18.2.2, the stationarity condition for such an equation is that the roots of the characteristic equation, $1 - D(z) = 0$, must lie outside the unit circle. For the present, we will assume that this is the case for the model we are considering and that $A(1) + D(1) < 1$. [This is stronger than the assumption needed to ensure stationarity in a higher-order autoregressive model; that would depend only on $D(L)$.] The implication is that the GARCH process is covariance stationary with $E[\epsilon_t] = 0$ (unconditionally), $\text{Var}[\epsilon_t] = \alpha_0/[1 - A(1) - D(1)]$, and $\text{Cov}[\epsilon_t, \epsilon_s] = 0$ for all $t \neq s$. This means that unconditionally the model is the classical regression model that we examined in Chapter 6.

The usefulness of this specification is that it allows the variance to evolve over time in a way that is much more general than the simple specification examined in Section 12.7. The comparison between simple finite-distributed lag models and the dynamic regression model discussed in Chapter 17 is analogous. For the example discussed in his paper, Bollerslev reports that although Engle and Kraft's (1983) ARCH(8) model for the rate of inflation in the GNP deflator appears to remove all ARCH effects, a closer look reveals GARCH effects at several lags. By fitting a GARCH (1,1) model to the same data, Bollerslev finds that the ARCH effects out to the same eight-period lag as fit by Engle and Kraft and that his observed GARCH effects are all satisfactorily accounted for.

18.5.1. Maximum Likelihood Estimation of the GARCH Model

Bollerslev describes a method of estimation based on the BHHH algorithm. As he shows, the method is relatively simple, although with the line search and first

[30]The conditions cannot be imposed a priori. In fact, there is no nonzero set of parameters that guarantees stability of *all* moments, even though the normal distribution has finite moments of all orders. As such, the normality assumption must be viewed as an approximation.

derivative method that he suggests, it probably involves more computation and more iterations than necessary. Following the suggestions of Harvey (1976), it turns out that there is a simpler way to estimate the GARCH model that is also very illuminating. It shows how this model is actually very similar to the more conventional model of multiplicative heteroscedasticity that we examined in Example 12.15. This is also essentially the technique used in Section 12.7, although we will simplify that presentation a bit here.

For normally distributed disturbances, the log-likelihood for a sample of T observations is

$$\begin{aligned}\ln L &= \sum_{t=1}^{T} -\frac{1}{2}\left[\ln(2\pi) + \ln \sigma_t^2 + \frac{\epsilon_t^2}{\sigma_t^2}\right] \\ &= \sum_{t=1}^{T} \ln f_t(\boldsymbol{\theta}) = \sum_{t=1}^{T} l_t(\boldsymbol{\theta}),^{31}\end{aligned}$$

where

$$\epsilon_t = y_t - \boldsymbol{\beta}'\mathbf{x}_t$$

and

$$\boldsymbol{\theta} = (\boldsymbol{\beta}', \alpha_0, \boldsymbol{\alpha}', \boldsymbol{\delta}')' = (\boldsymbol{\beta}', \boldsymbol{\gamma}')'.$$

18.5.1a. Estimating the Variance Parameters. Derivatives of $\ln L$ are obtained by summation. The first derivatives with respect to the variance parameters are

$$\begin{aligned}\frac{\partial l_t}{\partial \boldsymbol{\gamma}} &= -\frac{1}{2}\left[\frac{1}{\sigma_t^2} - \frac{\epsilon_t^2}{(\sigma_t^2)^2}\right]\frac{\partial \sigma_t^2}{\partial \boldsymbol{\gamma}} \\ &= \frac{1}{2}\left(\frac{1}{\sigma_t^2}\right)\frac{\partial \sigma_t^2}{\partial \boldsymbol{\gamma}}\left(\frac{\epsilon_t^2}{\sigma_t^2} - 1\right) \\ &= \frac{1}{2}\left(\frac{1}{\sigma_t^2}\right)\mathbf{g}_t v_t.\end{aligned} \tag{18-26}$$

Note that $E[v_t] = 0$. Using the notation defined above, we have

$$\begin{aligned}\frac{\partial^2 l_t}{\partial \boldsymbol{\gamma}\,\partial \boldsymbol{\gamma}'} &= \frac{1}{2}v_t\left\{\frac{\partial[(1/\sigma_t^2)\mathbf{g}_t]}{\partial \boldsymbol{\gamma}'}\right\} + \frac{1}{2}\left(\frac{1}{\sigma_t^2}\right)\mathbf{g}_t\left\{\frac{\partial[(\epsilon_t^2/\sigma_t^2) - 1]}{\partial \boldsymbol{\gamma}'}\right\} \\ &= \frac{1}{2}v_t\left(\frac{\partial[(1/\sigma_t^2)\mathbf{g}_t]}{\partial \boldsymbol{\gamma}'}\right) - \frac{1}{2}\left(\frac{\mathbf{g}_t}{\sigma_t^2}\right)\left(\frac{\epsilon_t^2}{\sigma_t^2}\right)\left(\frac{\mathbf{g}_t}{\sigma_t^2}\right)'.\end{aligned} \tag{18-27}$$

We will return to the computation of the derivatives $\mathbf{g}_t$ later. Suppose, for now, that there are no regression parameters. Newton's method for estimating

[31] There are three minor errors in Bollerslev's derivation that we note here to avoid the apparent inconsistencies. In his (22), $\frac{1}{2}h_t$ should be $\frac{1}{2}h_t^{-1}$. In (23), $-2h_t^{-2}$ should be $-h_t^{-2}$. In (28), $h\,\partial h/\partial\omega$ should, in each case, be $(1/h)\,\partial h/\partial\omega$. [In his (8), $\alpha_0\alpha_1$ should be $\alpha_0 + \alpha_1$, but this has no implications for our derivation.]

the variance parameters would be

$$\hat{\gamma}^{i+1} = \hat{\gamma}^{i} - \mathbf{H}^{-1}\mathbf{g},$$

where $\mathbf{H}$ indicates the Hessian and $\mathbf{g}$ is the first derivatives vector. Following Harvey's suggestion (see Example 12.15), we will use the method of scoring instead. To do this, we make use of $E[v_t] = 0$ and $E[\epsilon_t^2/\sigma_t^2] = 1$. After taking expectations in (18-27), the iteration reduces to

$$\hat{\gamma}^{i+1} = \hat{\gamma}^{i} + \left[\sum_t \frac{1}{2}\left(\frac{\mathbf{g}_t}{\sigma_t^2}\right)\left(\frac{\mathbf{g}_t}{\sigma_t^2}\right)'\right]^{-1}\left[\sum_t \frac{1}{2}\left(\frac{\mathbf{g}_t}{\sigma_t^2}\right)v_t\right].$$

Notice that this is exactly equation (12-35). For this part of the iteration, we would obtain the update for the estimate of the variance parameters as the vector of slopes in a linear regression of $v_{*_t} = (1/\sqrt{2})v_t$ on regressors $\mathbf{w}_{*_t} = (1/\sqrt{2})\mathbf{g}_t/\sigma_t^2$. That is,

$$\begin{aligned}\hat{\gamma}^{i+1} &= \hat{\gamma}^{i} + [\mathbf{W}_*'\mathbf{W}_*]^{-1}\mathbf{W}_*'\mathbf{v}_* \\ &= \hat{\gamma}^{i} + [\mathbf{W}_*'\mathbf{W}_*]^{-1}\left(\frac{\partial \ln L}{\partial \boldsymbol{\gamma}}\right),\end{aligned} \tag{18-28}$$

where row t of $\mathbf{W}_*$ is $\mathbf{w}_{*_t}'$. As in Example 12.15, the iteration has converged when the slope vector is zero, which happens when the first derivative vector is zero. When the iterations are complete, the estimated asymptotic covariance matrix is simply

$$\text{Est. Asy. Var}[\hat{\gamma}] = [\hat{\mathbf{W}}_*'\hat{\mathbf{W}}_*]^{-1}$$

based on the estimated parameters. Note that this matrix is close to, but not quite the same as, the BHHH estimator. It is instructive to make the difference explicit. From the derivation above,

$$\mathbf{W}_*'\mathbf{W}_* = \sum_{t=1}^{T}\left[\left(\frac{1}{\sqrt{2}}\right)\frac{\mathbf{g}_t}{\sigma_t^2}\right]\left[\left(\frac{1}{\sqrt{2}}\right)\frac{\mathbf{g}_t}{\sigma_t^2}\right]'. \tag{18-29}$$

From the first derivatives in (18-26), the BHHH estimator would be the inverse of

$$\mathbf{B}'\mathbf{B} = \sum_{t=1}^{T} v_t^2\left[\frac{1}{2}\frac{\mathbf{g}_t}{\sigma_t^2}\right]\left[\frac{1}{2}\frac{\mathbf{g}_t}{\sigma_t^2}\right]'. \tag{18-30}$$

But $E[v_t^2] = 2$, so the expectations of these two matrices are the same.

18.5.1b. Estimating the Regression Parameters. The usefulness of the derivation just given is that $E[\partial^2 \ln L/\partial\boldsymbol{\gamma}\,\partial\boldsymbol{\beta}']$ is, in fact, zero. Since the expected Hessian is block diagonal, applying the method of scoring to the full parameter vector can proceed in two parts, exactly as it did in Example 12.15 for the multiplicative heteroscedasticity model. That is, the updates for the mean and variance parameters vectors can be computed separately.

Consider then the slope parameters, $\boldsymbol{\beta}$. The relevant first derivative is

$$\frac{\partial l_t}{\partial \boldsymbol{\beta}} = \frac{\epsilon_t \mathbf{x}_t}{\sigma_t^2} + \frac{1}{2}\left(\frac{1}{\sigma_t^2}\right) v_t \left(\frac{\partial \sigma_t^2}{\partial \boldsymbol{\beta}}\right). \quad \textbf{(18-31)}$$

For convenience, denote $\partial\sigma_t^2/\partial\boldsymbol{\beta}$ as $\mathbf{d}_t$. Then the second derivatives are

$$\frac{\partial^2 l_t}{\partial \boldsymbol{\beta}\,\partial \boldsymbol{\beta}'} = -\left(\frac{1}{\sigma_t^2}\right)\mathbf{x}_t\mathbf{x}_t' - \left(\frac{1}{\sigma_t^2}\right)^2 \epsilon_t \mathbf{x}_t \mathbf{d}_t' - \frac{1}{2}\left(\frac{1}{\sigma_t^2}\right) v_t \mathbf{d}_t \mathbf{d}_t' + \frac{1}{2}\left(\frac{1}{\sigma_t^2}\right) v_t \left(\frac{\partial \mathbf{d}_t}{\partial \boldsymbol{\beta}'}\right) + \frac{1}{2}\left(\frac{1}{\sigma_t^2}\right) \mathbf{d}_t \left(\frac{\partial v_t}{\partial \boldsymbol{\beta}'}\right). \quad \textbf{(18-32)}$$

Recall that $v_t = (\epsilon_t^2/\sigma_t^2) - 1$, so

$$\frac{\partial v_t}{\partial \boldsymbol{\beta}'} = -2\left(\frac{1}{\sigma_t^2}\right)\epsilon_t \mathbf{x}_t' - \left(\frac{1}{\sigma_t^2}\right)\left(\frac{\epsilon_t^2}{\sigma_t^2}\right)\mathbf{d}_t'.$$

Since $\mathbf{d}_t$ is not a function of current innovations and $E(\epsilon_t) = E(v_t) = 0$, only the first term in (18-32) and the second term in $\partial v_t/\partial\boldsymbol{\beta}'$ have nonzero expectation (conditioned on ψ_t). Also, $E[\epsilon_t^2/\sigma_t^2] = 1$. Collecting terms, we are left with

$$E\left[\frac{\partial^2 l_t}{\partial \boldsymbol{\beta}\,\partial \boldsymbol{\beta}'}\right] = -\left(\frac{1}{\sigma_t^2}\right)\mathbf{x}_t\mathbf{x}_t' - \frac{1}{2}\left(\frac{1}{\sigma_t^2}\right)^2 \mathbf{d}_t\mathbf{d}_t'.$$

The same type of modified scoring method as used earlier produces the iteration

$$\begin{aligned} \hat{\boldsymbol{\beta}}^{i+1} &= \hat{\boldsymbol{\beta}}^{i} + \left[\sum_{t=1}^{T} \frac{\mathbf{x}_t\mathbf{x}_t'}{\sigma_t^2} + \frac{1}{2}\left(\frac{\mathbf{d}_t}{\sigma_t^2}\right)\left(\frac{\mathbf{d}_t}{\sigma_t^2}\right)'\right]^{-1} \left[\sum_{t=1}^{T} \frac{\mathbf{x}_t\epsilon_t}{\sigma_t^2} + \frac{1}{2}\left(\frac{\mathbf{d}_t}{\sigma_t^2}\right) v_t\right] \\ &= \hat{\boldsymbol{\beta}}^{i} + \left[\sum_{t=1}^{T} \frac{\mathbf{x}_t\mathbf{x}_t'}{\sigma_t^2} + \frac{1}{2}\left(\frac{\mathbf{d}_t}{\sigma_t^2}\right)\left(\frac{\mathbf{d}_t}{\sigma_t^2}\right)'\right]^{-1} \left(\frac{\partial \ln L}{\partial \boldsymbol{\beta}}\right) \\ &= \hat{\boldsymbol{\beta}}^{i} + \mathbf{h}^{i}. \end{aligned} \quad \textbf{(18-33)}$$

This has been referred to as a **double-length regression.** [See Orme (1990) and Davidson and MacKinnon (1993, Chapter 14).] The update vector $\mathbf{h}^i$ is the vector of slopes in an augmented or double-length generalized regression,

$$\mathbf{h}^i = [\mathbf{C}'\boldsymbol{\Omega}^{-1}\mathbf{C}]^{-1}[\mathbf{C}'\boldsymbol{\Omega}^{-1}\mathbf{a}], \quad \textbf{(18-34)}$$

where $\mathbf{C}$ is a $2T \times K$ matrix whose first T rows are the $\mathbf{X}$ from the original regression model and whose next T rows are $(1/\sqrt{2})\mathbf{d}_t'/\sigma_t^2$, $t = 1, \ldots, T$; $\mathbf{a}$ is a $2T \times 1$ vector whose first T elements are ϵ_t and whose next T elements are $(1/\sqrt{2})v_t$, $t = 1, \ldots, T$; and $\boldsymbol{\Omega}$ is a diagonal matrix with $1/\sigma_t^2$ in positions $1, \ldots, T$ and ones below observation T. At convergence, $[\mathbf{C}'\boldsymbol{\Omega}^{-1}\mathbf{C}]^{-1}$ provides the asymptotic covariance matrix for the MLE. The resemblance to the familiar result for the generalized regression model is striking, but note that this is based on the double-length regression.

18.5.1c. Computing the Derivatives. It remains to formulate the computation of $\mathbf{g}_t$ and $\mathbf{d}_t$. These are as follows:

$$\frac{\partial \sigma_t^2}{\partial \boldsymbol{\gamma}} = \mathbf{g}_t = \mathbf{z}_t + \sum_{i=1}^{p} \delta_i \mathbf{g}_{t-i}.$$

[Recall that $\mathbf{z}_t$ is defined after (18-25).] Starting values are needed to begin this recursion. Bollerslev suggests that the presample variances and squared disturbances be estimated with $s^2 = \mathbf{e}'\mathbf{e}/T$, which would be based on the current parameter estimates. Therefore,

$$\mathbf{z}_0 = \mathbf{z}_1 = \cdot \cdot \cdot = [1, s^2, s^2, \ldots]'.$$

The derivative may be written as

$$\mathbf{g}_t = \mathbf{z}_t + \mathbf{G}_t \boldsymbol{\delta},$$

where $\mathbf{G}_t$ is a $(1 + q + p) \times p$ matrix whose p columns are, at observation t, the p previous observations on $\mathbf{g}$. It is now necessary to estimate the presample values of $\mathbf{g}_t$. If the GARCH process were at a constant value (defined by $\mathbf{z}_0$) for many periods prior to the sample, then $\mathbf{g}$, being a sum of previous $\mathbf{z}$'s, would be also. By substitution, we would have

$$\mathbf{g}_0 = \mathbf{z}_0 + \delta_1 \mathbf{g}_0 + \delta_2 \mathbf{g}_0 + \cdot \cdot \cdot + \delta_p \mathbf{g}_0,$$

or

$$\mathbf{g}_0 = \frac{1}{1 - \delta_1 - \delta_2 - \cdot \cdot \cdot - \delta_p} \mathbf{z}_0 = \frac{1}{1 - D(1)} \mathbf{z}_0.$$

The earlier values would be the same. Any presample columns in $\mathbf{G}_t$ can be set equal to $\mathbf{g}_0$. As the summation progresses, columns are shifted rightward in $\mathbf{G}_t$ with the leftmost one replaced at the end of the computation with the current value of $\mathbf{g}_t$ obtained in anticipation of the next observation. A similar procedure can be used to compute

$$\begin{aligned} \frac{\partial \sigma_t^2}{\partial \boldsymbol{\beta}} = \mathbf{d}_t &= -2 \sum_{j=1}^{q} \alpha_j \mathbf{x}_{t-j} \epsilon_{t-j} + \sum_{j=1}^{p} \delta_j \mathbf{d}_{t-j} \\ &= \mathbf{E}_t \boldsymbol{\alpha} + \mathbf{D}_t \boldsymbol{\delta}. \end{aligned} \tag{18-35}$$

$\mathbf{E}_t$ is a $K \times q$ matrix whose jth column is $-2\mathbf{x}_{t-j}\epsilon_{t-j}$, and $\mathbf{D}_t$ is a $K \times p$ matrix whose p columns are the p previous observations on $\mathbf{d}_t$. The matrices $\mathbf{E}_t$ and $\mathbf{D}_t$ can be computed in a summation in the same fashion as $\mathbf{G}_t$ shown earlier. This recursion is simpler to initialize, since presample values of ϵ_t may be set to their expectation of zero. Thus, any presample columns in $\mathbf{E}_t$ and $\mathbf{D}_t$ can be filled with columns of zeros.

18.5.1d. Summary. The iteration is done simply by computing the update vectors to the current parameters as defined above. An important consideration is that to apply the scoring method, the estimates of $\boldsymbol{\beta}$ and $\boldsymbol{\gamma}$ are updated simultaneously. That is, one does not use the updated estimate of $\boldsymbol{\gamma}$ in (18-28) to update the weights for the GLS regression to compute the new $\boldsymbol{\beta}$ in (18-33). The same estimates (the results of the prior iteration) are used on the right-hand sides of both (18-28) and (18-33). The remaining problem is to obtain starting values for the iterations. One obvious choice is **b**, the OLS estimator, for $\boldsymbol{\beta}$, $\mathbf{e}'\mathbf{e}/T = s^2$ for α_0, and zero for all the remaining parameters. The OLS slope vector will be consistent under all specifications. A useful alternative in this context would be to start $\boldsymbol{\alpha}$ at the vector of slopes in the least squares regression of e_t^2, the squared OLS residual, on a constant and q lagged values.[32] As discussed below, an LM test for the presence of GARCH effects is then a by-product of the first iteration. In principle, the updated result of the first iteration is an **efficient two-step estimator** of all the parameters. But having gone to the full effort to set up the iterations, nothing is gained by not iterating to convergence. One virtue of allowing the procedure to iterate to convergence is that the resulting log-likelihood function can be used in likelihood ratio tests.

18.5.2. Pseudo–Maximum Likelihood Estimation

We now consider an implication of nonnormality of the disturbances. Suppose that the assumption of normality is weakened to only

$$E[\epsilon_t \mid \psi_t] = 0,$$

$$E\left[\frac{\epsilon_t^2}{\sigma_t^2} \mid \psi_t\right] = 1,$$

and

$$E\left[\frac{\epsilon_t^4}{\sigma_t^4} \mid \psi_t\right] = \kappa, \quad \textit{a finite value},$$

where σ_t^2 is as defined earlier. Now the normal log-likelihood function is inappropriate. In this case, the nonlinear (ordinary or weighted) least squares estimator would have the properties discussed in Chapter 11. It would be more difficult to compute than the MLE discussed earlier, however. It has been shown [see White (1982a) and Weiss (1982)] that the *pseudo-MLE* obtained by maximizing the same log-likelihood as if it were correct produces a consistent estimator despite the misspecification.[33] The asymptotic covariance matrices for the parameter estimates must be adjusted, however.

[32]A test for the presence of q ARCH effects against none can be carried out by carrying TR^2 from this regression into a table of critical values for the chi-squared distribution. But in the presence of GARCH effects, this procedure loses its validity.

[33]White (1982a) gives some additional requirements for the true underlying density of ϵ_t. Gourieroux et al. (1984) also consider the issue. Under the assumptions given, the expectations of the matrices in (18-27) and (18-32) remain the same as under normality. The consistency and asymptotic normality of the pseudo-MLE can be argued under the logic of GMM estimators.

The general result for cases such as this one [see Gourieroux et al. (1984)] is that the appropriate asymptotic covariance matrix for the pseudo-MLE of a parameter vector $\boldsymbol{\theta}$ would be

$$\text{Asy. Var}[\hat{\boldsymbol{\theta}}] = \mathbf{H}^{-1}\mathbf{F}\mathbf{H}^{-1}, \tag{18-36}$$

where

$$\mathbf{H} = -E\left[\frac{\partial^2 \ln L}{\partial \boldsymbol{\theta}\, \partial \boldsymbol{\theta}'}\right]$$

and

$$\mathbf{F} = E\left[\left(\frac{\partial \ln L}{\partial \boldsymbol{\theta}}\right)\left(\frac{\partial \ln L}{\partial \boldsymbol{\theta}'}\right)\right]$$

(that is, the BHHH estimator), and ln L is the utilized but inappropriate log-likelihood function. For present purposes, **H** and **F** are still block diagonal, so we can treat the mean and variance parameters separately. In addition, $E[v_t]$ is still zero, so the second derivative terms in both blocks are quite simple. (The parts involving $\partial^2\sigma_t^2/\partial\boldsymbol{\gamma}\,\partial\boldsymbol{\gamma}'$ and $\partial^2\sigma_t^2/\partial\boldsymbol{\beta}\,\partial\boldsymbol{\beta}'$ fall out of the expectation.) Taking expectations and inserting the parts produces the corrected asymptotic covariance matrix for the variance parameters:

$$\text{Asy. Var}[\hat{\boldsymbol{\gamma}}_{\text{PMLE}}] = [\mathbf{W}_*'\mathbf{W}_*]^{-1}\mathbf{B}'\mathbf{B}[\mathbf{W}_*'\mathbf{W}_*]^{-1},$$

where the matrices are defined in (18-29) and (18-30). For the slope parameters, the adjusted asymptotic covariance matrix would be

$$\text{Asy. Var}[\hat{\boldsymbol{\beta}}_{\text{PMLE}}] = [\mathbf{C}'\boldsymbol{\Omega}^{-1}\mathbf{C}]^{-1}\left[\sum_{t=1}^{T}\mathbf{b}_t\mathbf{b}_t'\right][\mathbf{C}'\boldsymbol{\Omega}^{-1}\mathbf{C}]^{-1},$$

where the outer matrix is defined in (18-34) and, from the first derivatives given in (18-29) and (18-35),

$$\mathbf{b}_t = \frac{\mathbf{x}_t\epsilon_t}{\sigma_t^2} + \frac{1}{2}\left(\frac{v_t}{\sigma_t^2}\right)\mathbf{d}_t.$$

18.5.3. Testing for GARCH Effects

The preceding development appears fairly complicated. In fact, it is not, since at each step, nothing more than a linear least squares regression is required. The intricate part of the computation is setting up the derivatives. On the other hand, it does take a fair amount of programming to get this far.[34] As Bollerslev suggests, it might be useful to test for GARCH effects first.

The simplest approach is to examine the squares of the least squares

[34]Since this procedure is available as a preprogrammed procedure in many computer programs, this warning might itself be overstated.

residuals. The autocorrelations of the squares of the residuals provide evidence about ARCH effects. An LM test of ARCH(q) against the hypothesis of no ARCH effects [ARCH(0), the classical model] can be carried out by computing $\chi^2 = TR^2$ in the regression of e_t^2 on a constant and q lagged values. The statistic has a limiting chi-squared distribution with q degrees of freedom. Values larger than the critical table value give evidence of the presence of ARCH (or GARCH) effects.

Bollerslev suggests a Lagrange multiplier statistic that is, in fact, surprisingly simple to compute. The LM test for GARCH(p, 0) against GARCH(p, q) can be carried out by referring T times the R^2 in the linear regression defined in (18-28) to the chi-squared critical value with q degrees of freedom. Note that this is precisely the statistic used in Section 12.7 for testing ARCH(1) against ARCH(0). There is, unfortunately, an indeterminacy in this test procedure. The test for ARCH(q) against GARCH(p, q) is exactly the same as that for ARCH(q) against ARCH($p + q$). For carrying out the test, one can use as starting values a set of estimates that includes $\boldsymbol{\delta} = \mathbf{0}$ and any consistent estimates for $\boldsymbol{\beta}$ and $\boldsymbol{\alpha}$. Then TR^2 for the regression at the initial iteration provides the test statistic.[35]

A number of recent papers have questioned the use of test statistics based solely on normality. Woolridge (1991) is a useful summary with several examples.

EXAMPLE 18.6 GARCH Model for Inflation

Bollerslev reports the results of a study of the implicit price deflator for GNP done by Engle and Kraft (1983) using an ARCH(8) model and his extension of it based on a GARCH(1, 1) model. Table 18.6 reports three sets of estimates for the model

$$\pi_1 = \beta_0 + \beta_1\pi_{t-1} + \beta_2\pi_{t-2} + \beta_3\pi_{t-3} + \beta_4\pi_{t-4} + \epsilon_t,$$

where

$$\pi_t = 100 \ln \frac{P_t}{P_{t-1}}.$$

The data used in the regressions are quarterly observations on the implicit price deflator for GNP from 1948.II to 1983.IV.

The first set of results are obtained by ordinary least squares. The least squares residuals give no evidence of autocorrelation out to lag 10, but the

[35]Bollerslev argues that in view of the complexity of the computations involved in estimating the GARCH model, it is useful to have a test for GARCH effects. This is a case (as are many other maximum likelihood problems) in which the apparatus for carrying out the test is the same as that for estimating the model, however. Having computed the LM statistic for GARCH effects, one can proceed to estimate the model just by allowing the program to iterate to convergence. There is no additional cost beyond waiting for the answer.

squares of the residuals show significant autocorrelations at lags of 1, 3, 7, 9, and 10. The LM test statistics for ARCH(1), ARCH(4), and ARCH(8) are all highly significant.

The declining linear lag model specified by Engle and Kraft (1983) is shown second. Note that there is a linear restriction in the model; the eight terms in the ARCH part of the model are actually functions of a single parameter. The values decline linearly from 0.179 to 0.022. The normalized residuals e_t/σ_t from the ARCH(8) model show, again, no evidence of autocorrelation, nor do their squares. The linear restriction of the linear lag model on the unrestricted ARCH(8) model appears not to be significant; the χ^2 value is 8.87, whereas the 95 percentile for the chi-squared distribution with seven degrees of freedom is 14.01. The ARCH(8) model therefore appears to have accounted adequately for the lagged effects in the conditional variance. But the LM test statistic for the inclusion of σ^2_{t-1} in the conditional variance is 4.57, which is significant at the 5 percent level.

The third set of estimates is for the GARCH(1, 1) model. The normalized residuals and their squares once again appear to be nonautocorrelated to lags of 10 periods. The LM test statistic for the additional ARCH terms, both singly and linearly restricted, is insignificant, as is the LM test statistic for another GARCH term in the model. [Recall, though, there is an equivalence in these tests, for example GARCH(1, 2) and GARCH(2, 1).] On this basis, the specification appears to be adequate.

Plots of the actual inflation rate and asymptotic confidence intervals for the one-step-ahead forecast errors are given in Bollerslev's paper for the predictions of the model estimated by least squares and by the GARCH(1, 1)

TABLE 18.6 Estimated Models of Inflation

	β_0	β_1	β_2	β_3	β_4
Classical model	0.240	0.552	0.177	0.232	−0.209
	(0.080)	(0.083)	(0.089)	(0.090)	(0.080)
	$\sigma^2 = 0.282$ (0.034)				
ARCH(8)	0.138	0.423	0.222	0.377	−0.175
	(0.059)	(0.081)	(0.108)	(0.078)	(0.104)
	$\sigma_t^2 = \underset{(0.033)}{0.058} + \underset{(0.265)}{0.808} \sum_{i=1}^{8} \left(\frac{9-i}{36}\right) \epsilon^2_{t-i}$				
GARCH(1, 1)	0.151	0.433	0.229	0.349	−0.162
	(0.060)	(0.081)	(0.110)	(0.077)	(0.104)
	$\sigma_t^2 = \underset{(0.006)}{0.007} + \underset{(0.070)}{0.135}\epsilon^2_{t-1} + \underset{(0.068)}{0.829}\sigma^2_{t-1}$				

Note: Asymptotic standard errors are given in parentheses.

model. The clear pattern is that in periods of very volatile inflation (the later 1940s and early to mid 1950s), the simple least squares regression is a visibly better predictor. The effect is reversed in the more stable period of the late 1950s and early 1970s.

EXERCISE

Data on the implicit deflator for GNP for 1950.I to 1983.IV are given in Table 18.1. Repeat the analysis of Section 18.5.4 using this subset of Engle and Kraft's data.

CHAPTER 19

Models with Discrete Dependent Variables

19.1. INTRODUCTION

There are many settings in which the phenomenon we seek to model is discrete rather than continuous. Consider, for example, modeling labor force participation, the decision of whether or not to make a major purchase, or the decision of which candidate to vote for in an election. For the first of these, intuition would suggest that factors such as age, education, marital status, number of children, and some economic data would be relevant in explaining whether an individual chooses to seek work or not in a given period. But something is obviously lacking if this is treated as the same sort of regression model we used to analyze consumption or the costs of production. In this chapter, we shall examine a variety of what have come to be known as **qualitative response (QR)** models. There are numerous different types that apply in different situations. What they have in common is that they are models in which the dependent variable is a discrete outcome, such as a "yes or no" decision, so that conventional regression methods are inappropriate.

This chapter is a lengthy but far from complete survey of topics in estimating *QR* models. Almost none of these models can be estimated with linear regression methods. Therefore, readers interested in the mechanics of estimation may want to review the material in Chapters 4 and 5 before continuing. In nearly all cases, the method of estimation is maximum likelihood. The various properties of maximum likelihood estimators were discussed in Chapter 4. We shall assume throughout this chapter that the necessary conditions behind the optimality properties of maximum likelihood estimators are met and therefore will not derive or establish these properties specifically for the QR models. Detailed proofs for most of these models can be found in surveys by Amemiya (1981), McFadden (1984), Maddala (1983), and Dhrymes (1984).

19.2. DISCRETE CHOICE MODELS

The general class of models we shall consider are those for which the dependent variable takes values 0, 1, 2, ... In a few cases, the values will themselves be meaningful, as in the following:

1. **Number of patents:** $y = 0, 1, 2, \ldots$ These are *count* data.

But in most of the cases we shall study, the values taken by the dependent variables are merely a coding for some qualitative outcome. Some examples are as follows:

2. **Labor force participation:** We equate "no" with 0 and "yes" with 1. These are qualitative choices. The zero/one coding is a mere convenience.
3. **Opinions of a certain type of legislation:** Let 0 represent "strongly opposed," 1 "opposed," 2 "neutral," 3 "support," and 4 "strongly support." These are **rankings,** and the values chosen are not quantitative but merely an ordering. The difference between the outcomes represented by 1 and 0 is not necessarily the same as that between 2 and 1.
4. **The occupational field chosen by an individual:** Let 0 be clerk, 1 engineer, 2 lawyer, 3 politician, and so on. These are merely categories, giving neither a ranking nor a count.
5. **Consumer choice among alternative shopping areas:** This has the same characteristics as example 4, but as we shall see, the appropriate model is a bit different.

None of these situations lends themselves readily to regression analysis. Nonetheless, in each case, we can construct models that link the decision or outcome to a set of factors, at least in the spirit of regression. Our approach will be to analyze each of them in the general framework of probability models:

$$\begin{aligned}\text{Prob(event } j \text{ occurs)} &= \text{Prob}(Y = j) \\ &= F[\text{relevant effects: parameters}].\end{aligned} \qquad \textbf{(19-1)}$$

It is convenient for our purposes to group the models into two broad categories, binomial and multinomial, depending on whether the outcome is the choice between two or more than two alternatives. The great majority of recent empirical work in economics has used models of binomial choice. As such, most of the material of this chapter will be devoted to them. The multinomial cases involve some new issues but are, for the most part, extensions of the binomial models. Within the multinomial models, we further divide the settings into unordered outcomes, such as those in examples 4 and 5, and ordered outcomes, such as those in examples 1 and 3. The latter have some of the familiar characteristics of regression models but involve some new complications as well. They are considered in Section 19.8.

19.3. MODELS FOR BINARY CHOICE

Models for explaining a binary (0/1) dependent variable typically arise in two contexts. In many cases, the analyst is essentially interested in a regression model in the same spirit as the models of Chapters 6 to 14. With data on the variable of interest and a set of covariates, the analyst is interested in specifying a relationship between the former and the latter, more or less along the lines of the models we have already studied. The example of voting behavior is typical. In other cases, the binary choice model arises in the context of a formal regression model in which the nature of the data observed dictate the special treatment of a binary choice model. In a model of the demand for tickets for a sporting event, in which the variable of interest is number of tickets, it could happen that the observation consists only of whether $(Y = 1)$ or not $(Y = 0)$ the sports facility was filled to capacity. It will generally turn out that the models and techniques used in both cases are the same. Nonetheless, it is useful to examine both of them.

19.3.1. The Regression Approach

To focus ideas, consider a model of labor force participation.[1] The respondent either works or seeks work $(Y = 1)$ or doesn't $(Y = 0)$ in the period in which our survey is taken. We believe that a set of factors, such as age, marital status, education, work history, and so on, gathered in a vector **x** explain the decision, so that

$$\begin{aligned} \text{Prob}(Y = 1) &= F(\boldsymbol{\beta}'\mathbf{x}) \\ \text{Prob}(Y = 0) &= 1 - F(\boldsymbol{\beta}'\mathbf{x}). \end{aligned} \tag{19-2}$$

The set of parameters $\boldsymbol{\beta}$ reflect the impact of changes in **x** on the probability. For example, among the factors that might interest us is the marginal effect of marital status on the probability of labor force participation. The problem at this point is to devise a suitable model for the right-hand side of the equation.

One possibility is a linear regression,

$$F(\mathbf{x}, \boldsymbol{\beta}) = \boldsymbol{\beta}'\mathbf{x}.$$

Since $E[y \mid \mathbf{x}] = F(\mathbf{x}, \boldsymbol{\beta})$, we can construct the regression model,

$$\begin{aligned} y &= E[y \mid \mathbf{x}] + (y - E[y \mid \mathbf{x}]) \\ &= \boldsymbol{\beta}'\mathbf{x} + \epsilon. \end{aligned} \tag{19-3}$$

But the **linear probability model** has a number of shortcomings. A minor complication arises because ϵ is heteroscedastic in a way that depends on $\boldsymbol{\beta}$. Since $\boldsymbol{\beta}'\mathbf{x} + \epsilon$ must equal 0 or 1, ϵ equals either $-\boldsymbol{\beta}'\mathbf{x}$ or $1 - \boldsymbol{\beta}'\mathbf{x}$, with probabilities

[1]Models for qualitative dependent variables can now be found in most disciplines in economics. Their most frequent use is in labor economics in the analysis of microlevel data sets, however.

$1 - F$ and F, respectively. Thus, you can easily show that

$$\text{Var}[\epsilon \mid \mathbf{x}] = \boldsymbol{\beta}'\mathbf{x}(1 - \boldsymbol{\beta}'\mathbf{x}). \tag{19-4}$$

Of course, absent any other problems, we could manage this with an FGLS estimator in the fashion of Chapter 12. For our purposes, though, a more serious flaw is that without some ad hoc tinkering with the disturbances, we cannot be assured that the predictions from this model will truly look like probabilities. We cannot constrain $\boldsymbol{\beta}'\mathbf{x}$ to the 0–1 interval. This produces both nonsense probabilities and negative variances. In view of this, and given the ready availability of convenient software for estimation, the linear model is becoming less frequently used except as a basis for comparison to some other more appropriate models.[2]

Our requirement, then, is a model that will produce predictions consistent with the underlying theory in (19-1). For a given regressor vector, we would expect

$$\lim_{\boldsymbol{\beta}'\mathbf{x}\to+\infty} \text{Prob}(Y = 1) = 1$$

and

$$\lim_{\boldsymbol{\beta}'\mathbf{x}\to-\infty} \text{Prob}(Y = 1) = 0. \tag{19-5}$$

See Figure 19.1. In principle, any proper, continuous probability distribution defined over the real line will suffice. The normal distribution has been used in many analyses, giving rise to the **probit** model,

$$\begin{aligned}\text{Prob}(Y = 1) &= \int_{-\infty}^{\boldsymbol{\beta}'\mathbf{x}} \phi(t)\,dt \\ &= \Phi(\boldsymbol{\beta}'\mathbf{x}).\end{aligned} \tag{19-6}$$

The function $\Phi(.)$ is a commonly used notation for the standard normal distribution. Partly because of its mathematical convenience, the logistic distribution,

$$\begin{aligned}\text{Prob}(Y = 1) &= \frac{e^{\boldsymbol{\beta}'\mathbf{x}}}{1 + e^{\boldsymbol{\beta}'\mathbf{x}}} \\ &= \Lambda(\boldsymbol{\beta}'\mathbf{x}),\end{aligned} \tag{19-7}$$

has also been used in many applications. We shall use the notation $\Lambda(.)$ to indicate the logistic cumulative distribution function. This model is called the **logit** model for reasons we shall discuss in the next section. (See Example 6.3 as

[2]The linear model is not beyond redemption. Aldrich and Nelson (1984) analyze the properties of the model at length. Judge et al. (1985) and Fomby et al. (1984) give interesting discussions of the ways we may modify the model to force internal consistency. But the fixes are sample dependent, and the resulting estimator, such as it is, may have no known sampling properties. Additional discussion of weighted least squares appears in Amemiya (1977b) and Mullahey (1990). Finally, its shortcomings notwithstanding, the linear probability model is applied by Caudill (1988) and Heckman and MacCurdy (1985).

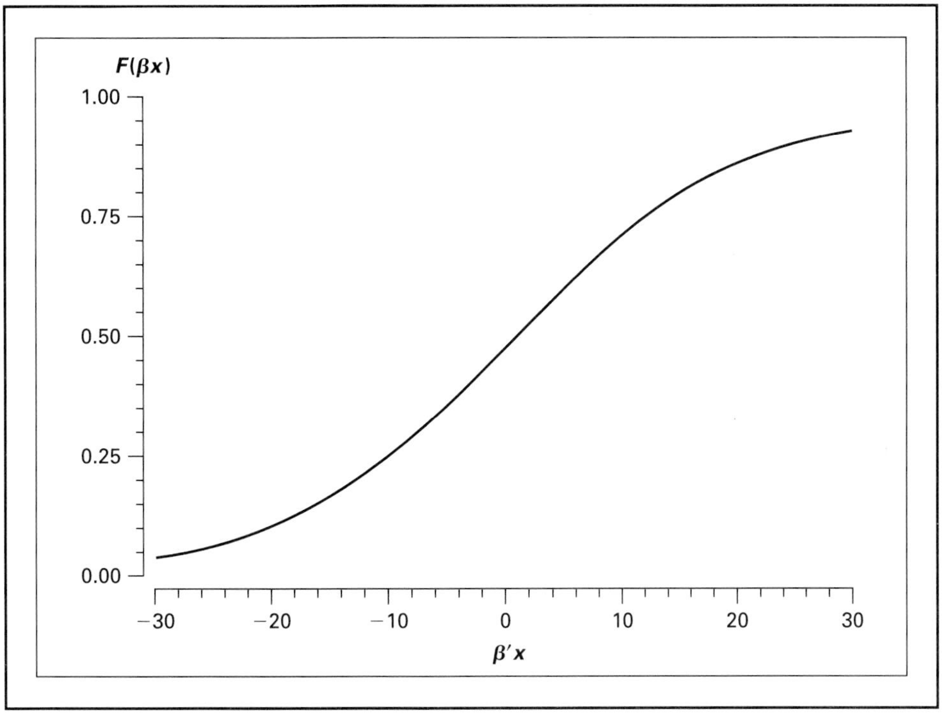

FIGURE 19.1 Model for a Probability.

well.) Other distributions have been suggested,[3] but in econometric applications the probit and logit models have been used almost exclusively.

The question of which distribution to use is a natural one. The logistic distribution is similar to the normal except in the tails, which are considerably heavier. (It more closely resembles a t distribution with seven degrees of freedom.) Therefore, for intermediate values of $\boldsymbol{\beta}'\mathbf{x}$ (say, between -1.2 and $+1.2$), the two distributions tend to give similar probabilities. The logistic distribution tends to give larger probabilities to $y = 0$ when $\boldsymbol{\beta}'\mathbf{x}$ is extremely small (and smaller probabilities to $y = 0$ when $\boldsymbol{\beta}'\mathbf{x}$ is very large) than the normal distribution. It is difficult to provide practical generalities on this basis, however, since they would require knowledge of $\boldsymbol{\beta}$. We should expect different predictions from the two models, however, if our sample contains (1) very few responses (Y's equal to 1) or very few nonresponses (Y's equal to 0) and (2) very wide variation in an important independent variable, particularly if (1) is also true. There are practical reasons for favoring one or the other in some cases for mathematical convenience, but it is difficult to justify the choice of one distribution or another on theoretical grounds. Amemiya (1981) discusses a number

[3]See, for example, Maddala (1983, pp. 27–32) and Aldrich and Nelson (1984).

of related issues, but as a general proposition, the question is unresolved. In most applications, it seems not to make much difference.

The probability model is a regression:

$$E[y \mid \mathbf{x}] = 0[1 - F(\boldsymbol{\beta}'\mathbf{x})] + 1[F(\boldsymbol{\beta}'\mathbf{x})] \\ = F(\boldsymbol{\beta}'\mathbf{x}). \tag{19-8}$$

Whatever distribution is used, it is important to note that the parameters of the model, like those of any nonlinear regression model, are not necessarily the marginal effects we are accustomed to analyzing. In general,

$$\frac{\partial E[y \mid \mathbf{x}]}{\partial \mathbf{x}} = \left\{\frac{dF(\boldsymbol{\beta}'\mathbf{x})}{d(\boldsymbol{\beta}'\mathbf{x})}\right\}\boldsymbol{\beta} \\ = f(\boldsymbol{\beta}'\mathbf{x})\boldsymbol{\beta}, \tag{19-9}$$

where $f(.)$ is the density function that corresponds to the cumulative distribution, $F(.)$. For the normal distribution, this is

$$\frac{\partial E[y \mid \mathbf{x}]}{\partial \mathbf{x}} = \phi(\boldsymbol{\beta}'\mathbf{x})\boldsymbol{\beta}, \tag{19-10}$$

where $\phi(t)$ is the standard normal density. For the logistic distribution,

$$\frac{d\Lambda[\boldsymbol{\beta}'\mathbf{x}]}{d(\boldsymbol{\beta}'\mathbf{x})} = \frac{e^{\boldsymbol{\beta}'\mathbf{x}}}{(1 + e^{\boldsymbol{\beta}'\mathbf{x}})^2} \\ = \Lambda(\boldsymbol{\beta}'\mathbf{x})[1 - \Lambda(\boldsymbol{\beta}'\mathbf{x})], \tag{19-11}$$

which is particularly convenient. Thus in the logit model,

$$\frac{\partial E[y \mid \mathbf{x}]}{\partial \mathbf{x}} = \Lambda(\boldsymbol{\beta}'\mathbf{x})[1 - \Lambda(\boldsymbol{\beta}'\mathbf{x})]\boldsymbol{\beta}. \tag{19-12}$$

It is obvious that these will vary with the values of $\mathbf{x}$. In interpreting the estimated model, it will be useful to calculate this at, say, the means of the regressors and, where necessary, other pertinent values. For convenience, it is worth noting that the same scale factor applies to all the slopes in the model.

A Computational Note: For computing marginal effects, one can evaluate the expressions at the sample means of the data or evaluate the marginal effects at every observation and use the sample average of the individual marginal effects. The functions are continuous, so Theorem 4.3 (the Slutsky theorem) applies; in large samples these will give the same answer. But that is not so in small or moderate sized samples. Current practice favors averaging the individual marginal effects when it is possible to do so.

EXAMPLE 19.1 Probability Models

The data listed in Table 19.1 were used by Spector and Mazzeo (1980) to analyze the effectiveness of a new method of teaching economics. The "dependent variable" for the study is GRADE, an indicator of whether students' grades on an examination improved after exposure to PSI, a new method of teaching eco-

TABLE 19.1 Data Used to Study Program Effectiveness

Obs.	*GPA*	*TUCE*	*PSI*	*GRADE*	*Obs.*	*GPA*	*TUCE*	*PSI*	*GRADE*
1	2.66	20	0	0	17	2.75	25	0	0
2	2.89	22	0	0	18	2.83	19	0	0
3	3.28	24	0	0	19	3.12	23	1	0
4	2.92	12	0	0	20	3.16	25	1	1
5	4.00	21	0	1	21	2.06	22	1	0
6	2.86	17	0	0	22	3.62	28	1	1
7	2.76	17	0	0	23	2.89	14	1	0
8	2.87	21	0	0	24	3.51	26	1	0
9	3.03	25	0	0	25	3.54	24	1	1
10	3.92	29	0	1	26	2.83	27	1	1
11	2.63	20	0	0	27	3.39	17	1	1
12	3.32	23	0	0	28	2.67	24	1	0
13	3.57	23	0	0	29	3.65	21	1	1
14	3.26	25	0	1	30	4.00	23	1	1
15	3.53	26	0	0	31	3.10	21	1	0
16	2.74	19	0	0	32	2.39	19	1	1

nomics. The other variables are GPA, the grade point average; TUCE, the score on a pretest that indicates entering knowledge of the material; and PSI, a binary variable indicator of whether the student was exposed to the new teaching method.

Table 19.2 presents four sets of parameter estimates. The slope parameters and derivatives were computed for four probability models: linear, probit, logit, and Weibull. The Weibull distribution is an asymmetric distribution with CDF

$$\text{Prob}(\text{GRADE} = 1 \mid \mathbf{x}) = 1 - \exp[-\exp(\boldsymbol{\beta}'\mathbf{x})].$$

TABLE 19.2 Estimated Probability Models

	Linear		*Logistic*		*Probit*		*Weibull*	
Variable	*Coefficient*	*Slope*	*Coefficient*	*Slope*	*Coefficient*	*Slope*	*Coefficient*	*Slope*
Constant	−1.498	—	−13.021	—	−7.452	—	−10.631	—
GPA	0.464	0.464	2.826	0.534	1.626	0.533	2.293	0.477
TUCE	0.010	0.010	0.095	0.018	0.052	0.017	0.041	0.009
PSI	0.379	0.379	2.379	0.499	1.426	0.468	1.562	0.325
$f(\boldsymbol{\beta}'\bar{\mathbf{x}})$	1.000		0.189		0.328		0.208	

The last three sets of estimates are computed by maximizing the appropriate log-likelihood function. Estimation is discussed in the next section, so standard errors are not presented here. The scale factor given in the last row is the density function evaluated at the means of the variables. Also, note that the slope given for PSI is the derivative, not the change in the function with PSI changed from 0 to 1 with other variables held constant.

A Computational Note: The appropriate marginal effect for a binary independent variable, say d, would be $\text{Prob}[Y = 1 \mid \bar{\mathbf{x}}_*, d = 1] - \text{Prob}[Y = 1 \mid \bar{\mathbf{x}}_*, d = 0]$, where $\bar{\mathbf{x}}_*$ denotes the means of all the other variables in the model. Simply taking the derivative with respect to the binary variable as if it were continuous provides an approximation that is often surprisingly accurate. In the preceding example, the difference in the two probabilities is $(0.5702 - 0.1057) = 0.4645$, whereas the approximation reported above is 0.468.

If one looked only at the coefficient estimates, it would be natural to conclude that the four models had produced radically different estimates. But a comparison of the columns of slopes shows that this is clearly wrong. The models are very similar; in fact, the logit and probit models results are nearly identical.

The data are moderately unbalanced between 0s and 1s for the dependent variable (21 and 11). As such, we might expect similar results for the probit and logit models. One indicator is a comparison of the coefficients. In view of the different variances of the distributions, 1 for the normal and $\pi^2/3$ for the logistic, we might expect to obtain comparable estimates by multiplying the probit coefficients by $\pi/\sqrt{3} \approx 1.8$. Amemiya (1981) found, through trial and error, that scaling by 1.6 instead produced better results. This proportionality result is frequently cited. The result in (19-9) may help to explain the finding. The index $\boldsymbol{\beta}'\mathbf{x}$ is not the random variable. (See Section 19.3.2.) The marginal effect in the probit model for, say, x_k is $\phi(\boldsymbol{\beta}_p'\mathbf{x})\beta_{pk}$, whereas that for the logit is $\Lambda(1 - \Lambda)\beta_{lk}$. (The subscripts p and l are for probit and logit). Amemiya suggests that his approximation works best at the center of the distribution, where $F = 0.5$, or $\boldsymbol{\beta}'\mathbf{x} = 0$ for either distribution. Suppose it is. Then $\phi(0) = 0.3989$ and $\Lambda(0)[1 - \Lambda(0)] = 0.25$. If the marginal effects are to be the same, then $0.3989\beta_{pk} = 0.25\beta_{lk}$, or $\beta_{lk} = 1.6\beta_{pk}$, which is the regularity observed by Amemiya. Note, though, as we depart from the center of the distribution, that the relationship will move away from 1.6. Since the logistic density descends more slowly than the normal, for unbalanced samples such as ours, the ratio of the logit coefficients to the probit coefficients will tend to be larger than 1.6. The ratios for the ones in Table 19.2 are closer to 1.7 than 1.6.

The computation of the derivatives of the conditional mean function is useful when the variable in question is continuous. But most applications contain at least one dummy variable, for which partial derivatives or marginal effects may not be meaningful. It turns out that the marginal effects suggested in

(19-9) generally produce a reasonable approximation to the change in the probability that Y equals 1 at a point such as the regressor means. But at the same time, we can analyze the effects of the dummy variable on the whole distributions by computing Prob($Y = 1$) over the range of $\boldsymbol{\beta}'\mathbf{x}$ (using the sample estimates) and with the two values of the binary variable. Example 19.2 illustrates for the probit model of Example 19.1.

EXAMPLE 19.2 Plotting Marginal Effects

Using the coefficients from the probit model in Table 19.2, we have the following probabilities as a function of GPA, at the mean of TUCE:

$$\begin{aligned} \text{PSI} &= 0\text{: Prob(GRADE} = 1) \\ &= \Phi[-7.45 + 1.62\text{GPA} + 0.052(21.938)] \\ \text{PSI} &= 1\text{: Prob(GRADE} = 1) \\ &= \Phi[-7.45 + 1.62\text{GPA} + 0.052(21.938) + 1.4263] \end{aligned}$$

Figure 19.2 shows these two functions plotted over the range of GRADE observed in the sample, 2.0 to 4.0. The effect of PSI on the probabilities is substantial. The marginal effect of PSI is the difference between the two functions, which ranges from only about 0.06 at GPA = 2 to about 0.50 at GPA of 3.5. This shows that the probability that a student's grade will increase after expo-

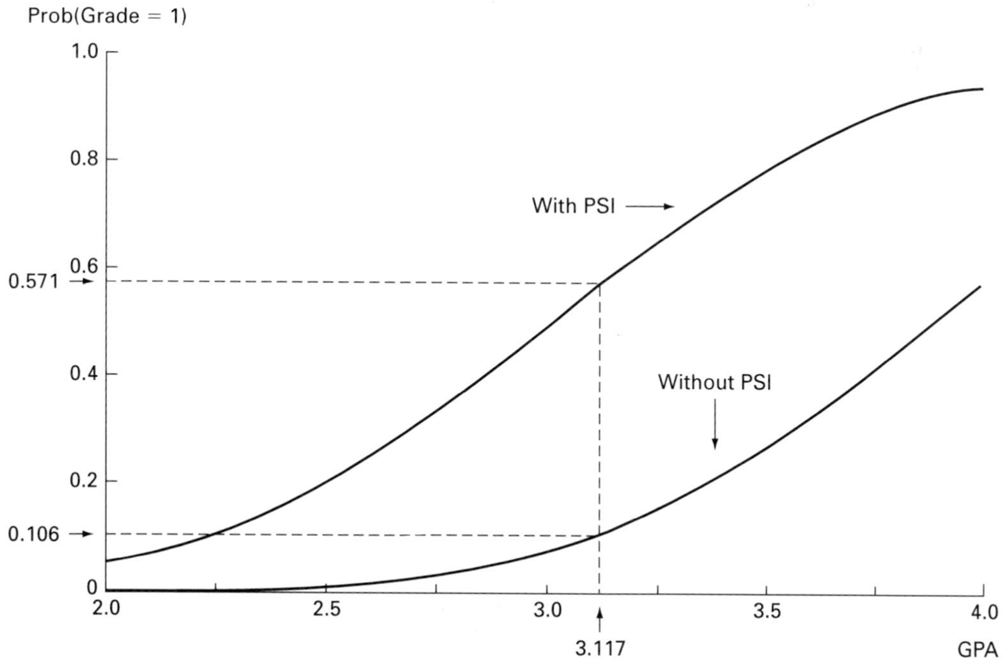

FIGURE 19.2 Effect of PSI on Predicted Probabilities.

sure to PSI is far greater for students with high GPAs than for those with low GPAs. At the sample mean of GPA of 3.117, the effect of PSI on the probability is 0.465. The simple derivative calculation of (19-9) is given in Table 19.2; the estimate is 0.468. But, of course, this does not show the wide range of differences displayed in Figure 19.2.

19.3.2. Index Function and Random Utility Models

Discrete dependent-variable models are often cast in the form of **index function models.** We view the outcome of a discrete choice as a reflection of an underlying regression. As an often-cited example, consider the decision to make a large purchase. The theory states that the consumer makes a marginal benefit-marginal cost calculation based on the utilities achieved by making the purchase and by not making the purchase, and using the money for something else. Since marginal benefit is obviously not observable, we model the difference between benefit and cost as an unobserved variable y^* such that

$$y^* = \boldsymbol{\beta}'\mathbf{x} + \epsilon.$$

We assume that ϵ has a standard logistic or a normal distribution with mean zero and variance one. We do not observe the net benefit of the purchase, only whether it is made or not. Therefore, our observation is

$$\begin{aligned} y &= 1 \quad \text{if } y^* > 0, \\ y &= 0 \quad \text{if } y^* \le 0. \end{aligned}$$

In this formulation, $\boldsymbol{\beta}'\mathbf{x}$ is called the **index function.**

Two aspects of this construction merit our attention. First, the assumption of unit variance is an innocent normalization. Suppose that we assume that the variance of ϵ is σ^2 instead and likewise multiply the coefficients by σ. Our observed data will be unchanged; y is 0 or 1, depending only on the sign of y^*, not on its scale. Second, the assumption of zero for the threshold is likewise innocent if the model contains a constant term.[4] Now the probability that $y = 1$ is

$$\begin{aligned} \text{Prob}(y^* > 0) &= \text{Prob}(\boldsymbol{\beta}'\mathbf{x} + \epsilon > 0) \\ &= \text{Prob}(\epsilon > -\boldsymbol{\beta}'\mathbf{x}). \end{aligned}$$

If the distribution is symmetric, as are the normal and logistic,

$$\begin{aligned} \text{Prob}(y^* > 0) &= \text{Prob}(\epsilon < \boldsymbol{\beta}'\mathbf{x}) \\ &= F(\boldsymbol{\beta}'\mathbf{x}). \end{aligned}$$

This provides an underlying structural model for the probability.

[4]Unless there is some compelling reason, binomial probability models should not be estimated without constant terms.

EXAMPLE 19.3 Structural Equations for a Probit Model

Nakosteen and Zimmer (1980) analyze a model of migration based on the following structure:[5] For individual i, the market wage that can be earned at the present location is

$$y_p^* = \boldsymbol{\beta}'\mathbf{x}_p + \epsilon_p.$$

Variables in the equation include age, sex, race, growth in employment, and growth in per capita income. If the individual migrates to a new location, his or her market wage would be

$$y_m^* = \boldsymbol{\gamma}'\mathbf{x}_m + \epsilon_m.$$

Migration, however, entails costs that are related both to the individual and to the labor market:

$$C^* = \boldsymbol{\alpha}'\mathbf{z} + u.$$

Costs of moving are related to whether the individual is self-employed and whether that person recently changed his or her industry of employment. They migrate if the benefit $y_m^* - y_p^*$ is greater than the cost C^*. The net benefit of moving is

$$\begin{aligned} M^* &= y_m^* - y_p^* - C^* \\ &= \boldsymbol{\gamma}'\mathbf{x}_m - \boldsymbol{\beta}'\mathbf{x}_p - \boldsymbol{\alpha}'\mathbf{z} + (\epsilon_m - \epsilon_p - u) \\ &= \boldsymbol{\delta}'\mathbf{w} + \epsilon. \end{aligned}$$

We could treat this as an ordinary regression except that M^* is unobservable. The individual either moves or does not. After the fact, we observe only y_m^* if the individual has moved or y_p^* if he or she has not. But we do observe that $M = 1$ for a move and $M = 0$ for no move. If the disturbances are normally distributed, this produces the probit model we analyzed earlier. Logistic disturbances produce the logit model instead.

An alternative interpretation of data on individual choices is provided by the **random utility model.** Suppose that, in the Nakosteen–Zimmer framework, y_m and y_p represent the individual's utility of two choices, which we might denote U^a and U^b. For another example, U^a might be the utility of rental housing and U^b that of home ownership. The observed choice between the two reveals which one provides the greater utility, but not the unobservable utilities. Hence, the observed indicator equals 1 if $U^a > U^b$ and 0 if $U^a \leq U^b$. A common formulation is the linear random utility model,

$$U^a = \boldsymbol{\beta}_a'\mathbf{x} + \epsilon_a \quad \text{and} \quad U^b = \boldsymbol{\beta}_b'\mathbf{x} + \epsilon_b. \tag{19-13}$$

[5]A number of other studies have also used variants of this basic formulation. Some important examples are Willis and Rosen (1979) and Robinson and Tomes (1982). The study by Tunali (1986) examined in Example 19.8 is another example.

Then if we denote by $Y = 1$ the consumer's choice of alternative a, we have

$$\begin{aligned}\text{Prob}[Y = 1 \mid \mathbf{x}] &= \text{Prob}[U^a > U^b] \\ &= \text{Prob}[\boldsymbol{\beta}_a'\mathbf{x} + \epsilon_a - \boldsymbol{\beta}_b'\mathbf{x} - \epsilon_b \mid \mathbf{x}] \\ &= \text{Prob}[(\boldsymbol{\beta}_a - \boldsymbol{\beta}_b)'\mathbf{x} + \epsilon_a - \epsilon_b > 0 \mid \mathbf{x}] \\ &= \text{Prob}[\boldsymbol{\beta}'\mathbf{x} + \epsilon > 0 \mid \mathbf{x}]\end{aligned} \qquad \textbf{(19-14)}$$

once again.

19.4. ESTIMATION AND INFERENCE IN BINARY CHOICE MODELS

With the exception of the linear probability model, estimation of binary choice models is usually based on the method of maximum likelihood. Each observation is treated as a single draw from a Bernoulli distribution (binomial with one draw). The model with success probability $F(\boldsymbol{\beta}'\mathbf{x})$ and independent observations leads to the joint probability, or likelihood function,

$$\text{Prob}(Y_1 = y_1, Y_2 = y_2, \ldots, Y_n = y_n) = \prod_{y_i=0} [1 - F(\boldsymbol{\beta}'\mathbf{x}_i)] \prod_{y_i=1} F(\boldsymbol{\beta}'\mathbf{x}_i). \qquad \textbf{(19-15)}$$

This can be conveniently written as

$$L = \prod_{i=1}^{n} [F(\boldsymbol{\beta}'\mathbf{x}_i)]^{y_i}[1 - F(\boldsymbol{\beta}'\mathbf{x}_i)]^{1-y_i}. \qquad \textbf{(19-16)}$$

This is the likelihood for a sample of n observations. Taking logs, we obtain

$$\ln L = \sum_{i=1}^{n} [y_i \ln F(\boldsymbol{\beta}'\mathbf{x}_i) + (1 - y_i)\ln(1 - F(\boldsymbol{\beta}'\mathbf{x}_i))].^{6} \qquad \textbf{(19-17)}$$

The first-order conditions for maximization require

$$\frac{\partial \ln L}{\partial \boldsymbol{\beta}} = \sum_{i=1}^{n} \left[\frac{y_i f_i}{F_i} + (1 - y_i)\frac{-f_i}{(1 - F_i)} \right] \mathbf{x}_i = \mathbf{0}. \qquad \textbf{(19-18)}$$

[In (19-18) and later, we will use the subscript i to indicate that the function has an argument $\boldsymbol{\beta}'\mathbf{x}_i$.] The choice of a particular form for F_i leads to the empirical model.

Unless we are using the linear probability model, the equations in (19-18) will be nonlinear and require an iterative solution. But both of the models we have looked at thus far are relatively straightforward to analyze. For the logit

[6] If the distribution is symmetric, as the normal and logistic are, then $1 - F(\boldsymbol{\beta}'\mathbf{x}) = F(-\boldsymbol{\beta}'\mathbf{x})$. Then there is a further simplification. Let $q = 2y - 1$. Then $\ln L = \Sigma_i \ln F(q_i \boldsymbol{\beta}'\mathbf{x}_i)$.

model, by inserting (19-7) and (19-11) in (19-18), we get, after a bit of manipulation, the necessary conditions

$$\frac{\partial \ln L}{\partial \boldsymbol{\beta}} = \sum_{i=1}^{n} (y_i - \Lambda_i)\mathbf{x}_i = \mathbf{0}. \tag{19-19}$$

Note that if $\mathbf{x}_i$ contains a constant term, the first-order conditions imply that the average of the predicted probabilities must equal the proportion of 1s in the sample.[7] This also bears some similarity to the least squares normal equations if we view the term $y_i - \Lambda_i$ as a residual.[8] For the normal distribution, the log-likelihood is

$$\ln L = \sum_{y_i=0} \ln[1 - \Phi(\boldsymbol{\beta}'\mathbf{x}_i)] + \sum_{y_i=1} \ln \Phi(\boldsymbol{\beta}'\mathbf{x}_i). \tag{19-20}$$

The first-order conditions for maximizing L are

$$\begin{aligned}\frac{\partial \ln L}{\partial \boldsymbol{\beta}} &= \sum_{y_i=0} \frac{-\phi_i}{1 - \Phi_i}\mathbf{x}_i + \sum_{y_i=1} \frac{\phi_i}{\Phi_i}\mathbf{x}_i \\ &= \sum_{i=1}^{n} \left(\frac{q_i\phi(q_i\boldsymbol{\beta}'\mathbf{x}_i)}{\Phi(q_i\boldsymbol{\beta}'\mathbf{x}_i)}\right)\mathbf{x}_i \\ &= \sum_{i=1}^{n} \lambda_i\mathbf{x}_i = \mathbf{0},\end{aligned} \tag{19-21}$$

where

$$q_i = 2y_i - 1.$$

For both models, Newton's method is a straightforward way to compute the parameter estimates. The actual second derivatives for the logit model are quite simple based on (19-17):

$$\mathbf{H} = \frac{\partial^2 \ln L}{\partial \boldsymbol{\beta}\, \partial \boldsymbol{\beta}'} = -\sum_i \Lambda_i(1 - \Lambda_i)\mathbf{x}_i\mathbf{x}_i'. \tag{19-22}$$

Since the second derivatives do not involve the random variable y_i, Newton's method is also the method of scoring for the logit model. Note that the Hessian is always negative definite, so the log-likelihood is globally concave. Newton's method will usually converge to the maximum of the log-likelihood in just a few iterations unless the data are especially badly conditioned.

The computation is slightly more involved for the probit model. A useful

---

[7]The same result holds for the linear probability model. Although regularly observed in practice, the result has not been verified for the probit model. A general result for the distributions for which the mean predicted probability will equal the sample proportions is given in Hein (1987).

[8]This sort of construction arises in many models. The first derivative of the log-likelihood with respect to the constant term produces the **generalized residual** in many settings. See, for example, Chesher et al. (1985).

simplification is obtained by using the variable $\lambda(y_i, \boldsymbol{\beta}'\mathbf{x}_i) = \lambda_i$ that is defined in (19-21). The second derivatives can be obtained using the result that for any z,

$$\frac{d\phi(z)}{dz} = -z\phi(z).$$

Then

$$\mathbf{H} = \frac{\partial^2 \ln L}{\partial \boldsymbol{\beta}\, \partial \boldsymbol{\beta}'} = \sum_{i=1}^{n} -\lambda_i(\lambda_i + \boldsymbol{\beta}'\mathbf{x}_i)\mathbf{x}_i\mathbf{x}_i'. \tag{19-23}$$

This is also negative definite for all values of $\boldsymbol{\beta}$. The proof is less obvious than for the logit model.[9] It suffices to note that the scalar part in the summation is $1 - \text{Var}[\epsilon \mid \epsilon < \boldsymbol{\beta}'\mathbf{x}]$ when $y = 1$ and $1 - \text{Var}[\epsilon \mid \epsilon > -\boldsymbol{\beta}'\mathbf{x}]$ when $y = 0$. In both cases, the variance is between 0 and 1, so the complement is as well.[10]

The asymptotic covariance matrix for the maximum likelihood estimator can be estimated by using the inverse of the Hessian evaluated at the maximum likelihood estimates. There are also two other estimators available. The Berndt, Hall, Hall, and Hausman estimator [see (4-52) and Example 4.23] would be

$$\mathbf{B} = \sum_i g_i^2 \mathbf{x}_i\mathbf{x}_i',$$

where $g_i = (y_i - \Lambda_i)$ for the logit model [see (19-19)] and $g_i = \lambda_i$ for the probit model [see (19-21)]. The third estimator would be based on the expected value of the Hessian. As we saw earlier, the Hessian for the logit model does not involve y_i, so $\mathbf{H} = E[\mathbf{H}]$. But because λ_i is a function of y_i [see (19-21)], this is not true for the probit model. Amemiya (1981) showed that for the probit model,

$$E\left[\frac{\partial^2 \ln L}{\partial \boldsymbol{\beta}\, \partial \boldsymbol{\beta}'}\right]_{\text{probit}} = \sum_{i=1}^{n} \lambda_{0i}\lambda_{i1}\mathbf{x}_i\mathbf{x}_i'. \tag{19-24}$$

Once again, the scalar part of the expression is always negative [see (19-21)]. The estimate of the asymptotic covariance matrix for the maximum likelihood estimates is then the negative inverse of whichever matrix is used to estimate the expected Hessian. Since the actual Hessian is generally used for the iterations, this is the usual choice. As we shall see below, though, for certain hypothesis tests, the BHHH estimator is a more convenient choice.

The predicted probabilities $F(\hat{\boldsymbol{\beta}}'\mathbf{x}) = \hat{F}$ and the estimated marginal effects $f(\hat{\boldsymbol{\beta}}'\mathbf{x}) \times \boldsymbol{\beta} = \hat{f}\hat{\boldsymbol{\beta}}$ are nonlinear functions of the parameter estimates. To compute standard errors, we can use the linear approximation approach (delta method) discussed in Section 6.7.5. For the predicted probabilities,

$$\text{Asy. Var}[\hat{F}] = [\partial \hat{F}/\partial \hat{\boldsymbol{\beta}}]'\mathbf{V}[\partial \hat{F}/\partial \hat{\boldsymbol{\beta}}]$$

[9] See, for example, Amemiya (1985, pp. 273–274) and Maddala (1983, p. 63).

[10] See Johnson and Kotz (1970) and Heckman (1979). We will make repeated use of this result in Chapter 20.

where

$$\mathbf{V} = \text{Asy. Var}[\hat{\boldsymbol{\beta}}].$$

The estimated asymptotic covariance matrix of $\hat{\boldsymbol{\beta}}$ can be any of the three described earlier. Let $z = \mathbf{x}'\hat{\boldsymbol{\beta}}$. Then the derivative vector is

$$[\partial\hat{F}/\partial\hat{\boldsymbol{\beta}}] = [d\hat{F}/dz][\partial z/\partial\hat{\boldsymbol{\beta}}] = \hat{f}\mathbf{x}.$$

Combining terms gives

$$\text{Asy. Var}[\hat{F}] = \hat{f}^2\mathbf{x}'\mathbf{V}\mathbf{x}.$$

This depends, of course, on the particular $\mathbf{x}$ vector used.

For the marginal effects, let $\hat{\boldsymbol{\gamma}} = \hat{f}\hat{\boldsymbol{\beta}}$. Then

$$\text{Asy. Var}[\hat{\boldsymbol{\gamma}}] = \left[\frac{\partial\hat{\boldsymbol{\gamma}}}{\partial\hat{\boldsymbol{\beta}}'}\right]\mathbf{V}\left[\frac{\partial\hat{\boldsymbol{\gamma}}}{\partial\hat{\boldsymbol{\beta}}'}\right]'.$$

The matrix of derivatives is

$$\hat{f}\left(\frac{\partial\hat{\boldsymbol{\beta}}}{\partial\hat{\boldsymbol{\beta}}'}\right) + \hat{\boldsymbol{\beta}}\left(\frac{d\hat{f}}{dz}\right)\left(\frac{\partial z}{\partial\hat{\boldsymbol{\beta}}'}\right) = \hat{f}\mathbf{I} + \left(\frac{d\hat{f}}{dz}\right)\hat{\boldsymbol{\beta}}\mathbf{x}'.$$

For the probit model, $df/dz = -z\phi$, so

$$\text{Asy. Var}[\hat{\boldsymbol{\gamma}}] = \phi^2[\mathbf{I} - (\boldsymbol{\beta}'\mathbf{x})\boldsymbol{\beta}\mathbf{x}']\mathbf{V}[\mathbf{I} - (\boldsymbol{\beta}'\mathbf{x})\boldsymbol{\beta}\mathbf{x}']'. \tag{19-25}$$

For the logit model, $\hat{f} = \hat{\Lambda}(1 - \hat{\Lambda})$, so

$$\frac{d\hat{f}}{dz} = (1 - 2\hat{\Lambda})\left(\frac{d\hat{\Lambda}}{dz}\right) = (1 - 2\hat{\Lambda})\hat{\Lambda}(1 - \hat{\Lambda}).$$

Collecting terms, we obtain

$$\text{Asy. Var}[\hat{\boldsymbol{\gamma}}] = [\Lambda(1 - \Lambda)]^2[\mathbf{I} + (1 - 2\Lambda)\boldsymbol{\beta}\mathbf{x}']\mathbf{V}[\mathbf{I} + (1 - 2\Lambda)\mathbf{x}\boldsymbol{\beta}']. \tag{19-26}$$

As before, the value obtained will depend on the $\mathbf{x}$ vector used.[11]

EXAMPLE 19.4 Estimates of Logit and Probit Models

Table 19.3 presents the estimated coefficients and marginal effects for the probit and logit models in Table 19.2. In both cases, the asymptotic covariance matrix is computed from the negative inverse of the actual Hessian of the log-likelihood.

For testing hypotheses about the coefficients, the full menu of procedures is available. The simplest method for a single restriction would be based on the usual t tests, using the standard errors from the information matrix. Using the normal distribution of the estimator, we would use the standard normal table

[11]For an application, see the study by Cecchetti (1986) discussed in Example 19.9.

TABLE 19.3 Estimated Coefficients and Standard Errors (Standard Errors in Parentheses)

	Logistic				*Probit*			
Variable	*Coefficient*	*t ratio*	*Slope*	*t ratio*	*Coefficient*	*t ratio*	*Slope*	*t ratio*
Constant	−13.021	−2.640	—	—	−7.452	−2.930	—	—
	(4.931)				(2.542)			
GPA	2.826	2.238	0.534	2.252	1.626	2.343	0.533	1.761
	(1.263)		(0.237)		(0.694)		(0.303)	
TUCE	0.095	0.672	0.018	0.685	0.052	0.617	0.017	0.587
	(0.142)		(0.026)		(0.084)		(0.029)	
PSI	2.379	2.234	0.449	2.284	1.426	2.397	0.468	1.695
	(2.234)		(0.197)		(0.595)		(2.276)	

rather than the t table for critical points. For more involved restrictions, it is possible to use the Wald test. For a set of restrictions $\mathbf{R}\boldsymbol{\beta} = \mathbf{q}$, the statistic is

$$W = (\mathbf{R}\hat{\boldsymbol{\beta}} - \mathbf{q})'\{\mathbf{R}(\text{Est. Asy. Var}[\hat{\boldsymbol{\beta}}])\mathbf{R}'\}^{-1}(\mathbf{R}\hat{\boldsymbol{\beta}} - \mathbf{q}).$$

EXAMPLE 19.5 Wald Test for a Subset of Coefficients

For testing the hypothesis that a subset of the coefficients, say the last L, are zero, the Wald statistic uses

$$\mathbf{R} = [\mathbf{0} \,|\, \mathbf{I}_L]$$

and $\mathbf{q} = \mathbf{0}$. Collecting terms, we find that the statistic is

$$W = \hat{\boldsymbol{\beta}}_L' \mathbf{V}_L^{-1} \hat{\boldsymbol{\beta}}_L\,, \tag{19-27}$$

where the subscript L indicates the subvector or submatrix corresponding to the L variables and $\mathbf{V}$ is the estimated asymptotic covariance matrix of $\hat{\boldsymbol{\beta}}$.

Likelihood ratio and Lagrange multiplier statistics can also be computed. The likelihood ratio statistic is

$$\text{LR} = -2[\ln \hat{L}_r - \ln \hat{L}],$$

where $\hat{L}_r$ and $\hat{L}$ are the log-likelihood functions evaluated at the restricted and unrestricted estimates, respectively. A common test, which is similar to the F test that all of the slopes in a regression are zero, is the likelihood ratio test that all the slope coefficients in the probit or logit model are zero. For this test, the constant term remains restricted. In this case, the unrestricted log-likelihood is the same for both probit and logit models,

$$\ln L_0 = n[P \ln P + (1 - P)\ln(1 - P)], \tag{19-28}$$

where P is the proportion of the observations that have dependent variable equal to 1.

EXAMPLE 19.6 Restricted Log Likelihoods

For the Spector and Mazzeo data, $P = 11/32$, so the restricted log-likelihoods is -20.5917. The unrestricted log-likelihoods for the probit and logit models are -12.819 and -12.890, respectively. The chi-squared statistics are therefore 15.546 for the probit model and 15.404 for the logit model. With 3 degrees of freedom, the critical value from the chi-squared table is 7.815, so the joint hypothesis that the coefficients on GPA, TUCE, and PSI are all zero is rejected.

It might be tempting to use the likelihood ratio test to choose between the probit and logit models. But there is no restriction involved, and the test is not valid for this purpose. To underscore the point, there is nothing in its construction to prevent the chi-squared statistic for this "test" from being negative.

The Lagrange multiplier test statistic is $\text{LM} = \mathbf{g}'\mathbf{V}\mathbf{g}$, where $\mathbf{g}$ is the first derivatives of the unrestricted model evaluated at the restricted parameter vector and $\mathbf{V}$ is any of the three estimators of the asymptotic covariance matrix of the maximum likelihood estimator. Davidson and MacKinnon (1984) find evidence that $E[\mathbf{H}]$ is the best of the three estimators to use, which gives

$$\text{LM} = \left(\sum_{i=1}^{n} g_i\mathbf{x}_i\right)'\left[\sum_{i=1}^{n} E[h_i]\mathbf{x}_i\mathbf{x}_i'\right]^{-1}\left(\sum_{i=1}^{n} g_i\mathbf{x}_i\right), \tag{19-29}$$

where

$$h_i = d^2 \ln F_i / d(\boldsymbol{\beta}'\mathbf{x}_i)^2.$$

For the logit model, when the hypothesis is that all the slopes are zero,

$$\text{LM} = nR^2,$$

where R^2 is the uncentered coefficient of determination in the regression of $(y_i - P)$ on $\mathbf{x}_i$ and P is the proportion of 1s in the sample. An alternative formulation based on the BHHH estimator, which we developed in Section 4.9.3c, is also convenient. For any of the models (probit, logit, Weibull, etc.), the first derivative vector can be written as

$$\frac{\partial \ln L}{\partial \boldsymbol{\beta}} = \sum_{i=1}^{n}\left(\frac{f_i}{F_i}\right)\mathbf{x}_i = \sum_{i=1}^{n} g_i\mathbf{x}_i = \mathbf{X}'\mathbf{G}\mathbf{i},$$

where $\mathbf{G}(n \times n) = \text{diag}[g_1, g_2, \ldots, g_n]$ and $\mathbf{i}$ is an $n \times 1$ column of 1s. The BHHH estimator of the Hessian is $(\mathbf{X}'\mathbf{G}'\mathbf{G}\mathbf{X})$, so the LM statistic based on this estimator is

$$\begin{aligned}\text{LM} &= n\left[\frac{1}{n}\mathbf{i}'(\mathbf{G}\mathbf{X})(\mathbf{X}'\mathbf{G}'\mathbf{G}\mathbf{X})^{-1}(\mathbf{X}'\mathbf{G}')\mathbf{i}\right]\\ &= n\left[\frac{1}{n}\mathbf{i}'\mathbf{D}(\mathbf{D}'\mathbf{D})^{-1}\mathbf{D}'\mathbf{i}\right]\\ &= nR_i^2,\end{aligned}$$

the uncentered coefficient of determination in a regression of a column of 1s on the first derivatives of the logs of the individual probabilities.

All the statistics listed here are asymptotically equivalent and are asymptotically distributed as chi-squared with degrees of freedom equal to the number of restrictions being tested. We consider some examples below.

19.4.1. Specification Tests in Binary Choice Models

In the classical regression model, we considered two important specification problems, the effect of omitted variables and the effect of heteroscedasticity. In the classical model, $\mathbf{y} = \mathbf{X}_1\boldsymbol{\beta}_1 + \mathbf{X}_2\boldsymbol{\beta}_2 + \boldsymbol{\epsilon}$, when least squares estimates $\mathbf{b}_1$ are computed omitting $\mathbf{X}_2$,

$$E[\mathbf{b}_1] = \boldsymbol{\beta}_1 + [\mathbf{X}_1'\mathbf{X}_1]^{-1}\mathbf{X}_1'\mathbf{X}_2\boldsymbol{\beta}_2.$$

Unless $\mathbf{X}_1$ and $\mathbf{X}_2$ are orthogonal, $\mathbf{b}_1$ is biased. If we ignore heteroscedasticity, although the least squares estimator is still unbiased and consistent, it is inefficient and the usual estimate of its sampling covariance matrix is inappropriate. Yatchew and Griliches (1984) have examined these same issues in the setting of the probit and logit models. Their general results are far more pessimistic. In the context of a binary choice model, they find the following:

1. If x_2 is omitted from a model containing x_1 and x_2,

$$\text{plim}\,\hat{\beta}_1 = c_1\beta_1 + c_2\beta_2,$$

   where c_1 and c_2 are complicated functions of the unknown parameters. The implication is that even if the omitted variable is uncorrelated with the included one, the coefficient on the included variable will be inconsistent.
2. If the disturbances in the underlying regression are heteroscedastic, the maximum likelihood estimators are inconsistent and the covariance matrix is inappropriate.

The second result is particularly troubling because the probit model is most often used with microeconomic data, which are frequently heteroscedastic.

Any of the three methods of hypothesis testing that were discussed above can be used to analyze these specification problems. The Lagrange multiplier test has the advantage that it can be carried out using the estimates from the restricted model, which sometimes brings a large saving in computational effort. This is especially true for the test for heteroscedasticity.[12]

To reiterate, the Lagrange multiplier statistic is computed as follows. Let the null hypothesis, H_0, be a specification of the model, and let H_1 be the alternative. For example, H_0 might specify that only variables $\mathbf{x}_1$ appear in the model, whereas H_1 might specify that $\mathbf{x}_2$ appears in the model as well. The statistic is

$$\text{LM} = \mathbf{g}_0'\mathbf{V}_0^{-1}\mathbf{g}_0,$$

[12]The results in this section are based on Davidson and MacKinnon (1984) and Engle (1984). A symposium on the subject of specification tests in discrete choice models is Blundell (1987).

where $\mathbf{g}_0$ is the vector of derivatives of the log-likelihood as specified by H_1 but evaluated at the maximum likelihood estimator of the parameters assuming that H_0 is true and $\mathbf{V}_0^{-1}$ is any of the three consistent estimators of the variance matrix of the maximum likelihood estimator under H_1, also computed using the maximum likelihood estimators based on H_0. The statistic is asymptotically distributed as chi-squared with degrees of freedom equal to the number of restrictions.

19.4.1a. Testing for Omitted Variables. The hypothesis to be tested is

$$\begin{aligned} H_0 &: y^* = \boldsymbol{\beta}_1'\mathbf{x}_1 \qquad\qquad + \epsilon, \\ H_1 &: y^* = \boldsymbol{\beta}_1'\mathbf{x}_1 + \boldsymbol{\beta}_2'\mathbf{x}_2 + \epsilon, \end{aligned} \tag{19-30}$$

so the test is of the hypothesis that $\boldsymbol{\beta}_2 = \mathbf{0}$. Examples 19.5 and 19.6 show how to carry out the Wald and LR tests. The Lagrange multiplier test would be carried out as follows:

1. Estimate the model in H_0 by maximum likelihood. The restricted coefficient vector is $[\hat{\boldsymbol{\beta}}, \mathbf{0}]$.
2. Let $\mathbf{x}$ be the compound vector, $[\mathbf{x}_1, \mathbf{x}_2]$.

The statistic is then computed according to (19-29). It is possible to show that this is equivalent to nR^2 in the regression of

$$r_i = y_i\sqrt{\frac{1 - F_i}{F_i}} + (y_i - 1)\sqrt{\frac{F_i}{1 - F_i}} \tag{19-31}$$

on

$$\mathbf{x}_i^* = \left[\frac{f_i}{\sqrt{F_i(1 - F_i)}}\right]\mathbf{x}_i.$$

Given the simplicity of (19-29) the appeal of this solution may be largely aesthetic. It is noteworthy, though, that in this case as in many others, the Lagrange multiplier is the coefficient of determination in a regression.[13]

19.4.1b. Testing for Heteroscedasticity. We use the general formulation analyzed by Harvey (1976),[14]

$$\text{Var}[\epsilon] = [\exp(\boldsymbol{\gamma}'\mathbf{z})]^2.^{15}$$

As noted by Davidson and MacKinnon, this test is not well suited to the logit model, so we will derive it specifically for the probit model. The model is

$$\begin{aligned} y^* &= \boldsymbol{\beta}'\mathbf{x} + \epsilon, \\ \text{Var}[\epsilon] &= [e^{\boldsymbol{\gamma}'\mathbf{z}}]^2. \end{aligned} \tag{19-32}$$

[13]The denominator in R^2 is *uncentered.*

[14]See Knapp and Seaks (1992) for an application.

[15]See Example 12.15.

The log-likelihood is

$$\ln L = \sum_{i=1}^{n}\left\{y_i \ln F\left(\frac{\boldsymbol{\beta}'\mathbf{x}_i}{\exp(\boldsymbol{\gamma}'\mathbf{z}_i)}\right) + (1-y_i)\ln\left[1 - F\left(\frac{\boldsymbol{\beta}'\mathbf{x}_i}{\exp(\boldsymbol{\gamma}'\mathbf{z}_i)}\right)\right]\right\}. \tag{19-33}$$

To be able to estimate all of the parameters, **z** cannot have a constant term. The derivatives are

$$\begin{aligned}\frac{\partial \ln L}{\partial \boldsymbol{\beta}} &= \sum_{i=1}^{n}\left[\frac{f_i(y_i - F_i)}{F_i(1-F_i)}\right]\exp(-\boldsymbol{\gamma}'\mathbf{z}_i)\mathbf{x}_i,\\ \frac{\partial \ln L}{\partial \boldsymbol{\gamma}} &= \sum_{i=1}^{n}\left[\frac{f_i(y_i - F_i)}{F_i(1-F_i)}\right]\exp(-\boldsymbol{\gamma}'\mathbf{z}_i)\mathbf{z}_i(-\boldsymbol{\beta}'\mathbf{x}_i).\end{aligned} \tag{19-34}$$

This is a difficult log-likelihood to maximize. But if the model is estimated assuming that $\boldsymbol{\gamma} = \mathbf{0}$, we can easily test for homoscedasticity. Let

$$\mathbf{w}_i = \begin{bmatrix}\mathbf{x}_i\\ (-\hat{\boldsymbol{\beta}}'\mathbf{x}_i)\mathbf{z}_i\end{bmatrix} \tag{19-35}$$

computed at the maximum likelihood estimator, assuming that $\boldsymbol{\gamma} = \mathbf{0}$. Then (19-29) can be used as usual for the Lagrange multiplier statistic.

Davidson and MacKinnon carried out a Monte Carlo study to examine the true sizes and power functions of these tests. As might be expected, the test for omitted variables is relatively powerful. The test for heteroscedasticity may well pick up some other form of misspecification, however, including perhaps the simple omission of **z** from the index function, so its power may be problematic. It is perhaps not surprising that the same problem arose earlier in our test for heteroscedasticity in the linear regression model.

EXAMPLE 19.7 Probit Model with Groupwise Heteroscedasticity

Table 19.4 presents estimates of the probit model of the earlier examples, now with a correction for heteroscedasticity of the form

$$\text{Var}[\epsilon_i] = \exp(\gamma \text{PSI}_i).$$

This produces a probit counterpart to the model of groupwise heteroscedasticity in the linear regression model that we examined in Section 15.3. When

TABLE 19.4 Estimated Coefficients

		Estimate	*Standard Error*	*Estimate*	*Standard Error*
Constant	β_1	−7.452	2.542	−12.6470	15.431
GPA	β_2	1.626	0.694	2.8094	3.0273
TUCE	β_3	0.052	0.084	0.10286	0.31032
PSI	β_4	1.426	0.595	1.7298	1.8023
PSI	γ	0.000	—	0.99998	1.374
Log *L*		−12.819		−11.992	

PSI equals 0, the variance is 1; when PSI equals 1, the variance is $\sigma^2 = e^\gamma$. (This model could be extended to G groups by using a set of G dummy variables for $\mathbf{z}$.)

The three tests for homoscedasticity give

$$\text{LR} = -2[-11.992 - (-12.819)] = 1.654,$$
$$\text{LM} = 4.086 \text{ based on the BHHH estimator},$$
$$\text{Wald} = \frac{(0.9999)^2}{1.374^2} = 1.654.$$

The tests for heteroscedasticity are contradictory. The critical value from the chi-squared distribution is 3.84, so based on the LR or Wald test, we would not reject $H_0: \gamma = 0$. But based on the LM test, we would. This is a borderline case and a small sample, so a result such as this should not be surprising.

The large standard errors and large coefficients in the extended model might suggest that the assumption of heteroscedasticity leads to a considerable distortion of the results. But this is deceiving. For the model with heteroscedasticity,

$$\frac{\partial \text{ Prob}(Y = 1)}{\partial x_k} = \phi\left[\frac{\boldsymbol{\beta}'\mathbf{x}}{\exp(\boldsymbol{\gamma}'\mathbf{z})}\right] \times \frac{\beta_k}{\exp(\boldsymbol{\gamma}'\mathbf{z})}.$$

For the model here, the means of the variables are [1.0, 3.117, 21.3, 0.4375]. Using the coefficient estimates given in Table 19.4, we obtain a marginal effect for GPA of 0.7631. The counterpart for the model without heteroscedasticity is given in Table 19.3; it is 0.533. So the estimated marginal effect of GPA is similar. We leave as an exercise the comparison for the other two variables.

19.4.2 Measuring Goodness of Fit

There have been many attempts to derive fit measures for the QR models.[16] At a minimum, one would want to report the maximized value of the log-likelihood function $\ln L$. Since the hypothesis that all the slopes in the model are zero is often interesting, the log-likelihood computed with only a constant term $\ln L_0$ [see (19-28)] should also be reported. An analog to the R^2 in a conventional regression model is the likelihood ratio index,

$$\text{LRI} = 1 - \frac{\ln L}{\ln L_0}.$$

The measure has an intuitive appeal in that it is bounded by 0 and 1. If all the slope coefficients are 0, it equals 0. There is no way to make LRI equal 1, although one can come close. If F_i is always 1 when y equals 1 and 0 when y equals 0, then $\ln L$ equals 0 (the log of 1) and LRI equals 1. It has been sug-

[16]See, for example, Cragg and Uhler (1970), Amemiya (1981), Maddala (1983), McFadden (1974), and Zavoina and McElvey (1975).

gested that this finding is indicative of a "perfect fit" and that LRI increases as the fit of the model improves. Unfortunately, values between 0 and 1 have no natural interpretation. If F_i is a proper pdf, then even with many regressors, the model cannot fit perfectly unless $\boldsymbol{\beta}'\mathbf{x}$ explodes to $+\infty$ or $-\infty$. As a practical matter, this does happen. But when it does, this is indicative of a flaw in the model, not a good fit.

A Computational Tip: If one of the regressors contains a value, say x^*, such that whenever this x is greater than x^*, y equals 1, and vice versa, and whenever this x is less than x^*, y equals 0, and vice versa, then the model will be a perfect predictor. This also holds if the sign of $\boldsymbol{\beta}'\mathbf{x}$ gives a perfect predictor of y for some $\boldsymbol{\beta}$.[17]

For example, careless researchers sometimes include as regressors dummy variables that are identical, or nearly so, to the dependent variable. In this case, the maximization procedure will break down precisely because $\boldsymbol{\beta}'\mathbf{x}$ is exploding during the iterations. Of course, this is not at all what we had in mind for a good fit.

A useful summary of the predictive ability of the model is a 2×2 table of the hits and misses of a prediction rule such as

$$\hat{y} = 1 \quad \text{if } \hat{F} > F^* \text{ and 0 otherwise.} \tag{19-36}$$

The usual threshold value is 0.5, on the basis that we should predict a 1 if the model says a 1 is more likely than a 0. It is important not to place too much emphasis on this measure of goodness of fit, however. Consider, for example, the naive predictor

$$\hat{y} = 1 \quad \text{if } P > 0.5 \text{ and 0 otherwise,} \tag{19-37}$$

where P is the proportion of 1s in the sample. This rule will always predict correctly $100P$ percent of the observations, which means that the naive model does not have zero fit. In fact, if the proportion of 1s in the sample is very high, it is possible to construct examples in which the second model will generate more correct predictions than the first! Once again, this is not a flaw in the model; it is a flaw in the fit measure.[18] The important element to bear in mind is that the coefficients of the estimated model are not chosen so as to maximize this (or any other) fit measure, as they are in the linear regression model in which **b** maximizes R^2. (The **maximum score** estimator discussed below addresses this issue directly.)

A second consideration is that 0.5, although the usual choice may not be a very good value to use for the threshold. If the sample is **unbalanced**—that is, has many more 1s than 0s, or vice versa—then by this prediction rule, it might never predict a 1 (or 0). To consider an example, suppose that in a sample of 10,000 observations, only 1000 have $Y = 1$. We know that the average pre-

---

[17]See McFadden (1984). If this condition holds, gradient methods *will* find that $\boldsymbol{\beta}$.

[18]See Amemiya (1981).

dicted probability in the sample will be 0.10. As such, it may require an extreme configuration of regressors even to produce an F of 0.2, to say nothing of 0.5. In such a setting, the prediction rule may fail every time to predict when $Y = 1$. The obvious adjustment is to reduce F^*. Of course, this comes at a cost. If we reduce the threshold F^* so as to predict $y = 1$ more often, we will increase the number of correct classifications of observations that do have $y = 1$, but we will also increase the number of times that we *incorrectly* classify as 1s observations that have $y = 0$.[19] In general, any prediction rule of the form in (19-36) will make two types of errors. It will incorrectly classify 0s as 1s and 1s as 0s. In practice, these errors need not be symmetric in the costs that result. For example, in a credit scoring model [see Boyes et al. (1989)], incorrectly classifying an applicant as a bad risk represents a missed opportunity, whereas incorrectly classifying a bad risk as a good one could lead to real and substantial costs. Changing F^* will always reduce the probability of one type of error while increasing the probability of the other. There is no correct answer as to the best value to choose. It depends on the setting and on the criterion function upon which the prediction rule depends.

EXAMPLE 19.8 Prediction with a Probit Model

Tunali (1986) estimated a probit model in a study of migration, subsequent remigration, and earnings for a large sample of observations of male members of household in Turkey. Among his results, he reports the following summary for a probit model:

		Predicted		
		D = 0	*D = 1*	*Total*
	D = 0	471	16	487
Actual	**D = 1**	183	20	203
	Total	654	36	690

The estimated model is highly significant, with a likelihood ratio test of the hypothesis that the coefficients (16 of them) are zero based on a chi-squared value of 69 with 16 degrees of freedom.[20] The model predicts 491 of 690, or 71.2 percent, of the observations correctly, although the likelihood ratio index is only 0.083. A naive model, which always predicts that $y = 0$ because $P < 0.5$, predicts 487 of 690, or 70.6 percent, of the observations correctly. This is hardly suggestive of no fit. The maximum likelihood estimator produces several signif-

[19]The technique of **discriminant analysis** is used to build a procedure around this consideration. In this setting, we consider not only the number of correct and incorrect classifications, but the cost of each type of misclassification.

[20]This actually understates slightly the significance of his model, as the preceding predictions are based on a bivariate model. The likelihood ratio test fails to reject the hypothesis that a univariate model applies, however.

icant influences on the probability but makes only four more correct predictions than the naive predictor.[21]

The likelihood ratio index is obviously related to the likelihood ratio statistic for testing the hypothesis that the coefficient vector is zero. Other similar fit measures have been proposed. Although they are suggestive, whether they have any relationship to maximizing any type of fit in the more familiar sense is a question that needs to be studied. The maximum likelihood estimator is *not* chosen so as to maximize a fitting criterion based on prediction of y, as it is in the classical regression (which maximizes R^2). It is chosen to maximize the joint density of the observed dependent variables. It remains an interesting question for research whether fitting y well or obtaining good parameter estimates is a preferable estimation criterion. Evidently, they are not necessarily compatible.

19.4.3 Analysis of Proportions Data

Data for the analysis of binary responses will be in one of two forms. The data we have considered thus far are **individual;** each observation consists of $[y_i, \mathbf{x}_i]$, the actual response of an individual and associated regressor vector. **Grouped data** usually consist of counts or proportions. Grouped data are obtained by observing the response of n_i individuals, all of whom have the same $\mathbf{x}_i$. The observed dependent variable will consist of the proportion P_i of the n_i individuals ij who respond with $y_{ij} = 1$. An observation is thus $[n_i, P_i, \mathbf{x}_i]$, $i = 1, \ldots, N$. Election data are typical.[22] In the grouped data setting, it is possible to use regression methods as well as maximum likelihood procedures to analyze the relationship between P_i and $\mathbf{x}_i$. The observed P_i is an estimate of the population quantity, $\pi_i = F(\boldsymbol{\beta}'\mathbf{x}_i)$. If we treat this as a simple problem in sampling from a Bernoulli population, then, from basic statistics, we have

$$P_i = F(\boldsymbol{\beta}'\mathbf{x}_i) + \epsilon_i = \pi_i + \epsilon_i,$$

where

$$E[\epsilon_i] = 0, \qquad \text{Var}[\epsilon_i] = \frac{\pi_i(1 - \pi_i)}{n_i}. \tag{19-38}$$

This heteroscedastic regression format suggests that the parameters could be estimated by a nonlinear weighted least squares regression. But there is a simpler way to proceed. Since the function $F(\boldsymbol{\beta}'\mathbf{x}_i)$ is strictly monotonic, it has an

---

[21]It is also noteworthy that nearly all the correct predictions of the maximum likelihood estimator are the 0s. It hits only 10 percent of the 1s in the sample.

[22]The earliest work on probit modeling involved applications of grouped data in laboratory experiments. Each observation consisted on n_i subjects receiving dosage x_i of some treatment, such as an insecticide, and a proportion P_i "responding" to the treatment, usually by dying. Finney (1971) and Cox (1970) are useful and important surveys of this literature.

inverse. (See Figure 19.1). Consider, then, a Taylor series approximation to this function around the point $\epsilon_i = 0$:

$$F^{-1}(P_i) = F^{-1}(\pi_i + \epsilon_i) \approx F^{-1}(\pi_i) + \left[\frac{dF^{-1}(\pi_i)}{d\pi_i}\right]\epsilon_i.$$

But $F^{-1}(\pi_i) = \boldsymbol{\beta}'\mathbf{x}_i$ and

$$\frac{dF^{-1}(\pi_i)}{d\pi_i} = \frac{1}{dF(\pi_i)/d\pi_i} = \frac{1}{f(\pi_i)},$$

so

$$F^{-1}(P_i) \approx \boldsymbol{\beta}'\mathbf{x}_i + \frac{\epsilon_i}{f_i}.$$

This produces a heteroscedastic linear regression,

$$F^{-1}(P_i) = z_i = \boldsymbol{\beta}'\mathbf{x}_i + u_i,$$

where

$$E[u_i] = 0 \quad \text{and} \quad \text{Var}[u_i] = \frac{F_i(1 - F_i)}{n_i f_i^2}. \qquad \textbf{(19-39)}$$

The inverse function for the logistic model is particularly easy to obtain. If

$$\pi_i = \frac{\exp(\boldsymbol{\beta}'\mathbf{x}_i)}{1 + \exp(\boldsymbol{\beta}'\mathbf{x}_i)},$$

then

$$\ln\left(\frac{\pi_i}{1 - \pi_i}\right) = \boldsymbol{\beta}'\mathbf{x}_i.$$

This function is called the **logit** of π_i, hence the name "logit" model. For the normal distribution, the inverse function $\Phi^{-1}(\pi_i)$, called the **normit** of π_i, must be approximated. The usual approach is a ratio of polynomials.[23]

Weighted least squares regression based on (19-39) produces the **minimum chi-squared estimates** of $\boldsymbol{\beta}$. Since the weights are functions of the unknown parameters, a two-step procedure is called for. As always, simple least squares at the first step produces consistent but inefficient estimates. Then the weights

$$w_i = \left[\frac{n_i\phi_i^2}{\Phi_i(1 - \Phi_i)}\right]^{1/2}$$

for the probit model and

$$w_i = [n_i\Lambda_i(1 - \Lambda_i)]^{1/2}$$

[23]See Abramovitz and Stegun (1971) and Section 5.2.3b. The function normit + 5 is called the **probit** of P_i. The term dates from the early days of this analysis, when the avoidance of negative numbers was a simplification with considerable payoff.

for the logit model, based on the first step estimates can be used for weighted least squares.[24] It has been shown that this estimator has the same properties as the maximum likelihood estimator. [See Amemiya (1985), pp. 275–280.]

Two complications arise in practice. The familiar result in (19-38) suggests that when the proportion is based on a large population, the variance of the estimator can be exceedingly low. This will resurface in implausibly low standard errors and high t ratios in the minimum chi-squared regression. Unfortunately, that is a consequence of the model.[25] The same result will emerge in maximum likelihood estimates based on proportions data. For grouped data, the log-likelihood is

$$\ln L = \sum_{i=1}^{n} n_i[P_i \ln F(\boldsymbol{\beta}'\mathbf{x}_i) + (1 - P_i)\ln(1 - F(\boldsymbol{\beta}'\mathbf{x}_i))].$$

Second, both the MLE and FGLS estimators break down if any of the proportions are 0 or 1. A number of ad hoc patches have been suggested; the one that seems to be most widely used is just to add or subtract a small constant, say 0.001, from the observed value when it is 0 or 1.

19.5. RECENT DEVELOPMENTS IN BINARY CHOICE MODELING

Qualitative response models have been a growth industry in econometrics. The recent literature, particularly in the area of panel data analysis, has produced a number of new techniques.

19.5.1. Random and Fixed Effects Models for Panel Data

The structural probit model for a possibly unbalanced panel of data would be written

$$y_{it}^* = \boldsymbol{\beta}'\mathbf{x}_{it} + \epsilon_{it}, \qquad \epsilon_{it} \sim N[0, 1], \quad i = 1, \ldots, n, t = 1, \ldots, T_i,$$
$$y_{it} = 1 \quad \text{if } y_{it}^* > 0, \text{ and 0 otherwise.}$$

If the ϵ_{it}'s are taken to be independent standard normal variables, then the panel nature of the data is irrelevant and the methods of the previous sections would apply. In this section, we will examine two approaches that have been suggested for modeling heterogeneity explicitly.[26]

---

[24]Simply using p_i and $f(F^{-1}(P_i))$ might seem to be a simple expedient in computing the weights. But this would be analogous to using y_i^2 instead of an estimate of σ_i^2 in a heteroscedastic regression. Fitted probabilities and, for the probit model, densities should be based on a consistent set of parameter values.

[25]Whether the proportion should, in fact, be considered as a single observation from a distribution of proportions is a question that arises in all these cases. It is unambiguous in the bioassay cases noted earlier. But the issue is less clear with election data, especially since in these cases, the n_i will represent most if not all the potential respondents in location i rather than a random sample of respondents.

[26]A survey on this set of results is given by Hsiao (1992).

The probit model does not lend itself well to the **fixed effects** treatment ($\epsilon_{it} = \alpha_i + \nu_{it}$) of Chapter 14. There is no feasible way to remove the heterogeneity, and with large numbers of cross-sectional units, estimation of the α_i's is intractable. Some progress has been made on a **random effects** specification. Ideally, we would like to specify that ϵ_{it} and ϵ_{is} are freely correlated within a group, but not across groups. But this will involve computing joint probabilities from a T_i variate normal distribution, which is problematic.[27] (We will return to this issue below.) A somewhat less general specification, which has the same structure as the random effects model of Chapter 14, has been implemented by Butler and Moffitt (1982). We will sketch the derivation to suggest how random effects are handled in discrete and limited dependent variable models such as this. Full details on estimation and inference may be found in Butler and Moffitt (1982) and Greene (1995a).

We specify

$$\epsilon_{it} = \nu_{it} + u_i$$

with both components normally distributed with zero means and independently of one another, so that

$$\text{Var}[\epsilon_{it}] = \sigma_\nu^2 + \sigma_u^2 = 1 + \sigma_u^2$$

and

$$\text{Corr}[\epsilon_{it}, \epsilon_{is}] = \rho = \sigma_u^2/(1 + \sigma_u^2).$$

The new free parameter is $\sigma_u^2 = \rho/(1 - \rho)$. Recall that in the cross-section case, the probability associated with an observation is

$$\text{Prob}[y_{it}] = \int_{-\infty}^{q_{it}\boldsymbol{\beta}'\mathbf{x}_{it}} f(\epsilon_{it})d\epsilon_{it} = \Phi[q_{it}(\boldsymbol{\beta}'\mathbf{x}_{it})],$$

where $q_{it} = 2y_{it} - 1$ is used to obviate having separate terms for $y_{it} = 0$ and 1. Because of the common u_i, the T_i observations in group i are jointly normally distributed with covariance matrix defined previously. The contribution of group i to the likelihood for the sample is

$$\begin{aligned} L_i &= \text{Prob}[y_{i1}, y_{i2}, \ldots, y_{iT_i}] \\ &= \int_{-\infty}^{q_{i1}\boldsymbol{\beta}'\mathbf{x}_{i1}} \int_{-\infty}^{q_{i2}\boldsymbol{\beta}'\mathbf{x}_{i2}} \cdots \int_{-\infty}^{q_{iT_i}\boldsymbol{\beta}'\mathbf{x}_{iT_i}} f(\epsilon_{i1}, \epsilon_{i2}, \ldots, \epsilon_{iT_i})d\epsilon_{iT_i} \cdots d\epsilon_{i2}d\epsilon_{i1}. \end{aligned}$$

The integration of the joint density, as it stands, is impractical. The special nature of the random effects model allows a simplification, however. We can

---

[27] A "limited information" approach based on the GMM estimation method has been suggested by Avery et al. (1983).

obtain the joint density of the ϵ_{it}'s by integrating u_i out of the joint density of $(\epsilon_{i1}, \ldots, \epsilon_{iT_i}, u_i), f(\epsilon_{i1}, \ldots, \epsilon_{iT_i}, u_i) = f(\epsilon_{i1}, \ldots, \epsilon_{iT_i} | u_i)f(u_i)$. So,

$$f(\epsilon_1, \epsilon_2, \ldots, \epsilon_{T_i}) = \int_{-\infty}^{+\infty} f(\epsilon_1, \epsilon_2, \ldots, \epsilon_{T_i} | u_i) f(u_i)\, du_i.$$

The advantage of this form is that conditioned on u_i, the ϵ_i's are independent, so

$$f(\epsilon_1, \epsilon_2, \ldots, \epsilon_{T_i}) = \int_{-\infty}^{+\infty} \prod_{t=1}^{T_i} f(\epsilon_{it} | u_i) f(u_i)\, du_i.$$

The density of u_i is $N[0, \rho/(1-\rho)]$. The conditional density of $\epsilon_{it} | u_i$ is $N[u_i, 1]$; conditioned on u_i, the only source of variation is v_{it}, which has variance 1. Combining all this and skipping a large amount of algebra [which may be found in Greene (1995a) and Butler and Moffitt (1982)], we may write the term for group i in the likelihood function as

$$L_i = \frac{1}{\sqrt{\pi}} \int_{-\infty}^{+\infty} e^{-r_i^2} \left\{ \prod_{t=1}^{T_i} \Phi[q_{it}(\boldsymbol{\beta}'\mathbf{x}_{it} + \theta r_i)] \right\} dr_i,$$

$$\theta = \sqrt{\frac{2\rho}{1-\rho}}.$$

The payoff to this manipulation is that this likelihood function involves only one dimensional integrals. The inner integrals are the CDF of the standard normal distribution, which are simple to obtain. The function in total, for all its complexity, is of the form

$$L_i = \frac{1}{\sqrt{\pi}} \int_{-\infty}^{+\infty} e^{-r_i^2} g(r_i)\, dr_i,$$

which is amenable to Gauss–Hermite quadrature for computation. (Gauss–Hermite quadrature is discussed in Section 5.4.2c.) The derivatives are likewise complex but computable by quadrature. The BHHH estimator is a natural choice for estimating the asymptotic covariance matrix for $[\hat{\boldsymbol{\beta}}, \hat{\theta}]$. An estimate of ρ is obtained from the result $\rho = \theta^2/(\theta^2 + 2)$, and a standard error can be obtained with the delta method.

The hypothesis of no cross-period correlation can be tested, in principle, using any of the three classical testing procedures we have discussed to examine the statistical significance of the estimated ρ.

A number of authors have found the Butler and Moffitt formulation to be a satisfactory compromise between a fully unrestricted model and the cross-section variant that ignores the correlation altogether. A recent application that includes both group and time effects is Tauchen et al.'s (1994) study of arrests and criminal behavior. The Butler and Moffitt approach has been criticized for the restriction of equal correlation across periods. But it does have a compelling virtue that the model can be efficiently estimated even with fairly large T_i using conventional computational methods. [See Greene (1995a, pp. 425–431).]

In contrast to the probit model, the logit model does lend itself to a *fixed effects* treatment (but not a random effects specification). A fixed effects logit model that accounts for the heterogeneity is

$$\text{Prob}(y_{it} = 1) = \frac{e^{\alpha_i + \boldsymbol{\beta}'\mathbf{x}_{it}}}{1 + e^{\alpha_i + \boldsymbol{\beta}'\mathbf{x}_{it}}}.$$

In this nonlinear model, it is not possible to sweep out the heterogeneity by taking differences or deviations from group means.[28] Chamberlain (1980) has suggested a different approach to estimating this model with data sets with large n and small T.[29] His suggestion, which was infeasible for the probit model, is that we consider the set of T observations for unit i as a group. The unconditional likelihood for the nT observations is

$$L = \prod_i \prod_t (F_{it})^{y_{it}}(1 - F_{it})^{1-y_{it}}.$$

Chamberlain suggests, instead, that we maximize the conditional likelihood function,

$$L^c = \prod_{i=1}^{n} \text{Prob}\left(Y_{i1} = y_{i1}, Y_{i2} = y_{i2}, \ldots, Y_{iT} = y_{iT} \,\middle|\, \sum_{t=1}^{T} y_{it}\right).$$

That is, the likelihood for each set of T observations is conditioned on the number of 1s in the set. It is useful to consider an example. Suppose that the sample consists of a large number of cross-sectional units, each observed in two periods, 1 and 2. The unconditional likelihood is

$$L = \prod_i \text{Prob}(Y_{i1} = y_{i1})\text{Prob}(Y_{i2} = y_{i2}).$$

The observations are independent, so the likelihood function is the product of the probabilities. For each pair of observations, we have the possibilities:

1. $y_{i1} = 0$ and $y_{i2} = 0$. Prob(0,0 | sum = 0) = 1.
2. $y_{i1} = 1$ and $y_{i2} = 1$. Prob(1,0 | sum = 2) = 1.

The ith term in L^c for either of these is just 1, so they contribute nothing to the

[28] In addition, even if it is possible to estimate the parameters, any desirable properties for the estimated individual effects, α_i, will depend on increasing T, which will not make sense in the typical panel. This will be particularly problematic for maximum likelihood estimators, whose only desirable properties are asymptotic. The solution, as Chamberlain suggests, is to remove the heterogeneity by some other means, and thereby finesse the problem of estimating the α_is.

[29] This technique is not limited to small T, but direct computation of the probability as shown below becomes unwieldy as T grows. A simple recursion greatly simplifies the computation, and T as high as 100 or more is feasible. See Krailo, M. and Pike, M., "Conditional Multivariate Logistic Analysis of Stratified Case-control Studies," *Applied Statistics*, 1984, pp. 95–103.

conditional likelihood function. When we take logs, these terms (and these observations) will drop out. But suppose that $y_{i1} = 0$ and $y_{i2} = 1$. Then,

3. $\text{Prob}(0, 1\,|\,\text{sum} = 1) = \dfrac{\text{Prob}(0, 1 \textit{ and } \text{sum} = 1)}{\text{Prob}(\text{sum} = 1)} = \dfrac{\text{Prob}(0, 1)}{\text{Prob}(0, 1) + \text{Prob}(1, 0)}.$

(The fourth probability would be obtained similarly.) Therefore, for this pair of observations, the conditional probability is

$$\frac{\dfrac{1}{1 + e^{\alpha_i + \boldsymbol{\beta}'\mathbf{x}_{i1}}}\dfrac{e^{\alpha_i + \boldsymbol{\beta}'\mathbf{x}_{i2}}}{1 + e^{\alpha_i + \boldsymbol{\beta}'\mathbf{x}_{i2}}}}{\dfrac{1}{1 + e^{\alpha_i + \boldsymbol{\beta}'\mathbf{x}_{i1}}}\dfrac{e^{\alpha_i + \boldsymbol{\beta}'\mathbf{x}_{i2}}}{1 + e^{\alpha_i + \boldsymbol{\beta}'\mathbf{x}_{i2}}} + \dfrac{e^{\alpha_i + \boldsymbol{\beta}'\mathbf{x}_{i1}}}{1 + e^{\alpha_i + \boldsymbol{\beta}'\mathbf{x}_{i1}}}\dfrac{1}{1 + e^{\alpha_i + \boldsymbol{\beta}'\mathbf{x}_{i2}}}} = \frac{e^{\boldsymbol{\beta}'\mathbf{x}_{i2}}}{e^{\boldsymbol{\beta}'\mathbf{x}_{i1}} + e^{\boldsymbol{\beta}'\mathbf{x}_{i2}}}.$$

By conditioning on the sum of the two observations, we have been able to remove the heterogeneity. Therefore, we can construct the conditional likelihood function as the product of these terms for the pairs of observations for which the two observations are (0, 1). Pairs of observations with 1 and 0 are included analogously. The product of the terms such as the preceding, for those observation sets for which the sum is not zero or T, constitutes the conditional likelihood. Maximization of the resulting function is straightforward and may be done by conventional methods.

As in the linear regression model, it is of some interest to test whether there is, indeed, heterogeneity. With homogeneity ($\alpha_i = \alpha$), there is no unusual problem, and the model can be estimated, as usual, as a logit model. It is not possible to test the hypothesis using the likelihood ratio test, however, because the two likelihoods are not comparable. (The conditional likelihood is based on a restricted data set.) None of the usual tests of restrictions can be used because the individual effects are never actually estimated. Hausman's (1978) specification test is a natural one to use here, however. Under the null hypothesis of homogeneity, both Chamberlain's conditional maximum likelihood estimator (CMLE) and the usual maximum likelihood estimator are consistent, but Chamberlain's is inefficient. (It fails to use the information that $\alpha_i = \alpha$, and it may not use all the data.) Under the alternative hypothesis, the unconditional maximum likelihood estimator is inconsistent,[30] whereas Chamberlain's estimator is consistent and efficient. The Hausman test can be based on the chi-squared statistic

$$\chi^2 = (\hat{\boldsymbol{\beta}}_{\text{CML}} - \hat{\boldsymbol{\beta}}_{\text{ML}})'(\text{Var[CML]} - \text{Var[ML]})^{-1}(\hat{\boldsymbol{\beta}}_{\text{CML}} - \hat{\boldsymbol{\beta}}_{\text{ML}}).$$

The estimated covariance matrices are those computed for the two maximum likelihood estimators. For the unconditional maximum likelihood estimator, the row and column corresponding to the constant term are dropped. A large value will cast doubt on the hypothesis of homogeneity. (There are K degrees of freedom for the test.) It is possible that the covariance matrix for the maxi-

[30]Hsaio (1992) derives the result explicitly for some particular cases.

mum likelihood estimator will be larger than that for the conditional maximum likelihood estimator. If so, the difference matrix in brackets is assumed to be a zero matrix, and the chi-squared statistic is therefore zero.

EXAMPLE 19.9 Fixed Effects in a Logit Model

Cecchetti (1986) applied Chamberlain's model in a study of the frequency of the price changes for a sample of 38 magazines observed over a 27-year period. The constant term for each magazine was allowed to change every 3 years, implying a total of 318 free parameters. The data were analyzed in 9-year subperiods, so a cross-section unit in our earlier notation consists of $T = 3$ periods. Since a price change could occur in any period, the sums of y_{it} were 0, 1, 2, or 3. The model included as regressors (1) the time since the last price change, (2) inflation since the last price change, (3) the size of the last price change, (4) current inflation, (5) industry sales growth, and (6) a measure of sales volatility. The most important determinants of the probability of a price change were found to be (1), (2), and (5). In none of Cecchetti's models was the Hausman statistic less than 40, indicating that the data did exhibit heterogeneity.

19.5.2. Semiparametric Analysis

In his survey of qualitative response models, Amemiya (1981) reports the following widely cited approximations for the linear probability (LP) model: Over the range of probabilities of 30 to 70 percent,

$$\hat{\boldsymbol{\beta}}_{\text{LP}} \approx 0.4\boldsymbol{\beta}_{\text{probit}} \text{ for the slopes},$$
$$\hat{\boldsymbol{\beta}}_{\text{LP}} \approx 0.25\boldsymbol{\beta}_{\text{logit}} \text{ for the slopes.}^{31}$$

Aside from confirming our intuition that least squares approximates the nonlinear model and providing a quick comparison for the three models involved, the practical usefulness of the formula is somewhat limited. Still, it is a striking result.[32] A recent series of studies has focused on reasons why the least squares estimates should be proportional to the probit and logit estimates. A related question concerns the problems associated with assuming that a probit model applies when, in fact, a logit model is appropriate or vice versa.[33] The approximation would seem to suggest that with this type of misspecification, we would, once again, obtain a scaled version of the correct coefficient vector. (Amemiya also reports the widely observed relationship $\hat{\boldsymbol{\beta}}_{\text{logit}} = 1.6\hat{\boldsymbol{\beta}}_{\text{probit}}$, which follows from the results above.)

Greene (1983a), building on Goldberger (1981), finds that if the probit

[31]An additional 0.5 is added for the constant term in both models.

[32]This does not imply that it is useful to report 2.5 times the linear probability estimates with the probit estimates for comparability. The linear probability estimates are already in the form of marginal effects, whereas the probit coefficients must be scaled *downward*. If the sample proportion happens to be close to 0.5, the right scale factor will be roughly $\phi[\Phi^{-1}(0.5)] = 0.3989$. But the density falls rapidly as P moves away from 0.5.

[33]See Ruud (1986) and Gourieroux et al. (1987).

model is correctly specified and if the regressors are themselves joint normally distributed, that the probability limit of the least squares estimator is a multiple of the true coefficient vector.[34] Greene's result is useful only for the same purpose as Amemiya's quick correction of OLS. Multivariate normality is obviously inconsistent with most applications. For example, nearly all applications include at least one dummy variable. Ruud (1982) and Cheung and Goldberger (1984), however, have shown that much weaker conditions than joint normality will produce the same proportionality result. For a probit model, Cheung and Goldberger require only that $E[\mathbf{x} \mid y^*]$ be linear in y^*. Several authors have built on these observations to pursue the issue of what circumstances will lead to proportionality results such as these. Ruud (1986) and Stoker (1986) have extended them to a very wide class of models that goes well beyond those of Cheung and Goldberger. Curiously enough, Stoker's results rule out dummy variables, but it is those for which the proportionality result seems to be most robust.[35]

19.5.3. The Maximum Score Estimator (MSCORE)

In Section 19.4.2, we discussed the issue of prediction rules for the probit and logit models. In contrast to the linear regression model, estimation of these binary choice models is not based on a fitting rule, such as the sum of squared residuals, which is related to the fit of the model to the data. The maximum score estimator *is* based on a fitting rule,

$$\text{Maximize}_{\boldsymbol{\beta}}\ S_{N\alpha}(\boldsymbol{\beta}) = \frac{1}{n}\sum_{i=1}^{n}[z_i - (1 - 2\alpha)\text{sgn}(\boldsymbol{\beta}'\mathbf{x}_i)].^{36}$$

The parameter α is a preset quantile, and $z_i = 2y_i - 1$. (So $z = -1$ if $y = 0$.) If α is set to $\frac{1}{2}$ then the maximum score estimator chooses the $\boldsymbol{\beta}$ to maximize the number of times that the prediction has the same sign as z. This matches our prediction rule in (19-36) with $F^* = 0.5$. So for $\alpha = 0.5$, maximum score attempts to maximize the number of correct predictions. Since the sign of $\boldsymbol{\beta}'\mathbf{x}$ is the same for all positive multiples of $\boldsymbol{\beta}$, the estimator is computed subject to the constraint that $\boldsymbol{\beta}'\boldsymbol{\beta} = 1$.

Since there is no log-likelihood function underlying the fitting criterion, there is no information matrix to provide a method of obtaining standard errors for the estimates. A method that is used to provide at least some idea of the sampling variability of the estimator is called **bootstrapping.** (See Section 5.3.4.) The method proceeds as follows. After the set of coefficients $\mathbf{b}_n$ is computed, B randomly drawn samples of m observations are drawn from the original data set *with replacement.* The bootstrap sample size m may be less than or

---

[34]The scale factor is estimable with the sample data, so under these assumptions, a method of moments estimator is available.

[35]See Greene (1983a).

[36]See Manski (1975, 1985, 1986) and Manski and Thompson (1986).

equal to n, the sample size. With each such sample, the maximum score estimator is recomputed, giving $\mathbf{b}_m(b)$. Then the **mean squared deviation matrix**

$$\mathbf{MSD(b)} = \frac{1}{B}\sum_{b=1}^{B}[\mathbf{b}_m(b) - \mathbf{b}_n][\mathbf{b}_m(b) - \mathbf{b}_n]'$$

is computed. The authors of the technique emphasize that this is not a covariance matrix.[37]

EXAMPLE 19.10 The Maximum Score Estimator

Table 19.5 presents maximum score estimates for Spector and Mazzeo's GRADE model using $\alpha = 0.4$ (found by trial and error). Note that they are quite far removed from the probit estimates. The estimates are extremely sensitive to the choice of α. Of course, there is no meaningful comparison of the coefficients, since the maximum score estimates are not the slopes of a conditional mean function. The prediction performance of the model is also quite sensitive to α, but this is to be expected.[38] Surprisingly enough, for these data, the maximum score approach does not predict the dependent variable quite as well as the probit model, although for this example, the difference is only a single observation. (The literature awaits a comparison of the prediction performance of the probit/logit (parametric) approaches and this semiparametric model.) The relevant scores for the two estimators are also given in the table.

TABLE 19.5 Maximum Score Estimator

		Maximum Score		*Probit*	
		Estimate	*Mean Square Dev.*	*Estimate*	*Standard Error*
Constant	β_1	−0.8492	0.7321	−7.4522	2.5420
GPA	β_2	0.01863	0.5349	1.6260	0.6939
TUCE	β_3	0.01104	0.08244	0.05173	0.08389
PSI	β_4	0.5276	0.59913	1.4264	0.5950

Maximum Score		Fitted 0	Fitted 1	Probit		Fitted 0	Fitted 1
Actual	0	20	1	Actual	0	18	3
	1	6	5		1	3	8

[37]Note that we are not yet agreed that $\mathbf{b}_n$ even converges to a meaningful vector, since no underlying probability distribution as such has been assumed. Once it is agreed that there is an underlying regression function at work, then a meaningful set of asymptotic results, including consistency can be developed. Manski et al. (op. cit.) and Kim and Pollard (1990) present a number of results. Even so, it has been shown that the bootstrap MSD matrix is useful for little more than descriptive purposes.

[38]The criterion function for choosing $\mathbf{b}$ is not continuous, and it has more than one optimum. Professor M. E. Bissey reported finding that the score function varies significantly between the local optima as well. [Personal correspondence to the author, University of York (1995).]

Semiparametric approaches such as this have the virtue that they do not make a possibly erroneous assumption about the underlying distribution. On the other hand, as seen in the example, this is no guarantee that the estimator will outperform the fully parametric estimator. One additional practical consideration is that semiparametric estimators such as this are very computation intensive. At present, the maximum score estimator is not usable for more than roughly 15 coefficients and perhaps 1500 to 2000 observations.[39] A third shortcoming of the approach is, unfortunately, inherent in its design. The parametric assumptions of the probit or logit produce a large amount of information about the relationship between the response variable and the covariates. In the final analysis, the marginal effects discussed earlier might well have been the primary objective of the study. That information is lost here.

19.5.4. A Kernel Estimator for a Nonparametric Regression Function

As noted, one unsatisfactory aspect of semiparametric formulations such as MSCORE is that the amount of information that the procedure provides about the population is limited; this is, after all, the purpose of dispensing with the firm (parametric) assumptions of the probit and logit models. Thus, in the preceding example, there is little that one can say about the population that generated the data based on the MSCORE "estimates" in the table. They do allow predictions of the response variable. But there is little information about any relationship between the response and the independent variables based on the "estimation" results. Even the mean-squared deviation matrix is suspect as an estimator of the asymptotic covariance matrix of the MSCORE coefficients.

The authors of the technique have proposed a secondary analysis of the results. Let

$$F_\beta(z_i) = E[y_i \mid \boldsymbol{\beta}'\mathbf{x}_i = z_i]$$

denote a smooth regression function for the response variable. Based on a parameter vector $\boldsymbol{\beta}$, the authors propose to estimate the regression by the **method of kernels** as follows. For the n observations in the sample and for the given $\boldsymbol{\beta}$ (e.g., $\mathbf{b}_n$ from MSCORE), let

$$z_i = \boldsymbol{\beta}'\mathbf{x}_i,$$
$$s = \left[\frac{1}{n}\sum_{i=1}^{n}(z_i - \bar{z})^2\right]^{1/2}.$$

For a particular value z^*, we compute a set of n weights using the **kernel function,**

$$w_i(z^*) = K[(z^* - z_i)/(\lambda s)],$$

[39]Communication from C. Manski to the author. The maximum score estimator has been implemented by Manski and Thompson (1986) and Greene (1995a).

where

$$K(r_i) = P(r_i)[1 - P(r_i)]$$

and

$$P(r_i) = [1 + \exp(-cr_i)]^{-1}.$$

The constant $c = (\pi/\sqrt{3})^{-1} \approx 0.55133$ is used to standardize the logistic distribution that is used for the kernel function. (See the discussion at the end of Example 19.1.) The parameter λ is a smoothing parameter. Large values will flatten the estimated function through $\bar{y}$, whereas values close to 0 will allow greater variation in the function but might cause it to be unstable. There is no good theory for the choice, but some suggestions have been made based on descriptive statistics. [See Wong (1983) and Manski (1986).] Finally, the function value is estimated with

$$F(z^*) \approx \frac{\sum_{i=1}^{n} w_i(z^*)y_i}{\sum_{i=1}^{n} w_i(z^*)}.$$

EXAMPLE 19.11 Nonparametric Regression

Figure 19.3 shows a plot of two estimates of the regression function for $E[\text{GRADE}\,|\,z]$. The coefficients are the MSCORE estimates given in Table 19.5. The plot is produced by computing fitted values for 100 equally spaced points in the range of $\mathbf{b}_n'\mathbf{x}$, which for these data and coefficients is $[-0.66229, 0.05505]$. The function is estimated with two values of the smoothing parameter, 1.0 and 0.3. As expected, the function based on $\lambda = 1.0$ is much flatter than that based on $\lambda = 0.3$. Unfortuntely, the results of the analysis are crucially dependent on the value assumed.

The nonparametric estimator displays a relationship between $\boldsymbol{\beta}'\mathbf{x}$ and $E[y_i]$. At first blush, this might suggest that we could deduce the marginal effects from this, but unfortunately, that is not the case. The coefficients in this setting are not meaningful, so all we can deduce from this is an estimate of the density, $f(z)$, by using first differences of the estimated regression function. It might seem, therefore, that the analysis has produced relatively little payoff for the effort. But this should come as no surprise if we reconsider the assumptions that we have made to reach this point. The only assumptions made thus far are that for a given vector of covariates $\mathbf{x}_i$ and coefficient vector $\boldsymbol{\beta}$ (that is, *any* $\boldsymbol{\beta}$), there exists a smooth function $F(\boldsymbol{\beta}'\mathbf{x}_i) = E[y_i\,|\,z_i]$. We have also assumed, at least implicitly, that the coefficients carry some information about the covariation of $\boldsymbol{\beta}'\mathbf{x}$ and the response variable. The technique will approximate any such function [see Manski (1986)].

There is a large and burgeoning literature on kernel estimation and nonparametric estimation in econometrics. [A recent application is Melenberg and van Soest (1996).] As this simple example suggests, with the radically different forms of the specified model, the information that is culled from the data

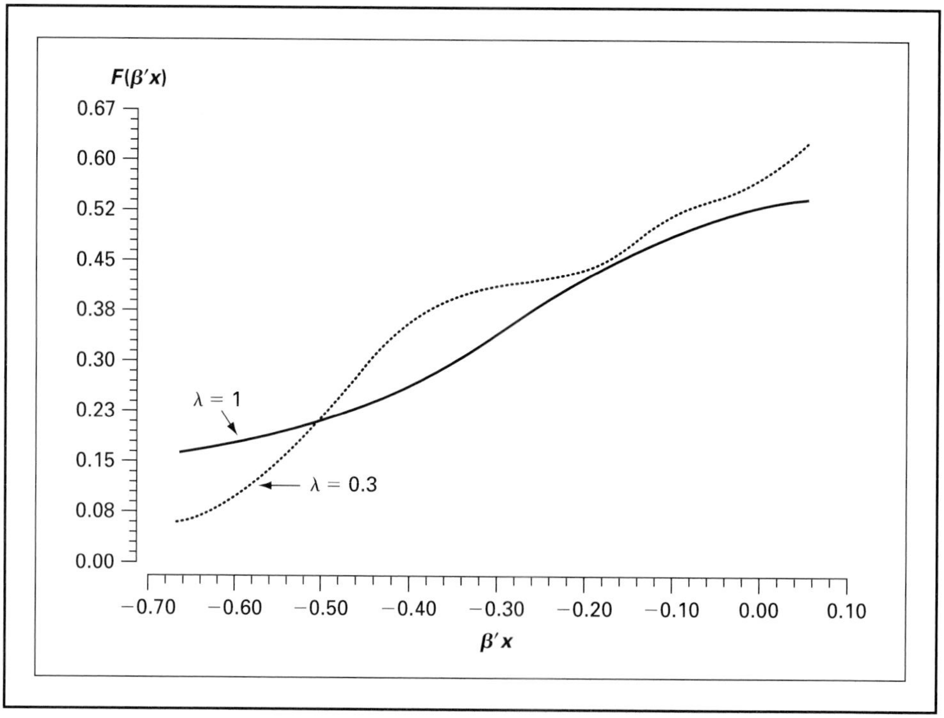

FIGURE 19.3 Nonparametric Regression.

changes radically as well. The general principle that this should make evident is that the fewer assumptions one makes about the population, the less precise the information that can be deduced by statistical techniques. That tradeoff is inherent in the methodology.

19.6. BIVARIATE AND MULTIVARIATE PROBIT MODELS

In Chapter 15, we analyzed a number of different multiple-equation extensions of the classical and generalized regression model. A natural extension of the probit model would be to allow more than one equation, with correlated disturbances, in the same spirit as the seemingly unrelated regressions model. The general specification for a two-equation model would be

$$
\begin{aligned}
y_1^* &= \boldsymbol{\beta}_1'\mathbf{x}_1 + \epsilon_1, \qquad y_1 = 1 \quad \text{if } y_1^* > 0, 0 \text{ otherwise,}\\
y_2^* &= \boldsymbol{\beta}_2'\mathbf{x}_2 + \epsilon_2, \qquad y_2 = 1 \quad \text{if } y_2^* > 0, 0 \text{ otherwise,}\\
E[\epsilon_1] &= E[\epsilon_2] = 0,\\
\text{Var}[\epsilon_1] &= \text{Var}[\epsilon_2] = 1,\\
\text{Cov}[\epsilon_1, \epsilon_2] &= \rho.
\end{aligned}
\tag{19-40}
$$

TABLE 19.6 Bivariate Probit Estimates

	Single Equation		*Bivariate*	
Public school				
Constant	−4.972	(3.996)	−4.764	(4.009)
Income	0.1537	(0.4495)	0.1149	(0.5958)
Taxes	0.6440	(0.5654)	0.6699	(0.7226)
School budget				
Constant	−0.6862	(4.009)	−0.3066	(3.850)
Income	0.9961	(0.4404)	0.9895	(0.4863)
Taxes	−1.2646	(0.5672)	−1.3080	(0.6748)
Years	−0.01644	(0.0147)	−0.0176	(0.0136)
ρ	0.0		0.137	(0.2303)
Log-likelihood	−40.0830 + −58.5006		−97.4117	

EXAMPLE 19.12 A Bivariate Probit Model

Greene (1984) reports estimates of a model of voter behavior in two decisions, whether to send at least one child to public school and whether to vote in favor of a school budget.[40] Regressors in the model were "income," "taxes" = property taxes paid, and "years" of residence in the community. The results in Table 19.6 were obtained using 95 observations.

19.6.1. Maximum Likelihood Estimation

The bivariate normal cdf is

$$\text{Prob}(X_1 < x_1, X_2 < x_2) = \int_{-\infty}^{x_2}\int_{-\infty}^{x_1} \phi_2(z_1, z_2, \rho)\, dz_1\, dz_2,$$

which we denote $\Phi_2(x_1, x_2, \rho)$. The density (which was given in Section 3.8) is

$$\phi_2(x_1, x_2, \rho) = \frac{e^{-(1/2)(x_1^2 + x_2^2 - 2\rho x_1 x_2)/(1-\rho^2)}}{2\pi(1-\rho^2)^{1/2}}.$$

To construct the log-likelihood, let $q_{i1} = 2y_{i1} - 1$ and $q_{i2} = 2y_{i2} - 1$. Thus, $q_{ij} = 1$ if $y_{ij} = 1$ and -1 if $y_{ij} = 0$ for $j = 1$ and 2. Now let

$$z_{ij} = \boldsymbol{\beta}_j' \mathbf{x}_{ij} \quad \text{and} \quad w_{ij} = q_{ij} z_{ij}, \quad j = 1, 2$$

and

$$\rho_{i*} = q_{i1} q_{i2} \rho.$$

Note the national convention. The subscript 2 is used to indicate the bivariate

[40]Data for the study are given in Pindyck and Rubinfeld (1981) and Rubinfeld (1977).

normal distribution in the density ϕ_2 and cdf Φ_2. In all other cases, the subscript 2 indicates the variables in the second equation in (19-40). As before, $\phi(.)$ and $\Phi(.)$ without subscripts denote the univariate standard normal density and cdf.

The probabilities that enter the likelihood function are

$$\text{Prob}(Y_1 = y_{i1}, Y_2 = y_{i2}) = \Phi_2(w_{i1}, w_{i2}, \rho_{i*}).$$

This accounts for all the necessary sign changes needed to compute probabilities for y's equal to 0 and 1. Thus,

$$\ln L = \sum_{i=1}^{n} \ln \Phi_2(w_{i1}, w_{i2}, \rho_{i*}).^{41} \qquad \textbf{(19-41)}$$

The derivatives of the log-likelihood then reduce to

$$\begin{aligned} \frac{\partial \ln L}{\partial \boldsymbol{\beta}_j} &= \sum_{i=1}^{n} \left(\frac{q_{ij} g_{ij}}{\Phi_2}\right) \mathbf{x}_{ij}, \quad j = 1, 2, \\ \frac{\partial \ln L}{\partial \rho} &= \sum_{i=1}^{n} \frac{q_{i1} q_{i2} \phi_2}{\Phi_2}, \end{aligned} \qquad \textbf{(19-42)}$$

where

$$g_{i1} = \phi(w_{i1})\Phi\left[\frac{w_{i2} - \rho_{i*} w_{i1}}{\sqrt{1 - \rho_{i*}^2}}\right] \qquad \textbf{(19-43)}$$

and the subscripts 1 and 2 in g_{i1} are reversed to obtain g_{i2}. (The derivative with respect to ρ is surprisingly simple.) Before considering the Hessian, it is useful to note what becomes of the preceding if $\rho = 0$. For $\partial \ln L/\partial \beta_1$, if $\rho = \rho_{i*} = 0$, g_{i1} reduces to $\phi(w_{i1})\Phi(w_{i2})$, ϕ_2 is $\phi(w_{i1})\phi(w_{i2})$, and Φ_2 is $\Phi(w_{i1})\Phi(w_{i2})$. Inserting these in (19-42) with q_{i1} and q_{i2} produces (19-21). Since $\Phi_2 = \Phi(w_{i1})\Phi(w_{i2})$ is not a function of ρ, $\partial \ln L/\partial \rho$ is zero.

The maximum likelihood estimates are obtained by simultaneously setting the three derivatives to zero. (See Example 5.6.) The second derivatives are relatively straightforward but tedious. Some simplifications are useful. Let

$$\begin{aligned} \delta_i &= \frac{1}{\sqrt{1 - \rho_{i*}^2}}, \\ v_{i1} &= \delta_i(w_{i2} - \rho_{i*} w_{i1}), \quad \text{so } g_{i1} = \phi(w_{i1})\Phi(v_{i1}), \\ v_{i2} &= \delta_i(w_{i1} - \rho_{i*} w_{i2}), \quad \text{so } g_{i2} = \phi(w_{i2})\Phi(v_{i2}). \end{aligned}$$

By multiplying it out, you can show that

$$\delta_i \phi(w_{i1})\phi(v_{i1}) = \delta_i \phi(w_{i2})\phi(v_{i2}) = \phi_2.$$

[41]To avoid further ambiguity, and for convenience, the observation subscript will be omitted from $\Phi_2 = \Phi_2(w_{i1}, w_{i2}, \rho_{i*})$ and from $\phi_2 = \phi_2(w_{i1}, w_{i2}, \rho_{i*})$.

Then

$$\frac{\partial^2 \ln L}{\partial \boldsymbol{\beta}_1\, \partial \boldsymbol{\beta}_1'} = \sum_{i=1}^{n} \mathbf{x}_{i1}\mathbf{x}_{i1}'\left[\frac{-w_{i1}g_{i1}}{\Phi_2} - \frac{\rho_{i*}\phi_2}{\Phi_2} - \frac{g_{i1}^2}{\Phi_2^2}\right],$$

$$\frac{\partial^2 \ln L}{\partial \boldsymbol{\beta}_1\, \partial \boldsymbol{\beta}_2'} = \sum_{i=1}^{n} q_{i1}q_{i2}\mathbf{x}_{i1}\mathbf{x}_{i2}'\left[\frac{\phi_2}{\Phi_2} - \frac{g_{i1}g_{i2}}{\Phi_2^2}\right],$$

$$\frac{\partial^2 \ln L}{\partial \boldsymbol{\beta}_1\, \partial \rho} = \sum_{i=1}^{n} q_{i2}\mathbf{x}_{i1}\frac{\phi_2}{\Phi_2}\left[\rho_{i*}\delta_i v_{i1} - w_{i1} - \frac{g_{i1}}{\Phi_2}\right],$$

$$\frac{\partial^2 \ln L}{\partial \rho^2} = \sum_{i=1}^{n} \frac{\phi_2}{\Phi_2}\left[\delta_i^2\rho_{i*}(1 - \mathbf{w}_i'\mathbf{R}_i^{-1}\mathbf{w}_i) + \delta_i w_{i1}w_{i2} - \frac{\phi_2}{\Phi_2}\right],$$

where $\mathbf{w}_i'\mathbf{R}_i^{-1}\mathbf{w}_i = \delta_i^2(w_{i1}^2 + w_{i2}^2 - 2\rho_{i*}w_{i1}w_{i2})$. (For $\boldsymbol{\beta}_2$, change the subscripts in $\partial^2 \ln L/\partial \boldsymbol{\beta}_1\, \partial \boldsymbol{\beta}_1'$ and $\partial^2 \ln L/\partial \boldsymbol{\beta}_1\, \partial \rho$ accordingly.) The complexity of the second derivatives for this model makes it an excellent candidate for the Berndt et al. estimator of the variance matrix of the maximum likelihood estimator.

Even though it is (almost) impossible to estimate higher-dimensional models, it is possible to test for correlation among the equations. The Lagrange multiplier test is a natural device in this setting. Under the null hypothesis that ρ equals zero, the model consists of independent probit equations, which can be estimated separately. Moreover, in the multivariate model, all the bivariate (or multivariate) densities and probabilities factor into the products of the marginals if the correlations are zero. This makes construction of the test statistic a simple matter of manipulating the results of the independent probits. The Lagrange multiplier statistic for testing $H_0{:}\,\rho = 0$ in a bivariate probit model is[42]

$$\text{LM} = \frac{g^2}{h},$$

where

$$g = \sum_{i=1}^{n} q_{i1}q_{i2}\frac{\phi(w_{i1})\phi(w_{i2})}{\Phi(w_{i1})\Phi(w_{i2})}$$

and

$$h = \sum_{i=1}^{n} \frac{[\phi(w_{i1})\phi(w_{i2})]^2}{\Phi(w_{i1})\Phi(-w_{i1})\Phi(w_{i2})\Phi(-w_{i2})}.$$

EXAMPLE 19.13 Testing for Correlation in the Bivariate Probit Model

Continuing the preceding example, we find that there are three ways in which we may test the hypothesis that ρ equals zero. A simple t test is equivalent to the Wald test. The square of the t ratio is the Wald statistic. Under the null hy-

[42]This is derived in Kiefer (1982).

pothesis, the log-likelihood is the sum of the log-likelihoods for the two independent probits. The Lagrange multiplier statistic is computed as shown earlier, using only the two independent probits. The results are

Wald statistic:	1.8947,
likelihood ratio:	2.3438,
Lagrange multiplier:	2.0581.

The critical value from the chi-squared table with one degree of freedom is 3.84. Therefore, all three statistics suggest that the hypothesis that ρ equals zero cannot be rejected.

There are several "marginal effects" one might want to evaluate in a bivariate probit model. For convenience in evaluating them, we will define a vector $\mathbf{x} = \mathbf{x}_1 \cup \mathbf{x}_2$ and let $\boldsymbol{\beta}_1'\mathbf{x}_1 = \boldsymbol{\gamma}_1'\mathbf{x}$. Thus, $\boldsymbol{\gamma}_1$ contains all the nonzero elements of $\boldsymbol{\beta}_1$ and possibly some zeros in the positions of variables in $\mathbf{x}$ that appear only in the other equation; $\boldsymbol{\gamma}_2$ is defined likewise. The bivariate probability is

$$\text{Prob}[y_1 = 1, y_2 = 1] = \Phi_2[\boldsymbol{\gamma}_1'\mathbf{x}, \boldsymbol{\gamma}_2'\mathbf{x}, \rho].$$

Signs are changed appropriately if the probability of the zero outcome is desired in either case. (See 19-41.) The marginal effects of changes in $\mathbf{x}$ on the probability are given by

$$\frac{\partial \Phi_2}{\partial \mathbf{x}} = g_1\boldsymbol{\gamma}_1 + g_2\boldsymbol{\gamma}_2,$$

where g_1 and g_2 are defined in (19-43). The familiar univariate cases will arise if $\rho = 0$, and effects specific to one equation or the other will be produced by zeros in the corresponding position in one or the other parameter vector. There are also some conditional mean functions to consider. The unconditional mean functions are given by the univariate probabilities:

$$E[y_j \mid \mathbf{x}] = \Phi(\boldsymbol{\gamma}_j'\mathbf{x}), \quad j = 1, 2,$$

so the analysis of (19-9) and (19-10) applies. One pair of conditional mean functions that might be of interest are

$$\begin{aligned} E[y_1 \mid y_2 = 1, \mathbf{x}] &= \text{Prob}[y_1 = 1 \mid y_2 = 1, \mathbf{x}] \\ &= \frac{\text{Prob}[y_1 = 1, y_2 = 1 \mid \mathbf{x}]}{\text{Prob}[y_2 = 1 \mid \mathbf{x}]} \\ &= \frac{\Phi_2(\boldsymbol{\gamma}_1'\mathbf{x}, \boldsymbol{\gamma}_2'\mathbf{x}, \rho)}{\Phi(\boldsymbol{\gamma}_2'\mathbf{x})} \end{aligned}$$

and similarly for $E[y_2 \mid y_1 = 1, \mathbf{x}]$. The marginal effects for this function are given by

$$\frac{\partial E[y_1 \mid y_2 = 1, \mathbf{x}]}{\partial \mathbf{x}} = \left(\frac{1}{\Phi(\boldsymbol{\gamma}_2'\mathbf{x})}\right)\left[g_1\boldsymbol{\gamma}_1 + \left(g_2 - \Phi_2\frac{\phi(\boldsymbol{\gamma}_2'\mathbf{x})}{\Phi(\boldsymbol{\gamma}_2'\mathbf{x})}\right)\boldsymbol{\gamma}_2\right].$$

Finally, one might construct the nonlinear conditional mean function

$$E[y_1 \mid y_2, \mathbf{x}] = \frac{\Phi_2[\boldsymbol{\gamma}_1'\mathbf{x}, (2y_2 - 1)\boldsymbol{\gamma}_2'\mathbf{x}, (2y_2 - 1)\rho]}{\Phi_{[}(2y_2 - 1)\boldsymbol{\gamma}_2'\mathbf{x}]}.$$

The derivatives of this function are the same as those above, with sign changes in several places if $y_2 = 0$ is the argument.

19.6.2. Extensions

19.6.2a. A Multivariate Probit Model. In principle, a multivariate model would extend (19-40) to more than two outcome variables just by adding equations. The practical obstacle to such an extension is primarily the evaluation of higher-order multivariate normal integrals. Some progress has been made on trivariate integration, but existing results are not sufficient to allow accurate and efficient evaluation for more than two variables in a sample of even moderate size.

An altogether different approach has recently been used with some success. Lerman and Manski (1981) suggested that one might approximate multivariate normal probabilities by random sampling. For example, to approximate $\text{Prob}(Y_1 > 1, Y_2 < 3, Y_3 < -1 \mid \rho_{12}, \rho_{13}, \rho_{23})$, we would simply draw random observations from this trivariate normal distribution (see Section 5.3.2c) and count the number of observations that satisfy the inequality. To obtain an accurate estimate of the probability, a quite large number of draws is required. The logic of the Manski–Lerman approach is sound, however. As discussed earlier—see Section 5.4.2e—recent developments have produced methods of producing quite accurate estimates of multivariate normal integrals based on this principle. The evaluation of multivariate normal integral is generally a much less formidable obstacle to the estimation of models based on the multivariate normal distribution.[43]

McFadden (1989) pointed out that for purposes of maximum likelihood estimation, accurate evaluation of probabilities is not necessarily the problem that needs to be solved. One can view the computation of the log-likelihood and its derivatives as a problem of estimating a mean. That is, in (19-41) and (19-42), the same problem arises if we divide by n. The idea is that even though the individual terms in the average might be in error, if the error has mean zero, it will average out in the summation. The important insight is, then, that if we can obtain probability estimates that only err randomly both positively and negatively, then it may be possible to obtain an estimate of the log-likelihood and its derivatives that is reasonably close to the one that would result from actually computing the integral. From a practical standpoint, it does not take inordinately large numbers of random draws to achieve this. This result, with the progress that has been made on Monte Carlo integration, has made feasible multivariate models that previously were intractable.

[43]Recent papers which propose improved methods of simulating probabilities include Pakes and Pollard (1989) and especially Börsch-Supan and Hajivassilou (1990), Geweke (1989), Keane (1994).

These observations do not imply that fully general, unrestricted T-variate models with free correlation matrices $\mathbf{R}$ are "in the tool kit." There remains a substantial obstacle to estimation of multivariate probit models. In any model that is estimated, however formulated, $\mathbf{R}$ must be a positive definite matrix. In models in which T is greater than 3, this imposes a substantial number of highly nonlinear inequality restrictions on the elements of $\mathbf{R}$. Note that in the Butler and Moffitt random effects formulation, $\mathbf{R} = \mathbf{I} + [\rho/(1-\rho)]\mathbf{ii}'$, which is positive definite if $-1 < \rho < 1$. Only one inequality constraint need be imposed during estimation, which is fairly simple. The corresponding problem for an unrestricted T-variate problem remains to be solved. The multivariate problems that have been solved in the received literature generally involve either trivariate models, for which the necessary restrictions are moderately simple to formulate explicitly, or T-variate problems in which $\mathbf{R}$ is tightly parameterized in terms of only a few underlying parameters for which constraints are easily imposed. The symposium on this subject in the November 1994 issue of the *Review of Economics and Statistics* presents discussion of this and a number of other topics.

19.6.2b. A Model with Censoring. There are situations in which the observed variables in the bivariate probit model are censored in one way or another. For example, in an evaluation of credit scoring models, Boyes et al. (1989) analyzed data generated by the following rule:

$$y_1 = 1 \quad \text{if individual } i \text{ defaults on a loan, 0 otherwise,}$$
$$y_2 = 1 \quad \text{if the individual is granted a loan, 0 otherwise.}$$

Greene (1993) applied the same model to y_1 = default on credit card loans, in which y_2 denotes whether an application for the card was accepted or not. For a given individual, y_1 is not observed unless y_2 equals 1. Thus, there are three types of observations in the sample with unconditional probabilities:[44]

$$\begin{aligned} y_2 &= 0: & \text{Prob}(Y_2 = 0) &= 1 - \Phi(\boldsymbol{\beta}_2'\mathbf{x}_2), \\ y_1 = 0, y_2 &= 1: & \text{Prob}(y_1 = 0, y_2 = 1) &= \Phi_2[-\boldsymbol{\beta}_1'\mathbf{x}_1, \boldsymbol{\beta}_2'\mathbf{x}_2, -\rho], \\ y_1 = 1, y_2 &= 1: & \text{Prob}(y_1 = 1, y_2 = 1) &= \Phi_2[\boldsymbol{\beta}_1'\mathbf{x}_1, \boldsymbol{\beta}_2'\mathbf{x}_2, \rho]. \end{aligned}$$

The log-likelihood function is based on these probabilities.[45]

19.7. LOGIT MODELS FOR MULTIPLE CHOICES

Some recent studies of multiple-choice settings include the following:

1. Hensher (1986), McFadden (1974), and many others have analyzed the travel mode of urban commuters.

---

[44]The model was first proposed by Wynand and van Praag (1981).

[45]Extensions of the bivariate probit model to other types of censoring are discussed in Poirier (1980) and Abowd and Farber (1982).

2. Schmidt and Strauss (1975a,b) and Boskin (1974) have analyzed occupational choice among multiple alternatives.
3. Terza (1985a) has studied the assignment of bond ratings to corporate bonds as a choice among multiple alternatives.

These are all distinct from the multivariate probit model we examined earlier. In that setting, there were several decisions, each between two alternatives. Here there is a single decision among two or more alternatives. We will examine two broad types of choice sets, **ordered** and **unordered.** The choice among means of getting to work, by car, bus, train, or bicycle, is clearly unordered. A bond rating is, by design, a ranking; that is its purpose. As we shall see, quite different techniques are used for the two types of models. Models for unordered choice sets are considered in this section. A model for ordered choices is described in Section 19.8.

Unordered-choice models can be motivated by a random utility model. For the ith consumer faced with J choices, suppose that the utility of choice j is

$$U_{ij} = \boldsymbol{\beta}'\mathbf{z}_{ij} + \epsilon_{ij}.$$

If the consumer makes choice j in particular, we assume that U_{ij} is the maximum among the J utilities. Hence, the statistical model is driven by the probability that choice j is made, which is

$$\text{Prob}(U_{ij} > U_{ik}) \quad \text{for all other } k \neq j.$$

The model is made operational by a particular choice of distribution for the disturbances. As before, two models have been considered, logit and probit. Because of the need to evaluate multiple integrals of the normal distribution, the probit model has found rather limited use in this setting. The logit model, in contrast, has been widely used in many fields, including economics, market research, transportation engineering, and so on. Let Y_i be a random variable that indicates the choice made. McFadden (1973) has shown that if (and only if) the J disturbances are independent and identically distributed with Weibull distribution,

$$F(\epsilon_{ij}) = \exp(e^{-\epsilon_{ij}}),$$

then

$$\text{Prob}(Y_i = j) = \frac{e^{\boldsymbol{\beta}'\mathbf{z}_{ij}}}{\sum_{j=1}^{J} e^{\boldsymbol{\beta}'\mathbf{z}_{ij}}}. \qquad \textbf{(19-44)}$$

This leads to what is called the **conditional logit** model.[46]

[46]It is occasionally labeled the **multinomial logit model,** but this conflicts with the usual name for the model discussed in the next section, which differs slightly. Although the distinction turns out to be purely artificial, we will maintain it for the present.

Utility depends on $\mathbf{x}_{ij}$, which includes aspects specific to the individual as well as to the choices. It is useful to distinguish them. Let $\mathbf{z}_{ij} = [\mathbf{x}_{ij}, \mathbf{w}_i]$. Then $\mathbf{x}_{ij}$ varies across the choices and possibly across the individuals as well. The components of $\mathbf{x}_{ij}$ are typically called the **attributes** of the choices. But $\mathbf{w}_i$ contains the **characteristics** of the individual and is, therefore, the same for all choices. If we incorporate this in the model, (19-44) becomes

$$\text{Prob}(Y_i = j) = \frac{e^{\boldsymbol{\beta}'\mathbf{x}_{ij} + \boldsymbol{\alpha}'\mathbf{w}_i}}{\sum_{j=1}^{J} e^{\boldsymbol{\beta}'\mathbf{x}_{ij} + \boldsymbol{\alpha}'\mathbf{w}_i}} = \frac{e^{\boldsymbol{\beta}'\mathbf{x}_{ij}} e^{\boldsymbol{\alpha}'_i\mathbf{w}_i}}{\sum_{j=1}^{J} e^{\boldsymbol{\beta}'\mathbf{x}_{ij}} e^{\boldsymbol{\alpha}'_i\mathbf{w}_i}}.$$

Terms that do not vary across alternatives—that is, those specific to the individual—fall out of the probability. Evidently, if the model is to allow individual specific effects, it must be modified. One method is to create a set of dummy variables for the choices and multiply each of them by the common **w**. We then allow the coefficient to vary across the choices instead of the characteristics. Analogously to the linear model, a complete set of interaction terms creates a singularity, so one of them must be dropped.

EXAMPLE 19.14 Attributes and Characteristics

A model of a shopping center choice by individuals might specify that the choice depends on attributes of the shopping centers such as number of stores and distance from the central business district, both of which are the same for all individuals, and income, which varies across individuals. Suppose that there were three choices. The three regressor vectors would be as follows:

Choice 1:	Stores	Distance	Income	0
Choice 2:	Stores	Distance	0	Income
Choice 3:	Stores	Distance	0	0

The data sets typically analyzed by economists do not contain mixtures of individual- and choice-specific attributes. Such data would be far too costly to gather for most purposes. When they do, the preceding framework can be used. For the present, it is useful to examine the two types of data separately and consider aspects of the model that are specific to the two types of applications.

19.7.1. The Multinomial Logit Model

To set up the model that applies when data are individual specific, it will help to consider an example.

EXAMPLE 19.15 Multinomial Logit Model for Occupational Choice

Schmidt and Strauss (1975a,b) estimated a model of occupational choice based on a sample of 1000 observations drawn from the Public Use Sample for three years, 1960, 1967, and 1970. For each sample, the data for each individual in the sample consist of the following:

1. *Occupation:* 1 = menial, 2 = blue collar, 3 = craft, 4 = white collar, 5 = professional.
2. *Regressors:* constant, education, experience, race, sex.

Schmidt and Strauss coded the outcomes 1, 2, 3, 4, and 5. For consistency with our earlier models, we will relabel them 0, 1, 2, 3, and 4. The model for occupational choice is, then,

$$\text{Prob}(Y_i = j) = \frac{e^{\boldsymbol{\beta}_j'\mathbf{x}_i}}{\sum_{k=0}^{4} e^{\boldsymbol{\beta}_k'\mathbf{x}_i}}. \qquad \textbf{(19-45)}$$

(With the recoding of outcomes 0, . . . , J, the binomial logit of Sections 19.3 and 19.4 is conveniently produced as the special case of $J = 1$.)

The model in (19-45) is a **multinomial logit model.**[47] The estimated equations provide a set of probabilities for the $J + 1$ choices for a decision maker with characteristics $\mathbf{x}_i$. Before proceeding, we must remove an indeterminacy in the model. If we define $\boldsymbol{\beta}_j^* = \boldsymbol{\beta}_j + \mathbf{q}$ for any vector $\mathbf{q}$, the identical set of probabilities result, as the terms involving $\mathbf{q}$ all drop out. A convenient normalization that solves the problem is to assume that $\boldsymbol{\beta}_0 = \mathbf{0}$. The probabilities are, therefore,

$$\begin{aligned}\text{Prob}(Y = j) &= \frac{e^{\boldsymbol{\beta}_j'\mathbf{x}_i}}{1 + \sum_{k=1}^{J} e^{\boldsymbol{\beta}_k'\mathbf{x}_i}} \quad \text{for } j = 1, 2, \ldots, J,\\ \text{Prob}(Y = 0) &= \frac{1}{1 + \sum_{k=1}^{J} e^{\boldsymbol{\beta}_k'\mathbf{x}_i}}.\end{aligned} \qquad \textbf{(19-46)}$$

The form of the binomial model examined in Section 19.4 results if $J = 1$. The model implies that we can compute J log-odds ratios

$$\ln\left[\frac{P_{ij}}{P_{i0}}\right] = \boldsymbol{\beta}_j'\mathbf{x}_i.$$

We could normalize on any other probability as well and obtain

$$\ln\left[\frac{P_{ij}}{P_{ik}}\right] = \mathbf{x}_i'(\boldsymbol{\beta}_j - \boldsymbol{\beta}_k).$$

From the point of view of estimation, it is useful that the odds ratio, P_j/P_k, does not depend on the other choices. This follows from the independence of disturbances in the original model. From a behavioral viewpoint, this is not so attractive. We shall return to this problem in Section 19.7.3.

---

[47]Nerlove and Press (1973).

Estimation of the multinomial logit model is straightforward. Newton's method will normally find a solution very readily unless the data are badly conditioned. The log-likelihood can be derived by defining, for each individual, $d_{ij} = 1$ if alternative j is chosen by individual i, and 0 if not, for the $J + 1$ possible outcomes. Then, for each i, one and only one of the d_{ij}'s is 1.[48] The log-likelihood is a generalization of that for the binomial probit or logit model:

$$\ln L = \sum_{i=1}^{n} \sum_{j=0}^{J} d_{ij} \ln \text{Prob}(Y_i = j).$$

The derivatives have the characteristically simple form

$$\frac{\partial \ln L}{\partial \boldsymbol{\beta}_j} = \sum_i [d_{ij} - P_{ij}]\mathbf{x}_i \quad \text{for } j = 1, \ldots, J.$$

The exact second derivatives matrix has J^2 $K \times K$ blocks,

$$\frac{\partial^2 \ln L}{\partial \boldsymbol{\beta}_j \partial \boldsymbol{\beta}_l'} = -\sum_{i=1}^{n} P_{ij}[\mathbf{1}(j = l) - P_{il}]\mathbf{x}_i\mathbf{x}_i'$$

where $\mathbf{1}(j = l)$ equals 1 if j equals l and 0 if not. Since the Hessian does not involve d_{ij}, these are the expected values, and Newton's method is equivalent to the method of scoring. The Berndt et al. method can be used instead by summing the outer products of the first derivatives. This will rarely be an improvement, however, because of the very simple form and global concavity of the log-likelihood. It is worth noting that the number of parameters in this model proliferates with the number of choices. This is unfortunate, as the typical cross section sometimes involves a fairly large number of regressors.

The coefficients in this model are difficult to interpret. It is tempting to associate $\boldsymbol{\beta}_j$ with the jth outcome, but this would be misleading. By differentiating (19-46), we find that the marginal effects of the attributes on the probabilities are

$$\boldsymbol{\delta}_j = \frac{\partial P_j}{\partial \mathbf{x}_i} = P_j[\boldsymbol{\beta}_j - \sum_{k=0}^{J} P_k\boldsymbol{\beta}_k] = P_j[\boldsymbol{\beta}_j - \overline{\boldsymbol{\beta}}]. \qquad \textbf{(19-47)}$$

Therefore, every subvector of $\boldsymbol{\beta}$ enters every marginal effect, both through the probabilities and through the weighted average that appears in $\boldsymbol{\delta}_j$. These can be computed from the parameter estimates. Although the usual focus is on the coefficient estimates, equation (19-47) suggests that there is at least some potential for confusion. Note, for example, that for any particular x_k, $\partial P_j/\partial x_k$ need not have the same sign as β_{jk}. Standard errors can be estimated using the delta method. (See Section 4.4.4.) For purposes of the computation, let $\boldsymbol{\beta} = [\mathbf{0}, \boldsymbol{\beta}_1', \boldsymbol{\beta}_2', \ldots, \boldsymbol{\beta}_j']'$. We include the fixed $\mathbf{0}$ vector for outcome 0 because al-

[48]If the data were in the form of proportions, such as market shares, then the appropriate log-likelihood and derivatives are obtained just by making $d_{ij} = n_i p_{ij}$.

though $\boldsymbol{\beta}_0 = \mathbf{0}$, $\boldsymbol{\gamma}_0 = -P_0\overline{\boldsymbol{\beta}}$, which is not $\mathbf{0}$. Note as well that Asy. Cov$[\hat{\boldsymbol{\beta}}_0, \hat{\boldsymbol{\beta}}_j] = \mathbf{0}$ for $j = 0, \ldots, J$. Then

$$\text{Asy. Var}[\hat{\boldsymbol{\delta}}_j] = \sum_{l=0}^{J}\sum_{m=0}^{J}\left(\frac{\partial \boldsymbol{\delta}_j}{\partial \boldsymbol{\beta}_l'}\right)\text{Asy. Cov}[\hat{\boldsymbol{\beta}}_l, \hat{\boldsymbol{\beta}}_m]\left(\frac{\partial \boldsymbol{\delta}_j'}{\partial \boldsymbol{\beta}_m}\right),$$

$$\frac{\partial \boldsymbol{\delta}_j}{\partial \boldsymbol{\beta}_l} = [\mathbf{1}(j = l) - P_l][P_j\mathbf{I} - \boldsymbol{\delta}_j\mathbf{x}'] - P_j[\boldsymbol{\delta}_l\mathbf{x}'].$$

Finding adequate fit measures in this setting presents the same difficulties as in the binomial models. As before, it is useful to report the log-likelihood. If the model contains no covariates, and no constant term, the log-likelihood will be

$$\ln L_c = \sum_{j=0}^{J} n_j \ln\left(\frac{1}{J+1}\right).$$

If the regressor vector includes a constant term, the restricted log-likelihood is

$$\ln L_0 = \sum_{j=0}^{J} n_j \ln\left(\frac{n_j}{n}\right) = \sum_{j=0}^{J} n_j \ln p_j,$$

where p_j is the sample proportion of observations that make choice j. If desired, the likelihood ratio index can also be reported. A useful table will give a listing of hits and misses of the prediction rule "predict $Y_i = j$ if $\hat{P}_j$ is the maximum of the predicted probabilities."[49]

19.7.2. The Conditional Logit Model

When the data consist of choice-specific attributes instead of individual-specific characteristics, the appropriate model is

$$\text{Prob}(Y_i = j) = \frac{e^{\boldsymbol{\beta}'\mathbf{z}_{ij}}}{\sum_{j=1}^{J} e^{\boldsymbol{\beta}'\mathbf{z}_{ij}}}. \qquad \textbf{(19-48)}$$

Here, in accordance with the convention in the literature, we let $j = 1, 2, \ldots, J$ for a total of J alternatives. The model is otherwise essentially the same as the multinomial logit. Even more care will be required in interpreting the parameters, however. Once again, an example will help to focus ideas.

EXAMPLE 19.16 Conditional Logit Model for Travel Mode Choice

Hensher (1986) estimated a model of mode choice for urban travel for a sample of Sydney commuters. The four choices were car/driver (C/D), car/passenger, train, and bus. For a basic model, the attributes were (1) a car/driver-

[49]Unfortunately, it is common for this rule to predict all observation with the same value in an unbalanced sample or a model with little explanatory power.

TABLE 19.7 Summary Statistics for Model Structure

	In-Vehicle Cost	*In-Vehicle Time*	*Walk Time*	*Wait Time*	*Number Choosing*
C/D	64.56	28.65	0.76	0.15	953
C/P	4.37	28.32	0.71	2.89	78
Train	98.23	43.84	10.50	8.37	279
Bus	81.61	38.15	7.47	7.11	145

C/D only: Parking cost = 26.59
Household business vehicles = 0.186
Percent travel cost paid for = 17.58

Source: Hensher (1986, p. 14). Standard deviations given by Hensher are omitted.

specific constant, (2) a car/passenger-specific constant, (3) a train-specific constant, (4) in-vehicle time (in minutes), (5) waiting time (in minutes), (6) walking time (in minutes), (7) in-vehicle costs, (8) parking cost, (9) number of household business vehicles required, and (10) percentage of travel cost covered by a nonhousehold source [(9) and (10) for C/D only]. The sample consists of 1455 observations. A summary of the data is given in Table 19.7. Hensher reports the results listed in Table 19.8.

At the sample means given here, the four predicted probabilities and predicted frequencies are given in Table 19.9.

In this model, the coefficients are not directly tied to the marginal effects. The marginal effects for continuous variables can be obtained by differentiating (19-48) with respect to **x** to obtain

$$\frac{\partial P_j}{\partial \mathbf{x}_k} = [P_j(\mathbf{1}(j = k) - P_k)]\boldsymbol{\beta}.$$

TABLE 19.8 Parameter Estimates (*t* Values in Parentheses)

(1)	0.8973	(4.86)	(2)	−2.2154	(−10.36)
(3)	1.3286	(9.10)	(4)	−0.0227	(−4.70)
(5)	−0.1336	(−6.68)	(6)	−0.0672	(−5.44)
(7)	−0.0063	(−5.03)	(8)	−0.0086	(−5.05)
(9)	0.4524	(1.83)	(10)	−0.0119	(3.71)

Log likelihood at $\beta = 0$ = −2017.1
Log likelihood (sample shares) = −1426.6
Log likelihood at convergence = −598.2

TABLE 19.9 Predicted Probabilities and Frequencies

	C/D	*C/P*	*Train*	*Bus*
Probability	0.88625	0.03799	0.01390	0.06186
Predicted N	1290	55	20	90
Actual N	953	78	279	145

Elasticities of Probabilities with Respect to In-Vehicle Cost

	Mode			
Attributes in	***C/D***	***C/P***	***Train***	***Bus***
C/D	−0.077	0.253	0.253	0.253
C/P	0.002	−0.013	0.002	0.002
Train	0.098	0.098	−0.231	0.098
Bus	0.042	0.042	0.042	−0.292

(To avoid cluttering the notation, we have dropped the observation subscript.) It is clear that through its presence in P_j and P_k, every attribute set $\mathbf{x}_j$ affects all the probabilities. Hensher suggests that one might prefer to report elasticities of the probabilities. These would be

$$\frac{\partial \ln P_j}{\partial \ln x_{km}} = x_{km}[\mathbf{1}(j = k) - P_k]\beta_k.$$

Since there is no ambiguity about the scale of the probability itself, whether one should report the derivatives or the elasticities is largely a matter of taste. Some of Hensher's elasticity estimates are presented in the previous example.

Estimation of the conditional logit model is simplest by Newton's method of the method of scoring. The log-likelihood is the same as for the multinomial logit model. Once again, we define $d_{ij} = 1$ if $Y_i = j$ and 0 otherwise. Then

$$\ln L = \sum_{i=1}^{n}\sum_{j=1}^{J} d_{ij} \ln \text{Prob}(Y_i = j).$$

Market share and frequency data are common in this setting. If the data are in this form, the only change needed is, once again, to define d_{ij} as the proportion or frequency. Because of the simple form of L, the gradient and Hessian have particularly convenient forms:

$$\frac{\partial \ln L}{\partial \boldsymbol{\beta}} = \sum_{i=1}^{n}\sum_{j=1}^{J} d_{ij}(\mathbf{x}_{ij} - \overline{\mathbf{x}}_i),$$

$$\frac{\partial^2 \ln L}{\partial \boldsymbol{\beta}\, \partial \boldsymbol{\beta}'} = -\sum_{i=1}^{n}\sum_{j=1}^{J} P_{ij}(\mathbf{x}_{ij} - \overline{\mathbf{x}}_i)(\mathbf{x}_{ij} - \overline{\mathbf{x}}_i)',$$

where

$$\overline{\mathbf{x}}_i = \sum_{j=1}^{J} P_{ij}\mathbf{x}_{ij}.$$

Once again, Newton's method and the method of scoring are equivalent and should converge readily. In this setting, the size of the estimation problem is independent of the number of choices. It is feasible to estimate a model for up to 100 or more alternatives. (Whether it is reasonable to model consumer choices with this many alternatives is a different question.) A data set constructed with more than a few choices is likely to be quite cumbersome. In this context, it is the data that proliferate with the number of choices, and far faster than the number of parameters did in the previous model. Every new choice added to the set adds a new row to the data set for every observation. For example, the four-outcome model requires $4 \times 1455 = 5820$ rows. Adding only one more alternative would add another 1455 rows of data.

The usual problems of fit measures appear here. The log-likelihood ratio and tabulation of actual versus predicted choices will be useful. There are two possible constrained log-likelihoods. Since the model cannot contain a constant term, the constraint $\boldsymbol{\beta} = \mathbf{0}$ renders all probabilities equal to $1/J$. The constrained log-likelihood for this constraint is then $L_c = -n \ln J$. Of course, it is unlikely that this hypothesis would fail to be rejected. Alternatively, we could fit the model with only the $J - 1$ choice-specific constants. This makes the constrained log-likelihood the same as in the multinomial logit model, $\ln L_0^* = \Sigma_j n_j \ln p_j$.

19.7.3. The Independence of Irrelevant Alternatives

We noted earlier that the odds ratios in the multinomial logit or conditional logit models are independent of the other alternatives. This is a convenient property as regards estimation, but it is not a particularly appealing restriction to place on consumer behavior. The property of the logit model whereby P_j/P_k is independent of the remaining probabilities is termed the **independence of irrelevant alternatives.** An example of the problem is suggested by Hensher's data. The model allocates 89 percent of the passengers to cars as drivers. Thus, the odds ratio between cars as drivers and buses is 0.89/0.06, or about 14.8 to 1. Suppose that we differentiate by type of car, domestic and foreign, and it happens to be an even split. We might expect the 89 percent of the population who drive to work to divide themselves evenly and the others to continue as they did before. Unfortunately, if they do, the odds between each car type and bus will fall to 7.4 to 1. To preserve the 14.8 to 1 odds ratio between cars and buses, half of the bus riders will be switched either to the train or to cars as passengers.

The independence assumption follows from the initial assumption that the disturbances are independent and homoscedastic. We will discuss below two models that have been developed to relax this assumption. Before doing so, we consider a test that has been developed for testing the validity of the assumption. Hausman and McFadden (1984) suggest that if a subset of the choice set truly is irrelevant, omitting it from the model altogether will not change parameter estimates systematically. Inclusion of these choices will be inefficient but will not lead to inconsistency. But if the remaining odds ratios are not truly independent of these alternatives, the parameter estimates obtained when these choices are eliminated will be inconsistent. This is the usual basis for Hausman's specification test. The statistic is

$$\chi^2 = (\hat{\boldsymbol{\beta}}_s - \hat{\boldsymbol{\beta}}_f)'[\hat{\mathbf{V}}_s - \hat{\mathbf{V}}_f]^{-1}(\hat{\boldsymbol{\beta}}_s - \hat{\boldsymbol{\beta}}_f),$$

where s indicates the estimators based on the restricted subset, f indicates the estimator based on the full set of choices, and $\hat{\mathbf{V}}_s$ and $\hat{\mathbf{V}}_f$ are the respective estimates of the asymptotic covariance matrices. The statistic is asymptotically distributed as chi-squared with K degrees of freedom.[50]

EXAMPLE 19.17 The Independence of Irrelevant Alternatives

In Example 19.16, are the odds ratios C/D to bus and C/D to train really independent of the presence of the C/P alternative? To use the Hausman test, we would eliminate choice 2, C/P, from the choice set and estimate a three-choice model. Since 78 respondents chose this mode, we would lose 78 observations. In addition, for every data vector left in the sample, the second attribute, which is the C/P dummy, would always be zero. Thus, this parameter could not be estimated. We would drop this variable. The test would be based on the two estimators of the nine remaining parameters.

19.7.4. Nested Logit Models

If the independence of irrelevant alternatives test fails, an alternative to the multinomial logit model will be needed. A natural alternative is a multivariate probit model:

$$U_j = \boldsymbol{\beta}'\mathbf{x}_j + \epsilon_j, \quad j = 1, \ldots, J, [\epsilon_1, \epsilon_2, \ldots, \epsilon_J] \sim N[\mathbf{0}, \boldsymbol{\Sigma}].$$

We had considered this model earlier but found that as a general model of consumer choice, its failings were the practical difficulty of computing the multinormal integral and estimation of an unrestricted correlation matrix. Hausman and Wise (1978) point out that for a model of consumer choice, the probit model may not be as impractical as it might seem. First, for J choices, the comparisons implicit in $U_j > U_k$ for $k \neq j$ involve the $J - 1$ differences, $\epsilon_j - \epsilon_k$. Thus, starting with a J-dimensional problem, we need only consider $(J - 1)$-order probabilities. Therefore, to come to a concrete example, a model with four choices requires only the evaluation of bivariate normal

[50]McFadden (1987) shows how this hypothesis can also be tested using a Lagrange multiplier test.

integrals, which, albeit still very complicated to estimate, is well within the received technology. For larger models, however, other specifications have proved more useful.

One way to relax the homoscedasticity assumption in the conditional logit model that also provides an intuitively appealing structure is to group the alternatives into subgroups that allow the variance to differ across the groups while maintaining the IIA assumption within the groups. This defines a **nested logit model.** To fix ideas, it is useful to think of this as a two-(or more) level choice problem (although, once again, the model arises as a modification of the stochastic specification in the original conditional logit model, not as a model of behavior). Suppose, then, that the J alternatives can be divided into L subgroups, such that the choice set can be written $[c_1, \ldots, c_J] = (c_{1|1}, \ldots, c_{J1|1}), \ldots, (c_{1|L}, \ldots, c_{JL|L})$. Logically, we may think of the choice process as that of choosing among the L choice sets, then making the specific choice within the chosen set. This produces a tree structure, which for two branches and, say, five choices might look as follows:

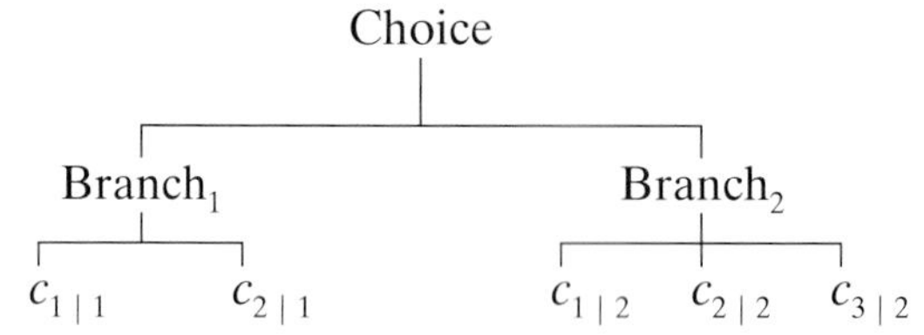

Suppose as well that the data consist of observations on the attributes of the choices $\mathbf{x}_{j|l}$ and attributes of the choice sets $\mathbf{z}_l$.

To derive the mathematical form of the model, we begin with the unconditional probability

$$\text{Prob}[\text{twig}_j, \text{branch}_l] = P_{jl} = \frac{e^{\boldsymbol{\beta}'\mathbf{x}_{j|l} + \boldsymbol{\gamma}'\mathbf{z}_l}}{\sum_{l=1}^{L}\sum_{j=1}^{J_l} e^{\boldsymbol{\beta}'\mathbf{x}_{j|l} + \boldsymbol{\gamma}'\mathbf{z}_l}}.$$

Now write this as

$$P_{jl} = P_{j|l}P_l = \left(\frac{e^{\boldsymbol{\beta}'\mathbf{x}_{j|l}}}{\sum_{j=1}^{J_l} e^{\boldsymbol{\beta}'\mathbf{x}_{j|l}}}\right)\left(\frac{e^{\boldsymbol{\gamma}'\mathbf{z}_l}}{\sum_{l=1}^{L} e^{\boldsymbol{\gamma}'\mathbf{z}_l}}\right)\frac{\left(\sum_{j=1}^{J_l} e^{\boldsymbol{\beta}'\mathbf{x}_{j|l}}\right)\left(\sum_{l=1}^{L} e^{\boldsymbol{\gamma}'\mathbf{z}_l}\right)}{\left(\sum_{l=1}^{L}\sum_{j=1}^{J_l} e^{\boldsymbol{\beta}'\mathbf{x}_{j|l} + \boldsymbol{\gamma}'\mathbf{z}_l}\right)}.$$

Define the **inclusive value** for the lth branch as

$$I_l = \ln \sum_{j=1}^{J_l} e^{\boldsymbol{\beta}'\mathbf{x}_{j|l}}.$$

Then, after canceling terms and using this result, we find

$$P_{j|l} = \frac{e^{\boldsymbol{\beta}'\mathbf{x}_{j|l}}}{\sum_{j=1}^{J_l} e^{\boldsymbol{\beta}'\mathbf{x}_{j|l}}},$$

$$P_l = \frac{e^{\boldsymbol{\gamma}'\mathbf{z}_l + \tau_l I_l}}{\sum_{l=1}^{L} e^{\boldsymbol{\gamma}'\mathbf{z}_l + \tau_l I_l}},$$

where the new parameters τ_l must equal 1 to produce the original model. Therefore, we use the restriction $\tau_l = 1$ to recover the conditional logit model, and the preceding just writes this model in another form. The **nested logit** model arises if this restriction is relaxed.

As before, the coefficients in the model are not directly interpretable. The derivatives that describe covariation of the attributes and probabilities are

$$\frac{\partial \ln \text{Prob}[\text{choice}_c, \text{branch}_b]}{\partial x(k) \text{ in choice } C \text{ and branch } B} = \{1(b = B)[1(c = C) - P_{C|B}] \\ + \tau_B[1(b = B) - P_B]P_C|B\}\beta_k.$$

The nested logit model has been extended to three and higher levels. The complexity of the model increases geometrically with the number of levels. But the model has been found to be extremely flexible, and is widely used for modeling consumer choice.

There are two ways to estimate the parameters of the nested logit model. A **limited information,** two-step maximum likelihood approach can be done as follows:

1. Estimate $\boldsymbol{\beta}$ by treating the choice within branches as a simple conditional logit model.
2. Compute the inclusive values for all the branches in the model. Estimate $\boldsymbol{\gamma}$ and the τ parameters by treating the choice among branches as a conditional logit model with attributes $\mathbf{z}_l$ and I_l.

Since this is a two-step estimator, the estimate of the asymptotic covariance matrix of the estimates at the second step must be corrected. [See Section 4.6, McFadden (1984), and Greene (1995a, Chapter 25).] For full information maximum likelihood (FIML) estimation of the model, the log-likelihood is

$$\ln L = \sum_{i=1}^{n} \ln[\text{Prob}(\text{twig}\,|\,\text{branch}) \times \text{Prob}(\text{branch})]_i.$$

The information matrix is not block diagonal in $\boldsymbol{\beta}$ and $(\boldsymbol{\gamma}, \boldsymbol{\tau})$, so FIML estimation will be more efficient than two-step estimation.[51]

[51]Until relatively recently, software for joint, full-information maximum likelihood estimation of all the parameters simultaneously was not widely available. This is no longer the case; there are several computer programs available for FIML estimation of nested logit models.

EXAMPLE 19.18 Nested Logit Model

Hensher and Greene [Greene (1995a)] report estimates of a model of travel mode choice for travel between Sydney and Melbourne, Australia. The data set contains 75 observations on choice among four alternatives, AIR, TRAIN, BUS, and CAR. The attributes used for their example were choice-specific constants and two continuous measures: GC, a measure of the generalized cost of the travel, constructed from measures of in-vehicle cost, and a wage-like measure times the amount of time spent traveling, TTIME, the travel time, and HINC, household income. They estimated a nested logit model, with two branches, FLY = (AIR) and GROUND = (TRAIN, BUS, CAR). Note that one of the branches has only a single choice, so the conditional probability, $P_{j|FLY} = P_{AIR|FLY} = 1$. The model is fit by both FIML and LIML methods. Parameter estimates are shown in Table 19.10.

Three sets of estimates are shown. The set marked "unconditional" are a conditional logit model for choice among four alternatives. The inclusive value parameter is constrained to 1.0 (by not including the inclusive value in the attributes.) The LIML estimates are computed in two steps. The standard errors at the second step are corrected for use of the two-step estimator. There are two tests for the nesting aspect available. The LR test between the first and second sets gives a chi-squared value of 2(65.73624 − 65.40806) = 0.65636, which is far less than the critical chi-squared value of 3.84. A second test can be based on the Wald statistic from the FIML estimates; $\chi^2 = (0.7758 - 1)^2/(0.24159)^2 = 0.86121$, which leads to the same conclusion.

To specify the nested logit model, it is necessary to partition the choice set into branches. Sometimes there will be a natural partition, such as in the example above, or in an example given by Maddala (1983), when the choice of residence is made first by community, then by dwelling type within the community. But in other instances, the partitioning of the choice set is ad hoc and leads to the troubling possibility that the results might be dependent on the branches so

TABLE 19.10 Nested Logit Models (Standard Errors in Parentheses)

	FIML Estimates		*Unconditional*		*LIML Estimates*	
β_{TRAIN}	3.8895	(0.52374)	3.6630	(0.70882)	3.5029	(1.0511)
β_{BUS}	1.0133	(1.5734)	0.84625	(0.97896)	−0.03645	(1.4389)
β_{GCOST}	−0.0233	(0.01026)	−0.01968	(0.007572)	−0.07256	(0.02121)
β_{TTIME}	−0.06356	(0.01337)	−0.06093	(0.015472)	−0.02071	(0.02723)
γ_{AIR}	3.8826	(1.1104)	3.3869	(1.1503)	−1.8367	(0.7478)
γ_{HINC}	0.02164	(0.01521)	0.02308	(0.01539)	0.03023	(0.01379)
τ	0.7758	(0.24159)	1.00000	(0.00000)	0.05578	(0.11453)
Log L	−65.40806		−65.73624		—	
Log L_0			−82.68496			

defined. (Many studies in this literature present several sets of results based on different specifications of the tree structure.) There is no well-defined testing procedure for discriminating among tree structures, so this is a problematic aspect of the model. Bhat (1995) and Allenby and Ginter (1995) have developed an extension of the conditional logit model that works around this difficulty. The model is based on

$$U_{ij} = \boldsymbol{\beta}'\mathbf{x}_{ij} + \epsilon_{ij}.$$

The model arises from the assumption that ϵ_{ij} has a homoscedastic extreme value distribution. The authors' proposed model simply relaxes the assumption of equal variances. Since the comparisons are all pairwise, one of the variances is set to 1.000; the same comparisons of utilities will result if all equations are multiplied by the same constant, so the indeterminacy is removed by setting one of the variances to 1. The model that remains, then, is exactly as before, with the additional assumption that $\text{Var}[\epsilon_{ij}] = \sigma_j$, with $\sigma_J = 1.0$. The resulting probabilities are shown in Example 5.5.

EXAMPLE 19.19 A Heteroscedastic Extreme Value Model

The model in the previous example was reestimated under these new assumptions. The results are shown in Table 19.11. This model is less restrictive than the nested logit model. To make them comparable, we note that in our example, we have assumed that $\sigma_{\text{AIR}} = 1.0$ and $\sigma_{\text{TRAIN}} = \sigma_{\text{BUS}} = \sigma_{\text{CAR}} = 1/\tau = 1.2899$. Thus, the HEV model relaxes two restrictions. The likelihood ratio test produces

TABLE 19.11 Estimates of a Heteroscedastic Extreme Value Model (Standard Errors in Parentheses)

	FIML Estimates	
β_{TRAIN}	3.8815	(0.52374)
β_{BUS}	2.0244	(1.5734)
β_{GCOST}	−0.04299	(0.01026)
β_{TTIME}	−0.48865	(0.01337)
γ_{AIR}	−4.5879	(1.1104)
γ_{HINC}	0.11568	(0.01521)
σ_{AIR}	0.2342	(0.21586)
σ_{TRAIN}	1.2553	(1.9105)
σ_{BUS}	2.4905	(4.7803)
σ_{CAR}	1.0000	(0.0000)
Log L	−61.63068	
Log L_0	−82.68496	

$$\chi^2[2] = -2[-61.63068 - (-65.40806)] = 9.73802.$$

The critical value from the table is 5.99, so the hypothesis of the nested logit model as a restriction on the HEV model is rejected. Recall that *conditioned* on the nested logit model, the hypothesis of the conditional logit model *was not* rejected.

As a final test of the IIA hypothesis, we refit the model with only the first four coefficients. The Hausman statistic with four degrees of freedom is 11.493. The critical value is 9.49, so the conclusion is once again that the conditional logit model is unduly restrictive for these data.

19.8. ORDERED DATA

Some multinomial-choice variables are inherently ordered. Examples that have appeared in the literature include the following:

1. Bond ratings.
2. Results of taste tests.
3. Opinion surveys.
4. The assignment of military personnel to job classifications by skill level.
5. Voting outcomes on certain programs.
6. The level of insurance coverage taken by a consumer: none, part, or full.
7. Employment: unemployed, part time, or full time.

In each of these cases, although the outcome is discrete, the multinomial logit or probit models would fail to account for the ordinal nature of the dependent variable.[52] Ordinary regression analysis would err in the opposite direction, however. Take the outcome of an opinion survey. If the responses are coded 0, 1, 2, 3, or 4, linear regression would treat the difference between a 4 and a 3 the same as that between a 3 and a 2, whereas in fact they are only a ranking.

The ordered probit and logit models have come into fairly wide use as a framework for analyzing such responses (Zavoina and McElvey, 1975). The model is built around a latent regression in the same manner as the binomial probit model. We begin with

$$y^* = \boldsymbol{\beta}'\mathbf{x} + \epsilon.$$

[52] In two papers, Beggs et al. (1981) and Hausman and Ruud (1986), the authors have begun to explore the possibility of using a richer specification of the logit model when respondents provide their rankings of the full set of alternatives in addition to the identity of the most preferred choice. This application falls somewhere between the conditional logit model and the ones we shall discuss here in that rather than provide a single choice among J either unordered or ordered alternatives, the consumer chooses one of the $J!$ possible orderings of the set of unordered alternatives.

As usual, y^* is unobserved. What we do observe is

$$
\begin{aligned}
y &= 0 \quad \text{if } y^* \le 0,\\
&= 1 \quad \text{if } 0 < y^* \le \mu_1,\\
&= 2 \quad \text{if } \mu_1 < y^* \le \mu_2,\\
&\ \vdots\\
&= J \quad \text{if } \mu_{J-1} \le y^*.
\end{aligned}
$$

This is a form of censoring. The μ's are unknown parameters to be estimated with $\boldsymbol{\beta}$. Consider, for example, an opinion survey. The respondents have their own intensity of feelings, which depends on certain measurable factors $\mathbf{x}$ and certain unobservable factors ϵ. In principle, they could respond to the questionnaire with their own y^* if asked to do so. Given only, say, five possible answers, they choose the cell that most closely represents their own feelings on the question.

As before, we assume that ϵ is normally distributed across observations. For the same reasons as in the binomial probit model (which is the special case of $J = 1$), we normalize the mean and variance of ϵ to 0 and 1. (The model can also be estimated with a logistically distributed disturbance. This is a trivial modification of the formulation and appears to make virtually no difference in practice.) With the normal distribution, we have the following probabilities:

$$
\begin{aligned}
\text{Prob}(y = 0) &= \Phi(-\boldsymbol{\beta}'\mathbf{x}),\\
\text{Prob}(y = 1) &= \Phi(\mu_1 - \boldsymbol{\beta}'\mathbf{x}) - \Phi(-\boldsymbol{\beta}'\mathbf{x}),\\
\text{Prob}(y = 2) &= \Phi(\mu_2 - \boldsymbol{\beta}'\mathbf{x}) - \Phi(\mu_1 - \boldsymbol{\beta}'\mathbf{x}),\\
&\ \vdots\\
\text{Prob}(y = J) &= 1 - \Phi(\mu_{J-1} - \boldsymbol{\beta}'\mathbf{x}).
\end{aligned}
$$

For all the probabilities to be positive, we must have

$$0 < \mu_1 < \mu_2 < \cdots < \mu_{J-1}.$$

Figure 19.4 shows the implications of the structure. It is evident that this is a generalization of the probit model we looked at earlier. The log-likelihood function and its derivatives can be obtained readily, and optimization can be done by the usual means.

As usual, the marginal effects of the regressors $\mathbf{x}$ on the probabilities are not equal to the coefficients. It is helpful to consider a simple example. Suppose that there are three categories. This implies only one unknown threshold parameter. The three probabilities are

$$
\begin{aligned}
\text{Prob}(y = 0) &= 1 - \Phi(\boldsymbol{\beta}'\mathbf{x}),\\
\text{Prob}(y = 1) &= \Phi(\mu - \boldsymbol{\beta}'\mathbf{x}) - \Phi(-\boldsymbol{\beta}'\mathbf{x}),\\
\text{Prob}(y = 2) &= 1 - \Phi(\mu - \boldsymbol{\beta}'\mathbf{x}).
\end{aligned}
$$

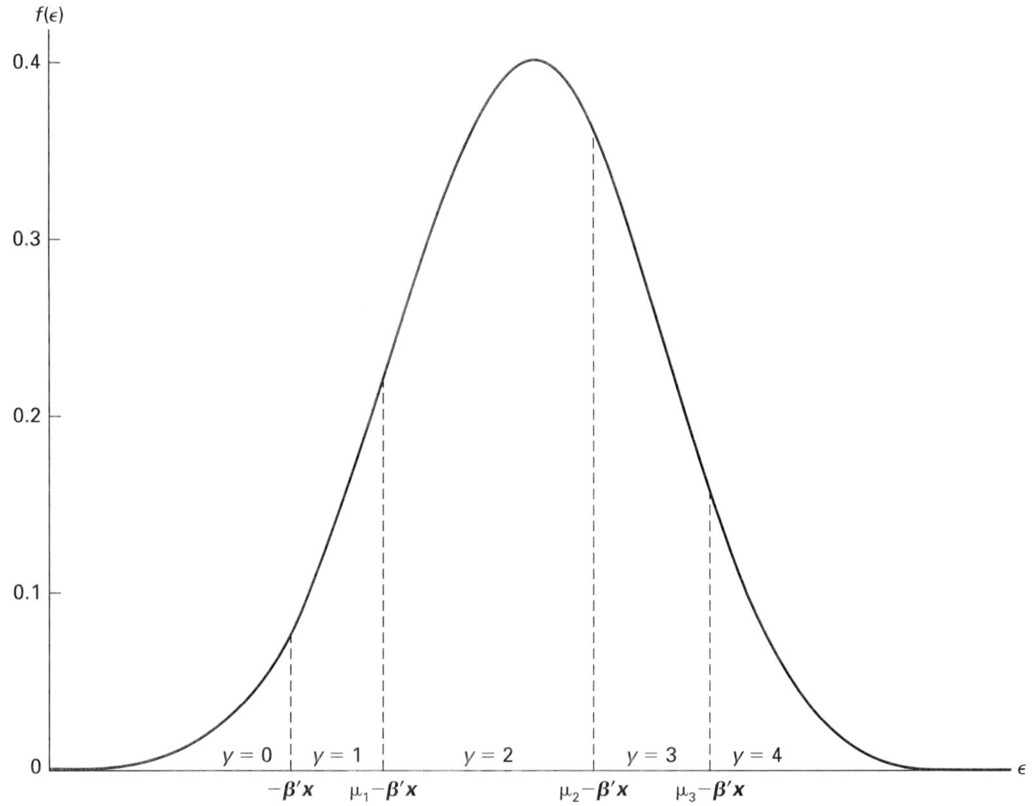

FIGURE 19.4 Probabilities in the Ordered Probit Model.

For the three probabilities, the marginal effects of changes in the regressors are

$$\frac{\partial \text{ Prob}[y = 0]}{\partial \mathbf{x}} = -\phi(\boldsymbol{\beta}'\mathbf{x})\boldsymbol{\beta},$$

$$\frac{\partial \text{ Prob}[y = 1]}{\partial \mathbf{x}} = [\phi(-\boldsymbol{\beta}'\mathbf{x}) - \phi(\mu - \boldsymbol{\beta}'\mathbf{x})]\boldsymbol{\beta},$$

$$\frac{\partial \text{ Prob}[y = 1]}{\partial \mathbf{x}} = \phi(\mu - \boldsymbol{\beta}'\mathbf{x})\boldsymbol{\beta}.$$

Figure 19.5 illustrates the effect. The probability distributions of y and y^* are shown in the solid curve. Increasing one of the x's while holding $\boldsymbol{\beta}$ and μ constant is equivalent to shifting the distribution slightly to the right, which is shown as the dashed curve. The effect of the shift is unambiguously to shift some mass out of the leftmost cell. Assuming that $\boldsymbol{\beta}$ is positive (for this x), this means that Prob($y = 0$) must decline. Alternatively, from the previous expression, it is obvious that the derivative of Prob($y = 0$) has the opposite sign from $\boldsymbol{\beta}$. By a similar logic, the change in Prob($y = 2$) [or Prob($y = J$) in the general case] must have the same sign as $\boldsymbol{\beta}$. Assuming that the particular $\boldsymbol{\beta}$ is positive,

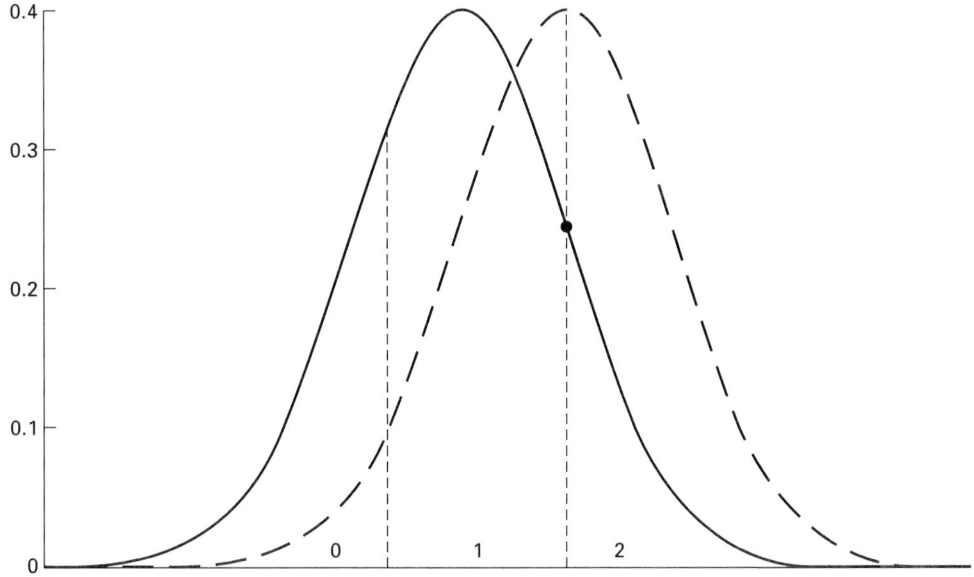

FIGURE 19.5 Effects of Change in x on Predicted Probabilities.

we are shifting some probability into the rightmost cell. But what happens to the middle cell is ambiguous. It depends on the two densities. In the general case, relative to the signs of the coefficients, only the signs of the changes in Prob($y = 0$) and Prob($y = J$) are unambiguous! The upshot is that we must be very careful in interpreting the coefficients in this model. This is the least obvious of all the models we have considered. Indeed, without a fair amount of extra calculation, it is quite unclear how the coefficients in the ordered probit model should be interpreted.[53]

EXAMPLE 19.20 Rating Assignments

Marcus and Greene (1985) estimated an ordered probit model for the job assignments of new Navy recruits. The Navy attempts to direct recruits into job classifications in which they will be most productive. The broad classifications the authors analyzed were technical jobs with three clearly ranked skill ratings: "medium skilled," "highly skilled," and "nuclear qualified/highly skilled." Since the assignment is partly based on the Navy's own assessment and needs and partly on factors specific to the individual, an ordered probit model was used with the following determinants: (1) ENSPE = a dummy variable indicating that the individual entered the Navy with an "A school" (technical training) guarantee, (2) EDMA = educational level of the entrant's mother, (3) AFQT

[53]This point seems uniformly to be overlooked in the received literature. Authors routinely report coefficients and t ratios, occasionally with some commentary about significant effects, but rarely suggest upon what or in what direction those effects are exerted.

= score on the Air Force Qualifying Test, (4) EDYRS = years of education completed by the trainee, (5) MARR = a dummy variable indicating that the individual was married at the time of enlistment, and (6) AGEAT = trainee's age at the time of enlistment. The sample size was 5641. The results are reported in Table 19.12. The extremely large t ratio on the AFQT score is to be expected, since it is a primary sorting device used to assign job classifications. To obtain the marginal effects of the continuous variables, we require the standard normal density evaluated at $-\boldsymbol{\beta}'\overline{\mathbf{x}} = -0.8479$ and $\mu - \boldsymbol{\beta}'\overline{\mathbf{x}} = 0.9421$. The predicted probabilities are $\Phi(0.8479) = 0.198$, $\Phi(0.9421) - \Phi(-0.8479) = 0.628$, and $1 - \Phi(0.9421) = 0.173$. (The actual frequencies were 0.25, 0.52, and 0.23.) The two densities are $\phi(-0.8479) = 0.278$ and $\phi(0.9421) = 0.255$. Therefore, the derivatives of the three probabilities with respect to AFQT, for example, are:

$$\frac{\partial P_0}{\partial \text{AFQT}} = (-0.278)0.039 = -0.01084,$$

$$\frac{\partial P_1}{\partial \text{AFQT}} = (0.278 - 0.255)0.039 = 0.0009,$$

$$\frac{\partial P_2}{\partial \text{AFQT}} = 0.255(0.039) = 0.00995.$$

Note that the marginal effects sum to zero; this follows from the requirement that the probabilities add to 1. This approach is not appropriate for evaluating the effect of a dummy variable. We can analyze a dummy variable by comparing the probabilities that result when the variable takes its two different values with those that occur with the other variables held at their sample means. For example, for the MARR variable, we have the results given in Table 19.13.

TABLE 19.12 Estimated Rating Assignment Equation

Variable	*Estimate*	*t ratio*	*Mean of Variable*
Constant	−4.34	—	—
ENSPA	0.057	1.7	0.66
EDMA	0.007	0.8	12.1
AFQT	0.039	39.9	71.2
EDYRS	0.190	8.7	12.1
MARR	−0.48	−9.0	0.08
AGEAT	0.0015	0.1	18.8
μ	1.79	80.8	—

TABLE 19.13 Marginal Effect of a Binary Variable

	$-\hat{\beta}'x$	$\hat{\mu} - \hat{\beta}'x$	*Prob[y = 0]*	*Prob[y = 1]*	*Prob[y = 2]*
MARR = 0	−0.8863	0.9037	0.187	0.629	0.184
MARR = 1	−0.4063	1.3837	0.342	0.574	0.084
Change			0.155	−0.055	−0.100

19.9 MODELS FOR COUNT DATA

The data on ship accidents by type and year of construction analyzed in Example 8.2 are typical of **count data.** (They are reproduced in Table 19.14.) In principle, we could analyze these data using multiple linear regression, as we did in Example 8.2. But, the preponderance of zeros and the small values and clearly discrete nature of the dependent variable suggest that we could improve on least squares and the linear model with a specification that accounts for these characteristics. The **Poisson regression model** has been widely used to study such data.

The Poisson regression model specifies that each y_i is drawn from a Poisson distribution with parameter λ_i, which is related to the regressors $\mathbf{x}_i$. The primary equation of the model is

$$\text{Prob}(Y_i = y_i) = \frac{e^{-\lambda_i}\lambda_i^{y_i}}{y_i!}, \quad y_i = 0, 1, 2, \ldots.$$

The most common formulation for λ_i is the **log-linear model,**

$$\ln \lambda_i = \boldsymbol{\beta}'\mathbf{x}_i.$$

It is easily shown that the expected number of events *per period* is given by

$$\begin{aligned} E[y_i \mid \mathbf{x}_i] &= \text{Var}[y_i \mid \mathbf{x}_i] = \lambda_i \\ &= e^{\boldsymbol{\beta}'\mathbf{x}_i} \end{aligned}$$

so

$$\frac{\partial E[y_i \mid \mathbf{x}_i]}{\partial \mathbf{x}_i} = \lambda_i \boldsymbol{\beta}.$$

With the parameter estimates in hand, this can be computed using any data vector desired.

In principle, the Poisson model is simply a nonlinear regression.[54] But it is

[54]We have estimated a Poisson regression model using two-step nonlinear least squares in Section 10.2.6 and Example 10.7.

far easier to estimate the parameters with maximum likelihood techniques. The log-likelihood function is

$$\ln L = \sum_{i=1}^{n}[-\lambda_i + y_i\boldsymbol{\beta}'\mathbf{x}_i - \ln y_i!].$$

The likelihood equations are

$$\frac{\partial \ln L}{\partial \boldsymbol{\beta}} = \sum_{i=1}^{n}(y_i - \lambda_i)\mathbf{x}_i = \mathbf{0}.$$

The Hessian is

$$\frac{\partial^2 \ln L}{\partial \boldsymbol{\beta}\, \partial \boldsymbol{\beta}'} = -\sum_{i=1}^{n}\lambda_i\mathbf{x}_i\mathbf{x}_i'.$$

The Hessian is negative definite for all $\mathbf{x}$ and $\boldsymbol{\beta}$. Newton's method is a simple algorithm for this model and will usually converge rapidly. At convergence, $[\Sigma_{i=1}^{n}\hat{\lambda}_i\mathbf{x}_i\mathbf{x}_i']^{-1}$ provides an estimate of the asymptotic covariance matrix for the parameter estimates. Given the estimates, the prediction for observation i is $\hat{\lambda}_i = \exp(\hat{\boldsymbol{\beta}}'\mathbf{x})$. A standard error for the prediction interval can be formed by using a linear Taylor series approximation. The estimated variance of the prediction will be $\hat{\lambda}_i^2\mathbf{x}_i'\mathbf{V}\mathbf{x}_i$, where $\mathbf{V}$ is the estimated asymptotic covariance matrix for $\hat{\boldsymbol{\beta}}$.

For testing hypotheses, the three standard tests are very convenient in this model. The Wald statistic is computed as usual. As in any discrete choice model, the likelihood ratio test has the intuitive form

$$\text{LR} = 2\sum_{i=1}^{n}\ln\left(\frac{\hat{P}_i}{\hat{P}_{\text{restricted},i}}\right),$$

where the probabilities in the denominator are computed with using the restricted model. Using the BHHH estimator for the asymptotic covariance matrix, the LM statistic is simply

$$\begin{aligned}\text{LM} &= \left[\sum_{i=1}^{n}\mathbf{x}_i'(y_i - \hat{\lambda}_i)\right]'\left[\sum_{i=1}^{n}\mathbf{x}_i\mathbf{x}_i'(y_i - \hat{\lambda}_i)^2\right]^{-1}\left[\sum_{i=1}^{n}\mathbf{x}_i(y_i - \hat{\lambda}_i)\right]\\ &= \mathbf{i}'\mathbf{G}(\mathbf{G}'\mathbf{G})^{-1}\mathbf{G}'\mathbf{i},\end{aligned}$$

where each row of $\mathbf{G}$ is simply the corresponding row of $\mathbf{X}$ multiplied by $e_i = (y_i - \hat{\lambda}_i), \hat{\lambda}_i$ is computed using the restricted coefficient vector, and $\mathbf{i}$ is a column of 1s.

EXAMPLE 19.21 Poisson Regression Model

The number of accidents per service month for a sample of ship types are listed in Table 19.14. The ships are of five types constructed in one of four periods. The observation is over two periods. Since ships constructed from 1975 to 1979 could not have operated from 1960 to 1974, there is one missing observation in each group. The second observation for group E is also missing, for reasons un-

TABLE 19.14 Ship Accident Data

	Ship Type					Year Constructed				Years Operated		Service	Accidents	
Type	*A*	*B*	*C*	*D*	*E*	*60–64*	*65–69*	*70–74*	*75–79*	*60–74*	*75–79*	*Months*	*Actual*	*Fitted*
1	1	0	0	0	0	1	0	0	0	1	0	127	0	0.210
1	1	0	0	0	0	1	0	0	0	0	1	63	0	0.153
1	1	0	0	0	0	0	1	0	0	1	0	1095	3	3.638
1	1	0	0	0	0	0	1	0	0	0	1	1095	4	5.341
1	1	0	0	0	0	0	0	1	0	1	0	1512	6	5.673
1	1	0	0	0	0	0	0	1	0	0	1	3353	18	18.468
1	1	0	0	0	0	0	0	0	1	1	0	—	—	—
1	1	0	0	0	0	0	0	0	1	0	1	2244	11	8.516
2	0	1	0	0	0	1	0	0	0	1	0	44882	39	43.129
2	0	1	0	0	0	1	0	0	0	0	1	17176	29	24.229
2	0	1	0	0	0	0	1	0	0	1	0	28609	58	55.132
2	0	1	0	0	0	0	1	0	0	0	1	20370	53	57.624
2	0	1	0	0	0	0	0	1	0	1	0	7064	12	15.373
2	0	1	0	0	0	0	0	1	0	0	1	13099	44	41.847
2	0	1	0	0	0	0	0	0	1	1	0	—	—	—
2	0	1	0	0	0	0	0	0	1	0	1	7117	18	15.666
3	0	0	1	0	0	1	0	0	0	1	0	1179	1	0.981
3	0	0	1	0	0	1	0	0	0	0	1	552	1	0.674
3	0	0	1	0	0	0	1	0	0	1	0	781	0	1.303
3	0	0	1	0	0	0	1	0	0	0	1	676	1	1.656
3	0	0	1	0	0	0	0	1	0	1	0	783	6	1.475
3	0	0	1	0	0	0	0	1	0	0	1	1948	2	5.388
3	0	0	1	0	0	0	0	0	1	1	0	—	—	—
3	0	0	1	0	0	0	0	0	1	0	1	274	1	0.522
4	0	0	0	1	0	1	0	0	0	1	0	251	0	0.386
4	0	0	0	1	0	1	0	0	0	0	1	105	0	0.237
4	0	0	0	1	0	0	1	0	0	1	0	288	0	0.888
4	0	0	0	1	0	0	1	0	0	0	1	192	0	0.869
4	0	0	0	1	0	0	0	1	0	1	0	349	2	1.216
4	0	0	0	1	0	0	0	1	0	0	1	1208	11	6.177
4	0	0	0	1	0	0	0	0	1	1	0	—	—	—
4	0	0	0	1	0	0	0	0	1	0	1	2051	4	7.226
5	0	0	0	0	1	0	0	0	1	0	1	45	0	0.235
5	0	0	0	0	1	1	0	0	0	0	1	—	—	—
5	0	0	0	0	1	0	1	0	0	1	0	789	7	3.612
5	0	0	0	0	1	0	1	0	0	0	1	437	7	2.937
5	0	0	0	0	1	0	0	1	0	1	0	1157	5	5.982
5	0	0	0	0	1	0	0	1	0	0	1	2161	12	16.400
5	0	0	0	0	1	0	0	0	1	1	0	—	—	—
5	0	0	0	0	1	0	0	0	1	0	1	542	1	2.834

explained by the authors.[55] The substantive variables in the model are number of accidents in the observation period and aggregate number of service months for the ship type by construction year for the period of operation.

Estimates of the parameters of a Poisson regression model are shown in Table 19.15. The model is

$$\ln E[\text{accident per month}] = \boldsymbol{\beta}'\mathbf{x}.$$

The model therefore contains the ship type, construction period, and operation period effects, and the aggregate number of months with a coefficient of 1.0.[56] The model is shown in Table 19.15, with sets of estimates for the full model and with the model omitting the type and construction period effects. Predictions from the estimated full model are shown in the last column of Table 19.14.

The hypothesis that the year of construction is not a significant factor in explaining the number of accidents is strongly rejected by the likelihood ratio test.

$$\chi^2 = 2[84.11514 - 68.41455] = 31.40118.$$

TABLE 19.15 Estimated Poisson Regressions (Standard Errors in Parentheses)

Mean Dependent Variable 10.47

Variable	*Full Model*		*No Ship Type Effect*		*No Period Effect*	
Constant	−6.4029	(0.2175)	−6.9470	(0.1269)	−5.7999	(0.1784)
Type = A						
Type = B	−0.5447	(0.1776)			−0.7437	(0.1692)
Type = C	−0.6888	(0.3290)			−0.7549	(0.3276)
Type = D	−0.0743	(0.2906)			−0.1843	(0.2876)
Type = E	0.3205	(0.2358)			0.3842	(0.2348)
60–64						
65–69	0.6959	(0.1497)	0.7536	(0.1488)		
70–74	0.8175	(0.1698)	1.0503	(0.1576)		
75–79	0.4450	(0.2332)	0.6999	(0.2203)		
Period = 60–74						
Period = 75–79	0.3839	(0.1183)	0.3875	(0.1181)	0.5001	(0.1116)
Log service	1.0000		1.0000		1.0000	
Log L	−68.41455		−80.20123		−84.11514	
G^2	38.96262		62.53596		70.34967	
R_p^2	0.94560		0.89384		0.90001	
R_d^2	0.93661		0.89822		0.88556	

[55]Data are from McCullagh and Nelder (1983). See Example 8.2 for details.

[56]When the length of the period of observation varies by observation by T_i, and the model is of the rate of occurrence of events *per unit of time,* then the mean of the observed distribution is $T_i\lambda_i$. This produces the coefficient of 1.0 on the number of periods of service in the model.

The critical chi-squared value for three degrees of freedom is 7.82. The ship type effect is likewise significant,

$$\chi^2 = 2[80.20123 - 68.41455] = 23.57336,$$

against a critical value for four degrees of freedom of 9.49. The LM tests for the two restrictions give the same conclusions, but much less strongly. The value is 12.544 for the ship type effect and 8.750 for the period effects.

19.9.1. Measuring Goodness of Fit

The Poisson model produces no natural counterpart to the R^2 in a linear regression model, as usual, because the conditional mean function is nonlinear and, moreover, because the regression is heteroscedastic. But many alternatives have been suggested.[57] A measure based on the standardized residuals is

$$R_p^2 = 1 - \frac{\sum_{i=1}^{n}\left[\frac{y_i - \hat{\lambda}_i}{\sqrt{\hat{\lambda}_i}}\right]^2}{\sum_{i=1}^{n}\left[\frac{y_i - \bar{y}}{\sqrt{\bar{y}}}\right]^2}.$$

This measure has the virtue that it compares the fit of the model with that provided by a model with only a constant term. But it can be negative, and it can fall when a variable is dropped from the model. For an individual observation, the **deviance** is

$$\begin{aligned} d_i &= 2[y_i \ln(y_i/\hat{\lambda}_i) - (y_i - \hat{\lambda}_i)] \\ &= 2[y_i \ln(y_i/\hat{\lambda}_i) - e_i], \end{aligned}$$

where, by convention, $0 \ln(0) = 0$. If the model contains a constant term, $\Sigma_{i=1}^{n} e_i = 0$. The sum of the deviances

$$G^2 = \sum_{i=1}^{n} d_i = 2\sum_{i=1}^{n} y_i \ln(y_i/\hat{\lambda}_i)$$

is reported as an alternative fit measure by some computer programs. This statistic will equal 0.0 for a model that produces a perfect fit. (Note that since y_i is an integer while the prediction is continuous, this could not happen.) Cameron and Windmeijer (1993) suggest that the fit measure based on the deviances,

$$R_d^2 = 1 - \frac{\sum_{i=1}^{n}\left[y_i \log\left(\frac{y_i}{\hat{\lambda}_i}\right) - (y_i - \hat{\lambda}_i)\right]}{\sum_{i=1}^{n}\left[y_i \log\left(\frac{y_i}{\bar{y}}\right)\right]}$$

---

[57]See the surveys by Cameron and Windmeijer (1993), Gurmu and Trivedi (1994), and Greene (1995b).

has a number of desirable properties. First, denote the log-likelihood function for the model in which ψ_i is used as the prediction (i.e., the mean) of y_i as $\ell(\psi_i, y_i)$. The Poisson model fit by MLE is, then, $\ell(\hat{\lambda}_i, y_i)$, the model with only a constant term is $\ell(\bar{y}, y_i)$, and a model that achieves a perfect fit (by predicting y_i with itself) is $\ell(y_i, y_i)$. Then

$$R_d^2 = \frac{\ell(\hat{\lambda}, y_i) - \ell(\bar{y}, y_i)}{\ell(y_i, y_i) - \ell(\bar{y}, y_i)}.$$

Both numerator and denominator measure the improvement of the model over one with only a constant term. The denominator measures the maximum improvement, since one cannot improve on a perfect fit. Hence, the measure is bounded by 0 and 1 and increases as regressors are added to the model.[58] We note, finally, the passing resemblance of R_d^2 to the "pseudo-R^2," or "likelihood ratio index" reported by some statistical packages (e.g., Stata),

$$R_{\text{LRI}}^2 = 1 - \frac{\ell(\hat{\lambda}_i, y_i)}{\ell(\bar{y}, y_i)}.$$

Many modifications of the Poisson model have been analyzed by economists.[59] In this and the next few sections, we will briefly examine a few of these.

19.9.2. Censoring and Truncation

There are cases in which a Poisson model would appear to apply, but the data are censored or truncated. (The difference is explored at length in Chapter 20.) For example, consider the answer to a questionnaire that asks, "How many trips to the doctor did you make in the last year?" The responses might be 0, 1, 2, 3 or more. These data are censored. Any observation greater than 3 is masked by being labeled a 3. Alternatively, we might consider a setting in which values of zero for the dependent variable were qualitatively different from the other values. For example, if the response variable is the number of trips to a particular recreational facility that were made in the last year, then zero might represent a qualitative decision not to visit the site, whereas values greater than zero represent one's choice of the number of visits to make, given that any visits at all would be made. In such a setting, it might make sense to confine attention to the nonzero observations, thereby truncating the distribution of responses. Models with these characteristics can be handled within the Poisson framework by using the laws of probability to modify the likelihood. For example, in the censoring case, the relevant probabilities that enter the log likelihood are

[58]Note that multiplying both numerator and denominator by 2 produces the ratio of two likelihood ratio statistics, each of which is distributed as chi-squared.

[59]There have been numerous surveys of models for count data, including Cameron and Trivedi (1986), Gurmu and Trivedi (1994), and Greene (1995b).

$$P_i = \text{Prob}(y_i = j) = \frac{e^{-\lambda_i}\lambda_i^j}{j!} \quad \text{if } y_i = 0, 1, 2,$$
$$P_i = \text{Prob}(y_i = 3) = 1 - \text{Prob}(y_i < 3) \quad \text{if } y_i = 3,$$
$$= 1 - [\text{Prob}(y_i = 0) + \text{Prob}(y_i = 1) + \text{Prob}(y_i = 2)].$$

The probabilities in the model with truncation above zero would be

$$\text{Prob}(y_i) = \frac{P_{y_i}}{1 - P_0} = \frac{e^{-\lambda_i}\lambda_i^{y_i}}{y_i!(1 - e^{-\lambda_i})}, \quad y_i = 1, 2, \ldots,$$

which is not appreciably more complicated to analyze than the basic Poisson model. A number of alternative cases are discussed by Terza (1985b), Mullahey (1986), Shaw (1988), Grogger and Carson (1991), Greene (1995b), and Lambert (1992).

19.9.3. Testing for Overdispersion

The Poisson model has been criticized because of its implicit assumption that the variance of y_i equals its mean. Many extensions of the Poisson model that relax this assumption have been proposed by Hausman et al. (1984), McCullagh and Nelder (1983), and Cameron and Trivedi (1986), to name but a few.

The first step in this extended analysis is usually a test for overdispersion in the context of the simple model. A number of authors have devised tests for "overdispersion" within the context of the Poisson model. [See Cameron and Trivedi (1990), Gurmu (1991), and Lee (1986).] We will consider three of the common tests, one based on a regression approach, one a conditional moment test, and a third, a Lagrange multiplier test, based on an alternative model. Conditional moment tests are developed in Section 11.6.2. It may be useful to review that material before working through Examples 19.22 and 19.23.

EXAMPLE 19.22 A Regression-Based Test for Overdispersion in the Poisson Model

In their presentation of the data used above, McCullagh and Nelder assert, without evidence, that there is overdispersion in the data. Some of their analysis follows on an assumption that the standard deviation of y_i is 1.3 times the mean. Cameron and Trivedi (1990) offer several different tests for overdispersion. A simple procedure used for testing the hypothesis

$$H_0\text{:Var}[y_i] = E[y_i],$$
$$H_1\text{:Var}[y_i] = E[y_i] + \alpha g(E[y_i])$$

is carried out by regressing

$$z_i = \frac{(y_i - \lambda_i)^2 - y_i}{\lambda_i\sqrt{2}},$$

where λ_i is the predicted value from the regression, on either a constant term or λ_i without a constant term. A simple t test of whether the coefficient is significantly different from zero tests H_0 versus H_1. For the data above, the t statistics for the two regressions are 0.572 and −0.483, respectively, so we do not reject H_0. But see Examples 19.23 and 19.24 for different approaches.

EXAMPLE 19.23 A Conditional Moment Test of Overdispersion

In the previous example, the hypothesis that $\text{Var}[y_i] = E[y_i]$ could not be rejected on the basis of a test that essentially formulated the alternative as $\text{Var}[y_i] = E[y_i] + g(E[y_i])$. That is a very specific type of overdispersion. Now we will consider the more general hypothesis that $\text{Var}[y_i]$ is completely given by $E[y_i]$. The alternative is that the variance is systematically related to the regressors in a way that is not completely accounted for by $E[y_i]$. Formally, we have $E[y_i] = \exp(\boldsymbol{\beta}'\mathbf{x}_i) = \lambda_i$. The null hypothesis is that $\text{Var}[y_i] = \lambda_i$ as well. We will test the hypothesis using the conditional moment test described in Section 11.6.2. The expected first derivatives and the moment restriction are

$$E[\mathbf{x}_i(y_i - \lambda_i)] = \mathbf{0} \quad \text{and} \quad E\{\mathbf{z}_i[(y_i - \lambda_i)^2 - \lambda_i]\} = \mathbf{0}.$$

To carry out the test, we do the following. Let $e_i = y_i - \hat{\lambda}_i$ and $\mathbf{z}_i = \mathbf{x}_i$ without the constant term.

1. Compute the Poisson regression by maximum likelihood.
2. Compute $\mathbf{r} = \Sigma_{i=1}^{n} \mathbf{z}_i[e_i^2 - \hat{\lambda}_i] = \Sigma_{i=1}^{n} \mathbf{z}v_i$ based on the maximum likelihood estimates.
3. Compute $\mathbf{M}'\mathbf{M} = \Sigma_{i=1}^{n} \mathbf{z}_i\mathbf{z}_i' v_i^2$, $\mathbf{D}'\mathbf{D} = \Sigma_{i=1}^{n} \mathbf{x}_i\mathbf{x}_i' e_i^2$, and $\mathbf{M}'\mathbf{D} = \Sigma_{i=1}^{n} \mathbf{z}_i\mathbf{x}_i' v_i e_i$.
4. Compute $\mathbf{S} = \mathbf{M}'\mathbf{M} - \mathbf{M}'\mathbf{D}(\mathbf{D}'\mathbf{D})^{-1}\mathbf{D}'\mathbf{M}$.
5. $C = \mathbf{r}'\mathbf{S}^{-1}\mathbf{r} = 26.555$. There are 8 degrees of freedom.

The 5 percent critical value from the chi-squared table is 15.50732. So the hypothesis is rejected. This conflicts with the Cameron and Trivedi result we found earlier. But this test is much more general, since the form of overdispersion is not specified here. That may explain the difference. Note that this affirms McCullagh and Nelder's conjecture.

EXAMPLE 19.24 A Lagrange Multiplier Test of Overdispersion

The next section presents the negative binomial model. This model relaxes the Poisson assumption that the mean equals the variance. The Poisson model is obtained as a parametric restriction on the negative binomial model, so a Lagrange multiplier test can be computed. In general, if an alternative distribution for which the Poisson model is obtained as a parametric restriction, such as the negative binomial model, can be specified, then a Lagrange multiplier statistic can be computed. The LM statistic is

$$\text{LM} = \frac{\sum_{i=1}^{n} \hat{w}_i[(y_i - \hat{\lambda}_i)^2 - y_i]}{\sqrt{2\sum_{i=1}^{n} \hat{w}_i^2 \hat{\lambda}_i^2}}.$$

The weight $\hat{w}_i$ depends on the assumed alternative distribution. For the negative binomial model discussed below, $\hat{w}_i$ equals 1.0. Thus, under this alternative, the statistic is particularly simple to compute:

$$\text{LM} = n(\mathbf{e}'\mathbf{e} - \bar{y})/(2\boldsymbol{\lambda}'\boldsymbol{\lambda})^{1/2}.$$

The main advantage of this test statistic is that one need only estimate the Poisson model to compute it.

For the Poisson regression results above, the value of the statistic is 46.4001. Once again, the hypothesis of the Poisson model is rejected.

19.9.4. Heterogeneity and the Negative Binomial Regression Model

The assumed equality of the conditional mean and variance functions is typically taken to be the major shortcoming of the Poisson regression model. Many alternatives have been suggested [see Hausman et al. (1984), Cameron and Trivedi (1986), Gurmu and Trivedi (1994), and Johnson and Kotz (1993) for some discussion.] The most common is the negative binomial model, which arises from a natural formulation of cross-section heterogeneity. We generalize the Poisson model by introducing an individual, unobserved effect into the conditional mean,

$$\begin{aligned} \log \mu_i &= \boldsymbol{\beta}'\mathbf{x}_i + \epsilon_i \\ &= \log \lambda_i + \log u_i, \end{aligned}$$

where the disturbance ϵ_i reflects either specification error as in the classical regression model or the kind of cross-sectional heterogeneity that normally characterizes microeconomic data. Then, the distribution of y_i conditioned on $\mathbf{x}_i$ *and* u_i (i.e., ϵ_i) remains Poisson with conditional mean and variance μ_i:

$$f(y_i \mid u_i) = \frac{e^{-\lambda_i u_i}(\lambda_i u_i)^{y_i}}{y_i!}.$$

The unconditional distribution $f(y_i \mid \mathbf{x}_i)$ is the expected value (over u_i) of $f(y_i \mid \mathbf{x}_i, u_i)$,

$$f(y_i \mid \mathbf{x}_i) = \int_0^\infty \frac{e^{-\lambda_i u_i}(\lambda_i u_i)^{y_i}}{y_i!} g(u_i)\, du_i.$$

The choice of a density for u_i defines the unconditional distribution. For mathematical convenience, a gamma distribution is usually assumed for $u_i =$

$\exp(\epsilon_i)$.[60] As in other models of heterogeneity, the mean of the distribution is unidentified if the model contains a constant term (because the disturbance enters multiplicatively) so $E[\exp(\epsilon_i)]$ is assumed to be 1.0. With this normalization,

$$g(u_i) = \frac{\theta^\theta}{\Gamma(\theta)} e^{-\theta u_i} u_i^{\theta-1}.$$

The density for y_i is then

$$\begin{aligned} f(y_i \mid \mathbf{x}_i) &= \int_0^\infty \frac{e^{-\lambda_i u_i}(\lambda_i u_i)^{y_i}}{y_i!} \frac{\theta^\theta u_i^{\theta-1} e^{-\theta u_i}}{\Gamma(\theta)} du_i \\ &= \frac{\theta^\theta \lambda_i^{y_i}}{\Gamma(y_i + 1)\Gamma(\theta)} \int_0^\infty e^{-(\lambda_i+\theta)u_i} u_i^{\theta+y_i-1} du_i \\ &= \frac{\theta^\theta \lambda_i^{y_i} \Gamma(\theta + y_i)}{\Gamma(y_i + 1)\Gamma(\theta)(\lambda_i + \theta)^{\theta+y_i}} \\ &= \frac{\Gamma(\theta + y_i)}{\Gamma(y_i + 1)\Gamma(\theta)} r_i^{y_i}(1 - r_i)^\theta, \quad \text{where } r_i = \frac{\lambda_i}{\lambda_i + \theta}, \end{aligned}$$

which is one form of the negative binomial distribution. The distribution has conditional mean λ_i and conditional variance $\lambda_i(1 + (1/\theta)\lambda_i)$. [This is model Negbin II in Cameron and Trivedi's (1986) presentation.] The negative binomial model can be estimated by maximum likelihood without much difficulty. A test of the Poisson distribution is often carried out by testing the hypothesis $\theta = 0$ using the Wald or likelihood ratio test. (The LM test is given in the preceding example.)

19.9.5. Poisson Models for Panel Data

The familiar approaches to accommodating heterogeneity in panel data have fairly straightforward extensions in the count data setting. [Hausman et al. (1984) give full details for these models.] We will examine them for the Poisson model. Hausman et al. also give results for the negative binomial model.

Consider first a fixed effects approach. The Poisson distribution is assumed to have conditional mean

$$\log \lambda_{it} = \boldsymbol{\beta}' \mathbf{x}_{it} + \alpha_i.$$

The approach used in the linear model of transforming y_{it} to group mean deviations does not remove the heterogeneity, nor does it leave a Poisson distribu-

[60]There is a minor error in Cameron and Trivedi (1986, p. 32) in that they state that ϵ, rather than $\exp(\epsilon)$, has a gamma density. The subsequent presentation is consistent with the latter.

tion for the transformed variable. An estimator that is not a function of the fixed effects is found by obtaining the joint distribution of $(y_{i1}, \ldots, y_{iT_i})$ conditional on their sum. For the Poisson model, this produces a close cousin to the logit model discussed earlier:

$$p\left(y_{i1}, y_{i2}, \ldots, y_{iT_i} \,\Big|\, \sum_{i=1}^{T_i} y_{it}\right) = \frac{\left(\sum_{t=1}^{T_i} y_{it}\right)!}{\left(\prod_{t=1}^{T_i} y_{it}!\right)} \prod_{t=1}^{T_i} p_{it}^{y_{it}},$$

where

$$p_{it} = \frac{e^{\boldsymbol{\beta}'\mathbf{x}_{it} + \alpha_i}}{\sum_{t=1}^{T_i} e^{\boldsymbol{\beta}'\mathbf{x}_{it} + \alpha_i}} = \frac{e^{\boldsymbol{\beta}'\mathbf{x}_{it}}}{\sum_{t=1}^{T_i} e^{\boldsymbol{\beta}'\mathbf{x}_{it}}}.$$

The contribution of group i to the conditional log-likelihood is

$$\log L_i = \sum_{t=1}^{T_i} y_{it} \log p_{it}.$$

The fixed effects approach has the same virtue in this setting as in the regression case. It is not necessary to assume that the effects, which are conditioned out and not estimated, are uncorrelated with the included, exogenous variables. If the uncorrelatedness of regressors and effects can be maintained, then the random effects model is an attractive alternative way to proceed. As before, the approach used in the linear regression model, partial deviations from the group means followed by generalized least squares (see Chapter 14), is not usable here. The approach used is to formulate the joint probability conditioned upon the heterogeneity, then integrate it out of the joint distribution. Thus, we form

$$p(y_{it}, \ldots, y_{iT_i} \mid u_i) = \prod_{t=1}^{T_i} p(y_{it} \mid u_i).$$

Then the random effect is swept out by obtaining

$$\begin{aligned} p(y_{i1}, \ldots, y_{iT_i}) &= \int_u p(y_{i1}, \ldots, y_{iT_i}, u_i)\, du_i \\ &= \int_u p(y_{i1}, \ldots, y_{iT_i} \mid u_i) g(u_i)\, du_i \\ &= E_u[p(y_{i1}, \ldots, y_{iT_i} \mid u_i)]. \end{aligned}$$

This is exactly the approach used earlier to condition the heterogeneity out of the Poisson model to produce the negative binomial model. If, as before, we take $p(y_{it}|u_i)$ to be Poisson with mean $\lambda_{it} = \exp(\boldsymbol{\beta}'\mathbf{x}_{it} + u_i)$ in which $\exp(u_i)$ is distributed as gamma with mean 1.0 and variance $1/\alpha$, then the preceding steps produce the negative binomial distribution,

$$p(y_{i1}, \ldots, y_{iT_i}) = \frac{\left[\prod_{t=1}^{T_i} \lambda_{it}^{y_{it}}\right]\Gamma\left(\theta + \sum_{t=1}^{T_i} y_{it}\right)}{\left[\Gamma(\theta)\prod_{t=1}^{T_i} y_{it}!\right]\left[\left(\sum_{t=1}^{T_i} y_{it}\right)!\right]\left[\left(\sum_{t=1}^{T_i} \lambda_{it}\right)^{\Sigma_{t=1}^{T_i} y_{it}}\right]} Q_i^{\theta}(1 - Q_i)^{\Sigma_{t=1}^{T_i} y_{it}},$$

where

$$Q_i = \frac{\theta}{\theta + \sum_{t=1}^{T_i} y_{it}}.$$

For estimation purposes, this is a negative binomial distribution for $Y_i = \Sigma_t y_{it}$ with mean $\Lambda_i = \Sigma_t \lambda_{it}$.

There is a mild preference in the received literature for the fixed effects estimators over the random effects estimators. The virtue of dispensing with the assumption of uncorrelatedness of the regressors and the group specific effects is substantial. On the other hand, the assumption does come at a cost. Since estimation of the fixed effects estimators requires them to be conditioned out, the probabilities and therefore the marginal effects cannot be computed. The coefficients in these models are of limited usefulness because of the nonlinearity of the conditional mean functions. Absent the probabilities, the only diagnostic measure is the weighted sum of squares, which is, for better or worse, purely ad hoc.

Brannas and Johanssen (1994) have suggested a semiparametric approach based on the GMM estimator by superimposing a very general form of heterogeneity on the Poisson model. They assume that conditioned on a random effect ϵ_{it}, y_{it} is distributed as Poisson with mean $\epsilon_{it}\lambda_{it}$. The covariance structure of ϵ_{it} is allowed to be fully general. For $t, s = 1, \ldots, T$, $\text{Var}[\epsilon_{it}] = \sigma_i^2$, $\text{Cov}[\epsilon_{it}, \epsilon_{js}] = \gamma_{ij}(|t - s|)$. For long time series, this is likely to have far too many parameters to be identified without some restrictions, such as first-order homogeneity ($\boldsymbol{\beta}_i = \boldsymbol{\beta}\ \forall\ i$), uncorrelatedness across groups,[61] [$\gamma_{ij}(.) = 0$ for $i \neq j$], groupwise homoscedasticity ($\sigma_i^2 = \sigma^2\ \forall\ i$), and nonautocorrelatedness [$\gamma(r) = 0\ \forall\ r \neq 0$]. With these assumptions, the estimation procedure they propose is similar to the procedures suggested earlier. If the model imposes enough restrictions, the parameters can be estimated by the method of moments. The authors discuss estimation of the model in its full generality.

[61]The authors suggest that their model can be adapted for unbalanced panels, that is, different numbers of observations in the groups. With this assumption, that would be straightforward, but without the uncorrelatedness across groups, this level of generality will be extremely difficult to achieve. The problem would be estimating the cross-group correlations with different numbers of observations in the two groups.

19.9.6. Hurdle and Zero-Altered Poisson Models

In some settings, the zero outcome of the data generating process is qualitatively different from the positive ones. Mullahey (1986) argued that this constituted a shortcoming of the Poisson (or negative binomial) model and suggested a "hurdle" model as an alternative.[62] In his formulation, a binary probability model determines whether a zero or a nonzero outcome occurs, then, in the latter case, a (truncated) Poisson distribution describes the positive outcomes. The model is

$$\begin{aligned}\text{Prob}[y_i = 0] &= e^{-\theta}\\ \text{Prob}[y_i = j] &= \frac{(1 - e^{-\theta})e^{-\lambda_i}\lambda_i^j}{j!(1 - e^{-\lambda_i})}, \quad j = 1, 2, \ldots .\end{aligned}$$

This formulation changes the probability of the zero outcome and scales the remaining probabilities so that all sum to 1. It adds a new restriction that $\text{Prob}[y_i = 0]$ no longer depends on the covariates, however. A natural next step, therefore, is to parameterize this probability. Mullahey suggests some formulations and applies the model to a sample of observations on daily beverage consumption.

Mullahey (1986), Heilbron (1989), Lambert (1992), Johnson and Kotz (1970), and Greene (1994) have analyzed an extension of the hurdle model in which the zero outcome can arise from one of two regimes.[63] In one regime, the outcome is always zero. In the other, the usual Poisson process is at work, which can produce the zero outcome or some other. In Lambert's application, she analyzes the number of defective items produced by a manufacturing process in a given time interval. If the process is under control, the outcome is always zero (by definition). If it is not under control, the number of defective items is distributed as Poisson and may be zero or positive in any period. The model at work is therefore

$$\begin{aligned}\text{Prob}[y_i = 0] &= \text{Prob}[\text{regime 1}] + \text{Prob}[y_i = 0 \mid \text{regime 2}]\text{Prob}[\text{regime 2}],\\ \text{Prob}[y_i = j] &= \text{Prob}[y_i = j \mid \text{regime 2}]\text{Prob}[\text{regime 2}], \quad j = 1, 2, \ldots .\end{aligned}$$

Let z denote a binary indicator of regime 1 ($z = 0$) or regime 2 ($z = 1$), and let y^* denote the outcome of the Poisson process in regime 2. Then the observed y is $z \times y^*$. A natural extension of the splitting model is to allow z to be determined by a set of covariates. These need not be the same as those that determine the conditional probabilities in the Poisson process. Thus, the model is

$$\begin{aligned}\text{Prob}[z_i = 1] &= F(\mathbf{w}_i, \gamma),\\ \text{Prob}[y_i = j \mid z_i = 1] &= \frac{e^{-\lambda_i}\lambda_i^j}{j!}.\end{aligned}$$

---

[62]For a similar treatment in a continuous data application, see Cragg (1971).

[63]The model is variously labeled the "With Zeros," or WZ, model [Mullahey (1986)], the "Zero Inflated Poisson," or ZIP, model [Lambert (1992)], and "Zero-Altered Poisson," or ZAP, model [Greene (1994)].

Note that the mean in this distribution is

$$E[y_i] = F \times 0 + (1 - F) \times E[y_i^* \mid y_i^* > 0]$$
$$= (1 - F) \times \frac{\lambda_i}{1 - e^{-\lambda_i}}.$$

Lambert (1992) and Greene (1994) consider a number of alternative formulations, including logit and probit models discussed in Sections 19.3 and 19.4, for the probability of the two regimes.

Both of these modifications substantially alter the Poisson formulation. First note that the equality of the mean and variance of the distribution no longer follows; both modifications induce overdispersion. On the other hand, the overdispersion does not arise from heterogeneity; it arises from the nature of the process generating the zeros. As such, an interesting identification problem arises in this model. If the data do appear to be characterized by overdispersion, it seems less than obvious whether it should be attributed to heterogeneity or to the regime splitting mechanism. Mullahey (1986) argues the point more strongly. He demonstrates that overdispersion will always induce excess zeros. As such, in a splitting model, we are likely to misinterpret the excess zeros as due to the splitting process instead of the heterogeneity.

It might be of interest to test simply whether there is a regime splitting mechanism at work or not. Unfortunately, the basic model and the zero-inflated model are not nested. Setting the parameters of the splitting model to zero, for example, does not produce Prob$[z = 0] = 0$. In the probit case, this probability becomes 0.5, which maintains the regime split. The preceding tests for over- or underdispersion would be rather indirect. What is desired is a test of non-Poissonness. An alternative distribution may (but need not) produce a systematically different proportion of zeros than the Poisson. Testing for a different distribution, as opposed to a different set of parameters, is a difficult procedure. Since the hypotheses are necessarily nonnested, the power of any test is a function of the alternative hypothesis and may, under some, be small. Vuong (1989) has proposed a test statistic for nonnested models that is well suited for this setting when the alternative distribution can be specified. Let $f_j(y_i \mid \mathbf{x}_i)$ denote the predicted probability that the random variable Y equals y_i under the assumption that the distribution is $f_j(y_i \mid \mathbf{x}_i)$, for $j = 1, 2$, and let

$$m_i = \log\left(\frac{f_1(y_i \mid \mathbf{x}_i)}{f_2(y_i \mid \mathbf{x}_i)}\right).$$

Then Vuong's statistic for testing the nonnested hypothesis of model 1 versus model 2 is

$$v = \frac{\sqrt{n}\left[\dfrac{1}{n}\sum_{i=1}^{n} m_i\right]}{\sqrt{\dfrac{1}{n}\sum_{i=1}^{n}(m_i - \overline{m})^2}}.$$

This is the standard statistic for testing the hypothesis that $E[m_i]$ equals 0. Vuong shows that v is asymptotically distributed as standard normal. As he notes, the statistic is bidirectional. If $|v|$ is less than 2, the test does not favor one model or the other. Otherwise, large values favor model 1 whereas small (negative) values favor model 2. Carrying out the test requires estimation of both models and computation of both sets of predicted probabilities.

In Greene (1994), it is shown that the Vuong test has some power to discern this phenomenon. The logic of the testing procedure is to allow for overdispersion by specifying a negative binomial count data process, then examine whether, *even allowing for the overdispersion*, there still appear to be excess zeros. In his application, that appears to be the case.

EXAMPLE 19.25 A Split Population Model for Major Derogatory Reports

In Example 10.7, we estimated a credit scoring model. The basic model predicts y_i, the number of major derogatory credit reports, as a function of $\mathbf{x}$ = [1, age, income, average expenditure]. The data for the model are listed in Table 10.8. Inspection of the data reveals a preponderance of zeros. Indeed, of 100 observations, 82 have $y_i = 0$, whereas of the remaining 18, ten have 1, three have 2, three have 3, one has 4, and one has 7. Thus, for a Poisson distribution, these data are actually a bit extreme. We propose to use Lambert's zero inflated Poisson model instead, with the Poisson distribution built around

$$\ln \lambda_i = \beta_1 + \beta_2 \text{ age} + \beta_3 \text{ income} + \beta_4 \text{ expenditure}$$

as in Example 10.7. For the splitting model, we use a logit model, with covariates $\mathbf{z}$ = [1, age, income, own/rent]. The estimates are shown in Table 19.16.

TABLE 19.16 Estimates of a Split Population Model

	Poisson and Logit Models		*Split Population Model*	
Variable	*Poisson for y*	*Logit for y > 0*	*Logit P(0/1)*	*Poisson for y*
Constant	−1.5481	3.5145	4.3256	1.3811
	(0.7176)	(1.1486)	(1.7781)	(1.0581)
Age	0.01201	−0.03595	−0.04045	−0.01164
	(0.01976)	(0.04278)	(0.04014)	(0.03292)
Income	0.22151	−0.09563	−0.72981	−0.06867
	(0.1010)	(0.20904)	(0.3978)	(0.20565)
Expend	−0.06663			−0.0058398
	(0.00192)			(0.002081)
Own/Rent		0.58010	0.49180	
		(0.79107)	(0.78964)	
Log L	−79.70854	−31.89901	−64.64649	
$\sum_{i=1}^{n} \hat{P}(0)$	82.9		83.5	

Vuong's diagnostic statistic appears to confirm intuition that the Poisson model does not adequately describe the data; the value is +6.118. On the other hand, if we examine the predictions of the model rather than the diagnostic, it appears that the Poisson model performs a bit better without the regime split.

EXERCISES

1. A binomial probability model is to be based on the following index function model:

$$\begin{aligned} y^* &= \alpha + \beta d + \epsilon, \\ y &= 1, \quad \text{if } y^* > 0, \\ y &= 0 \quad \text{otherwise.} \end{aligned}$$

The only regressor, d, is a dummy variable. The data consist of 100 observations that have the following:

		y	
		0	1
d	0	24	28
	1	32	16

Obtain the maximum likelihood estimators of α and β, and estimate the asymptotic standard errors of your estimates. Test the hypothesis that β equals zero by using a Wald test (asymptotic t test) and a likelihood ratio test. Use the probit model and then repeat, using the logit model. Do your results change? [Hint: Formulate the log-likelihood in terms of α and $\delta = \alpha + \beta$.]

2. Suppose that a linear probability model is to be fit to a set of observations on a dependent variable y that takes values 0 and 1, and a single regressor x that varies continuously across observations. Obtain the exact expressions for the least squares slope in the regression in terms of the mean(s) and variance of x, and interpret the result.

3. Given the data set

y	1	0	0	1	1	0	0	1	1	1
x	9	2	5	4	6	7	3	5	2	6

estimate a probit model and test the hypothesis that x is not influential in determining the probability that y equals 1.

4. Construct the Lagrange multiplier statistic for testing the hypothesis that all the slopes (but not the constant term) equal zero in the binomial logit model. Prove that the Lagrange multiplier statistic is nR^2 in the regression of $(y_i - P)$ on the x's, where P is the sample proportion of 1s.

5. We are interested in the ordered probit model. Our data consist of 250 observations, of which the response are

y	0	1	2	3	4
n	50	40	45	80	35

Using the preceding data, obtain maximum likelihood estimates of the unknown parameters of the model. [Hint: Consider the probabilities as the unknown parameters.]

6. The following hypothetical data give the participation rates in a particular type of recycling program and the number of trucks purchased for collection by 10 towns in a small mid-Atlantic state:

Town	*Trucks*	*Participation (%)*
1	160	11
2	250	74
3	170	8
4	365	87
5	210	62
6	206	83
7	203	48
8	305	84
9	270	71
10	340	79

The town of Eleven is contemplating initiating a recycling program but wishes to achieve a 95 percent rate of participation. Using a probit model for your analysis,

(a) How many trucks would the town expect to have to purchase in order to achieve their goal? [Hint: See Section 19.4.3.] Note that you will use $n_i = 1$.

(b) If trucks cost \$20,000 each, is a goal of 90 percent reachable within a budget of \$6.5 million? (That is, should they *expect* to reach the goal?)

(c) According to your model, what is the marginal value of the 301st truck in terms of the increase in the percentage participation?

7. A data set consists of $n = n_1 + n_2 + n_3$ observations on y and x. For the first n_1 observations, $y = 1$ and $x = 1$. For the next n_2 observations, $y = 0$ and $x = 1$. For the last n_3 observations, $y = 0$ and $x = 0$. Prove that neither (19-19) nor (19-21) has a solution.

8. Data on t = strike duration and x = unanticipated industrial production for a number of strikes in each of 9 years are given in Table 20.7. Use the Poisson regression model discussed in Section 19.8 to determine whether x is a significant determinant of the *number of strikes* in a given year.

CHAPTER 20

Limited Dependent Variable and Duration Models

20.1. INTRODUCTION

This chapter is concerned with truncation and censoring.[1] The effect of truncation occurs when sample data are drawn from a subset of a larger population of interest. For example, studies of income based on incomes above or below some poverty line may be of limited usefulness for inference about the whole population. This is essentially a characteristic of the distribution from which the sample data are drawn. Censoring is a more common problem in recent studies. To continue the example, suppose that instead of being unobserved, incomes below the poverty line are reported as if they were *at* the poverty line. The censoring of a range of values of the variable of interest introduces a distortion into conventional statistical results similar to that of truncation. Unlike truncation, however, censoring is essentially a defect in the sample data. Presumably, if they were not censored, the data would be a representative sample from the population of interest.

This chapter will discuss four broad topics: truncation, censoring, a form of truncation called the *sample selection problem,* and a class of models called *duration models.* Although most empirical work on the first three involves censoring rather than truncation, we will study the simpler model of truncation first. It provides most of the theoretical tools we need to analyze models of censoring and sample selection. The fourth topic, on models of duration—When will a spell of unemployment or a strike end?—could reasonably stand alone. It does in countless articles and a library of books.[2] We include our introduction to this subject in this chapter because in most applications, duration

[1]Five surveys of these topics are Dhrymes (1984), Maddala (1977b, 1983, 1984), and Amemiya (1984). The last is part of a symposium on censored and truncated regression models.

[2]For example, Lancaster (1990).

modeling involves censored data and it is thus convenient to treat duration here (and because we are nearing the end of our survey and yet another chapter seems unwarranted).

20.2. TRUNCATION

In this section, we are concerned with inferring the characteristics of a population from a sample drawn from a restricted part of that population.

EXAMPLE 20.1 A Truncated Distribution

"The typical 'upper affluent American' . . . makes \$142,000 per year . . . . The people surveyed had household income of at least \$100,000."[3] Does this statistic tell us anything about the "typical American"? As it stands, it probably does not (popular impressions notwithstanding). The article goes on to state, "If you're in that category, pat yourself on the back—only 2 percent of American households make the grade, according to the survey."

20.2.1. Truncated Distributions

For our purposes, a **truncated distribution** is the part of an untruncated distribution that is above or below some specified value. For instance, in Example 20.1, we are given a characteristic of the distribution of incomes above \$100,000. This is, of course, only a part of the full distribution of incomes.

THEOREM 20.1: Density of a Truncated Random Variable. *If a continuous random variable x has pdf f(x) and a is a constant,*

$$f(x \mid x > a) = \frac{f(x)}{\text{Prob}(x > a)}.^{4}$$

The proof follows from the definition of conditional probability. This amounts merely to scaling the density so that it integrates to one over the range above a.

EXAMPLE 20.2 Truncated Uniform Distribution

If x has a uniform distribution $U(0, 1)$,

$$f(x) = 1, \quad 0 \leq x \leq 1.$$

For truncation at $x = \frac{1}{3}$,

[3]*New York Post* (1987).

[4]The case of truncation from above instead of below is handled in an analogous fashion and does not require any new results.

$$f\left(x \mid x > \frac{1}{3}\right) = \frac{f(x)}{\text{Prob}(x > \frac{1}{3})} = \frac{1}{(\frac{2}{3})} = \frac{3}{2}, \quad \frac{1}{3} \le x \le 1.$$

Most recent applications use the **truncated normal distribution.** If x has a normal distribution with mean μ and standard deviation σ, then

$$\begin{aligned}\text{Prob}(x > a) &= 1 - \Phi\left(\frac{a - \mu}{\sigma}\right) \\ &= 1 - \Phi(\alpha),\end{aligned}$$

where $\alpha = (a - \mu)/\sigma$ and $\Phi(.)$ is the standard normal cdf. The density of the truncated normal distribution is then

$$\begin{aligned}f(x \mid x > a) &= \frac{f(x)}{1 - \Phi(\alpha)} \\ &= \frac{(2\pi\sigma^2)^{-1/2} e^{-(x-\mu)^2/(2\sigma^2)}}{1 - \Phi(\alpha)} \\ &= \frac{\dfrac{1}{\sigma}\phi\left(\dfrac{x - \mu}{\sigma}\right)}{1 - \Phi(\alpha)},\end{aligned}$$

where $\phi(.)$ is the standard normal pdf. The **truncated standard normal distribution,** with $\mu = 0$ and $\sigma = 1$, is illustrated for $a = -0.5, 0$, and 0.5 in Figure 20.1. For convenience in what follows, we shall call a random variable whose distribution is truncated a **truncated random variable.**

20.2.2. Moments of Truncated Distributions

We are usually interested in the mean and variance of the truncated random variable. These would be obtained in the usual fashion:

$$E[x \mid x > a] = \int_a^\infty x f(x \mid x > a)\, dx$$

for the mean and likewise for the variance.

EXAMPLE 20.3 Moments of the Truncated Uniform Distribution

For the uniformly distributed random variable in Example 20.2,

$$E\left[x \mid x > \frac{1}{3}\right] = \int_{1/3}^{1} x\left(\frac{3}{2}\right) dx = \frac{2}{3}.$$

For a variable distributed uniformly between L and U, the variance is $(U - L)^2/12$. Thus,

$$\text{Var}[x \mid x > \tfrac{1}{3}] = \tfrac{1}{27}.$$

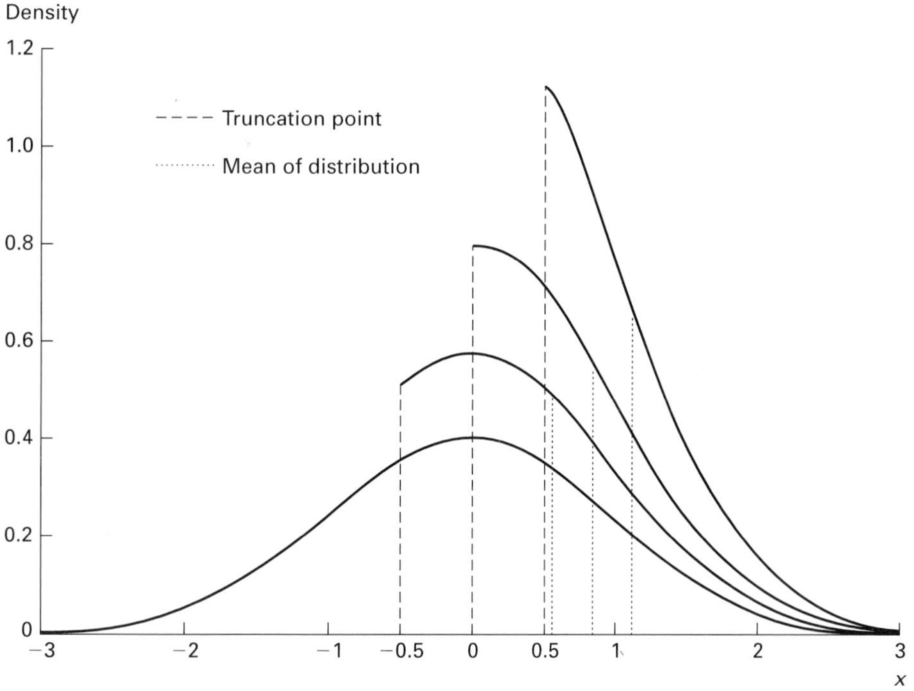

FIGURE 20.1 Truncated Normal Distributions.

The mean and variance of the untruncated distribution are $\frac{1}{2}$ and $\frac{1}{12}$, respectively.

Example 20.3 illustrates two results.

1. If the truncation is from below, the mean of the truncated variable is greater than the mean of the original one. If the truncation is from above, the mean of the truncated variable is smaller than the mean of the original one.
2. Truncation reduces the variance compared with the variance in the untruncated distribution.

Henceforth, we shall use the terms **truncated mean** and **truncated variance** to refer to the mean and variance in the truncated distribution.

For the truncated normal distribution, we have the following theorem:[5]

THEOREM 20.2: Moments of the Truncated Normal Distribution. *If* $x \sim N[\mu, \sigma^2]$ *and a is a constant,*

$$E[x \mid \text{truncation}] = \mu + \sigma\lambda(\alpha), \quad \textbf{(20-1)}$$

$$\text{Var}[x \mid \text{truncation}] = \sigma^2[1 - \delta(\alpha)], \quad \textbf{(20-2)}$$

where $\alpha = (a - \mu)/\sigma$,

---

[5]Details may be found in Johnson and Kotz (1970, p. 81).

$$\lambda(\alpha) = \phi(\alpha)/[1 - \Phi(\alpha)] \quad \text{if truncation is } x > a, \tag{20-3a}$$

$$\lambda(\alpha) = -\phi(\alpha)/\Phi(\alpha) \quad \text{if truncation is } x < a, \tag{20-3b}$$

and

$$\delta(\alpha) = \lambda(\alpha)[\lambda(\alpha) - \alpha]. \tag{20-4}$$

An important result is

$$0 < \delta(\alpha) < 1 \quad \text{for all values of } \alpha.$$

This implies point 2 on page 951. A result that we will use at several points below is $d\phi(\alpha)/d\alpha = -\alpha\phi(\alpha)$. The function $\lambda(\alpha)$ is called the **inverse Mills ratio.** The function (20-3a) is also the **hazard function** for the distribution. The mean of the truncated standard normal distribution is a function of the truncation point as shown in Figure 20.2. A useful way to view truncation is in terms of the probability that x is less than a, which we shall call the **degree of truncation.** This is an increasing function of a. As this probability rises, a greater proportion of the distribution is being discarded, and the mean rises accordingly. Figure 20.3 shows the relationship between $E[x\,|\,x > a]$ and $\text{Prob}[x > a]$ for the standard normal distribution.

EXAMPLE 20.4 Moments of a Truncated Lognormal Distribution

Continuing Example 20.1, since the degree of truncation in the sample is 98 percent, the \$142,000 is probably quite far from the mean in the full population.

Suppose that incomes in the population are lognormally distributed.[6] Then the log of income has a normal distribution with, say, mean μ and standard deviation σ. Let $y = \ln x$. Two useful numbers for this example are $\ln 100 = 4.605$ and $\ln 142 = 4.956$. Suppose that the survey is large enough for us to treat the sample average as the true mean. The article states that

$$E[y\,|\,y > 4.605] = 4.956.$$

It also tells us that $\text{Prob}[y > 4.605] = 0.02$. From Theorem 20.2,

$$E[y\,|\,y > 4.605] = \mu + \frac{\sigma\phi(\alpha)}{1 - \Phi(\alpha)},$$

where

$$\alpha = \frac{4.605 - \mu}{\sigma}.$$

But we know that $\Phi(\alpha) = 0.98$, so $\alpha = \Phi^{-1}(0.98) = 2.054$. Continuing, then,

$$\text{(a) } 2.054\sigma = 4.605 - \mu.$$

In addition, given $\alpha = 2.054$, $\phi(\alpha) = \phi(2.054) = 0.0484$. From (20-1), then,

$$4.956 = \mu + \sigma\left(\frac{0.0484}{0.02}\right)$$

[6]See Section 3.4.4.

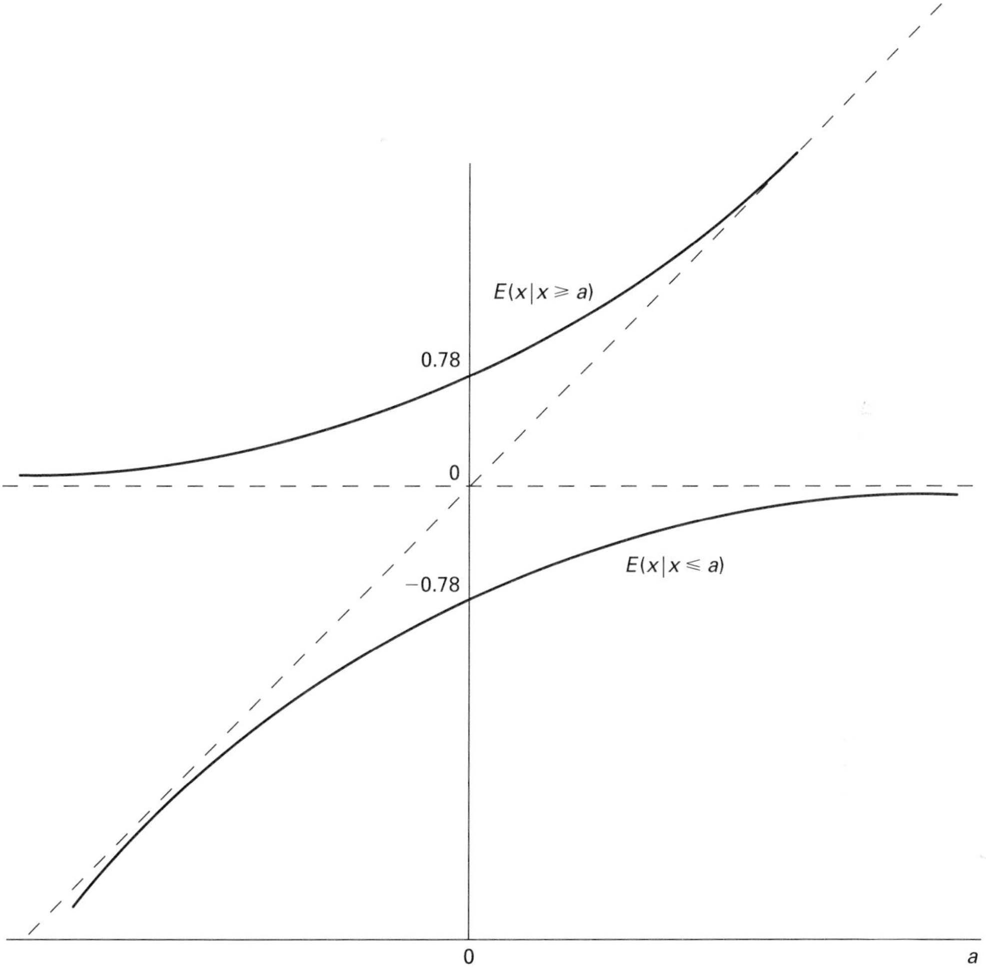

FIGURE 20.2 Mean of the Truncated Normal Distribution.

or

$$\text{(b) } 4.956 = \mu + 2.420\sigma.$$

The solutions to (a) and (b) are

$$\mu = 2.635 \quad \text{and} \quad \sigma = 0.959.$$

To obtain the mean income, we use the result that if $z \sim N[\mu, \sigma^2]$, then $E[e^z] = e^{\mu+\sigma^2/2}$. Inserting our values for μ and σ gives $E[z] = \$22{,}087$.[7]

---

[7]The 1987 *Statistical Abstract of the United States* lists average household income across all groups for the United States as about $25,000.

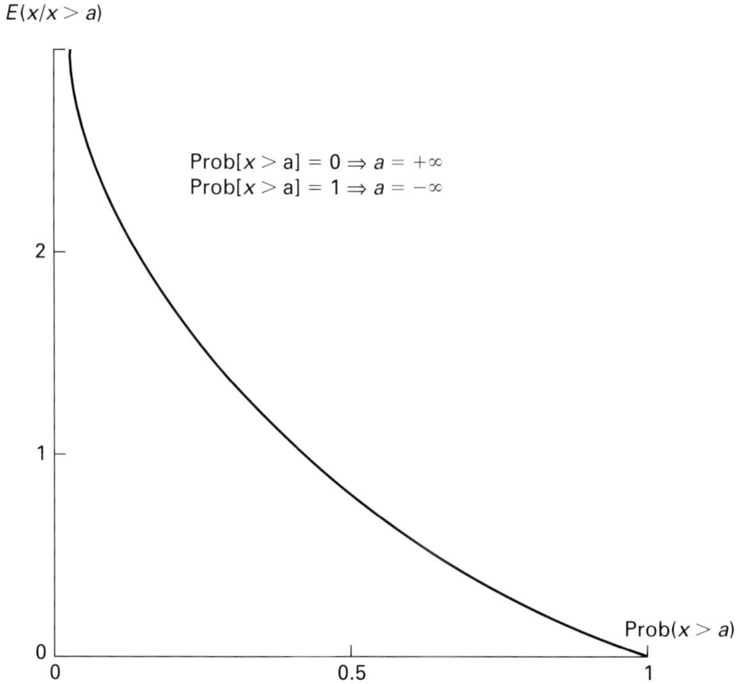

FIGURE 20.3 Conditional Mean as a Function of the Degree of Truncation.

20.2.3. The Truncated Regression Model

In the model of the earlier examples, we now assume that

$$\mu = \boldsymbol{\beta}'\mathbf{x}_i,$$

the deterministic part of the classical regression model. Then

$$y_i = \boldsymbol{\beta}'\mathbf{x}_i + \epsilon_i,$$

where

$$\epsilon_i \sim N[0, \sigma^2],$$

so that

$$y_i \mid \mathbf{x}_i \sim N[\boldsymbol{\beta}'\mathbf{x}_i, \sigma^2].$$

We are interested in the distribution of y_i given that y_i is greater than the truncation point a. This is precisely the model described in Theorem 20.2. It follows that

$$E[y_i \mid y_i > a] = \boldsymbol{\beta}'\mathbf{x}_i + \sigma \frac{\phi[(a - \boldsymbol{\beta}'\mathbf{x}_i)/\sigma]}{1 - \Phi[(a - \boldsymbol{\beta}'\mathbf{x}_i)/\sigma]}. \qquad \textbf{(20-5)}$$

The conditional mean is therefore a nonlinear function of $\mathbf{x}$ and $\boldsymbol{\beta}$.

The marginal effects in this model *in the subpopulation* can be obtained by writing

$$E[y_i \mid y_i > a] = \boldsymbol{\beta}'\mathbf{x}_i + \sigma\lambda(\alpha_i), \qquad \textbf{(20-6)}$$

where now $\alpha_i = (a - \boldsymbol{\beta}'\mathbf{x}_i)/\sigma$. Then

$$\begin{aligned}\frac{\partial E[y_i \mid y_i > a]}{\partial \mathbf{x}_i} &= \boldsymbol{\beta} + \sigma\left(\frac{d\lambda_i}{d\alpha_i}\right)\frac{\partial \alpha_i}{\partial \mathbf{x}_i} \\ &= \boldsymbol{\beta} + \sigma(\lambda_i^2 - \alpha_i\lambda_i)\left(\frac{-\boldsymbol{\beta}}{\sigma}\right) \\ &= \boldsymbol{\beta}(1 - \lambda_i^2 + \alpha_i\lambda_i) \\ &= \boldsymbol{\beta}(1 - \delta(\alpha_i)).\end{aligned} \qquad \textbf{(20-7)}$$

Note the appearance of the truncated variance. Since the truncated variance is between 0 and 1, we conclude that for every element of $\mathbf{x}_i$, the marginal effect is less than the corresponding coefficient. There is a similar **attenuation** of the variance. In the subpopulation $y_i > a$, the regression variance is not σ^2 but

$$\text{Var}[y_i \mid y_i > a] = \sigma^2[1 - \delta(\alpha_i)].$$

Whether the marginal effect in (20-7) or the coefficient $\boldsymbol{\beta}$ itself is of interest depends on the intended inferences of the study. If the analysis is to be confined to the subpopulation, (20-7) is of interest. If the study is intended to extend to the entire population, however, it is the coefficients $\boldsymbol{\beta}$ that are actually of interest.

EXAMPLE 20.5 Marginal Effects in a Truncated Regression

Hausman and Wise (1977) estimated an earnings equation for low-income families.[8] The truncation in their model is from above, with thresholds at poverty levels defined as a function of family size. Their model links the log of earnings to education, a score on an intelligence test, a union membership dummy variable, the number of months in vocational training, a dummy variable equal to one if the individual reported having an illness that limited the ability to work, and age. The assumption implicit in the model is that there is a linear equation connecting these variables in the full population that we seek to study, using data drawn from the subpopulation of people with incomes below the poverty levels. The discussion of the estimates in the article appears to indicate particular attention to the group from which the sample is drawn, not the population at large. (A set of estimates is presented in Example 20.7.)

[8] A similar set of results is presented in Crawford (1975).

20.2.3a. Least Squares Estimation. We now consider estimation of the parameters of the truncated regression. One's first inclination might be to use ordinary least squares. For the subpopulation from which the data are drawn, we could write (20-6) in the form

$$\begin{aligned} y_i \mid y_i > a &= E[y_i \mid y_i > a] + u_i \\ &= \boldsymbol{\beta}'\mathbf{x}_i + \sigma\lambda_i + u_i, \end{aligned} \quad \textbf{(20-8)}$$

where u_i is y_i minus its conditional expectation. By construction, u_i has a zero mean, but it is heteroscedastic:

$$\text{Var}[u_i] = \sigma^2(1 - \lambda_i^2 + \lambda_i\alpha_i) = \sigma^2(1 - \delta_i),$$

which is a function of $\mathbf{x}_i$. If we estimate (20-8) by ordinary least squares regression of $\mathbf{y}$ on $\mathbf{X}$, we have omitted a variable, the nonlinear term λ_i. All the biases that arise because of an omitted variable can be expected.

Without some knowledge of the distribution of $\mathbf{x}$, it is not possible to determine how serious the bias is likely to be. A result obtained by Cheung and Goldberger (1984) is broadly suggestive. If $E[\mathbf{x} \mid y]$ in the full population is a linear function of y, then

$$\text{plim } \mathbf{b} = \boldsymbol{\beta}\tau$$

for some proportionality constant τ. This is consistent with the widely observed (albeit rather rough) proportionality relationship between least squares estimates of this model and consistent maximum likelihood estimates.[9] The proportionality result appears to be quite general. In applications, it is usually found that, compared with consistent maximum likelihood estimates, the OLS estimates are biased toward zero. (See Example 20.7.)

20.2.3b. Maximum Likelihood Estimation. As specified in Theorem 20.1,

$$f(y_i) = \frac{\dfrac{1}{\sigma}\,\phi[(y_i - \boldsymbol{\beta}'\mathbf{x}_i)/\sigma]}{1 - \Phi[(a - \boldsymbol{\beta}'\mathbf{x}_i)/\sigma]}.$$

The log-likelihood is the sum of logs of these densities:

$$\begin{aligned} \ln L = -\frac{n}{2}[\ln(2\pi) + \ln \sigma^2] - \frac{1}{2\sigma^2}\sum_{i=1}^{n}(y_i - \boldsymbol{\beta}'\mathbf{x}_i)^2 \\ - \sum_{i=1}^{n}\ln\left[1 - \Phi\left(\frac{a - \boldsymbol{\beta}'\mathbf{x}_i}{\sigma}\right)\right]. \end{aligned} \quad \textbf{(20-9)}$$

[9] See the appendix in Hausman and Wise (1977) and Greene (1983b) as well.

Maximization, although rather involved because of the extreme nonlinearity of the function, is straightforward in principle using the methods of Chapter 5. After a small amount of manipulation, the necessary conditions for maximizing (20-9) reduce to

$$\frac{\partial \ln L}{\partial \begin{pmatrix} \boldsymbol{\beta} \\ \sigma^2 \end{pmatrix}} = \sum_{i=1}^{n} \begin{pmatrix} \left[\dfrac{y_i - \boldsymbol{\beta}'\mathbf{x}_i}{\sigma^2} - \dfrac{\lambda_i}{\sigma} \right] \mathbf{x}_i \\ -\dfrac{1}{2\sigma^2} + \dfrac{(y_i - \boldsymbol{\beta}'\mathbf{x}_i)^2}{2\sigma^4} - \dfrac{\alpha_i \lambda_i}{2\sigma^2} \end{pmatrix} = \sum_{i=1}^{n} \mathbf{g}_i = \mathbf{0}, \qquad \textbf{(20-10)}$$

where $\alpha_i = (a - \boldsymbol{\beta}'\mathbf{x}_i)/\sigma$ and $\lambda_i = \phi(\alpha_i)/[1 - \Phi(\alpha_i)]$. The Hessian for this model is quite involved. Hausman and Wise suggest using the Berndt et al. estimator during the iterations and to obtain the standard errors instead. This involves summing the outer product of the vectors in (20-10) that are written by individual observation to suggest the computation involved. But as shown in the next example, Olsen's (1978) reparameterization greatly simplifies the problem.

EXAMPLE 20.6 Reparameterized Log-Likelihood

Olsen's (1978) suggested reparameterization brings a quite remarkable simplification to this model. We will examine the standard case of truncation from below at $a = 0$. Let $\theta = 1/\sigma$ and let $\boldsymbol{\gamma} = (1/\sigma)\boldsymbol{\beta}$. Then the log-likelihood function becomes

$$\begin{aligned}
\ln L &= \frac{n}{2}[\ln(2\pi) + n \ln \theta] - \frac{1}{2}\sum_{i=1}^{n}(\theta y_i - \boldsymbol{\gamma}'\mathbf{x}_i)^2 - \sum_{i=1}^{n} \ln \Phi(\boldsymbol{\gamma}'\mathbf{x}_i) \\
\frac{\partial \ln L}{\partial \boldsymbol{\gamma}} &= \sum_{i=1}^{n} (\epsilon_i - \lambda_i)\mathbf{x}_i \\
\frac{\partial \ln L}{\partial \theta} &= \sum_{i=1}^{n} \left(\frac{1}{\theta} + \epsilon_i y_i\right) \\
\frac{\partial^2 \ln L}{\partial \begin{pmatrix} \boldsymbol{\gamma} \\ \theta \end{pmatrix} \partial(\boldsymbol{\gamma}'\,\theta)} &= -\sum_{i=1}^{n} \left[(1 - \delta_i) \begin{pmatrix} \mathbf{x}_i \\ y_i \end{pmatrix} (\mathbf{x}_i\; y_i) + \begin{pmatrix} \mathbf{0} & \mathbf{0} \\ \mathbf{0}' & 1/\theta^2 \end{pmatrix} \right].
\end{aligned}$$

where $\epsilon_i = (\theta y_i - \boldsymbol{\gamma}'\mathbf{x}_i)$, $\alpha_i = \boldsymbol{\gamma}'\mathbf{x}_i$, and $\delta_i = \lambda_i(\lambda_i + \alpha_i)$. In this form, the actual Hessian and Newton's method are the preferred approaches to estimation. The maximization of this log-likelihood function is routine. After estimation of $[\boldsymbol{\gamma}, \theta]$, estimates of $[\boldsymbol{\beta}, \sigma]$ can be recovered as $\hat{\boldsymbol{\beta}} = (1/\hat{\theta})\hat{\boldsymbol{\gamma}}$ and $\hat{\sigma} = 1/\hat{\theta}$. The asymptotic covariance matrix can be estimated as $\mathbf{JVJ}'$, where $\mathbf{V}$ is the negative inverse of the estimated Hessian and **J** is the estimate of the derivatives matrix,

$$\mathbf{J} = \begin{bmatrix} \dfrac{\partial \boldsymbol{\beta}}{\partial \boldsymbol{\gamma}'} & \dfrac{\partial \boldsymbol{\beta}}{\partial \theta} \\ \dfrac{\partial \sigma}{\partial \boldsymbol{\gamma}'} & \dfrac{\partial \sigma}{\partial \theta} \end{bmatrix} = \begin{bmatrix} \dfrac{1}{\theta}\mathbf{I} & \dfrac{-1}{\theta^2}\boldsymbol{\gamma} \\ \mathbf{0}' & \dfrac{-1}{\theta^2} \end{bmatrix}.$$

EXAMPLE 20.7 Estimates of a Truncated Regression Model

Hausman and Wise report the estimates listed in Table 20.1 for the study described in the previous example. Standard errors are given in parentheses. The authors used 684 observations. The marginal effects are computed using (20-7), with an assumed income cutoff of $5,002. In the study, this was used for a family of four. The scale factor for the marginal effects is 0.2456. Since the dependent variable is measured in logarithms, the effects are given in percentages. (The authors did not present these marginal effects.)

The authors note, for example, that "if we interpret the coefficient on education as the rate of return to a year of education, we find that it is quite low, approximately 1.6 percent" (p. 926). (The coefficient 0.0165 is reported for a model with a different specification for the age variable.) The surrounding discussion is obviously directed at low-income people in the sample, for which, in view of (20-7), their observation rather understates the case. Their estimate of the return to a year of education *for the low-income people in their sample* is closer to about 0.4 percent.

TABLE 20.1 Estimated Earnings Equation

	Least Squares	*Maximum Likelihood*	*Mean of X*	*Marginal Effect (%)*
Constant	8.2030 (0.0910)	9.1023 (0.0255)	1.00	
Education	0.0095 (0.0057)	0.0146 (0.0070)	8.76	0.36
IQ	0.0016 (0.0016)	0.0061 (0.0048)	33.5	0.14
Training	0.0022 (0.0016)	0.0065 (0.0031)	3.27	0.14
Union	0.0900 (0.0305)	0.2463 (0.0887)	0.56	
Illness	−0.0761 (0.0378)	−0.2259 (0.1069)	0.21	
Age	−0.0030 (0.0018)	−0.0162 (0.0053)	36.7	−0.39
σ	0.391	0.168	$\sigma_{y\mid x} = 0.306$	

20.3. CENSORED DATA

A very common problem in microeconomic data is censoring of the dependent variable. When the dependent variable is censored, values in a certain range are all transformed to (or reported as) a single value.[10]

EXAMPLE 20.8 Censored Random Variable

We are interested in the number of tickets *demanded* for events at a certain arena. Our only measure is the number actually *sold*. Whenever an event sells out, however, we know that the actual number demanded is larger than the number sold. The number of tickets demanded is censored when it is transformed to obtain the number sold.

Some other examples that have appeared in the empirical literature are as follows:[11]

1. Household purchases of durable goods,[12]
2. The number of extramarital affairs,[13]
3. The number of hours worked by a woman in the labor force,[14]
4. The number of arrests after release from prison,[15]
5. Household expenditure on various commodity groups,[16]
6. Vacation expenditures.[17]

Each of these studies analyzes a dependent variable that is zero for a significant fraction of the observations. Conventional regression methods fail to account for the qualitative difference between *limit* (zero) observations and *nonlimit* (continuous) observations.

20.3.1. The Censored Normal Distribution

The relevant distribution theory for a censored variable is similar to that for a truncated one. Once again, we focus on the normal distribution, as nearly all the received work has been based on an assumption of normality. We also assume that the censoring point is zero, although this is only a convenient normalization.

In a truncated distribution, only the part of distribution above $y = 0$ is relevant to our computations. To make the distribution integrate to one, we

---

[10] See, for example, Section 19.9.2 for an application in a discrete choice model.

[11] More extensive listings may be found in Amemiya (1984) and Maddala (1983).

[12] Tobin (1958).

[13] Fair (1977, 1978).

[14] Quester and Greene (1982).

[15] Witte (1980).

[16] Jarque (1987).

[17] Melenberg and van Soest (1996).

scale it up by the probability that an observation in the untruncated population falls in the range that interests us. When data are censored, the distribution *that applies to the sample data* is a mixture of discrete and continuous distributions. Figure 20.4 shows the effects.

To analyze this distribution, we define a new random variable y transformed from the original one, y^*, by

$$\begin{aligned} y &= 0 \quad \text{if } y^* \leq 0, \\ y &= y^* \quad \text{if } y^* > 0. \end{aligned}$$

The distribution that applies if $y^* \sim N[\mu, \sigma^2]$ is $\text{Prob}(y = 0) = \text{Prob}(y^* \leq 0) = \Phi\left(-\frac{\mu}{\sigma}\right) = 1 - \Phi\left(\frac{\mu}{\sigma}\right)$, and if $y^* > 0$, y has the density of y^*.

This distribution is a mixture of discrete and continuous parts. The total probability is 1, as required, but instead of scaling the second part, we simply assign the full probability in the censored region to the censoring point, in this case, zero.

THEOREM 20.3: Moments of the Censored Normal Variable. *If* $y^* \sim N[\mu, \sigma^2]$ *and* $y = a$ *if* $y^* \leq a$ *or else* $y = y^*$, *then*

$$E[y] = \Phi a + (1 - \Phi)(\mu + \sigma\lambda)$$

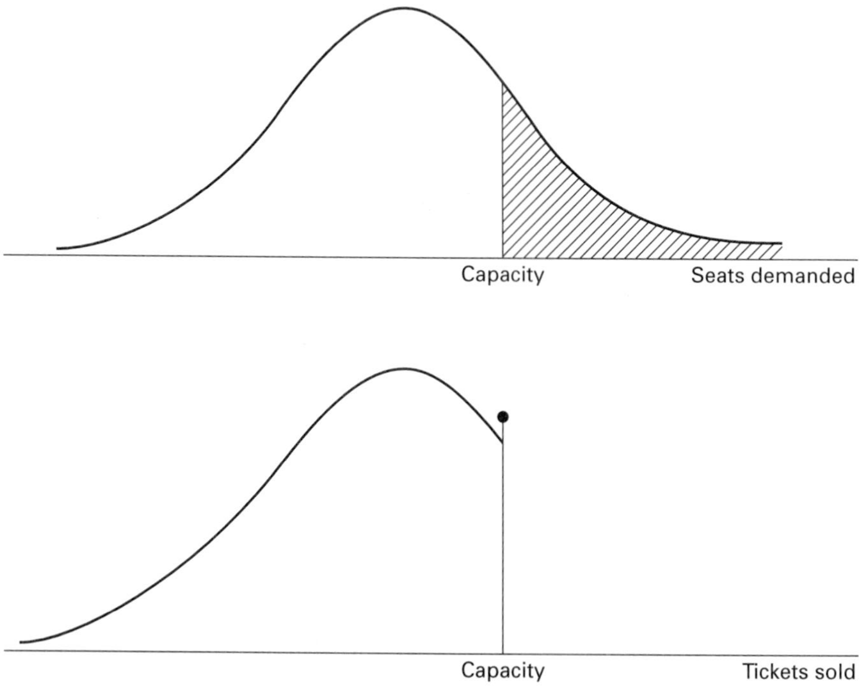

FIGURE 20.4 Partially Censored Distribution.

and

$$\text{Var}[y] = \sigma^2(1 - \Phi)[(1 - \delta) + (\alpha - \lambda)^2\Phi],$$

where $\Phi[(a - \mu)/\sigma] = \Phi(\alpha) = \text{Prob}(y^* \le a) = \Phi$, $\lambda = \phi/(1 - \Phi)$ and $\delta = \lambda^2 - \lambda\alpha$.

Proof: *For the mean,*

$$\begin{aligned} E[y] &= \text{Prob}(y = a) \times E[y \mid y = a] + \text{Prob}(y > a) \times E[y \mid y > a] \\ &= \text{Prob}(y^* \le a) \times a + \text{Prob}(y^* > a) \times E[y^* \mid y^* > a] \\ &= \Phi a + (1 - \Phi)(\mu + \sigma\lambda) \end{aligned}$$

using Theorem 20.2.

For the variance, we use a counterpart to the decomposition in (3-70), that is, Var[y] = E[conditional variance] + Var[conditional mean], *and Theorem 20.2.*

$$\begin{aligned} E[\text{conditional variance}] &= \Phi\text{Var}[y \mid y = a] + (1 - \Phi)\,\text{Var}[y \mid y > a] \\ &= \Phi 0 + (1 - \Phi)\,\text{Var}[y^* \mid y^* > a] \\ &= (1 - \Phi)\sigma^2(1 - \delta). \\ \text{Var}[\text{conditional mean}] &= \Phi\{a - E[y]\}^2 + (1 - \Phi)\{E[y \mid y > a] - E[y]\}^2 \\ &= \Phi\{a - \Phi a - (1 - \Phi)(\mu + \sigma\lambda)\}^2 \\ &\quad + (1 - \Phi)\{(\mu + \sigma\lambda) - \Phi a \\ &\quad - (1 - \Phi)(\mu + \sigma\lambda)\}^2 \\ &= \Phi\{(1 - \Phi)(a - \mu - \sigma\lambda)\}^2 \\ &\quad + (1 - \Phi)\{\Phi(a - \mu - \sigma\lambda)\}^2. \end{aligned}$$

In the second term, a squared −1 has been dropped. Substitute $a - \mu = \sigma\alpha$ *and collect terms to obtain*

$$\begin{aligned} \text{Var}[\text{conditional mean}] &= \{\Phi(1 - \Phi)^2 + (1 - \Phi)\Phi^2\}\sigma^2(\alpha - \lambda)^2 \\ &= \Phi(1 - \Phi)\sigma^2(\alpha - \lambda)^2. \end{aligned}$$

Finally, the sum is

$$\text{Var}[y] = \sigma^2(1 - \Phi)[(1 - \delta) + (\alpha - \lambda)^2\Phi].$$

For the special case of $a = 0$, the mean simplifies to

$$E[y \mid a = 0] = \Phi\left(\frac{\mu}{\sigma}\right)(\mu + \sigma\lambda), \quad \text{where } \lambda = \frac{\phi(\mu/\sigma)}{\Phi(\mu/\sigma)}.$$

For censoring of the upper part of the distribution instead of the lower, it is only necessary to reverse the role of Φ and $1 - \Phi$ and redefine λ as in Theorem 20.2.

EXAMPLE 20.9 Censored Distribution

To continue Example 20.8, suppose that the arena in question has 20,000 seats and, in a recent season, sold out 25 percent of the time. If the average attendance, including sellouts, was 18,000, what are the mean and standard deviation of the demand for seats? According to Theorem 20.3, the 18,000 is an estimate of

$$E[\text{sales}] = 20{,}000(1 - \Phi) + [\mu + \sigma\lambda]\Phi.$$

Since this is censoring from above, rather than below, $\lambda = -\phi(\alpha)/\Phi(\alpha)$. The argument of Φ, ϕ, and λ is $\alpha = (20{,}000 - \mu)/\sigma$. If 25 percent of the events are sellouts, $\Phi = 0.75$. Inverting the standard normal at 0.75 gives $\alpha = 0.675$. In addition, if $\alpha = 0.675$, then $-\phi(0.675)/0.75 = \lambda = -0.424$. This provides a pair of equations in μ and σ:

$$18{,}000 = 0.25(20{,}000) + 0.75(\mu - 0.424\sigma)$$

and

$$0.675\sigma = 20{,}000 - \mu.$$

The solutions are $\sigma = 2426$ and $\mu = 18{,}362$.

For comparison, suppose that we were told that the mean of 18,000 applies only to the events that were *not* sold out and that, on average, the arena sells out 25 percent of the time. Now our estimates would be obtained from the equations

$$18{,}000 = \mu - 0.424\sigma$$

and

$$0.675\sigma = 20{,}000 - \mu.$$

The solutions are $\sigma = 1820$ and $\mu = 18{,}772$.

20.3.2. The Censored Regression Model — Tobit Analysis

The regression model based on the preceding discussion is referred to as the **censored regression model** or the **tobit model.**[18] The regression is obtained by making the mean in the preceding correspond to a classical regression model. The general formulation is usually given in terms of an index function,

$$\begin{aligned} y_i^* &= \boldsymbol{\beta}'\mathbf{x}_i + \epsilon_i, \\ y_i &= 0 \quad \text{if } y_i^* \leq 0, \\ y_i &= y_i^* \quad \text{if } y_i^* > 0. \end{aligned} \qquad \textbf{(20-11)}$$

There are potentially three conditional mean functions to consider, depending on the purpose of the study. For the index variable, sometimes called the *latent variable*, $E[y_i^*]$ is $\boldsymbol{\beta}'\mathbf{x}_i$. If the data are always censored, however, this

[18]This is in reference to Tobin (1958), where the model was first proposed.

will usually not be useful. Consistent with Theorem 20.3, for an observation randomly drawn from the population, which may or may not be censored,

$$E[y_i \mid \mathbf{x}_i] = \Phi\left(\frac{\boldsymbol{\beta}'\mathbf{x}_i}{\sigma}\right)(\boldsymbol{\beta}'\mathbf{x}_i + \sigma\lambda_i),$$

where

$$\lambda_i = \frac{\phi(\boldsymbol{\beta}'\mathbf{x}_i/\sigma)}{\Phi(\boldsymbol{\beta}'\mathbf{x}_i/\sigma)}. \tag{20-12}$$

Finally, if we intend to confine our attention to uncensored observations, the results of the previous section apply.[19] It is an unresolved question which of these functions should be used for computing predicted values from this model. Intuition suggests that $E[y_i \mid \mathbf{x}_i]$ is correct, but authors differ on this point. For the setting in Example 20.8, for predicting the number of tickets sold, say, to plan for an upcoming event, the censored mean is obviously the relevant quantity. On the other hand, if the objective is to study the need for a new facility, the mean of the latent variable y_i^* would be more interesting.

There are differences in the marginal effects in the models as well. For the index variable,

$$\frac{\partial E[y_i^* \mid \mathbf{x}_i]}{\partial \mathbf{x}_i} = \boldsymbol{\beta}.$$

But for y, given the censoring, the marginal effect is only[20]

$$\frac{\partial E[y_i \mid \mathbf{x}_i]}{\partial \mathbf{x}_i} = \boldsymbol{\beta}\Phi\left(\frac{\boldsymbol{\beta}'\mathbf{x}_i}{\sigma}\right).$$

Once again, which one is relevant depends on the purpose of the estimates.

McDonald and Mofitt (1980) suggested a useful decomposition of $\partial E[y_i^* \mid \mathbf{x}_i]/\partial \mathbf{x}_i$,

$$\frac{\partial E[y_i \mid \mathbf{x}_i]}{\partial \mathbf{x}_i} = \boldsymbol{\beta} \times [\Phi_i(1 - \lambda_i(\alpha_i + \lambda_i)) + \phi_i(\alpha_i + \lambda_i)],$$

where

$$\Phi_i = \Phi(\boldsymbol{\beta}'\mathbf{x}_i/\sigma) = \Phi(\alpha_i)$$

and

$$\lambda_i = \phi_i/\Phi_i.$$

[19] This does not mean that limit observations should be discarded, since this just produces the truncated regression setting. This is no more amenable to least squares than the censored data model.

[20] The result that the marginal effect is obtained by scaling the parameters by the probability in the uncensored region carries over to more general settings as well. Rosett and Nelson (1975) and Nakamura and Nakamura (1983) consider a model with censoring on both ends of the distribution. For a model in which values of y^* less than or equal to a are reported as a and values greater than or equal to b are reported as b, $\partial E[y_i \mid \mathbf{x}_i]/\partial \mathbf{x}_i = \boldsymbol{\beta} \times \text{Prob}(a \le y_i^* \le b) = \boldsymbol{\beta}[\Phi((b - \boldsymbol{\beta}'\mathbf{x}_i)/\sigma) - \Phi((a - \boldsymbol{\beta}'\mathbf{x}_i)/\sigma)]$.

Taking the two parts separately, this decomposes the slope vector into

$$\frac{\partial E[y_i \mid \mathbf{x}_i]}{\partial \mathbf{x}_i} = \text{Prob}[y_i > 0]\frac{\partial E[y_i \mid \mathbf{x}_i, y_i > 0]}{\partial \mathbf{x}_i} + E[y_i \mid \mathbf{x}_i, y_i > 0]\frac{\partial \text{Prob}[y_i > 0]}{\partial \mathbf{x}_i}.$$

Thus, a change in $\mathbf{x}_i$ has two effects. It affects the conditional mean of y_i^* in the positive part of the distribution, and it affects the probability that the observation will fall in that part of the distribution.

EXAMPLE 20.10 Estimated Tobit Equations for Hours Worked

In their study of the number of hours worked in a survey year by a large sample of wives, Quester and Greene (1982) were interested in whether wives whose marriages were statistically more likely to dissolve hedged against that possibility by spending, on average, more time working.[21] They reported the tobit estimates given in Table 20.2. The last figure in the table implies that a very large proportion of the women reported zero hours, so least squares regression would be inappropriate.

TABLE 20.2 Tobit Estimates of an Hours-Worked Equation

	White Wives		*Black Wives*	
	Coefficient	***Slope***	***Coefficient***	***Slope***
Constant	−1803.13 (−8.64)		−2753.87 (−9.68)	
Small kids	−1324.84 (−19.78)	−385.89	−824.19 (−10.14)	−376.53
Education difference	−48.08 (−4.77)	−14.00	22.59 (1.96)	10.32
Relative wage	312.07 (5.71)	90.90	286.39 (3.32)	130.93
Second marriage	175.85 (3.47)	51.51	25.33 (0.41)	11.57
Mean divorce probability	417.39 (6.52)	121.58	481.02 (5.28)	219.75
High divorce probability	670.22 (8.40)	195.22	578.66 (5.33)	264.36
σ	1559	618	1511	826
Sample size	7459		2798	
Proportion working	0.29		0.46	

[21] In a not completely unrelated study done at roughly the same time, Fair (1978) applied the tobit model to a study of the allocation of leisure time between spouse and paramour.

The figures in parentheses are the ratio of the coefficient estimate to the estimated asymptotic standard error. The dependent variable is hours worked in the survey year. "Small kids" is a dummy variable indicating whether there were children in the household. The "education difference" and "relative wage" variables compare husband and wife on these two dimensions. The wage rate used for wives was predicted using a previously estimated regression model and is thus available for all individuals, whether working or not. "Second marriage" is a dummy variable. Divorce probabilities were produced by a large microsimulation model presented in another study.[22] The variables used here were dummy variables indicating "mean" if the predicted probability was between 0.01 and 0.03 and "high" if it was greater than 0.03. The "slopes" are the marginal effects described earlier.

Note the marginal effects compared with the tobit coefficients. Likewise, the estimate of σ is quite misleading as an estimate of the standard deviation of hours worked.

The effects of the divorce probability variables were as expected and were quite large. One of the questions raised in connection with this study was whether the divorce probabilities could reasonably be treated as independent variables. It might be that for these individuals, the number of hours worked was a significant determinant of the probability.

20.3.3. Estimation

Estimation of this model is very similar to that of truncated regression. The tobit model has become so routine, and been incorporated in so many computer packages, that despite formidable obstacles in years past, estimation is now essentially on the level of ordinary linear regression.[23] The log-likelihood for the censored regression model is

$$\ln L = \sum_{y_i > 0} -\frac{1}{2}\left[\ln(2\pi) + \ln\sigma^2 + \frac{(y_i - \boldsymbol{\beta}'\mathbf{x}_i)^2}{\sigma^2}\right] + \sum_{y_i = 0} \ln\left[1 - \Phi\left(\frac{\boldsymbol{\beta}'\mathbf{x}_i}{\sigma}\right)\right]. \tag{20-13}$$

The two parts correspond to the classical regression for the nonlimit observations and the relevant probabilities for the limit observations, respectively. This is a nonstandard type of likelihood, since it is a mixture of discrete and continuous distributions. In a seminal paper, Amemiya (1973b) showed that despite the complications, proceeding in the usual fashion to maximize ln L would produce an estimator with all of the familiar desirable properties assumed for MLEs.

---

[22] Orcutt et al. (1976).

[23] See Hall (1984).

The log-likelihood function is fairly involved, but Olsen's (1978) reparameterization (see Example 20.6) simplifies things considerably. With $\boldsymbol{\gamma} = \boldsymbol{\beta}/\sigma$ and $\theta = 1/\sigma$, the log-likelihood is

$$\ln L = \sum_{y_i>0} -\frac{1}{2}[\ln(2\pi) - \ln\theta^2 + (\theta y_i - \boldsymbol{\gamma}'\mathbf{x}_i)^2] + \sum_{y_i=0} \ln[1 - \Phi(\boldsymbol{\gamma}'\mathbf{x}_i)]. \tag{20-14}$$

The results in this setting are now very similar to those for the truncated regression in Example 20.6. As before, the Hessian is always negative definite, so Newton's method is simple to use and usually converges quickly. After convergence, the original parameters can be recovered using $\sigma = 1/\theta$ and $\boldsymbol{\beta} = \boldsymbol{\gamma}/\theta$. The asymptotic covariance matrix for these estimates can be obtained from that for the estimates of $[\boldsymbol{\gamma}, \theta]$ using $\text{Asy. Var}[\hat{\boldsymbol{\beta}}, \hat{\sigma}] = \mathbf{J}\,\text{Asy. Var}[\hat{\boldsymbol{\gamma}}, \hat{\theta}]\mathbf{J}'$, where $\mathbf{J}$ was given in the earlier example.

Researchers often compute ordinary least squares estimates despite their inconsistency. Almost without exception, it is found that the OLS estimates are smaller in absolute value than the MLEs. A striking empirical regularity is that the maximum likelihood estimates can often be approximated by dividing the OLS estimates by the proportion of nonlimit observations in the sample.[24]

Although ordinary least squares is demonstrably inconsistent in this setting, a number of consistent alternatives to maximum likelihood estimation have been proposed. One possibility is to apply nonlinear least squares to the conditional mean function of either the tobit model using the full sample or to the truncated regression using only the nonlimit observations.[25] A second possibility is to use Heckman's two-step correction to ordinary least squares, which is described in Section 20.4.[26]

EXAMPLE 20.11 Least Squares Versus Maximum Likelihood

For their second regression in Example 20.10, Quester and Greene also obtained the least squares results listed in Table 20.3.

The marginal effects in the model are obtained by scaling the maximum likelihood estimates by $\hat{\Phi} = 0.4568 = \Phi(\hat{\boldsymbol{\beta}}'\overline{\mathbf{x}}/\hat{\sigma})$. The scale factor for the least squares estimates is $1/P$, where P is the proportion of nonlimit observations in the sample, 0.4601. There are two things to note. First, as expected, the scaled least squares coefficients closely resemble the consistent maximum likelihood estimates. Second, the marginal effects estimated for the tobit model rather closely resemble the least squares estimates. We recall the discussion of nonlinear regression models in Chapter 10. The slopes of the highly nonlinear conditional mean function in this model appear to be approximated rather well by the OLS estimates.

[24] This is explored further in Greene (1980b), Goldberger (1981), and Cheung and Goldberger (1984).

[25] See Amemiya (1985, Chap. 10).

[26] See Heckman (1979), Wales and Woodland (1980), Greene (1981), Stapleton and Young (1981), Paarsch (1984), and Nelson (1984).

TABLE 20.3 Estimated Hours Equation

Variable	*MLE*	*Marginal Effect*	*Least Squares*	*Scaled Least Squares*
Small kids	−824.19	−376.53	−352.63	−766.59
Education difference	22.59	10.32	11.47	24.93
Relative wage	286.39	130.93	123.95	269.46
Second marriage	25.33	11.57	13.14	28.57
Mean divorce probability	481.02	219.75	219.22	476.57
High divorce probability	578.66	264.36	244.17	530.80

20.3.4. Some Issues in Specification

Two issues that commonly arise in microeconomic data, heteroscedasticity and nonnormality, have been analyzed at length in the tobit setting.[27]

20.3.4a. Heteroscedasticity. Maddala and Nelson (1975), Hurd (1979), Arabmazar and Schmidt (1982a, b), and Brown and Moffitt (1982) all have varying degrees of pessimism regarding how inconsistent the maximum likelihood estimator will be when heteroscedasticity occurs. Not surprisingly, the degree of censoring is the primary determinant. Unfortunately, all the analyses have been carried out in the setting of very specific models—for example, involving only a single dummy variable or one with groupwise heteroscedasticity—so the primary lesson is the very general conclusion that heteroscedasticity emerges as an obviously serious problem.

One can approach the heteroscedasticity problem directly. Petersen and Waldman (1981) present the computations needed to estimate a tobit model with heteroscedasticity of several types. Replacing σ with σ_i in the log-likelihood function and including σ_i^2 in the summations produces the needed generality. Specification of a particular model for σ_i provides the empirical model for estimation.

EXAMPLE 20.12 Multiplicative Heteroscedasticity in the Tobit Model

Petersen and Waldman analyzed the volume of short interest in a cross section of common stocks. The regressors included a measure of the market component of heterogeneous expectations as measured by the firm's BETA coefficient; a company-specific measure of heterogeneous expectations, NONMARKET; the NUMBER of analysts making earnings forecasts for the company;

[27]Two recent symposia that contain numerous results on these subjects are Blundell (1987) and Duncan (1986b). An application that explores these two issues in detail is Melenberg and van Soest (1996).

the number of common shares to be issued for the acquisition of another firm, MERGER; and a dummy variable for the existence of OPTIONs. They report the results listed in Table 20.4 for a model in which the variance is assumed to be of the form $\sigma_i^2 = \exp(\boldsymbol{\alpha}'\mathbf{x}_i)$. The values in parentheses are the ratio of the coefficient to the estimated asymptotic standard error.

The effect of heteroscedasticity on the estimates is extremely large. A test of the hypothesis that $\boldsymbol{\alpha} = \mathbf{0}$ (except for the constant term) can be based on the likelihood ratio statistic. For these results, the statistic is $-2[-547.3 - (-466.27)] = 162.06$. This is asymptotically distributed as chi-squared with five degrees of freedom. The sample value exceeds the critical value in the table, so the hypothesis can be rejected.

In the preceding example, we carried out a likelihood ratio test against the hypothesis of homoscedasticity. It would be desirable to be able to carry out the test without having to estimate the unrestricted model. A Lagrange multiplier test can be used for that purpose. Consider the heteroscedastic tobit model in which we specify that

$$\sigma_i^2 = \sigma^2 e^{\boldsymbol{\alpha}'\mathbf{w}_i}. \tag{20-15}$$

This is a fairly general model that includes many familiar ones as special cases. The null hypothesis of homoscedasticity is $\boldsymbol{\alpha} = \mathbf{0}$. (We used this specification in the probit model in Section 19.4.1b and in the linear regression model in Example 12.15.) After some algebra, the necessary conditions for maximization of the log-likelihood *under the null hypothesis of homoscedasticity* reduce to the

TABLE 20.4 Estimates of a Tobit Model

	Homoscedastic	*Heteroscedastic*	
	β	β	α
Constant	−18.28	−4.11	−0.47
	(5.10)	(3.28)	(0.60)
BETA	10.97	2.22	1.20
	(3.61)	(2.00)	(1.81)
NONMARKET	0.65	0.12	0.08
	(7.41)	(1.90)	(7.55)
NUMBER	0.75	0.33	0.15
	(5.74)	(4.50)	(4.58)
MERGER	0.50	0.24	0.06
	(5.90)	(3.00)	(4.17)
OPTION	2.56	2.96	0.83
	(1.51)	(2.99)	(1.70)
Log *L*	−547.30	−466.27	
Sample size	200	200	

following, in which subscripts are used to indicate partial differentiation of the log-likelihood:

$$\ln L_{\boldsymbol{\beta}} = \sum_{i=1}^{n} a_i \mathbf{x}_i, \qquad \ln L_{\sigma}^2 = \sum_{i=1}^{n} b_i, \qquad \ln L_{\boldsymbol{\alpha}} = \sum_{i=1}^{n} \sigma^2 b_i \mathbf{w}_i,$$

where z_i is 1 if y_i is positive and 0 otherwise,

$$\begin{aligned} a_i &= z_i\left(\frac{\epsilon_i}{\sigma^2}\right) + (1 - z_i)\left(\frac{(-1)\lambda_i}{\sigma}\right), \\ b_i &= z_i\left(\frac{(\epsilon_i^2/\sigma^2 - 1)}{2\sigma^2}\right) + (1 - z_i)\left(\frac{(\boldsymbol{\beta}'\mathbf{x}_i)\lambda_i}{2\sigma^3}\right), \\ \lambda_i &= \frac{\phi(\boldsymbol{\beta}'\mathbf{x})}{1 - \Phi_i}. \end{aligned} \tag{20-16}$$

The sums are taken over all observations, and all functions involving unknown parameters (ϵ, ϕ, $\boldsymbol{\beta}'\mathbf{x}_i$, λ_i, etc.) are evaluated at the restricted (homoscedastic) maximum likelihood estimates. To construct the Lagrange multiplier statistic, we use the Berndt et al. estimator for the information matrix. Under the null hypothesis, at the maximum likelihood estimates, $\ln L_{\boldsymbol{\beta}}$ and $\ln L_{\sigma}^2$ are both zero. Therefore, the statistic can be computed as

$$\text{LM} = \ln L_{\boldsymbol{\alpha}}' \mathbf{Q}_{\boldsymbol{\alpha\alpha}'} \ln L_{\boldsymbol{\alpha}}, \tag{20-17}$$

where $\ln L_{\boldsymbol{\alpha}}$ is as above and $\mathbf{Q}_{\boldsymbol{\alpha\alpha}'}$ is the lower right block in

$$\mathbf{Q} = \left[\sum_{i=1}^{n} \begin{bmatrix} a_i^2\mathbf{x}_i\mathbf{x}_i' & a_i b_i \mathbf{x}_i & \sigma^2 a_i b_i \mathbf{x}_i \mathbf{w}_i' \\ a_i b_i \mathbf{x}_i' & b_i^2 & \sigma^2 b_i^2 \mathbf{w}_i' \\ \sigma^2 a_i b_i \mathbf{w}_i \mathbf{x}_i' & \sigma^2 b_i^2 \mathbf{w}_i & \sigma^4 b_i^2 \mathbf{w}_i \mathbf{w}_i' \end{bmatrix}\right]^{-1}.$$

As often happens with LM statistics, there is a simple way to construe this one as the R^2 in a regression. Let $\mathbf{g}_i = [a_i\mathbf{x}_i, b_i, \sigma^2 b_i \mathbf{w}_i]$ define the ith row of a derivatives matrix $\mathbf{G}$. Then $\mathbf{Q} = [\mathbf{G}'\mathbf{G}]^{-1}$. Also, when they are evaluated at the restricted MLEs, the sums of the derivatives defined above are

$$\sum_{i=1}^{n} \mathbf{g}_i = \begin{bmatrix} \ln L_{\boldsymbol{\beta}} \\ \ln L_{\sigma^2} \\ \ln L_{\boldsymbol{\alpha}} \end{bmatrix} = \begin{bmatrix} \mathbf{0} \\ 0 \\ \ln L_{\boldsymbol{\alpha}} \end{bmatrix},$$

so

$$\text{LM} = \mathbf{i}'\mathbf{G}[\mathbf{G}'\mathbf{G}]^{-1}\mathbf{G}'\mathbf{i} = nR^2$$

in the regression of a column of ones on the $K + 1 + P$ derivatives of the log-likelihood function for the model with multiplicative heteroscedasticity, evaluated at the estimates from the restricted model. (If there were no limit observations, it would reduce to the Breusch–Pagan statistic discussed in Chapter 12.) Given the maximum likelihood estimates of the tobit model coefficients, it is quite simple to compute. The statistic is asymptotically distributed as chi-squared with degrees of freedom equal to the number of variables in $\mathbf{w}_i$.

20.3.4b. Misspecification of Prob[$y^* < 0$]. In an early study in this literature, Cragg (1971) proposed a somewhat more general model in which the probability of a limit observation is independent of the regression model for the nonlimit data. One can imagine, for instance, the decision on whether or not to purchase a car as being different from the decision on how much to spend on the car, having decided to buy one. A related problem raised by Fin and Schmidt (1984) is that in the tobit model, a variable that increases the probability of an observation being a nonlimit observation also increases the mean of the variable. They cite as an example loss due to fire in buildings. Older buildings might be more likely to have fires, so that $\partial\ \text{Prob}[y_i > 0]/\partial\ \text{age}_i > 0$, but because of the greater value of newer buildings, incur smaller losses when they do, so that $\partial E[y_i \mid y_i > 0]/\partial\ \text{age}_i < 0$. This would require the coefficient on age to have different signs in the two functions. This is impossible in the tobit model because they are the same coefficient.

A more general model that accommodates these objections is as follows.

1. Decision equation:

$$\begin{aligned} \text{Prob}[y_i^* > 0] &= \Phi(\boldsymbol{\gamma}'\mathbf{x}_i), \qquad & z_i &= 1 \quad \text{if } y_i^* > 0, \\ \text{Prob}[y_i^* \le 0] &= 1 - \Phi(\boldsymbol{\gamma}'\mathbf{x}_i), \qquad & z_i &= 0 \quad \text{if } y_i^* \le 0. \end{aligned} \tag{20-18}$$

2. Regression equation for nonlimit observations:

$$E[y_i \mid z_i = 1] = \boldsymbol{\beta}'\mathbf{x}_i + \sigma\lambda_i,$$

according to Theorem 20.2.

This is a combination of the truncated regression model of Section 20.2 and the univariate probit model of Chapter 19, which suggests a method of analyzing it. The tobit model of this section arises if $\boldsymbol{\gamma}$ equals $\boldsymbol{\beta}/\sigma$. The parameters of the decision equation can be estimated independently using the truncated regression model of Section 20.2. A recent application is Melenberg and van Soest (1996).

Fin and Schmidt considered testing the restriction of the tobit model. Based only on the tobit model, they devised a Lagrange multiplier statistic that, although a bit cumbersome algebraically, can be computed without great difficulty. If one is able to estimate the truncated regression model, the tobit model, and the probit model separately, there is a simpler way to test the hypothesis. The tobit log-likelihood is the sum of the log-likelihoods for the truncated regression and probit models. [To show this, add and subtract $\Sigma_{y_i=1} \ln \Phi(\boldsymbol{\beta}'\mathbf{x}_i/\sigma)$ in (20-13). This produces (20-9) for the truncated regression model plus (19-20) for the probit model.] Therefore, a likelihood ratio statistic can be computed using

$$\lambda = -2[\ln L_T - (\ln L_P + \ln L_{TR})],$$

where

$$\begin{aligned} L_T &= \text{likelihood for the tobit model in (20-13), with the same coefficients,} \\ L_P &= \text{likelihood for the probit model in (19-20), fit separately,} \\ L_{TR} &= \text{likelihood for the truncated regression model in (20-9), fit separately.} \end{aligned}$$

20.3.4c. Nonnormality. Nonnormality is an especially difficult problem in this setting. It has been shown that if the underlying disturbances are not normally distributed, the usual estimator based on (20-13) is inconsistent. Research is ongoing both on alternative estimators and on methods for testing for this type of misspecification.[28]

One approach to the estimation is to use an alternative distribution. Kalbfleisch and Prentice (1980) present a unifying treatment that includes several distributions such as the exponential, lognormal, and Weibull. (Their primary focus is on survival analysis in a medical statistics setting. This is an interesting convergence of the techniques in very different disciplines.) Of course, assuming some other specific distribution does not necessarily solve the problem and may make it worse. A preferable alternative would be to devise an estimator that is robust to changes in the distribution. Powell's (1981, 1984) least absolute deviations (LAD) estimator appears to offer some promise.[29] The main drawback to its use is its computational complexity. An extensive application of the LAD estimator is Melenberg and van Soest (1996). Although estimation in the nonnormal case is relatively difficult, testing for this failure of the model is worthwhile to assess the estimates obtained by the conventional methods. Among the tests that have been developed are Hausman tests, Lagrange multiplier tests,[30] and conditional moment tests.[31] The conditional moment tests are described in the next section.

To employ a Hausman test, we require an estimator that is consistent and efficient under the null hypothesis but inconsistent under the alternative—the tobit estimator with normality—and an estimator that is consistent under both hypotheses but inefficient under the null hypothesis. For estimation of $\boldsymbol{\beta}$, this requires a robust estimator of $\boldsymbol{\beta}$, which restores the difficulties of the previous paragraph. Nelson (1981) and Ruud (1982) simplified the problem by considering, instead of $\boldsymbol{\beta}$, $\text{Prob}[y > 0]$ from the marginal distribution of y and $E[(1/n)\mathbf{X}'\mathbf{y}]$, both of which can be estimated using sample moments. Recent applications [e.g., Melenberg and van Soest (1996)] have used the Hausman test to compare the tobit/normal estimator with Powell's consistent, but inefficient (robust), LAD estimator.

Another approach to testing is to embed the normal distribution in some other distribution, then use an LM test for the normal specification. Ruud (1984, 1986) suggested a modification of the normal CDF,

$$\text{Prob}[\epsilon_i < t] = F(t) = \Phi(t + \delta_0 + \delta_1 t^2 + \delta_2 t^3).$$

A nonzero δ_0 offsets the median of the distribution from zero, whereas δ_1 and δ_2 create the nonnormality more generally. The standard model results if

[28]See Duncan (1983, 1986b), Goldberger (1983), and Fernandez (1986). We will examine one of the tests more closely in the following section.

[29]See Duncan (1986a,b) for a symposium on the subject and Amemiya (1984). Additional references are Newey et al. (1990) and Robinson (1988).

[30]Bera and Jarque (1981, 1982).

[31]See, for example, Nelson (1981).

$\boldsymbol{\delta} = (0, 0, 0)$. In computing the probabilities, based on $F(t)$, $\boldsymbol{\beta}'\mathbf{x}_i$ will play the role of t. If the model contains a constant term, δ_0 will not be identified, so for the case we are considering here, the normalization $\delta_0 = 0$ would be imposed. Chesher and Irish (1987) have devised an LM test of normality in the tobit model based on **generalized residuals** that is equivalent to an LM test of $\delta_1 = \delta_2 = 0$ in this model. In many models, including the tobit model, Chesher and Irish's generalized residuals can be computed as the derivatives of the log-densities with respect to the constant term, so

$$e_i = \frac{1}{\sigma^2}\left[z_i(y_i - \boldsymbol{\beta}'\mathbf{x}_i) + (1 - z_i)\sigma\left(\frac{\phi_i}{1 - \Phi_i}\right)\right],$$

where z_i is defined in (20-18). This is an estimate of ϵ_i that accounts for the censoring in the distribution. By construction, $E[e_i] = 0$, and if the model actually does contain a constant term, then $\Sigma_{i=1}^{n} e_i \equiv 0$ since this is the first of the necessary conditions for the MLE. The test is then carried out by regressing a column of 1s on $\mathbf{a}_i = [e_i\mathbf{x}_i, b_i, e_i^3, e_i^4 - 3e_i^2]$, where b_i is defined in (20-16). Note that the first $K + 1$ variables in $\mathbf{a}_i$ are the derivatives of the tobit log-likelihood. Let $\mathbf{A}$ be the $n \times (K + 3)$ matrix with ith row equal to $\mathbf{a}_i'$. Then $\mathbf{A} = [\mathbf{G}, \mathbf{M}]$, where the $K + 1$ columns of $\mathbf{G}$ are the derivatives of the tobit log-likelihood and the two columns in $\mathbf{M}$ are the last two variables in $\mathbf{a}_i$. Then the chi-squared statistic is nR^2 as usual; that is,

$$\text{LM} = \mathbf{i}'\mathbf{A}(\mathbf{A}'\mathbf{A})^{-1}\mathbf{A}'\mathbf{i}.$$

But the necessary conditions that define the MLE are $\mathbf{i}'\mathbf{G} = \mathbf{0}$, so the first $K + 1$ elements of $\mathbf{i}'\mathbf{A}$ are zero. Using (2-66), then, the LM statistic becomes

$$\text{LM} = \mathbf{i}'\mathbf{M}[\mathbf{M}'\mathbf{M} - \mathbf{M}'\mathbf{G}(\mathbf{G}'\mathbf{G})^{-1}\mathbf{G}'\mathbf{M}]^{-1}\mathbf{M}'\mathbf{i}.$$

This is a chi-squared statistic with two degrees of freedom. Note the similarity to (20-17), where a test for homoscedasticity is carried out by the same method. As emerges so often in this framework, the test of the distribution actually focuses on the skewness and kurtosis of the residuals.

20.3.4d. Conditional Moment Tests. Pagan and Vella (1989) (see, as well, Ruud (1984)) describe a set of conditional moment tests of the specification of the tobit model.[32,33] We will consider three:

[32]Their survey is quite general and includes other models, specifications, and estimation methods. We will consider only the simplest cases here. The reader is referred to their paper for formal presentation of these results.

[33]Developing specification tests for the tobit model has been a popular enterprise. A sampling of the received literature includes Nelson (1981), Bera et al. (1982), Chesher and Irish (1987), Chesher et al. (1985), Gourieroux et al. (1984, 1987), Newey (1986), Rivers and Vuong (1988), Horowitz and Neumann (1989), and Pagan and Vella (1989). Newey (1985a,b) are useful references on the general subject of conditional moment testing. More general treatments of specification testing are Godfrey (1988) and Ruud (1984).

1. The variables $\mathbf{z}$ have not been erroneously omitted from the model.
2. The disturbances in the model are homoscedastic.
3. The underlying disturbances in the model are normally distributed.

For the third of these, we will take the standard approach of examining the third and fourth moments, which for the normal distribution are 0 and $3\sigma^4$, respectively.[34] The underlying motivation for the tests can be made with reference to the regression part of the tobit model in (20-11),

$$y_i^* = \boldsymbol{\beta}'\mathbf{x}_i + \epsilon_i.$$

Neglecting for the moment that we only observe y_i^* subject to the censoring, the three hypotheses imply the following expectations:

1. $E[\mathbf{z}_i(y_i - \boldsymbol{\beta}'\mathbf{x}_i)] = \mathbf{0}$,
2. $E\{\mathbf{z}_i[(y_i - \boldsymbol{\beta}'\mathbf{x}_i)^2 - \sigma^2]\} = \mathbf{0}$,
3. $E[(y_i - \boldsymbol{\beta}'\mathbf{x}_i)^3] = 0$ and $E[(y_i - \boldsymbol{\beta}'\mathbf{x}_i)^4 - 3\sigma^4] = 0$.

In (1), the variables in $\mathbf{z}_i$ would be one or more variables not already in the model. We are interested in assessing whether they should be or not. In (2), presumably, although not necessarily, $\mathbf{z}_i$ would be the regressors in the model. For the present, we will assume that y^* is observed directly, without censoring. That is, we will construct the CM tests for the classical linear regression model. Then we will go back to the necessary step and make the modification needed to account for the censoring of the dependent variable.

Conditional moment tests are described in Section 11.6.2. To review, for a model estimated by maximum likelihood, the statistic is

$$C = \mathbf{i}'\mathbf{M}[\mathbf{M}'\mathbf{M} - \mathbf{M}'\mathbf{G}(\mathbf{G}'\mathbf{G})^{-1}\mathbf{G}'\mathbf{M}]^{-1}\mathbf{M}'\mathbf{i},$$

where the rows of $\mathbf{G}$ are the terms in the gradient of the log-likelihood function, $(\mathbf{G}'\mathbf{G})^{-1}$ is the BHHH estimator of the asymptotic covariance matrix of the MLE of the model parameters, and the rows of $\mathbf{M}$ are the individual terms in the sample moment conditions. [Several occurrences of the sample size in (11-54) will cancel out.] Note that this is the same construction as the LM statistic just discussed. The difference is in how the rows of $\mathbf{M}$ are constructed.

For a regression model without censoring, the sample counterparts to the moment restrictions in (1) to (3) would be

$$\mathbf{r}_1 = \frac{1}{n}\sum_{i=1}^{n}\mathbf{z}_i e_i, \quad \text{where } e_i = y_i - \mathbf{b}'\mathbf{x}_i \text{ and } \mathbf{b} = (\mathbf{X}'\mathbf{X})^{-1}\mathbf{X}'\mathbf{y},$$

$$\mathbf{r}_2 = \frac{1}{n}\sum_{i=1}^{n}\mathbf{z}_i(e_i^2 - s^2), \quad \text{where } s^2 = \frac{\mathbf{e}'\mathbf{e}}{n},$$

$$\mathbf{r}_3 = \frac{1}{n}\sum_{i=1}^{n}\begin{bmatrix} e_i^3 \\ e_i^4 - 3s^4 \end{bmatrix}.$$

[34]See Example 4.26 and Section 10.5.4.

For the positive observations, we observe y^*, so the observations in **M** are the same as for the classical regression model, that is,

1. $\mathbf{m}_i = \mathbf{z}_i(y_i - \boldsymbol{\beta}'\mathbf{x}_i)$,
2. $\mathbf{m}_i = \mathbf{z}_i[(y_i - \boldsymbol{\beta}'\mathbf{x}_i)^2 - \sigma^2]$,
3. $\mathbf{m}_i = [(y_i - \boldsymbol{\beta}'\mathbf{x}_i)^3, (y_i - \boldsymbol{\beta}'\mathbf{x}_i)^4 - 3\sigma^4]'$.

For the limit observations, these are replaced with their expected values, conditioned on $y = 0$, which means that $y^* \leq 0$ or $\epsilon_i \leq -\boldsymbol{\beta}'\mathbf{x}$. Let $q_i = (\boldsymbol{\beta}'\mathbf{x}_i)/\sigma$ and $\lambda_i = \phi_i/(1 - \Phi_i)$. Then from (20-2), (20-3b), and (20-4),

1. $\mathbf{m}_i = \mathbf{z}_i E[(y_i^* - \boldsymbol{\beta}'\mathbf{x}_i)\,|\,y = 0] = \mathbf{z}_i(\boldsymbol{\beta}'\mathbf{x}_i - \sigma\lambda_i) - \boldsymbol{\beta}'\mathbf{x}_i = \mathbf{z}_i(-\sigma\lambda_i)$.
2. $\mathbf{m}_i = \mathbf{z}_i E[(y_i^* - \boldsymbol{\beta}'\mathbf{x}_i)^2 - \sigma^2\,|\,y = 0] = \mathbf{z}_i[\sigma^2(1 + q_i\lambda_i) - \sigma^2] = \mathbf{z}_i(\sigma^2 q_i\lambda_i)$.

($E[\epsilon_i^2\,|\,y = 0]$ is not the variance, since the mean is not zero.) For the third and fourth moments, we simply reproduce Pagan and Vella's results. [See also Greene (1995a, pp. 618–619).]

3. $\mathbf{m}_i = \sigma^3\lambda_i[-(2 + q_i^2), \sigma q_i(3 + q_i^2)]'$.

These are the remaining terms needed to compute **M**.

20.4. SELECTION – INCIDENTAL TRUNCATION

The topic of sample selection, or *incidental truncation*, has been the subject of an enormous recent literature, both theoretical and applied.[35] This analysis combines both of the previous topics.

EXAMPLE 20.13 Incidental Truncation

In the high-income survey discussed in Examples 20.1 and 20.4, respondents were also included in the survey if their net worth, not including their homes, was at least \$500,000. Suppose that the survey of incomes was based *only* on people whose net worth was at least \$500,000. This is a form of truncation, but not quite the same as in Section 20.2. This selection criterion does not necessarily exclude individuals whose incomes at the time might be quite low. Still, one would expect that, on average, individuals with a high net worth would have a high income as well. Thus, the average income in this subpopulation would, in all likelihood, also be misleading as an indication of the income of the typical American. The data in such a survey would be incidentally truncated, or nonrandomly selected.

Recent econometric studies of nonrandom sampling have analyzed the deleterious effects of sample selection on the properties of conventional esti-

[35] The four surveys noted in the introduction to this chapter provide fairly extensive, although far from exhaustive, lists of the studies. Recent studies that suggest the likely direction of future development are Heckman (1990), Manski (1989, 1990, 1995), and Newey et al. (1990).

mators such as least squares; have produced a variety of alternative estimation techniques; and, in the process, have yielded a rich crop of empirical models. In some cases, the analysis has led to a reinterpretation of earlier results.

20.4.1. Incidental Truncation in a Bivariate Distribution

Suppose that y and z have a bivariate distribution with correlation ρ. We are interested in the distribution of y given that z exceeds a particular value. Intuition suggests that if y and z are positively correlated, the truncation of z should push the distribution of y to the right. As before, we are interested in (1) the form of the incidentally truncated distribution and (2) the mean and variance of the incidentally truncated random variable. Since it has dominated the empirical literature, we will focus on the bivariate normal distribution.[36]

The truncated *joint* density of y and z is

$$f(y, z \mid z > a) = \frac{f(y, z)}{\text{Prob}(z > a)}.$$

To obtain the incidentally truncated marginal density for y, we would then integrate z out of this expression. The moments of the incidentally truncated normal distribution are given in Theorem 20.4.[37]

Theorem 20.4: MOMENTS OF THE INCIDENTALLY TRUNCATED BIVARIATE NORMAL DISTRIBUTION. *If y and z have a bivariate normal distribution with means μ_y and μ_z, standard deviations σ_y and σ_z, and correlation ρ, then*

$$\begin{aligned} E[y \mid z > a] &= \mu_y + \rho\sigma_y\lambda(\alpha_z), \\ \text{Var}[y \mid z > a] &= \sigma_y^2[1 - \rho^2\delta(\alpha_z)], \end{aligned} \qquad \textbf{(20-19)}$$

where

$$\alpha_z = (a - \mu_z)/\sigma_z, \lambda(\alpha_z) = \phi(\alpha_z)/[1 - \Phi(\alpha_z)], \quad \text{and} \quad \delta(\alpha_z) = \lambda(\alpha_z)[\lambda(\alpha_z) - \alpha_z].$$

Note that the expressions involving z are precisely analogous to the moments of the truncated distribution of x given in Theorem 20.2. If the truncation is $z < a$, we make the replacement $\lambda(\alpha_z) = -\phi(\alpha_z)/\Phi(\alpha_z)$.

As expected, the truncated mean is pushed in the direction of the correlation if the truncation is from below and in the opposite direction if it is from above. In addition, the incidental truncation reduces the variance, as both $\delta(\alpha)$ and ρ^2 are between 0 and 1.

20.4.2. Regression in a Model of Selection

To motivate a regression model that corresponds to the results in Theorem 20.4, we consider two examples.

---

[36]We will reconsider the issue of the normality assumption in Section 20.4.5.

[37]Much more general forms of the result that apply to multivariate distributions are given in Johnson and Kotz (1974). See also Maddala (1983, pp. 266–267).

EXAMPLE 20.14 A Model of Labor Supply

A simple model of female labor supply that has been examined in many studies consists of two equations:[38]

1. *Wage equation.* The difference between a person's *market wage*, what she could command in the labor market, and her *reservation wage*, the wage rate necessary to make her choose to participate in the labor market, is a function of characteristics such as age and education, as well as, for example, number of children and where a person lives.
2. *Hours equation.* The desired number of labor hours supplied depends on the wage, home characteristics such as whether there are small children present, marital status (see Example 20.9), and so on.

The problem of truncation surfaces when we consider that the second equation describes desired hours, but an actual figure is observed only if the individual is working. We infer from this that the market wage exceeds the reservation wage. Thus, the hours variable in the second equation is incidentally truncated.

EXAMPLE 20.15 A Migration Model

Example 20.3 presents a model of migration analyzed by Nakosteen and Zimmer. That model fits precisely into the framework described earlier. Briefly, the equations of the model are

$$\begin{aligned} &\text{net benefit of moving:} && M_i^* = \boldsymbol{\gamma}'\mathbf{w}_i + u_i, \\ &\text{income if moves:} && I_{i1} = \boldsymbol{\beta}_1'\mathbf{x}_{i1} + \epsilon_{i1}, \\ &\text{income if stays:} && I_{i0} = \boldsymbol{\beta}_0'\mathbf{x}_{i1} + \epsilon_{i0}. \end{aligned}$$

One component of the net benefit is the market wage individuals could achieve if they move, compared with what they could obtain if they stay. Therefore, among the determinants of the net benefit are factors that also affect the income received in either place. An analysis of income in a sample of migrants must account for the incidental truncation of the mover's income on a positive net benefit. Likewise, the income of the stayer is incidentally truncated on a nonpositive net benefit. The model implies an income after moving for all observations, but we observe it only for those who actually do move.

To put the preceding examples in a general framework, let the equation that determines the sample selection be

$$z_i^* = \boldsymbol{\gamma}'\mathbf{w}_i + u_i,$$

and let the equation of primary interest be

$$y_i = \boldsymbol{\beta}'\mathbf{x}_i + \epsilon_i.$$

[38]See, for example, Heckman (1976). This strand of literature begins with an exchange by Gronau (1974) and Lewis (1974).

The sample rule is that y_i is observed only when z_i^* is greater than zero. Suppose, as well, that ϵ_i and u_i have a bivariate normal distribution with zero means and correlation ρ. Then we may insert these in Theorem 20.4 to obtain the model *that applies to the observations in our sample*:

$$\begin{aligned} E[y_i \mid y_i \text{ is observed}] &= E[y_i \mid z_i^* > 0] \\ &= E[y_i \mid u_i > -\boldsymbol{\gamma}'\mathbf{w}_i] \\ &= \boldsymbol{\beta}'\mathbf{x}_i + E[\epsilon_i \mid u_i > -\boldsymbol{\gamma}'\mathbf{w}_i] \\ &= \boldsymbol{\beta}'\mathbf{x}_i + \rho\sigma_\epsilon\lambda_i(\alpha_u) \\ &= \boldsymbol{\beta}'\mathbf{x}_i + \beta_\lambda\lambda_i(\alpha_u), \end{aligned}$$

where $\alpha_u = -\boldsymbol{\gamma}'\mathbf{w}_i/\sigma_u$ and $\lambda(\alpha_u) = \phi(\boldsymbol{\gamma}'\mathbf{w}_i/\sigma_u)/\Phi(\boldsymbol{\gamma}'\mathbf{w}_i/\sigma_u)$. So,

$$\begin{aligned} y_i \mid z_i^* > 0 &= E[y_i \mid z_i^* > 0] + v_i \\ &= \boldsymbol{\beta}'\mathbf{x}_i + \beta_\lambda\lambda_i(\alpha_u) + v_i. \end{aligned}$$

Least squares regression using the observed data—for instance, OLS regression of hours on its determinants, using only data for women who are working—produces inconsistent estimates of $\boldsymbol{\beta}$. Once again, we can view the problem as an omitted variable. Least squares regression of y on $\mathbf{x}$ *and* λ would produce consistent estimates, but if λ is omitted, the specification error of an omitted variable is committed. Finally, note that the second part of Theorem 20.4 implies that even if λ_i were observed, least squares would be inefficient. The disturbance v_i is heteroscedastic.

The marginal effect of the regressors on y_i *in the observed sample* consists of two components. There is the direct effect on the mean of y_i, which is $\boldsymbol{\beta}$. In addition, for a particular independent variable, if it appears in the probability that z_i^* is positive, it will influence y_i through its presence in λ_i. The full effect of changes in a regressor that appears in both $\mathbf{x}_i$ and $\mathbf{w}_i$ on y is

$$\frac{\partial E[y_i \mid z_i^* > 0]}{\partial x_{ik}} = \beta_k - \gamma_k\left(\frac{\rho\sigma_\epsilon}{\sigma_u}\right)\delta_i(\alpha_u),$$

where

$$\delta_i = \lambda_i^2 + \alpha_i\lambda_i.^{39}$$

Suppose that ρ is positive and $E[y_i]$ is greater when z_i^* is positive than when it is negative. Since $0 < \delta_i < 1$, the additional term serves to reduce the marginal effect. The change in the probability affects the mean of y_i in that the mean in the group $z_i^* > 0$ is higher. The second term in the derivative compensates for this effect, leaving only the marginal effect of a change *given that* $z_i^* \geq 0$ *to begin with*. Consider Example 20.15, and suppose that education affects both the probability of migration and the income in either state. If we suppose that the income of migrants is higher than that of otherwise identical people who do

[39] We have reversed the sign of α_μ in (20-19) since $a = 0$, and $\alpha = \boldsymbol{\gamma}'\mathbf{w}/\sigma_M$ is somewhat more convenient. Also, as such, $\partial\lambda/\partial\alpha = -\delta$.

not migrate, the marginal effect of education has two parts, one due to its influence in increasing the probability of the individual's entering a higher-income group and one due to its influence on income within the group. As such, the coefficient on education in the regression overstates the marginal effect of the education of migrants and understates it for nonmigrants. The sizes of the various parts depend on the setting. It is quite possible that the magnitude, sign, and statistical significance of the effect might all be different from those of the estimate of $\boldsymbol{\beta}$, a point that appears frequently to be overlooked in empirical studies.

In most cases, the selection variable z^* is not observed. Rather, we observe only its sign. To consider our two examples, we typically observe only whether a woman is working or not working or whether an individual migrated or not. We can infer the sign of z^*, but not its magnitude, from such information. Since there is no information on the scale of z^*, the disturbance variance in the selection equation cannot be estimated. (We encountered this problem in Chapter 19 in connection with the probit model.) Thus, we reformulate the model as follows:

selection mechanism: $z_i^* = \boldsymbol{\gamma}'\mathbf{w}_i + u_i$, $z_i = 1$ if $z_i^* > 0$ and 0 otherwise; $\text{Prob}(z_i = 1) = \Phi(\boldsymbol{\gamma}'\mathbf{w}_i)$ and $\text{Prob}(z_i = 0) = 1 - \Phi(\boldsymbol{\gamma}'\mathbf{w}_i)$.

regression model: $y_i = \boldsymbol{\beta}'\mathbf{x}_i + \epsilon_i$ observed only if $z_i = 1$, $(u_i, \epsilon_i) \sim$ bivariate normal $[0, 0, 1, \sigma_\epsilon, \rho]$.

Suppose that, as in many of these studies, z_i and $\mathbf{w}_i$ are observed for a random sample of individuals, but y_i is observed only when $z_i = 1$. This is precisely the model we examined earlier, with

$$E[y_i \mid z_i = 1] = \boldsymbol{\beta}'\mathbf{x} + \rho\sigma_\epsilon\lambda(\boldsymbol{\gamma}'\mathbf{w}).$$

20.4.3. Estimation

The parameters of the sample selection model can be estimated by maximum likelihood.[40] This is quite cumbersome, however, and an alternative procedure due to Heckman (1979) is usually used instead. Heckman's two-step estimation procedure is as follows:[41]

1. Estimate the probit equation by maximum likelihood to obtain estimates of $\boldsymbol{\gamma}$. For each observation in the selected sample compute $\hat{\lambda}_i = \phi(\hat{\boldsymbol{\gamma}}\mathbf{w}_i)/\Phi(\hat{\boldsymbol{\gamma}}\mathbf{w}_i)$ and $\hat{\delta}_i = \hat{\lambda}_i(\hat{\lambda}_i + \hat{\boldsymbol{\gamma}}\mathbf{w}_i)$.
2. Estimate $\boldsymbol{\beta}$ and $\beta_\lambda = \rho\sigma_\epsilon$ by least squares regression of y on $\mathbf{x}$ and $\hat{\lambda}$.

[40] See Greene (1995a).

[41] Perhaps in a mimicry of the "tobit" estimator described earlier, this procedure has come to be known as the "Heckit" estimator.

EXAMPLE 20.16 The Migration Model (Continued)

Nakosteen and Zimmer (1980) applied the model of Example 20.15 to a sample of 9223 individuals with data for 2 years (1971 and 1973) sampled from the Social Security Administration's Continuous Work History Sample. Over the period, 1078 individuals migrated and the remaining 8145 did not. The independent variables in the migration equation were as follows:

$$SE = \text{self-employment dummy variable; 1 if yes,}$$
$$\Delta EMP = \text{rate of growth of state employment,}$$
$$\Delta PCI = \text{growth of state per capita income,}$$
$$\mathbf{x} = \text{AGE, RACE (nonwhite = 1), SEX (female = 1),}$$
$$\Delta SIC = \text{1 if individual changes industry.}$$

The earnings equations included ΔSIC and SE. The authors reported the results given in Table 20.5. The figures in parentheses are asymptotic t ratios.

It is possible to obtain consistent estimates of the individual parameters ρ and σ_ϵ. At each observation, the true variance of the disturbance would be

$$\sigma_i^2 = \sigma_\epsilon^2(1 - \rho^2\delta_i).$$

TABLE 20.5 Estimated Earnings Equations

	Migration	*Migrant Earnings*	*Nonmigrant Earnings*
Constant	−1.509	9.041	8.593
SE	−0.708 (−5.72)	−4.104 (−9.54)	−4.161 (−57.71)
ΔEMP	−1.488 (−2.60)	—	—
ΔPCI	1.455 (3.14)	—	—
AGE	−0.008 (−5.29)	—	—
RACE	−0.065 (−1.17)	—	—
SEX	−0.082 (−2.14)	—	—
ΔSIC	0.948 (24.15)	−0.790 (−2.24)	−0.927 (−9.35)
λ	—	0.212 (0.50)	0.863 (2.84)

The average variance for the sample would converge to

$$\operatorname{plim} \frac{1}{n}\sum_{i=1}^{n} \sigma_i^2 = \sigma_\epsilon^2(1 - \rho^2\overline{\delta}).$$

This is what is estimated by the least squares residual variance $\mathbf{e}'\mathbf{e}/n$. For the square of the coefficient on λ, we have

$$\operatorname{plim} b_\lambda^2 = \rho^2\sigma_\epsilon^2,$$

whereas based on the probit results we have

$$\operatorname{plim} \frac{1}{n}\sum_{i=1}^{n} \hat{\delta}_i = \overline{\delta}.$$

Then we can obtain a consistent estimator of σ_ϵ^2 using

$$\hat{\sigma}_\epsilon^2 = \frac{1}{n}\mathbf{e}'\mathbf{e} + \hat{\overline{\delta}} b_\lambda^2.$$

Finally, an estimate of ρ^2 is obtained as

$$\hat{\rho}^2 = \frac{b_\lambda^2}{\hat{\sigma}_\epsilon^2}.$$

This provides a complete set of estimates of the model's parameters.[42]

To test hypotheses, an estimate of the asymptotic covariance matrix of $[\mathbf{b}', b_\lambda]$ is needed. We have two problems to contend with. First, we can see in Theorem 20.4 that the disturbance term in

$$(y_i \mid z_i = 1) = \boldsymbol{\beta}'\mathbf{x}_i + \rho\sigma_\epsilon\lambda_i + v_i \tag{20-20}$$

is heteroscedastic:

$$\operatorname{Var}[v_i] = \sigma_\epsilon^2(1 - \rho^2\delta_i).$$

Second, there are unknown parameters in λ_i. Suppose that we assume for the moment that λ_i and δ_i are known (i.e., we do not have to estimate $\boldsymbol{\gamma}$). For convenience, let $\mathbf{x}_i^* = [\mathbf{x}_i, \lambda_i]$, and let $\mathbf{b}^*$ be the least squares coefficient vector in the regression of y on $\mathbf{x}^*$ in the selected data. Then, using the appropriate form of the variance of ordinary least squares in a heteroscedastic model from Chapter 12, we would have to estimate

$$\begin{aligned}\operatorname{Var}[\mathbf{b}^*] &= \sigma_\epsilon^2[\mathbf{X}_*'\mathbf{X}_*]^{-1}\left[\sum_{i=1}^{n}(1 - \rho^2\delta_i)\mathbf{x}_i^*\mathbf{x}_i^{*\prime}\right][\mathbf{X}_*'\mathbf{X}_*]^{-1} \\ &= \sigma_\epsilon^2[\mathbf{X}_*'\mathbf{X}_*]^{-1}[\mathbf{X}_*'(\mathbf{I} - \rho^2\boldsymbol{\Delta})\mathbf{X}_*][\mathbf{X}_*'\mathbf{X}_*]^{-1},\end{aligned}$$

[42]Note that $\hat{\rho}^2$ is not a sample correlation and, as such, is not limited to [0, 1]. See Greene (1981) for discussion.

where $\mathbf{I} - \rho^2\mathbf{\Delta}$ is a diagonal matrix with $(1 - \rho^2\delta_i)$ on the diagonal. Without any other complications, this could be computed fairly easily using $\mathbf{X}$, the sample estimates of σ_ϵ^2 and ρ^2, and the assumed known values of λ_i and δ_i.

The parameters in $\boldsymbol{\gamma}$ do have to be estimated using the probit equation. Rewrite (20-20) as

$$(y_i \mid z_i = 1) = \boldsymbol{\beta}'\mathbf{x}_i + \beta_\lambda\lambda_i + v_i + \beta_\lambda(\hat{\lambda}_i - \lambda_i).$$

In this form, we see that in the preceding expression, we have ignored both an additional source of variation in the compound disturbance and correlation across observations; the same estimate of $\boldsymbol{\gamma}$ is used to compute $\hat{\lambda}$ for every observation. Heckman has shown that the earlier covariance matrix can be appropriately corrected by adding a term inside the brackets,

$$\mathbf{Q} = \hat{\rho}^2(\mathbf{X}_*'\hat{\mathbf{\Delta}}\mathbf{W})\text{Est. Var}[\hat{\boldsymbol{\gamma}}](\mathbf{W}'\hat{\mathbf{\Delta}}\mathbf{X}_*) = \hat{\rho}^2\mathbf{F}\hat{\mathbf{V}}\mathbf{F}',$$

where $\hat{\mathbf{V}} = \text{Est. Asy. Var}[\hat{\boldsymbol{\gamma}}]$, the estimator of the asymptotic covariance of the probit coefficients. Any of the estimators in (19-20) to (19-24) may be used to compute $\hat{\mathbf{V}}$. The complete expression is

$$\text{Var}[\mathbf{b}, b_\lambda] = \hat{\sigma}_\epsilon^2[\mathbf{X}_*'\mathbf{X}_*]^{-1}[\mathbf{X}_*'(\mathbf{I} - \hat{\rho}^2\hat{\mathbf{\Delta}})\mathbf{X}_* + \mathbf{Q}][\mathbf{X}_*'\mathbf{X}_*]^{-1}.$$ [43]

20.4.4. Treatment Effects

The basic model of selectivity outlined earlier has been extended in an impressive variety of directions.[44] An interesting application that has found wide use is the measurement of treatment effects and program effectiveness.

An earnings equation that accounts for the value of a college education is

$$\text{earnings}_i = \boldsymbol{\beta}'\mathbf{x}_i + \delta C_i + \epsilon_i,$$

where C_i is a dummy variable indicating whether or not the individual attended college. The same format has been used in any number of other analyses of programs, experiments, and treatments. The question is: Does δ measure the value of a college education (assuming that the rest of the regression model is correctly specified)? The answer is no if the typical individual who chooses to go to college would have relatively high earnings whether or not he or she went to college. The problem is one of self-selection. If our observation is correct, least squares estimates of δ will actually overestimate the treatment effect. The same observation applies to estimates of the treatment effects in other settings in which the individuals themselves decide whether or not they will receive the treatment.

---

[43]This formulation is derived in Greene (1981). Note that the Murphy and Topel results for two-step estimators given in Theorem 10.3 would apply here as well. Asymptotically, this would give the same answer. The Heckman formulation has become standard in the literature.

[44]For a survey, see Maddala (1983).

To put this in a more familiar context, suppose that we model program participation (e.g., whether or not the individual goes to college) as

$$C_i^* = \boldsymbol{\gamma}'\mathbf{w}_i + u_i,$$
$$C_i = 1 \quad \text{if } C_i^* > 0, 0 \text{ otherwise.}$$

We also suppose that, consistent with our previous conjecture, u_i and ϵ_i are correlated. Coupled with our earnings equation, we find that

$$\begin{aligned} E[y_i \mid C_i = 1] &= \boldsymbol{\beta}'\mathbf{x}_i + \delta + E[\epsilon_i \mid C_i = 1] \\ &= \boldsymbol{\beta}'\mathbf{x}_i + \delta + \rho\sigma_\epsilon \lambda(\boldsymbol{\gamma}'\mathbf{w}_i) \end{aligned} \tag{20-21}$$

once again. Evidently, a viable strategy for estimating this model is to use the two-step estimator discussed earlier. The net result will be a different estimate of δ that will account for the self-selected nature of program participation. For nonparticipants, the counterpart to (20-21) is

$$E[y_i \mid C_i = 0] = \boldsymbol{\beta}'\mathbf{x}_i + \rho\sigma_\epsilon \left[\frac{-\phi(\boldsymbol{\gamma}'\mathbf{w}_i)}{1 - \Phi(\boldsymbol{\gamma}'\mathbf{w}_i)}\right].$$

The difference in expected earnings between participants and nonparticipants is, then,

$$E[y_i \mid C_i = 1] - E[y_i \mid C_i = 0] = \delta + \rho\sigma_\epsilon \left[\frac{\phi_i}{\Phi_i(1 - \Phi_i)}\right].$$

If the selectivity correction λ_i is omitted from the least squares regression, this difference is what is estimated by the least squares coefficient on the treatment dummy variable. But since (by assumption) all terms are positive, we see that least squares overestimates the treatment effect. Note, finally, that simply estimating separate equations for participants and nonparticipants does not solve the problem. In fact, this would be equivalent to estimating the two regressions of Example 20.15 by least squares, which, as we have seen, would lead to inconsistent estimates of both sets of parameters.

There are many variations of this model in the recent empirical literature. They have been applied to the analysis of education,[45] the Head Start program,[46] and a host of other settings.[47] This is a particularly important strand of literature as the use of dummy variable models to analyze treatment effects and program participation has a long history in empirical economics. This analysis has called into question the interpretation of a number of received studies.

---

[45]Willis and Rosen (1979).

[46]Goldberger (1972b).

[47]A useful summary of the issues is Barnow et al. (1981). See also Maddala (1983) for a long list of applications. A related application is the switching regression model. See, for example, Quandt (1982, 1988).

20.4.5. The Normality Assumption

Recent research has cast some skepticism on the selection model based on the normal distribution. [See Goldberger (1983) for an early salvo in this literature.] Among the findings are that the parameter estimates are surprisingly sensitive to the distributional assumption that underlies the model. Of course, this in itself does not invalidate the normality assumption, but it does call its generality into question. On the other hand, the received evidence is compelling that sample selection, in the abstract, raises serious problems, distributional questions aside. The most recent literature—for example, Duncan (1986b), Manski (1989, 1990), and Heckman (1990)—has suggested some promising approaches based on robust and nonparametric estimators. These obviously have the virtue of greater generality. Unfortunately, the cost is that these approaches generally are quite limited in the breadth of the models they can accommodate. That is, one might gain the robustness of a nonparametric estimator at the cost of being unable to make use of the rich set of accompanying variables usually present in the panels to which selectivity models are often applied. For example, the nonparametric bounds approach of Manski (1990) is defined for two regressors. Other methods [e.g., Duncan (1986b)] allow more elaborate specification. The upshot is that the issue remains unsettled. For better or worse, the empirical literature on the subject continues to be dominated by Heckman's original model built around the joint normal distribution.

20.4.6. Selection in Qualitative Response Models

The problem of sample selection has appeared in other settings besides the linear regression model. In Section 19.6.2b, we saw, for example, an application of what amounts to a model of sample selection in a bivariate probit model; a binary response variable $y_i = 1$ if an individual defaults on a loan is observed only if a related variable z_i equals 1 (the individual is granted a loan). Greene's (1992) application to credit card applications and defaults is similar.

A current strand of literature has sought to construct a model of sample selection for count data models.[48] Terza (1995) models the phenomenon as a form of heterogeneity in the Poisson model. We write

$$y_i \mid \epsilon_i \sim \text{Poisson}(\lambda_i),$$
$$\ln \lambda_i \mid \epsilon_i = \boldsymbol{\beta}'\mathbf{x}_i + \epsilon_i.$$

Then the sample selection is similar to that discussed in the previous sections, with

$$z_i^* = \boldsymbol{\gamma}'\mathbf{w}_i + u_i,$$
$$z_i = 1 \quad \text{if } z_i^* > 0, 0 \text{ otherwise}$$

[48]See, for example, Bockstael et al. (1990), Smith (1988), Brannas (1995), Greene (1994, 1995c), Weiss (1995), and Terza (1995).

and $[\epsilon_i, u_i]$ have a bivariate normal distribution with the same specification as in our earlier model. As before, we assume that $[y_i, \mathbf{x}_i]$ are only observed when $z_i =$ 1. Thus, the manifest effect of the selection is to affect the mean (and variance) of y_i, although the effect on the distribution is unclear. In the observed data, y_i no longer has a Poisson distribution. Terza shows that under these assumptions,

$$E[y_i \mid \mathbf{x}_i, z_i = 1] = e^{\boldsymbol{\beta}'\mathbf{x}_i} e^{\sigma_\epsilon^2/2}\left[\frac{\Phi(\theta + \boldsymbol{\alpha}'\mathbf{w}_i)}{\Phi(\boldsymbol{\gamma}'\mathbf{w}_i)}\right] = e^{\boldsymbol{\beta}_0'\mathbf{x}_i}\tau_i(\theta, \boldsymbol{\gamma}) = \lambda_i^0 \tau_i(\theta, \boldsymbol{\gamma}), \tag{20-22}$$

where $\theta = \rho\sigma_\epsilon$. Since $\partial\Phi(\theta + \boldsymbol{\gamma}'\mathbf{w}_i)/\partial\theta = \phi(\theta + \boldsymbol{\gamma}'\mathbf{w}_i) > 0$ and $\theta = \rho\sigma_\epsilon$, if ρ is positive, the selection has the effect of increasing the mean, as might be expected.

Since the exact distribution remains to be derived, maximum likelihood is not feasible. But (20-22) does define a nonlinear regression that can be estimated by nonlinear least squares. Terza suggests a two-step analog to the Heckman estimator discussed previously: (1) estimate $\boldsymbol{\gamma}$ using the probit model for z and (2) using the selected subsample, estimate $\boldsymbol{\beta}_0$ and θ using nonlinear least squares; the constant term in $\boldsymbol{\beta}_0$ will estimate that in $\boldsymbol{\beta}$ plus $\frac{1}{2}\sigma_\epsilon^2$, whereas all other elements will be the same. The Murphy and Topel results of Theorem 10.3 can be applied to estimate the asymptotic covariance matrix. In the notation of Theorem 10.3, $\sigma^2\mathbf{V}_b$ is the conventionally computed estimator for the asymptotic covariance matrix of $[\hat{\boldsymbol{\beta}}_0, \hat{\theta}]$ and $\mathbf{V}_c$ is the estimated asymptotic covariance matrix for the estimated coefficients of the probit model $\mathbf{c}$. For the remaining matrices in the computation,

$$\mathbf{x}_i^0 = \lambda_i^0\begin{bmatrix}\tau_i(\theta, \boldsymbol{\gamma})\mathbf{x}_i \\ \partial\tau_i(\theta, \boldsymbol{\gamma})/\partial\theta\end{bmatrix} \quad \text{and} \quad \mathbf{V}_b = \left[\sum_{i=1}^{n} \mathbf{x}_i^0\mathbf{x}_i^{0\prime}\right]^{-1},$$

$$\frac{\partial\tau_i(\theta, \boldsymbol{\gamma})}{\partial\theta} = \frac{\phi(\theta + \boldsymbol{\gamma}'\mathbf{w}_i)}{\Phi(\boldsymbol{\alpha}'\mathbf{w}_i)} = \tau_{i\theta}(\theta, \boldsymbol{\gamma}),$$

$$\frac{\partial h(.)}{\partial\boldsymbol{\gamma}} = \lambda_i^0\frac{\partial\tau(\theta, \boldsymbol{\gamma})}{\partial\boldsymbol{\gamma}} = \lambda_i^0\left[\left(\frac{\phi(\theta + \boldsymbol{\gamma}'\mathbf{w}_i)}{\Phi(\boldsymbol{\gamma}'\mathbf{w}_i)}\right) + \tau_i(\theta, \boldsymbol{\gamma})\left(\frac{\phi(\boldsymbol{\gamma}'\mathbf{w}_i)}{\Phi(\boldsymbol{\gamma}'\mathbf{w}_i)}\right)\right]\mathbf{w}_i = r_i\mathbf{w}_i,$$

$$\frac{\partial g(.)}{\partial\boldsymbol{\gamma}} = \left(\frac{\phi(\boldsymbol{\gamma}'\mathbf{w}_i)}{\Phi(\boldsymbol{\gamma}'\mathbf{w}_i)}\right)\mathbf{w}_i.$$

20.5. MODELS FOR DURATION DATA[49]

Intuition might suggest that the longer a strike persists, the more likely it is that it will end within, say, the next week. Or is it? It seems equally plausible to suggest that the longer a strike has lasted, the more difficult must be the problems that led to it in the first place, and hence the *less* likely it is that it will end in

[49]Analysis of duration is a fairly new but rapidly growing area in econometrics. There are a large number of highly technical articles but relatively few accessible sources for the uninitiated. A particularly useful introductory survey is Kiefer (1988), upon which we have drawn heavily for this section. Other useful sources are Kalbfleisch and Prentice (1980), Heckman and Singer (1984a), and Lancaster (1990).

the next short time interval. A similar kind of reasoning could be applied to spells of unemployment or the interval between conceptions. In each of these cases, it is not only the duration of the event, per se, that is interesting, but also the likelihood that the event will end in "the next period" given that it has lasted as long as it has.

The analysis of duration data comes fairly recently to the economics literature. Analysis of the length of *time until failure* has interested engineers for decades. For example, the models discussed in the next section were applied to the durability of electric and electronic components long before economists discovered their usefulness. Likewise, the analysis of *survival times*—for example, the length of survival after the diagnosis of a disease or after an operation such as a heart transplant—has long been a staple of biomedical research. Social scientists have recently applied the same body of techniques to strike duration, length of unemployment spells, intervals between conception, time until business failure, length of time between arrests, length of time from purchase until a warranty claim is made, intervals between purchases, and so on.

This section will give a brief introduction to the econometric analysis of duration data. As usual, we will restrict our attention to a few straightforward, relatively uncomplicated techniques and applications, primarily to introduce terms and concepts. The reader can then wade into the literature to find the extensions and variations. We will concentrate primarily on what are known as parametric models. These apply familiar inference techniques and provide a convenient departure point. Alternative approaches are considered at the end of the discussion.

20.5.1. Duration Data

The variable of interest in the analysis of duration is the length of time that elapses from the beginning of some event either until its end or until the measurement is taken, which may precede termination. Observations will typically consist of a cross section of durations, $t_1, t_2, \ldots, t_n$. The process being observed may have begun at different points in calendar time. For example, the strike duration data examined in the next section are drawn from nine different years.

Censoring is a pervasive and usually unavoidable problem in the analysis of duration data. The common cause is that the measurement is made while the process is ongoing. An obvious example can be drawn from medical research. Consider analyzing the survival times of heart transplant patients. Although the beginning times may be known with precision, at the time of the measurement, observations on any individuals who are still alive are necessarily censored. Likewise, samples of spells of unemployment drawn from surveys will probably include some individuals who are unemployed at the time the survey is taken. For these individuals, duration, or survival, is at least the observed t_i, but not equal to it. Estimation must account for the censored nature of the data for the same reasons as considered in Section 20.3. The consequences of ignoring censoring in duration data are not unlike those that arise in regression analysis.

In a conventional regression model that characterizes the conditional mean and variance of a distribution, the regressors can be taken as fixed characteristics at the point in time or for the individual for which the measurement is taken. When measuring duration, the observation is implicitly on a process that has been under way for a length of time, $[0, t)$. If the analysis is conditioned on a set of covariates (the counterparts to regressors) $\mathbf{x}_t$, the duration is implicitly a function of the entire time path of the variable $\mathbf{x}(t)$, $t = [0, t)$, which may have changed during the interval. For example, the observed duration of employment in a job may be a function of the individual's rank in the firm. But their rank may well have changed several times between the time they were hired and when the observation was made. As such, observed rank at the end of the job tenure is not necessarily a complete description of the individual's rank *while they were employed*. Likewise, marital status, family size, and amount of education are all variables that can change during the duration of unemployment, and which one would like to account for in the duration model. The treatment of **time varying covariates** is a considerable complication.[50]

20.5.2. A Regression-like Approach — Parametric Models of Duration

We will use the term *spell* as a catchall for the different duration variables we might measure. Spell length is represented by the random variable T. A simple approach to duration analysis would be to apply regression analysis to the sample of observed spells. By this device, we could characterize the expected duration, perhaps conditioned on a set of covariates whose values were measured at the end of the period. We could also assume that conditioned on an $\mathbf{x}$ that has remained fixed from $T = 0$ to $T = t$, t has a normal distribution, as we commonly do in regression. We could then characterize the probability distribution of observed duration times. But normality turns out not to be particularly attractive in this setting for a number of reasons, not least of which is that duration is positive by construction, while a normally distributed variable can take negative values. (*Log*normality turns out to be a palatable alternative, but it is only one among a long roster of contenders.)

20.5.2a. Theoretical Background. Suppose that the random variable T has a continuous probability distribution $f(t)$, where t is a realization of T. The cumulative probability is

$$F(t) = \int_0^t f(s)\, ds = \text{Prob}(T \leq t).$$

We will usually be more interested in the probability that the spell is of length *at least t*, which is given by the **survival function,**

$$S(t) = 1 - F(t) = \text{Prob}(T \geq t).$$

[50]See Petersen (1986) for one approach to this problem.

Consider the question raised in the introduction: Given that the spell has lasted until time t, what is the probability that it will end in the next short interval of time, say Δ? This is

$$l(t, \Delta) = \text{Prob}(t \leq T \leq t + \Delta \,|\, T \geq t).$$

A useful function for characterizing this aspect of the distribution is the **hazard rate,**

$$\begin{aligned}\lambda(t) &= \lim_{\Delta \to 0} \frac{\text{Prob}(t \leq T \leq t + \Delta \,|\, T \geq t)}{\Delta} \\ &= \lim_{\Delta \to 0} \frac{F(t + \Delta) - F(t)}{\Delta S(t)} \\ &= \frac{f(t)}{S(t)}.\end{aligned}$$

Roughly, the hazard rate is the rate at which spells are completed after duration t, given that they last at least until t. As such, the hazard function gives an answer to our original question.

Given the way our question was posed at the outset, we might prefer to model the hazard function rather than the density, the CDF, or the survival function. Clearly, all four functions are related. The hazard function is

$$\lambda(t) = \frac{-d \ln S(t)}{dt}$$

and

$$f(t) = S(t)\lambda(t).$$

Another useful function is the **integrated hazard function**

$$\Lambda(t) = \int_0^t \lambda(s)\, ds,$$

for which

$$S(t) = e^{-\Lambda(t)},$$

so

$$\Lambda(t) = -\ln S(t).$$

The integrated hazard function is generalized residual [Chesher and Irish (1987)] in this setting.

20.5.2b. Models of the Hazard Rate. For present purposes, the hazard function is more interesting than the survival rate or the density. Indeed, based on the previous results, one might consider modeling the hazard function directly, rather than the survival function, then for purposes of estimation, integrating backward to obtain the density. For example, the base case for many analyses is a hazard rate that does not vary over time. That is, $\lambda(t)$ is a constant λ. This is characteristic of a process that has no memory; the *conditional* probability of "failure" in a given short interval is the same regardless of when the observation is made. Thus,

$$\lambda(t) = \lambda.$$

From the earlier definition, we obtain the simple differential equation,

$$\frac{-d \ln S(t)}{dt} = \lambda.$$

The solution is

$$\ln S(t) = k - \lambda t,$$

or

$$S(t) = Ke^{-\lambda t},$$

where K is the constant of integration. The condition that $S(0) = 1$ implies that $K = 1$, and the solution is

$$S(t) = e^{-\lambda t}.$$

This is the exponential distribution, which has been used to model the time until failure of electronic components, precisely because of the memoryless property of the distribution. Estimation of λ is simple, since with an exponential distribution, $E[t] = 1/\lambda$. The maximum likelihood estimate of λ would be $1/\bar{t}$.

A natural extension might be to model the hazard rate as a linear function, $\lambda(t) = \alpha + \beta t$. Then $\Lambda(t) = \alpha t + \frac{1}{2}\beta t^2$ and $f(t) = \lambda(t)S(t) = \lambda(t) \exp[-\Lambda(t)]$.[51] With an observed sample of durations, estimation of α and β is, at least in principle, a straightforward problem in maximum likelihood. [Kennan (1985) used a similar approach.]

A distribution whose hazard function slopes upward is said to have **positive duration dependence.** For such distributions, the likelihood of failure at time t, conditional upon duration up to time t, is increasing in t. The opposite case is that of decreasing hazard or **negative duration dependence.** Our question in the introduction about whether the strike is more or less likely to end at time t given that it has lasted until time t can be framed in terms of positive or negative duration dependence. The assumed distribution has a considerable bearing on the answer. If one is unsure at the outset of the analysis whether the data can be characterized by positive or negative duration dependence, it is counterproductive to assume a distribution that displays one characteristic or

---

[51]To avoid a negative hazard function, one might depart from $\lambda(t) = \exp[g(t, \boldsymbol{\theta})]$, where $\boldsymbol{\theta}$ is the vector of parameters to be estimated.

the other over the entire range of t. Thus, the exponential distribution and our suggested extension could be problematic.

The literature contains a cornucopia of choices for duration models, including normal, inverse normal [inverse Gaussian; see Lancaster (1990)], lognormal, F, gamma, Weibull (which is a popular choice), and many others.[52] To illustrate the differences, we will examine a few of the simpler ones. Table 20.6 lists the hazard functions and survival functions for four commonly used distributions.

All these are distributions for a nonnegative random variable. Their hazard functions display very different behaviors. The hazard function for the exponential distribution is constant, that for the Weibull is monotonically increasing or decreasing depending on p, and the hazards for lognormal and log-logistic distributions first increase, then decrease. Which among these or the many alternatives is likely to be best in any application is uncertain.

20.5.2c. Maximum Likelihood Estimation. The parameters λ and p of these models can be estimated by maximum likelihood. For observed duration data, $t_1, t_2, \ldots, t_n$, the log-likelihood function can be formulated and maximized in the ways we have become familiar with in earlier chapters. Censored observations can be incorporated exactly as in Section 20.3 for the tobit model. [See (20-13).] As such,

$$\ln L = \sum_{\text{uncensored observations}} \ln f(t \mid \boldsymbol{\theta}) + \sum_{\text{censored observations}} \ln S(t \mid \boldsymbol{\theta}),$$

where $\boldsymbol{\theta} = (\lambda, p)$. For some distributions, it is convenient to formulate the log-likelihood function in terms of $f(t) = \lambda(t)S(t)$ so that

$$\ln L = \sum_{\text{uncensored observations}} \lambda(t \mid \boldsymbol{\theta}) + \sum_{\text{all observations}} \ln S(t \mid \boldsymbol{\theta}).$$

TABLE 20.6 Some Survival Distributions

Distribution	*Hazard Function, $\lambda(t)$*	*Survival Function, $S(t)$*
Exponential	λ,	$S(t) = e^{-\lambda t}$
Weibull	$\lambda p(\lambda t)^{p-1}$,	$S(t) = e^{-(\lambda t)^p}$
Lognormal	$f(t) = (p/t)\phi[p \ln(\lambda t)]$	$S(t) = \Phi[-p \ln(\lambda t)]$
	[ln t is normally distributed with mean $-\ln\lambda$ and standard deviation $1/p$.]	
Log-logistic	$\lambda(t) = \lambda p(\lambda t)^{p-1}/[1 + (\lambda t)^p]$,	$S(t) = 1/[1 + (\lambda t)^p]$
	[ln t has a logistic distribution with mean $-\ln\lambda$ and variance $\pi^2/(3p^2)$.]	

Note: These formulations differ slightly from Kiefer's. His formulation of the Weibull hazard is $\lambda(t) = \gamma p t^{p-1}$, so his γ corresponds to our λ^p. We follow the convention of Kalbfleisch and Prentice (1980).

[52] Three sources that contain numerous specifications are Kalbfleisch and Prentice (1980), Cox and Oakes (1985), and Lancaster (1990).

Inference about the parameters can be done in the usual way. Either the BHHH estimator or actual second derivatives can be used to estimate asymptotic standard errors for the estimates.[53]

EXAMPLE 20.17 Log-Linear Survival Models for Strike Duration

The strike duration data given in Kennan (1985, pp. 14–16) have become a familiar standard for the demonstration of hazard models. Table 20.7 lists the durations in days of 62 strikes that commenced in June of the years 1968 to 1976. Each involved at least 1000 workers and began at the expiration or reopening of a contract. Kennan reported the actual duration. In his survey, Kiefer, using the same observations we use in the next section, censored the data at 80 days to demonstrate the effects of censoring. We have kept the data in their original form; the interested reader is referred to Kiefer for further analysis of the censoring problem.[54] The variable x reported with the strike duration data is a measure of unanticipated aggregate industrial production net of seasonal and trend components. It is computed as the residual in a regression of the log of industrial production in manufacturing on time, time squared, and monthly dummy variables.

Parameter estimates for the four duration models are given in Table 20.8. The estimate of the median of the survival distribution is obtained by solving the equation $S(t) = 0.5$. For example, for the Weibull model,

TABLE 20.7 Strike Duration Data

Year	x	*Strike Durations (days)*										
1968	0.01138	7	9	13	14	26	29	52	130			
1969	0.02299	9	37	41	49	52	119					
1970	−0.03957	3	17	19	28	72	99	104	114	152	153	216
1971	−0.05467	15	61	98								
1972	0.00535	2	25	85								
1973	0.07427	3	10									
1974	0.06450	1	2	3	3	3	4	8	11	22		
		23	27	32	33	35	43	43	44	100		
1975	−0.10443	5	49									
1976	−0.00700	2	12	12	21	21	27	38	42	117		

[53]The transformation $w = p(\ln t + \ln \lambda)$ for these distributions greatly facilitates maximum likelihood estimation. For example, for the Weibull model, by defining $w = p(\ln t + \ln \lambda)$, we obtain the very simple density $f(w) = \exp[w - \exp(w)]$. Therefore, by using $\ln t$ instead of t, we greatly simplify the log-likelihood function. Details for these and several other distributions may be found in Kalbfleisch and Prentice (1980, pp. 56–60). The Weibull distribution is examined in detail in the next section.

[54]Our statistical results are nearly the same as Kiefer's despite the censoring.

TABLE 20.8 Estimated Duration Models (Estimated Standard Errors in Parentheses)

	λ	p	*Median Duration*
Exponential	0.02344	1.00000	29.571
	(0.002979)	(0.00000)	(3.5224)
Weibull	0.02439	0.92083	27.54275
	(0.00354)	(0.11086)	(3.9969)
Log-logistic	0.04153	1.33148	24.07853
	(0.00707)	(0.17201)	(4.10188)
Lognormal	0.04514	0.77206	22.15175
	(0.00806)	(0.08865)	(3.95395)

$$S(M) = 0.5 = e^{-(\lambda M)^p}$$

or

$$M = \frac{1}{\lambda}(\ln 2)^{1/p}.$$

For the exponential model, $p = 1$. For the lognormal and log-logistic models, $M = 1/\lambda$. The delta method is then used to estimate the standard error of this function of the parameter estimates. (See Section 4.4.4.) All these distributions are skewed to the right. As such, $E[t]$ is greater than the median. For the exponential and Weibull models, $E[t] = [1/\lambda]\Gamma[(1/p) + 1]$; for the normal, $E[t] = (1/\lambda)[\exp(1/p^2)]^{1/2}$.

The implied hazard functions are shown in Figure 20.5.

20.5.2d. Exogenous Variables. One limitation of the models given above is that external factors are not given a role in the survival distribution. The addition of "covariates" to duration models is fairly straightforward, although the interpretation of the coefficients in the model is less so. Consider, for example, the Weibull model. (The extension to other distributions will be direct.) Let

$$\lambda_i = e^{-\boldsymbol{\beta}'\mathbf{x}_i},$$

where $\mathbf{x}_i$ is a constant term and a set of variables that are assumed not to change from time $T = 0$ to the "failure time," $T = t$. Making λ a function of a set of regressors is equivalent to changing the units of measurement on the time axis. For this reason, these models are sometimes called "accelerated failure time" models. Note, as well, that in all the models listed (and generally), the regressors do not bear on the question of duration dependence, which is a function of p. Let $\sigma = 1/p$ and let $\delta_i = 1$ if the spell is completed and $\delta_i = 0$ if it is censored. Finally, let

$$w_i = p \ln(\lambda_i t_i) = \frac{1}{\sigma}(\ln t_i - \boldsymbol{\beta}'\mathbf{x}_i).$$

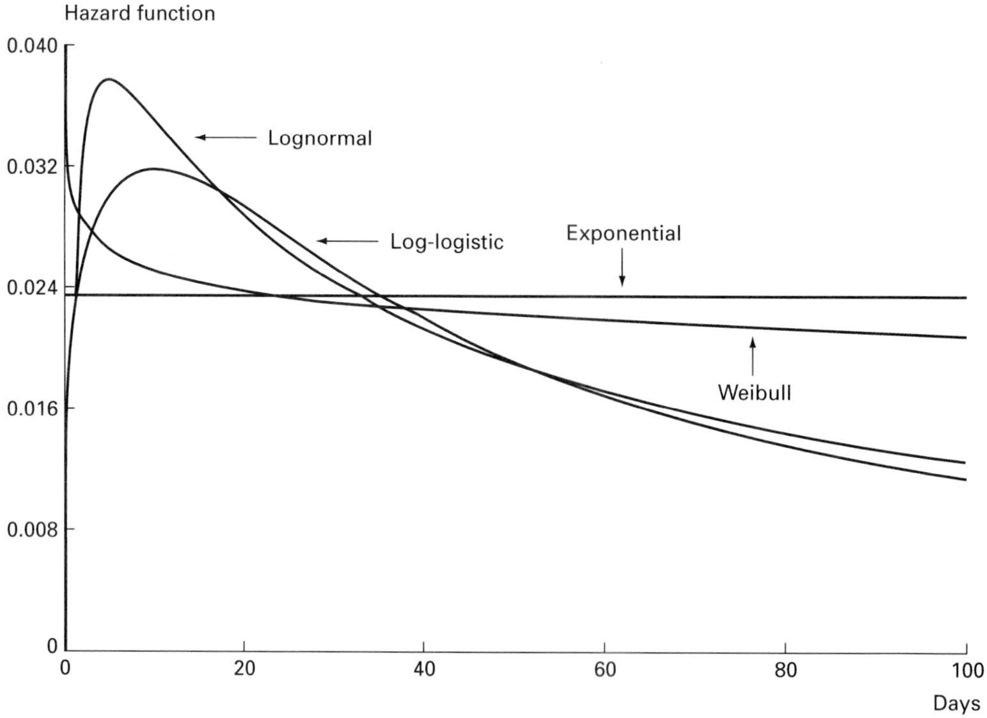

FIGURE 20.5 Hazard Function.

By making the change of variable, we find that

$$f(w_i) = \left(\frac{1}{\sigma}\right)\exp(w_i - e^{w_i})$$

and

$$S(w_i) = \exp(-e^{w_i}).$$

The log-likelihood is

$$\ln L = \sum_{i=1}^{n} [\delta_i \ln f(w_i) + (1 - \delta_i)\ln S(w_i)],$$

which reduces to

$$\ln L = \sum_{i} [\delta_i(w_i - \ln \sigma) - e^{w_i}].$$

(Many other distributions, including the others in Table 20.6, simplify in the same way.) The derivatives are obtained by using $\partial w_i/\partial\sigma = -w_i/\sigma$ and $\partial w_i/\partial\boldsymbol{\beta} = -\mathbf{x}_i/\sigma$. These can be equated to zero using the methods described in

Chapter 5. The individual terms can also be used to form the BHHH estimator of the asymptotic covariance matrix for the estimates.[55] The Hessian is also simple to derive, so Newton's method could be used instead.[56]

Note that the hazard function generally depends on t, p, and $\mathbf{x}$. The sign of the estimated coefficient suggests the direction of the effect of the variable on the hazard function when the hazard is monotonic. But in those cases, such as the log-logistic, in which the hazard is nonmonotonic, even this may be ambiguous. The magnitudes of the effects may also be difficult to interpret in terms of the hazard function. But in a few cases, we do get a regression-like interpretation. In the Weibull and exponential models, $E[t \mid \mathbf{x}_i] = \exp(\boldsymbol{\beta}'\mathbf{x}_i)\Gamma[(1/p) + 1]$, whereas for the log-normal and log-logistic models, $E[\ln t \mid \mathbf{x}_i] = \boldsymbol{\beta}'\mathbf{x}_i$. In these cases, β_k is the derivative (or a multiple of the derivative) of this conditional mean. For some other distributions, the conditional median of t is easily obtained. Other cases are discussed by Kiefer (1988) and Kalbfleisch and Prentice (1980).

EXAMPLE 20.18 Weibull Model with a Covariate

With the industrial production variable included as a covariate, the estimated Weibull model is

$$-\ln \lambda = \underset{(0.1394)}{3.7772} - \underset{(2.973)}{9.3515x}, \qquad p = \underset{(0.1217),}{1.00288}$$

$$\text{median strike length} = 27.35\ (3.667)\ \text{days}, \qquad E[t] = 39.83\ \text{days}.$$

Note that the Weibull model is now almost identical to the exponential model ($p = 1$). Since the hazard conditioned on x is approximately equal to λ_i, it follows that the hazard function is increasing in "unexpected" industrial production. A 1 percent increase in x leads to a 9.35 percent increase in λ, which since $p \approx 1$ translates into a 9.35 percent decrease in the median strike length or about 2.6 days. (Note that $M = \ln 2/\lambda$.)

20.5.2e. Specification Analysis. There is no direct counterpart to the set of regression residuals with which to assess the validity of the specification of the duration model. The coefficients themselves can be analyzed with the familiar trinity of tests that we have used previously for analyzing maximum likelihood estimates. In most parametric models of duration, maximum likelihood estimation is fairly routine, so the choice among Wald, Lagrange multiplier, or likelihood ratio tests can be based on convenience. But an assessment of the overall specification of the model is more difficult. The integrated hazard

[55] Note that the log-likelihood function has the same form as that for the tobit model in Section 20.3. By just reinterpreting the nonlimit observations in a tobit setting, we can, therefore, use this framework to apply a wide range of distributions to the tobit model. [See Greene (1995a) and references given therein.]

[56] See Kalbfleisch and Prentice (1980) for numerous other examples.

function provides one useful measure. Regardless of the specification, under the hypothesis of the model, the sample of observations on $S(t \mid \theta)$, computed at the true parameter values, will have a uniform distribution. This is an application of the fundamental probability transform: Let $F(t)$ denote the CDF of t, and let $z = F(t)$. Then $t = F^{-1}(z)$, and the CDF of z is $F(z) = F[F^{-1}(z)] = z$, which is the CDF of the standard uniform distribution. If $F(t) \sim U[0, 1]$, so is $S(t) = 1 - F(t)$. As such, one possible check on the specification of the model would be to see if the sample of estimated survival rates computed from the model looks like a sample from the uniform distribution. The usual approach is to use, instead, the

$$\textbf{generalized residual} = \epsilon = \Lambda(t \mid \boldsymbol{\theta}) = -\ln S(t \mid \boldsymbol{\theta}).$$

This transformation of a $U(0, 1)$ variable will have CDF

$$F(\epsilon) = 1 - e^{-\epsilon},$$

which is the CDF of an exponential variable with parameter $\lambda = 1$. With this in hand, a rough check on the specification of the model can be done by examining the moments of the generalized residuals. The theoretical values for the unit exponential distribution, in the absence of censoring, based on $E[\epsilon^r] = r!$, would be 1, 1, 2, and 9 for the mean and the next three central moments. The first is imposed by the maximization of the log likelihood, but the other moment restrictions could be tested using, for example, the methods in Section 20.3.4c. The conditional moment test is derived in general terms in Kiefer (1985b) and Sharma (1989). (See Section 11.6.2 for additional details on conditional moment tests.) The precise test procedure for our Weibull model, based on Pagan and Vella's (1989) results (see Section 20.3.4c), is detailed in Jaggia (1991).

EXAMPLE 20.19 A Conditional Moment Test for the Weibull Distribution

The generalized residuals for the Weibull model are

$$e_i = [\exp(-\hat{\boldsymbol{\beta}}'\mathbf{x}_i)t_i]^{\hat{p}}.$$

The sample mean is 1.0 as expected. The theoretical moments which we can use for a specification test are

$$\begin{aligned}
\mu_2' &= E[\epsilon^2] = 2,\\
\mu_3' &= E[\epsilon^3] = 6,\\
\mu_4' &= E[\epsilon^4] = 24,\\
\mu_*' &= E[\ln \epsilon] = \Psi(1) = -0.5772.
\end{aligned}$$

Jaggia suggests two tests, one based on μ_2' and μ_*' and one based on μ_2', μ_3', and μ_4'. Both tests are based on Pagan and Vella's results for conditional moment tests. The test statistic is

$$\chi^2[2 \text{ or } 3] = \mathbf{i'M[M'M - M'D(D'D)^{-1}D'M]^{-1}M'i},$$

where

$$\mathbf{i} = n \times 1 \text{ column of 1s } (n = 62),$$
$$\mathbf{M} = n \times J \text{ matrix with } i\text{th row} = \text{individual term in the moment.}$$

For the first test, the sample moment is

$$\mathbf{m} = \frac{1}{62} \sum_{i=1}^{62} \begin{bmatrix} e_i^2 - 2 \\ \ln e_i - \Psi(1) \end{bmatrix}.$$

The transpose of the ith term is the ith row in $\mathbf{M}$. For the second test, the ith row in $\mathbf{M}$ is

$$\mathbf{M}^i = [e_i^2 - 2, e_i^3 - 6, e_i^4 - 24].$$

The matrix $(\mathbf{D}'\mathbf{D})^{-1}$ is the estimator of the asymptotic covariance matrix of the parameter estimators. For the Weibull model, the parameters are $\boldsymbol{\theta}' = [\beta_1, \beta_2, p]$. The estimates are given in Example 20.18. This is the BHHH estimator of the asymptotic covariance matrix. The log-likelihood is given in Section 20.5.2d. The derivatives of the individual terms in $\ln L = \Sigma_{i=1}^{n} \ln f_i$ are

$$\frac{\partial \ln f_i}{\partial \boldsymbol{\theta}'} = \frac{1}{\sigma} \begin{bmatrix} \mathbf{x}_i(e_i^{w_i} - \delta_i) - \mathbf{0} \\ w_i(e_i^{w_i} - \delta_i) - \delta_i \end{bmatrix}'.$$

This gives the ith row of $\mathbf{D}$. The values of the two test statistics are 50.2285 and 60.6528. The critical values from the chi-squared table are 5.99 for the first and 7.82 for the second, so these results cast doubt on the specification of the Weibull model. (Jaggia reaches the same conclusion using all 566 of Kennan's observations.)

Other approaches to specification analysis are suggested by Kiefer (1985a, 1988), Lancaster and Chesher (1985), Chesher et al. (1985), Lawless (1982), and Lancaster (1990).

20.5.2f. Heterogeneity. The problem of heterogeneity in duration models can be viewed essentially as the result of an incomplete specification. Individual specific covariates are intended to incorporate observation specific effects. But if the model specification is incomplete and if systematic individual differences in the distribution remain after the observed effects are accounted for, then inference based on the improperly specified model is likely to be problematic. We have already encountered several settings in which the possibility of heterogeneity mandated a change in the model specification; the fixed and random effects regression, logit, and probit models all incorporate observation-specific effects. Indeed, all the failures of the linear regression model discussed in the preceding chapters can be interpreted as a consequence of heterogeneity arising from an incomplete specification.

There are a number of ways of extending duration models to account for heterogeneity. The strictly nonparametric approach of the Kaplan–Meier estimator is largely immune to the problem, but it is also rather limited in how much information can be culled from it. One direct approach is to model heterogeneity in the parametric model. Suppose that we posit a survival function conditioned on the individual specific effect v_i. We treat the survival function as $S(t_i \mid v_i)$. Then add to that a model for the unobserved heterogeneity $f(v_i)$. (Note that this is a counterpart to the incorporation of a disturbance in a regression model and follows the same procedures that we used in the Poisson model with random effects.) Then

$$S(t) = E_v[S(t \mid v)] = \int_v f(v) S(t \mid v)\, dv.$$

The gamma distribution is frequently used for this purpose.[57] Consider, for example, using this device to incorporate heterogeneity into the Weibull model we used earlier. As is typical, we assume that v has a gamma distribution with mean 1 and variance $\theta = 1/k$. Then

$$f(v) = \frac{k^k}{\Gamma(k)} e^{-kv} v^{k-1}$$

and

$$S(t \mid v) = e^{-(v\lambda t)^p}.$$

After a bit of manipulation, we obtain the unconditional distribution,

$$S(t) = \int_0^\infty f(v) S(t \mid v)\, dv = [1 + \theta(\lambda t)^p]^{-1/\theta}.$$

The limiting value, with $\theta = 0$, is the Weibull survival model, so $\theta = 0$ corresponds to $\text{Var}[v] = 0$, or no heterogeneity.[58] The hazard function for this model is

$$\lambda(t) = \lambda p(\lambda t)^{p-1}[S(t)]^\theta,$$

which shows the relationship to the Weibull model.

This is a common approach to parametric modeling of heterogeneity. In an important paper on this subject, Heckman and Singer (1984b) argued that this approach tends to overparameterize the survival distribution and can lead to rather serious errors in inference. They gave some dramatic examples to make the point. They also expressed some concern that researchers tend to choose the distribution of heterogeneity more on the basis of mathematical convenience than on any sensible economic basis.

---

[57]See, for example, Hausman et al. (1984), who use it to incorporate heterogeneity in the Poisson regression model. The application is developed in Section 19.9.5.

[58]For the strike data analyzed earlier, the maximum likelihood estimate of θ is 0.0004, which suggests that at least in the context of the Weibull model, heterogeneity does not appear to be a problem.

20.5.3. Other Approaches

The parametric models are attractive for their simplicity. But by imposing as much structure on the data as they do, the models may distort the estimated hazard rates. It may be that a more accurate representation can be obtained by imposing fewer restrictions.

The Kaplan–Meier **product limit estimator** is a strictly empirical approach to survival and hazard function estimation. Assume that the observations on duration are sorted in ascending order, so that $t_1 \leq t_2$ and so on and, for now, that no observations are censored. Suppose, as well, that there are K distinct survival times in the data, denoted T_k; K will equal n unless there are ties. Let n_k denote the number of individuals whose observed duration is at least T_k. The set of individuals whose duration is at least T_k is called the **risk set** at this duration. (We borrow, once again, from biostatistics, where the risk set is those individuals still "at risk" at time T_k). Thus, n_k is the size of the risk set at time T_k. Let h_k denote the number of observed spells completed at time T_k. An empirical estimate of the survivor function would be

$$\hat{S}(T_k) = \frac{n_k - h_k}{n_k}.$$

The estimator of the hazard rate is

$$\hat{\lambda}(T_k) = \frac{h_k}{n_k}.$$

Corrections are necessary for observations that are censored. Lawless (1982), Kalbfleisch and Prentice (1980), Kiefer (1988), and Greene (1995a) give details.

EXAMPLE 20.20 Kaplan–Meier Hazard Function Estimates

The estimates of $\lambda(t)$ and $S(t)$ are tabulated in Kiefer (1988, p. 658). Figures 20.6 and 20.7 show the estimated survival and hazard functions.

Cox's (1972) approach to the **proportional hazard** model is another popular method of analyzing the effect of covariates on the hazard rate. The model specifies that

$$\lambda(t_i) = e^{-\boldsymbol{\beta}'\mathbf{x}_i}\lambda_0(t_i).$$

The function λ_0 is the "baseline" hazard; this is the individual heterogeneity. In principle, this is a parameter for each observation that must be estimated. Cox's **partial likelihood** estimator provides a method of estimating $\boldsymbol{\beta}$ without requiring estimation of λ_0. The estimator is somewhat similar to Chamberlain's estimator for the logit model with panel data in that a conditioning operation is used to remove the heterogeneity. (See Section 19.5.1.) Suppose that the sample contains K distinct exit times, $T_1, \ldots, T_K$. For any time T_i, the risk set, denoted R_i is all individuals whose exit time is at least T_i. The risk set is defined with respect to any moment in time T as the set of individuals who have not yet

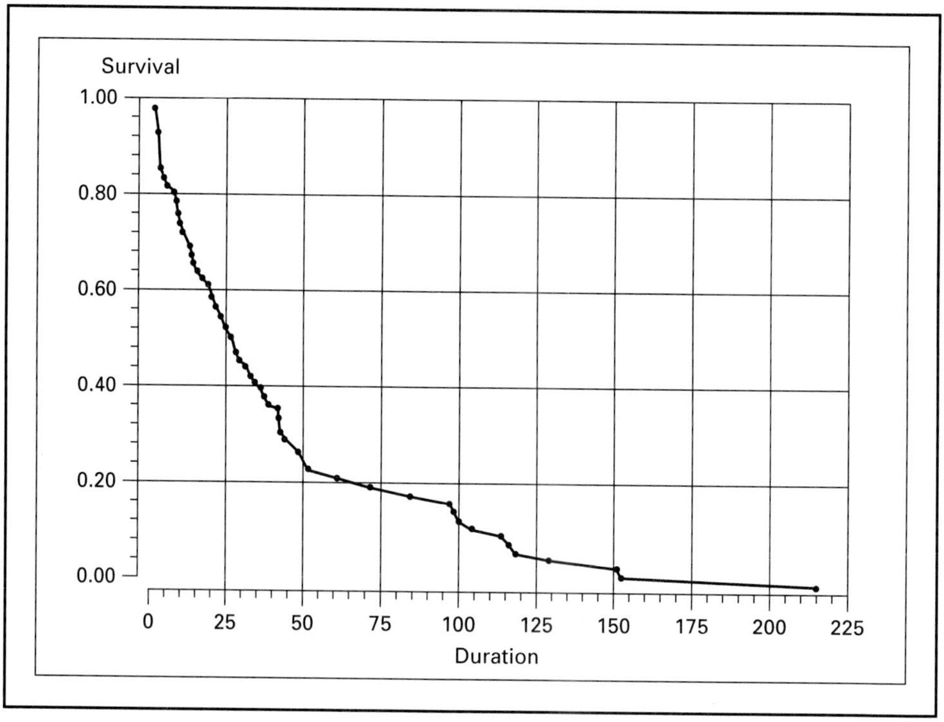

FIGURE 20.6 Estimated Survival Function.

FIGURE 20.7 Estimated Hazard Function.

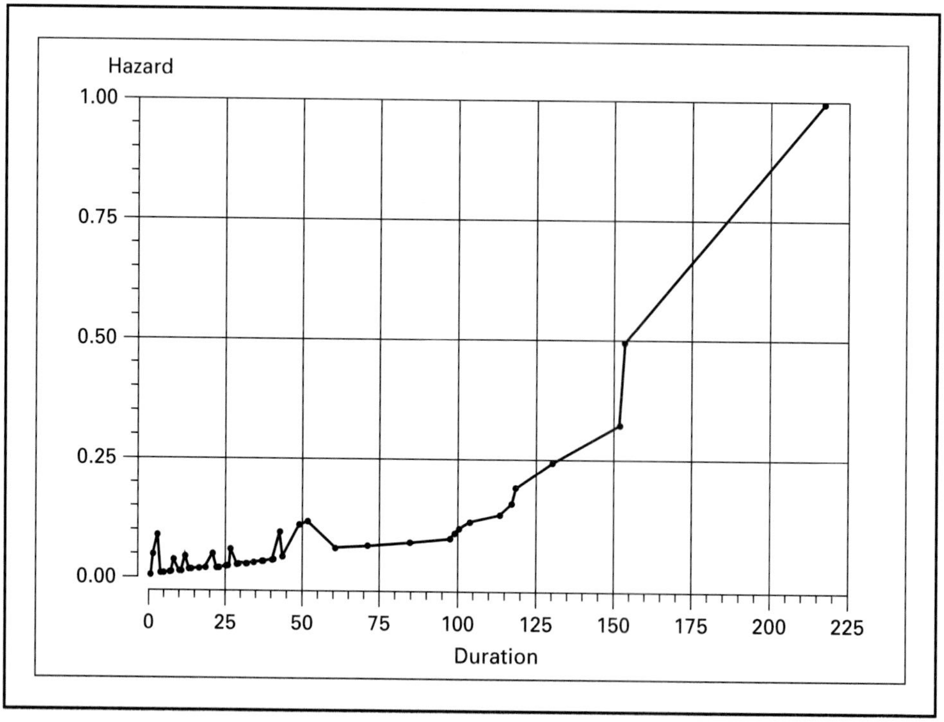

exited just prior to that time. For every individual j in risk set R_i, $t_j \geq T_i$. The probability that an individual exits at time T_i *given that exactly one individual exits at this time* (this is the counterpart to the conditioning in the binary logit model in Chapter 19) is

$$\text{Prob}[t_j = T_i \,|\, \text{risk set}_i] = \frac{e^{\boldsymbol{\beta}'\mathbf{x}_i}}{\sum_{j \in R_i} e^{\boldsymbol{\beta}'\mathbf{x}_j}}.$$

Thus, the conditioning sweeps out the baseline hazard functions. For the simplest case in which exactly one individual exits at each distinct exit time and there are no censored observations, the partial log-likelihood is

$$\ln L = \sum_{i=1}^{K} \left[\boldsymbol{\beta}'\mathbf{x}_i - \sum_{j \in R_i} e^{\boldsymbol{\beta}'\mathbf{x}_j} \right].$$

If m_i individuals exit at time t_i, the contribution to the log-likelihood is the sum of the terms for each of these individuals.

EXAMPLE 20.21 Proportional Hazard Model

The proportional hazard model does not have a constant term. (The baseline hazard is an individual specific constant.) For the strike data, the estimate of β is -9.0726, with an estimated standard error of 3.225. This is very similar to the estimate obtained for the Weibull model in Example 20.19.

The proportional hazard model is a common choice for modeling durations as it is a reasonable compromise between the Kaplan–Meier estimate and the possibly excessively structured parametric models. Hausman and Han (1990) and Mayer (1988), among others have devised other "semiparametric" specifications for hazard models.

EXERCISES

1. The following 20 observations are drawn from a censored normal distribution:

3.8396	7.2040	0.00000	0.00000	4.4132	8.0230
5.7971	7.0828	0.00000	0.80260	13.0670	4.3211
0.00000	8.6801	5.4571	0.00000	8.1021	0.00000
1.2526	5.6016				

The applicable model is

$$y_i^* = \mu + \epsilon_i ,$$
$$y_i = y_i^* \quad \text{if } \mu + \epsilon_i > 0, 0 \text{ otherwise,}$$
$$\epsilon_i \sim N[0, \sigma^2].$$

All exercises in this section are based on the preceding. The OLS estimator of μ in the context of this tobit model is simply the sample mean. Compute the mean of all 20 observations. Would you expect this estimator to over- or underestimate μ? If we consider only the nonzero observations, the truncated regression model applies. The sample mean of the nonlimit observations is the least squares estimator in this context. Compute it and then comment on whether this should be an overestimate or an underestimate of the true mean.

2. We now consider the tobit model that applies to the full data set.
   (a) Formulate the log-likelihood for this very simple tobit model.
   (b) Reformulate the log-likelihood in terms of $\theta = 1/\sigma$ and $\gamma = \mu/\sigma$. Then derive the necessary conditions for maximizing the log-likelihood with respect to θ and γ.
   (c) Discuss how you would obtain the values of θ and γ to solve the problem in part b.
   (d) Obtain the maximum likelihood estimators of μ and σ.
3. Using only the nonlimit observations, repeat Exercise 2 in the context of the truncated regression model.
4. Estimate μ and σ by using the method of moments estimator outlined in Example 20.4. Compare your results with those in the previous exercises.
5. Continuing to use the data in Exercise 1, consider once again only the nonzero observations. Suppose that the sampling mechanism is as follows: y^* and another normally distributed random variable z have population correlation 0.7. The two variables, y^* and z, are sampled jointly. When z is greater than zero, y is reported. When z is less than zero, both z and y are discarded. Exactly 35 draws were required to obtain the preceding sample. Estimate μ and σ. [Hint: Use Theorem 20.4.]

Appendix Tables

TABLE 1 Cumulative Normal Distribution. Table Entry Is $\Phi(z) = \text{Prob}[Z \leq z]$.

z	.00	.01	.02	.03	.04	.05	.06	.07	.08	.09
0.0	.5000	.5040	.5080	.5120	.5160	.5199	.5239	.5279	.5319	.5359
0.1	.5398	.5438	.5478	.5517	.5557	.5596	.5636	.5675	.5714	.5753
0.2	.5793	.5832	.5871	.5910	.5948	.5987	.6026	.6064	.6103	.6141
0.3	.6179	.6217	.6255	.6293	.6331	.6368	.6406	.6443	.6480	.6517
0.4	.6554	.6591	.6628	.6664	.6700	.6736	.6772	.6808	.6844	.6879
0.5	.6915	.6950	.6985	.7019	.7054	.7088	.7123	.7157	.7190	.7224
0.6	.7257	.7291	.7324	.7357	.7389	.7422	.7454	.7486	.7517	.7549
0.7	.7580	.7611	.7642	.7673	.7704	.7734	.7764	.7794	.7823	.7852
0.8	.7881	.7910	.7939	.7967	.7995	.8023	.8051	.8078	.8106	.8133
0.9	.8159	.8186	.8212	.8238	.8264	.8289	.8315	.8340	.8365	.8389
1.0	.8413	.8438	.8461	.8485	.8508	.8531	.8554	.8577	.8599	.8621
1.1	.8643	.8665	.8686	.8708	.8729	.8749	.8770	.8790	.8810	.8830
1.2	.8849	.8869	.8888	.8907	.8925	.8944	.8962	.8980	.8997	.9015
1.3	.9032	.9049	.9066	.9082	.9099	.9115	.9131	.9147	.9162	.9177
1.4	.9192	.9207	.9222	.9236	.9251	.9265	.9279	.9292	.9306	.9319
1.5	.9332	.9345	.9357	.9370	.9382	.9394	.9406	.9418	.9429	.9441
1.6	.9452	.9463	.9474	.9484	.9495	.9505	.9515	.9525	.9535	.9545
1.7	.9554	.9564	.9573	.9582	.9591	.9599	.9608	.9616	.9625	.9633
1.8	.9641	.9649	.9656	.9664	.9671	.9678	.9686	.9693	.9699	.9706
1.9	.9713	.9719	.9726	.9732	.9738	.9744	.9750	.9756	.9761	.9767
2.0	.9772	.9778	.9783	.9788	.9793	.9798	.9803	.9808	.9812	.9817
2.1	.9821	.9826	.9830	.9834	.9838	.9842	.9846	.9850	.9854	.9857
2.2	.9861	.9864	.9868	.9871	.9875	.9878	.9881	.9884	.9887	.9890
2.3	.9893	.9896	.9898	.9901	.9904	.9906	.9909	.9911	.9913	.9916
2.4	.9918	.9920	.9922	.9925	.9927	.9929	.9931	.9932	.9934	.9936
2.5	.9938	.9940	.9941	.9943	.9945	.9946	.9948	.9949	.9951	.9952
2.6	.9953	.9955	.9956	.9957	.9959	.9960	.9961	.9962	.9963	.9964
2.7	.9965	.9966	.9967	.9968	.9969	.9970	.9971	.9972	.9973	.9974
2.8	.9974	.9975	.9976	.9977	.9977	.9978	.9979	.9979	.9980	.9981
2.9	.9981	.9982	.9982	.9983	.9984	.9984	.9985	.9985	.9986	.9986
3.0	.9987	.9987	.9987	.9988	.9988	.9989	.9989	.9989	.9990	.9990
3.1	.9990	.9991	.9991	.9991	.9992	.9992	.9992	.9992	.9993	.9993
3.2	.9993	.9993	.9994	.9994	.9994	.9994	.9994	.9995	.9995	.9995
3.3	.9995	.9995	.9995	.9996	.9996	.9996	.9996	.9996	.9996	.9997
3.4	.9997	.9997	.9997	.9997	.9997	.9997	.9997	.9997	.9997	.9998

TABLE 2 Ordinates of the Standard Normal Density. Table Entry Is $\phi(z)$.

z	.00	.01	.02	.03	.04	.05	.06	.07	.08	.09
0.0	.3989	.3989	.3989	.3988	.3986	.3984	.3982	.3980	.3977	.3973
0.1	.3970	.3965	.3961	.3956	.3951	.3945	.3939	.3932	.3925	.3918
0.2	.3910	.3902	.3894	.3885	.3876	.3867	.3857	.3847	.3836	.3825
0.3	.3814	.3802	.3790	.3778	.3765	.3752	.3739	.3725	.3712	.3697
0.4	.3683	.3668	.3653	.3637	.3621	.3605	.3589	.3572	.3555	.3538
0.5	.3521	.3503	.3485	.3467	.3448	.3429	.3410	.3391	.3372	.3352
0.6	.3332	.3312	.3292	.3271	.3251	.3230	.3209	.3187	.3166	.3144
0.7	.3123	.3101	.3079	.3056	.3034	.3011	.2989	.2966	.2943	.2920
0.8	.2897	.2874	.2850	.2827	.2803	.2780	.2756	.2732	.2709	.2685
0.9	.2661	.2637	.2613	.2589	.2565	.2541	.2516	.2492	.2468	.2444
1.0	.2420	.2396	.2371	.2347	.2323	.2299	.2275	.2251	.2227	.2203
1.1	.2179	.2155	.2131	.2107	.2083	.2059	.2036	.2012	.1989	.1965
1.2	.1942	.1919	.1895	.1872	.1849	.1826	.1804	.1781	.1758	.1736
1.3	.1714	.1691	.1669	.1647	.1626	.1604	.1582	.1561	.1539	.1518
1.4	.1497	.1476	.1456	.1435	.1415	.1394	.1374	.1354	.1334	.1315
1.5	.1295	.1276	.1257	.1238	.1219	.1200	.1182	.1163	.1145	.1127
1.6	.1109	.1092	.1074	.1057	.1040	.1023	.1006	.0989	.0973	.0957
1.7	.0940	.0925	.0909	.0893	.0878	.0863	.0848	.0833	.0818	.0804
1.8	.0790	.0775	.0761	.0748	.0734	.0721	.0707	.0694	.0681	.0669
1.9	.0656	.0644	.0632	.0620	.0608	.0596	.0584	.0573	.0562	.0551
2.0	.0540	.0529	.0519	.0508	.0498	.0488	.0478	.0468	.0459	.0449
2.1	.0440	.0431	.0422	.0413	.0404	.0396	.0387	.0379	.0371	.0363
2.2	.0355	.0347	.0339	.0332	.0325	.0317	.0310	.0303	.0297	.0290
2.3	.0283	.0277	.0270	.0264	.0258	.0252	.0246	.0241	.0235	.0229
2.4	.0224	.0219	.0213	.0208	.0203	.0198	.0194	.0189	.0184	.0180
2.5	.0175	.0171	.0167	.0163	.0158	.0154	.0151	.0147	.0143	.0139
2.6	.0136	.0132	.0129	.0126	.0122	.0119	.0116	.0113	.0110	.0107
2.7	.0104	.0101	.0099	.0096	.0093	.0091	.0088	.0086	.0084	.0081
2.8	.0079	.0077	.0075	.0073	.0071	.0069	.0067	.0065	.0063	.0061
2.9	.0060	.0058	.0056	.0055	.0053	.0051	.0050	.0048	.0047	.0046
3.0	.0044	.0043	.0042	.0040	.0039	.0038	.0037	.0036	.0035	.0034
3.1	.0033	.0032	.0031	.0030	.0029	.0028	.0027	.0026	.0025	.0025
3.2	.0024	.0023	.0022	.0022	.0021	.0020	.0020	.0019	.0018	.0018
3.3	.0017	.0017	.0016	.0016	.0015	.0015	.0014	.0014	.0013	.0013
3.4	.0012	.0012	.0012	.0011	.0011	.0010	.0010	.0010	.0009	.0009

TABLE 3 Percentiles of the Student's t Distribution. Table Entry Is x Such That $\text{Prob}[t_n \le x] = P$.

P n	.750	.900	.950	.975	.990	.995
1	1.000	3.078	6.314	12.71	31.82	63.66
2	0.817	1.886	2.920	4.303	6.965	9.925
3	0.766	1.638	2.354	3.182	4.541	5.841
4	0.741	1.533	2.132	2.777	3.747	4.604
5	0.727	1.476	2.015	2.571	3.365	4.032
6	0.718	1.440	1.943	2.447	3.143	3.708
7	0.711	1.415	1.895	2.365	2.998	3.500
8	0.706	1.397	1.860	2.306	2.897	3.355
9	0.703	1.383	1.833	2.262	2.822	3.250
10	0.700	1.372	1.813	2.228	2.764	3.169
11	0.698	1.363	1.796	2.201	2.718	3.106
12	0.696	1.356	1.782	2.179	2.681	3.055
13	0.694	1.350	1.771	2.161	2.650	3.012
14	0.693	1.345	1.762	2.145	2.624	2.977
15	0.691	1.341	1.753	2.132	2.602	2.947
16	0.691	1.337	1.746	2.120	2.584	2.921
17	0.689	1.333	1.740	2.110	2.567	2.898
18	0.688	1.330	1.734	2.101	2.552	2.879
19	0.688	1.328	1.729	2.093	2.539	2.861
20	0.687	1.326	1.725	2.086	2.528	2.845
21	0.687	1.323	1.721	2.080	2.518	2.831
22	0.686	1.321	1.717	2.074	2.508	2.819
23	0.686	1.319	1.714	2.069	2.500	2.807
24	0.686	1.318	1.711	2.064	2.492	2.797
25	0.685	1.316	1.708	2.060	2.485	2.787
26	0.684	1.315	1.706	2.056	2.479	2.779
27	0.684	1.314	1.704	2.052	2.473	2.771
28	0.683	1.313	1.701	2.048	2.467	2.763
29	0.683	1.311	1.699	2.045	2.462	2.756
30	0.683	1.311	1.697	2.042	2.457	2.750
35	0.682	1.307	1.690	2.030	2.438	2.724
40	0.681	1.303	1.684	2.021	2.423	2.705
45	0.680	1.301	1.680	2.014	2.412	2.690
50	0.680	1.299	1.676	2.009	2.403	2.678
60	0.679	1.296	1.671	2.000	2.390	2.660
70	0.679	1.294	1.667	1.994	2.381	2.648
80	0.679	1.292	1.664	1.990	2.374	2.639
90	0.678	1.291	1.662	1.987	2.368	2.632
100	0.677	1.290	1.660	1.984	2.364	2.626
∞	0.674	1.282	1.645	1.960	2.326	2.576

TABLE 4 Percentiles of the Chi-Squared Distribution. Table Entry Is c Such That $\text{Prob}[\chi_n^2 \le c] = P$.

Pn	*.005*	*.010*	*.025*	*.050*	*.100*	*.250*	*.500*	*.750*	*.900*	*.950*	*.975*	*.990*	*.995*
1	0.00004	0.0002	0.001	0.004	0.02	0.10	0.46	1.32	2.71	3.84	5.02	6.63	7.89
2	0.01	0.02	0.05	0.10	0.21	0.58	1.39	2.77	4.61	5.99	7.38	9.21	10.60
3	0.07	0.12	0.22	0.35	0.59	1.21	2.37	4.11	6.25	7.82	9.35	11.34	12.84
4	0.21	0.30	0.49	0.71	1.06	1.92	3.36	5.39	7.78	9.49	11.14	13.28	14.86
5	0.41	0.56	0.83	1.15	1.61	2.68	4.35	6.63	9.24	11.07	12.83	15.09	16.75
6	0.68	0.87	1.24	1.64	2.21	3.46	5.35	7.84	10.64	12.59	14.45	16.81	18.55
7	0.99	1.24	1.69	2.17	2.83	4.25	6.35	9.04	12.02	14.07	16.01	18.48	20.28
8	1.35	1.65	2.18	2.73	3.49	5.07	7.34	10.22	13.36	15.51	17.54	20.09	21.96
9	1.74	2.09	2.70	3.33	4.17	5.90	8.34	11.39	14.68	16.92	19.02	21.67	23.59
10	2.16	2.56	3.25	3.94	4.87	6.74	9.34	12.55	15.99	18.31	20.48	23.21	25.19
11	2.60	3.05	3.82	4.57	5.58	7.59	10.34	13.70	17.28	19.68	21.92	24.72	26.76
12	3.07	3.57	4.40	5.23	6.30	8.44	11.34	14.85	18.55	21.03	23.34	26.22	28.30
13	3.57	4.11	5.01	5.89	7.04	9.30	12.34	15.98	19.81	22.36	24.74	27.69	29.82
14	4.07	4.66	5.63	6.57	7.79	10.17	13.34	17.12	21.07	23.69	26.12	29.14	31.32
15	4.60	5.23	6.26	7.26	8.55	11.04	14.34	18.25	22.31	25.00	27.49	30.58	32.80
16	5.14	5.81	6.91	7.96	9.31	11.91	15.34	19.37	23.54	26.30	28.85	32.00	34.27
17	5.70	6.41	7.57	8.67	10.09	12.79	16.34	20.49	24.77	27.59	30.19	33.41	35.72
18	6.26	7.01	8.23	9.39	10.86	13.68	17.34	21.61	25.99	28.87	31.53	34.81	37.16
19	6.84	7.63	8.91	10.12	11.65	14.56	18.34	22.72	27.20	30.14	32.85	36.19	38.58
20	7.43	8.26	9.59	10.85	12.44	15.45	19.34	23.83	28.41	31.41	34.17	37.57	40.00
21	8.03	8.90	10.28	11.59	13.24	16.35	20.34	24.93	29.62	32.67	35.48	38.93	41.40
22	8.64	9.54	10.98	12.34	14.04	17.24	21.34	26.04	30.81	33.93	36.78	40.29	42.80
23	9.26	10.20	11.69	13.09	14.85	18.14	22.34	27.14	32.01	35.17	38.08	41.64	44.18
24	9.89	10.86	12.40	13.85	15.66	19.04	23.34	28.24	33.20	36.42	39.37	42.98	45.56
25	10.52	11.52	13.12	14.61	16.47	19.94	24.34	29.34	34.38	37.65	40.65	44.32	46.93

Pn	*.005*	*.010*	*.025*	*.050*	*.100*	*.250*	*.500*	*.750*	*.900*	*.950*	*.975*	*.990*	*.995*
26	11.16	12.20	13.84	15.38	17.29	20.84	25.34	30.44	35.56	38.89	41.92	45.64	48.29
27	11.81	12.88	14.57	16.15	18.11	21.75	26.34	31.53	36.74	40.11	43.19	46.96	49.65
28	12.46	13.56	15.31	16.93	18.94	22.66	27.34	32.62	37.92	41.34	44.46	48.28	50.99
29	13.12	14.26	16.05	17.71	19.77	23.57	28.34	33.71	39.09	42.56	45.72	49.59	52.34
30	13.79	14.95	16.79	18.49	20.60	24.48	29.34	34.80	40.26	43.77	46.98	50.89	53.67
31	13.70	15.04	17.11	19.01	21.31	25.46	30.50	36.00	41.33	44.70	47.73	51.38	53.94
32	14.37	15.74	17.87	19.80	22.15	26.37	31.50	37.08	42.49	45.91	48.98	52.67	55.26
33	15.05	16.45	18.62	20.59	22.99	27.29	32.50	38.17	43.65	47.12	50.22	53.96	56.59
34	15.73	17.16	19.38	21.39	23.83	28.21	33.50	39.25	44.81	48.32	51.46	55.25	57.90
35	16.42	17.88	20.14	22.19	24.68	29.13	34.50	40.33	45.97	49.52	52.70	56.53	59.21
36	17.11	18.60	20.91	22.99	25.52	30.05	35.50	41.41	47.12	50.71	53.94	57.81	60.52
37	17.81	19.33	21.68	23.80	26.37	30.97	36.50	42.49	48.27	51.91	55.17	59.08	61.83
38	18.51	20.06	22.45	24.61	27.22	31.89	37.50	43.57	49.42	53.10	56.39	60.35	63.13
39	19.22	20.79	23.22	25.42	28.08	32.81	38.50	44.65	50.57	54.29	57.62	61.62	64.42
40	19.92	21.53	24.00	26.23	28.93	33.73	39.50	45.72	51.71	55.47	58.84	62.88	65.71
41	20.64	22.27	24.78	27.05	29.79	34.66	40.50	46.80	52.86	56.66	60.06	64.14	67.00
42	21.35	23.01	25.57	27.87	30.65	35.58	41.50	47.87	54.00	57.84	61.28	65.40	68.29
43	22.07	23.76	26.35	28.69	31.51	36.51	42.50	48.95	55.14	59.02	62.49	66.65	69.57
44	22.79	24.51	27.14	29.51	32.37	37.44	43.50	50.02	56.27	60.19	63.70	67.91	70.84
45	23.52	25.26	27.93	30.34	33.23	38.37	44.50	51.09	57.41	61.37	64.91	69.15	72.12
46	24.25	26.02	28.72	31.16	34.10	39.29	45.50	52.16	58.55	62.54	66.12	70.40	73.39
47	24.98	26.77	29.52	31.99	34.96	40.22	46.50	53.23	59.68	63.72	67.32	71.64	74.66
48	25.71	27.53	30.32	32.82	35.83	41.15	47.50	54.30	60.81	64.89	68.53	72.88	75.92
49	26.45	28.30	31.12	33.65	36.70	42.08	48.50	55.37	61.94	66.05	69.73	74.12	77.19
50	27.19	29.06	31.92	34.49	37.57	43.02	49.50	56.44	63.07	67.22	70.92	75.35	78.45

TABLE 5 95th Percentile of the F Distribution. Table Entry Is f Such That $\text{Prob}[F_{n_1,n_2} \leq f] = .95$.

n_1 = Degrees of Freedom for the Numerator

n_2	*1*	*2*	*3*	*4*	*5*	*6*	*7*	*8*	*9*
1	161.	200.	216.	225.	230.	234.	237.	239.	241.
2	18.5	19.0	19.2	19.2	19.3	19.3	19.4	19.4	19.4
3	10.1	9.55	6.54	9.12	5.89	8.94	5.63	8.85	5.49
4	7.71	6.94	6.59	6.39	6.26	6.16	6.09	6.04	6.00
5	6.61	5.79	5.41	5.19	5.05	4.95	4.88	4.82	4.77
6	5.99	5.14	4.76	4.53	4.39	4.28	4.21	4.15	4.10
7	5.59	4.74	4.35	4.12	3.97	3.87	3.79	3.73	3.68
8	5.32	4.46	4.07	3.84	3.69	3.58	3.50	3.44	3.39
9	5.12	4.26	3.86	3.63	3.48	3.37	3.29	3.23	3.18
10	4.96	4.10	3.71	3.48	3.33	3.22	3.14	3.07	3.02
11	4.84	3.98	3.59	3.36	3.20	3.10	3.01	2.95	2.90
12	4.75	3.89	3.49	3.26	3.11	3.00	2.91	2.85	2.80
13	4.67	3.81	3.41	3.18	3.03	2.92	2.83	2.77	2.72
14	4.60	3.74	3.34	3.11	2.96	2.85	2.77	2.70	2.65
15	4.54	3.68	3.29	3.06	2.90	2.79	2.71	2.64	2.59
16	4.49	3.63	3.24	3.01	2.85	2.74	2.66	2.59	2.54
17	4.45	3.59	3.20	2.97	2.81	2.70	2.62	2.55	2.50
18	4.41	3.56	3.16	2.93	2.77	2.66	2.58	2.51	2.46
19	4.38	3.52	3.13	2.90	2.74	2.63	2.54	2.48	2.42
20	4.35	3.49	3.10	2.87	2.71	2.60	2.52	2.45	2.39
21	4.32	3.47	3.07	2.84	2.69	2.57	2.49	2.42	2.37
22	4.30	3.44	3.05	2.82	2.66	2.55	2.46	2.40	2.34
23	4.28	3.42	3.03	2.80	2.64	2.53	2.44	2.38	2.32
24	4.26	3.40	3.01	2.78	2.62	2.51	2.42	2.36	2.30
25	4.24	3.39	2.99	2.76	2.60	2.49	2.41	2.34	2.28
26	4.23	3.37	2.98	2.74	2.59	2.48	2.39	2.32	2.27
27	4.22	3.36	2.96	2.73	2.57	2.46	2.37	2.31	2.25
28	4.20	3.34	2.95	2.72	2.56	2.45	2.36	2.29	2.24
29	4.18	3.33	2.94	2.70	2.55	2.43	2.35	2.28	2.22
30	4.17	3.32	2.92	2.69	2.53	2.42	2.34	2.27	2.21
35	4.12	3.27	2.88	2.64	2.49	2.37	2.29	2.22	2.16
40	4.08	3.23	2.84	2.61	2.45	2.34	2.25	2.18	2.13
45	4.06	3.21	2.81	2.58	2.42	2.31	2.22	2.15	2.10
50	4.05	3.18	2.79	2.56	2.40	2.29	2.20	2.13	2.07
60	4.00	3.15	2.76	2.53	2.37	2.26	2.17	2.10	2.04
70	3.98	3.13	2.74	2.50	2.35	2.23	2.14	2.07	2.02
80	3.96	3.11	2.72	2.49	2.33	2.22	2.13	2.06	2.00
90	3.95	3.10	2.71	2.47	2.32	2.20	2.11	2.04	1.99
100	3.94	3.09	2.70	2.46	2.31	2.19	2.10	2.03	1.98
∞	3.84	3.00	2.60	2.37	2.21	2.10	2.01	1.94	1.88

n_1 = ***Degrees of Freedom for the Numerator***

10	*12*	*15*	*20*	*30*	*40*	*50*	*60*	∞
242.	244.	246.	248.	250.	251.	251.	252.	254.
19.4	19.4	19.4	19.5	19.5	19.5	19.5	19.5	19.5
8.79	8.74	5.32	8.66	8.62	8.59	8.58	8.57	8.83
5.97	5.91	5.86	5.80	5.75	5.72	5.70	5.69	5.63
4.74	4.68	4.62	4.56	4.50	4.46	4.44	4.43	4.37
4.06	4.00	3.94	3.88	3.81	3.78	3.75	3.74	3.67
3.64	3.58	3.51	3.45	3.38	3.34	3.32	3.31	3.23
3.35	3.28	3.22	3.15	3.08	3.04	3.02	3.01	2.93
3.14	3.07	3.01	2.94	2.86	2.83	2.80	2.79	2.71
2.98	2.91	2.85	2.78	2.70	2.66	2.64	2.62	2.54
2.85	2.79	2.72	2.65	2.57	2.53	2.51	2.49	2.40
2.75	2.69	2.62	2.54	2.47	2.43	2.40	2.39	2.30
2.67	2.60	2.53	2.46	2.38	2.34	2.31	2.30	2.21
2.60	2.54	2.46	2.39	2.31	2.27	2.24	2.22	2.13
2.54	2.48	2.40	2.33	2.25	2.21	2.18	2.16	2.07
2.49	2.43	2.35	2.28	2.19	2.15	2.12	2.11	2.01
2.45	2.38	2.31	2.23	2.15	2.10	2.08	2.06	1.96
2.41	2.34	2.27	2.19	2.11	2.06	2.04	2.02	1.92
2.38	2.31	2.24	2.16	2.07	2.03	2.00	1.98	1.88
2.35	2.28	2.20	2.13	2.04	1.99	1.97	1.95	1.84
2.32	2.25	2.18	2.10	2.01	1.97	1.94	1.92	1.81
2.30	2.23	2.15	2.07	1.99	1.94	1.91	1.89	1.78
2.28	2.20	2.13	2.05	1.96	1.91	1.89	1.87	1.76
2.26	2.18	2.11	2.03	1.94	1.89	1.86	1.84	1.73
2.24	2.17	2.09	2.01	1.92	1.87	1.84	1.82	1.71
2.22	2.15	2.07	1.99	1.90	1.85	1.82	1.80	1.70
2.21	2.13	2.06	1.97	1.89	1.84	1.81	1.79	1.68
2.19	2.12	2.04	1.96	1.87	1.82	1.79	1.77	1.66
2.18	2.11	2.03	1.95	1.86	1.81	1.78	1.75	1.65
2.17	2.09	2.02	1.93	1.84	1.79	1.76	1.74	1.62
2.12	2.04	1.96	1.88	1.79	1.74	1.70	1.68	1.57
2.08	2.00	1.92	1.84	1.75	1.69	1.66	1.64	1.51
2.05	1.98	1.90	1.81	1.71	1.66	1.63	1.60	1.48
2.03	1.95	1.87	1.79	1.69	1.63	1.60	1.58	1.45
1.99	1.92	1.84	1.75	1.65	1.60	1.56	1.54	1.39
1.97	1.89	1.81	1.72	1.62	1.57	1.53	1.51	1.36
1.95	1.88	1.79	1.70	1.60	1.55	1.51	1.48	1.34
1.94	1.86	1.78	1.69	1.59	1.53	1.49	1.47	1.32
1.93	1.85	1.77	1.68	1.57	1.52	1.48	1.45	1.30
1.83	1.75	1.67	1.57	1.46	1.39	1.34	1.31	1.00

TABLE 6 99th Percentiles of the F Distribution. Table Entry Is f Such That Prob[$F_{n_1,n_2} \leq f$] = .99.

n_1 = *Degrees of Freedom for the Numerator*

n_2	1	2	3	4	5	6	7	8	9
1	4052	5000	5403	5625	5724	5859	5928	5982	6023
2	98.5	99.0	99.2	99.3	99.3	99.3	99.4	99.4	99.4
3	34.1	30.8	21.3	28.7	19.0	27.9	27.7	27.5	27.3
4	21.2	18.0	16.7	16.0	15.5	15.2	15.0	14.8	14.7
5	16.3	13.3	12.1	11.4	11.0	10.6	10.5	10.3	10.2
6	13.7	10.9	9.78	9.15	8.75	8.47	8.26	8.10	7.98
7	12.2	9.55	8.45	7.85	7.46	7.19	6.99	6.84	6.72
8	11.3	8.65	7.59	7.01	6.63	6.37	6.18	6.03	5.91
9	10.6	8.02	6.99	6.42	6.06	5.80	5.61	5.47	5.35
10	10.0	7.56	6.55	6.00	5.64	5.39	5.20	5.06	4.94
11	9.65	7.21	6.22	5.67	5.32	5.07	4.89	4.74	4.63
12	9.33	6.93	5.95	5.41	5.06	4.82	4.64	4.50	4.39
13	9.07	6.70	5.74	5.21	4.86	4.62	4.44	4.30	4.19
14	8.86	6.51	5.56	5.04	4.69	4.46	4.28	4.14	4.03
15	8.68	6.36	5.42	4.89	4.56	4.32	4.14	4.01	3.90
16	8.53	6.23	5.29	4.77	4.44	4.20	4.03	3.89	3.78
17	8.40	6.11	5.18	4.67	4.34	4.10	3.93	3.79	3.68
18	8.29	6.01	5.09	4.58	4.25	4.01	3.84	3.71	3.60
19	8.19	5.93	5.01	4.50	4.17	3.94	3.77	3.63	3.52
20	8.10	5.85	4.94	4.43	4.10	3.87	3.70	3.57	3.46
21	8.02	5.78	4.88	4.37	4.04	3.81	3.64	3.51	3.40
22	7.95	5.72	4.82	4.31	3.99	3.76	3.59	3.45	3.35
23	7.88	5.66	4.76	4.26	3.94	3.71	3.54	3.41	3.30
24	7.82	5.61	4.72	4.22	3.90	3.67	3.50	3.36	3.26
25	7.77	5.57	4.68	4.18	3.86	3.63	3.46	3.32	3.22
26	7.72	5.53	4.64	4.14	3.82	3.59	3.42	3.29	3.18
27	7.68	5.49	4.60	4.11	3.79	3.56	3.39	3.26	3.15
28	7.64	5.45	4.57	4.07	3.75	3.53	3.36	3.23	3.12
29	7.60	5.42	4.54	4.04	3.73	3.50	3.33	3.20	3.09
30	7.56	5.39	4.51	4.02	3.70	3.47	3.31	3.17	3.07
35	7.41	5.27	4.40	3.91	3.59	3.37	3.20	3.07	2.96
40	7.31	5.18	4.31	3.83	3.51	3.29	3.12	2.99	2.89
45	7.23	5.11	4.25	3.77	3.46	3.23	3.07	2.94	2.83
50	7.17	5.06	4.20	3.72	3.41	3.19	3.02	2.89	2.79
60	7.08	4.98	4.13	3.65	3.34	3.12	2.95	2.82	2.72
70	7.01	4.92	4.07	3.60	3.29	3.07	2.91	2.78	2.67
80	6.96	4.88	4.04	3.56	3.26	3.04	2.87	2.74	2.64
90	6.93	4.85	4.01	3.54	3.23	3.01	2.85	2.72	2.61
100	6.90	4.82	3.98	3.51	3.21	2.99	2.82	2.70	2.59
∞	6.63	4.61	3.78	3.32	3.02	2.80	2.64	2.51	2.41

n_1 = *Degrees of Freedom for the Numerator*								
10	***12***	***15***	***20***	***30***	***40***	***50***	***60***	∞
6056	6106	6157	6209	6261	6287	6302	6313	6366
99.4	99.4	99.4	99.5	99.5	99.5	99.5	99.5	99.5
27.2	27.1	26.9	26.7	26.5	26.4	26.4	26.3	26.1
14.6	14.4	14.2	14.0	13.8	13.8	13.7	13.6	13.5
10.1	9.89	9.72	9.55	9.38	9.29	9.24	9.20	9.02
7.88	7.72	7.56	7.40	7.23	7.14	7.09	7.06	6.88
6.62	6.47	6.31	6.16	5.99	5.91	5.86	5.82	5.65
5.81	5.67	5.52	5.36	5.20	5.12	5.07	5.03	4.86
5.26	5.11	4.96	4.81	4.65	4.57	4.52	4.48	4.31
4.85	4.71	4.56	4.41	4.25	4.17	4.12	4.08	3.91
4.54	4.40	4.25	4.10	3.94	3.86	3.81	3.78	3.60
4.30	4.16	4.01	3.86	3.70	3.62	3.57	3.54	3.36
4.10	3.96	3.82	3.67	3.51	3.43	3.38	3.34	3.17
3.94	3.80	3.66	3.51	3.35	3.27	3.22	3.18	3.00
3.81	3.67	3.52	3.37	3.22	3.13	3.08	3.05	2.87
3.69	3.55	3.41	3.26	3.10	3.02	2.97	2.93	2.75
3.59	3.46	3.31	3.16	3.00	2.92	2.87	2.84	2.65
3.51	3.37	3.23	3.08	2.92	2.84	2.79	2.75	2.57
3.43	3.30	3.15	3.00	2.85	2.76	2.71	2.68	2.49
3.37	3.23	3.09	2.94	2.78	2.70	2.64	2.61	2.42
3.31	3.17	3.03	2.88	2.72	2.64	2.58	2.55	2.36
3.26	3.12	2.98	2.83	2.67	2.58	2.53	2.50	2.31
3.21	3.08	2.93	2.78	2.62	2.54	2.48	2.45	2.26
3.17	3.03	2.89	2.74	2.58	2.49	2.44	2.40	2.21
3.13	2.99	2.85	2.70	2.54	2.45	2.40	2.36	2.17
3.10	2.96	2.82	2.66	2.50	2.42	2.36	2.33	2.13
3.06	2.93	2.78	2.63	2.47	2.38	2.33	2.29	2.10
3.03	2.90	2.75	2.60	2.44	2.35	2.30	2.26	2.06
3.01	2.87	2.73	2.58	2.41	2.33	2.27	2.24	2.03
2.98	2.84	2.70	2.55	2.39	2.30	2.25	2.21	2.01
2.88	2.74	2.60	2.45	2.28	2.19	2.14	2.10	1.91
2.80	2.67	2.52	2.37	2.20	2.12	2.06	2.02	1.81
2.74	2.61	2.47	2.31	2.15	2.06	2.00	1.96	1.75
2.70	2.56	2.42	2.27	2.10	2.01	1.95	1.91	1.68
2.63	2.50	2.35	2.20	2.03	1.94	1.88	1.84	1.60
2.59	2.45	2.31	2.15	1.98	1.89	1.83	1.79	1.53
2.55	2.42	2.27	2.12	1.94	1.85	1.79	1.75	1.49
2.53	2.39	2.25	2.09	1.92	1.82	1.76	1.72	1.48
2.50	2.37	2.22	2.07	1.89	1.80	1.74	1.69	1.43
2.32	2.18	2.04	1.88	1.70	1.57	1.51	1.46	1.00

TABLE 7a Durbin–Watson Statistic: 1 Percent Significance Points of *dL* and *dU*

	$k' = 1$		$k' = 2$		$k' = 3$		$k' = 4$		$k' = 5$	
n	*dL*	*dU*	*dL*	*dU*	*dL*	*dU*	*dL*	*dU*	*dL*	*dU*
6	0.390	1.142	—	—	—	—	—	—	—	—
7	0.435	1.036	0.294	1.676	—	—	—	—	—	—
8	0.497	1.003	0.345	1.489	0.229	2.102	—	—	—	—
9	0.554	0.998	0.408	1.389	0.279	1.875	0.183	2.433	—	—
10	0.604	1.001	0.466	1.333	0.340	1.733	0.230	2.193	0.150	2.690
11	0.653	1.010	0.519	1.297	0.396	1.640	0.286	2.030	0.193	2.453
12	0.697	1.023	0.569	1.274	0.449	1.575	0.339	1.913	0.244	2.280
13	0.738	1.038	0.616	1.261	0.499	1.526	0.391	1.826	0.294	2.150
14	0.776	1.054	0.660	1.254	0.547	1.490	0.441	1.757	0.343	2.049
15	0.811	1.070	0.700	1.252	0.591	1.464	0.488	1.704	0.391	1.967
16	0.844	1.086	0.737	1.252	0.633	1.446	0.532	1.663	0.437	1.900
17	0.874	1.102	0.772	1.255	0.672	1.432	0.574	1.630	0.480	1.847
18	0.902	1.118	0.805	1.259	0.708	1.422	0.613	1.604	0.522	1.803
19	0.928	1.132	0.835	1.265	0.742	1.415	0.650	1.584	0.561	1.767
20	0.952	1.147	0.863	1.271	0.773	1.411	0.685	1.567	0.598	1.737
21	0.975	1.161	0.890	1.277	0.803	1.408	0.718	1.554	0.633	1.712
22	0.997	1.174	0.914	1.284	0.831	1.407	0.748	1.543	0.667	1.691
23	1.018	1.187	0.938	1.291	0.858	1.407	0.777	1.534	0.698	1.673
24	1.037	1.199	0.960	1.298	0.882	1.407	0.805	1.528	0.728	1.658
25	1.055	1.211	0.981	1.305	0.906	1.409	0.831	1.523	0.756	1.645
26	1.072	1.222	1.001	1.312	0.928	1.411	0.855	1.518	0.783	1.635
27	1.089	1.233	1.019	1.319	0.949	1.413	0.878	1.515	0.808	1.626
28	1.104	1.244	1.037	1.325	0.969	1.415	0.900	1.513	0.832	1.618
29	1.119	1.254	1.054	1.332	0.988	1.418	0.921	1.512	0.855	1.611
30	1.133	1.263	1.070	1.339	1.006	1.421	0.941	1.511	0.877	1.606
31	1.147	1.273	1.085	1.345	1.023	1.425	0.960	1.510	0.897	1.601
32	1.160	1.282	1.100	1.352	1.040	1.428	0.979	1.510	0.917	1.597
33	1.172	1.291	1.114	1.358	1.055	1.432	0.996	1.510	0.936	1.594
34	1.184	1.299	1.128	1.364	1.070	1.435	1.012	1.511	0.954	1.591
35	1.195	1.307	1.140	1.370	1.085	1.439	1.028	1.512	0.971	1.589
36	1.206	1.315	1.153	1.376	1.098	1.442	1.043	1.513	0.988	1.588
37	1.217	1.323	1.165	1.382	1.112	1.446	1.058	1.514	1.004	1.586
38	1.227	1.330	1.176	1.388	1.124	1.449	1.072	1.515	1.019	1.585
39	1.237	1.337	1.187	1.393	1.137	1.453	1.085	1.517	1.034	1.584
40	1.246	1.344	1.198	1.398	1.148	1.457	1.098	1.518	1.048	1.584
45	1.288	1.376	1.245	1.423	1.201	1.474	1.156	1.528	1.111	1.584
50	1.324	1.403	1.285	1.446	1.245	1.491	1.205	1.538	1.164	1.587
55	1.356	1.427	1.320	1.466	1.284	1.506	1.247	1.548	1.209	1.592
60	1.383	1.449	1.350	1.484	1.317	1.520	1.283	1.558	1.249	1.598
65	1.407	1.468	1.377	1.500	1.346	1.534	1.315	1.568	1.283	1.604
70	1.429	1.485	1.400	1.515	1.372	1.546	1.343	1.578	1.313	1.611
75	1.448	1.501	1.422	1.529	1.395	1.557	1.368	1.587	1.340	1.617
80	1.466	1.515	1.441	1.541	1.416	1.568	1.390	1.595	1.364	1.624
85	1.482	1.528	1.458	1.553	1.435	1.578	1.411	1.603	1.386	1.630
90	1.496	1.540	1.474	1.563	1.452	1.587	1.429	1.611	1.406	1.636
95	1.510	1.552	1.489	1.573	1.468	1.596	1.446	1.618	1.425	1.642
100	1.522	1.562	1.503	1.583	1.482	1.604	1.462	1.625	1.441	1.647
150	1.611	1.637	1.598	1.651	1.584	1.665	1.571	1.679	1.557	1.693
200	1.664	1.684	1.653	1.693	1.643	1.704	1.633	1.715	1.623	1.725

Source: N. E. Savin and K. J. White, "The Durbin–Watson Test for Serial Correlation with Extreme Sample Sizes of Many Regressors," *Econometrica,* 45(8), Nov. 1977, pp. 1992–1995.

Note: k' is the number of regressors excluding the intercept.

k' = 6		*k'* = 7		*k'* = 8		*k'* = 9		*k'* = 10	
dL	*dU*	*dL*	*dU*	*dL*	*dU*	*dL*	*dU*	*dL*	*dU*
—	—	—	—	—	—	—	—	—	—
—	—	—	—	—	—	—	—	—	—
—	—	—	—	—	—	—	—	—	—
—	—	—	—	—	—	—	—	—	—
—	—	—	—	—	—	—	—	—	—
0.124	2.892	—	—	—	—	—	—	—	—
0.164	2.665	0.105	3.053	—	—	—	—	—	—
0.211	2.490	0.140	2.838	0.090	3.182	—	—	—	—
0.257	2.354	0.183	2.667	0.122	2.981	0.078	3.287	—	—
0.303	2.244	0.226	2.530	0.161	2.817	0.107	3.101	0.068	3.374
0.349	2.153	0.269	2.416	0.200	2.681	0.142	2.944	0.094	3.201
0.393	2.078	0.313	2.319	0.241	2.566	0.179	2.811	0.127	3.053
0.435	2.015	0.355	2.238	0.282	2.467	0.216	2.697	0.160	2.925
0.476	1.963	0.396	2.169	0.322	2.381	0.255	2.597	0.196	2.813
0.515	1.918	0.436	2.110	0.362	2.308	0.294	2.510	0.232	2.714
0.552	1.881	0.474	2.059	0.400	2.244	0.331	2.434	0.268	2.625
0.587	1.849	0.510	2.015	0.437	2.188	0.368	2.367	0.304	2.548
0.620	1.821	0.545	1.977	0.473	2.140	0.404	2.308	0.340	2.479
0.652	1.797	0.578	1.944	0.507	2.097	0.439	2.255	0.375	2.417
0.682	1.766	0.610	1.915	0.540	2.059	0.473	2.209	0.409	2.362
0.711	1.759	0.640	1.889	0.572	2.026	0.505	2.168	0.441	2.313
0.738	1.743	0.669	1.867	0.602	1.997	0.536	2.131	0.473	2.269
0.764	1.729	0.696	1.847	0.630	1.970	0.566	2.098	0.504	2.229
0.788	1.718	0.723	1.830	0.658	1.947	0.595	2.068	0.533	2.193
0.812	1.707	0.748	1.814	0.684	1.925	0.622	2.041	0.562	2.160
0.834	1.698	0.772	1.800	0.710	1.906	0.649	2.017	0.589	2.131
0.856	1.690	0.794	1.788	0.734	1.889	0.674	1.995	0.615	2.104
0.876	1.683	0.816	1.776	0.757	1.874	0.698	1.975	0.641	2.080
0.896	1.677	0.837	1.766	0.779	1.860	0.722	1.957	0.665	2.057
0.914	1.671	0.857	1.757	0.800	1.847	0.744	1.940	0.689	2.037
0.932	1.666	0.877	1.749	0.821	1.836	0.766	1.925	0.711	2.018
0.950	1.662	0.895	1.742	0.841	1.825	0.787	1.911	0.733	2.001
0.966	1.658	0.913	1.735	0.860	1.816	0.807	1.899	0.754	1.985
0.982	1.655	0.930	1.729	0.878	1.807	0.826	1.887	0.774	1.970
0.997	1.652	0.946	1.724	0.895	1.799	0.844	1.876	0.789	1.956
1.065	1.643	1.019	1.704	0.974	1.768	0.927	1.834	0.881	1.902
1.123	1.639	1.081	1.692	1.039	1.748	0.997	1.805	0.955	1.864
1.172	1.638	1.134	1.685	1.095	1.734	1.057	1.785	1.018	1.837
1.214	1.639	1.179	1.682	1.144	1.726	1.108	1.771	1.072	1.817
1.251	1.642	1.218	1.680	1.186	1.720	1.153	1.761	1.120	1.802
1.283	1.645	1.253	1.680	1.223	1.716	1.192	1.754	1.162	1.792
1.313	1.646	1.284	1.682	1.256	1.716	1.227	1.746	1.199	1.785
1.338	1.653	1.312	1.683	1.285	1.714	1.259	1.745	1.232	1.777
1.362	1.657	1.337	1.685	1.312	1.714	1.287	1.743	1.262	1.773
1.383	1.661	1.360	1.687	1.336	1.714	1.312	1.741	1.288	1.769
1.403	1.666	1.381	1.690	1.358	1.715	1.336	1.741	1.313	1.767
1.421	1.670	1.400	1.693	1.378	1.717	1.357	1.741	1.335	1.765
1.543	1.708	1.530	1.722	1.515	1.737	1.501	1.752	1.468	1.767
1.613	1.735	1.603	1.746	1.592	1.575	1.582	1.768	1.571	1.779

Continued on next page

TABLE 7a — *Continued*

	k′ = *11*		*k′* = *12*		*k′* = *13*		*k′* = *14*		*k′* = *15*	
n	*dL*	*dU*	*dL*	*dU*	*dL*	*dU*	*dL*	*dU*	*dL*	*dU*
16	0.060	3.446	—	—	—	—	—	—	—	—
17	0.084	3.286	0.053	3.506	—	—	—	—	—	—
18	0.113	3.146	0.075	3.358	0.047	3.557	—	—	—	—
19	0.145	3.023	0.102	3.227	0.067	3.420	0.043	3.601	—	—
20	0.178	2.914	0.131	3.109	0.092	3.297	0.061	3.474	0.038	3.639
21	0.212	2.817	0.162	3.004	0.119	3.185	0.084	3.358	0.055	3.521
22	0.246	2.729	0.194	2.909	0.148	3.084	0.109	3.252	0.077	3.412
23	0.281	2.651	0.227	2.822	0.178	2.991	0.136	3.155	0.100	3.311
24	0.315	2.580	0.260	2.744	0.209	2.906	0.165	3.065	0.125	3.218
25	0.348	2.517	0.292	2.674	0.240	2.829	0.194	2.982	0.152	3.131
26	0.381	2.460	0.324	2.610	0.272	2.758	0.224	2.906	0.180	3.050
27	0.413	2.409	0.356	2.552	0.303	2.694	0.253	2.836	0.208	2.976
28	0.444	2.363	0.387	2.499	0.333	2.635	0.283	2.772	0.237	2.907
29	0.474	2.321	0.417	2.451	0.363	2.582	0.313	2.713	0.266	2.843
30	0.503	2.283	0.447	2.407	0.393	2.533	0.342	2.659	0.294	2.785
31	0.531	2.248	0.475	2.367	0.422	2.487	0.371	2.609	0.322	2.730
32	0.558	2.216	0.503	2.330	0.450	2.446	0.399	2.563	0.350	2.680
33	0.585	2.187	0.530	2.296	0.477	2.408	0.426	2.520	0.377	2.633
34	0.610	2.160	0.556	2.266	0.503	2.373	0.452	2.481	0.404	2.590
35	0.634	2.136	0.581	2.237	0.529	2.340	0.478	2.444	0.430	2.550
36	0.658	2.113	0.605	2.210	0.554	2.310	0.504	2.410	0.455	2.512
37	0.680	2.092	0.628	2.186	0.578	2.282	0.528	2.379	0.480	2.477
38	0.702	2.073	0.651	2.164	0.601	2.256	0.552	2.350	0.504	2.445
39	0.723	2.055	0.673	2.143	0.623	2.232	0.575	2.323	0.528	2.414
40	0.744	2.039	0.694	2.123	0.645	2.210	0.597	2.297	0.551	2.386
45	0.835	1.972	0.790	2.044	0.744	2.118	0.700	2.193	0.655	2.269
50	0.913	1.925	0.871	1.987	0.829	2.051	0.787	2.116	0.746	2.182
55	0.979	1.891	0.940	1.945	0.902	2.002	0.863	2.059	0.825	2.117
60	1.037	1.865	1.001	1.914	0.965	1.964	0.929	2.015	0.893	2.067
65	1.087	1.845	1.053	1.889	1.020	1.934	0.986	1.980	0.953	2.027
70	1.131	1.831	1.099	1.870	1.068	1.911	1.037	1.953	1.005	1.995
75	1.170	1.819	1.141	1.856	1.111	1.893	1.082	1.931	1.052	1.970
80	1.205	1.810	1.777	1.844	1.150	1.878	1.122	1.913	1.094	1.949
85	1.236	1.803	1.210	1.834	1.184	1.866	1.158	1.898	1.132	1.931
90	1.264	1.798	1.240	1.827	1.215	1.856	1.191	1.886	1.166	1.917
95	1.290	1.793	1.267	1.821	1.244	1.848	1.221	1.876	1.197	1.905
100	1.314	1.790	1.292	1.816	1.270	1.841	1.248	1.868	1.225	1.895
150	1.473	1.783	1.458	1.799	1.444	1.814	1.429	1.830	1.414	1.847
200	1.561	1.791	1.550	1.801	1.539	1.813	1.528	1.824	1.518	1.836

Source: N. E. Savin and K. J. White, "The Durbin–Watson Test for Serial Correlation with Extreme Sample Sizes of Many Regressors," *Econometrica*, 45(8), Nov. 1977, pp. 1992–1995.

Note: *k′* is the number of regressors excluding the intercept.

k′ = 16		*k′* = 17		*k′* = 18		*k′* = 19		*k′* = 20	
dL	***dU***	***dL***	***dU***	***dL***	***dU***	***dL***	***dU***	***dL***	***dU***
—	—	—	—	—	—	—	—	—	—
—	—	—	—	—	—	—	—	—	—
—	—	—	—	—	—	—	—	—	—
—	—	—	—	—	—	—	—	—	—
—	—	—	—	—	—	—	—	—	—
0.035	3.671	—	—	—	—	—	—	—	—
0.050	3.562	0.032	3.700	—	—	—	—	—	—
0.070	3.459	0.046	3.597	0.029	3.725	—	—	—	—
0.092	3.363	0.065	3.501	0.043	3.629	0.027	3.747	—	—
0.116	3.274	0.085	3.410	0.060	3.538	0.039	3.657	0.025	3.766
0.141	3.191	0.107	3.325	0.079	3.452	0.055	3.572	0.036	3.682
0.167	3.113	0.131	3.245	0.100	3.371	0.073	3.490	0.051	3.602
0.194	3.040	0.156	3.169	0.122	3.294	0.093	3.412	0.068	3.524
0.222	2.972	0.182	3.098	0.146	3.220	0.114	3.338	0.087	3.450
0.249	2.909	0.208	3.032	0.171	3.152	0.137	3.267	0.107	3.379
0.277	2.851	0.234	2.970	0.196	3.087	0.160	3.201	0.128	3.311
0.304	2.797	0.261	2.912	0.221	3.026	0.184	3.137	0.151	3.246
0.331	2.746	0.287	2.858	0.246	2.969	0.209	3.078	0.174	3.184
0.357	2.699	0.313	2.808	0.272	2.915	0.233	3.022	0.197	3.126
0.383	2.655	0.339	2.761	0.297	2.865	0.257	2.969	0.221	3.071
0.409	2.614	0.364	2.717	0.322	2.818	0.282	2.919	0.244	3.019
0.434	2.576	0.389	2.675	0.347	2.774	0.306	2.872	0.268	2.969
0.458	2.540	0.414	2.637	0.371	2.733	0.330	2.828	0.291	2.923
0.482	2.507	0.438	2.600	0.395	2.694	0.354	2.787	0.315	2.879
0.505	2.476	0.461	2.566	0.418	2.657	0.377	2.748	0.338	2.838
0.612	2.346	0.570	2.424	0.528	2.503	0.488	2.582	0.448	2.661
0.705	2.250	0.665	2.318	0.625	2.387	0.586	2.456	0.548	2.526
0.786	2.176	0.748	2.237	0.711	2.298	0.674	2.359	0.637	2.421
0.857	2.120	0.822	2.173	0.786	2.227	0.751	2.283	0.716	2.338
0.919	2.075	0.886	2.123	0.852	2.172	0.819	2.221	0.786	2.272
0.974	2.038	0.943	2.082	0.911	2.127	0.880	2.172	0.849	2.217
1.023	2.009	0.993	2.049	0.964	2.090	0.934	2.131	0.905	2.172
1.066	1.984	1.039	2.022	1.011	2.057	0.983	2.097	0.955	2.135
1.106	1.965	1.080	1.999	1.053	2.033	1.027	2.068	1.000	2.104
1.141	1.948	1.116	1.979	1.091	2.012	1.066	2.044	1.041	2.077
1.174	1.934	1.150	1.963	1.126	1.993	1.102	2.023	1.079	2.054
1.203	1.922	1.181	1.949	1.158	1.977	1.136	2.006	1.113	2.034
1.400	1.863	1.385	1.880	1.370	1.897	1.355	1.913	1.340	1.931
1.507	1.847	1.495	1.860	1.484	1.871	1.474	1.883	1.462	1.896

TABLE 7b Durbin–Watson Statistic: 5 Percent Significance Points of *dL* and *dU*

	k′ = 1		*k′* = 2		*k′* = 3		*k′* = 4		*k′* = 5	
n	*dL*	*dU*	*dL*	*dU*	*dL*	*dU*	*dL*	*dU*	*dL*	*dU*
6	0.610	1.400	—	—	—	—	—	—	—	—
7	0.700	1.356	0.467	1.896	—	—	—	—	—	—
8	0.763	1.332	0.559	1.777	0.368	2.287	—	—	—	—
9	0.824	1.320	0.629	1.699	0.455	2.128	0.296	2.588	—	—
10	0.879	1.320	0.697	1.641	0.525	2.016	0.376	2.414	0.243	2.822
11	0.927	1.324	0.758	1.604	0.595	1.928	0.444	2.283	0.316	2.645
12	0.971	1.331	0.812	1.579	0.658	1.864	0.512	2.177	0.379	2.506
13	1.010	1.340	0.861	1.562	0.715	1.816	0.574	2.094	0.445	2.390
14	1.045	1.350	0.905	1.551	0.767	1.779	0.632	2.030	0.505	2.296
15	1.077	1.361	0.946	1.543	0.814	1.750	0.685	1.977	0.562	2.220
16	1.106	1.371	0.982	1.539	0.857	1.728	0.734	1.935	0.615	2.157
17	1.133	1.381	1.015	1.536	0.897	1.710	0.779	1.900	0.664	2.104
18	1.158	1.391	1.046	1.535	0.933	1.696	0.820	1.872	0.710	2.060
19	1.180	1.401	1.074	1.536	0.967	1.685	0.859	1.848	0.752	2.023
20	1.201	1.411	1.100	1.537	0.998	1.676	0.894	1.828	0.792	1.991
21	1.221	1.420	1.125	1.538	1.026	1.669	0.927	1.812	0.829	1.964
22	1.239	1.429	1.147	1.541	1.053	1.664	0.958	1.797	0.863	1.940
23	1.257	1.437	1.168	1.543	1.078	1.660	0.986	1.785	0.895	1.920
24	1.273	1.446	1.188	1.546	1.101	1.656	1.013	1.775	0.925	1.902
25	1.288	1.454	1.206	1.550	1.123	1.654	1.038	1.767	0.953	1.886
26	1.302	1.461	1.224	1.553	1.143	1.652	1.062	1.759	0.979	1.873
27	1.316	1.469	1.240	1.556	1.162	1.651	1.084	1.753	1.004	1.861
28	1.328	1.476	1.255	1.560	1.181	1.650	1.104	1.747	1.028	1.850
29	1.341	1.483	1.270	1.563	1.198	1.650	1.124	1.743	1.050	1.841
30	1.352	1.489	1.284	1.567	1.214	1.650	1.143	1.739	1.071	1.833
31	1.363	1.496	1.297	1.570	1.229	1.650	1.160	1.735	1.090	1.825
32	1.373	1.502	1.309	1.574	1.244	1.650	1.177	1.732	1.109	1.819
33	1.383	1.508	1.321	1.577	1.258	1.651	1.193	1.730	1.127	1.813
34	1.393	1.514	1.333	1.580	1.271	1.652	1.208	1.728	1.144	1.808
35	1.402	1.519	1.343	1.584	1.283	1.653	1.222	1.726	1.160	1.803
36	1.411	1.525	1.354	1.587	1.295	1.654	1.236	1.724	1.175	1.799
37	1.419	1.530	1.364	1.590	1.307	1.655	1.249	1.723	1.190	1.795
38	1.427	1.535	1.373	1.594	1.318	1.656	1.261	1.722	1.204	1.792
39	1.435	1.540	1.382	1.597	1.328	1.658	1.273	1.722	1.218	1.789
40	1.442	1.544	1.391	1.600	1.338	1.659	1.285	1.721	1.230	1.786
45	1.475	1.566	1.430	1.615	1.383	1.666	1.336	1.720	1.287	1.776
50	1.503	1.585	1.462	1.628	1.421	1.674	1.378	1.721	1.355	1.771
55	1.528	1.601	1.490	1.641	1.452	1.681	1.414	1.724	1.374	1.768
60	1.549	1.616	1.514	1.652	1.480	1.689	1.444	1.727	1.408	1.767
65	1.567	1.629	1.536	1.662	1.503	1.696	1.471	1.731	1.438	1.767
70	1.583	1.641	1.554	1.672	1.525	1.703	1.494	1.735	1.464	1.768
75	1.598	1.652	1.571	1.680	1.543	1.709	1.515	1.739	1.487	1.770
80	1.611	1.662	1.586	1.688	1.560	1.715	1.534	1.743	1.507	1.772
85	1.624	1.671	1.600	1.696	1.575	1.721	1.550	1.747	1.525	1.774
90	1.635	1.679	1.612	1.703	1.589	1.726	1.566	1.751	1.542	1.776
95	1.645	1.687	1.623	1.709	1.602	1.732	1.579	1.755	1.557	1.778
100	1.654	1.694	1.634	1.715	1.613	1.736	1.592	1.758	1.571	1.780
150	1.720	1.746	1.706	1.760	1.693	1.774	1.679	1.788	1.665	1.802
200	1.758	1.778	1.748	1.789	1.738	1.799	1.728	1.810	1.718	1.820

Source: N. E. Savin and K. J. White, "The Durbin–Watson Test for Serial Correlation with Extreme Sample Sizes of Many Regressors," *Econometrica,* 45(8), Nov. 1977, pp. 1992–1995.

Note: k′ is the number of regressors excluding the intercept.

k′ = 6		k′ = 7		k′ = 8		k′ = 9		k′ = 10	
dL	*dU*	*dL*	*dU*	*dL*	*dU*	*dL*	*dU*	*dL*	*dU*
—	—	—	—	—	—	—	—	—	—
—	—	—	—	—	—	—	—	—	—
—	—	—	—	—	—	—	—	—	—
—	—	—	—	—	—	—	—	—	—
—	—	—	—	—	—	—	—	—	—
0.203	3.005	—	—	—	—	—	—	—	—
0.268	2.832	0.171	3.149	—	—	—	—	—	—
0.328	2.692	0.230	2.985	0.147	3.266	—	—	—	—
0.389	2.572	0.286	2.848	0.200	3.111	0.127	3.360	—	—
0.447	2.472	0.343	2.727	0.251	2.979	0.175	3.216	0.111	3.438
0.502	2.388	0.398	2.624	0.304	2.860	0.222	3.090	0.155	3.304
0.554	2.318	0.451	2.537	0.356	2.757	0.272	2.975	0.198	3.184
0.603	2.257	0.502	2.461	0.407	2.667	0.321	2.873	0.244	3.073
0.649	2.206	0.459	2.396	0.456	2.589	0.369	2.783	0.290	2.974
0.692	2.162	0.595	2.339	0.502	2.521	0.416	2.704	0.336	2.885
0.732	2.124	0.637	2.290	0.547	2.460	0.461	2.633	0.380	2.806
0.769	2.090	0.677	2.246	0.588	2.407	0.504	2.571	0.424	2.734
0.804	2.061	0.715	2.208	0.628	2.360	0.545	2.514	0.465	2.670
0.837	2.035	0.751	2.174	0.666	2.318	0.584	2.464	0.506	2.613
0.868	2.012	0.784	2.144	0.702	2.280	0.621	2.419	0.544	2.560
0.897	1.992	0.816	2.117	0.735	2.246	0.657	2.379	0.581	2.513
0.925	1.974	0.845	2.093	0.767	2.216	0.691	2.342	0.616	2.470
0.951	1.958	0.874	2.071	0.798	2.188	0.723	2.309	0.650	2.431
0.975	1.944	0.900	2.052	0.826	2.164	0.753	2.278	0.682	2.396
0.998	1.931	0.926	2.034	0.854	2.141	0.782	2.251	0.712	2.363
1.020	1.920	0.950	2.018	0.879	2.120	0.810	2.226	0.741	2.333
1.041	1.909	0.972	2.004	0.904	2.102	0.836	2.203	0.769	2.306
1.061	1.900	0.994	1.991	0.927	2.085	0.861	2.181	0.795	2.281
1.080	1.891	1.015	1.979	0.950	2.069	0.885	2.162	0.821	2.257
1.097	1.884	1.034	1.967	0.971	2.054	0.908	2.144	0.845	2.236
1.114	1.877	1.053	1.957	0.991	2.041	0.930	2.127	0.868	2.216
1.131	1.870	1.071	1.948	1.011	2.029	0.951	2.112	0.891	2.198
1.146	1.864	1.088	1.939	1.029	2.017	0.970	2.098	0.912	2.180
1.161	1.859	1.104	1.932	1.047	2.007	0.990	2.085	0.932	2.164
1.175	1.854	1.120	1.924	1.064	1.997	1.008	2.072	0.945	2.149
1.238	1.835	1.189	1.895	1.139	1.958	1.089	2.002	1.038	2.088
1.291	1.822	1.246	1.875	1.201	1.930	1.156	1.986	1.110	2.044
1.334	1.814	1.294	1.861	1.253	1.909	1.212	1.959	1.170	2.010
1.372	1.808	1.335	1.850	1.298	1.894	1.260	1.939	1.222	1.984
1.404	1.805	1.370	1.843	1.336	1.882	1.301	1.923	1.266	1.964
1.433	1.802	1.401	1.837	1.369	1.873	1.337	1.910	1.305	1.948
1.458	1.801	1.428	1.834	1.399	1.867	1.369	1.901	1.339	1.935
1.480	1.801	1.453	1.831	1.425	1.861	1.397	1.893	1.369	1.925
1.500	1.801	1.474	1.829	1.448	1.857	1.422	1.886	1.396	1.916
1.518	1.801	1.494	1.827	1.469	1.854	1.445	1.881	1.420	1.909
1.535	1.802	1.512	1.827	1.489	1.852	1.465	1.877	1.442	1.903
1.550	1.803	1.528	1.826	1.506	1.850	1.484	1.874	1.462	1.898
1.651	1.817	1.637	1.832	1.622	1.847	1.608	1.862	1.594	1.877
1.707	1.831	1.697	1.841	1.686	1.852	1.675	1.863	1.665	1.874

Continued on next page

TABLE 7b — *Continued*

	$k' = 11$		$k' = 12$		$k' = 13$		$k' = 14$		$k' = 15$	
n	dL	dU	dL	dU	dL	dU	dL	dU	dL	dU
16	0.098	3.503	—	—	—	—	—	—	—	—
17	0.138	3.378	0.087	3.557	—	—	—	—	—	—
18	0.177	3.265	0.123	3.441	0.078	3.603	—	—	—	—
19	0.220	3.159	0.160	3.335	0.111	3.496	0.070	3.642	—	—
20	0.263	3.063	0.200	3.234	0.145	3.395	0.100	3.542	0.063	3.676
21	0.307	2.976	0.240	3.141	0.182	3.300	0.132	3.448	0.091	3.583
22	0.349	2.897	0.281	3.057	0.220	3.211	0.166	3.358	0.120	3.495
23	0.391	2.826	0.322	2.979	0.259	3.128	0.202	3.272	0.153	3.409
24	0.431	2.761	0.362	2.908	0.297	3.053	0.239	3.193	0.186	3.327
25	0.470	2.702	0.400	2.844	0.335	2.983	0.275	3.119	0.221	3.251
26	0.508	2.649	0.438	2.784	0.373	2.919	0.312	3.051	0.256	3.179
27	0.544	2.600	0.475	2.730	0.409	2.859	0.348	2.987	0.291	3.112
28	0.578	2.555	0.510	2.680	0.445	2.805	0.383	2.928	0.325	3.050
29	0.612	2.515	0.544	2.634	0.479	2.755	0.418	2.874	0.359	2.992
30	0.643	2.477	0.577	2.592	0.512	2.708	0.451	2.823	0.392	2.937
31	0.674	2.443	0.608	2.553	0.545	2.665	0.484	2.776	0.425	2.987
32	0.703	2.411	0.638	2.517	0.576	2.625	0.515	2.733	0.457	2.840
33	0.731	2.382	0.668	2.484	0.606	2.588	0.546	2.692	0.488	2.796
34	0.758	2.355	0.695	2.454	0.634	2.554	0.575	2.654	0.518	2.754
35	0.783	2.330	0.722	2.425	0.662	2.521	0.604	2.619	0.547	2.716
36	0.808	2.306	0.748	2.398	0.689	2.492	0.631	2.586	0.575	2.680
37	0.831	2.285	0.772	2.374	0.714	2.464	0.657	2.555	0.602	2.646
38	0.854	2.265	0.796	2.351	0.739	2.438	0.683	2.526	0.628	2.614
39	0.875	2.246	0.819	2.329	0.763	2.413	0.707	2.499	0.653	2.585
40	0.896	2.228	0.840	2.309	0.785	2.391	0.731	2.473	0.678	2.557
45	0.988	2.156	0.938	2.225	0.887	2.296	0.838	2.367	0.788	2.439
50	1.064	2.103	1.019	2.163	0.973	2.225	0.927	2.287	0.882	2.350
55	1.129	2.062	1.087	2.116	1.045	2.170	1.003	2.225	0.961	2.281
60	1.184	2.031	1.145	2.079	1.106	2.127	1.068	2.177	1.029	2.227
65	1.231	2.006	1.195	2.049	1.160	2.093	1.124	2.138	1.088	2.183
70	1.272	1.986	1.239	2.026	1.206	2.066	1.172	2.106	1.139	2.148
75	1.308	1.970	1.277	2.006	1.247	2.043	1.215	2.080	1.184	2.118
80	1.340	1.957	1.311	1.991	1.283	2.024	1.253	2.059	1.224	2.093
85	1.369	1.946	1.342	1.977	1.315	2.009	1.287	2.040	1.260	2.073
90	1.395	1.937	1.369	1.966	1.344	1.995	1.318	2.025	1.292	2.055
95	1.418	1.929	1.394	1.956	1.370	1.984	1.345	2.012	1.321	2.040
100	1.434	1.923	1.416	1.948	1.393	1.974	1.371	2.000	1.347	2.026
150	1.579	1.892	1.564	1.908	1.550	1.924	1.535	1.940	1.519	1.956
200	1.654	1.885	1.643	1.896	1.632	1.908	1.621	1.919	1.610	1.931

Source: N. E. Savin and K. J. White, "The Durbin–Watson Test for Serial Correlation with Extreme Sample Sizes of Many Regressors," *Econometrica*, 45(8), Nov. 1977, pp. 1992–1995.

Note: k' is the number of regressors excluding the intercept.

k′ = 16		k′ = 17		k′ = 18		k′ = 19		k′ = 20	
dL	dU	dL	dU	dL	dU	dL	dU	dL	dU
—	—	—	—	—	—	—	—	—	—
—	—	—	—	—	—	—	—	—	—
—	—	—	—	—	—	—	—	—	—
—	—	—	—	—	—	—	—	—	—
—	—	—	—	—	—	—	—	—	—
0.058	3.705	—	—	—	—	—	—	—	—
0.083	3.619	0.052	3.731	—	—	—	—	—	—
0.110	3.535	0.076	3.650	0.048	3.753	—	—	—	—
0.141	3.454	0.101	3.572	0.070	3.678	0.044	3.773	—	—
0.172	3.376	0.130	4.494	0.094	3.604	0.065	3.702	0.041	3.790
0.205	3.303	0.160	3.420	0.120	3.531	0.087	3.632	0.060	3.724
0.238	3.233	0.191	3.349	0.149	3.460	0.112	3.563	0.081	3.658
0.271	3.168	0.222	3.283	0.178	3.392	0.138	3.495	0.104	3.592
0.305	3.107	0.254	3.219	0.208	3.327	0.166	3.431	0.129	3.528
0.337	3.050	0.286	3.160	0.238	3.266	0.195	3.368	0.156	3.465
0.370	2.996	0.317	3.103	0.269	3.208	0.224	3.309	0.183	3.406
0.401	2.946	0.349	3.050	0.299	3.153	0.253	3.252	0.211	3.348
0.432	2.899	0.379	3.000	0.329	3.100	0.283	3.198	0.239	3.293
0.462	2.854	0.409	2.954	0.359	3.051	0.312	3.147	0.267	3.240
0.492	2.813	0.439	2.910	0.388	3.005	0.340	3.099	0.295	3.190
0.520	2.774	0.467	2.868	0.417	2.961	0.369	3.053	0.323	3.142
0.548	2.738	0.495	2.829	0.445	2.920	0.397	3.009	0.351	3.097
0.575	2.703	0.522	2.792	0.472	2.880	0.424	2.968	0.378	3.054
0.600	2.671	0.549	2.757	0.499	2.843	0.451	2.929	0.404	3.013
0.626	2.641	0.575	2.724	0.525	2.808	0.477	2.892	0.430	2.974
0.740	2.512	0.692	2.586	0.644	2.659	0.598	2.733	0.553	2.807
0.836	2.414	0.792	2.479	0.747	2.544	0.703	2.610	0.660	2.675
0.919	2.338	0.877	2.396	0.836	2.454	0.795	2.512	0.754	2.571
0.990	2.278	0.951	2.330	0.913	2.382	0.874	2.434	0.836	2.487
1.052	2.229	1.016	2.276	0.980	2.323	0.944	2.371	0.908	2.419
1.105	2.189	1.072	2.232	1.038	2.275	1.005	2.318	0.971	2.362
1.153	2.156	1.121	2.195	1.090	2.235	1.058	2.275	1.027	2.315
1.195	2.129	1.165	2.165	1.136	2.201	1.106	2.238	1.076	2.275
1.232	2.105	1.205	2.139	1.177	2.172	1.149	2.206	1.121	2.241
1.266	2.085	1.240	2.116	1.213	2.148	1.187	2.179	1.160	2.211
1.296	2.068	1.271	2.097	1.247	2.126	1.222	2.156	1.197	2.186
1.324	2.053	1.301	2.080	1.277	2.108	1.253	2.135	1.229	2.164
1.504	1.972	1.489	1.989	1.474	2.006	1.458	2.023	1.443	2.040
1.599	1.943	1.588	1.955	1.576	1.967	1.565	1.979	1.554	1.991

TABLE 8 Five Percent Significance Points of $\partial_{4,L}$ and $\partial_{4,U}$ for Regressions With Quarterly Dummy Variables ($k = k' + 1$)

	$k' = 1$		$k' = 2$		$k' = 3$		$k' = 4$		$k' = 5$	
n	$d_{4,L}$	$d_{4,U}$	$d_{4,L}$	$d_{4,U}$	$d_{4,L}$	$d_{4,U}$	$d_{4,L}$	$d_{4,U}$	$d_{4,L}$	$d_{4,U}$
16	0.774	0.982	0.662	1.109	0.549	1.275	0.435	1.381	0.350	1.532
20	0.924	1.102	0.827	1.203	0.728	1.327	0.626	1.428	0.544	1.556
24	1.036	1.189	0.953	1.273	0.867	1.371	0.779	1.459	0.702	1.565
28	1.123	1.257	1.050	1.328	0.975	1.410	0.898	1.487	0.828	1.576
32	1.192	1.311	1.127	1.373	1.061	1.443	0.993	1.511	0.929	1.587
36	1.248	1.355	1.191	1.410	1.131	1.471	1.070	1.532	1.013	1.598
40	1.295	1.392	1.243	1.442	1.190	1.496	1.135	1.550	1.082	1.609
44	1.335	1.423	1.288	1.469	1.239	1.518	1.189	1.567	1.141	1.620
48	1.369	1.451	1.326	1.493	1.281	1.537	1.236	1.582	1.191	1.630
52	1.399	1.475	1.359	1.513	1.318	1.554	1.276	1.595	1.235	1.639
56	1.426	1.496	1.389	1.532	1.351	1.569	1.312	1.608	1.273	1.648
60	1.449	1.515	1.415	1.548	1.379	1.583	1.343	1.619	1.307	1.656
64	1.470	1.532	1.438	1.563	1.405	1.596	1.371	1.629	1.337	1.664
68	1.489	1.548	1.459	1.577	1.427	1.608	1.396	1.639	1.364	1.671
72	1.507	1.562	1.478	1.589	1.448	1.618	1.418	1.648	1.388	1.678
76	1.522	1.574	1.495	1.601	1.467	1.628	1.439	1.656	1.411	1.685
80	1.537	1.586	1.511	1.611	1.484	1.637	1.457	1.663	1.431	1.691
84	1.550	1.597	1.525	1.621	1.500	1.646	1.475	1.671	1.449	1.696
88	1.562	1.607	1.539	1.630	1.515	1.654	1.490	1.677	1.466	1.702
92	1.574	1.617	1.551	1.639	1.528	1.661	1.505	1.684	1.482	1.707
96	1.584	1.626	1.563	1.647	1.541	1.668	1.519	1.690	1.496	1.712
100	1.594	1.634	1.573	1.654	1.552	1.674	1.531	1.695	1.510	1.717

Source: K. F. Wallis, "Testing for Fourth Order Autocorrelation in Quarterly Regression Equations," *Econometrica,* 40(4), July 1972, p. 623.

References

Abowd, J., and H. Farber. "Job Queues and Union Status of Workers." *Industrial and Labor Relations Review*, 35, 1982, pp. 354–367.

Abramovitz, M., and I. Stegun. *Handbook of Mathematical Functions*. New York: Dover Press, 1971.

Adelman, F., and I. Adelman. "The Dynamic Properties of the Klein–Goldberger Model." *Econometrica*, 27, 1959, pp. 596–625.

Afifi, T., and R. Elashoff. "Missing Observations in Multivariate Statistics." *Journal of the American Statistical Association*, 61, 1966, pp. 595–604.

Afifi, T., and R. Elashoff. "Missing Observations in Multivariate Statistics." *Journal of the American Statistical Association*, 62, 1967, pp. 10–29.

Ahn, S., and P. Schmidt. "Efficient Estimation of Models for Dynamic Panel Data Models," *Journal of Econometrics*, 68, 1, 1995, pp. 5–28.

Aigner, D. "MSE Dominance of Least Squares with Errors of Observation." *Journal of Econometrics*, 2, 1974, pp. 365–372.

Aigner, D., K. Lovell, and P. Schmidt. "Formulation and Estimation of Stochastic Frontier Production Models." *Journal of Econometrics*, 6, 1977, pp. 21–37.

Aitchison, J., and J. Brown. *The Lognormal Distribution with Special Reference to Its Uses in Economics*. New York: Cambridge University Press, 1969.

Aitken, A. "On Least Squares and Linear Combinations of Observations." *Proceedings of the Royal Statistical Society*, 55, 1935, pp. 42–48.

Akaike, H. "Information Theory and an Extension of the Maximum Likelihood Principle." In B. Petrov and F. Csake, eds., *Second International Symposium on Information Theory*. Budapest: Akademiai Kiado, 1973.

Albert, J., and S. Chib. "Bayesian Analysis of Binary and Polytomous Response Data." *Journal of the American Statistical Association*, 88, 1993a, pp. 669–679.

Albert, J., and S. Chib. "Bayes Inference via Gibbs Sampling of Autoregressive Time Series Subject to Markov Mean and Variance Shifts." *Journal of Business and Economic Statistics*, 11, 1993b, pp. 1–15.

Aldrich, J., and F. Nelson. *Linear Probability, Logit, and Probit Models*. Beverly Hills: Sage Publications, 1984.

Ali, M., and C. Giaccotto. "A Study of Several New and Existing Tests for Heteroscedasticity in the General Linear Model." *Journal of Econometrics*, 26, 1984, pp. 355–374.

Allenby, G., and J. Ginter. "The Effects of In-Store Displays and Feature Advertising on Consideration Sets." *International Journal of Research in Marketing*, 12, 1995, pp. 67–80.

Almon, S. "The Distributed Lag Between Capital Appropriations and Expenditures." *Econometrica*, 33, 1965, pp. 178–196.

Alvarez, R., G. Garrett, and P. Lange. "Government Partisanship, Labor Organization, and Macroeconomic Performance." *American Political Science Review*, 85, 1991, pp. 539–556.

Amemiya, T. "The Estimation of Variances in a Variance-Components Model." *International Economic Review*, 12, 1971, pp. 1–13.

Amemiya, T. "Regression Analysis When the Variance of the Dependent Variable Is Proportional to the Square of Its Expectation." *Journal of the American Statistical Association*, 68, 1973a, pp. 928–934.

Amemiya, T. "Regression Analysis When the Dependent Variable Is Truncated Normal." *Econometrica*, 41, 1973b, pp. 997–1016.

Amemiya, T. "A Note on a Heteroscedastic Model." *Journal of Econometrics*, 6, 1977a, pp. 365–370.

Amemiya, T. "Some Theorems in the Linear Probability Model." *International Economic Review*, 18, 1977b, pp. 645–650.

Amemiya, T. "The Estimation of a Simultaneous Equation Generalized Probit Model." *Econometrica*, 46, 1978, pp. 1193–1205.

Amemiya, T. "Qualitative Response Models: A Survey." *Journal of Economic Literature*, 19, 4, 1981, pp. 481–536.

Amemiya, T. "Tobit Models: A Survey." *Journal of Econometrics*, 24, 1984, pp. 3–63.

Amemiya, T. *Advanced Econometrics*. Cambridge: Harvard University Press, 1985.

Amemiya, T., and K. Morimune. "Selecting the Optimal Order of Polynomial in the Almon Distributed Lag." *Review of Economics and Statistics*, 56, 1974, pp. 378–386.

Anderson, T. *The Statistical Analysis of Time Series*. New York: John Wiley and Sons, 1971.

Anderson, T., and C. Hsiao. "Estimation of Dynamic Models with Error Components." *Journal of the American Statistical Association*, 76, 1981, pp. 598–606.

Anderson, T., and C. Hsiao. "Formulation and Estimation of Dynamic Models Using Panel Data." *Journal of Econometrics*, 18, 1982, pp. 67–82.

Anderson, T., and H. Rubin. "Estimation of the Parameters of a Single Equation in a Complete System of Stochastic Equations." *Annals of Mathematical Statistics*, 20, 1949, pp. 46–63.

Anderson, T., and H. Rubin. "The Asymptotic Properties of Estimators of the Parameters of a Single Equation in a Complete System of Stochastic Equations." *Annals of Mathematical Statistics*, 21, 1950, pp. 570–582.

Anderson, R., and J. Thursby. "Confidence Intervals for Elasticity Estimators in Translog Models." *Review of Economics and Statistics*, 68, 1986, pp. 647–657.

Andrews, D. "A Robust Method for Multiple Linear Regression." *Technometrics*, 16, 1974, pp. 523–531.

Aneuryn-Evans, G., and A. Deaton. "Testing Linear Versus Logarithmic Regression Models." *Review of Economic Studies*, 47, 1980, pp. 275–291.

Arabmazar, A., and P. Schmidt. "An Investigation into the Robustness of the Tobit Estimator to Nonnormality." *Econometrica*, 50, 1982a, pp. 1055–1063.

Arabmazar, A., and P. Schmidt. "Further Evidence on the Robustness of the Tobit Estimator to Heteroscedasticity." *Journal of Econometrics*, 17, 1982b, pp. 253–258.

Arellano, M. "Computing Robust Standard Errors for Within-Groups Estimators." *Oxford Bulletin of Economics and Statistics*, 49, 1987, pp. 431–434.

Arellano, M. "A Note on the Anderson-Hsiao Estimator for Panel Data." *Economics Letters*, 31, 1989, pp. 337–341.

Arellano, M., and S. Bond. "Some Tests of Specification for Panel Data: Monte Carlo Evidence and an Application to Employment Equations." *Review of Economics and Statistics*, 58, 1991, pp. 277–297.

Arellano, M., and O. Bover. "Another Look at the Instrumental Variables Estimation of Error Components Models." *Journal of Econometrics*, 68, 1, 1995, pp. 29–52.

Arrow, K., H. Chenery, B. Minhas, and R. Solow. "Capital-Labor Substitution and Economic Efficiency." *Review of Economics and Statistics*, 45, 1961, pp. 225–247.

Avery, R., L. Hansen, and J. Hotz. "Multiperiod Probit Models and Orthogonality Condition Estimation." *International Economic Review*, 24, 1983, pp. 21–35.

Baille, R. "The Asymptotic Mean Squared Error of Multistep Prediction From the Regression Model with Autoregressive Errors." *Journal of the American Statistical Association*, 74, 1979, pp. 175–184.

Balestra, P., and M. Nerlove. "Pooling Cross Section and Time Series Data in the Estimation of a Dynamic Model: The Demand for Natural Gas." *Econometrica*, 34, 1966, pp. 585–612.

Baltagi, B. "Pooling Under Misspecification, Some Monte Carlo Evidence on the Kmenta and Error Components Techniques." *Econometric Theory*, 2, 1986, pp. 429–441.

Baltagi, B. *Econometric Analysis of Panel Data*. New York: John Wiley and Sons, 1995.

Barnow, B., G. Cain, and A. Goldberger. "Issues in the Analysis of Selectivity Bias." In E. Stromsdorfer and G. Farkas, eds., *Evaluation Studies Review Annual*, vol. 5, Beverly Hills: Sage Publications, 1981.

Barten, A. "Maximum Likelihood Estimation of A Complete System of Demand Equations." *European Economic Review*, Fall, 1, 1969, pp. 7–73.

Basmann, R. "On Finite Sample Distributions of Generalized Classical Linear Identifiability Test Statistics." *Journal of the American Statistical Association*, 55, 1960, pp. 650–659.

Bazzara, M., and C. Shetty. *Nonlinear Programming—Theory and Algorithms*. New York: John Wiley and Sons, 1979.

Beach, C., and J. MacKinnon. "A Maximum Likelihood Procedure for Regression with Autocorrelated Errors." *Econometrica*, 46, 1978a, pp. 51–58.

Beach, C., and J. MacKinnon. "Full Maximum Likelihood Estimation of Second-Order Autoregressive Error Models." *Journal of Econometrics*, 7, 1978b, pp. 187–198.

Beck, N., and J. Katz. "What to Do (and Not to Do) with Time-Series-Cross-Section Data in Comparative Politics." *American Political Science Review*, 89, 1995, pp. 634–647.

Beck, N., J. Katz, R. Alvarez, G. Garrett, and P. Lange. "Government Partisanship, Labor Organization, and Macroeconomic Performance: A Corrigendum." *American Political Science Review*, 87, 4, 1993, pp. 945–948.

Beggs, J. "Time Series Analysis in Pooled Cross Sections." *Econometric Theory*, 2, 1986, pp. 331–349.

Beggs, S., S. Cardell, and J. Hausman. "Assessing the Potential Demand for Electric Cars." *Journal of Econometrics*, 17, 1981, pp. 19–20.

Bellman, R. *Introduction to Matrix Analysis*. New York: McGraw-Hill, 1970.

Belsley, D. "On the Efficient Computation of the Nonlinear Full-Information Maximum Likelihood Estimator." Technical Report Number 5, Center for Computational Research in Economics and Management Science, Vol. 2, Cambridge, Mass., 1980.

Belsley, D. *Conditioning Diagnostics, Collinearity, and Weak Data in Regression*. New York: John Wiley and Sons, 1991.

Belsley, D., E. Kuh, and R. Welsch. *Regression Diagnostics: Identifying Influential Data and Sources of Collinearity*. New York: John Wiley and Sons, 1980.

Ben-Porath, Y. "Labor Force Participation Rates and Labor Supply." *Journal of Political Economy*, 81, 1973, pp. 697–704.

Bera, A., and C. Jarque. "Efficient Tests for Normality, Heteroscedasticity, and Serial Independence of Regression Residuals." *Economics Letters*, 6, 1980a, pp. 255–259.

Bera, A., and C. Jarque. "Model Specification Tests: A Simultaneous Approach." *Journal of Econometrics*, 20, 1980b, pp. 59–82.

Bera, A., and C. Jarque. "Efficient Tests for Normality, Heteroscedasticity, and Serial Independence of Regression Residuals: Monte Carlo Evidence." *Economics Letters*, 7, 1981, pp. 313–318.

Bera, A., and C. Jarque. "Model Specification Tests: A Simultaneous Approach." *Journal of Econometrics*, 20, 1982, pp. 59–82.

Bera, A., C. Jarque, and L. Lee. "Testing for the Normality Assumption in Limited Dependent Variable Models." Mimeo, Department of Economics, University of Minnesota, 1982.

Berndt, E. *The Practice of Econometrics*. Reading, Mass. : Addison-Wesley, 1990.

Berndt, E., and L. Christensen. "The Translog Function and the Substitution of Equipment, Structures, and Labor in U.S. Manufacturing, 1929–1968." *Journal of Econometrics*, 1, 1973, pp. 81–114.

Berndt, E., B. Hall, R. Hall, and J. Hausman. "Estimation and Inference in Nonlinear Structural Models." *Annals of Economic and Social Measurement*, 3/4, 1974, pp. 653–665.

Berndt, E., and E. Savin. "Conflict Among Criteria for Testing Hypotheses in the Multivariate Linear Regression Model." *Econometrica*, 45, 1977, pp. 1263–1277.

Berndt, E., and D. Wood. "Technology, Prices, and the Derived Demand for Energy." *Review of Economics and Statistics*, 57, 1975, pp. 376–384.

Berzeg, K. "The Error Components Model: Conditions for the Existence of Maximum Likelihood Estimates." *Journal of Econometrics*, 10, 1979, pp. 99–102.

Bhargava, A. and J. Sargan. "Estimating Dynamic Random Effects Models from Panel Data Covering Short Periods." *Econometrica*, 51, 1983, pp. 221–236.

Bhat, C. "A Heteroscedastic Extreme Value Model of Intercity Mode Choice." Working Paper, Department of Civil Engineering, University of Massachusetts, Amherst, 1995, (forthcoming *Transportation Research*), 1995.

Blackley, R., Follain, J., and J. Ondrich. "Box-Cox Estimation of Hedonic Models: How Serious Is the Iterative OLS Variance Bias?" *Review of Economics and Statistics*, 66, 1984, pp. 348–353.

Blanchard, O. "Why Does Money Affect Output? A Survey." Working Paper No. 2285, National Bureau of Economic Research, Cambridge, 1987.

Blundell, R., ed. "Specification Testing in Limited and Discrete Dependent Variable Models." *Journal of Econometrics*, 34, 1/2, 1987, pp. 1–274.

Bock, M., T. Yancey, and G. Judge. "The Statistical Consequences of Preliminary Test Estimators in Regression." *Journal of the American Statistical Association*, 68, 1972, pp. 109–116.

Bockstael, N., I. Strand, K. McConnell, and F. Arsanjani. "Sample Selection Bias in the Estimation of Recreation Demand Functions: An Application to Sport Fishing." *Land Economics*, 66, 1990, pp. 40–49.

Bollerslev, T. "Generalized Autoregressive Conditional Heteroscedasticity." *Journal of Econometrics*, 31, 1986, pp. 307–327.

Boot, J., and G. deWitt. "Investment Demand: An Empirical Contribution to the Aggregation Problem." *International Economic Review*, 1, 1960, pp. 3–30.

Börsch-Supan, A., and V. Hajivassiliou. "Smooth Unbiased Multivariate Probability Simulators for Maximum Likelihood Estimation of Limited Dependent Variable Models." *Journal of Econometrics*, 58, 3, 1993, pp. 347–368.

Boskin, M. "A Conditional Logit Model of Occupational Choice." *Journal of Political Economy*, 82, 1974, pp. 389–398.

Box, G., and D. Cox. "An Analysis of Transformations." *Journal of the Royal Statistical Society*, Series B, 1964, pp. 211–264.

Box, G., and G. Jenkins. *Time Series Analysis: Forecasting and Control*, 2nd ed. San Francisco: Holden Day, 1984.

Box, G., and M. Muller. "A Note on the Generation of Random Normal Deviates." *Annals of Mathematical Statistics*, 29, 1958, pp. 610–611.

Box, G., and D. Pierce. "Distribution of Residual Autocorrelations in Autoregressive Moving Average Time Series Models." *Journal of the American Statistical Association*, 65, 1970, pp. 1509–1526.

Box, G., and Tiao, G. "Modelling Multiple Time Series with Applications." *Journal of the American Statistical Association*, 76, 1981, pp. 802–816.

Boyes, W., D. Hoffman, and S. Low. "An Econometric Analysis of the Bank Credit Scoring Problem." *Journal of Econometrics*, 40, 1989, pp. 3–14.

Boyles, R. "On the Convergence of the EM Algorithm," *Journal of the Royal Statistical Society*, Series B, 45, 1, 1983, pp. 47–50.

Brannas, K. "Explanatory Variables in the ARMA Count Data Model." Working Paper No. 381, Department of Economics, University of Umea, Sweden, 1995.

Brannas, K. and P. Johanssen. "Panel Data Regressions for Counts." Manuscript, Department of Economics, University of Umea, Sweden, 1994.

Breslaw, J. "Evaluation of Multivariate Normal Probabilities Using a Low Variance Simulator." *Review of Economics and Statistics*, 76, 1994, pp. 673–682.

Breusch, T. "Testing for Autocorrelation in Dynamic Linear Models." *Australian Economic Papers*, 17, 1978, pp. 334–355.

Breusch, T., and A. Pagan. "A Simple Test for Heteroscedasticity and Random Coefficient Variation." *Econometrica*, 47, 1979, pp. 1287–1294.

Breusch, T., and A. Pagan. "The LM Test and Its Applications to Model Specification in Econometrics." *Review of Economic Studies*, 47, 1980, pp. 239–254.

Bridge, J. *Applied Econometrics*. Amsterdam: North Holland, 1971.

Brown, C., and R. Moffitt. "The Effect of Ignoring Heteroscedasticity on Estimates of the Tobit Model." Mimeo, University of Maryland, Department of Economics, June 1982.

Brown, R. "The Identification Problem in Systems Nonlinear in the Variables." *Econometrica*, 51, 1983, pp. 175–196.

Brown, R., J. Durbin, and J. Evans. "Techniques for Testing the Constancy of Regression Relationships Over Time." *Journal of the Royal Statistical Society*, Series B, 37, 1975, pp. 149–172.

Brundy, J., and D. Jorgenson. "Consistent and Efficient Estimation of Systems of Simultaneous Equations by Means of Instrumental Variables." *Review of Economics and Statistics*, 53, 1971, pp. 207–224.

Buse, A. "Goodness of Fit in Generalized Least Squares Estimation." *American Statistician*, 27, 1973, pp. 106–108.

Buse, A. "The Likelihood Ratio, Wald, and Lagrange Multiplier Tests: An Expository Note." *American Statistician*, 36, 1982, pp. 153–157.

Butler, J., and R. Moffitt. "A Computationally Efficient Quadrature Procedure for the One Factor Multinomial Probit Model." *Econometrica*, 50, 1982, pp. 761–764.

Cameron, A., and P. Trivedi. "Econometric Models Based on Count Data: Comparisons and Applications of Some Estimators and Tests." *Journal of Applied Econometrics*, 1, 1986, pp. 29–54.

Cameron, A., and P. Trivedi. "Regression Based Tests for Overdispersion in the Poisson Model." *Journal of Econometrics*, 46, 1990, pp. 347–364.

Cameron, C., and F. Windmeijer. "*R*-Squared Measures for Count Data Regression Models with Applications to Health Care Utilization." Working Paper No. 93-24, Department of Economics, University of California, Davis, 1993.

Campbell, J., and P. Perron. "Pitfalls and Opportunities: What Macroeconomists Should Know About Unit Roots." National Bureau of Economic Research, Macroeconomics Conference, Cambridge, February 1991.

Carlin, B. and S. Chib. "Bayesian Model Choice via Markov Chain Monte Carlo." *Journal of the Royal Statistical Society*, Series B, 57, 1995, pp. 408–417.

Casella, G., and E. George. "Explaining the Gibbs Sampler." *American Statistician*, 46, 3, 1992, pp. 167–174.

Caudill, S. "An Advantage of the Linear Probability Model over Probit or Logit." *Oxford Bulletin of Economics and Statistics*, 50, 1988, pp. 425–427.

Caves, D., L. Christensen, and M. Trethaway. "Flexible Cost Functions for Multiproduct Firms." *Review of Economics and Statistics*, 62, 1980, pp. 477–481.

Cecchetti, S. "The Frequency of Price Adjustment: A Study of the Newsstand Prices of Magazines." *Journal of Econometrics*, 31, 1986, pp. 255–274.

Chamberlain, G. "Omitted Variable Bias in Panel Data: Estimating the Returns to Schooling." *Annales de L'Insee,* 30/31, 1978, pp. 49–82.

Chamberlain, G. "Analysis of Covariance with Qualitative Data." *Review of Economic Studies*, 47, 1980, pp. 225–238.

Chamberlain, G. "Panel Data." In Z. Griliches and M. Intriligator, eds., *Handbook of Econometrics*, Amsterdam: North Holland, 1983.

Chamberlain, G. "Asymptotic Efficiency in Estimation with Conditional Moment Restrictions." *Journal of Econometrics*, 34, 1987, pp. 305–334.

Chamberlain, G., and E. Leamer. "Matrix Weighted Averages and Posterior Bounds." *Journal of the Royal Statistical Society*, Series B, 1976, pp. 73–84.

Chambers, R. *Applied Production Analysis: A Dual Approach.* New York: Cambridge University Press, 1988.

Chesher, A., and M. Irish. "Residual Analysis in the Grouped Data and Censored Normal Linear Model." *Journal of Econometrics*, 34, 1987, pp. 33–62.

Chesher, A., T. Lancaster, and M. Irish. "On Detecting the Failure of Distributional Assumptions." *Annales de L'Insee*, 59/60, 1985, pp. 7–44.

Cheung, C., and A. Goldberger. "Proportional Projections in Limited Dependent Variable Models." *Econometrica*, 52, 1984, pp. 531–534.

Chib, S. "Bayes Regression for the Tobit Censored Regression Model." *Journal of Econometrics*, 51, 1992, pp. 79–99.

Chib, S., and E. Greenberg. "Markov Chain Monte Carlo Simulation Methods in Econometrics." Manuscript, Olin School of Business, Washington University in St. Louis, 1995.

Chow, G. "Tests of Equality Between Sets of Coefficients in Two Linear Regressions." *Econometrica*, 28, 1960, pp. 591–605.

Christensen, L., and W. Greene. "Economies of Scale in U.S. Electric Power Generation." *Journal of Political Economy*, 84, 1976, pp. 655–676.

Christensen, L., D. Jorgenson, and L. Lau. "Transcendental Logarithmic Utility Functions." *American Economic Review*, 65, 1975, pp. 367–383.

Cochrane, D., and G. Orcutt. "Application of Least Squares Regression to Relationships Containing Autocorrelated Error Terms." *Journal of the American Statistical Association*, 44, 1949, pp. 32–61.

Conniffe, D. "Covariance Analysis and Seemingly Unrelated Regression Equations." *American Statistician*, 36, 1982a, pp. 169–171.

Conniffe, D. "A Note on Seemingly Unrelated Regressions." *Econometrica*, 50, 1982b, pp. 229–233.

Conway, D., and H. Roberts. "Reverse Regression, Fairness and Employment Discrimination." *Journal of Business and Economic Statistics*, 1, 1, 1983, pp. 75–85.

Cooley, T., and S. LeRoy. "Atheoretical Macroeconomics: A Critique." *Journal of Monetary Economics*, 16, 1985, pp. 283–308.

Cooper, P. "Two Approaches to Polynomial Distributed Lag Estimation." *American Statistician*, 26, 1972, pp. 32–35.

Cornwell, C., and P. Schmidt. "Panel Data with Cross Sectional Variation in Slopes as Well as in Intercept." Econometrics Workshop Paper No. 8404, Michigan State University, Department of Economics, 1984.

Coulson, N., and R. Robins. "Aggregate Economic Activity and the Variance of Inflation: Another Look." *Economics Letters*, 17, 1985, pp. 71–75.

Cox, D. "Tests of Separate Families of Hypotheses." *Proceedings of the Fourth Berkeley Symposium on Mathematical Statistics and Probability*, Vol. 1, Berkeley: University of California Press, 1961.

Cox, D. "Further Results on Tests of Separate Families of Hypotheses." *Journal of the Royal Statistical Society*, Series B, 24, 1962, pp. 406–424.

Cox, D. *Analysis of Binary Data*. London: Methuen, 1970.

Cox, D. "Regression Models and Life Tables." *Journal of the Royal Statistical Society*, Series B, 34, 1972, pp. 187–220.

Cox, D., and D. Oakes. *Analysis of Survival Data*. New York: Chapman and Hall, 1985.

Cragg, J. "On the Relative Small-Sample Properties of Several Structural-Equation Estimators." *Econometrica*, 35, 1967, pp. 89–110.

Cragg, J. "Some Statistical Models for Limited Dependent Variables with Application to the Demand for Durable Goods." *Econometrica*, 39, 1971, pp. 829–844.

Cragg, J. "Estimation and Testing in Testing in Time Series Regression Models with Heteroscedastic Disturbances." *Journal of Econometrics*, 20, 1982, pp. 135–157.

Cragg, J. "More Efficient Estimation in the Presence of Heteroscedasticity of Unknown Form." *Econometrica*, 51, 1983, pp. 751–763.

Cragg, J., and R. Uhler. "The Demand for Automobiles." *Canadian Journal of Economics*, 3, 1970, pp. 386–406.

Cramér, H. *Mathematical Methods of Statistics*. Princeton: Princeton University Press, 1948.

Cramer, J. S. "Efficient Grouping, Regression and Correlation in Engel Curve Analysis." *Journal of the American Statistical Association*, 59, 1964, pp. 233–250.

Crawford, D. "Estimating Earnings Functions from Truncated Samples." Discussion Paper 287-75, Institute For Research on Poverty, University of Wisconsin, 1975.

Cumby, R., J. Huizinga, and M. Obstfeld. "Two-step, Two Stage Least Squares Estimation in Models with Rational Expectations." *Journal of Econometrics*, 21, 1983, pp. 333–355.

Davidson, R., and J. MacKinnon. "Several Tests for Model Specification in the Presence of Alternative Hypotheses." *Econometrica*, 49, 1981, pp. 781–793.

Davidson R., and J. MacKinnon. "Convenient Specification Tests for Logit and Probit Models." *Journal of Econometrics*, 25, 1984, pp. 241–262.

Davidson, R., and J. MacKinnon. "Testing Linear and Loglinear Regressions Against Box–Cox Alternatives." *Canadian Journal of Economics*, 18, 1985, pp. 499–517.

Davidson, J., and J. MacKinnon. *Estimation and Inference in Econometrics*. New York: Oxford University Press, 1993.

Deaton, A. "Demand Analysis." In Z. Griliches and M. Intriligator, eds., *Handbook of Econometrics*, Amsterdam: North Holland, 1983.

Deaton, A., and J. Muellbauer. *Economics and Consumer Behavior*. New York: Cambridge University Press, 1980b.

Dempster, A., N. Laird, and D. Rubin. "Maximum Likelihood Estimation from Incomplete Data via the EM Algorithm." *Journal of the Royal Statistical Society*, Series B, 39, 1977, pp. 1–38.

Desai, M. *Applied Econometrics*. New York: McGraw-Hill, 1976.

Dezhbaksh, H. "The Inappropriate Use of Serial Correlation Tests in Dynamic Linear Models." *Review of Economics and Statistics*, 72, 1990, pp. 126–132.

Dhrymes, P. "Efficient Estimation of Distributed Lags with Autocorrelated Errors." *International Economic Review*, 10, 1969, pp. 47–67.

Dhrymes, P. *Distributed Lags: Problems of Estimation and Formulation*. San Francisco: Holden Day, 1971.

Dhrymes, P. *Mathematics for Econometrics*. Needham, MA: Springer-Verlag, 1974.

Dhrymes, P. "Limited Dependent Variables." In Z. Griliches and M. Intriligator, eds., *Handbook of Econometrics*, vol. 2, Amsterdam: North Holland, 1984.

Dickey, D., W. Bell, and R. Miller. "Unit Roots in Time Series Models: Tests and Implications." *American Statistician*, 40, 1, 1986, pp. 12–26.

Dickey, D. and W. Fuller. "Distribution of the Estimators for Autoregressive Time Series with a Unit Root." *Journal of the American Statistical Association*, 74, 1979, pp. 427–431.

Dickey, D., and W. Fuller. "Likelihood Ratio Tests for Autoregressive Time Series with a Unit Root." *Econometrica*, 49, 1981, pp. 1057–1072.

Dickey, D., D. Jansen, and D. Thornton. "A Primer on Cointegration with an Application to Money and Income." *Federal Reserve Bank of St. Louis, Review*, 73, 2, 1991, pp. 58–78.

Dielman, T. *Pooled Cross-Sectional and Time Series Data Analysis*. New York: Marcel-Dekker, 1989.

Diewert, E. "Applications of Duality Theory." In M. Intriligator and D. Kendrick, *Frontiers in Quantitative Economics*, Amsterdam: North Holland, 1974.

Domowitz, I., and C. Hakkio. "Conditional Variance and the Risk Premium in the Foreign Exchange Market." *Journal of International Economics*, 19, 1985, pp. 47–66.

Don, F., and J. Magnus. "On the Unbiasedness of the Iterated GLS Estimator," *Communications in Statistics*, 1980, pp. 519–527.

Doran, H., and Griffiths, W. "Inconsistency of the OLS Estimator of the Partial Adjustment—Adaptive Expectations Model." *Journal of Econometrics*, 6, 1978, pp. 133–146.

Draper, N., and D. Cox. "On Distributions and Their Transformation to Normality." *Journal of the Royal Statistical Society*, Series B, 31, 1969, pp. 472–476.

Draper, N., and H. Smith. *Applied Regression Analysis*. New York: John Wiley and Sons, 1980.

Duncan, G. "Sample Selectivity as a Proxy Variable Problem: On the Use and Misuse of Gaussian Selectivity Corrections." *Research in Labor Economics*, Supplement 2, 1983, pp. 333–345.

Duncan, G. "A Semiparametric Censored Regression Estimator." *Journal of Econometrics*, 31, 1986a, pp. 5–34.

Duncan, G., ed. "Continuous/Discrete Econometric Models with Unspecified Error Distribution." *Journal of Econometrics*, 32, 1, 1986b, pp. 1–187.

Durbin, J. "Errors in Variables." *Review of the International Statistical Institute*, 22., 1954, pp. 23–32.

Durbin, J. "Testing for Serial Correlation in Least Squares Regression When Some of the Regressors Are Lagged Dependent Variables." *Econometrica*, 38, 1970, pp. 410–421.

Durbin, J., and G. Watson. "Testing for Serial Correlation in Least Squares Regression—I." *Biometrika*, 37, 1950, pp. 409–428.

Durbin, J., and G. Watson. "Testing for Serial Correlation in Least Squares Regression—II." *Biometrika*, 38, 1951, pp. 159–178.

Durbin, J., and G. Watson. "Testing for Serial Correlation in Least Squares Regression—III." *Biometrika*, 58, 1971, pp. 1–42.

Dwivedi, T., and K. Srivastava. "Optimality of Least Squares in the Seemingly Unrelated Regressions Model." *Journal of Econometrics*, 7, 1978, pp. 391–395.

Edlefson, L., and S. Jones. *Gauss*. Kent, WA: Aptech Systems, 1985.

Efron, B. "Bootstrapping Methods: Another Look at the Jackknife." *Annals of Statistics*, 7, 1979, pp. 1–26.

Eicker, F. "Limit Theorems for Regressions with Unequal and Dependent Errors." In L. LeCam, and J. Neyman, *Proceedings of the Fifth Berkeley Symposium on Mathematical Statistics and Probability*, Berkeley: University of California Press, 1967, pp. 59–82.

Enders, W. *Applied Econometric Time Series*. New York, John Wiley and Sons, 1995.

Engle, R. "Autoregressive Conditional Heteroscedasticity with Estimates of the Variance of United Kingdom Inflations." *Econometrica*, 50, 1982, pp. 987–1008.

Engle, R. "Estimates of the Variance of U.S. Inflation Based on the ARCH Model." *Journal of Money, Credit, and Banking*, 15, 1983, pp. 286–301.

Engle, R. "Wald, Likelihood Ratio, and Lagrange Multiplier Tests in Econometrics." In Z. Griliches and M. Intriligator, eds., *Handbook of Econometrics*, vol. 2, Amsterdam: North Holland, 1984.

Engle, R., and C. Granger. "Co-integration and Error Correction: Representation, Estimation and Testing." *Econometrica*, 35, 1987, pp. 251–276.

Engle, R., D. Hendry, and J. Richard. "Exogeneity," *Econometrica*, 51, 1983, pp. 277–304.

Engle, R., and D. Kraft. "Multiperiod Forecast Error Variances of Inflation Estimated from ARCH Models." In A. Zellner, ed., *Applied Time Series Analysis of Economic Data*, Washington D.C.: Bureau of the Census, 1983.

Engel, R., and B. Yoo. "Forecasting and Testing in Cointegrated Systems." *Journal of Econometrics*, 35, 1987, pp. 143–159.

Evans, G., and N. Savin. "Testing for Unit Roots: I." *Econometrica*, 49, 1981, pp. 753–779.

Evans, G., and N. Savin. "Testing for Unit Roots: II." *Econometrica*, 52, 1984, pp. 1241–1269.

Fair, R. "The Estimation of Simultaneous Equations Models with Lagged Endogenous Variables and First Order Serially Correlated Errors." *Econometrica*, 38, 1970, pp. 507–516.

Fair, R. "Efficient Estimation of Simultaneous Equations with Autoregressive Errors by Instrumental Variables." *Review of Economics and Statistics*, 54, 1972, pp. 444–449.

Fair, R. "A Note on Computation of the Tobit Estimator." *Econometrica*, 45, 1977, pp. 1723–1727.

Fair, R. "A Theory of Extramarital Affairs." *Journal of Political Economy*, 86, 1978, pp. 45–61.

Fair, R. *Specification and Analysis of Macroeconomic Models*. Cambridge: Harvard University Press, 1984.

Farebrother, R. "The Durbin–Watson Test for Serial Correlation When There Is No Intercept in the Regression." *Econometrica*, 48, 1980, pp. 1553–1563.

Feldstein, M. "Multicollinearity and the MSE of Alternative Estimators." *Econometrica*, 41, 1973, pp. 337–346.

Fernandez, L. "Nonparametric Maximum Likelihood Estimation of Censored Regression Models." *Journal of Econometrics*, 32, 1986, pp. 35–57.

Fin, T., and P. Schmidt. "A Test of the Tobit Specification Against an Alternative Suggested by Cragg." *Review of Economics and Statistics*, 66, 1984, pp. 174–177.

Finney, D. *Probit Analysis*. Cambridge: Cambridge University Press, 1971.

Fisher, F. "Tests of Equality Between Sets of Coefficients in Two Linear Regressions: An Expository Note." *Econometrica*, 28, 1970, pp. 361–366.

Fisher, F. *The Identification Problem in Econometrics*. New York: Krieger, 1976.

Fletcher, R. *Practical Methods of Optimization*. New York: John Wiley and Sons, 1980.

Fomby, T., C. Hill, and S. Johnson. "An Optimal Property of Principal Components in the Context of Restricted Least Squares." *Journal of the American Statistical Association*, 73, 1978, pp. 191–193.

Fomby, T., C. Hill, and S. Johnson. *Advanced Econometric Methods*. Needham, MA: Springer-Verlag, 1984.

Friedman, M. *A Theory of the Consumption Function*. Princeton: Princeton University Press, 1957.

Frisch, R. "Editorial." *Econometrica*, 1, 1933, pp. 1–4.

Frisch, R. and F. Waugh. "Partial Time Regressions as Compared with Individual Trends." *Econometrica*, 1, 1933, pp. 387–401.

Frost, P. "Some Properties of the Almon Lag Technique When One Searches for Degree of Polynomial and Lag." *Journal of the American Statistical Association*, 70, 1975, pp. 606–612.

Fuller, W. *Introduction to Statistical Time Series*. New York: John Wiley and Sons, 1976.

Fuller, W., and G. Battese. "Estimation of Linear Models with Crossed-Error Structure." *Journal of Econometrics*, 2, 1974, pp. 67–78.

Gabrielsen, A. "Consistency and Identifiability." *Journal of Econometrics*, 8, 1978, pp. 261–263.

Gallant, A. *Nonlinear Statistical Models*. New York: John Wiley and Sons, 1987.

Gallant, A., and A. Holly. "Statistical Inference in an Implicit Nonlinear Simultaneous Equation in the Context of Maximum Likelihood Estimation." *Econometrica*, 48, 1980, pp. 697–720.

Gallant, R., and H. White. *A Unified Theory of Estimation and Inference for Nonlinear Dynamic Models*. Oxford: Basil Blackwell, 1988.

Galpin, J., and Hawkins, D. "The Use of Recursive Residuals in Checking Model Fit in Linear Regression." *American Statistician*, 38, 1984, pp. 94–105.

Garber, S., and S. Klepper. "Extending the Classical Normal Errors in Variables Model," *Econometrica*, 48, 1980, pp. 1541–1546.

Garber, S., and D. Poirier. "The Determinants of Aerospace Profit Rates." *Southern Economic Journal*, 41, 1974, pp. 228–238.

Gaver, K., and M. Geisel. "Discriminating Among Alternative Models: Bayesian and Non-Bayesian Methods." In P. Zarembka, ed., *Frontiers in Econometrics*, New York: Academic Press, 1974.

Gelfand, A., and A. Smith. "Sampling Based Approaches to Calculating Marginal Densities," *Journal of the American Statistical Association,* 85, 1990, pp. 972–985.

Geweke, J. "Inference and Causality in Econometric Time Series Models." In Z. Griliches and M. Intriligator, eds., *Handbook of Econometrics*, vol. 2, Amsterdam: North Holland, 1984.

Geweke, J. "Exact Inference in the Inequality Constrained Normal Linear Regression Model." *Journal of Applied Econometrics*, 2, 1986, pp. 127–142.

Geweke, J. "Antithetic Acceleration of Monte Carlo Integration in Bayesian Inference." *Journal of Econometrics*, 38, 1988, pp. 73–90.

Geweke, J. "Bayesian Inference in Econometric Models Using Monte Carlo Integration." *Econometrica*, 57, 1989, pp. 1317–1340.

Geweke, J., M. Keane, and D. Runkle. "Alternative Computational Approaches to Inference in the Multinomial Probit Model." *Review of Economics and Statistics*, 76, 1994, pp. 609–632.

Geweke, J., and R. Meese. "Estimating Regression Models of Finite But Unknown Order." *International Economic Review*, 22, 1981, pp. 55–70.

Geweke, J., R. Meese, and W. Dent. "Comparing Alternative Tests of Causality in Temporal Systems: Analytic Results and Experimental Evidence." *Journal of Econometrics*, 21, 1983, pp. 161–194.

Giles, D., and M. King. "Fourth Order Autocorrelation: Further Significance Points for the Wallis Test." *Journal of Econometrics*, 8, 1978, pp. 255–259.

Gleick, J. *Chaos: Making a New Science*. New York: Penguin, 1987.

Glesjer, H. "A New Test for Heteroscedasticity." *Journal of the American Statistical Association*, 64, 1969, pp. 316–323.

Godfrey, L. "Testing Against General Autoregressive and Moving Average Error Models When the Regressors Include Lagged Dependent Variables." *Econometrica*, 46, 1978b, pp. 1293–1302.

Godfrey, L. *Misspecification Tests in Econometrics*. Cambridge: Cambridge University Press, 1988.

Godfrey, L., and D. Poskitt. "Testing the Restrictions of the Almon Lag Technique." *Journal of the American Statistical Association*, 70, 1975, pp. 105–108.

Godfrey, L. G., and M. R. Wickens. "Tests of misspecification using locally equivalent alternative models." In G. C. Chow and P. Corsi, eds., *Evaluating the Reliability of Econometric Models*, New York: John Wiley and Sons, 1982, pp. 71–99.

Goffe, W., G. Ferrier, and J. Rodgers. "Global Optimization of Statistical Functions with Simulated Annealing." *Journal of Econometrics*, 60, 1/2, 1994, pp. 65–100.

Goldberger, A. "Best Linear Unbiased Prediction in the Generalized Regression Model." *Journal of the American Statistical Association*, 57, 1962, pp. 369–375.

Goldberger, A. *Econometric Theory*. New York: John Wiley and Sons, 1964.

Goldberger, A. "Estimation of a Regression Coefficient Matrix Containing a Block of Zeroes." SSRI, EME, Number 7002, University of Wisconsin, 1970.

Goldberger, A. "Selection Bias in Evaluating Treatment Effects: Some Formal Illustrations." Discussion Paper 123-72, Institute for Research on Poverty, University of Wisconsin, Madison, 1972b.

Goldberger, A. "Linear Regression After Selection." *Journal of Econometrics*, 15, 1981, pp. 357–366.

Goldberger, A. "Abnormal Selection Bias." In S. Karlin, T. Amemiya, and L. Goodman, eds., *Studies in Econometrics, Time Series, and Multivariate Statistics*, New York: Academic Press, 1983.

Goldberger, A. "One-Sided and Inequality Tests for a Pair of Means." No. 8629, Social Science Research Institute, University of Wisconsin, Madison, 1986.

Goldberger, A. *A Course in Econometrics*. Cambridge: Harvard University Press, 1991.

Goldfeld, S. "The Demand for Money Revisited." *Brookings Papers on Economic Activity*, Washington, D.C., Brookings Institution, 3, 1973.

Goldfeld, S., and R. Quandt. "Some Tests for Homoscedasticity." *Journal of the American Statistical Association*, 60, 1965, pp. 539–547.

Goldfeld, S., and R. Quandt. "Nonlinear Simultaneous Equations: Estimation and Prediction." *International Economic Review*, 9, 1968, pp. 113–136.

Goldfeld, S., and R. Quandt. *Nonlinear Methods in Econometrics*. Amsterdam: North Holland, 1971.

Goldfeld, S., and R. Quandt. "GQOPT: A Package for Numerical Optimization of Functions." Department of Economics, Princeton University, 1972.

Goldfeld, S., R. Quandt, and H. Trotter. "Maximization by Quadratic Hill Climbing." *Econometrica*, 1966, pp. 541–551.

Gordon, R., ed. *The American Business Cycle.* Chicago: National Bureau of Economic Research, 1986.

Gourieroux, C., and A. Monfort. "Testing Non-Nested Hypotheses." In Z. Griliches, and M. Intriligator, eds., *Handbook of Econometrics*, vol. 4, Amsterdam: North Holland, 1994.

Gourieroux, C., A. Monfort, E. Renault, and A. Trognon. "Generalized Residuals." *Journal of Econometrics*, 34, 1987, pp. 5–32.

Gourieroux, C., A. Monfort, and A. Trognon. "Pseudo Maximum Likelihood Methods: Applications to Poisson Models." *Econometrica*, 52, 1984, pp. 701–720.

Granger, C. "Investigating Causal Relations by Econometric Models and Cross-Spectral Methods." *Econometrica*, 37, 1969, pp. 424–438.

Granger, C., and P. Newbold. "Spurious Regressions in Econometrics." *Journal of Econometrics*, 2, 1974, pp. 111–120.

Granger, C., and P. Newbold. *Forecasting Economic Time Series*. New York: Academic Press, 1977.

Granger, C., and M. Watson. "Time Series and Spectral Methods in Econometrics." In Z. Griliches and M. Intriligator, eds., *Handbook of Econometrics*, vol. 2, Ch. 17, Amsterdam: North Holland, 1984.

Greenberg, E. and C. Webster. *Advanced Econometrics: A Bridge to the Literature*. New York: John Wiley and Sons, 1983.

Greene, W. "Maximum Likelihood Estimation of Econometric Frontier Functions." *Journal of Econometrics*, 13, 1980a, pp. 27–56.

Greene, W. "On the Asymptotic Bias of the Ordinary Least Squares Estimator of the Tobit Model." *Econometrica*, 48, 1980b, pp. 505–514.

Greene, W. "Sample Selection Bias as a Specification Error: Comment." *Econometrica*, 49, 1981, pp. 795–798.

Greene, W. "Estimation of Limited Dependent Variable Models by Ordinary Least Squares and the Method of Moments." *Journal of Econometrics*, 21, 1983a, pp. 195–212.

Greene, W. "Simultaneous Estimation of Factor Substitution, Economies of Scale, and Non-Neutral Technical Change." In A. Dogramaci, ed. *Econometric Analyses of Productivity*, Boston: Kluwer-Nijoff, 1983b.

Greene, W. "Estimation of the Correlation Coefficient in a Bivariate Probit Model Using the Method of Moments." *Economics Letters*, 16, 1984, pp. 285–291.

Greene, W. "A Gamma Distributed Stochastic Frontier Model." *Journal of Econometrics*, 46, 1990, pp. 141–163.

Greene, W. "A Statistical Model for Credit Scoring." Working Paper No. EC-92-29, New York University, Department of Economics, Stern School of Business, 1992.

Greene, W. "Accounting for Excess Zeros and Sample Selection in Poisson and Negative Binomial Regression Models." Working Paper No. EC-94-10, Department of Economics, Stern School of Business, New York University, 1994.

Greene, W. *LIMDEP, Version 7.0: User's Manual*. Bellport, NY: Econometric Software, 1995a, pp. 234–241.

Greene, W. "Count Data." Manuscript, Department of Economics, Stern School of Business, New York University, 1995b.

Greene, W. "Sample Selection in the Poisson Regression Model." Working Paper No. EC-95-6, Department of Economics, Stern School of Business, New York University, 1995c.

Greene, W., and T. Seaks. "The Restricted Least Squares Estimator: A Pedagogical Note." *Review of Economics and Statistics*, 73, 1991, pp. 563–567.

Greenstadt, J. "On the Relative Efficiencies of Gradient Methods." *Mathematics of Computation*, 1967, pp. 360–367.

Grether, D., and G. Maddala. "Errors in Variables and Serially Correlated Disturbances in Distributed Lag Models." *Econometrica*, 41, 1973, pp. 255–262.

Griliches, Z. "Hybrid Corn: An Exploration in the Economics of Technological Change." *Econometrica*, 25, 1957, pp. 501–522.

Griliches, Z. "A Note on Serial Correlation Bias in Estimates of Distributed Lags." *Econometrica*, 26, 1961a, pp. 65–73.

Griliches, Z. "Hedonic Price Indexes for Automobiles: An Econometric Analysis of Quality Change." Government Price Statistics, Hearings, U.S. Congress, Joint Economic Committee, January 24, 1961b.

Griliches, Z. "Distributed Lags: A Survey." *Econometrica*, 35, 1967, pp. 16–49.

Griliches, Z. "Economic Data Issues." In Z. Griliches and M. Intriligator, eds., *Handbook of Econometrics*, vol. 3, Amsterdam: North Holland, 1986.

Griliches, Z., G. Maddala, R. Lucas, and N. Wallace. "Notes on Estimated Aggregate Quarterly Consumption Functions." *Econometrica*, 30, 1962, pp. 491–500.

Griliches, Z. and P. Rao. "Small Sample Properties of Several Two Stage Regression Methods in the Context of Autocorrelated Errors." *Journal of the American Statistical Association*, 64, 1969, pp. 253–272.

Grogger, J., and R. Carson. "Models for Truncated Counts," *Journal of Applied Econometrics*, 6, 1991, pp. 225–238.

Gronau, R. "Wage Comparisons: A Selectivity Bias," and Lewis, H., "Comments on Selectivity Biases in Wage Comparisons." *Journal of Political Economy*, 82, 1974, pp. 1119–1155.

Grunfeld, Y. "The Determinants of Corporate Investment." Unpublished Ph.D. thesis, Department of Economics, University of Chicago, 1958.

Grunfeld, Y., and Z. Griliches. "Is Aggregation Necessarily Bad?" *Review of Economics and Statistics*, 42, 1960, pp. 1–13.

Guilkey, D. "Alternative Tests for a First-Order Vector Autoregressive Error Specification." *Journal of Econometrics*, 2, 1974, pp. 95–104.

Guilkey, D., K. Lovell, and R. Sickles. "A Comparison of the Performance of Three Flexible Functional Forms." *International Economic Review*, 24, 1983, pp. 591–616.

Guilkey, D., and P. Schmidt. "Estimation of Seemingly Unrelated Regressions with Vector Autoregressive Errors." *Journal of the American Statistical Association*, 1973, pp. 642–647.

Guilkey, D., and P. Schmidt. "Extended Tabulations for Dickey–Fuller Tests." *Economics Letters*, 31, 1989, pp. 355–358.

Gujarati, D. *Basic Econometrics*, 3rd ed. New York, McGraw-Hill, 1995.

Gurmu, S. "Tests for Detecting Overdispersion in the Positive Poisson Regression Model." *Journal of Business and Economic Statistics*, 9, 1991, pp. 215–222.

Gurmu, S., and P. Trivedi. "Recent Developments in Models of Event Counts: A Survey," Department of Economics, Indiana University, Manuscript, 1994.

Haavelmo, T., "The Statistical Implications of a System of Simultaneous Equations," *Econometrica*, 11, 1943, pp. 1–12.

Hadley, G. *Linear Algebra*. Reading, MA: Addison-Wesley, 1961.

Haitovsky, Y. "Missing Data in Regression Analysis." *Journal of the Royal Statistical Society*, Series B, 1968, pp. 67–82.

Hajivassiliou, V. "Smooth Simulation Estimation of Panel Data LDV Models." Department of Economics, Yale University, 1990.

Hajivassiliou, V., D. McFadden, and P. Ruud. "Simulation of Multivariate Normal Orthant Probabilities: Methods and Programs." Discussion Paper No. 1021, Yale University, Cowles Foundation, 1992.

Hall, B. "TSP Version 4.0 Reference Manual." Stanford: TSP International, 1982.

Hall, B. "Software for the Computation of Tobit Model Estimates." *Journal of Econometrics*, 24, 1984, pp. 215–222.

✓Hamilton, J. *Time Series Analysis*. Princeton: Princeton University Press, 1994.

Hannan, E., and R. Terrell. "Testing for Serial Correlation After Least Squares Regression." *Econometrica*, 1966, pp. 646–660.

Hansen, L. "Large Sample Properties of Generalized Method of Moments Estimators." *Econometrica*, 50, 1982, pp. 1029–1054.

Hansen, L., and K. Singleton. "Efficient Estimation of Asset Pricing Models with Moving Average Errors." Mimeo, Department of Economics, Carnegie Mellon University, 1988.

Harvey, A. "Estimating Regression Models with Multiplicative Heteroscedasticity." *Econometrica*, 44, 1976, pp. 461–465.

Harvey, A. *Forecasting, Structural Time Series Models and the Kalman Filter*. New York: Cambridge University Press, 1989.

Harvey, A. *The Econometric Analysis of Time Series*, 2nd ed. Cambridge: MIT Press, 1990.

Harvey, A. and G. Collier. "Testing for Functional Misspecification in Regression Analysis." *Journal of Econometrics*, 6, 1977, pp. 103–119.

Harvey, A. and I. McAvinchey. "On the Relative Efficiency of Various Estimators of Regression Models with Moving Average Disturbances." In E. Charatsis, ed., Proceedings of the Econometric Society European Meetings, Athens, 1979, Amsterdam: North Holland, 1981.

Harvey, A., and G. Phillips. "A Comparison of the Power of Some Tests for Heteroscedasticity in the General Linear Model." *Journal of Econometrics*, 2, 1974, pp. 307–316.

Hatanaka, M. "An Efficient Estimator for the Dynamic Adjustment Model with Autocorrelated Errors." *Journal of Econometrics*, 2, 1974, pp. 199–220.

Hatanaka, M. "Several Efficient Two-Step Estimators for the Dynamic Simultaneous Equations Model With Autoregressive Disturbances." *Journal of Econometrics*, 4, 1976, pp. 189–204.

Hausman, J. "An Instrumental Variable Approach to Full-Information Estimators for Linear and Certain Nonlinear Models." *Econometrica*, 43, 1975, pp. 727–738.

Hausman, J. "Specification Tests in Econometrics." *Econometrica*, 46, 1978, pp. 1251–1271.

Hausman, J. "Specification and Estimation of Simultaneous Equations Models." In Z. Griliches, and M. Intriligator, eds., *Handbook of Econometrics*, Amsterdam: North Holland, 1983.

Hausman, J., B. Hall, and Z. Griliches. "Economic Models for Count Data with an Application to the Patents-R&D Relationship." *Econometrica*, 52, 1984, pp. 909–938.

Hausman, J., and A. Han. "Flexible Parametric Estimation of Duration and Competing Risk Models." *Journal of Applied Econometrics*, 5, 1990, pp. 1–28.

Hausman, J. and D. McFadden. "A Specification Test for the Multinomial Logit Model." *Econometrica*, 52, 1984, pp. 1219–1240.

Hausman, J., and P. Ruud. "Specifying and Testing Econometric Models for Rank Ordered Data With an Application to the Demand for Mobile and Portable Telephones." Working Paper No. 8605, University of California, Berkeley, Department of Economics, 1986.

Hausman, J., and W. Taylor. "Panel Data and Unobservable Individual Effects." *Econometrica*, 49, 1981, pp. 1377–1398.

Hausman, J., and D. Wise. "Social Experimentation, Truncated Distributions, and Efficient Estimation." *Econometrica*, 45, 1977, pp. 919–938.

Hausman, J., and D. Wise. "A Conditional Probit Model for Qualitative Choice: Discrete Decisions Recognizing Interdependence and Heterogeneous Preferences." *Econometrica*, 46, 1978, pp. 403–426.

Heckman, J. "The Common Structure of Statistical Models of Truncation, Sample Selection, and Limited Dependent Variables and a Simple Estimator for Such Models." *Annals of Economic and Social Measurement*, 5, 1976, pp. 475–492.

Heckman, J. "Dummy Endogenous Variables in a Simultaneous Equation System." *Econometrica*, 46, 1978, pp. 931–959.

Heckman, J. "Sample Selection Bias as a Specification Error." *Econometrica*, 47, 1979, pp. 153–161.

Heckman, J. "Varieties of Selection Bias." *American Economic Review*, 80, 1990, pp. 313–318.

Heckman, J., and T. MaCurdy. "A Simultaneous Equations Linear Probability Model." *Canadian Journal of Economics*, 18, 1985, pp. 28–37.

Heckman, J., and B. Singer. "Econometric Duration Analysis." *Journal of Econometrics*, 24, 1984a, pp. 63–132.

Heckman, J., and B. Singer. "A Method for Minimizing the Impact of Distributional Assumptions in Econometric Models for Duration Data." *Econometrica*, 52, 1984b, pp. 271–320.

Heckman, J., and R. Willis. "Estimation of a Stochastic Model of Reproduction: An Econometric Approach." In N. Terleckyj, ed., *Household Production and Consumption*, New York: National Bureau of Economic Research, 1976.

Heilbron, D. "Generalized Linear Models for Altered Zero Probabilities and Overdispersion in Count Data." Technical Report, Department of Epidemiology and Biostatistics, University of California, San Francisco, 1989.

Hein, D. "Predicted and Actual Frequencies in Binomial Response Models." *Economics Letters*, 23, 1987, pp. 104–107.

Hendry, D. "Econometrics: Alchemy or Science?" *Economica*, 47, 1980, pp. 387–406.

Hendry, D. "Monte Carlo Experimentation in Econometrics." In Z. Griliches and M. Intriligator, eds., *Handbook of Econometrics*, Vol. 2, Amsterdam: North Holland, 1984.

Hendry, D., A. Pagan, and J. Sargan. "Dynamic Specification." In Z. Griliches and M. Intriligator, eds., *Handbook of Econometrics*, Vol. 2, Amsterdam: North Holland, 1984.

Hensher, D. "Simultaneous Estimation of Hierarchical Logit Mode Choice Models." Working Paper No. 24, MacQuarie University, School of Economic and Financial Studies, 1986.

Hildebrand, G., and T. Liu. *Manufacturing Production Functions in the United States*. Ithaca: Cornell University Press, 1957.

Hildreth, C., and W. Dent. "An Adjusted Maximum Likelihood Estimator." In W. Saelkert, ed., *Econometrics and Economic Theory: Essays in Honor of Jan Tinbergen*, London: Macmillan, 1974, pp. 3–25.

Hildreth, C., and C. Houck. "Some Estimators for a Linear Model with Random Coefficients." *Journal of the American Statistical Association*, 63, 1968, pp. 584–595.

Hildreth, C., and J. Lu. "Demand Relations with Autocorrelated Disturbances." Technical Bulletin No. 276, Michigan State University Agricultural Experiment Station, 1960.

Hite, S. *Women and Love*. New York: Alfred A. Knopf, 1987.

Holtz-Eakin, D., W. Newey, and H. Rosen. "Estimating Vector Autoregressions with Panel Data." *Econometrica*, 56, 6, 1988, pp. 1371–1395.

Horn, D., A. Horn, and G. Duncan. "Estimating Heteroscedastic Variances in Linear Models." *Journal of the American Statistical Association*, 70, 1975, pp. 380–385.

Horowitz, J., and G. Neumann. "Specification Testing in Censored Regression Models." *Journal of Applied Econometrics*, 4(S), 1989, pp. S35–S60.

Hsiao, C. "Some Estimation Methods for a Random Coefficient Model." *Econometrica*, 43, 1975, pp. 305–325.

Hsiao, C. "Identification." In Z. Griliches and M. Intriligator, eds., *Handbook of Econometrics*, Amsterdam: North Holland, 1983.

Hsiao, C. *Analysis of Panel Data*. New York: Cambridge University Press, 1986.

Hsiao, C. "Logit and Probit Models." In L. Matyas and P. Sevestre, eds., *The Econometrics of Panel Data: Handbook of Theory and Applications*, 2nd ed. Dordrecht: Kluwer-Nijoff, 1996.

Hurd, M. "Estimation in Truncated Samples When There Is Heteroscedasticity." *Journal of Econometrics*, 11, 1979, pp. 247–258.

Husby, R. "A Nonlinear Consumption Function Estimated from Time Series and Cross Section Data," *Review of Economics and Statistics*, 53, 1971, pp. 76–79.

Im, E. "Unequal Numbers of Observations and Partial Efficiency Gain." *Economics Letters*, 46, 1994, pp. 291–294.

Jaggia, S. "Tests of Moment Restrictions in Parametric Duration Models." *Economics Letters*, 37, 1991, pp. 35–38.

James, W., and C. Stein. "Estimation with Quadratic Loss." In J. Neyman, ed., *Proceedings of the Fourth Berkeley Symposium on Mathematical Statistics and Probability*, vol. 1, 1961, Berkeley: University of California Press, pp. 361–379.

Jarque, C. "An Application of LDV Models to Household Expenditure Analysis in Mexico." *Journal of Econometrics*, 36, 1987, pp. 31–54.

Jennrich, R. I. "The Asymptotic Properties of Nonlinear Least Squares Estimators." *Annals of Statistics*, 2 1969, pp. 633–643.

Jobson, J. and W. Fuller. "Least Squares Estimation When the Covariance Matrix and Parameter Vector Are Functionally Related." *Journal of the American Statistical Association*, 75, 1980, pp. 176–181.

Johansen, S. "Statistical Analysis of Cointegration Vectors," *Journal of Economic Dynamics and Control*, 12, 1988, pp. 231–254.

Johansen, S., and K. Juselius. "Maximum Likelihood Estimation and Inference on Cointegration, with Applications for the Demand for Money." *Oxford Bulletin of Economics and Statistics*, 52, 1990, pp. 169–210.

Johnson, N., and S. Kotz. *Distributions in Statistics, Continuous Univariate Distributions*—2. New York: John Wiley and Sons, 1970.

Johnson, N., and S. Kotz, *Distributions in Statistics—Continuous Multivariate Distributions*. New York: John Wiley and Sons, 1974.

Johnson, N., and S. Kotz. *Distributions in Statistics—Discrete Distributions*, 2nd ed. New York: John Wiley and Sons, 1993.

Johnston, J. *Econometric Methods*. New York: McGraw-Hill, 1984.

Joreskog, K. "A General Method for Estimating a Linear Structural Equation System." In A. Goldberger, and O. Duncan, *Structural Equation Models in the Social Sciences*, New York: Academic Press, 1973.

Joreskog, K., and G. Gruvaeus. "A Computer Program for Minimizing a Function of several Variables." Research Bulletin Number 70-14, Educational Testing Services, 1970.

Joreskog, K., and D. Sorbom. "LISREL V User's Guide." Chicago: National Educational Resources, 1981.

Jorgenson, D. "Rational Distributed Lag Functions." *Econometrica*, 34, 1966, pp. 135–149.

Jorgenson, D. "Econometric Methods for Modeling Producer Behavior." In Z. Griliches and M. Intriligator, *Handbook of Econometrics*: vol. 3, Amsterdam: North Holland, 1983.

Judge, G., and M. Bock. *The Statistical Implications of Pre-Test and Stein Rule Estimators in Econometrics*. Amsterdam: North Holland, 1978.

Judge, G., and M. Bock. "Biased Estimation." In Z. Griliches and M. Intriligator, eds., *Handbook of Econometrics*, vol. 1, Amsterdam: North Holland, 1983.

Judge, G., C. Hill, W. Griffiths, and T. Lee. *The Theory and Practice of Econometrics*. New York: John Wiley and Sons, 1985.

Judge, G., C. Hill, W. Griffiths, T. Lee, and H. Lutkepol. *An Introduction to the Theory and Practice of Econometrics*. New York: John Wiley and Sons, 1982.

Judge, G., and T. Yancey. "Sampling Properties of An Inequality Restricted Estimator." *Economics Letters*, 4, 1981, pp. 327–333.

Just, R., and R. Pope. "Stochastic Specification of Production Functions and Economic Implications." *Journal of Econometrics*, 7, 1978, pp. 67–86.

Kakwani, N. "The Unbiasedness of Zellner's Seemingly Unrelated Regression Equation Estimators." *Journal of the American Statistical Association*, 62, 1967, pp. 141–142.

Kalbfleisch, J. and R. Prentice. *The Statistical Analysis of Failure Time Data*. New York: John Wiley and Sons, 1980.

Kalman, R. "A New Approach to Linear Filtering and Prediction Problems." *Journal of Basic Engineering, Transactions ASME*, Series D, 82, 1960, pp. 35–45.

Kamlich, R. and S. Polachek. "Discrimination: Fact or Fiction? An Examination Using an Alternative Approach." *Southern Economic Journal*, October 1982, pp. 450–461.

Keane, M. "A Computationally Practical Simulation Estimator for Panel Data." *Econometrica*, 62, 1, 1994, pp. 95–116.

Kelejian, H. "Missing Observations in Multivariate Regression—Efficiency of a First Order Method." *Journal of the American Statistical Association*, 64, 1969, 1609–1616.

Kelejian, H. "Two-Stage Least Squares and Econometric Systems Linear in Parameters but Nonlinear in the Endogenous Variables." *Journal of the American Statistical Association*, 66, 1971, pp. 373–374.

Kelly, J. "Linear Cross Equation Constraints and the Identification Problem." *Econometrica*, 43, 1975, pp. 125–140.

Kennan, J. "The Duration of Contract Strikes in U.S. Manufacturing." *Journal of Econometrics*, 28, 1985, pp. 5–28.

Kennedy, W., and J. Gentle. *Statistical Computing*. New York: Marcel Dekker, 1980.

Keynes, J. *The General Theory of Employment, Interest, and Money*. New York: Harcourt, Brace, and Jovanovich, 1936.

Kiefer, N. "Testing for Independence in Multivariate Probit Models." *Biometrika*, 69, 1982, pp. 161–166.

Kiefer, N. ed. "Econometric Analysis of Duration Data." *Journal of Econometrics*, 28, 1, 1985a, 1–169.

Kiefer, N. "Specification Diagnostics Based on Laguerre Alternatives for Econometric Models of Duration." *Journal of Econometrics*, 28, 1985b, pp. 135–154.

Kiefer, N. "Economic Duration Data and Hazard Functions." *Journal of Economic Literature*, 26, 1988, pp. 646–679.

Kiefer, N., and Salmon, M. "Testing Normality in Econometric Models." *Economics Letters*, 11, 1983, pp. 123–127.

Kim, H., and J. Pollard. "Cube Root Asymptotics." *Annals of Statistics*, March 1990, pp. 191–219.

King, M. "The Durbin–Watson Test for Serial Correlation: Bounds for Regressions with Trend and/or Seasonal Dummy Variables." *Econometrica*, 49, 1981, pp. 1571–1581.

Kiviet, J. "On Bias, Inconsistency, and Efficiency of Some Estimators in Dynamic Panel Data Models." *Journal of Econometrics*, 68, 1, 1995, pp. 63–78.

Klein, L. *Economic Fluctuations in the United States 1921–1941.* New York: John Wiley and Sons, 1950.

Klein, L. *An Introduction to Econometrics.* Englewood Cliffs: Prentice-Hall, Inc. 1962.

Klepper, S., and E. Leamer. "Consistent Sets of Estimates for Regressions with Errors in All Variables." *Econometrica*, 52, 1983, pp. 163–184.

Kmenta, J. In "On Estimation of the CES Production Function," *International Economic Review*, 8, 1967, pp. 180–189.

Kmenta, J. *Elements of Econometrics.* New York: Macmillan, 1986.

Kmenta, J., and R. Gilbert. "Small Sample Properties of Alternative Estimators of Seemingly Unrelated Regressions." *Journal of the American Statistical Association*, 63, 1968, pp. 1180–1200.

Kmenta, J., and W. Oberhofer. "Estimation of Standard Errors of the Characteristic Roots of a Dynamic Econometric Model." *Econometrica*, 41, 1973, pp. 171–177.

Knapp, L., and T. Seaks. "An Analysis of the Probability of Default on Federally Guaranteed Student Loans." *Review of Economics and Statistics*, 74, 1992, pp. 404–411.

Kobayashi, M. "A Bounds Test of Equality Between Sets of Coefficients in Two Linear Regressions When Disturbance Variances are Unequal." *Journal of the American Statistical Association*, 81, 1986, pp. 510–514.

Koenker, R., and G. Bassett. "Regression Quantiles." *Econometrica*, 46, 1978, pp. 107–112.

Koenker, R., and G. Bassett. "Robust Tests for Heteroscedasticity Based on Regression Quantiles." *Econometrica*, 50, 1982, pp. 43–61.

Kosobud, R. "A Note on a Problem Caused by the Assignment of Missing Data in Sample Survey." *Econometrica*, 31, 1963, pp. 562–563.

Koyck, L. *Distributed Lags and Investment Analysis.* Amsterdam: North Holland, 1954.

Lahiri, K., and D. Egy. "Joint Estimation and Testing for Functional Form and Heteroscedasticity." *Journal of Econometrics*, 15, 1981, pp. 299–307.

Lahiri, K., and P. Schmidt. "On the Estimation of Triangular Structural Systems." *Econometrica*, 46, 1978, pp. 1217–1221.

Lambert, D. "Zero-Inflated Poisson Regression, with an Application to Defects in Manufacturing." *Technometrics*, 34, 1, 1992, pp. 1–14.

Lancaster, T. *The Analysis of Transition Data.* New York: Cambridge University Press, 1990.

Lancaster, T., and A. Chesher. "Residual Tests and Plots with a Job Matching Illustration." *Annales de L'Insee,* 59/60, 1985, pp. 47–70.

Landers, A. "Survey," *Chicago Tribune*, 1980, passim.

Lawless, J. *Statistical Models and Methods for Lifetime Data.* New York: John Wiley and Sons, 1982.

Leamer, E. *Specification Searches: Ad Hoc Inferences with Nonexperimental Data.* New York: John Wiley and Sons, 1978.

Lee, L. "Estimation of Error Components Models with ARMA(p,q) Time Component - An Exact GLS Approach." No. 78–104, University of Minnesota, Center for Economic Research, 1978a.

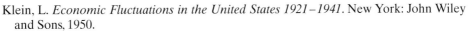

Lee, L. "Specification Tests for Poisson Regression Models." *International Economic Review*, 27, 1986, pp. 689–706.

Lee, L., and W. Griffiths. "The Prior Likelihood and Best Linear Unbiased Prediction in Stochastic Coefficient Linear Models." Working Paper No. 1, University of New England Working Papers in Econometrics and Applied Statistics, 1979.

Lerman, R., and C. Manski. "On the Use of Simulated Frequencies to Approximate Choice Probabilities." In C. Manski and D. McFadden, eds., *Structural Analysis of Discrete Data with Econometric Applications*, Cambridge: MIT Press, 1981.

Levi, M. "Errors in the Variables in the Presence of Correctly Measured Variables." *Econometrica*, 41, 1973, pp. 985–986.

Lewis, H. "Comments on Selectivity Biases in Wage Comparisons." *Journal of Political Economy*, 82, 1974, pp. 1119–1155.

Lillard, L., and R. Willis. "Dynamic Aspects of Earning Mobility." *Econometrica*, 46, 1978, pp. 985–1012.

Litterman, R. "Techniques of Forecasting Using Vector Autoregressions." Working Paper No. 15, Federal Reserve Bank of Minneapolis, 1979.

Litterman, R. "Forecasting with Bayesian Vector Autoregressions—Five Years of Experience." *Journal of Business and Economic Statistics*, 4, 1986, pp. 25–38.

Liu, T. "Underidentification, Structural Estimation, and Forecasting." *Econometrica*, 28, 1960, pp. 855–865.

Ljung, G., and G. Box. "On a Measure of Lack of Fit in Time Series Models." *Biometrika*, 66, 1979, pp. 265–270.

Longley, J. "An Appraisal of Least Squares Programs from the Point of the User." *Journal of the American Statistical Association*, 62, 1967, pp. 819–841.

MacKinnon, J., and H. White. "Some Heteroscedasticity Consistent Covariance Matrix Estimators with Improved Finite Sample Properties." *Journal of Econometrics*, 19, 1985, pp. 305–325.

MacKinnon, J., H. White, and R. Davidson. "Tests for Model Specification in the Presence of Alternative Hypotheses; Some Further Results." *Journal of Econometrics*, 21, 1983, pp. 53–70.

MaCurdy, T. "The Use of Time Series Processes To Model the Error Structure of Earnings in a Longitudinal Data Analysis." *Journal of Econometrics*, 18, 1982, pp. 83–114.

Maddala, G. "The Use of Variance Components Models in Pooling Cross Section and Time Series Data." *Econometrica*, 39, 1971, pp. 341–358.

Maddala, G. *Econometrics*. New York: McGraw-Hill, 1977a.

Maddala, G. "Limited Dependent Variable Models Using Panel Data." *Journal of Human Resources*, 22, 1977b, pp. 307–338.

Maddala, G. *Limited Dependent and Qualitative Variables in Econometrics*. New York: Cambridge University Press, 1983.

Maddala, G. "Disequilibrium, Self-Selection, and Switching Models." In Z. Griliches and M. Intriligator, eds., *Handbook of Econometrics*, Amsterdam: North Holland, 1984.

Maddala, G. *Introduction to Econometrics*, 2nd ed. New York: Macmillan, 1992.

Maddala, G. *The Econometrics of Panel Data,* vols. 1 and 2. Brookfield, VT: E. E. Elgar, 1993.

Maddala, G., and F. Nelson. "Specification Errors in Limited Dependent Variable Models." Working Paper 96, National Bureau of Economic Research, Cambridge, 1975.

Maeshiro, A. "On the Retention of the First Observations in Serial Correlation Adjustment of Regression Models." *International Economic Review*, 20, 1979, pp. 259–265.

Magnus, J. "Maximum Likelihood Estimation of the Generalized Regression Model with Unknown Parameters in the Disturbance Covariance Matrix." *Journal of Econometrics*, 7, 1978, pp. 281–312.

Magnus, J., and H. Neudecker. *Matrix Differential Calculus with Applications in Statistics and Econometrics*. New York: John Wiley and Sons, 1988.

Malinvaud, E. *Statistical Methods of Econometrics*. Amsterdam: North Holland, 1970.

Mann, H., and A. Wald. "On the Statistical Treatment of Linear Stochastic Difference Equations." *Econometrica*, 11, 1943, pp. 173–220.

Manski, C. "The Maximum Score Estimator of the Stochastic Utility Model of Choice." *Journal of Econometrics*, 3, 1975, pp. 205–228.

Manski, C. "Semiparametric Analysis of Discrete Response: Asymptotic Properties of the Maximum Score Estimator." *Journal of Econometrics*, 27, 1985, pp. 313–333.

Manski, C. "Operational Characteristics of the Maximum Score Estimator." *Journal of Econometrics*, 32, 1986, pp. 85–100.

Manski, C. "Anatomy of the Selection Problem." *Journal of Human Resources*, 24, 1989, pp. 343–360.

Manski, C. "Nonparametric Bounds on Treatment Effects." *American Economic Review*, 80, 1990, pp. 319–323.

Manski, C. *Analog Estimation Methods in Econometrics*. London: Chapman and Hall, 1992.

Manski, C. *Identification Problems in Econometrics*. Cambridge: Harvard University Press, 1995.

Manski, C., and S. Thompson. "MSCORE: A Program for Maximum Score Estimation of Linear Quantile Regressions from Binary Response Data." Mimeo, University of Wisconsin, Madison, Department of Economics, 1986.

Manski, C., and S. Thompson. "Estimation of Best Predictors of Binary Response." *Journal of Econometrics*, 40, 1989, pp. 97–124.

Mariano, R. "Analytical Small-Sample Distribution Theory in Econometrics: The Simultaneous Equations Case." *International Economic Review*, 23, 1982, pp. 503–534.

Marcus, A., and W. Greene. "The Determinants of Rating Assignment and Performance." Working Paper CRC528, Center for Naval Analyses, 1985.

Matyas, L., and P. Sevestre, eds. *The Econometrics of Panel Data: Handbook of Theory and Applications*, 2nd ed. Dordrecht: Kluwer-Nijoff, 1996.

McAleer, M., G. Fisher, and P. Volker. "Separate Misspecified Regressions and the U.S. Long-Run Demand for Money Function." *Review of Economics and Statistics*, 64, 1982, pp. 572–583.

McAleer, M., A. Pagan, and P. Volker. "What Will Take the Con Out of Econometrics?" *American Economic Review*, 75, 1985, pp. 293–307.

McCallum, B. "Relative Asymptotic Bias from Errors of Omission and Measurement." *Econometrica*, 40, 1972, pp. 757–758.

McCullagh, P., and J. Nelder. *Generalized Linear Models*. New York: Chapman and Hall, 1983.

McCulloch, J. "On Heteros*edasticity." *Econometrica*, 53, 2, 1985, p. 483.

McDonald, J., and R. Moffitt. "The Uses of Tobit Analysis." *Review of Economics and Statistics*, 62, 1980, pp. 318–321.

McElroy, M. "Goodness of Fit for Seemingly Unrelated Regressions: Glahn's $R^2_{y.x}$ and Hooper's $\bar{r}^2$." *Journal of Econometrics*, 6, 1977, pp. 381–387.

McFadden, D. "Conditional Logit Analysis of Qualitative Choice Behavior." In P. Zarembka, ed., *Frontiers in Econometrics*, New York: Academic Press, 1973.

McFadden, D. "The Measurement of Urban Travel Demand." *Journal of Public Economics*, 3, 1974, pp. 303–328.

McFadden, D. "Econometric Analysis of Qualitative Response Models." In Z. Griliches and M. Intriligator, eds., *Handbook of Econometrics*, vol. 2, Amsterdam: North Holland, 1984.

McFadden, D. "Regression Based Specification Tests for the Multinomial Logit Model." *Journal of Econometrics*, 34, 1987, pp. 63–82.

McFadden, D. "A Method of Simulated Moments for Estimation of Discrete Response Models Without Numerical Integration." *Econometrica*, 57, 1989, pp. 995–1026.

McFadden, D., and W. Newey. "Asymptotic Properties of Nonlinear Estimators." Mimeo, Department of Economics, MIT, 1988.

McFadden, D., and P. Ruud. "Estimation by Simulation." *The Review of Economics and Statistics*, 76, 1994, pp. 591–608.

Melenberg, B., and A. van Soest. "Parametric and Semi-Parametric Modelling of Vacation Expenditures." *Journal of Applied Econometrics*, 11, 1, 1996, pp. 59–76.

Messer, K., and H. White. "A Note on Computing the Heteroscedasticity Consistent Covariance Matrix Using Instrumental Variable Techniques." *Oxford Bulletin of Economics and Statistics*, 46, 1984, pp. 181–184.

Meyer, B. "Semiparametric Estimation of Hazard Models." Northwestern University, Department of Economics, 1988.

Mills, T. *Time Series Techniques for Economists*. New York: Cambridge University Press, 1990.

Mizon, G., and J. Richard. "The Encompassing Principle and its Application to Testing Nonnested Models." *Econometrica*, 54, 1986, pp. 657–678.

Mullahey, J. "Specification and Testing of Some Modified Count Data Models." *Journal of Econometrics*, 33, 1986, pp. 341–365.

Mullahey, J. "Weighted Least Squares Estimation of the Linear Probability Model, Revisited." *Economics Letters*, 32, 1990, pp. 35–41.

Mundlak, Y. "On the Pooling of Time Series and Cross Sectional Data." *Econometrica*, 46, 1978, pp. 69–86.

Murphy, K., and R. Topel. "Estimation and Inference in Two Step Econometric Models." *Journal of Business and Economic Statistics*, 3, 1985, pp. 370–379.

Nakamura, A., and M. Nakamura. "On the Relationships Among Several Specification Error Tests Presented by Durbin, Wu, and Hausman." *Econometrica*, 49, 1981, pp. 1583–1588.

Nakamura, A., and M. Nakamura. "Part-Time and Full Time Work Behavior of Married Women: A Model with a Doubly Truncated Dependent Variable." *Canadian Journal of Economics*, 1983, pp. 229–257.

Nakosteen, R., and M. Zimmer. "Migration and Income: The Question of Self-Selection." *Southern Economic Journal*, 46, 1980, pp. 840–851.

Nelder, J., and R. Mead. "A Simplex Method for Function Minimization." *Computer Journal*, 7, 1965, pp. 308–313.

Nelson, C., and H. Kang. "Pitfalls in the Use of Time as an Explanatory Variable in Regression." *Journal of Business and Economic Statistics*, 2, 1984, pp. 73–82.

Nelson, C., and C. Plosser. "Trends and Random Walks in Macroeconomic Time Series: Some Evidence and Implications." *Journal of Monetary Economics*, 10, 1982, pp. 139–162.

Nelson, F. "A Test For Misspecification in the Censored Normal Model." *Econometrica*, 49, 1981, pp. 1317–1329.

Nelson, F. "Efficiency of the Two-Step Estimator for Models with Endogenous Sample Selection." *Journal of Econometrics*, 24, 1984, pp. 181–196.

Nerlove, M. "Returns to Scale in Electricity Supply." In C. Christ, ed., *Measurement in Economics: Studies in Mathematical Economics and Econometrics in Memory of Yehuda Grunfeld*, Stanford: Stanford University Press, 1963.

Nerlove, M. "Further Evidence on the Estimation of Dynamic Relations From a Time Series of Cross Sections." *Econometrica*, 39, 1971a, pp. 359–382.

Nerlove, M. "A Note on Error Components Models." *Econometrica*, 39, 1971b, pp. 383–396.

Nerlove, M. "Lags in Economic Behavior." *Econometrica*, 40, 1972, pp. 221–251.

Nerlove, M., and F. Diebold. "Unit Roots in Economic Time Series: A Selective Survey." In T. Bewley, ed., *Advances in Econometrics*, vol. 8, New York: JAI Press, 1990.

Nerlove, M., and S. Press. "Univariate and Multivariate Log-Linear and Logistic Models." RAND–R1306-EDA/NIH, Santa Monica, 1973.

Nerlove, M., and K. Wallis. "Use of the Durbin–Watson Statistic in Inappropriate Situations." *Econometrica*, 34, 1966, pp. 235–238.

New York Post. "America's New Big Wheels of Fortune," May 22, 1987, p. 3.

Newey, W. "A Method of Moments Interpretation of Sequential Estimators." *Economics Letters*, 14, 1984, pp. 201–206.

Newey, W. "Maximum Likelihood Specification Testing and Conditional Moment Tests." *Econometrica*, 53, 1985a, pp. 1047–1070.

Newey, W. "Generalized Method of Moments Specification Testing." *Journal of Econometrics*, 29, 1985b, pp. 229–256.

Newey, W. "Specification Tests for Distributional Assumptions in the Tobit Model." *Journal of Econometrics*, 34, 1986, pp. 125–146.

Newey, W., J. Powell, and J. Walker. "Semiparametric Estimation of Selection Models." *American Economic Review*, 80, 1990, pp. 324–328.

Newey, W., and K. West. "A Simple Positive Semi-Definite, Heteroscedasticity and Autocorrelation Consistent Covariance Matrix." *Econometrica*, 55, 1987a, pp. 703–708.

Newey, W., and K. West. "Hypothesis Testing with Efficient Method of Moments Estimation." *International Economic Review*, 28, 1987b, pp. 777–787.

Nicholls, D., A. Pagan, and R. Terrell. "The Estimation and Use of Models with Moving Average Disturbance Terms: A Survey." *International Economic Review*, 16, 1975, pp. 113–134.

Nickell, S. "Biases in Dynamic Models with Fixed Effects." *Econometrica*, 49, 1981, pp. 1417–1426.

Oberhofer, W., and J. Kmenta. "A General Procedure for Obtaining Maximum Likelihood Estimates in Generalized Regression Models." *Econometrica*, 42, 1974, pp. 579–590.

Ohtani, K., and M. Kobayashi. "A Bounds Test for Equality Between Sets of Coefficients in 2 Linear Regression Models Under Heteroscedasticity." *Econometric Theory*, 2, 1986, pp. 220–231.

Ohtani, K., and T. Toyoda. "Estimation of Regression Coefficients After a Preliminary Test for Homoscedasticity." *Journal of Econometrics*, 12, 1980, pp. 151–159.

Ohtani, K., and T. Toyoda. "Small Sample Properties of Tests of Equality Between Sets of Coefficients in Two Linear Regressions Under Heteroscedasticity." *International Economic Review*, 26, 1985, pp. 37–44.

Olsen, R. "A Note on the Uniqueness of the Maximum Likelihood Estimator in the Tobit Model." *Econometrica*, 46, 1978, pp. 1211–1215.

Orcutt, G., S. Caldwell, and R. Wertheimer. *Policy Exploration Through Microanalytic Simulation*. Washington, D.C.: Urban Institute, D.C., 1976.

Orme, C. "Double and Triple Length Regressions for the Information Matrix Test and Other Conditional Moment Tests." Mimeo, University of York, UK, Department of Economics, 1990.

Ouliaris, S., J. Park, and P. Phillips. "Testing for a Unit Root in the Presence of a Maintained Trend." In B. Raj, ed., *Advances in Econometrics and Modeling*, Needham, MA: Kluwer Nijoff, 1989.

Paarsch, H. "A Monte Carlo Comparison of Estimators for Censored Regression Models." *Journal of Econometrics*, 24, 1984, pp. 197–214.

Pagan, A. "Some Consequences of Viewing LIML as an Iterated Aitken Estimator," *Economics Letters*, 3, 1979, pp. 369–372.

Pagan, A., and A. Hall. "Diagnostic Tests as Residual Analysis." *Econometric Reviews*, 2, 1983, pp. 159–218.

Pagan, A., and D. Nicholls. "Estimating Prediction Errors and Their Standard Deviations Using Constructed Variables." *Journal of Econometrics*, 24, 1984, pp. 293–310.

Pagan, A. and F. Vella. "Diagnostic Tests for Models Based on Individual Data: A Survey." *Journal of Applied Econometrics*, 4, Supplement, 1989, pp. S29–S59.

Pagan, A., and M. Wickens. "A Survey of Some Recent Econometric Methods." *Economic Journal*, 99, 1989, pp. 962–1025.

Pagano, M., and M. Hartley. "On Fitting Distributed Lag Models Subject to Polynomial Restrictions." *Journal of Econometrics*, 16, 1981, pp. 171–198.

Pakes, A., and D. Pollard. "Simulation and the Asymptotics of Optimization Estimators." *Econometrica*, 57, 1989, pp. 1027–1058.

Pal, M. "Consistent Moment Estimators of Regression Coefficients in the Presence of Errors in Variables." *Journal of Econometrics*, 14, 1980, pp. 666–668.

Park, R. "Estimation with Heteroscedastic Error Terms." *Econometrica*, 34, 1966, p. 888.

Park, R. "Efficient Estimation of a System of Regression Equations When Disturbances Are Both Serially and Contemporaneously Correlated." *Journal of the American Statistical Association*, 62, 1967, pp. 500–509.

Park, R., and B. Mitchell. "Estimating the Autocorrelated Error Model with Trended Data." *Journal of Econometrics*, 13, 1980, pp. 185–201.

Perron, P. "Testing for a Unit Root in a Time Series with a Changing Mean." *Journal of Business and Economic Statistics*, 8, 1990, pp. 153–162.

Pesaran, H. "On the General Problem of Model Selection." *Review of Economic Studies*, 41, 1974, pp. 153–171.

Pesaran, H., and A. Deaton. "Testing Non-Nested Nonlinear Regression Models." *Econometrica*, 46, 1978, pp. 677–694.

Petersen, D., and D. Waldman. "The Treatment of Heteroscedasticity in the Limited Dependent Variable Model." Mimeo, University of North Carolina, Chapel Hill, November 1981.

Petersen, T. "Fitting Parametric Survival Models with Time Dependent Covariates." *Journal of the Royal Statistical Society*, Series C (Applied Statistics), 35, 1986, pp. 281–288.

Phillips, P. "Exact Small Sample Theory in the Simultaneous Equations Model." In Z. Griliches, and M. Intriligator, eds., *Handbook of Econometrics*, vol. 1, Amsterdam: North Holland, 1983.

Phillips, P. "Understanding Spurious Regressions." *Journal of Econometrics*, 33, 1986, pp. 311–340.

Phillips, P., and S. Ouliaris. "Asymptotic Properties of Residual Based Tests for Cointegration." *Econometrica*, 58, 1990, pp. 165–193.

Phillips, P., and P. Perron. "Testing for a Unit Root in Time Series Regression." *Biometrika*, 75, 1988, pp. 335–346.

Pindyck, R., and D. Rubinfeld. *Econometric Models and Economic Forecasts*. New York: McGraw-Hill, 1981.

Poirier, D. *The Econometrics of Structural Change*. Amsterdam: North Holland, 1974.

Poirier, D. "The Effect of the First Observation in Regression Models with First-Order Autoregressive Disturbances." *Applied Statistics*, 27, 1978a, pp. 67–68.

Poirier, D. "The Use of the Box - Cox Transformation in Limited Dependent Variable Models." *Journal of the American Statistical Association*, 73, 1978b, pp. 284–287.

Poirier, D. "Partial Observability in Bivariate Probit Models." *Journal of Econometrics*, 12, 1980, pp. 209–217.

Poirier, D. "Frequentist and Subjectivist Perspectives on the Problems of Model Building in Economics, (with discussion)." *Journal of Economic Perspectives*, 2, 1988, pp. 121–144.

Poirier, D., ed. "Bayesian Empirical Studies in Economics and Finance." *Journal of Econometrics*, 49, 1991.

Poirier, D. *Intermediate Statistics and Econometrics*. Cambridge: MIT Press, 1995, pp. 1–217.

Poirier, D., and A. Melino. "A Note on the Interpretation of Regression Coefficients Within a Class of Truncated Distributions." *Econometrica*, 46, 1978, pp. 1207–1209.

Powell, J. "Least Absolute Deviations Estimation For Censored and Truncated Regression Models." Technical Report 356, Stanford University, IMSSS, 1981.

Powell, J. "Least Absolute Deviations Estimation for the Censored Regression Model." *Journal of Econometrics*, 25, 1984, pp. 303–325.

Powell, M. "An Efficient Method for Finding the Minimum of a Function of Several Variables Without Calculating Derivatives." *Computer Journal*, 1964, pp. 165–172.

Prais, S., and H. Houthakker. *The Analysis of Family Budgets*. New York: Cambridge University Press, 1955.

Prais, S., and C. Winsten. "Trend Estimation and Serial Correlation." Cowles Commission Discussion Paper Number 383, Chicago, 1954.

Press, W., B. Flannery, S. Teukolsky, and W. Vetterling. *Numerical Recipes: The Art of Scientific Computing*. Cambridge: Cambridge University Press, 1986.

Quandt, R. "Econometric Disequilibrium Models." *Econometric Reviews*, 1, 1982, pp. 1–63.

Quandt, R. "Computational Problems and Methods." In Z. Griliches and M. Intriligator, eds., *Handbook of Econometrics*, vol. 1, Amsterdam: North Holland, 1983.

Quandt, R. *The Econometrics of Disequilibrium*. New York: Basil Blackwell, 1988.

Quandt, R., and J. Ramsey. "Estimating Mixtures of Normal Distributions and Switching Regressions." *Journal of the American Statistical Association*, 73, December 1978, pp. 730–738.

Quester, A., and W. Greene. "Divorce Risk and Wives' Labor Supply Behavior." *Social Science Quarterly*, 63, 1982, pp. 16–27.

Raferty, A., and S. Lewis. "How Many Iterations in the Gibbs Sampler?" In J. Berger, J. Bernardo, A. Dawid, and F. Smith, *Bayesian Statistics* Oxford: Clarendon Press, 1992.

Raj, B., and B. Baltagi, eds. *Panel Data Analysis*. Heidelberg: Physica-Verlag, 1992.

Ramsey, J. "Classical Model Selection Through Specification Error Tests," in P. Zarembka, ed., *Frontiers in Econometrics*. Academic Press, 1974.

Rao, C. *Linear Statistical Inference and Its Applications*. New York: John Wiley and Sons, 1973.

Revankar, N. "Some Finite Sample Results in the Context of Two Seemingly Unrelated Regression Equations." *Journal of the American Statistical Association*, 69, 1974, pp. 187–190.

Revankar, N. "Use of Restricted Residuals in SUR Systems: Some Finite Sample Results." *Journal of the American Statistical Association*, 71, 1976, pp. 183–188.

Rice, P., and K. Smith. "An Econometric Model of the Petroleum Industry." *Journal of Econometrics*, 6, 1977, pp. 263–287.

Ridder, G., and T. Wansbeek. "Dynamic Models for Panel Data." In R. van der Ploeg, ed., *Advanced Lectures in Quantitative Economics*, New York: Academic Press, 1990, pp. 557–582.

Riersol, O. "Identifiability of a Linear Relation Between Variables Which Are Subject to Error." *Econometrica*, 18, 1950, pp. 375–389.

Rivers, D., and Q. Vuong. "Limited Information Estimators and Exogeneity Tests for Simultaneous Probit Models." *Journal of Econometrics*, 39, 1988, pp. 347–366.

Roberts, G. "Convergence Diagnostics of the Gibbs Sampler." In J. Bernardo et al., eds., *Proceedings of the Fourth Valencia International Conference on Bayesian Statistics*, New York: Oxford University Press, 1992, pp. 775–782.

Robinson, C., and N. Tomes. "Self Selection and Interprovincial Migration in Canada." *Canadian Journal of Economics*, 15, 1982, pp. 474–502.

Robinson, P. "Semiparametric Econometrics: A Survey." *Journal of Applied Econometrics*, 3, 1988, pp. 35–51.

Rosett, R., and F. Nelson. "Estimation of the Two-Limit Probit Regression Model." *Econometrica*, 43, 1975, pp. 141–146.

Rubin, H. "Consistency of Maximum Likelihood Estimators in the Explosive Case." In T. Koopmans, ed., *Statistical Inference in Dynamic Economic Models*, New York: John Wiley and Sons, 1950.

Rubinfeld, D. "Voting in a Local School Election: A Micro Analysis." *Review of Economics and Statistics*, 59, 1977, pp. 30–42.

Rutemiller, H., and D. Bowers. "Estimation in a Heteroscedastic Regression Model." *Journal of the American Statistical Association*, 63, 1968, pp. 552–557.

Ruud, P. "Specification Errors in Limited Dependent Variable Models." Ph.D. thesis, Department of Economics, Massachusetts Institute of Technology, 1981.

Ruud, P. "A Score Test of Consistency." Manuscript, Department of Economics, University of California, Berkeley 1982.

Ruud, P. "Tests of Specification in Econometrics." *Econometric Reviews*, 3, 1984, pp. 211–242.

Ruud, P. "Consistent Estimation of Limited Dependent Variable Models Despite Misspecification of the Distribution." *Journal of Econometrics*, 32, 1986, pp. 157–187.

Ruud, P. "Extensions of Estimation Methods Using the EM Algorithm." *Journal of Econometrics*, 49, 1991, pp. 305–341.

Ruud, P. "Sufficient Conditions for the Consistency of Maximum Likelihood Estimation Despite, Misspecification of Distribution in Multinomial Discrete Choice Models." *Econometrica*, 51, 1, 1993, pp. 225–228.

Salem, D., and T. Mount. "A Convenient Descriptive Model of the Income Distribution." *Econometrica*, 42, 6, 1974, pp. 1115–1128.

Salkever, D. "The Use of Dummy Variables to Compute Predictions, Prediction Errors, and Confidence Intervals." *Journal of Econometrics*, 4, 1976, pp. 393–397.

Savin, E. and K. White. "The Durbin–Watson Test for Serial Correlation With Extreme Sample Sizes or Many Regressors." *Econometrica*, 45, 1977, pp. 1989–1996.

Schmidt, P. "The Asymptotic Distribution of Dynamic Multipliers." *Econometrica*, 41, 1973, pp. 161–164.

Schmidt, P. "The Algebraic Equivalence of the Oberhofer-Kmenta and Theil-Boot Formulae for the Asymptotic Variance of a Characteristic Root of a Dynamic Econometric Model." *Econometrica*, 42, 1974d, pp. 591–592.

Schmidt, P. *Econometrics*. New York: Marcel Dekker, 1976.

Schmidt, P. "Estimation of Seemingly Unrelated Regressions with Unequal Numbers of Observations," *Journal of Econometrics*, 5, 1977, pp. 365–377.

Schmidt, P. "A Note on Dynamic Simulation Forecasts and Stochastic Forecast-Period Exogenous Variables." *Econometrica*, 46, 1978, pp. 1227–1230.

Schmidt, P. "Frontier Production Functions." *Econometric Reviews*, 4, 2, 1986, pp. 289–328.

Schmidt, P., and R. Sickles. "On the Efficiency of the Almon Lag Technique." *International Economic Review*, 16, 1975, pp. 792–795.

Schmidt, P., and R. Sickles. "Some Further Evidence on the Use of the Chow Test Under Heteroscedasticity." *Econometrica*, 45, 1977, pp. 1293–1298.

Schmidt, P., and R. Strauss. "The Prediction of Occupation Using Multiple Logit Models." *International Economic Review*, 16, 1975a, pp. 471–486.

Schmidt, P., and R. Strauss. "Estimation of Models with Jointly Dependent Qualitative Variables: A Simultaneous Logit Approach." *Econometrica*, 43, 1975b, pp. 745–755.

Schmidt, P., and R. Waud. "The Almon Lag Technique and the Monetary Versus Fiscal Policy Debate." *Journal of the American Statistical Association*, 68, 1973, pp. 11–19.

Seaks, T. and K. Layson. "Box-Cox Estimation with Standard Econometric Problems." *Review of Economics and Statistics*, 65, 1983, pp. 160–164.

Sharma, S. "Specification Diagnostics for Econometric Models of Duration." Mimeo, Department of Economics, University of California at Los Angeles, 1989.

Shaw, D. "'On-Site Samples' Regression Problems of Nonnegative Integers, Truncation, and Endogenous Stratification." *Journal of Econometrics*, 37, 1988, pp. 211–223.

Shephard, R. *The Theory of Cost and Production*. Princeton: Princeton University Press, 1970.

Sims, C. "Money, Income, and Causality." *American Economic Review*, 62, 1972, pp. 540–552.

Sims, C. "Exogeneity and Causal Ordering in Macroeconomic Models." *New Methods in Business Cycle Research: Proceedings from a Conference*, Federal Reserve Bank of Minneapolis, 1977, pp. 23–43.

Sims, C. "Macroeconomics and Reality." *Econometrica*, 48, 1, 1980, pp. 1–48.

Smith, R., and R. Blundell. "An Exogeneity Test for a Simultaneous Equation Tobit Model with an Application to Labor Supply." *Econometrica*, 54, 1986, pp. 679–685.

Smith, V. "Selection and Recreation Demand." *American Journal of Agricultural Economics*, 70, 1988, pp. 29–36.

Solow, R. "Technical Change and the Aggregate Production Function." *Review of Economics and Statistics*, 39, 1957, pp. 312–320.

Spector, L., and M. Mazzeo. "Probit Analysis and Economic Education." *Journal of Economic Education*, 11, 1980, pp. 37–44.

Spencer, D. and K. Berk. "A Limited Information Specification Test." *Econometrica*, 49, 1981, pp. 1079–1085.

Spitzer, J. "A Fast and Efficient Method for Estimation of Parameters in Models with the Box–Cox Transformation." *Journal of the American Statistical Association*, 77, 1982a, pp. 760–766.

Spitzer, J. "A Primer on Box–Cox Estimation." Review of Economics and Statistics, 64, 1982b, pp. 307–313.

Spitzer, J. "Variance Estimates in Models with the Box–Cox Transformation: Implications for Estimation and Hypothesis Testing." *Review of Economics and Statistics*, 66, 1984, pp. 645–652.

Stapleton, D., and D. Young. "Censored Normal Regression with Measurement Error on the Dependent Variable." Discussion Paper 81-30, Department of Economics, University of British Columbia, 1981.

Stern, S. "Two Dynamic Discrete Choice Estimation Problems and Simulation Method Solutions." *Review of Economics and Statistics*, 76, 1994, pp. 695–702.

Stock, J. "Unit Roots, Structural Breaks, and Trends." In R. Engle and D. McFadden, eds., *Handbook of Econometrics*, vol. 4, Amsterdam: North Holland, 1994.

Stock, J., and M. Watson, "Testing for Common Trends." *Journal of the American Statistical Association*, 83, 1988, pp. 1097–1107.

Stoker, T. "Consistent Estimation of Scaled Coefficients." *Econometrica*, 54, 1986, pp. 1461–1482.

Stone, R. *The Measurement of Consumers' Expenditure and Behaviour in the United Kingdom,* 1920–1938. Cambridge: Cambridge University Press, 1954a.

Stone, R. "Linear Expenditure Systems and Demand Analysis: An Application to the Pattern of British Demand." *Economic Journal*, 64, 1954b, pp. 511–527.

Strang, G. *Linear Algebra and Its Applications*. New York: Academic Press, 1988.

Strickland, A., and L. Weiss. "Advertising, Concentration, and Price Cost Margins." *Journal of Political Economy*, 84, 1976, pp. 1109–1121.

Stuart, A., and S. Ord. *Kendall's Advanced Theory of Statistics.* New York: Oxford University Press, 1989.

Suits, D. "Dummy Variables: Mechanics vs. Interpretation." *Review of Economics and Statistics* 66, 1984, pp. 177–180.

Swamy, P. "Efficient Inference in a Random Coefficient Regression Model." *Econometrica*, 38, 1970, pp. 311–323.

Swamy, P. *Statistical Inference in Random Coefficient Regression Models*. New York: Springer-Verlag, 1971.

Swamy, P. "Linear Models with Random Coefficients." In P. Zarembka, ed., *Frontiers in Econometrics*, New York: Academic Press, 1974.

Tanner, M. *Tools for Statistical Inference*, 2nd ed. New York: Springer-Verlag, 1993.

Tauchen, H., A. Witte, and H. Griesinger. "Criminal Deterrence: Revisiting the Issue with a Birth Cohort." *Review of Economics and Statistics*, 3, 1994, pp. 399–412.

Taylor, L. "Estimation by Minimizing the Sum of Absolute Errors." In P. Zarembka, ed., *Frontiers in Econometrics*, New York: Academic Press, 1974.

Taylor, W. "Small Sample Properties of a Class of Two Stage Aitken Estimators." *Econometrica*, 45, 1977, pp. 497–508.

Terza, J. "Ordinal Probit: A Generalization." *Communications in Statistics*, 14, 1985a, pp. 1–12.

Terza, J. "A Tobit Type Estimator for the Censored Poisson Regression Model." *Economics Letters*, 18, 1985b, pp. 361–365.

Terza, J. "Estimating Count Data Models with Endogenous Switching: Sample Selection and Endogenous Treatment Effects." Working Paper No. 4-95-14, Department of Economics, Penn State University, 1995 (forthcoming, *Journal of Econometrics*).

Theil, H. *Economic Forecasts and Policy*. Amsterdam: North Holland, 1961.

Theil, H. *Principles of Econometrics*. New York: John Wiley and Sons, 1971.

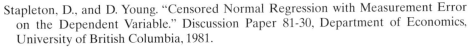

Theil, H. "Linear Algebra and Matrix Methods in Econometrics." In Z. Griliches and M. Intriligator, eds., *Handbook of Econometrics*, vol. 1, New York: North Holland, 1983.

Theil, H., and J. Boot. "The Final Form of Econometric Equation Systems." *Review of the International Statistical Institute*, 30, 1962, pp. 136–152.

Theil, H., and A. Goldberger. "On Pure and Mixed Estimation in Economics." *International Economic Review*, 2, 1961, pp. 65–78.

Theil, H., and A. Nagar. "Testing the Independence of Regression Disturbances." *Journal of the American Statistical Association*, 52, 1961, pp. 793–806.

Thomson, M. "Some Results on the Statistical Properties of an Inequality Constrained Least Squares Estimator in a Linear Model with Two Regressors." *Journal of Econometrics*, 19, 1982, pp. 215–231.

Thursby, J. "Misspecification, Heteroscedasticity, and the Chow and Goldfeld–Quandt Tests." *Review of Economics and Statistics*, 64, 1982, pp. 314–321.

Tobin, J. "Estimation of Relationships for Limited Dependent Variables." *Econometrica*, 26, 1958, pp. 24–36.

Toyoda, T., and K. Ohtani. "Testing Equality Between Sets of Coefficients After a Preliminary Test for Equality of Disturbance Variances in Two Linear Regressions." *Journal of Econometrics*, 31, 1986, pp. 67–80.

Trivedi, P., and A. Pagan. "Polynomial Distributed Lags: A Unified Treatment." *Economic Studies Quarterly*, 30, 1979, pp. 37–49.

Tunali, I. "A General Structure for Models of Double Selection and an Application to a Joint Migration/Earnings Process with Remigration." *Research in Labor Economics*, 8, 1986, pp. 235–282.

United States Bureau of the Census, *Public Use Samples of Basic Records from the 1970 Census*. U.S. Government Printing Office, Washington, D.C., 1972.

United States Department of Commerce. *Statistical Abstract of the United States*. Government Printing Office, Washington, D.C., 1979.

United States Department of Commerce, National Income and Product Accounts, BEA. *Survey of Current Business: Business Statistics, 1984*. Washington, D.C., 1984.

United States Government Printing Office. *Economic Report of the President, 1983*. Washington, D.C., 1983.

United States Government Printing Office. *Economic Report of the President, 1986*. Washington, D.C., 1986.

United States Government Printing Office. *Economic Report of the President, 1987*. Washington, D.C., 1987.

United States Government Printing Office. *Economic Report of the President, 1994*. Washington, D.C., 1994.

Veall, M. "Bootstrapping the Probability Distribution of Peak Electricity Demand." *International Economic Review*, 28, 1987, pp. 203–212.

Veall, M. "Bootstrapping the Process of Model Selection: An Econometric Example." *Journal of Applied Econometrics*, 7, 1992, pp. 93–99.

Vinod, H. "Bootstrap, Jackknife, Resampling, and Simulation Methods: Applications in Econometrics." In G. Maddala, C. Rao, and H. Vinod, eds., *Handbook of Statistics: Econometrics*, vol. 11, Chap. 11, Amsterdam: North Holland, 1993.

Vinod, H. and B. Raj. "Economic Issues in Bell System Divestiture: A Bootstrap Application." *Journal of the Royal Statistical Society*, Series C, Applied Statistics, 37, 2, 1994, pp. 251–261.

Vuong, Q. "Likelihood Ratio Tests for Model Selection and Non-Nested Hypotheses." *Econometrica*, 57, 1989, pp. 307–334.

Waldman, D. "A Note on the Algebraic Equivalence of White's Test and a Variant of the Godfrey/Breusch-Pagan Test for Heteroscedasticity." *Economics Letters*, 13, 1983, pp. 197–200.

Wales, T., and A. Woodland. "Sample Selectivity and the Estimation of Labor Supply Functions." *International Economic Review*, 21, 1980, pp. 437–468.

Wallace, T., and A. Hussain. "The Use of Error Components in Combining Cross Section with Time Series Data." *Econometrica*, 37, 1969, pp. 55–72.

Wallace, T., and C. Toro-Vizcarrondo. "Tables for the Mean Squared Error Test for Exact Linear Restrictions in Regression." *Journal of the American Statistical Association*, 1969, pp. 1649–1663.

Wallis, K. "Testing for Fourth Order Autocorrelation in Quarterly Regression Equations." *Econometrica*, 40, 1972, pp. 617–636.

Wang, H. "Applications of Tests of Nonnested Models." Ph.D. dissertation, Department of Economics, State University of New York, Stony Brook, 1996.

Watson, M. "Vector Autoregressions and Cointegration." In R. Engle and D. McFadden eds., *Handbook of Econometrics*, vol. 4, Amsterdam: North Holland, 1994.

Waugh, F. "The Place of Least Squares in Econometrics." *Econometrica*, 29, 1961, pp. 386–396.

Weiss, A. "Asymptotic Theory for ARCH Models: Stability, Estimation, and Testing." Discussion Paper 82–36, Department of Economics, University of California, San Diego, 1982.

Weiss, A. "Simultaneity and Sample Selection in Poisson Regression Models." Manuscript, Department of Economics, University of Southern California, 1995.

White, H. "Using Least Squares to Approximate Unknown Regression Functions." *International Economic Review*, 21, 1, 1980a, pp. 149–170.

White, H. "A Heteroscedasticity-Consistent Covariance Matrix Estimator and a Direct Test for Heteroscedasticity." *Econometrica*, 48, 1980b, pp. 817–838.

White, H. "Maximum Likelihood Estimation of Misspecified Models." *Econometrica*, 53, 1982a, pp. 1–16.

White, H., ed. "Model Specification." *Journal of Econometrics*, 20, 1, 1982b, pp. 1–157.

White, H., ed. "Non-Nested Models." *Journal of Econometrics*, 21, 1, 1983, pp. 1–160.

White, H. *Asymptotic Theory for Econometricians*. New York: Academic Press, 1984.

White, H. *Estimation, Inference, and Specification Analysis*. New York: Cambridge University Press, 1994.

White, K. *SHAZAM, Version 7*. Department of Economics, University of British Columbia, Vancouver, 1993.

Wickens, M. "A Note on the Use of Proxy Variables." *Econometrica*, 40, 1972, pp. 759–760.

Willis, R., and S. Rosen. "Education and Self-Selection." *Journal of Political Economy*, 87, 1979, pp. S7–S36.

Witte, A. "Estimating an Economic Model of Crime with Individual Data." *Quarterly Journal of Economics*, 94, 1980, pp. 57–84.

Wong, W. "On the Consistency of Cross Validation in Kernel Nonparametric Regression." *The Annals of Statistics*, 11, 1983, pp. 1136–1141.

Woolridge, J. "Specification Testing and Quasi-Maximum Likelihood Estimation." *Journal of Econometrics*, 48, 1/2, 1991, pp. 29–57.

Working, E. "What Do Statistical Demand Curves Show?" *Quarterly Journal of Economics*, 41, 1926, pp. 212–235.

Wu, C. "On the Convergence Properties of the EM Algorithm." *Annals of Statistics*, 11, 1983, pp. 95–103.

Wu, D. "Alternative Tests of Independence Between Stochastic Regressors and Disturbances." *Econometrica*, 41, 1973, pp. 733–750.

Wynand, P., and B. Van Praag. "The Demand For Deductibles in Private Health Insurance: A Probit Model with Sample Selection." *Journal of Econometrics*, 17, 1981, pp. 229–252.

Yatchew, A., and Z. Griliches. "Specification Error in Probit Models." *Review of Economics and Statistics*, 66, 1984, pp. 134–139.

Zarembka, P. "Functional Form in the Demand for Money." *Journal of the American Statistical Association*, 63, 1968, pp. 502–511.

Zarembka, P. "Transformations of Variables in Econometrics." In P. Zarembka, ed., *Frontiers in Econometrics*, Boston: Academic Press, 1974.

Zavoina, R., and W. McElvey. "A Statistical Model for the Analysis of Ordinal Level Dependent Variables." *Journal of Mathematical Sociology*, Summer 1975, pp. 103–120.

Zellner, A. "An Efficient Method of Estimating Seemingly Unrelated Regressions and Tests of Aggregation Bias." *Journal of the American Statistical Association*, 57, 1962, pp. 500–509.

Zellner, A. "Estimators for Seemingly Unrelated Regression Equations: Some Exact Finite Sample Results." *Journal of the American Statistical Association*, 58, 1963, pp. 977–992.

Zellner, A., ed. *Readings in Economic Statistics and Econometrics*. Boston: Little, Brown, 1968.

Zellner, A. *Introduction to Bayesian Inference in Econometrics*. New York: John Wiley and Sons, 1971.

Zellner, A. "Statistical Analysis of Econometric Models." *Journal of the American Statistical Association*, 74, 1979, pp. 628–643.

Zellner, A. *Basic Issues in Econometrics*. Chicago: University of Chicago Press, 1984.

Zellner, A. "Bayesian Econometrics." *Econometrica*, 53, 1985, pp. 253–269.

Zellner, A., and M. Geisel. "Analysis of Distributed Lag Models with Application to the Consumption Function." *Econometrica*, 38, 1970, pp. 865–888.

Zellner, A., and D. Huang. "Further Properties of Efficient Estimators for Seemingly Unrelated Regression Equations." *International Economic Review*, 3, 1962, pp. 300–313.

Zellner, A., and C.-K. Min. "Gibbs Sampler Convergence Criteria." Unpublished manuscript, Graduate School of Business, University of Chicago, 1992.

Zellner, A., and N. Revankar. "Generalized Production Functions." *Review of Economic Studies*, 37, 1970, pp. 241–250.

Zellner, A., and A. Siow. "Posterior Odds Ratios for Selected Regression Hypotheses (with Discussion)." In J. Bernardo, M. DeGroot, D. Lindley, and A. Smith, eds., *Bayesian Statistics*, Valencia: University Press, 1980.

Zellner, A., and H. Theil. "Three Stage Least Squares: Simultaneous Estimation of Simultaneous Equations." *Econometrica*, 30, 1962, pp. 63–68.

Indexes

AUTHOR INDEX

A

B

C

D

E

F

G

H

I

J

Q

R

S

T

U

V

W

Y

Z

SUBJECT INDEX

A

C

D

E

F

G

H

K

L

M

T

U

V

W

Y

Z